# THE EUROPEAN UNION AND CHINA, 1949–2008

This book is a comprehensive reference book and commentary on basic documents about relations between the EU and the People's Republic of China from 1949 to the present. It contains all significant official and unofficial documents in English and Chinese about EU–China relations since the founding of the PRC in 1949. Since the opening-up of China in 1979, and especially after the establishment of the EU in 1992, relations between the EU and China have developed apace. Today the EU and China are 'strategic partners', with a very broad-based relationship, extending far beyond trade to encompass a growing number of important economic, political, social and cultural domains. The relationship is certain to gain in importance with increasing globalisation, EU expansion, Chinese membership of the World Trade Organisation, the renewal and development of China, and changes in the international trading system and international politics. This book provides an indispensable foundation for teaching, research, policy-making and advising on EU–China relations. It includes both documents originally published in English and English translations of documents previously available only in Chinese, Essential to every library, it will also be required reading for students, teachers, researchers, policy-makers, legal practitioners and government officials in the EU, China, the United States and elsewhere.

Volume 3 in the China and International Economic Law Series

**China and International Economic Law Series**

*Editors-in-General: Wenhua Shan, Qing Zhang and Xin Zhang*

**Volume 1.** The Legal Framework of EU-China Investment Relations: A Critical Appraisal *Wenhua Shan*

**Volume 2.** International Trade Regulation in China: Law and Policy *Xin Zhang*

# The European Union and China, 1949–2008

## Basic Documents and Commentary

Francis Snyder

•HART•
PUBLISHING

OXFORD AND PORTLAND, OREGON
2009

Published in North America (US and Canada) by

Hart Publishing
c/o International Specialized Book Services
920 NE 58th Avenue, Suite 300
Portland, OR 97213-3786
USA
Tel: +1 503 287 3093 or toll-free: (1) 800 944 6190
Fax: +1 503 280 8832
E-mail: orders@isbs.com
Website: www.isbs.com



Hart Publishing Ltd, 16C Worcester Place, Oxford OX1 2JW
Telephone: +44 (0)1865 517530 Fax: +44 (0)1865 510710
E-mail: mail@hartpub.co.uk
Website: http://www.hartpub.co.uk

British Library Cataloguing in Publication Data
Data Available

ISBN: 978-1-84113-724-7

Typeset by Forewords, Oxford
Printed and bound in Great Britain by
Lightning Source UK Ltd

*To my students all over the world,*
*especially in China and Europe,*
*who continue to teach me so much*
*about relations between China and the European Union*

# Publisher's Note

The author and publisher gratefully acknowledge the authors and publishers of the documents which appear in this book, and in particular, the following for permission to reprint the documents indicated by the numbers below

**BBC Monitoring and BBC Written Archives Centre:** 1.25, 1.26.

**Beijing Review:** 1.11–1.15, 1.17–1.19, 1.22–1.24.

**European Commission:** 1.28, 1.29, 2.1–2.13, 3.1–3.7, 3.13, 3.14, 3.18–3.21, 4.1–4.14, 4.16–4.19, 5.1–5.20. 5.22–5.24, 6.1–6.78.1–8.7, 9.1–9.5. Only European Community legislation printed in the paper edition of the Official Journal of the European Union is deemed authentic. For documents downloaded from the EUR-Lex database, the following indicates the source and copyright holder: http://eur-lex.europa.eu, © European Communities, 1998-2008.

**Hamburg Chamber of Commerce:** 3.17 (http://www.hamburg-summit.com/hamburg-summit/pdfs/2006/SpeechWenJiabao130906.pdf).

**Ministry of Foreign Affairs:** 3.9, 3.10, 3.16.

**Official Web Portal of the Central People's Government, People's Republic of China:** 3.15.

**Portuguese Presidency of the EU:** 4.15 (http://www.eu2007.pt/UE/vEN/Noticias_Documentos/20071017UEChina.htm).

**Unknown source:** 5.21.

**Forum for Trade and Economic Cooperation between China and the Portuguese-speaking Countries:** 8.8, 8.9.

**WTO:** 9.6 (http://www.wto.org/english/thewto_e/countries_e/china_e.htm)

**Xinhua News Agency, People's Republic of China:** 1.1–1.10, 1.16, 1.20, 1.21, 1.27, 3.8, 3.11, 3.12.

# Acknowledgements

Preparing a book of basic documents and commentary on relations between the European Union and China since 1949 bears a strong resemblance to train travel from Beijing to Chengdu. The way is long, there are many good companions, the food is often excellent, and the closer one approaches the destination, the greater the distance left behind. But there is one striking difference: the train arrives at Chengdu, but a book of this kind is never definitively finished, even when it is delivered to the publisher. EU–China relations constitute a continuing process, not a fixed journey. For their companionship, suggestions and contribution to making my participation in this process so stimulating and enjoyable, I am grateful to many friends, colleagues and students (not discrete categories), as well as to numerous institutions. Here it is possible to thank only a small proportion of those to whom gratitude is due. I hope that those who have participated in the making of this book, but whose names are not included for reasons of space, will accept its publication as a small token of my appreciation for their help.

For stimulating, encouraging and then reawakening my interest in China, I wish to thank two mentors: Jerome A Cohen, then Professor of Law and Director of the Center for East Asian Legal Studies, Harvard Law School, who first taught me Chinese law, accepted me as his research assistant and integrated me into his research team many years ago when I was a student at Harvard Law School; and more recently the late Wang Tieya, then Professor of International Law at Peking University Law School, who graciously acted as my host during my first visits to Peking University. I am also grateful to the late Emile Noël, who, while President of the European University Institute in Florence, did much to encourage my research on EU–China relations. Preparing this book has been a philosophical as well as an academic experience, and on many occasions I have reflected on the lives and the academic and professional contributions of these three people who helped to shape my interest in China and its relations with Europe.

Among the colleagues from whom I have learned most about EU–China relations, I am deeply grateful to Song Ying, Associate Professor at Peking University Law School and Associate Director of the PKU Centre for European Studies; Zhou Hong, Professor and Director of the Institute for European Studies at the Chinese Academy of Social Sciences, Beijing; Cheng Weidong, Associate Professor and Head of the Law and Politics Division, Chinese Academy of Social Sciences, Beijing; and Dai Bingran, Emeritus Professor of Economics, Jean Monnet Chair and Emeritus Director of the Centre for European Studies, Fudan University. I owe a special debt to Cheng Weidong for his moral and intellectual support after changes in circumstances and other responsibilities made it impossible for us to realise our original plan to prepare this book together.

During work on this book, I have had the good fortune to benefit from the support of the following institutions (in alphabetical order): Chinese Academy of Social Sciences (CASS), Beijing; the College of Europe (Bruges and Warsaw [Natolin]); Institute of European Studies of Macau (IEEM); London School of Economics (LSE); University of Macau; Université Paul Cézanne Aix-Marseille III, in particular the Centre d'Etudes et de Recherches Internationales et Communautaires (CERIC) (UMR CNRS 6201) and the Faculté de Droit et de Science Politique ; Peking University Law School and the Centre for European Studies at Peking University; Tsinghua Law School, Tsinghua University, Beijing; and Wissenschaftskolleg zu Berlin (Institute for Advanced Study, Berlin). For this institutional support, I am grateful in particular to the following individuals (in alphabetical order of their institutions): at the CASS: Zhou Hong and Cheng Weidong, respectively Director and Head of the Law and Politics Division, Institute for European Studies; at the College of Europe: Paul Demaret and Robert Picht, respectively Rector and former Vice-Rector; at the IEEM: Maria do Céu Esteves and José Luis de Sales Marques, successive Presidents of the IEEM; at the LSE: Simon Roberts, Robert Reiner, Christopher Greenwood and Hugh Collins, successive Convenors of the LSE Law Department; at the University of Macau: Manuel Trigo, formerly Dean of the Law Faculty, his successor Zheng Lingliang, Associate Dean Liu Gaolong, and Paulo Canelas de Castro, Co-ordinator of the Master's Programme in European, International and Comparative Law; at the Université Paul Cézanne Aix-Marseille III: Jacques Bourrinet, founder and first Director of the CERIC, as well as Rostane Mehdi and Sandrine Maljean-Dubois, currently Director and Adjunct Director, respectively, of the CERIC, and the late Agnès Teyssot-Castelan, Administrator of the CERIC, together with Jacques Mestre and Marc Pena, successive Deans of the Faculté de Droit et de Science Politique; at Peking University: Zhu Suli, Li Ming and Yin Ming, respectively Dean, Executive Dean and Administrator, Peking University Law School, and Li Qiang, Song Ying and Zhu Tianbiao, respectively Director and Associate Directors, Centre for European Studies, as well as Wu Zhipan, formerly Dean of PKU Law School; at Tsinghua Law School: Wang Chenguang, Zhang Chenying and Yang Rujun, respectively Dean and the successive Heads of the Foreign Affairs Office; and at the Wissenschaftskolleg zu Berlin: Wolf Lepenies and Joachim Nettelbeck, formerly Rector and (then and currently) Secretary, respectively.

Many other people helped to make this book possible, through documents, conversations, comments and other kinds of intellectual and moral support. While any list would be incomplete, I wish to thank especially (in alphabetical order), in addition to people already mentioned, Kai Anderson, Dai Bingran, Jacques Bourgeois, Paulo Canelas de Castro, Mick Cox, Paul Demaret, Bhimla Dheermojee, Bentham Fong, Florence Giorgi, Inge Govaere, Carol Harlow, Valérie Hauspie, Hu Kehua, Nico Krisch, Jacqueline Lastenhouse-Bury, Clara Lei, Jimmy Leung, Li Ming, Li Qiang, Liu Fei, Gabriella Lombardo, Luo Haocai, Imelda Maher, Catherine Manthorpe, Jing Men, Michael Oliver, Peng Xu, Rao Geping, Simon Roberts, Christopher Ross, José Luis de Sales Marques, Shao Jingchun, Brendan Smith, Colin Scott, Rima Sondaite Van Soest, Nicolas Triart, Wang Chenguang, Wu Changqi, Wu Zhipan, Yang Zugong, Zhang Qi, Zhu Suli, colleagues in the 2001–2002 Globalisation Working Group at the Wissenschaftskolleg zu Berlin, participants in the London

School of Economics–Peking University Summer School in 2006 and 2007, and participants in the Law and Public Policy course in 2006 and 2007 as part of the Executive Public Policy Training Programme offered by the London School of Economics together with Peking University, Sciences Po Paris and the School of International and Public Affairs at Columbia University.

A series of workshops, conferences and networks punctuated, stimulated and directly informed the preparation of this book. I am pleased to acknowledge the contribution of the following meetings, organising institutions and sources of financial support: ESF/SCSS Exploratory Workshop, 'The Strategic Use of European Law and its Implications for Labour Market Relations in the EU and China: Transnational Companies, International Production Networks and Small and Medium-Sized Enterprises', which I organised under the aegis of the European Institute and the Law Department, London School of Economics, with financial support from the European Science Foundation, 12–13 December 2003; 'Journées d'étude sur les nouvelles configurations normatives européennes', organised by the Centre d'Etudes et de Recherches Internationales et Communautaires (CERIC), Faculté de Droit et de Science Politique, Université Paul Cézanne Aix-Marseille III, with financial support from the European Commission, Aix-en-Provence, 17–18 July 2005; 5th International Workshop for Young Scholars (WISH)/5ème Rencontre Internationale des Jeunes Chercheurs (RIJC), 'The European Union, India and China: Strategic Partners in a Changing World'/'L'Union européenne, l'Inde et la Chine: Parténaires stratégiques dans un monde en mutation', organised by the *European Law Journal*, of which I serve as Editor-in-Chief, together with the CERIC and the College of Europe (Warsaw [Natolin], with sponsorship from the Centre for European Studies of Peking University, Tsinghua Law School and the Institute of European Studies of the Chinese Academy of Social Sciences, Beijing, with financial support from the European Commission, *European Law Journal,* Blackwell Publishers and the Faculté de Droit et de Science Politique of the Université Paul Cézanne Aix-Marseille III, held in Aix-en-Provence, 17–18 November 2006; and the continuing ESRC EU–China–WTO Research Seminar Network, of which I serve as coordinator, and which has been held at the London School of Economics periodically since 2003, supported by the UK Economic and Social Research Council.

I thank the following for allowing me to present papers or lectures which contributed directly to this book: the ESF Exploratory Workshop and the CERIC Journées d'étude (with Cheng Weidong), already mentioned, as well as the Academy of International Trade Law (Macao), Chinese Academy of Social Sciences, College of Europe (Bruges), College of Europe (Warsaw [Natolin]), the University of Hull, London School of Economics, Université Paul Cézanne Aix-Marseille III, Peking University Law School, Peking University European Studies Centre, Peking University Soft Law Centre and Tsinghua Law School, Tsinghua University. I am grateful for comments and suggestions received on these occasions.

For the full texts of various documents, I am indebted to the British Library of Political and Economic Science at the London School of Economics, the Library of the School of Oriental and African Studies (SOAS) at the University of London, the University of Leeds Brotherton Library holdings of series of news, news analysis and translation on China since 1949, and the European Commission and the Council of the European Union in Brussels. Special thanks are due to the staff of the LSE, SOAS and Brotherton libraries, and particularly to Ms Xiyi Huang, Faculty Team Librarian at the Brotherton Library, University of Leeds, for her help in locating the text of many historical documents, and to Yin Xiao for preparing these documents in useable form. The websites of the European Commission, both in Brussels and at the Commission Delegation in Beijing, provided invaluable information on EU documents. For additional EU documents, I thank INFODOC at the Directorate General for Information of the European Parliament, in particular Didier Vanden Bemden and Andrée Grégoire; Historical Archives of the European Commission, especially Luisa Palla; and the Historical Archives of the Council of the European Union, especially Manfred Leutner and Stéphane Gierts; and the China Desk Officers in the European Commission in DG External Relations as well as numerous other Directorates-General of the European Commission for providing documents concerning specific sectors. I owe a special debt of gratitude to Rima Sondaite Van Soest, European Commission, DG External Relations, H2-China, Taiwan, Hong Kong, Macao & Mongolia, for her advice, persistence and effectiveness in tracking down numerous documents. For Chinese-language documents, I am indebted not only to Yin Xiao and to the Brotherton Library in Leeds, but also to the websites of the Ministry of Commerce and the Ministry of Foreign Affairs, People's Republic of China, Beijing. For documents on the Forum for Economic and Trade Cooperation between China and the Portuguese-Speaking Countries, I wish to thank José Luis de Sales Marques, Jimmy Leong and the Secretariado Permanente do Fórum para a Cooperação Económica e Comercial entre a China e os Países de Língua Portuguesa (Macau).

For research assistance I am grateful to (in alphabetical order) Bao Yongqing, Gildo Espada, Hou Feng, Hu Kehua, Wu Qianlan, Gulrez Yazdani and Zhang Yuanyuan, and especially to Magda Salykova and Yin Xiao. I thank Zhang Yuanyuan and particularly Yin Xiao for translating relevant documents from Chinese to English. I am very grateful to Gildo Espada for providing a first draft of translations of documents from Portuguese to English; the final translation of such documents is my own. Translations from French to English are my own.

This book would not have been feasible without the cooperation of institutions in the EU and China. In addition to universities and research institutes, several other institutions and their staff played an indispensable role in the project. The European Commission awarded me a Jean Monnet Chair *ad personam*, specialising in relations between the EU and China. This enabled me to devote time to the project, including extended stays at Peking University and Tsinghua University. The Directorate-General for External Relations (DG Relex) and the Directorate-General for External Trade (DG Trade) were unfailingly helpful in discussions. Periodic discussions at the Ministry of Commerce (Mofcom) and contacts with the Ministry of Foreign Affairs of the People's Republic of China in Beijing contributed a great deal to the book. I wish to thank all the officials from the European Commission and from the Chinese Ministry of Commerce and Ministry of Foreign Affairs who contributed to the making of this book. I do not include all their names here, but I hope they will accept this recognition of their help.

Inter-institutional cooperation constitutes an important part of EU–China relations. The book not only testifies to this cooperation; it has also benefited from it. In addition to discussions with staff of several EU–China programmes, I have had the pleasure of participating directly in several major programmes concerned with higher and professional education, especially the development of European studies in China, including Hong Kong Special Administrative Region and Macao Special Administrative Region. In 1997, the University of Hong Kong invited me as Distinguished Visiting Professor at their Law Faculty. This visit enabled me to give lectures on European law at most if not all of the universities in Hong Kong, as well as several in mainland China. I am grateful to the Law Faculty of the University of Hong Kong for their generosity and support and to my hosts in several Chinese universities and research institutes, including the Guangdong Academy of Social Sciences. Since 1997 I have been actively involved in the development of European studies, especially of EU law, not only in mainland China but in Macao, both at the Institute of European Studies of Macau (IEEM) and at the University of Macau. My thanks to them for enabling me to contribute to European studies in Macau and to the EU–Macau Cooperation Programme in the Legal Field. In 1998, I was the first high-level Robert Schuman Professor under the EU–China Higher Education Cooperation Programme. I am indebted to the Programme, its Directors and also to my host institution, the Chinese Academy of Social Sciences, Beijing, and especially to Zhou Hong, the Director of the CASS Institute of European Studies. From 2000 to 2004 I served on the Programme Advisory Group of the EU–China Legal and Judicial Cooperation Programme. My responsibility concerned pedagogical matters and helping to select Chinese judges and prosecutors for training in the EU. Apart from meetings and seminars in Europe, I visited Beijing for interviews and seminars on numerous occasions. I am grateful to the Programme, including the British Council, the lead contractor, and to Stephen Forbes, the European Director, and Ni Jing, the Chinese Co-Director, for their help and support. Most recently, the EU–China European Studies Centres Programme from 2005 to 2007 has contributed greatly to my knowledge of EU–China relations. In this framework, I acted as coordinator for EU partners (LSE, CERIC) in consortia led by Peking University and by the University of Wuhan, respectively, and served on several occasions as Visiting Professor at the Centre for European Studies and the Law School at Peking University. The EU–China European Studies Centres Programme Office in Beijing also invited me to give a short training course on research methods and teaching methodology in EU law to teachers of EU law from all over China; I express my thanks to the Programme directors and the participants.

Financial support for the project came from the European Commission Jean Monnet Programme in the form of a Jean Monnet Chair, the London School of Economics and the LSE Law Department, and the China Scholarship Council. The China Scholarship Council kindly awarded me a Chinese Culture Research Fellowship in 2006–2007. I am very grateful to Chang Quansheng of the Education Section, Embassy of the People's Republic of China in the United Kingdom, and Wang Chenguang, Dean of Tsinghua Law School, my host institution for the Fellowship, for their kindness and support. The book would have taken considerably longer without their help.

For their patience, understanding and efficiency, I owe a great debt to Richard Hart, Rachel Turner, Mel Hamill and their colleagues at Hart Publishing in Oxford.

This is not my first book to appear under the Hart imprint, and every time I have been impressed and delighted with the spirit of cooperation between publisher and author which characterises Richard Hart and his colleagues.

My son, Jasper, made numerous contributions to this book, for which I am very grateful.

Most of all, I owe an enormous debt of gratitude to my wife, Anne-Lise, for her support, understanding, tolerance and music during the preparation of this book. The final stages in writing any book are intense, sometimes exhilarating, and sometimes difficult; and now we can rejoice in the fact that life, a process even larger than EU–China relations, continues.

Finally, I am very grateful to my students, past and present, in Europe and China, who have helped me to learn about EU–China relations and to whom this book is dedicated.

Despite the generous help of many friends and colleagues, and the support of numerous institutions, all responsibility for any shortcomings in the conception and organisation of this book, the selection and presentation of documents and the commentary is my own. All suggestions for improvement are welcome.

Francis Snyder
Aix-en-Provence
London
Beijing
19 February 2008

# Contents

# List of Abbreviations

| | |
|---|---|
| Bartke (1973) | W Bartke, *Agreements of the People's Republic of China with Other Countries, 1969–1972* (Hamburg, Institüt für Asienkunde, 1973) |
| Bartke (1992) | W Bartke, *The Agreements of the People's Republic of China with Foreign Countries, 1949–1990* (Munich, KG Sauer Verlag for the Institute of Asian Affairs, Hamburg, 2nd revised and enlarged edition, 1992) |
| C | Chinese language |
| Chiu | H Chiu, *Agreements of the People's Republic of China: A Calendar of Events, 1966–1980* (New York, Praeger Publishers, 1981) |
| DS | Dokumentensammlung (Collection of Documents: Chung-hua jen-min kung-ho-kuo tui-wai kuan-hai wen chien-chi, with reference to Verträge des Volksrepublic China, Institut für Asienkunde, Hamburg |
| E | English language |
| FBIS | Foreign Broadcast Information Service (Washington, DC) |
| HPCh | Handbook on People's China, Beijing |
| JMJP | Jen-min jih-pao (People's Daily, Peking [Beijing] |
| Johnston and Chiu | DM Johnston and H Chiu, *Agreements of the People's Republic of China, 1949–1967: A Calendar* (Cambridge, MA, Harvard University Press, 1968 |
| NCNA | New China News Agency, Beijing |
| NCNA Peking | New China (Hsin-hua) New Agency (English language service), Daily news release (Peking) |
| PR | *Peking Review;* since 1 January 1979, renamed *Beijing Review* (see Chiu, viii) |
| SCMP | Survey China Mainland Press (US Consulate, Hong Kong) |
| V | Verträge des Volksrepublik China, Institut für Asienkunde, Hamburg |

# List of Tables

# List of Documents

# Introduction

This book is a comprehensive reference work of basic documents and commentary about relations between the European Union (EU) and the People's Republic of China (PRC, China) from 1949 to the beginning of 2008. Many of the current EU Member States have long had diplomatic and commercial relations with China, even leaving aside the extensive pre-twentieth-century history of relations between China and Europe. Diplomatic relations between the European Economic Community (EEC) and China started in 1975. Subsequently, these relations expanded as part of the EEC's common commercial policy and China's economic reforms. Since the opening-up of China in 1979, relations between the EU and China have developed apace, especially after the establishment of the EU in 1992 and China's accession to membership of the World Trade Organization (WTO) in 2001. Today the EU and China are 'strategic partners', with a very broad-based relationship, extending far beyond trade to encompass a growing number of important economic, political, social and cultural domains. The relationship is certain to gain in importance with increasing globalisation— especially foreign investment and financial interdependence, EU expansion, the re-emergence and development of China, Chinese membership of WTO, and changes in the international trading system and international politics. Through an extensive range of documents, the book bears witness to these developments. It provides a solid foundation for teaching, research, policy-making and advising on EU–China relations today and in the future.

Until now, basic documents on EU–China relations have been scattered among many sources and have not been readily available, even to the specialist. This is so despite the excellent websites of the EU, especially the European Commission, and of the PRC, notably the Ministry of Foreign Affairs and the Ministry of Commerce. This book is designed to fill the gap. Its principal aim is to provide a book of basic documents and commentary on EU–China relations, both bilateral and within the multilateral legal framework of the WTO. It contains most, if not all, significant official and unofficial documents in English and Chinese about bilateral EU–China relations since the founding of the PRC in 1949. It includes published and previously unpublished documents in English and documents previously available only in Chinese, French or Portuguese; the latter have been translated into English. The commentary introduces the documents briefly and sets them in a wide context. Special effort has been made to achieve a balanced presentation of both EU and Chinese documents and viewpoints, so far as possible in a book based mainly on official documents. The book does not include the text of EU or Chinese legislation, though footnotes refer to some of the most important relevant EC or EU acts. This book is therefore not a general textbook on EU–China relations, even though as a collection of basic documents with associated commentary it serves as a useful basis for such a work.[1] Selective references are given in the footnotes, but the text does not give exhaustive references to relevant secondary literature. This literature is vast, and much is readily available on the Internet or in numerous secondary sources.

The book is organised roughly according to the chronological development of EU–China relations. Within this chronological framework, the chapters are organised according to different types of policy instruments. This criterion is more useful and more easily comprehensible than a strictly legal criterion would be; in any event, legal characteristics, such as the name of a document or the distinction between legally binding and non-legally binding documents, emerge clearly from the chapter titles. The criterion used here has several advantages. It reflects most closely the perspectives of the two parties, the EU and China. It also emphasises the coherence of relatively discrete policy areas, despite differences in the nomenclature of policy instruments used in a specific area. Finally, it facilitates the task of the reader in locating documents concerning a specific subject matter or area of policy, thus making the book easier to read or consult.

Each chapter begins with a brief introduction explaining its purpose, scope and contents. The introduction to the chapter sets the documents in a broader context. Each chapter then gives a list of the basic documents in tabular form, with full references to the documents and related material. The full texts of the most important documents, so far as possible, are included in the chapter. Not all documents listed in a table, however, are given in full text. These include some documents with very long, technical annexes because, despite their legal, political or economic significance, such documents would make the book far too long and, in any event, they can be found elsewhere, in libraries or on the Internet. In addition, other documents that are technical amendments of a basic document but do not alter the basic text are also not given in full. A few primary documents are not available to the public; this is noted in the text, and another document on the same topic is included in the text instead. I have aimed to provide complete references to all documents where possible, so that interested readers can locate the documents for themselves if they are not included in complete form here.

[1] Currently there is no comprehensive study of EU–China relations from 1949 to the present, taking into account both European and Chinese perspectives. In English, for European studies of specific periods, see H Kapur, *Distant Neighbours: China and Europe* (London, Pinter Publishers, 1990) [1949–1989]; H Kapur, *China and the European Economic Community: The New Connection* (Dordrecht, Martinus Nijhoff, 1986) [1957–early 1980s]; D Shambaugh (ed), *China and Europe: 1949–1995* (Contemporary China Institute, School of Oriental and African Studies, University of London, Research Notes and Studies, vol 11, 1996) [brief overview of the period from 1949–1995]; RL Edmonds (ed), *China and Europe since 1978: A European Perspective*, published as *The China Quarterly Special Issues New Series*, vol 2 (Cambridge, Cambridge University Press, 2002) [political and economic relations between Europe and China 1978–2000]. An assessment of American, European and Japanese scholarship on Chinese economy, politics and foreign and security policies may be found in R Ash, D Shambaugh and S Takagi (eds), *China Watching: Perspectives from Europe, Japan and the United States* (London, Routledge, 2007). Reviews of China–Europe relations including contributions by Chinese as well as European and American scholars are S Crossick and E Reuter (eds), *China-EU: A Common Future* (Singapore, World Scientific, 2007) and D Shambaugh, E Sandschneider and H Zhou (eds), *China–Europe Relations: Perspectives, Policies and Prospects* (London, Routledge, 2008). For a Chinese perspective (in English) on the period 1949–2001, see X Chen, 'From Political Alliance in China's Conception to Comprehensive Partnership in Building: The Relations between China and the European Community/European Union' (Dissertation, Universität Tübingen, 2003). For a recent review see J Men, 'Chinese Perceptions of the European Union' (2006) 12 *European Law Journal* 788. See also (2007) 13(6) *European Law Journal*, special issue on 'The European Union, India and China'.

Chapter 1 concerns the period from the founding of the People's Republic of China in 1949 to the establishment of diplomatic relations between the EEC and China in 1975. It consists of documents on the establishment of diplomatic relations by individual European countries with China.

Chapter 2 focuses on the development since 1975 of the bilateral legal framework for EU–China relations concerning trade in general and trade in textiles in particular. All trade and textiles agreements between the EU and China are grouped in a single chapter partly because these agreements are interrelated and partly for ease of reference. As of the time of writing, the 1985 Trade and Economic Cooperation Agreement between the European Economic Community (EEC; now the European Community, EC) and the People's Republic of China constitutes the bilateral legal framework for EU–China relations. Currently, however, the EU and China are negotiating a new agreement.

Chapter 3 traces the development of the general policy framework for EU–China relations, starting with the first ever policy document (issued by the EU) on the subject in 1995 and ending with the most recent documents available at the time of writing. It presents EU and Chinese policy documents and selected speeches by Chinese leaders about EU–China relations from 1995 until 2007.[2] It enables the reader to trace the evolution of EU and Chinese policies about EU–China relations up to the present.

Within the legal framework of the 1985 bilateral agreement, and within the political framework of the series of policy papers, the EU and China have used several institutional forms to develop their relationship and to expand the range of fields of cooperation. Chapters 4 and 5 concern policy instruments which for the most part are in the form of 'soft law', in the sense of documents which in principle are not legally binding but which nevertheless may have practical and even legal effects.[3] Chapter 6 concentrates on legally binding bilateral agreements in areas other than trade or textiles.

Chapter 4 focuses on a group of policy instruments and institutions which often are known collectively as political dialogues. The group comprises summit meetings and policy dialogues. The former include annual summits from the first summit in 1998 up to the tenth summit in 2007. The latter are concerned with general policies, notably human rights and arms, which cut across EU–China relations as a whole. They are frequently called 'informal' mechanisms, because they are usually not consecrated in legal form or legally binding. However, they are highly institutionalised as important parts of the EU–China relationship today; it is necessary to emphasise the word 'today' because instruments concerning such highly controversial topics as human rights or arms can change.

Chapter 5 deals with another group of soft law policy instruments, namely sectoral dialogues, joint declarations and memoranda of understanding (MOUs). These

[2] Speeches by EU Commissioners or other EU officials are on the whole not included. In the EU, policy papers are the main expression of general policy, whereas in China there is only one policy paper on the EU. Speeches by leaders are (and remain) relatively more important expressions of policy in China than in the EU. These differences in the expression of policy reflect differences in political and administrative organisation in the EU and China.

[3] For this definition, see F Snyder, 'The Effectiveness of European Community Law: Institutions, Processes, Tools and Techniques' (1993) 56 *The Modern Law Review* 19, 32.

instruments are 'vertical' instruments limited to specific economic sectors or sub-sectors or particular areas of social policy, in contrast to the general 'horizontal' political dialogues, the impact of which cuts across all EU–China relations. In other words, sectoral dialogues are instruments of economic and social regulation. Sometimes specific instruments, such as dialogues, joint declarations or MOUs, overlap or are intertwined. As with political dialogues, they are not legally binding in themselves but nonetheless may have practical and even legal effects. These policy instruments form the core of a very wide range of EU–China relations today.

Chapter 6 concerns bilateral agreements between the EU and China between 1999 and the present, except for agreements concerning trade and textiles. These agreements represent a 'second generation' of bilateral agreements between the EU and China, as they extend EU–China relations beyond the long extent fields of trade and textiles into maritime transport, customs cooperation, tourist groups, science and technology, space satellites and nuclear fusion. In contrast to the documents discussed in Chapters 4 and 5, the agreements that are the subject of Chapter 6 are legally binding.

Chapter 7 concerns the very wide range of cooperation projects by means of which the EU and China have expanded and deepened their relationship in recent years. It also shows that the EU Member States continue to play a very important role in European relations with China.

Chapter 8 treats EU relations with Hong Kong and Macao. Hong Kong and Macao are special administrative regions within the Chinese 'one country, two systems' arrangement. Each has responsibility for its external trade. Each is separately a member of the WTO. This chapter presents policy papers and bilateral agreements concerning these two special administrative regions of the PRC.

Chapter 9 presents documents on EU–China relations within the framework of the WTO. Since Chinese accession in 2001, the WTO has provided the multilateral legal framework for EU–China relations in many fields. The EU and China cooperate within other international organisations, such as the United Nations and its subsidiary bodies, or international standardisation organisations. However, the WTO is of special significance in EU–China relations because of the overwhelming importance of trade in the development of relations between the EU and China.

In their relations, the EU and China have tended to focus on different themes at different periods of time. The organisation of the book conveys both the chronological development and the dramatic expansion of EU–China relations from 1949 to the present. The structure of the book should allow the reader to see at a glance, in general terms, how EU–China relations have developed over that period. To recap, these relations started with the establishment of diplomatic relations between individual European countries and China. Then the European Economic Community (EEC, now the EC) and China concluded bilateral agreements on trade, especially trade in textiles. Subsequently a series of policy papers set a framework for broader relations. On the EU side, the European Commission prepared communications to the Council of the European Union (formerly the Council of Ministers) and the European Parliament. On the Chinese side, a policy paper in 2003, together with several speeches by Chinese leaders, were the principal expression of policies toward the EU.

Within this evolving framework, the EU and China concluded a series of bilateral agreements on an increasing variety of topics, going far beyond trade. They also agreed on more informal arrangements, more political than legal but sometimes with legal consequences, on an extremely broad range of subjects. Together with policy papers, the summits and other political dialogues, memoranda of understanding, sectoral dialogues and joint declarations provided a framework for, contributed to and stimulated a large number of cooperation projects. Relations between the EU and China were not limited to mainland China; they also concerned the special administrative regions of Hong Kong and Macao and, so far as the General Agreement on Tariffs and Trade (GATT) is concerned, Taiwan. Before and after the accession of the People's Republic of China to the WTO in 2001, the EU and China concluded bilateral agreements in the shadow of WTO law. Currently, at the time of writing, the EU and China are negotiating a new bilateral legal framework for their relationship, taking account of the development of EU–China relations since 1949 as well as their shared membership of the WTO.[4]

For the present purposes, 'China' includes both mainland China and the special administrative regions of Hong Kong and Macao; only one document concerns Taiwan, and this deals with the inclusion of Taiwan in the GATT as the separate customs territory of Taiwan, Penghu, Kinmen and Matsu. 'European Union' refers to the European Communities established in the 1950s, as well as to the European Union created in 1992. The European Communities include the European Coal and Steel Community (ECSC, now absorbed into the European Community, or EC), established by the 1951 Treaty of Paris; the European Economic Community (EEC, now called the EC), established by the 1957 Treaty of Rome; and the European Atomic Energy Community (EAEC, or Euratom), established by another 1957 Treaty of Rome. The European Union was established as a legal entity only by the Maastricht Treaty on European Union in 1992. It was based on the three European Communities existing at the time together with other forms of cooperation established by the Treaty. The subsequent Treaty of Amsterdam and Treaty of Nice retained this basic structure. From the legal standpoint, most, albeit not all, of the documents in the book concern the EC. At the time of writing (February 2008), foreign economic relations lie within the legal competence of the EC, not the EU. The EU currently lacks the legal personality required to enter into legally binding agreements, though the European Commission, in the name of the EU, has issued numerous policy papers and has established a wide variety of informal dialogues with China. In most areas of foreign trade, the EC has exclusive legal competence; in some policy fields, the EC shares competence with the EC Member States. The Treaty of Lisbon, still to be ratified, replaces the EC with the EU. The EU will have legal personality. It will also have exclusive competence in all matters of foreign trade, though not in all matters concerning economic cooperation. The Treaty of Lisbon thus will be taken into account in the current EU–China negotiations for a new bilateral agreement and will help to shape EU–China relations in the future.

[4] The European Community and its Member States separately are founding members of the WTO. Lacking legal personality and competence in the field of international trade until the Treaty of Lisbon, which at the time of writing is still to be ratified, the EU is not a WTO member. The People's Republic of China has been a WTO member since 11 December 2001.

# 1

# Diplomatic Relations, 1949–1975: From New China and New Europe to Diplomatic Relations between China and the EEC

## INTRODUCTION

The People's Republic of China, or 'New China' (hereafter China or PRC), was founded on 1 October 1949. Seven months later, the declaration by French Foreign Minister Robert Schuman on 9 May 1950 initiated the 'New Europe' as a process of legal, economic, social and political integration.[1] Twenty-five years later, in 1975, China and the European Economic Community (EEC) established diplomatic relations, after the start of the EEC's common commercial policy and following the normalisation of relations between China and the USA. During the decades between 1949 and 1975, however, numerous Western European countries, both current and future Member States of the EEC, established diplomatic (and other) relations with China. This chapter presents basic documents concerning the diplomatic relations between these Western European countries and China from 1949 to 1975.[2]

[1] The Schuman Declaration led to the 1951 Treaty of Paris establishing the European Coal and Steel Community, followed by two 1957 Treaties of Rome establishing the European Economic Community and the European Atomic Energy Community, respectively, and culminating later in the 1992 Maastricht Treaty on European Union, as amended so far by the Treaties of Amsterdam (1997) and Nice (2001) and, still to come at the time of writing, the Treaty of Lisbon.

[2] In constructing a comprehensive list of basic documents on diplomatic relations between European countries and China for this period, I have relied on two groups of indexes of documents. One group, the most comprehensive in its references to sources, is the product of research at Harvard Law School. It consists of DM Johnston and H Chiu, *Harvard Studies in East Asian Law, vol 3. Agreements of the People's Republic of China, 1949–1967: A Calendar* (Cambridge, MA, Harvard University Press, 1968) and the follow-up volume, H Chiu, *Agreements of the People's Republic of China: A Calendar of Events, 1966–1980* (New York, Praeger Publishers, 1981). The other group of sources, the fruit of research at the Institüt für Asienkunde Hamburg, includes W Bartke, *Agreements of the People's Republic of China with Other Countries, 1969–1972* (Hamburg, Institüt für Asienkunde, 1973) and W Bartke, *The Agreements of the People's Republic of China with Foreign Countries, 1949–1990* (Munich, KG Sauer Verlag for the Institute of Asian Affairs, Hamburg, 2nd revised and enlarged edn, 1992). These sources are calendars or lists of agreements. They do not contain the full text of any agreements. For the full texts of various documents, I are indebted to the British Library of Political and Economic Science at the London School of Economics and the University of Leeds Brotherton Library holdings of series of news, news analysis and translation on China since 1949. I am especially grateful to Ms Xiyi Huang, Faculty Team Library, Brotherton Library, University of Leeds.

The chapter includes documents on the establishment and development of diplomatic relations between China and the 27 current Member States of the European Union. Diplomatic relations were usually concluded by a joint communiqué. Often the full text of such agreements is simply not available in publicly printed form. Writing in 1973, Bartke noted that

> [t]he People's Republic of China's former habit of publishing the full text of the agreements was discontinued almost a decade ago. What can be found in Chinese and other authentic sources is substantially only the heading of the agreements.[3]

The thorough index by Johnston and Chiu does not even list

> strictly diplomatic agreements—such as agreements to establish diplomatic relations, to exchange ambassadors, and to raise missions to the status of embassies.[4]

Chiu notes that these joint communiqués are

> never signed or issued subject to ratification, so it may be presumed that their entry into force is automatic upon signature or issuance.[5]

As a result, the objective of the chapter is to present such documents as are available outside of diplomatic archives and thus to outline the pattern of establishment of diplomatic relations between European countries and China. Nevertheless, with a few exceptions, it has been possible to locate virtually all relevant documents.

In order to present as comprehensive a picture as possible of EU–China relations, all the current Member States are included. With this in mind, it is useful to briefly trace the history of European integration, so that readers will have clearly in view the entire range of European countries concerned before a more detailed chronological presentation of the establishment of diplomatic relations between specific European countries and China.

More than a year after the founding of the PRC, six Western European countries signed, in Paris on 18 April 1951, the treaty establishing the European Coal and Steel Community (ECSC). 'The Six' comprised France, Germany, Italy, Belgium, Netherlands and Luxembourg. On 25 March 1957, in Rome, the same European countries signed the treaties establishing the European Economic Community (EEC) and the European Atomic Energy Community (EAEC or Euratom). The UK, Denmark and Ireland joined the three Communities as of 1973, followed by Greece in 1979 and Spain and Portugal in 1986. On 7 February 1992, these 12 Member States of the three European Communities, meeting at Maastricht in the Netherlands, signed the Treaty on European Union. This treaty created the European Union (EU), based on the European Communities supplemented by intergovernmental cooperation in the fields of foreign policy and justice and home affairs. In 1995, the EU expanded to encompass Austria, Finland and Sweden. The Maastricht Treaty was amended by the Treaties of Amsterdam (1997) and Nice (2001). The Czech Republic, Cyprus, Estonia, Latvia, Lithuania, Hungary, Malta, Poland, Slovakia and Slovenia joined in 2004. Bulgaria and Romania became Member States of the EU on 1 January 2007. At

[3] Bartke (1973), *ibid*, 5 (Note by the Institute of Asian Affairs).
[4] Johnston and Chiu, above n 2, ix.
[5] Chiu, above n 2, vi–vii.

the time of writing (September 2007), the EU Member States have agreed but not yet ratified the Treaty of Lisbon, amending the Nice Treaty.

The establishment of diplomatic relations between these Western European countries and China occurred in several waves.[6] We can distinguish four generations: the first generation in 1949, immediately following the establishment of the PRC; a second generation in the early 1950s; a third generation during the period between the end of the Korean War until the Cultural Revolution (1954–1964); and a fourth generation just before and in the years following the normalisation of relations between the USA and China (1970–1979).

## FIRST GENERATION, 1949

Immediately following the foundation of the PRC in 1949, countries which then were part of the USSR or the Soviet bloc concluded diplomatic relations with China. Table 1 shows this first generation of diplomatic relations.

These countries, now EU Member States, included the Baltic countries of Estonia, Latvia and Lithuania as then part of the former USSR (see Document 1.1). The first generation also included other countries of the Soviet bloc, namely Bulgaria (see Document 1.2), Romania (see Document 1.3), Czechoslovakia (now the Czech Republic and Slovakia; see Document 1.4), Hungary (see Document 1.5), Poland (see Document 1.6), the German Democratic Republic (see Document 1.7) and Romania (see Document 1.7). In addition, it included Slovenia (document not available), which then was part of the Socialist Federal Republic of Yugoslavia.

These documents emphasise the successful struggle for liberation by the Central People's Government as represented in the establishment of the PRC, its claimed mandate as the expression of the overwhelming majority of the Chinese people and the contribution which diplomatic relations could make to the success of a democratic, peaceful and socialist bloc. During this period, as subsequently, the establishment of diplomatic relations often provided a basis for the conclusion of other agreements, though some countries also concluded agreements with China before establishing diplomatic relations.[7]

### Document 1.1: Establishment of Diplomatic Relations between the USSR, including Estonia, Latvia and Lithuania, and China, 1949

**USSR**[8]

People's Daily 4th October 1949 p1

[6] On the development of Chinese foreign policy, see Wang Jisi, 'International Relations Theory and the Study of Chinese Foreign Policy: A Chinese Perspective', in TW Robinson and D Shambaugh (eds), *Chinese Foreign Policy: Theory and Practice* (Oxford, Clarendon Press, 1994) 481.

[7] Compare Johnston and Chiu with Chiu, above n 2.

[8] Translated from Chinese.

**Table 1.1: The First Generation of Diplomatic Relations between European Countries and China, 1949**

| Date of signing or issue | Country | Effective date[a] | Place of signature or issuance[b] | Instrument | Subject matter[c] | Source: Bartke[d] | Source: Chiu[e] | Source of document published in this book |
|---|---|---|---|---|---|---|---|---|
| 3.10.1949 | Estonia [as part of USSR] | | | Communiqué | | Bartke, pp 163, 172 give: DS1,p 5f (V5 p 353f) | | USSR-PRC text in *People's Daily*, 4 October 1949, p 1 |
| 3.10.1949 | Latvia [as part of USSR* | | | Communiqué | | Bartke, pp 163,172 give: DS1 p 5f (V5 p 353f) | | USSR-PRC text in *People's Daily*, 4 October 1949, p 1 |
| 3.10.1949 | Lithuania [as part of USSR] - see also next row | | | Communiqué | | Bartke, pp 163, 172 give: DS1,p 5f (V5 p 353f) | | USSR-PRC text in *People's Daily*, 4 October 1949, p 1 |
| 14.9.1991 | Lithuania | | Vilnius | Joint communiqué | Establishment of diplomatic relations | | | *Summary of World Broadcasts (SWB)*, FE/1178 A2/1, 16 September 1991 |
| 4.10.1949 | Bulgaria | | ** | Communiqué | | Bartke pp 21, 24 give: DS1, pp 6–7 | | *People's Daily*, 5 October 1949, p 1 (translated from Chinese by Yin Xiao) |
| 5.10.1949 | Romania | | | News report | | Bartke, pp 154, 158 give: DS1, p 7f (V5 p 321f) | | *People's Daily*, 6 October 1949, p 1 (translated from Chinese by Yin Xiao) |

**Table 1.1: continued**

| Date of signing or issue | Country | Effective date[a] | Place of signature or issuance[b] | Instrument | Subject matter[c] | Source: Bartke[d] | Source: Chiu[e] | Source of document published in this book |
|---|---|---|---|---|---|---|---|---|
| 6.10.1949 | Czech Republic [as Czechoslovakia | | | Communiqué | | Bartke, pp 38,42 give: DS1, pp 10–11 (V5, pp 471–2) | | *People's Daily,* 8 October 1949, p 1 (translated from Chinese by Yin Xiao) |
| 6.10.1949 | Hungary | | | Communiqué | | Bartke, pp 78, 82 give: DS1 p 8f (V5, p 520f) | | *People's Daily,* 8 October 1949, p 1 (translated from Chinese by Yin Xiao) |
| 6.10.1949 | Slovakia: as Czechoslovakia | | | Communiqué | | Bartke, pp 38,42 give: DS1, pp 10–11 (V5, pp 471–2) | | *People's Daily,* 8 October 1949, p 1 (translated from Chinese by Yin Xiao) |
| 7.10.1949 | Poland | | | Communiqué | | Bartke, pp 146, 152 give: DS1 p 11f (V5 p 282f) | | *People's Daily,* 8 October 1949, p 1 (translated from Chinese by Yin Xiao) |
| 27.10.1949 | Germany as DDR (GDR) | | | Exchange of notes | | Bartke,pp 58,63 give: DS1, pp 14–15 (V5 pp 96–7) | | *People's Daily,* 3 November 1949, p 1 (translated from Chinese by Yin Xiao) |
| | Slovenia [as part of SFRY] | | | | | | | |

**Table 1.1: footnotes**

Abbreviations for English-language sources: FBIS, Foreign Broadcast Information Service, Washington, DC; PR, used by Chiu to indicate source of documents but not mentioned in his list of abbreviations; perhaps it means: JPRS, Joint Publications Research Service, Washington, DC; SCMP, Survey China Mainland Press, US Consultate, Hong Kong.

[a]Effective date presumed to be same as date of signing unless otherwise noted.

[b]Unknown unless otherwise indicated.

[c]Establishment of diplomatic relations unless otherwise noted.

[d]Above n 2.

[e]Chiu, above n 2, p viii states 'Where the full text is available at the source, an initial (in parentheses indicates the language in which the text is given . . . References not followed by an initial indicate that the information given at the source is limited. In many of these cases there is little to be learned by consulting the sources beyond what is already provided in the calendar entry'.

Government of USSR Officially Recognizes PRC
Decided to Establish Diplomatic Relations with PRC and to Exchange Ambassadors
Minister Zhou Cables Reply to Gromyko Expressing Warm Welcome

*Xinhua News Agency Beijing 3rd October*

After Foreign Minister of the Central Government of the People's Republic of China Zhou En-lai sent the Proclamation of Chairman Mao Ze-dong in the form of official letter to the governments of foreign countries in the afternoon of 1st October, the Government of the Soviet Union has received the Proclamation and on 2nd October at 21:45 hours wired a Note signed by Gromyko to Foreign Minister Zhou En-lai, stating that the Government of the Soviet Union has decided to establish diplomatic relations between the two countries and to exchange ambassadors. Gromyko's Note says:

Beijing the Central Government of the People's Republic of China
Foreign Minister Mr. Zhou En-Lai:

The Government of the Union of Soviet Socialist Republics has received the Proclamation issued by the Central People's Government of China dated on 1st October, with the proposal of establishing diplomatic relations between the People's Republic of China and the Soviet Union. The Government of the Soviet Union, after examining the proposal of the Central People's Government of China, based on the consistent wish to establish truly friendly relations with the Chinese people, and the confidence that the Central People's Government of China represents the will of the overwhelming majority of the Chinese people, hereby notifies Your Excellency: the Government of Soviet Union decides to establish diplomatic relations between the Soviet Union and the People's Republic of China and to exchange ambassadors.

Andrei Gromyko
Vice Foreign Minister of the Soviet Union
Entrusted by the Government of the Soviet Union
2nd October 1949 21:45

*Xinhua News Agency Beijing 3rd October*

Foreign Minister of the People's Republic of China Zhou En-lai cables Moscow a reply in a Note to Vice Foreign Minister of the Soviet Union Gromyko today, expressing warm welcome the immediate establishment of diplomatic relations between the two big countries of China and the USSR and the exchange of ambassadors. Minister Zhou's cable reads:

Moscow the Union of Soviet Socialist Republics
Vice Foreign Minister Mr. Andrei Gromyko:

I, on behalf of the Central People's Government of the People's Republic of China, have the honor of having received Your Excellency's cable dated 2nd October notifying the decision of the Government of the Soviet Union to establish diplomatic relations between the Soviet Union and the People's Republic of China. The Central People's Government of the People's Republic of China has strong confidence in the deep friendliness that the Government of the Soviet Union has for the Chinese people. The Chinese Government and the Chinese people are infinitely elated today as the USSR is the first friendly country who recognizes the People's Republic of China. I notify Your Excellency hereby that: The Central People's Government of the People's Republic of China warmly welcomes immediate establishment of diplomatic relations between the People's Republic of China and the Soviet Union and exchange of ambassadors.

Zhou En-lai
Foreign Minister
Central People's Government of the People's Republic of China
Beijing, 3rd October 1949

## Document 1.2: Establishment of Diplomatic Relations between Bulgaria and China, 1949

**BULGARIA**[9]

People's Daily 5th October 1949 pl

Government of Bulgaria Accepts Chairman Mao's Proclamation Wish to Establish Diplomatic Relations with PRC Minister Zhou Cables Reply Stating Warm Welcome

*Xinhua News Agency, Beijing 4th October*

Foreign Ministry of the People's Republic of China Zhou En-lai received today a note from the Foreign Minister of the People's Republic of Bulgaria Boptomov. He, in reply to the Official Letter of our Foreign Minister, Zhou En-lai dated 1st October, states the wish to establish diplomatic relations with the People's Republic of China and to exchange diplomatic representatives. The full text of the note is as follows:

Beijing the Central Government of the People's Republic of China
Foreign Minister Mr. Zhou En-Lai:

This telegram hereby confirms that The Government of the People's Republic of Bulgaria has received the Proclamation issued by the Central People's Government of the People's Republic of China dated on 1st October. The Bulgarian Government, after examining the proposal of the Central People's Government of the People's Republic of China concerning the establishment of diplomatic relations with foreign countries, based on the wish of the Bulgarian people, and the belief that the struggle and success of the Chinese People is shared by the advanced and peace-loving forces of the whole world, and the confidence that the Central People's Government of China represents the will of all Chinese people, hereby decides to establish diplomatic relations between the People's Republic of Bulgaria and the People's Republic of China and to exchange diplomatic representatives.

Vladimir Boptomov
Foreign Minister
People's Republic of Bulgaria
Sofia, 3rd October 1949

[9] Translated from Chinese.

*Xinhua News Agency Beijing 4 October*

Foreign Minister of the Central People's Government of the People's Republic of China Zhou En-Lai cables a reply in a note today to the Foreign Minister of the People's Republic of Bulgaria, Boptomov, to warmly welcome the establishment of Sino-Bulgarian diplomatic relations. The full text of the note is as follows:

Sofia the People's Republic of Bulgaria
Foreign Minister Mr. Vladimir Boptomov:

I, on behalf of the Central People's Government of the People's Republic of China, have the honour of having received Your Excellency's cable, dated 3rd October, notifying the decision of the Government of the People's Republic of Bulgaria to establish diplomatic relations between the People's Republic of Bulgaria and the People's Republic of China and to exchange diplomatic representatives. I notify your Excellency that: The Central People's Government of the People's Republic of China warmly welcomes and immediately establishes diplomatic relations between the People's Republic of China and the People's Republic of Bulgaria and exchanges diplomatic representatives.

Zhou En-lai
Foreign Minister
Central People's Government of the People's Republic of China
Beijing, 4th October 1949

## Document 1.3: Establishment of Diplomatic Relations between Romania and China, 1949

**ROMANIA**[10]

People's Daily 6th October 1949 p1

**China and Romania Establish Diplomatic Relations**
Romania Sends Note to PRC, Minister Zhou Cables Reply Stating Warm Welcome

*Xinhua News Agency, Beijing 5 October*

Foreign Minister of the People's Republic of China Zhou En-lai received today a note from the Foreign Minister of the People's Republic of Romania, Ana Boke, dated 3rd October, notifying the decision of the People's Republic of Romania to establish diplomatic relations with the People's Republic of China. The full text of the note is as follows:

Beijing Foreign Ministry of the Central Government of the People's Republic of China
Foreign Minister Zhou En-Lai:

The Government of the People's Republic of Romania and the Romania people have been taking note with welcome of the proclamation of the founding of the People's Republic of China and the election of the Central People's Government headed by Mao Ze-dong. The Government of the People's Republic of Romania, after examining the proposal contained in the Proclamation of the Central People's Government of China, dated 1st October, has decided to establish diplomatic relations between the People's

[10] Translated from Chinese.

Republic of Romania and the People's Republic of China. We firmly believe that the relations will make special contribution to the consolidation of the democratic, peaceful and socialist bloc, led by our common great friend the Soviet Union and to its undertakings of fights against imperialism and for peace, national independence and democracy.

Ana Boke
Foreign Minister
People's Republic of Romania
Bucharest, 3rd October 1949

*Xinhua News Agency Beijing 5th October*

Foreign Minister of the Central People's Government of the People's Republic of China Zhou En-Lai cables a reply in a Note today to Foreign Minister of the People's Republic of Romania Ana Boke, to warmly welcome the establishment of Sino-Romanian diplomatic relations. The full text of the Note is as follows:

Bucharest Foreign Ministry of the People's Republic of Romania
Minister Ana Boke:

I, on behalf of the Central People's Government of the People's Republic of China, have the honour of having received Your Excellency's cable, dated 3rd October, notifying the decision of the Government of the People's Republic of Romania to establish diplomatic relations between the People's Republic of Romania and the People's Republic of China. I notify Your Excellency hereby, that the Central People's Government of the People's Republic of China warmly welcomes immediate establishment of diplomatic relations between the People's Republic of China and the People's Republic of Romania and decides to exchange diplomatic representatives.

Zhou En-lai
Foreign Minister
Central People's Government of the People's
Republic of China
Beijing, 5th October 1949

## Document 1.4: Establishment of Diplomatic Relations between Czechoslovakia (now Czech Republic and Slovakia) and China, 1949

### CZECHOSLOVAKIA[11]

People's Daily 8th October 1949 p1

*Xinhua News Agency, Beijing 6th October*

Foreign Minister of the People's Republic of China Zhou En-lai today receives a Note from Foreign Minister of the Republic of Czechoslovakia ... dated 5th October, notifying the decision of the Republic of Czechoslovakia to establish diplomatic relations with the People's Republic of China. The full text of the Note is as follows:

Beijing Central People's Government of China
Foreign Minister Mr. Zhou En-Lai:

[11] Translated from Chinese.

The Government of the Republic of Czechoslovakia welcomes with excitement the content of the Proclamation of the Central People's Government of China, which demonstrates the will of the Chinese People, which has been proved in their heroic struggle, and the true establishment of freedom and independence. Based on the common ground of the great ideal of our two great nations, our Government decides to establish diplomatic relations between the Republic of Czechoslovakia and the People's Republic of China.

… …
Vice Premier and Acting Foreign Minister
Cables
On behalf of the Government of the Republic of Czechoslovakia

*Xinhua News Agency Beijing 6th October*

Foreign Minister of the People's Republic of China Zhou En-Lai today sends a reply in a note to the Foreign Minister of the Republic of Czechoslovakia, …, to welcome the establishment of Sino-Czechoslovakian diplomatic relations. The full text of the note is as follows:

Prague Government of the Republic of Czechoslovakia
Acting Foreign Minister Mr. … …:

I, on behalf of the Central People's Government of the People's Republic of China, have the honour of having received Your Excellency's cable dated 5th October. I am greatly pleased to be informed that your Government has decided to establish diplomatic relations between the Republic of Czechoslovakia and the People's Republic of China. I hereby notify Your Excellency that: the Central People's Government of the People's Republic of China warmly welcomes the immediate establishment of diplomatic relations between the People's Republic of China and the Republic of Czechoslovakia and decides to exchange diplomatic representatives.

Zhou En-lai
Foreign Minister
Central People's Government of the People's Republic of China
Beijing, 6th October 1949

## Document 1.5: Establishment of Diplomatic Relations between Hungary and China, 1949

### HUNGARY[12]

People's Daily 8th October 1949 p1

*Xinhua News Agency, Beijing 6' October*

Foreign Ministry of the People's Republic of China Zhou En-lai receives today a Note from Foreign Minister of the People's Republic of Hungary, … …, dated 4th October, notifying

12 Translated from Chinese.

the decision of the People's Republic of Hungary to establish diplomatic relations with the People's Republic of China. The full text of the note is as follows:

Beijing Foreign Minister of the People's Republic of China
Mr. Zhou En-Lai:

The Hungarian people are paying attention, with utmost sympathy, to the Chinese people's heroic struggle for freedom under the leadership of Mao Ze-dong. The achievement of fighting against internal and foreign oppressors by millions of Chinese labourers is glorious. The achievement ensures the freedom and possibility for the people's democratic development, and makes the overwhelming majority of the Chinese people prepare for founding the Central People's Government of the People's Republic of China. The Hungarian people and their Government hold that the founding of the People's Republic of China is a contribution, with historical meanings, to the international peace, and warmly congratulate the new central government of the Chinese people. In the mean time, they consider that the People's Government represents the overwhelming majority of the Chinese people, and is willing to consolidate and enhance the friendship and cooperation of our peoples. The Government of the People's Republic of Hungary, after examining the Proclamation of the Central People's Government of the People's Republic of China, dated 1st October, considers that the Government of the People's Republic of China is the sole legal government of China, and would like to take the opportunity to establish diplomatic relations of our two countries.

… …
Foreign Minister
People' s Republic of Hungary
Budapest, 4th October 1949

*Xinhua News Agency Beijing 6 October*

Foreign Minister of the People's Republic of China Zhou En-Lai today sends a reply in a Note to Foreign Minister of the People's Republic of Hungary … …, to welcome Hungary and China to establish diplomatic relations. The full text of the note is as follows:

Budapest Government of the People's Republic of Hungary Foreign Minister …:

I, on behalf of the Central People's Government of the People's Republic of China, have the honor of having received Your Excellency's cable, dated 4th October, notifying the decision of your Government to establish diplomatic relations between the People's Republic of Hungary and the People's Republic of China. I notify Your Excellency hereby that, the Central People's Government of the People's Republic of China warmly welcomes immediate establishment of diplomatic relations between the People's Republic of China and the People's Republic of Hungary and decides to exchange diplomatic representatives.

Zhou En-lai
Foreign Minister
Central People's Government of the People's
Republic of China
Beijing, 6th October 1949

[13] Translated from Chinese.

## Document 1.6: Establishment of Diplomatic Relations between Poland and China, 1949

### POLAND[13]

People's Daily 8th October 1949 p1

*Xinhua News Agency, Beijing 7th October*

Foreign Ministry of the People's Republic of China Zhou En-lai today receives a Note from Vice Foreign Minister of the Republic of Poland, …, dated 5th October, notifying the decision of the Republic of Poland to establish diplomatic relations with the People's Republic of China. The full text of the note is as follows:

> Beijing Foreign Ministry of the Central People's Government of the People's Republic of China
> Foreign Minister Mr. Zhou En-Lai:
>
> This is to confirm that the Republic of Poland has received the Proclamation of the Central People's Government of China, dated 1st October, and the proposal of establishing diplomatic relations between the People's Republic of China and the Republic of Poland. The position of the Polish Government towards the Chinese people is well-known. The Polish Government consistently shares the same stand with people of all countries for their rights of independence and self-determination. The heroic struggle that has been taken by the Chinese people for decades, in the aim of freedom from the oppression of domestic reactionaries and foreign imperialists, wins limitless sympathy and warm support of the Polish people. This heroic struggle sets an example to encourage all people who love freedom and peace to take the way of struggle.
>
> Mr. Minister, I am delighted that the successful struggle for freedom and democracy of the Chinese people is approaching an end. On behalf of the Government of my country, I notify you [that we] agree to establish diplomatic relations between the Republic of Poland and the People's Republic of China.
>
> I firmly believe that, between the Peoples of our two countries and the Governments of the Republic of Poland and the People's Republic of China, strong friendly links and economic and cultural relations will be established. This will be a great progress in consolidating world peace and all nations' security and prosperity.
>
> Vice Foreign Minister
> People's Republic of Poland
> Signed and issued on behalf of Foreign Minister
> Warsaw, 5th October 1949

*Xinhua News Agency Beijing 7th October*

Foreign Minister of the People's Republic of China Zhou En-Lai today cabled a reply in a note to Vice Foreign Minister of the Republic of Poland, … …, to warmly welcome the establishment of diplomatic relations by the Republic of Poland with China. The full text of the note is as follows:

> Foreign Ministry of the Republic of Poland
> Vice Minister … …:

I, on behalf of the Central People's Government of the People's Republic of China, have the honour of having received Your Excellency's cable dated 5th October and am very pleased to be informed that your Government has decided to establish diplomatic relations between the Republic of Poland and the People's Republic of China. I notify Your Excellency hereby that: the Central People's Government of the People's Republic of China warmly welcomes immediate establishment of diplomatic relations between the People's Republic of China and the Republic of Poland and decides to exchange ambassadors.

Zhou En-lai
Foreign Minister
Central People's Government of the People's Republic of China
Beijing, 7th October 1949

## Document 1.7: Establishment of Diplomatic Relations between the German Democratic Republic and China, 1949

### GERMANY, DEMOCRATIC REPUBLIC[14]

People's Daily 3rd November 1949 p1

German Foreign Minister Replied Minister Zhou En-lai
Welcoming Establishment of Sino-German Diplomatic Relation
Asserting 'It Is Turning Point in History of Relations of Chinese–German Peoples and Will Make Great Contribution to Maintain and Strengthen World Peace'

*Xinhua News Agency Beijing 2nd November*

Minister Zhou of Chinese Foreign Ministry received a reply, cabled by the Foreign Minister of the Democratic Republic of Germany, …, dated 27th October. The cable extended a welcome to Minister Zhou's note, dated 25th October, informing the decision of establishing Sino-German diplomatic relations. …'s reply is as follows:

Foreign Ministry of the People's Republic of China Minister Mr. Zhou En-lai:

On the occasion of the proclamation of the founding of the Democratic Republic of Germany and of the formation of the Provisional Government, we, the Provisional Government of the Republic of Germany, have the great honour to have received your congratulatory cable, and to be informed of the decision of the Central People's Government of the People's Republic of China to establish diplomatic relations with the Democratic Republic of Germany and to exchange diplomatic representatives.

Exactly as mentioned in your cable, the founding of the Democratic Republic of Germany not only accords with the pressing wish of all the German people, but also is welcomed by people who wish for lasting peace around the globe. The Provisional Government of the Democratic Republic of Germany and all German people are very delighted by your cable.

The democratic force of the German people is constantly paying close attention to, and deep sympathy for the great Chinese people in their heroic struggle against home and

[14] Translated from Chinese.

foreign enemies in the aim of winning liberation, and congratulates sincerely the establishment of the diplomatic relations between the two countries and the friendly relations created hereafter with the People's Republic of China.

The victory of battles achieved by the Chinese people in striving for self-liberation has strengthened the confidence of all people who desire integration and independence, and assure their causes of justice, with the support of the peace-loving force of all the people around the world, to an end of victory.

I, on behalf of the Provisional Government of the Democratic Republic of Germany, pledge to you the wish of establishing diplomatic relations between our two countries on the friendly basis of mutual respect and equality. This decision manifests the turning point with decisive meanings in the history of relations of Sino-German peoples. The relations of our two peoples will make an enormous contribution to maintaining and consolidating peace.

…… …

Foreign Minister
Democratic Republic of Germany

## SECOND GENERATION, 1950

In 1950, a second generation of countries, comprising Denmark, Finland and Sweden, established diplomatic relations with China (see Table 1.2). In contrast to the majority of countries in Western Europe, these Scandinavian countries were not involved in the Korean War and did not follow the US policy of non-recognition and containment of China at that time. From the Chinese standpoint, recognition of these European countries, as well as of the countries in the first generation, was part of the policy of 'two camps', one aspect of which was the policy of 'lean to one side', that is choosing to establish relations with some countries rather than others in the divided bipolar Cold War world.[15] In all, 14 of the current 27 EU Member States can trace their diplomatic relations with China back to the early years of the PRC, even though these relations originated, in some cases, from the fact that the current EU Member State was an integral part of the USSR or, in other cases, from the fact that the current Member State then was part of the Soviet bloc: in both instances the establishment of diplomatic relations with China formed part of USSR foreign policy.

The PRC government news agency reported the conclusion of negotiations and the dispatch of ambassadors. The documents regarding the establishment of diplomatic relations by this second generation of countries and China (except for Finland, for which no document appears to be available) are as follows:

[15] See Wang Jisi, above n 6; see also Mao Zedong, 'Is it Right to "Learn to One Side"? (December 8, 1956)' in *Mao Zedong on Diplomacy*, compiled by The Ministry of Foreign Affairs of the People's Republic of China and the Party Literature Research Center under the Central Committee of the Communist Party of China (Beijing, Foreign Languages Press, 1st edn 1998, 2nd printing 2007) 215.

**Table 1.2: The Second Generation of Diplomatic Relations between European Countries and China, 1950**

| Date of signing or issue | Country | Effective date[a] | Place of signature or issuance[b] | Instrument | Subject matter[c] | Source: Bartke[d] | Source: Chiu[e] | Source of document published in this book |
|---|---|---|---|---|---|---|---|---|
| 9.1.1950 | Denmark | | | Exchange of letters | | Bartke pp. 43,44 give: DS1, pp 21–2 | | People's Daily, 9 May 1950 (translated from Chinese by Yin Xiao) |
| 9.5.1950 | Sweden | | | Communiqué | | Bartke, pp 180, 181 give: Handbook on People's China, Beijing | | People's Daily, 9 May 1950, p 1 (translated from Chinese by Yin Xiao) |
| 28.10.1950 | Finland | | | Exchange of notes | | Bartke, p 50 gives: V3, p. 21 | | |

See Table 1.1 for footnotes and abbreviations.

## Document 1.8: Establishment of Diplomatic Relations between Denmark and China, 1950

**DENMARK**[16]

People's Daily 9th May 1950 p1

**China and Denmark Establish Diplomatic Relations**
Exchanges Envoys Geng Biao and …

*Xinhua News Agency 10th May*

The Danish Government, on 9th January of this year, proclaimed the wish to establish diplomatic relations with the People's Republic of China. Minister Zhou En-lai, of the Chinese Foreign Ministry, on 14th January cabled a reply to the Foreign Minister of the Danish Government, …, to express the same wish, and invite the Danish Government to dispatch representatives to Beijing in order to carry out negotiations concerning preliminary and procedural issues of establishing Sino-Danish diplomatic relations. The representative of negotiation, dispatched by the Danish Government … as provisional Charge d'Affairs, arrived in Beijing on 26th February and immediately began the negotiation concerned. Now the negotiation is finished smoothly. The Governments of China and Denmark have reached the following agreement: the Danish Government dispatches … as envoy to the People's Republic of China, and the Central Government of the People's Republic of China dispatches General Geng Biao as envoy of the People's Republic of China to Denmark.

## Document 1.9: Establishment of Diplomatic Relations between Sweden and China, 1950

**SWEDEN**[17]

People's Daily 9th May 1950 p1

**China and Sweden Establish Diplomatic Relations**
Exchanges Ambassadors of Geng Biao and …

*Xinhua News Agency 9th May*

The Swedish Government on 14th January of this year proclaimed the wish to establish diplomatic relations with the People's Republic of China. Minister Zhou En-lai, of the Chinese Foreign Ministry, on 18 January cabled a reply to Minister … … of Foreign Ministry of the Swedish Government to express the same wish, and invite representatives from the Swedish Government to Beijing to carry out negotiations concerning preliminary and procedural issues. The representative of negotiation dispatched by Swedish Government … as provisional charge d'affaires arrived in Beijing on 26th February and immediately began the negotiation concerned. Now the negotiation is finished. The Swedish Government dispatches … as Ambassador to the People's Republic of China, and the Central Government of the People's Republic of China dispatches General Geng Biao as Ambassador of the People's Republic of China to Sweden.

16 Translated from Chinese.
17 Translated from Chinese.

**Table 1.3: The Third Generation of Relations between European Countries and China, 1954–1964**

| Date of signing or issue | Country | Effective date[a] | Place of signature or issuance[b] | Instrument | Subject matter[c] | Source: Bartke[d] | Source: Chiu[e] | Source of document published in this book |
|---|---|---|---|---|---|---|---|---|
| 17.6.1954 | Great Britain | | | Agreement | | Bartke, pp 70, 73 give: DS3 p 107 (V3 p 91) | | |
| 19.11.1954 | Netherlands | | | Exchange of notes | | Bartke, pp 126, 127 give: DS3 p 188 (V3 p 59) | | |
| 15.8.1960 | Cyprus | | | News report | Recognition | Bartke pp. 37, 38 give: JMJP 16.8.1960 | | *People's Daily*, 16 August 1960, p 1 (translated from Chinese by Yin Xiao) |
| 27.1.1964 | France | | | Joint communiqué | | Bartke, pp 51, 57 give: JMJP, 28.1.1964 | | *Beijing Review*, vol. 7, no 5, 31 January 1964, p 10 |

See Table 1.1 for footnotes and abbreviations.

## THIRD GENERATION, 1954–1964

A third generation began after the Korean War and the break in relations between China and the Soviet Union, and ended after the Great Leap Forward and before the Cultural Revolution (see Table 1.3). In 1954 Great Britain (no document available) and the Netherlands (no document available) established diplomatic relations with China on the level of chargé d'affaires. In August 1960, on achieving independence from the UK, Cyprus immediately recognised the PRC (see Document 1.10). In January 1964, as part of President Charles de Gaulle's policy of building a foreign policy independent of the USA, France became the first major Western European power to establish diplomatic relations on the level of exchange of ambassadors with China (see Document 1.11).[18] Hence, in this second period, one country (France) which was then a Member State of the European Communities established diplomatic relations with China, as did three other countries which subsequently became Member States.

### Document 1.10: Diplomatic Recognition of Cyprus by China, 1960

**CYPRUS**[19]

People's Daily 16th August 1960 p1

Premier Zhou and Minister Chen Cable to Congratulate the Founding of Republic of Cyprus

**PRC Acknowledges Republic of Cyprus**

*Xinhua News Agency 15th August 1960*

Premier of the People's Republic of China Zhou En-lai today cables President of the Republic of Cyprus Archbishop Makarios III to congratulate the proclaimed independence of Cyprus. The text of the cable is as follows:

Your Eminence President of the Republic of Cyprus Archbishop Makarios:

Hearing with happiness the news of the proclamation of independence of Cyprus, I, solemnly, on behalf of the Government and People of the People's Republic of China, extend cordial congratulations to Your Eminence and, through Your Eminence, to the Government and People of the Republic of Cyprus. I wish the Cypriot People more achievement in enhancing national unity and upholding national independence. I wish your great country prosperity and happiness for your people.

Zhou En-lai
Premier of the State Council
People's Republic of China
Beijing, 15th August 1960

18 See also Mao Zedong, 'We Greatly Appreciate France's Independent Policy' in *Mao Zedong on Diplomacy, ibid*, 415.

19 Translated from Chinese.

*Xinhua News Agency 15th August 1960*

Foreign Minister of the People's Republic of China Chen Yi today telegrams Foreign Minister of the Republic of Cyprus, Nikos Kaladeodis, to congratulate the proclaimed independence of Cyprus, and to inform him of the decision of the Chinese Government to acknowledge the Republic of Cyprus. The text of the telegram is as follows:

Your Excellency Foreign Minister of the Republic of Cyprus, Mr Nikos Kaladeodis:

On the occasion of the proclaimed independence of Cyprus, I solemnly, on behalf of the Government of the People's Republic of China, extend cordial congratulations to Your Excellency. I have the honour to notify Your Excellency that the People's Republic of China has decided to recognise the Republic of Cyprus. I wish that the acknowledgement by our government of your country will help the advancement of the friendly relations between the two countries of China and Cyprus.

Chen Yi
Foreign Minister
People's Republic of China
Beijing, 15th August 1960

## Document 1.11: Diplomatic Recognition of China by France, 1964

**FRANCE**

Beijing Review Vol.7 No.5 January 31st, 1964 p10

Sino-French Joint Communiqué

Following is the joint communiqué issued by the Government of the People's Republic of China and the Government of the French Republic on January 27 on the establishment of diplomatic relations between China and France. – Ed.

The Government of the People's Republic of China and the Government of the French Republic have decided in mutual agreement to establish diplomatic relations.

For this purpose, the two Governments have agreed to appoint their ambassadors within three months.

## FOURTH GENERATION, 1970–1979

In July 1971 US National Security Advisory Henry Kissinger made his secret visit to China, followed by President Nixon's visit to China in February 1972. China resumed its seat in the United Nations Security Council in October 1971. Nixon's visit culminated on 27 February 1972 in a joint communiqué between the USA and the PRC (the Shanghai Communiqué), which began the normalisation of USA–China

**Table 1.4: The Fourth Generation of Diplomatic Relations between European Countries and China, 1970–1979**

| Date of signing or issue | Country | Effective date[a] | Place of signature or issuance[b] | Instrument | Subject matter[c] | Source: Bartke[d] | Source: Chiu[e] | Source of document published in this book |
|---|---|---|---|---|---|---|---|---|
| 26.5.1971 | Austria | 28.5.1971 | Bucharest | Joint communiqué | Establishment of diplomatic relations | Bartke, p 11 gives: NCNA, 28.5.1971 | Chiu p 57 gives: 'TYC 18:4 (C ); JMJP 5/28/71 (C ); PR 14, 23:11 (6/4/71) (E); NCNA Peking 5/27/71; SCMP 4913:83 (6/8/71) (E) | *Beijing Review*, vol. 14, no. 23, 4 June 1971, p 11 |
| 25.10.1971 | Belgium | 25.10.1971 | Paris | Joint communiqué | Establishment of diplomatic relations | Bartke, pp 15, 17 give: NCNA, 26.10.1971 | Chiu p 64 gives: 'TYC 18:13 (C); JMJP 10/27/71 (C ); PR 14.44:4 (10/29/71); NCNA Peking 10/26/71); SCMP 5007:165 (11/4/71)(E) | *Beijing Review*, vol. 14, no. 44, 29 October 1971, p 4 |
| 14.12.1971 | Cyrpus | 14.12.1971 | | Communiqué | Establishment of diplomatic relations | Bartke, p 37, 38 give: NCNA, 12.1.1971 | Chiu p 68 gives: 'TYC 18:28 (C ); JMJP 1/13/72 (C ); PR 15.3:3 (1/21/72) (E); NCNA Peking 1/12/72; SCMP 5060:33 (1/14/72 (E) | *People's Daily*, 16 August 1960, p 1 (translated from Chinese by Yin Xiao) |
| 11.10.1972 | Germany as BRD (GFR) | 11.10.1972 | Beijing | Joint communiqué | Establishment of diplomatic relations and exchange of ambassadors | Bartke, pp 58, 63 give: NCNA, 11.10.1972 | Chiu p 82 gives: 'TYC 19:31 (C ); JMJP 10/12/72 (C ); PR 15.42:4 (10/20/72) (E); NCNA Peking 10/11/72; SCMP 5421:108 (10/25/72 (E) | *Beijing Review*, 15,42, 20 January 1972, p 4 [full text in Chinese in *People's Daily*, 12 October 1972, p 1] |

**Table 1.4: Continued**

| Date of signing or issue | Country | Effective date[a] | Place of signature or issuance[b] | Instrument | Subject matter[c] | Source: Bartke[d] | Source: Chiu[e] | Source of document published in this book |
|---|---|---|---|---|---|---|---|---|
| 13.3.1972 | Great Britain | | | Agreement | | Bartke, pp 70, 73 give: NCNA, 13.3.1972 | Chiu | *Beijing Review,* vol. 15, no. 11, 17 March 1972, p 3 [full text in Chinese in *People's Daily,* 14 March 1972, p 1] |
| 5.6.1972 | Greece | 5.6.1972 | Tirana | Joint communiqué | Establishment of diplomatic relations | Bartke, p 74 gives: NCNA, 5.6.1972 | Chiu p 77 gives: 'TYC 19:18 (C ); JMJP 6/6/72 (C ); PR 15.23:3 (6/9/72) (E); NCNA Peking 6/5/72; SCMP 5155:146 (6/16/72( (E)ì | *Beijing Review,* vol. 15, no. 23, 9 June 1971, pp 3-4 [full text in Chinese in *People's Daily,* 6 June 1972, p 1] |
| 22.6.1979 | Ireland | | New York | Joint communiqué | Establishment of diplomatic relations | Bartke, p 89 gives: NCNA, 18.6.1979 | Chiu p 184 gives ' JMJP 6/24/79; PR 22. 26:7 (6/29/79); NCNA Peking 6/23/79; FBIS (1) 124:G1 (6/26/79) (E) | *People's Daily,* 11 March 1973, p 1 (translated from Chinese by Yin Xiao), [see also: *Summary of World Broadcasts (SWB)*, FE/6152/A1/a, 27 June 1979] |
| 6.11.1970 | Italy | 6.11.1970 | Beijing | Joint communiqué | Establishment of diplomatic relations | Bartke, pp 90, 92 give: NCNA, 6.11.1970 | Chiu p 50 gives: 'TYC 17:2 (C ); JMJP 11/7/70 (C ); PR 13.46:6 (11/13/70) (E); NCNA Peking 11/6/70; SCMP 4779:26 (11/16/70) (E)' | *Beijing Review,* vol. 13, no. 46, 13 November 1970, p 6 |

**Table 1.4: Continued**

| Date of signing or issue | Country | Effective date[a] | Place of signature or issuance[b] | Instrument | Subject matter[c] | Source: Bartke[d] | Source: Chiu[e] | Source of document published in this book |
|---|---|---|---|---|---|---|---|---|
| 13.11.1972 | Luxem-bourg | 16.11.1972 | Moscow | Joint communiqué | Establishment of diplomatic relations | Bartke, p 111 gives: NCNA, 16.11.1972 | Chiu p 85 gives: 'TYC 19:15 (C ); JMJP 11/17/72 (C ); PR 15.47:4 (11/24/72) (E); NCNA Peking 11/16/72; SCMP 5264:85 (11/28/72) (E)' | *Beijing Review*, vol. 15, no. 47, 24 November 1972, p 4 [full text in Chinese in *People's Daily*, 24 November 1972] |
| 16.5.1972 | Netherla nds | 18.5.1972 | Beijing | Joint communiqué | Raising level of diplomatic relations from offices of chargés d'affaires to embassies as from 5.18.1972 (Chiu p 76) | Bartke, pp 126, 127 give: DS3 p 188 (V3 p.59) | Chiu p 76 gives: 'TYC 19:24 (C ); JMJP 5/17/72 (C ); PR 15.21:20 (5/26/72) (E); NCNA Peking 5/17/72; SCMP 5142:217 (5/26/72)(E) | *Beijing Review*, vol. 15, no. 21, 26 May 1972, p 20 [full text in Chinese in *People's Daily*, 17 May 1972, p 1] |
| 8.2.1979 | Portugal | | | Communiqué | | Bartke, p 153 gives: NCNA 8.2.1979 | | *People's Daily*, 8 February 1979, p 1 (translated from Chinese by Yin Xiao) |

**Table 1.4: Continued**

| Date of signing or issue | Country | Effective date[a] | Place of signature or issuance[b] | Instrument | Subject matter[c] | Source: Bartke[d] | Source: Chiu[e] | Source of document published in this book |
|---|---|---|---|---|---|---|---|---|
| 9.3.1973 | Spain | 9.3.1973 | Paris | Joint communiqué | Establishment of diplomatic relations (Chiu p 296) | Bartke, pp 173, 174 give: NCNA 10.3.1973 | Chiu p 92 gives: 'TYC 20:4 (C ); JMJP 3/11/73 (C ); PR 16.11:3 (3/16/73) (E); NCNA Peking 3/10/73; SCMP 5388:115 (3/21/73) (E) | *People's Daily,* 11 March 1973, p 1 (translated from Chinese by Yin Xiao); see also *Beijing Review,* vol. 16, no. 11, 16 March 1973, p 3 [full text of this summary in Chinese in *People's Daily,* 11 March 1973, p 1] |

See Table 1.1 for footnotes and abbreviations.

relations.[20] In the wake of normalisation, 10 European countries concluded diplomatic relations with China (see Table 1.4). These included five countries which were already EEC Member States: Italy (1970: see Document 1.12), Belgium (1971: see Document 1.13), the German Federal Republic (1971: see Document 1.14), Luxembourg (1972: see Document 1.15) and Ireland (1979: see Document 1.16). The fourth generation also included five other countries: Austria (1971: see Document 1.17), Greece (see 1972: Document 1.18), Malta (1972: see Document 1.19), Spain (1973: see Document 1.20) and Portugal (1979: see Document 1.21). A third group of countries in the fourth generation comprised three countries which upgraded their existing relations with China. Cyprus, having recognised China in 1960, established diplomatic relations with China in 1971 (see Document 1.22). Great Britain (see Document 1.23) and the Netherlands (see Document 1.24) upgraded their relations with China from chargé d'affaires to ambassador status in 1972. Finally, two of the Baltic states, which earlier had entered into diplomatic relations as part of the USSR, established diplomatic ties with China in 1991 as independent states, first Latvia (see Document 1.25) and then Lithuania (see Document 1.26).

In contrast to earlier generations of diplomatic relations, the fourth generation of agreements stated expressly that the relations were to be governed by the principles of mutual respect for sovereignty and territorial integrity, non-interference in each other's internal affairs, and sovereignty and mutual benefit.[21] Also for the first time, the European partners expressly affirmed their recognition of the government of the People's Republic of China as the sole legal government of China. Following the 'One China Principle', they committed themselves to not establishing official relations with Taiwan.

## Document 1.12: Establishment of Diplomatic Relations between Italy and China, 1970

### ITALY

Beijing Review Vol.13 No.46 November 13th, 1970 p6

Joint Communiqué of Government of People's Republic of China and Government of Republic of Italy on Establishment of Diplomatic Relations between China and Italy

In accordance with the principles of mutual respect for sovereignty and territorial integrity, non-interference in each other's internal affairs, equality and mutual benefit, the Government of the People's Republic of China and the Government of the Republic of Italy have decided upon mutual recognition and the establishment of diplomatic relations, effective on November 6, 1970, and the exchange of ambassadors within three months.

20 The USA established diplomatic relations with the PRC by a Joint Communiqué issued in Beijing, only on 16 December 1978, with effect from 1 January 1979. See Chiu, above n 6, 176, who refers to the following sources: JMJP 12/17/78/C; POR 21.51:8 (12/12/78) (E); NCNA Peking 12/16/78; FBIS(1).243:A1 (12/12/78) (E).

21 These principles are part of the Five Principles of Peaceful Co-existence, originally articulated by Chinese Premier Zhou Enlai in negotiations with India concerning Tibet in 1954 and since then constant elements of Chinese foreign policy. See Ministry of Foreign Affairs of the People's Republic of China, 'China's Initiation of the Five Principles of Peaceful Co-Existence', 17 November 2000, available at http://www.fmprc.gov.cn/ziliao/3602/3604/tl8053.htm (accessed 23 January 2005).

The Chinese Government reaffirms that Taiwan is an inalienable part of the territory of the People's Republic of China. The Italian Government takes note of this statement of the Chinese Government.

The Italian Government recognizes that the Government of the People's Republic of China is the sole legal government of China.

The Chinese Government and the Italian Government have decided, through consultation, to provide all necessary assistance for the establishment and the performance of the functions of embassies in their respective capitals, on the basis of equality and mutual benefit and in accordance with international practice.

## Document 1.13: Establishment of Diplomatic Relations between Belgium and China, 1971

**BELGIUM**

Beijing Review Vol.14 No.44 October 29th, 1971 p4

Joint Communiqué on the Establishment of Diplomatic Relations between the People's Republic of China and Belgium

Joint Communiqué on the Establishment of Diplomatic Relations between the People's Republic of China and the Kingdom of Belgium

In accordance with the principles of mutual respect for sovereignty and territorial integrity, non-interference in each other's internal affairs, equality and mutual benefit, the Government of the People's Republic of China and the Royal Government of Belgium have decided upon mutual recognition and the establishment of diplomatic relations effective on October 25, 1971, and the exchange of ambassadors within three months.

The Chinese Government reaffirms that Taiwan is an inalienable part of the territory of the People's Republic of China. The Belgian Government takes note of this statement of the Chinese Government.

The Belgian Government recognizes that the Government of the People's Republic of China is the sole legal Government of China.

The Chinese Government and the Belgian Government have decided, through consultation, to provide all necessary assistance for the establishment and performance of the functions of embassies in their respective capitals on the basis of equality and mutual benefit and in accordance with international practice.

(Signed)
Huang Chen
Ambassador of the People's
Republic of China to France

(Signed)
Robert Rothschild
Ambassador of the Kingdom
of Belgium to France

Done in Paris, October 25, 1971

## Document 1.14: Establishment of Diplomatic Relations between the German Federal Republic and China, 1971

### GERMANY, FEDERAL REPUBLIC[22]

Beijing Review Vol.15 No.42 January 20th, 1972 p4

People's Republic of China and Federal Republic of Germany Establish Diplomatic Relations: Joint Communiqué

The Government of the People's Republic of China and the Government of the Federal Republic of Germany decided, on October 11, 1972, to establish diplomatic relations and to exchange ambassadors within a short time.

| | |
|---|---|
| For the Government of the People's Republic of China | For the Government of the Federal Republic of Germany |
| (Signed) | (Signed) |
| Chi Peng-fei | Walter Schiele |

Done in duplicate in Peking on October 11, 1972 in Chinese and German Languages.

## Document 1.15: Establishment of Diplomatic Relations between Luxembourg and China, 1972

### LUXEMBOURG[23]

Beijing Review Vol.15 No.47 November 24th, 1972 p4

China and Luxembourg Establishment of Diplomatic Relations

The Governments of China and Luxembourg, after friendly consultations, issued on November 16 a joint Communiqué on the establishment of diplomatic relations between the two countries. The communiqué said:

'The Government of the People's Republic of China and the Government of the Grand Duchy of Luxembourg have decided to grant each other recognition and to establish diplomatic relations as from November 16, 1972.

The two Governments declare that their relations will be governed by the principles of mutual respect for sovereignty and territorial integrity, non-interference in each other's internal affairs, and equality and mutual benefit.

The Government of the Grand Duchy of Luxembourg confirms its recognition of the Government of the People's Republic of China as the sole legal Government of China.'

22 Full text in Chinese is available in *People's Daily* 12th October 1972 p1. In the Chinese text, the place, time, and versions of signature are stated as the second paragraph as 'Signed in Beijing on 11th October 1972, with the official text in two copies, each written in Chinese and German.' The titles of both signatories given in the Joint Communiqué are respectively 'Representative'.

23 Full text in Chinese is available in *People's Daily*. The signatories and the signing place and time are given as 'Ambassador of the People's Republic of China to the USSR Liu Quan-xin' and 'Ambassador of the Duchy of Luxembourg to the USSR … …'; and 'Moscow 13th November 1972'.

## Document 1.16: Establishment of Diplomatic Relations between Ireland and China, 1979

**IRELAND**[24]

People's Daily

Joint Communiqué on Establishment of Diplomatic Relations between the People's Republic of China and Ireland

Xinhua News Agency Beijing 23rd June

The People's Republic of China and Ireland decide to establish diplomatic relations. The full text of the Joint Communiqué of establishment of diplomatic relations is as follows:

> The Government of the People's Republic of China and the Government of Ireland decided to establish ambassadorial diplomatic relations and to exchange ambassadors.
>
> The Irish Government recognizes that the Government of the People's Republic of China is the sole legal Government of China.
>
> The governments of the two countries agree to develop the friendly cooperative relations between the two countries on the basis of the principles of mutual respect for sovereignty and territorial integrity, non-interference in each other's internal affairs, equality and mutual benefit including trade promotion.
>
> The governments of the two countries decide, through consultations, that, on the basis of equality and mutual benefit, and in accordance with international practice, they will provide necessary assistance for the construction of embassies and the performance of their missions in their respective capitals.

Lai Ya-li
(Signature)
Ambassador Extraordinary and
Plenipoteniary of the People's Republic of China to
the United Nations

Paul John Gerrard Keating
(Signature)
Ambassador Extraordinary and
Plenipotentiary of Ireland to
the United Nations

New York, 22nd June 1979

## Document 1.17: Establishment of Diplomatic Relations between Austria and China, 1971

**AUSTRIA**

Beijing Review Vol.14 No.23 June 4th, 1971 p11

Joint Communiqué on the Establishment of Diplomatic Relations between the People's Republic of China and the Republic of Austria

In accordance with the principles of mutual respect for sovereignty and territorial integrity, non-interference in each other's internal affairs, equality and mutual benefit, the

[24] Translated from Chinese.

Government of the People's Republic of China and the Government of the Republic of Austria have decided upon mutual recognition and the establishment of diplomatic relations effective on May 28, 1971, and the exchange of ambassadors within six months.

The Chinese Government respects the status of neutrality of the Republic of Austria.

The Austrian Government recognizes the Government of the People's Republic of China as the sole legal Government of China.

The Chinese Government and the Austrian Government have agreed to provide all necessary assistance for the establishment and the performance of the functions of embassies in their respective capitals on the basis of equality and mutual benefit and in accordance with international practice.

(Signed)
Chang Hai-feng
Ambassador of the People's
Republic of China to Romania

(Signed)
Eduard Tschoep
Ambassador of the Republic
of Austria to Romania

Bucharest, May 26, 1971

## Document 1.18: Establishment of Diplomatic Relations between Greece and China, 1972

**GREECE**[25]

Beijing Review Vol.15 No.23 June 9th, 1971 pp3-4

Diplomatic Relations Established Between China and Greece

Chinese Ambassador to the People's Republic of Albania, Liu Chen-hua, and the Greek Ambassador to the People's Republic of Albania, ... ..., signed a joint Communiqué on the establishment of diplomatic relations between the People's Republic of China and the Kingdom of Greece, in Tirana on June 5. The communiqué said:

> 'In accordance with the principles of mutual respect for sovereignty and territorial integrity, non-interference in each other's internal affairs and equality and mutual benefit, the Government of the People's Republic of China and the Royal Government of Greece have decided to recognize each other and establish diplomatic relations as from June 5, 1972, and to exchange ambassadors within six months.
>
> The Greek Government recognizes that the Government of the People's Republic of China is the sole legal Government of China.
>
> The Chinese Government reaffirms that Taiwan is an inalienable part of the territory of the People's Republic of China. The Greek Government takes note of this position of the Chinese Government.
>
> The Chinese and Greek Governments have decided, through consultation, to provide each other with all necessary assistance for the establishment and the performance of the functions of embassies in their respective capitals, on the basis of equality and mutual benefit and in accordance with international practice.'

25 Full text in Chinese available in *People's Daily* 6th June 1972 p1.

## Document 1.19: Establishment of Diplomatic Relations between Malta and China, 1972

### MALTA[26]

Beijing Review Vol.15 No.9 March 3rd, 1972 p3

Diplomatic Relations Established Between China and Malta

A joint communiqué on the establishment of diplomatic relations between the Government of the People's Republic of China and the Government of Malta was issued on February 25. The joint communiqué said:

'In accordance with the principles of mutual respect for sovereignty and territorial integrity, non-interference in each other's internal affairs and equality and mutual benefit, the Government of the People's Republic of China and the Government of Belgium have decided upon mutual recognition and the establishment of diplomatic relations as from January 31, 1972 and have agreed upon the exchange of ambassadors within a short time.

The Maltese Government recognizes the Government of the People's Republic of China as the sole legal Government of China.

The Chinese Government reaffirms that Taiwan Province is an inalienable part of the territory of the People's Republic of China. The Government of Malta takes note of this statement of the Chinese Government.

The Chinese Government supports the Government and People of Malta in their efforts to safeguard national independence and sovereignty and to develop a self-contained economy devoted to peace.

The Chinese Government and the Maltese Government have decided to provide each other with all necessary assistance for the establishment and the performance of the functions of the diplomatic missions in their respective capitals on the basis of equality and mutual benefit and in accordance with international practice.'

The communiqué was signed on January 31 in Rome by Shen Ping, representative of the Chinese Government and Ambassador to Italy, and Carmel John Mallia, representative of the Maltese Government and Ambassador to Italy.

## Document 1.20: Establishment of Diplomatic Relations between Spain and China, 1973

### SPAIN[27]

People's Daily 11th March 1973 p1

Joint Communiqué on the Establishment of Sino-Spanish Diplomatic Relations by Government of the People's Republic of China and Government of Kingdom of Spain

26 Full text in Chinese is available in *People's Daily* 26th February 1972 p1.
27 Translated from Chinese.

*Xinhua New Agency 10th March 1973*

Joint Communiqué on the Establishment of Sino-Spanish Diplomatic Relations by Government of the People's Republic of China and Government of Kingdom of Spain

The Government of the People's Republic of China and the Government of the Kingdom of Spain decide to establish ambassadorial-level diplomatic relations effective from 9th March 1973 and to exchange of ambassadors within three months.

The two governments will maintain their diplomatic relations in accordance with the principles of mutual respect for sovereignty and territorial integrity, non-interference in each other's internal affairs, equality and mutual benefit.

The Spanish Government recognizes that the Government of the People's Republic of China is the sole legal Government of China, acknowledges the Chinese Government's position that Taiwan is a province of the People's Republic of China, and decides to remove its official representative institutions from Taiwan before 10 April 1973.

The Government of the People's Republic of China and the Government of the Kingdom of Spain, on the basis of equality and mutual benefit and in accordance with international practice, will provide necessary assistance for the construction of embassies, accommodations of the staff of embassies and the performance of their missions in their respective capitals.

Huang Zhen
(Signature)
Ambassador Extraordinary and
Plenipotentiaryof the
People's Republic of China
to the Republic of France

… …
(Signature)
Ambassador Extraordinary and
Plenipotentiary of the
Kingdom of Spain
to the Republic of France

Paris, 9th March 1973

## Document 1.21: Establishment of Diplomatic Relations between Portugal and China, 1979

**PORTUGAL**[28]

People's Daily 8th February 1979 p1

Joint Communiqué on Establishment of Sino-Portuguese Diplomatic Relations

*Xinhua News Agency Beijing 8$^{th}$ February*

The Government of the People's Republic of China and the Government of the Republic of Portugal decide to establish diplomatic relations from 8th February 1979. The full text of the Joint Communiqué is as follows:

The Government of the People's Republic of China and the Government of the Republic of Portugal decide to establish ambassadorial-level diplomatic relations from 8th February 1979 and to exchange of ambassadors within three months.

28 Translated from Chinese.

The two governments will maintain their diplomatic relations in accordance with the principles of mutual respect for sovereignty and territorial integrity, non-interference in each other's internal affairs and equality and mutual benefit.

The Government of the Republic of Portugal recognizes that the Government of the People's Republic of China is the sole legal Government of China and that Taiwan is an integral part of the People's Republic of China. The Government of the Republic of Portugal proclaims that it has terminated diplomatic relations with Taiwan since January 1975.

The Chinese and Portuguese governments decide, through consultations, that, on the basis of equality and mutual benefit, and in accordance with international practice, they will provide all necessary assistance for the other to construct the embassy and to perform the missions in their respective capitals.

Hai Ke-hua
(Signature)
Ambassador Extraordinary and
Plenipotentiary of the
People's Republic of China
to the Republic of France

… …
(Signature)
Ambassador Extraordinary and
Plenipotentiary of the
Republic of Portugal
to the Republic of France

Paris, 8th February 1979

## Document 1.22: Establishment of Diplomatic Relations between Cyprus and China, 1971

**CYPRUS[29]**

Beijing Review Vol.15 No.3 January 21st, 1972 p3

China and Cyprus Establish Diplomatic Relations

The communiqué issued on January 12 on the establishment of diplomatic relations between the People's Republic of China and the Republic of Cyprus stated:

'The Government of the People's Republic of China and the Government of the Republic of Cyprus, in conformity with the interest and desire of the people of the two countries, have decided to establish diplomatic relations at the ambassadorial level with immediate effect.

The Chinese government and the people firmly support the government and people of the Republic of Cyprus in their just struggle against foreign intervention and interference in any form and for the complete independence, sovereignty, unity and the territorial integrity of Cyprus.

The government of the Republic of Cyprus recognizes that the government of the People's Republic of China is the sole legal government representing the entire Chinese people.

The two governments are firmly opposed to imperialism, colonialism and neocolonialism. The two governments agree to develop the diplomatic relations, friendship and

[29] Full text in Chinese is available in *People's Daily* 13th January 1972 p1.

cooperation between the two countries on the basis of the principles of mutual respect for sovereignty and territorial integrity, non-interference in each other's internal affairs, equality and mutual benefit and peaceful coexistence.'

The communiqué was signed in New York on December 14, 1971 by Chiao Kuna-hua, Vice-Minister of Foreign Affairs of the People's Republic of China, and Spyros Kyprianou, Minister of Foreign Affairs of the Republic of Cyprus . . .

## Document 1.23: Upgrading of Diplomatic Relations between Great Britain and China, 1972

### GREAT BRITAIN[30]

Beijing Review Vol.15 No. 11 March 17th, 1972 p3

China and Britain to Exchange Ambassadors

Vice-Minister of Foreign Affairs of the People's Republic of China Chiao Kuan-hua and British Charge D'Affaires to the People's Republic of China, J.M. Addis, duly authorized by their respective Governments, held negotiations on March 13, 1972 and reached an agreement on the exchange of ambassadors between the two countries. Following is the text of the Joint Communiqué on the Agreement between the People's Republic of China and the United Kingdom of Great Britain and Northern Ireland on an Exchange of Ambassadors:

'1. Both confirming the principles of mutual respect for sovereignty and territorial integrity, non-interference in each other's internal affairs, equality and mutual benefit, the Government of the People's Republic of China and the Government of the United Kingdom have decided to raise the level of their respective diplomatic representatives in each other's capitals from charges d'affaires to ambassadors, as from March 13, 1972.

2. The Government of the United Kingdom, acknowledging the position of the Chinese Government that Taiwan is a province of the People's Republic of China, has decided to remove its official representation in Taiwan on March 13, 1972.

3. The government of the United Kingdom recognizes the government of the People's Republic of China as the sole legal government of China.

The Government of the People's Republic of China appreciates the above stand of the Government of the United Kingdom.'

## Document 1.24: Upgrading of Diplomatic Relations between the Netherlands and China, 1972

### NETHERLANDS[31]

Beijing Review Vol.15 No.21 May 26, 1972 p20

30 Full text in Chinese is available in *People's Daily* 14th March 1972 p1. The Joint Communiqué was signed in Beijing.

31 Full text in Chinese is available in *People's Daily* 17th May 1972 p1. The Chinese version has one extra paragraph at the beginning of the Joint Communiqué which says: 'The Government of the People's Republic of China and the Government of the Kingdom of Netherlands have made friendly consultation through the meeting of their extraordinarily appointed representatives in Beijing.'

China and Netherlands Raise Level of Diplomatic Relations

The Representative of the Government of the People's Republic Chiao Kuan-hua, Vice-Minister of Foreign Affairs, and the representative of the Government of the Kingdom of the Netherlands J.J. Derksen, Ambassador Extraordinary and Plenipotentiary, held consultations in Peking under the authorization of their respective Governments and signed a joint Communiqué on May 16 on raising the level of diplomatic relations between the two countries. The communiqué stated:

'The two sides have reviewed the relations between the two Governments and the two peoples since 1950. Both Governments confirm the principles of mutual respect for sovereignty and territorial integrity, non-interference in each other's internal affairs and equality and mutual benefit, and hold that further development of the relations between the two countries on the basis of these principles is to the mutual benefit of the two countries and the two peoples.

The Government of the People's Republic of China and the Government of the Kingdom of the Netherlands have agreed to raise the level of their respective diplomatic missions in two countries from offices of charges d'afffaire to embassies as from May 18, 1972.

The Chinese Government reaffirms that Taiwan is a province of the People's Republic of China. The Government of the Kingdom of the Netherlands respects this position of the Chinese Government and reaffirms that it recognizes that the Government of the People's Republic of China is the sole legal Government of China.

The Governments of the Kingdom of the Netherlands holds that the principles of peaceful coexistence should imply non-interference in each other's internal affairs, not only between countries and groups of countries of different socio-political systems, but equally between countries belonging to an alliance and having identical or similar socio-political systems. The Government of the People's Republic of China appreciates this position of the Governments of the Kingdom of the Netherlands.'

## Document 1.25: Establishment of Diplomatic Relations between Latvia and China, 1991

**LATVIA**

SWB FE/1177 A2/1 14th September 1991

Communique on Establishment of Diplomatic Ties between China and Latvia

*Xinhua News Agency, Peking domestic service in Chinese 1044 gmt 12 Sep 91*

'Full text' of the joint communiqué on the establishment a/diplomatic relations between the PRC and the Republic of Latvia (FE/1176 i [5])

Joint Communiqué on the Establishment of Diplomatic Relations between the PRC and the Republic of Latvia:

In accordance with the interests and wishes of the people of the two countries, the PRC government and the government of the Republic of Latvia have decided to establish ambassador level diplomatic relations as of 12th September 1991.

Governments of the two countries agree to develop friendly and cooperative relations between the two countries on the basis of the principles of mutual respect for sovereignty and territorial integrity, non-aggression, non-interference in each other's internal affairs, equality and mutual benefit, and peaceful coexistence.

The government of the Republic of Latvia recognizes that the PRC government is the only legitimate government of China, and that Taiwan is an inalienable part of Chinese territory. The government of the Republic of Latvia commits itself to not establishing official relations and not conducting official interchanges with Taiwan.

The PRC government supports the Republic of Latvia government's efforts to safeguard its national independence and to develop its economy.

The governments of the two countries agree, on the basis of equality and mutual benefit and in accordance with international practice, to provide all necessary assistance to each other's diplomatic representatives in carrying out their duties.

(Signed)
Tian Zengpei
Representative of the PRC govern-ment

(Signed)
Sandra Kalniete
Representative of the government
of the Republic of Latvia

Dated: 12th September 1991, in Riga. CHN=B

## Document 1.26: Establishment of Diplomatic Relations between Lithuania and China, 1991

**LITHUANIA**

SWB FE/1178 A2/1 16th September 1991

Communiqué on Estabishment of Diplomatic Ties between China and Lithuania

*Xinhua News Agency, Peking, in English 1019 gmt 14 Sep 91*

Chinese Vice Foreign Minister Tian Zengpei and his Lithuanian counterpart V. Katkus signed in the Lithuanian capital of Vilnius a joint communiqué on the establishment of diplomatic relations between the countries.

The government of the People's Republic of China and the government of the Republic of Lithuania in conformity with the interests and desires of the two peoples, have decided to establish diplomatic relations at the ambassadorial level as of 14 September 1991, the communiqué said.

The two governments, it said have agreed to develop the friendly relations and cooperation between the two countries on the basis of the principles [of] mutual respect for sovereignty and territorial integrity, mutual non-aggression, non-interference in each other's internal affairs, equality and mutual benefit and peaceful coexistence.

The government of the Republic of Lithuania recognizes the government of the People's Republic of China as the sole legal government of China and Taiwan as an unalienable part of the Chinese territory, the communiqué pointed out, adding the government of the

Republic of Lithuania undertakes the obligation not to establish official relations or engage in official contacts with Taiwan.

It said the government of the People's Republic of China supports the legal government of the Republic of Lithuania, in its efforts to safeguard state independence and develop the economy.

The two sides expressed their desire to cooperate in the economic, scientific and technological, cultural, judicial and other fields. They will exchange views on major political problems and international issues including the process of disarmament, the communiqué said.

It said the two governments have agreed to provide each other with all necessary assistance for the performance of the functions of their diplomatic representative on the basis of equality and mutual benefit in accordance with international practice.

The government of the People's Republic of China fully supports the application of the Republic of Lithuania for membership at the United Nations, the communiqué said. CHN-B

## EEC–CHINA RELATIONS, 1975

These concerns on the Chinese side were echoed in relations between China and the European Economic Community. In autumn 1973, Sir Christopher Soames, then Vice-President of the European Commission in charge of foreign affairs, visited Beijing on a personal invitation from the Chinese Ambassador in London. Subsequently, in May 1975, he again visited Beijing, this time on the formal invitation from the Chinese Institute for Foreign Relations transmitted to the Commission by the Chinese Embassy in Brussels. His statement on behalf of the EEC that the EEC had no relations with Taiwan cleared the way for the establishment of diplomatic relations.[32] Document 1.27 is an extract from the Chinese report of this meeting.[33]

The representative of the Commission subsequently informed the Member States via the Committee of Permanent Representatives (CoRePer) of the intention of the Chinese government to accredit an ambassador to the European Economic Community.[34] On 7 July 1975, Mr Emile Noël, the Secretary-General of the Commission of the European Communities, notified Mr Nicolas Hommel, then Secretary General of the Council of the European Communities, that the Chinese Embassy in Belgium had informed the Commission on 26 June 1975 of its wish to accredit HE Mr Li Lien-Pi, then Chinese Ambassador to Belgium, as its Head of Mission to the European

[32] See H Kapur, *China and the European Economic Community: The New Connection* (Dordrecht, Martinus Nijhoff, 1986) 29, 44 note 29.

[33] For further details, see *Bulletin of the EC*, 5–1975, paras 1201–5, and 9–1975, paras 2343–4; *9th General Report on the activities of the European Communities* (Official of Official Publications of the European Communities, Luxembourg, 1975) 298.

[34] Extrait du projet de compte-rendu sommaire de la 769ème réunion du Comité des Représentants permanents', Bruxelles, les 7–12/5/75, Doc: 643/75 (RP/CRS 16), point 41. 'Divers', in the file 'Représentation de la République populaire de Chine auprès des Communautés européennes: accréditation du chef de mission', Temp File No 40281, Historical Archives of the Council of the European Union, Brussels, consulted 18 February 2008.

Communities, that the Commission had agreed on the accreditation with regard to the ECSC and that it was prepared to agree to the accreditation also with regard to the EEC and the EAEC following agreement by the Council, which was legally responsible for foreign affairs of these two Communities. The Council gave its agreement on 12 August 1975. On 1 September 1975, the Chinese Minister of Foreign Affairs notified the President of the Council of Ministers of the European Communities that HE Mr Li Lien-Pi had been named Head of the Mission of the People's Republic of China to the European Economic Community (see Document 1.28). On 15 September 1975, HE Mr Li Lien-Pi presented his letters of credence as first Head of Mission for the People's Republic of China to the European Economic Community, with effect as of 16 September 1975 (see Document 1.29). Such accreditation took effect also with regard to the ECSC and the EAEC.[35]

With regard to foreign trade, the EEC assumed the legal competences previously held by its Member States following the end of the transitional period in European integration and the establishment of the EEC's common commercial policy. During the same period, China was nearing the end of the Cultural Revolution. Mao Zedong was ill and died in 1976. The establishment of diplomatic relations between the EEC and China was an expression of converging interests and provided a basis for the conclusion of agreements on trade in general and textiles in particular (see Chapter 2).

## Document 1.27: EEC and China Intend to Establish Diplomatic Relations, 1975

People's Daily, 11th May, 1975 p1[36]

**China and European Economic Community Establish Official Relations**

Vice Chairman Soames declared to confirm, as already declared by the Commission, EEC does not maintain any official relations or reach any agreements with Taiwan

*New China News Agency 11th May 1975*

Vice Chairman of the Commission of the European Economic Community (EEC) Christopher Soames and his party left Beijing to visit Guangzhou in the morning of 9th May.

Vice Chairman Soames and his six-member party, including Director-General Wellenstein from the Foreign Relations of the EEC Commission, arrived in Beijing on 4th May, with the invitation from Chinese People's Institute of Foreign Relations to visit China.

Premiere Zhou En-lai and Vice Premier Li Xian-nian met Vice Chairman Soames and his party on separate occasions and had friendly talks with them. Foreign Minister Qian Guan-hua met Vice Chairman Soames and his party. The two sides broadly exchanged views upon international issues and the issues regarding bilateral relations between China and the EEC. Both agreed to establish official relations between the People's Republic of China and the European Economic Community. The Chinese government decided to dispatch representative to the EEC.

35 This paragraph is based on documents in the file 'Représentation de la République populaire de Chine auprès des Communautés européennes: accréditation du chef de mission', Temp File No 40281, Historical Archives of the Council of the European Union, Brussels, consulted 18 February 2008.

36 Translated from Chinese.

In the afternoon of 8th May, Vice Chairman Soames hosted a press conference in Beijing. He announced that both sides had agreed to establish official diplomatic relations, and made statement about Taiwan: 'Concerning the issue of Taiwan, the Foreign Minister reiterated China's well-known position in this regard, namely, the government of the People's Republic of China is the sole legal government of China, and Taiwan is an integral part of Chinese territory. He emphasized the importance they attach, and inquired about the standpoint of the Community, in particular, whether the Community has any official relations with Taiwan.

> 'I explained that, to recognize a country is beyond the scope of duties of the EEC, yet I indicated to the Minister that, all Community member countries recognize the government of the People's Republic of China as the sole legal government and adopt positions acceptable to the People's Republic. According to these positions, I confirm that, as stated by the Commission spokesman in Brussels on 30th April, the EEC does not maintain any official relations or establish any agreements with Taiwan.'

At the night of 8th May, Vice Chairman Soames hosted a farewell banquet. When addressing the relations between the EEC and China, he said: 'I feel honored that I can play a part for initiating the development of our new relations. I hope and believe that the new relation will have true significance.' 'We Europeans give our salute to the People's Republic of China. Both our two societies have recovered lately from the shadow of civil war and international wars. We both are proud of respecting our long past and are confident in looking ahead into the future.'

Foreign Trade Minister Li Qian delivered a speech at the banquet that Mr. Soames was the first official representative from the EEC who visited China. His visit promoted new advancement of the relations between China and the EEC.

He said, 'Since the founding of the EEC, there has been a growing tendency towards unity between the western European countries. They withstand external pressure and interference, and safeguard their sovereignty and independence with unremitting efforts. This is a positive factor in the changing international situation.'

Minister Li Qian also remarked: 'We are willing to witness that the EEC and the third world develop better relations. It is our belief that, if all counties that are subject to the invasion, interference and control by the super-powers unite together, they will surely defeat the superpowers' conspiracy of seeking global hegemony.'

Vice Chairman Soames and his party will leave Guangzhou for Europe on 11th May.

## Document 1.28: Chinese Appointment of the First Ambassador of the People's Republic of China to the European Economic Community, 1975

Appointment of the First Ambassador of the People's Republic of China to the European Economic Community
(Translation)

Beijing, 1 September 1975

Mr President,

I have the honour to inform you that Mister Li Lien-pi, Ambassador Extraordinary and Plenipotentiary of the People's Republic of China to the Kingdom of Belgium, has been appointed Head of the Mission of the People's Republic of China to the European Economic Community.

Accept, Mr President, the assurances of my highest consideration.

(signed) Kiao Kouan-houa
Minister of Foreign Affairs of the
People's Republic of China

His Excellency Mr Mariano Rumor
President of the Council of Ministers
of the European Communities,
Brussels

**Document 1.29: Accreditation of the First Ambassador of the People's Republic of China to the European Economic Community, 1975**

**Official Journal of the European Communities No C 224/1, 1st October 1975**

I
(Information)
COUNCIL AND COMMISSION
Missions of third countries

The President of the Council and the President of the Commission of the European Communities received His Excellency Ambassador Li Lien-Pi who presented to them his letters of credence in his capacity as Ambassador, Head of the Mission of the People's Republic of China to the European Economic Community (EEC), with effect from 16 September 1975.

## CONCLUSION

The Cold War shaped the four generations of the establishment of diplomatic relations between European countries and China more than any other single factor. It conditioned the initiation and development of the successive waves of diplomatic initiatives, from the former Soviet bloc countries, the Nordic countries and the EEC Member States to the EEC itself. It was not only a fundamental element in the development of European integration; it also provided the context for the establishment of diplomatic relations between the EEC and China. The development of diplomatic relations between European countries and China between 1949 to the late 1970s bore its unmistakeable imprint.

Today, both the European Community and all 27 EU Member States have diplomatic relations with China. Table 1.5 summarises these diplomatic relations by alphabetical order of the EC or EU Member State. The EC, like the EU, is a divided-power system, in which legal competences are divided between the EC and the Member States. Relations between the EU and China can therefore be seen as a projection on the international plane of the distribution of competences between the

**Table 1.5: Diplomatic Relations between the EC and its Member States, on the one hand, and China, on the other hand, as of 2007**

| Country | Date of signing or issue | Effective date[a] | Place of signature or issuance[b] | Instrument | Subject matter[c] | Source: Bartke[d] | Source: Chiu[e] | Source of document published in this book |
|---|---|---|---|---|---|---|---|---|
| Austria | 26.5.1971 | 28.5.1971 | Bucharest | Joint communiqué | Establishment of diplomatic relations | Bartke p 11 gives: NCNA, 28.5.1971 | Chiu p 57 gives: 'TYC 18:4 (C ); JMJP 5/28/71 (C ); PR 14, 23:11 (6/4/71) (E); NCNA Peking 5/27/71; SCMP 4913:83 (6/8/71) (E) | *Beijing Review*, vol. 14, no. 23, 4 June 1971, p 11 |
| Belgium | 25.10.1971 | 25.10.1971 | Paris | Joint communiqué | Establishment of diplomatic relations | Bartke pp 15, 17 give: NCNA, 26.10.1971 | Chiu p 64 gives: 'TYC 18:13 (C ); JMJP 10/27/71 (C ); PR 14.44:4 (10/29/71); NCNA Peking 10/26/71); SCMP 5007:165 (11/4/71)(E) | *Beijing Review*, vol. 14, no. 44, 29 October 1971, p 4 |
| Bulgaria | 4.10.1949 | | ** | Communiqué | | Bartke pp 21, 24 give: DS1, pp 6–7 | | *People's Daily*, 5 October 1949, p 1 (translated from Chinese by Yin Xiao) |
| Cyprus | 15.8.1960 | | | News report | Recognition | Bartke pp 37, 38 give: JMJP 16.8.1960 | | *People's Daily*, 16 August 1960, p 1 (translated from Chinese by Yin Xiao) |

**Table 1.5: Continued**

| Country | Date of signing or issue | Effective date[a] | Place of signature or issuance[b] | Instrument | Subject matter[c] | Source: Bartke[d] | Source: Chiu[e] | Source of document published in this book |
|---|---|---|---|---|---|---|---|---|
| Cyprus | 14.12.1971 | 14.12.1971 | | Communiqué | Establishment of diplomatic relations | Bartke p 37, 38 give: NCNA, 12.1.1971 | Chiu p 68 gives: 'TYC 18:28 (C ); JMJP 1/13/72 (C ); PR 15.3:3 (1/21/72) (E); NCNA Peking 1/12/72; SCMP 5060:33 (1/14/72 (E) | *Beijing Review*, vol. 15, no. 3, 21 January 1972, p 3 [full text in Chinese in People's Daily, 13 January 1972, p 1] |
| Czech Republic [as Czechosl ovakia | 6.10.1949 | | | Communiqué | | Bartke, pp 38,42 give: DS1, pp 10–11 (V5, pp 471–2) | | *People's Daily,* 8 October 1949, p 1 (translated from Chinese by Yin Xiao) |
| Denmark | 9.1.1950 | | | Exchange of letters | | Bartke pp 43,44 give: DS1, pp 21–22 | | *People's Daily*, 9 May 1950 (translated from Chinese by Yin Xiao) |
| Estonia [as part of USSR] | 3.10.1949 | | | Communiqué | | Bartke, pp 163, 172 give: DS1,p 5f (V5 p 353f) | | USSR-PRC text in *People's Daily*, 4 October 1949, p 1 |
| Finland | 28.10.1950 | | | Exchange of notes | | Bartke, p 50 gives: V3, p 21 | | |

**Table 1.5: Continued**

| Country | Date of signing or issue | Effective date[a] | Place of signature or issuance[b] | Instrument | Subject matter[c] | Source: Bartke[d] | Source: Chiu[e] | Source of document published in this book |
|---|---|---|---|---|---|---|---|---|
| France | 27.1.1964 | | | Joint communiqué | | Bartke, pp 51, 57 give: JMJP, 28.1.1964 | | *Beijing Review,* vo. 7, no 5, 31J anuary 1964, p 10 |
| Germany as DDR (GDR) | 27.10.1949 | | | Exchange of notes | | Bartke,pp 58,63 give: DS1, pp 14–15 (V5 pp 96–7) | | *People's Daily,* 3 November 1949, p 1 (translated from Chinese by Yin Xiao) |
| Germany as BRD (GFR) | 11.10.1972 | 11.10.1972 | Beijing | Joint communiqué | Establishment of diplomatic relations and exchange of ambassadors | Bartke, pp 58, 63 give: NCNA, 11.10.1972 | Chjiu p 82 gives: 'TYC 19:31 (C ); JMJP 10/12/72 (C ); PR 15.42:4 (10/20/72) (E); NCNA Peking 10/11/72; SCMP 5421:108 (10/25/72 (E) | *Beijing Review,* 15,42, 20 January 1972, p 4 [full text in Chinese in *People's Daily,* 12 October 1972, p 1] |
| Great Britain | 17.6.1954 | | | Agreement | | Bartke, pp 70, 73 give: DS3 p 107 (V3 p.91) | Chiu | |
| Great Britain | 13.3.1972 | | | Agreement | | Bartke, pp 70,, 73 give: NCNA, 13.3.1972 | Chiu | *Beijing Review,* vol. 15, no. 11, 17 March 1972, p 3 [full text in Chinese in *People's Daily,* 14 March 1972, p 1] |

**Table 1.5: Continued**

| Country | Date of signing or issue | Effective date[a] | Place of signature or issuance[b] | Instrument | Subject matter[c] | Source: Bartke[d] | Source: Chiu[e] | Source of document published in this book |
|---|---|---|---|---|---|---|---|---|
| Greece | 5.6.1972 | 5.6.1972 | Tirana | Joint communiqué | Establishment of diplomatic relations | Bartke, p 74 gives: NCNA, 5.6.1972 | Chiu p 77 gives: 'TYC 19:18 (C ); JMJP 6/6/72 (C ); PR 15.23:3 (6/9/72) (E); NCNA Peking 6/5/72; SCMP 5155:146 (6/16/72( (E)i | *Beijing Review,* vol. 15, no. 23, 9 June 1971, pp 3–4 [full text in Chinese in *People's Daily,* 6 June 1972, p 1] |
| Hungary | 6.10.1949 | | | Communiqué | | Bartke, pp 78, 82 give: DS1 p.8f (V5, p 520f) | | *People's Daily,* 8 October 1949, p 1 (translated from Chinese by Yin Xiao) |
| Ireland | 22.6.1979 | | New York | Joint communiqué | Establishment of diplomatic relations | Bartke, p 89 gives: NCNA, 18.6.1979 | Chiu p 184 gives ' JMJP 6/24/79; PR 22. 26:7 (6/29/79); NCNA Peking 6/23/79; FBIS (1) 124:G1 (6/26/79) (E) | *People's Daily,* 11 March 1973, p 1 (translated from Chinese by Yin Xiao), [see also: *Summary of World Broadcasts (SWB)*, FE/6152/A1/a, 27 June 1979] |
| Italy | 6.11.1970 | 6.11.1970 | Beijing | Joint communiqué | Establishment of diplomatic relations | Bartke, pp 90, 92 give: NCNA, 6.11.1970 | Chiu p 50 gives: 'TYC 17:2 (C ); JMJP 11/7/70 (C ); PR 13.46:6 (11/13/70) (E); NCNA Peking 11/6/70; SCMP 4779:26 (11/16/70) (E)' | *Beijing Review,* vol. 13, no. 46, 13 November 1970, p 6 |

**Table 1.5: Continued**

| Country | Date of signing or issue | Effective date[a] | Place of signature or issuance[b] | Instrument | Subject matter[c] | Source: Bartke[d] | Source: Chiu[e] | Source of document published in this book |
|---|---|---|---|---|---|---|---|---|
| Latvia [as part of USSR* | 3.10.1949 | | | Communiqué | | Bartke, pp 163,172 give: DS1 p.5f (V5 p.353f) | | USSR-PRC text in *People's Daily*, 4 October 1949, p 1 |
| Latvia | 12.9.1991 | | Riga | Joint communiqué | Establishment of diplomatic relations | | | *Summary of World Broadcasts (SWB)*, FE/1177 A2/1, 14 September 1991 |
| Lithuania [as part of USSR] | 3.10.1949 | | | Communiqué | | Bartke, pp 163, 172 give: DS1,p 5f (V5 p 353f) | | USSR-PRC text in *People's Daily*, 4 October 1949, p 1 |
| Lithuania | 14.9.1991 | | Vilnius | Joint communiqué | Establishment of diplomatic relations | | | *Summary of World Broadcasts (SWB)*, FE/1178 A2/1, 16 September 1991 |
| Luxem-bourg | 13.11.1972 | 16.11.1972 | Moscow | Joint communiqué | Establishment of diplomatic relations | Bartke, p 111 gives: NCNA, 16.11.1972 | Chiu p 85 gives: 'TYC 19:15 (C ); JMJP 11/17/72 (C ); PR 15.47:4 (11/24/72) (E); NCNA Peking 11/16/72; SCMP 5264:85 (11/28/72) (E)' | *Beijing Review,* vol. 15, no. 47, 24 November 1972, p 4 [full text in Chinese in *People's Daily,* 24 November 1972] |

**Table 1.5: Continued**

| Country | Date of signing or issue | Effective date[a] | Place of signature or issuance[b] | Instrument | Subject matter[c] | Source: Bartke[d] | Source: Chiu[e] | Source of document published in this book |
|---|---|---|---|---|---|---|---|---|
| Malta | 31.1.1972 | 31.1.1972 | Rome | Joint communiqué | Establishment of diplomatic relations | Bartke, p 114 gives NCNA 25.2.1972 | Chiu p 70 gives: 'TYC 19:4 (C ); JMJP 2/26/72 (C ); PR 15.9:3 (3/3/72) (E); NCNA Peking 2/25/72; SCMP 5088:133 (3/8/72) (E)' | *Beijing Review,* vol. 15, no. 9, 3 March 1972, p 3 [full text in Chinese in *People's Daily,* 26 February 1972, p 1] |
| Nether-lands | 19.11.1954 | | | Exchange of notes | | Bartke, pp 126, 127 give: DS3 p 188 (V3 p.59) | | |
| Nether-lands | 16.5.1972 | 18.5.1972 | Beijing | Joint communiqué | Raising level of diplomatic relations from offices of chargés d'affaires to embassies as from 5.18.1972 (Chiu p 76) | Bartke, pp 126, 127 give: DS3 p 188 (V3 p.59) | Chiu p 76 gives: 'TYC 19:24 (C ); JMJP 5/17/72 (C ); PR 15.21:20 (5/26/72) (E); NCNA Peking 5/17/72; SCMP 5142:217 (5/26/72)(E) | *Beijing Review,* vol. 15, no. 21, 26 May 1972, p 20 [full text in Chinese in *People's Daily,* 17 May 1972, p 1] |
| Poland | 7.10.1949 | | | Communiqué | | Bartke, pp 146, 152 give: DS1 p 11f (V5 p 282f) | | *People's Daily, 8 October 1949, p 1* (translated from Chinese by Yin Xiao) |

**Table 1.5: Continued**

| Country | Date of signing or issue | Effective date[a] | Place of signature or issuance[b] | Instrument | Subject matter[c] | Source: Bartke[d] | Source: Chiu[e] | Source of document published in this book |
|---|---|---|---|---|---|---|---|---|
| Portugal | 8.2.1979 | | | Communiqué | | Bartke, p 153 gives: NCNA 8.2.1979 | | *People's Daily,* 8 February 1979, p 1 (translated from Chinese by Yin Xiao) |
| Romania | 5.10.1949 | | | News report | | Bartke, pp 154, 158 give: DS1, p 7f (V5 p 321f) | | *People's Daily,* 6 October 1949, p 1 (translated from Chinese by Yin Xiao) |
| Slovakia: as Czechoslovakia | 6.10.1949 | | | Communiqué | | Bartke, pp 38,42 give: DS1, pp 10–11 (V5, pp 471–2) | | *People's Daily,* 8 October 1949, p 1 (translated from Chinese by Yin Xiao) |
| Slovenia | | | | | | | | |
| Spain | 9.3.1973 | 9.3.1973 | Paris | Joint communiqué | Establishment of diplomatic relations (Chiu p 296) | Bartke, pp 173, 174 give: NCNA 10.3.1973 | Chiu p 92 gives: 'TYC 20:4 (C ); JMJP 3/11/73 (C ); PR 16.11:3 (3/16/73) (E); NCNA Peking 3/10/73; SCMP 5388:115 (3/21/73) (E) | *People's Daily,* 11 March 1973, p 1 (translated from Chinese by Yin Xiao); see also *Beijing Review,* vol. 16, no. 11, 16 March 1973, p 3 [full text of this summary in Chinese in *People's Daily,* 11 March 1973, p 1] |

**Table 1.5: Continued**

| Country | Date of signing or issue | Effective date[a] | Place of signature or issuance[b] | Instrument | Subject matter[c] | Source: Bartke[d] | Source: Chiu[e] | Source of document published in this book |
|---|---|---|---|---|---|---|---|---|
| Sweden | 9.5.1950 | | | Communiqué | | Bartke, pp 180, 181 gives: *Handbook on People's China,* Beijing | | *People's Daily,* 9 May 1950 , p 1 (translated from Chinese by Yin Xiao) |

See Table 1.1 for footnotes and abbreviations.

EC and its Member States. The EU/EC law principle of attributed competences runs like a bright line through Europe–China relations today, as we will see in later chapters. In this context, the establishment of diplomatic relations between the EEC and China in 1975 built on earlier contacts. Nevertheless, it

> can be regarded as the first [formal] step towards a closer relationship which can hardly fail to be of considerable significance both to the People's Republic of China and to the European Community.[37]

[37] The quotation is adapted from the report of Sir Christopher Soames's visit to Beijing in May 1975: see *Bulletin of the EC*, 5–1975, para 1205.

# 2

# Bilateral Agreements on Trade and Textiles, 1975–Present: From the Establishment of Diplomatic Relations through Chinese Accession to the World Trade Organization

## INTRODUCTION

Following the establishment of diplomatic relations in 1975, the EEC/EC and China concluded a number of bilateral agreements on trade in general or on trade in textiles. After the death of Mao Zedong in 1976, Deng Xiaoping started market-oriented economic reforms and the 'opening up' of China to the outside world. In December 1978, he officially launched the 'Four Modernizations', embracing agriculture, industry, science and technology and national defence. This programme of reform stressed self-reliance, import substitution and growth led by exports and foreign trade. As part of the reform, China concluded a series of bilateral agreements with the EEC. These early agreements were exclusively concerned with trade or trade and economic cooperation in general, or with trade in textiles in particular, which were the main subjects of common interest at the time. They provided the legal normative framework for EEC and later EU—China relations from the late 1970s until 2001, when they were complemented or replaced by the law of the World Trade Organization (WTO).

Starting in the early 1990s, however, this legal framework proved too narrow to encompass the rapidly developing relations between the EU and China. This was due largely to the expansion of EC competences following the 1992 Maastricht Treaty on European Union, the transformation of China as a result of economic reforms, increasing foreign direct investment in China from the EU and elsewhere, and the elaboration by the EU and China of more coherent overall policies toward each other. China joined the WTO in late 2001. The WTO provided a new legal framework for EU–China trade relations. It did not directly affect the EU–China bilateral agreement on trade in general until recently, but it had an immediate and substantial impact on their bilateral agreements regarding trade in textiles.

After China acceded to the WTO, trade in textiles between the EU and China was governed by WTO law, notably the WTO Agreement on Textiles and Clothing (ATC). The ATC provided for a ten-year transitional period for the gradual removal of quotas on trade in textiles. The transitional period started on 1 January 1995, when the WTO was established, and ended on 31 December 2004. Before the end of the transitional period both the EU and China took steps to avoid major disruptions in textiles trade, but a significant disagreement broke out after 1 January 2005. The negotiations of the parties resulted in two essential legal documents, which are included in this chapter.

The chapter focuses on bilateral agreements concerning trade in general and trade specifically in textiles since 1975, including those textile agreements between the EU and China since Chinese accession to the WTO.[1] The broadening and deepening of EU–China relations after 1992 also resulted in a number of bilateral agreements in other fields.[2] Chapter 6 deals with these other agreements, many of which fall within the scope of the currently applicable 1985 Agreement on Trade and Economic Cooperation, which is being renegotiated at the time of writing (February 2008) but which has not yet been concluded.

1 Numerous EC domestic laws have an important effect on China, just as numerous Chinese domestic laws affect the EU. On the EU side, examples include EC antidumping law, food safety law, environmental law and technical standards. See, eg the basic EC antidumping legislation, Council Regulation (EC) No 384/96, [1996] OJ L56/1, consolidated version, available at http://europa.eu.int/eur-lex/en/consleg/main/1996/en_1996R0384_index.html (accessed 24 June 2007); the EU Food Law, Regulation (EC) 178/2002 of the European Parliament and the Council of 28 January 2002 laying down the general principles and requirements of food law, establishing the European Food Safety Authority and laying procedures in matters of food safety, [2002] OJ L31/1; the WEEE Directive, Directive 2002/96/EC of the European Parliament and the Council of 27 January 2003 on waste electrical and electronic equipment, [2003] OJ L37/24; the RoHS Directive, Directive 2002/95/EC of the European Parliament and the Council of 27 January 2003 on the restriction of the use of certain hazardous substances in electrical and electronic equipment, [2003] OJ L37/19; and the recent REACH legislation on chemicals, especially the basic Regulation (EC) No 1907/2006 of 18 December 2006 concerning the Registration, Evaluation, Authorisation and Restriction of Chemicals (REACH) establishing a European chemicals agency [partial title], as corrected, [2007] OJ L136/3. However, this book focuses on bilateral agreements. It therefore does not include EC legislation, or autonomous measures, adopted by the EC alone, or analogous measures adopted by the People's Republic of China.

2 EC autonomous measures include legislation, in addition to antidumping law, which is concerned solely with international trade. An example which has had a great effect on EU –China relations is the EC's Generalised Scheme of Preferences, established in 1971. China has been the largest beneficiary. Due to its large market share for specific products, however, it would have lost its preferential status under proposed reforms: see World Bank Press Review, 'New GSP Scheme Explained', published on the website of TRALAC (Trade Law Centre for Southern Africa), http://www.tralac.org/scripts/content.php?id=3008 (accessed 24 September 2007). For current arrangements, see Council Regulation (EC) No 980/2005 of 27 June 2005 applying a scheme of generalised tariff preferences, [2005] OJ L169/1. China is not included on the list of beneficiary countries of 'GSP plus': see Commission Decision 2005/924/EC of 21 December 2005 on the list of beneficiary countries which qualify for the special incentive arrangement for sustainable development and good governance, provided for by Art 26(e) of Council Regulation (EC) No 980/2005 applying a scheme of generalised tariff preferences, [2005] OJ L337/50. The GSP Users Guide is available at http://ec.europa.eu/trade/issues/global/gsp/gspguide.htm. See also Communication from the Commission to the Council, the European Parliament and the European Economic and Social Committee, 'Developing Countries, International Trade and Sustainable Development: the Function of the Community's Generalised System of Preferences (GSP) for the Ten-year Period from 2006 to 2015', COM(2004) 461 final (Brussels, 7 July 2004); European Parliament Resolution on the Communication from the Commission to the Council, the European Parliament and the European Economic Social Committee, 'Developing Countries, International Trade and Sustainable Development: the Function of the Community's Generalised System of Preferences (GSP) for the Ten-year Period from 2006 to 2015 (COM(2004)461)', [2005] OJ C166E/65; Opinion of the European Economic and Social Committee on the 'Generalised System of Preferences (GSP)', [2004] OJ C110/34. On the effect of WTO law on the EC's GSP, see European Communities, 'Conditions for the Granting of Tariff Preferences to Developing Countries', WT/ABS246/AB/R (adopted 20 April 2004), analysed at http://www.worldtradelaw.net/dsc/ab/ec-preferences (accessed 29 September 2007).

## TRADE AGREEMENTS

Between 1975 and 2001 the EEC and China concluded two trade agreements (see Table 2.1).

**Table 2.1: Trade Agreements between the EEC and China, 1975–2001**

| Measure/agreement | Source | Adoption by EEC | Source |
|---|---|---|---|
| Trade Agreement between the European Economic Community and the People's Republic of China (see Document 2.1) | OJ L123, 11.5.1978, p 2 | Council Regulation (EEC) No 946778 of 2 May 1978 concerning the conclusion of the Trade Agreement between the European Economic Community and the People's Republic of China | OJ L123, 11.5.78, p 1 |
| Agreement on Trade and Economic Cooperation between the European Economic Community and the People's Republic of China (see Document 2.2) | OJ L250 19.9.1985, p 2 | Council Regulation (EEC) No 2616/85 of 16 September 1985 concerning the conclusion of a Trade and Economic Cooperation Agreement between the European Economic Community and the People's Republic of China | OJ L250 19.9.1985, p 1 |

The first was concluded in 1978. The 1978 Trade Agreement (Document 2.1) was very general in nature, simply expressing the determination of the parties to create favourable conditions for trade, to seek to improve the structure of their trade and to examine suggestions by the other party for the purpose of facilitating trade. Each accorded the other limited most-favoured-nation treatment. The parties undertook to make every effort to foster expansion of and balance in trade, with China to give favourable consideration to EEC imports and the EEC to strive for increasing liberalisation of imports from China. Reflecting the fact that Chinese market reforms were only just beginning, the parties stated that trade shall be effected at market-related prices and rates. The Agreement also created an EEC–China Joint Committee for Trade, to meet once a year, alternately in Beijing and Brussels. Among its tasks were to monitor the Agreement and examine any problems which might arise.

## Document 2.1: 1978 Trade Agreement

**Trade Agreement between the European Economic Community and the People' s Republic of China**

*Official Journal L 123, 11/05/1978 P. 0002*
*Greek special edition: Chapter 11 Volume 9 P. 0200*

TRADE AGREEMENT between the European Economic Community and the People's Republic of China

THE COUNCIL OF THE EUROPEAN COMMUNITIES
and
THE GOVERNMENT OF THE PEOPLE'S REPUBLIC OF CHINA,

DESIRING to develop economic relations and trade between the European Economic Community and the People's Republic of China on the basis of equality and the mutual advantage of the two Contracting Parties and to give a new impetus to their relations,

HAVE DECIDED TO CONCLUDE THIS AGREEMENT THE TERMS OF WHICH ARE AS FOLLOWS:

Article 1

The two Contracting Parties will endeavour, within the framework of their respective existing laws and regulations, to promote and intensify trade between them.

To this end they confirm their determination:

(a) to take all appropriate measures to create favourable conditions for trade between them;

(b) to do all they can to improve the structure of their trade in order to diversify it further; and

(c) to examine, each for its own part and in a spirit of goodwill, any suggestions made by the other Party, in particular in the Joint Committee, for the purpose of facilitating trade between them.

Article 2

1. In their trade relations the two Contracting Parties shall accord each other most-favoured-nation treatment in all matters regarding:

(a) customs duties and charges of all kinds applied to the import, export, re-export or transit of products, including the procedures for the collection of such duties or charges;

(b) regulations, procedures and formalities concerning customs clearance, transit, warehousing and transhipment of products imported or exported;

(c) taxes and other internal charges levied directly or indirectly on products or services imported or exported;

(d) administrative formalities for the issue of import or export licences.

2. Paragraph 1 of this Article shall not apply in the case of:

(a) advantages accorded by either Contracting Party to States which together with it are members of a customs union or free trade area;

(b) advantages accorded by either Contracting Party to neighbouring countries for the purpose of facilitating border trade;

(c) measures which either Contracting Party may take in order to meet its obligations under international commodity agreements.

Article 3

The two Contracting Parties will make every effort to foster the harmonious expansion of their reciprocal trade and to help, each by its own means, to attain a balance in such trade.

Should an obvious imbalance arise, the matter must be examined within the Joint Committee so that measures can be recommended in order to improve the situation.

Article 4

1. The People's Republic of China will give favourable consideration to imports from the European Economic Community. To this end the competent Chinese authorities will ensure that Community exporters have the possibility of participating fully in opportunities for trade with China.

2. The European Economic Community will strive for an increasing liberalization of imports from the People's Republic of China. To this end it will endeavour progressively to introduce measures extending the list of products for which imports from China have been liberalized and to increase the amounts of quotas. The procedure for implementation will be examined within the framework of the Joint Committee.

Article 5

1. The two Contracting Parties shall exchange information on any problems that may arise with regard to their trade and shall open friendly consultations, with the intention of promoting trade, for the purpose of seeking mutually satisfactory solutions to those problems. Each of the two Contracting Parties will ensure that no action is taken before consultations are held.

2. In an exceptional case, however, where the situation does not admit any delay, either Contracting Party may take measures, but must endeavour as far as possible to hold friendly consultations before doing so.

3. Each Contracting Party will ensure that, when taking the measures referred to in paragraph 2, the general objectives of this Agreement are not prejudiced.

Article 6

The two Contracting Parties undertake to promote visits by persons, groups and delegations from economic, trade and industrial circles, to facilitate industrial and technical exchanges and contacts connected with trade and to foster the organization of fairs and exhibitions by both sides and the relevant provision of services. As far as possible they must grant each other the facilities concerning the above activities.

Article 7

Trade in goods and the provision of services between the two Contracting Parties shall be effected at market-related prices and rates.

Article 8

The Contracting Parties agree that payments for transactions shall be made, in accordance with their respective existing laws and regulations, in currencies of the Member States of the Community, Renminbi or any convertible currency accepted by the two parties concerned in the transactions.

Article 9

1. An EEC-China Joint Committee for Trade shall be set up, comprising representatives of the European Economic Community on the one hand and representatives of the People's Republic of China on the other.

2. The tasks of the Joint Committee shall be as follows:

- to monitor and examine the functioning of this Agreement,
- to examine any questions that may arise in the implementation of this Agreement,
- to examine problems that could hinder the development of trade between the Contracting Parties,
- to examine means and new opportunities of developing trade between the Contracting Parties and other problems relating to their trade,

and

- to make recommendations that may help to attain the objectives of this Agreement.

3. The Joint Committee shall meet once a year, in Brussels and Peking alternately. Extraordinary meetings may be convened by mutual agreement, at the request of either Contracting Party. The office of chairman of the Joint Committee shall be held by each of the two Contracting Parties in turn. Where both Parties consider it necessary, the Joint Committee may set up working parties to assist it in its work.

Article 10

As far as the European Economic Community is concerned, this Agreement shall apply to the territories in which the Treaty establishing the European Economic Community is applied, and under the conditions laid down in that Treaty.

Article 11

This Agreement shall enter into force on the first day of the month following the date on which the Contracting Parties have notified each other of the completion of the legal procedures necessary for this purpose. It is concluded for a period of five years. The Agreement shall be tacitly renewed from year to year provided that neither Contracting Party notifies the other Party in writing of its denunciation of the Agreement six months before the date of expiry.

However, the Agreement may be amended by mutual consent of the two Contracting Parties in order to take account of new situations.

Til bekræftelse heraf har undertegnede, som er behørigt befuldmægtigede hertil, underskrevet denne aftale.

Zu Urkund dessen haben die hierzu gehörig befugten Unterzeichneten dieses Abkommen unterschrieben.

In witness whereof, the undersigned, being duly authorized thereto, have signed this Agreement.

En foi de quoi, les soussignés, dûment habilités à cette fin, ont signé le présent accord.

In fede di che, i sottoscritti, debitamente abilitati a tale fine, hanno firmato il presente accordo.

Ten blijke waarvan de ondergetekenden, naar behoren daartoe gemachtigd, deze Overeenkomst hebben ondertekend.

Udfærdiget i Bruxelles, den tredje april nitten hundrede og otteoghalvfjerds i to eksemplarer på dansk, engelsk, fransk, italiensk, nederlandsk, tysk og kinesisk, hvilke tekster alle har samme gyldighed.

Geschehen zu Brüssel am dritten April neunzehnhundertachtundsiebzig in zwei Urschriften in dänischer, deutscher, englischer, französischer, italienischer, niederländischer und chinesischer Sprache, wobei jeder Wortlaut gleichermaßen verbindlich ist.

Done at Brussels on the third day of April in the year one thousand nine hundred and seventy-eight, in two copies in the Danish, Dutch, English, French, German, Italian and Chinese languages, each text being equally authentic.

Fait à Bruxelles, le trois avril mil neuf cent soixante-dix-huit, en deux exemplaires, en langues allemande, anglaise, danoise, française, italienne, néerlandaise et chinoise, chacun de ces textes faisant également foi.

Fatto a Bruxelles, il tre aprile millenovecentosettantotto, in due esemplari nella lingua danese, francese, inglese, italiana, olandese, tedesca e cinese, ciascuno di questi testi facente ugualmente fede.

Gedaan te Brussel, op drie april negentienhonderd achtenzeventig, in twee exemplaren, in de Deense, Duitse, Engelse, Franse, Italiaanse, Nederlandse en Chinese taal, zijnde alle teksten gelijkelijk authentiek.

For Rådet for De europæiske Fællesskaber

Für den Rat der Europäischen Gemeinschaften

For the Council of the European Communities

Pour le Conseil des Communautés européennes

Per il Consiglio delle Comunità europee

Voor de Raad van de Europese Gemeenschappen

For regeringen for Den kinesiske Folkerepublik

Für die Regierung der Volksrepublik China

For the Government of the People's Republic of China

Pour le gouvernement de la république populaire de Chine

Per il governo della Repubblica popolare cinese

Voor de Regering van de Volksrepubliek China

In 1985 the EEC and China replaced the 1978 Agreement with a new, more general agreement. The 1985 Agreement on Trade and Economic Cooperation (TEC Agreement; Document 2.2) was broader than its predecessor. It encompassed both trade and economic cooperation, in particular in industry and mining, agriculture, science and technology, energy, transport and communication, environmental protection and cooperation in third countries. It provided that each party, within the framework of its respective laws, would promote greater, mutually beneficial investment. It carefully preserved the powers of the EEC Member States to undertake bilateral economic cooperation activities in China and to conclude new economic cooperation agreements with China. It also preserved the Joint Committee. The 1985 TEC Agreement remains the general bilateral legal framework for EU–China trade today. Negotiations are currently underway to replace it with a broader, up-to-date agreement.

## Document 2.2: Agreement on Trade and Economic Cooperation between the European Economic Community and the People's Republic of China, 1985

**Agreement on Trade and Economic Cooperation between the European Economic Community and the People's Republic of China—1985**

THE COUNCIL OF THE EUROPEAN COMMUNITIES,

THE GOVERNMENT OF THE PEOPLE'S REPUBLIC OF CHINA,

NOTING with satisfaction the development of friendly relations between the European Economic Community and the People's Republic of China,

CONSIDERING that the Trade Agreement between the European Economic Community and the People's Republic of China, signed on 3 April 1978, has been satisfactorily applied,

INSPIRED by their common will to introduce a new stage into their commercial and economic relations,

DESIRING on the basis of equality and mutual advantage, to intensify and diversify their trade and actively develop economic and technical cooperation in line with their mutual interests,

HAVE DECIDED TO CONCLUDE THIS AGREEMENT, THE TERMS OF WHICH ARE AS FOLLOWS:

Article 1

The two Contracting Parties will endeavour, within the framework of their respective existing laws and regulations, and in accordance with the principles of equality and mutual advantage:

- to promote and intensify trade between them;
- to encourage the steady expansion of economic cooperation.

## CHAPTER 1
## Trade Cooperation

Article 2

The two Contracting Parties confirm their determination:

(a) to take all appropriate measures to create favourable conditions for trade between them;

(b) to do their utmost to improve the structure of their trade in order to diversify it further;

(c) to examine, each for its own part and in a spirit of goodwill, any suggestions made by the other Party, in particular in the Joint Committee, for the purpose of facilitating trade between them.

Article 3

1. In their trade relations, the two Contracting Parties shall accord each other most-favoured-nation treatment in all matters regarding:

(a) customs duties and charges of all kinds applied to the import, export, re-export, or transit of products, including the procedures for the collection of such duties or charges;

(b) regulations, procedures and formalities concerning customs clearance, transit, warehousing and transhipment of products imported or exported;

(c) taxes and other internal charges levied directly or indirectly on products or services imported or exported;

(d) administrative formalities for the issue of import or export licences.

2. Paragraph 1 shall not apply in the case of:

(a) advantages accorded by either Contracting Party to States which together with it are members of a customs union or free trade area;

(b) advantages accorded by either Contracting Party to neighbouring countries for the purpose of facilitating border trade;

(c) measures which either Contracting Party may take in order to meet its obligations under international commodity agreements. Article 4

The two Contracting Parties will make every effort to foster the harmonious expansion of their reciprocal trade and to help, each by its own means, to attain a balance in such trade.

Should an obvious imbalance arise, the matter must be examined within the Joint Committee so that measures can be recommended in order to improve the situation.

Article 5

1. The People's Republic of China will give favourable consideration to imports from the European Economic Community. To this end, the competent Chinese authorities will ensure that Community exporters have the possibility of participating fully in opportunities for trade with China.

2. The European Economic Community will strive for an increasing liberalization of imports from the People's Republic of China. To this end it will endeavour progressively to introduce measures extending the list of products for which imports from China have been liberalized and to increase the amounts of quotas. The procedure for implementation will be examined within the framework of the Joint Committee.

Article 6

1. The two Contracting Parties shall exchange information on any problems that may arise with regard to their trade and shall open friendly consultations, with the intention of promoting trade, for the purpose of seeking mutually satisfactory solutions to those problems. Each of the two Contracting Parties will ensure that no action is taken before consultations are held.

2. In an exceptional case, however, where the situation does not admit any delay, either Contracting Party may take measures, but must endeavour as far as possible to hold friendly consultations before doing so.

3. Each Contracting Party will ensure that when it takes the measures referred to in paragraph 2, the general objectives of this Agreement are not prejudiced.

Article 7

The two Contracting Parties undertake to promote visits by persons, groups and delegations from economic, trade and industrial circles, to facilitate industrial and technical exchanges and contracts connected with trade and to foster the organization of fairs and exhibitions by both sides and the relevant provision of services. As far as possible, they must grant each other the necessary facilities for the above activities.

Article 8

Trade in goods and the provision of services between the two Contracting Parties shall be effected at market-related prices and rates.

Article 9

The two Contracting Parties agree that payments for transactions shall be made, in accordance with their respective existing laws and regulations, in currencies of the Member States of the Community, Renminbi or any convertible currency accepted by the two parties concerned in the transactions.

## CHAPTER II
## Economic cooperation

Article 10

Within the limits of their respective competence, and with the main aims of encouraging the development of industry and agriculture in the European Economic Community and in the People's Republic of China, of diversifying their economic links, encouraging scientific and technological progress, opening up new sources of supply and new markets, helping to develop their economies and raise their respective standards of living, the two Contracting Parties agree to develop economic cooperation in all the spheres subject to common accord, and in particular:

- industry and mining;

- agriculture, including agro-industry;
- science and technology;
- energy;
- transport and communication;
- environmental protection;
- cooperation in third countries.

Article 11

According to their needs and within the means at their disposal and as far as they are able, the two Contracting Parties shall encourage the application of the various forms of industrial and technical cooperation, for the benefit of their undertakings or organizations. In order to attain the objectives of this Agreement, the two Contracting Parties shall endeavour to facilitate and promote, among other activities:

- joint production and joint ventures;
- common exploitation;
- the transfer of technology;
- cooperation between financial institutions;
- visits, contact and activities designed to promote cooperation between individuals, delegations and economic organizations;
- the organization of seminars and symposia;
- consultancy services;
- technical assistance, including the training of staff;
- a continuous exchange of information relevant to commercial and economic cooperation.

Article 12

1. In order to attain the objectives of this Agreement, the two Contracting Parties shall agree, within the framework of their respective laws, rules and policies, to promote and encourage greater and mutually beneficial investment.

2. In addition, the Parties undertake to improve the existing favourable investment climate in particular through encouraging the extension, by and to the Member States of the Community and by and to the People's Republic of China, of investment promotion and protection arrangements based on the principles of equity and reciprocity.

Article 13

In view of the difference in the two Contracting Parties' levels of development, the European Economic Community is prepared, within the context of its development aid activities, within the means at its disposal, and in accordance with its rules, to continue its development activities in the People's Republic of China.

It confirms its willingness to examine the possibility of stepping up and diversifying these activities.

Article 14

Without prejudice to the relevant provisions of the Treaties establishing the European Communities, this Agreement and any action taken thereunder shall in no way affect the powers of any of the Member States of the Communities to undertake bilateral activities with the People's Republic of China in the field of economic cooperation and conclude, where appropriate, new economic cooperation agreements with the People's Republic of China.

**CHAPTER III**
**Joint committee**

Article 15

1. The two Contracting Parties shall set up, under this Trade and Economic Cooperation Agreement, a Joint Committee comprising representatives of the European Economic Community on the one hand and representatives of the People's Republic of China on the other.

2. The tasks of the Joint Committee shall be as follows:

- to monitor and examine the functioning of this Agreement and review the various cooperation schemes implemented;
- to examine any questions that may arise in the implementation of this Agreement;
- to examine problems that could hinder the development of trade and economic cooperation between the two Contracting Parties;
- to examine means and new opportunities of developing trade and economic cooperation;
- to make recommendations that may help to attain the objectives of this Agreement, in the areas of common interest.

3. The Joint Committee shall meet once a year, in Brussels and Beijing alternately. Extraordinary meetings may be convened by mutual agreement, at the request of either Contracting Party. The office of chairman of the Joint Committee shall be held by each of the two Contracting Parties in turn. Where both Parties consider it necessary, the Joint Committee may set up working parties to assist it in its work.

**CHAPTER IV**
**Final provisions**

Article 16

As far as the European Economic Community is concerned, this Agreement shall apply to the territories in which the Treaty establishing the European Economic Community is applied and under the conditions laid down in that Treaty. Article 17

This Agreement replaces the Trade Agreement between the European Economic Community and the People's Republic of China of 3 April 1978, which entered into force on 1 June 1978.

Article 18

This Agreement shall enter into force on the first day of the month following the date on which the Contracting Parties have notified each other of the completion of the legal procedures necessary for this purpose. It is concluded for a period of five years. The Agreement shall be tacitly renewed from year to year provided that neither Contracting Party notifies

**Table 2.2: EEC–China Agreements on Trade in Textiles, 1979–2000**

| Agreement | Adoption by EEC/EC | Implementation by EEC/EC | Period of application |
|---|---|---|---|
| Agreement between the European Economic Community and the People's Republic of China on trade in textile products (1979) [official version not published till 1986], OJ L389, 31.12.1986, p 2 [text of Agreement not available; see text in this book of EEC implementing regulation, Council Regulation (EEC) No 3061/79] [see document 2.3] | Council Decision 86/669/EEC of 8 April 1986 concerning the conclusion of the Agreement between the European Economic Community and the People's Republic of China on trade in textile products, the Protocol of Adaptation and the Supplementary Protocol thereto , OJ L389, 31.12.1986, p. 1 | Council Regulation (EEC) No 3061/79 of 20 December 1979 on common rules for imports of certain textile products originating in the People's Republic of China, OJ L345,, 31.12. 1979, p. 1; extended by Council Regulation (EEC) No 109/84 amending Regulation (EEC) No 3061/79 on common rules for imports of certain textile products originating in the People's Republic of China, OJ L15, 18.1.1984, p. 1 | 1979 –31.12.1984 as extended |
| Additional Protocol to the Agreement between the European Economic Community and China on Trade in Textiles consequent on the Accession of the Hellenic Republic to the Community (1981), official version not published till 1986, OJ L389, 31.12.1986, p. 2 [not included in this book] | | | |
| Supplementary Protocol to the 1979 Agreement [not included in this book] | | Council Regulation (EEC) No 2072/84 of 29 June 1984 on common rules for imports of certain textile products originating in the People's Republic of China, OJ L198, 27.7.1984, p. 1 | 1.1.1984–31.12.1988 |

**Table 2.2: Continued**

| Agreement | Adoption by EEC/EC | Implementation by EEC/EC | Period of application |
|---|---|---|---|
| Additional Protocol to the Agreement between the European Economic Community and the People's Republic of China on trade in textile products consequent on the accession of the Kingdom and Spain and the Portuguese Republic to the Community , OJ L125, 14.5.1987, p. [not included in this book] | Council Decision No 87/265/EEC of 11 May 1987 concerning the conclusion of an Additional Protocol to the Agreement between the European Economic Community and the People's Republic of China on trade in textile products consequent on the accession of the Kingdom of Spain and the Portuguese Republic to the Community, OJ L125, 14.5.1987, p. 42 | Council Regulation (EEC) No 4136/86 of 22 December 1986 on common rules for imports of certain textile products originating in third countries, OJ L383, 31.12.1986, p. 1 | |
| Agreement between the European Economic Community and the People's Republic of China on trade in textile products – Protocol A – Protocol B – Protocol C – Protocol D – Protocol E – Agreed Minutes – Exchange of Notes, OJ L380, 31.12.1988, p. 2 [see document 2.4] | Council Decision No 88/656/EEC of 19 December 1988 concerning the provisional application of the Agreement between the European Economic Community and the People's Republic of China on trade in textile products, OJ L380, 31.12.1988, p. 1; Council Decision 90/647/EEC of 24 September 1990 concerning the conclusion of the Agreement between the European Economic Community and the People's Republic of China on trade in textile products, OJ L352 15.12.1990, p. 1 | Council Regulation (EEC) 2135/89 of 12 June 1989 on common rules for imports of certain textile products originating in the People's Republic of China, OJ L212 1989, p. 1; see also Commission Communication concerning the first Agreement between the European Economic Community and the People's Republic of China on trade in textile products not covered by the MFA bilateral agreement on trade in textile products initialled on 9 December 1988, OJ C66, 17.3.1995, p. 2 | Provisional application from 1.1.1989; Council Decision 90/647/EEC then approved, on behalf of the EEC, the 1988 Textiles Agreement, which continued in force |

**Table 2.2: Continued**

| Agreement | Adoption by EEC/EC | Implementation by EEC/EC | Period of application |
|---|---|---|---|
| Agreed Minute amending the Agreement between the European Economic Community and the People's Republic of China on trade in textile products, OJ L96, 12.4.1990, p. 88 [not included in this book] | | Council Decision 90/175/EEC of 2 April 1990 concerning the provisional application of the Agreed Minute amending the Agreement between the European Economic Community and the People's Republic of China on trade in textile products, OJ L96, 12.4.1990, p. 87 | From 1.1.1990 |
| Agreement in the form of an exchange of letters amending the Agreement between the European Economic Community and the People's Republic of China on trade in textile products – Agreed Minutes – Notes verbales – Exchange of notes, OJ L410, 31.12.1992 p. 103 (unofficial translation) [not included in this book] | | | 1.1.1993–31.12.1994, with automatic extension till 31.12.1995, unless notified otherwise, except if WTO ATC is concluded and enters into force earlier |

**Table 2.2: Continued**

| Agreement | Adoption by EEC/EC | Implementation by EEC/EC | Period of application |
|---|---|---|---|
| Agreement in the form of an Exchange of Letters between the European Community and the People's Republic of China amending the 1988 MFA | | | |
| Agreement between the European Economic Community and the People's Republic of China on trade in textile products to take into account the expected accession of the Republic of Austria, the Republic of Finland and the Kingdom of Sweden to the European Union – Exchange of Notes, OJ L94, 26.4.1995, p. 107 (unofficial translation) [not included in this book] | | | |

**Table 2.2: Continued**

| Agreement | Adoption by EEC/EC | Implementation by EEC/EC | Period of application |
|---|---|---|---|
| Agreement between the European Economic Community and the People's Republic of China on trade in textile products not covered by the MFA bilateral agreement on trade in textile products intialled on 9 December 1988 as extended and modified by the exchange of letters initialled on 8 December 1992 – Protocol A – Protocol B – Protocol of Understanding concerning the implementation of Article 12 of the Agreement – Agreed Minute, OJ L104, 6.5.1995, p. 2 (unofficial translation) [see document 2.5] | | Council Decision 95/155/EC OF 10 April 1995 on the provisional application of the Agreement between the European Community and the People's Republic of China on trade in textile products not covered by the MFA bilateral agreement on trade in textile products initialled on 9 December 1988 as extended and modified by the Exchange of Letters initialled on 8 December 1992, OJ L104, 6.5.1995, p. 1 | |
| Agreement on the modification of certain provisions of the 1988 MFA bilateral Agreement on trade in textile products between the European Community and the People's Republic of China, OJ L261, 31.10.1995, p. 2 [see document 2.6] | Council Decision 95/440/EC of 13 June 1995 on the conclusion of the Agreement between the European Community and the People's Republic of China on the modification of certain provisions of the 1988 MFA bilateral Agreement on trade in textile products between the European Community and the People's Republic of China, OJ L261, 31.10.1995, p. 1 | | Following signature; provisional application as of the date of initialing |

**Table 2.2: Continued**

| Agreement | Adoption by EEC/EC | Implementation by EEC/EC | Period of application |
|---|---|---|---|
| Agreement in the form of an Exchange of Letters between the European Community and the People's Republic of China amending the Agreement between the European Economic Community and the People's Republic of China on trade in textile products as last amended by Agreements initialled on 14 December 1994 – Agreed Minute, OJ L81, 30.3.1996, p. 318 (unofficial translation) [see document 2.7] | | Council Decision 96/225/EC of 22 December 1995 on the provisional application of certain bilateral agreements between the European Community and certain third countries on trade in textile products (Bulgaria, the People's Republic of China, Czech Republic, Slovakia), OJ L81, 30.3.1996, p. 310 | Till 31.12.1998 |
| Agreement in the form of an exchange of letters between the European Community and the People's Republic of China amending the Agreement between the European Economic Community and the People's Republic of China on trade in textile products as last amended by Agreements initialled on 13 December 1995 – Agreed Minutes, OJ L12, 16.1.1999, p. 28 [see document 2.8] | Council Decision 199/36/EC of 21 December 1998 on the provisional application of the Agreement in the form of an exchange of letters between the European Community and the People's Republic of China amending the Agreement between the European Economic Community and the People's Republic of China on trade in textile products, OJ L12, 16.1.1999, p. 27 | Provisional application from 1.1.1999 | |

**Table 2.2: Continued**

| Agreement | Adoption by EEC/EC | Implementation by EEC/EC | Period of application |
|---|---|---|---|
| Agreement in the form of an exchange of letters between the European Community and the People's Republic of China initialled in Beijing on 6 December 1999 amending the Agreement between the European Economic Community and the People's Republic of China on trade in textile products as last amended by an agreement initialled on 20 November 1999 and amending the Agreement between the European Community and the People's Republic of China initialled on 19 January 1995 on trade in textile products not covered by the MFA bilateral Agreement, OJ L345, 31.12.1999, p. 2 [see document 2.9] | | Council Decision 1999/876/EC of 21 December 1999 on the provisional application of the Agreement in the form of an Exchange of Letters amending the Agreements between the European Community and the People's Republic of China on trade in textile products, OJ L345, 31.12.1999, p. 1 | Applicable till 31.12.2000 |

**Table 2.2: Continued**

| Agreement | Adoption by EEC/EC | Implementation by EEC/EC | Period of application |
|---|---|---|---|
| Agreement in the form of an Exchange of Letters between the European Community and the People's Republic of China initialled in Beijing on 19 May 2000 amending the Agreement between them on trade in textile products and amending the Agreement between them initialled on 19 January 1995 on trade in textile products not covered by the MFA bilateral Agreement – Protocol A, OJ L314, 14.12.2000, p. 14 [see document 2.10] | Council Decision 2000/787/EC of 23 November 2000 on the signing, on behalf of the European Community, of the Agreement in the form of an Exchange of Letters between the European Community and the People's Republic of China initialled in Beijing on 19 May 2000 amending the Agreement between them on trade in textile products and amending the Agreement between them initialled on 19 January 1995 on trade in textile products not covered by the MFA bilateral Agreement, and authorising its provisional application, OJ L314, 14.12.2000, p 13 | | Application from 21.11.2000 |
| China's accession to the WTO – First and second stage of integration under the Agreement on textiles and clothing, OJ C356, 14.12.2001, p. 4 [see document 2.11] | | Removal of certain quantitative restrictions as from 11.12.2001, date of PRC accession to WTO | |
| Notice on the application of Article 10a of Council Regulation (EEC) No 3030(93 concerning a textiles specific safeguard clause [see document 2.12] [see also Chapter 7] | OJ EC C101, 27.4.2005, p. 2 | | |

**Table 2.2: Continued**

| Agreement | Adoption by EEC/EC | Implementation by EEC/EC | Period of application |
|---|---|---|---|
| Memorandum of Understanding (MOU) Between the European Commission and the Ministry of Commerce of the People's Republic of China on the Export of Certain Chinese Textile and Clothing Products to the European Union (Shanghai Agreement) [see document 2.13] | Source: Europa Rapid Press Releases, Reference: MEMO/05/201, 12.6.2005 | Commission Regulation (EC) No 1084/2005 of 8 July 2005 amending Annexes II, III and V to Council Regulation (EEC) No 3030/93 on common rules for imports of certain textile products from third countries, OJ 9.7.2005 L177(19 | Signed Shanghai, 10.6.2005 |
| Minutes of the consultations regarding the establishment of transitional flexibility measures on the Memorandum of Understanding between the European Commission and the Ministry of Commerce of the People's Republic of China on the export of certain Chinese textile and clothing products to the EU, Beijing 5.9.2005 [see document 2.14] | | Commission Regulation (EC) No 1478/2005 of 12 September 2005 amending Annexes V, VI and VIII to Council Regulation (EEC) no 3030/93 on common rules for imports of certain textile products from third countries, OJ 13.9.2005 L236/2 | Signed Beijing, 1.9.2005 |

the other Party in writing of its denunciation of the Agreement six months before the date of expiry.

However, the Agreement may be amended by mutual consent of the two Contracting Parties in order to take account of new situations.

## TEXTILES AGREEMENTS

Starting in 1979, the EEC and China also concluded a series of agreements on trade in textiles, designed mainly to protect the European market.

During the late 1970s until 1995, international trade in textiles was governed mainly by the Agreement Regarding International Trade in Textiles, the Multi-fibre Arrangement (MFA). Succeeding a series of earlier textiles agreements, the MFA was adopted within the framework of the GATT in 1974. The EEC participated in and signed the MFA; China did not accede to the MFA until 1984. In 1979, the EEC and China concluded their first bilateral textiles agreement. The 1979 Textiles Agreement (Document 2.3) was concluded outside the MFA but was consistent with it. It replaced a system of annual export quotas. It was amended on the accession of Greece, a Supplementary Protocol was concluded in 1979, and the Agreement and Protocols were amended on the accession of Spain and Portugal to the EEC.

### Document 2.3: 1979 Textiles Agreement between the EEC and China as implemented by EEC Council Regulation (EEC) No 3061/79

**Council Regulation (EEC) No 3061/79 of 20 December 1979 on common rules for imports of certain textile products originating in the People's Republic of China**

*Official Journal L 345, 31/12/1979 P. 0001–0051*
*Greek special edition: Chapter 11 Volume 17 P. 0096*

++++

(1) OJ No L 365, 27. 12. 1978, p. 1.

(2) OJ No L 148, 26. 6. 1968, p. 1.

(3) OJ No L 307, 30. 11. 1977, p. 1.

(4) OJ No L 307, 30. 11. 1977, p. 42.

COUNCIL REGULATION (EEC) No 3061/79

of 20 December 1979

on common rules for imports of certain textile products originating in the People's Republic of China

THE COUNCIL OF THE EUROPEAN COMMUNITIES,

Having regard to the Treaty establishing the European Economic Community, and in particular Article 113 thereof,

Having regard to the proposal from the Commission,

Whereas the Community has negotiated an Agreement with the People's Republic of China (hereinafter referred to as "China") on trade in textile products;

Whereas the Community and China decided that the provisions of that Agreement will be fully implemented as from 1 January 1980 until 31 December 1983;

Whereas it is necessary, with a view to implementing the Agreement and to take account of its particularities, to establish specific common rules for imports of certain textile products originating in China;

Whereas, in order to apply quantitative limits in conformity with the Agreement negotiated with China, it is necessary to establish a special management procedure; whereas it is desirable that such common management system be decentralized by allocating the quantitative limits among the Member States, and that the import authorizations be issued by the Member States' authorities in accordance with the double-checking system defined in the Agreement;

Whereas, in order to ensure the best possible utilization of the quantitative limits, they should be allocated in accordance with the requirements of the Member States and with the quantitative objectives established by the Council; whereas, however, the extent of the disparities existing in the conditions for imports of these products into the Member States and the particularly sensitive position of the Community textiles industry mean that the said conditions can be standardized only gradually; whereas for these reasons allocation of supplies cannot immediately be effected on the basis of requirements alone;

Whereas it is also necessary to introduce efficient and rapid procedures for altering quantitative limits and their allocation to take account of the development of trade flows, needs for additional imports and the Community's obligations under the Agreement with China;

Whereas, in the case of products not subject to quantitative limitation, the Agreement provides for a consultation procedure whereby, under certain conditions, agreement can be sought with China on the introduction of quantitative limits; whereas it is necessary to provide a procedure whereby the Community may introduce quantitative limits pending the conclusion of such consultation or as a result of such consultations or where such consultations do not lead to agreement;

Whereas it is therefore necessary to lay down a rapid and efficient procedure for introducing such quantitative limits and concluding arrangements with China;

Whereas, for practical reasons, it is convenient to make use, for the purposes enumerated above, of the management committee already set up by Council Regulation (EEC) No 3059/78 of 21 December 1978 on common rules for imports of certain textile products originating in third countries (1),

HAS ADOPTED THIS REGULATION:

Article 1

1. This Regulation shall apply to imports into the Community of the textile products listed in Annex I and originating in China.

2. The description and identification of the products listed in Annex I shall be those used in the nomenclature of the Common Customs Tariff and in the nomenclature of goods for the external trade statistics of the Community and the statistics of trade between Member States (NIMEXE), without prejudice to Article 3 (4).

3. Subject to provisions of this Regulation the import into the Community of the textile products referred to in paragraph 1 shall not be subject to quantitative restrictions or measures having equivalent effect to such restrictions.

Article 2

1. The origin of the products referred to in Article 1 (1) shall be determined in accordance with the rules in force in the Community.

2. The procedures for control of the origin of the products referred to in Article 1 (1) are laid down in Annexes III and VI.

Article 3

1. The import into the Community of the textile products listed in Annex IV, originating in China and shipped between 1 January 1980 and 31 December 1983, shall be subject to the annual quantitative limits laid down in that Annex.

2. The release for free circulation in the Community of imports subject to the quantitative limits referred to in paragraph 1 shall be subject to the presentation of an import authorization or equivalent document issued by the Member States authorities in accordance with Article 10.

3. The authorized imports shall be charged against the quantitative limits laid down for the year in which the products are shipped in China.

4. The definition of quantitative limits laid down in Annex IV and the categories of products to which they apply shall be adapted in accordance with the procedure laid down in Article 14 where this proves necessary to ensure that any subsequent amendment to the nomenclature of the Common Customs Tariff or the nomenclature of goods for the external trade statistics of the Community and the statistics of trade between Member States (NIMEXE) does not result in a reduction of such quantitative limits.

5. Exports of all textile products originating in China, including handloom and folklore products covered by the categories referred to in Article 1, shall be subject to a double-checking system, as described hereinafter.

6. Where imports into the Community of textile products listed in Annex I and originating in China are effected at abnormally low prices, the provisions of Annex IX shall apply.

7. In the case of products subject to quantitative limits established in the Agreement or fixed subsequently pursuant to Article 11 of this Regulation, the provisions of Annex V shall apply, subject to the provisions of paragraph 6 and of Article 5 (3) and (4)

8. Imports of products not subject to such quantitative limits shall be conditional upon the presentation of an import document issued in the manner set out in Annex V for the issue of import licences, subject to the provisions of paragraph 6 and of Article 11, in particular paragraph 7 thereof. The import document shall be granted on presentation of a shipment certificate issued by the competent Chinese authorities and corresponding to the specimen set out in Annex VII.

9. An importer's declaration or application submitted for the purpose of obtaining an import authorization or import document shall be accompanied by the corresponding export licence or shipment certificate and, where a Member State so requests, by a copy of the contract of purchase, or equivalent proof of price.

Article 4

1. Imports of products not subject to quantitative limitation before 1 January 1980 which were in the course of shipment to the Community before that date shall not be subject to the quantitative limits referred to in Article 3 provided they were shipped from China before 1 January 1980 and were released for free circulation in the Community before 1 April 1980.

2. The release for free circulation of products the import of which was subject to quantitative limitation before 1 January 1980 and which were shipped before the said date shall continue from that date to be subject to the presentation of the same import documents, and to the same import conditions, as before 1 January 1980.

Article 5

1. The quantitative limits referred to in Article 3 shall not apply to products admitted into the customs territoty of the Community under the arrangements for inward processing or other suspensive arrangements, provided that they are declared to be for re-export under such a system outside the said territory in the same state or after processing.

The subsequent release for free circulation of the products referred to in the first subparagraph shall be subject to the quantitative limits referred to in Article 3 and to the presentation of an import authorization or equivalent document issued in accordance with Article 3 (2) and the products so released shall be charged against the quantitative limit established for the year for which the export licence was issued.

2. Where the authorities in the Member States establish that imports of textile products have been charged against a quantitative limit fixed pursuant to Article 3 and that these products have subsequently been re-exported outside the Community, they shall inform the Commission thereof and issue additional import authorizations for the same products and the same quantities in accordance with Article 3 (2).

Imports effected under cover of such authorizations shall not be charged against the quantitative limit for the current year or the following year.

3. Any quantitative limit, except for categories 2 and 3, established in Annex IV or any level resulting from the application of the rates specified in Article 11 (2) and (3), may be exceeded by 10% as long as the imports causing this excess are imports of cottage industry and folklore products as defined in Annex VIII, originating in China.

4. The provisions of the above paragraph shall apply only to products accompanied by a certificate drawn up by the Chinese authorities in conformity with the specimen set out in the appendix to Annex VIII and which fulfil the conditions laid down in Annex VIII.

Article 6

In order that the Community textile and clothing industry may benefit from the utilization of all the quantitative limits established in Annex IV, and in particular those established for categories 2, 3 and 37, and in order to contribute to the improvement of supplies to these industries of raw silk, silk waste, angora and cashmere, the Commission shall, at the request of one or more Member States, submit to the Chinese authorities before 1 December of each Agreement year a list of interested manufacturing and processing companies, and, where appropriate, the quantities of products requested by the companies concerned.

Article 7

1. The quantitative limits introduced pursuant to Article 11 shall be allocated in such a way as to ensure the improved utilization of these quantitative limits and to attain progressively a more balanced penetration of the markets by means of improved burden-sharing between the Member States.

2. The allocation of the quantitative limits referred to in paragraph 1 shall be adapted in accordance with the procedure laid down in Article 14 and according to the criteria defined in paragraph 1 where this proves necessary, particularly in view of trends in patterns of trade, in order to ensure their improved utilization.

Article 8

1. China may, after notifying the Commission in advance, utilize the shares allocated to Member States in the following ways:

(a) Advance utilization during any given year of a portion of a share established for the following year shall be authorized for each category of products up to 5% of the share for the year of actual utilization.

Such advance imports shall be deducted from the corresponding shares established for the following year.

(b) Carry-over of amounts not utilized during any given year to the corresponding share for the following year shall be authorized up to 5% of the share for the year of actual utilization.

However, for each of the categories of products subject to quantitative limitations, carry-over of quantities unused in 1979 shall be authorized up to 10% of the quantitative limits for 1980.

For categories to which the arrangement described in the above subparagraph is applied, no advance use shall be authorized during 1980.

(c) Transfers of quantities in Group 1 categories shall be made only as follows:

- transfers from category 1 to categories 2 and 3 shall be authorized up to 5% of the share established for the category to which the listed transfer is made,
- transfers between categories 2 and 3 are governed by the provisions of the appendix to Annex IV,
- transfers between categories 4, 5, 6, 7 and 8 shall be authorized up to 5% of the share established for the category to which the transfer is made.

Transfers of quantities into the different categories in Groups II, III, IV and V may be made from any category in Groups I, II, III, IV and V subject to a maximum of 5% of the share established for the category to which the transfer is made.

The table of equivalence applicable to the abovementioned transfers is given in Annex I.

2. In the event of recourse by China to the provisions of paragraph 1, the Commission shall notify the authorities of the Member State concerned which shall authorize the imports in question in accordance with the double-checking system defined in Annexes V and VI.

3. Where a Member State's share has been increased by the application of paragraph 1, or of Article 9, or where further possibilities for imports into that Member State have been created under Article 9, such increases or further import possibilities shall not be taken into account for the purposes of applying paragraph 1 in the current year or subsequent years.

Article 9

1. Member States which find that they require additional imports for their internal consumption or which consider that their share may not be fully utilized shall notify the Commission accordingly.

2. The quantitative limits laid down in Article 3 may be increased in accordance with the procedure laid down in Article 14 where it appears that additional imports are required.

3. At the request of a Member State which finds that it requires additional imports, either on the occasion of fairs of where it has issued import authorizations or equivalent documents for up to 80% of its national share, the Commission may, after oral or written consultations with the Member States within the Committee referred to in Article 13, open up additional possibilities for imports into that Member State.

In an emergency, the Commission shall open consultations within the Committee within five working days following receipt of the request from the Member State concerned and shall take a decision within 15 working days calculated from the same date.

Article 10

1. The authorities of the Member States shall issue the import authorizations or equivalent documents provided for in Article 3 (2) up to the amount of their shares, taking into account the measures taken pursuant to Articles 5, 7, 8 and 9.

2. The import authorizations or equivalent documents shall be issued in accordance with Annexes V and VI.

3. The quantities of products covered by the import authorizations or equivalent documents provided for in Article 3 shall be charged against the share of the Member State which issued those authorizations or documents.

Article 11

1. The following provisions shall apply, under the conditions enumerated hereinafter, to the importations into the Community of textile products listed in Annex I, originating in China and not subject to the quantitative limits referred to in Article 3.

2. The Commission—on its own initiative or at the request of a Member State—can request the opening of consultations with China in order to reach agreement on a suitable level of limitation for any category of products when it finds, through the system of double-checking, that the total volume covered by the shipment certificates issued by the Chinese authorities for the category in question in an Agreement year is above to reach or exceed the level resulting from the application of the following percentages:

- 0.2% if the category is in Group I,

- 1.5% if the category is in Group II,
- 5% if the category is in Group III, IV and V,

to the preceding calendar year's total imports into the Community of products in the same category, subject to the provisions of paragraph 10.

3. Such consultation with China can also be requested in order to reach agreement on a suitable level of regional limitation for any category of products when it is found that the total volume covered by shipment certificates issued by the Chinese authorities in an Agreement year for any category of product is about to reach or exceed, in relation to the total quantities calculated for the whole Community according to the percentage specified in paragraph 2 above, the relevant percentages set out for the regions of the Community in the table below:

| | |
|---|---|
| Germany | 28.5% |
| Benelux | 10.5% |
| France | 18.5% |
| Italy | 15% |
| Denmark | 3% |
| Ireland | 1% |
| United Kingdom | 23.5% |

4. For products subject to quota under the autonomous import arrangements in effect at the time of initialling of the Agreement, such consultations shall be initiated within eight days of a request by a Member State.

For other products, the decision to hold consultations shall be taken in accordance with the procedure referred to in Article 14.

This decision must be taken within 15 working days from such a request. Where the outcome of this decision is that consultations should be opened, this shall happen within eight working days of the decision to do so.

5. Pending the result of the consultations and within five working days from the date on which the request for them was notified to China in accordance with paragraph 8, a quantitative limit shall be established for imports into the Community or, at the request of Member States, into one or more regions, at a level not lower than that notified in the request for consultations, nor that resulting from the application of the rate referred to in paragraph 2, nor the level of imports in 1978 of products of the same category originating in China.

Such limits will remain in force until replaced by a definitive limit introduced after the consultation has taken place or until it is decided, after the consultation and in accordance with the provisions of this Article, that no that no definitive limit should be introduced.

6. The introduction of a quantitative limit does not preclude the import of products covered by this quantitative limit but shipped from China before the date on which the request for consultations was notified to China. Notice of this date will be given by a Commission communication published without delay in the Official Journal of the European Communities.

7. In the case of products subject to quota under the autonomous import arrangements in effect at the time of the initialling of the Agreement with China, a Member State may, where the conditions set out in paragraph 3 are fulfilled, suspend the issue of import documents provided that the suspension is brought to the attention of the Commission within seven working days of the date on which such an import document was requested by an importer. The importer must in turn be informed without delay. When the quantitative limit referred to in paragraph 5 is established, the issue of import documents will be resumed within and up to the level of the quantitative limit in question, subject always to the provisions of paragraph 6.

8. Where consultations are opened with China, the Commission may request that China with effect from the date of notification of the request for consultations and pending a mutually satisfactory solution suspend or limit at the level indicated by the Commission its exports of the category of products in question to the Community or to one or more regions thereof.

The consultations with China may lead to the conclusion of an arrangement between China and the Community, which shall stipulate that the quantitative limits applied shall be administered in accordance with the double-checking system.

The consultations shall be conducted in accordance with the following rules:

- the Commission shall notify China of the request for consultations,
- the request for consultations shall be followed within a reasonable period and in any event within 15 days of the notifiction, by a report setting out the conditions which, in the Commission's opinion, justify the submission of such a request,
- the Commission shall initiate consultations within one month at the latest of notification of the request, with a view to reaching agreement or a mutually acceptable conclusion within one month at the latest.

9. Should the Community and China fail to reach a satisfactory solution within the time limit set out above, imports of the category of products in question may be made subject to definitive quantitative limits at an annual level not lower than that reached by imports of the said products and indicated in the request for consultations.

10. Where, for a particular category of products, the provisions of paragraph 2 are applied, the level which shall be taken into consideration shall be the highest level reached in respect of the category of products in question in either of the last two years preceding the year of application of the measure establishing a quantitative limit.

11. Where the development of total imports into the Community of a product which is subject to a quantitative limit fixed in accordance with paragraphs 5 to 9 renders it necessary, the annual level of that quantitative limit shall be increased, after consultation with China in accordance with the procedure laid down in paragraph 8, to ensure compliance with the conditions set out in paragraphs 2 and 3.

12. Quantitative limits established pursuant to this Article shall be the subject of a Commission Regulation and shall be administered in accordance with Articles 3 to 10.

Article 12

1. In respect of each quantitative limit set out in Annex IV, Member States shall notify the Commission, within the first 10 days of each month, of the total quantities, in the

appropriate units and by country of origin and category of products, for which import authorizations have been issued during the preceding month.

2. In respect of the textile products in Annexes I and II, Member States shall notify the Commission monthly, within 30 days following the end of each month, of the total quantities imported during that month, by NIMEXE code and in the units, including where appropriate supplementary units, of the NIMEXE code.

The imports shall be broken down in accordance with the statistical procedures in force; they shall be expressed in terms of quantity and value in order to permit an assessment of the evolution of the trade balance in textile products with China.

3. Member States shall notify the Commission monthly within 30 days following the end of each month, of the quantities, in the appropriate units and category of products, of products specified in paragraph 1 of Annex VIII.

4. In order to enable market trends in the products covered by this Regulation to be monitored, Member States shall communicate to the Commission, before 31 March each year, statistical data for the preceding year on exports. The statistical data relating to the production and consumption of each product shall be forwarded under arrangements to be determined subsequently pursuant to the procedure laid down in Article 14.

5. Where the nature of the products or particular circumstances so require, the Commission may, at the request of a Member State or on its own initiative, alter the time limits for communicating the abovementioned information under the procedure laid down in Article 14.

6. Member States shall notify the Commission, under conditions set in accordance with the procedure laid down in Article 14 of all other particulars deemed under that procedure to be necessary in order to ensure compliance with the obligations agreed between the Community and China.

Article 13

Where reference is made to the procedure defined in Article 14, the Committee referred to in that Article shall, for the purpose and duration of this Regulation, be the "Textile Committee" set up under Article 14 of Council Regulation (EEC) No 3059/78.

Article 14

1. Where reference is made to the procedure defined in this Article, the chairman, on his own initiative or at the request of a Member State, shall refer the matter to the Committee.

2. The Commission representative shall submit draft measures to the Committee. The Committee shall deliver an opinion on the draft measures within a period which may be fixed by the chairman depending on the degree of urgency of the matters to be examined. The Committee shall decide by a majority of 41 votes, the votes of the Member States being weighted as specified in Article 148 (2) of the Treaty. The chairman shall not vote.

3. (a) The Commission shall adopt the measures proposed where they are in conformity with the Commitee's opinion.

(b) Where the measures proposed are not in conformity with the Committee's opinion, or where no opinion has been given, the Commission shall submit to the Council without delay a proposal for the measures to be taken. The Council shall act by a qualified majority.

(c) Should the Council fail to take a decision within one month of the date on which the proposal was laid before it, the Commission shall adopt the proposed measures.

Article 15

The chairman may, on his own initiative or at the request of one of the Member States' representatives, consult the Committee about any other matter relating to the operation of this Regulation.

Article 16

The Member States shall inform the Commission forthwith of all measures taken pursuant to this Regulation and of all laws, regulations or administrative provisions concerning arrangements for the import of the products covered by this Regulation.

Article 17

Any amendments or adjustments to the Annexes to this Regulation which may be necessary to take into account any amendment or the expiry of the Agreement with China or the conclusion, amendment or expiry of any further arrangement with China or amendments made to Community rules on statistics, or customs arrangements or common import arrangements, shall be adopted in accordance with the procedure laid down in Article 14.

Article 18

This Regulation shall enter into force on 1 January 1980.

It shall apply until 31 December 1983.

This Regulation shall be binding in its entirety and directly applicable in all Member States.

Done at Brussels, 20 December 1979.

For the Council

The President

J. TUNNEY

ANNEX I

referred to in Article 1

Where the expression " babies " garments' is used, this is meant also to cover girls' garments up to and including commercial size 86.

When the constitutive material of the products of categories 1 to 114 is not specifically mentioned these products are to be taken to be made exclusively of wool or of fine animal hair, of cotton or of synthetic or artificial textile fibres.

GROUP I

| Category | Description | NIMEXE code (1979) | Table of equivalence | |
|---|---|---|---|---|
| | | | pieces/kg | g/piece |

| | | | | |
|---|---|---|---|---|
| 1 | Cotton yarn not put up for retail sale | 55.05-13; 19; 21; 25; 27; 29; 33; 35; 37; 41; 45; 46; 48; 52; 58; 61; 65; 67; 69; 72; 78; 92; 98 | | |
| 2(1) | Woven fabrics of cotton, other than gauze, terry fabrics, narrow woven fabrics, pile fabrics, chenille fabrics, tulle and other net fabrics: | 55.09-01; 02; 03; 04; 05; 11; 12; 13; 14; 15; 16; 17; 19; 21; 29; 31; 33; 35; 37; 38; 39; 41; 49; 51; 52; 53; 54; 55; 56; 57; 59; 61; 63; 64; 65; 66; 67; 68; 69; 70; 71; 72; 73; 74; 76; 77; 78; 81; 82; 83; 84; 86; 87; 92; 93; 97 | | |
| | a) Of which other than unbleached or bleached | 55.09-03; 04; 05; 51; 52; 53; 54; 55; 56; 57; 59; 61; 63; 64; 65; 66; 67; 70; 71; 81; 82; 83; 84; 86; 87; 92; 93; 97 | | |
| 3 | Woven fabrics of synthetic fibres (discontinuous or waste) other than narrow woven fabrics, pile fabrics (including terry fabrics) and chenille fabrics: | 56.07-01; 04; 05; 07; 08; 11; 13; 14; 16; 17; 18; 21; 23; 24; 26; 27; 28; 32; 33; 34; 36 | | |
| | a) Of which other than unbleached or bleached | 56.07-01; 05; 07; 08; 13; 14; 16; 18; 21; 23; 26; 27; 28; 33; 34; 36 | | |
| 4 | Shirts, T-shirts, lightweight fine knit roll, polo' or turtle necked jumpers and pullovers, undervests and the like, knitted or crocheted, not elastic or rubberized, other than babies' garments of cotton or synthetic textile fibres; T-shirts and lightweight fine knit roll, polo or turtle necked jumpers and pullovers, of regenerated textile fibres, other than babies' garments | 60.04-19; 20; 22; 23; 24; 26; 41; 50; 58; 71; 79; 89 | 6.48 | 154 |
| 5 | Jerseys, pullovers, slip-overs, waistcoats, twinsets, cardigans, bedjackets and jumpers, knitted or crocheted, not elastic or rubberized, of wool, of cotton or of man-made textile fibres | 60.05-01; 27; 28; 29; 30; 33; 36; 37; 38 | 4.53 | 221 |

| | | | | |
|---|---|---|---|---|
| 6 | Men's and boys' woven breeches, shorts and trousers (including slacks) | 61.01-62; 64; 66; 72; 74; 76 | 1.76 | 568 |
| | Women's, girls' and infants' woven trousers and slacks | 61.02-66; 68; 72 | | |
| 7 | Blouses and shirt-blouses, knitted or crocheted (not elastic or rubberized), or woven, for women, girls and infants | 60.05-22; 23; 24; 25<br>61.02-78; 82; 84 | 5.55 | 180 |
| 8 | Men's and boys' shirts, woven | 61.03-11; 15; 19 | 4.60 | 217 |

(1) Category 2 includes cotton fabrics (absorbent gauze), not impregnated or coated with pharmadental substances, talling within heading no 30.04 of the Common Customs Tariff.

GROUP II

| Category | Description | NIMEXE code (1979) | Table of equivalence | |
|---|---|---|---|---|
| | | | pieces/kg | g/piece |
| 9 | Woven cotton terry fabrics | 55.08-10; 30; 50; 80 | | |
| | Toilet and kitchen linen of woven cotton terry fabrics | 62.02-71 | | |
| 10 | Gloves, mittens and mitts, knitted or crocheted, not elastic or rubberized, impregnated or coated with artificial plastic materials | 60.02-40 | 10.14 pairs | 99 |
| 11 | Gloves, mittens and mitts, knitted or crocheted, not elastic or rubberized, other than those of category 10 | 60.02-50; 60; 70; 80 | 24.6 pairs | 41 |
| 12 | Stockings, under stockings, socks, ankle-socks, sockettes and the like, knitted or crocheted, not elastic or rubberized, other than women's stockings of synthetic textile fibres | 60.03-11; 19; 20; 27; 30; 90 | 24.3 pairs | 41 |
| 13 | Men's and boys' underpants and briefs, women's, girls' and infants' (other than babies') knickers and briefs, knitted or crocheted, not elastic or rubberized, of cotton or synthetic textile fibres | 60.04-48; 56; 75; 85 | 17 | 59 |

| | | | | |
|---|---|---|---|---|
| 14A | Men's and boys' coats of impregnated, coated, covered or laminated woven fabric | 61.01-01 | 1.0 | 1000 |
| 14B | Men's and boys' woven overcoats, raincoats and other coats, cloaks and capes, other than those of category 14A | 61.01-41; 42; 44; 46; 47 | 0.72 | 1389 |
| 15A | Women's, girls' and infants' coats of impregnated, coated, covered or laminated woven fabric | 61.02-05 | 1.1 | 909 |
| 15B | Women's, girls' and infants' woven overcoats, raincoats and other coats, cloaks and capes, jackets and blazers, other than garments of category 15A | 61.02-31; 32; 33; 35; 36; 37; 39; 40 | 0.84 | 1190 |
| 16 | Men's and boys' woven suits (including coordinate suits consisting of two or three pieces, which are ordered, packed, consigned and normally sold together), excluding ski suits | 61.01-51; 54; 57 | 0.80 | 1250 |
| 17 | Men's and boys' woven jackets and blazers (excluding waister jackets) | 61.01-34; 36; 37 | 1.43 | 700 |
| 18 | Men's and boy's woven under garments other than shirts | 61.03-51; 55; 59; 81; 85; 89 | | |
| 19 | Handkerchiefs of woven fabric, of a value of not more than 15 EUA / kg net weight | 61.05-30; 99 | 55.5 | 18 |
| 20 | Bed linen, woven | 62.02-11; 19 | | |
| 21 | Parkas; anoraks, windcheaters, waister jackets and the like, woven | 61.01-29; 31; 32; 61.02-25; 26; 28 | 2.3 | 435 |
| 22 | Yarn of discontinuous or waste synthetic fibres, not put up for retail sale | 56.05-03; 05; 07; 09; 11; 13; 15; 19; 21; 23; 25; 28; 32; 34; 36; 38; 39; 42; 44; 45; 46; 47 | | |
| | a) Of which acrylic | 56.05-21; 23; 25; 28; 32; 34; 36 | | |
| 23 | Yarn of discontinuous or waste regenerated fibres, not put up for retail sale | 56.05-51; 55; 61; 65; 71; 75; 81; 85; 91; 95; 99 | | |
| 24 | Men's and boys' pyjamas, knitted or crocheted, of cotton or of synthetic textile fibres | 60.04-47; 73 | 2.8 | 357 |

| | | | | |
|---|---|---|---|---|
| 25 | Women's, girls' and infants' (other than babies') knitted or crocheted pyjamas and nightdresses, of cotton or synthetic fibres | 60.04-51; 53; 81; 83 | 4.3 | 233 |
| 26 | Women's, girls' and infants' (other than babies') woven and knitted or crocheted dresses | 60.05-41; 42; 43; 44<br>61.02-48; 52; 53; 54 | 3.1 | 323 |
| 27 | Women's, girls' and infants' (other than babies') woven and knitted or crocheted skirts, including divided skirts | 60.05-51; 52; 54; 58<br>61.02-57; 58; 62 | 2.6 | 385 |
| 28 | Knitted or crocheted trousers (except shorts) other than babies' | 60.05-61; 62; 64 | 1.61 | 620 |
| 29 | Women's, girls' and infants' (other than babies') woven suits, and costumes (including coordinate suits consisting of two or three pieces which are ordered, packed, consigned and normally sold together), excluding ski suits | 61.02-42; 43; 44 | 1.37 | 730 |
| 30A | Women's, girls' and infants' woven pyjamas and nightdresses | 61.04-11; 13; 18 | 4.0 | 250 |
| 30B | Women's, girls' and infants' (other than babies') woven undergarments, other than pyjamas and nightdresses | 61.04-91; 93; 98 | | |
| 31 | Brassières, woven, knitted or crocheted | 61.09-50 | 182 | 55 |

GROUP III

| Category | Description | NIMEXE code (1979) | Table of equivalence | |
|---|---|---|---|---|
| | | | pieces/kg | g/piece |
| 32 | Woven pile fabrics and chenille fabrics (other than terry fabrics of cotton and narrow woven fabrics), of wool, of cotton or of man-made textile fibres | 58.04-07; 11; 15; 18; 41; 43; 45; 61; 63; 67; 69; 71; 75; 77; 78 | | |
| 33 | Woven fabrics of strip or the like of polyethylene or polypropylene, less than 3 m wide; woven sacks of such strip or the like | 51.04-06<br>62.03-96 | | |

| | | | | |
|---|---|---|---|---|
| 34 | Woven fabrics of strip or the like of polyethylene or polypropylene, 3 m or more wide | 51.04-08 | | |
| 35 | Woven fabrics of synthetic textile fibres (continuous), other than those for tyres and those containing elastomeric yarn | 51.04-11; 13; 15; 17; 18; 21; 23; 25; 26; 27; 28; 32; 34; 36; 42; 44; 46; 48 | | |
| | a) Of which other than unbleached or bleached | 51.04-15; 17; 18; 23; 25; 26; 27; 28; 32; 34; 42; 44; 46; 48 | | |
| 36 | Woven fabrics of regenerated textile fibres (continuous), other than those for tyres and those containing elastomeric yarn | 51.04-56; 58; 62; 64; 66; 72; 74; 76; 82; 84; 86; 88; 89; 93; 94; 95; 96; 97; 98 | | |
| | a) Of which other than unbleached or bleached | 51.04-58; 62; 64; 72; 74; 76; 82; 84; 86; 88; 89; 94; 95; 96; 97; 98 | | |
| 37 | Woven fabrics of regenerated textile fibres (discontinuous or waste), other than narrow woven fabrics, pile fabrics(including terry fabrics) and chenille fabrics | 56.07-37; 42; 44; 48; 52; 53; 54; 57; 58; 62; 63; 64; 66; 72; 73; 74; 77; 78; 82; 83; 84; 87 | | |
| | a) Of which other than unbleached or bleached | 56.07-37; 44; 48; 52; 54; 57; 58; 63; 64; 66; 73; 74; 77; 78; 83; 84; 87 | | |
| 38A | Knitted or crocheted synthetic curtain fabrics including net curtain fabric | 60.01-40 | | |
| 38B | Net curtains | 62.02-09 | | |
| 39 | Woven table linen, toilet and kitchen linen, other than of cotton terry fabric | 62.02-41; 43; 47; 65; 73; 77 | | |
| 40 | Woven curtains (other than net curtains) and furnishing articles | 62.02-81; 89 | | |
| 41 | Yarn of synthetic textile fibres (continuous), not put up for retail sale, other than non-textured single yarn untwisted or with a twist of not more than 50 turns for metre | 51.01-05; 07; 08; 09; 11; 13; 16; 18; 21; 23; 26; 28; 32; 34; 38; 42; 44; 48 | | |

| | | | | |
|---|---|---|---|---|
| 42 | Yarn of regenerated textile fibres (continuous), not put up for retail sale, other than single yarn of viscose rayon untwisted or with a twist of not more than 250 turns per metre and single non-textured yarn of any acetate | 51.01-50; 61; 64; 66; 71; 76; 80 | | |
| 43 | Yarn of man-made fibres (continuous), put up for retail sale | 51.03-10; 20 | | |
| 44 | Woven fabrics of synthetic textile fibres (continuous), containing elastomeric yarn | 51.04-05 | | |
| 45 | Woven fabrics of regenerated textile fibres (continuous), containing elastomeric yarn | 51.04-54 | | |
| 46 | Carded or combed sheep's or lambs' wool or other fine animal hair | 53.05-10; 22; 29; 32; 39 | | |
| 47 | Yarn of carded sheep's or lambs' wool (woollen yarn) or of carded fine animal hair, not put up for retail sale | 53.06-21; 25; 31; 35; 51; 55; 71; 75<br>53.08-11; 15 | | |
| 48 | Yarn of combed sheep's or lambs' wool (worsted yarn) or of combed fine animal hair, not put up for retail sale | 53.07-01; 09; 21; 29; 40; 51; 59; 81; 89<br>53.08-21; 25 | | |
| 49 | Yarn of sheep's or lambs' wool or of fine animal hair, put up for retail sale | 53.10-11; 15 | | |
| 50 | Woven fabrics of sheep's or lambs' wool or of fine animal hair | 53.11-01; 03; 07; 11; 13; 17; 20; 30; 40; 52; 54; 58; 72; 74; 75; 82; 84; 88; 91; 93; 97 | | |
| 51 | Carded or combed cotton | 55.04-00 | | |
| 52 | Cotton yarn put up for retail sale | 55.06-10; 90 | | |
| 53 | Cotton gauze | 55.07-10; 90 | | |
| 54 | Regenerated textile fibres (discontinuous or waste), carded or combed | 56.04-21; 23; 25; 29 | | |
| 55 | Synthetic textile fibres (discontinuous or waste), carded or combed | 56.04-11; 13; 15; 16; 17; 18 | | |
| 56 | Yarn of synthetic textile fibres (discontinuous or waste), put up for retail sale | 56.06-11; 15 | | |

| | | | | |
|---|---|---|---|---|
| 57 | Yarn of regenerated textile fibres (discontinuous or waste), put up for retail sale | 56.06-20 | | |
| 58 | Carpets, carpeting and rugs, knotted (made up or not) | 58.01-01; 11; 13; 17; | | |
| 59 | Woven, knitted or crocheted carpets, carpeting, rugs, mats and matting, and 'Kelem', 'Schumacks' and 'Karamanie' rugs and the like (made up or not) | 58.02-12; 14; 17; 18; 19; 30; 43; 49; 90 | | |
| | Floor coverings of felt | 59.02-01; 09 | | |
| 60 | Tapestries, hand made | 58.03-00 | | |
| 61 | Narrow woven fabrics not exceeding 30 cm in width with selvedges (woven, gummed or made otherwise) on both edges, other than woven labels and the like; bolduc | 58.05-01; 08; 30; 40; 51; 59; 61; 69; 73; 77; 79; 90 | | |
| 62 | Woven labels, badges and the like, not embroidered, in the piece, in strips or cut to shape or size | 58.06-10; 90 | | |
| | Chenille yarn (including flock chenille yarn), gimped yarn (other than metallized yarn and gimped horsehair yarn); braids and ornamental trimmings in the piece; tassels, pompons and the like | 58.07-31; 39; 50; 80 | | |
| r | Tulle and other net fabrics (but not including woven, knitted or crocheted fabrics), plain | 58.08-11; 15; 19; 21; 29 | | |
| | Tulle and other net fabrics (but not including woven, knitted or crocheted fabrics), figured; hand or mechanically made lace, in the piece, in strips or in motifs | 58.09-11; 19; 21; 31; 35; 39; 91; 95; 99 | | |
| | Embroidery, in the piece, in strips or in motifs | 58.10-21; 29; 41; 45; 49; 51; 55; 59 | | |
| 63 | Knitted or crocheted fabric, not elastic or rubberized, of synthetic textile fibres, containing elastofibres | 60.01-30 | | |
| | Knitted or crocheted fabric, elastic or rubberized | 60.06-11; 18 | | |

| | | | | |
|---|---|---|---|---|
| 64 | Rachel lace and long-pile fabric (imitation fur), knitted or crocheted, not elastic or rubberized, of synthetic textile fibres | 60.01-51; 55 | | |
| 65 | Knitted or crocheted fabrics, not elastic or rubberized, other than those of categories 38 A, 63 and 64 | 60.01-01; 10; 62; 64; 65; 68; 72; 74; 75; 78; 81; 89; 92; 94; 96; 97 | | |
| 66 | Travelling rugs and blankets | 62.01-10; 20; 81; 85; 93; 95 | | |
| 67 | Clothing accessories and other articles (except garments), knitted or crocheted, not elastic or rubberized | 60.05-94; 95; 96; 97; 98; 99 | | |
| | Articles (other than bathing costumes) of knitted or crocheted fabric, elastic or rubberized | 60.06-92; 96; 98 | | |

GROUP IV

| Category | Description | NIMEXE code (1979) | Table of equivalence | |
|---|---|---|---|---|
| | | | pieces/kg | g/piece |
| 68 | Babies' under garments of knitted or crocheted fabrics, not elastic or rubberized | 60.04-02; 03; 04; 06; 07; 08; 10; 11; 12; 14 | | |
| 69 | Women's, girls' and infants' knitted or crocheted petticoats and slips, of synthetic textile fibres, other than babies' garments | 60.04-54 | 7.8 | 128 |
| 70 | Panty-hose (tights) | 60.04-31; 33; 34 | 30.4 | 33 |
| 71 | Babies' knitted outer garments | 60.05-06; 07; 08; 09 | | |
| 72 | Knitted swimwear | 60.05-11; 13; 15 60.06-91 | 10 | 100 |
| 73 | Track suits of knitted or crocheted fabric, not elastic or rubberized | 60.05-16; 17; 19 | 1.67 | 600 |

| | | | | |
|---|---|---|---|---|
| 74 | Women's, girls' and infants' (other than babies') suits and costumes (including coordinate suits consisting of two or three pieces which are ordered, packed, consigned and normally sold together), of knitted or crocheted fabric, not elastic or rubberized, excluding ski suits | 60.05-71; 72; 73; 74 | 1.54 | 650 |
| 75 | Men's and boys' suits (including coordinate suits consisting of two or three pieces which are ordered, packed, consigned and normally sold together), of knitted or crocheted fabric, not elastic or rubberized, excluding ski suits | 60.05-66; 68 | 0.80 | 1 250 |
| 76 | Men's and boys' woven industrial and occupational clothing | 61.01-13; 15; 17; 19 | | |
| | Women's, girls' and infants' woven aprons, smock-overalls and other industrial and occupational clothing (whether or not also suitable for domestic use) | 61.02-12; 14 | | |
| 77 | Women's stockings of synthetic textile fibres | 60.03-24; 26 | 40 pairs | 25 |
| 78 | Men's and boys' woven bath robes, dressing gowns, smoking jackets and similar indoor wear and other outer garments, except garments of categories 6, 14A, 14B, 16, 17, 21, 76 and 79 | 61.01-09; 24; 25; 26; 92; 94; 96 | | |
| 79 | Woven swimwear | 61.01-22; 23<br>61.02-16; 18 | 8.3 | 120 |
| 80 | Babies' woven garments | 61.02-01; 03<br>61.04-01; 09 | | |
| 81 | Women's, girls' and infants' woven bath robes, dressing gowns, bed jackets and similar indoor wear and other outer garments, except garments of categories 6, 7, 15A, 15B, 21, 26, 27, 29, 76, 79 and 80 | 61.02-07; 22; 23; 24; 86; 88; 92 | | |

| | | | | |
|---|---|---|---|---|
| 82 | Under garments, other than babies', knitted or crocheted, not elastic or rubberized, of wool, of fine animal hair or of regenerated textile fibres | 60.04-38; 60 | | |
| 83 | Outer garments, knitted or crocheted, not elastic or rubberized, other than garments of categories 5, 7, 26, 27, 28, 71, 72, 73, 74 and 75 | 60.05-04; 76; 77; 78; 79; 88; 90; 91; 92 | | |
| 84 | Shawls, scarves, mufflers, mantillas, veils and the like, other than knitted or crocheted | 61.06-30; 40; 50; 60 | | |
| 85 | Ties, bow ties and cravats, other than knitted or crocheted | 61.07-30; 40; 90 | 17.9 | 56 |
| 86 | Corsets, corset-belts, suspender-belts, braces, suspenders, garters and the like (including such articles of knitted or crocheted fabric), other than brassieres, whether or not elastic | 61.09-20; 30; 40; 80 | 8.8 | 114 |
| 87 | Gloves, mittens, mitts, stockings, socks and sockettes, not being knitted or crocheted goods | 61.10-00 | | |
| 88 | Made up accessories for articles of apparel (for example, dress shields, shoulder and other pads, belts, muffs, sleeve protectors, pockets), other than knitted or crocheted | 61.11-00 | | |
| 89 | Handkerchiefs of woven cotton fabric, of a value of more than 15 EUA/kg net weight | 61.05-20 | 59 | 17 |

GROUP V

| Category | Description | NIMEXE code (1979) | Table of equivalence | |
|---|---|---|---|---|
| | | | pieces/kg | g/piece |
| 90 | Twine, cordage, ropes and cables, of synthetic textile fibres, plaited or not | 59.04-11; 13; 15; 17; 18 | | |
| 91 | Tents | 62.04-23; 73 | | |
| 92 | Woven fabrics of man-made textile fibres and rubberized textile woven fabrics, for tyres | 51.04-03; 52<br>59.11-15 | | |

| | | | | |
|---|---|---|---|---|
| 93 | Sacks and bags, of a kind used for the packing of goods, of woven fabrics, other than made from polyethylene or polypropylene strip | 62.03-93; 95; 97; 98 | | |
| 94 | Wadding and articles of wadding; textile flock and dust and mill neps | 59.01-07; 12; 14; 15; 16; 18; 21; 29 | | |
| 95 | Felt and articles of felt, whether or not impregnated or coated, other than floor coverings | 59.02-35; 41; 47; 51; 57; 59; 91; 95; 97 | | |
| 96 | Bonded fibre fabrics, similar bonded yarn fabrics, and articles of such fabrics, whether or not impregnated or coated, other than clothing and clothing accessories | 59.03-11; 19; 30 | | |
| 97 | Nets and netting made of twine, cordage or rope, and made up fishing nets of yarn, twine, cordage or rope | 59.05-11; 21; 29; 91; 99 | | |
| 98 | Other articles made from yarn, twine, cordage, rope or cables, other than textile fabrics, articles made from such fabrics and articles of category 97 | 59.06-00 | | |
| 99 | Textile fabrics coated with gum or amylaceous substances, of a kind used for the outer covers of books and the like; tracing cloth; prepared painting canvas; buckram and similar fabrics for hat foundations and similar uses | 59.07-10; 90 | | |
| 100 | Textile fabrics impregnated, coated, covered or laminated with preparations of cellulose derivatives or of other artificial plastic materials | 59.08-10; 51; 61; 71; | | |
| 101 | Twine, cordage, ropes and cables, plaited or not, other than of synthetic textile fibres | 59.04-80 | | |

| | | | | |
|---|---|---|---|---|
| 102 | Linoleum and materials prepared on a textile base in a similar manner to linoleum, whether or not cut to shape or of a kind used as floor coverings; floor coverings consisting of a coating applied on a textile base, cut to shape or not | 59.10-10; 31; 39 | | |
| 103 | Rubberized textile fabrics other than rubberized knitted or crocheted goods, excluding fabrics for tyres | 59.11-11; 14; 17; 20 | | |
| 104 | Textile fabrics, impregnated or coated, other than those of categories 99, 100, 102 and 103; painted canvas being theatrical scenery, studio backcloths or the like | 59.12-00 | | |
| 105 | Elastic fabrics and trimmings (other than knitted or crocheted goods) consisting of textile materials combined with rubber threads | 59.13-01; 11; 13; 15; 19; 32; 34; 35; 39 | | |
| 106 | Wicks, of woven, plaited or knitted textile materials, for lamps, stoves, lighters, candles and the like; tubular knitted gas-mantle fabric and incandescent gas mantles | 59.14-00 | | |
| 107 | Textile hosepiping and similar tubing, with or without lining, armour or accessories of other materials | 59.15-10; 90 | | |
| 108 | Transmission, conveyor or elevator belts or belting, of textile material, whether or not strengthened with metal or other material | 59.16-00 | | |
| 109 | Woven tarpaulins, sails, awnings and sunblinds | 62.04-21; 61; 69 | | |
| 110 | Woven pneumatic mattresses | 62.04-25; 75 | | |
| 111 | Camping goods, woven, other than pneumatic mattresses and tents | 62.04-29; 79 | | |
| 112 | Other made-up textile articles, woven, excluding those of categories 113 and 114 | 62.05-10; 30; 93; 98 | | |

| | | | | |
|---|---|---|---|---|
| 113 | Floor cloths, dish cloths, dusters and the like, other than knitted or crocheted | 62.05-20 | | |
| 114 | Textile fabrics and textile articles of a kind commonly used in machinery or plant | 59.17-10; 29; 31; 39; 49; 51; 59; 71; 79; 91; 93; 95; 99 | | |

ANNEX II
referred to in Article 12 (2)

| Category | Description | NIMEXE code (1979) | Units |
|---|---|---|---|
| 115 | Flax or ramie yarn, not put up for retail sale | 54.03-10; 31; 35; 37; 39; 50; 61; 69 | Tonnes |
| 116 | Flax or ramie yarn, put up for retail sale | 54.04-10; 90 | Tonnes |
| 117 | Woven fabrics of flax or of ramie | 54.05-21; 25; 31; 35; 38; 51; 55; 61; 68 | Tonnes |
| 118 | Bed linen, of flax or ramie, other than knitted or crocheted | 62.02-15 | Tonnes |
| 119 | Table linen, toilet linen and kitchen linen of flax or ramie, other than knitted or crocheted | 62.02-61; 75 | Tonnes |
| 120 | Curtains (including net curtains) and other furnishing articles, of flax or ramie, other than knitted or crocheted | 62.02-01; 87 | Tonnes |
| 121 | Twine, cordage, ropes and cables, plaited or not, of flax or ramie | 59.04-60 | Tonnes |
| 122 | Sacks and bags, of a kind used for the packing of goods, used, of flax or sisal, other than knitted or crocheted | 62.03-91 | Tonnes |
| 123 | Woven pile fabrics and chenille fabrics, of flax or ramie, other than narrow woven fabrics; shawls, scarves, mufflers, mantillas, veils and the like, of flax or ramie, other than knitted or crocheted | 58.04-80<br>61.06-90 | Tonnes |
| 124 | Synthetic staple fibre | 56.01-11; 13; 15; 16; 17; 18<br>56.02-11; 13; 15; 19<br>56.03-11; 13; 15; 19 | Tonnes |
| 125 | Synthetic filament yarn | 51.01-14; 25<br>51.02-12; 13; 15; 22; 24, 28 | Tonnes |
| 126 | Regenerated staple fibre | 56.01-21; 23; 25; 29<br>56.02-21; 23; 25; 29<br>56.03-21; 23; 25; 29 | Tonnes |

| | | | |
|---|---|---|---|
| 127 | Regenerated filament yarn | 51.01-62; 73<br>51.02-41; 49 | Tonnes |
| 128 | Coarse hair, carded or combed | 53.05-50 | Tonnes |
| 129 | Coarse hair yarns | 53.09-10; 20 | Tonnes |
| 130A | Thrown silk | 50.04-10; 90<br>50.07-10 | Tonnes |
| 130B | Spun silk yarns | 50.05-10; 90; 99<br>50.07-90; 99 | Tonnes |
| 131 | Sisal yarns | 57.07-90 | Tonnes |
| 132 | Paper yarns | 57.07-20 | Tonnes |
| 133 | Hemp, etc., yarns | 57.07-01; 03; 07 | Tonnes |
| 134 | Metallized yarns | 52.01-10; 90 | Tonnes |
| 135 | Fabrics of coarse hair | 53.12-00 | Tonnes |
| 136 | Silk fabrics | 50.09-01; 20; 31; 39; 41; 42; 44; 45; 47; 48; 61; 62; 64; 66; 69; 80<br>59.17-21 | Tonnes |
| 137 | Pile fabrics of silk, etc. | 58.04-05<br>58.05-20 | Tonnes |
| 138 | Fabrics of hemp, etc., and paper | 57.11-10; 20; 90 | Tonnes |
| 139 | Fabrics of metal yarns | 52.02-00 | Tonnes |
| 140 | Knitted fabric of other fibres | 60.01-98 | Tonnes |
| 141 | Blankets of other fibres | 62.01-99 | Tonnes |
| 142 | Carpets of sisal, hemp, etc. | 58.02-20; 60; 80 | Tonnes |
| 143A | Clothing of non-MFA fibres, knitted | 60.04-09; 16; 29<br>60.05-21; 26; 31; 32; 39; 49; 75; 80; 93 | Tonnes |
| 143B | Clothing of non-MFA fibres, woven | 61.01-38; 48; 58; 68; 78; 98<br>61.02-34; 41; 45; 47; 55; 64; 74; 76; 94<br>61.05-91<br>61.06-10<br>61.07-10 | Tonnes |
| 144 | Felt of coarse hair | 59.02-45 | Tonnes |
| 145 | Cordage of abaca | 59.04-20 | Tonnes |
| 146A | Sisal baler and binder twine | 59.04-31 | Tonnes |
| 146B | Other sisal twine and cordage | 59.04-35; 38 | Tonnes |
| 146C | Jute binder and baler twine | 59.04-70 | Tonnes |
| 147 | Silk waste, carded or combed | 50.03-90 | Tonnes |
| 148A | Jute yarns | 57.06-11; 15; 30 | Tonnes |
| 148B | Coir yarns | 57.07-10 | Tonnes |
| 149A | Jute fabrics, 150 to 230 cm wide, unbleached | 57.10-61 | Tonnes |
| 149B | Jute fabrics, over 230 cm wide, unbleached | 57.10-65 | Tonnes |

| | | | |
|---|---|---|---|
| 149C | Jute fabrics, over 150 cm wide, finished | 57.10-70 | Tonnes |
| 150A | Jute fabrics, under 150 cm wide and weighing not more than310 g, and sacks therefrom | 57.10-21; 29<br>62.03-13 | Tonnes |
| 150B | Jute fabrics, under 150 cm wide and weighing 310 to 500 g, and sacks therefrom | 57.10-31; 39<br>62.03-15 | Tonnes |
| 150C | Jute fabrics, under 150 cm wide and weighing more than 500 g, and sacks therefrom | 57.10-50<br>62.03-17 | Tonnes |
| 151A | Coir carpets | 58.02-11 | Tonnes |
| 151B | Jute carpets | 58.02-50 | Tonnes |
| 152 | Jute felt | 59.02-31 | Tonnes |
| 153 | Jute sacks | 62.03-11 | Tonnes |
| 154 | Natural raw fibres | 50.01-00<br>50.02-00<br>50.03-10<br>53.01-10; 20; 30; 40<br>53.02-10; 51; 59; 93; 95 97<br>53.03-01; 03; 20; 30; 9[illegible] 95<br>53.04-00<br>54.01-10; 21; 25; 30; 40 70<br>54.02-00<br>55.01-10; 90<br>55.02-10; 90<br>55.03-10; 30; 50; 90<br>57.01-20; 50<br>57.02-00<br>57.03-10; 30; 50<br>57.04-10; 30; 50 | Tonnes |

ANNEX III (referred to in Article 2)

ORIGIN

Article 1

1. Products listed in Annex I, originating in China, may be imported into the Community in accordance with the arrangements established by this Regulation on production of a certificate of origin conforming to the specimen attached to Annex VI.

2. The certificate of origin shall be issued by the competent governmental authorities of China if the products in question can be considered products originating in that country within the meaning of the relevant rules in force in the Community.

3. However, products listed in Annex I other than those falling within Group I or II may be imported into the Community in accordance with the arrangements established by the Regulation on production of a declaration by the exporter or supplier on the invoice, or, where there is no invoice, on another commercial document relating to the products in

question, to the effect that the said products originate in the supplying country where the declaration is made within the meaning of the relevant rules in force within the Community.

4. Where different criteria for determining origin are fixed in respect of products falling within a single category and a single tariff heading, the certificate or declaration must include a description of the goods which is sufficiently detailed to allow assessment of the criterion on the basis of which the certificate was issued or the declaration made.

Article 2

The discovery of slight discrepancies between the entries made in the certificate of origin and those made in the documents produced to the customs office for the purpose of carrying out the formalities for importing the product shall not ipso facto cast doubt upon the statements in the certificate.

Article 3

1. Subsequent verification of certificates of origin shall be carried out at random, or whenever the competent Community authorities have reasonable doubt as to the authenticity of the certificate or as to the accuracy of the information regarding the true origin of the products in question.

In such cases the competent authorities in the Community shall return the certificate of origin or a copy thereof to the competent governmental authority of China giving, where appropriate, the reasons of form or substance for an enquiry. If the invoice has been submitted, such invoice or a copy thereof shall be attached to the certificate or its copy. The authorities shall also forward any information that has been obtained suggesting that the particulars given on the said certificate are inaccurate.

2. The provisions of paragraph 1 above shall also be applicable to subsequent verifications of the declarations of origin referred to in Article 1 (3) of this Annex.

3. The results of the subsequent verifications carried out in accordance with paragraphs 1 and 2 shall be communicated to the competent authorities of the Community within three months at the latest.

4. Should such verifications reveal abuse or major irregularities in the use of declarations of origin, the Member State concerned shall inform the Commission of this fact. The Commission shall pass the information on to the other Member States.

At the request of a Member State or at the initiative of the Commission, the Committee on Origin shall, as soon as possible and in accordance with the procedure specified in Article 13 of Regulation (EEC) No 802/68 (2), examiné whether it is desirable to require the production of a certificate of origin, in accordance with Article 1 (1) and (2), in respect of the products concerned and China.

The decision shall be taken in accordance with the procedure specified in Article 14 of Regulation (EEC) No 802/68.

5. For the purpose of subsequent verification of certificates of origin, copies of the certificates as well as any export documents referring to them shall be kept for at least two years by the competent governmental authority of China.

6. Random recourse to the procedure specified in this Article must not constitute an obstacle to the release for home use of the products in question.

Article 4

1. The movement certificates and Forms EUR.1 and EUR.2 and the certificates of origin Form A and Forms APR presented at the time of importation into the Community in order to obtain a tariff preference shall be accepted in place of the proof of origin stipulated in Article 1.

2. The proof of origin referred to in Article 1 shall not be required where goods are accompanied by a certificate conforming to the specimen and complying with the conditions set out in Regulation (EEC) No 2635/77 (3) or (EEC) No 2636/77 (4) or in the corresponding provisions which are to replace the said Regulations.

3. Paragraph 2 shall also apply to goods accompanied by a certificate conforming to the specimen and complying with the conditions set out in Annex VII to this Regulation.

4. Non-commercial imports exempt from production of the documents referred to in paragraph 1 in accordance with the provisions of the preferential arrangements concerned shall not be subject to the provisions of this Annex.

## ANNEX IV

When the constitutive material of the products of categories 1 to 114 is not specifically mentioned these products are to be taken to be made exclusively of wool or of fine animal hair, of cotton or of synthetic or artificial textile fibres.

The breakdown between Member States of the quantitative limits for 1981, 1982 and 1983 is published for the purposes of information, and its definitive version shall be the subject of a Community Regulation at the beginning of each of those years.

| Category | CCT heading No | NIMEXE code (1979) | Description | Third countries | Member States | Units | Quantitative limits from 1 January to 31 December | | | |
|---|---|---|---|---|---|---|---|---|---|---|
| | | | | | | | 1980 | 1981 | 1982 | 1983 |
| 1 | 55.05 | 55.05-13; | Cotton yarn, not put up for retail sale | China | D | Tonnes | 1 226 | 1 228 | 1 230 | 1 232 |
| | | 19; 21; 25; 27; 29; 33; | | | F | | 504 | 509 | 513 | 517 |
| | | 35; 37; 41; 45; 46; 48; | | | I | | 103 | 104 | 105 | 106 |
| | | 52; 58; 61; 65; 67; 69; | | | BNL | | 137 | 138 | 140 | 142 |
| | | 72; 78; 92; 98 | | | UK | | 61 | 62 | 63 | 64 |
| | | | | | IRL | | 87 | 89 | 91 | 93 |
| | | | | | DK | | 50 | 51 | 52 | 53 |
| | | | | | EEC | | 2 168 | 2 181 | 2 194 | 2 207 |
| 2 (1) | 55.09 | | Other woven fabrics of cotton: | China (2) | D | Tonnes | 2 705 | 2 725 | 2 745 | 2 765 |
| | | | | | F | | 4 672 | 4 682 | 4 692 | 4 702 |
| | | 55.09-01; 02; 03; 04; 05; 11; 12; 13; 14; 15; 16; 17; 19; 21; 29; 31; 33; 35; 37; 38; 39; 41; 49; 51; 52; 53; 54; 55; 56; 57; 59; 61; 63; 64; 65; 66; 67; 68; 69; 70; 71; 72; 73; 74; 76; 77; 78; 81; 82; 83; 84; 86; 87; 92; 93; 97 | Woven fabrics of cotton, other than gauze, terry fabrics, narrow woven fabrics, pile fabrics, chenille fabrics, tulle and other net fabrics: | | I | | 1 717 | 1 724 | 1 731 | 1 738 |
| | | | | | BNL | | 3 155 | 3 177 | 3 199 | 3 221 |
| | | | | | UK | | 3 837 | 3 874 | 3 911 | 3 948 |
| | | | | | IRL | | 492 | 495 | 498 | 501 |
| | | | | | DK | | 1 523 | 1 526 | 1 529 | 1 532 |
| | | | | | EEC | | 18 101 | 18 203 | 18 305 | 18 407 |

(1) Category 2 includes cotton fabrics (absorbent gauze), not impregnated or coated with pharmaceutical substances, falling within heading No 30.04 of the Common Customs Tariff.
(2) See Appendix.

| Category | CCT heading No | NIMEXE code (1979) | Description | Third countries | Member States | Units | Quantitative limits from 1 January to 31 December | | | |
|---|---|---|---|---|---|---|---|---|---|---|
| | | | | | | | 1980 | 1981 | 1982 | 1983 |
| 2 (cont) | | 55.09-03; 04; 05; 51; 52; 53; 54; 55; 56; 57; 59; 61; 63; 64; 65; 66; 67; 70; 71; 81; 82; 83; 84; 86; 87; 92; 93; 97 | a) Of which other than unbleached or bleached | China | D | Tonnes | 271 | 272 | 275 | 277 |
| | | | | | F | | 467 | 468 | 469 | 470 |
| | | | | | I | | 172 | 172 | 173 | 174 |
| | | | | | BNL | | (1) | (1) | (1) | (1) |
| | | | | | UK | | 384 | 387 | 391 | 395 |
| | | | | | IRL | | 49 | 50 | 50 | 50 |
| | | | | | DK | | 152 | 153 | 153 | 153 |
| 3 | 56.07A | | Woven fabrics of man-made fibres(discontinuous or waste): | China (1) | D | Tonnes | 278 | 286 | 294 | 302 |
| | | | | | F | | 129 | 138 | 147 | 157 |
| | | | | | I | | 201 | 203 | 205 | 206 |
| | | | A. Of synthetic textile fibres: | | BNL | | 2 263 | 2 266 | 2 269 | 2 272 |
| | | 56.07-01; 04; 05; 07; 08; 11; 13; 14; 16; 17; 18; 21; 23; 24; 26; 27; 28; 32; 33; 34; 36 | Woven fabrics of synthetic fibres(discontinuous or waste) other than narrow woven fabrics, pile fabrics (including terry fabrics) and chenille fabrics: | | UK | | 40 | 40 | 40 | 40 |
| | | | | | IRL | | 51 | 52 | 53 | 54 |
| | | | | | DK | | 62 | 64 | 66 | 69 |
| | | | | | EEC | | 3 024 | 3 049 | 3 074 | 3 100 |
| | | 56.07-01; 05; 07; 08; 13; 14; 16; 18; 21; 23; 26; 27; 28; 33; 34; 36 | a) Of which other than unbleached or bleached | China | D | Tonnes | 28 | 29 | 29 | 30 |
| | | | | | F | | 13 | 14 | 15 | 16 |
| | | | | | I | | 20 | 20 | 20 | 21 |
| | | | | | BNL | | (1) | (1) | (1) | (1) |
| | | | | | UK | | 4 | 4 | 4 | 4 |
| | | | | | IRL | | 5 | 5 | 5 | 5 |
| | | | | | DK | | 6 | 6 | 7 | 7 |

(1) See Appendix.

| Category | CCT heading No | NIMEXE code (1979) | Description | Third countries | Member States | Units | Quantitative limits from 1 January to 31 December 1980 | 1981 | 1982 | 1983 |
|---|---|---|---|---|---|---|---|---|---|---|
| 4 | 60.04 | | Under garments, knitted or crocheted, not elastic or rubberized; | China | D | 1 000 pieces | 1 183 | 1 215 | 1 246 | 1 278 |
| | B I | 60.04-19; 20; 22; | Shirts, T-shirts, lightweight fine | | F | | 1 351 | 1 371 | 1 390 | 1 410 |
| | II a) | 23; 24; 26; 41; 50; | knit roll, polo or turtle necked | | I | | 623 | 657 | 699 | 743 |
| | b) | 58; 71; 79; 89 | jumpers and pullovers, undervests | | BNL | | 427 | 453 | 478 | 503 |
| | c) | | and the like, knitted or crocheted, | | UK | | 511 | 557 | 603 | 652 |
| | IV b) 1 aa) | | not elastic or rubberized, other than | | IRL | | 19 | 21 | 24 | 27 |
| | dd) | | babies' garments, of cotton or | | DK | | 78 | 86 | 94 | 103 |
| | 2 ee) | | synthetic textile fibres; T-shirts and | | | | | | | |
| | d) 1 aa) | | lightweight fine knit roll, polo or | | EEC | | 4 192 | 4 360 | 4 534 | 4 716 |
| | dd) | | turtle necked jumpers and | | | | | | | |
| | 2 dd) | | pullovers, of regenerated textile fibres, other than babies' garmentsc | | | | | | | |
| 5 | 60.05 | 60.05-01; 27; 28; | Outer garments and other articles, | China | D | 1 000 pieces | 1 465 1 508 | 1 551 | 1 596 | |
| | A I | 29; 30; 33; 36; 37; | knitted or crocheted, not elastic or | | | | | | | |
| | II b) 4 bb) 11 | 38 | rubberized: | | F | | 714 | 745 | 777 | 810 |
| | aaa) | | A. Outer garments and clothing | | I | | 639 | 667 | 700 | 734 |
| | bbb) | | accessories: | | BNL | | 394 | 408 | 481 | 435 |
| | ccc) | | Jerseys, pullovers, slip-overs, | | UK | | 1 077 (1) | 1 126 | 1 175 | 1 226 |
| | ddd) | | waistcoats, twinsets, cardigans, | | IRL | | 24 | 26 | 28 | 30 |
| | 22 bbb) | | bedjackets and jumpers, knitted or | | DK | | 65 | 74 | 84 | 94 |
| | ccc) | | crocheted, not elastic or rubberized, | | | | | | | |
| | ddd) | | of wool, of cotton or of man-made | | EEC | | 4 378 (1) | 4 554 | 4 736 | 4 925 |
| | eee) | | textile fibres– | | | | | | | |
| 6 | 61.01 B V d) | 61.01-62; 64; 66; | Men's and boys' outer garments: | China | D | 1 000 pieces | 2 757 | 2 815 | 2 874 | 2 933 |
| | 1 | 72; 74; 76 | Women's, girls' and infants' outer | | | | | | | |
| | 2 | 61.02-66; 68; 72 | garments: | | F | | 892 | 942 | 992 | 1 044 |
| | 3 | | B. Other: Men's and boys' woven | | I | | 491 | 528 | 563 | 611 |
| | c) 1 | | breeches, shorts and trousers | | BNL | | 862 (1) | 884 | 906 | 929 |
| | 2 | | (including slacks); women's, girls' | | UK | | 209 | 231 | 254 | 273 |
| | 3 | | and infants' woven trousers and | | IRL | | 31 | 34 | 38 | 42 |
| | 61.02 B II e) | | slacks, of wool, of cotton or of | | DK | | 295 | 297 | 299 | 301 |
| | 6 aa) | | man-made textile fibres | | | | | | | |
| | bb) | | | | EEC | | 5 537 | 5 731 | 5 932 | 6 139 |
| | cc) | | | | | | | | | |

| Category | CCT heading No | NIMEXE code (1979) | Description | Third countries | Member States | Units | Quantitative limits from 1 January to 31 December | | | |
|---|---|---|---|---|---|---|---|---|---|---|
| 7 | 60.05 | | Outer garments and other articles, | China | D | 1 000 pieces | 654 | 658 | 662 | 666 |
| | A II b) 4 aa) 22 | | knitted or crocheted, not elastic or | | F | | 223 | 226 | 229 | 232 |
| | 33 | | rubberized: | | I | | 267 | 274 | 282 | 290 |
| | 44 | | A. Outer garments and clothing ac - | | BNL | | 122 | 124 | 125 | 127 |
| | 55 | | cessories: | | UK | | 157 | 162 | 167 | 172 |
| | | | II. Other | | IRL | | 20 | 20 | 21 | 21 |
| | | | | | DK | | 51 | 52 | 53 | 54 |
| | 61.02 | | Women's, girl's and infant's outer | | EEC | | 1 494 | 1 516 | 1 539 | 1 562 |
| | B II e) 7 bb) | | garments: | | | | | | | |
| | cc) | | | | | | | | | |
| | dd) | | B. Other: | | | | | | | |
| | | 60.05-22; | Blouses and shirt blouses, knitted, | | | | | | | |
| | | 23; 24; 25 | crocheted (not elastic or | | | | | | | |
| | | | rubberized), | | | | | | | |
| | | | or woven, for women, girls and | | | | | | | |
| | | 61.02-78; 82; 84 | infants, of wool, of cotton or of | | | | | | | |
| | | | man - made textile fibres | | | | | | | |
| 8 | 61.03 | | Men's and boy's under garments, | China | D | 1 000 pieces | 3 327 | 3 354 | 3 381 | 3 408 |
| | A | | including collars, shirt fronts and | | F | | 580 | 581 | 581 | 582 |
| | | | cuffs: | | I | | 553 | 577 | 602 | 628 |
| | | 61.03-11: | Men's and boy's shirts, woven, of | | BNL | | 480 | 490 | 500 | 510 |
| | | | | | UK | | 773 | 801 | 830 | 859 |
| | | 15; 19 | wool, of cotton or of man-made | | IRL | | 37 | 38 | 40 | 41 |
| | | | | | DK | | 396 | 397 | 398 | 399 |
| | | | textile fibres | | EEC | | 6 146 | 6 238 | 6 332 | 6 427 |
| 9 | 55.08 | | Terry-towelling and similar terry | China | D | Tonnes | 768 | 780 | 796 | 810 |
| | | | [illegible] | | [illegible] | | [illegible] | [illegible] | [illegible] | [illegible] |
| | | | Bed linen, table linen, toilet linen | | I | | 269 | 290 | 305 | 328 |
| | 62.02 | | and kitchen linen, curtains and | | BNL | | 104 | 120 | 137 | 156 |
| | B III a) I | | other furnishing articles: | | UK | | 340 | 378 | 421 | 461 |
| | | | | | IRL | | 12 | 14 | 16 | 18 |
| | | | B. Other: | | DK | | 251 | 252 | 253 | 254 |
| | | 55.08-10; | Woven cotton terry fabrics; toilet | | EEC | | 1 918 | 2 034 | 2 156 | 2 285 |
| | | 30; 50; 80 | and kitchen linen of woven cotton | | | | | | | |
| | | 62.02-71 | terry fabrics | | | | | | | |

| Category | CCT heading No | NIMEXE code (1979) | Description | Third countries | Member States | Units | Quantitative limits from 1 January to 31 December 1980 | 1981 | 1982 | 1983 |
|---|---|---|---|---|---|---|---|---|---|---|
| 10 | 60.02 | 60.02-40 | Gloves, mittens and mitts, knitted or crocheted, not elastic or rubberized: | China (1) | D | 1 000 pairs | 1 751 | 1 804 | 1 858 | 1 913 |
| | A | | Gloves, mittens and mitts, knitted or crocheted, not elastic or rubberized, impregnated or coated with artificial plastic materials | | UK | | 639 (1) | 658 | 677 | 698 |
| 12 | 60.03 | 60.03-11; 19; | Stockings, under stockings, socks, ankle – socks, sockettes and the like, knitted or crocheted, not elastic rubberized: | China | D | 1 000 pairs | 841 | 912 | 990 | 1 077 |
| | A | 20; 27; 30; 90 | | | F | | 4 504 | 4 526 | 4 549 | 4 572 |
| | B I | | | | I | | 307 | 352 | 398 | 446 |
| | II b) | | | | BNL | | 996 | 1 017 | 1 040 | 1 060 |
| | C | | Other than women's stockings of synthetic textile fibres | | UK | | 577 | 702 | 830 | 962 |
| | D | | | | IRL | | 18 | 23 | 25 | 28 |
| | | | | | DK | | 220 | 230 | 240 | 250 |
| | | | | | EEC | | 7 463 | 7 762 | 8 072 | 8 395 |
| 14 B | 61.01 | 61.01-41; 42; | Men's and boys' outer garments: | China | D | 1 000 pieces | 46 | 47 | 48 | 49 |
| | B V b) 1 | 44; 46; 47 | | | I | | 19 | 20 | 20 | 21 |
| | 2 | | Men's and boys' woven overcoats, raincoats and other coats, cloaks and capes, other than those of category 14 A, of wool, of cotton or of man - made textile fibres | | UK | | 14 | 15 | 15 | 16 |
| | 3 | | | | IRL | | 1 | 1 | 1 | 1 |
| 15 B | 61.02 | 61.02-31; 32; | Women's girls' and infants' outer garments: | China | I | 1 000 pieces | 23 | 23 | 24 | 25 |
| | B II e) 1 aa) | 33; 35; 36; 37; | | | IRL | | 3 | 3 | 3 | 3 |
| | bb) | 39; 40 | | | | | | | | |
| | cc) | | B. Other: | | | | | | | |
| | 2 aa) | | Women's, girls' and infants' woven overcoats, raincoats and other coats, cloaks and capes, jackets and blazers, other than garments of category 15 A, of wool, of cotton or of man-made textile fibres | | | | | | | |
| | bb) | | | | | | | | | |
| | cc) | | | | | | | | | |

(1) See Appendix.

| Category | CCT heading No | NIMEXE code (1979) | Description | Third countries | Member States | Units | Quantitative limits from 1 January to 31 December | | | |
|---|---|---|---|---|---|---|---|---|---|---|
| | | | | | | | 1980 | 1981 | 1982 | 1983 |
| 17 | 61.01 | | Men's and boy's outer garments: | China | I | 1 000 pieces | 21 | 21 | 22 | 23 |
| | B V a) 1 | | | | UK | | 36.7 | 37.8 | 39.0 | 40.1 |
| | 2 | 61.01-34; | Men's and boys' woven jackets | | | | | | | |
| | 3 | 36; 37 | (excluding waister jackets) and blaz - ers, or wool, of cotton or of man - made textile fibres | | | | | | | |
| 18 | 61.03 | | Men's and boys' under garments, | China | D | Tonnes | 51 | 53 | 55 | 56 |
| | B | | including collars, shirt fronts and cuffs: | | F | | 41 | 42 | 44 | 45 |
| | C | | | BNL | | 12 | 13 | 13 | 14 | |
| | | 61.03-51; 55; 59; 81; 85; 89 | Men's and boys' woven under garments other than shirts, of wool, of cotton or of man-made textile fibres | | UK | | 72 | 74 | 76 | 79 |
| 19 | 61.05 | | Handkerchiefs: | China (1) | D | 1 000 pieces | 13 442 | 13 889 | 14 350 | 14 806 |
| | B I | | | | F | | 2 558 | 2 910 | 3 305 | 3 737 |
| | III | | B. Other: | | I | | 7 896 | 8 059 | 8 258 | 8 451 |
| | | | | | BNL | | 11 630 | 11 687 | 11 745 | 11 804 |
| | | 61.05-30; | Handkerchief of woven fabric, of a | | UK | | 4 552 | 5 156 | 5 730 | 6 347 |
| | | 99 | value of not more than 15 EUA / kg | | IRL | | 117 | 133 | 154 | 174 |
| | | | net weight | | DK | | 1 635 | 1 668 | 1 702 | 1 735 |
| | | | | | EEC | | 41 830 | 43 504 | 45 244 | 47 054 |
| 23 | 56.05 | | Yarn of man-made fibres (discontinuous or waste), not put up for retail sale: | China | BNL | Tonnes | 1 751 | 1 804 | 1 858 | 1 913 |
| | B | | B. Of regenerated textile fibres: | | | | | | | |
| | | 56.05 51 55; 61; 65; 71; 75; 81; 85; 91; 95; 99 | Yarn of discontinuous or waste regenerated fibres, not put up for retail sale | | | | | | | |

(1) See Appendix.

| Category | CCT heading No | NIMEXE code (1979) | Description | Third countries | Member States | Units | Quantitative limits from 1 January to 31 December 1980 | 1981 | 1982 | 1983 |
|---|---|---|---|---|---|---|---|---|---|---|
| 32 | ex 58.04 | 58.04-07; 11; 15; 18; 41; 43; 45; 61; 63; 67; 69; 71; 75; 77; 78 | Woven pile fabrics and chenille fabrics (other than terry towelling or similar terry fabrics of cotton falling within heading No 55.08 and fabrics falling within heading No 58.05): | China | D | Tonnes | 569 | 588 | 614 | 640 |
| | | | | | F | | 372 | 385 | 400 | 416 |
| | | | | | I | | 275 | 290 | 306 | 322 |
| | | | | | BNL | | 114 | 128 | 146 | 167 |
| | | | | | UK | | 310 | 354 | 391 | 430 |
| | | | | | IRL | | 35 | 35 | 35 | 36 |
| | | | Woven pile fabrics and chenille fabrics (other than terry fabrics of - cotton and narrow woven fabrics), of wool, of cotton or of man-made textile fibres | | DK | | 101 | 102 | 103 | 104 |
| | | | | | EEC | | 1 776 | 1 882 | 1 995 | 2 115 |
| 37 | 56.07 B | 56.07-37; 42; 44; 48; 52; 53; 54; 57; 58; 62; 63; 64; 66; 72; 73; 74; 77; 78; 82; 83; 84; 87 56.07-3744; 48; 52; 54; 57; 5863; 64; 66; 73; 74; 77; 78; 83; 84; 87 | Woven fabrics of man-made fibres (discontinuous or waste): | China | D | Tonnes | 1 442 | 1 491 | 1 538 | 1 588 |
| | | | | | F | | 467 | 523 | 585 | 650 |
| | | | | | I | | 556 | 610 | 666 | 725 |
| | | | B. Of regenerated textile fibres: | | BNL | | 518 | 535 | 555 | 573 |
| | | | Woven fabrics of regenerated textile fibres (discontinuous or waste) other than narrow woven fabrics, pile fabrics– (including terry fabrics) and chenille fabrics: | | UK | | 573 | 654 | 744 | 842 |
| | | | | | IRL | | 36 | 40 | 43 | 47 |
| | | | | | DK | | 829 | 833 | 837 | 841 |
| | | | | | EEC | | 4 421 | 4 686 | 4 968 | 5 266 |
| | | | a) Of which other than unbleached or bleached | China | D | Tonnes | 433 | 447 | 461 | 476 |
| | | | | | F | | 142 | 161 | 181 | 203 |
| | | | | | I | | 167 | 183 | 199 | 218 |
| | | | | | BNL | | 155 | 161 | 167 | 172 |
| | | | | | UK | | 170 | 192 | 218 | 244 |
| | | | | | IRL | | 11 | 12 | 13 | 14 |
| | | | | | DK | | 249 | 250 | 251 | 252 |
| | | | | | EEC | | 1 327 | 1 406 | 1 490 | 1 579 |
| 39 | 62.02 B II a) c) | 62.02-41; 43; 47; 65; 73; 77 | Bed linen, table linen, toilet linen and kitchen linen; curtains and other furnishing articles: | China (1) | D | Tonnes | 900 | 943 | 992 | 1 041 |
| | | | | | F | | 531 (1) | 564 | 598 | 636 |
| | | | | | I | | 444 (1) | 472 | 500 | 529 |
| | | | | | BNL | | 420 | 433 | 445 | 457 |
| | III a) 2 c | | B. Other: | | UK | | 194 | 244 | 302 | 371 |
| | | | | | IRL | | 19 | 24 | 27 | 30 |
| | | | Woven table linen, toilet and kitchen linen, other than of cotton terry fabric | | DK | | 70 | 78 | 87 | 94 |
| | | | | | EEC | | 2 578 | 2 758 | 2 951 | 3 158 |

(1) See Appendix.

| Category | CCT heading No | NIMEXE code (1979) | Description | Third countries | Member States | Units | Quantitative limits from 1 January to 31 December | | | |
|---|---|---|---|---|---|---|---|---|---|---|
| | | | | | | | 1980 | 1981 | 1982 | 1983 |
| 59 | 58.02<br>ex A<br>B<br><br>ex 59.02<br>A | <br><br><br><br><br><br><br><br>58.02-12;<br>14; 17; 18;<br>19; 30; 43;<br>49; 90<br><br>59.02-01; 09 | Other carpets, carpeting, rugs, mats and matting, and 'Kelem', 'Schumacks' and 'Karamanie' rugs and the like (made up or not):<br>Felt and articles of felt, whether or not impregnated or coated:<br>A. Felt in the piece or simply cut to rectangular shape:<br>Woven, knitted or crocheted carpets, carpeting, rugs, mats and matting, and 'Kelem', 'Schumacks' and 'Karamanie' rugs and the like (made up or not); floor covering, of felt | China | F | Tonnes | 152 | 160 | 168 | 176 |
| 76 | 61.01<br>B I<br>61.02<br>B II a) | <br><br><br><br><br>61.01-13;<br>15; 17; 19<br><br>61.02-12; 14 | Men's and boys' outer garments:<br>Women's, girls' and infants' outer garments:<br>B. Other:<br>Men's and boys' woven industrial and occupational clothing; women's girls' and infants' woven aprons, smock-overalls and other industrial and occupational clothing (whether or not also suitable for domestic use), of wool, of cotton or of man-made textile fibres | China | F<br>BNL | Tonnes | 84<br>51 | 88<br>54 | 93<br>57 | 97<br>60 |
| 78 | 61.01<br>A II<br><br>B III<br><br>V f) 1 | <br><br>61.01-09;<br><br>24; 25; 25;<br><br>92; 94; 96 | Men's and boys' outer garments:<br>Men's and boys' woven bath robes, dressing gowns, smoking jackets and similar indoor wear and other outer garments, except garments of categories 6, 14 A, 14 B, 16, 17, 21, 76 and 79, of wool, of cotton or of man-made textile fibres | China (1) | F | Tonnes | 200 | 209 | 220 | 231 |

(1) See Appendix.

Appendix to Annex IV

| Category | Supplier country | Provisions | | | | |
|---|---|---|---|---|---|---|
| 2 | China | Possibility of transfer with category 3 of up to 40% of the category to which the transfer is made, except Benelux, where the category is merged with category 3. | | | | |
| 2 a) | China | The following levels apply to Benelux for the category combined with category 3 a) (tonnes): | | | | |
| | | 1980 | 1981 | 1982 | 1983 | |
| | | 202 | 204 | 206 | 208 | |
| 3 | China | Possibility of transfer with category 2 of up to 40% of the category to which the transfer is made, except Benelux, where the category is merged with category 2. | | | | |
| 3 a) | China | See category 2 a). | | | | |
| 5 | China | The following sub-limits apply within the quantitative limits prescribed in the Annex for the Community and the United Kingdom: | | | | |
| | | Jerseys and pullovers of fine wool and animal hair (pieces): | | | | |
| | | | 1980 | 1981 | 1982 | 1983 |
| | | EEC | 41 600 | 43 300 | 45 000 | 46 800 |
| | | UK | 9 400 | 9 700 | 10 000 | 10 400 |
| 6 | China | The following sub-limits apply within the quantitative limits prescribed in the Annex for Benelux: | | | | |
| | | Long trousers (1 000 pieces): | | | | |
| | | 1980 | 1981 | 1982 | 1983 | |
| | | 410 | 420 | 430 | 440 | |
| 10 | China | The quantitative limits prescribed in the Annex include gloves, mittens and mitts, knitted or crocheted, not elastic or rubberized, of category 11, of wool, of cotton or of man-made fibres. | | | | |
| | | The following sub-limits apply within the quantitative limits prescribed in the Annex for the United Kingdom: | | | | |
| | | Knitted gloves, mittens and mitts of category 10 (coated or impregnated) (pairs): | | | | |
| | | 1980 | 1981 | 1982 | 1983 | |
| | | 20 600 | 21 200 | 21 900 | 22 500 | |
| Category | Supplier country | Provisions | | | | |
| 19 | China | The quantitative limits prescribed in the Annex include cotton handkerchiefs of category 89. | | | | |

| | | |
|---|---|---|
| 39 | China | The quantitative limits prescribed in the Annex include bed linen of category 20. |
| | | The following sum-limits apply within the quantitative limits prescribed in the Annex for France: |
| | | Household linen other than embroidered (tonnes): |
| | | 1980 1981 1982 1983 |
| | | 129 137 147 157 |
| | | The following sub-limits apply within the quantitative limits prescribed in the Annex for Benelux: |
| | | Bed linen (tonnes): |
| | | 1980 1981 1982 1983 |
| | | 32 34 37 39 |
| 78 | China | The quantitative limits prescribed in the Annex include other women's outerwear of category 81. |

For Germany 26% of all the quantitative limits prescribed in the Annex are reserved for use as the Berlin Fair.

ANNEX V
referred to in Article 3

DOUBLE CHECKING SYSTEM

Article 1

The competent government authorities of China shall issue an export licence in respect of all consignments of textile products subject to the quantitative limits established in Annex IV, up to the level of the said limits and the corresponding shares.

Article 2

1. The export licence shall conform to the specimen appended to Annex VI and may also contain a translation into another language. It must certify inter alia that the quantity of goods in question has been set off against the quantitative limit and the share established for the category of the product concerned.

2. Importers shall not be obliged to import the total quantity covered by an import authorizations or document in a single consignment.

Article 3

The validity of import authorizations granted by the authorities of the Member States shall be subject to the validity of and the quantities indicated in the export licences issued by the competent authorities of China on the basis of which the import authorizations were granted.

Article 4

Exports shall be set off against the quantitative limits and shares established for the year for which the export licence has been issued.

Article 5

1. The authorities of the Memeber State designated on the export licence as the country of destination shall issue an import licence automatically within a maximum of five working days of the presentation by the importer of the original of the corresponding export licence, subject to the provisions of Article II of this Regulation.

2. The import authorizations shall be valid for six months.

3. The import authorizations shall be valid only in the Member State which issued them.

4. The importer's declaration or request shall only mention or contain:

(a) the identification of the importer and exporter;

(b) the country of origin and possibly the country of export and purchase;

(3) a description of the product including:

_ its commercial designation,

_ the category of the product,

_ a description of the goods in accordance with the tariff heading and / or the reference number of the nomenclature of goods for the external trade statistics;

(d) the quantity in the appropriate unit;

(e) the value;

(f) possibly dates of payment and delivery and a copy of the bill of lading and of the purchase contract;

(g) date and number of the export licence;

(h) any internal code used for administrative purposes;

(i) date and signature of importer.

Article 6

Import authorizations or equivalent documents shall be issued without discrimination to any importer in the Community wherever the place of his establishment may be in the Community, without prejudice to compliance with the other conditions required under current rules.

Article 7 1. Should the authorities of a Member State find that the total volume covered by the export licences issued by China for a given category exceeds the share established for that category, the said authorities shall suspend the issue of import authorizations or equivalent documents and immediately inform both the authorities of China and the Commission.

2. The Commission shall immediately initiate consultations with the authorities of China.

## ANNEX VI

## FORM AND RULES FOR COMPLETION OF EXPORT LICENCES, SHIPMENT CERTIFICATES AND CERTIFICATES OF ORIGIN; COMMON PROVISIONS

Article 1

Export licences, shipment certificates and certificates of origin shall be made out in English or French.

If they are completed by hand, entries must be in ink and in printscript.

Export licences, shipment certificates and certificates of origin may comprise additional copies duly indicated as such.

The documents shall measure 210 by 297 mm. The paper used must be white writing paper, sized, not containing mechanical pulp and weighing not less than 25 g / m2. Each part shall have a printed guillochepattern background making any falsification by mechanical or chemical means apparent to the eye. Each document shall bear a serial number, whether or not printed, by which it can be identified.

Article 2

The export licence shipment certificate and the certificate or origin may be issued after the shipment of the products to which they relate. In such cases they must bear the endorsement " délivré aa posteriori " or " issued retrospectively ".

Article 3

In the event of theft, loss or destruction of an export licence, shipment certificate or a certificate of origin, the exporter may apply to the competent governmental authority which issued the document for a duplicate to be made out on the basis of the export documents in his possession. The duplicate licence or certificate issued in this way must bear the endorsement " duplicata " or " duplicate ".

The duplicate must bear the date of the original licence or certificate.

Article 4

The Commission shall supply the Member States' authorities with the names and addresses of the authorities in China competent to issue certificates of origin and export licences or shipment certificates, together with specimens of stamps used by those authorities.

| | | |
|---|---|---|
| 1 Exporter (name, full address, country)<br>Exportateur (nom, addresse complète, pays) | ORIGINAL | 2 No |
| | 3 Quota year<br>Année contingentaire | 4 Category number<br>Numéro de catégorie |
| | | |
| 5 Consignee (name, full address, country)<br>Destinataire (nom, addresse complète, pays) | CERTIFICATE OF ORIGIN<br>(Textile products) | |
| | | |
| | CERTIFICAT D'ORIGINE<br>(produits textiles) | |
| | 6 Country of origin<br>Pays d'origine | 7 Country of destination<br>Pays de destination |
| | | |
| 8 Place and date of shipment – Means of transport<br>Lieu et date d'embarquement – Moyen de transport | 9 Supplementary details<br>Données supplémentaires | |
| | | |
| 10 Marks and numbers – Number and kind of packages – Description of goods<br>Marques et numéros – Nombre et nature des colis – Désignation des marchandises | 11 Quantity (1)<br>Quantité (1) | 12 FOB Value (2)<br>Valeur fob (2) |
| | | |
| | | |
| | | |
| | | |
| | | |
| 13 CERTIFICATION BY THE COMPETENT AUTHORITY – VISA DE L'AUTORITE COMPETENTE | | |
| I, the undersigned, certify that the goods described above originated in the country shown in box No 6, in accordance with the provisions in force in the European Economic Community | | |
| Je soussigné certifie que les marchandises désignées ci-dessus sont originaires du pays figurant dans la case 6, conformément aux dispositions en vigueur dans la Communauté économique européenne. | | |
| | | |

| | | |
|---|---|---|
| 14 Competent authority (name, full address, country)<br>Autorité compétente (nom, addresse complète, pays) | At – À..., | on – le |
| | (Signature) | (Stamp – Cachet) |

(1) Show net weight (kg) and also quantity in the unit prescribed for category where other than net weight – Indiquer le poids net en kilogrammes ainsi que la quantité dans l'unité prévue pour la catégorie si cette unité n'est pas le poids net.

(2) In the currency of the sale contract – Dans la monnaie du contract de vente.

| | | |
|---|---|---|
| 1 Exporter (name, full address, country)<br>Exportateur (nom, addresse complète, pays) | ORIGINAL | 2 No |
| | 3 Quota year<br>Année contingentaire | 4 Category number<br>Numéro de catégorie |
| | | |
| 5 Consignee (name, full address, country)<br>Destinataire (nom, addresse complète, pays) | EXPORT LICENCE<br>(Textile products) | |
| | | |
| | LICENCE D'EXPORTATION<br>(produits textiles) | |
| | 6 Country of origin<br>Pays d'origine | 7 Country of destination<br>Pays de destination |
| | | |
| 8 Place and date of shipment – Means of transport<br>Lieu et date d'embarquement – Moyen de transport | 9 Supplementary details<br>Données supplémentaires | |
| | | |
| 10 Marks and numbers – Number and kind of packages – Description of goods<br>Marques et numéros – Nombre et nature des colis – Désignation des marchandises | 11 Quantity (1)<br>Quantité (1) | 12 FOB Value (2)<br>Valeur fob (2) |
| | | |
| | | |
| | | |
| | | |
| 13 CERTIFICATION BY THE COMPETENT AUTHORITY – VISA DE L'AUTORITE COMPETENTE | | |

| | | |
|---|---|---|
| I, the undersigned, certify that the goods described above have been charged against the quantitative limit established for the year shown in box No 3 in respect of the category shown in box No 4 by the provisions regulating trade in textile products with the European Economic Community. | | |
| Je soussigné certifie que les marchandises désignées ci-dessus ont été imputées sur la limite quantitative fixée pour l'année indiquée dans la case 3 pour la catégorie désignée dans la case 4 dans le cadre des dispositions régissant les échanges de produits textiles avec la Communauté économique européenne. | | |
| | | |
| 14 Competent authority (name, full address, country)<br>Autorité compétente (nom, addresse complète, pays) | At – À...,<br>(Signature) | on – le<br>(Stamp – Cachet) |

(1) Show net weight (kg) and also quantity in the unit prescribed for category where other than net weight – Indiquer le poids net en kilogrammes ainsi que la quantité dans l'unité prévue pour la categorie si cette unité n'est pas le poids net.

(2) In the currency of the sale contract – Dans la monnaie du contract de vente.

## ANNEX VII

| | | |
|---|---|---|
| 1 Exporter (name, full address, country)<br>Exportateur (nom, addresse complète, pays) | ORIGINAL | 2 No |
| | 3 Quota year<br>Année contingentaire | 4 Category number<br>Numéro de catégorie |
| | | |
| 5 Consignee (name, full address, country)<br>Destinataire (nom, addresse complète, pays) | SHIPMENT CERTIFICATE<br>(Textile products) | |
| | | |
| | CERTIFICAT D'EMBARQUEMENT<br>(produits textiles) | |
| | 6 Country of origin<br>Pays d'origine | 7 Country of destination<br>Pays de destination |
| | | |
| 8 Place and date of shipment – Means of transport<br>Lieu et date d'embarquement – Moyen de transport | 9 Supplementary details<br>Données supplémentaires | |
| | | |

| | | |
|---|---|---|
| 10 Marks and numbers – Number and kind of packages – Description of goods<br>Marques et numéros – Nombre et nature des colis – Désignation des marchandises | 11 Quantity (1)<br>Quantité (1) | 12 FOB Value (2)<br>Valeur fob (2) |
| | | |
| | | |
| | | |
| | | |
| 13 CERTIFICATION BY THE COMPETENT AUTHORITY – VISA DE L'AUTORITE COMPETENTE | | |
| I, the undersigned, certify that the goods described above are intended for export in the framework of the provisions regulating trade in textile products with the European Economic Community. | | |
| Je soussigné certifie que les marchandises désignées ci-dessus sont destinées à étre exportées dans le cadre des dispositions régissant les échanges de produits textiles avec la Communauté économique européenne. | | |
| | | |
| 14 Competent authority (name, full address, country)<br>Autorité compétente (nom, addresse complète, pays) | At – À...,<br><br>(Signature) | on – le<br><br>(Stamp – Cachet) |

(1) Show net weight (kg) and also quantity in the unit prescribed for category where other than net weight – Indiquer le poids net en kilogrammes ainsi que la quantité dens l'unité prévue pour la catégorie si cette unité n'est pas le poids net.

(2) In the currency of the sale contract – Dans la monnaie du contrat de vente.

## ANNEX VIII
referred to in Article 5 (3)

1. For the purpose of the Agreement with China, cottage industry and folklore products are defined as follows:

(a) garments traditionally made by hand in the cottage industry of China from fabrics and sewn solely by hand without the aid of any machine;

(b) other textile articles traditionally made by hand in the cottage industry of China from fabrics woven on hand or foot operated looms; being fabrics of a kind traditionally made in the cottage industry of China, and sewn solely by hand without the aid of any machine;

(c) traditional folklore handicraft textile products of China as defined in a list to be agreed between the two Parties.

2. The provisions of Article 5 (3) apply only in respect of products covered by a certificate conforming to the specimen appendixed to this Annex and issued by the competent authorities of China.

Appendix to Annex VIII

<table>
<tr><td rowspan="2">1 Exporter (name, full address, country)<br>Exportateur (nom, adresse complète, pays)</td><td colspan="2">ORIGINAL 2 NO</td></tr>
<tr><td colspan="2">CERTIFICATE in regard to TEXTILE HANDICRAFTS and TRADITIONAL TEXTILEPRODUCTS, OF THE COTTAGE INDUSTRY, issued in confirmity with endunder the conditions regulating trade in textile products with the EuropeanEconomic Community</td></tr>
<tr><td>3 Consignee (name, full address, country)<br>Destinataire (nom, adresse complète, pays)</td><td colspan="2">CERTIFICAT relatif aux PRODUCTS TEXTILES FAITS A LA MAIN, et aux PRODUCTS TEXTILES RELEVANT DU FOLKLORE TRADITIONNEL, DE FABRICATION ARTISANALE, délivré en conformité avec et sous les conditionsrégissant les échanges de produits textiles avec la Communauté économique européenne</td></tr>
<tr><td></td><td>4 Country of origin<br>Pays d'origine</td><td>5 Country of destination<br>Pays de destination</td></tr>
<tr><td></td><td></td><td></td></tr>
<tr><td>6 Place and date of shipment – Means of transport<br>Lieu et date d'embarquement – Moyen de transport</td><td colspan="2">7 Supplementary details<br>Données supplémentaires</td></tr>
<tr><td></td><td></td><td></td></tr>
<tr><td></td><td></td><td></td></tr>
<tr><td>8 Marks and numbers – Number and kind of packages – Description of goods<br>Marques et numéros – Nombre et nature des colis – Désignation des marchandises</td><td>9 Quantity<br>Quantité</td><td>10 FOB Value (1)<br>Valeur fob (1)</td></tr>
<tr><td></td><td></td><td></td></tr>
<tr><td colspan="3">11 CERTIFICATION BY THE COMPETENT AUTHORITY – VISA DE L'AUTORITE COMPETENTE</td></tr>
</table>

| |
|---|
| I, the undersigned, certify that the consignment described above includes only the following traditional textile products of the cottage industry of the country shown in box No 4: |
| a) garments obtained manually from fabrics and sewn solely by hand without the aid of any machine (2); |
| b) other textile articles obtained manually from the fabrics woven on hand or foot operated looms and sewn solely by hand without the aid of any machine (handicrafts) (2); |
| c) traditional folklore handicraft textile products as defined in the list agreed between the European Economic Community and the country shown in box No 4. |
| Je soussigné certifie que l'envoi décrit ci-dessus contient exclusivement les produits textiles suivants relevant traditionnellement de la fabrication artisanale du pays figurant dans la case 4: |
| a) vêtements obtenus manuellement à partir de tissus et cousus uniquement à la main sans l'aide d'une machine (2); |
| b) autres articles textiles obtenus manuellement à partir de tissus tissés sur des métiers actionnés à la main ou au pied et cousus uniquement à la main sans l'aide d'une machine (handicrafts) (2); |
| c) produits textiles relevant du folklore traditionnel comme définis dans la liste convenue entre la Communauté économique européenne et le pays indiqué dans la case 4. |

| | | |
|---|---|---|
| 12 Competent authority (name, full address, country) Autorité compétente (nom, adresse complète, pays) | | |
| | At – À..., | on – le |

| | | |
|---|---|---|
| | (Signature) | (Stamp – Cachet) |

(1) In the currency of the sale contract – Dans la monnaie du contrat de vente.

(2) Delete as appropriate – Biffer la (les) mention (s) inutile (s).

## ANNEX IX
referred to in Article 3 (6)

1. At the request of a Member State which considers that a given textile product covered by categories 1 to 114 set out in Annex I is being imported from China at prices lower than those generally charged for like products, sold under normal commercial conditions by other exporting countries on the market of the Member State concerned, the Commission may request that consultations should be initiated with China.

2. The Member State requesting the application of this provision shall communicate the facts justifying the measure to the Commission.

3. In critical circumstances, the competent authorities of Member States may suspend the issue of import authorizations or import documents until such time as a mutually acceptable solution is found within the framework of the consultations specified in paragraph 1.

When the 1979 Agreement and Protocols expired in 1988, the EEC and China concluded a new Textiles Agreement (see Document 2.4). It provided a system of quotas for Chinese textile exports to the EEC, except for products declared for re-export out of the EC and cottage industry fabrics. For products not subject to quotas, the Agreement retained the 'basket exit mechanism': if imports from China exceeded specified percentages of all imports of the product in preceding years, the EEC could request consultations and, if these failed, eventually introduce annual quotas. The 1988 Agreement also included a double-checking system of export licences and import licences, as well as anti-circumvention provisions. The Agreement was amended in 1990 and again in 1992. The 1992 Agreement extended the validity of the 1988 Agreement automatically up to 31 December 1995 unless otherwise either party notified the other at least six months before 31 December 1994 or unless the Uruguay Round ATC was concluded and entered into force earlier.

### Document 2.4: 1988 Textiles Agreement between the EEC and China

**Agreement between the European Economic Community and the People's Republic of China on trade in textile products—Protocol A—Protocol B—Protocol C—Protocol D—Protocol E—Agreed Minutes—Exchange of Notes**

*Official Journal L 380, 31/12/1988 P. 0002–0073*
*L 352 15/12/1990 P. 0002*

Initialled at Brussels on 9 December 1988

THE COUNCIL OF THE EUROPEAN COMMUNITIES,

of the one part, and

THE GOVERNMENT OF THE PEOPLE'S REPUBLIC OF CHINA

of the other part,

DESIRING to promote, with a view to permanent cooperation and in conditions providing every security for trade, the orderly and equitable development of trade in textile products between the European Economic Community (hereinafter referred to as 'the Community') and the People's Republic of China (hereinafter referred to as 'China'),

RESOLVED to take the fullest possible account of the serious economic and social problems at present affecting the textile industry in both importing and exporting countries, and in particular, to eliminate real risks of market disruption on the market of the Community and real risks of disruption to the textile trade of China,

HAVING REGARD to the Arrangement regarding International Trade in Textiles (hereinafter referred to as 'the Geneva Arrangement'), and in particular Article 4 thereof, and to the conditions set out in the Protocol extending the Arrangement,

HAVING REGARD to the Trade and Economic Cooperation Agreement between the Community and China,

HAVE DECIDED to conclude this Agreement and to this end have designated as their Plenipotentiaries:

THE COUNCIL OF THE EUROPEAN COMMUNITIES:

THE GOVERNMENT OF THE PEOPLE'S REPUBLIC OF CHINA:

WHO HAVE AGREED AS FOLLOWS:

## I. General provisions

Article 1

The Parties recognize and confirm that without prejudice to the rights and obligations under the Trade and Economic Cooperation Agreement between the Community and China the conduct of their mutual trade in textile products shall be governed by the provisions of this Agreement.

Article 2

1. Trade in textile products listed in Annex I and originating within the Contracting Parties shall be liberalized

for the duration of this Agreement under the conditions set out therein.

2. Trade in textile products listed in Annex II and originating within the Contracting Parties shall be covered by this Agreement solely for the purposes of application of the provisions making explicit reference to that Annex.

3. Subject to the provisions of this Agreement, the Community undertakes, in respect of the products listed in Annex I, to suspend the application of quantitative import restrictions currently in force and not to introduce new quantitative restrictions under Article 3 of the Geneva Arrangement.

4. Measures having equivalent effect to quantitative restrictions on the importation into the Community of the products listes in Annex I shall be prohibited.

## II. Arrangements for exports to the Community

Article 3

1. China agrees to establish and maintain for each calendar year quantitative limits on its exports to the Community in accordance with Annex III. Such exports shall be subject to a double-checking system specified in Protocol A.

2. In administering the quantitative limits referred to in paragraph 1, China shall ensure that the Community textile industry shall benefit from utilization of the said limits.

More particularly, as regards categories 2, 3 and 37 China undertakes to reserve, as a priority, 50% of the quantitative limits concerned for industry users during one hundred and fifteen days beginning on 1 January of each year. For this purpose, contracts made with the industry during the period in question shall be taken into consideration.

3. To facilitate the implementation of these provisions the Community shall provide the competent Chinese authorities, before the end of each year, with a list of interested manufacturers and processors and, if possible, of the quantity of products requested for each firm. To this end, the firms concerned are invited to make direct contact with the relevant

Chinese bodies by 15 February of the following year, in order to make their purchasing intentions known.

Article 4

1. Imports into the Community of textile products covered by this Agreement shall not be subject to the quantitative limits established in Annex III, provided that they are declared to be for re-export outside the Community in the same state or after processing, within the framework of the administrative system of control which exists within the Community.

However, the release for home use of products imported under the conditions referred to above shall be subject to the production of an export licence issued by the Chinese authorities, and to proof of origin in accordance with the provisions of Protocol A.

2. Where the Community authorities ascertain that imports of textile products have been set off against a quantitative limit established under this Agreement, but that the products have subsequently been re-exported outside the Community, the authorities concerned shall inform the Chinese authorities within four weeks of the quantities involved and authorize imports of identical quantities of the same products, which shall not be set off against the quantitative limit established under this Agreement for the current or the following year.

3. Exports of cottage industry fabrics woven on hand- or foot-operated looms, garments or other made-up articles obtained manually from such fabrics and of traditional folklore handicraft products shall not be subject to quantitative limits, provided that these products meet the conditions laid down in Protocol B.

4. China and the Community recognize the special and differential character of re-imports of textile products into the Community after processing in China.

Provided that they are effected in accordance with the regulations on economic outward processing in force in the Community, these re-imports are not subject to the quantitative limits set out in Annex III when they are subject to the specific arrangements laid down in Protocol E.

Article 5

1. In any Agreement year advance use of a portion of the quantitative limit established for the following Agreement year is authorized for each category of products up to 5% of the quantitative limit for the current Agreement year.

Amounts delivered in advance shall be deducted from the corresponding quantitative limits established for the following Agreement year.

2. Carry-over to the corresponding quantitative limit for the following Agreement year of the amounts not used during any Agreement year is authorized for each category of products up to 7% of the quantitative limit for the current Agreement year.

3. Transfers in respect of categories in Group I shall not be made from any category except as follows:

- transfers between Categories 2 and 3 and from Category 1 to Categories 2 and 3 may be made up to 7% of the quantitative limits for the category to which the transfer is made,
- transfers between Categories 4, 5, 6, 7, and 8 may be made up to 7% of the quantitative limit for the category to which the transfer is made.

Transfers into any category in Groups II and III may be made from any category or categories in Groups I, II and III up to 7% of the quantitative limit for the category to which the transfer is made.

4. The table of equivalence applicable to the transfers referred to above is given in Annex I to this Agreement.

5. The increase in any category of products resulting from the cumulative application of the provisions in paragraphs 1, 2 and 3 above during an Agreement year shall not exceed 17%.

6. Prior notification shall be given by the authorities of China in the event of recourse to the provisions of paragraphs 1, 2 and 3 above.

Article 6

1. Exports of textile products not listed in Annex III to this Agreement may be made subject to quantitative limits by China on the conditions laid down in the following paragraphs.

2. Where the Community finds, under the system of administrative control set up, that the level of imports of products in a given category not listed in Annex III originating in China exceeds, in relation to the preceding years total imports into the Community from all sources of products in that category, the following rates:

- 5% for categories of products in Group II,
- 10% for categories of products in Group III,

it may request the opening of consultations in accordance with the procedure described in Article 16 of this Agreement, with a view to reaching agreement on an appropriate restraint level for the products in such category.

The Community shall authorize the importation of products of the said category shipped from China before the date on which the request for consultations was submitted.

3. Pending a mutually satisfactory solution, China undertakes to limit exports of the products in the category concerned to the Community or to the regions of the Community market specified by the Community for a provisional period of three months from the date on which the request for consultations is made. Such provisional limit shall be established at 25% of the level of imports reached during the calendar year preceding that in which imports exceeded the level resulting from the application of the formula set out in paragraph 2, and gave rise to the request for consultation, or 25% of the level resulting from the application of the formula set out in paragraph 2, whichever is the higher.

4. Should the Parties be unable in the course of consultations to reach a satisfactory solution within the period specified in Article 16, paragraph 2, the Community shall have the right to introduce a definitive quantitative limit at an annual level not lower than the level resulting from the application of the formula set out in paragraph 2, or 106% of the level of imports reached during the calendar year preceding that in which imports exceeded the level resulting from the application of the formula set out in paragraph 2 and gave rise to the request for consultations, whichever is the higher.

The annual level so fixed shall be revised upwards after consultations in accordance with the procedure referred to in Article 16, with a view to fulfilling the conditions set out in paragraph 2, should the trend of total imports into the Community of the product in question make this necessary.

5. The limits introduced under paragraph 2 or paragraph 4 may in no case be lower than the level of imports of products in that category originating in China in 1988.

6. Quantitative limits may also be established by the Community on a regional basis in accordance with the provisions of Protocol C.

7. The annual growth rate for the quantitative limits introduced under this Article shall be determined in accordance with the provisions of Protocol D.

8. The provisions of this Article shall not apply where the percentages specified in paragraph 2 have been reached as a result of a fall in total imports into the Community, and not as a result of an increase in exports of products originating in China.

9. In the event of the provisions of paragraphs 2, 3 or 4 being applied, China undertakes to issue export certificates for products covered by contracts concluded before the introduction of the quantitative limit, up to the volume of the quantitative limit fixed.

10. Up to the date of communication of the statistics referred to in Article 15 paragraph 6, the provisions of paragraph 2 of this Article shall apply on the basis of the annual statistics previously communicated by the Community.

11. The provisions of this Agreement which concern exports of products subject to the quantitative limits established in Annex III shall also apply to products for which quantitative limits are introduced under this Article.

Article 7

1. China and the Community agree to cooperate fully in preventing the circumvention of this Agreement by transhipment, re-routing or whatever other means.

2. Where information available to the Community as a result of the investigations carried out in accordance with the procedures set out in Protocol A constitutes evidence that products of Chinese origin subject to quantitative limits established under this Agreement have been transhipped, re-routed or otherwise imported into the Community in circumvention of this Agreement, the Community may request the opening of consultations in accordance with the procedures described in Article 16, with a view to reaching agreement on an equivalent adjustment of the corresponding quantitative limits established under this Agreements.

3. Pending the result of the consultations referred to in paragraph 2, China shall, as a precautionary measure, if so requested by the Community, make the necessary arrangements to ensure that adjustments of quantitative limits liable to be agreed following the consultations referred to in paragraph 2 may be carried out for the quota year in which the request to open consultations in accordance with paragraph 2 was made, or for the following year if the quota for the current year is exhausted, where clear evidence of circumvention is provided.

4. Should the parties be unable in the course of consultations to reach a satisfactory solution within the period specified in Article 16 paragraph 2, the Community shall have the right, where clear evidence of circumvention has been provided, to deduct from the quantitative limits established under this Agreement amounts equivalent to the products of Chinese origin.

Article 8

1. China shall endeavour to ensure that exports of textile products covered by this Agreement are spaced out as evenly as possible over the year, due account being taken in particular of seasonal factors.

2. Should there be an excessive concentration of imports of any products belonging to a category subject to quantitative limits under this Agreement, the Community may request consultations in accordance with the procedure specified in Article 16 with a view to remedying this situation.

Article 9

In the event of denunciation of this Agreement as provided for in Article 20 paragraph 3, the quantitative limits established in Annex III shall be reduced on a pro rata basis.

Article 10

1. Portions of the quantitative limits established in Annex III not used in one region of the Community may be reallocated to another region in accordance with the procedures in force in the Community.

The Community undertakes to examine with care and reply within four weeks to any request made for reallocation by China. In the event of agreement on such reallocation, the flexibility provisions set out in Article 5 shall continue to be applicable to the levels of the original allocation.

2. After 1 June of each year of application of the Agreement, China may transfer, subject to prior notification to the Community, the unused quantities of the regional quota-shares of a Community quantitative limit, set out in Annex III, to the quota-shares of the same limit of other regions of the Community provided that the regional quota-share from which the transfer is made is utilized by less than 80%, and up to the amount of the following percentages of the quota-share to which the transfer is made:

- 4% in the first year of application of the Agreement,
- 8% in the second year of application of the Agreement,
- 16% in the third year of application of the Agreement.

The percentage in the fourth year of application of the Agreement shall be determined following consultations between the Parties.

3. Should it appear in any given region of the Community that additional supplies are required, the Community may, where measures taken pursuant to paragraph 2 are inadequate to cover those requirements, authorize the importation of amounts greater than those stipulated in Annex III.

Article 11

1. China undertakes to take such measures as are required to make possible the export of the minimum annual quantities laid down in Annex IV of the products listed in that Annex. The Parties will examine each year the possibilities of increasing these quantities in the light of the needs of Community industry and China's export possibilities.

2. In administering exports of the products referred to in paragraph 1, China undertakes to give favourable consideration, taking into account its export possibilities, to request from the Community textile industry with a view to meeting its needs.

For this purpose, the Community may submit to the Chinese authorities before the end of each year a list of interested manufacturers and processors and, if possible, the quantities of products requested by each of the firms in question.

3. The Contracting Parties are agreed that transactions in the products listed in Annex IV shall be carried out in accordance with Articles 8 and 9 of the Trade and Economic Cooperation Agreement taking account of market practice and normal trade flows.

III. Imports into China

Article 12

1. In return for the increased opportunities for the export of Chinese textile products to the Community, China shall encourage and facilitate the importation on its market of textile products originating in the Community listed in annexes I and II. To this end China will take such measures as are necessary to avoid exacerbating and if possible to reduce, during the period of application of the Agreement, the disequilibrium in its textile trade balance with the Community.

2. Where a need for additional supplies arises, and in particular a need leading to the diversification of imports of textile products into China, preference will be given to imports of products originating in the Community referred to in paragraph 1 and offered on terms meeting the conditions set out in Articles 8 and 9 of the Trade and Economic Cooperation Agreement.

Article 13

1. The two Parties agree to examine the trend of trade in textile products and garments each year, in the framework of the consultations provided for in Article 16 and on the basis of the statistics referred to in Article 15.

2. If the Community finds that the provisions of Article 12 paragraph 2 of this Agreement place it in an unfavourable position as compared with a third country, it may request consultations with China in accordance with the procedure specified in Article 16 with a view to taking appropriate action consistent with the rights and obligations under the Trade and Economic Cooperation Agreement.

IV. Common provisions

Article 14

1. The classification of the products covered by this Agreement is based on the tariff and statistical nomenclature and on the Common Customs Tariff of the Community (hereinafter called the 'combined nomenclature', or in abbreviated form 'CN').

Any amendment to the combined nomenclature (CN) made in accordance with the procedures in force in the Community, concerning categories of products covered by this Agreement or any decision relating to the classification of goods shall not have the effect of reducing any quantitative limit introduced pursuant to this Agreement.

2. The origin of the products covered by this Agreement shall be determined in accordance with the rules in force in the Community.

Any amendment to these rules of origin shall be communicated by China and shall not have the effect of reducing any quantitative limit established in Annex III.

The procedures for control of the origin of the products referred to above are laid down in Protocol A.

Article 15

1. China shall supply the Community with precise statistical information on all export licences issued for categories of textile products subject to the quantitative limits set out in Annex III, expressed in quantities and in terms of value and broken down by Member State of the Community, as well as on all certificates issued by the Chinese authorities for products referred to in Article 4 paragraph 3 and subject to the provisions of Protocol B.

2. The Community shall likewise transmit to the Chinese authorities precise statistical information on import authorizations or documents issued by the Community authorities and import statistics for products covered by the system referred to in Article 6 paragraph 2.

3. The information referred to above shall, for all categories of products, be transmitted before the end of the second month following the quarter to which the statistics relate.

4. Upon request by the Community, China shall supply import statistics for all products covered by Annexes I and II.

5. Should it be found on analysis of the information exchanged that there are significant discrepancies between the returns for exports and those for imports, consultations may be initiated in accordance with the procedure specified in Article 16 of this Agreement.

6. For the purpose of applying the provisions of Article 6, the Community undertakes to provide the Chinese authorities before 15 April of each year with the preceding year's statistics on imports of all textile products covered by this Agreement, broken down by supplying country and Community Member State.

Article 16

1. A Textile Committee (hereinafter referred to as the 'Committee') made up of representatives of the Contracting Parties shall be set up, its members being appointed by the Joint Committee provided for in Article 15 of the Trade and Economic Cooperation Agreement.

The Committee shall deal with matters raised for consultation under the terms of this Agreement, in accordance with the procedure set out in paragraph 2 below, and with any problem arising from the application of the Agreement.

2. The consultation procedures referred to in this Agreement shall be governed by the following rules:

- any request for consultations shall be notified in writing to the other Party,
- the request for consultations shall be followed within a reasonable period (and in any case not later than 15 days following the notification) by a statement setting out the reasons and circumstances which, in the opinion of the requesting Party, justify the submission of such a request,

- the Parties shall enter into consultations within one month at the latest of notification of the request, with a view to reaching agreement on a mutually acceptable conclusion within one further month at the latest.

3. The Community may request consultations in accordance with paragraph 2 when it ascertains that during a particular year of application of the Agreement difficulties arise in the Community or one of its regions from a sharp and substantial increase, by comparison to the preceding year, in imports of a given category of Group I subject to the quantitative limits set out in Annex III.

Article 17

The two Contracting Parties undertake to promote the exchange of visits by persons, groups and delegations from business, trade and industry, to facilitate contracts in the industrial, commercial and technical fields connected with trade in textile products and garments and to assist in the organization of fairs and exhibitions of mutual interest.

Article 18

Pending the entry into force in China of national legislation on intellectual property, the two Parties, at the request of either of them, shall hold consultations in accordance with the procedure laid down in Article 16 for the purpose of finding an equitable solution in any dispute relating to the protection of marks, designs or models of articles of apparel and textile products.

V. Final provisions

Article 19

As regards the Community, this Agreement shall apply to the territories in which the Treaty establishing the European Economic Community is applied under the conditions laid down in that Treaty.

Article 20

1. This Agreement shall enter into force on the first day of the month following the date of its signature. It shall be applicable until 31 December 1992.

2. This Agreement shall apply with effect from 1 January 1989.

3. Either Party may at any time propose modifications to this Agreement or denounce it, provided that at least six months' notice is given. In that event, the Agreement shall come to an end on the expiry of the period of notice.

4. The Annexes and Protocols to this Agreement and the Agreed Minutes and letters joined thereto, shall form an integral part thereof.

Article 21

This Agreement shall be drawn up in two copies in the Danish, Dutch, English, French, German, Greek, Italian, Portuguese, Spanish and Chinese languages, each of these texts being equally authentic.

*ANNEX I*

**LIST OF PRODUCTS REFERRED TO IN ARTICLE 1 (1)**

1. When the constitutive material of the products of categories 1 to 114 is not specifically mentioned, these products are to be taken to be made exclusively of wool or of fine hair, of cotton or of man-made fibres.

2. Garments which are not recognizable as being garments for men or boys or as being garments for women or girls are classified with the latter.

3. Where the expression 'babies' garments' is used, this is meant also to cover girls' garments up to and including commercial size 86.

GROUP I A

| Category | CN code 1988 | Description | Table of equivalence | |
|---|---|---|---|---|
| | | | pieces/kg | g/piece |
| (1) | (2) | (3) | (4) | (5) |
| 1 | 5204 11 00 | Cotton yarn, not put up for retail sale | | |
| | 5204 19 00 | | | |
| | 5205 11 00 | | | |
| | 5205 12 00 | | | |
| | 5205 13 00 | | | |
| | 5205 14 00 | | | |
| | 5205 15 10 | | | |
| | 5205 15 90 | | | |
| | 5205 21 00 | | | |
| | 5205 22 00 | | | |
| | 5205 23 00 | | | |
| | 5205 24 00 | | | |
| | 5205 25 10 | | | |
| | 5205 25 30 | | | |
| | 5205 25 90 | | | |
| | 5205 31 00 | | | |
| | 5205 32 00 | | | |
| | 5205 33 00 | | | |
| | 5205 34 00 | | | |
| | 5205 35 10 | | | |
| | 5205 35 90 | | | |
| | 5205 41 00 | | | |
| | 5205 42 00 | | | |
| | 5205 43 00 | | | |
| | 5205 44 00 | | | |
| | 5205 45 10 | | | |
| | 5205 45 30 | | | |
| | 5205 45 90 | | | |
| | 5206 11 00 | | | |
| | 5206 12 00 | | | |
| | 5206 13 00 | | | |
| | 5206 14 00 | | | |
| | 5206 15 10 | | | |
| | 5206 15 90 | | | |
| | 5206 21 00 | | | |
| | 5206 22 00 | | | |
| | 5206 23 00 | | | |
| | 5206 24 00 | | | |
| | 5206 25 10 | | | |
| | 5206 25 90 | | | |
| | 5206 31 00 | | | |
| | 5206 32 00 | | | |
| | 5206 33 00 | | | |

| (1) | (2) | (3) | (4) | (5) |
|---|---|---|---|---|
| 1 *(cont'd)* | 5206 34 00 | | | |
| | 5206 35 10 | | | |
| | 5206 35 90 | | | |
| | 5206 41 00 | | | |
| | 5206 42 00 | | | |
| | 5206 43 00 | | | |
| | 5206 44 00 | | | |
| | 5206 45 10 | | | |
| | 5206 45 90 | | | |
| | ex 5604 90 00 | | | |
| 2 | 5208 11 10 | Woven fabrics of cotton, other than gauze, terry fabrics, narrow woven fabrics, pile fabrics, chenille fabrics, tulle and other net fabrics: | | |
| | 5208 11 90 | | | |
| | 5208 12 11 | | | |
| | 5208 12 13 | | | |
| | 5208 12 15 | | | |
| | 5208 12 19 | | | |
| | 5208 12 91 | | | |
| | 5208 12 93 | | | |
| | 5208 12 95 | | | |
| | 5208 12 99 | | | |
| | 5208 13 00 | | | |
| | 5208 19 00 | | | |
| | 5208 21 10 | | | |
| | 5208 21 90 | | | |
| | 5208 22 11 | | | |
| | 5208 22 13 | | | |
| | 5208 22 15 | | | |
| | 5208 22 19 | | | |
| | 5208 22 91 | | | |
| | 5208 22 93 | | | |
| | 5208 22 95 | | | |
| | 5208 22 99 | | | |
| | 5208 23 00 | | | |
| | 5208 29 00 | | | |
| | 5208 31 00 | | | |
| | 5208 32 11 | | | |
| | 5208 32 13 | | | |
| | 5208 32 15 | | | |
| | 5208 32 19 | | | |
| | 5208 32 91 | | | |
| | 5208 32 93 | | | |
| | 5208 32 95 | | | |
| | 5208 32 99 | | | |
| | 5208 33 00 | | | |
| | 5208 39 00 | | | |
| | 5208 41 00 | | | |
| | 5208 42 00 | | | |
| | 5208 43 00 | | | |
| | 5208 49 00 | | | |
| | 5208 51 00 | | | |
| | 5208 52 10 | | | |
| | 5208 52 90 | | | |
| | 5208 53 00 | | | |
| | 5208 59 00 | | | |
| | 5209 11 00 | | | |
| | 5209 12 00 | | | |
| | 5209 19 00 | | | |
| | 5209 21 00 | | | |
| | 5209 22 00 | | | |
| | 5209 29 00 | | | |
| | 5209 31 00 | | | |
| | 5209 32 00 | | | |
| | 5209 39 00 | | | |
| | 5209 41 00 | | | |
| | 5209 42 00 | | | |
| | 5209 43 00 | | | |

| (1) | (2) | (3) | (4) | (5) |
|---|---|---|---|---|
| 2 *(cont'd)* | 5209 49 10<br>5209 49 90<br>5209 51 00<br>5209 52 00<br>5209 59 00<br><br>5210 11 10<br>5210 11 90<br>5210 12 00<br>5210 19 00<br>5210 21 10<br>5210 21 90<br>5210 22 00<br>5210 29 00<br>5210 31 10<br>5210 31 90<br>5210 32 00<br>5210 39 00<br>5210 41 00<br>5210 42 00<br>5210 49 00<br>5210 51 00<br>5210 52 00<br>5210 59 00<br><br>5211 11 00<br>5211 12 00<br>5211 19 00<br>5211 21 00<br>5211 22 00<br>5211 29 00<br>5211 31 00<br>5211 32 00<br>5211 39 00<br>5211 41 00<br>5211 42 00<br>5211 43 00<br>5211 49 11<br>5211 49 19<br>5211 49 90<br>5211 51 00<br>5211 52 00<br>5211 59 00<br><br>5212 11 10<br>5212 11 90<br>5212 12 10<br>5212 12 90<br>5212 13 10<br>5212 13 90<br>5212 14 10<br>5212 14 90<br>5212 15 10<br>5212 15 90<br>5212 21 10<br>5212 21 90<br>5212 22 10<br>5212 22 90<br>5212 23 10<br>5212 23 90<br>5212 24 10<br>5212 24 90<br>5212 25 10<br>5212 25 90<br><br>ex 5811 00 00<br><br>ex 6308 00 00 * | | | |

| (1) | (2) | (3) | (4) | (5) |
|---|---|---|---|---|
| 2 a) | 5208 31 00<br>5208 32 11<br>5208 32 13<br>5208 32 15<br>5208 32 19<br>5208 32 91<br>5208 32 93<br>5208 32 95<br>5208 32 99<br>5208 33 00<br>5208 39 00<br>5208 41 00<br>5208 42 00<br>5208 43 00<br>5208 49 00<br>5208 51 00<br>5208 52 10<br>5208 52 90<br>5208 53 00<br>5208 59 00 | a) Of which:<br>Other than unbleached or bleached | | |
| | 5209 31 00<br>5209 32 00<br>5209 39 00<br>5209 41 00<br>5209 42 00<br>5209 43 00<br>5209 49 10<br>5209 49 90<br>5209 51 00<br>5209 52 00<br>5209 59 00 | | | |
| | 5210 31 10<br>5210 31 90<br>5210 32 00<br>5210 39 00<br>5210 41 00<br>5210 42 00<br>5210 49 00<br>5210 51 00<br>5210 52 00<br>5210 59 00 | | | |
| | 5211 31 00<br>5211 32 00<br>5211 39 00<br>5211 41 00<br>5211 42 00<br>5211 43 00<br>5211 49 11<br>5211 49 19<br>5211 49 90<br>5211 51 00<br>5211 52 00<br>5211 59 00 | | | |
| | 5212 13 10<br>5212 13 90<br>5212 14 10<br>5212 14 90<br>5212 15 10<br>5212 15 90<br>5212 23 10<br>5212 23 90<br>5212 24 10<br>5212 24 90<br>5212 25 10<br>5212 25 90 | | | |
| | ex 5811 00 00 | | | |
| | ex 6308 00 00 | | | |

| (1) | (2) | (3) | (4) | (5) |
|---|---|---|---|---|
| 3 | 5512 11 00 | Woven fabrics of synthetic fibres (discontinuous or waste) other than narrow woven fabrics, pile fabrics (including terry fabrics) and chenille fabrics | | |
| | 5512 19 10 | | | |
| | 5512 19 90 | | | |
| | 5512 21 00 | | | |
| | 5512 29 10 | | | |
| | 5512 29 90 | | | |
| | 5512 91 00 | | | |
| | 5512 99 10 | | | |
| | 5512 99 90 | | | |
| | 5513 11 10 | | | |
| | 5513 11 30 | | | |
| | 5513 11 90 | | | |
| | 5513 12 00 | | | |
| | 5513 13 00 | | | |
| | 5513 19 00 | | | |
| | 5513 21 10 | | | |
| | 5513 21 30 | | | |
| | 5513 21 90 | | | |
| | 5513 22 00 | | | |
| | 5513 23 00 | | | |
| | 5513 29 00 | | | |
| | 5513 31 00 | | | |
| | 5513 32 00 | | | |
| | 5513 33 00 | | | |
| | 5513 39 00 | | | |
| | 5513 41 00 | | | |
| | 5513 42 00 | | | |
| | 5513 43 00 | | | |
| | 5513 49 00 | | | |
| | 5514 11 00 | | | |
| | 5514 12 00 | | | |
| | 5514 13 00 | | | |
| | 5514 19 00 | | | |
| | 5514 21 00 | | | |
| | 5514 22 00 | | | |
| | 5514 23 00 | | | |
| | 5514 29 00 | | | |
| | 5514 31 00 | | | |
| | 5514 32 00 | | | |
| | 5514 33 00 | | | |
| | 5514 39 00 | | | |
| | 5514 41 00 | | | |
| | 5514 42 00 | | | |
| | 5514 43 00 | | | |
| | 5514 49 00 | | | |
| | 5515 11 10 | | | |
| | 5515 11 30 | | | |
| | 5515 11 90 | | | |
| | 5515 12 10 | | | |
| | 5515 12 30 | | | |
| | 5515 12 90 | | | |
| | 5515 13 11 | | | |
| | 5515 13 19 | | | |
| | 5515 13 91 | | | |
| | 5515 13 99 | | | |
| | 5515 19 10 | | | |
| | 5515 19 30 | | | |
| | 5515 19 90 | | | |
| | 5515 21 10 | | | |
| | 5515 21 30 | | | |
| | 5515 21 90 | | | |
| | 5515 22 11 | | | |
| | 5515 22 19 | | | |
| | 5515 22 91 | | | |
| | 5515 22 99 | | | |
| | 5515 29 10 | | | |
| | 5515 29 30 | | | |

| (1) | (2) | (3) | (4) | (5) |
|---|---|---|---|---|
| 3<br>*(cont'd)* | 5515 29 90<br>5515 91 10<br>5515 91 30<br>5515 91 90<br>5515 92 11<br>5515 92 19<br>5515 92 91<br>5515 92 99<br>5515 99 10<br>5515 99 30<br>5515 99 90 | | | |
| | 5803 90 30 | | | |
| | ex 5905 00 70 | | | |
| | ex 6308 00 00 | | | |
| 3 a) | 5512 19 10<br>5512 19 90<br>5512 29 10<br>5512 29 90<br>5512 99 10<br>5512 99 90 | a) Of which:<br>Other than unbleached or bleached | | |
| | 5513 21 10<br>5513 21 30<br>5513 21 90<br>5513 22 00<br>5513 23 00<br>5513 29 00<br>5513 31 00<br>5513 32 00<br>5513 33 00<br>5513 39 00<br>5513 41 00<br>5513 42 00<br>5513 43 00<br>5513 49 00 | | | |
| | 5514 21 00<br>5514 22 00<br>5514 23 00<br>5514 29 00<br>5514 31 00<br>5514 32 00<br>5514 33 00<br>5514 39 00<br>5514 41 00<br>5514 42 00<br>5514 43 00<br>5514 49 00 | | | |
| | 5515 11 30<br>5515 11 90<br>5515 12 30<br>5515 12 90<br>5515 13 19<br>5515 13 99<br>5515 19 30<br>5515 19 90<br>5515 21 30<br>5515 21 90<br>5515 22 19<br>5515 22 99<br>5515 29 30<br>5515 29 90<br>5515 91 30<br>5515 91 90 | | | |

| (1) | (2) | (3) | (4) | (5) |
|---|---|---|---|---|
| 3 a) *(cont'd)* | 5515 92 19<br>5515 92 99<br>5515 99 30<br>5515 99 90<br><br>5803 90 30<br><br>ex 5905 00 70<br><br>ex 6308 00 00 | | | |

GROUP I B

| (1) | (2) | (3) | (4) | (5) |
|---|---|---|---|---|
| 4 | 6105 10 00<br>6105 20 10<br>6105 20 90<br>6105 90 10<br><br>6109 10 00<br>6109 90 10<br>6109 90 30<br><br>6110 20 10<br>6110 30 10 | Shirts, T-shirts, lightweight fine knit roll, polo or turtle necked jumpers and pullovers (other than of wool or fine animal hair), undervests and the like, knitted or crocheted | 6,48 | 154 |
| 5 | 6101 10 90<br>6101 20 90<br>6101 30 90<br><br>6102 10 90<br>6102 20 90<br>6102 30 90<br><br>6110 10 10<br>6110 10 31<br>6110 10 39<br>6110 10 91<br>6110 10 99<br>6110 20 91<br>6110 20 99<br>6110 30 91<br>6110 30 99 | Jerseys, pullovers, slip-overs, waistcoats, twinsets, cardigans, bed-jackets and jumpers (other than jackets and blazers), anoraks, windcheaters, waister jackets and the like, knitted or crocheted | 4,53 | 221 |
| 6 | 6203 41 10<br>6203 41 90<br>6203 42 31<br>6203 42 33<br>6203 42 35<br>6203 42 90<br>6203 43 19<br>6203 43 90<br>6203 49 19<br>6203 49 50<br><br>6204 61 10<br>6204 62 31<br>6204 62 33<br>6204 62 35<br>6204 63 19<br>6204 69 19 | Men's or boys' woven breeches, shorts other than swimwear and trousers (including slacks); women's or girls woven trousers and slacks, of wool, of cotton or of man-made fibres | 1,76 | 568 |
| 7 | 6106 10 00<br>6106 20 00<br>6106 90 10<br><br>6206 20 00<br>6206 30 00<br>6206 40 00 | Women's or girls' blouses, shirts and shirt-blouses, whether or not knitted or crocheted, of wool, cotton or man-made fibres | 5,55 | 180 |
| 8 | 6205 10 00<br>6205 20 00<br>6205 30 00 | Men's or boys' shirts, other than knitted or crocheted, of wool, cotton or man-made fibres | 4,60 | 217 |

GROUP II A

| (1) | (2) | (3) | (4) | (5) |
|---|---|---|---|---|
| 9 | 5802 11 00<br>5802 19 00<br>ex 6302 60 00 | Terry towelling and similar woven terry fabrics of cotton; toilet linen and kitchen linen, other than knitted or crocheted, of terry towelling and woven terry fabrics, of cotton | | |
| 20 | 6302 21 00<br>6302 22 90<br>6302 29 90<br>6302 31 10<br>6302 31 90<br>6302 32 90<br>6302 39 90 | Bed linen, other than knitted or crocheted | | |
| 22 | 5508 10 11<br>5508 10 19<br>5509 11 00<br>5509 12 00<br>5509 21 10<br>5509 21 90<br>5509 22 10<br>5509 22 90<br>5509 31 10<br>5509 31 90<br>5509 32 10<br>5509 32 90<br>5509 41 10<br>5509 41 90<br>5509 42 10<br>5509 42 90<br>5509 51 00<br>5509 52 10<br>5509 52 90<br>5509 53 00<br>5509 59 00<br>5509 61 10<br>5509 61 90<br>5509 62 00<br>5509 69 00<br>5509 91 10<br>5509 91 90<br>5509 92 00<br>5509 99 00 | Yarn of staple or waste synthetic fibres, not put up for retail sale | | |
| 22 a) | 5508 10 19<br>5509 31 10<br>5509 31 90<br>5509 32 10<br>5509 32 90<br>5509 61 10<br>5509 61 90<br>5509 62 00<br>5509 69 00 | a) Of which acrylic | | |
| 23 | 5508 20 10<br>5510 11 00<br>5510 12 00<br>5510 20 00<br>5510 30 00<br>5510 90 00 | Yarn of staple or waste artificial fibres, not put up for retail sale | | |

| (1) | (2) | (3) | (4) | (5) |
|---|---|---|---|---|
| 32 | 5801 10 00<br>5801 21 00<br>5801 22 00<br>5801 23 00<br>5801 24 00<br>5801 25 00<br>5801 26 00<br>5801 31 00<br>5801 32 00<br>5801 33 00<br>5801 34 00<br>5801 35 00<br>5801 36 00<br><br>5802 20 00<br>5802 30 00 | Woven pile fabrics and chenille fabrics (other than terry towelling or terry fabrics of cotton and narrow woven fabrics) and tufted textile surfaces, of wool, of cotton or of man-made textile fibres | | |
| 32 a) | 5801 22 00 | a) Of which:<br>Cotton corduroy | | |
| 39 | 6302 51 10<br>6302 51 90<br>6302 53 90<br>ex 6302 59 00<br>6302 91 10<br>6302 91 90<br>6302 93 90<br>ex 6302 99 00 | Table linen, toilet and kitchen linen, other than knitted or crocheted, other than of terry towelling or similar terry fabrics of cotton | | |

GROUP II B

| (1) | (2) | (3) | (4) | (5) |
|---|---|---|---|---|
| 12 | 6115 12 00<br>6115 19 10<br>6115 19 90<br>6115 20 11<br>6115 20 90<br>6115 91 00<br>6115 92 00<br>6115 93 10<br>6115 93 30<br>6115 93 99<br>6115 99 00 | Panty-hose and tights, stockings, understockings, socks, ankle-socks sockettes and the like, knitted or crocheted, other than for babies including stockings for varicose veins, other than products of category 70 | 24,3 pairs | 41 |
| 13 | 6107 11 00<br>6107 12 00<br>6107 19 00<br><br>6108 21 00<br>6108 22 00<br>6108 29 00 | Men's or boys' underpants and briefs, women's or girls' knickers and briefs, knitted or crocheted, of wool, cotton or man-made fibres | 17 | 59 |
| 14 | 6201 11 00<br>ex 6201 12 10<br>ex 6201 12 90<br>ex 6201 13 10<br>ex 6201 13 90<br><br>6210 20 00 | Men's or boys' woven overcoats, raincoats and other coats, cloaks and capes, of wool, of cotton or of man-made textile fibres (other than parkas) (of category 21) | 0,72 | 1 389 |
| 15 | 6202 11 00<br>ex 6202 12 10<br>ex 6202 12 90<br>ex 6202 13 10<br>6202 13 90<br><br>6204 31 00<br>6204 32 90<br>6204 33 90<br>6204 39 19<br><br>6210 30 00 | Women's or girls' woven overcoats, raincoats and other coats, cloaks and capes; jackets and blazers, of wool, of cotton or of man-made textile fibres (other than parkas) (of category 21) | 0,84 | 1 190 |
| 16 | 6203 11 00<br>6203 12 00<br>6203 19 10<br>6203 19 30<br>6203 21 00<br>6203 22 90<br>6203 23 90<br>6203 29 19 | Men's or boys' suits and ensembles, other than knitted or crocheted, of wool, of cotton or of man-made fibres, excluding ski suits | 0,80 | 1 250 |
| 17 | 6203 31 00<br>6203 32 90<br>6203 33 90<br>6203 39 19 | Men's or boys' jackets and blazers, other than knitted or crocheted, of wool, of cotton or of man-made fibres | 1,43 | 700 |
| 18 | 6207 11 00<br>6207 19 00<br>6207 21 00<br>6207 22 00<br>6207 29 00<br>6207 91 00 | Men's or boys' singlets and other vests, underpants, briefs, nightshirts, pyjamas, bathrobes, dressing gowns and similar articles, other than knitted or crocheted | | |

| (1) | (2) | (3) | (4) | (5) |
|---|---|---|---|---|
| 18<br>*(cont'd)* | 6207 92 00<br>6207 99 00 | | | |
| | 6208 11 00<br>6208 19 10<br>6208 19 90<br>6208 21 00<br>6208 22 00<br>6208 29 00<br>6208 91 10<br>6208 91 90<br>6208 92 10<br>6208 92 90<br>6208 99 00 | Women's or girls' singlets and other vests, slips, petticoats, briefs, panties, nightdresses, pyjamas, négligés, bathrobes, dressing gowns and similar articles, other than knitted or crocheted | | |
| 19 | 6213 20 00<br>6213 90 00 | Handkerchiefs, other than knitted or crocheted | 59 | 17 |
| 21 | ex 6201 12 10<br>ex 6201 12 90<br>ex 6201 13 10<br>ex 6201 13 90<br>6201 91 00<br>6201 92 00<br>6201 93 00<br><br>ex 6202 12 10<br>ex 6202 12 90<br>ex 6202 13 10<br>ex 6202 13 90<br>6202 91 00<br>6202 92 00<br>6202 93 00 | Parkas; anoraks, windcheaters, waister jackets and the like, other than knitted or crocheted, of wool, of cotton or man-made fibres | 2,3 | 435 |
| 24 | 6107 21 00<br>6107 22 00<br>6107 29 00<br>6107 91 00<br>6107 92 00<br>ex 6107 99 00 | Men's or boys' nightshirts, pyjamas, bathrobes, dressing gowns and similar articles, knitted or crocheted | 3,9 | 257 |
| | 6108 31 10<br>6108 31 90<br>6108 32 11<br>6108 32 19<br>6108 32 90<br>6108 39 00<br>6108 91 00<br>6108 92 00<br>6108 99 10 | Women's or girls' nightdresses, pyjamas, négligés, bathrobes, dressing gowns and similar articles, knitted or crocheted | | |
| 26 | 6104 41 00<br>6104 42 00<br>6104 43 00<br>6104 44 00<br><br>6204 41 00<br>6204 42 00<br>6204 43 00<br>6204 44 00 | Women's or girls' dresses, of wool, of cotton or man-made fibres | 3,1 | 323 |
| 27 | 6104 51 00<br>6104 52 00<br>6104 53 00<br>6104 59 00 | Women's or girls' skirts, including divided skirts | 2,6 | 385 |

| (1) | (2) | (3) | (4) | (5) |
|---|---|---|---|---|
| 27 *(cont'd)* | 6204 51 00<br>6204 52 00<br>6204 53 00<br>6204 59 10 | | | |
| 28 | 6103 41 10<br>6103 41 90<br>6103 42 10<br>6103 42 90<br>6103 43 10<br>6103 43 90<br>6103 49 10<br>6103 49 91<br><br>6104 61 10<br>6104 61 90<br>6104 62 10<br>6104 62 90<br>6104 63 10<br>6104 63 90<br>6104 69 10<br>6104 69 91 | Trousers, bib and brace overalls, breeches and shorts (other than swimwear), knitted or crocheted, of wool, of cotton or man-made fibres | 1,61 | 620 |
| 29 | 6204 11 00<br>6204 12 00<br>6204 13 00<br>6204 19 10<br>6204 21 00<br>6204 22 90<br>6204 23 90<br>6204 29 19 | Women's or girls' suits and ensembles, other than knitted or crocheted, of wool, of cotton or man-made fibres, excluding ski suits | 1,37 | 730 |
| 31 | 6212 10 00 | Brassières, woven, knitted or crocheted | 18,2 | 55 |
| 68 | 6111 10 90<br>6111 20 90<br>6111 30 90<br>ex 6111 90 00<br><br>ex 6209 10 00<br>ex 6209 20 00<br>ex 6209 30 00<br>ex 6209 90 00 | Babies' garments and clothing accessories, excluding babies' gloves, mittens and mitts of categories 10 and 87, and babies' stockings, socks and sockettes, other than knitted or crocheted, of category 88 | | |
| 73 | 6112 11 00<br>6112 12 00<br>6112 19 00 | Track suits of knitted or crocheted fabric, of wool, of cotton or of man-made textile fibres | 1,67 | 600 |
| 76 | 6203 22 10<br>6203 23 10<br>6203 29 11<br>6203 32 10<br>6203 33 10<br>6203 39 11<br>6203 42 11<br>6203 42 51<br>6203 43 11<br>6203 43 31<br>6203 49 11<br>6203 49 31<br><br>6204 22 10<br>6204 23 10<br>6204 29 11 | Men's or boys' industrial or occupational clothing, other than knitted or crocheted;<br>Women's or girls' aprons, smock-overalls and other industrial or occupational clothing, other than knitted or crocheted | | |

| (1) | (2) | (3) | (4) | (5) |
|---|---|---|---|---|
| 76<br>*(cont'd)* | 6204 32 10<br>6204 33 10<br>6204 39 11<br>6204 62 11<br>6204 62 51<br>6204 63 11<br>6204 63 31<br>6204 69 11<br>6204 69 31<br><br>6211 32 10<br>6211 33 10<br>6211 42 10<br>6211 43 10 | | | |
| 77 | ex 6211 20 00 | Ski suits, other than knitted or crocheted | | |
| 78 | 6203 41 30<br>6203 42 59<br>6203 43 39<br>6203 49 39<br><br>6204 61 80<br>6204 61 90<br>6204 62 59<br>6204 62 90<br>6204 63 39<br>6204 63 90<br>6204 69 39<br>6204 69 50<br><br>6210 40 00<br>6210 50 00<br><br>6211 31 00<br>6211 32 90<br>6211 33 90<br>6211 41 00<br>6211 42 90<br>6211 43 90 | Garments, other than knitted or crocheted, excluding garments of categories 6, 7, 8, 14, 15, 16, 17, 18, 21, 26, 27, 29, 68, 72, 76 and 77 | | |
| 83 | 6101 10 10<br>6101 20 10<br>6101 30 10<br><br>6102 10 10<br>6102 20 10<br>6102 30 10<br><br>6103 31 00<br>6103 32 00<br>6103 33 00<br>ex 6103 39 00<br><br>6104 31 00<br>6104 32 00<br>6104 33 00<br>ex 6104 39 00<br><br>ex 6112 20 00<br><br>6113 00 90<br><br>6114 10 00<br>6114 20 00<br>6114 30 00 | Overcoats, jackets, blazers and other garments, including ski suits, knitted or crocheted, excluding garments of categories 4, 5, 7, 13, 24, 26, 27, 28, 68, 69, 72, 73, 74, 75 | | |

GROUP III A

| (1) | (2) | (3) | (4) | (5) |
|---|---|---|---|---|
| 33 | 5407 20 11 | Woven fabrics of synthetic filament yarn obtained from strip or the like of polyethylene or polypropylene, less than 3 m wide | | |
| | 6305 31 91<br>6305 31 99 | Sacks and bags, of a kind used for the packing of goods, not knitted or crocheted, obtained from strip or the like | | |
| 34 | 5407 20 19 | Woven fabrics of synthetic filament yarn, obtained from strip or the like of polyethylene or polypropylene, 3 m or more wide | | |
| 35 | 5407 10 00<br>5407 20 90<br>5407 30 00<br>5407 41 00<br>5407 42 10<br>5407 42 90<br>5407 43 00<br>5407 44 10<br>5407 44 90<br>5407 51 00<br>5407 52 00<br>5407 53 10<br>5407 53 90<br>5407 54 00<br>5407 60 10<br>5407 60 30<br>5407 60 51<br>5407 60 59<br>5407 60 90<br>5407 71 00<br>5407 72 00<br>5407 73 10<br>5407 73 91<br>5407 73 99<br>5407 74 00<br>5407 81 00<br>5407 82 00<br>5407 83 10<br>5407 83 90<br>5407 84 00<br>5407 91 00<br>5407 92 00<br>5407 93 10<br>5407 93 90<br>5407 94 00<br>ex 5811 00 00<br>ex 5905 00 70 | Woven fabrics of synthetic fibres (continuous), other than those for tyres of category 114 | | |
| 35 a) | 5407 42 10<br>5407 42 90<br>5407 43 00<br>5407 44 10<br>5407 44 90<br>5407 52 00<br>5407 53 10<br>5407 53 90<br>5407 54 00<br>5407 60 30<br>5407 60 51<br>5407 60 59<br>5407 60 90 | a) Of which:<br>Other than unbleached or bleached | | |

| (1) | (2) | (3) | (4) | (5) |
|---|---|---|---|---|
| 35 a)<br>*(contd)* | 5407 72 00<br>5407 73 10<br>5407 73 91<br>5407 73 99<br>5407 74 00<br>5407 82 00<br>5407 83 10<br>5407 83 90<br>5407 84 00<br>5407 92 00<br>5407 93 10<br>5407 93 90<br>5407 94 00<br><br>ex 5811 00 00<br><br>ex 5905 00 70 | | | |
| 36 | 5408 10 00<br>5408 21 00<br>5408 22 10<br>5408 22 90<br>5408 23 10<br>5408 23 90<br>5408 24 00<br>5408 31 00<br>5408 32 00<br>5408 33 00<br>5408 34 00<br><br>ex 5811 00 00<br><br>ex 5905 00 70 | Woven fabrics of continuous artificial fibres, other than those for tyres of category 114 | | |
| 36 a) | 5408 10 00<br>5408 22 10<br>5408 22 90<br>5408 23 10<br>5408 23 90<br>5408 24 00<br>5408 32 00<br>5408 33 00<br>5408 34 00<br><br>ex 5811 00 00<br><br>ex 5905 00 70 | a) Of which:<br>Other than unbleached or bleached | | |
| 37 | 5516 11 00<br>5516 12 00<br>5516 13 00<br>5516 14 00<br>5516 21 00<br>5516 22 00<br>5516 23 10<br>5516 23 90<br>5516 24 00<br>5516 31 00<br>5516 32 00<br>5516 33 00<br>5516 34 00<br>5516 41 00<br>5516 42 00<br>5516 43 00<br>5516 44 00<br>5516 91 00 | Woven fabrics of artificial staple fibres | | |

| (1) | (2) | (3) | (4) | (5) |
|---|---|---|---|---|
| 37 *(cont'd)* | 5516 92 00<br>5516 93 00<br>5516 94 00<br><br>5803 90 50<br><br>ex 5905 00 70 | | | |
| 37 a) | 5516 12 00<br>5516 13 00<br>5516 14 00<br>5516 22 00<br>5516 23 10<br>5516 23 90<br>5516 24 00<br>5516 32 00<br>5516 33 00<br>5516 34 00<br>5516 42 00<br>5516 43 00<br>5516 44 00<br>5516 92 00<br>5516 93 00<br>5516 94 00<br><br>5803 90 50<br><br>ex 5905 00 70 | a) Of which:<br>Other than unbleached or bleached | | |
| 38 A | 6002 43 11<br>6002 93 10 | Knitted or crocheted synthetic curtain fabric including net curtain fabric | | |
| 38 B | ex 6303 91 00<br>ex 6303 92 90<br>ex 6303 99 90 | Net curtains, other than knitted or crocheted | | |
| 40 | ex 6303 91 00<br>ex 6303 92 90<br>ex 6303 99 90<br><br>6304 19 10<br>ex 6304 19 90<br>6304 92 00<br>ex 6304 93 00<br>ex 6304 99 00 | Woven curtains (including drapes), interior blinds, curtain and bed valances and other furnishing articles, other than knitted or crocheted, of wool, of cotton or of man-made fibres | | |
| 41 | 5401 10 11<br>5401 10 19<br><br>5402 10 10<br>5402 10 90<br>5402 20 00<br>5402 31 10<br>5402 31 30<br>5402 31 90<br>5402 32 00<br>5402 33 10<br>5402 33 90<br>5402 39 10<br>5402 39 90<br>5402 49 10<br>5402 49 91<br>5402 49 99<br>5402 51 10<br>5402 51 30 | Yarn of synthetic filament (continuous), not put up for retail sale, other than non-textured single yarn untwisted or with a twist of not more than 50 turns per metre | | |

| (1) | (2) | (3) | (4) | (5) |
| --- | --- | --- | --- | --- |
| 41 *(cont'd)* | 5402 51 90<br>5402 52 10<br>5402 52 90<br>5402 59 10<br>5402 59 90<br>5402 61 10<br>5402 61 30<br>5402 61 90<br>5402 62 10<br>5402 62 90<br>5402 69 10<br>5402 69 90<br><br>ex 5604 20 00<br>ex 5604 90 00 | | | |
| 42 | 5401 20 10<br><br>5403 10 00<br>5403 20 10<br>5403 20 90<br>ex 5403 32 00<br>5403 33 90<br>5403 39 00<br>5403 41 00<br>5403 42 00<br>5403 49 00<br><br>ex 5604 20 00 | Yarn of continuous man-made fibres, not put up for retail sale:<br>Yarn of artificial fibres; yarn of artificial filaments, not put up for retail sale, other than single yarn of viscose rayon untwisted or with a twist of not more than 250 turns per metre and single non-textured yarn of cellulose acetate | | |
| 43 | 5204 20 00<br><br>5207 10 00<br>5207 90 00<br><br>5401 10 90<br>5401 20 90<br><br>5406 10 00<br>5406 20 00<br><br>5508 20 90<br><br>5511 30 00 | Yarn of man-made filament, yarn of staple artificial fibres, cotton yarn, put up for retail sale | | |
| 46 | 5105 10 00<br>5105 21 00<br>5105 29 00<br>5105 30 10<br>5105 30 90 | Carded or combed sheep's or lambs' wool or other fine animal hair | | |
| 47 | 5106 10 10<br>5106 10 90<br>5106 20 11<br>5106 20 19<br>5106 20 91<br>5106 20 99<br><br>5108 10 10<br>5108 10 90 | Yarn of carded sheep's or lambs' wool (woollen yarn) or of carded fine animal hair, not put up for retail sale | | |
| 48 | 5107 10 10<br>5107 10 90<br>5107 20 10<br>5107 20 30 | Yarn of combed sheep's or lambs' wool (worsted yarn) or of combed fine animal hair, not put up for retail sale | | |

| (1) | (2) | (3) | (4) | (5) |
|---|---|---|---|---|
| 48 *(cont'd)* | 5107 20 51<br>5107 20 59<br>5107 20 91<br>5107 20 99<br><br>5108 20 10<br>5108 20 90 | | | |
| 49 | 5109 10 10<br>5109 10 90<br>5109 90 10<br>5109 90 90 | Yarn of sheep's or lambs' wool or of fine animal hair, put up for retail sale | | |
| 50 | 5111 11 00<br>5111 19 10<br>5111 19 90<br>5111 20 00<br>5111 30 10<br>5111 30 30<br>5111 30 90<br>5111 90 10<br>5111 90 91<br>5111 90 93<br>5111 90 99<br><br>5112 11 00<br>5112 19 10<br>5112 19 90<br>5112 20 00<br>5112 30 10<br>5112 30 30<br>5112 30 90<br>5112 90 10<br>5112 90 91<br>5112 90 93<br>5112 90 99 | Woven fabrics of sheep's or lambs' wool or of fine animal hair | | |
| 51 | 5203 00 00 | Cotton, carded or combed | | |
| 53 | 5803 10 00 | Cotton gauze | | |
| 54 | 5507 00 00 | Staple artificial fibres, including waste, carded, combed or otherwise processed for spinning | | |
| 55 | 5506 10 00<br>5506 20 00<br>5506 30 00<br>5506 90 10<br>5506 90 91<br>5506 90 99 | Synthetic staple fibres, including waste, carded or combed or otherwise processed for spinning | | |
| 56 | 5508 10 90<br><br>5511 10 00<br>5511 20 00 | Yarn of staple synthetic fibres (including waste), put up for retail sale | | |
| 58 | 5701 10 10<br>5701 10 91<br>5701 10 93<br>5701 10 99<br>5701 90 10<br>5701 90 90 | Carpets, carpetines and rugs, knotted (made up or not) | | |

| (1) | (2) | (3) | (4) | (5) |
|---|---|---|---|---|
| 59 | 5702 10 00<br>5702 31 10<br>5702 31 30<br>5702 31 90<br>5702 32 10<br>5702 32 90<br>5702 39 10<br>5702 41 10<br>5702 41 90<br>5702 42 10<br>5702 42 90<br>5702 49 10<br>5702 51 00<br>5702 52 00<br>ex 5702 59 00<br>5702 91 00<br>5702 92 00<br>ex 5702 99 00<br><br>5703 10 10<br>5703 10 90<br>5703 20 11<br>5703 20 19<br>5703 20 91<br>5703 20 99<br>5703 30 11<br>5703 30 19<br>5703 30 51<br>5703 30 59<br>5703 30 91<br>5703 30 99<br>5703 90 10<br>5703 90 90<br><br>5704 10 00<br>5704 90 00<br><br>5705 00 10<br>5705 00 31<br>5705 00 39<br>ex 5705 00 90 | Carpets and other textile floor coverings, other than the carpets of category 58 | | |
| 60 | 5805 00 00 | Tapestries, hand-made, of the type Gobelins, Flanders, Aubusson, Beauvais and the like, and needleworked tapestries (for example, petit point and cross stitch) made in panels and the like by hand | | |
| 61 | ex 5806 10 00<br>5806 20 00<br>5806 31 10<br>5806 31 90<br>5806 32 10<br>5806 32 90<br>5806 39 00<br>5806 40 00 | Narrow woven fabrics, and narrow fabrics (bolduc) consisting of warp without weft assembled by means of an adhesive, other than labels and similar articles of category 62<br><br>Elastic fabrics and trimmings (not knitted or crocheted), made from textile materials assembled from rubber thread | | |
| 62 | 5606 00 91<br>5606 00 99<br><br>5804 10 11<br>5804 10 19<br>5804 10 90<br>5804 21 10<br>5804 21 90<br>5804 29 10<br>5804 29 90<br>5804 30 00 | Chenille yarn (including flock chenille yarn), gimped yarn (other than metallized yarn and gimped horsehair yarn):<br><br>Tulle and other net fabrics but not including woven, knitted or crocheted fabrics, hand or mechanically-made lace, in the piece, in strips or in motifs | | |

| (1) | (2) | (3) | (4) | (5) |
| --- | --- | --- | --- | --- |
| 62 *(cont'd)* | 5807 10 10<br>5807 10 90 | Labels, badges and the like of textile materials, not embroidered, in the piece, in strips or cut to shape or size, woven | | |
| | 5808 10 00<br>5808 90 00 | Braids and ornamental trimmings in the piece; tassels pompons and the like | | |
| | 5810 10 10<br>5810 10 90<br>5810 91 10<br>5810 91 90<br>5810 92 10<br>5810 92 90<br>5810 99 10<br>5810 99 90 | Embroidery, in the piece, in strips or in motifs | | |
| 63 | 5906 91 00<br>ex 6002 10 10<br>6002 10 90 | Knitted or crocheted fabric of synthetic fibres containing by weight 5 % or more of elastomeric yarn and knitted or crocheted fabric containing by weight 5 % or more of rubber thread | | |
| | ex 6002 30 10<br>6002 30 90<br>ex 6001 10 00<br>6002 20 31<br>6002 43 19 | Raschel lace and long-pile fabric of synthetic fibres | | |
| 65 | 5606 00 10<br>ex 6001 10 00<br>6001 21 00<br>6001 22 00<br>6001 29 10<br>6001 91 10<br>6001 91 30<br>6001 91 50<br>6001 91 90<br>6001 92 10<br>6001 92 30<br>6001 92 50<br>6001 92 90<br>6001 99 10<br>ex 6002 10 10<br>6002 20 10<br>6002 20 39<br>6002 20 50<br>6002 20 70<br>ex 6002 30 10<br>6002 41 00<br>6002 42 10<br>6002 42 30<br>6002 42 50<br>6002 42 90<br>6002 43 31<br>6002 43 33<br>6002 43 35<br>6002 43 39<br>6002 43 50<br>6002 43 91<br>6002 43 93<br>6002 43 95<br>6002 43 99<br>6002 91 00<br>6002 92 10<br>6002 92 30<br>6002 92 50 | Knitted or crocheted fabric other than those of categories 38 A and 63, of wool, of cotton or of man-made fibres | | |

| (1) | (2) | (3) | (4) | (5) |
|---|---|---|---|---|
| 65<br>*(cont'd)* | 6002 92 90<br>6002 93 31<br>6002 93 33<br>6002 93 35<br>6002 93 39<br>6002 93 91<br>6002 93 99 | | | |
| 66 | 6301 10 00<br>6301 20 91<br>6301 20 99<br>6301 30 90<br>ex 6301 40 90<br>ex 6301 90 90 | Travelling rugs and blankets, other than knitted or crocheted, of wool, of cotton or of man-made fibres | | |

GROUP III B

| (1) | (2) | (3) | (4) | (5) |
|---|---|---|---|---|
| 10 | 6111 10 10<br>6111 20 10<br>6111 30 10<br>ex 6111 90 00<br><br>6116 10 10<br>6116 10 90<br>6116 91 00<br>6116 92 00<br>6116 93 00<br>6116 99 00 | Gloves, mittens and mitts, knitted or crocheted | 17<br>pairs | 59 |
| 67 | 5807 90 90<br><br>6113 00 10<br><br>6117 10 00<br>6117 20 00<br>6117 80 10<br>6117 80 90<br>6117 90 00<br><br>6301 20 10<br>6301 30 10<br>6301 40 10<br>6301 90 10<br><br>6302 10 10<br>6302 10 90<br>6302 40 00<br>ex 6302 60 00<br><br>6303 11 00<br>6303 12 00<br>6303 19 00<br><br>6304 11 00<br>6304 91 00<br><br>ex 6305 20 00<br>ex 6305 39 00<br>ex 6305 90 00<br>6305 31 10<br><br>6307 10 10<br>6307 90 10 | Knitted or crocheted clothing accessories other than for babies; household linen of all kinds, knitted or crocheted; curtains (including drapes) and interior blinds, curtain or bed valances and other furnishing articles knitted or crocheted; knitted or crocheted blankets and travelling-rugs, other knitted or crocheted articles including parts of garments or of clothing accessories | | |
| 67 a) | 6305 31 10 | a) Of which:<br>Sacks and bags of a kind used for the packing of goods, made from polyethylene or polypropylene strip | | |
| 69 | 6108 11 10<br>6108 11 90<br>6108 19 10<br>6108 19 90 | Women's or girls' slips and petticoats, knitted or crocheted | 7,8 | 128 |
| 70 | 6115 11 00<br>6115 20 19<br>6115 93 91 | Panty-hose and tights of synthetic fibres, measuring per single yarn less than 67 decitex (6,7 tex)<br>Women's full-length hosiery of synthetic fibres | 30,4<br>pairs | 33 |

| (1) | (2) | (3) | (4) | (5) |
|---|---|---|---|---|
| 72 | 6112 31 10<br>6112 31 90<br>6112 39 10<br>6112 39 90<br>6112 41 10<br>6112 41 90<br>6112 49 10<br>6112 49 90<br><br>6211 11 00<br>6211 12 00 | Swimwear, of wool, of cotton or of man-made fibres | 9,7 | 103 |
| 74 | 6104 11 00<br>6104 12 00<br>6104 13 00<br>ex 6104 19 00<br>6104 21 00<br>6104 22 00<br>6104 23 00<br>ex 6104 29 00 | Women's or girls knitted or crocheted suits and ensembles, of wool, of cotton or man-made fibres, excluding ski suits | 1,54 | 650 |
| 75 | 6103 11 00<br>6103 12 00<br>6103 19 00<br>6103 21 00<br>6103 22 00<br>6103 23 00<br>6103 29 00 | Men's or boys' knitted or crocheted suits and ensembles, of wool, of cotton or of man-made fibres, excluding ski suits | 0,80 | 1 250 |
| 84 | 6214 20 00<br>6214 30 00<br>6214 40 00<br>6214 90 10 | Shawls, scarves, mufflers, mantillas, veils and the like other than knitted or crocheted, of wool, of cotton or man-made fibres | | |
| 85 | 6215 20 00<br>6215 90 00 | Ties, bow ties and cravats not knitted or crocheted, of wool, of cotton or man-made fibres | 17,9 | 56 |
| 86 | 6212 20 00<br>6212 30 00<br>6212 90 00 | Corsets, corset-belts, suspender belts, braces, suspenders, garters and the like, and parts thereof, whether or not knitted or crocheted | 8,8 | 114 |
| 87 | 6216 00 00<br><br>ex 6209 10 00<br>ex 6209 20 00<br>ex 6209 30 00<br>ex 6209 90 00 | Gloves, mittens and mitts, not knitted or crocheted | | |
| 88 | 6217 10 00<br>6217 90 00<br><br>ex 6209 10 00<br>ex 6209 20 00<br>ex 6209 30 00<br>ex 6209 90 00 | Stockings, socks and sockettes, not knitted or crocheted; other clothing accessories, parts of garments or of clothing accessories, other than for babies, other than knitted or crocheted | | |

| (1) | (2) | (3) | (4) | (5) |
|---|---|---|---|---|
| 90 | 5607 41 00<br>5607 49 11<br>5607 49 19<br>5607 49 90<br>5607 50 11<br>5607 50 19<br>5607 50 30<br>5607 50 90 | Twine, cordage, ropes and cables of synthetic fibres, plaited or not | | |
| 91 | 6306 21 00<br>6306 22 00<br>6306 29 00 | Tents | | |
| 93 | ex 6305 20 00<br>ex 6305 39 00 | Sacks and bags, of a kind used for the packing of goods of wover fabrics, other than made from polyethylene or polypropylene strip | | |
| 94 | 5601 10 10<br>5601 10 90<br>5601 21 10<br>5601 21 90<br>5601 22 10<br>5601 22 91<br>5601 22 99<br>5601 29 00<br>5601 30 00 | Wadding of textile materials and articles thereof; textile fibres, not exceeding 5 mm in length (flock), textile dust and mill neps | | |
| 95 | 5602 10 19<br>5602 10 31<br>5602 10 39<br>5602 10 90<br>5602 21 00<br>5602 29 90<br>5602 90 00<br>ex 5807 90 10<br>ex 5905 00 70<br>6210 10 10<br>6307 90 91 | Felt and articles thereof, whether or not impregnated or coated, other than floor coverings | | |
| 96 | 5603 00 10<br>5603 00 91<br>5603 00 93<br>5603 00 95<br>5603 00 99<br>ex 5807 90 10<br>ex 5905 00 70<br>6210 10 91<br>6210 10 99<br>ex 6301 40 90<br>ex 6301 90 90<br>6302 22 10<br>6302 32 10<br>6302 53 10<br>6302 93 10<br>6303 92 10<br>6303 99 10 | Non-woven fabrics and articles of such fabrics, whether or not impregnated, coated, covered or laminated | | |

| (1) | (2) | (3) | (4) | (5) |
|---|---|---|---|---|
| 96 *(cont'd)* | ex 6304 19 90<br>ex 6304 93 00<br>ex 6304 99 00<br>ex 6305 39 00<br>6307 10 30<br>ex 6307 90 99 | | | |
| 97 | 5608 11 11<br>5608 11 19<br>5608 11 91<br>5608 11 99<br>5608 19 11<br>5608 19 19<br>5608 19 31<br>5608 19 39<br>5608 19 91<br>5608 19 99<br>5608 90 00 | Nets and netting made of twine, cordage or rope and made up fishing nets of yarn, twine, cordage or rope | | |
| 98 | 5609 00 00<br>5905 00 10 | Other articles made from yarn, twine, cordage, rope or cables, other than textile fabrics, articles made from such fabrics and articles of category 97 | | |
| 99 | 5901 10 00<br>5901 90 00 | Textile fabrics coated with gum or amylaceous substances, of a kind used for the outer covers of books and the like; tracing cloth; prepared painting canvas; buckram and similar stiffened textile fabrics of a kind used for hat foundations | | |
| | 5904 10 00<br>5904 91 10<br>5904 91 90<br>5904 92 00 | Linoleum, whether or not cut to shape; floor coverings consisting of a coating or covering applied on a textile backing, whether or not cut to shape; | | |
| | 5906 10 10<br>5906 10 90<br>5906 99 10<br>5906 99 90 | Rubberized textile fabrics, not knitted or crocheted, excluding those for tyres | | |
| | 5907 00 00 | Textile fabrics otherwise impregnated or coated; painted canvas being theatrical scenery, studio back-cloths or the like, other than of category 100 | | |
| 100 | 5903 10 10<br>5903 10 90<br>5903 20 10<br>5903 20 90<br>5903 90 10<br>5903 90 91<br>5903 90 99 | Textile fabrics impregnated, coated, covered or laminated with preparations of cellulose derivatives or of other artificial plastic materials | | |
| 101 | ex 5607 90 00 | Twine, cordage, ropes and cables, plaited or not, other than of synthetic fibres | | |
| 109 | 6306 11 00<br>6306 12 00<br>6306 19 00<br>6306 31 00<br>6306 39 00 | Tarpaulins, sails, awnings, and sunblinds | | |

| (1) | (2) | (3) | (4) | (5) |
|---|---|---|---|---|
| 110 | 6306 41 00<br>6306 49 00 | Woven pneumatic mattresses | | |
| 111 | 6306 91 00<br>6306 99 00 | Camping goods, woven, other than pneumatic mattresses and tents | | |
| 112 | 6307 20 00<br>ex 6307 90 99 | Other made up textile articles, woven, excluding those of categories 113 and 114 | | |
| 113 | 6307 10 90 | Floor cloths, dish cloths and dusters, other than knitted or crocheted | | |
| 114 | 5902 10 10<br>5902 10 90<br>5902 20 10<br>5902 20 90<br>5902 90 10<br>5902 90 90<br><br>5908 00 00<br><br>5909 00 10<br>5909 00 90<br><br>5910 00 00<br><br>5911 10 00<br>ex 5911 20 00<br>5911 31 11<br>5911 31 19<br>5911 31 90<br>5911 32 10<br>5911 32 90<br>5911 40 00<br>5911 90 10<br>5911 90 90 | Woven fabrics and articles for technical uses | | |

*ANNEX II*

**referred to in Article 2 (2)**

GROUP IV

| Category | CN code | Description | Table of equivalence | |
|---|---|---|---|---|
| | | | pieces/kg | g/piece |
| (1) | (2) | (3) | (4) | (5) |
| 115 | 5306 10 11<br>5306 10 19<br>5306 10 31<br>5306 10 39<br>5306 10 50<br>5306 10 90<br>5306 20 11<br>5306 20 19<br>5306 20 90<br>5308 90 11<br>5308 90 13<br>5308 90 19 | Flax or ramie yarn | | |
| 117 | 5309 11 11<br>5309 11 19<br>5309 11 90<br>5309 19 10<br>5309 19 90<br>5309 21 10<br>5309 21 90<br>5309 29 10<br>5309 29 90<br>5311 00 10<br>5803 90 90<br>5905 00 31<br>5905 00 39 | Woven fabrics of flax or of ramie | | |
| 118 | 6302 29 10<br>6302 39 10<br>6302 29 30<br>6302 52 00<br>ex 6302 59 00<br>6302 92 00<br>ex 6302 99 00 | Bed linen, table linen, toilet linen and kitchen linen, of flax or ramie, other than knitted or crocheted | | |
| 120 | ex 6303 99 90<br>6304 19 30<br>ex 6304 99 00 | Curtains (including drapes), interior blinds, curtain and bed valances and other furnishing articles, not knitted or crocheted, of flax or ramie | | |
| 121 | ex 5607 90 00 | Twine, cordage, ropes and cables, plaited or not, of flax or ramie | | |
| 122 | ex 6305 90 00 | Sacks and bags, of a kind used for the packing of goods, used, of flax, other than knitted or crocheted | | |
| 123 | 5801 90 10<br>6214 90 90 | Woven-pile fabrics and chenille fabrics of flax or ramie, other than narrow woven fabrics<br>Shawls, scarves, mufflers, mantillas, veils and the like, of flax or ramie, other than knitted or crocheted | | |

GROUP V

| (1) | (2) | (3) | (4) | (5) |
|---|---|---|---|---|
| 124 | 5501 10 00<br>5501 20 00<br>5501 30 00<br>5301 90 00<br>5303 10 11<br>5303 10 19<br>5303 10 90<br>5303 20 00<br>5303 30 00<br>5303 40 00<br>5303 90 10<br>5303 90 90<br>5505 10 10<br>5505 10 30<br>5505 10 50<br>5505 10 70<br>5505 10 90 | Synthetic staple fibres | | |
| 125 A | 5402 41 10<br>5402 41 30<br>5402 41 90<br>5402 42 00<br>5402 43 10<br>5402 43 90 | Synthetic filament yarn (continuous) not put up for retail sale, other than yarn of category 41 | | |
| 125 B | 5404 10 10<br>5404 10 90<br>5404 90 11<br>5404 90 19<br>5404 90 90<br>ex 5604 20 00<br>ex 5604 90 00 | Monofilament, strip (artificial straw and the like) and imitation catgut of synthetic materials | | |
| 126 | 5502 00 10<br>5502 00 90<br>5504 10 00<br>5504 90 00<br>5505 20 00 | Artificial staple fibres | | |
| 127 A | 5403 31 00<br>ex 5403 32 00<br>5403 33 10 | Yarn of artificial filaments (continuous) not put up for retail sale, other than yarn of category 42 | | |
| 127 B | 5405 00 00 | Monofilament, strip (artificial straw and the like) and imitation catgut of artificial textile materials | | |
| 128 | 5105 40 00 | Coarse animal hair, carded or combed | | |
| 129 | 5110 00 00 | Yarn of coarse animal hair or of horsehair | | |
| 130 A | 5004 00 10<br>5004 00 90<br>5006 00 10 | Silk yarn other than yarn spun from silk waste | | |

| (1) | (2) | (3) | (4) | (5) |
|---|---|---|---|---|
| 130 B | 5005 00 10<br>5005 00 90<br>5006 00 90 | Silk yarn other than of category 130 A; silk-worm gut | | |
| 131 | 5308 90 90 | Yarn of other vegetable textile fibres | | |
| 132 | 5308 30 00 | Paper yarn | | |
| 133 | 5308 20 10<br>5308 20 90 | Yarn of true hemp | | |
| 134 | 5605 00 00 | Metallized yarn | | |
| 135 | 5113 00 00 | Woven fabrics of coarse animal hair or of horsehair | | |
| 136 | 5007 10 00<br>5007 20 10<br>5007 20 21<br>5007 20 31<br>5007 20 39<br>5007 20 41<br>5007 20 51<br>5007 20 59<br>5007 20 61<br>5007 20 69<br>5007 20 71<br>5007 90 10<br>5007 90 30<br>5007 90 50<br>5007 90 90<br>5803 90 10<br>ex 5903 00 90<br>ex 5911 20 00 | Woven fabrics of silk or of silk waste | | |
| 137 | ex 5801 90 90<br>ex 5806 10 00 | Woven pile fabrics and chenille fabrics and narrow woven fabrics of silk, or of silk waste | | |
| 138 | 5311 00 90<br>ex 5905 00 90 | Woven fabrics of paper yarn and other textile fibres other than of ramie | | |
| 139 | 5809 00 00 | Woven fabrics of metal threads or of metallized yarn | | |
| 140 | ex 6001 10 00<br>6001 29 90<br>6001 99 90<br>6002 20 90<br>6002 49 00<br>6002 99 00 | Knitted or crocheted fabric of textile material other than wool or fine animal hair, cotton or man-made fibres | | |
| 141 | ex 6301 90 90 | Travelling rugs and blankets of textile material other than wool or fine animal hair, cotton or man-made fibres | | |

| (1) | (2) | (3) | (4) | (5) |
|---|---|---|---|---|
| 142 | ex 5702 39 90<br>ex 5702 49 90<br>ex 5702 59 00<br>ex 5702 99 00<br>ex 5705 00 90 | Carpets and other textile floor coverings of sisal, of other fibres of the Agave family or of Manila hemp | | |
| 144 | 5602 10 35<br>5602 29 10 | Felt of coarse animal hair | | |
| 145 | 5607 30 00<br>ex 5607 90 00 | Twine, cordage, ropes and cables plaited or not abaca (Manila hemp) or of true hemp | | |
| 146 A | ex 5607 21 00 | Binder or baler twine for agricultural machines, of sisal or other fibres of the Agave family | | |
| 146 B | ex 5607 21 00<br>5607 29 10<br>5607 29 90 | Twine, cordage, ropes and cables of sisal or other fibres of the Agave family, other than the products of category 146 A | | |
| 146 C | 5606 10 00 | Twine, cordage, ropes and cables, whether of not plaited or braided, of jute or of other textile bast fibres of heading No 5303 | | |
| 147 | 5003 90 00 | Silk waste (including cocoons unsuitable for reeling), yarn waste and garnetted stock, other than not carded or combed | | |
| 148 A | 5307 10 10<br>5307 10 90<br>5307 20 00 | Yarn of jute or of other textile bast fibres of heading No 5303 | | |
| 148 B | 5308 10 00 | Coir yarn | | |
| 149 | 5310 10 90<br>ex 5310 90 00 | Woven fabrics of jute or of other textile bast fibres of a width of more than 150 cm | | |
| 150 | 5310 10 10<br>ex 5310 90 00<br>6305 10 90 | Woven fabrics of jute or of other textile bast fibres of a width of not more than 150 cm<br>Sacks and bags, of a kind used for the packing of goods, of jute or of other textile bast fibres, other than used | | |
| 151 A | 5702 20 00 | Floor coverings of coconut fibres (coir) | | |
| 151 B | ex 5702 39 90<br>ex 5702 49 90<br>ex 5702 59 00<br>ex 5702 99 00 | Carpets and other textile floor coverings, of jute or of other textile bast fibres, other than tufted or flocked | | |
| 152 | 5602 10 11 | Needle loom felt of jute or of other textile bast fibres not impregnated or coated, other than floor coverings | | |
| 153 | 6305 10 10 | Used sacks and bags, of a kind used for the packing of goods, of jute or of other textile bast fibres of heading No 5303 | | |

| (1) | (2) | (3) | (4) | (5) |
|---|---|---|---|---|
| 154 | 5001 00 00 | Silk-worm cocoons suitable for reeling | | |
| | 5002 00 00 | Raw silk (not thrown) | | |
| | 5003 10 00 | Silk waste (including cocoons unsuitable for reeling), yarn waste and garnetted stock, not carded or combed | | |
| | 5101 11 00<br>5101 19 00<br>5101 21 00<br>5101 29 00<br>5101 30 00 | Wool not carded or combed | | |
| | 5102 10 10<br>5102 10 30<br>5102 10 50<br>5102 10 90<br>5102 20 00 | Fine or coarse animal hair, not carded or combed | | |
| | 5103 10 10<br>5103 10 90<br>5103 20 10<br>5103 20 91<br>5103 20 99<br>5103 30 00 | Waste of wool or of fine or coarse animal hair, including yarn waste but excluding garnetted stock | | |
| | 5104 00 00 | Garnetted stock of wool or of fine or coarse animal hair | | |
| | 5301 10 00<br>5301 21 00<br>5301 29 00<br>5301 30 10<br>5301 30 90 | Flax, raw or processed but not spun: flax tow and waste (including yarn waste and garnetted stock) | | |
| | 5305 91 00<br>5305 99 00 | Ramie and other vegetable textile fibres raw or processed but not spun: tow, noils and waste, other than coir and abaca of heading No 5304 | | |
| | 5201 00 10<br>5201 00 90 | Cotton, not carded or combed | | |
| | 5202 10 00<br>5202 91 00<br>5202 99 00 | Cotton waste (including yarn waste and garnetted stock) | | |
| | 5302 10 00<br>5302 90 00 | True hemp *(Cannabis sativa L.)*, raw or processed but not spun: tow and waste of true hemp (including yarn waste and garnetted stock) | | |
| | 5305 21 00<br>5305 29 00 | Abaca (Manila hemp or *Musa textilis Nee*), raw or processed but not spun: tow, noils and waste of abaca (including yarn waste and garnetted stock) | | |
| | 5303 10 00<br>5303 90 00 | Jute and other textile bast fibres (excluding flax, true hemp and ramie), raw or processed but not spun: tow and waste of true hemp (including yarn waste and garnetted stock) | | |
| | 5304 10 00<br>5304 90 00 | Other vegetable textile fibres, raw or processed but not spun: tow, noils and waste of such fibres (including yarn waste and garnetted stock) | | |
| | 5305 11 00<br>5305 19 00<br>5305 91 00<br>5305 99 00 | | | |
| 156 | 6106 90 30<br>ex 6110 90 90 | Blouses and pullovers knitted or crocheted of silk or silk waste for women and girls | | |
| 157 | 6101 90 10<br>6101 90 90 | | | |
| | 6102 90 10<br>6102 90 90 | | | |
| | ex 6103 39 00<br>6103 49 99 | | | |

| (1) | (2) | (3) | (4) | (5) |
|---|---|---|---|---|
| 157 *(cont'd)* | ex 6104 19 00<br>ex 6104 29 00<br>ex 6104 39 00<br>ex 6104 49 00<br>6104 69 99<br>6105 90 90<br>6106 90 50<br>6106 90 90<br>ex 6107 99 00<br>6108 99 90<br>6109 90 90<br>6110 90 10<br>6110 90 90<br>ex 6111 90 00<br>6114 90 00 | Garments, knitted or crocheted, other than those of categories 1 to 123 and of category 156 | | |
| 159 | 6204 49 10<br>6206 10 00<br>6214 10 00<br>6215 10 00 | Dresses, blouses and shirt-blouses, not knitted or crocheted, of silk or silk waste<br>Shawls, scarves, mufflers, mantillas, veils and the like, not knitted or crocheted, of silk or silk waste<br>Ties, bow ties and cravats of silk or silk waste | | |
| 160 | 6213 10 00 | Handkerchiefs of silk or silk waste | | |
| 161 | 6201 19 00<br>6201 99 00<br>6202 19 00<br>6202 99 00<br>6203 19 90<br>6203 29 90<br>6203 39 90<br>6203 49 90<br>6204 19 90<br>6204 29 90<br>6204 39 90<br>6204 49 90<br>6204 59 90<br>6204 69 90<br>6205 90 10<br>6205 90 90<br>6206 90 10<br>6206 90 90<br>ex 6211 20 00<br>6211 39 00<br>6211 49 00 | Garments, not knitted or crocheted, other than those of categories 1 to 123 and category 159 | | |

*ANNEX III*

**COMMUNITY AND REGIONAL QUANTITATIVE LIMITS**

The allocation of Community limits among regions of the Community will be communicated to China in accordance with the rules in force in the Community.

The product descriptions together with the relevant CN codes are reproduced in Annex I.

Each quantitative limit established for Germany in this Annex, with the exception of Categories 18, 23, 26, 67, 73, 76 and 83, contains a sub-ceiling amounting to 19 % of the quantitative limit in question for use exclusively at the Berlin Fair.

**Community limits**

| Category | Description | Unit | Year | Quantitative limit |
|---|---|---|---|---|
| 1 | Cotton yarn not put up for retail sale | tonnes | 1989<br>1990<br>1991<br>1992 | 3 300<br>3 366<br>3 433<br>3 502 |
| 2 (2) | Woven fabrics of cotton, other than gauze, terry fabrics, narrow woven fabrics, pile fabrics, chenille fabrics, tulle and other net fabrics: | tonnes | 1989<br>1990<br>1991<br>1992 | 23 100 (1)<br>23 562 (1)<br>24 033 (1)<br>24 514 (1) |
| 2A (3) | Of which: other than unbleached or bleached | tonnes | 1989<br>1990<br>1991<br>1992 | 2 872<br>2 927<br>2 984<br>3 042 |
| 3 (2) | Woven fabrics of synthetic fibres (discontinuous or waste) other than narrow woven fabrics, pile fabrics (including terry fabrics) and chenille fabrics | tonnes | 1989<br>1990<br>1991<br>1992 | 4 750<br>4 893<br>5 039<br>5 190 |
| 3A (3) | Of which: other than unbleached or bleached | tonnes | 1989<br>1990<br>1991<br>1992 | 570<br>587<br>605<br>623 |

(1) The following additional quantities may be exported to the EEC by China:

| | | | |
|---|---|---|---|
| Fabrics of category 2 below 115 cm in width | tonnes | 1989<br>1990<br>1991<br>1992 | 1 230<br>1 255<br>1 280<br>1 305 |
| Fabrics of category 2 for medical gauze (CN codes 5208 11 10 and 5208 21 10) | tonnes | 1989<br>1990<br>1991<br>1992 | 1 700<br>1 734<br>1 769<br>1 804 |

(2) Possibility of transfer to and from category 3 of up to 40 % of the category to which the transfer is made, except for Benelux, where such transfers are possible up to 100 %.

(3) For Benelux, categories 2A and 3A are combined.

| Category | Description | Unit | Year | Quantitative limit |
|---|---|---|---|---|
| 4 (1) | Shirts, T-shirts, lightweight fine knit roll, polo or turtle necked jumpers and pullovers (other than of wool or fine animal hair), undervests and the like, knitted or crocheted | 1 000 pieces | 1989<br>1990<br>1991<br>1992 | 32 800<br>34 440<br>36 162<br>37 970 |
| 5 (3) | Jerseys, pullovers, slip-overs, waistcoats, twinsets, cardigans, bed-jackets and jumpers (other than jackets and blazers), anoraks, wind-cheaters, waister jackets and the like, knitted or crocheted | 1 000 pieces | 1989<br>1990<br>1991<br>1992 | 8 250 (2)<br>8 580 (2)<br>8 923 (2)<br>9 280 (2) |
| 6 | Men's or boys' woven breeches, shorts (other than swimwear) and trousers (including slacks); women's or girl's woven trousers and slacks, of wool, of cotton or of man-made fibres | 1 000 pieces | 1989<br>1990<br>1991<br>1992 | 9 650 (4)<br>10 036 (4)<br>10 437 (4)<br>10 855 (4) |
| 7 | Women's or girl's blouses, shirts and shirt-blouses, whether or not knitted or crocheted, of wool, cotton or of man-made fibres | 1 000 pieces | 1989<br>1990<br>1991<br>1992 | 2 850 (5)<br>2 964 (5)<br>3 083 (5)<br>3 206 (5) |

(1) For the purpose of setting off exports against the agreed quantitative limits a conversion rate of 5 garments (other than babies' garments) of a maximum commercial size of 130 cm, for 3 garments whose commercial size exceeds 130 cm may be applied for up to 5 % of the quantitative limits.

(2) These figures include the following quantities reserved for European industry for a period of 180 days each year:
1989: 100 000 pieces
1990: 104 000 pieces
1991: 108 000 pieces
1992: 112 000 pieces

(3) For products of category 5 (other than anoraks, windcheaters, waister jackets and the like) of fine animal hair, the following sublimits apply within the quantitative limits established for category 5:

| | EEC of which | *United Kingdom* |
|---|---|---|
| 1989: | 90 000 pieces | 20 000 pieces |
| 1990: | 94 000 pieces | 21 000 pieces |
| 1991: | 97 000 pieces | 22 000 pieces |
| 1992: | 101 000 pieces | 23 000 pieces |

For the United Kingdom, these sublimits also cover the same products made of wool.

(4) These figures include the following quantities reserved for European industry for a period of 180 days each year:
1989: 300 000 pieces
1990: 312 000 pieces
1991: 324 000 pieces
1992: 337 000 pieces
The following additional quantities or shorts (CN codes 6203 41 90, 6203 42 90, 6203 43 90 and 6203 49 50) may be exported to the EEC by China:
1989: 850 000 pieces
1990: 884 000 pieces
1991: 919 000 pieces
1992: 956 000 pieces
The following sublimits for long trousers apply within the quantitative limits established for Benelux:
1989: 576 000 pieces
1990: 599 000 pieces
1991: 623 000 pieces
1992: 648 000 pieces

(5) These figures include the following quantities reserved for European industry for a period of 180 days each year:
1989: 300 000 pieces
1990: 312 000 pieces
1991: 324 000 pieces
1992: 337 000 pieces

| Category | Description | Unit | Year | Quantitative limit |
|---|---|---|---|---|
| 8 | Men's or boys' shirts, other than knitted or crocheted, of wool, cotton or man-made fibres | 1 000 pieces | 1989<br>1990<br>1991<br>1992 | 9 000 (¹)<br>9 270 (¹)<br>9 548 (¹)<br>9 835 (¹) |
| 9 | Terry towelling and similar woven terry fabrics of cotton; toilet linen and kitchen linen, other than knitted or crocheted, of terry towelling and woven terry fabrics, of cotton | tonnes | 1989<br>1990<br>1991<br>1992 | 3 624<br>3 841<br>4 072<br>4 316 |
| 10 | Gloves, mittens and mitts, knitted or crocheted | 1 000 pairs | 1989<br>1990<br>1991<br>1992 | 42 500 (²)<br>44 625 (²)<br>46 856 (²)<br>49 199 (²) |
| 12 | Panty-hose and tights; understockings, stockings, socks, ankle-socks, sockettes and the like, knitted or crocheted, other than for babies, including stockings for varicose veins, other than products of category 70 | 1 000 pairs | 1989<br>1990<br>1991<br>1992 | 14 299<br>15 014<br>15 765<br>16 553 |
| 18 | Men's or boys' singlets and other vests, underpants, briefs, nightshirts, pyjamas, bathrobes, dressing gowns and similar articles other than knitted or crocheted;<br>Women's or girls' singlets and other vests, slips, petticoats, briefs, panties, nightshirts, nightdresses, pyjamas, négligés, bathrobes, dressing gowns and similar articles, other than knitted or crocheted | tonnes | 1989<br>1990<br>1991<br>1992 | 3 300<br>3 465<br>3 638<br>3 820 |
| 19 | Handkerchiefs, other than knitted or crocheted | 1 000 pieces | 1989<br>1990<br>1991<br>1992 | 68 630<br>72 062<br>75 665<br>79 448 |
| 20/39 | Bed linen, other than knitted or crocheted<br>Table linen, toilet and kitchen linen, other than knitted or crocheted, other than of terry towelling or similar terry fabrics of cotton | tonnes | 1989<br>1990<br>1991<br>1992 | 6 100 (³)<br>6 405 (³)<br>6 725 (³)<br>7 062 (³) |

(¹) These figures include the following quantities reserved for European industry for a period of 180 days each year:
1989: 300 000 pieces
1990: 309 000 pieces
1991: 318 000 pieces
1992: 328 000 pieces

(²) The following sublimits apply within the quantitative limits established for the United Kingdom: Knitted gloves, mittens and mitts, coated, impregnated or covered with plastics (CN code 6116 10 10):
1989: 280 000 pairs
1990: 294 000 pairs
1991: 309 000 pairs
1992: 324 000 pairs

(³) The following sublimits apply within the quantitative limits established for France, for table linen, toilet and kitchen linen, not embroidered:
1989: 244 tonnes
1990: 256 tonens
1991: 269 tonnes
1992: 282 tonnes

The following sublimits for bed linen apply within the quantitative limits established for Benelux and Spain:

| | *Benelux* | *Spain* |
|---|---|---|
| 1989: | 61 tonnes | 66 tonnes |
| 1990: | 64 tonnes | 69 tonnes |
| 1991: | 67 tonnes | 73 tonnes |
| 1992: | 721 tonnes | 76 tonnes |

| Category | Description | Unit | Year | Quantitative limit |
|---|---|---|---|---|
| 21 (²) | Parkas, anoraks, windcheaters, waister jackets and the like, other than knitted or crocheted, of wool, cotton or man-made fibres | 1 000 pieces | 1989<br>1990<br>1991<br>1992 | 6 500 (¹)<br>6 825 (¹)<br>7 166 (¹)<br>7 525 (¹) |
| 22 | Yarn of staple or waste synthetic fibres, not put up for retail sale | tonnes | 1989<br>1990<br>1991<br>1992 | 10 500 (³)<br>11 130 (³)<br>11 798 (³)<br>12 506 (³) |
| 23 | Yarn of staple or waste artificial fibres, not put up for retail sale | tonnes | 1989<br>1990<br>1991<br>1992 | 7 250<br>7 685<br>8 146<br>8 635 |
| 26 | Women's or girls' dressed, of wool, cotton or man-made fibres | 1 000 pieces | 1989<br>1990<br>1991<br>1992 | 3 200 (⁴)<br>3 360 (⁴)<br>3 528 (⁴)<br>3 704 (⁴) |
| 32 | Woven pile fabrics and chenille fabrics (other than terry towelling or terry fabrics of cotton and narrow woven fabrics) and tufted textile surfaces, of wool, of cotton or of man-made textile fibres | tonnes | 1989<br>1990<br>1991<br>1992 | 2 968<br>3 116<br>3 272<br>3 436 |
| 37 | Woven fabrics of artificial staple fibres | tonnes | 1989<br>1990<br>1991<br>1992 | 8 600<br>9 116<br>9 663<br>10 243 |
| 37 A | Of which:<br>Other than unbleached or bleached | tonnes | 1998<br>1990<br>1991<br>1992 | 2 580<br>2 735<br>2 899<br>3 073 |
| 73 (²) | Track suits of knitted or crocheted fabric, of wool, cotton or of man-made textile fibres | 1 000 pieces | 1989<br>1990<br>1991<br>1992 | 2 050<br>2 153<br>2 260<br>2 373 |
| 76 | Men's or boys' industrial or occupational clothing, other than knitted or crocheted;<br>Women's or girls' aprons, smock-overalls and other industrial or occupational clothing, other than knitted or crocheted | tonnes | 1989<br>1990<br>1991<br>1992 | 3 250 (⁵)<br>3 413 (⁵)<br>3 583 (⁵)<br>3 762 (⁵) |

(¹) These figures include the following quantities reserved for European industry for a period of 180 days each year:
1989: 300 000 pieces
1990: 315 000 pieces
1991: 315 000 pieces
1992: 347 000 pieces

(²) For the purpose of setting off exports against the agreed quantitative limits a conversion rate of 5 garments (other than babies' garments) of a maximum commercial size of 130 cm, for 3 garments whose commercial size exceeds 130 cm may be applied for up to 5 % of the quantitative limits.

(³) The following sublimits apply within the quantitative limits established for the United Kingdom, for acrylic yarn (CN codes 5508 10 19, 5509 31 10, 5509 31 90, 5509 32 10, 5509 32 90, 5509 61 10, 5509 61 90, 5509 62 00, 5509 69 00):
1989: 150 tonnes
1990: 159 tonnes
1991: 169 tonnes
1992: 179 tonnes

(⁴) These figures include the following quantities reserved for Euopean industry for a period of 180 days each year:
1989: 150 000 pieces
1990: 158 000 pieces
1991: 165 000 pieces
1992: 174 000 pieces

(⁵) These figures include the following quantities reserved for German industry for a period of 180 days each year:
1989: 100 tonnes
1990: 105 tonnes
1991: 110 tonnes
1992: 116 tonnes

**Regional Limits**

| Category | Description | Unit | Member States | Quantitative Limits | | | |
|---|---|---|---|---|---|---|---|
| | | | | 1989 | 1990 | 1991 | 1992 |
| 13 | Men's or boys' underpants and briefs, women's or girls' knickers and briefs, knitted or crocheted, of wool, cotton or man-made fibres | 1 000 pieces | D<br>F<br>BNL<br>UK<br>IRL | 10 886<br>2 622<br>2 791<br>36 549<br>488 | 11 430<br>2 753<br>2 931<br>38 376<br>512 | 12 002<br>2 891<br>3 077<br>40 295<br>538 | 12 602<br>3 035<br>3 231<br>42 310<br>565 |
| 15 | Women's or girls' woven overcoats, and other coats, cloaks and capes; jackets and blazers, of wool, of fibres (other than parkas of category 21) | 1 000 pieces | F<br>BNL | 445 (1)<br>187 | 467 (1)<br>196 | 491 (1)<br>206 | 515 (1)<br>217 |
| 16 | Men's or boys' suits and ensembles, other than knitted or crocheted, of wool, of cotton or of man-made fibres, excluding ski suits | 1 000 pieces | F<br>I<br>UK | 300<br>4 500<br>225 | 315<br>4 725<br>236 | 331<br>4 961<br>248 | 347<br>5 209<br>260 |
| 24 (2) | Men's or boys' nightshirts, pyjamas, bathrobes, dressing gowns and similar articles, knitted or crocheted;<br>Women's or girls' nightdresses, pyjamas, négligés, bathrobes, dressing gowns and similar articles, knitted or crocheted | 1 000 pieces | D<br>F<br>I<br>BNL<br>UK | 4 900<br>840<br>435<br>384<br>513 | 5 145<br>882<br>457<br>403<br>539 | 5 402<br>926<br>480<br>423<br>566 | 5 672<br>972<br>504<br>445<br>594 |
| 27 | Women's or girls' skirts, including divided skirts | 1 000 pieces | UK | 320 | 336 | 353 | 370 |
| 29 | Women's or girls' suits and ensembles, other than knitted or crocheted, of wool, of cotton or of man-made fibres, excluding ski suits | 1 000 pieces | F<br>I | 185<br>240 | 194<br>252 | 204<br>265 | 214<br>278 |
| 31 | Brassières, woven, knitted or crocheted | 1 000 pieces | F<br>BNL<br>UK | 1 700<br>600<br>650 | 1 785<br>630<br>683 | 1 874<br>662<br>717 | 1 968<br>695<br>752 |
| 33 | Woven fabrics of synthetic filament yarn obtained from strip of the like of polyethylene or polypropylene, less than 3 m wide;<br>Sacks and bags, of a kind used for packing of goods, not knitted or crocheted, obtained from strip or the like | tonnes | F<br>BNL<br>UK<br>IRL | 630<br>4 300<br>875<br>650 | 662<br>4 515<br>919<br>683 | 695<br>4 741<br>965<br>717 | 729<br>4 978<br>1 013<br>752 |
| 36 | Woven fabrics of continuous artificial fibres, other than those for tyres of category 114 | tonnes | F | 350 | 368 | 386 | 405 |
| 40 | Woven curtains (including drapes), interior blinds, curtain and bed valances and other furnishing articles, other than knitted or crocheted, of wool, of cotton or of man-made fibres | tonnes | I | 625 | 663 | 702 | 744 |
| 59 | Carpets and other textile floor coverings, other than carpets of category 58 | tonnes | F | 247 | 262 | 278 | 294 |

| Category | Description | Unit | Member States | Quantitative Limits | | | |
|---|---|---|---|---|---|---|---|
| | | | | 1989 | 1990 | 1991 | 1992 |
| 66 | Travelling rugs and blankets, other than knitted or crocheted, of wool, or cotton or of man-made fibres | tonnes | I | 501 | 531 | 563 | 597 |
| 67 | Knitted or crocheted clothing accessories other than for babies; household linen of all kinds, knitted or crocheted; curtains (including drapes) and interior blinds, curtain or bed valances and other furnishing articles, knitted or crocheted; knitted or crocheted blankets and travelling rugs; other knitted or crocheted articles including parts of garments or of clothing accessories | tonnes | D<br>F | 1 004<br>800 | 1 064<br>848 | 1 128<br>899 | 1,196<br>953 |
| 67A | Of which: sacks and bags of a kind used for the packing of goods, made from polyethylene or polypropylene strip | tonnes | F | 300 | 318 | 337 | 357 |
| 68 | Babies' garments and clothing accessories, excluding babies' gloves, mittens and mitts of categories 10 and 87 and babies' stockings, socks and sockettes, other than knitted or crocheted, of category 88 | tonnes | F<br>UK | 950 (³)<br>355 | 998 (³)<br>373 | 1,047 (³)<br>391 | 1,100 (³)<br>411 |
| 78 | Garments, other than knitted or crocheted, excluding garments of categories 6, 7, 8, 14, 15, 16, 17, 18, 21, 26, 27, 29, 68, 72, 76 and 77 | tonnes | F<br>I | 280<br>260 | 297<br>276 | 315<br>292 | 333<br>310 |
| 83 | Overcoats, jackets, blazers and other garments, including ski suits, knitted or crocheted, excluding garments of categories 4, 5, 7, 13, 24, 26, 27, 28, 68, 69, 72, 73, 74, 75 | tonnes | D<br>F | 150<br>105 | 158<br>110 | 165<br>116 | 174<br>122 |
| 87 | Gloves, mittens and mitts, not knitted or crocheted | tonnes | F<br>UK | 235<br>120 | 247<br>126 | 259<br>132 | 272<br>139 |
| 91 | Tents | tonnes | F<br>BNL | 420 (⁴)<br>250 | 445 (⁴)<br>265 | 472 (⁴)<br>281 | 500 (⁴)<br>298 |

(1) These figures include the following quantities reserved for French industry for a period of 180 days each year:
1989: 178 000 pieces
1990: 187 000 pieces
1991: 196 000 pieces
1992: 206 000 pieces

(2) For the purpose of setting off exports against the agreed quantitative limits a conversion rate of 5 garments (other than babies' garments) of a maximum commercial size of 130 cm, for 3 garments whose commercial size exceeds 130 cm may be applied for up to 5 % of the quantitative limits.

(3) These figures include the following quantities reserved for French industry for a period of 180 days each year:
1989: 380 tonnes
1990: 399 tonnes
1991: 419 tonnes
1992: 440 tonnes

(4) These figures include the following quantities reserved for French industry for a period of 180 days each year:
1989: 55 tonnes
1990: 58 tonnes
1991: 62 tonnes
1992: 66 tonnes

ANNEX IV
referred to in Article 11 ASSURED PROVISION BY CHINA OF TEXTILE RAW MATERIALS

Minimum quantities which China undertakes to reserve for the Community each year:

Silk

Raw silk (CN code 5002 00 00): 3 000 tonnes

Waste silk (CN codes 5003 10 00 and 5003 90 00): ([1])

Fine animal hair

Angora (CN code 5102 10 10): 700 tonnes

Cashmere (CN code ex 5102 10 50): 500 tonnes

([1]) China will accord favorable consideration to Community economic operators, within the limits of availability.

PROTOCOL A

TITLE I
CLASSIFICATION

Article 1

1. The competent authorities of the Community undertake to inform China of any changes in the combined nomenclature (CN) before the date of their entry into effect in the Community.

2. The competent authorities of the Community undertake to inform China of any decisions relating to the classification of products subject to the Agreement within one month of their adoption at the latest. Such communication shall include:

(a) a description of the products concerned;

(b) the relevant category and the related CN codes;

(c) the reasons which have led to the decision.

3. Where a decision on classification results in a change of classification practice or a change of category of any product subject to the Agreement, the competent authorities of the Community shall provide 30 days' notice, from the date of the Community's communication, before the decision is put into effect. Products shipped before the date of application of the decision shall remain subject to the earlier classification practice, provided that the goods in question are presented for importation into the Community within 60 days of that date.

4. Where a Community decision on classification resulting in a change of classification practice or a change of categorization of any product subject to the Agreement affects a category subject to restraint, the two Parties agree to enter into consultations in accordance with the procedures described in Article 16 paragraph 1 of the Agreement with a view to honouring the obligation under the second subparagraph of Article 14 paragraph 1 of the Agreement and mitigating any disruptive effects which might arise from such a Community decision.

Article 2

In case of divergent opinions between China and the competent Community authorities at the point of entry into the Community on the classification of products covered by the present Agreement, classification shall provisionally be based on indications provided by the Community, pending consultations in accordance with Article 16 with a view to reaching agreement on definitive classification of the product concerned.

TITLE II
ORIGIN

Article 3

1. Products originating in China for export to the Community in accordance with the arrangements established by this Agreement shall be accompanied by a certificate of Chinese origin conforming to the model annexed to this Protocol.

2. The certificate of origin shall be issued by the competent governmental authorities of China if the products in question can be considered products originating in that country within the meaning of the relevant rules in force in the Community.

3. However, the products in Group III may be imported into the Community in accordance with the arrangements established by this Agreement on production of a declaration by the exporter on the invoice or other commercial document relating to the products to the effect that the products in question originated in China within the meaning of the relevant rules in force in the Community.

4. The certificate of origin referred to in paragraph 1 shall not be required for import of goods covered by a certificate of origin Form A or Form APR completed in accordance with the relevant Community rules in order to qualify for generalized tariff preferences.

Article 4

Where different criteria for determining origin are laid down for products falling within the same category, certificates or declarations of origin shall contain a sufficiently detailed description of the goods to enable the criterion to be determined on the basis of which the certificate was issued or the declaration drawn up.

Article 5

The discovery of slight discrepancies between the statements made in the certificate of origin and those made in the documents produced to the customs office for the purpose of carrying out the formalities for importing the product shall ipso facto cast doubt upon the statements in the certificate.

TITLE III
DOUBLE CHECKING SYSTEM FOR CATEGORIES OF PRODUCTS WITH QUANTITATIVE LIMITS

Section I
Exportation

Article 6

The competent authorities of China shall issue an export licence in respect of all consignments from China of textile products referred to in Annex III, up to the relevant quantitative limits as may be modified by Articles 5, 9 and 10 of the Agreement and of textile products subject to any definitive or provisional quantitative limits established as a result of the application of Article 6 of the Agreement.

Article 7

1. The export licence shall conform to the model annexed to this Protocol. It must certify inter alia that the quantity of the product in question has been set off against the quantitative limit prescribed for the category of the product in question.

2. Each export licence shall cover only one of the categories of products listed in Annex III of this Agreement. It may be used for one or more consignments of the products in question.

3. Where the conversion rate provided for in Annex III is applied the following note must be inserted in box 9 of the export licence: 'conversion rate for garments of a commercial size not exceeding 130 cm is to be applied'.

4. Where the provisions of Article 3 (2) and Annex III of the Agreement concerning quantities reserved for industry are applied, the following note must be inserted in box 9 of the export licence: 'quantitites reserved for industry'.

Article 8

The competent Community authorities must be notified forthwith of the withdrawal or alteration of any export licence already issued.

Article 9

1. Exports shall be set off against the quantitative limits established for the year in which shipment of the goods has been effected, even if the export licence is issued after such shipment.

2. For the purpose of applying paragraph 1, shipment of the goods is considered to have taken place on the date of their loading on to the exporting aircraft, vehicle or vessel.

Article 10

The presentation of an export licence, in application of Article 12, shall be effected not later than 31 March of the year following that in which the goods covered by the licence have been shipped.

Section II
Importation

Article 11

Importation into the Community of textile products subject to quantitative limits shall be subject to the presentation of an import authorization or document.

Article 12

1. The competent Community authorities shall issue such import authorization or document automatically within five working days of the presentation by the importer of the original of the corresponding export licence.

The import authorization or document shall be valid for six months.

2. The competent Community authorities shall cancel the already issued import authorization or document if the corresponding export licence has been withdrawn.

However, if the competent Community authorities have not been notified of the withdrawal or cancellation of the export licence until after the products have been imported into the Community, the quantities involved shall be set off against the quantitative limit for the category and the quota year in question.

Article 13

1. If the competent Community authorities find that the total quantities covered by export licences issued by China for a particular category in any Agreement year exceed the quantitative limit established in Annex III for that category, as may be modified by Articles 5, 9 and 10 of the Agreement, or any definitive or provisional limit established under Article 6 of the Agreement, the said authorities may suspend the further issue of import authorizations or documents. In this event, the competent Community authorities shall immediately inform the authorities of China and the special consultation procedure set out in Article 16 of the Agreement shall be initiated forthwith.

2. Exports of Chinese origin not covered by Chinese export licences issued in accordance with the provisions of this Protocol may be refused the issue of import authorizations or documents by the competent Community authorities.

However, if the import of such products is allowed into the Community by the competent Community authorities, the quantities involved shall not be set off against the appropriate quantitative limits set out in Annex III or established as a result of the application of Article 6 of the Agreement, without the express agreement of China.

TITLE IV
FORM AND PRODUCTION OF EXPORT LICENCES AND CERTIFICATES OF ORIGIN, AND COMMON PROVISIONS

Article 14

1. The export licence and the certificate of origin may comprise additional copies duly indicated as such. They shall be made out in English or French. If they are completed by hand, entries must be in ink and in block capitals.

These documents shall measure 210×297 mm. The paper used must be white writing paper, sized, not containing mechanical pulp and weighing not less than 25 g/m². Each part shall have a printed guilloche-pattern background making any falsification by mechanical or chemical means apparent to the eye.

If the documents have several copies only the top copy which is the original shall be printed with the guilloche-pattern background. This copy shall be clearly marked as 'original' and the other copies as 'copy'. Only the original shall be accepted by the competent authorities in the Community as being valid for the purposes of export to the Community in accordance with the arrangements established by this Agreement.

2. Each document shall bear a standardized serial number, whether or not printed, by which it can be identified. This number shall be composed of the following elements:

two letters identifying China as follows: CN,

two letters identifying countries of destination as follows:

BL: Benelux

DE: Federal Republic of Germany

DK: Denmark

EL: Greece

ES: Spain

FR: France

GB: United Kingdom

IE: Ireland

IT: Italy

PT: Portugal

- a one-digit number identifying quota year, corresponding to the last figure in year, e.g. 9 for 1989,
- a two-digit number running consecutively from 01 to 99 identifying the issuing office,
- a five-digit number running consecutively from 00001 to 99999 allocated to the country of destination.

3. The competent authorities in China shall satisfy themselves that the goods exported correspond to the statements given in the export licence and certificate of origin.

Article 15

The export licence and certificate of origin may be issued after the shipment of the products to which they relate. In such cases they shall bear either the endorsement 'délivré a posteriori' or the endorsement 'Issued retrospectively'.

Article 16

1. In the event of theft, loss or destruction of an export licence or a certificate of origin, the exporter may apply to the competent governmental authority which issued the document for a duplicate to be made out on the basis of the export documents in his possession. The duplicate of any such certificate or licence so issued shall bear the endorsement 'duplicata'.

2. The duplicate must bear the date of the original export licence or certificate of origin.

TITLE V
ADMINISTRATIVE COOPERATION

Article 17

The Community and China shall cooperate closely to implement the provisions of this Agreement. To this end, contacts and exchanges of views (including on technical matters) shall be facilitated by both Parties.

Article 18

In order to ensure that the Agreement is properly applied, the Community and China assist each other in checking the authenticity and accuracy of export licences and certificates of origin isued or declarations made under this Protocol.

Article 19

China shall send the Commission of the European Communities the names and addresses of the governmental authorities competent for the issue and verification of export licences and certificates of origin together with specimens of the stamps used by these authorities. China shall also notify the Commission of any change in this information.

Article 20

1. Subsequent verification of certificates of origin or export licences shall be carried out at random, or whenever

the competent Community authorities have reasonable doubt as to the authenticity of the certificate or licence or as to the accuracy of the information regarding the products in question.

2. In such cases the competent authorities in the Community shall return the certificate of origin or export licence or a copy thereof to the competent governmental authority in China giving, where appropriate, the reasons of form or substance for an enquiry. If the invoice has been submitted, such invoice or a copy thereof shall be attached to the certificate or licence or its copy. The authorities shall also forward any information that has been obtained suggesting that the particulars given on the said certificate or licence are inaccurate.

3. The provisions of paragraph 1 shall be applicable to subsequent verfications of the declarations of origin referred to in Article 3 of this Protocol.

4. The results of the subsequent verifications carried out in accordance with paragraphs 1 and 2 shall be communicated to the competent authorities of the Community within three months at the latest. The information communicated shall indicate whether the disputed certificate or licence applied to the goods actually exported and whether these goods are eligible for export in accordance with the arrangements established by this Agreement. The information shall also include, at the request of the Community, copies of all documentation necessary to determine the facts fully and in particular the true origin of the goods.

Should such verifications reveal systematic irregularities in the use of declarations of origin, the Community may subject imports of the products in question to the provisions of Article 3 paragraph 1 and 2 of this Protocol.

5. For the purpose of subsequent verification of certificates of origin, copies of the certification as well as any export documents referring to them shall be kept for at least a period of two years by the competent governmental authority in China.

6. Recourse to the random verification procedure specified in this Article must not constitute an obstacle to the release for home use of the products in question.

Article 21

1. Where the verification procedure referred to in Article 20 or where information available to the Community or to China indicates or appears to indicate that the provisions of this Agreement are being contravened, both parties shall cooperate closely and with appropriate urgency to prevent such contravention.

2. To this end China shall, on this own initiative or at the request of the Community, carry out appropriate enquiries or arrange for such enquiries to be carried out concerning operations which are or appear to the Community to be in contravention of this Agreement. China shall communicate the results of these enquiries to the Community together with any other pertinent information enabling the true origin of the goods to be determined.

3. By agreement between the competent Community authorities and the competent Chinese authorities, officials designated by the Community may be present at the enquiries referred to above.

4. In pursuance of the cooperation referred to in paragraph 1, China and the Community shall exchange any information considered by either Party to be of use in preventing the provisions of the Agreement. These exchanges may include information on textile production in China and on trade in textile products of a kind covered by this Agreement between China and other countries, particulary where the Community has reasonable grounds to consider that the products in question may be in transit across the territory of China prior to their importation into the Community. This information shall include at the request of the Community copies of all relevant documentation.

5. Where it is established that the provisions of this Agreement have been contravened, China and the Comunity may agree to take such measures as are necessary to prevent a recurrence of such contravention.

*Annex to Protocol A, Article 3 (1)*

1 Exporter (name, full address, country)
Exportateur (nom, adresse complète, pays)

**ORIGINAL**

2 No

3 Quota year
Année contingentaire

4 Category number
Numéro de catégorie

5 Consignee (name, full address, country)
Destinataire (nom, adresse complète, pays)

**CERTIFICATE OF ORIGIN**
**(Textile products)**

**CERTIFICAT D'ORIGINE**
**(Produits textiles)**

6 Country of origin
Pays d'origine

7 Country of destination
Pays de destination

8 Place and date of shipment – Means of transport
Lieu et date d'embarquement – Moyen de transport

9 Supplementary details
Données supplémentaires

10 Marks and numbers – Number and kind of packages – DESCRIPTION OF GOODS
Marques et numéros – Nombre et nature des colis – DÉSIGNATION DES MARCHANDISES

11 Quantity (¹)
Quantité (¹)

12 FOB Value (²)
Valeur fob (²)

13 CERTIFICATION BY THE COMPETENT AUTHORITY – VISA DE L'AUTORITÉ COMPÉTENTE

I, the undersigned, certify that the goods described above originated in the country shown in box No 6, in accordance with the provisions in force in the European Economic Community.

**Je soussigné certifie que les marchandises désignées ci-dessus sont originaires du pays figurant dans la case 6, conformément aux dispositions en vigueur dans la Communauté économique européenne.**

14 Competent authority (name, full address, country)
Autorité compétente (nom, adresse complète, pays)

At – À ........................................, on – le ........................

(Signature) (Stamp – Cachet)

(¹) Show net weight (kg) and also quantity in the unit prescribed for category where other than net weight – Indiquer le poids net en kilogrammes ainsi que la quantité dans l'unité prévue pour la catégorie si cette unité n'est pas le poids net.
(²) In the currency of the sale contract – Dans la monnaie du contrat de vente.

*Annex to Protocol A, Article 7 (1)*

1 Exporter (name, full address, country)
Exportateur (nom, adresse complète, pays)

**ORIGINAL**

2 **No**

3 Quota year
Année contingentaire

4 Category number
Numéro de catégorie

5 Consignee (name, full address, country)
Destinataire (nom, adresse complète, pays)

**EXPORT LICENCE**
**(Textile products)**

**LICENCE D'EXPORTATION**
**(Produits textiles)**

6 Country of origin
Pays d'origine

7 Country of destination
Pays de destination

8 Place and date of shipment – Means of transport
Lieu et date d'embarquement – Moyen de transport

9 Supplementary details
Données supplémentaires

10 Marks and numbers – Number and kind of packages – DESCRIPTION OF GOODS
Marques et numéros – Nombre et nature des colis – DÉSIGNATION DES MARCHANDISES

11 Quantity (¹)
Quantité (¹)

12 FOB value (²)
Valeur fob (²)

13 CERTIFICATION BY THE COMPETENT AUTHORITY – VISA DE L'AUTORITÉ COMPÉTENTE

I, the undersigned, certify that the goods described above have been charged against the quantitative limit established for the year shown in box No 3 in respect of the category shown in box No 4 by the provisions regulating trade in textile products with the European Economic Community.

Je soussigné certifie que les marchandises désignées ci-dessus ont été imputées sur la limite quantitative fixée pour l'année indiquée dans la case 3 pour la catégorie désignée dans la case 4 dans le cadre des dispositions régissant les échanges de produits textiles avec la Communauté économique européenne.

14 Competent authority (name, full address, country)
Autorité compétente (nom, adresse complète, pays)

At – À ........................................, on – le ........................

(Signature) (Stamp – Cachet)

(¹) Show net weight (kg) and also quantity in the unit prescribed for category where other than net weight – Indiquer le poids net en kilogrammes ainsi que la quantité dans l'unité prévue pour la catégorie si cette unité n'est pas le poids net.
(²) In the currency of the sale contract – Dans la monnaie du contrat de vente.

PROTOCOL B

1. The exemption provided for in Article 4 (3) of the Agreement in respect of the cottage industry products shall apply only to the following products:

(a) fabrics woven on hand- or foot-operated looms, being fabrics of a kind traditionally made in the cottage industry of China;

(b) garments or other textile articles of a kind traditionally made in the cottage industry of China obtained manually from the fabrics referred to above and sewn exclusively by hand without the aid of any machine;

(c) traditional folklore textile products of China made by hand in the cottage industry of China as defined in the list agreed between both Parties and annexed to this Protocol.

2. Exemption shall be granted only for products accompanied by a certificate issued by the competent Chinese authorities in accordance with the specimen annexed to this Protocol. Such certificates shall state the grounds on which exemption is based and shall be accepted by the competent Community authorities provided that they are satisfied that the products concerned conform to the conditions set out in this Protocol. Certificates covering the products referred to in paragraph (c) above shall bear a conspicuous stamp: 'FOLKLORE'. In case of divergent opinion between China and the competent Community authorities at the point of entry into the Community as to the nature of such products, consultations shall be held within one month with a view to resolving such divergences. Should imports of any of the above products reach such proportions as to cause difficulties to the Community, the two Parties shall open consultations forthwith in accordance with the procedure laid down in Article 16 of the Agreement with a view to finding a quantitative solution to the problem.

3. The provisions of Title IV and V of Protocol A shall apply 'mutatis mutandis' to the products referred to in paragraph 1 of this Protocol.

ANNEX to Protocol B
TRADITIONAL FOLKLORE TEXTILE PRODUCTS OBTAINED IN THE COTTAGE INDUSTRY OF CHINA ARE IDENTIFIED IN THE ANNEXED LIST

This list covers the following kinds of products (and other items as may be agreed upon by both parties from time to time):

A. Products of hand-made lace traditional of China

1. Crochet lace:

Simply by means of a crochet hook, different products are obtained (piano covers, scarves, tablecloths, bedspreads, doilies, shawls, traycloths, curtains, lace in the piece, bedcovers, sofa covers, cushion covers and insertions for these articles) with traditional designs of Shandong (Shantung), Shanghai and Shantou (Swatow).

2. Tsimou lace:

This is a traditional and a special characteristic craft produced in Tsimou county, Shandong (Shantung) province. Cotton or man-made fibre threads are worked by hand according to paper sketches of flora, vases, fishes, birds and other traditional Chinese designs, joined and sewn on to a piece of cotton or man-made fibre woven fabrics, thus producing articles such as traycloths, cushion covers, piano covers, tablecloths, bedspreads, doilies, shawls, lace in the piece, bed covers, sofa covers and insertions for these articles.

3. Gou-gou lace:

This is another traditional type of heavy-work hand-made lace typical of Shandong (Shantung), made of coarser cotton or man-made fibre threads, thus producing articles such as shawls, traycloths, cushion covers, curtains, piano covers, doilies, tablecloths, bedspreads, sofa covers, lace in the piece, bed covers and insertions for these articles.

4. Gingzhoufu lace:

This is a very fine type of lace made by hand in different traditional designs. It takes months, and sometimes years to make one set of this type of tablecloth and napkins. It is a typical product of Shandong (Shantung), producing articles such as lace in the piece, shawls, traycloths, cushion covers, piano covers, tablecloths, bedspreads, sofa covers, doilies, bed covers and insertions for these articles.

5. Rongcheng lace:

This is the finest and most elaborate kind of Chinese lace. It is made in the traditional way in Shandong (Shantung). Unlike Xiaoshan lace, the whole design is finished in one piece thus producing articles such as lace in the piece, shawls, traycloths, cushion covers, piano covers, doilies, tablecloths, bedspreads, sofa covers, scarves, bed covers and insertions for these articles.

6. Filite lace:

This is also called mesh-hole lace, made of strong cotton or man-made fibre threads, hand worked in the same manner as nets into different traditional designs, thus obtaining lace in the piece, sofa covers, doilies, gloves, cushion covers, piano covers, tablecloths, curtains, bed covers, traycloths, shawls, bedspreads and insertions for these articles. It is a typical product of Shantou (Swatow) and Fujian.

7. Tatting lace:

This is another kind of hand-made lace in the traditional designs made from high quality cotton or man-made fibre threads, simply obtained by means of a specially made tiny shuttle, thus producing lace in the piece, shawls, traycloths, cushion covers, piano covers, tablecloths, bedspreads and doilies, bed covers, sofa covers and insertions for these articles. It is typical of Shandong (Shantung) and Shantou (Swatow).

8. Batten lace:

This is another type of heavy lace made by hand from cotton or man-made fibre threads which are worked into strips of different shapes. These strips are then joined together according to a prepared sketch or inserted into cloth, thus producing lace in the piece, shawls, traycloths, cushion covers, tablecloths, bedspreads, doilies, bed covers, sofa covers, piano covers and insertions for these articles. The designs correspond to the traditional ones of Shandong (Shantung).

9. Bangchui lace:

Cotton or man-made fibre threads are hand worked according to a predetermined sketch by craftsmen making use of dozens of tiny spindles. For an elaborate design more than 100 spindles may be used. The final products in traditional designs are available in the form of lace in the piece, shawls, traycloths, cushion covers, piano covers, bed covers, tablecloths, bedspreads, doilies, sofa covers and insertions for these articles. It is a traditional and typical product of Shandong (Shantung).

10. Xiaoshan lace:

This is a kind of lace made with tens of thousands of fine cotton threads. It is first worked into small pieces according to patterns on a paper sketch, which is later discarded. By sewing together by hand these small pieces, lace in the piece, shawls, traycloths, cushion covers, tablecloths, doilies, bedspreads, sofa covers, piano covers, bed covers and insertions for these articles in traditional designs of Xiaoshan are obtained.

11. Wangkou lace:

The material used is cotton or man-made fibre threads. The lace is available in different numbers of holes per inch. Traditional designs are then braided through the mesh holes. Lace in the piece, doilies, shawls, traycloths, cushion covers, piano covers, tablecloths, bedspreads, net curtains, bed covers, sofa covers and insertions for these articles are so obtained traditionally in Shandong (Shantung).

12. Hand knitted lace (Needle point lace):

By means of a pair of knitting needles, lace in the piece, shawls, traycloths, curtains, sofa covers, cushion covers, piano covers, tablecloths, bed covers, bedspreads, doilies and insertions for these articles are obtained by hand in traditonal elaborate designs. It is a typical product of Shandong (Shantung), Shanghai, Tianjin (Tientsin) and Liaoning.

B. Products largely embroidered by hand in the following traditional techniques of China

1. Cut work and embroidery:

Traditional designs of Shanghai, Shantou (Swatow), Shandong (Shantung) are embroidered by hand on to cotton or man-made woven fabrics. After embroidery, some parts of the cloth are cut away by hand, so making traditional designs on cushion covers, bed sheets, scarves, sunblinds, handkerchiefs, tablecloths, bedspreads, doilies, pillowcases, shawls, traycloths, bed covers, sofa covers, curtains, guest towels, piano covers, aprons. This type of product also presents drawn work and stuffed embroidery.

2. Embroidery organdy:

Various kinds of hand embroidery in traditional Chinese designs and colours, typical of Beijing (Peking) and Shantou (Swatow) are carried out on fine translucent cotton woven fabrics, thus producing traycloths, sofa covers, cushion covers, piano covers, aprons, scarves, tablecloths, bed covers, curtains, bedsheets, pillowcases, shawls, bedspreads, guest towels, handkerchiefs, doilies.

3. Multi-coloured embroidery:

This is a typical kind of hand-embroidered work, specially distinguished for its elaborate traditional colour combination and designs. It is further matched with various kinds of drawn and punch work. This technique is typical of Shanghai, Beijing (Peking), Guangdong (Kwangtung), Tianjin (Tientsin), Fujian and Shandong (Shantung), producing traycloths, cushion covers, bedsheets, scarves, tablecloths, bed covers, curtains, pillowcases, shawls, bedspreads, guest towels, aprons, doilies, sofa covers, piano covers, handkerchiefs.

C. Products obtained by the traditional Chinese technique 'applique and embroidery'

This technique involves the previous cutting by hand of coloured cloth into traditional floral or geometrical designs which are then sewn by hand on to cotton or man-made woven fabrics. Large hand embroideries in traditional colours and designs are always included in this technique, producing traycloths, handkerchiefs, place mats, cushion covers, scarves, tablecloths, bedsheets, bed covers, shawls, bedspreads, sofa covers, piano covers, guest towels, aprons, pillowcases, doilies, curtains.

D. Products presenting important traditional Chinese designs obtained by hand by the 'cross stitch' technique

Cross stitches are made by hand on cotton or man-made woven fabrics with colour-fast threads without a pattern drawn on the fabric, simply by counting the numbers of weft and warp. This technique is typical of Zhejiang (Chekiang), Beijing (Peking) and Shantou (Swatow), producing bedsheets, doilies, cushion covers, handkerchiefs, scarves, tablecloths, bedspreads bed covers, shawls, sofa covers, piano covers, guest towels, aprons, pillowcases, doilies, curtains.

E. Hand-made needle point tapestry

These are among the famous and traditional hand-made products of China, typical of Shanghai and Shandong (Shantung). Double ply woollen yarns are worked by hand into cotton canvas by needle point stitches to form various traditional designs frequently of a pictorial character, such as landscapes, scenic historic sites, animals, etc.

F. Wax-dyeing products (Fabrics and made-up articles)

Wax-dyeing is a traditional method and also a cultural heritage of long standing in Guizhou and Sichuan provinces. With special instruments beeswax is used to draw traditional designs on cotton or man-made woven fabrics. After soaking in dye, the wax melts away and the drawings are revealed. These fabrics are used for producing curtains, doilies, scarves, sofa covers, tablecloths, bedspreads, bedsheets, and aprons.

G. Products made by hand painting

These products belong to the traditional art of China. Typical largely elaborated designs are hand painted on the pillowcases, bedsheets, shawls, scarves, tablecloths, place mats, curtains, bedspreads and sofa covers of various kinds of woven fabrics by artists. Every painting is different and completely done by hand.

H. Hand-knotted carpets and rugs

These are made from wool or other animal-hair yarn. Knots most commonly used are Senna or Persian knots and Ghiordes or Turkish knots. Chinese hand-knotted carpets enjoy a long history. The traditional patterns used are common to China and occasionally to neighbouring regions of North and Central Asia and mainly consist of typical stylized flora, animals, popular daily necessities, Chinese characters and geometrical motifs.

I. Hand-hooked carpets and rugs

These carpets are made by the insertion by hand of textile yarns by means of hooks into a pre-existing woven fabric, thus producing loops or, if the hooks are combined with a cutting device, also operated by hand, to form cut pile.

J. Hand-woven carpets and rugs

These are carpets woven on a wooden or iron loom operated by hand with or without tuft piles. These carpets are essentially Chinese Kelem carpets and Tibetan rugs with traditional Chinese patterns.

K. Blouses and shirt-blouses

These are woven garments largely embroidered by hand with traditional Chinese designs and colours.

L. Pullovers and cardigans

These are knitted or crocheted neither elastic nor rubberized traditional Chinese textile garments. They are largely embroidered by hand with various unique Chinese floral designs and colours.

M. Bed blankets, bed covers, bedsheets, bedspreads, pillowcases, tablecloths, cushion covers, doilies, shawls, sofa covers, curtains, guest towels, piano covers, aprons, scarves, handkerchiefs, traycloths and embroidery on woven fabrics in the piece intended to be made up into these articles

These textile products are made of artificial silk or of a mixture of natural silk and rayon and are largely embroidered by hand with traditional Chinese designs and colours.

N. Open-work knitted or crocheted articles entirely made by hand

These are garments and other traditional textile products of China.

1. The garments consist of pullovers, cardigans, waistcoats, blouses, dresses, sets of pullover plus skirt.

2. The other articles consist of shawls, traycloths, curtains, sofa covers, cushion covers, piano covers, handbags,

scarves, tablecloths, bedspreads, doilies and gloves.

O. Patchwork cotton waistcoats and jackets

The patchwork cotton waistcoat is a kind of traditional decorative garment which spreads far and wide among the masses of Hunghe River Valley of China. It has the following characteristics:

(a) the outside is a piece of material made up of bits of cloth of various sizes, shapes and colours. The inside is of cotton or man-made fibre, padded by hand. The lining is one piece of grey cloth. The waistcoat is sleeveless, completely open at the front and fastened by means of toggles.

(b) flowers, animals and insects and sometimes geometrical patterns are its main designs and all of these designs are patched by hand. Definition for jacket is the same as for the waistcoat except that it has long sleeves.

P. Handicraft 'tying and dyeing' fabrics

The fabrics are tied with threads as per the desired design and dyed; the threads are cut off after the fabrics have been dyed, and the pattern comes out. The main fabrics used are made of cotton and other vegetable fibre, man-made fibre and their blend.

Imports of products of category 97 made by hand are by analogy governed by the provisions set out for imports of products referred to in Protocol B, providing that they conform to the definition given below:

'Hand-knotted fishing nets, nettings, net shopping bags made directly of twine, cordage or rope.

Hand-knotted made-up fishing nets made of yarn, twine, cordage or rope.'

*Annex to Protocol B*

1 Exporter (name, full address, country)
Exportateur (nom, adresse complète, pays)

**ORIGINAL**

2 No

**CERTIFICATE in regard to HANDLOOMS, TEXTILE HANDICRAFTS and TRADITIONAL TEXTILE PRODUCTS, OF THE COTTAGE INDUSTRY, issued in conformity with and under the conditions regulating trade in textile products with the European Economic Community**

**CERTIFICAT relatif aux TISSUS TISSÉS SUR MÉTIERS À MAIN, aux PRODUITS TEXTILES FAITS À LA MAIN, et aux PRODUITS TEXTILES RELEVANT DU FOLKLORE TRADITIONNEL, DE FABRICATION ARTISANALE, délivré en conformité avec et sous les conditions régissant les échanges de produits textiles avec la Communauté économique européenne**

3 Consignee (name, full address, country)
Destinataire (nom, adresse complète, pays)

4 Country of origin
Pays d'origine

5 Country of destination
Pays de destination

6 Place and date of shipment — Means of transport
Lieu et date d'embarquement — Moyen de transport

7 Supplementary details
Données supplémentaires

8 Marks and numbers — Number and kind of packages — DESCRIPTION OF GOODS
Marques et numéros — Nombre et nature des colis — DÉSIGNATION DES MARCHANDISES

9 Quantity
Quantité

10 FOB Value (¹)
Valeur fob (¹)

11 CERTIFICATION BY THE COMPETENT AUTHORITY — VISA DE L'AUTORITÉ COMPÉTENTE

I, the undersigned, certify that the consignment described above includes only the following textile products of the cottage industry of the country shown in box No 4:
a) fabrics woven on looms operated solely by hand or foot (handlooms) (²)
b) garments or other textile articles obtained manually from the fabrics described under a) and sewn solely by hand without the aid of any machine (handicrafts) (²)
c) traditional folklore handicraft textile products made by hand, as defined in the list agreed between the European Economic Community and the country shown in box No 4.

Je soussigné certifie que l'envoi décrit ci-dessus contient exclusivement les produits textiles suivants relevant de la fabrication artisanale du pays figurant dans la case 4:
a) tissus tissés sur des métiers actionnés à la main ou au pied (handlooms) (²)
b) vêtements ou autres articles textiles obtenus manuellement à partir de tissus décrits sous a) et cousus uniquement à la main sans l'aide d'une machine (handicrafts) (²)
c) produits textiles relevant du folklore traditionnel fabriqués à la main, comme définis dans la liste convenue entre la Communauté économique européenne et le pays indiqué dans la case 4.

12 Competent authority (name, full address, country)
Autorité compétente (nom, adresse complète, pays)

At — À .................................................., on — le ..................................

(Signature)

(Stamp — Cachet)

(¹) In the currency of the sale contract — Dans la monnaie du contrat de vente.
(²) Delete as appropriate — Biffer la (les) mention(s) inutile(s).

**List of traditional folklore textile products obtained in the cottage industry of China**

| Products | Paragraphs giving details of the products | Denomination of the products | No of photographs | Categories for non-folk products | CN codes 1988 |
|---|---|---|---|---|---|
| 1. PRODUCTS OF HAND-MADE LACE (paragraphs A 1 to A 12) | A 1 to A 12 | LACE IN THE PIECE | 20 | 62 | 5804 30 00 |
| 2. PRODUCTS LARGELY EMBROIDERED BY HAND (paragraphs B, C, D, M) | | TABLE LINEN: | | 39 | 6302 51 10<br>6302 51 90<br>6301 53 90<br>ex 6302 59 00 |
| | A 1 to A 12, B, C, D, M | — tablecloths | 2, 6, 8, 10, 14, 15, 17, 21, 24, 25, 26, 40, 42, 43, 77 | | |
| | A 1 to A 12, B, C, D, M | — doilies | | | |
| | A 1 to A 12, B, C, M | — traycloths | 36, 41 | | |
| | C | — place mats | 35 | | |
| | | BED LINEN: | | 20 | 6302 21 00<br>6302 22 90<br>6302 29 90<br>6302 31 10<br>6302 31 90 |
| | B, C, D, M | — Pillowcases | 39 | | |
| | B, C, D, M | — Bed sheets | 39 | | |
| | M | BLANKETS | 78 | 66 | 6301 20 91<br>6301 20 99<br>6301 30 90<br>ex 6301 40 90<br>ex 6301 90 90 |
| | B, C, D, M | TOILET LINEN: | | 39 | 6302 91 10<br>6302 91 90<br>6302 93 90<br>ex 6302 99 00 |
| | | — guest towels, other than of terry towelling and similar terry fabrics | 23 | | |
| | M | EMBROIDERY ON WOVEN FABRICS IN THE PIECE | 83 | 62 | 5810 91 10<br>5810 91 90<br>5810 92 10<br>5810 92 90<br>5810 99 10<br>5810 99 90 |
| | B, C, D, M | CURTAINS AND OTHER FURNISHING ARTICLES: | | 40 | 6303 91 00<br>ex 6303 92 90<br>ex 6303 99 90<br>6304 19 10<br>ex 6304 19 90<br>6304 92 00<br>ex 6304 93 00<br>ex 6304 99 00 |
| | A 1, A 3, A 6, A 12, B, C, D, M | — curtains | 4, 9 | | |
| | A 1 to A 12, B, C, D, M | — bedspreads | 3, 5, 7, 12, 13, 16, 18, 19 | | |
| | A 1 to A 12, B, C, D, M | — sofa covers | 4 | | |
| | A 1 to A 12, B, C, D, M | — piano covers | 22, 28 | | |
| | A 1 to A 12, B, C, D, M | — bed covers | 83 | | |
| | A 1 to A 12, B, C, D, M | — cushion covers | 79, 80 | | |
| | 81 | — sunblinds | 27 | 109 | 6306 11 00<br>6306 12 00<br>6306 19 00 |

| Products | Paragraphs giving details of the products | Denomination of the products | No of photographs | Categories for non-folk products | CN codes 1988 |
|---|---|---|---|---|---|
| (1. and 2.) PRODUCTS OF HAND-MADE LACE OR LARGELY EMBROIDERED BY HAND *(cont'd)* | A 11 | NET CURTAINS | | 38 B | ex 6303 91 00<br>ex 6303 92 90<br>ex 6303 99 90 |
| | B, C, D, M | HANDKERCHIEFS | 30, 31 | 19 | 6213 20 00<br>6213 90 00 |
| | A 1 to A 12 | INSERTIONS | 1 | 62 | 5804 30 00 |
| | A 6 | GLOVES | 11 | 87 | 6216 00 00 |
| | A 1 to A 12, B, C, D, M | SHAWLS AND SCARVES | 81, 82 | 84 | 6214 20 00<br>6214 30 00<br>6214 40 00<br>6214 90 10 |
| | B, C, D | APRONS | | 76 | 6211 42 10<br>6211 43 10 |
| 3. OPEN WORK HAND-KNITTED OR HAND-CROCHETED PRODUCTS, OTHER THAN GARMENTS | N 2 | TABLE LINEN:<br>— traycloths<br>— tablecloths<br>— doilies | 94, 95 | 57 | 6302 40 00 |
| | | CURTAINS AND OTHER FURNISHING ARTICLES: | | 67 | |
| | | — piano covers | | | 6304 91 00 |
| | | — cushion covers | | | |
| | | — curtains | | | 6303 11 00<br>6303 12 00<br>6303 19 00 |
| | | — bedspreads | | | 6304 11 00 |
| | | — sofa covers | | | |
| | | SHAWLS AND SCARVES | | 67 | |
| | | NET CURTAINS | | 67 | 6303 11 00<br>6303 12 00<br>6303 19 00 |
| | | GLOVES | 96 | 10 | 6116 91 00<br>6116 92 00<br>6116 93 00 |
| | | HANDBAGS | 97, 98 | 67 | 6307 90 10 |
| 4. HAND-MADE NEEDLE POINT TAPESTRY | E | TAPESTRY | 44 to 56 | 60 | 5805 00 00 |
| 5. WAX-DYEING PRODUCTS WOVEN | F | TABLE LINEN:<br>— table/cloths<br>— doilies | 58 | 39 | 6302 51 10<br>6302 51 90<br>6302 53 90<br>ex 6302 59 90 |
| | | BED LINEN:<br>— bed sheets | | 20 | 6302 31 10<br>6302 31 90<br>6302 32 90<br>6302 39 90 |

| Products | Paragraphs giving details of the products | Denomination of the products | No of photographs | Categories for non-folk products | CN codes 1988 |
|---|---|---|---|---|---|
| 5. WAX-DYEING PRODUCTS WOVEN *(cont'd)* | | CURTAINS AND OTHER FURNISHING ARTICLES: | | 40 | |
| | | — sofa covers | | | 6304 92 00<br>ex 6304 93 00<br>ex 6304 99 00 |
| | | — bedspreads | | | 6304 19 10<br>ex 6304 19 90 |
| | | — curtains | | | ex 6303 91 00<br>ex 6303 92 90<br>ex 6303 99 90 |
| | | APRONS | 57, 59 | 76 | ex 6211 42 10<br>6211 43 10 |
| | | SCARVES | | 84 | 6214 20 00<br>6214 30 00<br>6214 40 00<br>6214 90 10 |
| | | FABRICS | | 2, 3, 35, 36 and 37 | As for the same categories in Annex I to the Agreement |
| 6. PRODUCTS MADE BY HAND PAINTING, WOVEN | G | TABLE LINEN: | | 39 | 6302 51 10<br>6302 51 90<br>6302 53 10<br>ex 6302 59 00 |
| | | — tablecloths | 60 | | |
| | | — place mats | | | |
| | | BED LINEN: | | 20 | |
| | | — bed sheets | | | 6302 31 10<br>6302 31 90<br>6302 32 90<br>6302 39 90 |
| | | CURTAINS AND OTHER FURNISHING ARTICLES: | | 40 | |
| | | — pillowcases | 61 | | 6304 92 00<br>ex 6304 93 00<br>ex 6304 99 00 |
| | | — curtains | | | ex 6303 91 00<br>ex 6303 92 90<br>ex 6302 99 90 |
| | | — bed spreads | | | 6304 19 10<br>ex 6304 19 90 |
| | | — sofa covers | | | 6304 92 00<br>ex 6304 93 00<br>ex 6304 99 00 |
| | | SHAWLS AND SCARVES | | 84 | 6214 20 00<br>6214 30 00<br>6214 40 00<br>6214 90 10 |
| 7. HAND-KNOTTED CARPETS AND RUGS | H | CARPETS, CARPETING AND RUGS, HAND-KNOTTED | 62 to 64 | 58 | 5701 10 10<br>5701 10 91<br>5701 10 93<br>5701 10 99<br>5701 90 10<br>5701 90 90 |

| Products | Paragraphs giving details of the products | Denomination of the products | No of photographs | Categories for non-folk products | CN codes 1988 |
|---|---|---|---|---|---|
| 8. HAND-HOOKED CARPETS AND RUGS | I | TUFTED CARPETS AND RUGS | 65, 66 | 59 | 5703 10 90<br>5703 20 90<br>5703 30 19<br>5703 30 99<br>5703 90 90 |
| 9. HAND-WOVEN CARPETS AND RUGS | J | — KELEM (KHILIN OR CILIM) RUGS AND THE LIKE<br>— OTHER CARPETS AND RUGS, WOVEN | 67, 68 | 59 | 5702 10 00 |
| 10. BLOUSES AND SHIRT-BLOUSES, WOVEN, LARGELY EMBROIDERED BY HAND | K | BLOUSES AND SHIRT-BLOUSES | 69 to 72 | 7 | 6206 20 00<br>6206 30 00<br>6206 40 00 |
| 11. PULLOVERS AND CARDIGANS, KNITTED OR CROCHETED, NEITHER ELASTIC NOR RUBBERIZED, LARGELY EMBROIDERED BY HAND | L | PULLOVERS AND CARDIGANS | 73 to 76 | 5 | 6110 10 10<br>6110 10 31<br>6110 10 39<br>6110 20 91<br>6110 20 99<br>6110 30 91<br>6110 30 99<br>(ex 6110 90 90) |
| 12. OPEN WORK, KNITTED OR CROCHETED, GARMENTS ENTIRELY MADE BY HAND | N 1 | PULLOVERS, CARDIGANS AND WAISTCOATS | 84 to 92 | 5 | 6110 10 10<br>6110 10 31<br>6110 10 39<br>6110 20 91<br>6110 20 99<br>6110 30 91<br>6110 30 99<br>(ex 6110 90 90) |
| | | BLOUSES | | 7 | 6106 10 00<br>6106 20 00<br>6106 90 10<br>(6110 90 90) |
| | | DRESSES | | 26 | 6104 41 00<br>6104 42 00<br>6104 43 00<br>6104 44 00 |
| | | 'SETS' PULLOVER PLUS SKIRT (WOMEN'S SUIT OR COORDINATE-SUIT) | 74 | | 6104 11 00<br>6104 12 00<br>6104 13 00 |
| 13. PATCHWORK COTTON WAISTCOATS AND JACKETS | O | WOVEN WAISTCOATS, OF COTTON | 99 | 78 | ex 6211 32 90<br>ex 6211 42 90 |
| | | WOVEN JACKETS, OF COTTON | | 15, 17 | 6203 32 90<br>6203 32 90 |
| 14. 'TYING AND DYEING' FABRICS | P | FABRICS | 100 | 2, 3, 35, 36 and 37 | As for the same categories in Annex I to the Agreement |

It is understood that dresses, gloves and shawls as illustrated on photos Nos 11, 85, 93 and 96 are hand-knitted or woven products representative of Chinese craft industry.

## PROTOCOL C

Pursuant to Article 6 (6) of the Agreement, a quantitative limit may be fixed on a regional basis where imports of a given product into any region of the Community in relation to the amounts determined in accordance with paragraph 2 of the said Article 6 exceed the following regional percentage:

| | |
|---|---|
| Germany | 25,5% |
| Benelux | 9,5% |
| France | 16,5% |
| Italy | 13,5% |
| Denmark | 2,7% |
| Ireland | 0,8% |
| United Kingdom | 21,0% |
| Greece | 1,5% |
| Spain | 7,5% |
| Portugal | 1,5% |

## PROTOCOL D

The annual growth rate for the quantitative limits introduced pursuant to Article 6 of the Agreement shall be determined as follows:

for products in categories falling within Groups II or III, the growth rate shall be fixed by agreement between the Parties in accordance with the consultation procedure established in Article 16 of the Agreement. Such growth rate may in no case be lower than the highest rate applied to corresponding products under bilateral agreements concluded under the Geneva Arrangement between the Community and other third countries having a level of trade equal to or comparable with that of China.

## PROTOCOL E

Re-imports in the sense of Article 4 paragraph 4 of this Agreement into the Community of products listed in the Annex to this Protocol shall be subject to the provisions of the Agreement except as specifically provided for by the particular provisions set out below:

1. Only re-imports into the Community subject to the specific quantitative limits set out in the Annex to this Protocol, as may be modified by the application of paragraphs 2 and 3, shall be considered re-imports in the sense of Article 4 paragraph 4.

2. Re-imports not covered by the Annex to this Protocol may be submitted to specific quantitative limits following consultations in accordance with the procedures set out in Article 16 of the Agreement, provided the products concerned are subject to the quantitative limits established under Annex III to the Agreement.

3. The Community may, at its own discretion, and bearing in mind the interest of both Parties, or in the framework of a request set out in Article 16 of the Agreement:

(a) examine the possibilities of transfers between categories and advance use or carry-over of portions of specific quantitative limits from one year to another;

(b) consider the scope for reallocating portions of any specific quantitative limits not used in one region of the Community to another region.

4. However the Community may automatically carry out the flexibilities in the sense of paragraph 3 up to the following extent:

(a) transfer between categories up to 20% of the share established for the category to which the transfer is made;

(b) carry-over of specific quantitative limits from one year to another up to 10,5% of the share for the year of actual utilization;

(c) advance use of specific quantitative limits from one year to another up to 7,5% of the share for the year of actual utilization.

5. The Community shall inform China of any measures taken pursuant to the preceding paragraphs.

6. Debiting against a specific quantitative limit referred to in paragraph 1 shall be carried out by the competent authorities of the Community at the time of issuing the prior authorization provided for by the Community regulation on economic outward processing, Regulation (EEC) N° 636/82. A specific quantitative limit shall be debited for the year in which a prior authorization is issued.

7. A certificate of origin shall be issued for all products covered by the present Protocol by China in accordance with the provisions of Protocol A of the Agreement, bearing a reference to the prior authorization referred to in paragraph 6 as evidence that the processing operation described in the prior authorization has been carried out in China.

8. The Community shall provide China with the names, addresses and the specimens of stamps used by the competent authorities of the Community for the issue of the prior authorizations referred to in paragraph 6.

9. Notwithstanding the provisions of paragraphs 1 to 8 above, China and the Community will continue to consult together to seek a mutually acceptable means to enable both parties to take advantage of the OPT provisions in the Agreement with a view to effective development of trade in textiles between China and the Community.

*Annex to Protocol E*

**OPT quantitative limits**

(In this Annex the product descriptions used in Annex I are given in abbreviated form)

| Category | Description | Units | Year | Quantitative limits EEC |
|---|---|---|---|---|
| 6 | Trousers and shorts, woven | 1 000 pieces | 1989<br>1990<br>1991<br>1992 | 1 200<br>1 272<br>1 348<br>1 429 |
| 7 | Blouses and shirt-blouses | 1 000 pieces | 1989<br>1990<br>1991<br>1992 | 350<br>371<br>393<br>417 |
| 8 | Woven shirts | 1 000 pieces | 1989<br>1990<br>1991<br>1992 | 1 000<br>1 045<br>1 092<br>1 141 |
| 21 | Parkas, anoraks and the like, woven | 1 000 pieces | 1989<br>1990<br>1991<br>1992 | 800<br>860<br>925<br>994 |

| Category | Description | Units | Year | Quantitative limits (D) |
|---|---|---|---|---|
| 26 | Dresses | 1 000 pieces | 1989<br>1990<br>1991<br>1992 | 600<br>645<br>693<br>745 |
| 76 | Industrial or occupational garments, woven | tonnes | 1989<br>1990<br>1991<br>1992 | 600<br>645<br>693<br>745 |

Agreed Minute concerning Article 11

In the course of the negotiations on the bilateral Textile Agreement between the European Economic Community and the People's Republic of China initialled on 9 December 1988, the delegation of the Community drew attention to difficulties experienced by importers and industrialists in the Community wishing to import angora, cashmere and raw and waste silk from China, concerning the implementation of commercial contracts.

The Chinese authorities undertake to endeavour, in consultation with the organisations responsible for the export of these products, to find remedies to these problems, and to ensure that the quality of the products is improved in order to meet the standards required by European industry.

The two delegations agreed that, in the event of any difficulties in provision and delivery of these fibres, consultations may be held with a view to finding a mutually satisfactory solution.

Head of Delegation of the People's Republic of China

Head of Delegation of the European Economic Community

Agreed Minute concerning Annex IV

In the course of the negotiations on the bilateral Textile Agreement between the European Economic Community and the People's Republic of China initialled on 9 December 1988, the delegation of the Community emphasized the importance it attached to European industries' access to supplies of Chinese raw silk. These industries require improved access to a quantity based on figures corresponding to the actual trade flows in recent years.

The Chinese delegation noted this request and will endeavour to supply additional quantities of raw silk to the industries in question according to the availability of supply.

The two delegations have agreed that, should problems arise in connection with supplies of raw silk, consultations will be held in order to resolve these problems.

Head of Delegation of the People's Republic of China

Head of Delegation of the European Economic Community

Agreed Minute

1. In the course of the negotiations on the bilateral Textile Agreement between the European Economic Community and the People's Republic of China initialled on 9 December 1988, the European Economic Community delegation drew attention to the administrative and economic difficulties which had in previous years arisen due to overshipments of products in certain categories in Annex III and for which licences have been issued.

2. The Chinese delegation confirmed that measures had been taken to ensure that the problems which had arisen in previous years would not be repeated under the Agreement initialled on

9 December 1988 and supplied details concerning the internal procedures which have been adopted. The Chinese delegation expressed confidence that the licensing system was now operating correctly.

3. The two sides agreed that should difficulties with overlicensing nevertheless arise, the consultations referred to in Article 13, paragraph 1 of Protocol A shall be initiated without

delay. In order to assist the Chinese authorities to initiate the internal procedures referred to in paragraph 2 above, the competent authorities in the Community will supply data concerning excess export licences presented.

Head of Delegation of the People's Republic of China

Head of Delegation of the European Economic Community

Agreed Minute

During the negotiations preceding the conclusion of the Textile Agreement on 9 December 1988, the delegation of the European Economic Community drew the attention of the Chinese delegation to the particular problems which have arisen in the Community markets due to imports from China of products of category 33. The Chinese delegation was unable at this stage to agree the introduction of a Community limit for these products.

In consequence, the two delegations have agreed that China will accord special consideration to any specific problems raised by the Community in respect of this category, and enter promptly into consultations with a view to finding an appropriate solution.

Head of Delegation of the People's Republic of China

Head of Delegation of the European Economic Community

Agreed Minute

The People's Republic of China and the European Economic Community agree that carry-over from the quantitative limits for the year 1988 of amounts not used during the year 1988 is authorized up to 7% of the corresponding quantitative limits for the year 1989. Anticipation of a portion of quantitative limits for the year 1989 is authorized up to 5% for any quantitative limit for the year 1988.

Head of Delegation of the People's Republic of China

Head of Delegation of the European Economic Community

Dear Mr. Hofmann,

I confirm that the Chinese authorities will give every assistance to European industrialists who wish to visit China in order to benefit from the access to the raw materials referred to in Annex IV to the Textile Agreement between the European Economic Community and China initialled on 9 December 1988, and in the Agreed Minute concerning Annex IV.

LI GOUDONG

Dear Mr. Hofmann,

Concerning category 2 (cotton fabrics), the two Parties have agreed that an additional quantity of 1 230 tonnes for fabrics below 115 cm in width may be exported by the People's Republic of China to the European Economic Community on the understanding that for the purposes of taking advantage of this additional facility, China will not in fact export fabrics above 100 cm in width.

I hereby declare that this is the understanding of the Chinese government.

LI GUODONG

Dear Mr. Hofmann,

I have the honour to confirm that China is willing to ensure the normal development of exports to the Community in respect of fabrics for medical gauze (CN codes 5208 11 10 and 5208 21 10), taking into account existing currents of trade, as well as specific solutions agreed upon in Brussels.

LI GUODONG

Dear Mr. Li Guodong,

Your delegation expressed particular concern about certain problems resulting from regional breakdown of the agreed Community restraint levels.

In case of difficulties concerning this problem the Community would enter into consultations in a constructive spirit with a view to finding a mutually acceptable solution.

G. HOFMANN

Exchange of Notes

The Mission of the People's Republic of China to the European Communities presents its compliments to the Directorate-General for External Relations of the Commission of the European Communities and has the honour to refer to the Agreement on textile products between the People's Republic of China and the Community initialled on 9 December 1988.

The Mission wishes to inform the Directorate-General that whilst awaiting the completion of the necessary procedures for the conclusion and the coming into force of the Agreement, the Government of the People's Republic of China is prepared to allow the provisions of the Agreement to apply de facto from 1 January 1989 if the Community is disposed to do likewise.

The Mission would be grateful if the Community would confirm its agreement to the foregoing.

The Mission of the People's Republic of China to the European Communities avails itself of this opportunity to renew to the Directorate-General for External Relations the assurance of its highest consideration.

Exchange of Notes

The Directorate-General for External Relations of the Commission of the European Communities presents its compliments to the Mission of the People's Republic of China to the European Communities and has the honour to refer to the Note of 20 December 1988 regarding the Agreement in textile products between the People's Republic of China and the Community initialled on 9 December 1988.

The Directorate-General for External Relations avails itself of this opportunity to renew to the Mission of the People's Republic of China to the European Communities the assurance of its highest consideration.

In 1995, the EC and China concluded a revised agreement on textile products not covered by the 1988 Agreement (see Document 2.5). The 1995 Agreement concerned mainly silk, as well as other textile products except those made of cotton, wool, fine animal hair and man-made fibres. It provided for quotas and a double-checking system, a basket-exit system for other products, advance use, provisions on anti-circumvention, inward processing and outward processing. It also required China to ensure that the Community textile industry benefited from the administration of the quotas and that the supply of raw materials to Community industry was made at conditions no less favourable than to Chinese domestic users. The agreement was concluded for two years with effect from 1 January 1995, with automatic extension for successive periods of one year unless otherwise notified.

### Document 2.5: 1995 EC–China Agreement on Trade in Textile Products not covered by the 1988 Agreement

**Agreement between the European Community and the People's Republic of China on trade in textile products not covered by the MFA bilateral Agreement on trade in textile products initialled on 9 December 1988 as extended and modified by the exchange of letters initialled on 8 December 1992—Protocol A—Protocol B—Protocol of Understanding concerning the implementation of article 12 of the Agreement—Agreed Minute Unofficial translation—Agreed Minutes—Exchange of Notes**

*Official Journal L 104, 06/05/1995 P. 0002–0029*

THE COUNCIL OF THE EUROPEAN UNION,

of the one part, and

THE GOVERNMENT OF THE PEOPLE'S REPUBLIC OF CHINA,

of the other part,

DESIRING to promote the orderly and equitable development of trade in textile products other than those made of cotton, wool, fine animal hair and man-made fibres, between the European Community (hereinafter referred to as 'the Community') and the People's Republic of China (hereinafter referred to as 'China'), with a view to strengthening cooperation and security for trade,

RESOLVED to take the fullest possible account of the serious economic and social problems at present affecting the textile industry in both importing and exporting countries and, in particular, to eliminate real risks of market disruption on the market of the Community and real risks of disruption to the textile trade of China,

HAVING REGARD to the Trade and Economic Cooperation Agreement between the Community and China,

HAVE DECIDED to conclude this Agreement and to this end have designated as their Plenipotentiaries:

THE COUNCIL OF THE EUROPEAN UNION:

THE GOVERNMENT OF THE PEOPLE'S REPUBLIC OF CHINA:

WHO HAVE AGREED AS FOLLOWS:

Article 1

1. The present Agreement covers the trade in textile raw materials and textile products, falling within Section XI of the combined nomenclature, that are listed in Annex I originating in the People's Republic of China.

2. Subject to the provisions of this or any subsequent Agreement, the Community undertakes, in respect of the products listed in Annex I, to suspend for the duration of this Agreement the application of quantitative import restrictions in force at the time of its initialling and not to introduce new quantitative restrictions, except as specified below.

3. Without prejudice to anti-dumping and countervailing measures, measures having equivalent effect to quantitative restrictions on the importation into the Community of the products listed in Annex I shall be prohibited for the duration of this Agreement.

Article 2

1. The classification of the products covered by this Agreement is based on the tariff and statistical nomenclature and on the Common Customs Tariff of the Community (hereinafter called the 'combined nomenclature' or in abbreviated form 'CN').

Any amendment to the combined nomenclature (CN) made in accordance with the procedures in force in the Community, concerning categories of products covered by this Agreement or any decision relating to the classification of goods shall not have the effect of reducing any quantitative limit introduced pursuant to this Agreement.

2. The origin of the products covered by this Agreement shall be determined in accordance with the rules in force in the Community.

Any amendment to these rules of origin shall be communicated to China and shall not have the effect of reducing any quantitative limit introduced pursuant to this Agreement.

The procedures for control of the origin of the products referred to above are laid down in Protocol A.

Article 3

1. China agrees to establish and maintain for each calendar year quantitative limits on its exports to the Community in accordance with Annex II. Such exports shall be subject to the double checking system specified in Protocol A.

2. In administering the quantitative limits referred to in paragraph 1 China shall ensure that the Community textile industry shall benefit from utilization of the said limits.

More particularly, as regards categories 156, 157, 159 and 161, China undertakes to reserve, as a priority, 23% of the quantitative limits concerned for users belonging to the Community textile industry during 90 days beginning on 1 January of each year.

To facilitate the implementation of these provisions, the Community shall provide the competent Chinese authorities, before the end of each year, with a list of interested manufacturers and processors and, if possible, of the quantity of products requested by each firm. To this end, the firms concerned are invited to make direct contact with the relevant Chinese bodies by 15 February of the following year in order to make their purchasing intentions known.

3. In the event of denunciation of this Agreement as provided for in Article 17 (3) the quantitative limits established in Annex II shall be reduced on a pro rata basis.

Article 4

1. Imports into the Community of textile products covered by this Agreement shall not be subject to the quantitative limits established in Annex II provided that they are declared to be for re-export outside the Community in the same state or after processing, within the framework of the administrative system of control which exists within the Community.

However, the release for home use within the Community of products imported under the conditions referred to above shall be subject to the production of an export licence issued by the Chinese authorities, and to proof of origin in accordance with the provisions of Protocol A.

2. Where the Community authorities ascertain that re-exports of textile products have been set off against a quantitative limit established under this Agreement, but that the products have subsequently been re-exported outside the Community, the authorities concerned shall inform the Chinese authorities within four weeks of the quantities involved and authorize imports of identical quantities of the same products which shall not be set off against the quantitative limit established under this Agreement for the current or the following year, as appropriate.

Article 5

1. China shall monitor its exports of products under restraint into the Community. Should a sudden and prejudicial change in traditional trade flows arise, the Community will be entitled to request consultations in order to find a satisfactory solution to those problems. Such consultations must be held within 15 working days of their being requested by the Community.

2. China shall endeavour to ensure that exports of textile products subject to quantitative limits into the Community are spaced out as evenly as possible over the year, due account being taken in particular of seasonal factors.

Article 6

1. China shall supply the Community with precise statistical information on all export licences issued for categories of textile products subject to the quantitative limits set out in Annex II, expressed in quantities and in terms of value and broken down by Member States of the Community.

2. The Community shall likewise transmit to the Chinese authorities precise statistical information on import authorization or documents issued by the Community authorities and import statistics for products covered by the quantitative limits set out in Annex II.

3. The information referred to in paragraphs 1 and 2 above shall, for all categories of products, be forwarded before the end of the month following the month to which the statistics relate.

4. Upon request by the Community, China shall supply import statistics for all products covered by Annex I.

5. Should it be found on analysis of the information exchanged that there are significant discrepancies between the returns for exports and those for imports, consultations may be initiated in accordance with the procedure specified in Article 14 of this Agreement.

6. For the purpose of applying the provisions of Article 7, the Community undertakes to provide the Chinese authorities before 15 April of each year with the preceding year's statistics on imports of all textile products covered by this Agreement, broken down by supplying country and Community Member States.

Article 7

1. Exports of textile products not listed in Annex II to this Agreement may be made subject to quantitative limits on the conditions laid down in the following paragraphs.

2. Where the Community finds, under the system of administrative control set up, that the level of imports of products in a given category not listed in Annex II originating in China, in relation to the preceding years' total imports into the Community from all sources of products in that category, reaches 25% for categories covering silk products and 10% for all the other products listed in Annex I, it may request the opening of consultations in accordance with the procedure described in Article 14 of this Agreement, with a view to reaching agreement on an appropriate restraint level for the products falling within such category.

The Community shall authorize the importation of products of the said category shipped from China before the date on which the request for consultations was submitted.

For the purposes of applying the provisions of this paragraph in the year 1995, the preceding year's total imports from all third countries shall be calculated on the basis of imports into the Community as constituted on 31 December 1994 and of imports into Austria, Finland and Sweden. Trade between the Community, Austria, Finland and Sweden, or between Austria, Finland and Sweden shall be excluded from this total.

3. Pending a mutually satisfactory solution, China undertakes to limit exports of the products in the category concerned to the Community or to those regions of the Community market specified by the Community for a provisional period of three months from the date on which the request for consultations is made. Such provisional limit shall be established at 25% of the level of imports reached during the calendar year preceding that in which imports exceeded the level resulting from the application of the formula set out in paragraph 2, and gave rise to the request for consultation, or 25% of the level resulting from the application of the formula set out in paragraph 2, whichever is the higher.

4. Should the Parties be unable in the course of consultations to reach a satisfactory solution within the period specified in Article 14 (1), the Community shall have the right to introduce a definitive quantitative limit at an annual level not lower than the level resulting from the application of the formula set out in paragraph 2, or 106% of the level of imports reached during the calendar year preceding that in which imports exceeded the level resulting from the application of the formula set out in paragraph 2 and gave rise to the request for consultations, whichever is the higher.

The annual level so fixed shall be revised upwards after consultations in accordance with the procedure referred to in Article 14 with a view to fulfilling the conditions set out in paragraph 2, should the trend of total imports into the Community of the products in question make this necessary.

5. The limits introduced under paragraph 2 or 4 may in no case be lower than the level of imports of products in that category originating in China in 1993.

6. The provisions of this Article shall not apply where the percentages specified in paragraph 2 have been reached as a result of a fall in total imports into the Community, and not as a result of an increase in exports of products originating in China.

7. In the event of the provisions of paragraph 2, 3 or 4 being applied, China undertakes to issue export licences for products covered by contracts concluded before the introduction of the quantitative limit, up to the volume of the quantitative limit fixed.

8. Up to the date of communication of the statistics referred to in Article 6 (6), the provisions of paragraph 2 of this Article shall apply on the basis of the annual statistics previously communicated by the Community.

9. The provisions of this Agreement which concern exports of products subject to the quantitative limits established in Annex II shall also apply to products for which quantitative limits are introduced pursuant to this Article.

Article 8

1. In any Agreement year advance use of a portion of the quantitative limit established for the following Agreement year is authorized for each category of products up to 1% of the quantitative limit for the current Agreement year, with a possibility to reach 5% after consultations in accordance with Article 14 (1).

Amounts delivered in advance shall be deducted from the corresponding quantitative limits established for the following Agreement year.

2. Carryover to the corresponding quantitative limit for the following Agreement year of the amounts not used during any Agreement year is authorized for each category of products up to 3% of the quantitative limit for the current Agreement year, with a possibility to reach 7% after consultations in accordance with Article 14.

3. Transfers between categories shall not be made except as follows:

- transfers between categories 156, 157, 159 and 161 may be made up to 1,5% of the quantitative limits for the category to which the transfer is made,
- transfers between the remaining categories may be made up to 6% of the quantitative limit for the category to which the transfer is made.

4. The increase in any category of products resulting from the cumulative application of the provisions of paragraphs 1, 2, and 3 during an Agreement year shall not exceed 14%.

5. The table of equivalence applicable to the transfers referred to above is given in Annex I to this Agreement.

6. Prior notification shall be given by the Chinese authorities in the event of recourse to the provisions of paragraphs 1, 2 and 3, at least 15 days in advance.

Article 9

1. China and the Community agree to cooperate fully in preventing the circumvention of this Agreement by transhipment, rerouting or whatever other means.

2. Where information available to the Community as a result of the investigations carried out in accordance with the procedures set out in Protocol A constitutes evidence that

products of Chinese origin subject to quantitative limits established under this Agreement have been transhipped, rerouted or otherwise imported into the Community in circumvention of this Agreement, the Community may request the opening of consultations in accordance with the procedures described in Article 14, with a view to reaching agreement on an equivalent adjustment of the corresponding quantitative limits established under this Agreement.

3. The two parties agree that in dealing with cases of circumvention the provisions of Article 5 of the Uruguay Round Agreement on Textiles and Clothing will be applied by the two parties, with the understanding that recourse to the TMB will become available as soon as both parties become Members of the WTO.

Article 10

The two Contracting Parties undertake to promote the exchange of visits by persons, groups and delegations from business, trade and industry, to facilitate contacts in the industrial, commercial and technical fields connected with trade in products and garments covered by the present Agreement and to assist in the organization of fairs and exhibitions of mutual interest.

The Contracting Parties, recognizing the need for an enhanced industrial cooperation for the products covered by this Agreement, will consult with a view to promoting action to encourage:

- investments that may promote increased integration between silk industries of both Parties and technological exchanges,
- the establishment of an arbitration body recognized by both industries to address possible disputes concerning the fulfilment of conditions and terms set out in contracts regarding in particular issues concerning the quantities and quality of products to be delivered,
- the establishment of a system of grading and standards for silk recognized by both industries and of appropriate common methods of testing.

Article 11

China and the Community recognize the special and differential character of reimports of textile products into the Community after processing in China.

Provided that they are effected in accordance with the Community regulations governing economic outward processing these reimports shall not be subject to the quantitative limits set out in Annex II when they are made in accordance with the specific arrangements laid down in Protocol B.

Article 12

China will ensure that the supply to the Community industry of raw materials shall be made at conditions not less favourable than to Chinese domestic users.

Article 13

China will ensure the respect of intellectual property rights on marks, designs and models belonging to Community operators. The two Parties, at the request of either of them, shall hold consultations in accordance with the procedure laid down in Article 14 for the purpose of finding an equitable solution to any dispute relating to the protection of intellectual property rights on products covered by this Agreement.

Article 14

1. Save where it is otherwise provided for in this Agreement, the consultation procedures referred to in this Agreement shall be governed by the following rules:

- any request for consultations shall be notified in writing to the other Party,
- the request for consultations shall be followed within a reasonable period (and in any case not later than 15 days following the notification) by a statement setting out the reasons and circumstances which, in the opinion of the requesting Party, justify the submission of such a request,
- the Parties shall enter into consultations within one month at the latest of notification of the request, with a view to reaching agreement on a mutually acceptable conclusion within one further month at the latest.

2. The Community may request consultations in accordance with paragraph 1 when it ascertains that during a particular year of application of the Agreement difficulties arise in the Community or one of its regions from a sharp and substantial increase in imports, by comparison to the preceding year.

Article 15

This Agreement shall be drawn up in two copies in the Danish, Dutch, English, Finnish, French, German, Greek, Italian, Portuguese, Spanish, Swedish and Chinese languages, each of these texts being equally authentic.

Article 16

As regards the Community, this Agreement shall apply to the territories in which the Treaty establishing the European Community is applied under the conditions laid down in that Treaty.

Article 17

1. This Agreement shall enter into force on the first day of the month following the date of its signature. It shall apply with effect from 1 January 1995 and be applicable for a duration of two years. Thereafter, its application shall be automatically extended for successive periods of one year unless either Party notifies the other at least six months in advance that it does not agree with the extension.

2. Should China become a Member of the World Trade Organization the restrictions in force shall be phased out in the framework of the Agreement on Textiles and Clothing of the Uruguay Round and notably the provisions of its Articles 2 (8), (13) and (14), 3 (2) (b) and 9.

3. Either Party may at any time propose modifications to this Agreement or denounce it, provided that at least six months' notice is given. In that event, the Agreement shall come to an end at the expiry of the period of notice.

4. The Annexes and Protocols to this Agreement and the Agreed Minutes joined thereto shall form an integral part thereof.

For the Government of the People's Republic of China

For the Council of the European Union

ANNEX I
(Referred to in Article 1 of the Agreement)

1. This Annex covers textile raw materials (categories 128 and 154), textile products other than those of wool and fine animal hair, cotton and man-made fibres, as well as man-made fibres and filaments and yarns of categories 124, 125 A, 125 B, 126, 127 A and 127 B.

2. Without prejudice to the rules for the interpretation of the combined nomenclature, the wording of the description of goods is considered to be of indicative value only, since the products covered by each category are determined, within this Annex, by CN codes. Where there is an 'ex' symbol in front of a CN code, the products covered in each category are determined by the scope of the CN code and by that of the corresponding description.

3. Garments which are not recognizable as being garments for men or boys or as being garments for women or girls are classified with the latter.

4. Where the expression 'babies' garments' is used, this is meant to cover garments up to and including commercial size 86.

>TABLE>

>TABLE>

>TABLE>

>TABLE>

>TABLE>

>TABLE>

ANNEX II

Annual Community quantitative limits referred to in Article 3 (1) (The product descriptions of the categories listed in this Annex are to be found in Annex I to this Agreement)

>

TABLE POSITION>

PROTOCOL A

TITLE I
CLASSIFICATION

Article 1

1. The competent authorities of the Community undertake to inform China of any changes in the combined nomenclature (CN) before the date of their entry into force in the Community.

2. The competent authorities of the Community undertake to inform the competent authorities of China of any decisions relating to the classification of products subject to the Agreement, within one month of their adoption at the latest. Such communication shall include:

(a) a description of the products concerned;

(b) the relevant category and the related CN codes;

(c) the reasons which have led to the decision.

3. Where a decision on classification results in a change of classification practice or a change of category of any product subject to the Agreement, the competent authorities of the Community shall provide 30 days' notice, from the date of the Community's communication, before the decision is put into effect. Products shipped before the date of entry into effect of the decision shall remain subject to the earlier classification practice, provided that the goods in question are presented for importation into the Community within 60 days of that date.

4. Where a Community decision on classification resulting in a change of classification practice or a change of categorization of any product subject to the Agreement affects a category subject to quantitative limits, the Contracting Parties agree to enter into consultation in accordance with the procedures described in Article 14 of the Agreement with a view to honouring the obligation under the second subparagraph of Article 2 (1) of the Agreement.

5. In case of divergent opinions between China and the competent Community authorities at the point of entry into the Community on the classification of products covered by the Agreement, classification shall provisionally be based on indications provided by the Community, pending consultations in accordance with Article 14 of the Agreement with a view to reaching agreement on definitive classification of the product concerned.

TITLE II
ORIGIN

Article 2

1. Products originating in China for export to the Community in accordance with the arrangements established by the Agreement shall be accompanied by a certificate of Chinese origin conforming to the model annexed to this Protocol.

2. The certificate of origin shall be certified by the competent Chinese authorities if the products in question can be considered to be products originating in that country within the meaning of the relevant rules in force in the Community.

Article 3

The certificate of origin shall be issued only on application having been made in writing by the exporter or, under the exporter's responsibility, by his authorized representative. The competent Chinese authorities shall ensure that the certificate of origin is properly completed and for this purpose they shall call for any necessary documentary evidence or carry out any check which they consider appropriate.

Article 4

Where different criteria for determining origin are laid down for products falling within the same category the certificates or declarations of origin must contain a sufficiently detailed description of the goods so as to enable the Chinese criterion to be determined, on the basis of which the certificate was issued or the declaration drawn up.

Article 5

The discovery of slight discrepancies between the statements made in the certificate of origin and those made in the documents produced to the customs office for the purpose of carrying out the formalities for importing the products shall not ipso facto cast doubt upon the statements in the certificate.

TITLE III
DOUBLE-CHECKING SYSTEM FOR THE CATEGORIES OF PRODUCTS SUBJECT TO COMMUNITY QUANTITATIVE LIMITS

Section I
Exportation

Article 6

The competent authorities of China shall issue an export licence in respect of all consignments from China of textile products referred to in Annex II, up to the relevant quantitative limits as may be modified by Article 3 (3), and Articles 8 and 9 of the Agreement, as well as of textile products subject to any definitive or provisional quantitative limits established as a result of the application of Article 7 of the Agreement.

Article 7

1. The export licence shall conform to the model annexed to this Protocol and it shall be valid for exports throughout the customs territory to which the Treaty establishing the European Community applies.

2. Each export licence must certify inter alia that the quantity of the product in question has been set off against the quantitative limit established for the category of the products concerned and shall only cover one of the categories of products subject to quantitative limits. It may be used for one or more consignments of the products in question.

Article 8

The competent authorities of the Community must be informed immediately of the withdrawal or modification of any export licence already issued.

Article 9

1. Exports shall be set off against the quantitative limits established for the year in which the shipment of the goods has been effected even if the export licence is issued after such shipment.

2. For the purpose of applying paragraph 1, shipment of the goods is considered to have taken place on the date of their loading onto the exporting aircraft, vehicle or vessel.

Article 10

The presentation of an export licence, in application of Article 12 hereafter, shall be effected not later than 31 March of the year following that in which the goods covered by the licence have been shipped.

Section II
Importation

Article 11

Importation into the Community of textile products subject to quantitative limits shall be subject to the presentation of an import authorization.

Article 12

1. The competent authorities of the Community shall issue the import authorization referred to in Article 11 within five working days of the presentation by the importer of the original of the corresponding export licence.

2. The import authorizations shall be valid for six months from the date of their issue for imports throughout the customs territory to which the Treaty establishing the European Community is applied.

3. The competent authorities of the Community shall cancel the import authorization already issued whenever the corresponding export licence has been withdrawn.

However, if the competent authorities of the Community are notified of the withdrawal or the cancellation of the export licence only after the importation of the products into the Community, the relevant quantities shall be set off against the quantitative limits established for the category and the quota year concerned.

Article 13

1. If the competent authorities of the Community find that the total quantities covered by export licences issued by the competent authorities of China for a particular category in any year exceed the quantitative limit established in accordance with Articles 3 and 7 of the Agreement for that category, as may be modified by Article 3 (3), and Articles 8 and 9 of the Agreement, the said authorities may suspend the further issue of import authorizations. In this event, the competent authorities of the Community shall immediately inform the authorities of China and the special consultation procedure set out in Article 14 of the Agreement shall be initiated forthwith.

2. Exports of products of Chinese origin subject to quantitative limits and not covered by Chinese export licences issued in accordance with the provisions of this Protocol may be refused an import authorization by the competent Community authorities.

However, without prejudice to Article 9 of the Agreement, if the import of such products is allowed into the Community by the competent authorities of the Community, the quantities involved shall not be set off against the appropriate quantitative limits established in Annex II or by virtue of Article 7, without the express agreement of the competent authorities of China.

TITLE IV
FORM AND PRODUCTION OF EXPORT CERTIFICATES AND CERTIFICATES OF ORIGIN, AND COMMON PROVISIONS CONCERNING EXPORTS TO THE COMMUNITY

Article 14

1. The export licence and the certificate of origin may comprise additional copies duly indicated as such. They shall be made out in English or French. If they are completed by hand, entries must be in ink and in printed script.

The documents shall measure 210 × 297 mm. The paper used shall be white writing paper, sized, not containing mechanical pulp, and weighing not less than 25 g/m². If the documents have several copies only the top copy, which is the original, shall be printed with the guilloche pattern background. This copy shall be clearly marked as 'original' and the other copies as 'copies'. Only the original shall be accepted by the competent authorities of the Community as being valid for the purpose of export to the Community in accordance with the provisions of the Agreement.

2. Each document shall bear a standardized serial number, whether or not printed, by which it can be identified.

This number shall be composed of the following elements:

- two letters identifying the exporting country as follows: CN,
- two letters identifying the intended Member State of customs clearance as follows:

AT = Austria

BL = Benelux

DE = Germany

DK = Denmark

EL = Greece

ES = Spain

FI = Finland

FR = France

GB = United Kingdom

IE = Ireland

IT = Italy

PT = Portugal

SE = Sweden

- a one-digit number identifying quota year, as follows:

1 for 1995; 2 for 1996; 3 for 1997 and so on,

- a two-digit number from 01 to 99, identifying the particular issuing office concerned in the exporting country,
- a five-digit number running consecutively from 00001 to 99999 allocated to the intended Member State of customs clearance.

Article 15

The export licence and the certificate of origin may be issued after the shipment of the products to which they relate. In such cases they must bear the endorsement 'délivré a posteriori' or 'issued retrospectively'.

Article 16

1. In the event of a theft, loss or destruction of an export licence or a certificate of origin the exporter may apply to the competent Chinese authorities which issued the document for a duplicate to be made out on the basis of the export documents in his possession. The duplicate of any such certificate or licence so issued shall bear the endorsement 'duplicata' or 'duplicate'.

2. The duplicate shall bear the date of the original export licence or certificate of origin.

TITLE V
ADMINISTRATIVE COOPERATION

Article 17

The Community and China shall cooperate closely in the implementation of the provisions of this Protocol. To this end, contacts and exchanges of views, including on technical matters, shall be facilitated by both Parties.

Article 18

In order to ensure the correct application of this Protocol, the Community and China offer mutual assistance for the checking of the authenticity and the accuracy of export licences and certificates of origin issued or of any declarations made within the terms of this Protocol.

Article 19

China shall transmit to the Commission of the European Community the names and addresses of the authorities competent to issue and verify the export licences and the certificates of origin, together with specimens of the stamps used by these authorities and specimen signatures of officials responsible for signing the export licences. China shall also notify the Community of any change in this information.

Article 20

1. Subsequent verification of certificates of origin or export licences shall be carried out at random, or whenever the competent Community authorities have reasonable doubt as to the authenticity of the certificate or licence or as to the accuracy of the information regarding the true origin of the products in question.

2. In such cases, the competent authorities in the Community shall return the certificate of origin or the export licence or a copy thereof to the competent Chinese authorities, giving, where appropriate, the reasons of form or substance which justify an enquiry. If the invoice has been submitted, such invoice or a copy thereof shall be attached to the certificate or to the licence or their copies. The authorities shall also forward any information that has been obtained suggesting that the particulars given on the said certificate or licence are inaccurate.

3. The results of the subsequent verifications carried out in accordance with paragraphs 1 and 2 shall be communicated to the competent authorities of the Community within three months at the latest. The information communicated shall indicate whether the disputed certificate, licence or declaration, applies to the goods actually exported and whether these goods are eligible for export under the arrangements established by the Agreement. The

information shall also include, at the request of the Community, copies of all the documentation necessary to fully determine the facts, and in particular the true origin of the goods.

4. For the purpose of subsequent verification of certificates of origin, copies of the certificates as well as any export documents referring to them shall be kept for at least two years by the competent Chinese authorities.

5. Recourse to the random verification procedure specified in this Article must not constitute an obstacle to the release for home use of the products in question.

Article 21

1. Where the verification procedure referred to in Article 20 or where information available to the competent authorities of the Community or of China indicates or appears to indicate that the provisions of this Agreement are being circumvented or infringed, the two contracting Parties shall cooperate closely and with the appropriate urgency in order to prevent or remedy any such circumvention or infringement.

2. To this end, the competent authorities of China shall, on their own initiative or at the request of the Community, carry out appropriate inquiries, or arrange for such inquiries to be carried out, concerning operations which are, or appear to the Community to be, in circumvention or infringement of the Agreement. China shall communicate the results of these inquiries to the Community, including any other pertinent information enabling the cause of the circumvention or infringement, including the true origin of the goods, to be determined.

3. By agreement between the Community and China, officials designated by the Community may be present at the inquiries referred to in paragraph 2.

4. In pursuance of the cooperation referred to in paragraph 1, the competent authorities of the Community and China shall exchange any information considered by either contracting Party to be of use in preventing or remedying circumvention or infringement of the provisions of the Agreement. These exchanges may include information on the production of textile products in China and on the trade in the type of products covered by this Agreement between China and third countries, particularly where the Community has reasonable grounds to consider that the products in question may be in transit across the territory of China prior to their importation into the Community. This information may include at the request of the Community copies of all available relevant documentation.

5. Where sufficient evidence shows that the provisions of the Agreement have been circumvented or infringed, the competent authorities of China and the Community may agree to take the measures set out in Article 9 (4) of the Agreement, and any other measures as are necessary to prevent a recurrence of such circumvention or infringement.

ANNEX to Protocol A, Article 2 (1)

>REFERENCE TO A FILM>

ANNEX to Protocol A, Article 7 (1): Model 1

>REFERENCE TO A FILM>

PROTOCOL B

Outward processing traffic (OPT) (Referred to in Article 11 of the Agreement)

1. Without prejudice to paragraph 2, only re-imports into the Community of products affected by the specific quantitative limits laid down in the Annex to this Protocol shall be considered re-imports within the meaning of Article 11 of the Agreement.

2. Re-imports not covered by the Annex to this Protocol may be made subject to specific quantitative limits following consultations in accordance with the procedures set out in Article 14 of the Agreement, provided the products concerned are subject to quantitative limits pursuant to the Agreement.

3. Having regard to the interests of both Parties, the Community may at its discretion, or in response to a request under Article 14 of the Agreement:

(a) examine the possibility of transferring from one category to another, using in advance or carrying over from one year to the next, portions of specific quantitative limits;

(b) consider the possibility of increasing specific quantitative limits.

4. However, the Community may apply automatically the flexibility rules set out in paragraph 3 within the following limits:

(a) transfers between categories may not exceed 20% of the quantity for the category to which the transfer is made;

(b) carry-over of a specific quantitative limit from one year to the next may not exceed 10,5% of the quantity set for the year of actual utilization;

(c) advance use of specific quantitative limits from one year to another may not exceed 7,5% of the quantity set for the year of actual utilization.

5. The Community shall inform China of any measures taken pursuant to the preceding paragraphs.

6. The competent authorities in the Community shall debit the specific quantitative limits referred to in paragraph 1 at the time of issue of the prior authorization required by Council Regulation (EC) No 3036/94 which governs economic outward processing arrangements. A specific quantitative limit shall be debited for the year in which a prior authorization is issued.

7. A certificate of origin made out by the organizations authorized to do so under Chinese law shall be issued, in accordance with Protocol A to the Agreement, for all products covered by this Protocol. This certificate shall bear a reference to the prior authorization mentioned in paragraph 6 as evidence that the processing operation it describes has been carried out in China.

8. The Community shall provide China with the names and addresses of, and specimens of the stamps used by, the competent authorities of the Community which issue the prior authorizations referred to in paragraph 6.

9. Without prejudice to the provisions of paragraphs 1 to 8, China and the Community shall continue consultations with a view to seeking a mutually acceptable solution enabling both Contracting Parties to benefit from the Agreement's provisions on outward processing traffic and so ensure the effective development of trade in textile products between China and the Community.

ANNEX to Protocol B (The product descriptions of the categories listed in this Annex are to be found in Annex I to the Agreement)

OPT QUOTAS

>TABLE>

PROTOCOL OF UNDERSTANDING CONCERNING THE IMPLEMENTATION OF ARTICLE 12 OF THE AGREEMENT

For the purpose of implementing Article 12 of the Agreement it is understood by both Parties that if exports of raw materials (products listed in the Annex to this Protocol) are made subject to specific measures, practices or policies (such as licences, guidances, fiscal, customs or others) such measures, practices or policies must not have for consequence that the conditions applying to the Community users become less favorable than those applied to users in China notably in terms of actual access and prices.

Consequently China shall abstain from any such measures, practices or policies that may result in double pricing.

The actual implementation of Article 12 of the Agreement as well as of the provisions of Article 11 of the bilateral Agreement on trade in textile products, shall be subject to periodic reviews. Should difficulties appear consultations will be held without delay with a view to solving the problems by appropriate action.

ANNEX to the Protocol of Understanding

>TABLE>

Agreed Minute

In the context of the Agreement between the European Community and the People's Republic of China the two Parties have agreed as follows:

1. In order to ensure the continuity of trade flows, and by derogation from Article 3 (1) of the Agreement, products listed in Annex II shipped from China after 31 December 1994 and subject, pursuant to Council Regulation (EC) No 517/94, to quantitative restrictions may be imported into the Community in 1995, without having to be accompanied by an export licence issued by the Chinese authorities, upon presentation of an import authorization issued after 31 December 1994 by the competent authorities of the Community pursuant to the provisions of the relevant Community regulation in force before the date of initialling of the present Agreement. Quantities thus imported in 1995 into the Community shall be set off against the quantitative limits established in Annex II to the Agreement and the levels for which export licences may be issued by the Chinese authorities for the year 1995 shall be reduced by equivalent quantities provided that the quantities for which import authorizations issued by the competent authorities of the Community are notified to China as soon as possible and not later than 28 February 1995.

2. Products listed in Annex II, not subject to quantitative restrictions in the Republic of Austria, the Republic of Finland and the Kingdom of Sweden before 1 January 1995, shall not be subject to the quantitative limits referred to in Article 3 (1) of the Agreement and to the double checking system specified in Protocol A provided that they have been shipped from the People's Republic of China to the Community before 1 January 1995, are

presented for importation in one of these Member States before 31 March 1995 and are exclusively destined for internal consumption in the concerned acceding country.

3. Taking into account the portion of 1995 quotas already allocated to importers by the competent authorities within the EC at the beginning of the year, and the consequences of such allocation for the export management of the Agreement in 1995, the parties agree to hold consultations, notably on reconciliation of figures, when necessary to deal with any difficulty and to ensure a cooperative implementation of the Agreement.

For the Delegation of the People's Republic of China

For the Delegation of the European Community

By the end of 1995 China was the largest supplier of textiles and clothing to the EC. Discussions were underway for China to accede to the WTO. With this in mind, the EC and China concluded an agreement to modify certain provisions of the 1988 MFA Bilateral Agreement (see Document 2.6). The new agreement was to serve as the basis of all notifications to the GATT/WTO as being the rates in force during the 12 month period prior to the entry into force of the ATC. In case China did not accede to the WTO before October 1995, the two parties would discuss the terms of a new bilateral agreement.

## Document 2.6: Agreement on the modification of certain provisions of the 1988 MFA Bilateral Agreement

**Agreement on the modification of certain provisions of the 1988 MFA bilateral Agreement on trade in textile products between the European Community and the People's Republic of China**

*Official Journal L 261 , 31/10/1995 P. 0002 – 0003*

AGREEMENT on the modification of certain provisions of the 1988 MFA bilateral Agreement on trade in textile products between the European Community and the People's Republic of China

Following discussions in December 1992 on the adaptation of growth and flexibility rates laid down in the 1988 MFA bilateral Agreement between China and the European Community, and the discussions in 1994 concerning the modifications of economic provisions of the Agreement, as envisaged in the exchange of letters between Sir Leon Brittan and Minister Wu Yi in view of China's accession to GATT/WTO, the two Parties have agreed that:

(a) the growth and flexibility rates set out in the bilateral agreement between China and the European Community are modified, as of 1 January 1993, as indicated in the Annex to this Agreement. This commitment reflects a compromise that takes into account the following elements:

(1) the fact that China has become the largest supplier of the EC in textiles and clothing;

(2) the perspective of China's accession to GATT/WTO;

(b) these modified rates will be the basis of all notifications to GATT/WTO, as being those in force during the 12 month period prior to the entry into force of the ATC (Uruguay Round Agreement on Textiles and Clothing);

(c) the actual application of the modified rates shall remain suspended until the date of China's accession to GATT/WTO;

(d) should China's accession to GATT/WTO not be completed during the first nine months of 1995, consultations will be held between the two Parties to discuss the terms of a bilateral Agreement governing the trade in textile products for1996 and subsequent years, to be based on the growth and flexibility rates not lower than those listed in the Annex attached to this Agreement;

(e) this Agreement shall enter into force on the first day of the month following its signature. It shall apply provisionally as of the date of its initialling.

For the Government of the People's Republic of China

For the Council of the European Union

ANNEX

TO THE AGREEMENT ON THE MODIFICATION OF THE 1988 MFA BILATERAL AGREEMENT ON TRADE IN TEXTILE PRODUCTS BETWEEN THE EUROPEAN COMMUNITY AND THE PEOPLE'S REPUBLIC OF CHINA

>TABLE>

>TABLE>

As China did not accede to the WTO in 1995, the EU and China concluded a further agreement (see Document 2.7). In addition to advance use and carry over of quota, it addressed the controversial issue of access by European companies to textiles raw materials in China, notably through an EC declaration that China's undertaking to reserve minimum quantities to Community industry or operaters could not be construed to affect other rights granted to European companies, such as national treatment.

### Document 2.7: 1996 Amendment to the 1988 Textiles Agreement

**Agreement in the form of an Exchange of Letters between the European Community and the People's Republic of China amending the Agreement between the European Economic Community and the People's Republic of China on trade in textile products as last amended by Agreements initialled on 14 December 1994—Agreed Minute Unofficial translation**

*Official Journal L 081, 30/03/1996 P. 0318–0389*

AGREEMENT in the form of an Exchange of Letters between the European Community and the People's Republic of China amending the Agreement between the European Economic Community and the People's Republic of China on trade in textile products as last amended by Agreements initialled on 14 December 1994

Letter from the Council of the European Union

Sir,

1. I have the honour to refer to the consultations held between our respective Delegations for the purpose of amending and extending the Agreement between the European

Economic Community and the People's Republic of China on trade in textile products initialled on 9 December 1988, as last amended by Agreement initialled on 14 December 1994 (hereinafter referred to as 'the Agreement').

2. As a result of the consultations, both Parties agreed to amend as of 1 January 1996 the following provisions of the Agreement:

2.1. The text of Article 5 is replaced by the following text:

'Article 5

1. In any Agreement year advance use of a portion of the quantitative limits established for the following Agreement year is authorized for each category of products up to 1% of the quantitative limit for the current Agreement year, with a possibility to reach 5% after consultations in conformity with Article 16, paragraph 2.

Amounts delivered in advance shall be deducted from the corresponding quantitative limits established for the following Agreement year.

2. Carryover to the corresponding quantitative limit for the following Agreement year of the amounts not used during Agreement year is authorized for each category of products up to 3% of the quantitative limit for the current Agreement year, with a possibility to reach 7% after consultations in conformity with Article 16, paragraph 2.

3. Transfers in respect of categories in Group I shall not be made from any category except as follows:

- Transfers between categories 2 and 3 may be made up to 4% of the quantitative limits for the category to which the transfer is made.
- Transfers from category 1 to categories 2 and 3 may be made up to 1% of the quantitative limits for the category to which the transfer is made.
- Transfers between categories 4 to 8 may be made up to 4% of the quantitative limits for the category to which the transfer is made.

Transfers into any categories in Groups II and III may be made from any category or categories in Groups I, II and III up to 6% of the quantitative limit for the category to which the transfer is made.

4. The table of equivalence applicable to the transfers referred to above is given in Annex I to this Agreement.

5. The increase in any category of products resulting from the cumulative application of the provisions in paragraphs 1, 2 and 3 above during an Agreement year shall not exceed 17%.

6. Prior notification shall be given by the authorities of China in the event of recourse to the provisions of paragraphs 1, 2 and 3 above.'

2.2. The Text of Article 11 is replaced by the following text:

'Article 11

1. China will ensure that the supply to the Community industry of raw materials shall be made at conditions not less favourable than to Chinese domestic users.

2. Without prejudice to paragraph 1, China undertakes to take such measures as are required to make possible the export of the minimum annual quantities laid down in Annex IV of the products listed in that Annex.

In administering exports of the products referred to in subparagraph 1, China undertakes to give favourable consideration, taking into account its export possibilities, to requests from the Community textile industry with a view to meeting its needs.

For this purpose, the Community may submit to the Chinese authorities before the end of each year a list of interested manufacturers and processors and, if possible, the quantities of products requested by each of the firms in question.

The Contracting Parties are agreed that transactions in the products listed in Annex IV shall be carried out in accordance with Articles 8 and 9 of the Trade and Economic Cooperation Agreement taking account of market practice and normal trade flows.'

2.3. The text of the second, third and fourth sentences of Article 20, paragraph 1, is replaced by the following text:

'It shall be applicable until 31 December 1998.'

2.4. Annex I which sets out the products concerned by the Agreement is replaced by Appendix 1 to this letter.

2.5. Annex III which sets out the quantitative restrictions for exports from the People's Republic of China to the European Community is replaced for the period from 1 January 1996 to 31 December 1998 by Appendix 2 to this letter.

2.6. Annex IV which sets out the minimum quantities of textile raw materials which the People's Republic of China undertakes to reserve for the European Community each year is replaced for the period from 1 January 1996 to 31 December 1998 by Appendix 3 to this letter.

2.7. The Annex to Protocol E which sets out the quantitative restrictions for economic outward processing operations is replaced for the period from 1 January 1996 to 31 December 1998 by Appendix 4 to this letter.

2.8. In the Joint Declaration on the Berlin Fair set out in Appendix 8 to the Agreement initialled on 8 December 1992 the reference to 'the years 1993, 1994, 1995' is replaced by the words 'the years 1996, 1997 and 1998'.

2.9. All references made in the Agreement to the 'European Economic Community' shall be read as being made to the 'European Community'.

2.10. All Agreed Minutes and Declarations annexed to this letter shall form an integral part of the Agreement.

3. Should the People's Republic of China become a Member of the World Trade Organization before the date of expiry of the Agreement, the restrictions in force shall be phased out in the framework of the WTO Agreement on Textiles and Clothing.

4. I should be obliged if you could kindly confirm the acceptance of your Government of the foregoing. Should this be the case, this Agreement in the form of an Exchange of Letters shall enter into force on the first day of the month following the day on which the Parties have notified each other that the legal procedures necessary to this end have been completed. In the meantime, it shall be applied provisionally from 1 January 1996 on conditions of reciprocity.

Please accept, Sir, the assurance of my highest consideration.

For the Council of the European Union

ANNEX I
PRODUCTS REFERRED TO IN ARTICLE 1

1. When the constitutive material of the products of categories 1 to 114 is not specifically mentioned, these products are to be taken to be made exclusively of wool or of fine hair, of cotton or of man-made fibres.

2. Garments which are not recognizable as being garments for men or boys or as being garments for women or girls are classified with the latter.

3. Where the expression 'babies' garments' is used, this is meant to cover garments up to and including commercial size 86.

>TABLE>

>TABLE>

>TABLE>

>TABLE>

>TABLE>

>TABLE>

ANNEX 1A

>TABLE>

Appendix 2

ANNEX III (The full product descriptions of the categories listed in this Annex are to be found in Annex I to the Agreement)

>TABLE>

Appendix 3

ANNEX IV (referred to in Article 11)

Assured provision by China of textile raw materials

Minimum quantities which China undertakes to reserve for the Community each year:

>TABLE>

Appendix 4

ANNEX TO PROTOCOL E

>TABLE>

Appendix 5

Agreed Minute

Delegations of the European Commission and the People's Republic of China met in Brussels on 12 and 13 December 1995 to hold consultations on the basis of Article 14 of the Agreement between the European Community and the People's Republic of China on trade in textile products not covered by the MFA bilateral Agreement, initialled on 19 January 1995.

At the end of discussions concerning the implementation of Protocol E to the Agreement it was agreed that the European Commission will give favourable consideration to requests made by the People's Republic of China to open specific quantitative limits for textile products resulting from outward economic processing in China.

On the same occasion it was recalled that re-imports into the Community of the above products will be carried out up to the quantitative limits which will be agreed for the concerned categories, provided that they will be effected in accordance with the regulations on economic outward processing in force in the Community.

For the Delegation of the People's Republic of China

For the Delegation of the European Commission

Appendix 6

DECLARATION BY THE EUROPEAN COMMUNITY CONCERNING ANNEX IV AND DECLARATION MADE BY CHINA IN RESPONSE

1. Declaration by the European Community

The Community declares that it considers that China's undertaking under Annex IV to the Agreement (to reserve minimum quantities of textile raw materials to the Community industry and operators) can in no way be construed or applied in such a way that will negatively affect the rights granted to Community operators under Article 11, paragraph 1, of the Agreement and Article 12 of the Agreement initialled on 19 January 1995.

2. Declaration made by China in response

The Chinese Delegation declares that it considers that export of textile raw materials by China to the European Community has been developing normally within the availability of supply and in conformity with demand as stipulated in the bilateral Agreement, and that the Chinese side has no intention to impose any restrictions.

Therefore, the Chinese Delegation maintains that there is no necessity for the European Community to raise this issue by making a unilateral declaration.

Letter from the Government of the People's Republic of China

I have the honour to acknowledge receipt of your letter of . . . which reads as follows:

'Sir,

I have the honour to refer to the consultations held between our respective Delegations for the purpose of amending and extending the Agreement between the European Economic Community and the People's Republic of China on trade in textile products initialled on 9 December 1988, as last amended by Agreement initialled on 14 December 1994 (hereinafter referred to as "the Agreement").

2. As a result of the consultations, both Parties agreed to amend as of 1 January 1996 the following provisions of the Agreement:

2.1. The text of Article 5 is replaced by the following text:

"Article 5

1. In any Agreement year advance use of a portion of the quantitative limits established for the following Agreement year is authorized for each category of products up to 1% of the quantitative limit for the current Agreement year, with a possibility to reach 5% after consultations in conformity with Article 16, paragraph 2.

Amounts delivered in advance shall be deducted from the corresponding quantitative limits established for the following Agreement year.

2. Carryover to the corresponding quantitative limit for the following Agreement year of the amounts not used during Agreement year is authorized for each category of products up to 3% of the quantitative limit for the current Agreement year, with a possibility to reach 7% after consultations in conformity with Article 16, paragraph 2.

3. Transfers in respect of categories in Group I shall not be made from any category except as follows:

- Transfers between categories 2 and 3 may be made up to 4% of the quantitative limits for the category to which the transfer is made.
- Transfers from category 1 to categories 2 and 3 may be made up to 1% of the quantitative limits for the category to which the transfer is made.
- Transfers between categories 4 to 8 may be made up to 4% of the quantitative limits for the category to which the transfer is made.

Transfers into any categories in Groups II and III may be made from any category or categories in Groups I, II and III up to 6% of the quantitative limit for the category to which the transfer is made.

4. The table of equivalence applicable to the transfers referred to above is given in Annex I to this Agreement.

5. The increase in any category of products resulting from the cumultative application of the provisions in paragraphs 1, 2 and 3 above during an Agreement year shall not exceed 17%.

6. Prior notification shall be given by the authorities of China in the event of recourse to the provisions of paragraphs 1, 2 and 3 above."

2.2. The Text of Article 11 is replaced by the following text:

"Article 11

1. China will ensure that the supply to the Community industry of raw materials shall be made at conditions not less favourable than to Chinese domestic users.

2. Without prejudice to paragraph 1, China undertakes to take such measures as are required to make possible the export of the minimum annual quantities laid down in Annex IV of the products listed in that Annex.

In administering exports of the products referred to in subparagraph 1, China undertakes to give favourable consideration, taking into account its export possibilities, to requests from the Community textile industry with a view to meetings its needs.

For this purpose, the Community may submit to the Chinese authorities before the end of each year a list of interested manufacturers and processors and, if possible, the quantities of products requested by each of the firms in question.

The Contracting Parties are agreed that transactions in the products listed in Annex IV shall be carried out in accordance with Articles 8 and 9 of the Trade and Economic Cooperation Agreement taking account of market practice and normal trade flows."

2.3. The text of the second, third and fourth sentences of Article 20, paragraph 1, is replaced by the following text:

"It shall be applicable until 31 December 1998."

2.4. Annex I which sets out the products concerned by the Agreement is replaced by Appendix 1 to this letter.

2.5. Annex III which sets out the quantitative restrictions for exports from the People's Republic of China to the European Community is replaced for the period from 1 January 1996 to 31 December 1998 by Appendix 2 to this letter.

2.6. Annex IV which sets out the minimum quantities of textile raw materials which the People's Republic of China undertakes to reserve for the European Community each year is replaced for the period from 1 January 1996 to 31 December 1998 by Appendix 3 to this letter.

2.7. The Annex to Protocol E which sets out the quantitative restrictions for economic outward processing operations is replaced for the period from 1 January 1996 to 31 December 1998 by Appendix 4 to this letter.

2.8. In the Joint Declaration on the Berlin Fair set out in Appendix 8 to the Agreement initialled on 8 December 1992 the reference to "the years 1993, 1994, 1995" is replaced by the words "the years 1996, 1997 and 1998".

2.9. All references made in the Agreement to the "European Economic Community" shall be read as being made to the "European Community".

2.10. All Agreed Minutes and Declarations annexed to this letter shall form an integral part of the Agreement.

3. Should the People's Republic of China become a Member of the World Trade Organization before the date of expiry of the Agreement, the restrictions in force shall be phased out in the framework of the WTO Agreement on Textiles and Clothing.

4. I should be obliged if you could kindly confirm the acceptance of your Government of the foregoing. Should this be the case, this Agreement in the form of an Exchange of Letters shall enter into force on the first day of the month following the day on which the Parties have notified each other that the legal procedures necessary to this end have been completed. In the meantime, it shall be applied provisionally from, 1 January 1996 on conditions of reciprocity.

Please accept, Sir, the assurance of my highest consideration.'

I have the honour to confirm that my Government is in agreement with the contents of your letter.

Please accept, Sir, the assurance of my highest consideration.

For the Government of the People's Republic of China

ANNEX I

PRODUCTS REFERRED TO IN ARTICLE 1

1. When the constitutive material of the products of categories 1 to 114 is not specifically mentioned, these products are to be taken to be made exclusively of wool or of fine hair, of cotton or of man-made fibres.

2. Garments which are not recognizable as being garments for men or boys or as being garments for women or girls are classified with the latter.

3. Where the expression 'babies' garments' is used, this is meant to cover garments up to and including commercial size 86.

>TABLE>

>TABLE>

>TABLE>

>TABLE>

>TABLE>

>TABLE>

ANNEX 1A

>TABLE>

Appendix 2

ANNEX III (The full product descriptions of the categories listed in this Annex are to be found in Annex I to the Agreement)

>TABLE>

Appendix 3

ANNEX IV (referred to in Article 11)

Assured provision by China of textile raw materials

Minimum quantities which China undertakes to reserve for the Community each year:

>TABLE>

Appendix 4

ANNEX TO PROTOCOL E

>TABLE>

Appendix 5

Agreed Minute

Delegations of the European Commission and the People's Republic of China met in Brussels on 12 and 13 December 1995 to hold consultations on the basis of Article 14 of the Agreement between the European Community and the People's Republic of China on trade in textile products not covered by the MFA bilateral Agreement, initialled on 19 January 1995.

At the end of discussions concerning the implementation of Protocol E to the Agreement it was agreed that the European Commission will give favourable consideration to requests made by the People's Republic of China to open specific quantitative limits for textile products resulting from outward economic processing in China.

On the same occasion it was recalled that re-imports into the Community of the above products will be carried out up to the quantitative limits which will be agreed for the concerned categories, provided that they will be effected in accordance with the regulations on economic outward processing in force in the Community.

For the Delegation of the People's Republic of China

For the Delegation of the European Commission

Appendix 6

DECLARATION BY THE EUROPEAN COMMUNITY CONCERNING ANNEX IV AND DECLARATION MADE BY CHINA IN RESPONSE

1. Declaration by the European Community

The Community declares that it considers that China's undertaking under Annex IV to the Agreement (to reserve minimum quantities of textile raw materials to the Community industry and operators) can in no way be construed or applied in such a way that will negatively affect the rights granted to Community operators under Article 11, paragraph 1, of the Agreement and Article 12 of the Agreement initialled on 19 January 1995.

2. Declaration made by China in response

The Chinese Delegation declares that it considers that export of textile raw materials by China to the European Community has been developing normally within the availability of supply and in conformity with demand as stipulated in the bilateral Agreement, and that the Chinese side has no intention to impose any restrictions.

Therefore, the Chinese Delegation maintains that there is no necessity for the European Community to raise this issue by making a unilateral declaration.

Appendix 7

AGREED MINUTE

1. Delegations of the European Community and the People's Republic of China met in Brussels from 12 to 13 December 1995 in accordance with Article 7 of the bilateral Agreement on Trade in Textiles initialled on 9 December 1988, as last amended by the Exchanges of Letters initialled on 14 December 1994, and with Articles 17 and 18 of Protocol A to the Agreement to resume the consultations held in Beijing from 30 October to 3 November and in Brussels from 27 November to 1 December 1995 on the question of the circumvention of the Agreement and the search for a satisfactory solution.

2. The Community Delegation in the course of the discussion recalled

(a) that by Notes Verbales of 9 February and 16 June 1995, the Community had transmitted to the Chinese authorities documents showing that the following pieces of textile products had been imported into the Community either under a false declaration of origin or illegally without being declared for customs clearance:

15 367 194 pieces of category 4,

304 040 pieces of category 6,

20 016 pieces of category 7,

15 438 pieces of category 8 and

9 000 pieces (2 tonnes) of category 78;

(b) that on the basis of the enquiries carried out in the territory of the Community and third countries, it had appeared that these products physically emanated from the territory of the People's Republic of China before either having been transhipped and imported into the Community under false declaration of origin or introduced illegally without being declared for customs clearance, that there were sufficient grounds to conclude that they had for origin the People's Republic of China, that they had been imported into the Community without having been set off against the quantitative limits established under the bilateral Agreement, and that they had, therefore, been imported into the Community in circumvention of the Agreement.

3. The Chinese Delegation, after having carried out enquiries on the circumvention cases presented by the European Commission in the territory of the People's Republic of China, agreed with respect to the following pieces of textile products on the Chinese origin:

13 077 778 pieces of category 4,

121 904 pieces of category 6,

20 016 pieces of category 7,

15 438 pieces of category 8 and

9 000 pieces (2 tonnes) of category 78.

The Chinese Delegation contested the Chinese origin in regard to 2 298 416 pieces of textile products of category 4 and 182 136 pieces of textile products of category 6.

4. The Chinese Delegation maintained that quota deductions should not be carried out in cases where the Community authorities have not demonstrated the intentional involvement of Chinese companies in the fraudulent importation into the Community.

5. The Community Delegation contested this opinion and maintained the view that, under the bilateral Agreement, nothing compelled the Community to demonstrate an active involvement of Chinese companies in order to seek an adjustment of the quantitative limits, equivalent to the quantities imported in circumvention of the Agreement.

6. As a consequence, the Delegation of the Community maintained that an adjustment be operated on the quantitative limits applicable to categories 4, 6, 7, 8 and 78.

7. While holding its positions unchanged, the Chinese Delegation accepted as a sign of goodwill that an adjustment be made on the 1995 quantitative limits applicable to categories 4, 6, 7, 8 and 78 as follows:

cat. 4: 13 077 778 pieces

cat. 6: 121 904 pieces

cat. 7: 20 016 pieces

cat. 8: 15 438 pieces

cat. 78: 9 000 pieces (2 tonnes)

8. In the course of consultations both parties reaffirmed the usefulness of strengthening cooperation in order to prevent circumvention of the provisions of the bilateral Agreement. Such cooperation should also provide for an exchange of information regarding Chinese exports to third countries and territories.

Brussels, 13 December 1995.

For the People's Republic of China

For the European Community

(1) For the purpose of setting off exports against the agreed quantitative limits a conversion rate of 5 garments (other than babies' garments) of a maximum commercial size of 130 cm, for 3 garments whose commercial size exceeds 130 cm may be applied for up to 5% of the quantitative limits.

(2) These figures include the following quantities reserved for European industry for a period of 180 days each year:

Discarding a TABLE

>TABLE>

(3) For products of category 5 (other than anoraks, windcheaters, waister jackets and the like) of fine animal hair, the following sublimits apply within the quantitative limits established for category 5:

Discarding a TABLE

>TABLE>

(4) These figures include the following quantities reserved for European industry for a period of 180 days each year:

Discarding a TABLE

>TABLE>

The following additional quantities of shorts (CN codes 6203 41 90, 6203 42 90, 6203 43 90 and 6203 49 50) may be exported to the EEC by China:

Discarding a TABLE

>TABLE>

(5) These figures include the following quantities reserved for the European industry for a period of 180 days each year:

Discarding a TABLE

>TABLE>

(6) These figures include the following quantities reserved for the European industry for a period of 180 days each year:

Discarding a TABLE

>TABLE>

(7) These figures include the following quantities reserved for the European industry for a period of 180 days each year:

Discarding a TABLE

>TABLE>

(8) These figures include the following quantities reserved for the European industry for a period of 180 days each year:

Discarding a TABLE

>TABLE>

(9) For the purpose of setting off exports against the agreed quantitative limits a conversion rate of 5 garments (other than babies' garments) of a maximum commercial size of 130 cm, for 3 garments whose commercial size exceeds 130 cm may be applied for up to 5% of the quantitative limits.

(10) For the purpose of setting off exports against the agreed quantitative limits a conversion rate of 5 garments (other than babies' garments) of a maximum commercial size of 130 cm, for 3 garments whose commercial size exceeds 130 cm may be applied for up to 5% of the quantitative limits.

(11) These figures include the following quantities reserved for European industry for a period of 180 days each year:

Discarding a TABLE

>TABLE>

(12) For the purpose of setting off exports against the agreed quantitative limits a conversion rate of 5 garments (other than babies' garments) of a maximum commercial size of 130 cm, for 3 garments whose commercial size exceeds 130 cm may be applied for up to 5% of the quantitative limits.

(13) These figures include the following quantities reserved for European industry for a period of 180 days each year:

Discarding a TABLE

>TABLE>

(14) For the purpose of setting off exports against the agreed quantitative limits a conversion rate of 5 garments (other than babies' garments) of a maximum commercial size of 130 cm, for 3 garments whose commercial size exceeds 130 cm may be applied for up to 5% of the quantitative limits.

(15) These figures include the following quantities reserved for European industry for a period of 180 days each year:

Discarding a TABLE

>TABLE>

(16) For products of category 5 (other than anoraks, windcheaters, waister jackets and the like) of fine animal hair, the following sublimits apply within the quantitative limits established for category 5:

Discarding a TABLE

>TABLE>

(17) These figures include the following quantities reserved for European industry for a period of 180 days each year:

Discarding a TABLE

>TABLE>

The following additional quantities of shorts (CN codes 6203 41 90, 6203 42 90, 6203 43 90 and 6203 49 50) may be exported to the EEC by China:

Discarding a TABLE

>TABLE>

(18) These figures include the following quantities reserved for the European industry for a period of 180 days each year:

Discarding a TABLE

>TABLE>

(19) These figures include the following quantities reserved for the European industry for a period of 180 days each year:

Discarding a TABLE

>TABLE>

(20) These figures include the following quantities reserved for the European industry for a period of 180 days each year:

Discarding a TABLE

>TABLE>

(21) These figures include the following quantities reserved for the European industry for a period of 180 days each year:

Discarding a TABLE

>TABLE>

(22) For the purpose of setting off exports against the agreed quantitative limits a conversion rate of 5 garments (other than babies' garments) of a maximum commercial size of 130 cm, for 3 garments whose commercial size exceeds 130 cm may be applied for up to 5% of the quantitative limits.

(23) For the purpose of setting off exports against the agreed quantitative limits a conversion rate of 5 garments (other than babies' garments) of a maximum commercial size of 130 cm, for 3 garments whose commercial size exceeds 130 cm may be applied for up to 5% of the quantitative limits.

(24) These figures include the following quantities reserved for European industry for a period of 180 days each year:

Discarding a TABLE

>TABLE>

(25) For the purpose of setting off exports against the agreed quantitative limits a conversion rate of 5 garments (other than babies' garments) of a maximum commercial size of 130

cm, for 3 garments whose commercial size exceeds 130 cm may be applied for up to 5% of the quantitative limits.

(26) These figures include the following quantities reserved for European industry for a period of 180 days each year:

Discarding a TABLE

>TABLE>

(27) China will accord favourable consideration to requests from Community economic operators for additional quantities, within the limits of availability.

(28) China will accord favourable consideration to requests from Community economic operators for additional quantities, within the limits of availability.

In 1998 the EU and China concluded a further textiles agreement (see Document 2.8). It aimed, on the European side, to ensure implementation of previously agreed provisions benefiting European industry, notably most-favoured-national treatment, national treatment and access to raw materials. At the time China was not yet a member of the WTO.

### Document 2.8: Agreement further amending the 1988 Textiles Agreement

**Agreement in the form of an exchange of letters between the European Community and the People's Republic of China amending the Agreement between the European Economic Community and the People's Republic of China on trade in textile products as last amended by Agreements initialled on 13 December 1995 – Agreed Minutes**

*OJ L 12, 16.1.1999, p. 28–71 (ES, DA, DE, EL, EN, FR, IT, NL, PT, FI, SV)*

AGREEMENT IN THE FORM OF AN EXCHANGE OF LETTERS between the European Community and the People's Republic of China amending the Agreement between the European Economic Community and the People's Republic of China on trade in textile products as last amended by Agreements initialled on 13 December 1995

Letter from the Council of the European Union

Sir,

1.1 have the honour to refer to the consultations held between our respective delegations for the purpose of amending and extending the Agreement between the European Economic Community and the People's Republic of China on trade in textile products initialled on 9 December 1988, as last amended by Agreements initialled on 13 December 1995 (hereinafter referred to as 'the Agreement').

2. As a result of the consultations, both Parties agreed to amend as of 1 January 1999 the following provisions of the Agreement:

2.1. The text of Article 12 shall be amended by the addition of the following paragraph:

'3. China confirms that the benefit of any concessions made or advantages extended by China to third states in respect of trade in textile and clothing products will be automatically and immediately extended also to the European Community on the basis of MFN in accordance with the provisions of Article 3 of the Trade and Economic Cooperation Agreement between the Parties.'

2.2. The text of the second sentence of Article 20(1) shall be replaced by the following:

'It shall be applicable until 31 December 1999.'

2.3. The text of Article 21 shall be replaced by the following:

'This Agreement shall be drawn up in two copies in the Danish, Dutch, English, Finnish, French, German, Greek, Italian, Portuguese, Spanish, Swedish and Chinese languages, each of these texts being equally authentic.'

2.4. Annex I which sets out the products concerned by the Agreement shall be replaced by Appendix 1 to this letter.

2.5. Annex III shall be replaced by Appendix 2 to this letter for the year 1999.

2.6. The Annex to Protocol E which sets out the quantitative restrictions for economic outward processing operations shall be replaced by Appendix 3 to this letter for the year 1999.

2.7. In the Joint Declaration on Berlin Fair set out in Appendix 8 to the Agreement initialled on 8 December 1992, the reference to 'the years 1993, 1994, 1995' shall be replaced by '1999'.

3. All agreed minutes and declarations annexed to this letter shall form an integral part of the Agreement.

4. Should the People's Republic of China become a Member of the World Trade Organisation before the date of expiry of this Agreement, the restrictions in force shall be phased out in the framework of the WTO Agreement on Textiles and Clothing and China's Protocol of Accession to the WTO.

5.1 should be obliged if you could kindly confirm the acceptance of your Government of the foregoing. Should this be the case, this Agreement in the form of an exchange of letters shall enter into force on the first day of the month following the day on which the Parties have notified each other that the legal procedures necessary to this end have been completed. In the meantime, it shall be applied provisionally from 1 January 1999 on conditions of reciprocity.

Please accept, Sir, the assurance of my highest consideration. For the Council of the European Union The President

APPENDIX 1

'ANNEX I PRODUCTS REFERRED TO IN ARTICLE 1

1. When the constitutive material of the products of categories 1 to 114 is not specifically mentioned, these products are to be taken to be made exclusively of wool or of fine hair, of cotton or of man-made fibres (1).

2. Garments which are not recognisable as being garments for men or boys or as being garments for women or girls are classified with the latter.

3. Where the expression "babies' garments" is used, this is meant to cover garments up to and including commercial size 86.

>TABLE>

>TABLE>

>TABLE>

>TABLE>

>TABLE>

>TABLE>

ANNEX IA

>TABLE>

(1) Where there is an "ex" symbol in front of a CN code, the products covered in each category are determined by the scope of the CN code and by that of the corresponding description.'

APPENDIX 2

'ANNEX III

(The full product descriptions of the categories listed in this Annex are to be found in Annex I to the Agreement)

COMMUNITY QUANTITATIVE LIMITS

>TABLE>

APPENDIX 3

'ANNEX TO PROTOCOL E
OUTWARD PROCESSING TRAFFIC COMMUNITY QUANTITATIVE LIMITS

>TABLE>

AGREED MINUTE CONCERNING ARTICLE 11

In the context of the Agreement in the form of an exchange of letters between the European Community and the People's Republic of China amending the Agreement between the European Economic Community and the People's Republic of China on trade in textile products as last amended by Agreements initialled on 13 December 1995, the European Community again raised the question of continuing difficulties in the implementation of provisions of Article 11 of the Agreement, in particular paragraph 1 thereof concerning supplies of raw materials from China at conditions not less favourable than to Chinese domestic users.

In this context, China outlined the measures which it had already taken to give effect to Article 11(1), and in particular to the increase in the reimbursement in VAT from 6 to 11% on the export of raw silk. China further undertook to examine all remaining charges and levies in order to ensure the implementation of Article 11(1).

The Parties agreed that, in the event of any difficulties in provision and delivery of raw materials, consultations may be held with a view to finding a mutually satisfactory solution.

For the European Community For the People's Republic of China

AGREED MINUTE ON THE INDUSTRY RESERVE

In the context of the Agreement in the form of an exchange of letters between the European Community and the People's Republic of China amending the Agreement between the European Economic Community and the People's Republic of China on trade in textile products as last amended by Agreements initialled on 13 December 1995, China took note of concerns expressed by the European Community regarding the implementation of Article 3(2) and (3) and the footnotes to Annex III setting out quantities reserved for European industry. With a view to strengthening a mutual understanding and cooperation in this field the Chinese side put forward the following account of the current procedure in force regarding the implementation of the industry reserve:

- the Chinese authorities will take the list of Community enterprises provided by the European Community authorities as being those users entitled to benefit from the industry reserve,
- Community industry will make contact with Chinese exporters with a view to entering into contracts with the Chinese manufacturers and exporters,
- the Chinese manufacturers or exporters will submit applications for use of the industry reserve together with the contracts to MOFTEC via the relevant foreign trade administrative bodies,
- within the limits of the reserve, MOFTEC will grant quota to Chinese manufacturers or exporters for the duration of the reserve, according to the relevant regulations,
- thereafter, the relevant foreign trade administrative bodies will issue export licences to allow the fulfilment of purchasing contracts for Community users notified on the lists provided by the Community authorities.

In this regard, the Chinese authorities undertake:

- to operate the system promptly and in a non-discriminatory manner,
- to provide the names and addresses of the relevant foreign trade administrative bodies,
- to provide texts of the relevant regulations as soon as they are available,
- to ensure that export licences under this system are identified as industry reserve,
- to supply separate statistical information concerning licences issued pursuant to these provisions,
- to cooperate with the European Community authorities to ensure that licences issued pursuant to these provisions are identified within the exchanges of information via the SIGL network.

The Parties agreed that, in the event of any difficulties in the application of the provisions relating to the 'industry reserve', consultations may be held with a view to finding a mutually satisfactory solution.

For the European Community For the People's Republic of China

Letter from the Government of the People's Republic of China

Sir,

I have the honour to acknowledge receipt of your letter which reads as follows:

Sir,

1. I have the honour to refer to the consultations held between our respective delegations for the purpose of amending and extending the Agreement between the European Economic Community and the People's Republic of China on trade in textile products initialled on 9

December 1988, as last amended by Agreements initialled on 13 December 1995 (hereinafter referred to as "the Agreement").

2. As a result of the consultations, both Parties agreed to amend as of 1 January 1999 the following provisions of the Agreement:

2.1. The text of Article 12 shall be amended by the addition of the following paragraph:

"3. China confirms that the benefit of any concessions made or advantages extended by China to third states in respect of trade in textile and clothing products will be automatically and immediately extended also to the European Community on the basis of MFN in accordance with the provisions of Article 3 of the Trade and Economic Cooperation Agreement between the Parties."

2.2. The text of the second sentence of Article 20(1), shall be replaced by the following text:

"It shall be applicable until 31 December 1999."

2.3. The text of Article 21 shall be replaced by the following text:

"This Agreement shall be drawn up in two copies in the Danish, Dutch, English, Finnish, French, German, Greek, Italian, Portuguese, Spanish, Swedish and Chinese languages, each of these texts being equally authentic."

2.4. Annex I which sets out the products concerned by the Agreement shall be replaced by Appendix 1 to this letter.

2.5. Annex III shall be replaced by Appendix 2 to this letter for the year 1999.

2.6. The Annex to Protocol E which sets out the quantitative restrictions for economic outward processing operations shall be replaced by Appendix 3 to this letter for the year 1999.

2.7. In the Joint Declaration on Berlin Fair set out in Appendix 8 to the Agreement initialled on 8 December 1992 the reference to "the years 1993, 1994,1995" shall be replaced by "1999".

3. All Agreed Minutes and Declarations annexed to this letter shall form an integral part of the Agreement.

4. Should the People's Republic of China become a Member of the World Trade Organisation before the date of expiry of this Agreement, the restrictions in force shall be phased out in the framework of the WTO Agreement on Textiles and Clothing and China's Protocol of Accession to the WTO.

5.1 should be obliged if you could kindly confirm the acceptance of your Government of the foregoing. Should this be the case, this Agreement in the form of an exchange of letters shall enter into force on the first day of the month following the day on which the Parties have notified each other that the legal procedures necessary to this end have been completed. In the meantime, it shall be applied provisionally from 1 January 1999 on conditions of reciprocity.'

I have the honour to confirm that my Government is in agreement with the contents of your letter.

Please accept, Sir, the assurance of my highest consideration.

For the Governmentof the People's Republic of China

APPENDIX 1

ANNEX I
PRODUCTS REFERRED TO IN ARTICLE 1

1. When the constitutive material of the products of categories 1 to 114 is not specifically mentioned, these products are to be taken to be made exclusively of wool or of fine hair, of cotton or of man-made fibres (1).

2. Garments which are not recognisable as being garments for men or boys or as being garments for women or girls are classified with the latter.

3. Where the expression "babies' garments" is used, this is meant to cover garments up to and including commercial size 86.

>TABLE>

>TABLE>

>TABLE>

>TABLE>

>TABLE>

>TABLE>

ANNEX IA

>TABLE>

(1) Where there is an "ex" symbol in front of a CN code, the products covered in each category are determined by the scope of the CN code and by that of the corresponding description.'

APPENDIX 2

'ANNEX III

(The full product descriptions of the categories listed in this Annex are to be found in Annex I to the Agreement)

COMMUNITY QUANTITATIVE LIMITS >TABLE>

APPENDIX 3

'ANNEX TO PROTOCOL E
OUTWARD PROCESSING TRAFFIC COMMUNITY QUANTITATIVE LIMITS

>TABLE>

AGREED MINUTE CONCERNING ARTICLE 11

In the context of the Agreement in the form of an exchange of letters between the European Community and the People's Republic of China amending the Agreement between the European Economic Community and the People's Republic of China on trade in textile products as last amended by Agreements initialled on 13 December 1995, the European Community again raised the question of continuing difficulties in the implementation of provisions of Article 11 of the Agreement, in particular paragraph 1 thereof concerning supplies of raw materials from China at conditions not less favourable than to Chinese domestic users.

In this context, China outlined the measures which it had already taken to give effect to Article 11(1), and in particular to the increase in the reimbursement in VAT from 6 to 11% on the export of raw silk. China further undertook to examine all remaining charges and levies in order to ensure the implementation of Article 11(1).

The Parties agreed that, in the event of any difficulties in provision and delivery of raw materials, consultations may be held with a view to finding a mutually satisfactory solution.

For the People's Republic of China For the European Community

AGREED MINUTE ON THE INDUSTRY RESERVE

In the context of the Agreement in the form of an exchange of letters between the European Community and the People's Republic of China amending the Agreement between the European Economic Community and the People's Republic of China on trade in textile products as last amended by Agreements initialled on 13 December 1995, China took note of concerns expressed by the European Community regarding the implementation of Article 3(2) and (3) and the footnotes to Annex III setting out quantities reserved for European industry. With a view to strengthening a mutual understanding and cooperation in this field the Chinese side put forward the following account of the current procedure in force regarding the implementation of the industry reserve:

- the Chinese authorities will take the list of Community enterprises provided by the European Community authorities as being those users entitled to benefit from the industry reserve,
- Community industry will make contact with Chinese exporters with a view to entering into contracts with the Chinese manufacturers and exporters,
- the Chinese manufacturers or exporters will submit applications for use of the industry reserve together with the contracts to MOFTEC via the relevant foreign trade administrative bodies,
- within the limits of the reserve, MOFTEC will grant quota to Chinese manufacturers or exporters for the duration of the reserve, according to the relevant regulations,
- thereafter, the relevant foreign trade administrative bodies will issue export licences to allow the fulfilment of purchasing contracts for Community users notified on the lists provided by the Community authorities.

In this regard, the Chinese authorities undertake:

- to operate the system promptly and in a non-discriminatory manner,
- to provide the names and addresses of the relevant foreign trade administrative bodies,
- to provide texts of the relevant regulations as soon as they are available,
- to ensure that export licences under this system are identified as industry reserve,
- to supply separate statistical information concerning licences issued pursuant to these provisions,
- to cooperate with the European Community authorities to ensure that licences issued pursuant to these provisions are identified within the exchanges of information via the SIGL network.

The Parties agreed that, in the event of any difficulties in the application of the provisions relating to the 'industry reserve', consultations may be held with a view to finding a mutually satisfactory solution.

For the People's Republic of China For the European Community

As the WTO negotiations neared an end, the EU and China updated and extended earlier textile agreements, pending China's accession to the WTO In late 1999 the EU and China concluded an agreement on both MFA and non-MFA textile products (see Document 2.9), amending and extending the early agreements until 31 December 2000.

### Document 2.9: 1999 Agreement on MFA and Non-MFA Textile Products

II

(Acts whose publication is not obligatory)

**COUNCIL DECISION of 21 December 1999 on the provisional application of the Agreement in the form of an Exchange of Letters amending the Agreements between the European Community and the People's Republic of China on trade in textile products (1999/876/EC)**

THE COUNCIL OF THE EUROPEAN UNION,

Having regard to the Treaty establishing the European Community, and in particular Article 133, in conjunction with Article 300(2), first sentence thereof,

Having regard to the proposal from the Commission,

Whereas:

(1) the Commission has negotiated on behalf of the Community an Agreement in the form of an Exchange of Letters between the European Community and the People's Republic of China amending the Agreement between the European Community and the People's Republic of China on trade in textile products, as last amended by the Agreement in the form of an Exchange of Letters initialled on 20 November 1998 and amending the Agreement between the European Community and the People's Republic of China initialled on 19 January 1995 on trade in textile products not covered by the MFA bilateral Agreement on trade in textile products;

(2) the Agreement in the form of an Exchange of Letters should be applied on a provisional basis from 1 January 2000 pending the completion of the procedures necessary for its conclusion, subject to reciprocal provisional application of the Agreement by the People's Republic of China,

HAS DECIDED AS FOLLOWS:

*Article 1*

The Agreement in the form of an Exchange of Letters between the European Community and the People's Republic of China initialled in Beijing on 6 December 1999 amending the Agreement between the European Economic Community and the People's Republic of China on trade in textile products as last amended by an Agreement initialled on 20

November 1999 and amending the Agreement between the European Community and the People's Republic of China initialled on 19 January 1995 on trade in textile products not covered by the MFA bilateral Agreement shall be applied on a provisional basis from 1 January 2000 pending its formal conclusion and subject to reciprocal provisional application of the Agreement in the form of an Exchange of Letters by the People's Republic of China.

The text of the Agreement in the Form of an Exchange of Letters is attached to this Decision.

*Article 2*

This Decision shall be published in the Official journal of the European Communities.

Done at Brussels, 21 December 1999.

For the Council
The President
T.HALONEN

**AGREEMENT IN THE FORM OF EXCHANGE OF LETTERS**
**between the European Community and the People's Republic of China initialled in Beijing on 6 December 1999 amending the Agreement between the European Economic Community and the People's Republic of China on trade in textile products as last amended by an agreement initialled on 20 November 1999 and amending the Agreement between the European Community and the People's Republic of China initialled on 19 January 1995 on trade in textile products not covered by the MFA bilateral Agreement**

A. *Letter from the Council of the European Union*

Sir,

1. I have the honour to refer to the consultations held between our respective delegations for the purpose of amending and extending both the Agreement between the European Economic Community and the People's Republic of China on trade in textile products initialled on 9 December 1988, as last amended by Agreements initialled on 20 November 1998 (hereinafter referred to as 'the MFA Agreement') and the Agreement between the European Community and the People's Republic of China initialled on 19 January 1995 on trade in textile products not covered by the MFA bilateral Agreement (hereinafter referred to as 'the non-MFA Agreement').

2. As a result of the consultations, both Parties agree to amend as of 1 January 2000 the following provisions of the MFA Agreement in order to ensure stability of trade while they continue their efforts to agree on the appropriate terms and conditions of an agreement governing future trade which, once applied by both Parties, will substitute for the present agreement:

2.1. The text of the second sentence of Article 20, paragraph 1 is replaced by the following text:

'It shall be applicable until 31 December 2000.'

2.2. Annex I which sets out the products concerned by the Agreement is replaced by Appendix 1 to this letter.

2.3. Annex III is replaced by Appendix 2 to this letter for the year 2000.

2.4. The Annex to Protocol E which sets out the quantitative restrictions for economic outward processing operations is replaced by Appendix 3 to this letter for the year 2000.

2.5. In the Joint Declaration on Berlin Fair set out in Appendix 8 to the Agreement initialled on 8 December 1992 the reference to 'the year 1999' is replaced by "the year 2000'.

3. As a result of the consultations, both Parties agree to amend as of 1 January 2000 the following

provisions of the non-MFA Agreement in order to ensure stability of trade while they continue their efforts to agree on the appropriate terms and conditions of an agreement governing future trade which, once applied by both Parties, will substitute for the present agreement:

3.1. The text of the second sentence of Article 17, paragraph 1, is replaced by the following text:

. 'It shall apply with effect from 1 January 1995 and be applicable until 31 December 2000.'

3.2. Annex I which sets out the products concerned by the Agreement is replaced by Appendix 4 to this letter.

3.3. Annex II is replaced by Appendix 5 to this letter for the year 2000.

3.4. The Annex to Protocol B is replaced by Appendix 6 for the year 2000.

4. All Agreed Minutes and Declarations annexed to this letter shall form an integral part of the relevant Agreement to which they refer.

5. Should the People's Republic of China become a Member of the World Trade Organisation before the date of expiry of this Agreement, the restrictions in force shall be phased out in the framework of the WTO Agreement on Textiles and Clothing and China's Protocol of Accession to the WTO.

6. I should be obliged if you could kindly confirm the acceptance of your Government of the foregoing. Should this be the case, this Agreement in form of Exchange of Letters shall enter into force on the first day of the month following the day on which the Parties have notified each other that the legal procedures necessary to this end have been completed. In the meantime, it shall be applied provisionally from 1 January 2000 on conditions of reciprocity.

Please accept, Sir, the assurance of my highest consideration.

For the Council of the European Union

B. *Letter from the Government of the People's Republic of China*

Sir,

I have the honour to acknowledge receipt of your letter of ... which reads as follows:

Sir,

1. I have the honour to refer to the consultations held between our respective delegations for the purpose of amending and extending both the Agreement between the European Economic Community and the People's Republic of China on trade in textile products initialled on 9 December 1988, as last amended by Agreements initialled on 20 November

1998 (hereinafter referred to as "the MFA Agreement") and the Agreement between the European Community and the People's Republic of China initialled on 19 January 1995 on trade in textile products not covered by the MFA bilateral Agreement (hereinafter referred to as "the non-MFA Agreement").

2. As a result of the consultations, both Parties agree to amend as of 1 January 2000 the following provisions of the MFA Agreement in order to ensure stability of trade while they continue their efforts to agree on the appropriate terms and conditions of an agreement governing future trade which, once applied by both Parties, will substitute for the present agreement:

2.1. The text of the second sentence of Article 20, paragraph 1 is replaced by the following text:

"It shall be applicable until 31 December 2000."

2.2. Annex I which sets out the products concerned by the Agreement is replaced by Appendix 1 to this letter.

2.3. Annex III is replaced by Appendix 2 to this letter for the year 2000.

2.4. The Annex to Protocol E which sets out the quantitative restrictions for economic outward processing operations is replaced by Appendix 3 to this letter for the year 2000.

2.5. In the Joint Declaration on Berlin Fair set out in Appendix 8 to the Agreement initialled on 8 December 1992 the reference to "the year 1999" is replaced by "the year 2000".

3. As a result of the consultations, both Parties agree to amend as of 1 January 2000 the following provisions of the non-MFA Agreement in order to ensure stability of trade while they continue their efforts to agree on the appropriate terms and conditions of an agreement governing future trade which, once applied by both Parties, will substitute for the present agreement:

3.1. The text of the second sentence of Article 17, paragraph 1, is replaced by the following text:

"It shall apply with effect from 1 January 1995 and be applicable until 31 December 2000."

3.2. Annex I which sets out the products concerned by the Agreement is replaced by Appendix 4 to this letter.

" 3.3. Annex II is replaced by Appendix 5 to this letter for the year 2000. 3.4. The Annex to Protocol B is replaced by Appendix 6 for the year 2000.

4. All Agreed Minutes and Declarations annexed to this letter shall form an integral part of the relevant Agreement to which they refer.

5. Should the People's Republic of China become a Member of the World Trade Organisation before the date of expiry of this Agreement, the restrictions in force shall be phased out in the framework of the WTO Agreement on Textiles and Clothing and China's Protocol of Accession to the WTO.

6. I should be obliged if you could kindly confirm the acceptance of your Government of the foregoing. Should this be the case, this Agreement in form of Exchange of Letters shall enter into force on the first day of the month following the day on which the Parties

have notified each other that the legal procedures necessary to this end have been completed. In the meantime, it shall be applied provisionally from 1 January 2000 on conditions of reciprocity.

Please accept, Sir, the assurance of my highest consideration.'

I have the honour to confirm that my Government is in agreement with the contents of your letter. Please accept, Sir, the assurance of my highest consideration.

For the Government of the People's Republic of China

*Appendix 1*

*'ANNEX I*

**PRODUCTS REFERRED TO IN ARTICLE 1**

1. When the constitutive material of the products of categories 1 to 114 is not specifically mentioned, these products are to be taken to be made exclusively of wool or of fine hair, of cotton or of man-made fibres ([1]).

2. Garments which are not recognisable as being garments for men or boys or as being garments for women or girls are classified with the latter.

3. Where the expression "babies' garments" is used, this is meant to cover garments up to and including commercial size 86.

GROUP I A

| Category | Description CN code 1999 | | | | | Table of equivalence | |
|---|---|---|---|---|---|---|---|
| | | | | | | pieces/kg | g/piece |
| (1) | (2) | | | | | (3) | (4) |
| 1 | Cotton yarn, not put up for retail sale | | | | | | |
| | 5204 11 00 | 5205 23 00 | 5205 42 00 | 5206 15 10 | 5206 34 00 | | |
| | 5204 19 00 | 5205 24 00 | 5205 43 00 | 5206 15 90 | 5206 35 00 | | |
| | | 5205 26 00 | 5205 44 00 | 5206 21 00 | 5206 41 00 | | |
| | 5205 11 00 | 5205 27 00 | 5205 46 00 | 5206 22 00 | 5206 42 00 | | |
| | 5205 12 00 | 5205 28 00 | 5205 47 00 | 5206 23 00 | 5206 43 00 | | |
| | 5205 13 00 | 5205 31 00 | 5205 48 00 | 5206 24 00 | 5206 44 00 | | |
| | 5205 14 00 | 5205 32 00 | | 5206 25 10 | 5206 45 00 | | |
| | 5205 15 10 | 5205 33 00 | 5206 11 00 | 5206 25 90 | | | |
| | 5205 15 90 | 5205 34 00 | 5206 12 00 | 5206 31 00 | ex 5604 90 00 | | |
| | 5205 21 00 | 5205 35 00 | 5206 13 00 | 5206 32 00 | | | |
| | 5205 22 00 | 5205 41 00 | 5206 14 00 | 5206 33 00 | | | |
| 2 | Woven fabrics of cotton, other than gauze, terry fabrics, pile fabrics, chenille fabrics, tulle and other net fabrics | | | | | | |
| | 5208 11 10 | 5208 22 99 | 5208 49 00 | 5209 31 00 | 5210 11 90 | | |
| | 5208 11 90 | 5208 23 00 | 5208 51 00 | 5209 32 00 | 5210 12 00 | | |
| | 5208 12 16 | 5208 29 00 | 5208 52 10 | 5209 39 00 | 5210 19 00 | | |
| | 5208 12 19 | 5208 31 00 | 5208 52 90 | 5209 41 00 | 5210 21 10 | | |
| | 5208 12 96 | 5208 32 16 | 5208 53 00 | 5209 42 00 | 5210 21 90 | | |
| | 5208 12 99 | 5208 32 19 | 5208 59 00 | 5209 43 00 | 5210 22 00 | | |
| | 5208 13 00 | 5208 32 96 | | 5209 49 10 | 5210 29 00 | | |
| | 5208 19 00 | 5208 32 99 | 5209 11 00 | 5209 49 90 | 5210 31 10 | | |
| | 5208 21 10 | 5208 33 00 | 5209 12 00 | 5209 51 00 | 5210 31 90 | | |
| | 5208 21 90 | 5208 39 00 | 5209 19 00 | 5209 52 00 | 5210 32 00 | | |
| | 5208 22 16 | 5208 41 00 | 5209 21 00 | 5209 59 00 | 5210 39 00 | | |
| | 5208 22 19 | 5208 42 00 | 5209 22 00 | | 5210 41 00 | | |
| | 5208 22 96 | 5208 43 00 | 5209 29 00 | 5210 11 10 | 5210 42 00 | | |

([1]) Where there is an "ex" symbol in front of a CN code, the products covered in each category are determined by the scope of the CN code and by that of the corresponding description.

| (1) | (2) | | | | | (3) | (4) |
|---|---|---|---|---|---|---|---|
| 2 *(cont'd)* | 5210 49 00 | 5211 29 00 | 5211 52 00 | 5212 14 90 | 5212 24 90 | | |
| | 5210 51 00 | 5211 31 00 | 5211 59 00 | 5212 15 10 | 5212 25 10 | | |
| | 5210 52 00 | 5211 32 00 | | 5212 15 90 | 5212 25 90 | | |
| | 5210 59 00 | 5211 39 00 | 5212 11 10 | 5212 21 10 | | | |
| | | 5211 41 00 | 5212 11 90 | 5212 21 90 | ex 5811 00 00 | | |
| | 5211 11 00 | 5211 42 00 | 5212 12 10 | 5212 22 10 | | | |
| | 5211 12 00 | 5211 43 00 | 5212 12 90 | 5212 22 90 | ex 6308 00 00 | | |
| | 5211 19 00 | 5211 49 10 | 5212 13 10 | 5212 23 10 | | | |
| | 5211 21 00 | 5211 49 90 | 5212 13 90 | 5212 23 90 | | | |
| | 5211 22 00 | 5211 51 00 | 5212 14 10 | 5212 24 10 | | | |
| 2 (a) | Of which: Other than unbleached or bleached | | | | | | |
| | 5208 31 00 | 5208 53 00 | 5210 31 10 | 5211 41 00 | 5212 15 90 | | |
| | 5208 32 16 | 5208 59 00 | 5210 31 90 | 5211 42 00 | 5212 23 10 | | |
| | 5208 32 19 | | 5210 32 00 | 5211 43 00 | 5212 23 90 | | |
| | 5208 32 96 | 5209 31 00 | 5210 39 00 | 5211 49 10 | 5212 24 10 | | |
| | 5208 32 99 | 5209 32 00 | 5210 41 00 | 5211 49 90 | 5212 24 90 | | |
| | 5208 33 00 | 5209 39 00 | 5210 42 00 | 5211 51 00 | 5212 25 10 | | |
| | 5208 39 00 | 5209 41 00 | 5210 49 00 | 5211 52 00 | 5212 25 90 | | |
| | 5208 41 00 | 5209 42 00 | 5210 51 00 | 5211 59 00 | | | |
| | 5208 42 00 | 5209 43 00 | 5210 52 00 | | ex 5811 00 00 | | |
| | 5208 43 00 | 5209 49 10 | 5210 59 00 | 5212 13 10 | | | |
| | 5208 49 00 | 5209 49 90 | | 5212 13 90 | ex 6308 00 00 | | |
| | 5208 51 00 | 5209 51 00 | 5211 31 00 | 5212 14 10 | | | |
| | 5208 52 10 | 5209 52 00 | 5211 32 00 | 5212 14 90 | | | |
| | 5208 52 90 | 5209 59 00 | 5211 39 00 | 5212 15 10 | | | |
| 3 | Woven fabrics of synthetic fibres (discontinuous or waste) other than narrow woven fabrics, pile fabrics (including terry fabrics) and chenille fabrics | | | | | | |
| | 5512 11 00 | 5513 22 00 | 5514 23 00 | 5515 13 19 | 5515 91 90 | | |
| | 5512 19 10 | 5513 23 00 | 5514 29 00 | 5515 13 91 | 5515 92 11 | | |
| | 5512 19 90 | 5513 29 00 | 5514 31 00 | 5515 13 99 | 5515 92 19 | | |
| | 5512 21 00 | 5513 31 00 | 5514 32 00 | 5515 19 10 | 5515 92 91 | | |
| | 5512 29 10 | 5513 32 00 | 5514 33 00 | 5515 19 30 | 5515 92 99 | | |
| | 5512 29 90 | 5513 33 00 | 5514 39 00 | 5515 19 90 | 5515 99 10 | | |
| | 5512 91 00 | 5513 39 00 | 5514 41 00 | 5515 21 10 | 5515 99 30 | | |
| | 5512 99 10 | 5513 41 00 | 5514 42 00 | 5515 21 30 | 5515 99 90 | | |
| | 5512 99 90 | 5513 42 00 | 5514 43 00 | 5515 21 90 | | | |
| | | 5513 43 00 | 5514 49 00 | 5515 22 11 | 5803 90 30 | | |
| | 5513 11 20 | 5513 49 00 | | 5515 22 19 | | | |
| | 5513 11 90 | | 5515 11 10 | 5515 22 91 | ex 5905 00 70 | | |
| | 5513 12 00 | 5514 11 00 | 5515 11 30 | 5515 22 99 | | | |
| | 5513 13 00 | 5514 12 00 | 5515 11 90 | 5515 29 10 | ex 6308 00 00 | | |
| | 5513 19 00 | 5514 13 00 | 5515 12 10 | 5515 29 30 | | | |
| | 5513 21 10 | 5514 19 00 | 5515 12 30 | 5515 29 90 | | | |
| | 5513 21 30 | 5514 21 00 | 5515 12 90 | 5515 91 10 | | | |
| | 5513 21 90 | 5514 22 00 | 5515 13 11 | 5515 91 30 | | | |
| 3 (a) | Of which: Other than unbleached or bleached | | | | | | |
| | 5512 19 10 | 5513 31 00 | 5514 31 00 | 5515 13 19 | 5515 92 99 | | |
| | 5512 19 90 | 5513 32 00 | 5514 32 00 | 5515 13 99 | 5515 99 30 | | |
| | 5512 29 10 | 5513 33 00 | 5514 33 00 | 5515 19 30 | 5515 99 90 | | |
| | 5512 29 90 | 5513 39 00 | 5514 39 00 | 5515 19 90 | | | |
| | 5512 99 10 | 5513 41 00 | 5514 41 00 | 5515 21 30 | ex 5803 90 30 | | |
| | 5512 99 90 | 5513 42 00 | 5514 42 00 | 5515 21 90 | | | |
| | | 5513 43 00 | 5514 43 00 | 5515 22 19 | ex 5905 00 70 | | |
| | 5513 21 10 | 5513 49 00 | 5514 49 00 | 5515 22 99 | | | |
| | 5513 21 30 | | | 5515 29 30 | ex 6308 00 00 | | |
| | 5513 21 90 | 5514 21 00 | 5515 11 30 | 5515 29 90 | | | |
| | 5513 22 00 | 5514 22 00 | 5515 11 90 | 5515 91 30 | | | |
| | 5513 23 00 | 5514 23 00 | 5515 12 30 | 5515 91 90 | | | |
| | 5513 29 00 | 5514 29 00 | 5515 12 90 | 5515 92 19 | | | |

GROUP I B

| (1) | (2) | (3) | (4) |
|---|---|---|---|
| 4 | Shirts, T-shirts, lightweight fine knit roll, polo or turtle necked jumpers and pullovers (other than of wool or fine animal hair), undervests and the like, knitted or crocheted<br><br>6105 10 00 · 6105 90 10 · 6109 90 10 · 6110 20 10<br>6105 20 10 · 6109 90 30 · 6110 30 10<br>6105 20 90 · 6109 10 00 | 6,48 | 154 |
| 5 | Jerseys, pullovers, slip-overs, waistcoats, twinsets, cardigans, bed-jackets and jumpers (other than jackets and blazers), anoraks, windcheaters, waister jackets and the like, knitted or crocheted<br><br>6101 10 90 · 6102 10 90 · 6110 10 10 · 6110 10 91 · 6110 20 99<br>6101 20 90 · 6102 20 90 · 6110 10 31 · 6110 10 95 · 6110 30 91<br>6101 30 90 · 6102 30 90 · 6110 10 35 · 6110 10 98 · 6110 30 99<br>6110 10 38 · 6110 20 91 | 4,53 | 221 |
| 6 | Men's or boys' woven breeches, shorts other than swimwear and trousers (including slacks); women's or girls' woven trousers and slacks, of wool, of cotton or of man-made fibres; lower parts of tracksuits with lining, other than category 16 or 29, of cotton or of man-made fibres<br><br>6203 41 10 · 6203 42 90 · 6204 61 10 · 6204 69 18 · 6211 43 42<br>6203 41 90 · 6203 43 19 · 6204 62 31<br>6203 42 31 · 6203 43 90 · 6204 62 33 · 6211 32 42<br>6203 42 33 · 6203 49 19 · 6204 62 39 · 6211 33 42<br>6203 42 35 · 6203 49 50 · 6204 63 18 · 6211 42 42 | 1,76 | 568 |
| 7 | Women's or girls' blouses, shirts and shirt-blouses, whether or not knitted or crocheted, of wool, cotton or man-made fibres<br><br>6106 10 00 · 6106 90 10 · 6206 20 00 · 6206 40 00<br>6106 20 00 · 6206 30 00 | 5,55 | 180 |
| 8 | Men's or boys' shirts, other than knitted or crocheted, of wool, cotton or man-made fibres<br><br>6205 10 00 · 6205 20 00 · 6205 30 00 | 4,60 | 217 |

GROUP II A

| (1) | (2) | (3) | (4) |
|---|---|---|---|
| 9 | Terry towelling and similar woven terry fabrics of cotton; toilet linen and kitchen linen, other than knitted or crocheted, of terry towelling and woven terry fabrics, of cotton<br><br>5802 11 00 5802 19 00 ex 6302 60 00 | | |
| 20 | Bed linen, other than knitted or crocheted<br><br>6302 21 00 6302 29 90 6302 31 90 6302 39 90<br>6302 22 90 6302 31 10 6302 32 90 | | |
| 22 | Yarn of staple or waste synthetic fibres, not put up for retail sale<br><br>5508 10 11 5509 21 90 5509 32 90 5509 52 10 5509 62 00<br>5508 10 19 5509 22 10 5509 41 10 5509 52 90 5509 69 00<br>5509 22 90 5509 41 90 5509 53 00 5509 91 10<br>5509 11 00 5509 31 10 5509 42 10 5509 59 00 5509 91 90<br>5509 12 00 5509 31 90 5509 42 90 5509 61 10 5509 92 00<br>5509 21 10 5509 32 10 5509 51 00 5509 61 90 5509 99 00 | | |
| 22 (a) | Of which acrylic<br><br>ex 5508 10 19 5509 31 10 5509 32 10 5509 61 10 5509 62 00<br>5509 31 90 5509 32 90 5509 61 90 5509 69 00 | | |
| 23 | Yarn of staple or waste artificial fibres, not put up for retail sale<br><br>5508 20 10 5510 11 00 5510 20 00 5510 90 00<br>5510 12 00 5510 30 00 | | |
| 32 | Woven pile fabrics and chenille fabrics (other than terry towelling or terry fabrics of cotton and narrow woven fabrics) and tufted textile surfaces, of wool, of cotton or of man-made textile fibres<br><br>5801 10 00 5801 24 00 5801 32 00 5801 36 00<br>5801 21 00 5801 25 00 5801 33 00<br>5801 22 00 5801 26 00 5801 34 00 5802 20 00<br>5801 23 00 5801 31 00 5801 35 00 5802 30 00 | | |
| 32 (a) | Of which: Cotton corduroy<br><br>5801 22 00 | | |
| 39 | Table linen, toilet linen and kitchen linen, other than knitted or crocheted, other than of terry towelling or similar terry fabrics of cotton<br><br>6302 51 10 6302 53 90 6302 91 10 6302 93 90<br>6302 51 90 ex 6302 59 00 6302 91 90 ex 6302 99 00 | | |

GROUP II B

| (1) | (2) | (3) | (4) |
|---|---|---|---|
| 12 | Panty-hose and tights, stockings, understockings, socks, ankle-socks, sockettes and the like, knitted or crocheted, other than for babies, including stockings for varicose veins, other than products of category 70<br>6115 12 00 6115 20 11 6115 91 00 6115 93 10 6115 93 99<br>6115 19 00 6115 20 90 6115 92 00 6115 93 30 6115 99 00 | 24,3 pairs | 41 |
| 13 | Men's or boys' underpants and briefs, women's or girls' knickers and briefs, knitted or crocheted, of wool, of cotton or of man-made fibres<br>6107 11 00 6107 19 00 6108 21 00 6108 29 00 ex 6212 10 10<br>6107 12 00 6108 22 00 | 17 | 59 |
| 14 | Men's or boys' woven overcoats, raincoats and other coats, cloaks and capes, of wool, of cotton or of man-made textile fibres (other than parkas) (of category 21)<br>6201 11 00 ex 6201 12 90 ex 6201 13 90 6210 20 00<br>ex 6201 12 10 ex 6201 13 10 | 0,72 | 1 389 |
| 15 | Women's or girls' woven overcoats, raincoats and other coats, cloaks and capes; jackets and blazers, of wool, of cotton or of man-made textile fibres (other than parkas) (of category 21)<br>6202 11 00 ex 6202 13 10 6204 31 00 6204 39 19<br>ex 6202 12 10 ex 6202 13 90 6204 32 90<br>ex 6202 12 90 6204 33 90 6210 30 00 | 0,84 | 1 190 |
| 16 | Men's or boys' suits and ensembles, other than knitted or crocheted, of wool, of cotton or of man-made fibres, excluding ski suits; men's or boys' tracksuits with lining, with an outer shell of a single identical fabric, of cotton or of man-made fibres<br>6203 11 00 6203 19 30 6203 23 80 6211 32 31<br>6203 12 00 6203 21 00 6203 29 18 6211 33 31<br>6203 19 10 6203 22 80 | 0,80 | 1 250 |
| 17 | Men's or boys' jackets and blazers, other than knitted or crocheted, of wool, of cotton or of man-made fibres<br>6203 31 00 6203 32 90 6203 33 90 6203 39 19 | 1,43 | 700 |
| 18 | Men's or boys' singlets and other vests, underpants, briefs, nightshirts, pyjamas, bathrobes, dressing gowns and similar articles, other than knitted or crocheted<br>6207 11 00 6207 21 00 6207 29 00 6207 91 90 6207 99 00<br>6207 19 00 6207 22 00 6207 91 10 6207 92 00<br>Women's or girls' singlets and other vests, slips, petticoats, briefs, panties, nightdresses, pyjamas, negligees, bathrobes, dressing gowns and similar articles, other than knitted or crocheted<br>6208 11 00 6208 21 00 6208 91 11 6208 92 00 ex 6212 10 10<br>6208 19 10 6208 22 00 6208 91 19 6208 99 00<br>6208 19 90 6208 29 00 6208 91 90 | | |

| (1) | (2) | (3) | (4) |
|---|---|---|---|
| 19 | Handkerchiefs, other than knitted or crocheted<br>6213 20 00   6213 90 00 | 59 | 17 |
| 21 | Parkas; anoraks, windcheaters, waister jackets and the like, other than knitted or crocheted, of wool, of cotton or of man-made fibres; upper parts of tracksuits with lining, other than category 16 or 29, of cotton or of man-made fibres<br>ex 6201 12 10   6201 91 00   ex 6202 12 10   6202 91 00   6211 32 31<br>ex 6201 12 90   6201 92 00   ex 6202 12 90   6202 92 00   6211 33 31<br>ex 6201 13 10   6201 93 00   ex 6202 13 10   6202 93 00   6211 42 31<br>ex 6201 13 90   ex 6202 13 90   6211 43 31 | 2,3 | 435 |
| 24 | Men's or boys' nightshirts, pyjamas, bathrobes, dressing gowns and similar articles, knitted or crocheted<br>6107 21 00   6107 29 00   6107 91 90   ex 6107 99 00<br>6107 22 00   6107 91 10   6107 92 00<br><br>Women's or girls' nightdresses, pyjamas, negligees, bathrobes, dressing gowns and similar articles, knitted or crocheted<br>6108 31 10   6108 32 11   6108 32 90   6108 91 10   6108 92 00<br>6108 31 90   6108 32 19   6108 39 00   6108 91 90   6108 99 10 | 3,9 | 257 |
| 26 | Women's or girls' dresses, of wool, of cotton or of man-made fibres<br>6104 41 00   6104 43 00   6204 41 00   6204 43 00<br>6104 42 00   6104 44 00   6204 42 00   6204 44 00 | 3,1 | 323 |
| 27 | Womens' or girls' skirts, including divided skirts<br>6104 51 00   6104 53 00   6204 51 00   6204 53 00<br>6104 52 00   6104 59 00   6204 52 00   6204 59 10 | 2,6 | 385 |
| 28 | Trousers, bib and brace overalls, breeches and shorts (other than swimwear), knitted or crocheted, of wool, of cotton or of man-made fibres<br>6103 41 10   6103 43 10   6104 61 10   6104 63 10<br>6103 41 90   6103 43 90   6104 61 90   6104 63 90<br>6103 42 10   6103 49 10   6104 62 10   6104 69 10<br>6103 42 90   6103 49 91   6104 62 90   6104 69 91 | 1,61 | 620 |
| 29 | Women's or girls' suits and ensembles, other than knitted or crocheted, of wool, of cotton or of man-made fibres, excluding ski suits; women's or girls' tracksuits with lining, with an outer shell of an identical fabric, of cotton or of man-made fibres<br>6204 11 00   6204 19 10   6204 23 80   6211 42 31<br>6204 12 00   6204 21 00   6204 29 18   6211 43 31<br>6204 13 00   6204 22 80 | 1,37 | 730 |
| 31 | Brassières, woven, knitted or crocheted<br>ex 6212 10 10   6212 10 90 | 18,2 | 55 |

| (1) | (2) | (3) | (4) |
|---|---|---|---|
| 68 | Babies' garments and clothing accessories, excluding babies' gloves, mittens and mitts of categories 10 and 87, and babies' stockings, socks and sockettes, other than knitted or crocheted, of category 88<br>6111 10 90 6111 30 90 ex 6209 10 00 ex 6209 30 00<br>6111 20 90 ex 6111 90 00 ex 6209 20 00 ex 6209 90 00 | | |
| 73 | Tracksuits of knitted or crocheted fabric, of wool, of cotton or of man-made textile fibres<br>6112 11 00 6112 12 00 6112 19 00 | 1,67 | 600 |
| 76 | Men's or boys' industrial or occupational clothing, other than knitted or crocheted<br>6203 22 10 6203 32 10 6203 42 11 6203 43 31 6211 32 10<br>6203 23 10 6203 33 10 6203 42 51 6203 49 11 6211 33 10<br>6203 29 11 6203 39 11 6203 43 11 6203 49 31<br>Women's or girls' aprons, smock overalls and other industrial or occupational clothing, other than knitted or crocheted<br>6204 22 10 6204 32 10 6204 62 11 6204 63 31 6211 42 10<br>6204 23 10 6204 33 10 6204 62 51 6204 69 11 6211 43 10<br>6204 29 11 6204 39 11 6204 63 11 6204 69 31 | | |
| 77 | Ski suits, other than knitted or crocheted<br>ex 6211 20 00 | | |
| 78 | Garments, other than knitted or crocheted, excluding garments of categories 6, 7, 8, 14, 15, 16, 17, 18, 21, 26, 27, 29, 68, 72, 76 and 77<br>6203 41 30 6204 61 80 6204 63 90 6210 50 00 6211 41 00<br>6203 42 59 6204 61 90 6204 69 39 6211 42 90<br>6203 43 39 6204 62 59 6204 69 50 6211 31 00 6211 43 90<br>6203 49 39 6204 62 90 6211 32 90<br>6204 63 39 6210 40 00 6211 33 90 | | |
| 83 | Overcoats, jackets, blazers and other garments, including ski suits, knitted or crocheted, excluding garments of categories 4, 5, 7, 13, 24, 26, 27, 28, 68, 69, 72, 73, 74, 75<br>6101 10 10 6102 20 10 6103 33 00 6104 33 00 6113 00 90<br>6101 20 10 6102 30 10 ex 6103 39 00 ex 6104 39 00<br>6101 30 10 6114 10 00<br>6103 31 00 6104 31 00 6112 20 00 6114 20 00<br>6102 10 10 6103 32 00 6104 32 00 6114 30 00 | | |

GROUP III A

| (1) | (2) | (3) | (4) |
|---|---|---|---|
| 33 | Woven fabrics of synthetic filament yarn obtained from strip or the like of polyethylene or polypropylene, less than 3 m wide<br>5407 20 11<br>Sacks and bags, of a kind used for the packing of goods, not knitted or crocheted, obtained from strip or the like<br>6305 32 81 6305 32 89 6305 33 91 6305 33 99 | | |
| 34 | Woven fabrics of synthetic filament yarn, obtained from strip or the like of polyethylene or polypropylene, 3 m or more wide<br>5407 20 19 | | |
| 35 | Woven fabrics of synthetic fibres (continuous), other than those for tyres of category 114<br>5407 10 00 5407 51 00 5407 61 90 5407 81 00 5407 94 00<br>5407 20 90 5407 52 00 5407 69 10 5407 82 00<br>5407 30 00 5407 53 00 5407 69 90 5407 83 00 ex 5811 00 00<br>5407 41 00 5407 54 00 5407 71 00 5407 84 00<br>5407 42 00 5407 61 10 5407 72 00 5407 91 00 ex 5905 00 70<br>5407 43 00 5407 61 30 5407 73 00 5407 92 00<br>5407 44 00 5407 61 50 5407 74 00 5407 93 00 | | |
| 35 (a) | Of which: Other than unbleached or bleached<br>ex 5407 10 00 5407 52 00 5407 69 90 5407 84 00 ex 5811 00 00<br>ex 5407 20 90 5407 53 00 5407 72 00 5407 92 00<br>ex 5407 30 00 5407 54 00 5407 73 00 5407 93 00 ex 5905 00 70<br>5407 42 00 5407 61 30 5407 74 00 5407 94 00<br>5407 43 00 5407 61 50 5407 82 00<br>5407 44 00 5407 61 90 5407 83 00 | | |
| 36 | Woven fabrics of continuous artificial fibres, other than those for tyres of category 114<br>5408 10 00 5408 22 90 5408 24 00 5408 33 00 ex 5811 00 00<br>5408 21 00 5408 23 10 5408 31 00 5408 34 00<br>5408 22 10 5408 23 90 5408 32 00 ex 5905 00 70 | | |
| 36 (a) | Of which: Other than unbleached or bleached<br>ex 5408 10 00 5408 23 10 5408 32 00 ex 5811 00 00<br>5408 22 10 5408 23 90 5408 33 00<br>5408 22 90 5408 24 00 5408 34 00 ex 5905 00 70 | | |
| 37 | Woven fabrics of artificial staple fibres<br>5516 11 00 5516 22 00 5516 32 00 5516 43 00 5516 94 00<br>5516 12 00 5516 23 10 5516 33 00 5516 44 00<br>5516 13 00 5516 23 90 5516 34 00 5516 91 00 5803 90 [illegible]0<br>5516 14 00 5516 24 00 5516 41 00 5516 92 00<br>5516 21 00 5516 31 00 5516 42 00 5516 93 00 ex 5905 00 [illegible]0 | | |
| 37 (a) | Of which: Other than unbleached or bleached<br>5516 12 00 5516 23 10 5516 33 00 5516 44 00 ex 5803 90 [illegible]0<br>5516 13 00 5516 23 90 5516 34 00 5516 92 00<br>5516 14 00 5516 24 00 5516 42 00 5516 93 00 ex 5905 00 [illegible]0<br>5516 22 00 5516 32 00 5516 43 00 5516 94 00 | | |

| (1) | (2) | (3) | (4) |
|---|---|---|---|
| 38 A | Knitted or crocheted synthetic curtain fabric including net curtain fabric<br>6002 43 11 6002 93 10 | | |
| 38 B | Net curtains, other than knitted or crocheted<br>ex 6303 91 00 ex 6303 92 90 ex 6303 99 90 | | |
| 40 | Woven curtains (including drapes, interior blinds, curtain and bed valances and other furnishing articles), other than knitted or crocheted, of wool, of cotton or of man-made fibres<br>ex 6303 91 00 ex 6303 99 90 6304 19 10 6304 92 00 ex 6304 99 00<br>ex 6303 92 90 ex 6304 19 90 ex 6304 93 00 | | |
| 41 | Yarn of synthetic filament (continuous), not put up for retail sale, other than non-textured single yarn untwisted or with a twist of not more than 50 turns per metre<br>5401 10 11 5402 20 00 5402 39 90 5402 52 00 5402 69 10<br>5401 10 19 5402 31 00 5402 49 10 5402 59 10 5402 69 90<br>5402 32 00 5402 49 91 5402 59 90<br>5402 10 10 5402 33 00 5402 49 99 5402 61 00 ex 5604 20 00<br>5402 10 90 5402 39 10 5402 51 00 5402 62 00 ex 5604 90 00 | | |
| 42 | Yarn of continuous man-made fibres, not put up for retail sale<br>5401 20 10<br><br>Yarn of artificial fibres; yarn of artificial filaments, not put up for retail sale, other than single yarn of viscose rayon untwisted or with a twist of not more than 250 turns per metre and single non-textured yarn of cellulose acetate<br>5403 10 00 ex 5403 32 00 5403 41 00 ex 5604 20 00<br>5403 20 10 5403 33 90 5403 42 00<br>5403 20 90 5403 39 00 5403 49 00 | | |
| 43 | Yarn of man-made filament of artificial staple fibres, cotton yarn, put up for retail sale<br>5204 20 00 5207 90 00 5401 20 90 5406 20 00 5511 30 00<br>5207 10 00 5401 10 90 5406 10 00 5508 20 90 | | |
| 46 | Carded or combed sheep's or lambs' wool or other fine animal hair<br>5105 10 00 5105 21 00 5105 29 00 5105 30 10 5105 30 90 | | |
| 47 | Yarn of carded sheep's or lambs' wool (woollen yarn) or of carded fine animal hair, not put up for retail sale<br>5106 10 10 5106 20 10 5106 20 99 5108 10 10<br>5106 10 90 5106 20 91 5108 10 90 | | |
| 48 | Yarn of combed sheep's or lambs' wool (worsted yarn) or of combed fine animal hair, not put up for retail sale<br>5107 10 10 5107 20 30 5107 20 91 5108 20 10<br>5107 10 90 5107 20 51 5107 20 99 5108 20 90<br>5107 20 10 5107 20 59 | | |

| (1) | (2) | (3) | (4) |
|---|---|---|---|
| 49 | Yarn of sheep's or lambs' wool or of combed fine animal hair, put up for retail sale<br>5109 10 10 5109 10 90 5109 90 10 5109 90 90 | | |
| 50 | Woven fabrics of sheep's or lambs' wool or of fine animal hair<br>5111 11 11 5111 19 39 5111 90 10 5112 19 11 5112 30 90<br>5111 11 19 5111 19 91 5111 90 91 5112 19 19 5112 90 10<br>5111 11 91 5111 19 99 5111 90 93 5112 19 91 5112 90 91<br>5111 11 99 5111 20 00 5111 90 99 5112 19 99 5112 90 93<br>5111 19 11 5111 30 10 5112 20 00 5112 90 99<br>5111 19 19 5111 30 30 5112 11 10 5112 30 10<br>5111 19 31 5111 30 90 5112 11 90 5112 30 30 | | |
| 51 | Cotton, carded or combed<br>5203 00 00 | | |
| 53 | Cotton gauze<br>5803 10 00 | | |
| 54 | Artificial staple fibres, including waste, carded, combed or otherwise processed for spinning<br>5507 00 00 | | |
| 55 | Synthetic staple fibres, including waste, carded or combed or otherwise processed for spinning<br>5506 10 00 5506 20 00 5506 30 00 5506 90 10 5506 90 90 | | |
| 56 | Yarn of synthetic staple fibres (including waste), put up for retail sale<br>5508 10 90 5511 10 00 5511 20 00 | | |
| 58 | Carpets, carpetines and rugs, knotted (made up or not)<br>5701 10 10 5701 10 93 5701 90 10<br>5701 10 91 5701 10 99 5701 90 90 | | |
| 59 | Carpets and other textile floor coverings, other than the carpets of category 58<br>5702 10 00 5702 51 00 5703 10 00 5703 30 51 5704 90 00<br>5702 31 00 5702 52 00 5703 20 11 5703 30 59<br>5702 32 00 ex 5702 59 00 5703 20 19 5703 30 91 5705 00 10<br>5702 39 10 5702 91 00 5703 20 91 5703 30 99 5705 00 30<br>5702 41 00 5702 92 00 5703 20 99 5703 90 00 ex 5705 00 90<br>5702 42 00 ex 5702 99 00 5703 30 11<br>5702 49 10 5703 30 19 5704 10 00 | | |
| 60 | Tapestries, hand-made, of the type Gobelins, Flanders, Aubusson, Beauvais and the like, and needlework tapestries (for example, petit point and cross stitch) made in panels and the like by hand<br>5805 00 00 | | |

| (1) | (2) | (3) | (4) |
|---|---|---|---|
| 61 | Narrow woven fabrics, and narrow fabrics (bolduc) consisting of warp without weft, assembled by means of an adhesive, other than labels and similar articles of category 62. Elastic fabrics and trimmings (not knitted or crocheted), made from textile materials assembled from rubber thread<br>ex 5806 10 00 5806 31 00 5806 32 90 5806 40 00<br>5806 20 00 5806 32 10 5806 39 00 | | |
| 62 | Chenille yarn (including flock chenille yarn), gimped yarn (other than metallised yarn and gimped horsehair yarn)<br>5606 00 91 5606 00 99<br>Tulle and other net fabrics but not including woven, knitted or crocheted fabrics, hand or mechanically-made lace, in the piece, in strips or in motifs<br>5804 10 11 5804 10 90 5804 21 90 5804 29 90<br>5804 10 19 5804 21 10 5804 29 10 5804 30 00<br>Labels, badges and the like of textile materials, not embroidered, in the piece, in strips or cut to shape or size, woven<br>5807 10 10 5807 10 90<br>Braids and ornamental trimmings in the piece; tassels, pompons and the like<br>5808 10 00 5808 90 00<br>Embroidery, in the piece, in strips or in motifs<br>5810 10 10 5810 91 10 5810 92 10 5810 99 10<br>5810 10 90 5810 91 90 5810 92 90 5810 99 90 | | |
| 63 | Knitted or crocheted fabric of synthetic fibres containing by weight 5% or more of elastomeric yarn and knitted or crocheted fabric containing by weight 5% or more of rubber thread<br>5906 91 00 ex 6002 10 10 ex 6002 30 10<br>6002 10 90 6002 30 90<br>Raschel lace and long-pile fabric of synthetic fibres<br>ex 6001 10 00 6002 20 31 6002 43 19 | | |
| 65 | Knitted or crocheted fabric other than those of categories 38 A and 63, of wool, of cotton or of man-made fibres<br>5606 00 10 6001 92 10 6002 20 70 6002 43 39 6002 92 90<br>6001 92 30 ex 6002 30 10 6002 43 50 6002 93 31<br>ex 6001 10 00 6001 92 50 6002 41 00 6002 43 91 6002 93 33<br>6001 21 00 6001 92 90 6002 42 10 6002 43 93 6002 93 35<br>6001 22 00 6001 99 10 6002 42 30 6002 43 95 6002 93 39<br>6001 29 10 6002 42 50 6002 43 99 6002 93 91<br>6001 91 10 ex 6002 10 10 6002 42 90 6002 91 00 6002 93 99<br>6001 91 30 6002 20 10 6002 43 31 6002 92 10<br>6001 91 50 6002 20 39 6002 43 33 6002 92 30<br>6001 91 90 6002 20 50 6002 43 35 6002 92 50 | | |
| 66 | Travelling rugs and blankets, other than knitted or crocheted, of wool, of cotton or of man-made fibres<br>6301 10 00 6301 20 99 ex 6301 40 90<br>6301 20 91 6301 30 90 ex 6301 90 90 | | |

GROUP III B

| (1) | (2) | (3) | (4) |
|---|---|---|---|
| 10 | Gloves, mittens and mitts, knitted or crocheted<br>6111 10 10 ex 6111 90 00 6116 10 80 6116 93 00<br>6111 20 10 6116 91 00 6116 99 00<br>6111 30 10 6116 10 20 6116 92 00 | 17 pairs | 59 |
| 67 | Knitted or crocheted clothing accessories other than for babies; household linen of all kinds knitted or crocheted; curtains (including drapes) and interior blinds, curtain or bed valances and other furnishing articles knitted or crocheted; knitted or crocheted blankets and travelling-rugs, other knitted or crocheted articles including parts of garments or of clothing accessories<br>5807 90 90 6117 80 90 6302 10 10 6303 19 00 ex 6305 32 90<br>6117 90 00 6302 10 90 6305 33 10<br>6113 00 10 6302 40 00 6304 11 00 ex 6305 39 00<br>6301 20 10 ex 6302 60 00 6304 91 00 ex 6305 90 00<br>6117 10 00 6301 30 10<br>6117 20 00 6301 40 10 6303 11 00 ex 6305 20 00 6307 10 10<br>6117 80 10 6301 90 10 6303 12 00 6305 32 11 6307 90 10 | | |
| 67 (a) | Of which: Sacks and bags of a kind used for the packing of goods, made from polyethylene or polypropylene strip<br>6305 32 11 6305 33 10 | | |
| 69 | Women's or girls' slips and petticoats, knitted or crocheted<br>6108 11 00 6108 19 00 | 7,8 | 128 |
| 70 | Panty-hose and tights of synthetic fibres, measuring per single yarn less than 67 decitex (6,7 tex<br>6115 11 00 6115 20 19<br><br>Women's full-length hosiery of synthetic fibres<br>6115 93 91 | 30,4 pairs | 33 |
| 72 | Swimwear, of wool, of cotton or of man-made fibres<br>6112 31 10 6112 39 90 6112 49 10 6211 11 00<br>6112 31 90 6112 41 10 6112 49 90 6211 12 00<br>6112 39 10 6112 41 90 | 9,7 | 103 |
| 74 | Women's or girls' knitted or crocheted suits and ensembles, of wool, of cotton or of man-made fibres, excluding ski suits<br>6104 11 00 6104 13 00 6104 21 00 6104 23 00<br>6104 12 00 ex 6104 19 00 6104 22 00 ex 6104 29 00 | 1,54 | 650 |

| (1) | (2) | (3) | (4) |
|---|---|---|---|
| 75 | Men's or boys' knitted or crocheted suits and ensembles, of wool, of cotton or of man-made fibres, excluding ski suits<br>6103 11 00 6103 19 00 6103 22 00 6103 29 00<br>6103 12 00 6103 21 00 6103 23 00 | 0,80 | 1 250 |
| 84 | Shawls, scarves, mufflers, mantillas, veils and the like other than knitted or crocheted, of wool, of cotton or of man-made fibres<br>6214 20 00 6214 30 00 6214 40 00 6214 90 10 | | |
| 85 | Ties, bow-ties and cravats not knitted or crocheted, of wool, of cotton or of man-made fibres<br>6215 20 00 6215 90 00 | 17,9 | 56 |
| 86 | Corsets, corset-belts, suspender belts, braces, suspenders, garters and the like, and parts thereof, whether or not knitted or crocheted<br>6212 20 00 6212 30 00 6212 90 00 | 8,8 | 114 |
| 87 | Gloves, mittens and mitts, not knitted or crocheted<br>ex 6209 10 00 ex 6209 20 00 ex 6209 30 00 ex 6209 90 00 6216 00 00 | | |
| 88 | Stockings, socks and sockettes, not knitted or crocheted; other clothing accessories, parts of garments or of clothing accessories, other than for babies, other than knitted or crocheted<br>ex 6209 10 00 ex 6209 30 00 6217 10 00<br>ex 6209 20 00 ex 6209 90 00 6217 90 00 | | |
| 90 | Twine, cordage, ropes and cables of synthetic fibres, plaited or not<br>5607 41 00 5607 49 19 5607 50 11 5607 50 30<br>5607 49 11 5607 49 90 5607 50 19 5607 50 90 | | |
| 91 | Tents<br>6306 21 00 6306 22 00 6306 29 00 | | |
| 93 | Sacks and bags, of a kind used for the packing of goods of woven fabrics, other than made from polyethylene or polypropylene strip<br>ex 6305 20 00 ex 6305 32 90 ex 6305 39 00 | | |
| 94 | Wadding of textile materials and articles thereof; textile fibres, not exceeding 5 mm in length (flock), textile dust and mill neps<br>5601 10 10 5601 21 10 5601 22 10 5601 22 99 5601 30 00<br>5601 10 90 5601 21 90 5601 22 91 5601 29 00 | | |
| 95 | Felt and articles thereof, whether or not impregnated or coated, other than floor coverings<br>5602 10 19 5602 10 90 5602 90 00 ex 5905 00 70 6307 90 91<br>5602 10 31 5602 21 00<br>5602 10 39 5602 29 90 ex 5807 90 10 6210 10 10 | | |

| (1) | (2) | (3) | (4) |
|---|---|---|---|
| 96 | Non-woven fabrics and articles of such fabrics, whether or not impregnated, coated, covered or laminated<br>5603 11 10 · 5603 91 90 · ex 5905 00 70 · 6302 32 10 · ex 6304 99 [illegible]0<br>5603 11 90 · 5603 92 10 · 6302 53 10<br>5603 12 10 · 5603 92 90 · 6210 10 91 · 6302 93 10 · ex 6305 32 [illegible]0<br>5603 12 90 · 5603 93 10 · 6210 10 99 · ex 6305 39 [illegible]0<br>5603 13 10 · 5603 93 90 · 6303 92 10<br>5603 13 90 · 5603 94 10 · ex 6301 40 90 · 6303 99 10 · 6307 10 [illegible]0<br>5603 14 10 · 5603 94 90 · ex 6301 90 90 · ex 6307 90 [illegible]9<br>5603 14 90 · ex 6304 19 90<br>5603 91 10 · ex 5807 90 10 · 6302 22 10 · ex 6304 93 00 | | |
| 97 | Nets and netting made of twine, cordage or rope and made up fishing nets of yarn, twine, cordage or rope<br>5608 11 11 · 5608 11 91 · 5608 19 11 · 5608 19 30 · 5608 90 [illegible]0<br>5608 11 19 · 5608 11 99 · 5608 19 19 · 5608 19 90 | | |
| 98 | Other articles made from yarn, twine, cordage, rope or cables, other than textile fabrics, articles made from such fabrics and articles of category 97<br>5609 00 00 · 5905 00 10 | | |
| 99 | Textile fabrics coated with gum or amylaceous substances, of a kind used for the outer covers of books and the like; tracing cloth; prepared painting canvas; buckram and similar stiffened textile fabrics of a kind used for hat foundations<br>5901 10 00 · 5901 90 00<br><br>Linoleum, whether or not cut to shape; floor coverings consisting of a coating or covering applied on a textile backing, whether or not cut to shape<br>5904 10 00 · 5904 91 10 · 5904 91 90 · 5904 92 00<br><br>Rubberised textile fabrics, not knitted or crocheted, excluding those for tyres<br>5906 10 00 · 5906 99 10 · 5906 99 90<br><br>Textile fabrics otherwise impregnated or coated; painted canvas being theatrical scenery, studio backcloths, other than of category 100<br>5907 00 10 · 5907 00 90 | | |
| 100 | Textile fabrics impregnated, coated, covered or laminated with preparations of cellulose derivatives or of other artificial plastic materials<br>5903 10 10 · 5903 20 10 · 5903 90 10 · 5903 90 99<br>5903 10 90 · 5903 20 90 · 5903 90 91 | | |
| 101 | Twine, cordage, ropes and cables, plaited or not, other than of synthetic fibres<br>ex 5607 90 00 | | |
| 109 | Tarpaulins, sails, awnings, and sun-blinds<br>6306 11 00 · 6306 12 00 · 6306 19 00 · 6306 31 00 · 6306 39 [illegible] | | |

| (1) | (2) | (3) | (4) |
|---|---|---|---|
| 110 | Woven pneumatic mattresses<br>6306 41 00 6306 49 00 | | |
| 111 | Camping goods, woven, other than pneumatic mattresses and tents<br>6306 91 00 6306 99 00 | | |
| 112 | Other made up textile articles, woven, excluding those of categories 113 and 114<br>6307 20 00 ex 6307 90 99 | | |
| 113 | Floor cloths, dish cloths and dusters, other than knitted or crocheted<br>6307 10 90 | | |
| 114 | Woven fabrics and articles for technical uses<br>5902 10 10 5902 10 90 5902 20 10 5902 20 90 5902 90 10 5902 90 90 5908 00 00 5909 00 10 5909 00 90 5910 00 00 5911 10 00 ex 5911 20 00 5911 31 11 5911 31 19 5911 31 90 5911 32 10 5911 32 90 5911 40 00 5911 90 10 5911 90 90 | | |

*ANNEX I A*

| Category | Description<br>CN code 1999 | Table of equivalence | |
|---|---|---|---|
| | | pieces/kg | g/piece |
| (1) | (2) | (3) | (4) |
| 163 | Gauze and articles of gauze put up in forms or packings for retail sale<br>3005 90 31' | | |

*Appendix 2*

'ANNEX III

(The full product descriptions of the categories listed in this Annex are to be found in Appendix 1 of this Agreement)

**COMMUNITY QUANTITATIVE LIMITS**

| Category | Units | 2000 | Category | Units | 2000 |
|---|---|---|---|---|---|
| 1 | tonnes | 3 943 | 20/39 | tonnes | 9 197 |
| 2 (*) | tonnes (1) | 28 890 | 21 (10) | 1 000 pieces (9) | 16 650 |
| of which 2A | tonnes | 3 731 | 22 | tonnes | 16 230 |
| 3 | tonnes | 5 918 | 23 | tonnes | 10 999 |
| of which 3A | tonnes | 743 | 24 (11) | 1 000 pieces | 42 508 |
| 4 (2) | 1 000 pieces | 78 476 | 26 | 1 000 pieces (12) | 5 191 |
| 5 (4) | 1 000 pieces (3) | 24 757 | 28 | 1 000 pieces | 66 953 |
| 6 | 1 000 pieces (5) | 26 229 | 29 | 1 000 pieces | 11 343 |
| 7 | 1 000 pieces (6) | 12 479 | 31 | 1 000 pieces | 69 137 |
| 8 | 1 000 pieces (7) | 17 535 | 32 | tonnes | 4 006 |
| 9 | tonnes | 5 842 | 33 (**) | tonnes | 26 373 |
| 10 | 1 000 pairs | 79 341 | 37 | tonnes | 13 553 |
| 12 | 1 000 pairs | 28 965 | of which 37A | tonnes | 4 017 |
| 13 | 1 000 pieces | 483 289 | 68 | tonnes | 19 584 |
| 14 | 1 000 pieces | 11 679 | 73 (13) | 1 000 pieces | 5 442 |
| 15 | 1 000 pieces (8) | 15 406 | 76 | tonnes (14) | 7 378 |
| 16 | 1 000 pieces | 15 668 | 78 | tonnes | 27 153 |
| 17 | 1 000 pieces | 10 699 | 83 | tonnes | 7 976 |
| 18 | tonnes | 5 801 | 97 | tonnes | 2 010 |
| 19 | 1 000 pieces | 99 588 | 163 | tonnes | 4 710 |

(*) Possibility of transfer to and from category 3 up to 40% of the category to which the transfer is made.
(**) Quantitative limits apply also to products declared for re-export outside the European Community.
(1) The following additional quantities may be exported to the EEC by China:

| | | | |
|---|---|---|---|
| Fabrics of category 2 below 115 cm in width | tonnes | 2000 | 1 395 |
| Fabrics of category 2 for medical gauze (CN codes 5208 11 10 and 5208 21 10) | tonnes | 2000 | 1 927 |

(2) For the purpose of setting off exports against the agreed quantitative limits a conversion rate of 5 garments (other than babies' garments) of a maximum commercial size of 130 cm, for 3 garments whose commercial size exceeds 130 cm may be applied for up to 5% of the quantitative limits.
(3) These figures include the following quantity reserved for European Industry for a period of 180 days, 41 000 pieces.
(4) For products of category 5 (other than anoraks, windcheaters, waister jackets and the like) of fine animal hair, the following sublimit applies within the quantitative limits estblished for category 5 2000: 229 000 pieces.
(5) These figures include the following quantity reserved for the European Industry for a period of 180 days, 1 149 000 pieces.
The following additional quantities of shorts (CN codes 6203 41 90, 6203 42 90, 6203 43 90 and 6203 49 50) may be exported to the EEC by China 2000: 1 142 000 pieces.

(6) These figures include the following quantity reserved for the European Industry for a period of 180 days, 691 000 pieces.
(7) These figures include the following quantity reserved for the European Industry for a period of 180 days, 1 117 000 pieces.
(8) These figures include the following quantity reserved for the European Industry for a period of 180 days, 312 000 pieces.
(9) These figures include the following quantity reserved for the European Industry for a period of 180 days, 1 008 000 pieces.
(10) For the purpose of setting off exports against the agreed quantitative limits a conversion rate of 5 garments (other than babies' garments) of a maximum commercial size of 130 cm, for 3 garments whose commercial size exceeds 130 cm may be applied for up to 5% of the quantitative limits.
(11) For the purpose of setting off exports against the agreed quantitative limits a conversion rate of 5 garments (other than babies' garments) of a maximum commercial size of 130 cm, for 3 garments whose commercial size exceeds 130 cm may be applied for up to 5% of the quantitative limits.
(12) These figures include the following quantity reserved for the European Industry for a period of 180 days, 339 000 pieces.
(13) For the purpose of setting off exports against the agreed quantitative limits a conversion rate of 5 garments (other than babies' garments) of a maximum commercial size of 130 cm, for 3 garments whose commercial size exceeds 130 cm may be applied for up to 5% of the quantitative limits.
(14) These figures include the following quantity reserved for the European Industry for a period of 180 days each year, 211 tonnes.'

*Appendix 3*

'*ANNEX TO PROTOCOL E*

OUTWARD PROCESSING TRAFFIC

**COMMUNITY QUANTITATIVE LIMITS**

| Category | Units | 2000 |
|---|---|---|
| 4 | 1 000 pieces | 295 |
| 5 | 1 000 pieces | 654 |
| 6 | 1 000 pieces | 2 310 |
| 7 | 1 000 pieces | 629 |
| 8 | 1 000 pieces | 1 442 |
| 13 | 1 000 pieces | 534 |
| 14 | 1 000 pieces | 595 |
| 15 | 1 000 pieces | 524 |
| 16 | 1 000 pieces | 966 |
| 17 | 1 000 pieces | 783 |
| 18 | tonnes | 134 |
| 21 | 1 000 pieces | 2 129 |
| 24 | 1 000 pieces | 141 |
| 26 | 1 000 pieces | 1 124 |
| 29 | 1 000 pieces | 116 |
| 31 | 1 000 pieces | 6 806 |
| 73 | 1 000 pieces | 257 |
| 76 | tonnes | 1 327 |
| 78 | tonnes | 68 |
| 83 | tonnes | 68' |

*Appendix 4*

'ANNEX I

1. This Annex covers textile raw materials (categories 128 and 154), textile products other than those of wool and fine animal hair, cotton and man-made fibres, as well as man-made fibres and filaments and yarns of categories 124, 125 A, 125 B, 126, 127 A and 127 B.

2. Without prejudice to the rules for the interpretation of the Combined Nomenclature, the wording of the description of goods is considered to be of indicative value only, since the products covered by each category are determined, within this Annex, by CN codes. Where there ist an "ex" symbol in front of a CN code, the products covered in each category are determined by the scope of the CN code and by that of the corresponding description.

3. Garments which are not recognisable as being garments for men or boys or as being garments for women or girls are classified with the latter.

4. Where the expression "babies' garments" is used, this is meant to cover garments up to and including commercial size 86.

GROUP I

| Category | Description<br>CN code 1999 | Table of equivalence | |
|---|---|---|---|
| | | pieces/kg | g/piece |
| (1) | (2) | (3) | (4) |
| ex 20 | Bed linen, other than knitted or crocheted<br>ex 6302 29 90 ex 6302 39 90 | | |
| ex 32 | Woven pile fabrics and chenille fabrics and tufted textile surfaces<br>ex 5802 20 00 ex 5802 30 00 | | |
| ex 39 | Table linen, toilet and kitchen linen, other than knitted or crocheted and other than those of category 118<br>ex 6302 59 00 ex 6302 99 00 | | |

GROUP II

| (1) | (2) | (3) | (4) |
|---|---|---|---|
| ex 12 | Panty-hose and tights, stockings, understockings, socks, ankle socks, sockettes and the like, knitted or crocheted, other than for babies<br>ex 6115 19 90 ex 6115 20 90 ex 6115 99 00 | 24,3 | 41 |
| ex 13 | Men's or boys' underpants and briefs, women's or girls' knickers and briefs, knitted or crocheted<br>ex 6107 19 00 ex 6108 29 00 ex 6212 10 10 | 17 | 59 |
| ex 14 | Men's or boys' woven overcoats, raincoats and other coats, cloaks and capes<br>ex 6210 20 00 | 0,72 | 1 389 |

| (1) | (2) | (3) | (4) |
|---|---|---|---|
| ex 15 | Women's or girls' woven overcoats, raincoats and other coats, cloaks and capes, jackets and blazers, other than parkas<br><br>ex 6210 30 00 | 0,84 | 1 190 |
| ex 18 | Men's or boys' singlets and other vests, underpants, briefs, nightshirts, pyjamas, bathrobes, dressing-gowns and similar articles, other than knitted or crocheted<br><br>ex 6207 19 00 ex 6207 29 00 ex 6207 99 00<br><br>Women's or girls' singlets and other vests, slips, petticoats, briefs, panties, nightdresses, pyjamas, negligees, bathrobes, dressing-gowns and similar articles, other than knitted or crocheted<br><br>ex 6208 19 90 ex 6208 29 00 ex 6208 99 00 ex 6212 10 10 | | |
| ex 19 | Handkerchiefs, other than those of silk and silk waste<br><br>ex 6213 90 00 | 59 | 17 |
| ex 24 | Men's or boys' nightshirts, pyjamas, bathrobes, dressing-gowns and similar articles, knitted or crocheted<br><br>ex 6107 29 00<br><br>Women's or girls' nightdresses, pyjamas, negligees, bathrobes, dressing-gowns and similar articles, knitted or crocheted<br><br>ex 6108 39 00 | 3,9 | 257 |
| ex 27 | Women's or girls' skirts, including divided skirts<br><br>ex 6104 59 00 | 2,6 | 385 |
| ex 28 | Trousers, bib and brace overalls, breeches and shorts (other than swimwear), knitted or crocheted<br><br>ex 6103 49 10 ex 6104 69 10 | 1,61 | 620 |
| ex 31 | Brassières, woven, knitted or crocheted<br><br>ex 6212 10 10 6212 10 90 | 18,2 | 55 |
| ex 68 | Babies' garments and clothing accessories, excluding babies' gloves, mittens and mitts of categories ex 10 and ex 87, and babies' stockings, socks and sockettes, other than knitted or crocheted, of category ex 88<br><br>ex 6209 90 00 | | |
| ex 73 | Tracksuits of knitted or crocheted fabric<br><br>ex 6112 19 00 | 1,67 | 600 |
| ex 78 | Woven garments of fabrics of heading Nos 5903, 5906 and 5907, excluding garments of categories ex 14 and ex 15<br><br>ex 6210 40 00 ex 6210 50 00 | | |
| ex 83 | Garments of knitted or crocheted fabrics of heading Nos 5903 and 5907 and ski suits, knitted or crocheted<br><br>ex 6112 20 00 ex 6113 00 90 | | |

GROUP III A

| (1) | (2) | (3) | (4) |
|---|---|---|---|
| ex 38 B | Net curtains, other than knitted or crocheted<br>ex 6303 99 90 | | |
| ex 40 | Woven curtains (including drapes, interior blinds, curtain and bed valances and other furnishing articles), other than knitted or crocheted<br>ex 6303 99 90 ex 6304 19 90 ex 6304 99 00 | | |
| ex 58 | Carpets, carpetines and rugs, knotted (made up or not)<br>ex 5701 90 10 ex 5701 90 90 | | |
| ex 59 | Carpets and other textile floor coverings, other than the carpets of categories ex 58, 142 and 151 B<br>ex 5702 10 00 ex 5702 59 00 ex 5702 99 00 ex 5703 90 10 ex 5703 90 90 ex 5704 10 00 ex 5704 90 00 ex 5705 00 90 | | |
| ex 60 | Tapestries, hand-made, of the type Gobelins, Flanders, Aubusson, Beauvais and the like, and needlework tapestries (for example, petit point and cross-stitch) made in panels and the like by hand<br>ex 5805 00 00 | | |
| ex 61 | Narrow woven fabrics, and narrow fabrics (bolduc) consisting of warp without weft, assembled by means of an adhesive, other than labels and similar articles of category ex 62 and of category 137<br>Elastic fabrics and trimmings (not knitted or crocheted), made from textile materials assembled from rubber thread<br>ex 5806 10 00 ex 5806 20 00 ex 5806 39 00 ex 5806 40 00 | | |
| ex 62 | Chenille yarn (including flock chenille yarn), gimped yarn (other than metallised yarn and gimped horsehair yarn)<br>ex 5606 00 91 ex 5606 00 99<br>Tulle and other net fabrics but not including woven, knitted or crocheted fabrics, hand or mechanically-made lace, in the piece, in strips or in motifs<br>ex 5804 10 11 ex 5804 10 19 ex 5804 10 90 ex 5804 29 10 ex 5804 29 90 ex 5804 30 00<br>Labels, badges and the like of textile materials, not embroidered, in the piece, in strips or cut to shape or size, woven<br>ex 5807 10 10 ex 5807 10 90<br>Braids and ornamental trimmings in the piece; tassels; pompons and the like<br>ex 5808 10 00 ex 5808 90 00<br>Embroidery, in the piece, in strips or in motifs<br>ex 5810 10 10 ex 5810 10 90 ex 5810 99 10 ex 5810 99 90 | | |

| (1) | (2) | (3) | (4) |
|---|---|---|---|
| ex 63 | Knitted or crocheted fabric of synthetic fibres containing by weight 5% or more of elastomeric yarn and knitted or crocheted fabric containing by weight 5% or more of rubber thread<br>ex 5906 91 00 ex 6002 10 10 ex 6002 10 90 ex 6002 30 10 ex 6002 30 90 | | |
| ex 65 | Knitted or crocheted fabric, other than those of category ex 63<br>ex 5606 00 10 ex 6002 10 10 ex 6002 30 10 | | |
| ex 66 | Travelling rugs and blankets, other than knitted or crocheted<br>ex 6301 10 00 ex 6301 90 90 | | |

GROUP III B

| (1) | (2) | (3) | (4) |
|---|---|---|---|
| ex 10 | Gloves, mittens and mitts, knitted or crocheted<br>ex 6116 10 20 ex 6116 10 80 ex 6116 99 00 | 17 pairs | 59 |
| ex 67 | Knitted or crocheted clothing accessories other than for babies; household linen of all kinds, knitted or crocheted; curtains (including drapes) and interior blinds, curtain or bed valances and other furnishing articles knitted or crocheted; knitted or crocheted blankets and travelling rugs, other knitted or crocheted articles including parts of garments or of clothing accessories<br>ex 5807 90 90 ex 6117 20 00 ex 6301 90 10 ex 6303 19 00 ex 6307 10 10<br>ex 6117 80 10 ex 6307 90 10<br>ex 6113 00 10 ex 6117 80 90 ex 6302 10 90 ex 6304 11 00<br>ex 6117 90 00 ex 6302 40 00 ex 6304 91 00<br>ex 6117 10 00 | | |
| ex 69 | Women's or girls' slips and petticoats, knitted or crocheted<br>ex 6108 19 00 | 7,8 | 128 |
| ex 72 | Swimwear<br>ex 6112 39 10 ex 6112 49 10 ex 6211 11 00<br>ex 6112 39 90 ex 6112 49 90 ex 6211 12 00 | 9,7 | 103 |
| ex 75 | Men's or boys' knitted or crocheted suits and ensembles<br>ex 6103 19 00 ex 6103 29 00 | 0,80 | 1 250 |
| ex 85 | Ties, bow-ties and cravats other than knitted or crocheted, other than those of category 159<br>ex 6215 90 00 | 17,9 | 56 |
| ex 86 | Corsets, corset-belts, suspender belts, braces, suspenders, garters and the like, and parts thereof, whether or not knitted or crocheted<br>ex 6212 20 00 ex 6212 30 00 ex 6212 90 00 | 8,8 | 114 |

| (1) | (2) | (3) | (4) |
|---|---|---|---|
| ex 87 | Gloves, mittens and mitts, not knitted or crocheted<br>ex 6209 90 00 ex 6216 00 00 | | |
| ex 88 | Stockings, socks and sockettes, not knitted or crocheted; other clothing accessories, parts of garments or of clothing accessories, other than for babies, other than knitted or crocheted<br>ex 6209 90 00 ex 6217 10 00 ex 6217 90 00 | | |
| ex 91 | Tents<br>ex 6306 29 00 | | |
| ex 94 | Wadding of textile materials and articles thereof; textile fibres, not exceeding 5 mm in length (flock), textile dust and mill neps<br>ex 5601 10 90 ex 5601 29 00 ex 5601 30 00 | | |
| ex 95 | Felt and articles thereof, whether or not impregnated or coated, other than floor coverings<br>ex 5602 10 19 ex 5602 29 90 ex 5807 90 10 ex 6307 90 91<br>ex 5602 10 39 ex 5602 90 00<br>ex 5602 10 90 ex 6210 10 10 | | |
| ex 97 | Nets and netting made of twine, cordage or rope and made up fishing nets of yarn, twine, cordage or rope<br>ex 5608 90 00 | | |
| ex 98 | Other articles made from yarn, twine, cordage, rope or cables, other than textile fabrics, articles made from such fabrics and articles of category ex 97<br>ex 5609 00 00 ex 5905 00 10 | | |
| ex 99 | Textile fabrics coated with gum or amylaceous substances, of a kind used for the outer covers of books and the like, tracing cloth; prepared painting canvas; buckram and similar stiffened textile fabrics of a kind used for hat foundations<br>ex 5901 10 00 ex 5901 90 00<br><br>Linoleum, whether or not cut to shape; floor coverings consisting of a coating or covering applied on a textile backing, whether or not cut to shape<br>ex 5904 10 00 ex 5904 91 10 ex 5904 91 90 ex 5904 92 00<br><br>Rubberised textile fabrics, not knitted or crocheted, excluding those for tyres<br>ex 5906 10 00 ex 5906 99 10 ex 5906 99 90<br><br>Textile fabrics otherwise impregnated or coated; painted canvas being theatrical scenery, studio backcloths, other than of category ex 100<br>ex 5907 00 10 ex 5907 00 90 | | |
| ex 100 | Textile fabrics, impregnated, coated, covered or laminated with preparations of cellulose derivatives or of other artificial plastic materials<br>ex 5903 10 10 ex 5903 20 10 ex 5903 90 10 ex 5903 90 99<br>ex 5903 10 90 ex 5903 20 90 ex 5903 90 91 | | |

| (1) | (2) | (3) | (4) |
|---|---|---|---|
| ex 109 | Tarpaulins, sails, awnings, and sun-blinds<br>ex 6306 19 00 ex 6306 39 00 | | |
| ex 110 | Woven pneumatic mattresses<br>ex 6306 49 00 | | |
| ex 111 | Camping goods, woven, other than pneumatic mattresses and tents<br>ex 6306 99 00 | | |
| ex 112 | Other made-up textile articles, woven, excluding those of categories ex 113 and ex 114<br>ex 6307 20 00 ex 6307 90 99 | | |
| ex 113 | Floor cloths, dish cloths and dusters, other than knitted or crocheted<br>ex 6307 10 90 | | |
| ex 114 | Woven fabrics and articles for technical uses, other than those of category 136<br>ex 5908 00 00 ex 5910 00 00 ex 5911 31 19 ex 5911 32 90 ex 5911 90 90<br>ex 5911 31 90 ex 5911 40 00<br>ex 5909 00 90 ex 5911 10 00 ex 5911 32 10 ex 5911 90 10 | | |

GROUP IV

| (1) | (2) | (3) | (4) |
|---|---|---|---|
| 115 | Flax or ramie yarn<br>ex 5306 10 10 5306 10 50 ex 5306 20 10 ex 5308 90 12<br>ex 5306 10 30 5306 10 90 5306 20 90 5308 90 19 | | |
| 117 | Woven fabrics of flax or ramie<br>ex 5309 11 10 5309 21 10 5311 00 10 ex 5905 00 30<br>5309 11 90 5309 21 90<br>ex 5309 19 00 ex 5309 29 00 5803 90 90 | | |
| 118 | Table linen, toilet linen and kitchen linen of flax or ramie, other than knitted or crocheted<br>6302 29 10 6302 39 30 ex 6302 59 00 ex 6302 99 00<br>6302 39 10 6302 52 00 6302 92 00 | | |
| 120 | Curtains (including drapes), interior blinds, curtain and bed valances and other furnishing articles, not knitted or crocheted, of flax or ramie<br>ex 6303 99 90 6304 19 30 ex 6304 99 00 | | |
| 121 | Twine, cordage, ropes and cables, plaited or not, of flax or ramie<br>ex 5607 90 00 | | |

| (1) | (2) | (3) | (4) |
|---|---|---|---|
| 122 | Sacks and bags, of a kind used for the packing of goods, used, of flax, other than knitted or crocheted<br>ex 6305 90 00 | | |
| 123 | Woven-pile fabrics and chenille fabrics of flax or ramie, other than narrow woven fabrics<br>5801 90 10<br>Shawls, scarves, mufflers, mantillas, veils and the like, of flax or ramie, other than knitted or crocheted<br>6214 90 90 | | |

GROUP V

| (1) | (2) | (3) | (4) |
|---|---|---|---|
| 124 | Synthetic staple fibres<br>5501 10 00 5501 90 90 5503 10 90 5503 90 10 5505 10 30<br>5501 20 00 5503 20 00 5503 90 90 5505 10 50<br>5501 30 00 5503 10 11 5503 30 00 5505 10 70<br>5501 90 10 5503 10 19 5503 40 00 5505 10 10 5505 10 90 | | |
| 125 A | Synthetic filament yarn (continuous) not put up for retail sale<br>ex 5402 41 00 5402 42 00 5402 43 00 | | |
| 125 B | Monofilament, strip (artificial straw and the like) and imitation catgut of synthetic materials<br>5404 10 10 5404 90 11 5404 90 90 ex 5604 20 00<br>5404 10 90 5404 90 19 ex 5604 90 00 | | |
| 126 | Artificial staple fibres<br>5502 00 10 ex 5502 00 80 5504 10 00 5505 20 00<br>ex 5502 00 40 5504 90 00 | | |
| 127 A | Yarn of artificial filaments (continuous) not put up for retail sale, single yarn or viscose rayon untwisted or with a twist of not more than 250 turns per metre and single non-textured yarn of cellulose acetate<br>5403 31 00 ex 5403 32 00 5403 33 10 | | |
| 127 B | Monofilament, strip (artificial straw and the like) and imitation catgut of artificial textile materials<br>5405 00 00 ex 5604 90 00 | | |
| 128 | Coarse animal hair, carded or combed<br>5105 40 00 | | |
| 129 | Yarn of coarse animal hair or of horsehair<br>5110 00 00 | | |

| (1) | (2) | (3) | (4) |
|---|---|---|---|
| 130 A | Silk yarn other than yarn spun from silk waste<br>5004 00 10 5004 00 90 5006 00 10 | | |
| 130 B | Silk yarn other than of category 130 A; silk-worm gut<br>5505 00 10 5006 00 90 ex 5604 90 00<br>5505 00 90 | | |
| 131 | Yarn of other vegetable textile fibres<br>5308 90 90 | | |
| 132 | Paper yarn<br>5308 30 00 | | |
| 133 | Yarn of true hemp<br>5308 20 10 5308 20 90 | | |
| 134 | Metallised yarn<br>5605 00 00 | | |
| 135 | Woven fabrics of coarse animal hair or of horsehair<br>5113 00 00 | | |
| 136 A | Woven fabrics of silk or of silk waste other than unbleached, scoured or bleached<br>5007 20 19 ex 5007 20 41 5007 20 69 5007 90 50<br>ex 5007 20 31 5007 20 59 5007 20 71 5007 90 90<br>ex 5007 20 39 5007 20 61 5007 90 30 | | |
| 136 B | Woven fabrics of silk or of silk waste other than those of category 136 A<br>5007 10 00 ex 5007 20 31 5007 20 51 5803 90 10 ex 5911 20 00<br>5007 20 11 ex 5007 20 39 5007 90 10<br>5007 20 21 ex 5007 20 41 ex 5905 00 90 | | |
| 137 | Woven pile fabrics and chenille fabrics and narrow woven fabrics of silk, or of silk waste<br>ex 5801 90 90 ex 5806 10 00 | | |
| 138 | Woven fabrics of paper yarn and other textile fibres other than of ramie<br>5311 00 90 ex 5905 00 90 | | |
| 139 | Woven fabrics of metal threads or of metallised yarn<br>5809 00 00 | | |
| 140 | Knitted or crocheted fabric of textile material other than wool or fine animal hair, cotton or man-made fibres<br>ex 6001 10 00 6001 99 90 6002 20 90 6002 99 00<br>6001 29 90 6002 49 00 | | |

| (1) | (2) | (3) | (4) |
|---|---|---|---|
| 141 | Travelling rugs and blankets of textile material other than wool or fine animal hair, cotton or man-made fibres<br>ex 6301 90 90 | | |
| 142 | Carpets and other textile floor coverings of sisal, of other fibres of the Agave family or of Manila hemp<br>ex 5702 39 90 ex 5702 59 00 ex 5705 00 90<br>ex 5702 49 90 ex 5702 99 00 | | |
| 144 | Felt of coarse animal hair<br>5602 10 35 5602 29 10 | | |
| 145 | Twine, cordage, ropes and cables plaited or not of abaca (Manila hemp) or of true hemp<br>5607 30 00 ex 5607 90 00 | | |
| 146 A | Binder or baler twine for agricultural machines, of sisal or other fibres of the Agave family<br>ex 5607 21 00 | | |
| 146 B | Twine, cordage, ropes and cables of sisal or other fibres of the Agave family, other than the products of category 146 A<br>ex 5607 21 00 5607 29 10 5607 29 90 | | |
| 146 C | Twine, cordage, ropes and cables, whether or not plaited or braided, of jute or of other textile bast fibres of heading No 5303<br>5607 10 00 | | |
| 147 | Silk waste (including cocoons unsuitable for reeling), yarn waste and garnetted stock, other than not carded or combed<br>5003 90 00 | | |
| 148 A | Yarn of jute or of other textile bast fibres of heading No 5303<br>5307 10 10 5307 10 90 5307 20 00 | | |
| 148 B | Coir yarn<br>5308 10 00 | | |
| 149 | Woven fabrics of jute or of other textile bast fibres of a width of more than 150 cm<br>5310 10 90 ex 5310 90 00 | | |
| 150 | Woven fabrics of jute or of other textile bast fibres of a width of not more than 150 cm; sacks and bags, of a kind used for the packing of goods, of jute or of other textile bast fibres, other than used<br>5310 10 10 ex 5310 90 00 5905 00 50 6305 10 90 | | |

| (1) | (2) | (3) | (4) |
|---|---|---|---|
| 151 A | Floor coverings of coconut fibres (coir)<br>5702 20 00 | | |
| 151 B | Carpets and other textile floor coverings, of jute or of other textile bast fibres, other than tufted or flocked<br>ex 5702 39 90 ex 5702 49 90 ex 5702 59 00 ex 5702 99 00 | | |
| 152 | Needle loom felt of jute or of other textile bast fibres not impregnated or coated, other than floor coverings<br>5602 10 11 | | |
| 153 | Used sacks and bags, of a kind used for the packing of goods, of jute or of other textile bast fibres of heading No 5303<br>6305 10 10 | | |
| 154 | Silk worm cocoons, suitable for reeling<br>5001 00 00<br>Raw silk (not thrown)<br>5002 00 00<br>Silk waste (including cocoons unsuitable for reeling), yarn waste and garnetted stock, not carded or combed<br>5003 10 00<br>Wool not carded or combed<br>5101 11 00 5101 19 00 5101 21 00 5101 29 00 5101 30 00<br>Fine or coarse animal hair, not carded or combed<br>5102 10 10 5102 10 30 5102 10 50 5102 10 90 5102 20 00<br>Waste of wool or fine or coarse animal hair, including yarn waste but excluding garnetted stock<br>5103 10 10 5103 20 10 5103 20 99<br>5103 10 90 5103 20 91 5103 30 00<br>Garnetted stock of wool or fine or coarse animal hair<br>5104 00 00<br>Flax, raw or processed but not spun: flax tow and waste (including yarn waste and garnetted stock)<br>5301 10 00 5301 21 00 5301 29 00 5301 30 10 5301 30 90<br>Ramie and other vegetable textile fibres, raw or processed but not spun: tow, noils and waste, other than coir and abaca of heading No 5304<br>5305 91 00 5305 99 00<br>Cotton, not carded or combed<br>5201 00 10 5201 00 90 | | |

| (1) | (2) | (3) | (4) |
|---|---|---|---|
| 154<br>*(cont'd)* | Cotton waste (including yarn waste and garnetted stock<br>5202 10 00 5202 91 00 5202 99 00<br>True hemp (*Cannabis sativa* L.) raw or processed but not spun; tow and waste of true hemp (including yarn waste and garnetted stock)<br>5302 10 00 5302 90 00<br>Abaca (Manila hemp or *Musa textilis* Nee), raw or processed but not spun: tow and waste of abaca (including yarn waste and garnetted stock)<br>5305 21 00 5305 29 00<br>Jute and other textile bast fibres (excluding flax, true hemp and ramie), raw or processed but not spun: tow and waste of jute or other textile bast fibres (including yarn waste and garnetted stock<br>5303 10 00 5303 90 00<br>Other vegetable textile fibres, raw or processed but not spun: tow and waste of such fibres (including yarn waste and garnetted stock)<br>5304 10 00 5305 11 00 5305 91 00<br>5304 90 00 5305 19 00 5305 99 00 | | |
| 156 | Blouses and pullovers knitted or crocheted of silk or silk waste for women and girls<br>6106 90 30 ex 6110 90 90 | | |
| 157 | Garments, knitted or crocheted, excluding garments of categories ex 10, ex 12, ex 13, ex 24, ex 27, ex 28, ex 67, ex 69, ex 72, ex 73, ex 75, ex 83 and 156<br>6101 90 10 6103 49 99 6105 90 90 6108 99 90 ex 6111 90 00<br>6101 90 90 6114 90 00<br>ex 6104 19 00 6106 90 50 6109 90 90<br>6102 90 10 ex 6104 29 00 6106 90 90<br>6102 90 90 ex 6104 39 00 6110 90 10<br>6104 49 00 ex 6107 99 00 ex 6110 90 90<br>ex 6103 39 00 6104 69 99 | | |
| 159 | Dresses, blouses and shirt-blouses, not knitted or crocheted, of silk or silk waste<br>6204 49 10 6206 10 00<br>Shawls, scarves, mufflers, mantillas, veils and the like, not knitted or crocheted, of silk or silk waste<br>6214 10 00<br>Ties, bow-ties and cravats of silk or silk waste<br>6215 10 00 | | |
| 160 | Handkerchiefs of silk or silk waste<br>6213 10 00 | | |
| 161 | Garments, not knitted or crocheted, excluding garments of categories ex 14, ex 15, ex 18, ex 31, ex 68, ex 72, ex 78, ex 86, ex 87, ex 88 and 159<br>6201 19 00 6203 19 90 6204 29 90 6205 90 10 ex 6211 20 00<br>6201 99 00 6203 29 90 6204 39 90 6205 90 90 6211 39 00<br>6203 39 90 6204 49 90 6211 49 00'<br>6202 19 00 6203 49 90 6204 59 90 6206 90 10<br>6202 99 00 6204 69 90 6206 90 90<br>6204 19 90 | | |

*Appendix 5*

'ANNEX II

(The full product descriptions of the categories listed in this Annex are to be found in Appendix 4 of this Agreement)

**COMMUNITY QUANTITATIVE LIMITS**

| Category | Units | 2000 |
|---|---|---|
| ex 13 (1) | 1 000 pieces | 714 |
| ex 18 (1) | tonnes | 946 |
| ex 20 (1) | tonnes | 43 |
| ex 24 (1) | 1 000 pieces | 180 |
| ex 39 (1) | tonnes | 403 |
| 115 | tonnes | 1 134 |
| 117 | tonnes | 539 |
| 118 | tonnes | 1 239 |
| 120 | tonnes | 488 |
| 122 | tonnes | 170 |
| 123 | tonnes | 83 |
| 124 | tonnes | 911 (2) |
| 125A | tonnes | 16 |
| 125B | tonnes | 39 |
| 126 | tonnes | 16 |
| 127A | tonnes | 26 |
| 127B | tonnes | 15 |
| 136A | tonnes | 389 |
| 140 | tonnes | 125 |
| 145 | tonnes | 26 |
| 146A | tonnes | 152 |
| 146B | tonnes | 231 |
| 151B | tonnes | 2 352 |
| 156 | tonnes | 3 073 |
| 157 | tonnes | 11 597 |
| 159 | tonnes | 4 152 |
| 160 | tonnes | 49 |
| 161 | tonnes | 14 864 |

(1) Categories marked by "ex" cover products other than those of wool or fine animal hairs, cotton or synthetic or artificial textile materials.

(2) This limit does not apply to fibers of polyvinyl alcohol falling within ex 5503 90 90.'

*Appendix 6*

'ANNEX TO PROTOCOL B

(the product descriptions of the categories listed in this Annex are to be found in Annex I to the Agreement)

OPT QUOTAS

**COMMUNITY QUANTITATIVE LIMITS FOR THE YEAR 2000**

| Category | Unit |
|---|---|
| 159 | 8,1 tonnes |
| 161 | 15,5 tonnes' |

A similar agreement was concluded in December 2000 (see Document 2.10). China's WTO membership was in sight, since by then China had concluded bilateral agreements on its WTO accession with both the USA and the EU (see Chapter 7). Consequently, the 2000 Agreement, which was to apply starting 21 November 2000, provided that quotas established under the EU–China bilateral agreements on textiles would, on China's accession to the WTO, be phased out in the framework of the WTO's ATC and China's Protocol on WTO Accession. It also stated the parties' agreement concerning EU notification to the WTO Textiles Monitoring Body of its textile quotas and programme for phasing them out within the framework of the ATC.

## Document 2.10: 2000 Agreement on MFA and Non-MFA Textile Products

**Agreement in the form of an Exchange of Letters between the European Community and the People's Republic of China initialled in Beijing on 19 May 2000 amending the Agreement between them on trade in textile products and amending the Agreement between them initialled on 19 January 1995 on trade in textile products not covered by the MFA bilateral Agreement—Protocol A**

*OJ L 314, 14.12.2000, p. 14–26 (ES, DA, DE, EL, EN, FR, IT, NL, PT FI, SV)*

Agreement in the form of an Exchange of Letters

between the European Community and the People's Republic of China initialled in Beijing on 19 May 2000 amending the Agreement between them on trade in textile products and amending the Agreement between them initialled on 19 January 1995 on trade in textile products not covered by the MFA bilateral Agreement

A. Letter from the Council of the European Union

Sir,

1. I have the honour to refer to the consultations held between our respective delegations for the purpose of amending and extending both the Agreement between the European Economic Community and the People's Republic of China on trade in textile products initialled on 9 December 1988, as last amended by an Agreement initialled on 6 December 1999 (hereinafter referred to as "the MFA Agreement") and the Agreement between the European Community and the People's Republic of China initialled on 19 January 1995 on trade in textile products not covered by the MFA bilateral Agreement, as last amended by an Agreement initialled on 6 December 1999 (hereinafter referred to as "the non-MFA Agreement").

2. As a result of the consultations, the Parties agreed to modify the MFA and non-MFA Agreements.

3. Should the People's Republic of China become a Member of the World Trade Organisation before the date of expiry of the MFA and non-MFA bilateral Agreements, the restrictions in force under those Agreements shall be phased out in the framework of the WTO Agreement on textiles and clothing and China's Protocol of Accession to the WTO.

4. Without prejudice to paragraph 3, and in particular without prejudice to safeguard provisions, the Parties recorded their mutual understanding on the following aspects concerning the notifications in respect of the restrictions under the MFA agreement to be made to the textiles monitoring body for the purposes of Article 2 of the Agreement on textiles and clothing:

(a) The European Union will notify to the textiles monitoring body the quantitative restrictions maintained under the MFA Agreement (save for those quantitative limits concerning products already included by the European Community in stages 1 or 2 of integration under the Agreement on textiles and clothing) at the levels agreed for the year during which China accedes to the WTO as being the restraint levels for the purposes of notification under Article 2(1) of the Agreement on textiles and clothing, detailing the quantitative limits contained in Annex III of the above agreement including the quantitative limits reserved for European industry within those amounts and the separate quantitative limits reserved for outward processing traffic and European fairs respectively.

(b) The European Union will notify to the textiles monitoring body the growth rates applicable to the restraint levels, and the relevant parts thereof, being those growth rates applied for the renewal of the MFA agreement for the year 2000.

(c) These growth rates will be increased by the growth on growth provisions of the Agreement on textiles and clothing for the second stage of integration beginning from 1 January of the year following accession, and, after 1 January 2002, by the growth on growth provisions for the third stage of integration.

(d) The European Union will notify the flexibility provisions contained in Article 5 of the MFA Agreement save for the cap on flexibilities contained in Article 5(5) as applying to the quantitative limits contained in Annex III of the above Agreement and to the limits set for European fairs.

5. Without prejudice to paragraph 3, and in particular without prejudice to safeguard provisions, the Parties recorded their mutual understanding on the following aspects concerning the notifications in respect of the restrictions under the non-MFA agreement to be made to the textiles monitoring body for the purposes of Article 3 of the Agreement on textiles and clothing:

(a) The European Community will notify to the textiles monitoring body the quantitative restrictions maintained under the non-MFA Agreement at the levels specified for the year during which China accedes to the WTO as being the restraint levels for the purposes of Article 3 of the Agreement on textiles and clothing, detailing the quantitative limits contained in Annex II of the non-MFA Agreement and the separate quantitative limits reserved for outward processing traffic.

(b) The Parties agree that pending liberalisation of the above quantitative restrictions the growth rates applied to them, and to the relevant parts thereof, for the renewal of the non-MFA agreement for the year 2000 will apply pending liberalisation of those restrictions and be included in the notification pursuant to Article 3 of the Agreement on textiles and clothing.

(c) The European Union will include the flexibility provisions contained in Article 8 of the non-MFA Agreement in its notification pursuant to Article 3 of the Agreement on textiles and clothing.

(d) The Parties agree that the European Community will align its programme in accordance Article 3(2) of the ATC to phase out the quantitative restrictions progressively to follow Annex I to this Agreement.

6. The Parties agreed that following China's WTO accession they would, pursuant to Article 2(17) of the Agreement on textiles and clothing, jointly notify to the textiles monitoring body the administrative arrangements contained in Annex II to this Agreement. The Parties agreed that the administrative arrangements would apply in respect of both the MFA Agreement and the non-MFA Agreement.

7. In the event that China accedes to the WTO after 31 December 2000 the Parties agree that both the MFA Agreement and the non-MFA Agreement will be automatically extended for a further period of one year to 31 December 2001, on the basis of the quantitative limits for the year 2000, together with all the relevant parts thereof including the quantities reserved for European industry, the quantities set for outward processing traffic and for European fairs, increased by the growth rates, if any, applied to the quantitative limits, and the relevant parts thereof, on the renewal of the MFA Agreement and the non-MFA Agreement for the year 2000.

8. I should be obliged if you could kindly confirm the acceptance of your Government of the foregoing. Should this be the case, this Agreement in form of an Exchange of Letters shall enter into force on the first day of the month following the day on which the Parties have notified each other that the legal procedures necessary to this end have been completed. In the meantime, it shall be applied provisionally on conditions of reciprocity.

Please accept, Sir, the assurance of my highest consideration.

For the Council of the European Union

ANNEX I
Phase-out schedule for the quantitative restrictions notified pursuant to Article 3 of the Agreement on textiles and clothing

>TABLE>

For those products that are to be phased out progressively in the above table the Parties agree that, dependent on progress in the removal by China of state trading in respect of silk products, the European Community will remove the restrictions on no less than 9 categories on 1 January 2002 and the restrictions on all remaining products no later than 1 January 2005. Either Party may at any time request consultations pursuant to the procedures provided for in the Administrative Arrangements agreed between the Parties concerning the application of the above provisions. In order to facilitate such consultations the competent authorities of the European Community will inform the Chinese authorities of any intention to make a notification in this regard to the textiles monitoring body.

ANNEX II
Administrative arrangements between the European Community and the People's Republic of China for notification to the textiles monitoring body under Article 2(17) of the Agreement on textiles and clothing

Article 1
Classification system

The classification of the products covered by these administrative arrangements is based on the tariff and statistical nomenclature of the European Community (the "Community") (hereinafter called the "Combined Nomenclature", or in abbreviated form "CN") and any amendments thereof.

Article 2
Determination of origin of covered products

1. The origin of the products covered by these administrative arrangements shall be determined in accordance with the rules in force in the Community and the procedures for control of the products set out in Protocol A.

2. If any amendment is made to the rules of origin, the Community shall, with the agreement of the People's Republic of China, take appropriate measures to avoid any possible consequent reduction of the People's Republic of China's ability to use the quantitative limits established under Article 2 of the Agreement on textiles and clothing (ATC).

Article 3
Double-checking

The People's Republic of China agrees to restrain its exports to the Community of the products described in the notifications of the Community to the textiles monitoring body (TMB) under Article 2(1) of the ATC to the limits set out therein as increased by the growth rates provided under Article 2 of the ATC and as may be modified by the flexibility provisions notified to the TMB under Article 2(1) of the ATC, until such time as these products are integrated into GATT 1994 under paragraphs 6, 8, or 9 of Article 2 of the ATC. Exports of restrained textile products shall be subject to a double-checking system specified in Protocol A.

Article 4
Industry reserve

Within the limits described in the notifications of the Community to the textiles monitoring body (TMB) under Article 2(1) of the Agreement on textiles and clothing (ATC) the People's Republic of China agrees to maintain a reserve open for Community industry for the quantities and for the periods specified in the footnotes to the notification.

To facilitate the implementation of these provisions the Community shall provide the competent Chinese authorities, before the end of each year, with a list of interested manufacturers and processors and, if possible, of the quantity of products requested for each firm. To this end, the firms concerned are invited to make direct contact with the relevant Chinese bodies by 15 February of the following year, in order to make their purchasing intentions known.

3. The Chinese authorities undertake to operate the system in such a way as to ensure the maximum possible utilisation of the industry reserve by Community industry consistent with market forces. In order to do so China undertakes to operate the system in a prompt and non-discriminatory manner; to provide the names and addresses of the relevant foreign trade administrative bodies; to provide texts of the relevant regulations as soon as they are available; to ensure that export licences under this system are identified as "industry reserve"; to supply separate statistical information concerning licences issued pursuant to these provisions; and, to cooperate with the European Community authorities to ensure that licences issued pursuant to these provisions are identified within the exchanges of information via the SIGL network established between the Community and China.

Article 5
Amounts reserved for use at European fairs

Within the limits described in the notifications of the Community to the textiles monitoring body (TMB) under Article 2(1) of the ATC the separate additional amounts specified for such purposes in the notification are reserved for use at trade fairs on the understanding that such amounts may be used exclusively at European Fairs. Such amounts may be modified by the flexibility provisions notified to the TMB under Article 2( ) of the ATC.

Article 6
Re-imports after OPT

The People's Republic of China and the Community recognise the special and differential character of re-imports of textile products into the Community after processing in the People's Republic of China. Such re-imports may be provided for outside the quantitative limits established under Article 2 of the ATC provided that they are effected in accordance with the regulations on economic outward processing in force in the Community.

Article 7
Imports to EC for re-export after processing

1. Exports to the Community of textile products covered by these administrative arrangements shall not be subject to quantitative limits established under Article 2 of the ATC, provided that they are declared to be for re-export outside the Community in the same state or after processing, within the framework of the administrative system of control which exists within the Community. However, the release for home use within the Community of products imported under the conditions referred to above shall be subject to the production of an export licence issued by the People's Republic of China authorities and to proof of origin, in accordance with the provisions of Protocol A.

2. Where the competent authorities in the Community have evidence that products exported from the People's Republic of China and set off by the People's Republic of China against a quantitative limit established under Article 2 of the ATC have been subsequently re-exported outside the Community, the authorities concerned shall notify the People's

Republic of China of the quantities involved. Upon receipt of such notification, the People's Republic of China may authorise exports for the current or the following year of identical quantities of products, within the same category, which shall not be set off against the quantitative limits established under Article 2 of the ATC.

Article 8
Cottage industry, handloom and folklore products

Cottage industry, handloom and folklore products fulfilling the definitions contained in Protocol B to the MFA Agreement shall be exempt from the quantitative restrictions established under Article 2 of the ATC provided they are accompanied by a certificate conforming to the model annexed to these administrative arrangements. In case of divergent opinions between China and the competent Community authorities at the point of entry into the Community as to the nature of such products consultations shall be held within one month with a view to resolving such difficulties. The Chinese authorities undertake not to issue certificates in respect of this exemption when exports of the products in question have exceeded 15 % of the quantitative limit for such a product established pursuant to Article 2 of the ATC.

Article 9
Operation of the SIGL system

The Parties agree that they will effect the management of licensing via the direct computer links established between the Community's SIGL system and the licensing computers of MOFTEC pursuant to the arrangements agreed between them.

Article 10
Statistical verification of carryover

The People's Republic of China shall provide the Community with export data showing the amounts of carryover available in any given year. The calculation of carry over will normally be effected pursuant to the information and data provided via the SIGL system. If substantial statistical differences exist between the export data from which the amount to be carried over is calculated and the Community's data the Community may, within the first 120 days of the following year, request consultations in accordance with the procedures referred to in Article 15(1) of these administrative arrangements on the amounts involved. Any such request shall be accompanied by full particulars of the alleged statistical differences. Where such a request is made, the portions carried over shall not be used until the parties have completed consultations. If no such request is made within a 120-day period, the portion carried over shall be presumed to have been calculated correctly.

Article 11
Exchange of statistical information

1. The People's Republic of China undertakes to supply the Community with precise statistical information on all export licences issued by the People's Republic of China authorities for all categories of textile products subject to the quantitative limits established under Article 2 of the ATC. The People's Republic of China shall set out in its periodical statistical reports the maximum export levels for each category subject to a quantitative limit established under Article 2 of the ATC and the rate of utilisation of these levels.

2. The Community shall likewise transmit to the People's Republic of China authorities precise statistical information on import documents issued by the Community authorities in respect of export licences issued by the People's Republic of China. This information shall, for all categories of products, be transmitted before the end of the second month following the quarter to which the statistics relate.

3. The Community shall transmit to the People's Republic of China authorities import statistics for products covered by Article 7(1) of these administrative arrangements.

4. Should it be found on analysis of the information exchanged above that there are significant discrepancies between the returns for exports and those for imports, consultations may be initiated in accordance with the procedure specified in Article 15(1) of these administrative arrangements. Any such consultations shall be resolved on the basis of the agreed descriptions of the products set out in the notification under Article 2(1) of the ATC.

5. The Parties agree that to the maximum extent possible such exchange of information shall be made via the computer links established between the Community's SIGL system and the licensing computers of MOFTEC as referred to in Article 9.

6. In any event, the information provided for in paragraph 1 shall, for all categories of products, be forwarded before the end of the month following the month to which the statistics relate and the information referred to in paragraph 3 shall, for all categories of products, be transmitted before the end of the third month following the quarter to which the statistics relate, unless they have already been exchanged by electronic means.

Article 12
Amendments to classification

1. The authorities of the People's Republic of China shall be informed of any amendment to the Combined Nomenclature or any decision, made in accordance with the procedures in force in the Community, relating to the classification of products covered by these administrative arrangements. Any such amendment or any decision which results in a modification of the classification of products covered by these administrative arrangements shall not have the effect of reducing the People's Republic of China's ability to use the quantitative limits established under Article 2 of the ATC. The procedures for the application of this paragraph are set out in Protocol A.

2. In case of divergent opinions between the People's Republic of China and the competent Community authorities at the point of entry into the Community on the classification of products subject to quantitative limits established under Articles 2 of the ATC, consultations in accordance with Article 15(1) of these administrative arrangements shall be held with a view to reaching agreement on the appropriate classification of the products concerned and to resolving any difficulties arising therefrom. For this purpose, the authorities of the People's Republic of China shall be informed by the competent authorities of the Community as soon as a case of divergent opinions on the classification of products arises. Pending agreement on the appropriate classification and in order to avoid disruption to trade, the products in question shall be imported on the basis of the classification indicated by the competent Community authorities at the point of entry, in conformity with the provisions of these administrative arrangements.

Article 13
Circumvention

1. The People's Republic of China and the Community agree to cooperate fully in preventing the circumvention of these administrative arrangements by transhipment, re-routing or whatever other means in accordance with Article 5 of the ATC.

2. Deduction of the relevant quantitative limits, once established pursuant to Article 5 of the ATC, shall, as a general rule, be effected by debiting an amount equivalent to the agreed amounts from the corresponding quantitative limits for the year in which the circumvention took place or for subsequent years, the timing and apportioning of such debiting being decided in consultation with the Community, to ensure that any debiting may be satisfactorily implemented.

3. The People's Republic of China confirms that its export control system permits the prompt debiting of the amounts agreed for such purposes to the corresponding quantitative limits established under Article 2 of the ATC and the previous bilateral Agreement.

4. Following China's accession to the WTO cases of circumvention taking place before accession will also be dealt with according to the above paragraphs.

Article 14
Regional concentration

1. The quantitative limits established under Article 2 of the ATC on imports into the Community of textile products of the People's Republic of China origin will not be broken down by the Community into regional shares.

2. Notwithstanding the above, for imperative technical or administrative reasons or to find a solution to economic problems resulting from regional concentration of imports, or in order to combat circumvention and fraud of the provisions of these administrative arrangements, the Community will establish for a limited period of time a specific management system in conformity with the principles of the internal market. Should the Community have recourse to this provision, the textile products covered by the corresponding export licences can only be put into free circulation in the region(s) of the Community indicated in those licences. Similarly, the products covered by the import licences can only be put into free circulation in the region(s) of the Community indicated in those licences. This provision was invoked by the Community as from 1 January 1993.

3. The Parties shall cooperate in order to prevent sudden and prejudicial changes in traditional trade flows resulting in regional concentration of direct imports into the Community.

4. The People's Republic of China shall monitor its exports of products under restraint into the Community. Should a sudden and prejudicial change in traditional trade flows arise, the Community will be entitled to request consultations in order to find a satisfactory solution to those problems. Such consultations shall be held in accordance with Article 15(1) of these administrative arrangements. The People's Republic of China, from the date of request for and pending the consultations, will not issue export licences that would further aggravate the problem.

5. However, if the Parties are unable to reach a satisfactory solution during the consultations, the People's Republic of China will, if so requested by the Community, respect temporary export limits for one or more regions of the Community. In such a case, these limits shall not preclude the importation into the region(s) concerned of products which

were shipped from the People's Republic of China on the basis of export licences obtained before the date of formal notification to the People's Republic of China by the Community about the introduction of the above limits. The Community shall inform the People's Republic of China of the technical and administrative measures that need to be introduced by both Parties so that implementation is in conformity with principles of the Internal Market.

6. The People's Republic of China shall endeavour to ensure that exports of textile products subject to quantitative limits established under Article 2 of the ATC into the Community are spaced out as evenly as possible over the year due account being taken in particular of seasonal factors.

7. The People's Republic of China shall endeavour not to deprive certain regions of the Community which have traditionally had relatively small shares of Community quotas of imports of products serving as inputs for their processing industry. The Community and the People's Republic of China shall hold consultations, should the need arise, in order to avert any problems which might occur in this respect.

Article 15
Consultations

1. Save where it is otherwise provided for in these administrative arrangements, the special consultation procedures referred to in these administrative arrangements shall be governed by the following rules:

- any request for consultations shall be notified in writing to the other Party, together with a statement setting out the reasons and circumstances which, in the opinion of the requesting Party, justify the submission of such a request;
- the Parties shall enter into consultations within one month at the latest of notification of the request, with a view to reaching agreement or a mutually acceptable conclusion within one further month at the latest.

2. If necessary, at the request of either of the Parties consultations shall be held on any problems arising from the application of these administrative arrangements. Any consultations held under this Article shall be approached by both Parties in a spirit of cooperation and with a desire to reconcile the differences between them.

Article 16
Quantitative limits notified under Article 3 of the ATC

The Parties agree that these administrative arrangements will apply "mutatis mutandis" to the quantitative limits notified by the European Community under Article 3 of the ATC.

PROTOCOL A

TITLE I
CLASSIFICATION

Article 1

1. The competent authorities of the Community undertake to inform the People's Republic of China of any changes in the Combined Nomenclature (CN) before the date of their entry into effect in the Community.

2. The competent authorities of the Community undertake to inform the People's Republic of China of any decisions relating to the classification of products subject to these administrative arrangements within one month of their adoption at the latest. Such communication shall include:

(a) a description of the products concerned;

(b) the relevant category and the related tariff and statistical references;

(c) the reasons which have led to the decision.

3. Where a decision on classification results in a change of classification practice or a change of category of any product subject to these administrative arrangements, the competent authorities of the Community shall provide 30 days' notice, from the date of the Community's communication, before the decision is put into effect. Products shipped before the date of application of the decision shall remain subject to the earlier classification practice, provided that the goods in question are presented for importation into the Community within 60 days of that date.

4. Where a Community decision on classification resulting in a change of classification practice or a change of categorisation of any product subject to these administrative arrangements affects a category subject to restraint, the Community undertakes to enter into consultations without delay in accordance with the procedures described in paragraph 1 of Article 15 of these administrative arrangements with a view to agreeing necessary adjustments to the appropriate quantitative limits established under Article 2 of the ATC and mitigating any disruptive effects which might arise from such a Community decision.

TITLE II
ORIGIN

Article 2

1. Products originating in the People's Republic of China for export to the Community in accordance with the arrangements established by these administrative arrangements shall be accompanied by a certificate of the People's Republic of China origin conforming to the model annexed to this Protocol.

2. The certificate of the People's Republic of China origin shall be issued by the competent governmental authorities of the People's Republic of China if the products in question can be considered products originating in that country within the meaning of the relevant rules in force in the Community.

3. The certificates of the People's Republic of China origin referred to in paragraph 1 shall not be required for products of Group III of the Community's system of categories. These may be imported into the Community in accordance with the arrangements set out in these administrative arrangements on production of a declaration by the exporter on the invoice or other commercial document relating to the products to the effect that the products in question originated in China within the meaning of the relevant rules in force in the Community.

4. The certificate of the People's Republic of China origin referred to in paragraph 1 shall not be required for import of goods covered by a certificate of origin Form A completed in accordance with the relevant Community rules in order to qualify for generalised tariff preferences.

Article 3

The discovery of slight discrepancies between the statements made in the certificate of origin and those made in the documents produced to the customs office for the purpose of carrying out the formalities for importing the product shall not ipso facto cast doubt upon the statements in the certificate.

TITLE III
DOUBLE-CHECKING SYSTEM FOR CATEGORIES OF PRODUCTS WITH QUANTITATIVE LIMITS

Section I
Exportation

Article 4

The competent authorities of the People's Republic of China shall issue an export licence in respect of all consignments from the People's Republic of China of textile products subject to quantitative limits established under Article 2 of the ATC, up to the relevant quantitative limits as increased by the growth rates provided under Article 2 of the ATC and as may be modified by the flexibility provisions notified to the TMB under Article 2(1) of the ATC, until such time as these products are integrated into GATT 1994 under paragraphs 6, 8 or 9 of Article 2 of the ATC.

Article 5

1. The export licence shall conform to the model annexed to this Protocol and it shall be valid for exports throughout the customs territory to which the Treaty establishing the European Community is applied.

2. Each export licence shall only cover one of the categories of products.

3. These provisions are without prejudice to any subsequent arrangements the Parties may enter into concerning the electronic transmission of information to replace the grant of export licences in paper form.

Article 6

The competent Community authorities must be notified forthwith of the withdrawal or alteration of any export licence already issued.

Article 7

1. Exports shall be set off against the quantitative limits established under Article 2 of the ATC for the year in which shipment of the goods has been effected, even if the export licence is issued after such shipment.

2. For the purpose of applying paragraph 1, shipment of the goods is considered to have taken place on the date of their loading on to the exporting aircraft, vehicle or vessel.

Article 8

The presentation of an export licence, in application of Article 10 below, shall be effected not later than 31 March of the year following that in which the goods covered by the export licence have been shipped.

Section II
Importation

Article 9

Importation into the Community of textile products subject to quantitative limits established under Article 2 of the ATC shall be subject to the presentation of an import authorisation or document.

Article 10

1. The competent Community authorities shall issue such import authorisation or document automatically within five working days of the presentation by the importer of the original of the corresponding export licence. The import authorisations shall be valid for six months from the date of their issue for imports throughout the customs territory to which the Treaty establishing the European Community is applied.

2. The competent Community authorities shall cancel the already issued import authorisation or document if the corresponding export licence has been withdrawn. However, if the competent Community authorities have not been notified of the withdrawal or cancellation of the export licence until after the products have been imported into the Community, the quantities involved shall be set off against the quantitative limit established under Article 2(1) of the ATC for the category and the quota year in question and the People's Republic of China shall be informed as soon as possible.

Article 11

1. If the competent Community authorities find that the total quantities covered by export licences issued by the People's Republic of China for a particular category in any given year exceed the quantitative limit established under Article 2 of the ATC for that category as increased by the growth rates provided under Article 2 of the ATC and as may be modified by the flexibility provisions notified to the TMB under Article 2(1) of the ATC, until such time as these products are integrated into GATT 1994 under paragraphs 6, 8 or 9 of Article 2 of the ATC, the said authorities may suspend the further issue of import authorisations or documents. In this event, the competent Community authorities shall immediately inform the authorities of the People's Republic of China and the special consultation procedure set out in Article 12(1) of these administrative arrangements shall be initiated forthwith.

2. Exports of restrained textile products of the People's Republic of China origin not covered by the People's Republic of China export licences issued in accordance with the provisions of this Protocol may be refused the issue of import authorisations or documents by the competent Community authorities. However, if the import of such products is allowed into the Community by the competent Community authorities, the quantities involved shall not be set off against the appropriate quantitative limits established under Article 2 of the ATC, without the express agreement of the People's Republic of China.

TITLE IV
FORM AND PRODUCTION OF EXPORT CERTIFICATES AND CERTIFICATES OF ORIGIN, AND COMMON PROVISIONS

Article 12

1. The export licence and the certificate of origin of the People's Republic of China may comprise additional copies duly indicated as such. They shall be made out in English or

French. If they are completed by hand, entries must be in ink and in printed script. These documents shall measure 210 x 297 mm. The paper used must be writing paper weighing not less than 25 g/m2. Only the original, clearly marked "original" shall be accepted by the competent authorities of the Community as being valid for the purposes of export to the Community in accordance with the arrangements established by these administrative arrangements.

2. Each export licence and certificate of the People's Republic of China origin shall bear a serial number, whether or not printed, by which it can be identified. The number for the export licence shall be standardised and composed of the following elements:

- two letters identifying the People's Republic of China as follows CN;
- two letters identifying the intended Member State of customs clearance as follows:

AT= Austria

BL= Benelux

DE= Germany

DK= Denmark

EL= Greece

ES= Spain

FI= Finland

FR= France

GB= United Kingdom

IE= Ireland

IT= Italy

PT= Portugal

SE= Sweden;

- a one-digit number identifying quota year, corresponding to the last figure in year, e.g. 7 for 1987;
- two spaces identifying the particular issuing office concerned in the People's Republic of China;
- a five-digit number running consequently from 00001 to 99999 allocated to the intended Member State of customs clearance.

Article 13

The export licence and certificate of origin may be issued after the shipment of the products to which they relate. In such cases they shall bear either the endorsement "délivré à posteriori" or the endorsement "issued retrospectively".

Article 14

1. In the event of theft, loss or destruction of an export licence or a certificate of origin, the exporter may apply to the competent governmental authority which issued the document

for a duplicate to be made out on the basis of the export documents in his possession. The duplicate of any such certificate or licence so issued shall bear the endorsement "duplicata".

2. The duplicate must bear the date of the original export licence or certificate of origin.

TITLE V
ADMINISTRATIVE COOPERATION

Article 15

The Community and the People's Republic of China shall cooperate closely to implement the provisions of these administrative arrangements. To this end, contacts and exchanges of views (including on technical matters) shall be facilitated by both parties, in particular to establish the authenticity and accuracy of documentation required under the provisions of these administrative arrangements.

Article 16

The People's Republic of China shall send to the Commission of the European Community the names and addresses of the governmental authorities competent for the issue and verification of export licences and certificates of origin together with specimens of the stamps used by these authorities. the People's Republic of China shall also notify the Commission of any change in this information.

Article 17

1. Verification of certificates of the People's Republic of China origin or export licences shall be carried out at random by the People's Republic of China authorities.

2. The competent Community authorities may request subsequent verification of certificates of the People's Republic of China origin or export licences at random or whenever they have reasonable doubt as to the authenticity of such certificates or licences or as to the accuracy of the information regarding the products in question. In such cases the competent authorities in the Community shall return the certificate of the People's Republic of China origin or export licence, or a copy thereof to the People's Republic of China authorities, giving, where appropriate, the reasons for an enquiry. If the invoice has been submitted, such invoice shall be attached to the certificate or licence or its copy. The authorities shall also forward any information that has been obtained suggesting that the particulars given on the said certificate or licence are inaccurate.

3. Should the results of the random verification referred to in paragraph 1 above reveal serious contravention of the provisions of these administrative arrangements, the People's Republic of China authorities shall notify the competent Community authorities of the results. Where the competent Community authorities have requested verification under paragraph 2 above, the results of such verification shall be communicated to the competent Community authorities within three months at the latest. The information communicated shall indicate whether the disputed certificate or licence applies to the goods actually exported and whether these goods are eligible for export in accordance with the arrangements established by these administrative arrangements. Where the competent Community authorities so request, the information communicated shall also include copies of such other available documentation as may facilitate the full determination of the facts and, in particular, the true origin of the goods.

4. For the purpose of subsequent verification of certificates of the People's Republic of China origin and export licences, copies of these together with relevant supporting documentation required to be lodged with the People's Republic of China authorities for the issue of such certificates or licences shall be kept for a period of at least two years by the People's Republic of China authorities.

Article 18

1. Where the verification procedure referred to in Article 17 above or where information available to the Community or to the People's Republic of China indicates or appears to indicate that the provisions of these administrative arrangements are being contravened, both parties shall cooperate closely and with appropriate urgency to prevent such contravention.

2. To this end, the People's Republic of China shall, on its own initiative or at the request of the Community, carry out appropriate enquiries or arrange for such enquiries to be carried out concerning operations which are or appear to be in contravention of these administrative arrangements. The People's Republic of China shall communicate the results of these enquiries to the Community together with such other available information as may facilitate the determination of the true origin of the goods.

3. By agreement between the Community and the People's Republic of China, officials designated by the Community may be present at the enquiries referred to in paragraph 2.

4. In pursuance of the cooperation referred to in paragraph 1, the People's Republic of China and the Community shall exchange any information considered by either party to be of use in preventing the contravention of the provisions of these administrative arrangements. These exchanges may include information on textile production in the People's Republic of China and on trade in textile products of a kind covered by these administrative arrangements between the People's Republic of China and other countries, particularly where the Community has reasonable grounds to consider that the products in question may be in transit across the territory of the People's Republic of China prior to their importation into the Community. This information shall include at the request of the Community copies of all relevant documentation. The People's Republic of China will provide such information as is available and in accordance with the People's Republic of China law.

5. The Community shall where appropriate at the request of the People's Republic of China cooperate jointly with the People's Republic of China in cases of circumvention which affect the People's Republic of China, in conformity with procedures in force in the Community.

6. Where it is established to the satisfaction of both parties that the provisions of these administrative arrangements have been contravened, the People's Republic of China and the Community agree to take all reasonable measures to prevent a recurrence of such contravention.

B. Letter from the Government of the People's Republic of China

Sir,

I have the honour to acknowledge receipt of your letter which reads as follows:

"1. I have the honour to refer to the consultations held between our respective delegations for the purpose of amending and extending both the Agreement between the European Economic Community and the People's Republic of China on trade in textile products initialled on 9 December 1988, as last amended by an Agreement initialled on 6 December 1999 (hereinafter referred to as 'the MFA Agreement') and the Agreement between the European Community and the People's Republic of China initialled on 19 January 1995 on trade in textile products not covered by the MFA bilateral Agreement, as last amended by an Agreement initialled on 6 December 1999 (hereinafter referred to as 'the non-MFA Agreement').

2. As a result of the consultations, the Parties agreed to modify the MFA and non-MFA Agreements.

3. Should the People's Republic of China become a Member of the World Trade Organisation before the date of expiry of the MFA and non-MFA bilateral Agreements, the restrictions in force under those Agreements shall be phased out in the framework of the WTO Agreement on textiles and clothing and China's Protocol of Accession to the WTO.

4. Without prejudice to paragraph 3, and in particular without prejudice to safeguard provisions, the Parties recorded their mutual understanding on the following aspects concerning the notifications in respect of the restrictions under the MFA agreement to be made to the textiles monitoring body for the purposes of Article 2 of the Agreement on textiles and clothing:

(a) The European Union will notify to the textiles monitoring body the quantitative restrictions maintained under the MFA Agreement (save for those quantitative limits concerning products already included by the European Community in stages 1 or 2 of integration under the Agreement on textiles and clothing) at the levels agreed for the year during which China accedes to the WTO as being the restraint levels for the purposes of notification under Article 2(1) of the Agreement on textiles and clothing, detailing the quantitative limits contained in Annex III of the above agreement including the quantitative limits reserved for European industry within those amounts and the separate quantitative limits reserved for outward processing traffic and European fairs respectively.

(b) The European Union will notify to the textiles monitoring body the growth rates applicable to the restraint levels, and the relevant parts thereof, being those growth rates applied for the renewal of the MFA agreement for the year 2000.

(c) These growth rates will be increased by the growth on growth provisions of the Agreement on textiles and clothing for the second stage of integration beginning from 1 January of the year following accession, and, after 1 January 2002, by the growth on growth provisions for the third stage of integration.

(d) The European Union will notify the flexibility provisions contained in Article 5 of the MFA Agreement save for the cap on flexibilities contained in Article 5(5) as applying to the quantitative limits contained in Annex III of the above Agreement and to the limits set for European fairs.

5. Without prejudice to paragraph 3, and in particular without prejudice to safeguard provisions, the Parties recorded their mutual understanding on the following aspects concerning the notifications in respect of the restrictions under the non-MFA agreement to be made to the textiles monitoring body for the purposes of Article 3 of the Agreement on textiles and clothing:

(a) The European Community will notify to the textiles monitoring body the quantitative restrictions maintained under the non-MFA Agreement at the levels specified for the year during which China accedes to the WTO as being the restraint levels for the purposes of Article 3 of the Agreement on textiles and clothing, detailing the quantitative limits contained in Annex II of the non-MFA Agreement and the separate quantitative limits reserved for outward processing traffic.

(b) The Parties agree that pending liberalisation of the above quantitative restrictions the growth rates applied to them, and to the relevant parts thereof, for the renewal of the non-MFA agreement for the year 2000 will apply pending liberalisation of those restrictions and be included in the notification pursuant to Article 3 of the Agreement on textiles and clothing.

(c) The European Union will include the flexibility provisions contained in Article 8 of the non-MFA Agreement in its notification pursuant to Article 3 of the Agreement on textiles and clothing.

(d) The Parties agree that the European Community will align its programme in accordance Article 3(2) of the ATC to phase out the quantitative restrictions progressively to follow Annex I to this Agreement.

6. The Parties agreed that following China's WTO accession they would, pursuant to of Article 2(17) of the Agreement on textiles and clothing, jointly notify to the textiles monitoring body the administrative arrangements contained in Annex II to this Agreement. The Parties agreed that the administrative arrangements would apply in respect of both the MFA Agreement and the non-MFA Agreement.

7. In the event that China accedes to the WTO after 31 December 2000 the Parties agree that both the MFA Agreement and the non-MFA Agreement will be automatically extended for a further period of one year to 31 December 2001, on the basis of the quantitative limits for the year 2000, together with all the relevant parts thereof including the quantities reserved for European industry, the quantities set for outward processing traffic and for European fairs, increased by the growth rates, if any, applied to the quantitative limits, and the relevant parts thereof, on the renewal of the MFA Agreement and the non-MFA Agreement for the year 2000.

8. I should be obliged if you could kindly confirm the acceptance of your Government of the foregoing. Should this be the case, this Agreement in form of an Exchange of Letters shall enter into force on the first day of the month following the day on which the Parties have notified each other that the legal procedures necessary to this end have been completed. In the meantime, it shall be applied provisionally on conditions of reciprocity."

I have the honour to confirm that my Government is in agreement with the contents of your letter and the annexes attached thereto.

Please accept, Sir, the assurance of my highest consideration.

For the Government of the People's Republic of China

The ATC provided for a ten-year period for the removal of textile quotas among WTO members. This transitional period started on 1 January 1995, when the WTO agreements entered into force but before China joined the WTO. By the time of Chinese accession, the first and second stages of integration had already been completed (see Document 2.11). Consequently, certain quantitative restrictions had already been removed as of 11 December 2001, when China acceded to WTO membership.

## Document 2.11: China's accession to the WTO: first and second stages of integration under the Agreement on Textiles and Clothing

**China's accession to the WTO**
**First and second stage of integration under the Agreement on textiles and clothing**

*Official Journal C 356 , 14/12/2001 P. 0004–0004 DA DE EL EN ES FI FR IT NL PT SV*

China's accession to the WTO
First and second stage of integration under the Agreement on textiles and clothing
(2001/C 356/03)

Following China's accession to the WTO on 11 December 2001, the European Community and the People's Republic of China have agreed to implement the removal of the quantitative restrictions on textile categories related to the first and second stage of integration on the same day. In addition, the quantitative restrictions maintained under the non-MFA Agreement will be removed as listed below.

As of that date, the abovementioned categories will no longer require the issue of export licences and will fall under the general provisions concerning certificates of origin. As a result these products will no longer require import authorisations for customs clearance, regardless of the date of shipment.

Categories for which quotas will be removed on 11 December

| Category | Phase-out for MFA categories |
|---|---|
| 19 | Following accession |
| 76 | Following accession |
| Category | Phase-out for non-MFA categories |
| 126 | Following accession |
| Category | Phase-out for categories bilaterally agreed |
| ex 13 | Following accession |
| ex 24 | Following accession |
| ex 39 | Following accession |
| 123 | Following accession |
| 124 | Following accession |
| 125 A | Following accession |
| 127 A | Following accession |
| 127 B | Following accession |
| 140 | Following accession |
| 151 B | Following accession |

As the sheer number of bilateral agreements between the EU and China demonstrates, trade in textiles has long been a subject of detailed regulation and also a source of disagreement between the EU and China. The transitional period under the ATC ended on 31 December 2004. Consequently, trade in textiles among WTO members, including the EC and China, was liberalised as of 1 January 2005, with one exception. The sole exception was the potential application of a textiles-specific safeguard clause (TSSC) set out in paragraph 242 of the China Accession Protocol (see Chapter 7). It provided that if imports of textiles 'threaten to impede, owing to market disruption, the orderly development of trade', the importing WTO member could request consultations and, on this request, the exporting WTO member (China) would hold textile shipments at no greater than 7.5% (6% for wool) above the amount entered during the first 12 months of the most recent 14 months preceding the month of request for consultations. If consultations failed to result in a mutually satisfactory solution, the importing WTO member could take appropriate action. However, no action was to remain in effect 'beyond one year without reapplication, unless otherwise agreed between the Community and China'. By means of this ambiguous formula, the WTO members hoped to avoid or minimise any trade conflicts.

Even before 31 December 2004, both the EU and China took steps to avoid, so far as possible, major disruptions in their trade in textiles due to the opening of the EU market. For example, the European Commission adopted a communication on 'The Future of the Textiles and Clothing Sector in the Enlarged European Union'.[3] It set up a high-level group which submitted a report on 'The Challenge of 2005—European Textiles and Clothing in a Quota Free Environment'.[4] The EU adapted its legislation on imports of textiles, including incorporating the TSSC (supplemented by reference to EU committee procedures) into its basic textiles import legislation.[5] It also established a system of surveillance for textile imports.[6] China established a tax and quotas on exports of textiles. The post-ATC situation was also discussed within the EU–China Trade Dialogue, established in early 2004. A special EU–China Textiles Dialogue was established on 6 May 2004. Its express aims were to 'secure a smooth transition to the post-quota environment' and 'to examine ways to avoid major disruptions' (see Chapter 4).

Nevertheless, once quotas ended, Chinese exports of textile products to EU importers, destined for EU retailers and consumers, increased dramatically. The parties sought to find a solution by informal consultations, but this was not sufficient. In the midst of the dispute, the European Commission issued a Notice interpreting the TSSC (see Document 2.12). It set forth the Commission's interpretation of the TSSC, established an early warning system, provided a set of guidelines for industry about possible recourse to the TSSC and laid down procedures for informal and

3 COM(2003) 649 final (Brussels, 29 October 2003).

4 See http://www.europa.eu.int/comm/enterprise/textile/documents/hlg_report_30-06-04.pdf (accessed 10 August 2004).

5 In January 2003, Council Regulation (EC) No 138/2003 amended Council Regulation (EEC) No 3030/93 by adding a new Art 10a which transposed into EC law para 242 of the WTO Working Party Report on China, [2003] OJ L23/1.

6 See Council Regulation (EC) No 2200/2004 of 31 December 2004 amending Council Regulation (EEC) Nos 3030/93 and 3285/94 as regards the common rules for imports of certain textile products from third countries, [2004] OJ L374/1.

formal consultations, investigations and potential action. Its most controversial aspect concerned 'other relevant factors', for example the impact of textile imports on small developing countries outside the EU, which the Commission could take into account in deciding whether or not to take action against imports. According to the Commission, the Notice was not legally binding, did not create any legal rights or obligations and constituted merely indicative guidelines on its intentions about textiles trade policy.

## Document 2.12: Commission Notice on the application of Article 10a of Council Regulation (EEC) No 3030/93 concerning a textiles specific safeguard clause

**Notice on the application of Article 10a of Council Regulation (EEC) No 3030/93 concerning a textiles specific safeguard clause**

*Official Journal C 101 , 27/04/2005 P. 0002 – 0015*

Notice on the application of Article 10a of Council Regulation (EEC) No 3030/93 concerning a textiles specific safeguard clause
(2005/C 101/02)

1. INTRODUCTION—OBJECTIVE OF THE GUIDELINES

The provisions of the textiles specific safeguard clause (hereafter "TSSC") contained in the Protocol of Accession of China to the WTO were incorporated into EU law by Council Regulation (EC) No 138/2003 [1], in the form of a new Article 10a inserted in Council Regulation (EEC) No 3030/93 [2]. The new Article 10a is almost a literal transcription of the language contained in China's Protocol of Accession to the WTO, the main addition being the establishment of the internal EU decision-making procedure, according to which decisions are adopted following what is called "comitology procedure" (cf. description further below).

Since its adoption, the provision has raised a number of questions of interpretation, and concerns have also been expressed regarding the need for the greatest possible transparency to be introduced in the procedures and for more predictability regarding the Commission policy on its implementation. The Commission, in response to these concerns, indicated in its communication on "Textiles and clothing after 2005" of 13 October 2004 [3] that it would make available "guidelines containing procedures and criteria that the Commission intends to follow, in conformity with the relevant Regulations adopted by the Council, for the application of safeguard clauses, in particular for the textiles-specific safeguard clause established in China's Protocol of Accession to the WTO". This communication contains an indication (hereafter called the "guidelines") of the way the Commission intends to apply the TSSC. Its purpose is therefore to inform interested parties of:

(a) the criteria for the application of the TSSC that the Commission considers should apply;

(b) the procedures for a diligent handling and examination of requests for the application of the TSSC, providing an opportunity for any interested parties to be involved in the process, that the Commission intends to apply.

The guidelines also explain the "early warning system", which the Commission intends to use to guide it in deciding whether to open an enquiry and consult intensively with China if certain "alert levels" are reached. This will be without prejudice to the actual application of the TSSC, which will depend on the conditions specified therein.

These guidelines are for the information of interested parties and do not constitute a legal instrument. They reflect the policy intention of the Commission to follow certain procedures and criteria for the application of the TSSC, and therefore should not lead to any legally legitimate expectations regarding the individual decisions that the Commission will adopt on the TSSC in conformity with the relevant regulations, and which will have to result from a case-by-case examination to ensure that any action under the TSSC is fully justified. Since the Commission has wide powers under the Community legislation for the application of the TSSC, these guidelines explain to interested parties how the Commission intends to exercise these powers.

## 2. DESCRIPTION OF THE SPECIFIC TEXTILES SAFEGUARD CLAUSE

The Report of the Working Party on the Accession of China to the WTO [4] attached to the Protocol of Accession of China to the WTO [5] introduced in its paragraph 242 a provision that would enable WTO Members to introduce safeguard measures vis-Ã -vis imports of textile and clothing (T&C) products from China, and this until the end of 2008 [6]. The main elements of the provision (reproduced in Annex 1) are the following:

(a) Conditions for invocation: the clause can be triggered "in the event a WTO Member believes that imports of Chinese origin of T&C products (…) were, due to market disruption, threatening to impede the orderly development of trade in these products".

(b) Safeguard measures contemplated. The clause is triggered by a request for consultations by the Member invoking the clause. There are two steps: (a) upon request of consultations, China agrees to limit its shipments to the country concerned in the relevant product category subject of the request to the amounts exported during the first 12 months of the most recent 14 months preceding the month in which the request for consultations was made, increased by 7,5 % (6 % for wool products); (b) in the absence of a mutually agreed solution, the WTO Member concerned may introduce quantitative limits for such amounts.

Such measures may be in force only for one year. However, the question whether they can be extended is subject to interpretation, as the text says that "no action taken under this paragraph shall remain in effect beyond one year without reapplication (…)", thus leaving open the possibility for a new application of the clause to the same products after the expiry of the year period.

It is worth noting that the TSSC is an exceptional provision of a transitional nature with no clear link with other safeguard provisions or procedures in the WTO. Its uniqueness, which implies that the approach followed in these guidelines cannot be applicable in other safeguard instruments, comes from the fact that it is destined to provide an additional means to facilitate the transition to the quotas-free regime that will be in force from the time of expiry of the WTO Agreement on Textiles and Clothing (ATC) on 31 December 2004, and taking into account the accession of China to the WTO seven years after the negotiations on the ATC concluded. It is also a particularly vaguely worded provision which can be applied with a relatively wide margin of discretion and little room for challenge in the WTO.

Its standards for application appear to be lower than those in force in the other WTO safeguard provisions. This may be attributable to the fact that the measures available under the

TSSC are more limited in scope (only quantitative limits) and duration (maximum one year) than those possible under other safeguard instruments.

## 3. TRANSPOSITION OF THE TSSC INTO EU LAW

The TSSC was implemented into Community law by Council Regulation (EC) No 138/2003 of 21 January 2003, which introduced a new Article 10a into Council Regulation (EEC) No 3030/93, in terms similar to the language contained in the Protocol (see Annex 2) and granted power to apply the mechanism to the Commission. The Commission thus is empowered to take the decisions, in consultation with the Textiles Committee, concerning the request for consultations (which triggers the imposition of self-limitations by China), acting at the request of a Member State or on its own initiative, and regarding the imposition of restrictions. It is this provision, in conjunction with general principles of Community law, that governs the application of TSSC in the Community.

Under Article 10a in Council Regulation (EEC) No 3030/93, whose legal provisions are also reproduced in Annex 2 [7], before the Commission requests formal consultations with China or before introducing restrictions, the Commission submits a draft of the measures proposed to the Textiles Committee, and adopts it subsequently if the Committee votes in favour by a qualified majority. In case of absence of qualified majority, the Commission submits to the Council a proposal without delay, after which the Council may reject, amend or revoke the Commission proposal by a qualified majority. However, if the Council fails to reach a position by a qualified majority within one month, then the Commission adopts the proposed measures. In case the Council opposed the measure by a qualified majority, then the Commission should re-examine it, and may then either make an amended proposal, resubmit its proposal, or present a legislative proposal; after the expiry of one month without a Council Decision, then the Commission should adopt the act.

This present Communication explains the criteria according to which decisions will be taken, which will be addressed in Section 4, and the procedures for the handling of complaints and in the decision-making, which will be addressed in Section 5. It also describes the "early warning system" designed to minimise the risk of market disruption and therefore having to resort to safeguards (Section 6). Finally, some levels of imports are indicated, below which the Commission does not intend, in principle, to invoke the safeguard clause (Section 7).

## 4. DEFINITIONS AND CRITERIA FOR THE APPLICATION OF THE TSSC

The TSSC can be applied when "imports into the Community of textile and clothing products originating in China and covered by the ATC threaten to impede, owing to market disruption, the orderly development of trade in those products". A number of key elements, as set out below, deserve explanation. This explanation should not be regarded as binding or authoritative; it merely sets out, for the benefit of interested parties, the Commission's understanding of these elements.

### (a) Causes of the disturbance

The cause of the disturbance—disorderly development of trade due to market disruption—has to be "imports of textile and clothing products originating from China and covered by the ATC". The origin of the products, as determined in accordance with the rules in force in the Community, is relevant, no matter if they come directly from China or through other intermediate territories. The products concerned must be covered by the WTO Agreement on Textiles and Clothing (ATC).

(b) "Threat to impede the orderly development of trade in textile and clothing products"

The TSSC was agreed in the WTO accession negotiations with China as an additional safeguard mechanism available in particular after liberalisation in the ATC has taken place, to take into account the very important production and export potential of China in textiles and clothing. In particular, its objective was to ensure a transition as smooth as possible to the quota-free trade environment prevailing in the sector from 2005. For this reason, the TSSC establishes as a trigger that the evolution of imports from China must "threaten to impede (...) the orderly development of trade" in textile and clothing products.

Such a concept has not been defined in WTO law or jurisprudence, nor is it found in EU legislation. In order to assess whether the "orderly development of trade" in textile and clothing products is being threatened, the Commission will take into account as a main indicator the existence of a rapid rise or surge in imports, in absolute or relative terms. A small percentage change cannot be considered sufficient to trigger the application of the TSSC. The increase must be rapid and steep, in a way that it can be considered as a significant alteration of trade patterns in a given product or group of products. It may concern the quantities imported, or the values of the products imported, or both. For instance, an increase of several tens of percentage points in products where China is already a dominant supplier—or by more in those cases where the quotas for China were low in relative terms—in a matter of a few months in 2005 as compared with the same period in 2004 can be considered as a rapid increase in imports.

In this context, increases such as those indicated in tables A and B of Section 6 can be considered as in principle "threatening to prevent the orderly development of trade in textile and clothing products". Conversely, the Commission will in principle consider that below certain rates of growth of imports, as indicated in Section 7, there is not such a "disorderly development of trade", as certain increased imports can be considered as a normal consequence of the elimination of quotas.

Such a rapid increase of imports need not be in absolute terms, it can also be in relative terms. However, the case for action to be envisaged if the increase is only in relative terms will obviously be weaker and more difficult to justify, except in case the imports took place under certain conditions (for instance in case of significant price drops or significant drops in exports to the EU from, for example, Euro Mediterranean or ACP partner countries), so as to "threaten to impede the orderly development of trade". In particular in cases of increased imports from China in relative or absolute terms which cannot be considered a surge in imports, a relevant factor to take into account will be the evolution of import prices, which will normally have to be assessed as average unit import prices as can be determined by import statistics. Significant drops of average unit import prices (especially if there is price undercutting as compared with other suppliers) combined with such increases in imports are likely to result in market disruption and constitute a threat to the "orderly development of trade".

(c) Market disruption

Drawing from the definitions and practice in other WTO and EC safeguard instruments [8], market disruption can be considered to exist, whenever imports of a product, or a category of products, are increasingly rapidly, either absolutely or relatively, or under such conditions, so as to be a significant cause of material injury, or threat of material injury, to the

Community industry. Factors to be taken into consideration in determining whether market disruption exists are inter alia the volume of imports concerned, the effect of such imports on prices for such products in the EU, and the effect of such imports on the EU industry producing these products.

In accordance with this internationally agreed definition of "market disruption", there is no need for actual injury to materialise, as in that case it would be too late for any measure to be effective, and therefore a threat of such injury can be sufficient. However, the threat of injury should be qualified and cannot be hypothetical: it should be imminent and appear from the current evolution of imports. In this respect, a requirement for the consideration of the existence of a threat of injury should be an actual rapid increase, in absolute or relative terms, of imports. A mere likelihood that such an increase may take place—for instance after the elimination of import quotas—should not be enough. Such a rapid increase in imports should be assessed in particular comparing the evolution of imports in a given relevant period (not shorter than 2 or 3 months) with a similar period in preceding years.

Another important element to take account is the evolution of import prices, as any significant drop of such prices or an undercutting of prices as compared for instance with other major suppliers can provide an indication of market disruption.

It should also be examined whether the volume of imports and their price have or will have a direct negative effect on the EU industry. The impact on upstream industry (e.g. spinning, weaving and knitting, or finishing industries) may also be relevant and should not be excluded in the assessment of injury or threat of injury to industry. All available relevant data will be used to assess the actual or expected impact on affected EU industry, such as, for instance, the evolution of production, market share, sales, employment, profitability and supply chain effects.

In order to take account of the multiplicity of products within and among categories in the textile and clothing sector, and the links and overlaps that may exist among them, it is considered appropriate to maintain flexibility to define on a case-by-case basis the products or groups of products concerned.

(d) Other relevant factors

One factor to be considered is the impact that a surge in imports from China may have on other suppliers and in particular on the more vulnerable and textile-dependent developing countries (small developing country economies, least developed and ACP countries, and in particular Southern and Eastern Mediterranean countries as they are part of the natural zone of competitiveness of the EU textile and clothing industry and are an important destination of both exports and investments of EU industry). A serious displacement from the EU market of traditional suppliers can constitute a sign that trade is being disturbed and have serious negative consequences that it may be appropriate to remedy, although safeguard action can be taken only if the criteria of "threat to prevent the orderly development of trade" and "market disruption", as explained in sub-sections (b) and (c) above, are met.

A positive determination that the conditions for the application of the TSSC have been met would in principle lead the Commission to request formal consultations with China under paragraph (a) of Article 10a. However, the Commission may decide otherwise in case the invocation of the TSSC would have important and tangible negative impact on the general interest of the Community (e.g. other industries—upstream or downstream—EU industry with investments in China, consumers or trade), which would clearly outweigh the positive consequences of action for industry.

5. PROCEDURES AND TIMETABLE FOR SAFEGUARD PROCEEDINGS

The Commission attaches great importance to the transparency and expediency in the handling of its trade instruments, so that when a Member State or other interested parties introduce a request for safeguard action, there are procedures to treat them in a way that all interested parties can be heard, decisions are adopted within a reasonable period of time and are properly motivated and communicated to the interested parties and to the public in general. Such transparency should result in greater predictability and certainty for trade and business, and make sure that decisions are taken in the best possible knowledge of all relevant factors and after having heard all relevant arguments. In cases of particular urgency, the Commission may decide, however, to expedite its procedures involving a shortening of the deadlines or a simplified and accelerated process of consultations, or take the necessary steps on the basis of the information available.

In order to achieve these objectives, the Commission intends to proceed as follows regarding the procedures for the implementation of the TSSC. Again, this must be regarded as an explanation, for the benefit of interested parties, of how the Commission intends to exercise its powers. It should not be regarded as binding or authoritative.

(a) Initiation of the procedure—Opening of an investigation and request for informal consultations with China

Before the invocation of the safeguard clause by requesting formal consultations with China, it is appropriate that the Commission will open an investigation in order to establish facts and request informal consultations with China in order to examine ways to avoid market disruption. This will be done under two hypotheses:

- at the request of a Member State,
- on the Commission's own initiative, which can be in two instances: when in application of the "early warning system" described in Section 6 certain "alert levels" are reached; or at the request of industry providing prima facie evidence of the need for safeguard.

The same procedures will apply to investigations initiated ex-officio or those initiated on the basis of requests.

(i) Initiation upon request from a Member State

In case a request contains sufficient prima facie evidence that the conditions for the application of the TSSC as spelt out in Section 4 are met, the Commission services will open an investigation and request informal consultations with the Chinese authorities.

Prima facie evidence is understood to exist when the request includes data and elements sufficiently pointing to the existence of market disruption, either at the EU level or at an appropriate lower geographical level, and the "disorderly development on trade" as defined in Section 4 of these guidelines. Such requests should, in principle, not be admissible if import levels are below those indicated in Section 7 of this document.

Requests may concern one or more product categories, or individual products within such categories.

The Commission will normally decide, within 15 calendar days from the reception of the request, whether to launch an investigation and request informal consultations or to reject the request. Any rejection of a request will give the reasons for its inadmissibility.

The Commission will, in principle, not accept for examination requests that constitute basically a repetition of previous requests that had been rejected, unless there were new elements that justify their presentation.

(ii) Initiation on the Commission own initiative

The Commission intends to initiate the procedures in two hypotheses:

- when, based on information collected under the imports monitoring system as detailed under Section 6 of these guidelines, the "alert levels" are exceeded;
- upon the presentation of sufficiently substantiated requests by parties which are directly affected by market disruption.

In this second hypothesis, for requests to be admissible, they should come from a body or group of enterprises within the EU sufficiently representative of the sector or product in question (this would not be the case, for instance, if there were two or more associations of manufacturers of the same products which held opposite views).

The Commission intends to apply to requests for safeguard action received from industry the procedures and criteria described in section (i) above.

(b) Publication of a notice and deadlines for comments

In case of the opening of an investigation, the Commission will publish without delay a notice of initiation of an investigation in the Official Journal ("OJ") of the European Union and in the first page of the web-site page of Directorate-General for Trade [9].

The notice in the OJ and in the web-site of Directorate-General for Trade will contain a summary of the basis for a safeguard investigation, including as appropriate the main elements of a request for safeguards that may have been presented, and invite all interested parties to make, within 21 calendar days, submissions with their views and providing relevant factual information. It will also specify the procedures and timetable to be followed by interested parties participating in the process.

(c) Investigation and informal consultations

The Commission will conduct an investigation to establish the facts within 60 days from the publication of the notice. This period can be extended once, in exceptional circumstances, by ten working days. The Commission will seek all information it deems to be necessary, including as appropriate by examining representations from interested parties to make a determination on whether to request formal consultations with China.

The Commission will disclose its findings to interested parties inviting additional comment and may also conduct hearings, if requested, of interested parties. The Commission will fix appropriate limits for this purpose. At the same time the investigation is opened the Commission will request informal consultations with China. The investigation and the informal consultations with China will be conducted simultaneously and within the deadline of 60 days.

(d) Decision to request formal consultations with China

The Commission will reach its decision on the basis of the information available at the end of the investigation, and will present to the Textiles Committee the results and conclusions of the investigations and of the informal consultations with China.

In case the Commission makes a positive determination regarding the applicability of the TSSC, it will without delay call a meeting of the Textiles Committee to seek its opinion on its intention to request formal consultations with China under paragraph (a) of the TSSC. The Commission will provide the Committee with a detailed factual statement of reasons and justifications for the request, together with "current data showing the existence or threat of market disruption and the role of products of Chinese origin in that disruption" [10]. The further steps in the procedure are those indicated in Article 17 of Council Regulation (EEC) No 3030/93 [11].

After consultation of the Textiles Committee and, as appropriate, completion of the procedures provided for in Article 17 of Council Regulation (EEC) No 3030/93, the Commission will, without undue delay, request formal consultations with China. Its determination and the reasons for the decision to request consultations will be published in a notice in the Official Journal of the European Union and in the first page of the web-site page of the Directorate General for Trade [12] and communicated to the party that made the request.

In case the Commission finds that the conditions for the application of the TSSC are not met, it will inform the complainant accordingly with an indication of the reasons of the decision, which will also be published in the OJ of the EU.

(e) Decisions and procedures in case of extreme urgency

In circumstances where delay would cause damage which it would be difficult to repair, the Commission may, after a preliminary determination that imports threaten to impede the orderly development of trade, request directly formal consultations with China without an investigation, or before the investigation is completed. This could be the case in particular if there is a surge of imports of such a significant magnitude that it is deemed obvious that the orderly development of trade is threatened and that such imports will cause significant material injury to the Community industry if action is not taken. Such request shall be made after consultation with the Textile Committee, in accordance with the procedures set out in Article 17 of Council Regulation (EEC) No 3030/93.

(f) Period of formal consultations with China

In accordance with the TSSC, China should from the receipt of the requests for consultations introduce self-restrictions in the exports. Should that not be the case within 15 calendar days from the request, the Commission will transmit, without delay, to the Textiles Committee the necessary proposals to remedy the situation; these should normally provide for the establishment of import limits calculated as provided for in Article 10a.1(a) of Council Regulation (EEC) No 3030/93.

The consultations period shall last 90 days from the receipt of the request for such consultations.

(g) Adoption of safeguard measures

If no mutually satisfactory solution is reached with China within the 90 day period specified in (f) above, and if it determines that the conditions set out in Section 4 are met, the Commission may impose a quantitative limit for the products under consideration. In this context the Commission will, without delay, call a meeting of the Textiles Committee to seek its opinion on a proposal to impose a quantitative limit for the relevant categories subject to the consultations. Such limit should also apply to imports of goods of Chinese origin, exported after the publication of the notice announcing formal consultations and shipped in excess of the quantities to which China should have limited itself in accordance with §242 of the Protocol of Accession. The further steps in the procedure are those indicated in Article 17 of Council Regulation (EEC) No 3030/93 [13].

Such a quantitative limit will be fixed at the amount of products of the concerned category that were imported into the EU during the first 12 months of the most recent 14 months preceding the month in which the request for consultations was made, increased by 7,5 % (or 6 % for wool product categories). Such limit will be effective for a period ending on 31 December of the year in which consultations were requested, or, where three months or less remained in the year at the time of the request for consultations, for a period ending 12 months after the request for consultations. Consultations with China should be continued during the term of the quantitative limit set up under this provision.

Such a decision, in accordance with the relevant procedures (Commission or Council), will be published in the OJ of the EU.

After the expiry of a safeguard measure on a given product, the procedures described in this section will be applicable for the introduction of new safeguards on the same products.

## 6. EARLY WARNING SYSTEM—EX-OFFICIO INITIATION OF INVESTIGATION AND REQUEST FOR INFORMAL CONSULTATIONS

In the light of past experience and in particular the development of imports from China in product categories liberalised in 2002, it would be appropriate to provide some guidance concerning the steps that the Commission will follow in order to give the highest possible degree of predictability for trade, to facilitate that imports from China evolve in a manner that avoids market disruption, and thus give maximum scope for finding acceptable solutions in a way that safeguard action is taken only as a last resort.

To pursue these objectives, the Commission will introduce an early warning system according to which, should the trend of imports from China show that there are indications that a "disorderly development of imports" is occurring or is imminent, and before invoking the safeguard clause, it would first ask for informal consultations with China and open an investigation on whether such imports may be causing market disruption. Only in cases where, despite such discussions, the trends in trade continued in such a way that the conditions for the application of the safeguard were met, the Commission would, using the procedures established in Council Regulation (EEC) No 3030/93, formally invoke the safeguard clause and therefore request formal consultations with China.

In any event, determinations to take safeguard action under the TSSC should be made on a case-by-case basis, after verification that the conditions for the application of the TSSC are met and—unless in cases of extreme urgency—following an investigation in line with the procedures outlined above.

On the basis of the monitoring of imports that it is carrying out in accordance with the provisions of Council Regulation (EEC) No 3030/93, the Commission will be examining regularly whether some indicative thresholds of actual imports [14] from China may be exceeded, either on a yearly basis or during a shorter period of time (in principle no less than 3 months) on a pro-rata temporis basis. In such cases, the Commission will establish contact with the Chinese authorities to examine the evolution of imports, its impact and the likelihood that the trends may continue. Such indicative thresholds, which contemplate very considerable increases over the quotas for China in 2004, have been determined, on a category by category basis, taking into account:

(a) The extent to which the quotas eliminated on 1 January 2005 were utilised also taking into account the relative position of other countries subject to quota in 2004.

(b) The share of total EU imports represented by imports from China as an indication or scope for expansion.

(c) The import penetration ratios and their evolution.

(d) The levels of EU production and their evolution.

(e) Other indicators concerning the situation of the market in the products concerned, such as the trends in consumption and prices.

The tables below give an indication of the growth of imports from China which, if reached, would in principle lead the Commission to open an investigation and request informal consultations with China:

TABLE A
Formula to determine the consultation levels

| Products whose imports from China represent as % of total EU imports in 2004 in volume | 2005 Increase over 2004 in % of 2004 imports | 2006 Increase over 2005 level in % of 2004 imports | 2007 Increase over 2006 level in % of 2004 imports | 2008 Increase over 2007 level in % of 2004 imports |
|---|---|---|---|---|
| 7,5 % or less | 100 % | 50 % | 50 % | 50 % |
| < 7,5 % to 20 % | 50 % | 50 % | 50 % | 50 % |
| < 20 % to 35 % | 30 % | 30 % | 30 % | 30 % |
| Over 35 % | 10 % | 10 % | 10 % | 10 % |

TABLE B
Consultation levels resulting from the application of the formula in Table A [NB: table to be developed on a category by category basis after application of the formula]

| Product category | Unit | Chinese 2004 imports EU-25 (thousands of units) | Chinese 2004 quota EU-25 (thousands of units) | Level 2005 | Level 2006 | Level 2007 | Level 2008 |
|---|---|---|---|---|---|---|---|
| 1—cotton yarn | tns | 3263 | 4770 | 9540 | 11925 | 14310 | 16695 |
| 2—cotton fabrics | tns | 34465 | 30556 | 51698 | 68930 | 86163 | 103395 |
| 3—synth. fabrics | tns | 10938 | 8088 | 21876 | 27345 | 32814 | 38283 |
| 4—T-shirts | pcs | 191473 | 126808 | 382946 | 478683 | 574419 | 670156 |
| 5—pullovers | pcs | 64324 | 39422 | 128648 | 160810 | 192972 | 225134 |
| 6—men's trousers | pcs | 75688 | 40913 | 151376 | 189220 | 227064 | 264908 |
| 7—blouses | pcs | 26035 | 17093 | 52070 | 65088 | 78105 | 91123 |

| | | | | | | | |
|---|---|---|---|---|---|---|---|
| 8—men's shirts | pcs | 40837 | 27723 | 61256 | 81674 | 102093 | 122511 |
| 9—terry towels | tns | 13538 | 6962 | 20307 | 27076 | 33845 | 40614 |
| 12—stockings + socks | prs | 131443 | 132029 | 264058 | 330073 | 396087 | 462102 |
| 13—men's underpants | pcs | 681114 | 586244 | 749225 | 817337 | 885448 | 953560 |
| 14—men's overcoats | pcs | 24326 | 17887 | 26759 | 29191 | 31624 | 34056 |
| 15—women overcoats | pcs | 35570 | 20131 | 46241 | 56912 | 67583 | 78254 |
| 16—men's suits | pcs | 17407 | 17181 | 19148 | 20888 | 22629 | 24370 |
| 17—jackets & blazers | pcs | 6063 | 13061 | 14367 | 15804 | 17241 | 18677 |
| 20—bed linen | tns | 7894 | 5681 | 15788 | 19735 | 23682 | 27629 |
| 22—synthetic fibre yarn | tns | 9364 | 19351 | 38702 | 48378 | 58053 | 67729 |
| 26—dresses | pcs | 8682 | 6645 | 17364 | 21705 | 26046 | 30387 |
| 28—trousers (other) | pcs | 102204 | 92909 | 132865 | 163526 | 194188 | 224849 |
| 29—women suits | pcs | 22541 | 15687 | 24796 | 27050 | 29304 | 31558 |
| 31—brassieres | pcs | 128272 | 96488 | 166754 | 205235 | 243717 | 282198 |
| 39—table + kitchen linen | tns | 7342 | 5681 | 11013 | 14684 | 18355 | 22026 |
| 78—other garments | tns | 31395 | 36651 | 40316 | 43981 | 47646 | 51311 |
| 83—overcoats | tns | 12039 | 10883 | 15651 | 19262 | 22874 | 26486 |
| 97—nets | tns | 3124 | 2861 | 4062 | 4999 | 5936 | 6873 |
| 163—medical gauze | tns | 8657 | 8481 | 9523 | 10388 | 11254 | 12120 |
| ex 20—bed linen silk | tns | 100 | 59 | 200 | 250 | 300 | 350 |
| 115—flax or ramie yarn | tns | 2727 | 1413 | 3545 | 4363 | 5181 | 6000 |
| 117—woven fabrics flax | tns | 1510 | 684 | 2264 | 3019 | 3774 | 4529 |
| 118—table bedlinen flax | tns | 2409 | 1513 | 2650 | 2891 | 3132 | 3373 |
| 122—sacks and bags flax | tns | 360 | 220 | 468 | 576 | 684 | 792 |
| 136A—woven fabrics silk | tns | 446 | 462 | 693 | 924 | 1155 | 1386 |

| | | | | | | | |
|---|---|---|---|---|---|---|---|
| 156—blouses, pullover silk | tns | 7291 | 3986 | 8020 | 8749 | 9478 | 10207 |
| 157—garmen ts knitted | tns | 17941 | 13738 | 19735 | 21529 | 23323 | 25117 |
| 159—blouses silk | tns | 3236 | 4352 | 4787 | 5222 | 5658 | 6093 |

The increases provided for the calculation of such levels are so important that, if they were exceeded, it could be considered in principle that there is a high likelihood that a "disorderly development of imports" is taking place. In case they were reached, either on a yearly basis or on a pro-rata basis over a period of in principle no less than 3 months [15], the Commission would launch an investigation to examine whether there are factors that may lead to the conclusion that the development of those imports prevent or not the "orderly development of imports" and whether the second condition for the application of the TSSC is met, i.e. market disruption in the sense of at least threat of injury to domestic industry. These thresholds would only trigger an investigation and informal consultations but would not be relevant in determining application of whether the TSSC is justified or not.

The consultations levels for 2006, 2007 and 2008 may be adjusted in the light of further examination and other factors that may come to the light subsequently.

The formula for the calculation of the consultation levels can be applied as appropriate for particular products determined at a level of aggregation below that of a product category. In that case, if imports from China exceeded the resulting levels on a yearly or on a pro-rata basis (in principle no less than 3 months), Commission could also, on its own initiative or at the request of a Member State or of an interested party, request informal consultations with China and open an enquiry.

Such levels therefore should be seen as an indication, which in case they are reached do not trigger any automatic application of the TSSC.

## 7. LEVELS BELOW WHICH, IN PRINCIPLE, NO TSSC ACTION SHOULD BE CONSIDERED

The Commission also considers that, in case some levels are not exceeded, there should in principle be no case for the invocation of the TSSC. This should be particularly the case when a Chinese expansion is moderate, taking into account their relative position in the EU market. In those instances, the Commission will consider that such increases are normal after the elimination of import quotas and therefore will in principle—i.e. unless evidence to the contrary is provided—consider that there is no "disorderly development of trade". These levels, which would provide already a considerable margin for expansion of Chinese exports to the EU, are indicated in the table below:

TABLE C
Formula to determine the minimum levels below which the TSSC will not be triggered

| Products whose imports from China represent as % of total EU imports in 2004 in volume | 2005Increase over 2004 in % of 2004 imports | 2006Increase over 2005 level in % of 2004 imports | 2007Increase over 2006 level in % of 2004 imports | 2008Increase over 2007 level in % of 2004 imports |
|---|---|---|---|---|

| | | | | |
|---|---|---|---|---|
| 7,5 % or less | 25 % | 25 % | 25 % | 25 % |
| < 7,5 % to 20 % | 20 % | 20 % | 20 % | 20 % |
| < 20 % to 35 % | 15 % | 15 % | 15 % | 15 % |
| Over 35 % | 10 % | 10 % | 10 % | 10 % |

TABLE D
Levels below which in principle the TSSC should not be invoked

| Product category | Unit | Chinese 2004 imports EU-25 (thousands of units) | Chinese 2004 quota EU-25 (thousands of units) | Level 2005 | Level 2006 | Level 2007 | Level 2008 |
|---|---|---|---|---|---|---|---|
| 1—cotton yarn | tns | 3263 | 4770 | 5963 | 7155 | 8348 | 9540 |
| 2—cotton fabrics | tns | 34465 | 30556 | 41358 | 48251 | 55144 | 62037 |
| 3—synth. fabrics | tns | 10938 | 8088 | 13673 | 16407 | 19142 | 21876 |
| 4—T-shirts | pcs | 191473 | 126808 | 239341 | 287210 | 335078 | 382946 |
| 5—pull-overs | pcs | 64324 | 39422 | 80405 | 96486 | 112567 | 128648 |
| 6—men's trousers | pcs | 75688 | 40913 | 94610 | 113532 | 132454 | 151376 |
| 7—blouses | pcs | 26035 | 17093 | 32544 | 39053 | 45561 | 52070 |
| 8—men's shirts | pcs | 40837 | 27723 | 49004 | 57172 | 65339 | 73507 |
| 9—terry towels | tns | 13538 | 6962 | 16246 | 18953 | 21661 | 24368 |
| 12—stocking s + socks | prs | 131443 | 132029 | 165036 | 198044 | 231051 | 264058 |
| 13—men's underpants | pcs | 681114 | 586244 | 749225 | 817337 | 885448 | 953560 |
| 14—men's overcoats | pcs | 24326 | 17887 | 26759 | 29191 | 31624 | 34056 |
| 15—women overcoats | pcs | 35570 | 20131 | 40906 | 46241 | 51577 | 56912 |
| 16—men's suits | pcs | 17407 | 17181 | 19148 | 20888 | 22629 | 24370 |
| 17—jackets & blazers | pcs | 6063 | 13061 | 14367 | 16326 | 18285 | 20245 |
| 20—bed linen | tns | 7894 | 5681 | 9868 | 11841 | 13815 | 15788 |
| 22—synth. fibre yarn | tns | 9364 | 19351 | 24189 | 29027 | 33864 | 38702 |
| 26—dresses | pcs | 8682 | 6645 | 10853 | 13023 | 15194 | 17364 |

| | | | | | | | |
|---|---|---|---|---|---|---|---|
| 28—trousers (other) | pcs | 102204 | 92909 | 117535 | 132865 | 148196 | 163526 |
| 29—women suits | pcs | 22541 | 15687 | 24796 | 27050 | 29304 | 31558 |
| 31—brassieres | pcs | 128272 | 96488 | 147513 | 166754 | 185994 | 205235 |
| 39—table + kitchen linen | tns | 7342 | 5681 | 8810 | 10279 | 11747 | 13216 |
| 78—other garments | tns | 31395 | 36651 | 40316 | 43981 | 47646 | 51311 |
| 83—overcoats | tns | 12039 | 10883 | 13845 | 15651 | 17457 | 19262 |
| 97—nets | tns | 3124 | 2861 | 3593 | 4062 | 4530 | 4999 |
| 163—medical gauze | tns | 8657 | 8481 | 9523 | 10388 | 11254 | 12120 |
| ex 20—bed linen silk | tns | 100 | 59 | 125 | 150 | 175 | 200 |
| 115—flax or ramie yarn | tns | 2727 | 1413 | 3136 | 3545 | 3954 | 4363 |
| 117—woven fabrics flax | tns | 1510 | 684 | 1812 | 2113 | 2415 | 2717 |
| 118—table bedlinen flax | tns | 2409 | 1513 | 2650 | 2891 | 3132 | 3373 |
| 122—sacks and bags flax | tns | 360 | 220 | 414 | 468 | 522 | 576 |
| 136A—woven fabrics silk | tns | 360 | 220 | 414 | 468 | 522 | 576 |
| 156—blouses, pullover silk | tns | 7291 | 3986 | 8020 | 8749 | 9478 | 10207 |
| 157—garments knitted | tns | 17941 | 13738 | 19735 | 21529 | 23323 | 25117 |
| 159—blouses silk | tns | 3236 | 4352 | 4787 | 5222 | 5658 | 6093 |

[1] OJ L 23, 28.1.2003, p. 1.

[2] OJ L 275, 8.11.1993, p. 3.

[3] "Textiles and clothing after 2005—the Recommendations of the High Level Group for textiles and clothing", COM(2004)668 final, of 13.10.2004.

[4] Document WT/MIN(01)3 of 10 November 2001.

[5] Document WT/L/432 of 23 November 2001.

[6] This paragraph is considered a part of the Protocol of Accession of China to the WTO, which in turn is an integral part of the WTO Agreement, cf. paragraph 2 of the Accession Protocol.

[7] Cf. Article 17 of Council Regulation (EEC) No 3030/93, which was amended by Council Regulation (EC) No 391/2001 of 26 February 2001.

[8] Cf. Article 2.1 of the WTO Agreement on Safeguards on the conditions for the application of safeguard measures, and paragraph 16.4 of the Protocol of Accession of China to the WTO (the Transitional Product Specific Safeguard Mechanism or TPSSM, Article 2.1 of Council Regulation (EC) No 427/2003 on a transitional product-specific safeguard mechanism for imports from China and Article 16.1 of Council Regulation (EC) No 3285/94 on the common rules for imports.

[9] Address: http://europa.eu.int/comm/trade/index_en.htm.

[10] Cf. first sub-paragraph of Article 10a).1.(a) of Council Regulation (EEC) No 3030/93 and paragraph 242(a) of the Report of the Working Party on the Accession of China to the WTO.

[11] See Annex 2.

[12] Address: http://europa.eu.int/comm/trade/index_en.htm.

[13] See Annex 2.

[14] Data on actual imports collected in accordance with Article 27 of Annex III of Council Regulation (EEC) No 3030/93. Should, however, such data not be available in a timely manner for reasons outside its control, the Commission may decide to start the procedure and open an investigation and request informal consultations with China if the data available from import licensing (cf. Article 25 of Annex III of Council Regulation (EEC) No 3030/93) indicate that imports from China are likely to exceed such "consultations levels".

[15] The calculation of the "consultation" or "alert" levels on a pro-rata basis should be done in such a way that, insofar as possible, seasonal aspects are taken into account. This may make it advisable to apply the formula for the calculation of the levels for the relevant period of the year to the imports of a comparable period of 2004.

ANNEX 1
Extract of the Report of the Working Party on the Accession of China

242. The representative of China agreed that the following provisions would apply to trade in textiles and clothing products until 31 December 2008 and be part of the terms and conditions for China's accession:

(a) In the event that a WTO Member believed that imports of Chinese origin of textiles and apparel products covered by the ATC as of the date the WTO Agreement entered into force, were, due to market disruption, threatening to impede the orderly development of trade in these products, such Member could request consultations with China with a view to easing or avoiding such market disruption. The Member requesting consultations would provide China, at the time of the request, with a detailed factual statement of reasons and justifications for its request for consultations with current data which, in the view of the requesting Member, showed: (1) the existence or threat of market disruption; and (2) the role of products of Chinese origin in that disruption;

(b) Consultations would be held within 30 days of receipt of the request. Every effort would be made to reach agreement on a mutually satisfactory solution within 90 days of the receipt of such request, unless extended by mutual agreement;

(c) Upon receipt of the request for consultations, China agreed to hold its shipments to the requesting Member of textile or textile products in the category or categories subject to these consultations to a level no greater than 7,5 per cent (6 per cent for wool product categories) above the amount entered during the first 12 months of the most recent 14 months preceding the month in which the request for consultations was made;

(d) If no mutually satisfactory solution were reached during the 90-day consultation period, consultations would continue and the Member requesting consultations could continue the limits under subparagraph (c) for textiles or textile products in the category or categories subject to these consultations;

(e) The term of any restraint limit established under subparagraph (d) would be effective for the period beginning on the date of the request for consultations and ending on 31 December of the year in which consultations were requested, or where three or fewer months remained in the year at the time of the request for consultations, for the period ending 12 months after the request for consultations;

(f) No action taken under this provision would remain in effect beyond one year, without reapplication, unless otherwise agreed between the Member concerned and China; and

(g) Measures could not be applied to the same product at the same time under this provision and the provisions of Section 16 of the Draft Protocol. The Working Party took note of these commitments.

ANNEX 2
Extract of provisions concerning the internal EU procedures for the adoption of decisions concerning the TSSC
Article 10a of Council Regulation (EEC) No 3030/93:

"Article 10a
Special safeguard provisions for China

1. Should imports into the Community of textiles and apparel products originating in China and covered by the (ATC) threaten to impede, owing to market disruption, the orderly development of trade in those products, such imports may, during the period ending on 31 December 2008, be made subject to specific safeguard measures under the following conditions:

(a) The Commission—acting at the request of a Member State or on its own initiative—shall open consultations with China with a view to easing or avoiding such market disruption. The request for consultation shall provide China with a detailed factual statement of reasons and justifications for the request, with current data showing the existence or threat of market disruption and the role of products of Chinese origin in that disruption. Consultations shall be commenced within 30 days of receipt of the request, the consultation period lasting 90 days from such receipt, unless extended by mutual agreement.

Upon receipt of the request for consultations China shall, during the period of consultation, hold its shipments to the Community of textile or textile products in the category or categories subject to the consultations, at a level no greater then 7,5 % (6 % for wool product categories) above the amount entered during the first 12 months of the most recent 14 months preceding the month in which the request for consultations was made.

(b) The Commission may, if no mutually satisfactory solution is reached during the 90-day consultation period, establish a quantitative limit for the category or categories subject to the consultations. The quantitative limit shall be set up on the basis of the level at which China held its shipments upon receipt of the Community's request for consultation. The term of this quantitative limit shall be effective for a period ending on 31 December of the year in which consultations were requested, or, where three months or less remained in the year at the time of the request for consultations, for a period ending 12 months after the request for consultations. Consultations with China shall be continued during the term of the quantitative limit set up under this provision.

(c) No action taken under this paragraph shall remain in effect beyond one year without reapplication, unless otherwise agreed between the Community and China. Measures shall not be applied to the same product at the same time under this paragraph and the provisions of Section 16 of the Protocol on the Accession of China to the WTO. Measures taken pursuant to point (b) shall be the subject of a Commission communication published without delay in the Official Journal of the European Communities.

2. The quantitative limits established pursuant to this Article shall not apply to products which have already been dispatched to the Community provided that they were shipped from the supplier country in which they originate for export to the Community before the date of notification of the request for consultations.

3. The measures provided for in this Article, including opening of consultations as provided for in paragraph 1(a), shall be adopted and implemented in accordance with the procedure laid down in Article 17."

Article 17 of Council Regulation (EEC) No 3030/93:

"Article 17
The textile committee

1. The Commission shall be assisted by a committee (hereinafter referred to as the "textile committee").

2. Where reference is made to this paragraph, Articles 5 and 7 of Decision 1999/468/EC shall apply. The period laid down in Article 5(6) of Decision 1999/468/EC shall be set at one month.

3. The textile committee shall adopt its rules of procedure."

Articles 5 and 7 of Council Decision 1999/468/EC [1]:

"Article 5
Regulatory procedure

1. The Commission shall be assisted by a regulatory committee composed of the representatives of the Member States and chaired by the representative of the Commission.

2. The representative of the Commission shall submit to the committee a draft of the measures to be taken. The committee shall deliver its opinion on the draft within a time-limit which the chairman may lay down according to the urgency of the matter. The opinion shall be delivered by the majority laid down in Article 205(2) of the Treaty in the case of decisions which the Council is required to adopt on a proposal from the Commission. The votes of the representatives of the Member States within the Committee shall be weighted in the manner set out in that Article. The chairman shall not vote.

3. The Commission shall, without prejudice to Article 8, adopt the measures envisaged if they are in accordance with the opinion of the committee.

4. If the measures envisaged are not in accordance with the opinion of the committee, or if no opinion is delivered, the Commission shall, without delay, submit to the Council a proposal relating to the measures to be taken and shall inform the European Parliament.

5. If the European Parliament considers that a proposal submitted by the Commission pursuant to a basic instrument adopted in accordance with the procedure laid down in Article 251 of the Treaty exceeds the implementing powers provided for in that basic instrument, it shall inform the Council of its position.

6. The Council may, where appropriate in view of any such position, act by qualified majority on the proposal, within a period to be laid down in each basic instrument but which shall in no case exceed three months from the date of referral to the Council.

If within that period the Council has indicated by qualified majority that it opposes the proposal, the Commission shall re-examine it. It may submit an amended proposal to the Council, re-submit its proposal or present a legislative proposal on the basis of the Treaty.

If on the expiry of that period the Council has neither adopted the proposed implementing act nor indicated its opposition to the proposal for implementing measures, the proposed implementing act shall be adopted by the Commission.

Article 7

1. Each committee shall adopt its own rules of procedure on the proposal of its chairman, on the basis of standard rules of procedure which shall be published in the Official Journal of the European Communities. Insofar as necessary existing committees shall adapt their rules of procedure to the standard rules of procedure.

2. The principles and conditions on public access to documents applicable to the Commission shall apply to the committees.

3. The European Parliament shall be informed by the Commission of committee proceedings on a regular basis. To that end, it shall receive agendas for committee meetings, draft measures submitted to the committees for the implementation of instruments adopted by the procedure provided for by Article 251 of the Treaty, and the results of voting and summary records of the meetings and lists of the authorities and organisations to which the persons designated by the Member States to represent them belong. The European Parliament shall also be kept informed whenever the Commission transmits to the Council measures or proposals for measures to be taken.

4. The Commission shall, within six months of the date on which this Decision takes effect, publish in the Official Journal of the European Communities, a list of all committees which assist the Commission in the exercise of implementing powers. This list shall specify, in relation to each committee, the basic instrument(s) under which the committee is established. From 2000 onwards, the Commission shall also publish an annual report on the working of committees.

5. The references of all documents sent to the European Parliament pursuant to paragraph 3 shall be made public in a register to be set up by the Commission in 2001."

[1] OJ L 184, 17.7.1999, p. 23.

On 10 June 2005 the EU and China reached the so-called 'Shanghai Agreement' (see Document 2.13). It limited 10 categories of Chinese textile exports to the EU to agreed levels until the end of 2007. The agreement was in the form of a Memorandum of Understanding, which, on ratification by the EU Member States, was transposed into EC law.[7]

### Document 2.13: The 'Shanghai Agreement', 10 June 2005

**Textile and footwear sector**
**Memorandum of Understanding (MOU) Between the European Commission and the Ministry of Commerce of the People's Republic of China on the Export of Certain Chinese Textile and Clothing Products to the European Union**
**12 June 2005**

In view of the comprehensive strategic partnership between the European Union (EU) and the People's Republic of China (PRC) and the development of their trade and economic ties, and with a view to provide the EU and Chinese textile industries with a stable and predictable trading environment,

The European Commission and the Ministry of Commerce of the People's Republic of China (hereinafter the two Sides), pursuant to the WTO principle of encouraging its Members to settle their differences by way of consultation, engaged in frank and friendly consultations on the export of certain Chinese textile and clothing products to the European Union until the end of the year 2008 in Shanghai, China on June 10, 2005 and reached the following understanding:

I—The European Commission agreed to handle the import of textile and clothing products under categories 2, 4, 5, 6, 7, 20, 26, 31, 39 and 115 originating in the People's Republic of China in accordance with Paragraphs II, III and IV of this MOU and to end the ongoing investigations concerning these products.

II—The Two Sides agreed that from June 11, 2005 to December 31, 2005, with regard to the following Categories, the quantity of Chinese exports to the EU (see Annex I) shall be calculated in accordance with the following methodology:

- Base: The base for Categories 4 and 115 shall be the actual imports into the EU originating in PRC from March 2004 to February 2005. The base for Categories 2, 5, 6, 7, 20, 26, 31 and 39 shall be the actual imports into the EU originating in PRC from April 2004 to March 2005.
- Growth rate: 12.5% for Categories 2, 20 and 39; 10% for Categories 4, 26, 31 and 115; and 8% for Categories 5, 6 and 7.
- Formula: Quantity=Base X (1 + Growth Rate) X 204 / 365.

III—The Two Sides agreed that in the year 2006, with regard to the following Categories, the quantity of Chinese exports to the EU (see Annex I) shall be calculated in accordance with the following methodology:

[7] See Commission Regulation (EC) No 1084/2005 of 8 July 2005 amending Annexes II, III and V to Council Regulation (EEC) No 3030/93 on common rules for imports of certain textile products from third countries, [2005] OJ L177, 19. On 7 June 2005, the Ministry of Commerce of the People's Republic of China adopted Decree No 13, 2005 on Provisional Administrative Measures on Textile Export (Temporary), which came into effect on 20 July 2005: see http://fec2.mofcom.gov.cn/aarticle/laws/200506.20050601240844, accessed 12 February 2008.

- Base: Estimated actual imports into the EU originating in PRC from January 1, 2005 to June 10, 2005 plus, for each Category, the quantity from June 11, 2005 to December 31, 2005 calculated in accordance with Paragraph II.
- Growth rate: 12.5% for Categories 2, 20 and 39; and 10% for Categories 4, 5, 6, 7, 26, 31 and 115.
- Formula: Quantity=Base X (1 + Growth Rate).

IV—The Two Sides agreed that in the year 2007, with regard to the following Categories, the quantity of Chinese exports to the EU (see Annex I) shall be calculated in accordance with the following methodology:

- Base: For each category, the quantity of the whole year 2006 calculated in accordance with Paragraph III.
- Growth rate: 12.5% for Categories 2, 20 and 39; and 10% for Categories 4, 5, 6, 7, 26, 31 and 115.
- Formula: Quantity=Base X (1 + Growth Rate).

The quantities resulting from the application of the methodology described in Paragraphs II, III and IV are indicated in Annex I.

V—Both Sides will put in place as soon as possible the necessary administrative arrangements for the management of the agreed import levels.

VI. The European Commission will exercise restraint concerning the application of EU rights under Paragraph 242 of the Report of the Working Party for the Accession of China to the WTO in the period 2005 to 2007 for textile and clothing products not covered by Paragraph I of the present Memorandum of Understanding, and for all textile and clothing products listed in Annex II in the year 2008. The two Sides stand ready to discuss promptly on any aspect regarding the implementation of this MOU.

VII. This MOU shall be submitted to the competent authorities for endorsement or approval.

(Signed) Peter MANDELSON (Signed) BO Xilai

Commissioner for External Trade
The European Commission

Minister of Commerce
The People's Republic of China

June 10, 2005 June 10, 2005

**Annex I**

| | | Rest of 2005 (from 11 June) | 2005 (total) | 2006 | 2007 |
|---|---|---|---|---|---|
| 5—pullovers | 1000 units | 68,974 | 181,549 | 199,704 | 219,674 |
| 6—men's trousers | 1000 units | 104,045 | 316,430 | 348,072 | 382,880 |
| 7—blouses | 1000 units | 24,761 | 73,176 | 80,493 | 88,543 |
| 4—T-shirts | 1000 units | 150,985 | 491,095 | 540,204 | 594,225 |
| 26—dresses | 1000 units | 7,959 | 24,547 | 27,001 | 29,701 |
| 31—brassières | 1000 units | 96,086 | 205,174 | 225,692 | 248,261 |
| 115—flax or ramie yarn | tons | 1,911 | 4,309 | 4,740 | 5,214 |
| 2—cotton fabrics | tons | 26,217 | 55,065 | 61,948 | 69,692 |
| 20—bed linen | tons | 6,451 | 14,040 | 15,795 | 17,770 |
| 39—table+kitchen linen | tons | 5,521 | 10,977 | 12,349 | 13,892 |

Though agreed on 10 June, the Shanghai Agreement was not published in the form of EU legislation until 8 July and came into force only on 11 July. In the intervening month, EU textile imports and Chinese textile exports, many of which had been ordered on the long-term contracts frequent in the industry, continued, resulting in an estimated 87 million pieces being blocked in EU ports. In order to resolve this problem, the EU and China again held consultations. The outcome of a further meeting in Beijing in September 2005 was another agreement (see Document 2.14). It modified the level of permitted imports in order to unblock the ports. About half of the increased amount resulted from 'agreed flexibilities', for example the transfer of quota amount from 2006 into 2005. The other half derived from a unilateral EU increase of import levels, namely additional quantities of permitted textile imports. The agreement also created a special reserve for cotton fabrics and established additional flexibility provisions, such as advance use, carry over and the possibility of transfer of quota amounts between different categories of textiles. The Memorandum of Understanding was transposed into a Commission Regulation by written procedure on 12 September and published in the EC Official Journal on 13 September 2005. It entered into force on 14 September, thus avoiding the problem of delay between international agreement and the entry into force of domestic EC law that undermined the Shanghai Agreement.[8]

[8] On 16 September 2005, the Ministry of Commerce of the People's Republic of China adopted Order No 20, 2005, on Provisional Administrative Measures on Textile Export. The Order came into force on 22 September 2005 and abolished the Provisional Administrative Measures on Textile Export (Temporary) (Ministry of Commerce Decree No 13, 2005): see http://www.fdi.gov.cn/pub/FDI.EN/Laws/GeneralLawsandRegulations/MinisterialRulings/P020060620324767652278.pdf, accessed 12 February 2008

## Document 2.14: Minutes of the consultations regarding the establishment of transitional flexibility measures on the Memorandum of Understanding between the European Commission and the Ministry of Commerce of the People's Republic of China on the export of certain Chinese textile and clothing products to the EU

**Minutes of the consultations regarding the establishment of transitional flexibility measures on the Memorandum of Understanding between the European Commission and the Ministry of Commerce of the People's Republic of China on the export of certain Chinese textile and clothing products to the EU**

In order to deal with certain implementing problems happening in 2005 and effectively implement the Memorandum of Understanding Between the European Commission and the Ministry of Commerce of the People's Republic of China on the Export of Certain Chinese Textile and Clothing Products to the European Union (hereinafter the MOU) signed on 11 June 2005, the Ministry of Commerce of the People's Republic of China and the European Commission (hereinafter both sides) held a friendly consultation in Beijing on 4-5 September 2005, the content of which is as follows:

1. Both sides agree that each of them shall take charge respectively for the quantities of goods of their own licensing. The EU side shall release the goods in accordance with the licences issued by both sides.

2. The EU agrees to take charge of those goods shipped from China between 11 June and 12 July 2005, for which in accordance with EU regulations it issued import licences to enter into the EU without limitations.

3. Both sides agree that China and the EU will take charge in equal parts of the goods blocked at the EU borders up to the date of signature of these minutes. The EU will allow the clearance through customs of goods blocked prior to the date of signature of these minutes, within the agreed levels.

4. Both sides agree that the EU side shall take charge of all the quantities shipped before 20 July in excess of the agreed levels and for which it has issued an import licence. Both sides agree that, except for the quantities laid down in Annex 1, the Chinese side will not be responsible for any new quantities that come out later on.

5. At the latest by 30 November 2005, the EU will inform China of the total sum of these goods of each category actually imported into the EU. At the latest by 31 January 2006, a final verification will be made.

6. Should the exports from China by 31 December 2005 be lower than the 2005 agreed import levels laid down in annex 1 of the MOU as amended by annex 1 to these minutes, the non-imported amounts will be carried over and added to the agreed import levels at the Chinese disposal corresponding to year 2006, regardless of paragraph 9.

7. China and EU will not issue more licenses for those categories that have exceeded the agreed import levels, or above the levels indicated in annex 1 of the MOU as amended by annex 1 to these minutes.

8. Both sides affirm that the EU licence issuing for goods shipped from 20 July 2005 will be conditional upon the issuing of Chinese license and transmission of relevant data in principle by electronic means.

Calculation of Annex I of MoU China

| | | 2005 | | | | | | | | 2006 | | | 2007 |
|---|---|---|---|---|---|---|---|---|---|---|---|---|---|
| Product category | | Imports March 04–Feb 05 | Imports April 04–March 05 | Imports Jan–April 2005 (customs) | Estimated imports 1 May till 10 June (Imports Jan–April /120*42 days) | growth rate 2005 % | (A or B + growth rate) | Quantities that can be imported from 11 June–31 Dec. 2005 (E/365*205 days) | Imports 2005 total (C+D+F) | growth rate 2006 % | Imports 2006 (total 2005 imports + growth rate) | Growth rate 2007 % | Imports 2007 (imports 2006 + growth rate) |
| | | A | B | C | D | | E | F | G | | | | |
| 4—T-shirts | 1000 units | 244.388 | | 251.933 | 88.176 | 10,0 | 268.827 | 150.985 | 491.094 | 10,0 | 540.204 | 10,0 | 594.224 |
| 115—flax or ramie yarn | tons | 3.094 | | 1.776 | 621 | 10,0 | 3.403 | 1.911 | 4.308 | 10,0 | 4.739 | 10,0 | 5.213 |
| 2—cotton fabrics | tons | | 41.493 | 21.369 | 7.479 | 12,5 | 46.679 | 26.217 | 55.066 | 12,5 | 61.949 | 12,5 | 69.692 |
| 5—pullovers | 1000 units | | 113.710 | 83.389 | 29.186 | 8,0 | 122.807 | 68.974 | 181.549 | 10,0 | 199.704 | 10,0 | 219.674 |
| 6—men's trousers | 1000 units | | 171.528 | 157.322 | 55.063 | 8,0 | 185.251 | 104.045 | 316.430 | 10,0 | 348.073 | 10,0 | 382.880 |
| 7—blouses | 1000 units | | 40.820 | 35.863 | 12.552 | 8,0 | 44.086 | 24.761 | 73.176 | 10,0 | 80.493 | 10,0 | 88.542 |
| 20—bed linen | tons | | 10.209 | 5.622 | 1.968 | 12,5 | 11.485 | 6.451 | 14.040 | 12,5 | 15.795 | 12,5 | 17.770 |
| 26—dresses | 1000 units | | 12.883 | 12.287 | 4.301 | 10,0 | 14.171 | 7.959 | 24.547 | 10,0 | 27.001 | 10,0 | 29.701 |
| 31—brassières | 1000 units | | 155.527 | 80.806 | 28.282 | 10,0 | 171.080 | 96.086 | 205.174 | 10,0 | 225.692 | 10,0 | 248.261 |
| 39—table+kitchen linen | tons | | 8.738 | 4.041 | 1.414 | 12,5 | 9.831 | 5.521 | 10.977 | 12,5 | 12.349 | 12,5 | 13.892 |

9. Both sides agree that China can, after confirmation by the Commission, effect during the validity of the MOU transfers between the levels agreed in the MOU to the extent and in the manner indicated in Annex 2.

10. Both sides agree to cooperate closely in the implementation of the MOU as amended by these minutes. To this effect, they commit to quickly finalise an administrative arrangement and to set up a working group composed of MOFCOM and Commission officials to deal with matters concerning the application of *the* MOU, and which will meet no less frequently than once a quarter.

11. Both sides affirm that the EU side shall check and release the shipments against the effective licenses and certificates of origin issued by the Chinese side from 2006.

12. Annex 1 and Annex 2 are an integral part of the Minutes, if there are any difference between MOU and the Minutes, the Minutes shall take precedence over the MOU.

13. These minutes shall be submitted to the competent authorities for endorsement or approval.

The European Commission Ministry of Commerce
The People's Republic of China

Beijing, 5 September 2005

Annex 1

= *Transfers from the 2006 levels (1000 pieces)*

- Cat. 5 – pullovers: 9,985 – New 2006 level: 189,719 (instead of 199,704)
- Cat. 6 -trousers: 9,149 – New 2006 level: 338,923 (instead of 348,072)
- Cat. 31 – brassieres: 5,810 – New 2006 level: 219,882 (instead of 225,692)

*Transfers from Cat. 2 – cotton fabrics in 2005 into the following categories:*

- Cat; 4 – T-shirts: 4,270,148 pieces – 658,973 kg of cat 2
- Cat. 5-pullovers: 13,824,000 pieces-5,124,580 kg of cat. 2
- Cat. 7 – blouses: 636,809 pieces – 114,740 kg of cat. 2
- Cat. 26 – dresses: 68,097 pieces – 21,967 kg of cat. 2
- Cat. 115 – flax/ramie yarn: 84,740 kg- 84,740 kg of cat. 2

Annex 2 – General flexibility provisions

- Advance utilisation: 5 %
- Carry-over: 7 %
- Transfers between categories 4, 5, 6, 7, 26 and 31:4%
- Transfers between categories 2, 20, 39 and 115:4%.

# 3

# Policy Papers and Related Documents, 1995–Present: From Trade to Strategic Partnership

## INTRODUCTION

In the early years after the establishment of diplomatic relations, China's partner on the European side was the European Economic Community (EEC). Relations between Europe and China focused on trade in general and on trade in textiles. The legal framework was the 1985 Agreement on Trade and Economic Cooperation, supplemented by specific agreements on textiles. The EEC had no legal competence concerning foreign policy, which remained within the power of the EEC Member States. A major change occurred with the 1992 Maastricht Treaty on European Union, which created the European Union (EU), endowed the European Council with a specific role, integrated foreign policy into the Treaty system in the form of an intergovernmental Common and Foreign Security Policy, renamed the EEC as the EC (European Community), and expanded the legal competences and thus policy fields of the EC. It provided a basis on the European side for the development of a broader, more coherent policy concerning China.

In China, the 'opening up' and economic reforms began in 1979. By the mid-1990s, the process of economic social transformation was well underway. After being interrupted following the 1989 Tian'anmen Square events, relations between the EU and China had resumed. Considerable progress had been made in the development of a comprehensive legal system. The first Foreign Trade Law was enacted in 1994.

These changes had a direct impact on relations between the EU and China. The progress of European integration and the reform of European treaties and institutions enabled the EU to build on the foundation of specialised bilateral agreements. Starting in 1994, the EU began to elaborate a more coherent and comprehensive policy concerning Asia in general and China in particular. The policy documents took the form of 'communications' by the European Commission, which since the early 1980s had employed communications as a means of setting out its policies and guidelines for action; such communications were not legally binding. The Commission occasionally produced other documents about its policy toward China. For its part, China has rarely published specific policy papers concerning a single country or region. In 2003, however, it published its first ever policy paper on Europe. Since then, this has been supplemented by major policy speeches by Chinese leaders. EU policies toward China and Chinese policies toward the EU developed partly in tandem, partly in reaction to each other and partly in response to other circumstances affecting one side or the other. The difference in the number and length of policy documents on the two sides testifies to the differences in institutional structure, policy-making processes, foreign policy and communication strategies in the EU and China.

Today, a series of policy documents is available to chart the evolution of EU–China relations since 1994. This chapter presents the most significant policy documents (see Table 3.1). They mark the development of the policy framework of EU–China relations. These documents established the parameters for legally binding or 'soft law' bilateral agreements, summits and dialogues, and cooperation programmes. They also shed light on EU–China relations at present and illuminate their possible development in the future.

The chapter is divided into three main parts, which treat the development of EU and China policy documents chronologically according to three phases. The first part deals with the period from 1994 to 2003, which we can call the period of 'exploration and construction'. The second part concerns the period from 2003 to 2006, a period of 'deepening and maturing'. The third part focuses on the period from 2006 to the present, which can be summarised as a period of 'managing partnership and competition'. Policy and other documents concerning Hong Kong and Macao are included in another chapter.

## EXPLORATION AND CONSTRUCTION, 1995–2003

In 1994 the European Commission set out its strategy for Asia (see Document 3.1). Its stated objectives were to maintain the EU's leading role in the world economy by strengthening its presence in Asia, to contribute to stability in Asia, to promote economic development and to contribute to the development of democracy, the rule of law and respect for human rights. Entitled 'Towards a New Asia Strategy', the document reviewed EU Asian policy thus far and set down new priorities to meet these objectives.

### Document 3.1: Commission Communication, 'Towards a New Asian Strategy' (1994)

Communication from the Commission to the Council
Towards a New Asia Strategy
Commission of the European Communities
COM(94) 314 final, Brussels, 13.07.94

**Executive Summary**

The rise of Asia is dramatically changing the world balance of economic power. By the year 2000, the World Bank estimates that half the growth in the global economy will come from East and Southeast Asia alone. This growth will ensure that by the year 2000 one billion Asians will have significant consumer spending power and of these, 400 million will have

**Table 3.1: EU and China Policy Papers, 1994–2007**

| Title | Document | Author | Place | Date | Reference number | Source | Related documents |
|---|---|---|---|---|---|---|---|
| Towards a New Asia Strategy [see Document 3.1] | Communcation from the Commission to the Council | Commission of the European Communities | Brussels | 13.7.1994 | COM(94)314 final | ec.europa.eu/europeaid/projects/asia-itc/downloads/towards_a_new_asia_strategy.pdf | |
| A Long Term Policy for China-Europe Relations [see Document 3.2] | Communication | Commission of the European Communities | Brussels | 1995 | COM(1995)2798 final | ec.europa.eu/external_relations/china/com95_279en.pdf - | European Parliament Resolution on the Commission Communication on a long term policy for China-Europe relations (COM(95)0279 C4-0288/95) |
| Building a Comprehensive Partnership with China [see Document 3.3] | Communication from the Commission | Commission of the European Communities | Brussels | 25.3.1998 | COM(1998)181 final | http://ec.europa.eu/external_relations/china/com_98/index.htm | |
| Implementation of the Communication 'Building a Comprehensive Partnership with China' [see Document 3.4] | Report from the Commission to the Council and the European Parliament | Commission of the European Communities | Brussels | 8.9.2000 | COM(2000)552 final | ec.europa.eu/external_relations/china/com_00_552/com2000_0552en01.pdf | |

**Table 3.1: Continued**

| Title | Document | Author | Place | Date | Reference number | Source | Related documents |
|---|---|---|---|---|---|---|---|
| EU Strategy towards China: Implementation of the 1998 Communication and Future Steps for a More Effective EU Policy [see Document 3.5] | Communication to the Council and the European Parliament | Commission of the European Communities | Brussels | 15.5.2001 | COM(2001)265 final | ec.europa.eu/external_relations/china/com01_265.pdf | |
| Europe and Asia: A Strategic Framework for Enhanced Partnerships [see Document 3.6] | Communication from the Commission | Commission of the European Communities | Brussels | 4.9.2001 | COM(2001) 469 final | database-dkkv.dyndns.org/eukavo/Commission/com2001_0469en01.pdf | |
| Country Strategy Paper: China [not included in this book] | Commission Working Document | Commission of the European Communities | Brussels | 1.3.2002 | IP/02/349 | http://ec.europa.eu/comm/external_relations/china/csp/index.htm | |

**Table 3.1: Continued**

| Title | Document | Author | Place | Date | Reference number | Source | Related documents |
|---|---|---|---|---|---|---|---|
| National Indicative Programme 2002–2004 [not included in this book] | National Indicative Programme | European Commission | Brussels | n.d. [2005] | | summary available in European Commission, Directorate-General for External Relations, 'National Indicative Programme 2005-2006', section 1.1.3 (Brussels, 2005) | |
| A Maturing Partnership - Shared Interests and Challenges in EU-China Relations (updating the European Commission's Communications on EU-China Relations of 1998 and 2001) [see Document 3.7] | Policy Paper for Transmission to the Council and the European Parliament | Commission of the European Communities | Brussels | 10.9.2003 | COM(2003)533 final | ec.europa.eu/external_relations/china/com_03_533/com_533_en.pdf | |

**Table 3.1: Continued**

| Title | Document | Author | Place | Date | Reference number | Source | Related documents |
|---|---|---|---|---|---|---|---|
| China's EU Policy Paper [see Document 3.8] | Policy Paper | Ministry of Foreign Affairs of the People's Republic of China | Beijing | 13.10.2003 | | http://www.fmprc.gov.cn/eng/wjb/zzjg/xos/dqzzywt/t27708.htm (visited 18.1.2005), http://english.peopledaily.com.cn/200310/13/print20031013_125906.html (accessed 30.10.2006) | |
| Vigorously Promoting Comprehensive Strategic Partnership between China and the European Union [see Document 3.9] | Speech at the China-EU Investment and Trade Symposium | H.E. WEN Jiabao, Premier of the State Council of the People's Republic of China | Brussels | 6.5.2004 | | http://www.chineseembassy.org/chn/wjb/zzjg/xos/dqzzywt/t94909.htm [in Chinese] (accessed 30.10.2006 | |
| Strengthening Partnership Through Increased Dialogue and Cooperation [see Document 3.10 | Speech at the Fifth Asia-Europe Meeting | H.E. WEN Jiabao, Premier of the State Council of the People's Republic of China | Hanoi | 8.10.2004 | | http://www.fmprc.gov.cn/eng/wjdt/zyjh/t164329.htm (accessed 30.10.2006) | |

**Table 3.1: Continued**

| Title | Document | Author | Place | Date | Reference number | Source | Related documents |
|---|---|---|---|---|---|---|---|
| A Strengthening of All-Round Cooperation and a Deepening of the Comprehensive Strategic Partnership between China and the European Union [see Document 3.11] | Speech to the China-EU Business Summit | H.E. WEN Jiabao, Premier of the State Council of the People's Republic of China | The Hague | 9.12. 2004 | | http://news.xinhuanet.com/world/2004-12/09/content_2314983.htm [in Chinese] (accessed 30.10.2006) | |
| Strengthening ASEM Economic and Financial Cooperation to Promote Common Development [see Document 3.12] | Speech at the Opening Ceremony of the Sixth ASEM Finance Ministers Meeting | H.E. WEN Jiabao, Premier of the State Council of the People's Republic of China | Tianjin | 26.6.2005 | | http://www.fmprc.gov.cn/eng/wjdt/zyjh/t202172.htm | |
| National Indicative Programme, 2005-2006: China [see Document 3.13] | National Indicative Programme | Commission of the European Communities | Brussels | 27.9.2004 | | http://ec.europa.eu/comm/external_relations/china/csp/index.htm (accessed 23.3.2007) | |

**Table 3.1: Continued**

| Title | Document | Author | Place | Date | Reference number | Source | Related documents |
|---|---|---|---|---|---|---|---|
| Summary of the Results of the Public Consultation on the China Communication [see Document 3.14] | | European Commission | Brussels | 7.9.2006 | European Commission, Directorate-General for Trade, G3-Sustainable development (including trade and environment); dialogue with civil society, DG Trade-G3/CS/RtB/saD(2006)10058, Brussels, 7.9.2006 | trade.ec.europa.eu/doclib/docs/2006/september/tradoc_130244.pdf | European Parliament, Committee on Foreign Affairs, Report on EU-China Relations (2005/2161(INI), Rapporteur: Bastiaan Belder, European Parliament, Session Document, Final A6-0257/2006, RR\367859EN.doc/PE 367.859v03-00 |
| Deepening Asia-Europe Cooperation to Jointly Meet Challenges [see Document 3.15] | Speech at the Sixth ASEM Summit | H.E. WEN Jiabao, Premier of the State Council of the People's Republic of China | Helsinki | 10.9.2006 | | http://www.fmprc.gov.cn/eng/wjdt/zyjh/t272762.htm, ,accessed 22.9.07 | |
| Enhance cooperation to promote win-win progress' [see Document 3.16] | Speech at the 2006 China-Europe Business Summit | H.E. WEN Jiabao, Premier of the State Council of the People's Republic of China | Helsinki | 12.9.2006 | | http://www.fmprc.gov.cn/eng/zxx/x/t272763.htm | |

**Table 3.1: Continued**

| Title | Document | Author | Place | Date | Reference number | Source | Related documents |
|---|---|---|---|---|---|---|---|
| The Hamburg Summit: China Meets Europe [see Document 3.17] | Speech at the Official Opening of the Hamburg Summit | H.E. WEN Jiabao, Premier of the State Council of the People's Republic of China | Hamburg | 13.9.2006 | | http://www.hamburg-summit.com/hamburg-summit/pdfs/2006/SpeechWenJiabao130906.pdf | |
| EU-China: Closer partners, growing responsibilities [see Document 3.18] | Communication to the Council and the European Parliament | Commission of the European Communities | Brussels | 24.10.2006 | COM(2006)631 final | eur-lex.europa.eu/LexUriServ/site/fr/com/2006/com2006_0631fr01.pdf - | Consultant Study on 'Future Opportunities and Challenges in EU-China Trade and Investment Relations, 2006-2010', commissioned by the European Commission,, 15.2.2007, available at http://ec.europa.eu/trade/issues/bilateral/countries/china/legis/index_en.htm |
| EU-China Trade and Investment: Competition and Partnership [see Document 3.19] | Commission Working Document, Policy Paper | Commission of the European Communities | Brussels | 24.10.2006 | COM(2006)632 final | http://eur-lex.europa.eu/LexUriServ/site/en/com/2006/com2006_0632en01.pdf | |

**Table 3.1: Continued**

| Title | Document | Author | Place | Date | Reference number | Source | Related documents |
|---|---|---|---|---|---|---|---|
| Global Europe: Europe's Trade Defence Instruments in a Changing Global Economy: A Green Paper for Public Consultation [see Document 3.20] | Communication | Commission of the European Communities | Brussels | 6.12.2006 | COM(2006)763 final | trade.ec.europa.eu/doclib/docs/2006/december/tradoc_131477.pdf | Council Conclusions: EU-China Strategic Partnership',in Council of the European Union, Press Release, 2771st Council Meeting, General Affairs and External Relations, External Relations, Brussels, 11-12 December 2006, President: Mr Erkki Tuomioja, Minister of Foreign Affairs of Finland, 16291/06 (Presse 353), availableat http://www.consilium.europa.eu/Newsroom accessed 21.9.2007 |
| Country Strategy Paper: China 2007-2013 [see Document 3.21] | Strategy Paper | European Commission | Brussels | 2006 | | http://www.fmprc.gov.cn/eng/wjdt/zyjh/t202172.htm | |

**Table 3.1: Continued**

| Title | Document | Author | Place | Date | Reference number | Source | Related documents |
|---|---|---|---|---|---|---|---|
| Multiannual Indicative Programme (MIP), 2007-2010 [not included in this book] | Multiannual Indicative Programme | European Commission | Brussels | 2006 | | http://ec.europa.eu/external_relations/china/csp/2007_mip_en.pdf | |

average disposable incomes as high, if not higher, than their European or US contemporaries.

The European Union needs therefore to accord Asia a higher priority than is at present the case.

The Union needs as a matter of urgency to strengthen its economic presence in Asia in order to maintain its leading role in the world economy. The establishment of a strong, co-ordinated presence in the different regions of Asia will allow Europe at the beginning of the 21st century to ensure that its interests are taken fully into account there.

Asia's growing economic weight is inevitably generating increasing pressures for a greater role in world affairs. At the same time the ending of the cold war has created a regional environment of unparalleled political fluidity. Consequently the European Union should seek to develop its political dialogue with Asia and should look for ways to associate Asia more and more in the management of international affairs, working towards a partnership of equals capable of playing a constructive and stabilising role in the world.

In order to seize these new opportunities the Union should seek to make a positive contribution to regional security dialogues and to follow closely developments in particular in the area of arms control and non-proliferation, regional disputes (Korea, Spratly, Kashmir) and the security of sea lanes. Matters relating to good governance, including human rights should also play an important role in the Union's relations with Asian countries

The success of Europe in taking advantage of the business opportunities in Asia largely depends upon decisions taken or not taken by the private sector. The Union's role is to pursue market opening for both goods and services and to overcome obstacles to European trade and investment by encouraging a favourable regulatory environment for business in Asia. Active participation by European companies on Asian markets it should be noted can contribute to providing qualified jobs for European workers.

To achieve its aims, the Union needs to adopt more pro-active strategies: emphasising fuller and increasingly targeted use of economic co-operation to promote European trade and investment. This can largely be achieved within present financial resources.

Reforms of previously centrally managed economies, such as China, India or Vietnam, are an extremely important aspect of the momentous changes sweeping across Asia. European participation in these changes both at the institutional and at the private sector level will contribute to reinforce mutual understanding and economic links.

The Union needs to conduct a co-ordinated programme of public relations in order to raise its profile in Asia.

By the year 2000, South Asia will still contain the single largest concentration of the world's poorest people, so development cooperation will remain as an instrument to contribute to the Asian governments' own efforts at poverty alleviation. Enhanced coordination between the Union and its Member States is required in order to achieve critical mass and the desired impact.

**I. Overall Objectives**

Asia defined. The term "Asia" is an over-simplification: Asia is not a single region. The 26 countries of Asia discussed in the present Communication have different cultural traditions and different social, economic and political profiles, even if industrialisation is making some of these differences less marked than in the past. (The 26 countries covered in this

Communication are grouped according to 3 geographic regions: The 8 countries and economies of East Asia (China, Japan, North and South Korea, Mongolia, Taiwan, Hong Kong, Macao); the 10 countries of Southeast Asia (Brunei, Indonesia, Malaysia, Philippines, Singapore, Thailand, Cambodia, Laos, Vietnam and Burma), and the 8 countries of South Asia (India, Pakistan, Bangladesh, Sri Lanka, Nepal, Bhutan, Maldives and Afghanistan). Relations with the 5 Central Asian republics are currently dealt with in the context of the CIS and are therefore not included here).

The main thrust of the present and future policy in Asia is related to economic matters. However, this major component of the Union policy has to be presented in the framework of the political and security balance of power in the region.

*Overall Objectives*

- To strengthen the Union's economic presence in Asia in order to maintain the Union's leading role in the world economy. The establishment of an important presence in Asia will allow Europe at the beginning of the 21$^{st}$ century to ensure that its interests are taken fully into account in this key region. Given the pace of growth in Asia, active participation by European companies can also contribute to providing qualified jobs for European workers.
- To contribute to stability in Asia by promoting international co-operation and understanding; the Union must to this end widen and deepen its political and economic relations with the countries in Asia.
- To promote the economic development of the less prosperous countries and regions in Asia. Given that Asia for the foreseeable future will continue to contain the world's largest concentration of poor people, the Union and its Member States will need to continue to contribute to poverty alleviation and sustainable growth.
- To contribute to the development and consolidation of democracy and the rule of law, and respect for human rights and fundamental freedoms in Asia.

*Priorities*

If the EU is to achieve these objectives, this will require a considerable effort to reorient existing policies and to move into new domains. The magnitude of this effort calls for a more efficient use of all available resources. Not least, this implies more coordination within the Union. This also calls for a set of clear policy priorities across Asia that can be followed up in a manner best suited to the individual circumstances of each country and region:

- To continue to strengthen the Union's bilateral relations with individual countries and regions in Asia.
- To raise the profile of Europe in Asia.
- To support efforts by Asian countries to cooperage at the regional and sub-regional level such as the ASEAN Regional Forum with a view to enhancing peace and security in the region and generally to strengthen the Union's relations with regional groups such as ASEAN or SAARC.
- To associate Asian countries in the management of international affairs and in particular to encourage them to play a more active role in multilateral actions with a view to maintaining international peace and security. To strengthen links with Asian countries in multilateral forums, and further encourage Asian participation in multilateral organisations.
- To pursue all actions necessary to ensure open markets and a non-discriminatory business environment conducive to an expansion of Euro-Asian trade and investments.

- To integrate into the open, market-based world trading system those Asian countries which are moving from state controls to market-oriented economies.
- To contribute to sustainable development and to poverty alleviation in the least prosperous countries of Asia.

## II. The EU's Existing Policy Instruments in its Relations with Asia

In proposing new strategies for Asia, the European Union does not start from a tabula rasa: the Union has already gained considerable experience in Asia:

### *Bilateral Relations*

Traditionally the EU conducts its bilateral co-operation with many countries and regions in Asia, as elsewhere, in the framework of Trade and Co-operation Agreements (see Annex III, Table 1).

The EU also has a structured political dialogue with most partners of the Asia region.

On a bilateral level, it is the case with Japan (on the basis of an EU-Japan Joint Declaration), China (recent exchange of letters between this country and the EU), India (on the basis of the joint political declaration of last December), Pakistan. With Sri Lanka, there has been an agreement of principle to initiate the dialogue, although it has not yet taken place. South Korea has requested a formalised arrangement.

At the regional level, the political dialogue takes place with ASEAN (there is no bilateral dialogue with individual members of ASEAN). There is provision for an annual EU-ASEAN meeting at the ministerial or senior officials level, and there is another ministerial level meeting every year in the framework of the ASEAN Post Ministerial Conference (PMC) where the EU is one of the dialogue partners, the others being the US, Canada, Australia, New Zealand, South Korea and Japan.

At an even broader level, the EU is taking part in the only collective regional security dialogue, the ASEAN Regional Forum (see page 9), which includes most Asian countries and will meet annually starting this year.

The political dialogue has mainly taken place at the ministerial or political director level, either in a Troika format or with the Presidency and the Commission.

Fifteen years ago the European Commission's only Delegation in Asia was in Tokyo. Today there are 10 delegations in Asia (see Annex III, Table 1 for list).

### *Multilateral Co-operation*

The Union is engaged in a wide-ranging dialogue with Asia within the UN system on subjects of common interest relating to international peace and security. The Union has in recent years greatly expanded its economic co-operation with Asian countries. This has not only happened in the context of the GATT where the role of Asian countries has increased considerably commensurate with their growing importance in world trade, but also in UN forums such as UNCED or CSD and in the OECD with Japan (and shortly Korea).

### *Commercial Policy*

The mainstay of the Union's Commercial policy, both in general and towards the countries of Asia, has always been an active commitment to trade liberalisation within the multilateral system with respect for all of the rules and commitments that this entails. Increased market access for the Union's exporters has been successfully pursued via the Uruguay Round and other actions at the multilateral level. The Union has also sought to improve market access for European business through its bilateral relations.

Trade promotion on a European level from Europe to Asian markets is undertaken, to various degrees, across the region. However, the main trade (and investment), promotion activities from Europe to Asia are made by the EU Member States acting individually.

The Union has at its disposal a number of trade policy instruments: antidumping measures and safeguard measures. These are in conformity with the Union's multilateral obligations and commitments that limit their use accordingly. With respect to textiles all existing restrictions under the MFA will be phased out over ten years as agreed in the Uruguay Round.

*Development Aid*

Between 1976 and 1991, the European Union disbursed aid worth more than 32 billion ECU to Asia. This makes the Union the second largest donor to Asia, after Japan but with three times more than the USA. Of the total amount disbursed by the Union, about 11% came from the budget line for Asia and Latin American countries administered by the Commission (see Annex III, Table 3). Only a small portion of this was allocated to, economic co-operation, the remainder going mainly to rural development projects and food aid. However effective this assistance may have been in the past, the need was felt to re-assess its effectiveness with a view to adapting the approach to the changed conditions in much of Asia.

An important start was made in the Developing Countries of Asia and Latin America Regulation of 1992. The Regulation foresees two main lines of co-operation:

(i) Development aid for the poorest countries and population groups and;

(ii) Economic co-operation with countries or regions with high growth potential.

Environmental issues have to be taken into account in both forms of co-operation. Economic co-operation, and this was the innovation in the regulation, is aimed at improving the business and regulatory environment in partner countries in order to stimulate two way trade and investments with the direct participation of the private sector to the benefit both of the Union and the partner country.

In 1991, the EC Council and its Member States adopted a resolution on human nights, democracy and development. On this basis, the EU gives high priority to specific agreed actions aimed at consolidating democracy and promoting human nights in some Asian countries. This kind of activity is increasingly diversified covering fields such as the support of elections, NGOs, free media, vulnerable groups, information on, and sensitivity to, human nights.

In 1993, despite the fact that for many years Asia has had many high growth developing countries, only 12% of the EU aid for Asia was committed to economic co-operation. The remainder was used for activities broadly intended to alleviate poverty (the main commitments went to South Asia). In both China and India the EU's largest activity undertaken in the 1980s was a dairy development project financed mainly out of the food aid budget.

Various forms of technical assistance and co-operation are financed from special budget lines for example for energy, the environment, tropical forests, science and technology, AIDS prevention and narcotics control.

Widespread support for Non-Governmental Organisations is available, including certain country-specific NGO funds (for example for Cambodia or Vietnam).

Humanitarian aid, refugee and emergency assistance are important contributions to the alleviation of suffering in Asia.

The Union is well aware of the importance to developing countries of access to its market. To this end, preferential market access has been unilaterally offered to Asian developing countries for many years under the EU's Generalised System of Preferences scheme. Indeed, the Asian countries are the main beneficiaries of the scheme, accounting for as much as 72% of imports by the Union under the scheme in 1992. On the 1 June 1994, the Commission adopted its Communication to the Council and the European Parliament relating to the revision and the updating of the principles to be followed in the elaboration of the new scheme to be applied for the period 1995 to 2004. The Commission will shortly table its proposals for the detailed operational scheme, more founded than in the past on the concept of development, which will be implemented on 1 January 1995.

Stabex was extended to Bangladesh and Nepal in 1987 under a five year scheme and to Burma in 1988. These are the only countries in Asia to have benefited from Stabex.

*Investment and Financial Facilities*

In addition to its contributions to balanced development within the Union, the European Investment Bank also finances investment projects in non-member countries. Since 1992, the EIB has extended its lending operations to the Asia and Latin America regions on an experimental basis. The scheme is open to countries there that have a co-operation agreement with the Union. An allocation of 250 million ECUs per year over three years is available for these countries. During the first year of operation, loans worth 100 million ECU were made to projects in Asia.

The European Community Investment Partners facility promotes joint ventures in Asian, Latin American and Mediterranean countries between local and European operators. Between 1988 and end 1993, 292 projects for a total ECIP financing of +/- 30 million ECU have been approved for Asia.

## III. The European Union's New Political Approach towards Asia

*1. The Justification for Closer Political Relations*

Introduction

The European Union is entrusted with the task of developing a common foreign and security policy to enable it to protect its interests and values as well as playing a constructive role in world politics.

The increase of the relative weight of Asia in the world economy will considerably reinforce the political weight of this region on the international political scene.

To keep Europe in its major role on the world stage it is imperative to take account of the emergence of these new Asian powers.

The maintenance of peace and stability in Asia is an important factor not only for the protection of the Union's interests in this region, including economic ones, but also for the respect of international obligations and agreements on which the Union itself depends for its security, e.g. regarding non-proliferation. It is therefore essential that the Union develop the capacity to play its proper role in the region.

1.1 Security Arrangements in Asia

Political and security relations between Asia and the major powers are undergoing a gradual but profound shift under the combined influence of rapidly spreading economic growth and the end of the Cold War.

From a security viewpoint the US remains the key player in the region and the current situation is characterised by a web of bilateral security arrangements between the United States and a number of Asian countries. At the present moment, no single Asian country or outside power appears to be in a position to take over the role of the US.

The US is in the process of developing a more pragmatic relationship with Asia. Whereas in the Cold War the US was prepared to subordinate its economic interests to the goal of containment, it is now focusing more and more on the economics of the relationship.

A further sign of such a shift in US policy towards Asia is the recent decision to extend (with a few exceptions) the MFN-treatment of Chinese exports into the US. The US thus uncoupled trade and human rights. This shift may also be regarded as a move towards a more long-term strategy aimed at influencing developments in China by further integrating China into world trade and economic relations.

Japan enjoys a privileged security relationship with the USA. The Japanese constitution renounces Japan's right to declare war and proscribes the use of Japanese forces outside Japan. Participation in certain international peacekeeping operations has, however, been possible.

In the wake of the Soviet collapse, Russia has tended to turn inwards and refrain from an active role, but remains a country to be reckoned with, notably with regard to developments in North Korea.

Pakistan, through its involvement in Afghanistan, and also China and India, are playing a significant role in former Soviet Central Asia, a key area for the stability and future development of Russia.

In the aftermath of World War II, Europe's former Asian colonies gained their independence leading to the almost complete withdrawal of European forces from the region. Hong Kong and Macau will revert to China in 1997 and 1999, respectively. As a result, the European influence on developments in Asia has for many years been exerted mainly through the medium of trade and investment, as well as development co-operation and cultural exchanges. It is to be noted, however, that some Member States still have wider interests in the region and maintain relationships that include a security component (e.g. the Five Power Defence Arrangement which links the UK with Malaysia and Singapore).

1.2 Political and Security Co-operation between Asian Countries

The reduction of tensions in the world has allowed the Asian countries to take the first modest step in the direction of developing an Asian identity and cultivating Asian approaches to Asian problems starting at the sub regional level.

The change in the "rapport de force" with non-Asian powers is translating into political confidence, notably and vocally among the countries of South East Asia, which no longer hesitate to question our moral values and our social systems.

Economic growth and imitation effects are having a dampening effect on intra-regional tensions: there is a shared perception in Asia that growth leads to prosperity, which in turn generates stability and security. But economic growth also makes it possible to expand military budgets: a number of countries, notably in South East Asia, have been active in developing their capabilities, especially in the naval field, and in spite of the soothing effects of economic growth, there remain a number of potentially serious regional flash points (Spratlys, Kashmir).

The first steps towards a regional security forum are taking place under the auspices of ASEAN, but at the same time there are signs that Asia is moving towards a classical balance of powers diplomacy.

The Union has a long-standing relationship with ASEAN. There is a formal EU-ASEAN agreement (1980). The EU participates in the annual ASEAN Post Ministerial Conference, which will now extend to the newly created regional security forum, the ARF (ASEAN Regional Forum). The ARF will be meeting for the first time this year. It encompasses most of the countries of Asia except North Korea and includes North America, the EU and Russia. In conformity with the principle of ASEAN itself, the discussions are to be consensus oriented and the participants clearly wish to avoid conflictual debate.

Although ARF may over time develop into the overall security forum for the Asian region, it is likely that sub-regional groupings may emerge to deal with specific problems, such as those of North East Asia. These sub-regional groupings may or may not operate in the framework of the ARF. The European experience gained from establishing and operating the CSCE may be of certain relevance in this connection.

### 1.3 Asia in Search of a Role in World Politics

With the increasing strength of Asia and individual Asian countries it is however inevitable that this region will wish to play a more prominent role on the world stage. Economic importance rather than military force will serve as a platform for its influence.

In connection with the debate on the restructuring of the United Nations Security Council it is already evident that Asia wants a stronger and also a permanent representation. It is well known that certain of the more important Asian countries feel entitled to a permanent seat in the Council. Considering the special responsibilities associated with being a permanent member of the Council this is a clear sign that these countries have the ambition to involve themselves in political questions relating not only to the Asian region but also beyond.

Another indication pointing in the same direction is the participation of certain Asian countries in international peacekeeping operations outside the Asian region. It is very much in the interest of the Union that the responsibilities of carrying out such operations be shared between as many countries as possible.

## *2. Characteristics of the new Political Approach towards Asia*

### 2.1 Strengthening the Political Dialogue with Asia

The political dialogue between the Union and Asia should develop within the following parameters.

The political dialogue must gain its legitimacy from the Council and from the European Parliament with the Commission playing the special role conferred upon it. The approach by the Council towards Asia is partly a reflection of the different historic relations between the individual Member States and the region, partly their present interest in strengthening such relations, often dictated by economic considerations. The Union's obligations, entered into under global arrangements also play an important role. The European Parliament has adjusted its structures and working methods to accommodate it's increased responsibility post-Maastricht. Its interparliamentary Delegations and sectoral committees, as well as ad hoc missions, have established contacts with all the major countries of the region.

Asia has on its side consistently advocated an outward looking European Union, which represents for the Asian countries a major source of income and investments. Asia has repeatedly encouraged Europe to show a greater interest in the region. The Asian countries have however refrained from being too specific in identifying the precise subjects that they would wish to elaborate further in a political dialogue with the Union. This may be explained by some uncertainty about how the Union works (representation), partly by a perception of the European Union as being a difficult partner to negotiate with (Uruguay Round).

The basic objective of the policies towards Asia in the coming years must therefore be to increase Asian interest in and knowledge of the Union and to demonstrate to the Asian countries the ability and commitment of Europe to make a positive contribution to the peaceful development and stability of the region. The EU should, in particular, develop its political dialogue with those countries in the region which are prepared and able to make a significant contribution to the maintenance of the region's peace and stability.

The European Union has already initiated a political dialogue with several Asian countries and group of countries and is in the process of developing dialogues with a number of others. The existing dialogues have typically consisted of a presentation of the general situation of the respective parties and discussions on regional and global problems. It might, however, be desirable to focus on specific subjects with appropriate preparation and follow-up. One way of achieving this would be to dedicate Troika meetings to agreed themes on which the parties would have sufficient time to elaborate.

In the future more effort should be spent on developing the political dialogue at expert level with a view to deepening the dialogue and if possible, making it more operational.

The Union participates in the ASEAN Regional Forum that provides for a wide-ranging dialogue on security concerns encompassing the greater part of Pacific Asia. The Union must follow the evolution of the ARF and develop ways for making its own particular contribution to the discussion of such matters.

### 2.2 Subjects for Political Discussion

#### *2.2.1 – Arms control and non-proliferation*

Rapid economic growth, territorial disputes, increasingly ambitious armament programmes, the potential for distrust in such a large region and the weakness of the multilateral organisations for political consultation are all factors which, could lead to regional conflicts in Asia capable of disrupting world equilibrium and thereby impinging on CFSP objectives.

Whereas global military expenditure fell by 20 % in 1993, such expenditure grew in East Asia alone.

The European Union considers policies on arms control and the non-proliferation of weapons of mass destruction (nuclear, chemical, biological, ballistic missiles) as important elements of the Common Foreign and Security Policy. These are probable areas for future joint action. The EU should explore the possibility of continuing or initiating dialogue on some of these points with the Asian countries.

The EU could focus these discussions on the following:

- **Conventional Arms.** The UN Conventional Arms Register was the result of a joint EC-Japan initiative and came properly into effect at the beginning of 1993. The gathering and publication of data are an essential measure of confidence where conventional arms transfer is concerned. The EU has already initiated a dialogue, which should be pursued, with many of the region's countries on the need to improve the register's coverage and efficiency.

At the 48th UN General Assembly, the 'international community began its reflection on the "Convention on prohibitions or restrictions on the use of certain conventional weapons which may be deemed to be excessively injurious or to have indiscriminate effect" in order to examine, in particular, an amendment to its Protocol II on anti-personnel mines. These negotiations will run to 1996. A successful outcome would be in the joint interest of the EU and the Asian countries given the use of such mines in conflicts in the region.

- The indefinite and unconditional extension of the NPT in 1995 is one of the CFSP's most important short-term objectives. The EU will continue its efforts to improve the Treaty's coverage. At the same time, the Union will make great diplomatic efforts with the countries of the region party to the Treaty to reach the objective of such an extension.
- **Strengthening the IAEA's Safeguards System.** The international tension brought about by North Korea's attitude on nuclear inspections underlines the need to reinforce the efficiency and maintain the credibility of the IAEA's safeguards system. This challenge for the international community also provides an opportunity for the EU and the Asian countries to co-operate.
- **Export Policies on the Export of Sensitive Goods and Technologies.** Given the industrial and commercial dynamism of the Asian countries and the deepening of their already well-developed technological abilities as suppliers, they are already major suppliers of goods and technologies which could be sensitive for the proliferation of weapons of mass destruction, whether in the chemical, ballistic, biological or nuclear sectors. (According to the IAEA, Asia is the only region in the world where there is an increase in the use of nuclear generators for domestic electricity supply with the number of nuclear power stations set to double from 70 in 1992 to 140 by 2010), A dialogue between the EU and Asia on the basis of objectives of non-proliferation and legitimate industrial, technological and trade development is of prime importance.
- **Conventions Prohibiting Chemical and Biological Weapons.** The rapid and concrete implementation of the obligations of the 1993 Convention Prohibiting Chemical Weapons and the strengthening of the terms of the 1972 Convention Prohibiting Biological Weapons are important short-term objectives for the EU with a view to consolidating the international nonproliferation and disarmament system. These topics could be appropriately pursued by the Union in its dialogue with its Asian partners.
- **Comprehensive Nuclear Test Ban Treaty.** The EU actively supports the efforts of the Disarmament Conference 'in Geneva to conclude a universal and verifiable treaty and should encourage its Asian partners to join in that support.

*2.2.2 – Human Rights*

The development and consolidation of democracy and the rule of law and respect for human rights and fundamental freedoms together form a major objective of the external policy of the European Union. Regarding human rights, the general approach of the EU is endorsement of existing international standards, as set down in the relevant international instruments, to which most or all Asian countries are signatories. In this respect, the Union should encourage all countries to become signatories of and to fully implement all relevant international instruments. The European Union pursues this objective, *inter alia, through dialogue guided by the Vienna Declaration and Programme of Action of the 1993 UN World Conference on Human Rights, to the success of which both the Union and the Asian countries have actively contributed.

In the first place the dialogue on human rights will predominantly be dealt with in its context and in appropriate forums both bilateral and multilateral, such as the UN Commission on Human Rights where the governments of the countries concerned are most likely to be under scrutiny.

The concept of the interrelationship between human rights, democracy and development, should be inspired by the assumption that economic development could bring about the progressive construction of civil society and thus improve the exercise of human rights, which in their turn could also be an important factor for development.

Emphasis should also be given to facilitating legislative and institutional reform, and, in this respect, technical training and granting of scholarships as well as visits and seminars could be envisaged.

*2.2.3 – Drugs*

The drug phenomenon constitutes a global problem and is today considered a major threat to the stability and democracy of societies confronted with it. Drug trafficking, drug production and drug consumption also presents a problem to Asian regions and has significant repercussions on the European economies and EU security and stability. The global aspect of the problem is widely recognised and the need for co-operation at international level is clearly voiced. The European Union therefore already initialised a dialogue on drug and drug related matters with some Asian countries such as India and China. This approach has to be pursued in order to enhance awareness of the drug problem at the highest political level. In fact the necessity for the systematic inclusion of the drugs question in the political dialogue has been stated and elaborated in the recent communication from the Commission to the Council and the European Parliament on a European Union Action Plan to Combat Drugs. The implementation of this drug plan has already been identified by the Corfu Council as a priority. The immediate objective of a political dialogue on drugs with Asian countries should be the improvement of the capacity and willingness of the countries concerned to commit themselves fully in the fight against drugs. A further aim will be the ratification by third countries of the three United Nation Conventions on narcotic drugs and psychotropic substances.

**IV. The European Union's New Trade & Co-operation Strategy towards Asia**

1. Justification for a New Trade & Co-operation Strategy

1.1 Economic growth in Asia

Europe's interests in Asia are:

(i) To benefit from the economic opportunities and to respond to the economic challenges in the region which contains the world's fastest growing countries, and which could represent between a quarter and a third of the world economy by the year 2000;

(ii) To integrate into the open, market-based world trading system those Asian countries such as China, India or Vietnam
which are moving from state controls to market-oriented economies;

(iii) And to assist in the enormous problem of poverty alleviation.

To secure these objectives, and to prepare for the growing role of the Asian powers in world affairs, the European Union needs to accord Asia a higher priority than it has done in the past. The Union also needs to re-assess its policies towards the countries and regions of Asia, moving from the defensive to the pro-active. This can only be achieved by the Union and its Member States in coordination and with the direct participation of the European private sector.

Characteristics of economic growth in Asia. Economic growth in the three regions of Asia has been extensively analysed and described (see Annex IV for economic profiles of the countries and regions of Asia). The main characteristics having direct implications for the European Union's new strategies are as follows:

- **Variations in growth:** Average GNP growth per capita in East Asia between 1965 and 1990 was 5.5%. Southeast Asia was not far behind but the average conceals important variations. East and Southeast Asia contain some of the world's richest countries to be sure, but they also contain some of its poorest (e.g. Mongolia, Burma, Cambodia, Laos or Vietnam). South Asia has on average had less rapid growth (1.8% over the same period), but there have also been important increases in wealth.
- **Rapid spread of growth:** Economic growth in Asia has spread very rapidly from one country, and from one region, to the next.

Given the above two points, European Union strategies will have to be flexible and modular in order to anticipate changes in all three regions of Asia, and they will have to be geared to the particular circumstances of the different countries and regions there.

Continued high growth in large parts of developing Asia. Despite the slowdown in Japan and in most of Europe (and in the US until 1993), the IMF reckons that Asian GNP will have grown on average by 44% between 1990 and 1995, (compared to 16% and 11% respectively for Latin America and Africa, and minus 32% for Eastern Europe and the former Soviet Union).

Growth of this order shows every sign of continuing and expanding; transforming as it does those countries and areas as yet untouched. There are signs that South Asia too could also enjoy higher growth in the next ten years, especially if the momentum of the restructuring process is maintained. However, South Asia will only succeed in substantially reducing poverty if economic growth there is matched by a significant reduction in birth rates.

Trade within Asia is growing rapidly, but growth trends within the three regions are very different (see graphs in Annex II). Here as elsewhere, East Asia has led the way: the increase in trade between East and Southeast Asia is striking. The proportion of trade between these two regions in 1991 (as compared to their trade with the rest of the world) was about the same as in NAFTA (42%) and this share was arrived at in a much shorter space of time. The jump in intra-trade is a "natural" development, i.e. it was achieved without formal trade arrangements and it is for the moment unlikely to lead to such arrangements. The growth of intra-Asian trade has led to a decline in dependence upon developed country markets in

North America and Europe to a degree never before seen. South Asia for the moment remains outside the growth in intra-regional Asian trade.

External trade plays a key role in both high speed and developing Asia's economic growth, although in varying degrees. The World Bank reckons that half the growth in world trade up to the year 2000 will be generated in East and Southeast Asia alone. This holds out enormous opportunities for the Union and can help create many new jobs.

Total East Asian trade doubled over the last decade. In 1992 it stood at one trillion ECU (of which Japan accounted for half). Trade in Southeast Asia has also grown, but not as rapidly: in 1991 it was 350 billion ECU. South Asia's total external trade ($50 billion) has only grown 25% over the same decade (the Union's two-way trade with all the countries of South Asia is only marginally larger than with Singapore).

Some countries in the region have a well-established record as free trading nations; others have only recently started to liberalise their trading regimes, while there are also countries that do not yet participate in international trade. Trade policy with an emphasis on defacto market access for both trade in goods and services will therefore be a key component in the Union's strategies towards not only developed Asia but also Asia's newly emerging markets.

In the area of trade the Union is, after the US, the most important market for the developing Asian countries, absorbing in 1993 as much as 128 billion ECU of exports or 27% of their total exports (see Annex III, Table 2). Without doubt, the Union has benefited as Union exports to these countries increased from 15 billion ECUs in 1980 to 93 billion ECUs in 1993, Concomitantly, the share of developing Asia in Union exports jumped from 7% to nearly 20%, thereby over-taking the 18% share of the US in total Union exports.

The inclusion of the EFTA countries in the Union will not greatly alter EU trade results with Asia countries since EFTA's trade with them is only about 10 to 15% of that of the Union (although individual EFTA countries hold important shares of specific Asian markets).

Foreign direct investment (FDI) play quantitatively and qualitatively an important role, in particular in East and Southeast Asia. The EU's relative share has declined steeply (between 1986 and 1992 only 10% of the region's FDI came from the Union), therefore the, Union's new strategy will emphasise investment promotion and the creation of favourable conditions for European investment in Asia.

Total FDI flows to these regions increased steadily during the eighties, with Japan being the long established leader of the three, followed by the US. Although Japan has the highest stock of cumulative FDI in Asia, since 1991, annual investments from Taiwan, Korea and Hong Kong have been at a higher level.

The impressive economic growth, especially in developing East Asia, should not prevent a critical assessment of its sustainability: high growth calls for adjustment (just as does low growth and stagnation, albeit adjustment of a different type). In the context of much of Asia this concerns in particular political liberalisation, as better paid, better fed people demand more individual freedom. The ability to address this issue in a satisfactory way will no doubt be of critical importance in sustaining economic growth in many Asian countries.

Sustaining high growth will also be determined by the ability to improve infrastructures, the lack of which can easily become a bottleneck to future growth.

Some countries need to invest heavily in mass education and the reform of their educational systems. This was one of the most important strategies for high growth and equitable income distribution in East Asia. All large countries in the region (China, India, the Philippines, Thailand, Indonesia and Vietnam) face severe regional imbalances as economic development has been in these countries first and foremost either concentrated in urban centres, or closely associated with one particular part of the country.

The environmental sustainability of unchecked rapid growth in the region is a source of growing concern with increasingly global dimensions. This applies not only to tropical forests, but also to the relatively low levels of energy efficiency in many countries of the region. Coupled with the relatively abundant supply of carbon rich fossil fuels (India, China) this is a problem that poses a particularly urgent challenge.

Market transition. Many countries of Asia are in the process of reforming their economies to make the transition from centrally planned to market based systems. Many are still hampered by large and inefficient state enterprises. The new strategies of the Union will be aimed to assist the ongoing reform process. It is after all in the enlightened self-interest of the Union to encourage the growth of new markets that are open and compete within the internationally agreed framework of the GATT.

Poverty also has its imperatives. Asia's future is not a homogenous picture of dynamic growth. A characteristic of high-speed growth in East and Southeast Asia was that it brought with it a dramatic increase in human welfare and huge reductions in poverty. The same is not so easily obtained in South Asia which in the year 2000 will still contain the single largest concentration of the world's poorest people. This represents more than just a brake on the South Asian countries' economic development and their potential as future markets for European business. People below the poverty line have higher fertility rates, greater vulnerability to disease and little option but to pursue short-term, environmentally degrading practices. These are challenges of global significance: poverty alleviation will therefore remain an important strand of the Union's Asia strategy.

1.2 Asia policies of Japan and the US

A re-evaluation of the EU's policies towards Asia cannot take place in a vacuum. All of the major international actors have an interest in the region, more so even than the EU whose interest is in the first instance primarily economic. The Union must therefore be aware of the ideas and actions of others if it is to safeguard its interests and maximise the potential of its own policies.

Japan's presence in East Asia and the role that it has played in the region's development is massive and on going. Aid, trade and investment links are very strong and have proved to be mutually beneficial. Recently there have been signs that Japan's relations with South Korea in particular are improving. In the case of China, after a slow start, economic links are becoming ever stronger. Southeast Asia is a major supplier of raw materials to Japan, and since 1985, Japan has relocated manufacturing capacity there on a scale unmatched by either Europe or the US. Japan is also intent on increasing its presence in South Asia; India is now a major recipient of Japanese ODA. In addition, Japanese direct investment in India has increased in recent years, albeit from a very low base. Japan is gradually assuming a higher profile throughout Asia, although it is careful to disassociate itself from the more assertive tone of some US or European pronouncements on human rights.

The United States has started to place increasing emphasis on its Asian Policy. The most obvious sign of this has been its active promotion of, and participation in, APEC (Asia Pacific Economic Co-operation). At this stage it is far from clear that this initiative has been successful. The recent trade dispute with Japan, a series of small disputes with Southeast

Asian countries and the question of China's MFN status all suggest that whilst the US wishes to increase its economic presence in the region, it has not yet found the optimum balance between the different policy strands. However, it is likely that away from "high politics", links between the respective business communities will be strengthened. 'The US is India's largest trading, partner with total bilateral trade of about half EU-India trade. India has been selected as one of the US Commerce department's "big ten emerging markets" (and a Section 301 target).

1.3 The need for new EU Strategies

Large parts of Asia are booming and market access is improving, but business there must be earned. The presumed dependence in all three main regions of Asia on Europe whether for their capital and know-how, or as a counter-balance to Japan and the USA, is less valid today than even five years ago. The reason for this is that Asia now has its own resources of capital, management and technological capacity.

It follows therefore that the European Union needs new pro-active strategies towards Asia. Above all it needs to strengthen its economic presence in Asia in order to maintain its leading role in the world economy. In doing so it is able to build upon the steps taken by individual EU members states to develop new strategies towards Asia.

*The costs of failing to develop pro-active strategies towards Asia.*

The Union stands to lose out on the economic miracle taking place there because of the strong competition: from Japan and the United States, and also increasingly from companies within the region's newly industrialised and capital rich countries such as Korea or Taiwan. To take the example of Japan, already Japanese companies are competing with each other to consolidate their position in Asian markets; they have invested heavily and are establishing the type of sales and distribution systems which European companies have found so hard to penetrate in Japan itself. If European companies are unable to take a full share of the world's main centre of growth in the next decade this will affect their profits and competitiveness, not only in Asian markets, but also world-wide.

If the Union loses out on the economic miracle taking place in Asia, this will have political costs, and at the very least it will exacerbate the calls for more defensive policies from those who view Asia as a threat rather than as a valuable partner, which in turn will further reduce the benefits to be gained from Asia, and so on, in a spiral of decline.

*Basis of New Strategies.*

Not the least significant aspect of the ongoing Asian transformation is that it represents the first achievement of sustained economic growth by a major area of the world outside of Europe or regions of European settlement. This means that the Union will not be able to take for granted automatic acceptance of European values and ways of doing things. Universal human rights are recognised in Asia as in Europe, but the manner in which these are advocated and defended is crucial. For its part, the Union favours a frank and open dialogue on these issues that should be developed as a necessary strand in the policy mix.

Economic growth in Asia has been market driven, taking place for the most part without formal regional structures. Therefore the Union's new strategies will be based upon an appreciation of the cultural, economic, social and political characteristics of each of the EU's individual partners in Asia.

The EU's strategies will also cover relations with regional groupings in Asia such as the ASEAN (Association of Southeast Asian Nations); SAARC (South Asia Association for Regional Co-operation); sub-regional arrangements such as the numerous cross-border "growth triangles" now emerging; and supra regional groups such as APEC (Asia Pacific Economic Co-operation), which link East Asia across the Pacific to the Americas and Australasia.

*2. Characteristics of the New EU Economic Strategy Towards Asia*

2.1 Economic policy implications

This section elaborates the specific policies and instruments required to achieve the policy objectives and the main policy implications within each of the domains. The individual design of policies will of course be country specific and must be elaborated in the light of their individual circumstances. The Union has a great deal of policy experience in Asia and must build upon its previous successes.

More and more countries within Asia are growing into economic and political powers and are becoming increasingly integrated into the world system. The EU's existing relations with them must be adapted to reflect the fact that we are all now partners in a global economy. It is therefore essential that the EU reinforces, or where it does not yet exist, establishes a non-confrontational dialogue of equals, to address questions of bilateral concern and also to consider jointly the growing number of global concerns. Most notably the maintenance of an open rule-based world trade system; preservation of public goods such as the environment and particular issues such as trade in narcotics or the prevention and cure of AIDS.

Closer consultation and dialogue can generate a greater understanding of each other's viewpoints and problems and facilitate the search for consensus solutions. This can in turn help to avert disputes and provide an environment, which is of benefit to business both in Europe and in Asia. The importance of such dialogue goes beyond the purely bilateral. If the Union can assist in the development of a consensus approach, this will feed into inter-regional initiatives (e.g. APEC) and smooth the path for work undertaken at the multilateral level, for example concerning the post Uruguay Round agenda.

The EU has a long-standing relation with ASEAN that remains a cornerstone of its dialogue with the region. The Union has welcomed the ASEAN Free Trade Agreement and indeed welcomes all such initiatives for regional co-operation provided they are consistent with the GATT-based multilateral trade system.

*2.1.1 – Raising the profile of Europe in Asia.*

The impact of certain actions can be greatly enhanced if individual Union actors join their forces. This applies as much to the business sector where the Union's image can act as an important selling point as to international forums. It also applies to cooperation programmes and activities, especially economic co-operation, which take place within a highly competitive environment.

A greater knowledge of the Union and its activities would increase the regard in which it is held in Asia. The EU should therefore provide much more information about Europe and make a much greater effort to explain the nature and objectives of EU policies in Asia. Greater efforts should also be made to provide information on European financed activities in Asia, especially economic cooperation (and also development projects). A wide range of different policies could fall within this domain.

*2.1.2 – Public information policy.*

In order to draw up a more efficient public information policy, a baseline all-media study of the European image in Asia is an essential prerequisite.

*2.1.3 – An enhanced visitors programme.*

Invitation of distinguished Asian politicians, journalists, academics and other leaders to Europe should be considered.

*2.1.4 – Strengthening Higher Education and training links with Asia.*

Including University Co-operation schemes targeted into specific technological, policy and management studies and emphasising the implementation of joint or mutually recognised post-graduate programmes, joint-research projects and university-industry cooperation activities. These will include, inter-alia, support to European and Asian Studies Centres and joint Management and Technical training programmes, implemented whenever possible with the active participation of European and Asian companies.

*2.1.5 – Encouraging decentralised.*

Co-operation between the institutions which are the basis of a pluralistic civil society. Such co-operation has in the context of the Union been a powerful force in the shaping of the European identity. With regard to the EU's relations with Asian countries, activities such as town twinning or cultural exchanges will be invaluable in an environment where there is a serious lack of knowledge and of mutual comprehension.

*2.1.6 – Improving European expertise in Asia.*

By supporting a network of European centres specialising in Asia (to share perspectives and expertise on Asia and to provide counsel and advice to European policy makers), and funding in countries such as Korea or China initiatives based on the EU's young executives programme in Japan.

2.2 Strengthening the European Economic Presence in Asia.

Economic co-operation is based upon the concept of mutual benefit, and as such is qualitatively different from development cooperation. This characteristic makes economic co-operation an important instrument in the EU's relations with many of the Asian countries, where the level of development is rapidly rising. It should be extended towards countries such as Korea for which at the moment it is not used.

There is also obviously scope to strengthen links in the fields of scientific co-operation and research and development, narcotics control, AIDS prevention and environmental co-operation. The Union is of course already active in these areas, but their potential needs to be exploited to the full.

Co-ordination with Member States and the private sector. The Union's co-operation in Asia will be complementary to that of the Member States. In order to achieve this and in order to increase the effectiveness of Union and Member State co-operation activities, greater co-ordination will have to take place between them in terms of policy co-ordination, operational co-ordination, including in the field; and co-ordination in multilateral forums. With regard to economic co-operation, the direct participation of the private sector is also a *sine* qua non.

The following activities (all of which contribute to economic co-operation in the broadest sense) are intended to ensure that European private sector is faced with a trading and investment environment which is conducive to economic growth and international trade. These activities will therefore promote European trade and investment in Asia.

*2.2.1 – Representations (lobbying).*

It is necessary to undertake all the appropriate steps to obtain from Asian partners' modifications of their legislation and administrative regulations that hamper the development of European trade and direct investments. Basic concerns include Standards and Quality Control, Intellectual Property Rights and the negotiation of Mutual Recognition Agreements on standards, testing and certification.

*2.2.2 – Providing expertise and policy advice.*

This applies to the ex-state trading countries of Asia which have embarked on structural economic reform, such as China, Mongolia, Vietnam or Laos, to assist them to set up the institutions, policies and laws to make a smooth transition to market-based economies (an example would be the EU market transition programme in Vietnam, the first major programme of this kind in Asia). Those countries who have not so embarked (Burma, North Korea), should be encouraged to do so as soon as political conditions permit.

Countries such as India and Pakistan who have already set about deregulating their economies should be assisted in these policies.

*2.2.3 – Promoting business co-operation between European companies and their Asian counterparts.*

This should be done by increasing information and by creating a favourable framework for industrial co-operation and notably for SMEs, through existing instrument.

Regarding the first point, information on trade and investments in both Europe and Asia, and improved information with regard to Asian markets and contracts, are required.

The opening of European Business Councils; Joint Investment Committees and especially European Business Information Centres (EBICs), are steps in the right direction, but more need to be opened (there are none as yet in China, ex-Indochina or Pakistan). The European Business Community in Tokyo and Seoul need to be supported. The role of the EBICs is to provide information on European and local market conditions, including trade and investment opportunities. They are established in close co-ordination with bilateral Chambers of Commerce and EU Member States' private sector representatives. To be successful, the EBICs also require backward linkages to European business associations and Chambers of Commerce and EU Industrial federations.

Second, a favourable framework for industrial co-operation which aims at creating a positive climate for EU investment and cooperation, should be initiated by launching concrete activities such as sectoral round tables, sufficiently horizontal industry-oriented training initiatives and pilot actions in the field of technological co-operation.

*2.2.4 – Establishing better links with European business associations and Chambers of Commerce.*

This could either be done by the formation of a business association at the European level as foreseen in the White Paper on Employment (e.g. "the Europe Asia Business

Association"), or by setting up a network with existing national associations. The objectives of such an association or network would be to promote economic co-operation between the European Union and the countries of Asia and to share perspectives and expertise on Asia and to provide counsel and advice to European policy makers.

*2.2.5 – Enhancing co-operation in the fields of science and technology and research and development.*

There is no doubt that such co-operation can have a positive effect upon the Union's economic presence within the region. To date the majority of the Union's efforts in this domain has either been co-operation with Japan, for example the new Forum on Science and Technology, or come under the Science and Technology for Development programmes. The recently approved Fourth Framework Programme (1994–98), Action 2, covers co-operation with third countries, especially developing countries and thus provides a means of enhancing scientific and technological co-operation with Asia. It would be important to reinforce these activities in so far as scientific co-operation in advanced fields such as information and communication technologies, industrial, and materials technologies and biotechnologies are concerned. A separate approach that merits a broader coverage is the establishment of European technology centres:

The funding available for international RTD co-operation under the 2nd Activity of the 4th Framework programme is relatively limited. Co-operative projects with Asia must, moreover, concentrate on areas where the co-operation will be beneficial to Community interests.

This being so, there may be scope for looking to other sources of funding, including under other policies of the Union, and other types of RTD co-operation. For example, it is particularly important to foster contact between young researchers of Asia and the Union as future leaders in the economic fields in their respective regions and therefore potential multipliers in terms of improving understanding and enhancing mutual interests.

*2.2.6 – Establishing European technology centres*

Especially in key sectors where Europe has a comparative advantage, e.g. the EC-Singapore Regional Institute for Environmental Technology which acts as a window for European research and development and services (in a sector which has equal salience both in dynamic and in developing Asia). Such windows for Europe-an R & D should be co-financed by the Union and the host country and may be based on institutional twinning. They should maintain close contact with other business facilitation activities such as the EBICs.

*2.2.7 – Supporting investment.*

The Union is lagging seriously behind other investors in the Asian boom (providing only 10% of inward FDI to East and Southeast Asia between 1986 and 1992). Many of the activities and instruments falling under economic co-operation (listed under points

IV.3.1 to 2.2.6 above) are therefore designed to support and promote European direct investment in Asia (one of the main tasks of the European Business Information Centres for example is to provide information on market and investment conditions in the Asian countries and regions in which they are established). In addition, the Union needs to promote direct investments by

Providing financial incentives for joint ventures and other forms of business tie-up (e.g. by using the European Community International Investment Partners scheme, ECIP, or the European Investment Bank or by sponsoring market research).

Supporting trade promotion. There is no need to duplicate Member State export efforts, but better co-ordination is needed to maintain an active presence on Asian markets as called for by the White Paper on Employment.

*2.2.8 – Co-operating to alleviate poverty*

Development Aid has traditionally been an important tool of the EU's policy, politically as well as economically and, at least for some countries, it will continue to be so.

East Asia has had an extraordinary success in reducing poverty by adopting outward oriented trade strategies, by importing foreign technologies and welcoming foreign investments. The Union supports this approach in its emphasis on economic co-operation.

Success can be claimed in alleviating poverty by South Asian governments and donors, including those of the European Union. But the problems are complex and, given the magnitude of the challenge and the limited resources available, aid needs to be constantly fine-tuned to ensure effective poverty alleviation. This will include emphasising support for policies which enable the poor to participate in growth by addressing barriers denying them access to opportunities, assets, credit or basic inputs, or by investing in the poor, for example by supporting primary education, health care (especially reproductive health care), preservation of the environment, supply of services to reduce urban slums and potable water supplies in poor regions.

Since the aid administered by the Commission only accounts for about 10% of the Union's total aid to Asia, in order to achieve maximum impact the Commission and the Member States need to enhance their co-ordination. In addition, in evaluating the impact of its aid, the Union needs to ensure that the balance between poverty alleviation and economic co-operation fits the changing conditions in Asia. Account will also have to be taken of the overall political conditions under which the aid is delivered to the recipient country in order to ensure maximum efficacy.

*2.2.9 – Enhanced co-operation in the field of the Environment*

Given the growing importance of international and economic relations in the field of the environment, it is important for there to be effective co-operation with the countries of the Asian region.

Within the resources available, the development of Community relations on the environment with countries in Asia need to be reinforced, Strong relations already exist with Japan and those with China and Korea are expected to move to a more formal footing in the medium term. The global nature of many environmental problems and the seventy of the problems in certain Asian countries, as well as the promises made by the Community at Rio necessitate an environmental dialogue with third countries.

*2.2.10 – Development of market for agricultural production*

Despite increasing agricultural production, there will be an increasing demand for imports of agricultural products, partly due to a change in diet. In the medium term these countries therefore will demand more cereals and livestock products from the world market. Therefore, there is a risk that import protection, for which Japan and Korea are striking examples, could spread even more in the region, although the commitments taken in the Uruguay Round will help to contain this kind of development. The European Union has an interest to be present on these markets with its agricultural products too, particularly processed ones.

**V. Conclusions**

The range of policies and instruments as set out in Parts II to IV above will be applied in a modular form which means that a coherent range of activities can be applied to different countries and regions in order to meet the interests of the European Union and its Member States, as well as the interests of the partner and recipient countries.

Individual components can be adjusted as countries evolve their economic structure (see Annex I, Table 2). In other words, the Union and its Member States should not seek to apply as many of the instruments as possible to as many countries in Asia as possible. This could only result in spreading of limited resources too thinly with a negative impact on both effectiveness and profile. It will be necessary therefore to prioritise both in terms of countries and in terms of sectors, and to apply different instruments to countries that are at different levels of development. The new strategy requires a comprehensive approach covering political, economic and cooperation aspects:

- The Union needs to accord Asia a higher priority and to deepen and extend its dialogue with Asian countries and regional groupings. This dialogue should be pursued both bilaterally and in the framework of multilateral organisations.
- The Union should, in particular, develop its political dialogue with those Asian countries which are prepared and able to make a significant contribution to the maintenance of peace and stability both within the region and globally. Arms control and non proliferation are of particular importance. The human rights issue form an integral part of the political dialogue.
- The Union should strengthen its relationship with regional and subregional security fora. The ASEAN Regional Forum is of particular note in that it allows for a wide-ranging dialogue on security concerns encompassing the greater part of Pacific Asia.
- The Union needs to place greater emphasis on market opening, for trade in goods and in services.
- The Union needs to select priority sectors for economic co-operation which reflect its own comparative advantage, e.g. banking, energy, environmental technologies, transport equipment, telecommunications, etc.
- The Union needs to help integrate into the open, market-based world trading system those Asian countries such as China, India, Vietnam or Pakistan which are moving from state controls to market-oriented economies.
- Greater emphasis should be placed on pro-active economic cooperation. Top priority for this type of co-operation should go to the newly emerging Asian markets, largely, but not exclusively in East and Southeast Asia, namely South Korea, China, Macao, Taiwan, Hong Kong, Indonesia, Malaysia, Pakistan, Philippines, Singapore, Thailand and India.
- The best experience of the Union and its Member States needs to be pooled in poverty alleviation strategies to focus on the population of those countries with major poverty problems, namely China, Mongolia, Cambodia, Laos, Vietnam, India, Bangladesh, Bhutan and Nepal (and Afghanistan and Burma when political conditions permit).

Within this broad framework, the first EU policy paper on China (see Document 3.2) aimed to set 'A Long Term Policy for China–Europe Relations'. Following the endorsement of a 'new Asian strategy' by the European Council summit in Essen, Germany, it sought to elaborate a strategy that recognised the international and regional economic and political impact of China's re-emergence. The pillars of the EU strategy were to be constructive engagement, commitment to human rights, ensuring the future of Hong Kong and Macao, supporting China's economic reform, supporting China's bid for membership of the World Trade Organization (WTO), targeted cooperation and increasing the profile of the EU in China. The 1995 Communication postulated the development of EU–China cooperation as a long-term EU policy goal.

**Document 3.2: Commission Communication, 'A Long Term Policy for China–Europe Relations' (1995)**

COMMUNICATION OF THE COMMISSION
A Long Term Policy for China–Europe Relations
COM(1993) 279 final

**A. INTRODUCTION**
**THE NEED FOR A LONG TERM POLICY FOR CHINA**

This Communication seeks to chart a long-run course for EU-China relations into the 21st century.

The rise of China is unmatched amongst national experiences since the Second World War. Japan has made its mark as an economic power, the Soviet Union survived essentially as a military power. China is increasingly strong in both the military-political and the economic spheres. China is in the midst of sustained and dramatic economic and social change at home. Abroad, China is becoming part of the world security and economic system at a time of greater economic interdependence and when global problems, from protection of the environment to nuclear non-proliferation, require coordinated commitment from governments worldwide. China is seeking integration into international structures: China has been a member of the IMF and the World Bank since the early 1980s; it participates in regional fora such as APEC, and is actively negotiating membership of the World Trade Organisation. China made an important contribution to the results of the World Conference on Human Rights held in Vienna in June 1993. China will also host a major UN conference on women in Beijing later this year.

It is 20 years since diplomatic relations were established between the EC and China, and 10 years since the signing of the existing Trade and Cooperation Agreement. The steady development of bilateral relations was interrupted by the 1989 Tiananmen Square events. Europe, like other major international partners of China, reacted with a range of sanctions. But the normalisation of relations, particularly in the past three years, has paved the way for a renewed surge in bilateral trade and investment. 1994 also saw major strides in bilateral cooperation and the establishment of a new arrangement for political dialogue.

The time has come to redefine the EU's relationship with China, in the spirit of the "new Asian strategy" endorsed by the Essen European Council. Europe must develop a long-term relationship with China that reflects China's worldwide, as well as regional, economic and political influence. Europe's relations with China are bound to be a cornerstone in Europe's external relations, both with Asia and globally. Europe needs an action-oriented, not a merely declaratory policy, to strengthen that relationship.

*A.1 THE RISE OF CHINA AND ITS GLOBAL AND REGIONAL IMPLICATIONS*

The rise of China represents enormous opportunities and challenges to the international system. The question is how China can share in the responsibilities and opportunities suited to its rapidly increasing power. China's political importance makes its stability of great concern both to its neighbours and to the world community at large. We believe that this stability is best served by political, economic and social reform in line with international norms.

The mere size of China, in terms of land and population, makes it impossible to address the central global issues of the 1990s without particular reference to the impact of China on their evolution and management. China is not only a nuclear power and a permanent member of the UN Security Council, but also one of the world's biggest arms producers and exporters. Her role across the whole security spectrum is central to global, as well as regional security.

Most observers, including the IMF and the World Bank, now believe that on the basis of purchasing power parities, the Chinese economy is similar in size to Japan and second only to the USA. Extrapolations of recent growth rates have led to forecasts of China becoming the biggest world economy in a generation's time. Although these estimates are subject to enormous margins of error, it is beyond dispute that after 15 years of economic reform, China's economy has already become one of the largest in the world.

China's size makes its impact on the physical environment unique. Despite its one-child policy, China's population increases by around 15 million people every year. But in addition, China's energy consumption is already second only to that of the USA. The consequences for the environment of such a huge country reaching western levels of consumption, and pollution, in the future are impossible to ignore. Hence the importance of China playing a full part in the wider policy exchange on such key issues as the environment, population, or health.

Although in the long term, the continued growth of China's economy could provide employment to its entire population, there is undoubtedly a short to medium term problem due to the substantial number of Chinese seeking to emigrate. With the possibilities for legal immigration to Western countries limited, trafficking of illegal immigrants has become increasingly prevalent. This not only affects North America; traffickers have also set up routed through Central America and the former Soviet Union towards Europe. It will be necessary to address the very real resultant problems in close cooperation with China.

China's size is also reflected in the multiplicity of players (central government agencies, both in Beijing and elsewhere, provincial and municipal authorities, emerging economic actors) who can influence Chinese policy and practice. In many respects, for example, Chinese provinces represent differing markets for EU exporters. Moreover, the rapid devolution of economic power is shifting responsibility for economic and trade policy-making and implementation to provincial level. This makes it all the more important to have firm commitments on the enforcement of China's international commitments at sub-national level, for example, during the WTO negotiations. It also makes it crucial to expand our bilateral trade and cooperation discussions to include provincial and local authorities which, de jure or de facto, are in charge of economic and trade policy in many fields.

### *A.2 CHINA'S IMPORTANCE FOR EUROPE*

To update EU policy towards China and better coordinate EU relations with this country, the European interests at stake must be clearly understood.

**Shared global and regional security interests** which will benefit from co-operative and responsible Chinese policy on all fronts, including adherence to the treaties governing nuclear and other weapons proliferation, an international drive to contain arms sales and encouragement of Chinese domestic political, economic and social reform in the interests of its people (20% of all people alive on the globe today). It is in everybody's interest including that of China itself – to see China demonstrating a cooperative and responsible attitude in the international community, whether as a signatory to UN Human Rights instruments and the Non-Proliferation Treaty, or by becoming a WTO Member and an active promoter of the post-Rio Summit environmental agenda at the heart of government policy.

**Shared interests on other global issues**: China should be engaged in dialogue and cooperation towards sustainable development and for the protection of the environment and global resources, scientific and technological development, the information society, demographic growth, poverty alleviation, the preservation of forests, addressing the problem of illegal immigration, and the control and eradication of disease, AIDS, drugs and crime.

**Global economic stability**: China's size and influence on world trade gives its economic policy global significance. It is in the world's interest, as well as China's, that the Chinese economy continues to grow and to open up, and that China takes its place as a major player in the world system of economic rules and policies. It is also essential to help China to participate fully in the rules-based system of the World Trade Organisation.

**Competitiveness**: in order for European industry to be globally competitive we must be present on the world's most dynamic markets. China is now the Union's fourth largest market and fourth largest supplier. China's market could become the largest in the world in many high tech sectors, from telecommunications to aircraft and from computers to energy. An active role for EU business in China, where US and Japanese competition is already fierce, is essential.

Given the breadth of these interests and the key role played by China, Europe must set itself the overriding general objective of promoting the fullest possible Chinese involvement in the international arena, whether on security, political, environmental, social or economic issues. We must also increase mutual understanding between Europeans and Chinese and raise the EU profile in China.

In addition, the influence of China's domestic evolution on its international policies cannot be ignored. EU interests will therefore be well served by supporting the development in China of institutions and a civil society based on the rule of law.

## B. POLITICAL RELATIONS: ENGAGING CHINA IN THE INTERNATIONAL COMMUNITY

### *B.1 CONSTRUCTIVE ENGAGEMENT*

China's own policy of a gradual opening up over recent years has been illustrated by its desire to join or rejoin international organisations and to intensify links with other key partners such as the United States and Japan. China now wishes to play the full part on the world stage that is appropriate for a country of its importance.

The EU is eager to see China sharing in the opportunities and responsibilities at the heart of the international community as China opens up to a freer flow of ideas and cooperation, both in the key Asian region and globally. We support the wholehearted participation of China in the international community. As the Commission stated in last year's review of European policy towards the region, we have an interest in a stable and peaceful Asia. China's decisions on how to employ its economic and military weight will have an essential impact on this.

Without exaggerating the role that the EU can play, we must use the opportunity offered by participation in regional fora and by bilateral dialogue to promote a responsible and constructive Chinese role in the region, including issues such as nuclear weapons on the Korean peninsular and territorial differences such as the Spratleys. As we recalled in March 1995, the EU believes in the peaceful and negotiated handling of such problems, whether in the South China Sea or elsewhere.

It is in the interests of Europe, and of the international community as a whole, to engage China in a political dialogue on disarmament and arms control issues. Nuclear Non-Proliferation, the missile technology control regime, the non-proliferation of chemical and biological weapons, conventional weapon sales, and control of trade in dual-use goods, should all be embraced in such a dialogue.

An ambitious new framework for bilateral political dialogue was set up in June 1994 to encourage this mutual goal of full Chinese participation in global affairs. Regular meetings between the EU Troika and China at ministerial level, as well as high level political consultations between the Commission and China, will continue. But these will now be supplemented by ad hoc Foreign Ministers' meetings, and twice yearly meetings, both between the Chinese Foreign Minister and the EU ambassadors in Beijing, and between the EU Presidency's Foreign Minister and the Chinese Ambassador in the EU Presidency capital. There will also be regular meetings of senior officials responsible for a range of policy areas. This dialogue should develop to include all issues of common interest and global significance. By the same token, with the ban of contacts between military personnel now lifted, the political and economic influence of the People's Liberation Army makes it appropriate to include the People's Liberation Army among potential dialogue partners.

These new arrangements have already made possible a sustained exchange of views, not only on respective internal developments, but on global and regional security interests, as well as human rights. All such matters can be examined in depth whilst continuing to respect the sovereignty of both parties. China and the EU can now discuss mutual interests and find common ground on the full range of political and security issues.

Collaboration should also be stepped up in dealing with the migratory consequences of a more open Chinese economy: in this respect, the EU and China should work together in fighting illegal immigration, taking into account existing principles and practices of readmission.

The EU welcomes opportunities to develop such a dialogue in a regional context. Links with the ASEAN Regional Forum are already well-established, and the Euro-Asia meeting in spring next year will provide an excellent opportunity for the EU and China to discuss mutual interests in the region.

*B.2 HUMAN RIGHTS*

A commitment to human rights and fundamental freedoms is at the heart of EU policy worldwide. Violations are not only a cause for concern in their own right, but because the

EU believes that espousal of international standards of human rights and acceptance of political liberalisation is vital for long-term social and political stability. The key criterion for pursuing human rights initiatives must be effectiveness, the impact that an initiative would have on the ground. For this reason, there is a danger that relying solely on frequent and strident declarations will dilute the message or lead to knee-jerk reactions from the Chinese government. To make progress, all the EU institutions should pursue human rights issues through a combination of carefully timed public statements, formal private discussions and practical cooperation.

The EU will pursue the issue of human rights through action on three levels. First, it will support potential efforts in China to open up and liberalise all areas of Chinese life, in different sections of society as well as different parts of the economy. These trends inevitably reinforce moves towards the development of a civil society based on the rule of law. Second, it will systematically and regularly continue to raise human rights issues in bilateral dialogue with China. Third, it will engage the international community in the dialogue through multilateral fora such as the United Nations. The framework for all these activities is clearly delineated by the common acceptance by both the EU and China of the Declaration and the Programme of Action of the World Conference on Human Rights of Vienna in June 1993[1].

There are already signs that the increasing exposure of all areas of Chinese life to the outside world is having a deep – if gradual – impact through social change and increased mutual understanding. EU policy is based on the well-founded belief that human rights tend to be better understood and better protected in societies open to the free flow of trade, investment, people, and ideas. As China continues its policy of opening up to the world, the EU will work to strengthen and encourage this trend. This is a major reason why the EU will continue to support the active participation of China in the international community in all fields of policy, political and economic, and to welcome China's increasing openness to dialogue. It is also an important reason for using the EC cooperation programme to encourage China's own efforts towards opening up, socially and economically.

The World Conference on Women in Beijing in September 1995 has focused attention on China as host, and Chinese policy in this area will inevitably come under particular scrutiny. The EU hopes for a successful outcome to the Conference, and looks forward to supporting China's efforts to build on the Conference in the years to come. In this context, the follow-up to the World Conference on Social Development, in Copenhagen in March 1995, should be mentioned. Such efforts to internationalise China are wholly consistent with a strong position on human rights – indeed they must be part of it and at the heart of a long-term strategy of engagement.

The EU institutions have consistently demonstrated their commitment to giving a clear message to China on human rights. In February 1995, the EU proposed a resolution before the UN Commission on Human Rights, summarising and deploring the violations which are still an everyday part of life in China. The resolution acknowledged the steps taken by China to reduce poverty and to reform the legal system. But reports of human rights violations by authorities at every level continue, with severe restrictions on the right of citizens to freedom of association, expression, and religion, as well as to due legal process and fair trial. China does not yet enjoy a fully impartial administration of justice and respect for the rule of law. Arrests of pro-democratic Chinese dissidents continue. With more than 50 minority groups in China, notably in the Autonomous Region of Tibet but also elsewhere, respect for the distinct cultural, ethnic, linguistic and religious identity of minorities also remains wholly inadequate.

The importance attached to human rights has been a consistent feature of the EU's policy towards China. Immediately after the Tiananmen Square events in June 1989, the EU imposed a number of sanctions which have been only gradually relaxed (a ban of arms sales is still in place). The Parliament has passed a number of resolutions on China and senior European Ministers and Commissioners consistently raise human rights when they meet their Chinese opposite numbers. In order to achieve maximum effectiveness, public statements have been reinforced by detailed discussions in private.

The EU must pursue a detailed dialogue on all aspects of human rights at every opportunity. The new and more systematic arrangements for political dialogue provide regular fora for exchanging views and deepening understanding on human rights issues. At the same time, effective concertation in the human rights debate at the international level is a prerequisite for a successful policy. The EU puts particular stress on the involvement of the international community through the UN Commission on Human Rights. The level of international support attracted for the resolution criticising the situation in China in February 1995 suggests that this approach is bearing fruit.

On top of all this, a new dialogue specifically devoted on human rights has recently been launched at China's suggestion. This dialogue centres on a biannual meeting between the EU troika and the Chinese government, which will not only improve the flow of information, but will also provide an opportunity for detailed discussion leading to concrete action.

Practical action is essential if this government-to-government dialogue is to be fully effective. The EU can promote practical cooperation, such as training and technical assistance in the legal and judicial fields, to back the efforts being made in China to establish a civil society based on the rule of law. Up till now, concrete action by the EU to encourage cooperation with individuals in the legal and judicial systems has been small-scale. The EU should henceforth coordinate with the Member States and the many active European NGOs to support the development of the rule of law in China.

### *B.3 HONG KONG MACAU*

The historical ties between Europe and Hong Kong and Macau inevitably mean that the European Union has taken a particular interest in the arrangements for the transfer of sovereignty to China.

The Council of Ministers has made clear the importance of implementing the principles contained formally in the two Joint Declarations signed by China and the United Kingdom and Portugal respectively. The high degree of autonomy guaranteed to the two Special Administrative Regions under the Declarations is of great importance to the well-being of the two Regions, and is recognised in Beijing to be in the interests of China. The Joint Declarations acknowledge that Hong Kong and Macau each have distinctive characteristics which need to be respected. Both territories already run their own affairs in economic and trade policy. The principle of continuity will govern the EU's relations with Hong Kong and Macau in the years leading up to the transfer of sovereignty and beyond.

Continued close relations with the EU are essential to both Hong Kong and Macau, and to Europe. Hong Kong is the EU's eleventh largest trading partner. Five of the Member States enjoy bilateral trade with Hong Kong of over 2 billion ECU. It is also a key destination for investment from across the EU Member States, with 40 EU banks and 45 insurance companies licensed in Hong Kong. Some 40,000 EU citizens are resident in Hong Kong.

The Commission's Office in Hong Kong responsible for relations with Hong Kong and Macau opened in 1993, and China has agreed that it will continue to operate as an independent entity after transfer of sovereignty. Equally, there will be no change in the functioning of the 1992 Trade and Cooperation Agreement with Macau. Relations in the WTO will continue, as Hong Kong and Macau both participate autonomously. Cooperation is already developing bilaterally on customs, standards, culture, university and business links. But the EU will also seek to take advantage of the particular opportunities offered by closer relations in the years to come:

- both territories have important roles to play as gateways to other regions of China, and can act as key facilitators for increased European trade and investment with China;
- the traditions of free trade and internationalism established by Hong Kong and Macau. These traditions serve as important examples for China and in the region as a whole, and suggest a continuing role for the territories as partners for the EU as the new WTO dialogue develops in the years to come.

### *B.4 PROPOSALS*

The European Union and China are both major global players. They should sustain a comprehensive, long-term bilateral dialogue. The EU's particular goals should include the following:

- to promote a dialogue on regional and global security issues which encourages full Chinese engagement in the international community through accession to all the key international instruments governing non-proliferation and arms control;
- to give practical support for the trend towards creating a reformed public management system in China based on civil society and the rule of law;
- to develop a programme of effective and coordinated cooperation in the legal and judicial fields;
- to support the principles of the Joint Declarations governing the transfer of sovereignty of Hong Kong and Macau.

## C. ECONOMIC AND TRADE RELATIONS: THE RISE OF NEW ECONOMIC POWER

The economic reform process launched by Deng Xiaoping sixteen years ago has dramatically changed the economic and social landscape in China. Despite its incremental nature it has exceeded all initial expectations.

It is in Europe's interests that this trend is accepted as irreversible. Although different opinions are still voiced in Beijing on the pace of reform, as well as on specific measures, there is widespread consensus among China's senior leaders about the necessity to deepen and broaden reforms to achieve the objective, enshrined in China's Constitution, of creating a "Socialist Market Economy" by the turn of the century (see Annex 1). This process has accelerated since 1992 to reach new areas, from banking and taxation to real estate and infrastructure. New sectors -and regions -have been opened to private, including foreign, activity. However, China still falls well short of having a full market economy, with adequate social protection including freedom of association for employees. Reform of state-owned industry, and the creation of a social security system to cope with its consequences, remain as key challenges for the future. The establishment of an effective legal framework, properly enforced, is an essential element in the process.

*C.1 A BOOMING ECONOMY*

Reform has changed the structure of China's economy beyond recognition. Collective, private and foreign-funded companies produce and sell well over half of China's industrial goods. Whilst over 80% of industrial output was subject to mandatory planning only ten years ago, the figure is now only 15%. The same is true for price controls, which affect less than 10% of retail sales at present. Public industry's share of total output has fallen from 77% to 44% and its share of retail sales to an even lower level. Although these figures should be treated cautiously, because production factor markets remain more controlled than goods markets in China, they clearly show a steady trend towards liberalisation of the economy.

China's macroeconomic performance since the launching of reforms can only be described as remarkable. GNP growth rates reached around 9% during the 1980s, and 12–13% in the last three years, with industrial output and investment growing at over 20% for several years. China's total trade rose from 20 $ billion to 237 $ billion between 1979 and 1994, growing twice as fast as output. Despite fluctuations, China's trade balance looks healthy and its foreign exchange reserves big enough to cope with a substantial foreign debt.

A shadow is cast on this generally rosy picture by an accelerating inflation rate. The reasons for this are structural, due to an undeveloped monetary policy and expansive fiscal policy. Other important structural imbalances exist which could undermine future development. Traditional disparities between the coastal and inland areas are widening rapidly, leading to massive migrations, infrastructure bottlenecks and environmental degradation. The inevitable transfer of production from public industry to the private sector and the slowing down of the agriculture sector could lead to massive unemployment.

The EU has much to offer to help China in its difficult process of transition. An exchange of experience and information could support China's efforts towards reform, whilst also increasing European knowledge about the modern Chinese economy. Training for economists has already been provided as part of the EC-China cooperation programme: an economic dialogue in areas such as monetary policy between officials could be the next step.

Another potential area for fruitful dialogue is social policy. An exchange would help to provide an important basis to discuss the evolution of social policy in the 1990s and beyond. Such a dialogue could include the development of internationally recognised labour standards, including International Labour Organisation standards in areas such as child and prison labour.

Another important element is the involvement of China with key international economic organisations. In the case of trade, this should mean WTO membership for China (see section C.3). But the importance of China to the world economy should also be acknowledged by other organisations. The decision by the May 1995 OECD Ministerial meeting to promote a new dialogue with China is to be welcomed; Europe should consider how to make a reality of these ties. The G-7 should also consider how the growing economic importance of China can be recognised in its deliberations.

The dramatic changes in the Chinese economy have inevitably had a great impact on EU-China trade with total two-way trade exceeding 30 billion ECU in 1993 and reaching an estimated 35 billion ECU for 1994.

EU-China trade has increased over fourteen-fold since the beginning of reform in China (see Annex 2). But EU exports have not kept pace with imports. The EU's trade surplus of the mid 1980s turned into a bilateral trade deficit, which has remained in the 8–10 billion

ECU range in the last four years. However, this is dwarfed by the US trade deficit with China and the proportion of EU imports covered by exports (55%) is much higher than that of the US (26% in 1993). Moreover, the EU share in the Chinese total imports grew from 11% to 15% in the first half of this decade, a better export performance than that of the US in the Chinese market (rising slowly to 12%) but less than the Japanese one (22%). Indeed, the EU market share in China is higher than that enjoyed by the Union in other parts of the Asian region.

The picture in the field of direct investment one of the crucial elements in China's reforms, is less bright for Europe. The EU share in total FDI in China (around 4%) remains far lower than its share in other emerging markets. EU companies are lagging clearly behind not only Hong Kong and other overseas Chinese but also US and Japanese companies.

EU (15) companies invested a total of 2.5 $ billion in the 1979–1993 period (7.3 $ billion pledged) in some 3,000 projects. This represents less than half of the investment of either US or Japanese companies. Although the average size of EU projects tends to be bigger than that of its competitors and some of them are the undisputed leaders in key sectors of China's industry (like automobiles, telecommunications, or pharmaceuticals) there is a clear perception, both within the Chinese, European and foreign business communities, that EU companies are being less dynamic than their competitors in the Chinese market – and are hence missing opportunities. This could not only have negative implications for future trade, but also weaken the EU's global competitiveness.

It is, of course, up to each company to evaluate the risks and rewards of such a difficult undertaking as a Chinese venture. The long term perspective adopted by big corporations, ready to incur short-term losses in order to gain a strategic presence, is usually not possible for SMEs. Smaller firms may on the other hand be able to take advantage of opportunities with shorter payback periods and narrower initial objectives : an attractive option in periods of uncertainty. The challenge for Europe is not to find the opportunities but simply to explore possible openings in China with as much energy as our main rivals.

At the very least, the EU should try to help EU companies to make well-informed investment decisions about the opportunities on offer in China by promoting better two-way information on investment conditions and opportunities, as well as direct business-to-business contacts.

### *C.2 A UNIQUE ECONOMIC SYSTEM*

Information and contacts will not, however, in themselves be sufficient to resolve the problems faced by those seeking to trade with China and make investments there.

China has over the last years made enormous strides to liberalise its trade regime and open its economy to the world. Tariffs have come down, trading rights have been granted to firms on a wider basis, the dual exchange rate has been unified, foreign investment has been attracted on a large scale, the basic framework for an effective judicial structure to handle property rights has been established.

Although these measures represent important steps forward, they are clearly insufficient to make the Chinese trade system compatible with internationally accepted rules. The right to import and export goods in China remains largely a state monopoly. Customs duties are prohibitive, particularly for many consumer products (and are applied in an ad hoc manner). Non-tariff measures such as licences and quotas abound. Exports continue to enjoy numerous unfairly favourable conditions, foreign currency controls remain a major obstacle, and new technical barriers are introduced to frustrate imports. Transparency remains a big problem due to unpublished administrative rules and orders, and secret trade plans on some products. These are only some examples: Annex 3 provides a full summary.

The EU's efforts to increase the WTO-compatibility of trade rules, and to improve market access and the investment environment in China, have focused on the multilateral negotiations for China's WTO membership and on bilateral trade meetings. The objective is a coherent and consistent one: to bring about the application of general internationally agreed trade principles, and at the same time to deal with specific issues of mutual concern.

### *C.3 MEMBERSHIP OF THE WORLD TRADE ORGANISATION*

As a founder member of the GATT and once more a major player on world markets, China's membership of the World Trade Organisation is in the interest of all trading nations. Since China's application to return to the GATT in July 1986, the EU has consistently sought to accelerate progress towards a decision on Chinese membership, based on conditions which will guarantee both China's ability to meet the extensive requirements of WTO membership and the integrity of the WTO system.

The EU has taken a leading role in the negotiation, in particular in establishing the principle that of the commitments that China would make when joining the WTO, most would be implemented on the date of membership, but some could be implemented under multilateral surveillance over a specified period of time after entry into the WTO. This general approach reflects a sympathetic understanding of the fact that China is a country that is rapidly developing, but, in important respects, has not yet become a developed economy with all the characteristics of a fully-fledged market-economy system.

Despite the stand-off in these negotiations in late 1994, the Commission continues to believe that the structure of the deal proposed by the European side last year, and later carried further by the Chairman of the GATT Working Party on China, remains valid. Both China and its trading partners must now show additional political commitment to progress if a deal is to be reached. The full integration of China into the WTO system is in the interest of all parties concerned: for WTO Members it would contribute to guaranteeing the continuation of China's reform process until a mature market economy is established, and for China it would guarantee that its goods and services have open access to export markets around the world. Although contacts have been relaunched in recent weeks, it remains to be seen whether substantive WTO negotiations can resume and a deal can soon be struck.

In our view, the key remaining issues are:

- commitments in the field of import tariffs. China should be ready to envisage binding its duties at levels which, at the end of an implementation period, would result in a weighted average tariff not higher than about twice the OECD average;
- initial commitments in the field of traded services across all sectors under negotiation. Commitments should not be undermined by geographical limitations, access specifications or other restrictions;
- the liberalisation of the foreign trade monopoly, if necessary with transitional provisions. An automatic right of individuals, both national and foreign, to engage in direct import or export trade in all products is a basic feature of the WTO system, but does not yet exist in China;
- adherence by China to the Tokyo Round Civil Aircraft Code and the Government Procurement Agreement. Chinese implementation of the Procurement Agreement will create opportunities abroad and cut government costs at home, and it could be implemented in stages;

- elimination by China of all WTO-inconsistent quotas or other non-tariff barriers, over a transitional period;
- making China's industrial policies WTO compatible;
- acceptance of appropriate provisions on other horizontal issues such as subsidies, standards, state-pricing, state trading and the elimination of export duties.
- the definition of an appropriate transitional trade defence mechanism, which could be invoked in cases of market disruption.

Beyond the requirements that aim to establish appropriate access to China's market as a balance for the effective access which Chinese exports and investments enjoy in the markets of WTO Members benefit, an essential precondition of any final deal must be firm Chinese adherence to the principle of non-discrimination. This will be a precondition for EU support of any successful WTO package.

The approach outlined above reflects the recognition of China's current transitional position in its suggested use of the technique of transitional periods. But it properly pays regard to the principle that there are some principles of the international trade order which are so fundamental that it is reasonable to expect their application by countries participating in that international trade order, whatever their stage of development.

*C.4 BILATERAL TRADE DISCUSSIONS*

Bilateral trade talks since 1992 have had three interrelated objectives: promoting China's economic and trade reforms, helping China into the multilateral trade system, and achieving better market access for European goods and services.

This dialogue was institutionalised in 1993 by an Economic and Trade Working Group. 1994 saw detailed, sectoral meetings on IPR, Agriculture, and Financial Services. This process should continue, with the expansion of trade talks to other sectors and their extension through discussions with sectoral Ministries, as the only way to achieve concrete results. One subject of possible future dialogue might be competition matters, as cooperation in this field will enhance the effectiveness of international trade.

The main results (Annex 3) so far have been solutions to specific issues, from trademark infringements to veterinary restrictions and other technical barriers. Although many of the EU bilateral requests are already being discussed in the framework of the WTO accession process, it has also been useful to discuss bilaterally key EU concerns.

A sustained trade dialogue has also enabled Europe to avoid any risk discrimination and to ensure that EU economic operators enjoy the same treatment as their competitors in China.

This has been particularly important in areas where the US and China have concluded bilateral agreements, like intellectual property, maritime transport, and market access. In each case, including the February 1995 IPR deal, China has formally undertaken to ensure equal treatment for EU persons and entities.

Bilateral discussions also give an opportunity to link trade issues and cooperation activities. For example, the EU-China industrial property technical assistance programme followed the signing of agreed minutes on IPR protection. In the case of IPR for example, the cooperation that is being provided may well prove essential in making it possible for China to apply on the ground the agreements that have been signed.

*C.5 PROPOSALS*

a) The EU should continue to strongly support reform as an integral part of its trade and cooperation.

b) The Commission is ready to engage with Chinese authorities in a dialogue on economic, social and monetary issues.

c) The EU should encourage dialogue between China and other key bodies such as the OECD, and raise the profile of China in debate in the G-7.

d) The EU should pursue China's entry into the WTO as soon as possible, under the right conditions, and monitor closely the implementation of China's WTO commitments.

e) In order to increase the effectiveness of our bilateral trade dialogue, the EU should:

- increase the frequency of the Economic and Trade Working Group meetings,
- consolidate the sectoral meetings in the three sectors, IPR, Agriculture and Financial Services, as permanent fora for in-depth discussions,
- expand these meetings to new sectors or subjects (like technical barriers to trade, consumer goods, in the transport sector, and on competition),
- develop contacts with sectoral ministries and provincial authorities,
- establish more links between trade and investment talks and cooperation activities (in sectors like standards and public procurement).

f) Direct investment in China is bound to be crucial both for ensuring access to this market and for bolstering the global competitiveness of EU industry. The EU therefore should to develop a new programme of business cooperation with China (see section D.2).

**D. COOPERATION**
**THE NEW PRIORITIES**

China is a vast country, and the EU has limited resources for cooperation. When China's importance is taken into account, the resources allocated to cooperation work with China have remained small. Under the basic budget lines for development aid and economic cooperation in Asia, under 20 million ECU was set aside each year during the period 1991–1994. This compares with some 90 million ECU for India, or 460 million ECU for the former Soviet Union countries under the TACIS programme in 1994.

*D.1 COOPERATION STRATEGY*

The following types of activity should be given priority:

- cooperation in areas of critical importance for the Chinese economy;
- cooperation which has a catalytic effect on best practice within the Chinese system;
- cooperation which bolsters reform.

EC cooperation should both be reinforced and more closely targeted on support for reform in all areas of Chinese society: reform to promote the integration of China into the world trade and investment system, reform of the underdeveloped and restrictive civil society in China, reform to bring China closer into the global information society, and reform to prevent further damage to the physical environment in China. The rural and urban poverty which remains a scourge for millions of Chinese and the need to feed such a huge population is at the heart of Chinese government policy, and underlies all EC cooperation.

Effectiveness and impact over the long term remain essential.

There are three key targets for EC-China cooperation:

- The Chinese government is acutely aware of the deficiencies in the skills base in China and of the enormous need for further human resource development as Chinese society and the Chinese economy evolve. This message is increasingly echoed by European entrepreneurs finding that their opportunities to expand in China are held back by the lack of appropriate skills in China. We need to identify a coherent European contribution in education and training. The EU should build on the China-Europe International Business School (CEIBS) in Shanghai to bring the best of European expertise, including community experience in education and training policy-making and programme development, to China. We need to identify partners in other provinces for initiatives to promote technical and vocational training, for which one option would be to follow the CEIBS format of a permanent centre to address skill shortages in fields from engineering to accountancy. On the university front, 60,000 students from China are in the US but only 6,000 in Europe: we must redouble our efforts in higher education.
- Economic and social reform should be encouraged through a more wide ranging programme of support to reforms touching on individual Chinese in different professions and walks of life. In particular the development of a fair and effectively working system for the administration of justice should be assisted and encouraged, stepping up judicial cooperation between the EU and its Member States on the one hand, and China on the other. One approach worth exploring would be to establish a cooperative programme in the legal and judicial field through an EU-wide exchange programme for young lawyers, judges and finally law enforcement officials. This would require careful coordination among Member States actors, but would provide (following language training) for internships at European civil, administrative and perhaps constitutional courts as well as selected law firms. A reciprocal programme for Europeans could be attractive in some areas of the project.
- The facilitation of cooperation between private sector actors by the EU and the Chinese government will support the healthy evolution of both economies. This conviction is at the core of a developing programme of business cooperation, with three central goals: to support the general evolution of the business environment in China, to develop new skills central to the management and administration of the modern Chinese economy, and to give direct encouragement to closer ties between EU and Chinese enterprises, through the provision of information and the facilitation of face-to-face contacts. Supporting the development of industrial cooperation with China should reinforce the presence of European operations in China and encourage new economic links. These objectives are already central to several existing initiatives, but have not kept pace with the growth in EU economic interests and opportunities in China.

These objectives can be pursued across a range of policy areas. Two areas of particular potential for future development are the environment, and scientific and technological cooperation:

- The environmental challenge faced by a rapidly developing China has been recognised by the Chinese government in its "Agenda 21" follow-up programme to the Rio Summit, with its accompanying list of specific projects leading to sustainable development. The problems faced by China in the environmental field are partly systemic -a low awareness of the long-term consequences of inaction – partly technological, and partly that China does not believe that it can afford the costs of high environmental standards. Of critical importance is the need to integrate environmental considerations into other areas of policy, such as economic planning. A new working group has been set up to discuss how the EU can best help Chinese efforts. We need to identify a coherent European contribution in a field where there is multiplicity of signals from the Chinese side. Our contribution must be defined clearly before it is launched and must make best use of EU expertise in environmental policy-making and technology, including clean energy technology. It is therefore essential that initiatives make full use of the willingness of European business to commit itself to a long-term technological partnership with China.

- Scientific and technological cooperation promotes an enabling environment for cooperation in general, as well as helping the search for science-based solutions to common global problems. S&T cooperation with China should therefore be pursued under the Community's Fourth Framework Programme so as to strengthen the European scientific and industrial base and to contribute to other Community cooperation with China. S&T cooperation should mobilise complementary skills from across Europe and China, supporting innovative research and promoting the development of human and institutional capital, with a particular emphasis on the training and mobility of young researchers.

*D.2 PROPOSALS*

The EC should step up its cooperation programme and ensure that it fits the economic and political realities of China in the 1990s.

In view of the limited resources available, it also requires a clear choice of priorities and concentration on them, rather than a dissipated efforts which would achieve less for China and render the EC's cooperation effort far less apparent within China.

Current financial resources are not sufficient to fulfil all these objectives, but increasing budgetary resources is not the only way to improve the effectiveness of EU action in China. The size of China makes it particularly worthwhile to ensure synergies between Member States and EU activities, as well as to concentrate resources. Cooperation should also be central to the objective of raising the profile of the EU in China, and of China in the EU. New cooperation work should have an information strategy as an explicit element for all major new projects (see section E.2).

Opportunities for EC-China cooperation should be sought in the following areas:

- Support for human resource development in China should follow the opening of the China-Europe International Business School with new initiatives at different levels, including: a programme to build ties and networks between individual higher education institutions in China and the EU and provide opportunities for Chinese students to benefit from European expertise, and a new programme of technical and vocational training targeted on the needs identified by economic operators in China.
- Economic and social reform should be pursued through training and technical assistance in sectors critical to reform. A second phase of the IPR training programme should shift the emphasis towards new areas such as copyrights and enforcement measures, and should be followed by new programmes in the areas of quality and standardisation, and public procurement. New cooperation should be organised to promote the development of civil society in China, and in particular to support the

evolution of the legal and judicial professions with a view to strengthening the rule of law in China.

- Action should continue to address rural and urban poverty and agricultural productivity through encouragement to the development of local economies. Initiatives need to be in tune with the needs of a rapidly changing China.
- EU business and technical expertise must be involved in a dialogue on the environment, with a transfer of EU expertise in environmental policy-making and technology relevant to Chinese circumstances in key sectors such as energy. We should promote exchanges of information on the environment between the Commission, the Member States and China; and improve communication with other organisations helping China to improve its environment.
- A new programme of business cooperation should bring together the commercial slant of much cooperation work and should be a key element in an intensified dialogue with the EU business community. This should have two new elements:
- promoting a two-way flow of relevant commercial information and support to EU and Chinese businessmen, through the establishment of a network of Business Information Centres in China, in provinces of China where existing business ties to China are scarce;
- facilitating direct business-to-business contacts in sectors of particular potential for industrial cooperation, through a coordinated programme of collaboration between enterprises and business to business trade or investment seminars, both in Europe and in China.
- Enhanced forms of scientific and technological cooperation under the Community's Fourth Framework Programme should be based on a continuing effort to promote high quality research in key areas of cooperation with China.

Projects which are not central to these objectives should be phased out or not renewed.

## E. COORDINATION AND INFORMATION

### *E.1 A POLICY APPROACH ADAPTED TO A CHANGING CHINA*

China is embarked on a period of change. Europe's policies, as outlined above, can both support the trend to reform in China and accommodate any uncertainties about the future direction of Chinese (and European) domestic policies. The development of the EU-China relationship must be a sustained long-term goal.

EU policy should seek to promote the objectives that have been described above in a comprehensive way, but should also be flexible enough to cope with unavoidable uncertainties in the future development of China. Most observers agree on the existence of a great variety of possible future economic, and in particular political, scenarios for the decades to come. But whatever temporary ups and downs come in the wake of trade quarrels or political differences, EU policy should never lose sight of its strategic interests in China.

The various programmes and instruments at the EU's disposal will always be small relative to a country of China's size. At the same time, several Member States are very active in areas like training, technical assistance, business facilitation, and the environment, all of which are priorities in EU policy. There is much to be gained by pooling experience and, if appropriate, resources in designing and implementing these common activities. If we do not cooperate, our voice will not be heard.

Several Chinese provinces have larger populations than the largest EU Member States. In addition, recent years have seen the proliferation of special economic zones and other development areas, as well as a devolution of economic power which has shifted responsibility for economic and trade policy-making and implementation to provincial level. Provincial authorities have wide powers across a variety of policy areas. The institutional interlocutors for the EU will always be the ministries in Beijing. But it is important for EU policy to acknowledge the importance of the provinces and for dialogue on some economic and cooperation issues to reach the provincial level.

The "Asia strategy" Communication called for a higher profile for the European Union in Asia. Given China's strong cultural identity and language, and given the shortcomings of its communication system and its sheer size, China presents a particular challenge.

The most important factor in the EU's image is our policy towards China. The deeper political dialogue now launched must be used to put a greater stress on the long-term common interests of the EU and China. The EU and China should gradually become more used to working together on a variety of policy issues and to debating key areas of mutual interest. A closer economic partnership will help to further the interests of Europe and China, already increasingly intertwined. Closer and better-focused cooperation will bring the work of the EU to a broader cross-section of society. But a more active information policy in China is essential to create a stronger profile for the EU.

In addition, the EU's activities in China too often go unnoticed in Europe, with many who might make a positive contribution or become more closely involved unaware of the opportunities. If a deeper partnership is to develop between Europeans and Chinese, openness and interest must be fostered on both sides. Informing the European public of the EU's activities should be seen as an inherent part of the Commission's responsibility to implement policy.

*E.2 PROPOSALS*

The impact of EU policy should be maximised by better coordination. This could be achieved by improving the links between the Member States, the Commission, and the private sector, both in Europe and in China:

- A China Experts Group (along the lines of the existing ones for Japan and Korea) could act as a forum for the exchange of ideas and information about China between experts from Member States' administrations and the Commission, across all policy areas.
- The possibility of closer coordination of cooperation activities in China with the Member States and other international organisations should also be explored more thoroughly. Cofinancing could bring benefits in pooling experience and strengths (the Commission only manages some 8% of total EU assistance to China, but offers grant financing rather than soft loans). A co-financing facility could be introduced to set aside a proportion of resources each year for joint projects with the Member States. Bringing together initiatives such as business service centres or cultural centres in one place could also help to consolidate the EU presence in China; "Europa Houses" in big provincial cities could house a number of different activities.
- An EU Business Council in Beijing, giving voice to EU businesses in China and taking advantage of existing networks both in China and in Europe, would help to articulate the views of the European business community and could act as an important input to policy formulation.
- Business, Commission and Member States should also be brought together in sectoral committees, to help effective monitoring not only of respect of China's WTO commitments but, more generally, of China's new commercial legislation.

- Business could also be more closely involved in sponsorship of EU-funded cooperation projects (as is already the case with the China-Europe International Business School in Shanghai). Certainly the close association of EU industry in cooperation is essential, not only to help target real industrial needs but also to ensure the strong link between EU initiatives and business which will keep such cooperation in tune with economic realities.

An information strategy for China could include a variety of initiatives to build up awareness of the EU in the media and amongst opinion-formers in China, and to foster awareness of EU initiatives amongst the wider European public:

Better targeted information products and intensified press and information activities. One way to reach an influential audience in both Europe and China would be to publish a professionally edited regular journal, like those already issued in the United States and Russia. Another, which requires a careful feasibility study, is the creation of European inputs to the growing Chinese electronic information society. There should also be a greater information component in cooperation work.

Better collaboration with Member States' cultural activities in China. The Council could invite Member States to include where possible a European element in their cultural initiatives in China.

Expansion of the current EU visitors programme under which the Commission invites media representatives and opinion-formers to Brussels and at least two Member States. Better networking of those involved in cooperation work.

Encouragement of the development of European Studies in China as part of the proposed programme of university cooperation (see section D.2), to build a better picture of the EU in China over the long term. Support to promote knowledge about China in Europe, through the development of research and networks between those engaged on Chinese studies in Europe. We also need to review the usefulness of European Documentation Centres in China.

## F. CONCLUSIONS

China is embarked on a period of change. Europe's policies, as outlined above, can both support the trend to reform in China and accommodate any uncertainties about the future. The development of the EU-China relationship must be a sustained long-term goal.

The rise of China presents China and the world with new challenges and opportunities. It is in Europe's interest that the current process of economic and social reform be encouraged and sustained. Europe and China need a long-term bilateral relationship in order to secure shared goals. Some such goals – such as the mutual interest in a smooth transition for Hong Kong and Macau -are based on ties of long standing. Others reflect new interests. But in both cases, Europe and China can work together in many practical ways: progress towards full integration in the world market economy, strengthening of civil society, poverty alleviation, environment protection, human resource development, scientific and technological development, the information society, trade and investment cooperation.

The Council is invited to:

- adopt the approach set out in this Communication;
  - encourage China to become fully integrated in the international community
  - widen political dialogue to include all issues of common interest and global significance

  - support China's WTO membership on the basis of clear commitments to create a fully-fledged market economy;
- contribute to reform inside China
  - pursue EU concerns on human rights and promoting the development of a civil society in China through support to the opening up of China, public and private bilateral ties, and international dialogue in multilateral fora
  - use cooperation to pursue the goals of human resource development, the promotion of economic and social reform, and cooperation between economic actors, including action in the field of the environment and science and technology;
- intensify ties between the European Union and China
  - develop commercial contacts to improve the business environment for EU business in China and to increase market access on a non-discriminatory basis
  - encourage contact between Europeans and Chinese, with a particular stress on business cooperation

The Council is invited to endorse the strategy outlined in this communication, and to invite the Commission, Member States, business and other actors to cooperate in pursuing the approach outlined. The Commission intends to move forward with the initiatives outlined in the months ahead.

## ANNEX 1: ECONOMIC REFORMS IN CHINA

Following the Third Plenum of the Chinese Communist Party's Eleventh Congress in December 1978, Deng Xiaoping led China on an ambitious reform process which has substantially changed the Chinese economic system as well as its relations with the world economy. This process has been neither smooth and steady nor the result of a clearly defined plan from above. On the contrary, it has been driven by a multitude of initiatives at various levels (central, local, individual), largely on a trial and error basis, and has resulted in an uneven path with several switches in focus and emphasis. Nevertheless, reforms have undoubtedly brought about a dramatic economic revitalisation and improved living standards.

Over the 16 years of this process, different phases can be identified:

a) **Launching of Reforms and emphasis on Agriculture** (December 1978 – September 1984): as seems logical in a country with some 800 million people living in the countryside, the first phase of reform focused on agriculture. The key measures included the raising of the prices paid by the state for farm goods and the introduction of a Contract Production Responsibility System, which replaced people's communes with the encouragement of individual productivity. In contrast, urban reform was only tentative. Perhaps the most significant step was the creation of Special Economic Zones to boost foreign investment in four coastal areas.

b) **Efforts towards creating a market economy** (October 1984 – September 1988): this phase tried to tackle the reform of state enterprises and price liberalisation, two key requirements for change. The objective was to separate ownership (public) and management through new legislation in areas like bankruptcy, and experiments in share holding and financial markets. In the area of price deregulation, progress was made for most consumer goods.

c) **Retrenchment** (October 1988-December 1991): this phase saw the Chinese authorities trying to regain control of an overheated economy by freezing prices, stopping reforms and slashing investment. But it appeared increasingly clear during this period that a decade of reform has substantially reduced the government's ability to control economic actors. However, reform was continued in areas such as prices and trade.

d) **Re-launching at higher speed** (since January 1992): the present phase, launched by Deng Xiaoping's trip to the South in January 1992, has drastically altered the political and economic climate, with a generalised rush towards accelerated reform in all areas of the economy, including areas like services or land use rights, previously little affected by reforms. Furthermore, new inland and Yangtze areas (like Nanjing, Wuhan and Chongqing) have opened for foreign trade and investment. New measures have been announced in the key areas of enterprise management and price liberalisation. The new Company Law entered into force in 1994. The reform of the banking system was launched and the new taxation system, including a VAT and a modified sharing of fiscal resources between Beijing and the provinces, were both enacted in 1994. The decision to abolish the official exchange rate and to allow the unified exchange rate to float (though controlled) in the swap markets, and the new taxation system, are the most recent and crucial reforms. Attempts to impose a credit squeeze had some effect during 1994, but the economy's momentum and growing provincial autonomy ensured that such attempts by the centre to slow the economy had only limited effect. Such reforms have been enshrined in China's Constitution under the new formula of socialist market economy.

*Macroeconomic Performance*

Since the launching of reforms, China has enjoyed a clear acceleration of GDP growth, averaging around 9% per year during the 1980s. Both industry and agriculture showed faster growth than in the past. Although output grew more rapidly in industry (12.6% annually during the 1980s) and especially in manufacturing, the acceleration in output growth was also dramatic in the agriculture sector. However, fast growth was accompanied by growing inflation. China had a long tradition of almost no inflation, but this trend changed abruptly with the liberalisation of production and prices, reaching a peak of over 18% in 1989.

Chinese economic performance since 1992 can only be describes as remarkable. GNP growth reached 12.8%, 13.4% and 11.8% in the last three years, with industrial output up by 13%, 20% and 21% respectively. Fixed investment surged by 29% last year. But inflation at around 25% in 1994, up from 15% in 1993, has aroused the traditional fears of overheating.

Another spectacular result of Chinese reforms has been the rapid growth of foreign trade. Since 1979 Chinese trade grew twice as fast as output, a clear outcome of China's new open-door policy. At the beginning of the reform period in 1978, total Chinese trade amounted to 20 $ billion and was roughly balanced. By 1994 this had surged to 237 $ billion. In addition, after trade deficits which reached as high as 15 $ billion in 1985, the Chinese trade balance went back to a surplus position in 1990. With the exception of a 12 $ billion deficit in 1993, China has enjoyed surpluses ever since, bolstered by what amounted to a devaluation of the Yuan at the time of currency unification in January 1994. This good performance in trade has helped to ease the foreign debt burden, which started to worry Chinese policy-makers during the 1980s, but now China has a very healthy foreign-exchange reserves at around 50 $ billion, even if foreign debt remains substantial at 80 $ billion.

*Structural Problems*

However, economic reform and booming trade has been concentrated in only a few Chinese provinces. With some exceptions, traditional regional imbalances in China between the rich and dynamic Southeast coastal areas (from Shanghai down to Canton) and the more backward North and West inland areas have been compounded since the beginning of reform. The establishment of five Special Economic Zones (Shenzhen, Zhuhai, Shantou, Xiamen and Hainan) followed by the "opening" to foreign investment of 14 coastal cities and the creation of Free Trade Zones and 5 Open Economic Zones accentuated the gap between the "two Chinas". The whole coast from North to South has progressively become an open zone that includes 11 provinces (292 cities and districts) which represent less than 5% of Chinese territory and around 17% of population, but which produce one third of China's GNP.

Other structural problems, like infrastructure bottlenecks and environmental degradation risk undermining sustainable long term economic growth in China. The problems of acute energy shortages, a transport system which is clearly inefficient and unable to meet demand, and primitive telecommunications, are bound to get worse as economic growth gathers speed and investment in these key sectors lags far behind. Environmental deterioration is already serious and, despite the government's awareness of the dangers of long-term damage, China's economic development strategy has focused on rapid wealth creation, leaving the consequences to be dealt with in the future.

Traditionally, China watchers used to focus on inflation as the most obvious signal not only of economic difficulties but also of political trouble ahead (and 1989 certainly proved them right). Recent figures have again pointed to overheating of the economy and growing urban inflation. Monetary policy rests on administered credit and not on interest rates or an open market policy. The recent negative interest rates make overheating a risk. Fiscal policy, and the protection of loss-making state owned enterprises, are also typically inflationary. A growing budget deficit (over 8% of GDP) and a rapidly expanding money supply are likely to exacerbate the problem. Unemployment could become a much more serious long-term problem, especially if reform of the inefficient state-owned sector gathers pace. Already, migration on a huge scale has taken place from the poor West to the coastal cities – some estimates have put this as high as 100 million people.

*The making of a "Socialist Market Economy" with Chinese characteristics*

The effects of over one decade of reform can be analysed in terms of the degree to which the market economy has developed in China, both as a way of organising production and as a way of matching supply and demand. In other words, what proportion of Chinese output is the result of mandatory planning (instead of individual decisions by companies) and what proportion of Chinese prices is controlled (instead of freely set by market forces). Evolution in company ownership is another key factor in assessing progress in reform.

a) **Planning versus market in output and prices**: the share of individual output which was the object of mandatory planning has been reduced sharply from around 80% in the early 1980s to just 17% in 1991. In other words, from an economy in which only 20% of industrial production escaped mandatory output targets, China moved to a new situation in which less than 20% of this output was under the strict control of the plan. Recent liberalisation has further reduced state production quotas. The hand of the state is still felt in China in numerous ways; but the crude influence of planning has been largely swept aside. The same trend towards liberalisation is noticeable in price determination. Some estimates indicate that the share of products under controlled prices has been reduced to 22% for agriculture, 20% for consumer goods and 36% for means of production. A new wave of liberalisation, announced during 1993, left only less than 10% of retail sales under state pricing.

b) **Ownership**: diversification in the ownership of production units, especially the growth of the non-state sector, is a clear indication of the development of a market economy. In 1978, 77.6% of industrial output and 54.6% of retail sales were in the hands of state companies. 1994 estimates put the output share of state-owned companies at 44% and their share of retail sales at only 41%. If we look at recent growth rates in the different sectors, the importance of the non-state sector is bound to continue its upward trend. Another feature has been the growing variety of different types of enterprise, from the township and village enterprises of the countryside to the burgeoning foreign invested joint ventures.

c) **Smashing the iron rice bowl**: the key to the Chinese reform process in the years to come is very probably going to be the sensitive issue of restructuring the huge, inefficient and loss-making state-owned industry, over 100,000 enterprises, of which about 11,000 are medium or large sized, employing some 100 million workers, of whom one-third could be made redundant. By 1994, some 40% of the state-owned companies were losing money (by official calculations). Their combined losses rose by 30% in 1994, and those still in the black saw a sharp decline in profits, leading to 4.7 $ billion of public subsidies (60% of the total public deficit). The debt chain between different companies is surging (some estimates put it at 69 $ billion) making restructuring of China's public industry all the more crucial but, also, more difficult.

Failure to tackle this sector will continue to undermine China's modernisation drive; but a destructive approach could have enormous social, economic and political consequences. Reform has so far been hesitant in this area. Besides a modest attempt at separating ownership and management (the contract management responsibility system) and partial separation of companies and the state by taxing profits and allowing some profit retention autonomy, few measures have really attacked the core of the problem When they have, like the Bankruptcy Law, they remain just a declaration of good intentions implemented only sporadically. This sector as a whole remains a serious brake on China's future development.

## ANNEX 2: EU-CHINA TRADE & INVESTMENT

### *EU-China Trade*

In parallel with China's booming total trade, the bilateral trade flows between the EU and China have also surged. Total bilateral trade in 1978 was only 2.4 billion ECU (EC -9), but by 1993 this had boomed to 30.8 billion ECU (EC-12). EU-China trade has increased almost thirteen-fold since the beginning of reform in China (see statistical annex).

The EC enjoyed a positive trade balance between 1983 and 1987, reaching a peak in 1985 with a 3.2 billion ECU trade surplus vis-à-vis China. Since 1988, however, the situation has changed dramatically. China enjoyed a 1.2 billion ECU trade surplus that year and from then until 1991, doubled it every single year. However, after growth in the surplus slowed in 1992, 1993 showed a reversal of the trend. EU exports grew by 65%, leading to the first reduction of our bilateral trade deficit since 1988, to 8.2 billion ECU. It should be noted that, in contrast, the US trade deficit vis-à-vis China continued to grow rapidly during 1992 – 1994, reaching 30 $ billion last year. But the available figures for 1994 indicate that China's bilateral trade surplus with the EU has started to grow again, and could have exceeded 10 billion ECU.

Of course, despite many efforts to analyse the reasons for discrepancies between EU and Chinese statistics, these remain significant. For example, Chinese figures showed a bilateral trade surplus for the EU of 2.4 $ million in 1993. Both Eurostat and a GATT statistics subgroup have explained these discrepancies as the result of differences over how to include Hong Kong re-export figures in the statistics.

Concerning trade by product category, EU exports continue to be concentrated in areas like machinery, both mechanical and electrical, transport equipment, and nuclear reactors, which amounted to over 65% of total EU exports to China in 1993. As for Chinese exports to the EC, the main items continue to be textiles and clothing (20% of the total), toys, electrical material, leather goods and footwear. These five categories together represent over 57% of total EC imports from China in 1993.

A longer term analysis of EU's trade performance in China shows the Community slightly losing market share in the Chinese import market during the 1980s. The EC (9) had a 12% share of Chinese imports in 1980, and the EC (10) reached a 13% share in 1985. But the EC (12) fell to 11% in 1990. However, this slight reduction compares favourably with the collapse of US (from 19% in 1980 to 8% in 1990) and Japanese (from 26% in 1980 to 10% in 1990) shares in the total of China's imports in the same period. Therefore, the US, the EU and Japan all lost market share in China during the 1980s, but the EU managed to retain its relative position much more successfully than its competitors. Recent figures suggest a growth in market share for the EU (around 15%), less dramatic than that of Japan, but more impressive than a stagnant US position. It is also worth noting that, in contrast to the US, the EU share of the Chinese market is higher than those enjoyed in other Asian markets such as the NICs, ASEAN or Japan.

A positive factor in China's surging exports to the EU has undoubtedly been the Community's GSP system. It should be noted that China has been, by far, the biggest beneficiary of the EU GSP in recent years. China's exports enjoying GSP benefits jumped from 2.1 billion ECU in 1988 to 6.6 billion ECU in 1992 and the Chinese share in the total benefits of the EC system went up from 13.7% to 22.2%, three times as much as the second beneficiary.

*Investment*

Foreign borrowing by China and foreign dorect investment in China have also been growing rapidly since the beginning of reforms. Foreign Direct Investment exploded in 1992 and 1993. In the period 1979–1992, China borrowed almost 75 $ billion (60 $ billion actually disbursed) and foreign companies set up 90,710 joint ventures, with a total value contracted of 110 $ billion and 36 $ billion actually used. FDI in China grew even more rapidly in 1993, reaching 111 $ billion of contracts and 25.8 $ billion actually used for the 83,000 new joint ventures established. Figures for 1994 showed a decrease in the amount of projects (47,490) and contracted FDI (much of which was simply Chinese capital going through Hong Kong to benefit from an advantageous FDI regime) but another growth in used foreign capital to over 33.8 $ billion. All in all, in the 1979–1994 period, over 221,000 of Joint Ventures have been created, over 301 $ billion have been pledged and over 95 $ billion actually invested in China. They employ some 12 million Chinese workers and they represent around 40% of China's total foreign trade.

Hong Kong and Macau companies are by far the biggest investors in China, with 114,147 projects, 150 $ billion of contracts and some 50 $ billion disbursed between 1979 and 1993. This represents around two-thirds of projects and contracts and three-quarters of used foreign capital. Taiwan comes second, increasing to 3/4 the share of FDI of Chinese origin. From the rest, the performance of the EU, USA and Japan in the period 1979–1993 can be summarised as follows:

| | Project | Contracts ($ million) | Used ($ million) |
|---|---|---|---|
| EU (12) | 2,741 | 6,952 | 2,442 |
| EU (15) | 3,070 | 7,319 | 2,549 |
| USA | 12,019 | 14,659 | 5,237 |
| JAPAN | 7,182 | 8,935 | 5,203 |

Therefore, EU investment lags behind that of the main competitors both in terms of number of joint ventures and capital invested. However, these figures show that the average size of EU projects tends to be bigger than those of other origin. Both the USA and Japan have invested a similar amount, 5 $ billion, to Taiwan, more that twice the EU figure. In terms of Member States, the biggest investors in China are:

| | Project | Contracts ($ million) | Used ($ million) |
|---|---|---|---|
| FRANCE | 547 | 920 | 602 |
| UK. | 616 | 3,018 | 578 |
| GERMANY | 569 | 1,458 | 527 |
| ITALY | 467 | 552 | 397 |

## ANNEX 3: EU-CHINA BILATERAL TRADE ISSUES

Following continuous pressure by China's trading partners, both bilaterally, and multilaterally in the GATT accession discussions, some improvements have been made to the Chinese trade system.

a) centralisation of foreign trade rules publication in a single office and publication of all existing rules to increase transparency (not yet fully implemented). The first ever Foreign Trade Law was adopted in May 1994 and entered into force in July (although some provisions seem not fully GATT-compatible);

b) lowering of certain custom duties;

c) reduction in the number of products subject to import licences or quotas as of June 1994, a total of 413 items were still subject to NTM's without renewal plans; abolition of import substitution policies and import and export planning;

d) elimination of the import regulatory tax, direct export subsidies and the import substitution policy;

e) elimination of the official exchange rate as of 1 January 1994 and unification of China's exchange rate at the swaps market rate, whose floating is controlled;

f) introduction of VAT, a uniform corporate tax and improved budget accounting rules;

g) conversion of some state owned enterprises to shareholding or limited liability companies, subcontracting of management of some remaining state owned enterprises, creation of a bankruptcy law.

Although these measures represent important step forward, they are clearly insufficient to make the Chinese trade system compatible with internationally accepted rules. Remaining problems include:

- Absence of transparency, certainty and uniformity
- Trade planning (plans which are often secret)
- Trade monopolies and other privileges of foreign trade corporations
- Foreign currency controls
- Very high customs tariffs
- Licensing system, quotas, tendering, and other import restrictions
- Tendering restrictions on imports
- Technical, veterinary and phytosanitary measures used not always in accordance with international rules
- Export subsidies (mostly indirect)
- Export taxes and restrictions
- Industrial policies which can have a severe impact on trade and investment conditions, for example in the automobile sector.

This list of measures clearly shows the dilemma for an exporter who has to face not only the classic deterrent of high customs duties and the requirement of an import licence, but also uncertainty about the rules applied, which are often unpublished and implemented on an ad hoc basis. Secret trade plans, import substitution policies carried out by the sectoral Ministries and foreign currency controls amount to a system which lacks transparency and certainty.

*Bilateral Trade Discussions*

A bilateral trade deficit of 8–10 billion ECU in the last four years deserves close analysis. Of course, bilateral trade imbalances are not a problem in themselves, but only if they reflect structures and practices which are not compatible with free and fair trade rules. We believe this is the case in China.

In order to deal more effectively with this problem, the Joint Committee, in its October 1991 meeting, decided to hold a Trade Experts' Meeting (which further evolved into a series of periodical discussions) to examine the specific problems hampering the adequate development of trade. The agendas of those meetings have included not only specific problems (phytosanitary and veterinary matters, industrial metals, footwear, silk, alcoholic beverages, services) but also horizontal issues (transparency, foreign exchange controls, etc.).

The purpose of these meetings was threefold. First, to increase mutual understanding on outstanding contentious issues and maintain pressure on the Chinese authorities to ease the existing problems; second to seek solutions to specific problems of EU interest; and finally, to avoid any discrimination that might result from China's deals with other partners, in particular with the US. Of course, most of the main issues of contention about access to the Chinese market are now being addressed also in the context of the negotiations on Chinese WTO accession.

The Joint Committee of April 1993 decided to set up a Working Group on Economic and Trade matters in order to institutionalise the on-going trade discussions. During the Joint Committee meeting of February 1994 it was decided to supplement the Economic and Trade Working Group with three sectoral meetings on Financial Services, IPR and Agriculture. Other sectors could be added in the future. This approach of backing up a global summary meeting on economic matters with detailed technical-level discussions is designed to ensure a realistic and fruitful dialogue: a genuine attempt to improve mutual understanding and facilitate economic ties between two important commercial partners.

The EU has raised bilaterally, a variety of sectoral issues in recent years.

- **Non-ferrous Metals** (notably the surge of imports at abnormally low prices which are at the origin of several anti-dumping procedures);
- **Silk Products** (in particular double pricing policies which lead to manufactured goods being sold by China more cheaply that the raw material);
- **Alcoholic Beverages** (the whole import regime, including the import monopoly, extremely high customs duties, unknown rules for trading and taxation, and unpublished import plans and quotas);
- **Financial Services** (limitation in the activities of foreign banks and insurance companies, possibility or establishment in areas like commerce, consulting and law firms);
- **Agriculture** (phytosanitary and veterinary measures which hamper trade in sectors like bovine meat, tobacco, and dairy products; discussion for concluding an administrative arrangement to govern phytosanitary and veterinary matters; and a request for an EC unit to be set up in the China Commodity Inspection Bureau);
- **IPR** (proper enforcement of existing legislation, notably infringements in the area of trademarks and unfair competition (counterfeiting and passing off), copyrights, as well as proper implementation of agreements on pipeline patent protection;
- **Shipping** (proper application of the 1992 Agreed Minutes, not yet fully achieved);
- **Technical Barriers** (the whole system remains non-transparent, mixing up private and public inspection and is not always based on international standards leading to trade obstacles as, for example, in the field of chemicals);
- **Taxation** (in particular the new VAT, which include discriminatory elements for foreign companies, and Consumption Tax);
- **National Treatment** for foreign-funded companies (constraints and discriminations affecting their operation in China).

Potential discrimination emerged after the US launched a first Section 301 investigation of the issue of intellectual property rights in 1991. A Memorandum of Understanding between the US and China provided for a substantial improvement in the level of patent and copyright protection in China. The MOU contained, however, provisions that would have discriminated against the Community. The subsequent dialogue with China led to an agreement on the subject, avoiding what could have been a major trade conflict. Discrimination of the Community vis-à-vis the US has also been prevented by negotiations in the area of maritime transport.

A second investigation under Section 301 was launched on the general question of access to the Chinese market for US exports. A compromise solution was finally reached and the US and China signed a Memorandum of Understanding on 10 October 1992 in which China agreed to publish all laws, regulations, rules, decrees, administrative guidance and policies affecting trade. Unpublished rules will no longer be enforceable and publication will be centralised in one official journal. In addition, China agreed to progressively reduce import restrictions, quotas, licensing requirements and controls; to give confirmation on the elimination of all import substitution rules and policies; to avoid the utilisation of veterinary and phytosanitary standards and testing requirements as import barriers, applying the same requirements to domestic and imported products; and to reduce tariffs on several products. It was clear that the benefits of the agreement would be enjoyed by all of China's trading partners, particularly in terms of transparency. But concern was expressed about one discriminatory element, a special provision allowing unrestricted importation of spare parts and kits only for US automobile joint ventures. The Chinese government accepted an exchange of letters whereby EU companies will enjoy exactly the same treatment, and agreed to consider EU's priority products for early liberalisation.

The recent US-China agreement on several IPR issues, most notably on copyright enforcement, is another step, as long as it is applied erga omnes, towards not only better Chinese legislation but, particularly, adequate enforcement of it. The Commission should make sure that EU products enjoy the same protection granted to US ones, de jure of course but particularly in practice, and that the provisions regarding joint ventures and market access are extended to EU companies and products.

*EC Import Regime*

Following the completion of the internal market, a review took place of the rules regulating a variety of nationally-set quotas, some 4,700 quotas on Chinese products were in place[2]. At the same time, this substantial liberalisation was only acceptable to European industry when accompanied by a minimum, of protection, in view of the unique nature of the Chinese economy and its consequent potential to disrupt the EU market in some sectors.

In the wake of the conclusion of the Uruguay Round, the abolition of all national QRs and the establishment of a few EU-wide was agreed. This new regime puts only seven product categories under quota (footwear, gloves, tableware and kitchenware, glassware, radio-broadcast receivers and toys) which represent around 13% of Chinese non-textile exports to the EU (in 1992). Other products will be subject to a surveillance regime with no quantitative limitation.

A new import regime was also established for Non-MFA textiles products, particularly silk and silk products. This autonomous regime has been negotiated with the Chinese and was soon transformed into a bilateral agreement.

It is clear that this new regime represents a substantial improvement on the old one, not only in terms of scope (volume of trade and number of products covered) but also in terms of transparency and certainty. In addition, the quota levels have been substantially raised in 1995 to take account both of enlargement and of specific problems in certain sectors.

## ANNEX 4: COOPERATION ACTIVITIES

*Financial and Technical Assistance*

The first project to be financed by the European Community came in 1984, just before the normalisation of cooperation activities through the Trade and Cooperation Agreement. A full-scale development aid programme developed in the wake of the signing of the Agreement in 1985. To the end of 1994, the EC financed a total of 25 development projects in China in the field of technical and financial assistance, by far the bulk of total resources devoted to relations with China. Projects have tended to combine expert advice on the spot, some training of Chinese in the EU, and support towards the modernisation of equipment. The projects have centred on the rural sector in its broadest sense, covering such varied fields as soil and water conservation, food processing and storage, as well as the improvement of crop yields. The programme was designed to spread the influence of the EC into a variety of sectors, and a variety of provinces. As a result, the programmes have touched on products as varied as citrus fruits and cashew nuts, shrimps and rubber. The geographical spread of activities has meant that the work has spread from Xinjiang in the west to Liaoning in the east, and from Jilin in the north to Hainan in the south.

One result has been that starting from scratch, an EC presence was established in diverse parts of China. The importance of the programme has also been given added force by the fact that few other foreign donors have entered the rural sector in China. However, in the face of such a vast country as China, the overall effect of a such a programme has necessarily been small. It has proved difficult to establish a national profile through the adoption of such a "bottom-up" strategy. In operational terms, the pooling of knowledge and experience between EU expert teams separated across the country has not been achieved. A further problem has been that at a time of rapid change in China, institutional partners sometimes find it difficult to fulfil their long-term commitments.

The largest single technical and financial assistance project in China has been the Dairy Development Project. The central aim of the project was to improve nutrition standards in China through supporting the dairy sector. First, EC milk powder and butter oil were made available to China at local prices. Then the proceeds were ploughed back into the development of the dairy industry in China. European experts from across the EC were sent to China to advise on the evolution of a sound dairy industry, cattle stocks were built up, and equipment was provided to enlarging the milk processing capability in China. The project was one of few foreign-funded projects in the heart of the Chinese rural sector, and the only EU project to have developed a network approach with true national scope and participation. The project promoted and modernised the dairy sector in 20 major municipalities and established a national strategy for the dairy sector. It set up structures and introduced new technology to ensure that the dairy products market and dairy production develop in tandem. A one year interim phase for the project agreed in 1994 involves 30 project areas and has moved away from supporting mainly milk processing capacity and the increase of cattle numbers towards strengthening the productivity of dairy farming and improving quality control throughout the dairy sector.

The Commission has now launched a feasibility study of a possible second phase. The study is examining the extension of the project to have an impact from the farm level right to the marketplace, addressing weaknesses such as quality control, hygiene and productivity to improve the responsiveness of the industry to the market. The commercial orientation of a second phase could include measures to promote the EU investment in the Chinese dairy sector.

To develop projects on such a national scale obviously requires greater resources and infrastructure. Another approach which has increasingly been adopted is to adopt a policy of institutional strengthening, supporting the development of policy at the centre. With this in mind, the China EC Centre for Agricultural Technology (CECAT) was established in Beijing. This Centre was set up to encourage the transfer of technology between the EC and China, and to consolidate the experience gained from the development aid of the EC and others over many years – to develop a centre of knowledge and know-how. CECAT seeks to spread the benefits of this work to as wide an audience as possible through seminars, special papers and audio-visual material, and by assisting European agro-businesses operating in the Chinese market. With current CECAT arrangements coming to an end next year, an assessment will be made to judge whether the Centre should continue on its current institutional footing for a second phase.

The objective of supporting minority populations in China has been pursued by defining projects in such a way that the benefits flow to minorities, for example by targeting regions or sectors in which minorities are concentrated. For example, an ongoing project to develop livestock in Qinghai province targets the upland areas, where farmers come largely from Tibetan stock.

*Economic Cooperation*

In parallel with the programme of technical and financial assistance, a programme of economic cooperation developed in the 1980s. This programme also sought to combine action at the local level with institutional strengthening at the centre.

During the late 1980s, the largest project at the micro level was a programme to support the modernisation of Chinese enterprises. This programme took advantage of consultancy expertise within the EU to address the particular needs of Chinese companies in transition. However, it proved difficult to ensure that the programme had a knock-on effect throughout the country, and its implementation was discontinued after 1989. A more successful attempt to strengthen the infrastructure of the Chinese economy came in the field of management education. From 1985, the China-Europe Management Institute (CEMI) offered management training to Chinese students, with European faculty teaching courses on management with an international focus. Its main task was the establishment of an MBA course, through which some 235 students have graduated. The MBA courses provided a new dimension to management training in China, a course with an international focus which quickly achieved an impressive reputation. CEMI also undertook research, producing publications and case studies, and in recent years placed a much greater emphasis on developing a range of management development courses, from which some 600 students have benefited since 1989. A variety of companies, from state owned companies to foreign joint ventures, were involved with CEMI, with close links to European companies. The CEMI MBA alumni can now be found in some of the most dynamic sectors of the Chinese economy. However, CEMI was not without its problems, notably poor facilities and a lack of independence which prevented it from establishing long-term stability and sustainability.

1994 saw the EU's efforts to develop management training in China enter a new phase. As the work of CEMI continued, it gradually became clear to the Commission, the Chinese government, and the business community in China and the EU that the time had come for a more ambitious attempt to address the severe shortage of Chinese managers trained to international standards. The result was the China-Europe International Business School (CEIBS), a fully-fledged business school set up in Shanghai in 1994. A partnership between a network of business schools in Europe and the Shanghai Jiaotong University, CEIBS is the first business school in China, offering international-level MBA and other courses to Chinese students from March 1995.

A permanent faculty source primarily in EU business schools will be built up, housed in a building constructed specifically for the school. CEIBS is an independent legal entity, managed through a Board of Directors in much the same way as a commercial joint venture, although it is non-profit making. The academic standard of the School is monitored and protected by an international group of scholars in an Academic Council, whilst sponsors of the project will influence the development of the School through an Advisory Council. Close links with the business community are central to CEIBS' philosophy, not only as sponsors but to ensure the continuing economic relevance of CEIBS's teaching to the modern Chinese economy. CEIBS symbolises a new concern to ensure that actions are properly in tune with the economic realities in China, as well as respecting the requirement that economic cooperation is of genuine mutual benefit.

Another element in the programme has been the provision of training to officials, where the EU could offer particular expertise and support. One example has been a programme of training for Chinese interpreters, to facilitate the internationalisation of key parts of the Chinese Ministry of Foreign Affairs and Ministry of Foreign Trade and Economic Cooperation. Since these interpreters later go on to policy-making roles in their ministries, the programme now includes an element to teach the interpreters about key issues concerning the European Union and the world trading system. Almost 150 interpreters have now benefited from intensive training at the Commission's Joint Interpreting and Conference Service. Another important example has been a programme of customs cooperation, aiming to facilitate trade by supporting the modernisation of customs authorities in China.

The complaints of the international community about standards of IPR protection in China are well known. But if China's efforts to develop an effective legal framework for IPR protection are to succeed, they will need technical assistance from the international community. With this in mind, the EU and the European Patent Office launched an industrial property training programme in China in 1993. The objective of the programme was not only to help bring Chinese legislation into line with international norms, but to assist the institutions in charge of implementing the laws, to encourage the development of an industrial property profession, and to improve awareness about the importance of effective IPR protection to the healthy development of a modern economy. So a variety of training schemes and symposia were organised for officials, lawyers, judges and businessmen, as well as the provision of key documentation.

Another example has been an ongoing programme to train economists from key ministries involved in economic reform in China. This has combined an introductory course on the economies of the EU and a series of seminars with a month-long stage in important economic institutions in Europe. The objective is to help economists learn more about the realities of how market economies function in Europe. Issues of particular interest to China and with a particular EU interest, such as regional policy or monetary policy, are given special weight in the programme. Other training has been organised in the field of accountancy and financial management, customs administration, and cooperation between statistical authorities.

Finally, a series of activities have been developed to encourage business-to-business contact, facilitating the establishment of business cooperation between entrepreneurs from China and from Europe. Such action has largely taken the form either of participation at trade fairs, or of organising business meetings and seminars with complementary participants "matched" in advance. A particular stress has been put on actions involving small and medium sized companies. European companies have also become increasingly interested in the possibilities for developing joint ventures in China offered by the European Community Investment Partners (ECIP) facility, which provides a variety of grants and loans to encourage European firms to establish joint ventures in several Asian countries, including China. Over 100 companies or organisations have taken advantage of the ECIP scheme to encourage EU joint ventures in China. China is now proving the most popular destination for ECIP applicants.

*Science and Technology Cooperation with China*

Scientific cooperation between the Community and China began in 1984. For some years, the programme of cooperation centred on short-term activities including seminars and training. But in recent years, the focus has shifted to the implementation of joint research activities with a high added value scientific content and involving research institutes on topics of mutual interest. More than 70 joint research projects have been funded, notably in biotechnology applied to agriculture and medicine, health, thermonuclear fusion, and environmental sciences including global change, earth observation and monitoring, which have established firm foundations for cooperation. In addition, several scientific workshops on these sectors have been organised in China, and more than 150 young scientists have received research grants to work in a variety of European institutions and laboratories. Cooperation in the area of biotechnology, one of the core areas for cooperation with China, is coordinated by the EC-China Biotechnology Centre, a joint initiative set up in 1991 to act as an information bureau and a catalyst for EU/China interaction.

The onset of the Fourth Framework Programme (1994–1998) has introduced new possibilities for scientific cooperation with China, supporting innovative research, mobilising complementary skills, developing human capital, training young researchers and generally fostering a culture of research.

*Other cooperation*

Cooperation has been undertaken in sectors of economic significance to EU business. Industrial cooperation has been developed in a number of areas of technological importance, with direct industrial projects (such as in the field of computer integrated manufacturing), promotion of the use of European standards and localisation of European products (such as in the field of software), as well as research cooperation in the industrial environment. An important programme of telecommunications cooperation has been defined and launched in close cooperation with the State Science and Technology Commission (SSTC), the Ministry of Posts and Telecommunications, the Ministry of Electronics and Industry and the Ministry of Radio, Film and TV, including institutional strengthening of the SSTC's own information network. This programme concerns two major long-term initiatives in areas of advanced technology, to support the use of the GSM standard for mobile communications, and to develop digital audio and video broadcasting technology. Energy cooperation began as early as 1981, and has sought to encourage the development of energy policy-making in China, with technical assistance to energy resource development and training in best practice. Amongst specific projects has been support for the gas industry in exploration and extraction techniques. In all of these cases, a genuine mutual interest has resulted from the transfer of technology and know-how to China through the use of European products, making such products progressively more familiar to the Chinese market.

But cooperation has not been limited to areas of interest to business. Following contact between European and Chinese universities in 1986, a small-scale programme in the field of higher education was organised. This built on a fledgling network of European studies bodies in Chinese universities (the Chinese Society for EC Studies), seven of which are now European Documentation Centres. An annual programme was developed made up of a summer school for Chinese students, with European lecturers teaching European studies, and a number of scholarships for Chinese doctoral-level students. In 1994, an initiative was also launched in the context of the EU's worldwide programme to combat AIDS/HIV and sexually transmitted diseases. The objective is to support the Chinese government's efforts to build up an administrative and medical infrastructure to combat these diseases.

1 As incorporated in the Resolution adopted by the General Assembly of the United Nations.
2 Regulation 3420/83.

On this foundation, the Commission in 1998 issued a new communication, entitled 'Building A Comprehensive Partnership with China' (Document 3.3). Its purpose was to update and intensify the policy laid down in the 1995 Communication. It sought to take account of the encouragement of China's reform represented in the 1997 XVth Party Congress marking the assumption of power by Jiang Zemin, increasing signs of China's growing role in international and regional affairs, the Asian financial crisis and, in the EU, the advent of the single currency and future enlargement. It set the aim of building a comprehensive partnership with China, going far beyond trade. The basic principles were to engage China further in the international community, to support its transition to an open society, to integrate China further into the world economy through trade and support for domestic reform, and to make the best use of the EU's scarce resources and raise the EU profile in China.

**Document 3.3: Commission Communication, 'Building A Comprehensive Partnership with China' (1998)**

COMMUNICATION OF THE COMMISSION
Building a Comprehensive Partnership with China
COM(1998) 181, Brussels, 25.03.1998

**Summary**

China's development since embracing economic reform under Deng Xiaoping twenty years ago has been remarkable. The country is undergoing a dramatic internal transformation from a centrally-planned economy, largely closed off to the world, towards an increasingly market-driven one engaged in global commerce. This has been accompanied by a significant evolution in China's civil society, even if the full respect for universal standards in the field of human rights remains incomplete.

In 1995, the European Union responded to the economic and political challenges posed by the changes in China by drawing up a comprehensive policy for the future development of the EU's relations with China. It adopted, in the spirit of the "new Asia strategy" endorsed by the Essen European Council, a *Communication on a long-term policy for China-Europe relations* that has served the EU well, providing a useful roadmap for the future.

Most of the initiatives within the 1995 strategic document are already underway, while others have yet to mature. The analytical foundations of the 1995 Communication still hold true, and it therefore remains the platform on which the EU's policy towards China is built. However, several developments of such significance have occurred since 1995 that the EU should respond by upgrading and intensifying that policy further.

Firstly, the Chinese Government recently gave its strongest endorsement of market reform and global integration since reform was launched in 1978. The XVth Chinese Communist Party Congress in 1997 ushered in the post-Deng era by endorsing an ambitious economic and social reform agenda for the next five years. This can be seen as a clear signal of China's intention to consolidate, accelerate and complete the transition already underway.

Secondly, China has become at once more assertive and more responsible in its foreign policy, both regionally and globally. China's role in promoting peace in Korea and Cambodia reflects its renewed commitment to the development of Asia as a whole. An unprecedented series of summits between China and some of its key world partners over the last year have demonstrated China's wish to be recognised as a world power while reflecting a common perception among these partners that constructive engagement with China should become a key policy priority. The smooth and successful handover of Hong Kong to Chinese sovereignty in July 1997 was a particularly clear expression of China's increasingly mature and responsible approach to its changing role in the region and on the world stage.

Thirdly, the financial crisis that began to spread across Asia in 1997 has exposed serious structural weaknesses in the economies of some of China's neighbours and will inevitably have some impact on China itself. It could be seen as an early warning for China since it highlighted the risks associated with certain aspects of the development paths followed by other Asian countries. The crisis underlines the need for further reform and liberalisation within China to guard against similar problems arising in its own economy.

Finally, the EU itself is changing in ways that will lead China to adjust its own strategic vision of the European continent. The EU stands on the threshold of a single currency and enlargement eastwards, and with the Treaty of Amsterdam has equipped itself with new means to assert itself on the world stage.

Such developments call both for long-term vision and for active engagement. Engaging China's emerging economic and political power, as well as integrating China into the international community, may prove one of the most important external policy challenges facing Europe and other partners in the 21st century.

This Communication seeks to meet that challenge by building upon the analysis of China's political and economic development set out in the 1995 document in order to set the priorities for a new, comprehensive EU-China partnership.

The new EU-China partnership will aim at:

- Engaging China further, through an upgraded political dialogue, in the international community
- Supporting China's transition to an open society based upon the rule of law and the respect for human rights
- Integrating China further in the world economy by bringing it more fully into the world trading system and by supporting the process of economic and social reform underway in the country
- Making Europe's funding go further
- Raising the EU's profile in China.

**A. Engaging China further in the international community**

China's emergence as an increasingly confident world power is of immense historic significance, both to Europe and to the international community as a whole. China has become a major partner in a world increasingly bound together by the forces of globalisation. The EU's prime objectives must be to see China integrated rapidly and fully into the international community, both politically and economically, and to support its transition towards an open society based upon the rule of law: this will facilitate both development in China and greater global stability.

The EU is committed to a strategy of comprehensive engagement with China. This should be achieved through a renewed and upgraded EU-China bilateral political dialogue, as well as through the greater involvement of China in both regional and multilateral initiatives of global interest.

*A.1 Upgrading the EU-China political dialogue*

China's willingness to play a greater role on the world stage has been demonstrated recently by an unprecedented series of bilateral summits with Japan, Russia and the US, giving each of these key partners the chance to display publicly their shared commitment to China.

Up until 1994, the EU's political dialogue with China was limited to short annual meetings in the margins of the United Nations General Assembly. The EU has steadily intensified this political dialogue, following an exchange of letters in 1994. The time has now come for the EU and China to raise the status of their relationship by holding annual summits at Head of State and Government level, encouraging contacts at ministerial level, and by holding meetings between Political Directors in a similar vein to contacts with other key partners. Annual EU-China Summits would put the EU-China relationship on a commensurate footing with the EU's approach towards other major international partners such as the US, Japan and Russia, raise the profile of the EU in China and vice versa, as well as injecting added momentum into the negotiation and resolution of key issues in the EU-China relationship.

*A.2 Building upon the ASEM process*

The Asia-Europe Meetings (ASEM) process, launched in Bangkok in 1996, has developed into a broad forum for in-depth consultations between European and Asian partners at political and expert level, and has stimulated a wide series of cooperation initiatives. By virtue of its informal nature and the variety of issues addressed in its framework, ASEM has added a new dimension to the EU-China relationship. China has taken a constructive approach in the process and has been particularly active in all ASEM economic cooperation initiatives.

Dialogue with China should be upgraded in the context of the EU's broader regional strategy towards Asia as embodied in ASEM. The EU should aim to encourage China's continued commitment to taking an active part in ASEM and the ASEM follow-up process. Promoting dialogue with China on sustainable development in the Asia region, addressing the issue of maritime security in the Asia region, combating illegal drugs trafficking, coping with the effects of the Asian financial crisis and addressing the issue of arms control and non-proliferation are prime examples where the EU should seek China's active involvement in ASEM.

*A.3 Addressing global issues*

Over recent years China has been forging a more coherent and outward-looking foreign policy to match its growing economic weight. The EU should build on this by encouraging China to play a proactive and responsible role in global issues.

The EU should engage China, a permanent member of the United Nations Security Council, in dialogue on major UN developments, in particular UN reform.

The EU should endeavour to raise issues related to China more regularly during G7/8 meetings. It should also work to intensify the increasingly substantial dialogue with China launched by the OECD in 1995.

China's status as a nuclear power gives particular importance to its disarmament and non-proliferation policy. In recent years, China has taken the welcome steps of joining the Nuclear Non-Proliferation Treaty, the Chemical Weapons Convention, the Biological Weapons Convention and the Zangger Committee (a nuclear export control regime), as well as respecting key provisions of the Missile Technology Control Regime. It also signed the Comprehensive Nuclear Test Ban Treaty. Continued support and encouragement should be given to Beijing's greater involvement in multilateral negotiations on such issues. Europe should also establish dialogue with China on the anti-personnel landmines issue, urging it to adopt a permanent export ban and to engage positively in the international process to eliminate these weapons.

Illegal immigration and international crime are issues of grave concern both to China and the EU. The EU should promote a substantial dialogue and encourage cooperation with China on combating illegal drug trafficking, money-laundering, organised crime and illegal immigration. Previous EU experience in other third countries on such issues could constitute a useful platform on which to consider launching specific cooperation initiatives in China.

The EU will continue to take every opportunity, within the political dialogue, to raise human rights issues in addition to the specific bilateral dialogue on human rights detailed in section B of this communication.

The way China's economy develops, its energy demand increases, and the pace of rapid industrialisation continues, is having a profound environmental impact at the national, regional, and global level. The EU should aim to ensure China's continued commitment to addressing world environmental challenges such as global warming and greenhouse gas emissions, not least through EU funded cooperation projects mentioned in section C2. In particular, the EU should encourage China's further involvement in the pursuit of global environmental objectives in the context of the 1992 Rio Earth Summit and its follow up, notably in the area of climate change.

*A.4 Fostering dialogue on Asian regional issues*

The EU has a role to play in maintaining stability in the Asian region through the non-violent resolution of conflicts there, notably as a participant in ASEAN-sponsored regional fora. China shares its frontiers with fourteen countries and has unresolved border disputes with some of them. The growing demand for a multilateral security dialogue in East Asia provides opportunities for Europe to increase its overall influence in the region. As the ASEAN Regional Forum (ARF)[1] develops further, and as China shows willingness to engage further in confidence-building measures in Asia, the EU should use this forum more systematically to discuss security issues with China.

Europe, a key contributor to the Korean Peninsula Economic Development Organisation (KEDO) and a major provider of food aid to North Korea, has a clear interest in the peaceful resolution of the Korean question, as does China. The Korean peninsula should be among key issues that feature in the EU's regular dialogue with China.

Likewise, the EU and China could consider launching a dialogue on other countries in the region, such as Cambodia, Vietnam and Burma, where China has strong influence.

China's increasing reliance on energy imports from Central Asia is bound to make it perceive stability in the region as a strategic priority. Given the EU's own strategic interest in Central Asia and privileged relationship with Russia, developments in Central Asia should be addressed at the appropriate time and in the appropriate forum.

Recent indications of an improvement in relations across the Taiwan Straits and the prospect of a more open and direct dialogue between Beijing and Taipei are encouraging. As before, the EU should welcome any steps which can be taken to further the process of peaceful reconciliation.

*A.5 Underpinning autonomy in Hong Kong and Macau*

Strong economic links and historical ties with Hong Kong and Macau make it inevitable that Europe will continue to take an active interest in the two territories, not least in view of the latter's handover in 1999. In the spirit of its 1997 Communication entitled *"The European Union and Hong Kong: Beyond 1997"*[2], the EU should seek to underpin further the autonomous responsibilities of the Hong Kong Special Administrative Region, following the smooth handover in July 1997 and the successful management of the post-handover period so far. The Commission will publish an annual report on EU-Hong Kong relations. It will also aim to ensure that the EC-Macau Trade and Cooperation Agreement remains fully implemented after Macau's handover to support Macau's autonomous responsibilities. Hong Kong and Macau have important roles to play as gateways to other regions of China, and the EU should develop bilateral cooperation initiatives with both territories.

The EU considers the continued expression of differing opinions through the media and other channels in Hong Kong to be a healthy sign of political maturity. The EU will continue to watch the electoral process in Hong Kong closely, placing particular emphasis on the EU's support for the eventual development of universal suffrage in the SAR.

Proposed initiatives:

- Propose annual EU-China Summits and other top-level meetings as well as EU-China Political Directors' meetings
- Enhance still further China's involvement in ASEM
- Cooperate on the future of the UN
- Raise awareness of China-related issues within G7, and encourage further dialogue between China and OECD
- Propose dialogue on non-proliferation and cooperate on reinforcing related export controls
- Urge China to integrate fully into the global arms control process, notably to introduce a permanent ban on the export of anti-personnel landmines
- Cooperate on combating drug trafficking, money-laundering, crime and illegal immigration
- Raise the issue of human rights within the political dialogue
- Develop dialogue on environment and sustainable development
- Discuss Asian regional security with China
- Develop dialogue with China on Korean peninsula, Central and South-East Asia
- Work to underpin autonomy of Hong Kong
- Ensure a smooth transfer of sovereignty in Macau in 1999 and develop cooperation with Macau

1) The ASEAN Regional Forum (ARF) was established in 1994 as a forum bringing together intra and extra regional powers to examine issues of security in the Asia-Pacific region with a view to maintain peace and stability. It comprises the nine ASEAN member States, the ten ASEAN dialogue partners (Australia, Canada, China, South Korea, United States, India, Japan, New Zealand, Russia and the European Union) and the two ASEAN observers (Cambodia and Papua New Guinea).
2) COM (97) 171 final, 23.04.1997.

**B. Supporting China's transition to an open society based on the rule of law and the respect for human rights**

China is still far from meeting internationally accepted standards on human rights. Serious shortcomings in China's human rights record remain, including in such areas as the suppression of freedoms among certain ethnic minorities and political dissidents, use of enforced prison labour, a still under-developed system of rule of law, and the extensive use of the death penalty. These remain matters of grave concern to the EU, its Institutions and public opinion at large.

Nonetheless, the situation of human rights in China has improved over the last twenty years. Economic reform has introduced greater freedom of choice in education, employment, housing, travel and other areas of social activity. China has passed new civil and criminal laws to protect citizens' rights and has signed several key instruments bringing the country closer to international norms. It has also taken steps to develop the electoral process at local level, allowing villagers to designate their local authorities.

A commitment to universally recognised human rights and fundamental freedoms lies at the heart of the EU's policy world-wide. Full respect for these principles is inextricably linked to economic development and prosperity, as well as the long-term social and political stability of any country.

The challenge for China now is to sustain economic growth and preserve social stability while creating an open society based on the rule of law. If Europe wishes to have a role in this process, it should continue to use all available channels to promote the cause of human rights in China in an active, sustained and constructive way. The resumption of the EU-China human rights dialogue without any pre-conditions gives the EU a real opportunity to pursue intense discussions which, coupled with specific cooperation projects, remains at present the most appropriate means of contributing to human rights in China.

*B.1 Promoting human rights through open debate…*

The EU believes in the merits of dialogue, in all appropriate fora, over confrontation. The EU and China should therefore tackle their differences in a frank, open and respectful manner.

An EU-China specific dialogue on human rights was launched in 1995 and interrupted in the Spring of 1996. Since its resumption in November 1997, China has shown a new-found willingness to engage in a serious and results-oriented dialogue. All subjects of concern, even the most sensitive ones, have been addressed during the discussions and the prospect of continued, regular dialogue has now been established. Furthermore, this dialogue has enabled the EU to obtain China's agreement in principle on a cooperation programme designed to strengthen the rule of law and promote civil, political, economic and social rights. Since the dialogue resumed, China has given a series of encouraging signals, including its decision to sign the UN Covenant on Economic, Social and Cultural Rights. China has also given an undertaking to examine the UN Covenant on Civil and Political Rights with a view to signing it, and has increased dialogue with the UN authorities in the field of human rights.

The EU will continue to urge China to sign and ratify the UN Covenant on Civil and Political Rights, to ratify the UN Covenant on Economic, Social and Cultural Rights and to fully implement both covenants. Furthermore, the EU will encourage enhanced cooperation with specialised UN bodies and raise all issues of concern, including the plight of certain Chinese citizens.

As it attaches great importance to the respect for the cultural, linguistic and religious identity of ethnic minorities, the EU will continue to raise issues relating to these matters in Tibet within the bilateral dialogue on human rights.

Finally, the Commission will continue to press, within the International Labour Organisation, for the ratification by all members, including China, of the ILO conventions on core labour standards, including those on freedom of association, the right to collective bargaining, the prohibition of forced labour, of exploitative child labour and anti-discrimination.

*B.2 ... and through cooperation*

The resumption of the EU-China dialogue on human rights has placed renewed emphasis on the constructive resolution of differences. This gives the European Union a chance to put its good intentions into practice and deliver tangible assistance. Two major priorities should be pursued:

- **Promoting the rule of law**. The EU should help China's efforts to develop a society based on the rule of law. Developing a sound and transparent legal framework, both in the civil and criminal sphere, providing rights to Chinese citizens – including the right to a fair trial – making them aware of those rights, and training lawyers and judges, would help achieve this goal as a first step. The EU is currently devising an ambitious programme of legal and judicial cooperation with these objectives in mind which will be discussed with Chinese authorities and ready for implementation by Autumn 1998.
- **Strengthening civil society**. The EU should aim to strengthen those practices which make up the fabric of a strong civil society. It should promote civil and political rights through initiatives such as the support for a training centre in China for officials engaged in the implementation of the village governance law. It could also allow for assistance to the most vulnerable groups in society, including ethnic minorities, women – as a follow up to the Beijing 1995 conference on Women – and children. Initiatives aimed at promoting consumers' rights and at supporting consumers' organisations could also be a way of strengthening civil society. The role of Non-Governmental Organisations in implementing projects aimed at strengthening civil society should be fully exploited.

Proposed initiatives:

- Urge China to sign, ratify and fully implement UN Covenants on human rights and ILO conventions on core labour standards
- Reinforce bilateral human rights dialogue with China
- Back up dialogue with concrete cooperation programmes
- Promote rule of law
- Strengthen civil society

**C. Integrating China further in the world economy**

The scale and speed of China's economic growth are making it one of Europe's major economic partners. China's trade with the world has almost doubled in value over the last five years, and it now runs a massive trade surplus both with Europe and with the United States. It has become the second largest recipient of foreign direct investment in the world after the United States, and the tenth largest trading nation. It is forecast by the World Bank to become one of the top three traders in the world by 2020.

China's unprecedented economic development has required a delicate balance between rapid economic growth, far-reaching reforms and the need to preserve social cohesion. This process has potential repercussions both for China and for the world economy, and it is in Europe's overwhelming interest that this transition be nurtured right through to its fruition, making China a strong, stable and open partner.

It is the EU's view that the objective of assisting China to become a global economic player fully integrated in the world economy and able to comply with common rules should be achieved through a combination of trade discussions and targeted cooperation initiatives. This strategic approach should seek to accelerate and consolidate China's integration into the world trading system while supporting the reforms that are so vital for China to thrive within that system.

*C.1 Bringing China into the world trading system*

EU-China trade has increased more than twenty-fold since the beginning of the reforms, making China the EU's third extra-European trading partner and creating vast potential for European trade and investment there. The EU's trade deficit with China reached 20 billion ECU in 1997, reflecting China's growing export capacity as well as the obstructive effect of market barriers in China itself. The EU should use all available channels, notably China's WTO accession process and the EU's bilateral trade negotiations, to iron out such barriers and help create an open Chinese economy that benefits European and global interests alike. Improving the climate for European investment in China should also be one of the EU's top objectives.

1.1. Supporting China's accession to the WTO

The EU remains one of the keenest advocates of China's early accession to the WTO. It will provide an important boost for China's economic reform and will signal strenghtened international confidence in the reform process. It will also cement China's place in the global economy and provide traders and investors with greater certainty when doing business in China. Furthermore, striking the right terms of accession for China will be a determining factor in the pace and scope of further multilateral trade Rounds.

Financial turbulence in Asia has triggered a crisis of confidence in several Asian economies which could have spillover effects in China. Against this background, China has a prime interest in demonstrating its continued commitment to the WTO accession process as a means of sustaining outside confidence in the fundamental health and dynamism of the economy. Closing markets or delaying reforms would be a misguided and counterproductive response to financial market instability.

China has made significant progress in recent years to liberalise its trade regime and open its economy to the world. Whether on tariff cuts, currency reform or the development of the legal system, the pace of change has been remarkable, and together, the EU and China are progressing towards a trade relationship which should culminate in China's membership of the WTO. However, for this goal to be achieved, sustained efforts still need to be made by China to respect the following commitments:

- Meet key WTO principles such as:

  **transparency**, including prompt publication of all relevant laws and regulations, clear licensing criteria and better identification of the authorities responsible for granting licences.

**national treatment**, notably by offering the same operational conditions to foreign companies as to domestic ones.

**non-discrimination** against EU companies vis-à-vis those of other trading partners.

- Offer real market access for industrial and agricultural goods by cutting tariffs significantly – including the removal of tariff "peaks" (duties of 15% and higher) and adherence to the Information Technology Agreement – and by removing all quotas, unjustified technical barriers to trade and other non-tariff measures. This should be achieved as a follow-up to the conceptual breakthrough negotiated by the European Commission with China in October 1997, in which a series of precise principles were agreed which provide clear parameters in which the negotiations on China's detailed tariff commitments are being pursued.
- Rapidly remove the current monopolies on foreign trade so that all Chinese or foreign nationals in China can engage in import and export.
- Provide substantial opening of China's services market in distribution, telecoms, financial services, professional services, tourism, travel and medical services. China is today moving into a new phase of economic development in which services will be the engine of future growth. Foreign companies would bring vast assets to China in terms of jobs, technology, on-the-job training and management skills.
- Open the financial sector (banking, securities and insurance) in a more systematic and comprehensive, if gradual, manner. This would boost China's long-term growth and outside confidence in the economy, and can be pursued without prompting uncontrollable capital movements and excessive volatility. It is also in China's interest to set up a proper regulatory framework and independent supervisory authority.
- Improve the conditions for foreign companies establishing in China. This includes removing all restrictions on the legal form of establishment (whether as a joint venture or a wholly-owned company), lifting geographic restrictions and those on the scope of permitted activity, and removing pre-establishment conditions. It also includes the removal of export performance requirements and export subsidies.
- Eliminate WTO-incompatible measures designed to promote priority industries.
- Rapid implementation of the WTO TRIPS Agreement and full enforcement and protection of intellectual property rights.
- Establish a transparent, open and competitive procurement regime. A key objective in this regard would be to secure China's membership of the WTO Agreement on Government Procurement as part of the WTO accession package. China has the largest procurement market in the world and failure to obtain access to that market would significantly reduce the overall value of the market access package.
- Join the WTO-related Civil Aircraft Code.

The EU's approach during the accession negotiations should continue to be characterised by the following features:

Firstly, the EU must negotiate resolutely to secure firm and viable market opening commitments commensurate with China's stage of development, potential and size, in order to make China's accession a lasting success.

Secondly, the EU has developed the concept that part of the final package may require the use of clearly defined transition periods for sectors where China needs to phase in its WTO obligations beyond the date of accession while adjusting its laws and practices. This approach has been put forward by the EU to respect China's own policy of implementing reforms gradually.

Thirdly, the EU should encourage China to anticipate accession by setting as an early priority the amendment of domestic laws and regulations that affect foreign investment, the aim being to make its investment regime less restrictive, more unified and its evolution more predictable.

Finally, the EU should be on hand to assist China as it makes the necessary adjustments, whether through cooperation or by offering practical assistance during the negotiations themselves. The EU is already drawing up a series of cooperation programmes designed to support China's reforms during and beyond the accession process, especially while it is adapting to WTO disciplines during transition periods. This initiative will include programmes to raise awareness of WTO principles – such as on intellectual property, public procurement, norms and standards, and customs – among Chinese officials at all levels of government and business executives, as well as aligning China's legislative and regulatory framework with WTO rules. WTO will also be a central theme in a broader training programme for the Chinese administration. Furthermore, the EU will develop a specific post-accession dialogue with China to ensure the implementation of its WTO commitments both during the phasing-in period and beyond.

The EU is ready to conclude the negotiations as soon as China shows it can offer genuine market opening, if necessary phased in gradually according to an agreed timetable, and ensure that the country becomes an open, proactive and forward-looking WTO member ready to participate in further liberalisation. Above all, China's WTO accession should not be seen as a new constraint imposed by the outside world on China, but rather as a supportive process which will strengthen its own internal reform programme.

1.2. Strengthening the bilateral trade agenda

The EU has a long history of trade relations with China, as embodied within the 1985 EC-China Trade and Cooperation Agreement and the EC-China Joint Committee meetings. Bilateral trade discussions should be pursued alongside the WTO process as an effective means of exchanging information and resolving bilateral issues. They provide a useful forum for ensuring strict adherence to the principle of non-discrimination, for example in fields such as maritime transport and financial services. Issues pursued within this bilateral dialogue should dovetail with the EU's Market Access Strategy, launched in 1996 to target the removal of obstacles to EU exports and investments world-wide. In parallel, the EU should use this bilateral channel to gain information concerning the implementation of China's WTO commitments and to ensure that these commitments are given concrete effect.

China is, by far, the main beneficiary of the EU's Generalised Scheme of tariff Preferences (GSP), with more than 30% of the value of all beneficiaries' imports in 1997. However, the implementation of the scheme's graduation mechanism (in which GSP advantages for certain sectors are withdrawn due to the high level of industrial development in those sectors) will necessarily reduce the advantages previously enjoyed by China. Nevertheless, the new GSP special incentive arrangements (social and environmental clauses), will allow beneficiary countries to obtain an additional preferential margin, provided they meet international standards of labour rights (International Labour Organisation standards on child labour, freedom of association and rights of bargaining) and environmental protection (International Timber Organisation standards on sustainable management of tropical forests). In the event of applications from China, the Commission will examine carefully if China meets the requested standards.

The European Commission has proposed amendments to the EC anti-dumping legislation vis-à-vis China that take account of the market reforms underway in the country. The proposal includes the removal of the label "non-market economy" which applies to China under the current legislation, by instituting a new case-by-case approach in anti-dumping proceedings whereby Chinese exporters, who are found to operate within clearly defined market economy conditions, will be granted market economy treatment. This means that the domestic prices and costs of such exporters will be used to establish normal value rather than information from a market analogue third country.

The proposal also introduces a more systematic approach to the granting of individual treatment and calculation of comparative advantage. The proposal will reflect the specific behaviour and operating conditions of individual firms, whilst at the same time acting as an incentive for further reforms among Chinese companies. As such, it will interact positively with the ongoing WTO accession negotiations.

The EU has confirmed to China that it is ready to phase out its quantitative restrictions on Chinese products as rapidly as China is able to remove its own. The removal of both sets of quantitative restrictions should be pursued as part of an overall market opening strategy and in the context of the WTO accession negotiations.

The Commission and Member States need to be fully updated at all stages on commercial legislation and administrative practice governing trade in goods and services in China. A strengthening of coordination and the regular exchange of detailed information between the Member States' Embassies and the Commission's Delegation in Beijing would make for a more efficient and focused bilateral trade dialogue.

1.3 Promoting investment

The development of Foreign Direct Investment (FDI) has been a key element of China's economic growth since it engaged in reforms in 1978. For several years, China has been the largest recipient of FDI among developing countries, and has now become the second largest recipient of FDI, after the United States. Investments originating in the Asia-Pacific region, notably from Hong Kong and Taiwan, dominate FDI in China, thus highlighting the regional dimension of China's integration into the world economy. The Asian financial crisis, which will reduce incoming FDI in China, makes it all the more important for China to further attract investment from its other partners, especially Europe and the United States.

The EU should aim at improving the investment environment for European companies in China. The construction of a sound and transparent regulatory framework for investment and a better enforcement of Chinese regulations on intellectual property rights are prime examples to achieve this objective.

The EU trade policy must be backed up by a comprehensive strategy to promote investment, as well as business and industrial cooperation with China, so as to strengthen the European presence in the Chinese market. The EU should launch such a strategy, focusing primarily on those industrial sectors – such as telecommunications, energy, environmental technology and services, transport and financial services – where Europe has a clear competitive advantage *(see also section C.2)*. The EU should strengthen the EU's export and investment promotion facilities for China, in particular the *European Community Investment Partners* (ECIP) programme, which aims at supporting the creation of joint-ventures between European and Chinese companies in China, and the *Asia-Invest* programme, which aims at helping European small and medium-sized enterprises identify potential partners in China. The EU should continue to devote particular attention to small and medium-sized enterprises in its business and investment promotion strategy in China.

1.4 Developing bilateral agreements

The EU-China trade dialogue could be further strengthened through the conclusion of specific bilateral agreements in areas of particular interest, such as:

- **Maritime transport**. A sectoral agreement on maritime transport, for which the Commission has a negotiating mandate, should aim to strengthen cooperation with China and improve market access conditions for European operators in China. The EU intends to base this agreement on the principles of freedom to provide maritime services, free access to cargo activities and unrestricted access to ancillary services. The agreement may provide for the establishment of a Working Party which could report to the Joint Committee set up under the EC-China Trade and Economic Cooperation Agreement.
- Air transport. The conclusion of a Memorandum of Understanding between the Commission, China and the European Association of Aeronautical Industry on Industrial Cooperation in the Aeronautical Sector could be a starting point for cooperation in the field of air safety, environment and infrastructure. This cooperation should be accompanied by the commencement of a dialogue in aviation matters.
- Nuclear trade and safety. The Commission should study the merits of negotiating a bilateral agreement with China in areas related to nuclear trade and nuclear safety in the framework of the Euratom Treaty. China's policy on nuclear non-proliferation is a key issue that should be taken into account in such an analysis.
- **Customs**. The Commission has been authorised to negotiate an agreement on customs cooperation and mutual administrative assistance. This will serve the dual purpose of facilitating trade between the EU and China on the one hand, and creating a framework through which to fight customs-related fraud on the other.
- Science and technology. A specific EU-China science and technology agreement should be concluded in order to enhance and expand cooperation in fields such as energy, environment, life sciences, material sciences, transport, telematics, information and communication technologies. It will strengthen the presence of European economic operators in China.

1.5 Making financial liberalisation and regulation go hand in hand

The creation of a sound financial environment is vital to sustain the confidence of investors and traders in China. The financial crisis that has struck some of China's neighbours in 1997 can be seen as an early warning signal from which China can learn. It throws into sharp relief the need for China to build a solid, transparent and open financial and banking system, and to make bank lending market-driven and commercially viable in order to avoid exposure to weaknesses similar to those of other Asian economies in future.

Together with the reform of its State-owned enterprises, China has embarked on an ambitious reform of its financial system. This includes the creation of a sound regulatory framework for financial activities. The EU fully supports this and is ready to offer China, through cooperation projects, its own expertise in financial regulation and prudential supervision. This should also be pursued through any initiative which could be taken within ASEM.

At the same time, the EU should seek to persuade China that liberalisation of its financial services markets – notably market access for foreign financial service providers in banking, insurance and securities – would strengthen the wider banking reforms. It would increase liquidity, prompt a more viable and effective allocation of credit within the economy, raise standards and increase available expertise, boosting jobs and growth in the process. An early commitment to include financial services within China's WTO offer would increase investor confidence at a time when it is severely lacking in some of China's neighbours. This would not entail any sudden exposure to market risk, as the EU has not suggested that China should introduce full freedom of capital movement in the near future.

1.6 Promoting the euro

The advent of Economic and Monetary Union makes it important for the EU to inform China of the major changes EMU will bring to its economic ties with Europe, as well as to the international financial system itself. In parallel with its commitment to the construction of a sound and open financial and banking system in China, the EU should establish a regular EU-China macro-economic dialogue. This dialogue should aim, *inter alia*, at informing China – which already has the world's second largest foreign currency reserves – about EMU and about the potential of the euro as a stable reserve currency.

Within the information campaign on the euro launched towards third countries, special attention should be given to China.

Proposed initiatives:

- Give continued impetus to WTO accession negotiations until a viable accession package is achieved
- Allow China to benefit from transition periods while certain sectors adapt to WTO obligations
- Offer China cooperation projects to help its economy adapt to WTO obligations
- Re-activate bilateral trade talks to exchange information and resolve issues of mutual concern
- Use bilateral trade talks to cement commitments made in the WTO process and improve synergy of these talks with the EU's market access strategy
- Adopt the Commission's proposed new anti-dumping regulation towards China and Russia
- Pursue gradual and reciprocal removal of EU and Chinese quantitative restrictions
- Develop a comprehensive EU investment promotion strategy and business and industrial cooperation in China
- Develop bilateral agreements in specific sectors
- Urge China to liberalise financial services in step with reform of its financial system and provide relevant EU expertise
- Inform China about the importance of the Euro as a stable reserve currency

*C.2. Supporting economic and social reform*

China's reforms are radically changing the economic and social landscape of the country. The pace of reform is impressive, but the process remains fragile and incomplete. The challenge for China is to pursue its economic transition whilst at the same time integrating the concept of sustainability into economic growth and guarding itself against social instability. The EU should therefore not just seek to negotiate the removal of trade and investment obstacles, but also help China build the institutions, policies, human resources, management techniques and other flanking instruments that constitute the fabric of a modern, outward-looking economy.

The resources available for this process will always be small in comparison with the needs. If the EU is to maximise the impact of these resources, cooperation needs to be concentrated on a small number of key objectives.

The five traditional pillars of EU-China cooperation set out in the 1995 Communication – human resources development, administrative and social reforms, business and industrial cooperation, environmental cooperation, rural and urban poverty alleviation – have stood the test of time through the successful implementation of a range of projects, and the principles behind the 1995 long-term strategy will continue to underpin the EU's approach to its cooperation programme. This approach was further developed in the EC-China Memorandum of Understanding on the programming of EC-China cooperation projects signed in Beijing in October 1997 between the Commission and the Chinese Authorities.

Given the pace of change in China, it is important to further update the objectives of the EU-China cooperation programme in keeping with the reforms taking place in China. The following specific priorities – to which must be added WTO-related cooperation projects (section C.1.1) and human rights cooperation projects (section B) – should be highlighted:

1. **Side-effects of company restructuring**. China is restructuring many of the State-Owned Enterprises (SOEs) which still form the core of its industry. This process of unprecedented scale and complexity could have major social and political side-effects. The EU should not try to address all aspects of a reform process of this magnitude, but rather focus on limited priorities, in close coordination with other donors, notably the World Bank. From its experience with restructuring and privatisation, both within the EU and in Central and Eastern Europe and the New Independant States, the EU would be well placed to offer its expertise as China introduces new models of ownership, corporate governance, accounting and management. The EU could also help China address welfare reform, which is one major fall-out of SOE restructuring since the Chinese welfare system in urban centres is largely taken care of by SOEs themselves. In keeping with China's desire to minimise the social side-effects of economic reform, and in order to contribute to urban poverty alleviation, the EU could help China in its search for new models of welfare, including medical care, social security, unemployment insurance and pensions.

2. **Financial reform**. China has wisely embarked on the reform of its financial system, whose fate is closely linked to that of the debt-ridden state-owned enterprises. A sound, transparent and market-driven banking system is indispensable for the creation of a sustainable economy. The EU – in close cooperation with both international and Member States' financial institutions responsible for financial supervision and prudential standards – should help China to develop the kind of rules, supervisory mechanisms and prudential standards that will enable it to guard against structural weaknesses exposed elsewhere during the Asian financial crisis.

3. **Industrial cooperation**. Sectoral cooperation schemes focusing on those sectors where EU industry has clear competitive and technological advantages and China has specific needs should be developed as a way of tackling issues such as regulation, the definition of common norms and standards, the development of mutually recognised certification procedures, the integration of cleaner production processes, as well as industrial and commercial training. Administrations, regulatory bodies, and industries from both sides should be involved in this exercise. Small and medium-sized enterprises should be encouraged to participate in this process. Priorities for forthcoming initiatives could include telecommunications, information technologies and aeronautics.

4. **Business dialogue**. The EU should support a greater involvement of European business and industry in China. A business dialogue should bring together EU executives and Chinese businessmen and policy-makers in order to increase awareness of China's

transition process and provide expertise on market reform. The results of this dialogue should also be used to identify further priorities for EU trade policy and cooperation initiatives.

5. **Legal and administrative reform**. The EU should back up its bilateral and multilateral trade negotiations with concrete assistance to China in reforming and modernizing the overall legal and administrative framework of its economy. Definition and enforcement of legislation – for example in intellectual property, company law and public procurement – as well as administrative organisation and management should be among the specific targets. The EU's continued support to the construction of a sound and competitive procurement regime would, in particular, increase industrial competitiveness and help China establish a modern and efficient public sector.

6. **Training**. Cooperation should help China strengthen its own training capacities by proposing modern professional training standards and practices. This should address the needs of both administration and industry. Vocational training programmes for industry would both help up-grade the quality of manpower in China and promote European management practices, technical know-how and standards, thus facilitating European investment. Likewise, training initiatives for public servants would help them face the challenges of a market-driven economy open to the world.

7. **Science and technology.** Scientific and technological cooperation should be used more actively as a means to strengthen European companies' position on the Chinese market as well as supporting China's own economic development. It should focus on agriculture, information and communication technologies, biotechnology, material sciences, transport, energy, the environment and natural resources. A specific EC-China Science and Technology Agreement should be negotiated rapidly *(see Section C I.4)*, and a web of partnerships should be created to allow the exchange of young scientists, managers and engineers in selected economic sectors.

8. **Environment**. China has become increasingly aware of the environmental cost of its former industrial model, and of its impact on the global environment. It is now seeking to reconcile rapid growth with sustainable production and consumption patterns. The EU should, along the lines set out in the *Communication on a Europe-Asia Cooperation Strategy in the Field of Environment* develop cooperation projects focusing on clean production methods, waste minimisation, environmental standards and training, and environmental management capacities as well as appropriate technology transfer. The EU should in particular help China integrate environmental priorities – such as the prevention of industrial pollution and greenhouse gas emissions, and the conservation of biological diversity – further into national economic policy-making processes and into development schemes at regional and local levels. Where desirable, and in line with the Chinese objective of reducing poverty, environmental conservation and poverty alleviation projects should be integrated together.

9. **Energy**. Europe should offer its environmental and energy know-how to China to help it develop efficient and clean industries and also to establish a presence in its potentially lucrative market for green technology, along the lines set out in the Commission's *Communication on a Europe-Asia Cooperation Strategy for Energy* Promoting energy efficiency, as well as developing clean coal technologies and alternative energy resources, notably natural gas, should be top priorities. The EU should seek to develop synergies with international financing institutions (IFIs) on these issues.

10. **Regional disparities, poverty alleviation and social cohesion**. Despite a significant rise in living standards, China is still a developing country. Rural and urban poverty are rife, China's vast floating population presents a serious threat to social stability and lasting economic prosperity, and disparities between advanced coastal regions and less developed inner provinces have become a key concern for both Chinese local and central authorities. The EU should help China accelerate the spread of prosperity across the country and improve regional and social cohesion through, inter alia, projects aimed at developing all communication links between coastal and less developed inland regions. This could in particular increase the attractiveness of inner regions for both Chinese and foreign investment.

Proposed initiatives:

- Provide expertise to reduce side-effects of company restructuring, notably welfare reform
- Provide expertise for financial sector reform
- Strengthen industrial and business cooperation
- Cooperate on legal and administrative framework
- Develop human resources cooperation with focus on professional training and exchange schemes
- Expand scientific and technological cooperation
- Promote sustainable development and help China integrate environmental policy concerns
- Foster transfer of know-how and technology in energy sector
- Develop cooperation to reduce regional disparities, alleviate poverty and improve social cohesion

**D. Making Europe's funding go further**

A comprehensive policy for relations with China needs to be backed up with the appropriate financial means to implement it. The EU's budgetary resources for China have more than tripled as a direct result of the policy launched in 1995, rising to around 70 million ECU per year up to 1999, from an annual average of 20 million ECU over the 1991–1994 period. This has enabled the EU to demonstrate its commitment to cooperation with China by pushing forward with the vast majority of new ideas proposed. As such, the current envelope appears sufficient at this stage to finance both the shorter and longer-term initiatives outlined in this Communication, so long as the budget is maintained for the 2000 to 2006 period.

Nevertheless, the EU should consider all possible avenues for improving the efficiency of its activities.

One key message of this Communication is that EU-funded cooperation programmes need to be even more closely linked with the EU's broader China policies. From the human rights dialogue through the WTO accession negotiations to questions relating to China's economic development, the EU should seize the chance to underscore its policies with concrete assistance projects where at all possible. The EU is emerging as one of the most important grant donors in China, and every effort should be deployed to maximise this advantage. Giving projects direct relevance to key policy objectives is one of the best ways of improving their efficiency. It is a simple exercise in value for money which could be achieved without increasing the overall budget allocated for China.

Like other international donors, the EU is continually looking for ways to improve the delivery of projects. So far, it has tended to concentrate on relatively high-budget programmes spread over several years. This maximises the impact of a cooperation budget which will remain small in relation to the needs of a country the size of China. Nevertheless, there are five important refinements that should be introduced:

Firstly, the EU faces an ever-increasing demand for supporting small but highly visible projects. Some of these initiatives – such as making European expertise available rapidly for the development of new legislation, professional training, networking with EU counterparts, organisation of seminars, and the production of information and communication material etc – have a potential impact going way beyond the small budget involved. The European Union should develop a facility whereby a selection of the very best of these smaller projects could be funded directly and rapidly from the Commission's Delegation in Beijing.

Secondly, synergy between the EU and Member States' cooperation programmes is still underdeveloped. Mechanisms for improving coordination, complementarity and possible joint projects should urgently be considered.

Thirdly, in view of the limits imposed by a relatively modest cooperation budget, the Commission has been exploring ways of collaborating more closely with international financing institutions. New opportunities have opened up for using EU grant-funded projects to prepare the way for larger funding from organisations such as the World Bank. In addition, the EU should envisage funding European experts in some of the Bank's policy related discussions with the Chinese government. This benefits all partners concerned and is particularly well suited to sectors like welfare reform, energy and the environment.

Fourthly, the European Investment Bank (EIB), which has a mandate for intervention in Asia up to the year 2000, has currently a modest degree of involvement in China. Up to now, it has launched one project – in the field of energy – with a budget of 50 Mecus. It appears, however, that there is room to improve the EIB's involvement in China within the existing mandate. This is even more important in the context of the World Bank's intention to scale down its development assistance through concessional financing and to abolish all concessional financing from 1999 onwards. The issue of the size and allocation of the EIB's financial envelope in Asia after the expiry of its present mandate remains open.

In order to ease the EIB's entry into China, make its lending more competitive and strengthen its implementing capacity, the Commission is ready to consider apportioning part of its cooperation budget to the EIB in order to fund feasibility studies and pre-investment analysis which would prepare the ground for EIB loans for projects of common interest implemented by institutional borrowers in China. An improved intervention of the EIB in China would increase the visibility of its cooperation work in China and raise the profile of its relations with the country more generally.

Fifthly, it is essential to continue close dialogue with the Chinese authorities in order to ensure that project development responds to shared objectives. This dialogue should encompass all phases of the project cycle, with particular attention put to the programming phase, as illustrated by the Memorandum of Understanding on programming of 1998 and 1999 cooperation signed in October 1997 between the Commission and the Chinese Authorities.

As a result of this dialogue, an early discussion and exchange of information with Member States on the basis of multi-annual programming would also contribute to increased synergies with Member States programmes. The same applies for the EIB, World Bank and other donors.

Proposed initiatives:

- Facilitate rapid funding of small, short-term projects out of Beijing
- Increase synergy between EU's China policy objectives and cooperation programmes
- Improve synergy with EU member states
- Investigate different means and approaches for collaboration with World Bank and other lenders
- Cooperate with EIB to expand EIB activities in China within existing mandate
- Strengthen regular dialogue with China on programming and project cycle, and ensure early information of Member States and IFIs

**E. Raising the profile of the European Union**

The reemergence of China is having a profound effect on public opinion. Few businesses, institutions or individual people outside China are not aware in some way of its rapidly growing profile on the world stage. For some it is perceived as an inexhaustible source of opportunities, others are more cautious in their assessment; most see it as a broadly positive development that requires a carefully balanced but decisive response from their public authorities, including the European Union. For such a response to be effective, it must be visible, not just in Europe, but in China and the world at large. Greater visibility will give the EU added weight in its dealings with China.

Close coordination within the EU itself will be needed if the EU is to raise its profile in China sucessfully. Annual summits and other high-level meetings with the Chinese leadership, of the kind recommended in section A.1 of this Communication, would go some way to improving visibility, and should be given adequate exposure to the media.

The EU should also upgrade its information policy towards China substantially. As a first step it should draw up its first-ever information strategy devoted solely to EU relations with China. The strategy should identify key target audiences within business, government, academia, NGOs, the media and other groups in order to diffuse information about the relationship. Such audiences should, where possible, be sought in China as well as in Europe. A new information strategy could include the following actions, among others:

Proposed initiatives:

- Set up a Commission Press and Information Service (SPI) in Beijing, to add to those already existing in Washington and Tokyo
- Expand the number of Chinese visitors travelling to Europe i.e. through the EU Visitors' Programme
- Increase the intensity of cultural exchange through schools, universities and other educational establishments
- Organise cultural initiatives such as exhibitions and explore means to develop future cooperation in the cultural field
- Increase the presence of the EU at conferences devoted to Chinese affairs and organise seminars and conferences on the subject of EU-China relations
- Expand cooperation with existing EU Studies Centres in Chinese universities and with the Chinese Society for EU Studies

**Conclusion**

China's growing political and economic self-confidence should serve as an incentive for the EU to engage the country more fully. Its growing strength has been matched, by and large, by a growing sense of responsibility. China's increasing assertiveness on the world stage therefore deserves a positive response from Europe. It also requires vision. This Communication seeks to set out that vision by laying the ground for a comprehensive partnership based on a set of specific, action-oriented initiatives.

The focal point of that vision must be to ensure the successful and lasting integration of China as an equal partner in the world economy. This should be coupled with an active commitment to creating a strong and open civil society based on fundamental freedoms and human rights, in step with China's move towards a market economy. China's WTO accession process, as well as the EU's bilateral trade agenda with China, remain key instruments, together with Europe's elaborate cooperation programme with China, to bring this to fruition. At the same time, the EU must be ready at short notice to adapt its policy to any unforeseen changes prompted by the speed and scope of China's transition.

Europe and China both stand on the threshold of critical change. This should give the former the added incentive to craft its own genuinely European strategy towards the latter.

Two years later, the Commission issued a report to the Council and the European Parliament on 'Implementation of the Communication "Building a Comprehensive Partnership with China"' (see Document 3.4). It reviewed the objectives of the 1998 Communication and the extent to which they had been met so far. Following the first and second EU–China summit meetings, it pointed in particular to the expansion of the EU's dialogues and other meetings with China, the promises and challenges of China's imminent accession to the WTO, and the review and expansion of EU–China cooperation programmes.

### Document 3.4: Commission Report, 'Implementation of the Communication "Building a Comprehensive Partnership with China"' (2000)

REPORT FROM THE COMMISSION TO THE COUNCIL
AND THE EUROPEAN PARLIAMENT
on the Implementation of the Communication
"Building a Comprehensive Partnership with China"
COM(2000) 552 final, Brussels 8.9.2000

**Executive Summary**

The main aims of the Commission's 1998 Communication <Building a Comprehensive Partnership with China>[1] were to engage China further in the international community, to support China's transition to an open society and to integrate China further into the global economy.

To achieve these aims, the Commission hoped, inter alia, to upgrade the political dialogue, encourage China's interest in ASEM and Asian regional issues, and strike the right terms for China's accession to the WTO. The Commission would also use the EU's experience and expertise to add value in assisting China's reform process, and to add human rights, the environment and sustainable development to the agenda.

Since the Communication was adopted, the EU-China relationship has greatly intensified. The first annual EU-China summits in 1998 and 1999 laid the groundwork for a more broadly based political dialogue. At the same time, an increasing succession of meetings and dialogues at all levels, and in numerous areas of concern both to the EU and to China, improved communication and promoted mutual understanding.

The agenda dialogue has been expanded to include regional security, economic and trade issues, and human rights. This could be broadened further, as noted in the 1998 Communication, to include other global issues such as illegal immigration and eventually drug-trafficking, money laundering and organised crime.

On 19 May 2000, the EU and China signed a Bilateral Agreement, paving the way for China's accession to the World Trading Organisation (WTO). Once China joins the WTO, a key challenge for the EU will be to develop mutually acceptable methods to monitor and assist with China's compliance with its WTO commitments. The EU will also continue to address remaining market access barriers.

The EU's Co-operation Programme with China has expanded steadily and now largely focuses on supporting sustainable development to assist China's overall reform process. The Programme's priorities and contents will be reviewed in order to keep up with the pace of constant change, as well as to improve the impact and visibility of EU assistance to China.

**Introduction**

On 25 March 1998, the European Commission adopted the Communication "*Building a Comprehensive Partnership with China*". The Communication was endorsed by the European Council of Ministers on 29 June 1998.

This Communication set out recommendations aimed at upgrading the EU's relationship with the People's Republic of China, and concluded "the Commission will regularly report to the Council and the European Parliament on the progress made in the implementation of the proposals of this Communication".

The production of this first report on the implementation of the new China strategy coincides with the twenty-fifth anniversary of the establishment of EC-China relations. It covers the period March 1998 to May 2000.

During the reporting period, the Chinese authorities have pursued structural reforms while continuing to promote economic growth. They have also taken steps to tackle corruption at all levels.

In 1999, GDP grew by 7,1%; lower growth than in recent, previous years. In the context of global trade, the Chinese Government enjoyed some successes, particularly the Sino-EU and Sino-US agreements on the conditions for China's accession to the WTO. On the domestic front, the restructuring of State Owned Enterprises remained at the core of the socio-economic reform agenda. During that period, the authorities dealt severely with democratic dissidents, religious groups and other movements

In reviewing the implementation of the recommendations, this report tries to identify, wherever possible, ways to take the EU-China partnership a further step forward.

The chapter headings A-E in this report correspond to those in the Communication itself.

**A. Engaging China further in the international community**

> "The EU is committed to a strategy of comprehensive engagement with China. This should be achieved through a renewed and upgraded EU-China bilateral political dialogue, as well as through the greater involvement of China in both regional and multilateral initiatives of global interest." COM (1998) 181, p. 5

*A.1 Upgrading the EU-China Political Dialogue*

The EU's own mechanisms and platforms for political dialogue with China developed fairly recently. The overall framework for the political dialogue was first formalised in 1994 through an exchange of letters, and the first-ever EU-China Summit, at heads of government level, took place on 2 April 1998 in London. It marked a response to China's increasing willingness to participate actively on the world stage. The second EU-China Summit took place on 21 December 1999, when President Prodi visited Beijing. These summits have provided a platform to give added momentum to the EU-China relationship, and to exchange views and raise issues of concern on political issues, human rights; economic and trade issues, including WTO accession; bilateral co-operation; and regional developments.

Meetings at Troika Foreign Minister level also took place in September 1998, March and September 1999, with the Chinese Foreign Minister.

Senior officials' meetings took place in October 1998 and June and October 1999, and provided opportunities to elicit Chinese views on regional issues such as ASEM; developments in the Korean peninsula; Japan; India-Pakistan relations; Indonesia and East Timor; Myanmar /Burma; and Taiwan.

Twice a year, EU Ambassadors in Beijing have had meetings with the Chinese Foreign Minister. In addition to the formal political dialogue, regular calls from the Troika Ambassadors on the Chinese Ministry of Foreign Affairs, as well as frequent, high-level, two-way visits, helped reinforce the EU-China political dialogue. In February 1998 and January 1999, Chinese Executive Vice-Prime Minister Li Lanqing and Vice-Premier Wu Bangguo, respectively, visited the European Commission. The President of the European Commission, Jacques Santer, visited China in November 1998. China's Prime Minister, Zhu Rongji, visited the Commission in Brussels on 11 July 2000. This was the first ever visit to the Commission by a Chinese Prime Minister.

The European Parliamentary Group with responsibility for Chinese affairs has met annually with members of the China National Peoples' Congress and there have been individual and group visits to China by MEPs. Further development of such contacts can only be valuable to the overall EU-China relationship.

Developments in China have also regularly featured on the agenda of the EU political dialogue with key partners such as the United States, Canada, Australia, Japan, India and Russia.

*A.2 Building upon the Asia-Europe Meetings (ASEM)*

The EU has encouraged China's integration in the ASEM process, covering a wide range of economic and political issues. China has taken a co-operative approach to ASEM since its launch and has been particularly keen on emphasising economic aspects -notably investment promotion. China has, however, taken a more cautious approach to discussing political issues. It took the welcome step of hosting an ASEM informal human rights seminar in Beijing in June 1999. It has also shown enthusiastic support to co-operation initiatives in fields such as science and technology. It initiated and hosted an *ASEM Science and Technology Ministerial Conference*, in October 1999 and will continue to play a leading role in this sector.

China has also actively participated in the *ASEM Trust Fund in* the financial sector and social policy reform processes, and contributed US$500,000 to the Fund.

*A.3 Addressing Global Issues*

During 1998, the EU engaged in an expert-level dialogue with China on arms control and non-proliferation. It is still at an early stage, but this dialogue has allowed useful exchanges of views on *the Comprehensive Test Ban Treaty*; the *Missile Technology Control Regime*; biological weapons, anti-personnel landmines; dual-use exports; and security developments in Asia. Although it is still too early to assess China's continuing interest in furthering this dialogue, it has nevertheless proved to be a useful confidence-building exercise.

The EU should now aim to examine broadening the scope of its political dialogue with China, to address issues of global interest such as the fight against drug trafficking, money-laundering, organised crime and illegal immigration, as noted in the Commission's 1998 Communication. These are all areas where the Union has been granted new responsibilities under the Amsterdam Treaty. For example, the situation of asylum-seekers from China has become a particular concern to some EU Member States, and an exchange of information between EU partners on the issue took place in 1999. The EU should assess China's readiness to engage in a specific dialogue in this field, and then explore opportunities for co-operation, as well as in others.

China has become a central player in the key international dialogues on several global environmental issues. Regular exchanges occur at several levels (including Ministerial) in the margins of international meetings, for example, on climate change. Chinese resources allocated to domestic measures to combat climate change are increasing as is Chinese enthusiasm concerning specific measures in the future to facilitate the transfer of climate change expertise and technology from the EU to China. The climate change dialogue in particular will become a major feature of EU-China relations over the coming years. Other global issues, notably the Conservation of Biological Diversity and protection of the Ozone Layer also feature as regular bilateral discussion items. These dialogues, as well as others on emerging global issues, will continue to be pursued vigorously by the Commission.

*A.4 Fostering Dialogue on Asian Regional Issues*

The EU took part in *Asean Regional Forum (ARF)* ministerial meetings in Manila in July 1998 and in Singapore in July 1999. The ARF has been able to play a positive role in the South China Sea dispute as well as in exchanging views on issues of regional concern such as the Korean peninsula. However, China has been reluctant to advance the ARF multilateral process any further, putting its traditional emphasis on bilateral diplomacy in its relations with Asian neighbours.

China regularly insists that its real influence on the Democratic People's Republic of Korea should not be exaggerated. It nevertheless remains a key ally and interlocutor of Pyongyang. Therefore, the situation in the Korean peninsula has been a major theme of the EU-China regional political dialogue. In this respect, the EU has urged China to maintain its positive role, particularly in the Four-Party Talks, and the two sides have shared views from their respective dialogues with the Democratic People's Republic of Korea.

During the reporting period, the EU has paid particular attention to the evolution of relations between China and Taiwan. In July 1999, the EU Presidency issued a declaration, on behalf of the EU, recalling the EU's adherence to the "one China" principle, underlining the need to resolve the question of Taiwan peacefully through constructive dialogue, and urging both sides to avoid taking steps or making statements which increase tension.

*A.5 Underpinning Autonomy in Hong Kong and Macau*

During the reporting period, the EU has closely followed the implementation of the Basic Laws of the two *Special Administrative Regions* of Hong Kong and Macau, particularly in relation to the autonomy and independence of the executive, legislative, and judiciary of the territories.

The EU's commitment to the proper functioning of these administrative and legal arrangements was clearly reaffirmed in January 1999 in the Commission's First Annual Report on the Hong Kong Special Administrative Region, which focused mainly on the development of democracy. *The EU-Hong Kong SAR Customs Co-operation Agreement*, which entered into force on 1st June 1999, also helped to underpin the independent functioning of the Hong Kong SAR economy. The Commission's Second Annual Report on Hong Kong, which was adopted on 18 May 2000, concentrated on Hong Kong's legal system and the "one China, two systems" principle, but also expressed some concern about the slow pace of introducing further democratisation.

The Commission released in November 1999 a Communication on "*The European Union and Macau: Beyond 2000*". Relations with Macau have been reinforced by the accreditation, to the European Community, of a Macau Economic and Trade Office in Brussels, and by the launching of several co-operation projects in Macau. EC-Macau Joint Committee meetings took place in 1998 and 1999, and there will be a further meeting in 2000. The provisions of the *EC-Macau Trade and Co-operation Agreement* have remained fully in force, after the transfer of sovereignty.

On 26 January 2000, the European Commission proposed a Council regulation to grant Hong Kong and Macau residents visa-free access to the EU.

**B. Supporting China's transition to an open society based on the rule of law and the respect for human rights**

> "The challenge for China now is to sustain economic growth and preserve social stability while creating an open society based on the rule of law. If Europe wishes to have a role in this process, it should continue to use all available channels to promote the cause of human rights in China in an active, sustained and constructive way." (*idem*, p. 9)

*B.1 Promoting Human Rights Through Open Dialogue…*

In recent years, economic reforms as well as the relaxation of some forms of State control in the social sphere have introduced an increased degree of self-determination for the individual in China. There have also been, since 1998, positive achievements with regard to China's participation in international human rights mechanisms. These include the visits of UN Human Rights Commissioner Mary Robinson to China in September 1998 and March 2000, and the signing by China of the *UN Covenant on Civil and Political Rights as well*, in October 1998. (China signed the *UN Covenant on Economic and Social Rights* one year earlier, in 1997.)

While there has been gradual improvement in economic and social rights, and progress towards the strengthening of the rule of law, there has been a lack of progress, and even a deterioration, in the area of civil and political rights. Repression of political dissidence, arbitrary detention conditions, the extensive use of the death penalty, the repression of ethnic minorities -including in Tibet, restrictions on religious freedom, rights of association and free speech, among others, continue to be major concerns for the EU.

The EU is also concerned at China's failure to observe internationally agreed core labour standards as set out in the relevant ILO Conventions and the ILO Declaration on Fundamental Principles and Rights at Work.

Regular rounds of this dialogue, held alternatively in China and Europe (in October 1998, February and October 1999, and February 2000), have provided a valuable platform to engage China on sensitive issues, channel EU concerns, provide arguments to the relevant Chinese authorities, and generate proposals for co-operation projects. Within this framework, the Chinese authorities have reported some progress on legal and judicial reform and have also expressed their readiness to address all sensitive issues in the formal dialogue -although this has not been matched so far by improvements on the ground. The EU has repeatedly emphasised the need to make the dialogue more results-oriented and better connected to decision-making in China.

In addition to the use of bilateral instruments such as the EU-China human rights dialogue, the EU has been eager to use multilateral fora to advance the cause of human rights in China. In 1998, 1999, and 2000, EU Member States decided not to table or co-sponsor a resolution on the human rights situation in China at the UN Commission on Human Rights (UNCHR) meeting in Geneva. However, in 1999 and again in 2000, the EU Presidency, in its opening statements to the $55^{th}$ and $56^{th}$ sessions of the UNCHR, expressed serious concern about the human rights situation in China.

During the reporting period, EU Heads of Mission in Beijing produced quarterly reports monitoring the human rights situation in China. The EU continues to raise the situation in Tibetatevery opportunity.

*B.2 and through co-operation*

Since the EU-China human rights dialogue started, the Commission has agreed to initiate a number of co-operation projects aimed at supporting and complementing the dialogue and improving, in practical terms, respect for human rights in the long term. This has involved, for example, the promotion of the rights of disabled persons and the setting up of the *EU-China Human Rights Small Projects Facility* to support small-scale initiatives in the human rights field.

Furthermore, several EU-China Human Rights Legal Seminars, open to the academic and NGO communities, have been held to complement the sessions of the official dialogue.

The *EU-China Legal and Judicial Programme* referred to under section C.2 below, was launched in March 2000 and will last for at least four years. It will underpin moves towards creating a society more firmly based on the rule of law and respect for human rights, by disseminating a better understanding of this concept among those professionals most closely involved in the Chinese legal system.

The *Village Governance* project aims to ensure the effective implementation of the law governing grass-roots village elections, thereby strengthening electoral practices and self-government at the village level. An international tender bidding process is currently under way.

The Commission intends, in 2000, to support human rights training courses at *Hong Kong University*. This project, building upon the Hong Kong SAR's unique expertise in the legal and judicial sphere, will offer training on human rights and legal issues to students from Asia, and in particular from the People's Republic of China.

Of particular importance for the foreseeable future is the effort to set up an EU-China Experts Network aimed at sharing experience with regard to the ratification and implementation of the two United Nations Human Rights Covenants.

**C. Integrating China further into the world economy**

> "It is the EU's view that the objective of assisting China to become a global economic player fully integrated in the world economy and able to comply with common rules should be achieved through a combination of trade discussions and targeted co-operation initiatives. This strategic approach should seek to accelerate and consolidate China's integration into the world trading system while supporting the reforms that are so vital for China to thrive within that system." (Idem, p. 11)

*C.1 Bringing China into the World Trading System*

The EU accounted for a significant and growing share of China's global trade surplus in 1998 and 1999. The Asian financial crisis affected Chinese exports in the region, and led to a diversion of Chinese exports from East and South East Asia towards Europe. The EU-China trade deficit increased from €24,4 billion in 1998 to more than €30 billion in 1999.

The large Chinese trade surplus, reflecting the growing strength of China's exports globally, is also assisted by persisting market access barriers in China, which impede trade and investment flows. For example, one factor of major concern to Industry is the unsatisfactory situation in China regarding Intellectual Property Rights. Removing these obstacles has therefore remained a priority for the EU, which aims to promote China's integration into the global economy and maximise the mutual benefits of bilateral trade and economic relations. The EU has pursued these goals both in its negotiations for China's accession to the World Trading Organisation (WTO), and through its bilateral commercial and economic consultations with China.

The negotiation of an agreement on China's accession to the WTO has been at the top of the EU's trade agenda for the past two years. The bilateral Sino-EU Agreement reached on 19 May 2000 therefore marks a major step forward in our trade relations. Coming in the wake of the Sino-US Agreement of November 1999, the Agreement with the EU virtually ensures that China will join the WTO early in 2001. The Commission and the Chinese authorities have agreed to step-by-step market opening in many areas, with implementation typically taking place within a three to five year period.

The EU-China Agreement will secure vastly improved access for EU (and other WTO member countries') firms to the Chinese market. Import tariffs and other non-tariff restrictions will be sharply and permanently reduced. WTO membership will consolidate and accelerate China's own efforts to promote transparency, fairness and openness across the board in China's own trade régime. And the WTO's independent and legally binding dispute settlement system will enable both sides to resolve trade problems quickly and effectively. In short, this Agreement greatly enhances the climate for European companies to export to, do business with and invest in, China. As a result, the EU and China can look forward positively to a reverse of the recently declining levels of Foreign Direct Investment (FDI) in China.

But beyond the commercial opportunities it will offer, WTO accession will have a substantial impact on economic reform and development in China. The EU was concerned throughout the negotiations to develop an assistance package that would foster gradual but lasting reform and sustainable development. Upon China's accession, it will be vital that all the required trade regime changes are implemented as scheduled. The EU is committed to working in partnership with China; in order to make this transition process as smooth as possible. The Commission will share its experience in the WTO with China, including offering to help China adapt its economy to meet WTO obligations, through the EU-China co-operation programme. Support for economic reform has already been earmarked as an area for future funding (see paragraph C.2 below)

WTO accession will bring another anchor for structural reform. Entering the world trading system will be a catalyst for Chinese firms to become more efficient, to show that they can compete on fair terms with the rest of the world. The Agreement will therefore also be good for Chinese companies and workers, as they draw the benefits of increasing foreign investment, and take on the most modern management practices and legal structures.

Progress in the accession talks had been accelerated in the course of 1999 through joint EUUS-China efforts, leading to the Sino-US agreement of November 1999. The EU was then keen to emphasise its own, specific interests in its own bilateral negotiations, aiming to ensure a level playing field for EU industry in China and to promote bilateral trade and investment flows.

Sino-European bilateral consultations on commercial issues, together with the WTO accession negotiations, have played, and will continue to play, an important role in resolving problems of mutual concern. The XVth meeting of the EU-China Joint Committee took place in June 1998. After China's accession to the WTO, both dialogues, bilateral and multilateral will be used to resolve trade issues such as regulatory problems, investment barriers, business environment for EU companies in China etc. It will also be an important forum for monitoring, and discussing possible differences of views about the scope and implementation of China's WTO undertakings.

Within the framework of the EU-China Joint Committee, the Commission intends to reassess, together with its Chinese partners, the existing mechanisms of the bilateral dialogue with a view to broadening, strengthening and adapting it to the new tasks facing China, after WTO accession. The Commission is considering opening up new channels of dialogue for specific areas such as industrial standards and certification procedures, sanitary and phytosanitary issues, securities markets regulation, and industrial affairs. Moreover, discussions regarding a maritime transport agreement have started and received ministerial endorsement on the occasion of the visit to the Commission of the responsible Chinese Minister, in July 1999. Exploratory talks on an EU-China customs co-operation agreement are also underway.

In addition, negotiations on an agreement between EURATOM and China on the peaceful use of nuclear energy are under consideration and there have been exploratory contacts with the Chinese authorities. Such an agreement would strengthen the long-term framework for nuclear co-operation between the EU and China, thereby facilitating existing and future trade, and encouraging mutually beneficial research, as well as ensuring the highest level of nonproliferation and of safety.

The EC antidumping regulation for transitional economies such as China was amended in 1998, in order to reflect market-driven changes in the country concerned. The new regulation introduced a case-by-case approach whereby Chinese exporters operating in a market environment are granted market economy treatment. This new regime has already been applied in a number of cases, resulting in the granting of market economy treatment to some Chinese firms. More and more Chinese companies will benefit from market economy treatment in the future, as the legislative framework for market economy conditions in China develops, and awareness of the relevant requirements increases.

The EC quantitative restrictions regime towards China was partially liberalised in 1998. No EU quotas were removed in 1999 in view of the situation of EU industries in the sectors concerned, and the lack of progress in the liberalisation of the Chinese quota regime. The progressive removal of quantitative restrictions on both sides is now to be part of China's WTO accession package, with quotas from both sides to be removed by 2005.

The EU has also developed some elements of a comprehensive investment promotion strategy and business co-operation in China, in support of the implementation of its market access strategy aimed at removing barriers to trade and investment in the Chinese market.

The *European Community Investment Partners* (ECIP) programme (which ended in 1999) sought to foster the presence of European small and medium size enterprises in emerging markets and proved very successful in China. At the end of 1998, 16% of all ECIP-funded initiatives were related to China, and resulted in the setting up of more than 60 joint ventures. Initiatives supported under the *Asia Invest* facility, which seeks to identify investment opportunities and partners in Asia, also developed in China in an encouraging way.

The Commission and the Chinese Council for the Promotion of International Trade (CCPIT) launched an "*EU-China Business Dialogue*" in 1998 with a view to fostering links between the European and Chinese business communities. It is expected that this informal process will expand further: a further round has been scheduled for 23 October 2000, in Beijing, at the same time as the annual EU-China Summit.

In October 1999, following several years of preparation, the EC Delegation in Beijing and locally based European companies launched the EU Chamber of Commerce in Beijing. This will underpin efforts to identify and help remove market access obstacles, and promote the European business presence in China. The Chamber is fully self-financing and already has more than 180 member companies.

*C.2 Supporting economic and social reform*

Supporting economic social reform has been the priority during the period concerned. China's expected accession to the WTO will force the pace of reform. The EU's co-operation efforts will continue to bring vital expertise where it is most needed.

Four existing projects, totalling EUR 22m,with WTO related objectives are outlined below:

- A programme in support of WTO accession to begin this autumn, will train Chinese officials responsible for implementing WTO commitments in a wide range of areas;
- A broad-based initiative to assist in the reform and restructuring of the financial services sector will begin at the end of the year;
- A project is already underway to cover the collection and provision of statistics;
- A programme aimed at fostering the development of a framework for transparent and nondiscriminatory public procurement will reach its completion shortly;
- A series of projects supporting the development of a modern and effective system for protecting Intellectual Property Rights has already begun.

In 1998 and 1999, EU-China co-operation focussed clearly on the priorities outlined in the Commission's 1998 Communication i.e., concentrating on assisting the economic and social reform process, in order to help foster the overall development of China.

In October 1998, the financing agreement for the *EU-China Legal and Judicial Co-operation Programme* was signed. This programme, launched in March 2000, comprises training and awareness raising activities for Chinese legal practitioners. It will train selected lawyers, judges and prosecutors in key areas of European legal practices. By helping to develop a sound, transparent, predictable legal system, and an accessible, efficient and fair judiciary, the programme will help moves towards a society more firmly based on respect for human rights. It will also improve the climate for European business and investment in China.

In order to reinforce the development of human resources in China and to promote people to people exchanges, the European Commission launched, in 1998, the *Junior Managers* programme, a training scheme aimed at sending junior European executives to China. It also set up an *EU-China Vocational Training Programme* which seeks to provide targeted regions with an improved range of vocational education and training services. In 1999, the *China-Europe International Business School (CEIBS)* inaugurated a new campus and launched a new phase in the development of the school, with the support of both the Commission and the Shanghai municipality. The CEIBS is now recognised as one of Asia's leading business schools.

In 1998, the Commission and interested academic organisations set up the Euro-*China Academic Network (ECAN)*, to foster inter-action between EU policy makers and the academic community, through thematic workshops and annual conferences.

In 1999, the Commission launched a five-year, large-scale *EU-China Scholarship 2000* project that will bring, starting from the 2000 academic year, two thousand Chinese post-graduates to study in European universities (studying, for example, economics and business studies, European studies and science and technology).

Also in 1999, in order to keep pace with the most recent concerns and core challenges of the Chinese reform process, the Commission started to define projects aimed at sharing experience with China on the reform of State-owned enterprises, as well as addressing the side-effects of this process (i.e. coping with unemployment and establishing a social security net).

The signature, in December 1998, of a *Scientific and Technological Co-operation Agreement*, has expanded the scope of EU-China co-operation in this sector. The Agreement entered into force in December 1999, and is expected to enable joint research in a wide range of topics under the EU's $5^{th}$ Framework Programme for RTD. It allows Chinese scientists to participate in EU thematic programs for R&D in industry related high technologies on a self-financing basis. It also provides the possibility of European scientists participating in Chinese R&D programmes, on a self-financed basis.

The S&T Agreement with China complements the ongoing joint research projects supported separately under the EU's INCO programme launched in 1999, and which focuses on sustainable development issues, and on China's continuing needs in agricultural development and healthcare, essential to the process of economic and social reform. Also within the framework of INCO, the Commission supported the 1998 launch of a China-Europe Biotechnology Network (to succeed the previously existing China-Europe Biotechnology centre) as a flexible instrument to foster greater co-operation in this key area.

The Environment has been a key priority of the European Commission's co-operation efforts in the last two years. Commission support for the China Council *Programme on Economic Planning and Environmental Protection*, seeking to promote integration of the environment into other policy areas in China, began in 1998 with input from sectoral experts, administrations and industry in the EU. The results of the Programme, due around

March 2001, are expected to feed into mainstream EC co-operation with China. The Commission has also supported the *Environmental Education Television Project for China*, using the televisual medium to promote environmental education across the country.

Given the accent on the environment, particularly the emphasis in the 10th Five Year Plan (2001–2005) on the development of an environmental industry sector there is much scope for developing important EU-China co-operative (and eventually commercial) opportunities in the coming period.

Since September 1999, European experts have been assisting Liaoning province in a large integrated environmental protection project, which includes improving energy efficiency and energy management. Energy has also been the main focus of training courses funded under the *Synergy* programme. More than 500 Chinese participants have attended training activities under this scheme in the last two years.

In 1998, at the request of the Chinese authorities, EU and Chinese experts jointly carried out an in-depth study on "*Energy Policy and Structure in the People's Republic of China*". This will help China define its priorities for energy policy under the 10th 5-year plan, for the period 2001–2005. The *Third Conference on EU-China Energy Co-operation*, held in Brussels in March 1999 and which included a large Chinese presence, discussed, amongst other issues, the results of the study. This will pave the way for further integration of energy considerations into EU-China environmental co-operation. In this respect, the 4th meeting of the EC-China Energy Working group, which took place in Beijing in March 2000, focussed the discussion on priority areas that could be included in a possible new EC-China Energy/Environment Programme, in which all relevant Chinese Government organisations would participate. In this respect, work is underway to explore how far the EU and China can co-operate in certain key areas, including cleaner coal, energy efficiency and promoting renewable sources of energy.

The Commission's Joint Interpreting and Conference Service operates its Chinese Interpreter-Training Programme which, over the past two years, has continued to train young Chinese Interpreters/Officials from the Ministries of Foreign Affairs and Trade and Economic Cooperation, as well as from, for example, Banks, Customs Authorities and Universities.

As in the past, the Commission has continued to provide support to small-scale development-aid projects, which have been launched by NGOs in the education, health, and sanitation sectors. The EU's support of NGOs does in itself contribute to the strengthening of civil society.

China is unique for a "developing" country. It has enjoyed an unprecedented high level of growth, which has brought prosperity to many areas. However, some mainly inland areas are lagging behind in growth terms. To counter this, China has set up a "National Poverty Alleviation Programme" and introduced a "Go West" policy to encourage national and foreign investors to invest in the poorer, western provinces. In addition China has become a donor of development assistance to other Asian countries.

EU assistance continues to focus on China's large-scale socio-economic reforms. In is in this area where the EU's assistance can add most value and thereby help China's own poverty reduction effort, in line with the EU's commitment to poverty alleviation worldwide.

**D. Making Europe's funding go further**

"One key message of this Communication is that EU-funded co-operation programmes need to be even more closely linked with the EU's broader China policies. From the human rights dialogue through the WTO accession negotiations to questions relating to China's economic development, the EU should seize the chance to underscore its policies with concrete assistance projects where at all possible." (*idem*, p. 22)

The Commission co-operation budget for China (under budget lines B7-300, B7-301 and B7707) amounted to €65 million per year in 1998 and 1999. This was rather modest given China's sheer size and the wide range of potential co-operation areas. However, the Commission has concentrated its financial resources on fewer projects, which are directly in line with the Chinese reform process, and on areas where the EU's action is the most efficient and visible, and can add most value. Concentration of activities will be essential to giving a critical mass effect to future EU projects, preserving delivery capacities, and addressing the current delays in the implementation of programmes (the attached Annex 1 shows the level of commitment and disbursement of EU aid to China in 1998 and 1999).

In order to facilitate and encourage short-term, small-size initiatives, an *EU-China Small Project Facility* was set up in 1998. This was operated in a decentralised manner by the EC Delegation in Beijing, allowed a rapid response to funding requests, and supported 23 projects. The continuation of this facility is currently under examination.

The Commission has consulted EU Member States prior to the launching of all large cooperation projects. It has sought, both in Brussels and in Beijing, to find synergies with Member State's own initiatives whenever possible. As a result, several EU projects have close links with projects carried out by Member States. In addition, the Commission, together with the Member States and China, co-funds the ASEM Trust Fund. The Commission has also established regular contacts with the European Investment Bank (EIB); the World Bank, and the United Nations Development Programme (UNDP). The Commission has co-operated with the UNDP in two projects, and is considering a joint initiative with the World Bank. The Chinese *Ministry of Foreign Trade and Economic Co-operation (MOFTEC)* has been, as in previous years, the partner organisation for programming, planning and decision-making on all EU-China co-operation.

In both 1998 and 1999, the Commission contributed emergency relief assistance to numerous victims of natural disasters following, for example, the earthquake in Hubei Province, torrential rains in various provinces and snowstorms in Tibet. Most of the funds were distributed through NGOs such as the Red Cross, Medecins Sans Frontieres and Save the Children. ECHO administered several EU humanitarian aid projects, totalling E1.1m.

In addition to the EU-China bilateral co-operation programme, China also benefits from EU regional co-operation projects in Asia.

**E. Raising the profile of the EU in China**

"Greater visibility will give the EU added weight in its dealings with China." (page 24)

The Commission has made significant efforts, in the last two years, to further enhance the visibility of the EU in China.

The *EU-China Higher Education Programme*, which mainly concentrates on those centres and professors teaching European studies in China, ensured that more than 400 scholars originating from different Chinese universities benefited from training in EU policy, economics and law.

The Commission and the EC Delegation in Beijing have organised several initiatives aimed at disseminating information on the Euro, including an important seminar on "the Euro and China – Into the 21st Century", which was held in Beijing in December last year.

Under the *EU-China Small Projects Facility*, activities such as a radio programme entitled "*Close to Europe*", and an awareness-raising seminar on "*EU-China: Partners in Progress*" have been implemented successfully.

The EC Delegation in Beijing, in addition to having its own web page, has launched a monthly "*Co-operation Flash*" report. In January this year, it also adopted a single cooperation logo to make EU-supported projects in China more easily recognisable.

**Conclusions and recommendations**

This report demonstrates that although EU-China relations have developed very significantly over the past two years, there is much scope to expand the relationship further.

In anticipation of China's imminent accession to the WTO, the EU needs to look ahead to see how this will affect our trade relations. China will require assistance to meet its WTO commitments. The Commission will continue to develop new channels of communication with the Chinese authorities, to monitor the implementation of China's WTO commitments, and to identify instances where China faces difficulties in adhering to these obligations. Implementation should be a matter of partnership, not a source of confrontation, and will need to involve members of the European business community more closely, as they will be best placed to identify whether or not China is meeting its obligations. The EU can then seek to help China overcome any difficulties through targeted, technical assistance and the strengthening of regulatory dialogues in key areas.

The EU remains committed to supporting the overall reform process in China through its Cooperation Programme. China's accession to the WTO will speed up and bring more pressure to bear on the need for reform and this, in turn, will impact upon the requirement for EU assistance.

Because of the magnitude of the challenges China faces, the Commission will also need to define further those areas that can benefit most from EU co-operation. It is clear, however, that the priorities will include socio-economic reform, human resources development, education, the environment, the promotion of human rights and the rule of law. The Commission's efforts will concentrate on sustainable development projects in the agreed priority areas, but the EU will continue to be flexible and ready to adapt to new challenges and changing situations, as and when they occur. In line with agreed EU policy on global poverty reduction, the Commission will also continue to bear in mind, when formulating new co-operation projects, that 11.5% of China's population still live in absolute poverty -with an income of less than USD 1.00 per day.

In accordance with the recently adopted European Community Development Policy, the EU will also improve delivery and better implementation of agreed projects.

The time is now ripe to explore whether we can broaden the dialogue into those areas where, as foreseen in the 1998 Communication, both the EU and China have an interest in exchanging views and working together. These areas should include, for example, the fight against illegal drug trafficking, organised crime, money-laundering and illegal immigration. These issues of global importance have long been of concern to the EU. They will be of increasing concern to China, particularly as Chinese leaders fully realise the challenges these issues pose to social stability. Some of these issues could, after exploratory talks with Member States, be included on the agenda of forthcoming sessions of the EU-China political dialogue, including the next EU-China Summit, scheduled to take place on 23 October 2000.

**Data on EC-China Co-operation Projects, Budget Lines B7-300 and 301**

| | Commitments € million | Number of projects committed | Payments made million |
|---|---|---|---|
| 1998 year | 56 | 26 | 15 |
| cumul. 31/12/98 | 0 | 92 | |
| 1999 year | 63 | 14 | 26 |
| cumul. 31/12/99 | 0 | 106 | |

**Details of Commitments for 1998 and 1999**

| EC-China Co-operation, '98 Programmes | | | |
|---|---|---|---|
| Themes / Names | Technical and Financial Assistance B7-300 | Economic Cooperation B7-301 | Human Rights B7-707 |
| **1. China** | | | |
| Small Project Facility | | 923.500 | |
| Admin. Of justice -semin. | | 16.970 | |
| EU technology transfer | | 49.840 | |
| EU-China Business Forum | | 20.500 | |
| Aeronaut. Prep. Mission | | 84.168 | |
| Ningxia Land Reclamation extension | 750.000 | | |
| Development of technical and vocational training | 15.100.000 | | |
| Programme on Legal Cooperation | 13.200.000 | | |
| WTO package | | 3.000.000 | |
| EU-China info pack | 36.000 | | |
| Legal seminar | | | 183.893 |
| Seminar on Women rights | | | 193.000 |
| Telecom -Mgmt. Training Cent. | | 413.400 | |
| Telecom -Itell. Transport System | | 400.000 | |
| Telecom -Health | | 174.700 | |
| Telecom -Interconnection | | 458.000 | |
| Vehicle emissions control | 838.344 | | |
| Biosafety Workshop | 51.400 | | |
| Aids Fellowships II | 402.875 | | |
| Support for Basic Education | 15.000.000 | | |
| WB -Education sector study | 33.000 | | |
| UNDP -solid waste disposal | 460.635 | | |
| TV-Environment broadcasts | 300.000 | | |

| | | | |
|---|---|---|---|
| SPF -human rights facility | | | 840.000 |
| Support to disabled federation | | | 980.000 |
| | | | |
| **2. Regional cooperation benefiting China** | | | |
| Europe/Asia Business Intern. Prog. | | 950.000 | |
| ASEM -Trust Fund | 3.750.000 | 3.750.000 | |
| ASEM -Asia/Euro Environ. Cent. | | 1.600.000 | |
| ASEM -visit Asian standards officials | 100.000 | | |
| | | | |
| **3. Macau** | | | |
| Macau tourism | | 700.000 | |
| Macau European Studies Institute | | 280.000 | |
| | | | |
| **4. Hong Kong** | | | |
| HK Monitor | | | 60.000 |
| | | | |
| **5. Expert missions** | | | |
| Contribution to framework contract | 150.000 | 2.100.000 | |
| Committed | 50.172.254 | 14.921.078 | 2.256.893 |

| EC-China cooperation '99 Programmes | | | |
|---|---|---|---|
| Themes / Names | Technical and Financial Assistance B7-300 | Economic Cooperation B7-301 | Human Rights B7-707 |
| **1. China** | | | |
| EU-China Relations Infopack – updating and reprinting | 40.000 | | |
| EU-China Legal Seminar in Bad Honnef, Germany -May 1999 | | | 115.840 |
| Contribution to framework contract 99-I | 150.000 | | |
| Aeronautics -Phase II Launch phase | | 520.000 | |
| 2nd Women Rights Seminar | | | 152.000 |

| | | | |
|---|---|---|---|
| Telecom Testing and Certification (EOTC) | | 310.000 | |
| SCIC -training of interpreters | 125.000 | | |
| EU-China Civil Aviation Cooperation – Phase I | | 4.111.000 | |
| HEPPAP* I -rider to Finance Agmt. | 197.850 | | |
| China-EU Public Administration Programme | 5.700.000 | | |
| Financial services initiative | 8.500.000 | | |
| Scholarship 2000 | 31.200.000 | | |
| Support to the CEIBS** phase II | | 10.950.000 | |
| | | | |
| **2. Macau** | | | |
| EC-Macau Cooperation Officer | | 450.000 | |
| Committed | 45.912.850 | 16.341.000 | 267.840 |

* Honghe Environmental Protection and Poverty Alleviation Project
** China-Europe International Business School (Shanghai)
[1] COM(1998) 181.

Less than one year later there followed another Commission Communication, dealing with 'EU Strategy towards China: Implementation of the 1998 Communication and Future Steps for a More Effective EU Policy' (see Document 3.5). It summarised the EU's earlier objectives, reviewed progress in meeting them and suggested specific actions for the short- and medium terms. Specific suggestions included integrating China further into the international community through intensified and more structured dialogue; supporting economic and social reforms toward a more open society; further integration of China into the world economy, including strengthening means of dealing with bilateral trade disputes; making better use of EU cooperation programmes in China, for example by means of a country strategy paper; and raising the EU's profile in China. In virtually all areas, the Commission emphasised the importance of additional EU technical assistance.

**Document 3.5: Commission Communication, 'EU Strategy towards China: Implementation of the 1998 Communication and Future Steps for a More Effective EU Policy' (2001)**

COMMUNICATION FROM THE COMMISSION TO THE COUNCIL AND THE EUROPEAN PARLIAMENT
EU Strategy towards China: Implementation of the 1998 Communication and Future Steps for a more Effective EU Policy
COM(2001) 265 final, Brussels 15.5.2001

## 1. EXECUTIVE SUMMARY

This Communication :

- Recalls the long term EU policy objectives as defined in 1998;
- presents developments over the past years in the EU, and China, and the new setting for EU-China relations;
- reports on the implementation of the 1998 policy;
- intends to contribute to a comprehensive and forward-looking review by the Union of its short and medium term objectives and of the dialogue and cooperation mechanisms in place for implementing EU policy towards China, identifying and making proposals on key issues where EU policy could usefully be adjusted and/or streamlined or where new elements could be added.

The Communication suggests ways of developing EU-China relations by defining concrete and practical short and medium term action points for EU policy to progress more effectively towards the long term aims defined in 1998.

Action points are intended to be as operational as possible. They should help set the agenda for focussed EU-China relations.

Key suggestions include:

- Engaging China further in the international community through a continued strengthening of the political dialogue by:
  —ensuring greater coherence and continuity in scheduling agreed talks at all levels,
  —targeted reinforcement of the expert level dialogue on specific issues of particular interest,
  —a commitment to ensure a better preparation of, and a link between, the dialogue at all levels,
  —better integration of interrelated global issues, and the consideration of producing occasional joint EU-China texts on issues of common concern in the margins of Summit meetings,
  —codifying the framework for the EU-China political dialogue.
  Supporting China's transition to an open society through:
  —a more focussed and results-oriented human rights dialogue, taking full account of the conclusions of the January 2001 General Affairs Council;
  —working with China to support relevant reforms under way;
  —implementing and preparing human rights-related assistance programmes in support of the rule of law and legal reform, economic, social, cultural as well as civil and political rights, and democracy;
  —programming and identifying new areas for EU assistance, such as the prevention of torture.
- Integrating China further in the world economy through:
  —the finalisation of China's WTO accession,
  —close monitoring of the correct implementation of China's WTO commitments,
  —implementing EU assistance programmes to make WTO accession a success,
  —strengthening existing sectoral dialogues and agreements in key areas (information society, environment, energy, science and technology) and develop new ones (enterprise policy, industrial standards and certification, customs, maritime transport, securities and competition policy),
  —strengthening EU-China business-to-business dialogue,
  —reinforcing efforts to deal with bilateral trade disputes.
- Making better use of EU co-operation programmes with China by:
  —reinforced long-term programming,
  —agreeing on a Country Strategy Paper,
  —focussing EC assistance activities in three main areas: promotion of sustainable development, encouragement of good governance initiatives and promotion of the rule of law, and support for economic and social reform with a view to supporting the efforts by China to ensure regional and social cohesion, the fight against poverty and the promotion of equal rights between men and women.
- Raising the EU's profile in China by strengthening all aspects of EU information policy vis-à-vis China.

The action points proposed are not exhaustive. They are intended as pointers for what could be undertaken over the coming years, building on what has been achieved so far.

## 2. INTRODUCTION

This Communication takes as its basis the Commission's 1998 Communication "Building a Comprehensive Partnership with China"[1] and the resulting Council conclusions of 29 June 1998 which stressed the Union's fundamental interest in strengthening relations with China.

Discussion in the Council during winter 2000/2001 indicated a consensus that EU global and long term objectives in relations with China as defined in 1998 remain largely valid. At the same time there was also consensus that there is scope for making EU policy more effective, by broadening dialogue and co-operation and fine-tuning existing instruments, taking into consideration developments that have taken place since 1998.

## 3. THE 1998 COMMUNICATION

The 1998 Commission Communication and Council Conclusions established the following aims for the EU-China relationship:

(i) Engaging China further, through an upgraded political dialogue, in the international community;

(ii) Supporting China's transition to an open society based upon the rule of law and the respect for human rights;

(iii) Integrating China further in the world economy by bringing it more fully into the world trading system and by supporting the process of economic social reform underway in the country, including in the context of sustainable development;

(iv) Making better use of existing European resources;

(v) Raising the EU's profile in China.

The Commission's report to the Council and the European Parliament of 8 September 2000[2] on the implementation of the 1998 Communication was a first stock-taking of EU policy.

The report noted that EU-China relations had intensified to a great extent as intended. The political dialogue had expanded, notably with the first EU-China Summits in 1998 and 1999. A bilateral EU-China agreement on China's WTO entry had been signed on 19 May 2000, paving the way for China's accession to the World Trade Organisation (WTO). And a technical assistance programme in support of WTO accession was about to begin. Trade and investment relations had intensified further. A *Scientific and Technological Co-operation Agreement* had been signed. EU support for Chinese environmental protection efforts and other important economic and social reform efforts had been strengthened. EU assistance programmes had been re-focused to match the 1998 policy objectives and a number of important projects in key areas of interest had been developed such as the *EU-China Legal and Judicial Co-operation Programme*, the *Training Programme on Village Governance*, the *EU-China Scholarship 2000* project, the *Junior Managers* programme and the *EU-China Vocational Training Programme*. In addition, a new campus of the *China-Europe International Business School (CEIBS)* had been inaugurated.

The report concluded that although EU-China relations had developed significantly there was scope for expanding the relationship further. This expansion has continued over the past year. Developments are reviewed under the overall aims in section IV.

## 4. THE NEW SETTING FOR EU-CHINA RELATIONS

Discussion of China in the framework of the Council in early 2001 revealed a consensus that the existing policy towards China and the EU's longer term aims in relations with China, as defined by the Commission Communication and the resulting Council Conclusions in 1998, remain basically valid. However, both objectives and instruments could and should be fine-tuned and operational goals for the short and medium term could be achieved by setting down action points in order to make EU policy more effective.

Several developments over the past years point to the need for fine-tuning the EU's policy towards China in 2001.

Firstly, there have been significant developments in the EU since 1998 which increasingly can and do affect relations with China, including the ratification and implementation of the Amsterdam Treaty, and the signing of the Nice Treaty and the adoption of a EU Charter on Fundamental Rights in December 2000. This reinforced the EU's Common Foreign and Security Policy (CFSP) and the European Security and Defence Policy (ESDP) as well as its Justice and Home Affairs (JHA) policy and other policy areas. The ongoing consolidation of EU integration makes the Union better equipped to engage China on an increasingly wide range of issues.

Secondly, there have been significant developments in China which need to be taken account of in re-focusing EU policy towards China, including China's increasingly assertive international role and growing political and economic weight. China is already the world's seventh largest trader, the second largest recipient of Foreign Direct Investment (FDI) and a major player in certain key economic sectors such as telecoms and the information society, and energy). In addition, China's continuing and far-reaching reform process is affecting ever more parts of Chinese society. Corruption and increasing disparities in regional development and in incomes are key concerns. The anticipated accession to the WTO will give added impetus to the pace of economic and social reform. However, it is also likely to give, at least in the short term, continued rise to both urban and rural unemployment, possibly straining China's social security system and adding to societal tensions. Increased internal and external migration over the past years illustrates the challenges. The general political situation in China is affected by upcoming leadership changes (16$^{th}$ Communist Party Congress in autumn 2002) and continued tensions over the issue of Taiwan.

Thirdly, there have been significant developments in EU-China relations which merit a brief review. These include the strengthened political dialogue, the opening of a dialogue on illegal migration and trafficking in human beings, the re-focusing of EU co-operation assistance to China with the new Country Strategy Paper, the strengthening of a number of important sectoral dialogues, as well as the growing importance of China as a trade and investment partner for the EU.

All these developments point to the scope and need for further enhancement of our engagement with China. China's opening over the past twenty years has created impressive economic growth which has improved the well-being of many Chinese people while also creating opportunities for European business. The wish to ensure sustained economic growth and development has fuelled reforms in general. But China's opening and joining the international community has always been fraught with difficulties and is likely to be so for many years. Nothing can be taken for granted. The reform process is not on permanent autopilot. It is in the EU's interests, both economic and political, to support an open China, the continuation of a smooth and ongoing reform process, and China's positive and constructive international engagement.

China is not always an easy partner for the EU. Its political system is unlike that of most other major third countries with which the EU has significant and growing relations, and EU concerns over key issues such as human rights affect and strain relations at times. But despite the difficulties involved, it is in the Union's own interest to engage China further. Globalisation means, among many other things, that a country the size of China is both part of the problem and the solution to all major issues of international and regional concern. Engagement means developing comprehensive relations which allow for working towards a common understanding on all issues of concern, in support of multilateral problem-solving wherever this applies on international and regional issues.

The development of EU-China relations necessitates a commitment by China at all levels. The necessary commitment at highest political level has been expressed clearly in recent EU-China Summit meetings. But the issues on the agenda for EU-China co-operation, be it illegal migration or the expansion of sectoral dialogues, will also need the full support of Chinese authorities at lower levels, including in the regions, as well as improved internal co-ordination in China between the various actors involved.

## 5. DEFINING ACTION POINTS FOR A MORE EFFECTIVE EU POLICY

### *5.1. Aim 1: Engaging China further in the international community*

The Context

Integrating China into the international community and encouraging China to work with the EU in addressing international, regional, and transnational challenges remains a priority for the Union. Many of the initiatives proposed in this respect in 1998 have been carried out. The political dialogue has been strengthened. Summit meetings are now held on an annual basis, foreign ministers meet regularly, as do Ambassadors and senior officials in Brussels, Beijing, New York and Geneva. There is also agreement in principle to hold regular talks at expert level on selected issues (CFSP Troika Working Groups). Although not always easy, the political dialogue between the EU and China has grown stronger, reflecting a mutual recognition of the need to clarify differences and identify ways of moving forward on all key issues of concern.

The importance of engaging China consistently and coherently on all issues of international concern reflects the recognition that China, as a UN Security Council member and a growing economic and political power can have significant influence on most major global issues, whether it is arms proliferation, illegal migration and trafficking in human beings, organised crime, money-laundering, or environmental degradation. Co-operation with China, bilaterally and within multilateral structures such as the UN, is crucial for ensuring that international advances are made in these important areas.

Although the political dialogue and the dialogue on global issues are particularly important to engage China further in the international community, the other dialogues covered elsewhere in this Communication also contribute to this aim.

Recent developments in EU-China relations

Over the past year further steps have been taken to develop the EU-China political dialogue. The third EU-China Summit held on 23 October 2000 was successful and confirmed a mutual interest in building ties further across the board. Additional impetus was given by the first meeting of the EU Political Directors Troika with China on 30 November in Beijing, allowing for a wide-ranging discussion of international and regional issues of mutual concern. In the area of illegal migration and trafficking in human beings, the first High Level Consultations between EU and Chinese officials were held in October 2000 in Brussels and February 2001 in Beijing. This followed up the exchange of letters between President Prodi and Prime Minister Zhu on the need to strengthen co-operation in this area, not least in the light of the Dover tragedy in June 2000 when 58 would-be Chinese illegal migrants perished.

The growing international importance of both China and the EU give the political dialogue and the more general dialogue on global issues particular relevance. Much can be done over the coming years to fine-tune and build on what has been achieved so far and make it more effective.

Action points

*Expansion of the political dialogue*

- Continue the newly established political dialogue at level of Political Directors on half-yearly basis.
- Schedule half-yearly Troika dialogue expert meetings with China in areas where there is already an agreement in principle for regular dialogue, such as Asian affairs, nonproliferation, conventional arms exports, disarmament, and consider adding UN affairs for half-yearly expert level discussions.
- Establish regular dialogue of Troika Political Counsellors in Beijing with the Chinese MFA on selected regional and international issues.
- Ensure an improved preparation of and follow-up to all political dialogue meetings,in particular Summit meetings, as well as a better link between the dialogue at different levels.
- Consider where it might be useful to issue occasional agreed texts (statements or minutes) after Summit meetings on key questions of common interest.
- Evaluate regularly in the Political and Security Committee the outcome and effectiveness of the EU-China political dialogue at all levels, and adjust it as necessary.
- Consider, in the light of evaluations, the possible expansion of the expert level dialogue to cover others issues (e.g. terrorism, regional affairs beyond Asia, others).
- Consider a codification of the framework for the strengthened EU-China political dialogue.

*Topics of the political dialogue*

- Give priority focus in the political dialogue to :
  —pursuing the Union's human rights concerns,
  —identifying practical ways of stepping up co-operation to promote further reconciliation between the two Koreas,
  —identifying practical ways of co-operating on Burma/Myanmar in support of UN efforts to encourage national reconciliation and to prevent Burma/Myanmar from becoming a source of regional insecurity, and drug-trafficking,
  —co-operation on strengthening the search for resolving territorial claims in the South China Sea through negotiations, including support for continued work on a Code of Conduct,
  —making clear the EU's strong interest in seeing the Taiwan issue resolved peacefully through dialogue,
  —supporting multilateral efforts to limit arms proliferation, exports and disarmament (MTCR code of conduct, safeguards, early entry into force of the Comprehensive

Nuclear Test-Ban Treaty, immediate commencement of negotiations on a Fissile Material Cut-Off Treaty, EU code of conduct on arms exports, July 2001 UN Conference on the illicit trade in small arms and light weapons and follow-up, supporting the Ottawa process on landmines),
—identifying ways of promoting engagement in multilateral security dialogues for conflict prevention on regional and international issues and making maximum use of existing fora for doing so (ASEM, ARF, UN),
—considering ways of further supporting UN peacekeeping operations,
—taking forward the EU-China dialogue on illegal migration and trafficking in human beings,
—stepping up co-operation to work towards the attainment of the goals and objectives adopted in major international conferences organised under UN auspices,
—ensuring awareness in the planning and preparation of political dialogue meetings that all policy areas are increasingly interrelated, including regional issues/security policy, international organisations/security policy/regional issues.

*Special Administrative Regions (SARs)*

- Continue to monitor developments in Hong Kong and Macao closely and to issue annual reports on each Special Administrative Region, drawing attention to the maintenance of the rule of law, fundamental freedoms and autonomy in each region, in accordance with their respective Basic Laws.

*Global issues*

- Continue and deepen the newly established dialogue on combating illegal migration and trafficking in human beings, focusing on practical ways of taking co-operation forward and aiming notably at easing the return of illegal Chinese migrants in EU Member States. Make use of 'best practices' established by China on this issue in co-operation with third countries, taking due account of human rights aspects and having in view the possible conclusion of a readmission agreement.
- Take forward other practical ways of strengthening co-operation on illegal migration such as intensified talks on the detection of forged documents and the illegal use of genuine documents, possible information campaigns, high level visits by Chinese central and regional officials to the EU and EU Member States, and workshops/seminars on other issues considered important for strengthened co-operation against illegal migration and trafficking in human beings.
- Consider ways of working together in the fight against organised crime.
- Increase efforts to better co-ordinate EU policies on global issues, not only between the Commission and Member States but also in areas where a more coherent and consistent policy could be achieved, including arms proliferation, drug trafficking, illegal migration and trafficking in human beings, organised crime, money-laundering, and environmental degradation.

*5.2. Aim 2: Supporting China's transition to an open society*

The Context

Supporting China's transition to an open society based on the rule of law and the respect for human rights is central to EU-China relations and will be so for years to come. There is much to do.

Living conditions for the majority of the Chinese population have improved in the last twenty years. Economic reform and liberalisation have introduced an increased degree of freedom and self-determination for the individual in the economic and social field.

There are also some indications that the construction of a more open legal system is under way in China. The importance of the rule of law in the process of China's modernisation and in view of the country's further integration into the international economy is recognised by the Chinese authorities and by the Chinese media. Progress has been achieved in the area of economic and social rights. Relevant provisions have been added to the Constitution in 1999. With respect to civil and political rights there is still a wide gap between generally accepted international standards and the human rights situation on the ground.

The EU and China are engaged in a human rights dialogue, which aims at improving the human rights situation by encouraging China to respect and promote human rights and fundamental freedoms and to co-operate with international human rights mechanisms. Since 1997, there have been ten official rounds of the dialogue.

Finally, small but important steps are also being taken to introduce a greater degree of democratisation at local level (direct elections in villages) which could be elevated to higher levels.

Recent developments in EU-China relations

Two sessions of the EU-China human rights dialogue were held over the past year, in September 2000 in Beijing and February 2001 in Stockholm. In addition two seminars were held in December 2000 in Paris on trade union rights and minor crimes, and in May 2001 in Beijing on the death penalty and the right to education. These allowed for in-depth discussions among officials and experts and clarified respective views and positions with a view to contributing to finding ways forward to address the EU's key concerns.

As noted in the General Affairs Council conclusions of 22 January 2001, the dialogue meetings are generally held in an atmosphere of openness, allowing a frank exchange on issues of particular concern to the EU, including: disregard for fundamental freedoms, arbitrary detention and re-education through labour, torture, the crackdown on pro-democracy activists, the situation of minorities and capital punishment.

More recently, the EU welcomed the decision by the People's Republic of China on 28 February to ratify the International Covenant on Economic, Social and Cultural Rights (ICESCR) which offers the prospect of greater respect of economic, social and cultural rights in China. The EU remains concerned, however, at China's proposed declaration with regard to article 8:1 (a) of the Covenant, to the effect that Chinese legislation takes precedence over the article of the Covenant, which guarantees the right to form and join a trade union of one's choice.

Overall, the European Union remains seriously concerned about the human rights situation in China and, as stated clearly in the GAC conclusions in January and March, while the EU-China human rights dialogue is the European Union's preferred channel for working to improve the situation in the various areas of concern it is clear that dialogue is an acceptable option only if progress is achieved on the ground. It is therefore imperative that the EU and China work together to promote the human rights situation in China, an effort which will not only help China's integration into the international community but also underpin economic reform and growth.

In support of the human rights dialogue the EU is funding a number of human rights-related assistance programmes in co-operation with China. Implementation of these projects, and preparation of new ones, has moved ahead over the past year and will continue to form an important part of the EU's effort to improve the human rights situation in China.

Action points

- Pursue the GAC conclusions of 22 January 2001 on the EU-China Human Rights Dialogue, focus the human rights dialogue better, assess it on a continuous basis, and identify ways of making it more effective and results-oriented, notably on the key issues of concern identified in the GAC conclusions, including co-operation with human rights mechanisms; guarantees for the protection of those prosecuted for a crime for which the death penalty could be imposed and restriction of the cases in which the death penalty can be imposed; reform of administrative detention; respect for the fundamental rights of all prisoners; untrammelled exercise of freedom of thought, conscience and religion, of the freedom of expression and of the freedom of assembly and of association. Identify ways of assisting China in implementing the recently ratified UN Covenant on Economic, Social and Cultural Rights and encourage China to take fully on board the provisions of the Covenant relating to freedom of association and urge China to respect internationally recognised core labour standards set out in the relevant International Labour Organisation Conventions.
- Continue encouraging China to ratify the UN Covenant on Political and Civil Rights.

Work with China to promote tentative steps towards reform relating to detention, the legal system and the range of criminal sanctions as well as initial reforms of the penal code and of the code of criminal procedure.

- Continue implementation and preparation of EU human rights-related assistance programmes addressing the rule of law and legal reform (EU-China Legal and Judicial Co-operation Programme), economic, social, cultural, civil and political rights (EU/China Network on the ratification and implementation of UN Covenants, Programme of support to economic, social and cultural rights in Yunnan Province, Chinese Disabled Persons Federation, EU-China Human Rights Small Project Facility, Scholarships for the Masters of Law course in Human Rights at the University of Hong Kong) and democracy (EU-China Training Programme on Village Governance).
- Undertake medium and long term strategy definition and programming of technical assistance and co-operation including defining appropriate human rights and democratisation priorities as part of the preparation of the Country Strategy Paper for co-operation with China. Subsequently identify possible new human rights-related projects, such as, for example, in the area of prevention of torture.

*5.3. Aim 3: Integrating China further in the world economy*

The Context

More than 20 years of remarkable economic growth have brought profound changes in the Chinese economy. China is now the world's $7^{th}$ largest trading nation, increasing its share of world trade to 3.9% in 2000. Total foreign trade grew by 31.5% to reach US$ 474 billion. Overall, China's economy, on a purchasing power parity basis, is on a par with that of Japan, just behind that of the US. It is attracting foreign direct investment (FDI) at a remarkable rate and is now the second largest recipient of FDI after the US, having overtaken the UK in 2000. Aggregate utilised FDI in 2000 amounted to around US$ 348.6

billion, with the total number of foreign invested firms reaching 364,345, while contracted FDI stood at US$ 676.7 billion. China is also becoming or has already become a player and a market of global importance in sectors such as the telecommunications, transport, energy and the environment.

EU-China trade has developed remarkably since China began its open-door policy in 1978. However, the EU's small trade surplus in the 1980s turned into a deficit in the 1990s, which reached a record level of €44.4 billion in 2000, an increase of almost 50% on the 1999 record deficit. In 2000 the EU was the largest foreign direct investor in China, excluding Hong Kong, with flows of contracted and utilised investment of over US$ 8.8 billion and about US$ 4.5 billion, respectively. However, despite these positive recent trends, the EU's share of FDI in China remains relatively low, compared to its share in other emerging markets.

China's integration into the world economy, with all that this implies for continued opening and reform, will be critical for building co-operative ties with China, deepening EU-China relations across the board, and furthering mutual EU and Chinese commercial interests. The EU and China have a fundamental shared interest in strengthening the rules-based multilateral trading system. In this regard, the importance of China's accession to the WTO cannot be overstated. It will lead to significant further market opening and it will ensure that China can actively participate as the world trading system prepares for further trade liberalisation in a forthcoming new Round. Accession is expected to boost confidence, generate domestic and foreign investment, and stimulate economic growth overall.

China remains committed to the continuation of its economic and social reform programme. Current challenges include the difficult and politically sensitive reform of the State Owned Enterprises (SOE) sector, of the financial system, especially the banking sector which has run up huge bad debts to the SOEs in particular, as well as of the social security system.

Unemployment continues to be exacerbated by the reform process as the reformed SOEs shed workers at an increasing rate. This adds to urban drift as large populations of unskilled and semi-skilled workers migrate to the main cities. China will also have to address increasing social and regional inequalities.

China is the world's second largest consumer of energy and the third largest producer. The size of its energy sector renders the country's energy policy and its potential impact on the world scene a matter of great international importance, particularly for air pollution and climate change.

Having detected the need to care for the natural environment in order to guarantee continuing prosperity, and having underlined a policy of sustainable development in its 10$^{th}$ Five-Year Plan (2001–2005), the reconciliation of rapid economic growth, changes and developments in society, and conservation of the environment has now become a top priority for China. The transfer of EU environmental knowledge, skills and technologies to China will become increasingly necessary if China is to achieve sustainable patterns of production and consumption, energy balance and other key targets, to optimise future economic evolution. Input from the EU will assist China's pursuit of better environmental performance, notably where there are global consequences, and/or a commonality of interests, e.g. climate change. EU expertise can help China to achieve its goals. First it must gain control over the causes of environmental degradation. Then, in the medium to longer term, it must reverse the damage and bring about environment improvements. China already has a vast array of national environmental protection standards and environmental regulations, but implementation remains weak. Currently devoting 0.93% of GDP to environmental protection spending, China has set a goal of increasing this to 1.2% by 2005 and 1.7% by 2010.

Progress towards availability to the Chinese authorities of reliable statistical information on external trade and employment, related to current statistical co-operation with the EC, will provide a future basis for effective monitoring and policy making.

Recent developments in EU-China relations

China's bilateral market access agreements with 3rd countries, including with the US in November 1999 and with the EU in May 2000, have paved the way for China's accession to the WTO. With all but one bilateral agreement concluded, a limited number of issues remain to be resolved. Discussions in the margins of the 23 October Summit resulted in the resolution of some outstanding bilateral EU-China issues, and meetings of the Geneva Working Party on China's accession in November and December 2000 and January 2001 allowed for breakthroughs in a number of areas. In January 2001, the EU submitted a comprehensive compromise proposal whose purpose was to solve all outstanding issues. WTO members are currently engaged with China with a view to overcoming the last remaining hurdles.

A meeting of the EU-China Joint Committee, held back-to-back with the Summit in October 2000 allowed for in-depth discussion of key bilateral trade and co-operation issues. Agreement in principle was reached to launch a dialogue on enterprise policy and regulation. A proposal by the Commission to broaden the scope of the existing Telecoms Working Group, by transforming it into an Information Society Working Group, covering also the regulatory framework for the sector, as well as new areas, was agreed with China.

Exploratory talks on a potential China-Euratom co-operation agreement on the peaceful use of nuclear energy were held in Beijing in November 2000, confirming mutual interest to proceed with preparations for the formal negotiations. A high-level meeting in November 2000 led to agreement that both sides will jointly prepare negotiations for an agreement on co-operation and mutual assistance in customs matters. A meeting of the Energy Working Group was held in March 2001 in Brussels. The Commission has proposed that the environment dialogue should be expanded to include policy issues.

Action points

*WTO, trade and investment*

- Finalise China's WTO accession as rapidly as possible.
- Closely monitor the implementation of China's WTO commitments. As a first step, urge China to bring its legislation, regulations and administrative structures, working practices and procedures into line with WTO requirements upon accession
- After accession, pursue specific dialogues and instruments for tracking WTO implementation with the Chinese authorities.
- Continue implementing the €22 million package of current WTO-related co-operation projects: WTO support phase one, financial services sector reform and restructuring, preparation and collection of statistics, transparency in public procurement, and the development of an effective IPR protection system.
- On China's accession, the EU stands ready to make an additional effort to help China adhere to its WTO commitments, complementing the existing package of projects.

- The EU and China should seek close co-operation for the development and liberalisation of world trade, in particular if a new Round can be launched at the WTO Ministerial Meeting in Qatar.
- Continue co-operation with, and support for, the newly created EU Chamber of Commerce in China, whose 200 members will be one of the most important means of monitoring adherence to WTO commitments.
- Support EU and Chinese companies in their EU-China Business Dialogue initiative. After two initial sessions in 1998 and 2000, this Dialogue is currently being reviewed to define its role in the light of China's forthcoming accession to WTO.

*Economic and Social Reform*

- Continue to encourage the reform process under way through contacts, dialogue at all levels, and co-operation.
- Define the best means of helping China develop an effective social security network through relevant co-operation activities.
- Promote an EU-China policy dialogue on education and human resource development. Develop and implement human resources development programmes targeted at key groups in China's reform process such as academics in business, law, politics, economics, science and technology, civil servants, young professionals, senior professionals and lawmakers, opinion leaders in media, etc., through the continuation and expansion of activities such as the EU-China Junior Managers programme and the Higher Education project.
- Establish an exchange of experience between both sides' authorities responsible for regional policy, with the objective of contributing to the establishment of a policy for reducing regional disparities in China.

*New sectoral dialogues*

- Pursue specific initiatives to establish dialogues with China on enterprise policy and regulation, industrial standards and certification, securities markets and competition policy.

*Telecom / Information Society*

- Transform the existing dialogue on telecommunications into a wider and deeper framework for a permanent and regular dialogue on the Information Society,covering,in addition to research and co-operation, the regulatory framework for the whole sector, including for new areas.
- Initiate an industrial dialogue on standards.
- Organise an EU-China Co-operation Forum on the Information Society in April 2002, to include an exhibition of European know-how in technology and services linked to the Information Society, an EU-China conference on the challenges of the Information Society and a series of business meetings, and other events as appropriate.

*Transport*

- Organise an information seminar on the GALILEO programme for global satellite navigation, positioning and timing in the course of 2001 and explore co-operation possibilities in this field.
- Begin exploratory talks with the Chinese in May 2001, to start negotiations for a bilateral maritime agreement, in view of the mandate given by the Council in 1998, to

improve the regulatory conditions under which maritime transport operations are carried out to and from China and to and from the European Community. The aim would be to establish provisions on the freedom to provide international maritime transport services and free access to the market, national treatment for European companies establishing in China, the unrestricted transfer of proceeds and investment, and the promotion of maritime cooperation.

*Customs co-operation*

- Continue preparatory talks with the Chinese side and begin negotiations for an agreement on co-operation and mutual assistance in customs matters.

*Environment*

- Review the existing work on environment carried out by the bilateral Environment Working Group and initiate a substantial and separate policy dialogue on environmental issues of mutual interest with the State Environmental Protection Administration (SEPA), regarding both the domestic and international domains, in order to exchange information to enhance domestic policy development and implementation. Explore how far the EU can assist China in integrating environmental considerations into other areas of policy; and forge fruitful partnerships to promote common interests within multilateral environmental agreements, where feasible.
- Assist China in developing suitable policies and strategies for, and conduct research cooperation in, the areas of sustainable forest management, sustainable land-use, land-planning and management, water resource management, sustainable energy production and marketing, air pollution and measures to combat climate change.
- Develop co-operation projects focusing on: cleaner production methods; waste minimisation and waste management; environmental skills training; development and application of environmental standards; upgrading environmental management capacities; transfer of environmental expertise and technologies transfer; environmental awareness.

*Energy*

- Establish a regulatory and policy dialogue. Develop further relevant co-operation projects notably encouraging know-how transfer, including a project to assist China in reducing the environmental impact of its energy production and consumption.
- Organise the 4th EU-China Conference on Energy Co-operation in Beijing on 18 June 2001, as well as further events, as appropriate.
- Develop co-operation on the peaceful use of nuclear energy, thereby helping to promote global nuclear non-proliferation. Prepare negotiating directives for a nuclear co-operation agreement. Launch of negotiations expected in late 2001 or early 2002.

*Science and Technology*

- Take the required steps to make the Science and Technology Agreement, which has been in force since December 1999, work more effectively, including allowing for greater participation of scientists in the other side's research and development programmes. In this context, a new fellowship scheme was implemented under the 5th EU Framework Programme enabling scientists from developing countries, including China, to participate more actively in selected projects; the Commission is proposing to expand this scheme significantly under the new EU Framework Programme.

- Consider ways to increase Chinese participation in projects approved under EU Science and Technology programmes to promote Sino-European S&T co-operation.The provision of information and assistance with applications, inter alia through the establishment in the course of 2001 of a joint EU-China office for the promotion of research co-operation, will be crucial in this respect. Encourage deeper co-operation between Chinese and European researchers in the framework of ASEM.
- Organise an EU-China S&T Conference in 2002.
- Assess the possibility of contributing to the organisation of an international conference on agricultural R&D in 2001 or early 2002, given the importance of the development of the agricultural sector to China's economy and social stability.

*Statistics*

- Engage the Chinese statistical authorities in a dialogue to further develop statistical cooperation. In particular, this would aim at strengthening the Chinese national statistical system and its capacity to produce reliable, accurate and timely data in the new rapidly developing economic and social fields.

*5.4. Aim 4: Making better use of existing European resources*

The Context

The EU's co-operation programme aims to support the Union's key overall aims in relations with China. The priority areas of intervention are: support to economic and social reform, promotion of sustainable development and environmental protection and promotion of good governance and the rule of law. Development of human resources is used as a key instrument in achieving the overall objectives of EU co-operation policy. At the same time, co-operation activities integrate the EU's general development co-operation priorities by incorporating poverty alleviation dimensions, regional and social cohesion within China, human rights and gender issues. The budget for the EU-China co-operation programme 2001–2005 should be around €250m.

Past experience has shown the clear need for improved project delivery. Concentration on fewer and larger projects, more flexibility and the creation of the Small Project facility to manage small projects quickly and efficiently have been first steps. The creation of EuropeAid Co-operation Office and the planned devolution of the project management cycle to the Delegation in Beijing are important reforms the Commission is undertaking to improve project delivery and donor co-ordination, and make better use of its resources, concentrating efforts at the policy level.

Recent developments in EU-China relations

The annual EU-China Joint Committee meeting in 2000 agreed that co-operation priorities for the near future (2001–2003) would include assistance in support of WTO accession, the fight against illegal migration and trafficking in human beings, social security reform, telecommunications/information society, environment, energy, and human resource development. It was also agreed that China's western provinces should benefit more from EU assistance and that China should be more involved with future planning and programming.

In January 2001 the responsibility for managing existing co-operation projects and those scheduled for commitment in 2001 was transferred from DG Relex to the EuropeAid Cooperation Office. This reform, together with the devolution of project management to delegations, including Beijing, and the concomitant reinforcement of staff resources at the delegations, is intended to ensure better co-ordination with co-operation programmes of other donors as well as improve and speed up the delivery of EU-China projects.

A Country Strategy Paper (CSP) is currently being drafted by the European Commission. It will define the overall objectives and the context as well as the key areas of intervention and the mechanisms of co-ordination with the beneficiary country and other donors. There will thus be a clear reference document and mission statement for EU-China assistance cooperation for the next few years. The CSP will give guidance to, and enhance the transparency of, EC assistance to China.

Action points

Finalise the CSP, ensuring close linkage between EC funded co-operation programmes and the EU's broader China policies, in particular development policy as presented by the Commission in May 2000, trade policy, the fight against global challenges and the Human Rights policy.

- On the basis of the CSP, develop co-operation activities in three main areas:
  —support to the economic and social reform process mainly through institutional strengthening and capacity building, human resources development, promotion of a sound business regulatory framework and the transfer of know-how and technology.
  —promotion of sustainable development aiming to achieve optimal balance between environmental protection, social development and economic growth.
  —encouragement of good governance initiatives and promotion of human rights and the rule of law.
- Reinforce co-ordination with Chinese authorities.
- Reinforce co-ordination, and explore possibilities for concrete, project-related cooperation with other donors, in particular EU Member States, International Financial Institutions and UN agencies.
- Continue to focus on large, but flexible projects in areas where the EU as a donor has a comparative advantage, designed in a way to concentrate on, and take account of, China's rapid development and shifting priorities.
- Improve flexibility of project design, allowing for annual adaptations of activities carried out, and the budgets allocated to them, in order to achieve projects' overall objectives in the optimum way.
- Implement devolution of the project management cycle to the Beijing Delegation as planned.

*5.5. Aim 5: Raising the EU's profile in China*

The Context

Raising the EU's profile in China remains a major challenge given the size of the country and the need to reach people at the regional, municipal and local levels, as China continues to devolve power in the economic and social sectors away from the centre in Beijing. The resources available for EU profile raising activities remain limited, but judicious use of modern technology will make it possible to reach many more people than previously. Five years ago, very few Chinese had private telephones and no ready access to the outside world. In 2001, the number of internet users is expected to reach 40 million and, by 2005, China will have an estimated 300 million users (compared to an estimated 200 million in the US).

The expanding EU-China relationship demands a better understanding of each partner by the other. Increasing openness and combined interests will require greater information exchanges. In addition, as China continues to open up to the world and as the EU expands its frontiers, there will be an increasing need for better and faster ways for disseminating information. The EU will need a proactive information policy, making good use of new technology, in addition to traditional people-to-people contacts and co-operation activities, to maintain a strong profile among so many sources of interest.

The EU's extensive activities in China continue to be little noticed in Europe, although an increasing number of joint European-Chinese research and commercial organisations are being set up in Brussels and elsewhere to take advantage of the growing interest in China. It will be an important factor in the EU-China relationship that the right messages about the EU's activities in China are disseminated within Europe, as well as in China, particularly as the EU approaches enlargement.

Recent developments in EU-China relations

- The Commission's external affairs web-sites have been upgraded in the past nine months and the number of documents available has increased from 4000 to almost 9000. The hit rate has grown from 700,000 to 1.8 million per month during the same period. The web-sites are therefore proving to be an efficient method of disseminating and promoting the EU's policies and programmes.
- The EU Visitors Programme has proved a valuable way of improving people-to-people contacts and visitor exchanges with a careful selection of key Chinese officials visiting the Commission and Member States to find out more about EU policies and programmes in a wide variety of areas.
- A group of 20 economic editors and reporters from China, Hong Kong and Macao participated in a week-long seminar in Brussels in 2000. The seminar concentrated on the Euro but also explained the roles and functions of the EU's various institutions to these influential journalists. The journalists concerned produced numerous articles on the EU in their various newspapers as a result.

Action points

- Improve knowledge and awareness of the European Union in China through the provision of systematic and up-to-date information on EU policies and activities and the dissemination of newly produced, up-to-date EU information materials, targeted to the media, opinion formers and key decision makers in China, and also to schools colleges and universities.
- Comprehensively update the Commission web-sites, including the Beijing Delegation web-site, and ensure the access and navigation systems are as harmonised and user-friendly as possible, and increase the number of links to related sites.
- Continue to make imaginative use of the EU Visitors Programme to bring important and key decision makers to Brussels and to Member States to learn about the EU and its individual members at first hand.
- Encourage and support alumni of EU co-operation programmes, such as the the EU-China Academic Network, the EU-China Junior managers programme and the EU-China Scholarship 2000 project, to establish alumni associations and networks in China, Asia and Europe.
- Raise awareness of EU co-operation with China in Europe,e.g.in the European business and academic communities, in order to support the momentum built up in China through various co-operation programmes (e.g. Junior Managers Programme).

- Encourage greater co-ordination and co-operation between Member States and the Commission's Delegation in Beijing when organising individual or joint cultural events.
- Maintain participation in seminars, workshops, meetings, Universities activities, NGO presentations etc., to inform participants of EU-China policies and actions more widely.

**6. CONCLUSION**

Relations with China will be a major opportunity and challenge for the EU for years to come. The long-term aims as defined in 1998 remain largely valid. This Communication has suggested ways of making EU policy more effective by defining short and medium term objectives and action points intended to give focus to EU-China interactions across the board with a view to the Union's long terms aims in relations with China.

Ultimately a successful relationship is based on two willing and committed partners. Building a comprehensive EU-China partnership will therefore require the commitment and engagement of both sides. Much has been achieved so far. But more needs to be done to develop the full potential of the relationship.

The challenge for the EU is to engage China comprehensively and coherently on all key issues identified in the 1998 and elaborated on in this Communication, in particular China's political and economic integration into the international community and the opening of China with the full respect of internationally recognised human rights standards and the rule of law.

A comprehensive partnership between the EU and China, both bilaterally and globally, will serve both EU and Chinese interests, politically and economically, and help improve the lives of citizens in Europe and China.

The opportunity for the EU is to promote its key interests in engaging China as a growing power by seeking positive and constructive solutions to major global issues, by contributing to improve the human rights situation in China, and by pursuing mutual commercial interests.

1 COM (1998) 181.
2 COM (2000) 552.

In September 2001, the first year of the new century, the European Commission published a new communication on its Asian strategy (see Document 3.6). Entitled 'Europe and Asia: A Strategic Framework for Enhanced Partnerships', this policy document updated the earlier EU strategy for Asia. It promoted the establishment of enhanced partnerships with Asian countries, using country strategy papers. This was to serve as a means of strengthening the EU's presence in the region and its international role consistently with its growing economic role as a result of past and future enlargements.

## Document 3.6: Commission Communication, 'Europe and Asia: A Strategic Framework for Enhanced Partnerships'

COMMUNICATION FROM THE COMMISSION
Europe and Asia: A Strategic Framework for Enhanced Partnerships
COM (2001) 469 final, Brussels 4.9.2001

**SUMMARY**

The Commission first set out an overall framework for EC relations with Asian countries in its 1994 Communication "Towards a New Asia Strategy". The present Communication updates that strategy, taking account of key developments in the intervening years, and establishing a comprehensive strategic framework for our relations with Asia and its subregions in the coming decade.

After commenting on the major economic, political and social changes in Asia, Europe and the world in recent years, the Communication takes stock of the development of EU-Asia relations since 1994. Our political dialogue with key partners in the region has intensified, and our trade and investment relations have expanded (notwithstanding the impact of the East Asian Crisis). There has been a modest growth in our development and economic cooperation with Asian countries. But much remains to be done, for example in deepening and broadening our political dialogue, in enhancing our bilateral trade and investment relations and strengthening our cooperation in the WTO, and in ensuring that our aid programmes in Asia can achieve their full potential. The degree of mutual awareness between our two regions remains insufficient.

Taking account of the above, the present Communication proposes that we should set an overall strategic framework for our relations with Asia in the coming decade based on the core objective of **strengthening the EU's political and economic presence across the region, and raising this to a level commensurate with the growing global weight of an enlarged EU**.

In particular, we should work to:

- contribute to peace and security in the region and globally, through a broadening of our engagement with the region;
- further strengthen our mutual trade and investment flows with the region;
- promote the development of the less prosperous countries of the region, addressing the root causes of poverty;
- contribute to the protection of human rights and to the spreading of democracy, good governance and the rule of law;
- build global partnerships and alliances with Asian countries, in appropriate international fora, to help address both the challenges and the opportunities offered by globalisation and to strengthen our joint efforts on global environmental and security issues;
- and help strengthen the awareness of Europe in Asia (and vice versa).

These general objectives and priorities are elaborated further in a series of specific action points for the region as a whole, and for each of the four key sub-regions (South Asia, South-East Asia, North-East Asia, Australasia).

This overall strategic framework (which may subsequently be amplified through specific subregional strategies as appropriate, as well as through the Country Strategy Papers focusing on development cooperation), will also serve as an important input for a proposed revision of the ALA Regulation in the first semester of 2002 (following on an overall evaluation now commencing). Looking forward, it will be important to take stock of progress on a regular basis, and it is suggested that the strategy may usefully be reviewed, and adapted as necessary, in five or six years' time.

For this strategic framework to be fully effective, it is essential that there is a proper consistency between the objectives being set, and the resources available to meet them. Our first priority is to ensure that the available resources are used in an effective and timely fashion, implementing fully the ongoing reform of our external assistance. Once this has been achieved, we will be better able to address the longer-term question of whether and to what extent the level of resources available for our cooperation activities with Asia should be increased.

In conclusion, the Communication emphasises that Asia is a crucial economic and political partner for Europe. More than ever before, the EU and its Asian partners should work together in addressing the global challenges which we both face, and the global opportunities which we should all be able to share. Our Asian partners are invited to reflect on their side on how we might address these issues together.

## 1. INTRODUCTION

In 1994, the Commission's Communication "Towards a New Asia Strategy"[1] set out for the first time an overall direction to be followed in our relations with Asia, and sought to build a more comprehensive and balanced framework for our relations with this vast region.

The 1994 Strategy paper covered South, South-East and North-East Asia. It emphasised the rapid economic changes that had taken place in the region over the previous decades, and the need to ensure an effective and proactive EU presence in the region. It set the key objectives of strengthening our economic presence in the region, contributing to its political stability through a broadening of our political and economic relations with the region as a whole, promoting the development of the less prosperous countries, and contributing to the spread of democracy, the rule of law, and human rights. It put forward eight key priorities to be addressed, including the continued strengthening of our bilateral relations, a raised profile of the EU in Asia, support for regional cooperation (with a view to enhancing peace and security), encouraging Asia to play a greater role in multilateral fora, ensuring open markets and a non-discriminatory business framework, encouraging the integration of state economies into the free market, contributing to sustainable development and poverty alleviation in the least prosperous countries, and the importance of ensuring a coordinated approach, across the EU, to our relations with the region.

This Strategy was subsequently elaborated further for specific countries or sectors in a number of more targeted Communications, touching for example on our relations with China, India, ASEAN, Indonesia, the ASEM process, and on the energy and environment sectors.[2]

Overall, the 1994 Asia Strategy has served us well (for an assessment of its implementation, see section 3 below). In many respects, the issues and responses identified there remain broadly valid today. However, the world has moved on since 1994, with significant economic and political changes both in Asia and in Europe, and with the acceleration of globalisation (and the intensification of the opportunities and challenges which that offers). In the coming years, the EU will experience a further transformation, with enlargement on the horizon, with the single market and single currency achieving their full potential and with a continued strengthening in EU policy coordination, both in foreign policy and in justice and home affairs policies.

The present Communication thus seeks to review and update our approach to Asia, to provide a new strategic framework which will address the changes since 1994, and to establish a coherent, comprehensive and balanced strategic approach for our relations with Asia in the coming decade.

## 2. ASIA AND EUROPE AT THE START OF THE 21ST CENTURY

### *2.1. Asia*

It has sometimes been suggested that even the term "Asia" may be a false concept, bestowing an artificial homogeneity on the vastly diverse economic and political geography of the region. But labels matter less than the reality which they represent, and it is the reality of Asia which is of essential importance for the EU. The present paper will take as its area of coverage the countries stretching from Afghanistan in the west to Japan in the east, and from China in the north to New Zealand in the south, plus all points between. It covers therefore those countries in South Asia, South-East Asia and North-East Asia which would meet any common definition of Asia (and which were covered in the 1994 Strategy). It also covers, for the first time, Australasia – given that the economic and political links of

***An Asian Snapshot*[4]**

| | | |
|---|---|---|
| *Population 3.3 billion (56% of world total)* | *GNP $7,440 billion (26% of world total)* | *$CO_2$ emissions 7.4 billion tonnes (33% of world total))* |
| | *Per capita incomes* | |
| *Cambodia $260* | *India $450* | *China $780* |
| *Malaysia $3,400* | *S Korea $8,490* | *Japan $32,230* |
| *Number of people living on less than $1 per day 800 million (66% of the world's poor people)* | | |
| *Asia's share of world trade 25.3% (developed Asia 14.2%, developing Asia 11.1%)* | | |
| *Asia's share of EC exports & imports 21.1% & 31.2% (developed Asia 10.6% & 13.0%, developing Asia 10.5% & 18.2%)* | | |

Australia and New Zealand with their neighbours to the north, and their geographic proximity, are sufficiently great that they should be treated here as part of the wider Asian and Asia-Pacific region[3].

Apart from the region's demographic and economic weight, Asia has been the cradle of several of the world's major religions, and its cultural richness is unparalleled. It is also the locus of several longstanding sources of tension or conflict (for example in Kashmir, Sri

Lanka, on the borders of Afghanistan, in Aceh and Mindanao, across the Taiwan Straits, in the South China Sea, and on the Korean peninsula). Several Asian states have a nuclear capability, and certain countries continue to cause concern in relation to the proliferation of weapons of mass destruction. Asia is also home to two-thirds of the world's poor, with 800 million people living on less than $1 per day, with food security, health, and access to basic services still ever-present issues in most of the lower-income countries of the region, and with serious disparities of income and opportunity still challenging many middle-income countries. Asia also has a critical role to play in addressing global, regional and local environmental challenges – reflecting the region's geographic, demographic and industrial weight, the importance of its natural resources and biodiversity, and the rapidity of economic and demographic change across the region. As an example, the region accounts for some 33% of global $CO_2$ emissions[5], and issues relating to climate change, energy consumption and efficiency, forest and watershed protection, and biodiversity are necessarily high on the regional and global agenda.

In recent decades certain parts of Asia, through diverse but effective development strategies, have experienced an economic transformation, improving the living standards of hundreds of millions of people (notwithstanding the East Asian Crisis of recent years). The social and environmental costs of such rapid change remain to be fully addressed, and Asia also faces the same global challenges as Europe, be they economic insecurity, environmental degradation, the scourge of AIDS, or transnational crime. Yet Asia has also benefited from the opportunities which globalisation offers, and many countries in the region have shown their ability to exploit these opportunities to the full.

There is also a massive diversity across Asia. The region includes three of the five largest countries in the world, in population terms (China, India, Indonesia), and some of the smallest (Brunei, Bhutan, the Maldives) – as well as two countries with the highest and lowest population densities in the world (Singapore and Mongolia respectively). It includes some of the richest countries in the world (Japan, Singapore, Australia), and some of the poorest (from Afghanistan to North Korea)[6]. There is a tremendously rich cultural and religious diversity across the region, reflecting the historic civilisations of South Asia, of South-East Asia, of China, Japan and Korea, and for that matter the multiple cultural heritages of Australasia. Yet this same diversity can also be a source of tension, with acute ethnic or religious divides in certain countries, which in some cases threaten to rip apart the fabric of society. There is also a massive political diversity across Asia, with Indonesia only recently emerged from a long period of "guided democracy", and with other countries which are still subject to military or theocratic dictatorships. Nor should one forget the considerable wealth of diversity (ethnic, social or cultural) within certain countries of the region, whether in India or China, in Indonesia, the Philippines or Burma/Myanmar.

Since the 1994 Strategy was written, Asia has changed considerably, both economically and politically. The growing economic optimism which had characterised East Asia for several decades received a major blow from the financial and economic crisis which erupted in 1997. Beginning with a financial collapse in Thailand, the crisis spread quickly across the whole region. Across most of East Asia the origins of the crisis lay both in internal issues of financial and corporate governance, debt management, and democratic accountability, and in external issues relating to cyclical demand for key exports, and to the mobility and volatility of short-term capital flows. Both the social and political impact of the crisis has been considerable, with several governments across the region falling as a result, and with Indonesia in particular experiencing the most severe economic and social strains.

A relatively rapid economic recovery has confirmed the underlying economic dynamism of the emerging economies of East Asia. Europe's own contribution to this recovery, in particular through keeping our markets open and building on the "trade and investment pledge" made at the second ASEM Summit in London in April 1998, has been of crucial importance. The changes in trade flows arising from the crisis have meant that the EU's trade deficit with Asia rose from €13.3 billion in 1996, to €121.5 billion in 2000.[7] The crisis has nonetheless underlined the imperative need for all the countries concerned (Japan no less than China and other emerging economies of the region[8]) to continue with a pro-active reform agenda, both in the financial and corporate sectors and in the field of social policy.[9]

In South Asia, notably in India, recent reforms have benefited the economy and supported a more modest but regular rate of growth. Such reforms must continue, and spread more widely across the region, if these countries are to take full advantage of the trade and investment opportunities available to them.

The political scene in Asia has also changed considerably in recent years. In the Sub-Continent, the ongoing tensions between India and Pakistan over Kashmir have now taken on a nuclear dimension. In South-East Asia, the political transition and economic crisis in Indonesia has helped lay a foundation for democratisation and improved governance, while also seeing an increase in centrifugal pressures which may threaten the integrity of the country. ASEAN has expanded its membership to include Burma/Myanmar, Cambodia and Laos, while East Timor, on the verge of becoming an independent state, may shortly apply to become ASEAN's eleventh member. In North-East Asia, President Kim Dae Jung's "Sunshine Policy" has brought a dramatic change to the prospects for peace on the Korean Peninsula, while China continues to pursue its internal economic and social reforms, and to exert an increasing economic and political influence across the region, becoming more assertive in the pursuit of its regional and global interests.

The late 1990s have also seen a marked increase in efforts at regional dialogue and cooperation, particularly in East Asia, with the birth of the "ASEAN plus 3" dialogue (and the earlier establishment of an East Asian presence in ASEM), with the gradual strengthening of the ARF as a confidence-building forum, and with increasing signs of a growing sense of East Asian identity (perhaps influenced in large part by a shared experience during the financial crisis). At the same time, ASEAN itself seems to have lost some of its momentum in recent years, partly reflecting Indonesia's preoccupation with internal concerns, partly reflecting the underlying difficulty of some of the issues with which ASEAN has been faced (for example in completing AFTA, in responding to the financial crisis, and in absorbing three new members). In South Asia, which in many respects remains distinct from the rest of the region, SAARC offers the opportunity of a broad regional cooperation with diversified aims, even if political tensions continue to hinder the establishment of a proposed "South Asia Free Trade Area", an essential step towards the insertion of that region into the international economic environment.

*2.2. Europe*

Compared with Asia, Europe has a similar total economic weight, though this is shared among a very much smaller, and richer, population. Europe, like Asia, draws benefit from a rich diversity of cultural and linguistic traditions, but our shared heritage (of conflict as well as of cooperation) has led us to undertake the most far-reaching exercise in regional integration in the world, with a single market uniting the European economic space, and since 1999 a single currency of global importance. This integration has also permitted us to benefit from more than 50 years of internal peace, and to prepare now to re-unite a broader Europe,

***An EU Snapshot***

| | | | |
|---|---|---|---|
| *EU 15* | *Population 375 million (6% of world total)* | *GNP $8,213 billion 28% of world total)* | *$CO_2$ emissions 3.1 billion tonnes (14% of world total)* |
| *Candidates* | *Population 168 million* | *GNP $556 billion* | *$CO_2$ emissions 1.0 billion tonnes* |
| *EU + Candidates* | *Population 544 million (9% of world total)* | *GNP $8,769 billion (30% of world total)* | *$CO_2$ emissions 4.1 billion tonnes (18% of world total)* |
| *Per capita incomes* | | | |
| *EU15 $21,877* | *Candidates $3,306* | *EU+Candidates $16,131* | |
| *EU 15 share of world trade* | | | |
| *EU Internal trade 23.3%* | *EU External trade 14.4%* | *EU total trade 37.7%* | |

previously divided by ideology. However, the 1990s also saw a series of murderous ethnic conflicts on the borders of the Union, which present the most serious threat to European peace and security since the end of the Cold War.

Europe itself has experienced considerable change in recent years. The birth of the European Union, with the Treaty of Maastricht in 1992, coincided with the effective completion of the Single Market launched in the 1980s. Since then, the launch of the euro in 1999 has created a full economic and monetary union covering most of our Member States, and launched a major new world currency. The EU's economic record has also improved significantly in recent years, with steady if moderate economic growth and low inflation, partly reflecting a new spirit of liberalisation and innovation across European industry, partly reflecting the economic and monetary discipline required for monetary integration (and also looking forward to taking full advantage of the opportunities offered by the emerging knowledge society). With sound macroeconomic fundamentals and on-going structural reforms, the EU and its Member States will provide an important pole of growth and stability in the global economy.

Preparations are currently well underway for the enlargement of the Union from 2003 onwards, with the eventual perspective of a European Union of up to twenty-eight members, and a population of 544 million. The EU's external relations have also been transformed as a result of the Maastricht and Amsterdam Treaties, with the creation in 1993 of a Common Foreign and Security Policy (and the strengthening of this policy from 1999 in building a European Security and Defence Policy), and the increasing importance of Justice and Home Affairs issues in our external relations (both in the first and third "pillars"). The Nice Treaty, when ratified, will further consolidate EU institutions and prepare the ground for enlargement. And the Commission itself has undergone significant change in recent years, with a re-focusing of our priorities and resources, and with an extensive reform underway in relation to the management of our external assistance.

*2.3. The global context*

As Asia and Europe have evolved, so has the global context in which we operate. "Globalisation" as such is hardly a new phenomenon, and the 18th and 19th centuries also saw rapid and far-reaching changes in the organisation of the world economy. What is new in recent years is the speed at which events in one part of the world influence conditions in another, and the intensity of our economic, political, and social interdependence. The East Asian Crisis may have brought home to the countries of the region their dependence on international capital flows, and emphasised again the importance of international trade as a motor of growth and recovery. But Europe also is subject to the same market disciplines, and needs to be no less vigilant on the need for good governance in the financial and corporate sector, or on the essential importance of responsive and affordable social policies.

This increasing global interdependence also brings with it increasing global responsibilities. The EU and its Asian partners have a shared interest in promoting peace and security at the global level, in enhancing the effectiveness of the UN, and in addressing global environmental challenges. It is also in our common interest to address the "dark side of globalisation", combatting transnational crime (including trafficking in women and children, the smuggling of illegal migrants, the drugs trade and money laundering) and terrorism, and addressing global scourges such as poverty and epidemic disease. HIV/AIDS in particular is spreading rapidly in parts of Asia, with a potentially severe economic impact on top of its terrible human costs.

Globalisation of course offers opportunities as well as challenges. Many Asian countries, particularly in East Asia, have benefitted greatly over several decades from a strong growth performance led by exports and by foreign investment (and the East Asian Crisis is likely to have represented only a temporary correction in this process). Europe's own growth record, slower and more mature than that of Asia, has itself been very largely dependent on foreign trade and investment, and on the success of the open and rules-based multilateral trading system established under the GATT and now the WTO.

It is in the imperative interest of both regions to see this system strengthened further, and in particular to see the early launch of a new Round of multilateral trade negotiations. These negotiations, on the basis of a comprehensive agenda including such key issues as investment and competition, will be crucial in helping revitalise growth in Asia in the aftermath of the financial crisis, and in particular in encouraging increased FDI flows to the region. The further strengthening of the multilateral trading system is even more important for the poorer countries of Asia, which would stand to lose most from any possible shift of emphasis from multilateralism towards plurilateral or bilateral trading arrangements – particularly if such arrangements turn out to be more trade-diverting than trade-creating, or if the poorer countries are simply left out.

It will therefore be in the joint interest of the EU and its Asian partners to work towards the further strengthening of the WTO, and for a further reduction in both tariff and non-tariff barriers around the world. The successful integration of China into the WTO will be crucial in this respect. At the same time, it will be essential for the developing countries of the region (no less than for developed countries) to build a sound policy framework to maximise the opportunities offered by globalisation. The risk otherwise is that the 800 million people living under the poverty line in Asia will become further marginalised.

It is likewise in our joint interest that the EU and its Asian partners work together to strengthen global efforts in relation to climate change, and the industrialised and industrialising countries in the region (particularly Japan, China, and India) have a crucial role to play in helping move forward the global environmental agenda. It must be acknowledged that major Asian countries are already undertaking significant steps to reduce greenhouse gas emissions, even without formal reduction or limitation commitments under the Kyoto Protocol. The EU, together with other industrial countries, should continue to support these efforts through technology transfer and related assistance as appropriate. Continued efforts to ensure a comprehensive global commitment to combating climate change will be of critical importance in protecting the interests of future generations in both our regions, and across the world.

Information has also become global in the 1990s, with the internet and email. The full effects of this information revolution have yet to be realised, but the scope which it offers for direct and immediate contact is already transforming our interaction with even the most distant regions of the world. Access to information will be a crucial determinant of any society's ability to respond to these new opportunities, and the closing of the "digital divide", both within and among our societies, will be of critical importance here.

## 3. RELATIONS BETWEEN THE EU AND ASIAN COUNTRIES: TAKING STOCK

The EU's relations with Asian countries have certainly evolved tremendously over recent years, and there is no doubt that the balanced and comprehensive approach called for in the 1994 Strategy has played an essential part in modernising our relations with this vast region. Much has been achieved since 1994, even if there is still a great potential for strengthening our relations further.

Since 1994, our **political dialogue** with key partners in the region has developed considerably, with new Summit dialogues in the Asia-Europe Meeting (ASEM) and with China, India, Japan and (soon) Korea, with the ongoing EU-ASEAN dialogue, including active EU participation in the ASEAN Regional Forum (ARF), and with continuing high-level contacts with Australia and New Zealand. The EU has continued to make an active contri-

> ***The EU and India : a partnership between the world's largest democracies***
>
> *The EU-India partnership reached a turning-point with our first Summit Meeting, in Lisbon in June 2000. The Summit agreed to build a coalition of interest in addressing global challenges such as the promotion of peace and security, the elimination of nuclear weapons, the fight against terrorism and international crime, and climate change, as well as setting an agenda to help us work together to fully utilise the huge economic and commercial potential of our respective markets, and reinforce our cooperation in the fields of research, science and technology.*[11]
>
> *The EU is also committed to work closely with India to address the challenge of eliminating poverty. Since 1994, EC support for social reform in India, particularly in the primary education and basic health sectors, has yielded impressive results.*

bution to peace and security issues in the region, for example in our assistance for the establishment of democratic government in Cambodia and East Timor, our support for refugees in and from Afghanistan, and in our support for the inter-Korean dialogue and our contribution to KEDO. The EU has also established an important human rights dialogue with China (and hopes to develop such a dialogue with North Korea); in Indonesia we are actively supporting efforts towards the strengthening of governance and civil society participation; and in relation to Burma/Myanmar and Pakistan the EU continues to encourage any opening towards democracy.

These are solid foundations on which we can build in enhancing our dialogue with the countries of the region. We should be able to discuss issues on which we may have differing views as well as identify areas of shared concern. We should emphasise areas where the EU and its Asian partners can work together in addressing the global challenges which face us all. And we should intensify joint efforts to strengthen the international institutions on which we all depend.

> ***The EU and Japan : expanding our cooperation***
>
> *Japan is the EU's second-largest export market (after the US), and a major investor in the EU. A healthy Japanese economy is of critical importance for our own prosperity as well as that of their regional neighbours. But our relations with Japan go far beyond the purely economic, with an increasing cooperation on global and regional issues, expressed in particular in the new "Action Plan" to be adopted at the 2001 EU-Japan Summit. Building on this, our task in the coming years will be to express this global partnership in concrete terms, whether in the political, economic or social field, both in multilateral institutions and in our bilateral relations.*

The institutional framework for our relations with Asian countries varies,[10] and only a few countries in the region have as yet entered into fully comprehensive ("third-generation") cooperation agreements with the EC. In this respect, Asia lags well behind other regions, such as Latin America, the Mediterranean and the CIS. Upgrading the institutional basis for our relations with key partners in Asia would allow for a more coherent approach to all relevant issues (in the political and security fields as well as on economic and development issues), would create a powerful stimulus for the intensification of our dialogue and cooperation in all areas, and would give a clear public signal of the commitment of both parties to raise our relationship to a new level.

Our **trade and investment** relations with Asia have expanded substantially, notwithstanding the substantial medium-term impact of the "East Asian Crisis" which erupted in 1997. In 2000 Asia accounted for 21.1% of total EU exports, making Asia our third-largest regional trading partner[12]. On the investment side Asia as a whole remained the fourth-largest regional investment destination for the EU, accounting for 6.8% of EU outward FDI flows and 9.2% of EU outward FDI stocks in 1999, the latest year for which figures are available.[13] However, the bulk of EU outward FDI continues to go to North America, and EU FDI flows to South East Asia in particular have not yet recovered from the East Asian Crisis. Both in our bilateral dialogue with key partners in the region, and in the WTO, the EU has worked consistently to reduce barriers to our two-way trade and investment and to enhance the institutional, legal and regulatory climate facing our economic operators. We have also made great efforts through our economic cooperation programmes such as Asia Invest to encourage European SMEs to better utilise the trade and investment opportunities available in Asia.

We must however strengthen further our dialogue and cooperation with Asia on trade and investment issues, and on broader macro-economic policy matters. Both in the WTO, and in our bilateral discussions with Asian partners, we should redouble our efforts to enhance the open multilateral framework for trade and investment, to remove non-tariff barriers to trade and investment, and to enhance the legal, regulatory and technical framework for our economic operators. We should continue our work to improve trade access for the poorest developing countries (a responsibility incumbent also on the more advanced developing countries in Asia). And we should build a stronger dialogue on economic and financial policy issues, sharing our own experience on regional macro-economic cooperation, and encouraging the broader use of the euro as an international currency.

Our cooperation funding for the developing countries in Asia has grown moderately in recent years, averaging some €438 million per year in 1996–2000 (development aid and economic cooperation combined), as against €363 million per year in 1991–1995. There has however been a significant evolution in terms of focus (with more than 80% of our development aid for Asia going to the low-income countries), while new programmes in mutually-beneficial economic cooperation have been introduced with particular interest for the more advanced countries in the region. Taking EC and Member-State aid efforts together, the EU continues to account for 30% of total ODA flows to Asia [14]

The bulk of this assistance has been focused on direct poverty-reduction measures, for example through support for the health and education sectors, rural development, and institutional capacity-building. The environment sector has also received significant support, with substantial programmes in areas such as forest protection, biodiversity, and environmental technology. Attention has also been paid to strengthening the economic links between our two regions, both in helping upgrade the trade and investment climate, and in promoting contact between economic operators in the two regions.

Much remains to be done, however, to ensure that EU aid programmes in Asia can achieve their full potential. The Commission has already launched a far-reaching reform of the management of our external assistance programmes, and the full and effective

**The EU and emerging East Asia: ASEAN and China**

*Growth has resumed in most of the emerging economies of East Asia following the economic crisis, and their ongoing transformation is changing the face of the region. The EU's political and economic relations with these countries have deepened considerably since 1994, accompanied by a broadening in our range of cooperation activities*

*Our relations with China continue to intensify, through frequent contacts at all levels, from annual Summits to expert meetings. The successful EU-ASEAN Ministerial Meeting in Vientiane in December 2000 set the scene for further strengthening this long-standing relationship, and the EU plays an increasingly active role in the ASEAN Regional Forum*

*The continued intensification of our relations with these countries, and the concrete results being achieved, will be a litmus test for EU-Asia relations in the coming years.*

implementation of these reforms will be an immediate priority for us. The allocation of our aid funding should fully reflect the focus on poverty reduction in the Commission's recent Communication on Development Policy.[15] We should strengthen our economic cooperation with Asia, in our mutual interest, and we should continue to ensure that environmental considerations are fully integrated within our cooperation activities, while strengthening our work in such key fields as energy, environmental technology and biodiversity.

The EC also provides substantial humanitarian assistance in Asia. Over the three years from 1998 to 2000, an average of €77.4m per year was provided in humanitarian assistance following natural or man-made disasters in Asia. This accounted for 12.8% of the EC's humanitarian assistance efforts world-wide. In the year 2000 alone, humanitarian assistance was provided to well over a dozen countries in Asia, according to needs. Particular efforts were made in relation to Afghanistan, Cambodia, India, Indonesia, North Korea, Mongolia, the Philippines, Thailand (Burmese refugees) and East Timor. At the beginning of this year a substantial contribution was made for the victims of the earthquake in Gujarat in India. Work on disaster prevention has also continued, with a second phase of the DipEcho programme funded in 2000.[16]

One element which does not seem to have evolved greatly is the degree of mutual awareness between our two regions, with stereotypes on both sides still casting Europe as introspective and old-fashioned, and Asia as a distant and exotic continent, presenting more challenges than opportunities. Much more needs to be done to raise the profile of Europe in Asia. It will be imperative to strengthen and expand the network of EC Delegations in the region.[17]

In addition, it will be important to strengthen our educational and cultural exchanges with the region (within our economic cooperation programmes), to broaden and intensify the range of seminars and conferences bringing together think-tanks and policy-makers from both regions, and to strengthen information and communications activities through our Delegations and through the Internet.

## 4. OBJECTIVES,PRIORITIES AND ACTION POINTS

### *4.1. General objectives and priorities*

The general policy objectives of the EU in its relations with Asia, as with other parts of the world, are set out in the EC and EU Treaties. To translate these general objectives into clear strategic priorities and action-points, our approach should be coherent and comprehensive, and should respond to the diversity of Asia. It should be realistic and focused, setting clear priorities which can be addressed within the resources available to us. It should emphasise the comparative advantage of the EU, and the value-added which we can offer – reflecting for example the EU's role as the largest single market in the world and the largest source of global FDI, and as the largest single source of ODA and of humanitarian assistance. It should also emphasise those areas where the EU's own experience and diversity may be of particular relevance in addressing issues such as regional cooperation and social policy.

In particular, our approach should reflect tomorrow's agenda, the forward-looking agenda of an enlarged European Union, and the implications of that for our relations with Asia in each of the three pillars. In this context, and taking account of the overall objectives of the EU, of the achievements and unfinished business of past years, and of the new challenges now to be faced, we can set one clear core objective to guide the future development of EU-Asia relations into the coming decade: we must focus on strengthening the EU's political and economic presence across the region, and raising this to a level commensurate with the growing global weight of an enlarged EU.

In order to meet this objective, we should in particular work to:

- contribute to peace and security in the region and globally, through a broadening of our engagement with the region;
- further strengthen our mutual trade and investment flows with the region;
- promote the development of the less prosperous countries of the region, addressing the root causes of poverty;

> *In our political and security relations with Asia, we should :*
>
> - *strengthen our engagement on regional and global security issues;*
> - *strengthen our dialogue and cooperation on conflict prevention issues;*
> - *and enhance our cooperation on justice and home affairs issues.*

- contribute to the spreading of democracy, good governance and the rule of law;
- build global partnerships and alliances with Asian countries, in appropriate international fora, to help address both the challenges and the opportunities offered by globalisation, and to strengthen our joint efforts on global environmental and security issues;
- and help strengthen the awareness of Europe in Asia (and vice versa)

### *4.2. Action points for the region as a whole*

**A**. In contributing to peace and security in the region and globally, the EU should work in particular to

- strengthen our engagement with Asia in relation to old and new global and regional security issues, both in our bilateral and regional relations, and in the UN framework. The EU should in particular play a pro-active role in regional cooperation fora such as the ARF, and in inter-regional dialogues such as ASEM;
- support conflict prevention efforts, and promote an enhanced sharing of experience between Europe and Asia concerning longer-term confidence-building measures. The Commission will in particular be guided by its recent Communication on conflict prevention,18 emphasising preventive action in a framework of international cooperation and coordination, and mobilising all Community instruments more effectively;
- strengthen our dialogue and cooperation with Asia in relation to justice and home affairs issues. Areas such as visa, asylum, immigration and other policies related to the free movement of persons are increasingly important in our relations with Asia as with other regions. In addition to addressing these issues, we should also strengthen our joint efforts to combat transnational crime, for example in areas such as the fight against drugs, trafficking in human beings, trafficking in arms, money-laundering, the exploitation of migrants, and fighting corruption.

**B**. In strengthening our mutual trade and investment flows with Asia, the EU should work in particular to:

- further develop our bilateral economic relations with Asian partners, in particular by strengthening our efforts to improve market access and investment conditions on both

> *In enhancing our economic and commercial links with Asian partners, we should :*
>
> - *work to strengthen our bilateral economic relations, reducing non-tariff barriers to trade and facilitating investment, and helping build a pro-development policy climate;*
> - *support cooperation between economic operators in our two regions;*
> - *strengthen our policy dialogue on economic and financial issues, and promote the use of the euro internationally;*
> - *continue to ensure favourable market access for the poorest developing countries;*
> - *Recognise the role of transport and energy in our trade relations as well as the impact of both sectors on the environment.*

sides, and by helping those countries which are seeking to build a business climate conducive to trade and investment. Intensified efforts to reduce technical barriers to trade, and to promote transparency and predictability in the legislative and regulatory context, will be of particular importance here. We should also work to strengthen our cooperation with regional groupings like ASEAN (which are a force for liberalisation and progress on trade and investment issues), and examine means of reinforcing our trade and investment links with the Asian countries in general;

- help strengthen private-sector cooperation between Europe and Asia, in our mutual interest, through support for contacts between economic operators in Europe (particularly SMEs) and in Asia. A particular attention should also be paid to the high-technology sectors which will help determine our common future, such as information and communications technology, transport and energy. The EIB will continue to play its role in supporting European investment in the region;

- strengthen our dialogue on economic and financial policy, and encourage sound policy reform in the financial and corporate sector. Europe's own experience in regional cooperation on economic and financial policy may be of particular interest to Asia, and we should in addition encourage Asia to take maximum advantage of the new possibilities offered by the euro.

> *In promoting development, the EU must work together with our Asian partners to :*
>
> - *help reduce poverty in the poorest developing countries of the region;*
> - *strengthen our dialogue on social policy issues;*
> - *while completing the reform of our own aid management.*

- enhance market access for the poorest developing countries, for example through the effective implementation of the recently agreed "Everything But Arms" initiative and the continued enhancement of our GSP system, and in line with existing EC policies. We should also encourage the middle-income countries in the region to strengthen their own contribution in this area.
- Take into account the essential role of transport in the continuation and development of trade between Europe and Asia and the growing inter-dependence of Europe and Asia in energy supply and demand. Furthermore, co-operation between Europe and Asia on energy use both in transport and in industry will be necessary in order to attempt to meet the climate change objectives of the Kyoto Protocol.

C. In promoting development in the region, the EU should in particular:

> *In contributing to democratisation, good governance and the rule of law, and respect for human rights we should strengthen our bilateral and multilateral dialogue with our Asian partners, encourage civil society dialogue, and ensure that human rights and governance issues are mainstreamed in our cooperation activities.*

- strengthen our efforts towards poverty reduction, particularly in the poorest countries of the region, and contribute to the achievement of the International Development Targets by 2015. This will be achieved through a strengthened focus on key poverty issues and new ways of working as set out in the Joint Commission and Council Statement on EC Development Policy;[19] themes of particular interest for Asia shall include trade and development, sector programmes in social areas (notably health and education), economic and social governance and institutional capacity-building, and the link between environmental conservation and poverty;
- strengthen our dialogue on social policy issues, sharing Europe's own experience in addressing the challenges of modernisation and globalisation. There is much to be gained from dialogue and exchange of best practice on the links between trade and social development, including the promotion of core labour standards.[20] There is no single "European model" of social governance, but Europe's own diversity, and our long experience of working to combine economic dynamism with social equity, may be of particular interest to many Asian partners;

- and pursue vigorously the reform of the management of EC external assistance,[21] ensuring that our scarce resources are used to the best possible effect;

**D**. In contributing to the spreading of democracy, good governance and the rule of law, and respect for human rights, we should, in line with the Commission's recent Communication on this subject[22]:

- work together with Asia to uphold the universality and indivisibility of human rights, and pursue a constructive dialogue both in bilateral fora (for example in our human rights dialogue with China), and in regional and multilateral fora, notably in the UN and its different agencies, in particular the ILO. We should also encourage the signing and ratification of the principal human rights instruments by those countries who have not yet done so;
- encourage the strengthening of civil society across the region, and promote a broader civil society dialogue between our two regions;
- and mainstream human rights and governance issues in our cooperation activities with Asia.

**E**. In building global partnerships and alliances with Asian partners, we should in particular:

- work together to strengthen our cooperation in the United Nations, for example in working for the early and comprehensive ratification of major international instruments such as the CTBT or the conventions on small arms and anti-personnel mines, and for a future global anti-corruption instrument; enhancing the non-proliferation regime and efforts to control other weapons of mass destruction; working for the reform of the UN system including a comprehensive reform of the Security Council in all its aspects; working to strengthen UN peacekeeping efforts through the support of a timely implementation of the recommendations contained in the Brahimi Report; and reinforcing the functioning of the UN system by encouraging a prompt and full payment by all partners of contributions based on the new scales of assessment including arrears;

*In building global partnerships with our Asian partners, we shall in particular work together to:*

- *strengthen the work of the United Nations and its different agencies;*
- *strengthen the open international trading system embodied in the WTO;*
- *safeguard the global environment;*
- *and combat global challenges while maximising global opportunities.*

- strengthen the open and rules-based international framework embodied in the WTO, both through building support for the early launching and successful completion of a comprehensive new Round of multilateral trade negotiations, and through working for the early accession of China and other Asian countries/economies who have yet to become members. A multilateral approach is the only realistic way forward in promoting our joint interests, and in safeguarding the particular interests of the poorest developing countries;
- address global, regional and local environmental challenges, working together in international fora to strengthen our joint efforts in relation to climate change and the

deterioration of the global commons, and in supporting efforts to promote sustainable resource management and to address urban and industrial environmental problems. Climate change, for example, poses a serious threat to a number of countries in Asia, and we should redouble our efforts to work with the more advanced developing countries in Asia on these issues. We should also take care to integrate environmental considerations into all areas of bilateral and inter-regional cooperation, including our scientific and technological cooperation efforts;

- strengthen our dialogue and cooperation with Asia in relation to global challenges, and in particular the fight against transnational crime, against terrorism, corruption, xenophobia, racism and fundamentalism of all kinds, and against epidemic disease (including HIV/AIDS in particular), while working also to enhance the access of the poorer countries in Asia to the global opportunities offered by new technologies, and helping diminish the knowledge and digital divides;
- and address the need for reinforced inter-regional scientific and technological cooperation to foster common analyses of and solutions to shared regional and global problems.

*In upgrading the EU's overall presence in Asia, we should:*

- *strengthen and expand the network of EC Delegations across the region;*
- *and work to strengthen educational and cultural exchanges between our two regions, and to promote enhanced civil society contacts and intellectual exchanges.*

F. In increasing the awareness of the EU in Asia, expressing better our economic and political presence in the region, and building on both the adoption of the single currency and the pursuit of a more effective common foreign and security policy, we should in particular:

- raise the EU's profile across Asia, strengthening and broadening our network of Delegations across the region, enhancing EU coordination at all levels, and intensifying information and communication efforts across the region. As indicated in the Commission's recent Communication on the development of the External Service,[23] and in addition to strengthening our existing Delegations (notably in the context of deconcentration of aid management), the Commission also proposes to open new Delegations in those countries where we are still under-represented politically, taking into account both trade and cooperation issues. In particular, it is proposed that new Delegations be opened in Malaysia and in Singapore, and in Cambodia, Laos and Nepal. Consideration will also be given to opening a trade representation office in Taiwan;
- work to strengthen educational, scientific and cultural exchanges with Asia, through support for enhanced cooperation between higher education institutions, an intensification of academic, research and student exchanges between our two regions, and the promotion of structural networks enabling mutually beneficial cooperation. Europe has a great deal to offer in the field of higher education[24] and scientific research, yet the great majority of Asian students studying abroad tend to go to North America or Australasia as a first priority. Equally, the number of European academics or students with links to Asia remains very small, while European Studies remains an underdeveloped field in most Asian countries;
- promote a strengthening and broadening of civil society partnerships between our two regions (whether among our parliamentary representatives, local authorities, NGOs,

youth associations, consumer groups, or professional associations), and an intensification of intellectual contacts and networking in relation to the challenges facing our two regions.

*4.3. Action points for the different regions of Asia*

The strategic priorities and action points described above set out a common foundation for relations between the EU and Asian countries across the board, and should guide us (mutatis mutandis) in developing our relations with Asia as a whole. Reflecting the underlying diversity of Asia, these general guidelines should be developed further for each of Asia's subregions and for our key partners across the region, both in our Country Strategies for development cooperation with individual developing countries, and in occasional Communications relating to our major partners. But it is already possible to indicate certain key issues to which emphasis must be given for each of the major regions of Asia.

> *In our relations with South Asia generally, we should strengthen our dialogue and cooperation on security issues, on economic and commercial issues, and on poverty reduction; priority will also be given to issues of human rights and conflict prevention.*
>
> *For India in particular, the strengthening of our bilateral cooperation on political, economic and social cooperation should go hand-in-hand with enhanced partnership on global issues.*

South Asia

The continuing tensions between India and Pakistan (and the imperative need to encourage progress towards nuclear disarmament, and the peaceful resolution of the Kashmir issue), as well as the threat to regional stability posed by terrorism, religious fundamentalism and ethnic conflict (notably for Afghanistan and Sri Lanka), illustrate the importance of political and security issues in the Sub-Continent. The EU should reflect more deeply on the major political challenges facing the region, and be ready to adopt a more assertive and forward-looking approach to its policy dialogue with the key countries in the region. India's role as a regional and global player, and the further enhancement of EU-India relations, will merit our special attention. An early restoration of parliamentary democracy in Pakistan will be a prime factor in paving the way for enhanced cooperation with that country.

Doubts regarding globalisation and a new WTO round have perhaps been greater in South Asia than elsewhere in the region. The EU should take this into account in preparing a comprehensive economic and commercial strategy towards South Asia, enhancing our dialogue with the countries of the region on trade and investment liberalisation and policy reform, and addressing the commercial concerns of both sides. Local strengths in high-tech sectors, and the ongoing economic reforms in India, should be used to encourage a greater focus on the Sub-Continent by European economic operators. Efforts towards stronger sub-regional economic cooperation within SAARC should be encouraged, as well as a stronger integration of South Asia within the broader Asian region (for example through a broadening of Asian participation in ASEM). The enhancement of mutual awareness between our two regions will continue to be a priority.

Support for poverty reduction efforts will be at the core of EU cooperation efforts. To maximise the impact of our limited resources, our work in areas such as health and education will increasingly focus on sectoral support and policy modernisation. We will work increasingly with regional and local authorities as well as national-level administrations. The role of NGOs will be crucial, and contacts between civil society groups in Europe and in the region should be encouraged. Trade development and economic reform will be given a special emphasis, since broader-based growth and an enhanced trade and investment climate will be essential for poverty reduction across the region. Coordination of EC and Member-States' cooperation efforts has already shown its efficacy in responding to the Gujarat earthquake, and this should serve as a best-practice model for the further strengthening of complementarity and concerted action among all EU donors.

South-East Asia

ASEAN, and the ASEAN Regional Forum, will continue to be the major focus of our political and security dialogue with South-East Asia, and it will be important for the EU to play a pro-active role in the ARF. More generally, our dialogue with ASEAN and its member

> *The EU-ASEAN relationship has since the 1970s been a constant factor in our partnerships with Asia. Recent developments in the region make it even more important to strengthen further our cooperation in all areas – political, economic & social. Particular attention will be given to enhancing mutual understanding and to developing global partnerships, as well as to the need to further strengthen our relations with key ASEAN partners.*

countries should help identify areas where ASEAN and the EU can work together on global security questions, and on global challenges such as drugs and transnational crime. We should continue to give full support to conflict prevention efforts within the region (for example in the Indonesian and Philippine archipelagos and in Burma/Myanmar), and to civil society efforts to promote transparency, good governance and the rule of law. And in our political dialogue with ASEAN and its member countries we should give attention to human rights issues.

In our economic relations with ASEAN and its member countries, we should work together to strengthen the WTO, to encourage trade and investment facilitation, and to help pursue financial and economic reform. Support for enhanced contact between economic operators in the two regions will be important, particularly in new-technology sectors. Efforts to enhance educational, intellectual and cultural links will likewise be strengthened.

For the low-income countries in the region, we should support those governments that are committed to reducing poverty, while in the more advanced economies a particular effort should be made to encourage social policy reform efforts, and to address urban and environmental issues. Support for improving the climate for trade and investment will make a crucial contribution to development and economic growth in all countries. Civil society efforts to address poverty, governance and social policy issues will continue to deserve our support, and dialogue among civil society groups in our two regions will be encouraged.

The further strengthening of our long-standing partnership with ASEAN will be a key priority in the coming years. This should be reflected both in a strengthened and comprehensive dialogue with ASEAN as a whole, and in the enhancement of our bilateral relations with key ASEAN partners. We should also provide active support for reinforced regional integration, on the basis of mutual solidarity within ASEAN.

Indonesia, as the largest country in the region (and the fourth most populous country in the world) will continue to exert a dominant influence across the region, and any further deterioration in the situation there could have the gravest effect on its neighbours. The EC will continue to apply the strategy spelt out in last year's Communication on Indonesia,[25] while reflecting further on how best to strengthen our political, economic and cooperation relations with that country.

North-East Asia

Strengthening our relations with China will be a major opportunity, and challenge, for the EU for years to come. China has firmly established itself as a regional power, and the Chinese economy, boosted by large inflows of foreign investment and technology, is rapidly moving up the technological ladder. China is already becoming a major competitor to developed economies in the region and beyond, and WTO accession will certainly bring a further increase in economic efficiency and competitiveness. This increasing economic power is likely to translate into growing Chinese assertiveness on the regional and international scene.

It is a clear EU interest to ensure that China plays a constructive and cooperative role both in the region and in the world. In building on our long-term aims for the bilateral relationship defined in 1998 and amplified in 2001,[26] we will therefore seek to engage China further on both bilateral and global issues. In particular, we will work to:

- ensure that China continues to develop in a sustainable way which will help it to play a constructive and cooperative role;
- engage China further in the international community, through a continued strengthening and focusing of our political dialogue;
- support China's transition to an open society through a more focused and results-oriented human rights dialogue, working with China to support relevant reforms;
- support China's integration in the world economy, by promoting its rapid accession to the WTO, using our assistance programmes and upgrading our dialogue in key policy areas to help make WTO accession and the social and economic reform process a success;
- and enhance the effectiveness of our assistance to China, focusing our programmes on three main areas: support to the reform process, promotion of sustainable development, scientific and technological cooperation[27], encouragement of good governance initiatives and promotion of the rule of law.

As regards the Hong Kong and Macao Special Administrative Regions (SARs), the EU will seek to ensure that the autonomy of the two SARs is upheld, within the "one country, two systems" principle enshrined in the Basic Laws of each SAR. This is a central plank of EU policy towards the territories and a major component of our relationship with China as a whole. The Commission policy documents of 1997 and 1999 regarding our relations with each Region[28] put our relations with the two SARs on a more permanent footing and committed the EU to observing developments and to producing annual reports on each.

Taiwan, which the EU recognises as a separate customs territory, but not as a sovereign state, is the EU's third-largest bilateral trading partner in Asia. Its pending accession to WTO should contribute to a further increase in trade and investment flows and related dialogues. The EU is convinced that the cross-straits issue can only be resolved peacefully, and on the basis of a constructive dialogue.

With respect to Japan, bilateral relations have developed considerably since the signing of the Joint Declaration in 1991, and a regular and wide-ranging dialogue has been established. This largely reflects a growing mutual awareness of shared interests, for instance in the continued health of the multilateral system, common challenges such as environmental degradation and the ageing society, and shared values such as the rule of law and human rights. The long economic stagnation in Japan has, however, caused concern from the point of view of possible adverse effects on the global economy and on growth prospects for developing countries in Asia, as well as depressing demand for EU exports and aggravating further the large bilateral imbalance. Moreover, cooperation between the EU and Japan in the field of foreign policy is growing, but could be considerably strengthened as recognised at the EU/Japan Summit in July 2000.

Against this background, priority actions include:

- the adoption of a joint action plan at the EU-Japan Summit in 2001, which will identify a set of cooperation initiatives giving political visibility and tangible content to the relationship over the coming decade. This will help us move from dialogue to closer policy coordination and concrete joint activities in the political and security, economic, justice and social fields;

> *In enhancing our relations with the countries of North-East Asia, we will in particular work to:*
>
> - *strengthen our engagement with China, and support its integration into the world economy and transition to an open society;*
> - *build an enhanced global and regional partnership with Japan on political, economic and social issues;*
> - *deepen our partnership with South Korea, while supporting the inter-Korean reconciliation process;*
> - *and strengthen our economic and commercial relations with the region as a whole, while encouraging necessary reforms.*

- a streamlined Regulatory Reform Dialogue with the aim of reviving the Japanese economy through opening markets further and stimulating inflows of direct investment from the EU;
- deepening EU/Japan cooperation at the multilateral level, both in the WTO with the immediate objective of launching a New Round at Doha, and in the field of environment, aiming at ratification and implementation of the Kyoto Protocol;
- encouraging Japan to engage further with its immediate neighbours in the fields of nonproliferation, human rights, rule of law, etc.

Major recent developments with respect to the Korean Peninsula have included the considerable steps forward in political liberalisation and economic reform in South Korea under President Kim Dae-Jung; the beginning of a thaw in inter-Korean relations with the "sunshine policy" of President Kim and his summit meeting last year with the North Korean President Kim Jong-il; and, in our bilateral relations, the coming into force on 1

*In enhancing relations with Australia and New Zealand, we will in particular work to*

- *expand our economic and commercial relations, while deepening our broader cooperation;*
- *and strengthen our cooperation on global and regional issues.*

April 2001 of the EU South Korea Framework Agreement and its attached political declaration, underlining the increasing strength of our economic and political relations, as well as the recent opening of diplomatic relations with the DPRK. Immediate priorities for action will include:

- encouragement to South Korea to persevere on the path of economic reform;
- continued support for the inter-Korean reconciliation process, developing the EU's own dialogue with North Korea on the basis of the principles decided by the Council in October and November 2000 (respect for human rights; non proliferation; economic reform). This will include a measured expansion of the Commission's assistance activities to help in the critical early stages of economic reform, and the encouragement of further opening by North Korea to the outside world;
- effective implementation of the Framework Agreement, including in particular the enhancement of our two-way trade and investment relations, together with appropriate cooperation initiatives in our mutual interest;
- continued cooperation with South Korea in the context of the WTO.

Australasia

Our relations with Australia and New Zealand have developed positively in recent years and are no longer dominated to the same extent as previously by agricultural trade issues. Indeed, these countries are now important overall trade and investment partners of the EU, and are increasingly important as political partners, representing a substantial force for stability in the broader Asia-Pacific region. At the multilateral level too, there is scope for the EU to deepen our cooperation with Australia and New Zealand.

Priorities for action include:

- further expanding two-way trade and investment, but, also seeking out worthwhile cooperation initiatives for instance in the fields of education, science and technology, research, development, migration policies, in order to deepen the relationship further.

*In further enhancing our regional dialogue with our Asian partners, notably within the ASEM framework, we will use this informal forum as a leading example of a successful EU-Asia partnership, addressing political, economic and social issues in a balanced and comprehensive fashion, based on mutual interest and equal partnership, and helping Europe and Asia to enhance their voice on the global stage. Enlarged participation in ASEM will further enhance its value, and its ability to promote regional stability, support multilateralism, raise mutual awareness, and strengthen the position and profile of the EU in Asia.*

- building stronger alliances at the multilateral level, most particularly in the WTO, with a view to launching a New Round at Doha, and in the field of environment with a view to ratifying and implementing the Kyoto Protocol.
- intensifying political and development assistance cooperation in the region.

Regional fora

In contrast to our relations with Latin America or with the Mediterranean or ACP countries, there is no one inter-regional forum in which Europe and Asia interact. The EU has a longstanding relationship with South-East Asia, through our partnership with ASEAN dating back to the late 1970s. In South Asia, we have worked to intensify our relations with SAARC since the 1990s. And with East Asia, the ASEM process has evolved rapidly since its beginnings in 1996.

The potential for strengthening EU-ASEAN and EU-SAARC relations has already been addressed elsewhere in this paper. The ARF (which has a particular interest as one of the rare regional fora with South Asian participation) will continue to increase in importance as its activities intensify, and the EU will certainly take a pro-active role in this essential forum.

The Commission has emphasised the importance which it attaches to the ASEM process[29], and the scope which it offers for enhancing Asia-Europe dialogue and cooperation on a basis of equal partnership and mutual respect. The ASEM process has offered an excellent example of inter-regional cooperation, and we will continue to work to ensure that it can make progress in each of its "three pillars" (political, economic and social). In particular, we should draw fully on ASEM's potential as a forum for an informal exchange of views promoting increased understanding and enhanced cooperation, and to use this to build concrete achievements in the various priority areas identified in the Asia-Europe Cooperation Framework adopted at the Seoul Summit. ASEM also offers an important opportunity to strengthen and broaden public engagement in Asia-Europe relations[30], and we should encourage parliamentary and civil society participation in this process.

The value of the ASEM process will be further enhanced through a broader participation. The Commission would welcome an enlargement of Asian participation in ASEM to include key representatives of the Sub-Continent, as well as Australia and New Zealand (just as the EU's participation in ASEM should in due course be enlarged in line with the enlargement of the Union itself). More generally, we shall continue to follow with interest the development of other regional fora in the broader Asia-Pacific region, such as APEC and ASEAN + 3, as well as of new sub-regional groupings such as the West Pacific Forum.

## 5. IMPLEMENTATION AND RESOURCES

In order to take account of the specificities of individual countries, it will of course be necessary to build on and amplify this framework through our sub-regional strategies,[31] and in Country Strategy Papers (which focus on development cooperation). It will also be essential to ensure that this framework is appropriately reflected in all aspects of the Commission's work, ensuring a coherent policy mix across all fields of activity. And a close and effective coordination among all EU partners will be a sine qua non for strengthening our relations with Asia, and for enhancing the profile of the EU in Asia.

The present document will in addition serve as an important input for the preparation of a revised legal basis for our cooperation with Asia. The present ALA Regulation[32] was adopted in 1992 (prior to the adoption of the Commission's first Asia Strategy). The Commission intends to review this Regulation in detail in the coming months, with a view to proposing an update during the first semester of 2002. It is probable that this new Regulation will be split into separate Regulations for Asia and for Latin America, to help provide for a more specific response to the particular context and needs of each region. An overall evaluation of ALA cooperation programmes is now being commenced, and this (together with the results of earlier evaluations) will be taken into account in appraising the directions to be followed in the new Regulations[33].

While the present Strategic Framework should serve as an effective guideline for our relations with Asia over the coming decade, it will be important to take stock of progress on a regular basis, and to respond flexibly to changing circumstances. A substantive review of the strategy in five or six years' time would be appropriate. Such a review should for example assess our achievements on the basis of certain simple (if largely qualitative) indicators, touching for example on such elements as the evolution of the EU's trade and investment relations with Asia, the impact of our policy dialogue and of our development programmes. the timing of this review, and the indicators against which progress should be measured, will be considered further during the preparation of the new Regulation.

In order for this Strategic Framework to be fully effective, it is essential that there is a proper consistency between the objectives being set, and the resources available to meet them (both in terms of staff and operational resources in headquarters and in the field, and in terms of the budgetary resources available for our cooperation programmes).

Our first and over-riding priority is to ensure that the available resources are used in an effective and timely fashion – a task to which the Commission has committed itself fully, and where the first fruits of the reform of the management of our external assistance are now being seen. It will be essential that the existing backlog of commitments and payments credits is absorbed, and that the new funds available each year are programmed effectively and committed promptly, if the European taxpayer and the intended beneficiaries are to be properly served. The EC, in partnership with the beneficiary countries, must focus its limited resources on a smaller number of simpler activities, targeted on the key priorities spelt out above, and ensure that these activities are implemented rapidly and effectively.

Once this has been achieved, we will be better able to address the longer-term question of whether and to what extent the level of resources available for our cooperation activities with Asia should be increased. The EC already devotes 80% of its cooperation funding for Asia to the poorest countries in the region.[34] But it is clear that these resources fall far short of giving an adequate response to the scale of the problems facing these countries. As was noted above, Asia accounts for half of the world's population, and for two-thirds of the world's poor. Yet the EC has allocated a very modest proportion of its total cooperation funding to Asia, and on a per capita basis the volume of EC aid funding going to Asia has been very much less than that for other regions of the developing world[35].

Such allocations of course reflect political choices (for example the priority which the EU gives to its near neighbours), as well as the historical evolution of the EU's aid programmes. In addition, the level of aid funding per se is far less important than the developmental impact of our trade and investment flows with the region. But once the reform process has been completed, and we are confident that the limited resources available are being used to their maximum effect, the EU should consider further the level of development cooperation funding which we allocate to Asia, taking account of the EU's financial perspectives and its global responsibilities, and of the overall context of the EU's external interventions.

## 6. CONCLUSIONS

Asian countries are a crucial economic and political partners for the EU. Quite apart from its economic and political weight, the region is also the locus of some of the world's most critical potential flash-points, and is home to the majority of the world's poor. Asia and Europe are increasingly subject to the same challenges and opportunities arising from globalisation. Yet too often these two regions may have seemed to be distant partners, focused more on their own concerns, or on their relations with other regions of the world, than on strengthening their mutual relations.

The Commission's 1994 Asia Strategy was a first effort to take an integrated, comprehensive and balanced view of the relations between the EU and its Asian partners. That strategy has helped considerably in re-focusing our relations with the region, but should now be updated to take account of the substantial changes in both regions since then, and of the further changes which are already on the horizon.

While acknowledging the sheer diversity of Asia, and the scale of the economic, political and cultural differences between and within the different constituent parts of the region as a whole, we can nevertheless identify one core objective which should guide us in further developing our relations with Asia. Over the coming decade, we should focus our efforts on strengthening the EU's political and economic presence in Asia, raising this to a level more commensurate with the growing global weight of an enlarged EU.

To achieve this central objective, we must:

- strengthen our engagement with Asia in the political and security fields;
- further strengthen our mutual trade and investment flows with the region;
- demonstrate our effectiveness as a partner in reducing poverty in Asia;
- contribute to the protection of human rights and to the spreading of democracy, good governance and the rule of law throughout the region;
- build global partnerships with key Asian partners, working together to address the global opportunities and challenges which face us all and to strengthen our joint efforts on global environmental and security issues;
- and strengthen further the mutual awareness between our two regions.

A number of concrete action points have been identified in this paper, in the political, economic and social dimensions, and with respect to our bilateral, regional and multilateral relations with Asia. More specific priorities have also been addressed as regards our relations with the different component regions of Asia, with regional powers such as India, Japan and China and other key partners such as ASEAN, Australia and Korea, and in inter-regional fora such as ASEM.

The implementation of this strategic framework, and its effectiveness in enhancing the relations between the EU and its Asian partners, will be kept under close review in the coming years. We must also ensure that the limited resources available for EC development and economic cooperation activities with Asia are used to their fullest effect, in order to highlight the potential for increasing these resources.

More than ever before, it will be imperative for the EU and its Asian partnersto work together in addressing the global challenges which we both face, and the global opportunities which we should all be able to share. The Commission for its part will make every effort to enhance our regional and global partnerships with Asia, and we would invite our Asian partners to reflect on their side on how we might address these issues together.

**ANNEX**

List of Acronyms

| | |
|---|---|
| ACP | African, Caribbean and Pacific countries |
| AFTA | ASEAN Free Trade Area |
| ALA | Asian and Latin American countries |
| APEC | Asia-Pacific Economic Cooperation |
| ARF | ASEAN Regional Forum |
| ASEAN | Association of South-East Asian Nations |
| ASEAN + 3 | ASEAN plus China, Japan and Korea |
| ASEM | Asia-Europe Meeting |
| CFSP | Common Foreign and Security Policy |
| CIS | Commonwealth of Independent States |
| CTBT | Comprehensive Test-Ban Treaty |
| DAC | Development Assistance Committee (OECD) |
| EC | European Community, |
| ESDP | European Security and Defence Policy |
| EU | European Union |
| FDI | Foreign Direct Investment |
| GATT | General Agreement on Tariffs and Trade |
| GSP | Generalised System of Preferences |
| KEDO | Korean Energy Development Organisation |
| LLDC | Least-Developed Countries |
| NAFTA | North American Free Trade Area |
| NGOs | non-governmental organisations |
| ODA | Official Development Assistance |
| SAARC | South Asian Association for Regional Cooperation |
| SARs | Special Administrative Regions (Hong Kong and Macau) |
| SMEs | small and medium enterprises |
| WTO | World Trade Organization |

**Asia, Population and GNP, 1999**

| | Population m. | GNP $ bn. | GNP per capita $ | GNP (PPP) $ bn. | GNP (PPP) per capita $ |
|---|---|---|---|---|---|
| **South Asia** | **1.330** | **575** | **432** | **2.658** | **1.998** |

| | | | | | |
|---|---|---|---|---|---|
| Afghanistan | 26,0 | ... | ... | ... | ... |
| Bangladesh | 128,0 | 47,0 | 370 | 188,3 | 1.475 |
| Bhutan | 0,8 | 0,4 | 510 | 1,2 | 1.496 |
| India | 998,0 | 442,2 | 450 | 2.144,1 | 2.149 |
| Maldives | 0,3 | 0,3 | 1.160 | 1,0 | 3.545 |
| Nepal | 23,0 | 5,1 | 220 | 28,5 | 1.219 |
| Pakistan | 135,0 | 64,0 | 470 | 236,8 | 1.757 |
| SriLanka | 19,0 | 15,7 | 820 | 58,0 | 3.056 |
| **South-East Asia** | **512** | **524** | **1.022** | **1.571** | **3.067** |
| Brunei | 0,3 | ... | ... | ... | ... |
| Burma | 45,0 | ... | ... | ... | ... |
| Cambodia | 12,0 | 3,0 | 260 | 15,1 | 1.286 |
| Indonesia | 207,0 | 119,5 | 580 | 505,0 | 2.439 |
| Laos | 5,0 | 1,4 | 280 | 8,8 | 1.726 |
| Malaysia | 23,0 | 77,3 | 3.400 | 180,8 | 7.963 |
| Philippines | 77,0 | 78,0 | 1.020 | 292,9 | 3.815 |
| Singapore | 3,0 | 95,4 | 29.610 | 87,1 | 27.024 |
| Thailand | 62,0 | 121,0 | 1.960 | 345,4 | 5.599 |
| Vietnam | 78,0 | 28,2 | 370 | 136,1 | 1.755 |
| | | | | | |
| **North-East Asia** | **1.480** | **5.908** | **3.993** | **7.989** | **5.400** |
| China | 1.250,0 | 980,2 | 780 | 4.112,2 | 3.291 |
| Hongkong | 7,0 | 161,7 | 23.520 | 144,0 | 20.939 |
| Macao | 0,5 | ... | ... | ... | ... |
| Chinese Taipei | 22,0 | 288,6 | 13.120 | ... | ... |
| Japan | 127,0 | 4.078,9 | 32.230 | 3.042,9 | 24.041 |
| N Korea | 23,0 | ... | ... | ... | ... |
| S Korea | 47,0 | 397,9 | 8.490 | 685,7 | 14.637 |
| Mongolia | 3,0 | 0,9 | 350 | 3,9 | 1.496 |
| | | | | | |
| **Australasia** | **23** | **434** | **18.848** | **490** | **21.291** |
| Australia | 19,0 | 380,8 | 20.050 | 426,4 | 22.448 |
| New Zealand | 4,0 | 52,7 | 13.780 | 63,3 | 16.566 |
| | | | | | |
| **Asia** | **3.345** | **7.440,2** | **2.224,3** | **12.707,5** | **3.799,1** |
| World | 5.975,0 | 29.232,1 | 4.890 | 38.804,9 | 6.490 |
| | | | | | |
| Asia% | 56,0% | 25,5% | | 32,7% | |

Source: World Bank, World Development Report 2000/2001

**EU and Candidates, Population and Income, 1999**

| | Population m. | GNP $ bn. | GNP per capita $ | GNP (PPP) $ bn. | GNP (PPP) per capita $ |
|---|---|---|---|---|---|
| **EU-15** | **375** | **8.213** | **21.877** | **7.842** | **20.890** |
| Austria | 8,0 | 210,0 | 25.970 | 192,5 | 23.808 |
| Belgium | 10,0 | 250,6 | 24.510 | 247,4 | 24.200 |
| Denmark | 5,0 | 170,3 | 32.030 | 129,1 | 24.280 |
| Finland | 5,0 | 122,9 | 23.780 | 109,6 | 21.209 |
| France | 59,0 | 1.427,2 | 23.480 | 1.293,8 | 21.897 |
| Germany | 82,0 | 2.079,2 | 25.350 | 1.837,8 | 22.404 |
| Greece | 11,0 | 124,0 | 11.770 | 153,8 | 14.595 |
| Ireland | 4,0 | 71,4 | 19.160 | 71,5 | 19.180 |
| Italy | 58,0 | 1.136,0 | 19.710 | 1.196,3 | 20.751 |
| Luxembourg | 0,4 | 19,3 | 44.640 | 16,5 | 38.247 |
| Netherlands | 16,0 | 384,3 | 24.320 | 364,3 | 23.052 |
| Portugal | 10,0 | 105,9 | 10.600 | 151,3 | 15.147 |
| Spain | 39,0 | 551,6 | 14.000 | 659,3 | 16.730 |
| Sweden | 9,0 | 221,8 | 25.040 | 184,4 | 20.824 |
| United Kingdom | 59,0 | 1.338,1 | 22.640 | 1.234,4 | 20.883 |
| | | | | | |
| **EU Candidates** | **168** | **556** | **3.306** | **1.249** | **7.427** |
| Bulgaria | 8,0 | 11,3 | 1.380 | 40,4 | 4.914 |
| Cyprus | 0,8 | 9,1 | 11.960 | 14,0 | 18.395 |
| Czech Republic | 10,0 | 52,0 | 5.060 | 126,3 | 12.289 |
| Estonia | 1,0 | 5,0 | 3.480 | 11,3 | 7.826 |
| Hungary | 10,0 | 46,8 | 4.650 | 105,5 | 10.479 |
| Latvia | 2,0 | 6,0 | 2.470 | 14,4 | 5.938 |
| Lithuania | 4,0 | 9,7 | 2.620 | 22,5 | 6.093 |
| Malta | 0,4 | 3,5 | 9.210 | 5,7 | 15.066 |
| Poland | 39,0 | 153,1 | 3.960 | 305,5 | 7.894 |
| Romania | 22,0 | 34,2 | 1.520 | 126,8 | 5.647 |
| Slovak Republic | 5,0 | 19,4 | 3.590 | 52,9 | 9.811 |
| Slovenia | 2,0 | 19,6 | 9.890 | 29,8 | 15.062 |
| Turkey | 64,0 | 186,3 | 2.900 | 394,1 | 6.126 |
| | | | | | |
| **EU + Candidates** | **544** | **8.769** | **16.131** | **9.091** | **16.724** |
| World | 5.975,0 | 29.232,1 | 4.890 | 38.804,9 | 6.490 |
| | | | | | |
| EU-15 % | 6,3% | 28,1% | | 20,2% | |
| EU + Candidates % | 9,1% | 30,0% | | 23,4% | |

**EU Trade with Asia and other regions, 1995–2000 (million euro)**

| | EU Exports | | | EU Imports | | | Balance | | Share | Share |
|---|---|---|---|---|---|---|---|---|---|---|
| | 2000 | 1995 | % pa 95–00 | 2000 | 1995 | % pa 95–00 | 2000 | 1995 | EU X 00 | EU X 95 |
| NORTH EAST ASIA | 121.859 | 86.177 | 7,2% | 218.260 | 111.093 | 14,5% | -96.402 | -24.916 | 13,0% | 15,0% |
| NE Asia (excl. Japan) | 77.162 | 53.281 | 7,7% | 133.255 | 56.794 | 18,6% | -56.093 | -3.513 | 8,2% | 9,3% |
| Japan | 44.697 | 32.896 | 6,3% | 85.005 | 54.299 | 9,4% | -40.308 | -21.403 | 4,8% | 5,7% |
| South Korea | 16.356 | 12.331 | 5,8% | 24.346 | 10.925 | 17,4% | -7.990 | 1.407 | 1,7% | 2,2% |
| China | 25.288 | 14.690 | 11,5% | 69.673 | 26.343 | 21,5% | -44.385 | -11.653 | 2,7% | 2,6% |
| Hong Kong | 20.243 | 15.796 | 5,1% | 11.708 | 7.156 | 10,3% | 8.536 | 8.640 | 2,2% | 2,8% |
| Macao | 178 | 137 | 5,4% | 858 | 532 | 10,0% | -680 | -395 | ... | ... |
| Taiwan | 14.851 | 10.112 | 8,0% | 26.499 | 11.756 | 17,7% | -11.648 | -1.643 | 1,6% | 1,8% |
| Mongolia | 65 | 49 | 5,5% | 50 | 31 | 9,9% | 14 | 18 | ... | ... |
| North Korea | 181 | 165 | 1,9% | 121 | 50 | 19,2% | 60 | 115 | ... | ... |
| ASEAN | 40.055 | 37.091 | 1,5% | 69.310 | 34.670 | 14,9% | -29.255 | 2.421 | 4,3% | 6,5% |
| Brunei | 272 | 625 | -15,3% | 129 | 263 | -13,3% | 143 | 362 | 0,0% | 0,1% |
| Indonesia | 4.397 | 5.854 | -5,6% | 10.833 | 6.109 | 12,1% | -6.436 | -254 | 0,5% | 1,0% |
| Malaysia | 8.380 | 7.939 | 1,1% | 16.887 | 9.156 | 13,0% | -8.507 | -1.217 | 0,9% | 1,4% |
| Philippines | 4.358 | 2.291 | 13,7% | 8.015 | 2.420 | 27,1% | -3.658 | -129 | 0,5% | 0,1% |
| Singapore | 14.720 | 10.904 | 6,2% | 15.853 | 8.760 | 12,6% | -1.133 | 2.144 | 1,6% | 1,9% |
| Thailand | 6.431 | 8.492 | -5,4% | 12.742 | 6.625 | 14,0% | -6.311 | 1.867 | 0,7% | 1,5% |
| Vietnam | 1.227 | 750 | 10,3% | 3.961 | 1.151 | 28,0% | -2.734 | -401 | 0,1% | 0,1% |
| Cambodia | 115 | 75 | 9,0% | 355 | 46 | 50,3% | -240 | 29 | ... | ... |
| Laos | 44 | 43 | 0,8% | 130 | 72 | 12,5% | -86 | -30 | | |
| Burma | 112 | 119 | -1,3% | 404 | 68 | 43,0% | -293 | 51 | ... | ... |

**EU Trade with Asia and other regions, 1995–2000 (continued)**

| | EU Exports | | | EU Imports | | | Balance | | Share | Share |
|---|---|---|---|---|---|---|---|---|---|---|
| | 2000 | 1995 | % pa 95–00 | 2000 | 1995 | % pa 95–00 | 2000 | 1995 | EU X 00 | EU X 95 |
| SOUTH ASIA | 17.660 | 12.828 | 6,6% | 20.240 | 12.159 | 10,7% | -2.579 | 669 | 1,9% | 2,2% |
| India | 13.304 | 9.440 | 7,1% | 12.342 | 7.796 | 9,6% | 962 | 1.644 | 1,4% | 1,6% |
| Pakistan | 1.905 | 2.045 | -1,4% | 2.602 | 1.979 | 5,6% | -697 | 67 | 0,2% | 0,4% |
| Sri Lanka | 1.575 | 720 | 16,9% | 1.891 | 930 | 15,2% | -317 | -210 | 0,2% | 0,1% |
| Nepal | 85 | 51 | 10,7% | 178 | 143 | 4,5% | -93 | -92 | 0,0% | 0,0% |
| Bangladesh | 695 | 495 | 7,0% | 3.046 | 1.260 | 19,3% | -2.351 | -765 | 0,1% | 0,1% |
| Maldives | 39 | 28 | 7,2% | 121 | 20 | 43,5% | -82 | 8 | ... | ... |
| Bhutan | 11 | 6 | 13,7% | 2 | 1 | 8,6% | 9 | 5 | ... | ... |
| Afghanistan | 46 | 43 | 1,4% | 57 | 29 | 14,4% | -11 | 13 | ... | ... |
| AUSTRALASIA | 17.857 | 12.287 | 7,8% | 11.130 | 6.672 | 10,8% | 6.727 | 5.615 | 1,9% | 2,1% |
| Australia | 15.694 | 10.500 | 8,4% | 8.730 | 4.975 | 11,9% | 6.965 | 5.526 | 1,7% | 1,8% |
| New Zealand | 2.140 | 1.786 | 3,7% | 2.386 | 1.697 | 7,1% | -247 | 89 | 0,2% | 0,3% |
| TOTALASIA | 197.431 | 148.384 | 5,9% | 318.940 | 164.593 | 14,1% | -121.509 | -16.210 | 21,1% | 25,9% |
| Developed Asia | 99.331 | 73.447 | 6,2% | 133.047 | 79.584 | 10,8% | -33.716 | -6.137 | 10,6% | 12,8% |
| Developing Asia | 98.100 | 74.937 | 5,5% | 185.893 | 85.010 | 16,9% | -87.793 | -10.073 | 10,5% | 13,1% |
| Europe excl. EU | 289.258 | 168.700 | 11,4% | 282.587 | 153.486 | 13,0% | 6.671 | 15.214 | 30,9% | 29,4% |
| Cand. Countries (13) | 150.415 | 70.658 | 16,3% | 117.012 | 55.468 | 16,1% | 33.403 | 15.190 | 16,1% | 12,3% |
| EEA + Switzerland | 98.107 | 69.776 | 7,1% | 106.188 | 69.929 | 8,7% | -8.081 | -153 | 10,5% | 12,2% |
| CIS | 27.568 | 20.820 | 5,8% | 54.227 | 24.931 | 16,8% | -26.660 | -4.111 | 2,9% | 3,6% |
| SE Europe | 9.619 | 5.486 | 11,9% | 4.539 | 2.763 | 10,4% | 5.079 | 2.723 | 1,0% | 1,0% |
| Other W. Europe | 3.550 | 1.960 | 12,6% | 620 | 396 | 9,4% | 2.930 | 1.564 | 0,4% | 0,3% |

**EU Trade with Asia and other regions, 1995–2000 (continued)**

| | EU Exports | | | EU Imports | | | Balance | | Share | Share |
|---|---|---|---|---|---|---|---|---|---|---|
| | 2000 | 1995 | % pa 95–00 | 2000 | 1995 | % pa 95–00 | 2000 | 1995 | EU X 00 | EU X 95 |
| NAFTA | 265.389 | 118.168 | 17,6% | 222.284 | 118.589 | 13,4% | 43.105 | -420 | 28,4% | 20,6% |
| US | 230.947 | 103.315 | 17,5% | 196.946 | 103.674 | 13,7% | 34.000 | -358 | 24,7% | 18,0% |
| Canada | 20.596 | 10.342 | 14,8% | 18.364 | 11.707 | 9,4% | 2.232 | -1.365 | 2,2% | 1,8% |
| Mexico | 13.846 | 4.511 | 25,1% | 6.973 | 3.208 | 16,8% | 6.873 | 1.303 | 1,5% | 0,8% |

**EU Trade with Asia and other regions, 1995–2000 (million euro)**

| | EU Exports | | | EU Imports | | | Balance | | Share | Share |
|---|---|---|---|---|---|---|---|---|---|---|
| | 2000 | 1995 | % pa 95–00 | 2000 | 1995 | % pa 95–00 | 2000 | 1995 | EU X 00 | EU X 95 |
| Other Regions | 160.186 | 108.320 | 8,1% | 157.466 | 87.392 | 12,5% | 2.720 | 20.928 | 17,1% | 18,9% |
| Mediterranean | 50.788 | 33.191 | 8,9% | 44.901 | 21.043 | 16,4% | 5.887 | 12.148 | 5,4% | 5,8% |
| South & Central | 40.357 | 27.884 | 7,7% | 41.326 | 27.222 | 8,7% | -969 | 662 | 4,3% | 4,9% |
| America Gulf | 31.055 | 20.983 | 8,2% | 28.336 | 11.482 | 19,8% | 2.719 | 9.501 | 3,3% | 3,7% |
| ACP | 37.987 | 26.262 | 7,7% | 42.904 | 27.645 | 9,2% | -4.917 | -1.383 | 4,1% | 4,6% |
| World (excl. intra-EU) | 935.733 | 573.277 | 10,3% | 1.022.671 | 545.253 | 13,4% | -86.937 | 28.024 | 100,0% | 100,0% |

Source: Eurostat

**World Trade Shares, 1999 (million euro)**

| | Imports | | Exports | | Total Trade | |
|---|---|---|---|---|---|---|
| | Total | % | Total | % | Total | % |
| WORLD (intra-EU excluded) | 4.164.100 | | 3.972.000 | | 8.136.100 | |
| intra-EU | 1.265.800 | | 1.332.800 | | 2.598.600 | |
| WORLD (intra-EU included) | 5.429.900 | 100,00 | 5.304.800 | 100,00 | 10.734.700 | 100,00 |
| EU (extra-EU) | 779.100 | 14,35 | 759.800 | 14,32 | 1.538.900 | 14,34 |
| EU (extra & intra-EU) | 2.044.900 | 37,66 | 2.092.600 | 39,45 | 4.137.500 | 38,54 |
| N.East ASIA | 731.427 | 13,47 | 877.155 | 16,54 | 1.608.582 | 14,98 |
| Japan | 291.555 | 5,37 | 393.334 | 7,41 | 684.888 | 6,38 |
| South Korea | 112.350 | 2,07 | 134.781 | 2,54 | 247.131 | 2,30 |
| China | 155.490 | 2,86 | 182.900 | 3,45 | 338.390 | 3,15 |
| Hong Kong | 168.562 | 3,10 | 163.066 | 3,07 | 331.628 | 3,09 |
| ASEAN | 289.654 | 5,33 | 346.953 | 6,54 | 636.607 | 5,93 |
| Indonesia | 27.163 | 0,50 | 53.663 | 1,01 | 80.826 | 0,75 |
| Malaysia | 61.449 | 1,13 | 79.332 | 1,50 | 140.781 | 1,31 |
| Philippines | 29.432 | 0,54 | 33.285 | 0,63 | 62.717 | 0,58 |
| Singapore | 104.216 | 1,92 | 107.649 | 2,03 | 211.865 | 1,97 |
| Thailand | 49.923 | 0,92 | 57.983 | 1,09 | 107.905 | 1,01 |
| Vietnam | 12.397 | 0,23 | 9.827 | 0,19 | 22.225 | 0,21 |
| South Asia | 68.236 | 1,26 | 53.768 | 1,01 | 122.003 | 1,14 |
| India | 42.102 | 0,78 | 36.787 | 0,69 | 78.890 | 0,73 |
| Pakistan | 9.661 | 0,18 | 7.918 | 0,15 | 17.579 | 0,16 |
| Sri Lanka | 6.218 | 0,11 | 4.019 | 0,08 | 10.237 | 0,10 |
| Nepal | 1.409 | 0,03 | 534 | 0,01 | 1.943 | 0,02 |
| Bangladesh | 7.837 | 0,14 | 4.241 | 0,08 | 12.078 | 0,11 |

**World Trade Shares, 1999 (continued)**

| | Imports | | Exports | | Total Trade | |
|---|---|---|---|---|---|---|
| | Total | % | Total | % | Total | % |
| ANZ | 80.968 | 1,49 | 64.004 | 1,21 | 144.971 | 1,35 |
| Australia | 67.486 | 1,24 | 52.548 | 0,99 | 120.033 | 1,12 |
| New Zealand | 13.482 | 0,25 | 11.456 | 0,22 | 24.938 | 0,23 |
| Total Asia | 1.170.284 | 21,55 | 1.341.880 | 25,30 | 2.512.163 | 23,40 |
| Developed Asia | 653.434 | 12,03 | 755.185 | 14,24 | 1.408.619 | 13,12 |
| Developing Asia | 516.850 | 9,52 | 586.695 | 11,06 | 1.103.545 | 10,28 |
| NAFTA | 1.351.291 | 24,89 | 998.721 | 18,83 | 2.350.012 | 21,89 |
| USA | 983.721 | 18,12 | 648.060 | 12,22 | 1.631.780 | 15,20 |
| Canada | 221.037 | 4,07 | 222.689 | 4,20 | 443.726 | 4,13 |
| Mexico | 146.533 | 2,70 | 127.973 | 2,41 | 274.506 | 2,56 |
| Other Regions | 429.833 | 7,92 | 409.663 | 7,72 | 839.496 | 7,82 |
| Mediterranean (excl Candidates) | 86.599 | 1,59 | 58.800 | 1,11 | 145.398 | 1,35 |
| Latin America (excl. Mexico) | 167.212 | 3,08 | 151.258 | 2,85 | 318.470 | 2,97 |
| Gulf | 78.125 | 1,44 | 109.855 | 2,07 | 187.980 | 1,75 |
| ACP (incl. S. Africa) | 97.897 | 1,80 | 89.751 | 1,69 | 187.648 | 1,75 |
| Europe (excl. EU) | 371.302 | 6,84 | 358.604 | 6,76 | 729.905 | 6,80 |
| Candidates (13) | 188.789 | 3,48 | 138.127 | 2,60 | 326.915 | 3,05 |
| EEA & other | 110.180 | 2,03 | 119.287 | 2,25 | 229.467 | 2,14 |
| CIS | 58.058 | 1,07 | 94.603 | 1,78 | 152.661 | 1,42 |
| SE Europe | 14.275 | 0,26 | 6.587 | 0,12 | 20.862 | 0,19 |

Source: IMF and Eurostat

**EU Foreign Direct Investment (extra-EU), 1995–1999**

| | €m. | % share | €m. | % share | €m. | % share | €m. | % share | €m. | % share | Averag e95–99 | % share |
|---|---|---|---|---|---|---|---|---|---|---|---|---|
| Global Total | 60.805 | 100,0% | 69.086 | 100,0% | 109.147 | 100,0% | 221.641 | 100,0% | 277.729 | 100,0% | 147.682 | 100,0% |
| NE Asia | 4.042 | 6,6% | 6.633 | 9,6% | 3.200 | 2,9% | 7.050 | 3,2% | 16.698 | 6,0% | 7.525 | 5,1% |
| Hong Kong | 1.325 | 2,2% | 1.247 | 1,8% | -51 | -0,0% | 2.519 | 1,1% | 4.481 | 1,6% | 1.904 | 1,3% |
| China | 715 | 1,2% | 1.650 | 2,4% | 1.893 | 1,7% | 603 | 0,3% | 1.109 | 0,4% | 1.194 | 0,8% |
| Japan | 1.243 | 2,0% | 2.474 | 3,6% | 1.275 | 1,2% | 719 | 0,3% | 8.921 | 3,2% | 2.926 | 2,0% |
| Korea | 366 | 0,6% | 347 | 0,5% | 217 | 0,2% | 2.686 | 1,2% | 1.627 | 0,6% | 1.049 | 0,7% |
| Taiwan | 393 | 0,6% | 915 | 1,3% | -134 | -0,1% | 523 | 0,2% | 560 | 0,2% | 451 | 0,3% |
| ASEAN 10 | 1.747 | 2,9% | 4.003 | 5,8% | 4.163 | 3,8% | -5.609 | -2,5% | -1.749 | -0,6% | 511 | 0,3% |
| Singapore | 467 | 0,8% | 1.534 | 2,2% | 2.002 | 1,8% | -8.870 | -4,0% | -5.787 | -2,1% | -2.131 | -1,4% |
| Malaysia | -56 | -0,1% | 658 | 1,0% | 404 | 0,4% | 1.061 | 0,5% | 768 | 0,3% | 567 | 0,4% |
| Thailand | 607 | 1,0% | 800 | 1,2% | 729 | 0,7% | 796 | 0,4% | 2.006 | 0,7% | 988 | 0,7% |
| Indonesia | 614 | 1,0% | 673 | 1,0% | 516 | 0,5% | 254 | 0,1% | 212 | 0,1% | 454 | 0,3% |
| Philippines | 95 | 0,2% | 327 | 0,5% | 364 | 0,3% | 784 | 0,4% | 700 | 0,3% | 454 | 0,3% |
| India | 339 | 0,6% | 342 | 0,5% | 621 | 0,6% | 867 | 0,4% | 1.146 | 0,4% | 663 | 0,4% |
| ANZ | 3.759 | 6,2% | 3.633 | 5,3% | 2.695 | 2,5% | 1.140 | 0,5% | 2.722 | 1,0% | 2.790 | 1,9% |
| Total Asia | 9.887 | 16,3% | 14.611 | 21,1% | 10.679 | 9,8% | 3.448 | 1,6% | 18.817 | 6,8% | 11.488 | 7,8% |
| Jap, Kor, Twn, ANZ | 5.761 | 9,5% | 7.369 | 10,7% | 4.053 | 3,7% | 5.068 | 2,3% | 13.830 | 5,0% | 7.216 | 4,9% |
| *As % Total Asia* | | *58,3%* | | *50,4%* | | *38,0%* | | *147,0%* | | *73,5%* | | *62,8%* |
| China, HKG, ASEAN, India | 4.126 | 6,8% | 7.242 | 10,5% | 6.626 | 6,1% | -1.620 | -0,7% | 4.987 | 1,8% | 4.272 | 2,9% |

**EU Foreign Direct Investment (extra-EU), 1995–1999 (continued)**

| | €m. | % share | €m. | % share | €m. | % share | €m. | % share | €m. | % share | Averag e95–99 | % share |
|---|---|---|---|---|---|---|---|---|---|---|---|---|
| *As % Total Asia* | | *41,7%* | | *49,6%* | | *62,0%* | | *-47,0%* | | *26,5%* | | *37,2%* |
| NAFTA | 33.668 | 55,4% | 27.383 | 39,6% | 52.626 | 48,2% | 139.858 | 63,1% | 187.578 | 67,5% | 88.223 | 59,7% |
| United States | 31.616 | 52,0% | 25.822 | 37,4% | 48.158 | 44,1% | 133.433 | 60,2% | 182.060 | 65,6% | 84.218 | 57,0% |
| Canada | 1.307 | 2,1% | 766 | 1,1% | 1.379 | 1,3% | 5.077 | 2,3% | 3.759 | 1,4% | 2.458 | 1,7% |
| Mexico | 745 | 1,2% | 795 | 1,2% | 3.089 | 2,8% | 1.348 | 0,6% | 1.759 | 0,6% | 1.547 | 1,0% |
| Europe extra EU | 9.628 | 15,8% | 12.928 | 18,7% | 20.822 | 19,1% | 36.590 | 16,5% | 20.782 | 7,5% | 20.150 | 13,6% |
| EFTA | 3.469 | 5,7% | 6.111 | 8,8% | 10.879 | 10,0% | 23.600 | 10,6% | 5.837 | 2,1% | 9.979 | 6,8% |
| Candidates | 5.913 | 9,7% | 6.130 | 8,9% | 7.885 | 7,2% | 12.028 | 5,4% | 14.117 | 5,1% | 9.215 | 6,2% |
| CIS | 246 | 0,4% | 687 | 1,0% | 2.058 | 1,9% | 962 | 0,4% | 828 | 0,3% | 956 | 0,6% |
| C & S America (excl Mexico) | 4.210 | 6,9% | 10.082 | 14,6% | 17.853 | 16,4% | 27.659 | 12,5% | 42.037 | 15,1% | 20.368 | 13,8% |
| ACP | 1.143 | 1,9% | 1.923 | 2,8% | 2.472 | 2,3% | 3.141 | 1,4% | 5.041 | 1,8% | 2.744 | 1,9% |
| Gulf, Iran, other MidEast | 486 | 0,8% | 427 | 0,6% | 966 | 0,9% | 2.816 | 1,3% | 2.629 | 0,9% | 1.465 | 1,0% |
| Mediterranea n (MMI) | 404 | 0,7% | 480 | 0,7% | 991 | 0,9% | 1.531 | 0,7% | -321 | -0,1% | 617 | 0,4% |

Source: Eurostat

**EC Financial and Technical Cooperation with Asia, 1976–2000 (million euro, commitments)**

| | Developmen t Coopn. 5-yr Total | Annual Av. | Economic Coopn. 5-yr Total | Annual Av. | Total 5-yr Total | Annual Av. |
|---|---|---|---|---|---|---|
| 1976–80 | 264,4 | 52,9 | | | 264,4 | 52,9 |
| 1981–85 | 703,4 | 140,7 | | | 703,4 | 140,7 |
| 1986–90 | 1.079,7 | 215,9 | | | 1.079,7 | 215,9 |
| 1991–95 | 1.627,9 | 325,6 | 189,0 | 37,8 | 1.816,9 | 363,4 |
| 1996–00 | 1.761,8 | 352,4 | 430,3 | 86,1 | 2.192,1 | 438,4 |
| Total 76–00 | 5.437,3 | | 619,3 | | 6.056,5 | |

Source: EC

**Total ODA flows to Asia*, 1989 and 1999 Global ODA flows, 1999 (million $, disbursements)**

| | 1988–89 av. | | 1998–99 av. | | 1999 | |
|---|---|---|---|---|---|---|
| EU | 4.741 | 39,4% | 4.812,6 | 30,4% | 26.756 | 47,5% |
| Japan | 4.549 | 37,8% | 8.053,2 | 50,9% | 15.323 | 27,2% |
| US | 1.170 | 9,7% | 1.452,6 | 9,2% | 9.[illegible]45 | 16,2% |
| Other DAC** | 1.576 | 13,1% | 1.489,0 | 9,4% | 5.[illegible]54 | 9,1% |
| Total | 12.036 | 100,0% | 15.807,4 | 100,0% | 56.378 | 100,0% |

Source: DAC

*Asia including South, South-East, North-East and Central Asia

**Other DAC members: Australia, Canada, New Zealand, Norway Switzerland

[1] COM(94) 314, 13 July 1994.

[2] For example, "A long-term policy for China-Europe Relations" (COM(95) 279, 5.07.95), "EU-India Enhanced Partnership" (COM(96) 275, 25.06.96), "Creating a New Dynamic in ASEAN-EU Relations" (COM(96) 314, 3.07.96), "Europe-Asia Cooperation Strategy for Energy" (COM(96) 308, 18.07.96), "The EU and Hong Kong : beyond 1997" (COM(97) 171, 23.04.97), "Perspectives and Priorities for the ASEM Process" (SEC(97) 1239, 26.06.97), "Europe-Asia Cooperation Strategy in the field of the Environment" (COM(97) 490, 13.10.97), "Building a comprehensive partnership with China" (COM(98) 181, 25/03/98), "The EU and Macau : beyond 2000" (COM(99) 484, 12/11/99), "Developing Closer Relations between Indonesia and the EU" (COM(00) 50, 2.02.00); "Perspectives and Priorities for the ASEM Process into the New Decade" (COM(00) 241, 18.4.00).

[3] This paper does not however cover certain other regions or countries which might geographically be considered as part of the wider Asia and Asia-Pacific region – Pacific Russia, Central Asia, the developing countries of the Pacific, nor the countries of the Gulf or the Near East. In varying degrees, these all have significant political and (sometimes economic), relationships with Asia as a whole, and an

understanding of these relationships is an essential part of the broader context of Asia. But in general the focus of their attention is elsewhere, and our relations with these countries are dealt with in a different context.

[4] Data here and in the "EU Snapshot" on a later page are taken from the World Bank Development Report 2000/2001 (population and income figures, year 1999, emission figures, year 1996) and from Eurostat (trade figures, year 2000).

[5] In 1996, Asia as a whole accounted for some 33% of global CO 2 emissions (compared with 23% from the US, and 14% from the EU). Within the Asian total, some 85% was accounted for by the five largest industrial and industrialising economies (China, Japan, India, South Korea and Australia).

[6] Eight Asian countries have been categorised as Least-Developed Countries (LLDCs) by the United Nations : Afghanistan, Bangladesh, Bhutan, the Maldives, Nepal, Burma/Myanmar, Cambodia, and Laos (in addition to Yemen, which is not covered in the present paper). North Korea, while not on the LLDC list, can also be considered as one of the poorest countries in the world.

[7] In 2000, the EU had a global trade deficit of €86.9 billion, representing a deficit of €121.5 billion with Asia (plus €26.7 billion with the CIS, €4.9 billion with ACP countries and €1.0 billion with South & Central America), and a surplus of €67.2 billion with the rest of the world.

[8] The continued recession in Japan has prevented that country from playing its traditional motor role in absorbing exports from elsewhere in the region, a role which for the moment at least has largely been taken over by the EU and the US.

[9] In this context, the EU also made a significant contribution in terms of policy advice following the Asian crisis, notably through the ASEM Trust Fund and the European Financial Expertise Network (EFEX).

[10] The EC is bound by comprehensive cooperation agreements (including clauses related to the commitment of both partners to human rights, democratic principles and the rule of law, and to the eventual suspension of the agreement) with five countries in Asia – Nepal, Laos, Cambodia, Bangladesh and South Korea; a similar agreement, not yet concluded or signed, has been negotiated with Pakistan. Similar agreements (but without a suspension clause) govern the EC's relations with four countries – India, Mongolia, Sri Lanka and Vietnam – and with Macao. An older style of cooperation agreement is still in force with nine of the member countries of ASEAN (Vietnam, Laos and Cambodia having acceded to this in addition to their separate, later bilateral agreements), and with China. Our relations with Australia, New Zealand and Japan are governed by Joint Declarations.

[11] The Commission adopted in July a draft Council decision for scientific and technological cooperation between the European Community and the Government of the Republic of India

[12] Asia, with 21.1% of our exports (extra-EU) in 2000, came after Europe outside the EU (30.9%) and NAFTA (28.4%), but accounted for more of our external trade than the Mediterranean, South & Central America, the Gulf and the ACP countries combined (17.1%).

[13] Asia's 6.8% share of EU outward FDI in 1999 put it in fourth place, after NAFTA (67.5%) and Central & South America (15.1%), and only a fraction behind Europe outside the EU (7.5%).

[14] In 1998–99, on average, EU donors as a whole accounted for 30.4% of total ODA flows to Asia, coming after Japan (50.9%) but well ahead of the USA (9.2%). This can be compared with an EU share of 47.5% of ODA flows world-wide, compared to 27.2% for Japan, and 16.2% for the USA. (DAC figures).

[15] "The European Community's Development Policy", COM(2000) 212, 26 April 2000.

[16] Asia was the third-largest beneficiary of EC humanitarian assistance in the period 1998–2000, coming after ex-Yugoslavia (36.8% of total commitments) and the ACP countries (24.4%), and followed by the CIS countries (7.9%), Middle East & North Africa (6.3%), and Latin America (6.1%).

[17] The EU currently has twelve Delegations in the region, in Colombo, Dhaka, Islamabad, New Delhi, Bangkok, Hanoi, Jakarta, Manila, Beijing (plus an Office in Hong Kong), Seoul, Tokyo, and Canberra. Two of these (Hanoi and Colombo) have been opened since 1994.

[18] "Conflict Prevention" (COM(2001) 211, 11 April 2001).

[19] Declaration of Development Council, November 2000.

[20] "Promoting core labour standards and improving social governance in the context of globalisation" (COM (2001) 416, 18.7.2001).

[21] "Reform of the Management of External Assistance" (SEC(2000) 814, 16 May 2000). 17

[22] "The EU's role in promoting human rights and democratisation in third countries" (COM(2001) 252, 8 May 2001).

[23] "The Development of the External Service" (COM(2001) 381, 03 July 2001).

[24] "Strengthening cooperation with third countries in the field of higher education (COM(2001)385, 18 July 2001".

[25] "Developing Closer Relations between Indonesia and the EU" (COM(00) 50, 2.02.00).

[26] The long-term aims spelt out in the Commission's 1998 Communication ("Building a comprehensive partnership with China" – COM(98) 181, 25.03.98) remain broadly valid today, and have been given

a more medium-term focus in our 2001 Communication – "Report on EU strategy towards China: implementation of the 1998 Communication and future steps for a more effective EU policy" (COM(2001) 265).

27 Agreement for scientific and technological cooperation between the European Community and the Government of the People's Republic of China (JO L6/40, 11.1.2000).

28 "The EU and Hong Kong: beyond 1997" (COM(97) 171, 23.04.97); "The EU and Macau: beyond 2000" (COM(1999) 484, 12.11.1999).

29 Most recently in the Commission Working Document "Perspectives and Priorities for the ASEM Process into the New Decade" (COM(00) 241, 18.4.00).

30 Useful work in these areas has already been taken forward, for example through ASEF (the Asia-Europe Foundation) and through independent NGO activities, and through AEBF (the Asia-Europe Business Forum).

31 As was done following the 1994 Strategy, it may be useful from time to time to prepare individual Communications on our relations with key partners in Asia, or on key themes in Asia-Europe relations.

32 Council Regulation (EEC) No 443/92 of 25 February 1992, on financial and technical assistance to, and economic cooperation with, the developing countries in Asia and Latin America.

33 Issues such as untying of aid, multiannual strategic programming, comitology shall be considered.

34 In 1996–2000, on average, 80% of EC development cooperation funding for Asia went to the poorest developing countries, including 32% for the least-developed countries in the region (Bangladesh, Bhutan, Cambodia, Laos, Nepal), and 48% for other low-income countries (India, Indonesia, Pakistan, Vietnam).

35 In 1998, out of a total of some €6.3 billion in EC cooperation funding disbursements, 7% was allocated to developing Asia (compared with 6% for Latin America, 9% for the CIS countries, 15% for the Mediterranean, and 32% for ACP countries). On a per capita basis EC disbursements for developing Asia represented some €0.15 per head (compared with €0.74 for Latin America, €1.94 for CIS countries, €3.31 for the Mediterranean countries, and €4.87 for the ACP countries). Figures from Cox & Chapman, "EC external cooperation programmes", Overseas Development Institute, London, 1999.

Within this framework, the Country Strategy Paper (CSP) for China 2002–2006, approved by the Commission on 25 February 2002, was released in March 2002.[1] Based mainly on the Commission's communications of 1998 and 2001, it was a multiannual planning and strategy document. It outlined specific means to support the EU's continuing objectives, namely to support China's reforms and to integrate China further into the world economy. The CSP gave special emphasis to ensuring the sustainability of economic social reforms, promoting sustainable development and encouraging good governance, the rule of law and development of civil society. All were to be supported by capacity building and technical assistance. The 2002–2004 National Indicative Programme (NIP) set out in detail the ways in which these objectives were to be achieved.[2]

## DEEPENING AND MATURING, 2003–2006

On 9 October 2003, the Commission issued a policy paper entitled 'A Maturing Partnership—Shared Interests and Challenges in EU–China Relations' (see Document

[1] The full text of this document is not included because of its length and technical nature. It may be found at http://ec.europa.eu/comm/external_relations/china/csp/index.htm (accessed 23 March 2007).

[2] The 2002–2004 NIP is not included in this book. For a summary, see European Commission, Directorate-General for External Relations, 'National Indicative Programme 2005–2006: China' (Brussels, 2005) s 1.1.3.

3.7). It was designed to update EU policy toward China and set the EU agenda for the next several years. Many changes had occurred on both sides since the previous communications: the euro was established, enlargement was imminent, the Chinese leadership had changed and new issues had emerged on the international scene. Sustainable development, peace and stability were major aims. The Commission proposed a policy of engagement, that is:

> developing comprehensive relations which allow for working towards a common understanding on all issues of concern, in support of multilateral problem-solving wherever this applies on international and regional issues.

This was to amount to a 'strategic partnership', 'a robust, enduring and mutually beneficial relationship of equals' built in particular around the EU's stake in China's successful transition, China's interest in the EU model of regional integration, and converging interests about the UN and the WTO. For the EU, the main priorities included continuing support of China's reforms, improvement of political dialogues including the human rights dialogue, extension of the EU cooperation programmes and raising the visibility of the EU in China.[3] The 2003 Communication was also intended to promote further reflection in China of its policy toward the EU, to be marked by the forthcoming Chinese policy paper on Europe.

## Document 3.7: Commission Policy Paper, 'A Maturing Partnership—Shared Interests and Challenges in EU–China Relations' (2003)

COMMISSION POLICY PAPER FOR TRANSMISSION TO THE COUNCIL AND THE EUROPEAN PARLIAMENT

**A maturing partnership – shared interests and challenges in EU-China relations**

(Updating the European Commission's Communications on EU-China relations of 1998 and 2001)

COM(2003) 533 final, Brussels 10.9.2003

**Executive Summary**

Much has changed in Europe, China and the world since the Commission's last policy paper was issued in early 2001. The Euro is now fully established, enlargement and major internal reforms are imminent, and the EU has taken on new responsibilities, notably in justice and home affairs (JHA) that have significant domestic and international impact. The draft European Security Strategy of June 2003 aims to reinforce the EU's Common Foreign and Security Policy, and recognises that China is one of the EU's major strategic partners. China has entered a new and challenging phase in its social and economic reform process. It has also become increasingly involved in world affairs, especially in multilateral fora, and is rapidly emerging as a major player in the world economy thanks to its dynamic growth and accession to the WTO. Moreover, a new generation of leaders has recently taken the reigns in Beijing and will be engaging the EU at the highest level for the first time at the EU-China summit in late October 2003. At the same time, both sides have to adapt to a fast moving international scene, with terrorism, weapons proliferation and other concerns, such as the

[3] On the extent to which these objectives were achieved as of April 2005, see European Commisison, External Relations Directorate General, Directorate Asia (except Japan and Korea), 'Note to File: Subject: China Action Points/Guidelines for Action—Stocktaking April 2005' (Brussels, FS D, 2005).

threat of SARS, rising to the top of the agenda. The sluggish world economy and concomitant negative trends in protectionism and regionalism also loom as potential threats to global trade and development.

Against this background, the EU and China have an ever-greater interest to work together as strategic partners to safeguard and promote sustainable development, peace and stability. Interests converge on many international governance issues, notably the importance both attach to the role of the UN in physical and environmental security and to that of the WTO, where both have much to gain from further trade liberalisation. Indeed, the growth in the bilateral trade relationship is striking: two-way trade exceeded €115 bn last year, making China Europe's third largest trading partner, albeit with a substantial surplus in China's favour. Moreover, EU firms remain important investors in China.

Mutually beneficial co-operation in the JHA, scientific and technical fields has also been growing apace in recent years, with a number of new agreements in process, and the EC's assistance programme continues at significant levels.

Europe thus has a major political and economic stake in supporting China's successful transition to a stable, prosperous and open country that fully embraces democracy, free market principles and the rule of law. The EU has much to offer here, stemming in part from its own experience in integrating accession countries from East and Central Europe.

Stock-taking is now required of our 2001 paper to take account of these developments and of new shared interests and challenges that lie ahead. It is also noteworthy that China will shortly be issuing its own strategic paper on relations with the EU, the first ever document of this kind.

This paper thus includes an assessment of what has been achieved, and proposals to update our approach which will help guide EU policy and action in the course of the next two to three years. On Governance, proposals are made to improve political dialogue through more clearly focussing existing mechanisms, which now cover regular sessions at six major levels, and to systematically address global and regional governance and security issues within these exchanges. The dialogue on illegal migration should be more results oriented and an agreement on the readmission of illegal migrants should be concluded soon.

Political dialogue should also continue to pay close attention to Human Rights in keeping with the tenets of a maturing partnership of the kind we now enjoy, and in the conviction that this is an integral part of ensuring sustainability of the reforms and long term stability. Measures to increase the efficiency and impact of the dedicated EU-China Human Rights dialogue include the raising of its level, greater focus on key issues, stronger continuity and follow-through on issues and individual cases, maximising synergies with existing bilateral Member State efforts, and raising the visibility and transparency of the dialogue. Moreover, China's developing civil society has an important role to play in protecting the welfare and rights of vulnerable people in general and in mitigating negative effects of reform.

In promoting China's economic opening at home and abroad, priorities are to work together to ensure success of the Doha Development Agenda, monitor and assist China's compliance with its WTO commitments, and monitor new regional agreements to ensure WTO-compatibility. The early signing of an 'Authorised Destination Status' agreement to facilitate Chinese tourism in Europe is a major priority. Negotiations on a long delayed customs agreement should begin as soon as possible.

Support for China's reform process and sectoral co-operation should be strengthened through: the launch of new dialogues and co-operation in the fields of intellectual property rights, sanitary standards, competition policy, industrial policy and human resource development; and through the reinforcement of existing dialogues and agreements on the regulation of industrial products, information society, environment, energy and scientific & technological co-operation. New agreements covering co-operation in research and related peaceful use of nuclear energy and on the EU's Galileo programme should be concluded.

The EU's co-operation programme, which supports activities in many of the above areas will follow the aims set out in the Country Strategy Paper approved in 2002, although the National Indicative Programme (NIP) is to be adjusted this year to take account of some operational changes. Outside of the NIP itself, China will continue to be a major beneficiary of the EU's regional co-operation and research programmes, where new initiatives, for example in the fight against SARS, will begin shortly.

The steering role of the EC-China Joint Committee should be reinforced not only as regards trade and co-operation matters, but also for the various sectoral dialogues.

Last but by no means least, new efforts to raise EU visibility in China are proposed, involving better understanding of the Chinese audience, the use of a few targeted messages and closer collaboration with EU Member States.

The course ahead is long and challenging, and given the depth and breadth of the partnership, it could not be otherwise. If it is to be successfully navigated, it is essential that there is full and lasting commitment from all players. On the EU side, close co-ordination of Union and Member State policies will be required and China will have to ensure that all branches and levels of its administration are on board. With the high stakes involved, we are confident that all involved will play their part.

## 1. INTRODUCTION

This policy paper is based on the Commission's 1998 Communication "Building a Comprehensive Partnership with China"[1] and the resulting Council conclusions which stressed the Union's fundamental interest in strengthening relations with China. They established the following aims for the EU-China relationship:

(i) Engaging China further, through an upgraded political dialogue, in the international community;

(ii) Supporting China's transition to an open society based upon the rule of law and the respect for human rights;

(iii) Integrating China further in the world economy by bringing it more fully into the world trading system and by supporting the process of economic and social reform underway in the country, including in the context of sustainable development;

(iv) Making better use of existing European resources;

(v) Raising the EU's profile in China.

The Commission undertook to report regularly about the progress made in implementing the proposals of this Communication. A first report was issued in September 2000.[2]

In June 2001, the Commission in its Communication "EU Strategy towards China: Implementation of the 1998 Communication and Future Steps for a more Effective EU Policy"[3] provided a review of EU policy and charted a course of short and medium term action points aimed to make progress towards the long term aims defined in 1998.

Discussions in the Council in the spring of 2003 confirmed that EU global and long term objectives in relations with China as defined in 1998 remained largely valid, and should be reaffirmed vis-à-vis the new Chinese leadership generation which took office in March 2003. The action plan put forward in the 2001 Communication had proved useful to maintain the momentum in the relationship, and should now be updated, in view of recent developments in the EU, China and the world at large.

The present policy paper addresses these aims, and reviews progress made in implementing the 1998 Communication and the 2001 plan of action points. Its objective is to provide further impetus for the relationship, and help guide EU policy and action over the next two to three years, taking account also of EU policy objectives towards the wider Asian region expressed in the Commission's 2001 Asia Strategy[4].

Finally, the paper intends to promote, the ongoing reflection in China about future policy towards the EU, which is to find expression in a policy paper later this year, the first ever of its kind in China's foreign relations. The appearance of this paper is evidence of the new importance China gives to the relationship.

## 2. A NEW MATURITY IN EU-CHINA RELATIONS

The last decade has seen a dynamic growth of the relationship between the EU and China. Relations which were once largely confined to the areas of trade and investment and financial/technical assistance have expanded to cover a multitude of sectors. A robust and regular political dialogue has been established. A number of sectoral agreements have been concluded, or are under negotiation. There are frequent and, in many cases, institutionalised, exchanges in areas ranging from global challenges such as the environment and illegal migration, through the field of basic and applied research and technological co-operation, to the regulatory framework in key sectors of the economy. EU assistance under the EC-China Co-operation Programme has been refocused on the EU's China policies in general. These changes have brought about a new maturity in the relationship, characterised by increasingly close policy co-ordination in many areas.

At the same time, events since 2001 – regarding the EU, regarding China, and in global affairs – create the need to take the partnership forward.

In the EU, the successful introduction of the Euro notes and coins at the beginning of 2002 was a landmark achievement in the history of European integration, soon to be followed by the EU's biggest enlargement ever in terms of scope and diversity, with ten new members set to accede on 1 May 2004. At the same time, the internal reform of the EU continues, with plans for an EU constitution under discussion.

These internal challenges notwithstanding, the EU cannot afford to be inward-looking. Internal developments in the EU as well as the European economy are closely entwined with developments on the world scene. Moreover, the world community expects the EU to play a role which is commensurate with its size and importance, not only in the economic area, but also on issues of global security and other global concerns. These expectations will grow further as the EU enlarges, and streamlines its constitutional structures.

The EU is striving to live up to these expectations. It has proven itself as a leading partner in the global coalition against terrorism in the aftermath of 11 September 2001, both through international action and through the use of its new powers in the field of Justice and Home Affairs. Following the reinforcement of its Common Foreign and Security Policy (CFSP) and European Security and Defence Policy (ESDP), the EU is playing an increasing role in areas such as conflict prevention and crisis management. The development of CFSP and

ESDP over the coming years will lead to an increasingly significant EU role in shaping and managing the world order. Key challenges and threats, and the EU's strategic objectives are summarised in the draft European Security Strategy.

China, on its side, has become an increasingly energetic player in world affairs. Buoyed by its dynamic economy, it is more and more becoming a locomotive for regional and global growth. Following its accession to WTO in December 2001, China is actively engaged in both the new round of multilateral negotiations under the WTO Doha Development Agenda and in regional integration initiatives. Internally, the process of economic and social reform is continuing, although it is facing growing challenges in the form of unemployment, social and regional disparities, corruption and threats to the stability of the financial and fiscal systems. The new – fourth – leadership generation which took office in March 2003 is expected to continue on the path of domestic reform and economic liberalisation. However, China's moves towards a more proactive and responsible foreign policy continue to be dominated by its focus on domestic stability and economic development.

Both the EU and China are, since 2001, engaged in a process of adaptation to a changing global environment. International terrorism, as well as growing concerns over the proliferation of weapons of mass destruction, have brought new types of international security concerns to the top of the global agenda. At the same time, global challenges such as climate change and environmental degradation, illegal migration, international crime, but also global health concerns such as HIV/AIDS which may pose a serious threat to China's long-term development, and severe acute respiratory syndrome (SARS), need to be addressed. Moreover, the sluggish state of the world economy is squeezing government budgets across the world, and has led to worrying trends of protectionism. Regional trade initiatives, which are proliferating, can be complementary to multilateral liberalisation and rule-making, but only if they are WTO-compliant and do not detract from the crucial negotiations under the WTO's Doha Development Agenda.

Faced with these developments, it is in the clear interest of the EU and China to work as strategic partners on the international scene. EU and Chinese interests converge on many issues of global governance, in particular as regards the key role of multilateral organisations and systems. Through a further reinforcement of their co-operation, the EU and China will be better able to promote these shared visions and interests, and thus to shore up their joint security and other interests in Asia and elsewhere.

Moreover, the stability and development of China itself is a key concern also of the EU. The EU has a clear stake in China's successful transition to a stable, prosperous and open country that fully embraces democracy, free market principles and the rule of law. It should thus do its utmost to support China's transition and reform processes by reinforcing cooperation and dialogue across the board. Notably, the EU's experience, not least that from the recent transition processes of many of the EU accession candidates, on how to adapt to the tremendous socio-economic challenges that opening and globalisation entail, and on the economic and societal models developed in the EU in response to these, should be exploited to the full. Similarly, the EU should intensify its efforts to help China address emerging sustainability challenges, particularly in the field of the environment. In the context of its support to China's transition, the EU should continue to speak out on its human rights concerns, and to encourage the rule of law and political reforms in China. These are issues which are sensitive for China, but also ones which are crucial to safeguard social stability in China and the sustainability of the reform process.

Developing a robust, enduring and mutually beneficial relationship of equals which covers all of these areas should be a major aim for both the EU and China in the coming years. A very positive start has been made. The following action points should help to keep relations on this course in the next few years. Realising them, and progressing towards the broader goal, will require the full commitment from all relevant players on both sides. On the EU side, it will be important to co-ordinate Member States' policies towards China to the maximum extent possible, so that the EU speaks with a single voice on all key issues of China policy. China, on its side, will need to ensure that all branches and levels of its administration are on board, and fully co-operate on the bilateral agenda.

## 3. CHARTING A COURSE FOR EU ACTION IN 2003 AND BEYOND

### *3.1 The EU and China: shared responsibilities in promoting global governance*

China is an increasingly important global player, interested in a stable and fair global environment which will allow it to pursue its course of economic development and internal reform. The EU expects China to contribute to global stability by gradually taking on more responsibility, commensurate with its political and economic weight, both in the bilateral and the multilateral context.

Given its particular position as a newly emerging power, China could notably play an important role in the common effort to reconcile the interests of developing and developed countries. The EU also looks towards China to use its considerable influence in Asia to promote peace and stability in the region, by taking a lead role in furthering regional integration and by helping to resolve pending regional conflicts.

The context

Chinese foreign policy has become progressively more proactive and constructive, with China increasingly engaged on both global issues and in regional dialogue, as in the case of the Korean Peninsula. In this context, China has expressed clear interest in strengthened political ties with the EU, and expects the EU to have clear joint policy lines on global issues of common concern.

EU and China share views on the importance of multilateral systems and rules for global governance, which includes the further strengthening of the United Nations system, its role in regional and global conflict resolution and in the co-ordination of actions addressing global concerns, from weapons control, through international terrorism, to climate change.

The EU-China political dialogue has become an increasingly important component of overall relations, and annual Summits have provided a strategic vision for the fast developing relationship.

The 2002 EU-China Summit confirmed the interest of both sides to further broaden and deepen the relationship in all areas, including through increased co-ordination and cooperation on global issues.

Implementation of action points in the 2001 Communication

In general, good progress has been achieved in the implementation of the concrete actions identified in the 2001 Communication.

*Political dialogue mechanisms*

EU-China political dialogue has developed further over the past two years. A new framework for reinforced dialogue was agreed between the two sides through an exchange of letters in June 2002.

In addition to high-level contacts, a number of lower-level dialogues have been established in the recent past, accentuating the gradual move from a relationship dominated by a top-down structure towards a relationship structure of multi-layered dialogues similar to the ones established with other major partners.

The newly-created political dialogue at the level of Political Directors has developed successfully and has proven a useful platform to prepare for, and follow-up on, ministerial-level Troikas and the Summits. Ministerial Troikas have been instrumental in ensuring high-level dialogue between Summits and to prepare for the Summits.

Meetings held every six months between the Chinese Foreign Minister and EU Ambassadors in Beijing, and corresponding meetings between the Foreign Minister of the country holding the EU Presidency and the Chinese Ambassador in that country, have enhanced communication flows, and been useful in addressing more day-to-day aspects of the relationship.

The mechanism of Troika dialogue expert meetings has been used in the area of non-proliferation and disarmament.

*Topics of the political dialogue*

Human rights concerns have been given priority focus and were systematically raised at the different levels within the political dialogue, in addition to the dedicated human rights dialogue with China *(see section 3.2)*.

Co-ordination was strengthened to promote the reconciliation and security on the Korean Peninsula, on the Burma/Myanmar issue, and on other regional questions.

The EU has also regularly reiterated its strong interest in, and insistence on, a peaceful resolution of the Taiwan issue through dialogue across the Taiwan Straits.

Developments in Hong Kong and Macau have been followed closely, with annual reports issued on both Special Administrative Regions, and particular attention given to developments in Hong Kong regarding the proposed national security legislation under Article 23 of the Basic Law, which may have consequences for the continuing exercise of freedoms and rights in Hong Kong.

Co-operation in the area of illegal migration and trafficking in human beings has been stepped up. Regular High Level Consultations in this area have built mutual confidence, and allowed for an increased exchange of information and on respective policies, legislation and concerns in this field. It was agreed that co-operation between both parties should be further enhanced. Expert visits have been exchanged between the EU and China, and seminars on the issue of forged documents held. Funds have been reserved by the EC for a specific cooperation programme, which should back up the dialogue. A joint seminar in November 2002 allowed the identification of some areas of common interest for project components

Illegal migration issues featured regularly on the agenda of political dialogue meetings, including the 2002 EU-China Summit. Readmission has been one of the key points of discussion since the launch of negotiations for an "Authorised Destination Status" agreement in February 2003. In November 2002, the Council authorised the Commission to negotiate a readmission agreement with China. Despite continued EU efforts, negotiations have not yet been launched.

The political dialogue has also followed up on multilateral efforts to limit arms proliferation, arms exports, and to promote disarmament.

Finally, there have been regular contacts on global environmental issues, including on climate change, at Ministerial level and in the margins of international conferences.

*New action points*

Raising the efficiency of the political dialogue

- Translate the agreement on reinforced political dialogue fully into practice. Better use should be made of the existing framework, stressing quality over quantity of the dialogue, thus achieving more consistency on the substance.
- Enhance the effectiveness of Ministerial Troikas in steering the political dialogue, while adjusting the mandates of these and other high-level EU-China fora to reflect the need for an effective co-ordination not only of the political dialogue, but also of other dialogue strands within the EU-China relationship at large (see section 4.).
- Hold more frequent ad hoc Troika political consultations at working level in Beijing to enhance continuity of our political dialogue with China between formal meetings, while at the same time increasing EU visibility.
- Maximise policy co-ordination with Member States on China, notably through regular exchanges in the framework of the Political and Security Committee. Such exchanges could be opened to China by inviting suitable Chinese counterparts to meetings on an ad hoc basis.
- Regularly include China as an item on the agenda of EU dialogue with third countries, such as the US, Russia, Japan and South Korea, in order to increase the convergence of EU and international policy vis-à-vis China.

EU priorities for the political dialogue

= Bilateral

- Stress human rights concerns as an essential component of the political dialogue.
- Encourage China and the Dalai Lama to further strengthen ongoing direct contacts with a view to finding a mutually acceptable solution to the question of Tibet in the context of ensuring a genuine autonomy for this region.
- Render High-level Consultations on illegal migration more concrete and result-oriented, including in the field of exchange of concrete information, and the setting-up of joint cooperation projects.
- Open negotiations on readmission of illegal migrants and conclude a readmission agreement with China.

- Follow up on Chinese request for closer co-operation on other Justice and Home Affairs issues, explore scope for co-operation on organised crime, money laundering and drug trafficking and production, including of synthetic drugs and drug precursors.
- Closely monitor developments in the Hong Kong and Macau Special Administrative Regions, notably as concerns the maintenance of the rule of law and safeguard of fundamental freedoms and autonomy, as enshrined in their Basic Laws.
- Stress EU insistence on a resolution of the Taiwan issue through peaceful dialogue, and underline the importance of growing economic ties for an improvement of the political climate; underline EU interest in closer links with Taiwan in non-political fields, including in multilateral contexts, in line with the EU's 'One-China' policy.

= Regional

- Strengthen co-operation on issues of mutual concern in the region in particular as regards to assuring peace and security on the Korean peninsula and on the Indian sub-continent, encouraging political reconciliation and reform in Burma/Myanmar and seeking resolution of the South China Sea issue.
- Promote a continued proactive stance by China in the ASEM (Asia-Europe Meeting) process, in consultations on international and regional security and other challenges within the ASEM political pillar, in building Asia-Europe understanding in the DDA negotiations under the economic pillar, and by fostering China's engagement in people-to-people contacts within the Dialogue on Cultures and Civilisations.
- Enhance consultations with China on the ASEAN Regional Forum (ARF), to reinforce the ARF's role on regional security issues, and promote co-operation on defence and on terrorism.
- Explore the possibility to establish an exchange of information between the EU and the Shanghai Co-operation Organisation (SCO), the permanent secretariat of which is to be established in Beijing.

= Global

- Include global governance issues regularly in the political dialogue with China and, where appropriate, consult with China in the early stages of EU policy development on these issues.
- Promote the development of a co-ordinated approach, and of joint EU-China policy initiatives, including, where possible, through joint declarations and demarches on issues of common interest both in the bilateral and multilateral context.
- Enhance co-operation to promote multilateral systems and rules for global governance, particularly the further strengthening of the United Nations system and its role in regional and global conflict resolution and co-ordination in addressing global concerns.

- Address global security, non proliferation/disarmament and arms control issues; reinforce dialogue on non proliferation topics, including on export control of dual use goods; encourage China to support the re-launch of the UN Conference on Disarmament, and to sign and ratify multilateral treaties and conventions such as the Comprehensive Test Ban Treaty and the Ottawa Convention on landmines.
- Explore the possibilities for reinforced dialogue with China on combating terrorism, with a view towards closer co-operation, including at the United Nations, while stressing the need to safeguard the human rights of ethnic minorities in China.
- Promote collaboration on global environmental challenges, including enhanced cooperation on the Kyoto protocol and climate change, and on follow-up to the World Summit on Sustainable Development.
- Launch the planned call for proposals on joint research into SARS under the Sixth EU Framework Programme for Research and Technological Development in which China is expected to be an important participant.

*3.2. Supporting China's transition to an open society based upon the rule of law and the respect for human rights*

Supporting China's transition to an open society based upon the rule of law remains an essential element of EU policy towards this country. This is particularly true in a period where China is engaged in substantial reforms, whose implementation requires the maintenance of societal stability. The EU believes that the respect for human rights, democratic accountability and the rule of law, as well as a democratic participation of citizens in decision-making processes, constitute the best guarantees for the long-term stability of a society and for the sustainability of a country's economic development, in China as elsewhere.

The context

In the domestic field, there are signs of improvements in relation to the establishment of the rule of law and the development of the legal system. The draft for a first ever civil code has been submitted to the National People's Congress. Legal training of judges has been strengthened. The rule of law has improved in the economic field, mainly as a consequence of China's accession to the WTO, but there has been no large-scale spill-over effect yet and "rule by law" generally still prevails. Tentative steps towards democratisation have continued, with the experiment of elections at township level, but there is no indication for a substantial change in the system of appointing leaders above village level in the near future.

Civil society is an area where significant developments have taken place in recent years. Whereas only few non-governmental organisations existed in China some years ago, a variety of grassroots organisations across the country now aspires to a role in policy making. They are taken more seriously by the government, but they still face important hurdles in realising their full potential.

However, a significant gap still exists between the current human rights situation in China and internationally accepted standards, in particular with respect to civil and political rights. As noted in the General Affairs Council conclusions of 18 March 2003, a number of serious EU concerns remain. China has still not ratified the UN International Covenant on

Civil and Political Rights. The practice of re-education through labour persists. The death penalty continues to be applied extensively, in particular in the context of the "strike hard" campaign. Freedom of expression, religion and association are still not guaranteed, in particular with respect to pro-democracy, labour and internet activists, and ethnic minorities, notably in Tibet and Xinjiang, are still deprived of their religious and cultural rights.

Implementation of action points in the 2001 Communication

Four sessions of the EU-China Human Rights dialogue have been held over the last two years. They have been complemented by four EU-China seminars on issues such as the death penalty, the prohibition and prevention of torture, the right to education, transparency and regulation of the mass media, the establishment of national human rights institutions, and of mechanisms for the implementation of economic, social and cultural rights.

The dialogue has allowed for detailed and frank exchanges of views on the different issues of concern. It has allowed the EU to obtain information on human rights in China, has raised awareness of Chinese decision-makers on international standards and EU best practices, and has helped to build mutual trust and confidence.

The dialogue has led to some positive developments. China has stated its engagement to enhance co-operation with UN Human Rights mechanisms, in particular with the UN High Commissioner for Human Rights, the special Rapporteurs on torture and on education, and the Chairman of the working group on arbitrary detention, although these commitments have yet to be fully realised. The dialogue has allowed for extensive exchanges of views on individual cases of human rights violations, and China's offer to provide information on individual cases between dialogue rounds is a welcome further step. Moreover, EC human rights-related assistance programmes have been implemented in a largely satisfactory manner, and China has shown readiness to envisage further projects, including on sensitive issues such as torture prevention in police and prison administration.

That said, a number of issues remain where the discussions have not yet allowed for meaningful progress. China has yet to provide a clear timetable for the ratification of the International Covenant on Civil and Political Rights. Although China has expressed its willingness to be more responsive to EU concerns regarding the use of the death penalty, administrative detention and torture, no substantial progress has been made in these fields, and longstanding EU requests to provide statistics on the use of the death penalty have not been answered. Substantial differences persist between the EU and China over the freedom of expression, religion and association. The same applies to the preservation and the promotion of the rights of minorities, in particular in Tibet and Xinjiang. The issue of North Korean refugees in China also remains an EU concern.

*New action points*

Dialogue and co-operation should continue to constitute the main EU approach to improving the human rights situation in China, although this should not exclude expressing comments and observations in other appropriate fora. But the dialogue will remain a credible option in the medium and long term only if effective progress is achieved on the ground. It will be essential to enhance the continuity of the dialogue. Complementing the dialogue, the EU will continue and intensify co-operation projects related to human rights and good governance, including under the European Initiative for Democracy and Human Rights under which China has become a focus country in 2003.

Moreover, at a time when China is engaged in major socio-economic reforms, support to the rule of law should not only imply top-down initiatives, but also grassroots action involving citizens, with a view to furthering ownership of the reforms. This is indeed a prerequisite if the reform is to be implemented in a stable and satisfactory manner. Civil society organisations, in whatever form, will therefore be increasingly needed, and of particular importance in supporting individuals and communities disadvantaged by the ongoing changes. The strengthening of civil society in China thus should be an EU priority.

Attention should also be given to the rights of workers who are among the most vulnerable groups in the context of the ongoing reforms. In this context, it is important to work toward strengthened co-operation between China and the ILO, aiming at adherence to the norms, conventions and recommendations of this organisation.

Human rights dialogue

- Upgrade the level of dialogue to vice-ministerial level, to enhance political impact and visibility.
- Focus on issues where there has been very little progress up to now, so as to allow for more meaningful discussion on key issues.
- Ensure better continuity through enhanced follow-up of issues and individual cases raised in formal dialogue meetings, notably by holding more regular working-level meetings in Beijing between the EU Troika and the Ministry of Foreign Affairs between dialogue sessions.
- Involve a wider variety of dialogue partners, and organise field visits outside Beijing.
- Maximise synergies with existing Member States' and other partners' human rights dialogues with China.
- Give as much visibility and transparency as possible to the dialogue, e.g. by briefing press, civil society and European Parliament after each session.
- In order to allow for a real two-way dialogue on human rights challenges in the EU and China, complement the dialogue with more expert exchanges, involving not only academics and NGOs, but also operational staff, such as police officials and prison staff.

Human rights/good governance-related co-operation programmes

- Focus on strengthening the understanding of law and legal processes by citizens and officials, together with training programmes for professionals, including lawyers, judges, prison and police officers.
- Share EU expertise on the compliance of domestic legislation with international standards.
- Continue promoting grass-roots democracy through support to China's experiments with direct suffrage.

- Extend co-operation programmes into new areas, such as the prevention of torture, freedom of expression and independent media, the promotion of minorities' rights, the International Criminal Court, the death penalty, and labour rights.
- Take into consideration the promotion of human rights, including economic, social and cultural rights and gender issues, as a cross-cutting theme throughout the EC-China Cooperation Programme.

Support to civil society

- Promote contacts and dialogue between European and Chinese civil society, in line with the recommendations resulting from the dialogue established between the European Economic and Social Committee and the China Economic and Social Council.
- Mitigate the negative impact of socio-economic reforms by supporting civil society organisations whose aim is to promote the rights and welfare of the most vulnerable groups in society.
- Provide assistance in these areas through major co-operation projects aiming in particular at building the capacity of the emerging civil society, establishing networks
- between European and Chinese civil society organisations, and encouraging Chinese NGOs to participate in international conferences open to civil society.

*3.3. Promoting China's economic opening at home and abroad*

The EU regards the successful and sustainable economic development of China as important and beneficial for the entire world. Its aim remains to contribute as much as possible to ensure that China masters successfully its transition to a stable, prosperous and open country. The EU thus is an ardent supporter of China's integration into the global economy, and has fully backed China's bid for WTO accession from the start. At the same time, it has sought to assist China in its internal reform process, and to help it in addressing the daunting challenges that this has brought. The EU offers open and liberal markets for Chinese exports, the transfer of European capital, technology and know-how that come with reinforced commercial ties, but also European experience and best practice in relevant economic, environmental and social sectors.

In turn, the EU looks towards China to act as a constructive and responsible player in the world economy, playing a role commensurate to its size and importance. The preservation and development of a liberal global trading system is in China's own long-term interest. Like all other major players, China should set an example by abstaining from protectionist reflexes, and help prevent them elsewhere. Having itself benefited significantly from globalisation, China should reciprocate by progressively opening its own economy, in line with its WTO accession commitments and beyond. China, as the EU, should do its utmost to help make the new round of WTO negotiations under the Doha Development Agenda (DDA) a success.

The context

China's process of integration into the world economy, launched in 1978, culminated in China's accession to the World Trade Organisation (WTO) on 11 December 2001, arguably one of the most momentous events in recent history, whose importance far transcends the realm of international trade. It not only buttresses China's position as a global trading power, but also cements the process of economic and social reform in China.

Progressive opening towards the world economy has made China one of the foremost beneficiaries of globalisation. In 2002, it became the world's fifth largest trader, with USD

620.8 bn worth of exports and imports, and with its foreign trade growing at 21.8%, a growth rate unrivalled by any major trading nation. China also overtook the US as the largest recipient of foreign direct investment (FDI) in the world, with new FDI inflows of USD 52.7 bn, up 12.5%.

China's economic achievements have made it the locomotive for economic growth in its region. Building on this, and also seeking to assuage fears at times linked to its ascendance, China is promoting ambitious initiatives for regional economic integration, notably the ASEAN + 1 scheme, which aims at the creation of a free trade area between the 10 ASEAN countries and China by 2010.

China has made considerable efforts to live up to its new role in the global economic system. To comply with its WTO accession commitments, it has cut tariffs across the board, and engaged in a thorough overhaul of laws and regulations. It has also launched a restructuring of government agencies responsible for economic issues. Nonetheless, a number of substantial concerns remain, in particular the lack of transparency in economic governance, overly restrictive and burdensome regulations in some sectors, the introduction of new non-tariff barriers, and the persistence of a protectionist culture favouring local industry, which could have the effect of limiting the very liberalisation which WTO entry was to bring about. More precisely, one year and a half after China's WTO accession, the EU concerns in terms of WTO implementation include notably the problems encountered regarding market access (allocation of quotas and tariff-rate quotas), services (financial services, telecommunication, construction), the enforcement of intellectual property rights and the respect of international standards (both industrial and in the sanitary and phytosanitary field).

Since its WTO accession, China has become an important player in the global trading system. It is playing an increasingly pro-active role in defending its interests in the ongoing DDA negotiations. Given China's stake in a dynamic and liberal trading system and its political objective of promoting a multipolar world governed by multilateral rules, it has an interest in a successful and timely conclusion of the Doha Round, resulting in further market opening, accommodation of developing countries' interests, and improved WTO rules. To make as much headway as possible in these negotiations, the EU closely co-operates with key players such as China to reach further convergence of views, seeking China's support particularly on rules-related issues, such as investment, competition, trade facilitation, and transparency in government procurement.

As the process of internal economic and social reform in China enters its most difficult phase, the enormous challenges for China in the years to come are becoming more apparent. Reform and opening have been accompanied by a significant rise in unemployment and underemployment. Disparities in regional economic development in income levels, and the rural-urban divide are reaching worrying levels. In spite of the considerable reduction in poverty associated with economic growth in recent years, China has still large numbers of poor people. In 1999 it was estimated that some 213 million Chinese, representing 17% of the population and 18% of the world's poor, were living on less than $1 per day. Serious weaknesses have yet to be tackled in the corporate and financial systems, as well as in the system of social security provision. Furthermore, the fiscal system is weighed down in the short-term by the need to maintain economic stimulus and in the long term by the need to improve social welfare.

Economic and trade relations between the EU and China have developed in step with the latter's emergence on the global economic scene. China in 2002 overtook Japan to become the EU's second-largest trading partner outside Europe, with a trade volume of over €115 bn. EU markets are open to China, as witnessed by the continuing increase in the EU's trade deficit with China, which topped €47 bn in 2002 and is by far the largest with any partner. The EU is also a major investor in China, with the stock of EU FDI at USD 34 bn at the end of 2002.[5]

The positive overall development of EU-China economic and trade relations puts into perspective the problems which have arisen in these areas. Nonetheless, the reinforcement of bilateral consultation mechanisms is necessary to ensure that bilateral problems, and concerns related to China's compliance with its WTO commitments, can be resolved rapidly and do not constrain the relationship. Enhanced regulatory dialogue will be important to overcome non-tariff barriers and facilitate bilateral trade. Full and timely implementation of China's WTO obligations and the removal of remaining market access obstacles will be crucial to ensure continued and balanced growth of two-way trade, and are key factors in attracting major new flows of European FDI in China.

Implementation of action points in the 2001 Communication

Good progress has been made in implementing the concrete actions identified in the 2001 Communication. An EU network has been created to track China's WTO implementation. There have also been regular and intensive consultations with the Chinese authorities on relevant issues. The EU Chamber of Commerce in China has become increasingly active and further increased its scope of activities, and has become a key interlocutor both for the EU and for the Chinese authorities. These instruments have allowed the EU to make progress on some important existing concerns.

In addition to regular dialogue on WTO and other trade issues, the Commission and Chinese authorities have launched a joint study process on areas which are on the agenda of the DDA negotiations, allowing for the identification of areas of common interest and of shared viewpoints.

Both sides have reinforced sectoral dialogue on questions of policy and regulation, focussing on sectors which are related to WTO, or affected by China's transition process. A dialogue on the regulation of industrial products, including standardisation and conformity assessment issues, was launched in October 2001. The existing Telecommunications Working Group in September 2001 was transformed into a broader Information Society Working Group whose remit now includes policy and the regulatory framework for the entire IS sector. A very successful EU-China Co-operation Forum on the Information Society was held in Beijing in April 2002. An environmental policy dialogue was initiated in September 2001. The scope of the existing Energy Working Group was extended to include policy issues. EU-China research co-operation under the 1999 S&T agreement has become increasingly successful, not least following the creation of the joint EU-China S&T Cooperation Promotion Office in Beijing in mid-2001; research projects involving China launched since 2000 have total budgets of over €94 million. In February 2003, China started negotiations to join the international ITER collaboration on the next major step for the development of fusion energy. Finally, first contacts have taken place on a possible new dialogue in the field of human resources development, including education, an area which is key to the success and sustainability of the reform process.

Progress has also been made towards new bilateral agreements in important fields. A maritime transport agreement, the EU's first such agreement with any third country was signed in December 2002, and has already been ratified by China. Good advances have been made in negotiating an agreement on "Authorised Destination Status", which will facilitate the visit of Chinese tourist groups to the EU. Negotiations for an agreement on co-operation in the field of satellite navigation, in the context of the European GALILEO programme, have started in May 2003, and a joint Sino-European satellite navigation co-operation centre has been opened in Beijing in February 2003. Exploratory discussions on an EU-China agreement on customs co-operation and mutual administrative assistance in customs matters have recently intensified following high-level discussions in June 2003. Beyond customs co-operation *per se,* an objective of mutual concern is to combat fraud and counterfeited goods. It is anticipated that the agreement will be concluded by early 2004. The Council in June 2003 adopted the negotiating directives for an agreement on research and related peaceful use of nuclear energy; formal negotiations will be launched very soon.

The EU has supported China's implementation of its WTO commitments, as well as its participation in the DDA negotiations through trade-related co-operation projects. In addition to ongoing projects focusing on capacity-building in China's government and administration, a new €15 million project will shortly be launched, the largest programme of this kind so far. The EC-China Co-operation Programme is also being used to complement the various sectoral dialogues, and to tackle challenges related to the process of economic and social reform.

<u>New action points</u>

- Streamline and optimise the structure of dialogue in the wider economic area, taking account of the reorganisation of the Chinese administration, with the aim of ensuring effective co-ordination of activities by relevant authorities on both sides in all the sectors referred to in this section.

*WTO, trade and investment*

- Reinforce bilateral dialogue and co-ordination related to the new round of multilateral negotiations under the WTO Doha Development Agenda, extending its coverage to all DDA issues, with the aim of facilitating China's participation in a forward looking WTO agenda, of building alliances in areas of mutual concern, and of jointly building bridges between developed and developing countries.
- Reinforce monitoring of the implementation of China's WTO commitments, inter alia by:
  – making the best use of available resources in the Commission and Member States by enhancing networking and information-sharing between missions in Beijing, but also between EU administrations in capitals;
  – enhanced co-ordination and information exchange with European industry and third countries;

- focusing not only on adaptation of Chinese laws and regulations to WTO rules, but also on their full and uniform implementation and enforcement by central, regional and local authorities;
- feeding into, and following up on, the EU's contributions to the annual WTO China Transitional Review Mechanism (TRM) exercise which provide a clear list of EU priorities as regards Chinese WTO implementation;
- assisting China in its WTO implementation efforts through visits, seminars, conferences, training and studies in the framework of relevant co-operation programmes.

• Strengthen dialogue with the Chinese administration on WTO implementation and bilateral trade and investment issues at all levels, to provide an effective system for early warning and real-time management of disputes.
• Monitor regional integration initiatives, such as ASEAN+1, as well as initiatives for bilateral free trade areas between China and third countries, safeguarding EU interests, ensuring that any new arrangements are fully compatible with WTO rules and frameworks, and that relevant efforts do not interfere with the DDA negotiations.
• Launch a dedicated dialogue on intellectual property rights issues with relevant Ministries and IPR agencies, given the continued pervasiveness of IPR infractions in China.
• Support the growth of the European Chamber of Commerce in China (EUCCC), the expansion of its scope of activities, as well as a stronger presence in the regions; promote the speedy integration of companies from new EU Member States into the EUCCC.
• Support possible initiatives by EU industry, notably the EUCCC, but also EU-based organisations, such as the EU-China Business Association (EUCBA), to facilitate mutual understanding and develop common business practices, as well as to establish a regular dialogue on trade and investment issues with Chinese government and industry, feeding into bilateral government-to-government dialogue.
• Reinforce trade-related co-operation programmes:
  - launch planned major projects in the area of WTO support and information society;
  - continue other, *ad hoc* actions such as WTO seminars with Commission participation;
  - review the role and weight of, and methods of delivery for, trade-related assistance in the National Indicative Programmes (NIPs) for 2002–2004 and 2005/2006, including in areas like trade and environment.
• Make better use of trade-related cooperation programmes to support EU-China dialogue in areas such as trade and investment, making best use of possibilities existing under relevant co-operation projects (e.g. round tables with business involvement foreseen in the ongoing Financial Services Project).
• Launch negotiations on an agreement on co-operation and mutual assistance in customs matters by the end of 2003, with a view to conclusion in 2004.

- Analyse China's formal request for full 'Market Economy Status' for the entire Chinese economy under the EC's antidumping instrument taking account of China's progress towards EU market economy criteria as documented in the request; continue to consider objectively the requests of individual Chinese companies for 'market economy' treatment in anti-dumping investigations.
- Make full use of the benefits that EU enlargement will bring for EU-China economic ties to deepen the relationship further, and allay groundless Chinese fears about a negative impact on trade flows; take account of the implications of enlargement by associating new EU Member States and their industries to the actions listed in this section.
- Examine China's request for special trade preferences under the special incentive arrangements for environmental protection of the EC's Generalised System of Preferences (GSP).

*Sectoral issues*

- Fully implement the successful dialogue on industrial products by closely involving industry and other interested parties, not least to deal effectively with potential technical barriers to trade on both sides.
- Strengthen the recently extended dialogue on the Information Society, to cover both information society and communications regulatory policy.
- Continue the efforts to resolve the current disputes on food safety issues. Building on these efforts, reinforce dialogue on sanitary and phytosanitary (SPS) issues, with the mutual aim of ensuring that trade takes place in the framework of standards which are based on science and agreed international rules. Implement SPS-related actions foreseen under planned trade-related cooperation programmes, and explore options for further support in this area. Pursue the initiative to establish a dialogue with China on competition policy.
- Conclude ongoing negotiations for an agreement on visa and related issues concerning visits of tourist groups from China (agreement on "Authorised Destination Status") by the end of 2003, thus facilitating EU-bound tourism by Chinese citizens.
- Strengthen existing policy dialogues on environment and energy, and complement them by implementing planned co-operation projects on environmental capacity-building and sustainable development. Through the Commission's participation in the China Council for International Co-operation on Environment and Development, help identify priorities for future co-operation in this area.
- Launch formal negotiations for a nuclear research co-operation agreement as soon as possible in 2003, with a view to a rapid conclusion of the agreement.
- Further expand co-operation under the 1999 EC-China Science and Technology Agreement, making best use of the new possibilities provided by the EC Sixth Framework Programme, including in areas such as biotechnology or the "Digital Olympics" initiative for Beijing 2008. Hold the second high-level "China-Europe S&T and Innovation Policy Forum" in Beijing in the second half of 2004.

- Support China's interest to join the ITER fusion research project, and continue negotiations for an agreement on the possible joint implementation of ITER, aiming at a conclusion by the end of 2003.
- Continue negotiations for an agreement on EU-China co-operation under the EU's GALILEO programme for global satellite navigation, aiming at a conclusion by the end of 2003. The objective is to bring China as a full partner to the programme, including investment through the Galileo Joint Undertaking.

*Economic and Social Reform*

- Continue supporting China's reform process across the board through dialogue and cooperation, including by making best possible use of experience from the comparable transition processes of EU accession candidates.
- Pursue the initiative to launch a policy dialogue in the field of education and human resources development, with the full involvement of the Ministry of Education.
- Establish exchanges of experience between relevant authorities on both sides responsible for regional policy, with a view to contributing to policies for reducing regional and urban/rural divides in China.
- Launch the planned co-operation project supporting social security reform, and develop new programmes in the area of human resources development.
- Establish a new dialogue on industrial policy, to contribute to the improvement of the competitiveness of businesses on both sides, and to enhance mutual understanding of regulatory frameworks on both sides.
- Promote exchanges in the area of macro-economic policy, e.g. on the Euro, exchange rate policies, China's economic reform process, and other issues of mutual interest.
- Make efforts to involve civil society more closely in existing and new exchanges, e.g. in the field of environmental protection.

*3.4. The EC-China Co-operation Programme – a mutually beneficial partnership underpinning EU objectives*

The context, and implementation of action points in the 2001 Communication

The China Country Strategy Paper (CSP) covering the period 2002–2006, and the National Indicative Programme (NIP) for 2002–2004 were approved by the Commission in February 2002, with indicative funding of up to €250 million for the period of the CSP. They represent a significant move towards an approach which is predicated on support for the EU's overall objectives in the framework of its China policy, albeit, in a mutually beneficial way.

In line with this policy, the CSP addresses the three following specific objectives, broadly designed to assist China in its reform process, while capitalising on the particular added value that the EC can provide when compared with other donors:

- Support for the social and economic reform process (WTO implementation, information society, social security reform, human resources development)
- Support for environmental protection and sustainable development (water resources, biodiversity protection), and
- Support for good governance and the rule of law (illegal migration, support to civil society).

In addition to ongoing co-operation activities under the national programme, which amount to approximately €260 million in terms of multi-annual financial commitments, it should be noted that China is a major participant in, and beneficiary of, a number of regional EC-financed Asian programmes. These include the EU-Asia Pro Eco Programme on the improvement of environmental performance in economic sectors; the Asia-Invest Programme promoting business partnerships; the Asia Information Technology and Communication Programme which co-finances mutually beneficial partnerships between Europe and Asia; and the Asia-Link Programme which promotes networking between higher education institutions.

Under these Asia-wide programmes, China is currently participating in between 35% and 50% of all proposals approved for financing, and is involved in activities for which the EC contribution amounts to some €21 million.

Considerable progress has been made in establishing the required environment for enhanced EU-China co-operation, in particular through the completion of the devolution of preparation and management responsibilities for bilateral projects from Commission Headquarters to the Delegation in Beijing, with the corresponding reinforcement of the Delegation's human resources, and through regular co-ordination with Member States and other donors. Furthermore, the focussing of the co-operation programme on a limited number of larger interventions in key sectors will in the longer term enhance programme effects and impact.

Some delays and difficulties in the implementation of the 2002–2004 NIP have however been encountered. These are in part related to the complexity and sensitivity of the issues to be addressed in the Chinese context – an example is the planned programme on illegal migration – and in part to the fact that the CSP/NIP programming approach to co-operation has not yet been fully internalised at all levels on the Chinese side, where improved inter-ministerial co-ordination and role definition is required.

This latter point is increasingly proving to be a constraint for programme implementation. The EC's principal Government interlocutor on co-operation matters is the Ministry of Commerce which has been the most appropriate focal point for the co-ordination of programme planning and implementation. However, with the current shift in orientation of the EC-China cooperation programme away from traditional development projects towards sectoral interventions which are increasingly aligned with EU policies, a greater degree of involvement of line Ministries is required. If the Ministry of Commerce is to continue in its co-ordinating role for the overall programme, more responsibilities should in general be devolved to line Ministries for the preparation and implementation of specific interventions.

While progress on NIP support for WTO implementation, the environment, and civil society remain broadly on track, the delays encountered in other areas will result in a concentration of activities toward the end of the NIP's duration. While the now-completed devolution exercise should result in more rapid commitments and implementation, this nevertheless constitutes an important challenge.

These elements will be taken into account under the Mid-Term Review of the CSP and NIP which is under way. While the CSP and the co-operation priorities stemming from it remain fully valid and responsive both to Community policies and to China's policies under its new leadership, an important review of the NIP is required in order make the necessary adjustments and to ensure that revised and attainable targets are defined.

*New action points*

- Complete the Mid-Term Review of the CSP and the 2002–2004 NIP during the second half of 2003.
- Prepare a new NIP for the period 2005–2006 by the first quarter of 2004, building on the experience gained in the implementation of the 2002–2004 NIP, while at the same time remaining focussed on the objectives specified in the overall framework of the 2002–2006 CSP. This will take account, inter alia, of Trade-Related Technical Assistance.
- Ensure appropriate consultation with the Chinese authorities in preparing the new NIP, in order to enhance ownership and facilitate implementation.
- Reconfirm with the Chinese authorities the multi-annual – as opposed to annual – programming approach under the CSP as the basis for EC co-operation.
- Promote improved co-ordination of project and programme preparation and implementation through the greater allocation of responsibilities to line ministries.
- Ensure a co-ordinated approach between the implementation of the NIP and the various related horizontal assistance programmes from which China benefits, notably the European Initiative for Democracy and Human Rights (EIDHR), and NGO budget lines.
- In view of the importance of the EC-China co-operation programme as a vehicle of support for the EU's China policy, strengthen dialogue on co-operation matters, notably in the wider context of the EU-China Joint Committee.

*3.5 Raising the EU's profile in China*

The development of EU-China relations requires better understanding between partners. Growth of relations, as well as changes on both sides, such as China's entry to WTO or the EU enlargement process, also require a review and adjustment of the EU's communication strategy. The increasing access of individual Chinese citizens to sources of information, through the development of information technologies, telecommunications and travel abroad, represents opportunities for enhanced EU visibility.

China's geopolitical vision of a multipolar world, and the Chinese perception of the EU as a partner of growing importance, also provide a favourable context for increased EU visibility. However, more needs to be done to raise EU visibility in China. The EC Delegation in Beijing, Member States as well as others, such as the European Chamber of Commerce have already made great efforts to raise the EU's profile through daily contacts, the dissemination of information and publications, and the organisation of public events.

To ensure the long-term sustainability of the EU-China relationship and the political dialogue, it is crucial that the EU becomes more visible in China, both to the general public and to its leadership. In this respect, emphasis should be put on a few key messages, for example:

- The EU, as a global player on the international stage, shares China's concerns for a more balanced international order based on effective multilateralism, and wants to engage China as a responsible power in the management of global issues.

- The EU stands for a set of common values, with democracy, human rights and peaceful resolution of conflicts through multilateral mechanisms at the core of it. Its unique raison d'être and institutions differentiate the EU from classical regional organisations.
- As a model of successful regional integration and of governance under the rule of law, the EU supports ongoing reforms in China and is ready to help China address current challenges of its economic and social transition.
- The EU is a major global trading power and market. It is willing to strengthen exchanges with China and to help China further integrate in the global economy.

Along with coherent messages, internal EU policy cohesion is vital to enhance EU visibility in China. Communication strategies and the EC-China Co-operation Programme should thus be closely linked to the EU's broader political objectives, in order to ensure overall policy coherence. It is equally important to ensure co-ordination of policies with Member States, including in the field of communication and co-operation.

To foster mutual understanding, efforts should be undertaken to promote people-to-people contacts, through increased tourist, educational and cultural exchanges.

The context, and implementation of action points in 2001 communication

Activities regarding information on the EU of the EC Delegation in Beijing have been intensified. Targeted communication actions such as an extensive Euro campaign have attracted wide coverage in China. Financial and staff resources are being reinforced, but remain limited. The web site of the Delegation has become fully operational in English and Chinese. Collective and individual visits to Brussels of Chinese journalists have continued. Most EU-China co-operation programmes also now include publicity activities.

People-to-people contacts, educational and cultural exchanges were also intensified. The EU Visitors Programme continues to be a valuable means to bring Chinese decision and opinion makers to Brussels to acquire first hand knowledge of Europe. The EC Delegation in Beijing strengthened links with academia through the organisation of round tables around visits by EU personalities, and the launching of the European Studies Centres Programme. In the cultural field, the EC Delegation and Member States have co-ordinated their participation in events such as Shanghai International Film Festival.

New action points

- Conduct a survey on public perceptions of the EU in China to identify information needs and gaps and help establish a targeted approach.
- Improve knowledge and awareness of the EU in China through the provision of comprehensive and up-to date information on EU policies, notably via Internet and audiovisual media, and with a special focus on enlargement and institutional developments within the EU, e.g. through an enlargement road show. Extend information activities beyond Beijing to China's major cities.
- Systematically issue press releases and/or hold press conferences in Beijing on the occasion of major meetings such as Summits, Joint Committees and sessions of the human rights dialogue. Try to find common ground with the Chinese side to issue joint statements, especially after EU-China Summits.

- Consider organising annual round tables alternatively in China and in the EU gathering Chinese and European journalists with EU personalities.
- Raise the level of co-ordination with Member States on information policy, to ensure that key EU messages are, whenever feasible, included in public parts of high level bilateral visits to China.
- Raise awareness in China of EU co-operation with China, e.g. through systematic inclusion of publicity activities in the scope of co-operation projects, field visits by journalists to projects, and increased project participation in business and academic fairs and exhibitions, including at regional level.
- Further reinforce people-to-people exchanges, by making use of co-operation activities to foster links between European and Chinese NGOs and social bodies, strengthening contacts with universities which provide European Studies courses, and developing cultural, educational and research initiatives in the framework of existing or planned EU programmes such as Erasmus World and the Marie Curie fellowships, while encouraging students, researchers, and Chinese universities to participate in such programmes.

## 4. IMPROVING THE MECHANISMS OF THE RELATIONSHIP

The expansion and strengthening of EU-China dialogue across the board has shown the need to streamline and further develop the current institutional structure of the relationship, in particular as regards the interaction between meetings at different levels and in the various areas, and emphasising quality over quantity of dialogue. Proposals have been made in the preceding sections for enhancing the effectiveness of dialogue in the political, economic and other fields. Experience proves that there is also a need for an effective high-level coordination of the entire breadth of EU-China relations, over and above improvements within the different strands of dialogue, and in keeping with the EU's overall aim of a comprehensive partnership with China in all areas. This general objective also militates in favour of increasing the profile and visibility of high-level meetings.

To this end, the following actions are proposed:

- Summits and meetings at ministerial level should focus on a limited set of strategic priorities. This will increase the strategic importance of EU-China Summits and Ministerials, allow for more free-flowing dialogue on selected topics, increase chances for concrete results, and in turn heighten their political visibility.
- The mandates of different high-level EU-China fora should be adjusted and clarified, to allow a better burden-sharing and division of responsibilities between them:
  - Summits should cover the whole breadth of the relationship. However, their agendas should be focussed to inject political momentum into the relationship and project a joint vision of world affairs, in the political and other fields.

- Foreign Ministers Troikas should cover political and human rights issues, but also, where appropriate, selected trade and sectoral issues.
- The steering role of the EC-China Joint Committee should be reinforced so as to cover the wider economic area, i.e. not only trade and investment issues, but also the fast expanding sectoral dialogue and the EC-China Co-operation Programme, thus maximising synergies between the three areas in question. To this end, the participation of relevant line ministries in the Joint Committee should be enhanced.
- Regional Directors Troikas should focus on EU and Asian economic and political integration, as well as on regional crises.
- Political Directors Troikas should cover political and other issues of global concern.

• To allow Summits to provide direction and stimulus to overall relations effectively, they should, wherever possible, be held on a stand-alone basis, rather than back-to-back with other events, in order to ensure adequate time appropriation and to increase visibility.
• For the same reason, and to provide a visible reflection of the increasing importance of the relationship, it could be considered to upgrade the level of Summits to presidential level.
• Chinese President Hu Jintao should be invited to visit Brussels in the near future, and reciprocal visits of senior EU leaders, including Commission President Prodi, to Beijing arranged, to give further expression to the growing political weight of the EU-China relationship.

***Annex 1***

**EU-China Dialogue**

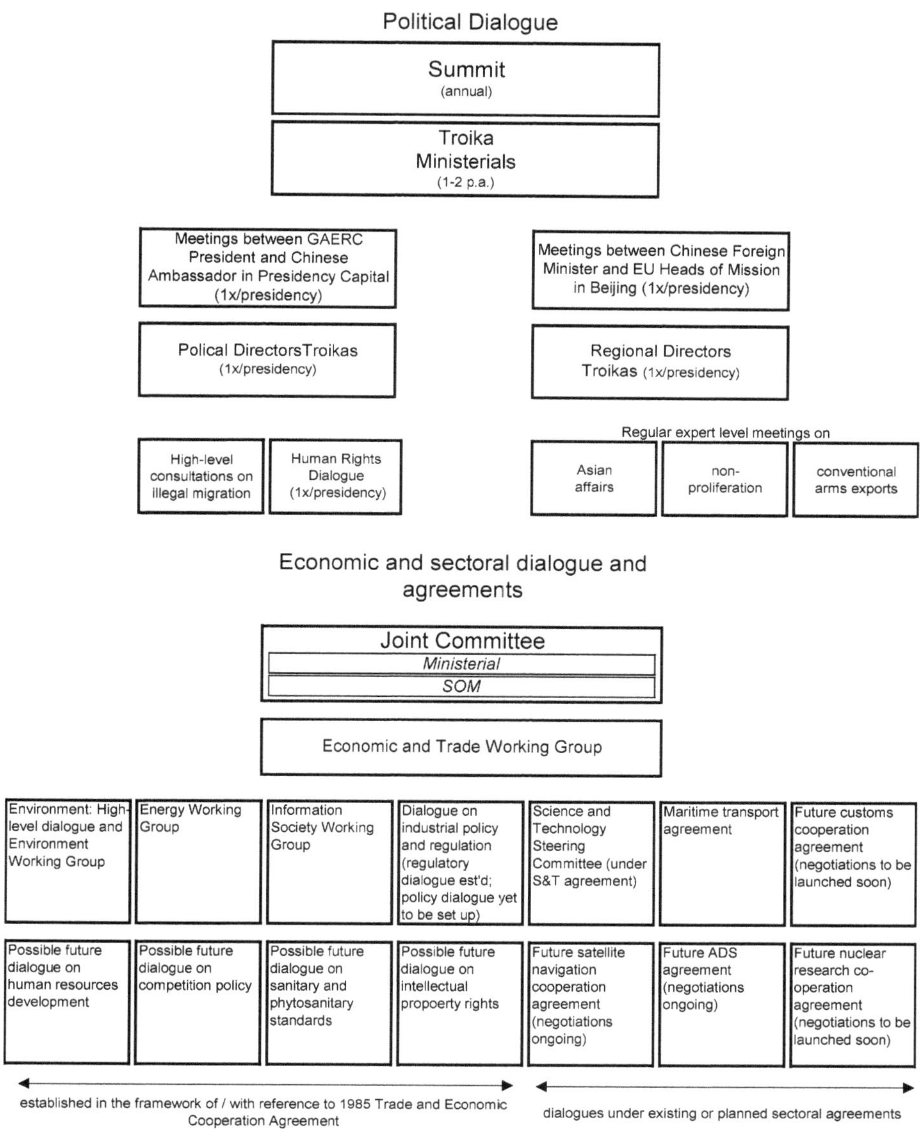

ANNEX 1

## EU trade with the world and China (€ million)

(exluding intra-EU trade)

Source: EUROSTAT (COMEXT)

### Total trade

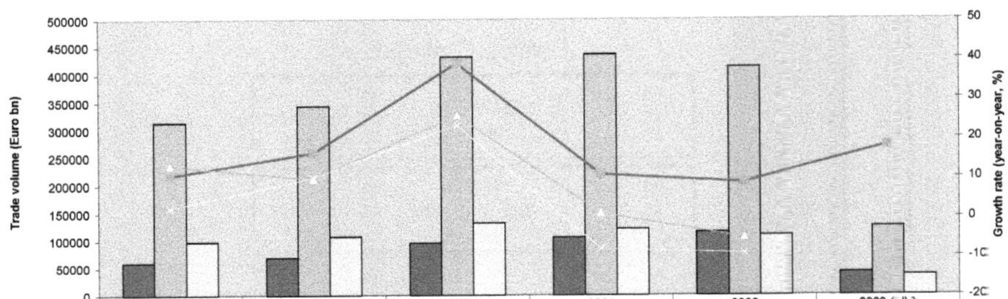


| | 1998 | 1999 | 2000 | 2001 | 2002 | 2003 ([illegible] IV) |
|---|---|---|---|---|---|---|
| China | 59.386 | 69.006 | 95.773 | 106.003 | 115.270 | 41.5[illegible]4 |
| US | 313.564 | 343.604 | 431.493 | 435.559 | 412.860 | 125.[illegible]2 |
| Japan | 97.609 | 107.284 | 132.068 | 121.218 | 109.966 | 36.5[illegible]3 |
| Growth (China) | 10,4 | 16,2 | 38,8 | 10,7 | 8,7 | 18,[illegible] |
| Growth (US) | 12,9 | 9,6 | 25,6 | 0,9 | -5,2 | |
| Growth (Japan) | 2,3 | 9,9 | 23,1 | -8,2 | -9,3 | |

### EU imports

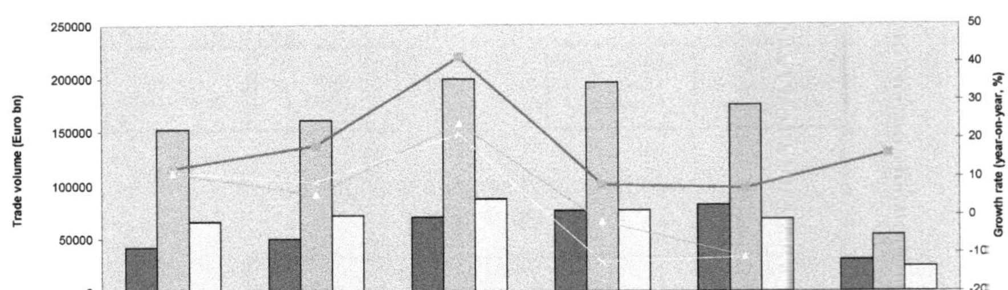


| | 1998 | 1999 | 2000 | 2001 | 2002 | 2003 ([illegible]IV) |
|---|---|---|---|---|---|---|
| China | 41.974 | 49.655 | 70.275 | 75.915 | 81.289 | 29.1[illegible]3 |
| US | 152.019 | 160.588 | 199.024 | 195.655 | 174.162 | 52.3[illegible]8 |
| Japan | 66.042 | 71.911 | 87.133 | 76.298 | 67.807 | 23.1[illegible]0 |
| Growth (China) | 12,4 | 18,3 | 41,5 | 8,0 | 7,1 | 16,[illegible] |
| Growth (US) | 11,2 | 5,6 | 23,9 | -1,7 | -11,0 | |
| Growth (Japan) | 11,3 | 8,9 | 21,2 | -12,4 | -11,1 | |

### EU exports

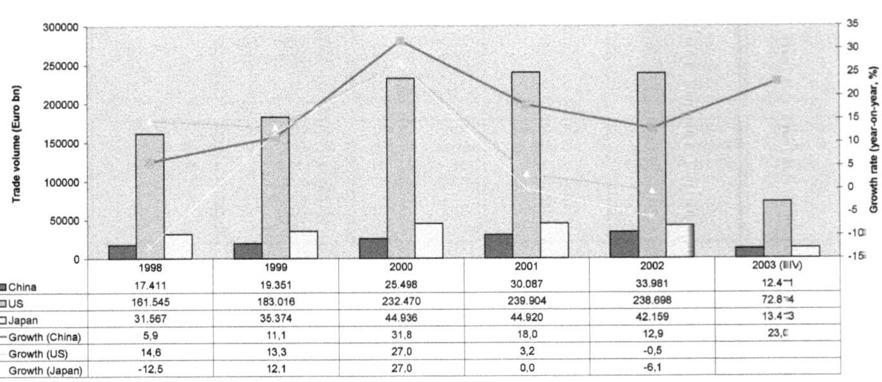


| | 1998 | 1999 | 2000 | 2001 | 2002 | 2003 ([illegible]IV) |
|---|---|---|---|---|---|---|
| China | 17.411 | 19.351 | 25.498 | 30.087 | 33.981 | 12.4[illegible] |
| US | 161.545 | 183.016 | 232.470 | 239.904 | 238.698 | 72.8[illegible]4 |
| Japan | 31.567 | 35.374 | 44.936 | 44.920 | 42.159 | 13.4[illegible]3 |
| Growth (China) | 5,9 | 11,1 | 31,8 | 18,0 | 12,9 | 23,[illegible] |
| Growth (US) | 14,6 | 13,3 | 27,0 | 3,2 | -0,5 | |
| Growth (Japan) | -12,5 | 12,1 | 27,0 | 0,0 | -6,1 | |

**China's trade with major partners (USD bn)**

Source: Chinese Government (MOFCCM / MOFTEC)

Total trade

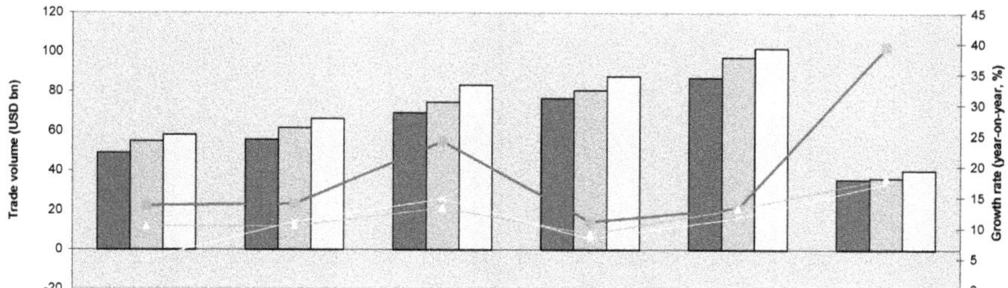


| | 1998 | 1999 | 2000 | 2001 | 2002 | 2003 (Jan.-April) |
|---|---|---|---|---|---|---|
| EU | 48,9 | 55,7 | 69,0 | 76,6 | 86,8 | 35,6 |
| US | 54,8 | 61,4 | 74,5 | 80,5 | 97,2 | 36,3 |
| Japan | 57,9 | 66,2 | 83,2 | 87,8 | 101,9 | 40,3 |
| Growth (EU) | 13,6 | 13,9 | 24,0 | 11,0 | 13,2 | 39,4 |
| Growth (US) | 11,9 | 12,0 | 21,2 | 8,1 | 20,8 | 36,3 |
| Growth (Japan) | -4,8 | 14,2 | 25,7 | 5,5 | 16,2 | 33,7 |

China's imports

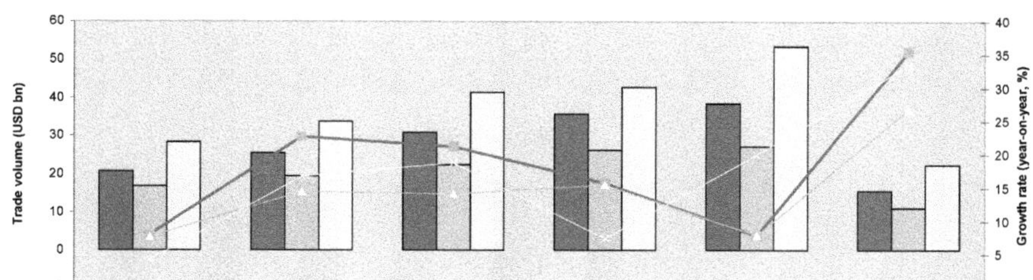


| | 1998 | 1999 | 2000 | 2001 | 2002 | 2003 (Jan.-April) |
|---|---|---|---|---|---|---|
| EU | 20,8 | 25,5 | 30,8 | 35,7 | 38,5 | 15,6 |
| US | 16,9 | 19,5 | 22,4 | 26,2 | 27,2 | 11,1 |
| Japan | 28,3 | 33,8 | 41,5 | 42,8 | 53,5 | 22,3 |
| Growth (EU) | 8,1 | 22,7 | 21,2 | 15,8 | 7,9 | 35,5 |
| Growth (US) | 3,6 | 15,4 | 14,8 | 17,2 | 3,9 | 36,9 |
| Growth (Japan) | -2,5 | 19,4 | 22,9 | 3,1 | 25,0 | 48,6 |

China's exports

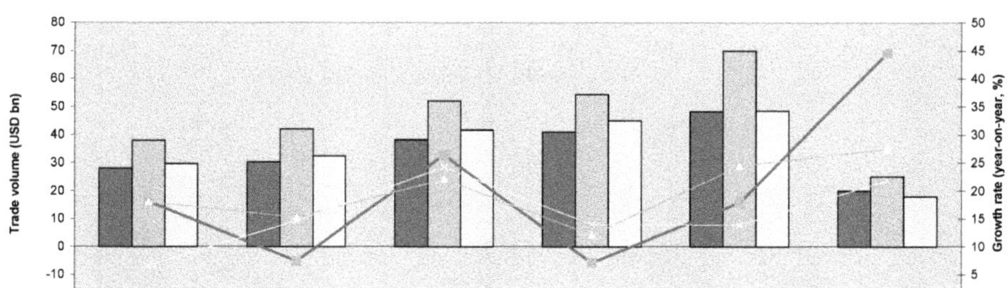


| | 1998 | 1999 | 2000 | 2001 | 2002 | 2003 (Jan.-April) |
|---|---|---|---|---|---|---|
| EU | 28,1 | 30,2 | 38,2 | 40,9 | 48,2 | 19,9 |
| US | 37,9 | 41,9 | 52,1 | 54,3 | 70,0 | 25,2 |
| Japan | 29,7 | 32,4 | 41,7 | 45,0 | 48,4 | 18,0 |
| Growth (EU) | 18,1 | 7,4 | 26,4 | 7,1 | 17,9 | 44,6 |
| Growth (US) | 16,0 | 10,5 | 24,2 | 4,2 | 28,9 | 34,9 |
| Growth (Japan) | -6,8 | 9,3 | 28,5 | 7,9 | 7,8 | 23,7 |

**Foreign Direct Investment (FDI) in China**

Source: Chinese Government (MOFCOM / MOFTEC)

New FDI inflows (USD bn)

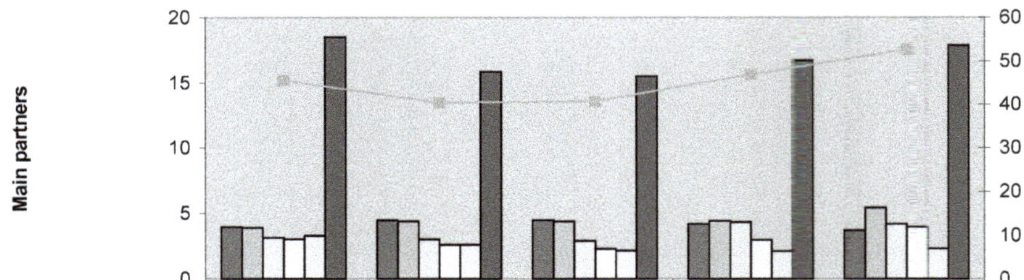


| | 1998 | 1999 | 2000 | 2001 | 2002 |
|---|---|---|---|---|---|
| EU | 4,0 | 4,5 | 4,5 | 4,2 | 3,7 |
| US | 3,9 | 4,4 | 4,4 | 4,4 | 5,4 |
| Japan | 3,2 | 3,0 | 2,9 | 4,3 | 4,2 |
| Taiwan | 3,0 | 2,6 | 2,3 | 3,0 | 4,0 |
| Singapore | 3,3 | 2,6 | 2,2 | 2,1 | 2,3 |
| Hong Kong* | 18,5 | 15,8 | 15,5 | 16,7 | 17,9 |
| Total | 45,6 | 40,4 | 40,7 | 46,9 | 52,7 |

Share in new FDI inflows

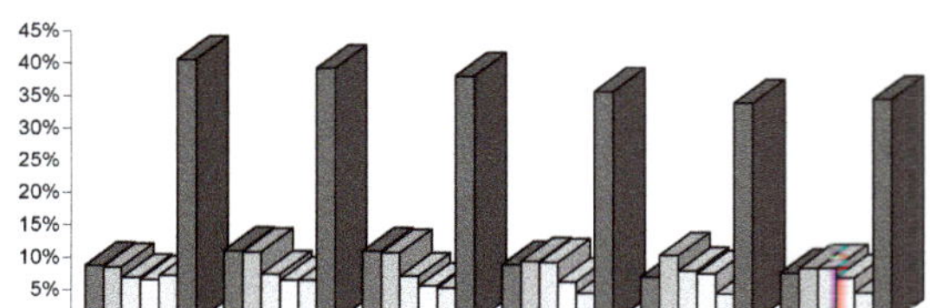


| | 1998 | 1999 | 2000 | 2001 | 2002 | 2003 (Jan.-March) |
|---|---|---|---|---|---|---|
| EU | 8,7% | 11,1% | 11,0% | 8,9% | 7,0% | 7,3% |
| US | 8,6% | 10,9% | 10,8% | 9,5% | 10,3% | 8,[illegible]% |
| Japan | 6,9% | 7,4% | 7,2% | 9,3% | 7,9% | 8,[illegible]% |
| Taiwan | 6,7% | 6,5% | 5,6% | 6,4% | 7,5% | 6,3% |
| Singapore | 7,2% | 6,5% | 5,3% | 4,6% | 4,4% | 4,3% |
| Hong Kong* | 40,6% | 39,2% | 38,1% | 35,7% | 33,9% | 34,[illegible]% |

Aggregate FDI (stocks, end of 2002)

(USD bn) (% share)

*) Chinese data on HK FDI are thought to be hugely exaggerated, as tax privileges offered to attract FDI prompt Chinese investors to export funds to Hong Kong and to repatriate them in the form of FDI. Moreover, large amounts of Taiwanese FDI pour into China through Hong Kong, skirting Taiwanese restrictions; Chinese figures capture only part of these (official figure for aggregate utilised Taiwanese FDI is 29 bn, but analysts estimates range from 70-100 bn).

**Annex 3: EU-China co-operation projects**

This list includes projects financed under the following budget titles and budget lines:

| | |
|---|---|
| B7-3 | Co-operation with Asian Developing Countries |
| B7-7 | European Initiative for Democracy and Human Rights (EIDHR) |
| B7-6000 | NGO co-financing |
| B7-6212 | Health, Population, Fight against HIV/AIDS |

**PROJECTS AND PROGRAMMES UNDER IMPLEMENTATION**

| Sector | Project | EC Grant (€) | Subtotal |
|---|---|---|---|
| General | EU-China Small Project Facility 2001/2005 | 8.000.000 | 8.000.000 |
| | China-Europe International Business School (Phase II) | 10.950.000 | 69.510.000 |
| | EU-China Junior Managers Training Programme | 11.640.000 | |
| | China Europe Public Administration Project (CEPA) | 5.700.000 | |
| Human Resource | EU-China Prog. for the Development of Vocational Training | 15.100.000 | |
| Development | Basic Education Project in Gansu Province | 15.000.000 | |
| | STD/HIV/AIDS Training Programme | 400.000 | |
| | Chinese Interpreters Training Programme 2001–2004 | 390.000 | |
| | European Studies Centres Programme (ESCP) | 10.330.000 | |
| | EU-China Legal and Judicial Co-operation Programme | 13.200.000 | 32.870.000 |
| | EU-China Village Governance Training Programme | 10.670.000 | |
| Rule of Law and Good | EU-China Intellectual Property Rights Co-operation Prog. | 5.600.000 | |
| Governance | China Human Rights Project Facility | 840.000 | |
| | EU-China Network on Human Rights Covenants | 1.730.000 | |
| | Co-op. in Economic Social and Cultural Rights in Yunnan | 830.000 | |
| | EU Support to China's Accession to the WTO | 3.600.000 | 48.170.000 |

| | | | |
|---|---|---|---|
| Economic and Social Reform | EU-China Financial Services Co-operation Project | 8.500.000 | |
| | EU-China Enterprise Reform Project | 8.500.000 | |
| | EU-China Civil Aviation Co-operation Project | 12.570.000 | |
| | Support for China's Integration into the World Trading System | 15.000.000 | |
| | EU-China Liaoning Integrated Environmental Programme | 37.000.000 | 87.800.000 |
| | Environmental Management Co-operation Project (EMCP) | 13.000.000 | |
| Environment | Vehicle Emmissions Control Project | 840.000 | |
| | Natural Forest Management Project | 16.500.000 | |
| | Energy and Environment Programme | 20.000.000 | |
| | Municipal Solid Waste Management Reform | 460.000 | |
| Rural and Agricultural | Pa-Nam Integrated Rural Development (Tibet) | 7.600.000 | 7.600 000 |
| | Improving Access to STD Services in Urban Areas in China | 1.070.000 | 6.320 000 |
| | Maternal and Child Health Care Project, Mid-West China | 880.000 | |
| | Child Welfare in Communities | 1.000.000 | |
| NGO Co-Financing and | Support to Health Policy in Disfavoured Regions of Wester China | 800.000 | |
| Health/Population | Rural Poverty Alleviation and CommunityCapacity Building | 500.000 | |
| | Yunnan Integrated Primary Health Care | 710.000 | |
| | Povert Alleviation for Communities in Western China | 750.000 | |
| | Sershul County Health Initiative, Sichuan Province | 110.000 | |
| | Leprosy Rehabilitation Programme | 500.000 | |
| Total: | | | 260.270.000 |

**REGIONAL PROGRAMMES IN WHICH CHINESE INSTITUTIONS ARE PARTICIPATING(1)**

| Category | Project | EC Grant (€) |
|---|---|---|
| Regional Programmes | Asia Pro Eco (2003 Call for Proposals, 1st Deadline) | 1.890.000 |
| | Asia-Link (2002 Call for proposals) | 4.930.000 |
| | Asia-Invest (1997–2002) | 9.130.000 |
| | Asia Urbs (2002 Call for Proposals) | 850.000 |
| | Asia IT & C (2002 Call for Proposals) | 4.480.000 |
| Total: | | 21.280.000 |

(1) Reference year 2003. China also participates in the ASEM Trust Fund II Regional Programme (total funding €20 million) and benfits from EC support to the Asia-Europe Foundation (total funding €3.5 million)

**PROJECTS AND PROGRAMMES UNDER PREPARATION**

| Category | Project | EC Grant (€) |
|---|---|---|
| Projects under preparation | Social Security Reform | Total indicative funding €135 million |
| | Information Society Human Resources Development | |
| | Environment Programmes | |
| | Information Technology Project | |
| | Support to Civil Society | |
| | Fight against Illegal Migration | |
| Total | | 135.000.000 |

1 COM (1998) 181
2 COM (2000) 552
3 COM (2001) 265
4 "Europe and Asia: A Strategic Framework for Enhanced Partnerships", COM (2001) 469.
5 Source: Chinese government (MOFCOM/MOFTEC).

A month later, on 13 October 2003, China issued its first ever policy paper on Europe (see Document 3.8). It defined the objectives of China's EU policy and outlined plans for bilateral cooperation for the next five years. It recognised that the EU 'is a major force in the world'. It also pointed out that 'there is no fundamental conflict of interest between China and the EU', despite differences of perspective or even disagreements due to history, culture, political system and economic development. China and the EU had many common interests, including market-building and market management, the construction and management of a new role in the world, an expansion of relations, the importance of domestic changes in China for EU–China relations, agreement that China's reforms needed support to be sustainable, the importance of Chinese membership of the WTO, multilateralism in global institutions and China's role in Asia. Consequently, the EU and China had established a 'full partnership'. On this basis, China's main objectives in its policy towards Europe were to develop political relations further by 'seeking common ground while reserving differences', to deepen economic cooperation and trade, and to increase cultural and people-to-people exchanges. Among other significant points, it noted the commitment of the EU and its Member States to the 'one-China principle' Following the issue of these two significant policy documents, the EU and China met in Beijing. They reviewed the two documents and identified areas for further dialogue and cooperation.[4]

## Document 3.8: China's EU Policy Paper

China's EU Policy Paper (full text)
October 2003

### Foreword

The international situation has been undergoing profound changes since the advent of the new century. The trend towards world multipolarity and economic globalisation is developing amid twists and turns. Peace and development remain the themes of our era. The world is hardly a tranquil place and mankind is still confronted with many serious challenges. However, preserving world peace, promoting development and strengthening cooperation, which is vital to the well-being of all nations, represents the common aspiration of all peoples and is an irreversible trend of history.

China is committed to turning herself into a well-off society in an all-round way and aspires for a favourable international climate. China will continue to pursue its independent foreign policy of peace and work closely with other countries for the establishment of a new international political and economic order that is fair and equitable, and based on the Five Principles of Peaceful Co-existence. China will, as always, respect diversity in the world and promote democracy in international relations in the interest of world peace and common development.

The European Union (EU) is a major force in the world. The Chinese Government appreciates the importance the EU and its members attach to developing relations with China. The present EU Policy Paper of the Chinese Government is the first of its kind and aims to highlight the objectives of China's EU policy, and outline the areas and plans of cooperation and related measures in the next five years so as to enhance China-EU all-round cooperation and promote a long-term and stable development of China-EU relations.

### Part One: Status and Role of the European Union

The creation and development of the European Union is an event of far-reaching significance following World War II. Since the launch of the European Coal and Steel Community in 1952, the EU has become what it is today through the stages of the Tax and Customs Union, the Single Market and the Economic and Monetary Union. Its integration in the foreign policy, defence and social fields has made headway. The Euro has been put to circulation successfully and a single area of justice is taking shape. The EU is now a strong and

[4] See European Commission, Directorate-General for External Relations, 'National Indicative Programme 2005–2006: China' (Brussels, 2005) s 1.1.2.

the most integrated community in the world, taking up 25 and 35 percent of the world's economy and trade respectively and ranking high on the world's list of per capita income and foreign investment.

In 2004, the EU will be enlarged to a total membership of 25. The new European Union would then cover much of Eastern and Western Europe with an area of four million square kilometers, a population of 450 million and a GDP of over 10 trillion US Dollars.

Despite its difficulties and challenges ahead, the European integration process is irreversible and the EU will play an increasingly important role in both regional and international affairs.

**Part Two: China's EU Policy**

China attaches importance to the role and influence of the EU in regional and international affairs. History proves that the establishment of diplomatic relations between China and the European Economic Community in 1975 has served the interests of both sides. Despite their twists and turns, China-EU relations as a whole have been growing stronger and more mature and are now on the track of a comprehensive and sound development. In 1998 China and the EU launched their annual summit mechanism. In 2001, the two sides established a full partnership. China and the EU have developed an ever closer consultation and fruitful cooperation in the political, economic, trade, scientific, cultural and educational fields. China-EU relations now are better than any time in history.

There is no fundamental conflict of interest between China and the EU and neither side poses a threat to the other. However, given their differences in historical background, cultural heritage, political system and economic development level, it is natural that the two sides have different views or even disagree on some issues. Nevertheless China-EU relations of mutual trust and mutual benefit cannot and will not be affected if the two sides address their disagreements in a spirit of equality and mutual respect.

The common ground between China and the EU far outweighs their disagreements. Both China and the EU stand for democracy in international relations and an enhanced role of the UN. Both are committed to combating international terrorism and promoting sustainable development through poverty elimination and environmental protection endeavours. China and the EU are highly complementary economically thanks to their respective advantages. The EU has a developed economy, advanced technologies and strong financial resources while China boasts steady economic growth, a huge market and abundant labour force. There is a broad prospect for bilateral trade and economic and technological cooperation. Both China and the EU member states have a long history and splendid culture each and stand for more cultural exchanges and mutual emulation. The political, economic and cultural common understanding and interaction between China and the EU offer a solid foundation for the continued growth of China-EU relations.

To strengthen and enhance China-EU relations is an important component of China's foreign policy. China is committed to a long-term, stable and full partnership with the EU. China's EU policy objectives are:

- To promote a sound and steady development of China-EU political relations under the principles of mutual respect, mutual trust and seeking common ground while reserving differences, and contribute to world peace and stability;
- To deepen China-EU economic cooperation and trade under the principles of mutual benefit, reciprocity and consultation on an equal basis, and promote common development;

- To expand China-EU cultural and people-to-people exchanges under the principle of mutual emulation, common prosperity and complementarity, and promote cultural harmony and progress between the East and the West.

**Part Three: Strengthen China-EU Cooperation in All Fields**

*I. The Political Aspect*

1. Strengthen the exchange of high-level visits and political dialogue

- Maintain close contacts and timely communication between the two sides at high levels through various means.
- Give full play to the functions of the China-EU annual summit by substantiating its content, stressing its practical results and strengthening bilateral coordination.
- Implement in real earnest China-EU agreement on political dialogue and constantly improve and strengthen mechanisms of regular and irregular consultations at all levels.
- Deepen relations with all EU members, including its new ones so as to maintain stability and continuity in the overall relationship between China and EU.

2. Strictly abide by the one-China principle

The one-China principle is an important political cornerstone underpinning China-EU relations. The proper handling of the Taiwan question is essential for a steady growth of China-EU relations. China appreciates EU and its members' commitment to the one-China principle and hopes that the EU will continue to respect China's major concerns over the Taiwan question, guard against Taiwan authorities' attempt to create "two Chinas" or "one China, one Taiwan" and prudently handle Taiwan-related issues. In this connection, it is important that the EU

- Prohibit any visit by any Taiwan political figures to the EU or its member countries under whatever name or pretext; not to engage in any contact or exchange of an official or governmental nature with Taiwan authorities.
- Not to support Taiwan's accession to or participation in any international organization whose membership requires statehood. Taiwan's entry into the WTO in the name of "separate customs territory of Taiwan, 'Penghu, Jinmen, Mazu" (or Chinese Taipei for short) does not mean any change in Taiwan's status as part of China. EU exchanges with Taiwan must be strictly unofficial and non-governmental.
- Not to sell to Taiwan any weapon, equipment, goods, materials or technology that can be used for military purposes.

3. Encourage Hong Kong and Macao's cooperation with EU

The Central Government of China supports and encourages the Hong Kong and Macao Special Administrative Regions in developing friendly relations and cooperation with the EU in accordance with the principle of "one country, two systems" and the provisions of the two Basic Laws and on the basis of equality and mutual benefit.

4. Promote the EU's understanding of Tibet

China encourages personages of various circles in the EU to visit Tibet and welcomes the support of the EU and its members to Tibet's economic, cultural, educational and social development and their cooperation with the autonomous region subject to full respect of China's laws and regulations. The Chinese side requests the EU side not to have any contact with the "Tibetan government in exile" or provide facilities to the separatist activities of the Dalai clique.

5. Continue the human rights dialogue

There are both consensus and disagreements between China and the EU on the question of human rights. The Chinese side appreciates the EU's persistent position for dialogue and against confrontation and stands ready to continue dialogue, exchange and cooperation on human rights with the EU on the basis of equality and mutual respect so as to share information, enhance mutual understanding and deepen cooperation in protecting, inter alia, citizens' social and cultural rights and the rights of the disadvantaged.

6. Strengthen international cooperation

- Enhance China-EU consultation and coordination on major international and regional hotspot issues.
- Strengthen China-EU cooperation at the UN and work together to uphold the UN's authority, promote its leading role in safeguarding world peace and facilitating economic and social development, particularly in helping developing countries eliminate poverty, improving global environment and drug control, and support UN's reform.
- Advance the process of Asia-Europe cooperation. China and the EU should work together to make ASEM a role model for inter-continental cooperation on the basis of equality, a channel for exchange between the oriental and occidental civilizations and a driving force behind the establishment of a new international political and economic order.
- Jointly combat terrorism. Both China and the EU are victims of terrorism and are strongly opposed to all forms of terrorism. Both sides are also opposed to any linkage between terrorism and any particular country, nation, ethnic group or religion. China and the EU should keep in close touch and cooperation on counter-terrorism.
- Jointly safeguard the international arms control, disarmament and non-proliferation regimes and step up consultation and coordination on the basis of mutual respect; strengthen exchange and cooperation on non-proliferation and export control and the prevention of weaponization of and arms race in outer space; jointly contribute to the resolution of the issue of anti-personnel landmines and explosive remnants of war; and enhance cooperation in implementing the international arms control treaties.

7. Enhance mutual understanding between Chinese and European legislative organs

The relations between the National People's Congress of China and the parliaments of EU member countries and the European Parliament are an important link in China-EU ties. The Chinese Government welcomes and supports the enhancement of exchange and dialogue between Chinese and European legislatures on the basis of mutual respect, deeper understanding, seeking common ground while shelving differences and developing cooperation.

8. Increase exchanges between political parties in China and the EU

The Chinese Government wishes to see an increase of exchange and cooperation between the Communist Party of China and all major EU political parties, parliamentary party groups and regional organizations of political parties on the basis of independence, complete equality, mutual respect and non-interference in each other's internal affairs.

*II. The Economic Aspect*

1. Economic Cooperation and Trade

China is committed to developing dynamic, long-term and stable economic cooperation and trade with the EU and expects the latter to become China's largest trading and investment partner.

To this end, it is important to:

- Give play to the mechanism of the economic and trade joint committee and step up economic and trade regulatory policy dialogue; give attention to updating the Trade and Economic Cooperation Agreement Between China and the European Union at an appropriate time; properly address irrational restrictions and technical barriers, ease restrictions on high-tech exports and tap the enormous potential of technological cooperation and trade in line with the WTO rules; grant China a full market economy status at an early date, reduce and abolish anti-dumping and other discriminatory policies and practices against China, and apply the Transitional Product-Specific Safeguard Mechanism (TPSSM) prudently; and compensate the Chinese side for its economic and trade losses which may arise due to the EU enlargement.
- Boost China-EU coordination and cooperation in the new round of WTO negotiations and work together for the success of the negotiations.
- Strengthen dialogue on investment, promote the establishment of bilateral investment-promotion institutions, energetically encourage and guide mutual investments between enterprises of the two sides, and expand cooperation between their small- and medium-sized enterprises; develop processing trade, contractual projects and labour cooperation of various kinds and encourage transnational business operation and internationalised production.
- China welcomes more EU development aid, especially in such fields as the environmental protection, poverty-alleviation, public health and hygiene and education. China also welcomes a stronger and more active role of the EU in human resources development, in particular, personnel training for China's central and western regions and build-up of China's capacity of participating in multilateral trading regime.
- Step up cooperation in the area of quality supervision, inspection and quarantine, establish appropriate consultation mechanisms and, subject to the principle of ensuring safety, security, hygiene, health and environmental protection, promptly address and resolve issues which may adversely affect market access of each other's products.
- Boost the customs cooperation and conclude a China-EU Customs Agreement in due course.

2. Financial Cooperation

China and the EU should launch a high-level financial dialogue mechanism, expand exchanges between their central banks on policies and deepen cooperation in preventing and managing financial crises and combating the financing of terrorism and money laundering. The Chinese side welcomes an expansion of China-related business by banks of the EU countries and hopes to see an appropriate settlement of the issue of Chinese financial institutions' access to the EU market.

The Chinese side will positively examine and consider applications of EU insurance institutions for business operation in China and improve its supervisory and regulatory regime in line with the Chinese insurance laws, regulations and statutes and China's WTO commitments.

Cooperation in securities legislation, market supervision and regulation, and investment operation will be strengthened and more EU securities institutions, fund management institutions and other institutional investors will be encouraged to enter into China's market. Chinese securities institutions will be encouraged to enter into the EU's securities market when conditions are ripe. In the meantime, Chinese enterprises will be strongly supported to raise funds in the EU's securities market.

3. Agricultural Cooperation

Exchanges between China and the EU in such fields as agricultural production, processing technology of agricultural produce and sustainable development will be intensified. The mechanism of the agricultural working group should be given a role to play. Bilateral cooperation between agricultural research institutes, universities and colleges as well as enterprises should be pushed forward. EU Enterprises are encouraged to take an active part in agricultural development in China's central and western regions and invest in such fields as agricultural high and new technologies, intensive processing of agricultural produce and development of agricultural infrastructure.

4. Environmental Cooperation

China-EU communication and cooperation in environmental protection should be stimulated and a mechanism of dialogue between the Chinese and EU environmental ministers launched. Framework documents on environmental cooperation should be formulated, and discussions held on the establishment of information network on environmental cooperation. Bilateral cooperation should be strengthened on such issues as environmental legislation and management, climate change, bio-diversity protection, bio-safety management, and trade and environment. Efforts should be made to jointly promote the implementation of the follow-up actions of the World Summit on Sustainable Development in Johannesburg. Non-governmental environmental protection organizations are encouraged to develop mutual exchanges. EU enterprises are encouraged to gain more access to Chinese environmental protection market through fair competition.

5. IT Cooperation

The Chinese side would like to see the EU participation in China's IT promotion. The mechanism of the EU-China working group on information society will be strengthened. Exchanges and dialogue will be conducted on strategies, policies, rules and regulations of information society. Trade in IT products and industrial and technological cooperation will be actively boosted. Greater exchanges in intellectual property rights and technical standards will be encouraged. Cooperation in the field of "Digital Olympics" will be promoted.

6. Energy Cooperation

China-EU cooperation will be expanded in such fields as energy structure, clean energy, renewable energy, and energy efficiency and saving. Exchanges on energy development policies will be promoted. Efforts will be made to ensure a successful EU-China Energy Conference. The energy working group mechanism will be strengthened. Training on energy technology and cooperation in demonstration projects will be boosted to promote application and transfer of technology.

7. Transport Cooperation

A mechanism of China-EU regular meeting will be set up within the framework of the China-EU Agreement on Maritime Transport. Cooperation in maritime transport and other maritime fields will be developed and coordination and cooperation in international organizations such as the International Maritime Organization (IMO) will be strengthened. Bilateral exchanges will be deepened and broadened in respect of policies of inland river transport, navigation safety and shipping standardization. Cooperation and exchanges in highway technology and management will be expanded. Dialogue and exchanges on highway transport legislation will be strengthened.

China-EU exchanges in civil aviation will be deepened. Chinese and EU enterprises are encouraged to strengthen their cooperation on production, technology, management and training.

*III. The Education, Science-Technology, Culture, Health and other Aspects*

1. Cooperation in Science and Technology

It is essential to promote China-EU scientific and technological cooperation on the basis of the principles of mutual benefit and reciprocity, sharing of results and protection of intellectual property rights. Joint development and cooperation on generic technologies and major technical equipment should be stepped up and Chinese institutions are encouraged to participate in the EU Framework Program for Research and Technological Development. China will, on the premise of equality and mutual benefit and a balance between interests and obligations, participate in the Galileo Program and enhance cooperation in international "big science" projects. Full play should be given to the role of the Scientific and Technologic Cooperation Steering Committee and efforts should be made to ensure a successful China-Europe Science & Technology and Innovation Policy Forum. Cooperation between scientific and technological intermediary agencies of the two sides as well as the interflow and training of scientific and technological human resources should be encouraged. Support should be given to Chinese and EU enterprises in their involvement in scientific and technological cooperation.

2. Cultural Exchange

China will be more open in cementing and deepening its exchange and cooperation with EU members in the cultural field and work towards a multi-level and all-dimensional framework of cultural exchanges between China and the European Union, EU members and their respective local governments, and between their peoples and business communities so as to make it easier for the people of China and the EU to get to know each other's fine cultures.

China will establish Chinese cultural centers in capitals of EU members and the EU headquarters – Brussels. On the basis of reciprocity and mutual benefit, China welcomes the set-up of cultural centers in Beijing by the EU side. China will encourage high quality cultural exchange activities and explore new modalities of cooperation in culture-related industries. Discussions will be held on the formation of a China-EU cultural cooperation consultation mechanism and the idea of jointly holding a China-EU cultural forum.

3. Cooperation in Education

Exchanges at all levels will be enhanced and expanded. It is necessary to establish a China-EU education cooperation consultation mechanism as appropriate and strengthen cooperation in areas including mutual recognition of academic credentials and degrees, exchange of students, language teaching, exchange of scholarships and teacher training. Work should be done to make a success of the China-Europe International Business School and bring forth more top professionals. The teaching of each other's languages should be encouraged and supported.

4. Cooperation in Health and Medical Care

Cooperation in the health sector should be strengthened, particularly in sharing experience of prevention and control of SARS, HIV/AIDS and other serious diseases. Efforts should be made to develop exchanges in clinical diagnosis and treatment, epidemiological investigation, analysis and surveillance, laboratory testing, R&D for medicines and vaccines, and training of medical personnel. Exploratory endeavor should be made for the establishment of a mechanism to keep each other informed and provide technical support in case of emergent public health hazards.

5. Press Exchange

Exchanges and cooperation will be boosted between the press and media communities of the two sides. Chinese and EU media agencies should be encouraged to enhance mutual understanding and give comprehensive and unbiased reports of each other. Relevant government departments or agencies of the two sides should enhance mutual contact and communication and share practices and experience in respect of government press release and the handling of government-media relations.

6. Personnel Exchange

People-to-people exchanges and those between non-governmental organizations of China and the EU should be encouraged. China is ready to conclude as early as possible agreement on designating EU countries as tourism destinations for outbound Chinese citizens incompliance with the principles of equality, reciprocity and mutual benefit.

China-EU consular cooperation should be strengthened and expanded. An early solution should be found through consultations to the problem of difficult access to entry visas by Chinese citizens and their impeded entry into EU countries. The legitimate rights and interests of travelers should be protected. Normal people-to-people exchanges between China and the EU should be ensured.

It is imperative to combat illegal migration and human trafficking, strictly enforce laws and crack down on illegal activities and crimes. The two sides should increase consultations and coordination and appropriately handle the question of repatriation and other issues arising therefrom.

*IV. The Social, Judicial and Administrative Aspects*

1. Cooperation in Labor and Social Security

China and the EU should strengthen cooperation on employment of legal immigrants and protection of the rights and interests of migrant workers and enhance coordination in international labor affairs. The two sides will negotiate and conclude a bilateral social security agreement and implement their joint social security cooperation program as well as broaden exchanges in social insurance of various kinds.

2. Exchange in Judicial Field

It is necessary to continue with the China-EU cooperation program in the legal and judicial fields based on equality and mutual respect, broaden related areas of cooperation, enhance exchanges in judicial reform and other key areas and explore cooperation with respect to administration of justice in combating cross border crimes. The two sides should do more in sharing experience of legal supervision and explore the possibility of establishing a mechanism of annual meeting between their high-level judicial officials.

3. Cooperation in Police Affairs

The Chinese side will establish and strengthen exchanges with relevant EU agencies and EUROPOL, broaden substantial cooperation with law-enforcement organs of EU members and step up coordination in case handling and information sharing within their respective legal framework. The two sides should support and actively participate in UN peacekeeping and other activities.

4. Cooperation in Public Administration

China and the EU should share experience in transforming government functions and deepening personnel management reform, discuss the establishment of a China-EU cooperation mechanism on personnel and administrative management and conduct exchanges in civil service system building and human resources development.

*V. The Military Aspect*

China and the EU will maintain high-level military-to-military exchanges, develop and improve, step by step, a strategic security consultation mechanism, exchange more missions of military experts, and expand exchanges in respect of military officers' training and defense studies.

The EU should lift its ban on arms sales to China at an early date so as to remove barriers to greater bilateral cooperation on defense industry and technologies.

Within this framework, HE Wen Jiabao, Premier of the State Council, made several important policy speeches during this period. On 6 May 2004, he gave a speech to the China–EU Investment and Trade Symposium in Brussels (see Document 3.9). The title of the speech was 'Vigorously Developing a Comprehensive Strategic Partnership between China and the European Union'. It stated that 'comprehensive' means 'the cooperation should be all-dimensional, wide-ranging and multi-layered'. 'Strategic' means 'the cooperation should be long-term and stable', 'transcend[ing] the differences in ideology and social system and . . . not subjected to the impacts of individual events that occur from time to time'. 'Partnership' means 'the cooperation should be equal-footed, mutually beneficial and win–win'. This was the first time that the basic terms of the new EU–China relationship were expressly defined. He recommended increasing the EU–China trade volume, increasing cooperation in high technology, promoting cooperation among small and medium-sized enterprises (SMEs), removing outdated barriers to trade, for example on high-tech exports, and improving and extending the mechanism of policy dialogues.

## Document 3.9: HE Premier Wen Jiabao, Speech to the China–EU Investment and Trade Symposium, Brussels, 6 May 2004, 'Vigorously Developing a Comprehensive Strategic Partnership between China and the European Union'

**Vigorously Developing a Comprehensive Strategic Partnership between China and the European Union**
Speech at the China-EU Investment and Trade Forum
by H.E. Wen Jiabao
Brussels, 6 May 2004

Your Excellency President Romano Prodi, Ladies and Gentlemen,

I am very pleased to attend this Investment and Trade Forum jointly sponsored by China's Ministry of Commerce and the Directorate General for Trade of the European Commission. Twenty-nine years ago today, China and the European Economic Community established official relations. The gathering here of so many businessmen on this auspicious occasion to discuss the vital matters of development and cooperation, is indeed a vivid illustration of the new dimension of China-EU ties.

During the past 29 years, China-EU relationship has withstood the test of time and evolving international situation, and has embarked on a course of mature, sound, and steady expansion. It is a shared view of the two sides to work for a comprehensive strategic partnership. By "comprehensive", it means that the cooperation should be all-dimensional, wide-ranging and multi-layered. It covers economic, scientific, technological, political and cultural fields, contains both bilateral and multilateral levels, and is conducted by both governments and non-governmental groups. By "strategic", it means that the cooperation should be long-term and stable, bearing on the larger picture of China-EU relations. It transcends the differences in ideology and social system and is not subjected to the impacts of individual events that occur from time to time. By "partnership", it means that the cooperation should be equal-footed, mutually beneficial and win-win. The two sides should base themselves on mutual respect and mutual trust, endeavour to expand converging interests and seek common ground on the major issues while shelving differences on the minor ones.

Committing themselves to developing such a new type of relationship at the beginning of the 21st century not only serves the mutual interests of China and the European Union but also contributes to peace, stability and development in our respective regions and the world at large.

The comprehensive strategic partnership between China and the EU is natural development necessitated by the facts of life and thus enjoys a solid foundation. First, the international situation has undergone stupendous and profound changes. Peace and development being the theme of the times offers a favourable international environment for the substantial expansion of China-EU relations. Second, both China and the EU follow courses of development suited to their characteristics and circumstances. The EU has continuously pushed for integration through union; while China, thanks to reform and opening-up, has moved into a new stage of building a well-off society in an all-round way. The two sides had no conflict of fundamental interest, and rather see their common interests growing steadily. Third, China and the EU are highly complementary economically. As the world's largest developing country, China enjoys a huge market potential and abundant human resources, and is advantageously placed in receiving international transfers of industries and technologies. The EU, on the other hand, is the world's largest developed economy with ample capital, advanced science and technology and a high degree of internationalisation. Such a complementarity prepares a solid groundwork for mutually beneficial cooperation between the two sides. Fourth, both China and the EU boast ancient histories and brilliant civilizations. Recognizing each other's cultural identity and conducting cultural exchanges of various forms provide a significant bridge for closer bond of China-EU relations. Fifth, the two sides have already accumulated sufficient experience in properly handling the disputes and ironing out their differences. Opting for dialogue and resisting confrontation not only reflects the existing maturity of the relationship but ensures its further healthy development in the days ahead.

My Government has all along viewed and cultivated China-EU relations from a strategic plane. Since the 1990's, Chinese leaders, such as Jiang Zemin and Hu Jintao, have visited EU member states on many occasions in an effort to advance the relations between China and the EU. We are pleased to note that since May 1, the EU has 25 members. The EU enlargement will make a key impact on European configuration and even the entire pattern of international relations. China has always supported European integration and looks forward to a more important role of the EU in European and international affairs. It is our hope that an enlarged EU would contribute to greater prosperity and stability in Europe and generate more opportunities for deeper ties between China and the EU.

A stronger China-EU comprehensive strategic partnership requires that we keep an eye on our long-term goals and tackle practical issues by planting our feet solidly on the day-to-day reality. Trade and Economic cooperation is part and parcel of China-EU relationship. To further expand China-EU economic ties, I would like to share my five-point recommendation as follows:

First, to make a bigger "cake". Both sides must work hard to tap their trade potential, expanding the trade scale and increasing the trade volume. At last year's China-EU Summit in Beijing, I proposed that our trade reach US$200 billion by the year 2013. Now this goal looks a bit too conservative, for our trade this year may likely top US$150 billion. It may not be a bad idea to have some leeway nonetheless.

Second, to step up cooperation in hi-tech area. The two sides should, while promoting cooperation in traditional areas of products procurement, technology transfer and investment, make vigorous efforts to push for joint R&D and cooperation in hi-tech area, with a view to developing internationally competitive products and opening up new markets.

Third, to promote cooperation among small and medium-sized businesses. While further enhancing existing cooperation among large enterprises, the two sides should help the small and medium-sized businesses to emerge as a vital player in China-EU economic partnership by putting in place necessary cooperation platform, providing information, financing and other needed services, and giving a full scope to the role of intermediary agencies.

Fourth, to remove out-dated barriers and obstacles. China will continue to faithfully honour its WTO commitments, stepping up protection of intellectual property rights and increasing the fairness and transparency of its trade and economic policies, laws and regulations. The EU is also expected to ease its restrictions on hi-tech exports to China, and lift its import bans that are inconsistent with WTO rules.

Fifth, to build and improve the consultation and dialogue mechanisms. The existing mechanisms, the Joint Committee on Economic and Trade Cooperation included, should be given full scope, with a view to properly addressing the problems, differences and other concerns of the two sides through friendly consultations. Prior to the adoption of major measures that may bear on the interests of the other side, greater attention should be paid to keep the partner informed and consulted so as to avoid complication of the problems. In addressing economic and trade issues at the multilateral level, consultation and coordination should be strengthened.

Ladies and Gentlemen,

It has been 25 years since we in China adopted the policy of reform and opening-up, and 3 years since our accession to WTO. Everyone who has been to China in these years could bear witness to the enormous economic and social transformation taking place there. In China, a socialist market economy has been basically put in place. The non-public sector of the economy, such as self-employed and private businesses, has grown rapidly, taking up a considerable share of the overall national economy. The pricing of more than 90% of the goods produced is done by the marketplace. The relevant policies, measures, laws and regulations are completely consistent with WTO, and nearly 3000 pieces of such documents have been made public after amendment for immediate implementation. With the transformation of government functions and deepening structural reform, the enterprise has become an independently managed economic entity. In addition to enjoying national treatment, China-based foreign-funded firms are entitled to, for example, tax privileges. China follows a market-based, single and regulated floating exchange rate regime, and is committed to improving its exchange rate forming mechanism. With the social security coverage expanding steadily, the rights and interests of working men and women in the areas of old-age pension, work-related injuries, medicare, unemployment benefits and others have been effectively guaranteed. I hope that our friends from the EU will take a full note of these facts, and recognize China's status as a full market economy at an early date. This would undoubtedly boost a fresh round of expansion in China-EU trade and economic cooperation.

At present, China's economy has entered the upward leg of another growth cycle. Economic restructuring is accelerating. The country's consumption pattern, driven by robust housing and car sales, has come into a new stage, allowing the overall national economy to grow at a fast and sustained speed. In 2003, with a GDP that grew by 9.1%, China became the world's 4th largest trader and 3rd largest importer. In the first quarter this year, our economy reported a 9.7% growth rate. It is estimated that by 2020 China's GDP would top US$4 trillion, with an annual import amounting to US$1 trillion. All in all, the rapid development of China's east coast, the advancement of China's west development strategy, the rejuvenation of Northeast China and other old industrial bases, and the 2008 Beijing Olympics and Shanghai World Expo 2010 would generate immense business opportunities for the business communities of the European Union.

China and Europe need each other in their respective pursuits of development. Right now, China-EU relationship finds itself at a fresh starting line, with a great deal to build upon and even more to look forward to. China and the European Union are made good and promising partners in trade and economic cooperation. As an old Chinese saying goes, "A truly wise man is apt at seizing opportunities rather than simply working out plans." I suppose none of us here would let go good opportunities, and I am sure you will strive for greater trade and economic cooperation between China and the EU and make a contribution to stronger China-EU comprehensive strategic partnership.

Thank you all.

On 8 October 2004, the Chinese Premier gave a speech in Hanoi to the Fifth Asia–Europe Meeting (ASEM), an increasingly important forum for EU–China relations (see Document 3.10). He pointed out that China and the EU shared many political interests and complemented each other economically. Emphasising the principles of mutual respect, equality, mutual benefit and non-interference in the each other's internal affairs, he made four propositions: to strengthen mutual trust through dialogue and consultation; to increase economic exchanges and promote regional economic growth and common prosperity; to develop new forms of cooperation and promote coordinated development throughout Asia; and to encourage both dialogue and the protection of cultural diversity in various countries. He also emphasised the importance of cooperation in the field of energy and the fundamental significance to China of the one-China policy concerning Taiwan.

## Document 3.10: HE Premier Wen Jiabao, Speech to the Fifth Asia–Europe Meeting, Hanoi, 8 October 2004, 'Strengthening Partnership Through Increased Dialogue and Cooperation'

**Strengthening Partnership Through Increased Dialogue and Cooperation**
Speech at the Fifth Asia-Europe Meeting, 2004/10/09
By H.E. WEN Jiabao
Premier of the State Council of the People's Republic of China
Hanoi, 8 October 2004

Mr. Chairman,

I wish to begin by thanking our host, the Vietnamese Government, for its thoughtful preparations and generous hospitality. I would also like to extend a warm welcome and sincere congratulations to the 13 new members on their formal accession to ASEM. I believe that with the concerted efforts of the 39 parties from Asia and Europe, this Summit will build on the achievements of the previous meetings and further the friendly and mutually beneficial Asia-Europe cooperation in the new circumstances.

Ever since its first Summit in 1996, ASEM has vigorously conducted political dialogue, economic cooperation and cultural exchanges, which have not only spurred the development of a new and comprehensive Asia-Europe partnership, but also promoted regional peace and development. As things stand now, both Asia and Europe are in a phase of robust growth. On the one hand, enjoying the world's most dynamic economic growth, Asia boasts rich resources, broad markets, and regional cooperation on the upswing. On the other, being the world's largest developed economy, the highly integrated EU abounds in capital and possesses sophisticated science and technology. The two regions, which are both renowned for their unique cultures, share political common ground in a wide range of areas and benefit from their economic complementarities. This has laid a solid foundation for more extensive and substantive dialogue and cooperation. The member states of an enlarged ASEM have a population of 2.4 billion, accounting for 40% of the world's total and produce over half of the world's GDP. Such an ASEM will play a more important role in international affairs.

The international situation is undergoing complex and profound changes in the new century. Peace and development remain the themes of our times. The trends of world multi-polarization and economic globalization are unfolding amidst twists and turns. Science and technology are advancing by leaps and bounds. The movement of industries and capital is picking up speed. Regional integration and cooperation are going in depth. The global economy has seen a good growth momentum. However, the world is far from tranquil and development uneven between regions. Destabilizing factors and uncertainties are on the increase in international relations. Regional conflicts sparked by ethnic and religious contradictions and boundary and territorial disputes crop up from time to time. Non-traditional security factors like terrorism, cross-border crimes, spread of infectious diseases and pollution of the environment have posed an ever-growing threat. In face of new opportunities and challenges, we should adhere to the principles of mutual respect, equality, mutual benefit and non-interference in each other's internal affairs, step up dialogue and cooperation in an all-round manner, gradually advance the ASEM process on the basis of consensus, substantiate and invigorate a new and comprehensive Asia-Europe partnership, and remain committed to the principle of openness at the same time, thus jointly contributing to world peace, development and progress. To this end, I wish to make the following propositions.

**1. Strengthening political mutual trust through dialogue and consultation.** Against the backdrop of a complex international situation, it serves the common interests of Asia and Europe to foster a favourable regional as well as international security environment. Both sides maintain that regional and global issues should be addressed through multilateral cooperation and international relations be democratized. We need to establish and improve dialogue and consultation mechanisms at various levels, strive to enhance mutual understanding and trust, increase sharing of experience and policy dialogues on regional cooperation, and have closer coordination in various multilateral forums including the United Nations in a joint endeavour to put in place a fair and rational new international political and economic order. We need to uphold the purposes and principles of the UN Charter, support necessary and reasonable reforms of the UN, help it strengthen its authority in handling international affairs and enhance its capacity to respond to threats and challenges. We need to carry out cooperation within the framework of ASEM, fend off and fight terrorism in all its manifestations and effectively counter such non-traditional security threats as weapons proliferation, illegal migration, cross-border crimes and HIV/AIDS.

**2. Increasing economic exchanges and promoting regional economic growth and common prosperity.** China is supportive of the Summit's focus on economic and trade cooperation and adopting Declaration on Closer ASEM Economic Partnership. We need to make the best use of ASEM's existing dialogue mechanisms, commit ourselves to open regionalism and increase the sharing of experience on regional economic integration. In the new round of multilateral trade negotiations, we need to have close consultation and coordination and push for an early and smooth completion of the Doha Agenda with a balance of interests of various parties. We need to deepen our cooperation within the framework of the ASEM Trade Facilitation Action Plan and ASEM Investment Promotion Action Plan, and remain committed to removing trade barriers and improving the investment climate. We need to give full play to the role of the Asia-Europe Business Forum, strengthen government-business interaction and communication and vigorously develop economic ties and trade. We need to promote cooperation between small and medium sized enterprises, explore new business opportunities and facilitate two-way trade and investment. China will host the ASEM Trade and Investment Exposition next year and welcomes the active participation of Asian and European business people.

**3. Opening new horizons for cooperation and promoting coordinated economic and social development in various countries.** Given Asian and European countries' uneven development levels, ASEM needs to actively carry out technical assistance and capacity building projects to narrow the development gap between ASEM members. In such areas as poverty reduction, social development, restructuring and public health, we need to give more support to the developing members in this region, particularly the poor, to help meet the UN's Millennium Development Goals. At the same time, we need to give more substance to our financial cooperation and support the development of the Asian Bond Market. We need to vigorously conduct policy dialogue and information-sharing on sustainable development and press ahead with our scientific and technological cooperation on forest protection and water management. We need to deepen our mutually beneficial cooperation on higher education and human resources development. In this way, a multi-tiered, multi-formed and wide-ranging Asia-Europe cooperation framework will gradually take shape.

**4. Actively conducting dialogues among civilizations and exchanges among cultures and respecting and preserving cultural diversity.** The continent of Asia and Europe, which is the home to us all, is the biggest continent on the earth. In the legend of ancient Greek, this area is deemed as the broad chest of the earth. The oriental civilizations in Asia and the occidental civilizations in Europe have added to each other's splendor in mankind's history. Either through the ancient "Silk Road" or today's information superhighway, the two sides' exchanges and mutual learning have never been interrupted, which has promoted progress and development in Asian and European countries. Against the backdrop of current international situation, it is significant to respect cultural diversity and encourage different civilizations to have dialogues on an equal footing and co-exit with tolerance. In this context, China, together with France, jointly sponsored the ASEM Declaration on Dialogue among Cultures and Civilizations for adoption at this Summit. We hope that countries in Asia and Europe will step up their coordination and cooperation in UNESCO and the UN as a whole, vigorously advance dialogue among civilizations in the international community, and improve international legislation in order to effectively preserve cultural diversity. Asian and European nations should actively go for cultural exchanges, forge close links between peoples on the two continents, and enhance the mutual understanding and friendship between youths in particular. China will host the Asia-Europe Young Political Leaders Forum next year to this end.

Mr. Chairman,

Twenty-six years of reform and opening-up have brought about sustained and rapid growth of our national economy and foreign trade. The system of socialist market economy has been improved gradually, which is open to the rest of the world in all directions, and a wide range of areas, and at multiple levels. Not long ago, ASEAN countries officially recognized China's full market economy status, signifying their acknowledgement of China's achievements in this regard. Committed to peaceful development, China will continue to press ahead with its reform and opening up and conscientiously honor its commitments upon its accession to the WTO. China's trade volume with ASEM members accounts for 47% of its total. The economic cooperation and trade between China and ASEAN has continued to develop rapidly. The enlarged EU has become the biggest trading partner of China. China's growth will provide enormous business opportunities for all countries and regions of the world, those in Asia and Europe included. China stands ready to further step up mutually beneficial cooperation with Asian and European countries and contribute to the stability and development in Asia and Europe and in the world at large.

Currently, energy price has become a source of worldwide concern and has impacted world economy. As a big producer and consumer of energy, China has long worked hard to improve energy efficiency, promote the diversification of energy sources and the cleanness in the use of energy. While equally stressing the importance of the production and consumption of energy and environmental protection, China has given priority to the saving of energy and gradually set up and improved petroleum reserve system with an aim to guarantee energy security. During the past 25 years, China has maintained a 9.4% economic growth rate with only 4.2% increase in energy consumption annually. However, the supply of energy in China is still faced with the problem of regional and seasonal shortage and there is still room for improvement for the energy-efficient technology. Therefore, China is willing to participate in the international energy cooperation in the protection, conservation of energy as well as the development of new energy.

The single biggest danger across Taiwan Straits is so-called "Taiwan Independence". The Chinese Government will seek peaceful reunification with utmost sincerity and effort but we will never allow the separation of Taiwan from the motherland. The question of Taiwan bears on the core interest of China as well as the feeling of 1.3 billion Chinese people. We appreciate the one-China policy of ASEM member countries that are all against Taiwan Independence, which is not only valuable support for China but also favorable for the stability across the Straits.

Thank you, Mr. Chairman.

On 9 December 2004, Premier Wen Jiabao gave a speech to the China–EU Business Summit in The Hague (see Document 3.11). It was entitled 'Strengthening All-round Cooperation and Deepening the Comprehensive Partnership between China and the European Union' or, in an alternative translation, 'Deepening the Sino-EU Relations and Strengthening the Comprehensive Cooperation'. Pointing out that EU–China relations had never before been so dynamic, he stated that the two sides were ready for further development since they had many common interests and no fundamental conflicts. The objective was to promote a broad strategic partnership, based on careful nurturing and on the principle of 'seek[ing] common ground on major issues while shelving differences on minor ones'. Both parties should seek all opportunities to increase bilateral cooperation. In his view, this would require the EU soon to recognise China's market economy status in antidumping cases and to liberalise exports of high-tech products. Describing China–EU relations as a comprehensive strategic partnership, he stressed that China was concerned with its own domestic challenges and did not pose a threat to other countries.

**Document 3.11: HE Premier Wen Jiabao, Speech to the China–EU Business Summit, The Hague, 9 December 2004, 'Strengthening All-round Cooperation and Deepening the Comprehensive Strategic Partnership between China and the European Union'**

Strengthening all-round cooperation and deepening the comprehensive strategic partnership between China and the European Union
Speech at the China-ELI industrial and commercial summit
by Chinese Premier Wen Jiabao
The Hague, Dec. 9.2004

Honorable Prime Minister Balkenende, Commissioner Mandelson, Ladies and Gentlemen,

I delivered a speech at the EU-China Trade and Investment Forum this May. during my visit to the headquarters of the European Union (EU). Today, I am glad to attend the China-EU industrial and commercial summit, to meet so many new and old friends. We gathered here with the aim to strengthen the friendship and cooperation between China and the EU. Hereby, I would like to discuss some key issues on developing the China-EU relationships together with you all.

Firstly, the China-EU relations have never been as dynamic and fruitful as they are today. The trade and exchange between the EU and China have a more than 2000 years' history, and of cause we passed through some tough periods. The establishment of new Chinese government in 1949 set up the foundation of developing equal and mutual beneficial relations between China and European countries. Upon the conclusion of the diplomatic relation between China and the EU as the milestone in 1975, the Sino-EU relation started a new page. The Chinese open-up policy provides additional impulse to the promotion of the relations. Today, the enlarged EU has become China's largest trading partner while China is the second largest trading partner to the EU. Some famous enterprises and brands are widely known all over the China. And China becomes the first non-EU country enjoying the full participation in the Galilei Project. The signature of China-EU Tourist Approved Destination Status (ADS) Agreement largely facilitates the people-to-people exchanges. All this shows that China-EU cooperation is wider in scope and better in content and the relationship has come into a new phase of maturity and sound and steady development

Secondly, China-EU relations are solidly based for further development as the two sides share interests in wide areas and there are no conflicts of fundamental interest between us. The two sides see eye to eye on a large number of major international issues and are highly complementary economically. The European Union could bring us ample capital, advanced science and technology and management experience, which are in need for China's modernization, while China enjoys a huge market potential and abundant human resources, which provide you with enormous business opportunities. Both China and the European Union boast ancient histories and brilliant civilizations and constitute an essential part of the world's culture diversification. Such a China-EU cooperation, based on shared interest, is most solid and enduring.

Thirdly, the objective of China-EU cooperation is to promote the comprehensive strategic partnership. The new type of relations between us will deliver greater benefits to both sides, but they also need our common nurturing. This requires that both sides constantly promote an all-round, wide-ranging and multi-level cooperation, making it long-term and stable. China and the EU shall stay in perpetual amity and common development with political trust, economic complementarity, cultural interactions and people-to-people exchanges.

Fourthly, we should follow some principles in developing China-EU relations. The first one is mutual respect and mutual trust. That means we should respect each party's course of development, transcends the differences in ideology and social system, enhance dialogue and exchange, and promote understanding and trust. The second one is equality and mutual benefit. At the same time of ensuring self interest. one shall also care about the other's favor on the basis of equal participation and fair competition. The third principle is to seek common ground on major issues while shelving differences on minor ones. We should face up to and deal with divergences faithfully, pay attention to the cooperation basis beyond the dissimilarities, and not be subjected to the impacts of individual events that occur from time to time. The last one refers to the win-win cooperation. We shall make good use of each one's advantage and benefit from the complementarity for the purpose of common prosperity.

Fifth, China and the EU will grasp opportunities to push forward bilateral ties in all fields. We should reinforce, through political and strategic security dialogue, the coordination and cooperation on international and regional issues of mutual interest; expand bilateral trade and investment scale, deepen communication and collaboration on multilateral trade sector; promote cooperation in technology sector and culture exchanges; and facilitate people-to-people friendly exchanges. 1 would like to point out here that the China-EU comprehensive strategic partnership will logically require that China's full market economy status be recognized at an early date and restrictions on exports of high-tech products to China be liberalized. It can only serve China-EU trade and economic exchanges and bring benefit to co-operation between our businesses communities.

Sixth, closer China-EU relations are conducive to the world. China and the EU are important forces for world peace and stability and both arc committed to multilateralism and actively promoting democracy and the rule of law in international relations. China, as the largest developing country in the world, and the EU, the largest group of developed countries in the world, should work to promote trade and economic cooperation on the basis of equality to the mutual benefit of both. That will significantly magnify development of economic globalization. China and the EU, the two important sponsors of cultural dialogue, both agree to protect the cultural diversity. The China-EU comprehensive strategic partnership is an open and constructive one. It is not an alliance, nor is it directed against any third party. Such a relationship not only serves the interest of each, but also contributes to peace, stability and global development.

Seventh, China-GU relations have a brilliant prospect. Next year, we will celebrate the 30th Anniversary of the China-EU Diplomatic Relations. During the 30 years, the cooperation between the two sides has been fruitful. Facing up to the future, China and EU are both on the key development period. China has set up the great objective of building a well-off society in an all-round way. The EU also endeavours to become the most active and competitive economic entity. This will provide the both sides with more development and cooperation opportunities. To promote the China-EU relations is well in line with the trends of economic globalization and global multilateralism. We believe that, by consolidating and promoting the comprehensive strategic partnership, the China-EU relations will round up to a new level.

Ladies and Gentlemen,

Mutual understanding is the basis of cooperation. By knowing better each other. China and EU could change those outdated ideologies and give away the misunderstandings. Chinese needs to know the Europe better and vice versa. Hereby, I would like to introduce you the present development in China.

Enormous economic and social transformation have been taking place since China adopted the policy of reform and opening-up 26 years ago. China has maintained a rapid and stable growth and the social atmosphere totally changed. Everybody who has been to China in these years could bear witness to the development and change. This year, Chinese economy keeps a rapid and stable development. The unstable elements emerged during the economic operations were effectively controlled and compromised due to the timely and prompt macro-regulation. We are fully confident in maintaining sustained growth next year and in the longer term beyond.

Most Europeans paid attention to Chinese economic developments, but they do not understand our progress in other fields, such as politic and social fields. China has almost set up the socialist market economy system. Our reform of political system is actively and gradually promoted. As a developing country, we carry out the people-oriented approach. We put on the priority of the right of survival and development and try the best to achieve social justice. Chinese government has helped more than 200 million peasants getting out of poverty, and provided over 20 million urban low-incomers with the lowest life guarantee, which makes an outstanding contribution to the global anti-poverty campaign. Democracy and fundamental rights has its historical development process in any country, it is not exceptional for the EU and China. We have already integrated the respect and protection of fundamental rights into the Constitution. The promotion of democracy and fundamental rights are ongoing together with the economic and social development.

There is no need to fear that the development of the "Chinese giant", since it will pose no threat to other countries. That fear is unfounded.

China is a big exporting country, as well as a big importing country. It is a country with 1.3 billion people and a huge internal market in a rapid developing process. It will not and is not able to rely only on its external market. This year, the total amount of imports and exports will reach 1100 billion US dollars, which includes 500 billion US dollars for imports. Among the exports, the products from the Wholly Foreign Owned Enterprises (WFOEs) and Sino-Foreign Joint Ventures occupy a large proportion. From January to October of this year, Chinese imports from the EU reaches 57.7 US dollars, an increase of 30% compared with the same period of last year. China will continue to honor its WTO commitments by further liberalizing trade in services, vigorously strengthening the protection of intellectual property rights and creating a fair, stable and transparent legal environment. China's development has already brought and will continue to bring tangible benefits to the rest of the world.

Like many other countries, China is also facing some resources and environment problems. But unlike some major resource-consuming countries, China is both a major consumer and a major producer of resources. To address these problems, China has developed a policy of relying mainly on domestic resources, working for both resource development and conservation. China is following a new road of industrialization and building a resource-conserving society through scientific and technological progress while vigorously promoting international cooperation in the energy, resources and environment sectors. We are sure to work out a course of durable development.

China is therefore sincere in pursuing peaceful development. It seeks to accelerate its self-development by pursuing and taking the advantage of the peaceful international environment. Meanwhile, its development would contribute to the world's peace and prosperity. In the contemporary history, Chinese people deeply suffered from aggression and oppression. So we know very well how precious the peace is. China does not pursue its development at the expense of other's interests. Instead, we rely primarily on our own efforts, taking advantage of our vast domestic market, abundant labour, huge pool of private savings and the enthusiasm of the people unleashed by reform. The sheer size of the challenges confronting China, a developing country with a population of one-plus billion people, trying to modernize and achieve prosperity, is not too difficult to imagine. It will take the hard work of generation after generation of the Chinese to make it a reality. It is no easy job for us to run our own affairs well. Given this, we will not pose any possible threat to anyone.

Ladies and Gentlemen,

The industry and commerce field was the first missionary of China-EU exchange. The Silk Road witnessed this great history. Till now, the industry and commerce is still the important driving force of promoting China-EU relations. On the right time in strengthening China-EU business exchange and cooperation, I hope that all the EU business leaders here present take a long-term view, seize the opportunities and make fresh contribution to push forward China-EU relations while seeking your own business success. The advancement of China's westward development strategy, the rejuvenation of Northeast China and other old industrial bases, and the 2008 Beijing Olympics and Shanghai World Expo 2010 would generate immense opportunities for the business communities of the European Union. I sincerely welcome European entrepreneurs to invest in China, and do your best, with a great deal to build on and even more to look forward to.

Thank you!

Chinese Premier Wen Jiabao gave a policy speech on 26 June 2005 on 'Strengthening ASEM Economic and Financial Cooperation to Promote Common Development' at the opening ceremony of the Sixth ASEM Finance Ministers Meeting in Tianjin (see Document 3.14). He recommended strengthening the dialogue and coordination on macroeconomic policies, increasing exchange on development experiences, deepening fiscal and financial cooperation, strengthening technical assistance and capacity building, and fostering win–win international cooperation. He also emphasised the Chinese policy of independently determined, gradual and controllable changes in the exchange rate for the Chinese currency RMB yuan.

## Document 3.12: HE Premier Wen Jiabao, Speech at the Opening Ceremony of the Sixth ASEM Finance Ministers Meeting, Tianjin, 26 June 2005, 'Strengthening ASEM Economic and Financial Cooperation to Promote Common Development'

**Strengthening ASEM Economic and Financial Cooperation**
**to Promote Common Development**

Speech at the Opening Ceremony of the Sixth ASEM Finance Ministers, Meeting
by Premier Wen Jiabao of China
26 June 2005

Distinguished Guests, Ladies and Gentlemen,

I would like to begin by expressing, on behalf of the Chinese Government, our warm congratulations on the opening of the Sixth ASEM Finance Ministers' Meeting (FMM) in Tianjin and our most sincere welcome to all the participants. This first finance ministers' meeting of an enlarged ASEM will be a good opportunity for you to explore strategies for ASEM economic and financial cooperation under the new situation and to discuss the major issues in the world economy. The meeting is anticipated to be fruitful and to produce two documents: a Chairman's Statement of the Sixth ASEM FMM and a Tianjin Initiative on Closer ASEM Economic and Financial Cooperation with a significant influence on advancing closer ASEM economic partnership.

The founding of ASEM is a strategic choice of Asia and Europe to step up exchanges and cooperation under the new international situation. Since the first ASEM meeting in 1996, Asia and Europe have been keen to conduct political dialogue, economic cooperation and scientific, technological and cultural exchanges, which has helped the growth of the new ASEM comprehensive partnership and contributed significantly to world peace and common development. Asia is by far the most dynamic economy in the world while the EU the world's largest developed economy. Their cooperation to mutual benefit has truly broad prospects. The enlarged ASEM, whose member countries have two fifths of the world's population and over half of the world's total GDP, will play an even greater role in world affairs. Since Asia and Europe both face important opportunities and new challenges under the new world situation, we need to strengthen cooperation in all areas to bring into play our respective advantages in a joint effort to surmount difficulties and risks and lift ASEM cooperation to a new high.

Ladies and Gentlemen,

Economic cooperation is the basis of the new ASEM comprehensive partnership. Fiscal and financial cooperation, as an important part of this cooperation, plays a crucial role. Asia and Europe must deepen their financial cooperation in this sector if they are to foster closer economic partnership, achieve win-win results and promote common development. To that end, I would like to make the following five recommendations:

First, strengthen dialogue and coordination on macro-economic policies. It is of great importance for Asian and European countries to regularly exchange economic and policy information through increased dialogue, communication and equal-footed consultation to jointly deal with risks and challenges facing the world economy. To promote sustainable and steady development of the world economy, we need to pool our efforts and adopt responsible macro-economic policies to maintain the stability of the major reserve currencies, curb big fluctuations in oil prices and prevent the rise of trade protectionism in all forms. The Chinese Government proposes to establish an ASEM Contingency Dialogue Mechanism for Emergent Economic and Financial Events within the framework of the ASEM FMM for the purpose of safeguarding economic and financial security.

Second, increase exchanges on development experience. We should have in-depth discussion on development paths and strategies and increase exchanges to share experience in regional integration and success stories in macro-economic regulations and restructuring under open conditions. Later this year, China and the United Kingdom will co-sponsor a "Fiscal Policy and Public Debts Forum" within the framework of the ASEM FMM. All the finance ministers of Asian and European countries and members of their financial communities are most welcome to take part in this Forum.

Third, deepen substantive cooperation in fiscal and financial sector. We should actively explore and advance fiscal and financial cooperation between Asia and Europe to develop the Asian regional bond market and support the role of the euro in maintaining international financial stability and promoting development so as to enhance the international standing of our two continents in the monetary and financial field. We should also give full scope to the positive role of the ASEM Trust Fund in assisting the underdeveloped members of ASEM in their financial reforms.

Fourth, strengthen technical assistance and financial capacity building. Given the uneven development between Asian and European countries, we should render greater support to the poor countries in the region through vigorous technical assistance so as to promote the realization of UN Millennium Development Goals. China, the European Commission and Austria will jointly launch an ASEM financial capacity-building project and entrust the Shanghai National Accounting Institute with its implementation.

Fifth, foster an environment for win-win international economic cooperation. We should, through our coordination and cooperation, promote the international community to pay more attention to the interests of the vast number of developing countries by way of substantially writing off their debts, increasing development aid and speeding up technology transfer. We should also facilitate the reform of the international financial and trade systems, promote an early conclusion of the WTO Doha round negotiations and call for innovative thinking in international development so as to establish a sound new international economic order.

Ladies and Gentlemen,

China has achieved sustained and rapid economic growth, markedly enhanced overall national strength and constantly improved people's life since its adoption of the reform and opening-up policy. During the past two years, we took some effective macro-economic measures to address the prominent problems in the economy and the Chinese economy has been in good shape. We will continue to take measures to further tackle the existing problems, with a view to achieving long-term, steady and fast growth of the Chinese economy. China's development largely depends on our own efforts, our own vast domestic market, abandonment labor resources and the implementation of the reform and opening-up policy. We are fully confident, capable and resourceful. We can overcome any difficulty and risk on the road ahead and reach our determined magnificent goal of social-economic development. China's development is conducive to the stability and prosperity of our region and peace and development of the whole world, and will not threaten or exert an adverse impact on any country.

Now, I would like to spend several minutes on the issue of RMB exchange rate which has been a focus of attention both at home and abroad. I have three points to make. First, it is the common understanding in the world that every country is entitled to choose the exchange rate mechanism and policy suitable to its own national conditions. Back in the early 1990s, China set its targets and tasks for the reform of RMB exchange rate mechanism. That is, to gradually establish a market-based and well-managed floating exchange rate system so as to keep RMB exchange rate basically stable at a reasonable and balanced level. Over the past decade and more, we have done a lot on the reform of RMB exchange rate mechanism and made important progress.

Second, keeping RMB exchange rate basically stable at a reasonable and balanced level is in the interests of economic development not only in China but also in neighboring countries and region as a whole, and contributes to the world financial stability and expansion of trade. This point was well illustrated during the Asian financial crisis in 1997, when the stable RMB helped alleviate the pain on our neighboring countries and regions and contribute to economic and financial stability and development in Asia and the whole world.

Third, we must uphold the principles of independent initiative, controllability and gradual progress in pursuing RMB exchange rate reform. By "independent initiative", we mean to independently determine the modality, content and timing of the reform in accordance with China's needs for reform and development. In the exchange rate reform, we should take account of its possible impact on the country's macro-economic stability, economic growth and job market, give consideration to the state of the financial system, the level of financial regulations, resilience of the enterprises and effect on foreign trade and keep an eye on the economic and financial performance of the neighboring countries and regions, and of the world as a whole. By "controllability", we mean to properly manage the changes in RMB exchange rate at the level of macro-regulations. We must push forward the reform but always stay on top of the changes, so as to prevent fluctuations in the financial market and economic instability. By "gradual progress", we mean to push forward the reform in a step-by-step manner. We must take into consideration both the present needs and the future development and guard against undue haste. In short, we need to continue improving the RMB exchange rate forming mechanism and develop an exchange rate system that is more market-oriented and more flexible. However, since this reform involves a wide range of areas and will have a far-reaching impact, it still requires a great deal of preparation to help create an enabling environment for all sides to sustain the possible impacts. Such a responsible attitude and practice of China will contribute to the stability and development of not only Chinese macro-economy but also the economy of the surrounding countries and the larger world.

Ladies and Gentlemen,

There is an old saying in China: "Distance cannot separate true friends who feel so close even when are thousands of miles apart." China and the other Asian countries are linked by common mountains and rivers and together they created the splendid Asian civilizations. The ancient and beautiful Silk Road is a witness to the Sino-European exchanges over thousands of years. Now, the mutually beneficial cooperation between China and other countries in Asia and Europe is entering a brand new stage. China has become a positive force for the economic development of Asia, Europe and the world as a whole. We will adhere to the road of peaceful development and remain committed to developing vigorous all-round cooperation featuring long-term stability with other countries in Asia and Europe. It is our hope that China and other countries in Asia and Europe will support each other and join hands to move forward.

May I conclude by wishing this ASEM FMM a complete success.

Thank you.

From the EU perspective, many of the details of the EU–China strategic partnership were set out in the European Commission in its National Indicative Programme (NIP) for China, 2005–2006 (see Document 3.13).[5] Despite its often highly technical nature, it is included here because it provides an extremely useful review of the recent CSP 2002–2006 and its relationship to the NIPs of 2002–2004 and 2005–2006, identifies clearly some important aspects of the progress and shortcomings of the CSP, shows how decisions are made between the EC and its Member States and between the EC and China, and indicates to some extent how general objectives set out in EU policy papers are implemented in practice. It thus forms a useful bridge between general policy documents and specific initiatives and actions, such as policy dialogues or cooperation programmes. The 2005–2006 NIP identified education, intellectual property protection, and good governance and rule of law as the main priorities for 2005, with an indicative budget of 250 million euros.

[5] The legal basis of the NIP for China was Council Regulation (EEC) NO 443/92 of 25 February 1992 on financial and technical assistance to, and economic cooperation with, the developing countries in Asia and Latin America (the ALA Regulation), [1992] OJ L52/1. For an evaluation of the ALA, see Consortium Eva-EU, 'Evaluation of the Council Regulation N 443/92 on Co-operation between the EC and ALA Countries: Final Report' (May 2002), available at http://ec.europa.eu/europaid/evaluation/reports/ala/951614.pdf (accessed 8 October 2007).

## Document 3.13: National Indicative Programme 2005–2006: China

EUROPEAN COMMISSION
NATIONAL INDICATIVE PROGRAMME, 2005–2006, CHINA

| | | |
|---|---|---|
| Country/Region | : | China |
| Budget years | : | 2005–2006 |
| Budget lines | : | 1910 |
| Legal base | : | ALA Regulation |
| | | Council Regulation (EEC) 443/92 of 25/02/92 |
| Cost of Order | : | €100 million |
| Programming Service | : | DG RELEX/H/2 |
| Head of Unit | : | James Moran |
| Co-ordinator | : | Richard Wilkinson |

### *1.1 INTRODUCTION*

#### 1.1.1 The legal framework

The present proposals have been formulated in accordance with the provisions of Council Regulation (EEC) 443/92 of 25th February 1992 on financial and technical assistance to, and economic co-operation with, the developing countries in Asia and Latin America (the ALA Regulation). The regulation is applicable to China.

Article 9 of the Regulation specifies that "Wherever possible, indicative five-year programming shall be established for each objective, country, or, if appropriate, region". Articles 14 and 15 of the Regulation furthermore specify that, before adoption, "…the indicative multiannual guidelines that apply to the main partner countries" shall be submitted by the Commission to a committee of Member State representatives (the ALA Committee) for its opinion.

The China Country Strategy Paper 2002–2006 constitutes the multiannual planning and strategy document, the objectives of which are reflected in the projects and programmes contained in the 2002–2004 and 2005–2006 National Indicative Programmes.

#### 1.1.2 The China 2002–2006 Country Strategy Paper (CSP)

The China 2002–2006 CSP was approved by the Commission on 25th February 2002. The cooperation strategy outlined in the CSP was largely built on the Commission's Communications of 1998 and 2001[1], and aims to support the implementation of the EU's wide policy objectives towards China. These include providing support for the continued reform and transition process; further integrating China into the world economy and the world trading system; supporting China's transition to an open society based upon the rule of law and respect for human rights; making better use of European resources notably through improved coordination with bilateral assistance from Member States; and raising the EU's profile in China.

These policy objectives were reiterated in the Commission's 2003 Policy Paper on China[2] which was issued one month before China's first ever policy paper on its relations with the EU. A seminar held in Beijing in February 2004 to jointly review both papers was successful in identifying areas for strengthened EU-China co-operation through dialogues and through the co-operation programme.

As a result of the CSP and the Policy Paper, the overall objectives of the co-operation programme are very much in line with the policy orientations that guide the development of the EU-China strategic partnership. As such, co-operation, where necessary, features in political dialogue with China, and often underpins activities in policy areas of mutual interest.

The China 2002–2006 CSP provides the policy objectives for EC assistance programmes to China for this period, with indicative funding of €250 million. On the basis of the analysis contained in the CSP the decision was taken that the EC co-operation programme should

focus on the three following areas: support for the social and economic reform process; the prevention of environmental degradation and the conservation of the natural environment; and support China's transition to an open society based on the rule of law and respect of human rights.

A summary of the objectives of the CSP is provided in Annex 3.1.

1.1.3 The China 2002–2004 National Indicative Programme (NIP)

The indicative financing for the 2002–2004 NIP amounts to €150 million. In line with the policy objectives defined in the 2002–2006 CSP, the China 2002–2004 NIP outlined the interventions foreseen for financing during the three-year period in question. These interventions are grouped in accordance with the three priority areas identified in the CSP and are as follows:

Priority Area 1: Support for the Social and Economic Reform Process

EU-China Programme to Support China's Integration into the World Trading System. This programme constitutes a follow-up to a previous EC-financed programme to assist China with the preparations for and process of accession to the World Trading Organisation (WTO). The overall objective of the programme is to support the further integration of China into the world economy, to assist the Chinese government with the implementation of its WTO obligations, and to increase China's capacity in the process of wider economic, regulatory, legal and administrative reform necessary for further trade liberalisation. The initial budgetary allocation of €15 million foreseen for the programme was committed in 2002, as foreseen, and the programme's implementation is now under way.

EU-China Information Society Project. This project, originally proposed for financing in 2002, is under preparation for financing in 2004 with the overall objective of promoting economic and social reform through the appropriate application of information and communications technology (ICT) to improve the effectiveness, efficiency, and accessibility of e-government services to citizens and businesses. The budget foreseen for the project is €15 million.

Social Security Reform Programme. This programme, also originally foreseen for financing in 2002, has been rolled forward for a proposed financing decision in 2004. With a financial allocation of €20 million under the NIP, the programme is presently being finalised, with the objective of developing co-operation in the domains of pensions, health and unemployment insurance through support for central policy development and the modernisation of delivery systems. European expertise will be tapped to provide effective support for institutional capacity building.

In the area of Human Resources Development, two interventions are under preparation for financing in 2004:

EU-China Managers Exchange and Training Programme. This programme draws on the experience gained in the previously-financed 'Junior Managers Exchange Programme'. With proposed financing of €17.2 million, the purpose of the programme is to meet the demand for EU-China co-operation in the profit and non-profit sectors in the areas of management and cultural exchange. The exchanges proposed will provide training in Europe for Chinese managers, capacity building for Chinese institutions, and training for EU managers to perform in the Chinese business environment. The programme is scheduled for financial commitment in 2004.

The 'Erasmus Mundus' China Window. The funding foreseen for this operation amounts to €9 million for commitment in 2004. The project aims to facilitate linkages between the EU and China in higher education, to enable Chinese students to complete postgraduate Masters Courses in Europe, to provide opportunities for Chinese scholars to undertake research and training assignments in Europe, and for universities to develop partnerships. The Project will be implemented directly through DG Education and Culture's (EAC) global Erasmus Mundus Programme.

Priority Area 2: Environment and Sustainable Development

A summary of China's environmental priorities is given in Annex 3.2.

Three interventions were originally foreseen in the NIP in this sector: environment policy support, biodiversity protection, and water resources conservation. The NIP nevertheless foresaw the possibility of consolidating programmes, as is in fact being done through the merging of the policy advice element into the two other interventions. The following two programmes are being prepared for financing in 2004:

EU-China Biodiversity Programme. The overall objective of the programme is to enable China to sustain or rehabilitate its ecosystems and to pursue its responsibilities under the relevant international conventions through the establishment of appropriate mechanisms for biodiversity management. The Programme will comprise policy advice and formulation, institutional strengthening, the promotion of environmental awareness at all levels, and the financing of biodiversity-related projects in a range of ecological and institutional systems in order to develop and improve coordinating mechanisms. The EC financing foreseen for the programme now amounts to €30 million.

River Basin management Programme. This programme, for which an EC contribution of €25 million is envisaged, is presently under appraisal in view of a commitment of funds in 2004. With the overall objective of improving integrated river basin management, various options are being examined, notably policy development and institutional capacity strengthening, and water and soil conservation in the upper Yangtse and Yellow Rivers, the former in close cooperation with the World Bank.

Priority Area 3: Good Governance and Strengthening of the Rule of Law

Two interventions were identified in the NIP for financing under this priority area:

EU-China Programme on Illegal Migration and Trafficking in Human beings. With €10 million foreseen in the NIP for commitment in 2002, the preparation of this programme has encountered severe difficulties, due to lack of agreement between the EU and Chinese sides on the scope and content. Conceived initially as a complementary activity to the ongoing EU-China dialogue on illegal migration, the scope of the proposed programme has been cut back to cover needs assessment visits to the EU, seminars on false supporting documentation, biometrics and return issues, research, and networks. Funding for the programme under the Mid-term Review has been reduced to less than €1 million. If agreement on the programme is not reached by the end of 2004 the financing will be dropped from the NIP.

EU-China Civil Society Co-operation Programme. The financing for this programme, as for the above programme on illegal migration, will be reduced, from €20 million originally foreseen in the NIP to €10 million. This reduction has come about mainly because of concerns over absorption capacity in the Chinese context, highlighted during the identification mission in 2003. A financing decision is foreseen for 2004 with programme objectives of improving the interaction between government and civil society, supporting the modification of legislation concerning NGOs, building capacity in Chinese civil society organisations and strengthening public participation in local decision making.

### *1.2 MID-TERM REVIEW (MTR) OF THE 2002–2006 CSP AND 2002–2004 NIP*

The MTR of the China CSP and NIP was carried out in 2003 in accordance with the four criteria defined by the General Affairs and External Relations Council (GAERC) of March 2003. These are given in paras. 1.2.1 to 1.2.4 below.

#### 1.2.1 Main political, economic and social developments in China

In 2003 the new Chinese leadership under President Hu Jintao introduced changes at the top in virtually all Ministries, notably in one of the EC's key partner Ministries, the Ministry of Foreign Trade and Economic Co-operation (MOFTEC), which became a new 'super-ministry' of commerce (MOFCOM).

It was noted the new leadership may want to give more attention to the social and environmental consequences of rapid economic growth, which China intends to maintain at around 7% p.a., and to give greater emphasis to governance issues, notably strengthening the rule of law. Fiscal and financial reform was also considered to be on the agenda. These issues are dealt with in the CSP, and were subsequently discussed at the Beijing seminar referred to under point 1.1.2 above.

While information on these changes is still being assessed, continuity of policy has been the watchword throughout the transition process, and it is unlikely that there will be major changes of course in the medium term.

Since 2002 China became increasingly active in the Asian region, playing an important role in diplomacy (e.g. the formation of the 'Shanghai Co-operation Organisation' and greater activism in ASEM) and in regional trade agreements, (e.g. the 'ASEAN + 1' Free Trade Agreement signed in November 2002). Relations with the US, at least prior to the Iraq imbroglio, were warming, with much activity on the trade and military fronts. However, events in 2003 cooled this process down somewhat, given China's stated preference to continue working within the UN framework on Iraq and (albeit muted) opposition to the US-led military involvement.

In 2004 trade tensions with the US have been on the rise, notably as a result of the record US trade deficit (US$ 135 billion in 2003) and its ramifications for the presidential election campaign.

China continues to make progress on poverty reduction and, based on UNDP analysis, will probably achieve most Millenium Development Goal targets by 2015. While on course nationally in this respect, the issue of growing inequality has to be addressed, and there is a need to work towards balanced regional economic growth. An overview of China's MDG status is given in Annex 3.3.

1.2.2 New EC/EU policy objectives and commitments

While the co-operation strategy was finalised in 2002, it nevertheless takes full account of relevant new EU policy objectives. There is a strong emphasis on Trade Related Technical Assistance through the programme to support China's integration into the world economy; migration issues are addressed in the formal Dialogue on Illegal Migration and under the cooperation programme referred to in para. 1.1.3 above; and co-operation in the environment sector constitutes a priority area under the NIP. The issue of counter-terrorism, while being raised with China in the framework of the Political Dialogue, is not the subject of co-operation activities, the subject being considered more appropriate for coverage in the multilateral framework. The CSP and NIP are thus considered to remain appropriate.

1.2.3 Results, performance, and lessons learned

The three priorities identified in the CSP/NIP, (support for social & economic reform, environmental and sustainable development and good governance and strengthening the rule of law) were considered to remain valid, and should not be changed.

However the review noted that progress in committing the NIP actions to support these priorities gave cause for concern. Four were scheduled for 2002 commitment but only one was committed (support for China's integration into the world trading system). The other three actions scheduled for financing in 2002 (social security reform, information society and illegal migration) were at various stages of preparation, and considered unlikely to be mature for financing until 2004. Further concern was expressed on the illegal migration programme where the Chinese side was showing little interest in the co-operation proposed. It was considered likely that the scope of this programme would have to be reduced.

It was noted that the two actions foreseen for commitment in 2003 (biodiversity protection and human resources development) would slip to 2004, and that some preparatory work remained to be done on the HRD programme, but with commitment in 2004 still likely.

Prospects for the two programmes foreseen for 2004 commitment (water resources conservation and support for civil society) remained good, but the overall picture of the NIP was one of serious 'back-end loading', with the bulk of the NIP funding remaining for 2004 commitment. While the then completed deconcentration process was considered to enable faster commitment and more efficient execution, this nevertheless constituted a major challenge.

1.2.4 Quality improvements

The delays encountered in the implementation of the 2002–2004 NIP can be attributed in part to the complexity of the programmes, the wide range of interlocutors that are frequently involved, and the difficulties encountered in co-ordination. The present programme apart, at the beginning of the 2002–2004 NIP there existed a very large volume of previously-financed projects and programmes which required considerable effort for launching and/or reinvigoration, and which continues to require substantial inputs for the purposes of monitoring and evaluation. An overview of the ongoing programme, financed mainly before the 20022004 NIP, is given in Annex 3.4[3]. This indicates the high volume of pre- 2002–2004 NIP funds presently under implementation. While the devolution exercise is now bearing its fruits, its implementation was demanding in terms of time and human resources. The benefits of devolution are witnessed by the substantial increase in co-operation disbursement figures which have risen from a pre-2003 annual average of some €28 million, to a projected figure of over €50 million for 2004.

Improvements in the quality of the programme have likewise been noted under the 2002–2004 NIP which constitutes a more focussed approach to the achievement of co-operation objectives with China than was the case under previous programmes. Further focussing, and flexibility, under the 2005–2006 NIP will however be required.

### *1.3 CONCLUSIONS OF THE MID-TERM REVIEW PROCESS*

#### 1.3.1 Validity of the Country Strategy Paper

The conclusion of the Mid-Term Review was that the co-operation objectives defined in the CSP, targeting interventions aimed at assisting China's economic and social reform programme, its sustainable environmental development, and its reforms in the area of good governance and the rule of law remain entirely valid.

The fast pace of change in China has highlighted the importance of these areas of cooperation in order to assist China with its efforts to ensure that the overall balance in its development is in kilter with its rapid economic growth. Furthermore, the EU has a clear stake in China's successful transition to a stable, prosperous and open country that embraces democracy, free market principles and the rule of law. The CSP is considered effective and appropriate in both these respects, and is moreover in line with the Commission's 2003 China Policy Paper.

#### 1.3.2 Implementation of the 2002–2004 NIP

The Mid-term Review of the NIP nevertheless concluded that certain modifications to the NIP were required in order to reflect the realities encountered during the preparation of the individual projects and programmes. A summary table is attached in Annex 3.5 indicating the modifications that are proposed. These can be summarised on a sector priority basis as follows:

The indicative funding foreseen in the NIP in the area of **Support to Social and Economic Reform** was originally €75 million. While at the time of the review it was proposed that this figure be maintained, it is now proposed that it be increased to €76.2 million to take account of proposed increased funding for human resources development. Proposals for this sub-sector have now been developed as indicated in para. 1.3.1 above, and the human resources development allocation will increase from €}25 million to €26.2 million with the financing of the two interventions foreseen, namely the Managers Exchange and Training Programme and the China window for participation in Erasmus Mundus. Other actions in the social and economic reform sector remain at their original indicative financing levels.

The original NIP indicative financing for the **Environment and Sustainable Development** sector amounted to €45 million for three interventions: policy support, biodiversity protection and water resources conservation. As indicated in para. 1.1.3 above, the first of these interventions is being consolidated into the two remaining programmes, resulting in a more focussed concentration of activities, while at the same time expanding the scope and financing (€45 to €55 million) to ensure higher impact.

The third sector of intervention, **Support for Good Governance and the Rule of Law**, has encountered considerable difficulties given the political sensitivities involved. The €10 million initially foreseen for illegal migration has been scaled down to €1 million, and the €20 million initially foreseen for civil society has been scaled down to €10 million.

### *1.4 THE CONSULTATION PROCESS*

1.4.1 Co-ordination with the Member States

Discussions with the Member States in Beijing has taken place on both the Mid-Term Review of the 2002–2004 NIP and the preparation of the 2005–2006 NIP. Summaries of those discussions are given in Annexes 3.6 and 3.7 respectively. There was broad agreement on the proposals.

1.4.2 Discussions with the Chinese Government

The Ministry of Commerce (MOFCOM) is the Chinese Government's principal interlocutor and co-ordinator for all matters related to grant assistance. Discussion with MOFCOM has taken place on both the Mid-Term Review of the 2002–2004 NIP and the preparation of the 2005–2006 NIP. Summaries of those discussions are given in Annexes 3.8 and 3.9 respectively. On the Mid-Term Review, while design and implementation of the actions under the first two priorities of the NIP have been satisfactory, it was confirmed that the original approach for actions under priority 3 (illegal migration and civil society) needed to be downscaled.

1.4.3 Consultations with non-state actors

A meeting was held in Beijing in November 2003 with a representative group of non-governmental organisations to explain and discuss the preparation of the 2005–2006 NIP, and ways in which civil society could play an active role in its implementation, notably through the NGO co-financing budget line, thematic budget lines, and Small Project Facilities administered by the delegation.

## 2 THE 2005–2006 NATIONAL INDICATIVE PROGRAMME

### *2.1 SUMMARY OF NIP PRIORITIES AND THEIR LINKS WITH THE CSP*

| | | CSP PRIORITY | | |
|---|---|---|---|---|
| 2005–2006 NIP Action | Social and Economic Reform | Environment and Sustainable Development | Good governance and the rule of law | Cross-sectoral |
| Higher Education | X | | | |
| IPR Co-operation Programme | X | | | |
| Governance and capacity building | | | X | |
| Support for sectoral dialogues and exchanges | | | | X |

While the 2005–2006 NIP does not include specific interventions in the area of the environment, the on-going and planned projects and programmes in this field will be implemented over the coming years and, with funding possibilities under the programme proposed under priority 4 (section 2.3.4 below), will provide continued and substantial support for this priority area of the 2002–2006 Country Strategy.

### *2.2 THE INDICATIVE BUDGET*

| 2005–2006 NIP Action | Range (€ mio) | Median (€ mio) |
|---|---|---|
| Higher Education | 45–55 | 50 |
| IPR Co-operation Programme | 9–11 | 10 |
| Governance and capacity building | 22–28 | 25 |
| Support for sectoral dialogues and exchanges | 4–6 | 5 |
| Reserve | 0 | 10 |
| TOTAL | | 100 |

### *2.3 PRIORITIES AND ACTIONS*

An overview of external assistance to China is given in Annex 3.10.

2.3.1 Priority 1 – Higher Education (Proposed allocation €45–55 million)

2.3.1.1 Background and justification

The CSP states that "Human resources development, the transfer of know-how and European standards and practices are horizontal tools which ensure sustainable development and long-term added value. Investment in minds rather than machines is a proven strategy to increase investment yields in general, and the results of a number of projects and programmes in China have proved the efficiency of this strategy".

The EC policy of giving high priority to co-operation in the field of human resource development is therefore seen as a key element of support to social and economic reform in China under the 2005–2006 NIP.

Education is put forward by the government as a key foundation for China's long-term development and its international competitiveness. In 2002 there were 16 million students, a figure 2.3 times higher than the 1997 figure, and several hundred higher education institutions have been merged to rationalise the university landscape. Universities have become more autonomous, and fewer now fall directly under the Ministry of Education's jurisdiction.

A major university development programme was initiated in 1992 with substantial central government funding, destined to project approximately one hundred centres of excellence in China's best universities to world-class level in their respective fields. This project enters its second, deepening phase in 2004.

In 1998 a further programme was launched, aiming at promoting nine top universities to world class level. In 2003 Beijing University, one of China's top universities, reformed its management, staff and career policy on the basis of a competitive model which is likely to be followed by other universities and susceptible to make Chinese teachers and researchers more competitive and productive.

Private schools, colleges, academies and universities are mushrooming. Demand for enrolment is very high, notably for those who can afford the fees and/or cannot pass the state entry examinations (there were 6.13 million candidates in 2003). In Shanghai alone there are about 1.800 such institutions with about 10% of all students enlisted in them. Some of those offer also high-demand degrees and contribute to the flexibility of the education market's supply side.

Since 2003, it has become more difficult for recent graduates (2.12 million in 2003) to find employment, so additional qualifications and international experience are sought after by the employers. It is only since the 1990s that graduates have to look for jobs themselves, as previously jobs were allocated to them by the state. Universities are not yet geared to the labour market.

In 2003 a regulation on co-operation with foreign education institutions was passed, to promote joint-venture schools and universities.

Basic education in rural China will remain another key government policy for the years to come, and while not covered in the present NIP, is addressed in an ongoing EC-financed basic education project.

Higher education in China is however heavily influenced by US concepts due to the perceived success of its education model, the quality of its universities, the high number of US alumni in influential policy and business positions, and the many educational opportunities that the United States provides for Chinese students. The Ministry of Education expressly wants to counterbalance this trend, and while recent US visa restrictions have somewhat changed this tendency, the relative ease of access to the US education system remains.

It may however be noted that, on 16$^{th}$ March 2004, the Commission issued a Communication proposing a directive and two recommendations 'on the admission of third-country nationals to carry out scientific research in the European Community.' One adopted, such instruments will facilitate the entry and stay of Chinese researchers in the EU.

China is keen to make its education sector more internationally diverse, compatible, and competitive through improved co-operation with European academic centres of excellence. In this context China is eager to engage in agreements with the Member States on mutual recognition of degrees. Some Member States have already concluded such agreements and others are negotiating. China also monitors the Bologna process and would like to get observer status.

This interest on the Chinese side is clearly made in China's October 2003 EU Policy Paper which calls for, *inter alia,* increased co-operation in education, and was reiterated at the EU-China Policy Paper Seminar (Beijing, February 2004) when both sides agreed to pursue the possibility of the creation of a 'China Window' in the Erasmus Mundus Programme.

The Erasmus Mundus Programme was established by decision of the European Parliament and Council on 5th December 2003 (Decision No 2317/2003/EC)[4], and covers the period 2004–2008 with a budget of €230 million. The timing of the proposal for a specific 'China Window' in the Programme is therefore most appropriate, coinciding as it does with the momentum being gathered under this major new world-wide European initiative in higher education.

The financing of a specific Erasmus Mundus 'China Window' under the 2005–2006 NIP would constitute a follow-up to the financing foreseen for the same purpose (€9 million) under the 2002–2004 NIP for which it is proposed that a financing decision be taken in the coming months. China's participation in the Erasmus Mundus Programme is seen as a logical follow-up to previous and ongoing EU-China human resources development projects and programmes in basic and vocational training, public administration, management, and European studies, and would constitute a complementary element to the high-level exchanges with China on education that are presently planned. The potential demand for Chinese participation in Erasmus Mundus is massive.

2.3.1.2 Objectives

The overall objective of this action is to provide support for China's economic and social reform programme and to strengthen the EU-China relationship in this area. In addition, the action would contribute substantially towards the improvement of political, economic, and cultural links between the EU and China, in full compliance with the spirit of the CSP.

The specific objectives of the action are to foster linkages between the EU and China in higher education through encouraging and enabling Chinese students to complete postgraduate studies in Europe.

2.3.1.3 Expected results

The expected results are Chinese postgraduates completing Masters degrees in Europe.

The programme is expected to have a considerable multiplier effect on future demand from China for European higher education, and, via personal links that the programme will create between Chinese students and their European counterparts, can be expected to foster future cooperation across the board. The specific 'China Window' will provide considerable 'additionality' to the Erasmus Mundus Programme, and, as the scholarships will offer opportunities to future political and economic decision-makers in China, sustained EU influence and visibility will be promoted.

2.3.1.4 Activities

Masters Courses at EU universities which have been designated by the overall Erasmus Mundus Programme as 'Erasmus Mundus Masters Courses' will be allocated a specific number of EC-funded scholarship grants for foreign students. The 'China Window' funding will be used to fund grants for Chinese students. University consortia and the EC will publicise the scholarship opportunities worldwide using a variety of media

Each university consortium running an Erasmus Mundus Masters Course will establish lists of the students (for attendance on its Erasmus Mundus Masters Course) considered eligible for scholarships. The selection criteria will be those adopted by the Erasmus Mundus Programme.

University consortia will submit an application for funding with their proposed scholarship lists to the EC for final approval, and the Chinese authorities will be informed accordingly.

2.3.1.5 Implementation

The Commission shall be responsible for the implementation of the activities to be financed in accordance with the procedures and standards defined for the overall Erasmus Mundus Programme.

It is foreseen that from 2005 onwards the European Commission will entrust the management of some Community programmes, including Erasmus Mundus, to an Executive Agency based in Brussels.

Part of the programme implementation will be undertaken by the university consortia that will be chosen to run the courses. They will carry out the initial selection of students for scholarships, put in place appropriate arrangements to host third country students and make payments to students.

The Commission Delegation in Beijing will co-operate with DG EAC in monitoring the specific 'China Window' funding under the programme.

2.3.1.6 Cross-cutting issues

An effort will be made to ensure an adequate gender balance of students.

2.3.1.7 Risks and assumptions

The risks and assumptions related to the programme are that information on opportunities under the Erasmus Mundus Programme reaches the targeted students; that EU universities remain competitive with other higher education providers; that there is support for the programme from the Chinese authorities; that students who receive scholarships will return to China and pursue high-level careers; and that their positive experiences in Europe are disseminated to others.

2.3.1.8 Main indicators

The main indicators will be the numbers of Chinese students participating in the programme, the quality of their performance, and the numbers of degrees awarded to them. More indirectly the indicators will be the overall numbers of Chinese students participating in higher education courses in the EU.

2.3.1.9 Estimated EC contribution

The estimated EC contribution to the specific 'China Window' in the Erasmus Mundus Programme is €45 to €55 million for the three academic years from 2006/2007 to 2008/2009. There is no financial contribution envisaged from the Chinese side, other than the cost of participation in monitoring activities.

2.3.1.10 Co-ordination

In order to preserve the necessary coherence between the activities of the programme and activities undertaken by other donors in the sector, regular meetings will take place with all interested parties, and in particular EU Members States' representatives in China, to ensure an open exchange of information, to avoid overlapping of activities and/or financing and to incorporate the lessons learnt by these other actors into the work of the programme.

Extensive consultation took place between the Commission and EU Member States in the preparation of the overall Erasmus Mundus Programme for which this programme provides additional funding for China, and will continue in the framework of the Erasmus Committee.

The Chinese Ministry of Education is the interlocutor on the programme for the Chinese government.

2.3.1.11 Indicative timeframe

It is intended that funds for the programme be committed in 2005 in order that scholarships for students may be awarded for the three academic years from 2006/2007 to 2008/2009.

2.3.2 Priority 2 – Intellectual Property Co-operation Programme (Proposed allocation €9–11 million)

2.3.2.1 Background and justification

This intervention is proposed under the first focal area of the 2002–2006 CSP which states that "Support for the social and economic reform process to ensure sustainable economic development and the fight against poverty, and China's integration in the world economy, with special emphasis on WTO implementation".

China has in recent years carried out considerable work to revise its intellectual property rights (IPR) laws and administrative regulations to bring them into line with the WTO's Agreement on Trade-Related Aspects of Intellectual Property Rights (TRIPs). This legislation has been extensively reviewed by the WTO in the framework of both the TRIPs Review Sessions and the Transitional Review Mechanism (TRM) foreseen in China's Accession Protocol.

While the Chinese framework of legislation protecting intellectual property is now generally in line with international standards, there remain considerable concerns over the continued high levels of infringements covering most types of rights and to a wide range of products.

Support to China in the area of legislative and administrative reform has been provided the EC-financed EU-China Intellectual Property Rights Co-operation Programme (1996–2004), with an EC contribution of €5.6 million, but much remains to be done in the field of IPR enforcement due to the largely non-deterrent penalties in current legislation, the sometimes ambiguous legal provisions, lack of clarity over the precise channels for enforcement, the need for improved co-ordination between enforcement bodies, and the need for training.

Some follow-up assistance on IPR issues is foreseen in the programme entitled 'Support to China's Integration into the World Trading System' financed with a €15 million EC contribution under the 2002–2004 NIP. Launched in 2004, two of the six components of this programme are designed in part to address IPR issues, albeit in a limited way, and with limited financing. These cover border enforcement in the context of import/export regulation, and general legislative, legal and judicial aspects of the implementation by China of WTO rules and commitments.

Chinese commitment to IPR protection and enforcement has been expressed at the highest level, notably by President Hu Jintao at the October 2003 EU-China Summit, as Chinese domestic industries themselves begin to be affected by counterfeiting of their own products. A commitment to hold a yearly formal "Structured EU-China IPR Dialogue" was made in October 2003. This dialogue will cover all aspects of the subject without sectoral limitation "...with the objective of improving communication and co-operation on the protection of IPRs and in view of the establishment of a long-term strategy on IPR enforcement to be supported by EU technical assistance programmes"[5]

Built on the experience of the prior EU-China IPR Co-operation programme, the new intervention should take account of the five following requirements:

- A need for a pragmatic and result-oriented approach. Considering the complexity of the infringement issue in China (tradition, social dimension, organised crime), the action should primarily focus on concerns for which rational solutions exist in the medium to long-term perspective.
- The need to develop a clearly targeted action. To this end, precise benchmarks and targets will be defined on which the action will principally focus.
- The need for flexibility so as to allow speedy response to needs as they arise.
- The need for close co-ordination with other donors and trade partners so as to avoid overlapping of activities with those of other stakeholders, and to maximise project impact, and
- The need to assist China to develop a regional Asian strategy. IP enforcement is a cross-border issue and the continued expansion of commercial activity via the internet exacerbates enforcement difficulties.

With this in view, it is intended that the IPR co-operation program under the 2005–2006 NIP should be complementary to previous and ongoing interventions and should focus on legislative aspects, judicial, public and administrative enforcement, co-ordination between agencies, and public awareness-building.

In all, the programme will have important synergies with the various political and sectoral commitments on IPR that have proliferated in EU-China relations over the last year, and with certain exchanges and agreements, such as the Galileo programme, where the protection of IPR has a direct impact on the scope of industrial co-operation.

2.3.2.2 Objectives

The overall objective of the programme is to contribute towards China's social and economic reform process.

The specific objective of the programme is to improve the efficiency of IPR administration in China through the provision of support to Chinese legislative, judicial, administrative, and enforcement agencies and institutions.

2.3.2.3 Expected results

The expected results of the programme are amongst others:

- Legislation and implementing regulations improved
- Chinese judges trained in critical issues such infringement identification, compensation, interlocutory injunction, rule of evidence, litigation procedure
- Improved efficiency of the principal agencies involved in IPR enforcement, such as, *inter alia*, the State Administration for Administration and Commerce, the Public Security Bureau and the Supreme People's Procurator, the People's Courts, and the State Intellectual Property Office
- Improved administrative capacity of relevant Chinese agencies such as the State Intellectual Property Office, the Chinese Trademark Office, and the National Copyright Administration of China, Customs, the State General Administration for Quality, Supervision, Inspection and Quarantine
- Improved procedures for handling IPR cases and co-ordination between agencies involved in IPR issues.
- Increased awareness of IPR issues.

2.3.2.4 Activities

The precise activities to be undertaken under the programme will be defined during the appraisal exercise, and will take account of other IPR interventions both planned and under implementation. Activities could include:

- the provision of training on the impact of legislation on enforcement and the role of IPR protection in promoting economic development
- the provision of assistance in the formulation of amendments to existing IPR legislation, particularly in the field of IPR enforcement
- the provision of specific training programmes and forums for Chinese judges on IPR issues
- the provision of education programs to improve the IPR knowledge in the police force
- the provision of assistance to the Public Security Bureau and the Supreme People's Procurator to establish comprehensive procedures for the handling of IPR cases and to co-ordinate their activities
- the provision of assistance to relevant administrative agencies in drafting regulations, introducing border control measures, setting up computer data networks, etc.
- the provision of assistance to ensure adequate co-ordination between agencies involved in IPR issues through a clear and fully integrated IPR enforcement strategy at central level
- awareness raising of consumers and of right holders
- support for the setting-up of an IPR Helpdesk by China, to provide information and assistance to interested companies.

2.3.2.5 Implementation

An identification mission will be launched in 2005 to formulate the programme and to provide the basis for detailed project appraisal. Key interlocutors for the formulation of the programme will include the authorities and institutions indicated under para. 2.4.2.3 above, and private sector actors.

2.3.2.6 Cross-cutting issues

As an action intended to assist with the development of the transparent and effective management of public affairs, there is a clear 'good governance' element to the programme which is in line with that priority identified in the CSP.

In addition, the enforcement of IPR is closely linked to the issue of consumer protection. In some areas, such as the pharmaceutical industry, counterfeiting can result in severe health hazards.

2.3.2.7 Risks and assumptions

The risks and assumptions associated with this programme are that:

- the Chinese Government remains committed to the implementation of IPR measures in accordance with the provisions of its accession to the WTO
- the authorities and agencies targeted for support under the programme are receptive to the assistance foreseen
- the required support inputs can be provided in a timely, responsive, and effective manner

2.3.2.8 Main indicators

Detailed programme indicators will be defined during the appraisal phase, but will be based on the benchmarks and targets to be established, and could include elements such as:

- registered numbers of IP infringements, counterfeiting and piracy
- numbers of IP criminal prosecutions, and levels of penalties
- commitment of the central administration to curb counterfeiting and piracy.

2.3.2.9 Estimated EC contribution

The EC contribution to the programme will be in the order of €9 to €11 million. Government counterpart funding of at least 50% of this amount is envisaged.

2.3.2.10 Co-ordination

Although China has established an IPR protection framework it is recognised that there is a lack of co-ordination on certain critical issues among the many agencies involved. It is therefore proposed that the co-ordination of IPR activities be supported in the framework of the programme. To this end assistance will be provided to the Chinese Government for the establishment of appropriate co-ordination mechanisms.

Further co-ordination with Member States and the donor community will be assured by the Commission Delegation in Beijing, and with the Member States by the Commission's headquarters.

2.3.2.11 Indicative timeframe

It is intended that funds for the programme be committed in 2006 and that the programme implementation period be defined at the time of programme identification and appraisal.

2.3.3 Priority 3 – Governance Capacity Building (Proposed allocation €22–28 million)

2.3.3.1 Background and justification

This programme is proposed under the third focal area of the 2002–2006 CSP which states that "Promoting good governance, the rule of law and human rights are key priorities of the EC Co-operation.

China has in recent years made considerable progress in modernising its laws and legal institutions. It has in place all the institutions of a formal legal system; a framework of laws and legislation, a national system of courts, a national prosecutorial system, accredited law schools, and an ever-growing legal profession. However, it is recognised that the capacity of China's legal and judicial system to effectively ensure adherence, compliance and enforcement of the law in an equitable manner is still limited.

EC support for legal and judicial reform in China is being provided under the 'EU-China Legal and Judicial Co-operation Programme' for which EC funding of €13.2 million has been provided for activities during the period 1999 to 2005. This programme was designed to develop a better understanding of the rule of law in China; to foster greater understanding of the concept of the rule of law among legal professionals and networking between them; to promote European legal systems as examples of best practice, and to improve awareness of the legal system in China and the rights that it confers. The programme adopted two main strategies to achieve these objectives: the provision of training opportunities for legal professionals (lawyers, judges, prosecutors and senior officials), and the provision of a financial facility through which small projects are being financed following calls for proposals.

A recent external evaluation of the programme has confirmed the relevance of the programme in the context of China's reform process, and serves to support the Chinese Government's proposal that co-operation in this area should be continued under the 2005–2006 NIP.

Civil society in China is still weak but is expanding. Institutional weaknesses, the disappearance of familiar organisational structures, the search for their practical and ideological replacements, and an increasing awareness of civil society's role have created the conditions for the creation of an increasingly autonomous civil society. New, home-grown NGOs have been created and provide valuable support to disadvantaged groups and have actively contributed to preventing social unrest.

The regulatory framework requires NGOs to be registered with the Ministry of Civil Affairs (MOCA) and/or local Civil Affairs Bureaux and imposes administrative controls. While some 244,000 NGOs are registered with MOCA, the largest group of civil society organisations is composed of the 1.3 to 2 million unregistered grassroots organisations. Foreign civil society organisations cannot register in China at present, other than by establishing a "foreign representative office".

Most grassroots NGOs generally perform less of a policy advocacy role and more of a social service and support role, though in spite of the regulatory intricacies and the poor understanding of the importance of a balanced relationship between the state and civil society, there are nevertheless political signs that a greater role for civil society is increasingly being recognised. The Government is increasingly conscious of the need to involve civil society in the process of resolving, in particular, social and environmental problems, and in this context further support for civil society could be envisaged.

In spite of certain improvements in recent years, particularly in respect of economic and social rights, the human rights situation in China remains a cause of concern. This is particularly so in the fields of civil and political rights. In March 2004 China added a clause to its Constitution to the effect that the State respects and protects human rights. While the immediate impact of this measure may be limited as Constitutional provisions are not directly enforceable in the legal system, it nevertheless represents an important political signal. Furthermore, the current leadership appears genuinely committed to governing China in a more responsive way, on the basis of the rule of law, in order to preserve social stability as disparities in income and opportunity deepen. Developments in the areas of the death penalty and administrative detention are not however seen as encouraging. Freedom of expression remains restricted (e.g. in the case of internet users) as does freedom of association, there are violations of the right to hold and manifest one's religion or belief, and there is a tendency to equate peaceful opposition with subversion of the state or terrorism and to repress it accordingly. There has been a certain loss of momentum in the area of cooperation with UN human rights mechanisms.

The permanent, six-monthly EU-China human rights dialogue is one of the EU's channels for working to improve the human rights situation in areas of concern. Furthermore, a number of projects funded under the European Initiative for Democracy and Human Rights are being implemented in China. These include, inter alia: The EU-China Network on the Human Rights Covenants; Strengthening the Defence of Death Penalty Cases in China; and The Human Rights Micro-Projects Programme. Further strengthening of EC support for human rights can be anticipated under the programme.

2.3.3.2 Objectives

The overall objective of the programme will be to support the Chinese Government in its efforts to develop a society based on the rule of law.

The specific objective of the programme will be to increase capacity for realising China's governance priorities.

2.3.3.3 Expected results

The expected result is that Chinese capacity in good governance will have been strengthened by the implementation of a series of activities focused on achieving structural and sustainable results. Management systems will have been improved, legislative skills increased, the quality of new legislation heightened, human resources development capacity enhanced, enforcement capacity reinforced, and the role of civil society strengthened.

The programme will also result in better human rights protection through strengthening of the rule of law, and enhanced transparency in legal procedure and practice.

Furthermore, for the programme to be considered successful, it should have enhanced the EU's capacity to interact at a high level on governance issues, through having strengthened links with key government, academic and civil society actors, as well as having increased donor coordination in this field.

2.3.3.4 Activities

Activities under the programme could be focused on some or all of the following areas:

1. Legislative Organs

The main focus under this component will be to improve the legal drafting capacity of key legislative actors in areas such as civil law, commercial law, corporate governance, criminal law, fiscal law, public health and sanitary law, environmental law, privacy and data protection laws, human rights law and administrative law. Key players could include the National People's Congress Standing Committee, line ministries, academic institutions and think thanks. Support may take the form of research and policy studies, acquisition of comparative legal materials, international technical advice, administrative co-operation, etc.

2. The Judicial and Administrative Systems

Concerning the judicial system, the achievements of the Legal and Judicial Co-operation Programme, which will end in mid-2005, will be consolidated and expanded. The focus of new actions would be less on training individual judiciary actors (prosecutors, magistrates), be it in the EU or in China, but more on reinforcing local institutions' capacity to ensure sustainable, high-quality human resources programmes. Possibilities for strengthening existing organisations such as the national and regional judges colleges or for supporting the establishment of new legal and/or judicial training institutions could be investigated.

Support could include human resources development actions such as curriculum and faculty development (including attention to non-legal skills such as communication and management techniques), support for specific training programmes organised by local institutions, in-service training, exchange programmes for legal scholars and high-ranking magistrates, twinning programmes between institutions, and seminars and workshops. Training in China would be given preference over training in the EU for general topics, though training in the EU may be more appropriate for more specialised legal and policy areas. The role of China's legal training institutions could be examined to identify additional needs and support requirements.

A further area of focus could be co-operation in the field of systemic capacity building. This may include supporting legal and administrative institutions' management capacity development, promoting reform to enhance governance capacity – for example procedures and systems for fiscal management, the management of procurators' offices and courts, improved co-ordination between actors, setting up data networks, etc.

Actions aimed at promoting access to justice and civil society scrutiny of the judicial system should be supported.

3. Law Enforcement Agencies

Considering the growing disparity between the developing legal and judicial apparatus and the actual enforcement of laws and regulations in China, reinforced co-operation in this field remains of particular relevance.

Actions could include strengthening capacity to enforce laws and regulations in specific fields such as labour and social standards, food quality and sanitary and phytosanitary standards, and environmental law. Actions complementary to the IPR Co-operation Programme could be envisaged. Actions may furthermore be identified to promote compliance with international standards and international best practice, for example in the areas of policing and prison management.

4. Capacity building for civil society

In addition to the three areas of intervention mentioned above, which mainly target the public sector, capacity-building measures focussed on civil society may be envisaged.

2.3.3.5 Implementation

The aim is to develop an integrated, dynamic, flexible and cost-effective programme which will allow the Commission and China to effectively and rapidly address needs in the governance field as they develop over the coming two years. The programme will be constructed so as to achieve maximum synergy with other donor initiatives and, where possible, activities will be supported by co-financing actions with other donors.

Chinese counterpart organisations could include, *inter alia*, the National People's Congress Standing Committee, the Ministry of Justice, the Supreme People's Procuatorate, the Supreme People's Court, specialised Government agencies, and civil society.

2.3.3.6 Cross-cutting issues

The principle cross-cutting issue targeted by the programme will be that of good governance through the provision of support for the effective management of public affairs.

The programme will seek to optimise integration of governance with the other two areas of the 2002–2006 CSP, namely social and economic reform and the environment and sustainable development. Civil society involvement in governance issues will be promoted across all components of the programme. Use of new technologies for information transfers and management systems will be promoted.

2.3.3.7 Risks and assumptions

The risks and assumptions associated with this action are that:

- political support and Government commitment to the process of legal and judicial reform continues
- the appropriate management structure is established
- the hosting capacity of selected training institutions is adequate
- respect for human rights, in particular in the area of law enforcement

2.3.3.8 Main indicators

The main indicators by which the impact and effectiveness of the support programme may be assessed are as follow:

- progress made in preparing improved legislation
- number of training programmes delivered
- outcome of evaluation of training programmes by participants and host institutions

2.3.3.9 Estimated EC contribution

The EC contribution to the programme will be made within the overall indicative allocation of €22–€28 million proposed for good governance under the 2005–2006 NIP when precise needs have been quantified and when the programme appraisal process has been completed. Government counterpart funding of up to 40% of this amount is envisaged.

2.3.3.10 Co-ordination

Overall responsibility for the co-ordination of activities under this action will lie with the Commission Delegation in Beijing. The preparation and implementation of programme activities will be the subject of exchanges between the Delegation, the Member States representatives.

The programme will be closely coordinated with other donors.

2.3.3.11 Indicative timeframe

It is proposed that funds be committed in 2006. The implementation period will be defined during the appraisal stage.

2.3.4 Priority 4 – Support for dialogues in the framework of the CSP (Proposed allocation €4–6 million)

2.3.4.1 Background and justification

The dialogues and exchanges between the Commission's various Directorates General and services and the Chinese Government are both wide and numerous, and are largely directly related to the objectives of the 2002–2006 CSP. All are supportive of China's development and in certain areas are closely linked to projects and programmes financed under the cooperation programme. In general they form an increasingly important element of the overall EU-China relationship. Examples of the areas covered by these dialogues include environmental issues, illegal migration, trade policy, information society, energy, education, space co-operation, etc. A table indicating the ongoing and planned dialogues and exchanges given in Annex 3.11.

The Chinese Government has shown a very keen interest in intensifying these dialogues, expanding them, and backing them up with concrete activities. The Commission shares this interest, and responds by providing regular contacts and exchanges with its Chinese counterparts. While these dialogues and exchanges can to some extent be supported by the Small Projects Facility under which support through calls for proposals can be given for small-scale projects related to China's reform programme, the overall needs are broader, and call for targeting on specific issues.

In both China's EU Policy Paper of October 2003 and the EC China Policy Paper of September 2003, a number of areas were identified where closer co-operation would be strengthened through exchanges of knowledge and best practice by way of co-operation between institutions and exchanges of experts. In the management of its reform process China is clearly interested in EU models as examples for its own development. In this context it may be noted that EU expertise and experience in a wide range of areas has been transferred to a number of transitional countries with considerable success.

In view of this demand from the Chinese side, and the EU objective of assisting China in its reform process, it is proposed to allocate funds under the 2005–2006 NIP for support to existing and future dialogues and exchanges in areas in which the Commission is engaged with the Chinese side and which clearly fall within the objectives of the CSP.

In designing projects and programmes under the 2002–2004 NIP an effort has been made to ensure that support for dialogues is or will be provided in the framework of existing or planned co-operation programmes. In some areas, notably in the environment, in information society, and in certain trade-related areas, this approach is already successful. However, previous experience shows that it is difficult to include new important topics or involve additional counterparts where not envisaged in the original project design. It is therefore necessary to provide additional support under this action where an existing programme or project is unable to respond to the specific requirements of the dialogue or exchange.

An example is the growing interest shown by the Chinese Government in establishing a dialogue on agriculture, particularly in the field of rural development. This is an area where EC experience could be beneficial to China, and where intensified exchanges can be anticipated.

The approach proposed would serve not only to assist China with its development efforts in the three specific areas defined in the CSP, but would also serve to align the co-operation programme more closely with the mainstream of the broader EU-China relationship, and enable it to respond to the dynamics of the relationship.

2.3.4.2 Objectives

The overall objective of the action is to provide support for China in its social and economic reform programme, in the area of the environment and sustainable development, and in the areas of good governance and the rule of law, in line with overall CSP priorities.

The specific objective is to provide closer and enhanced co-operation between the EU and China in development-related areas in which the EU has particular experience and expertise.

2.3.4.3 Expected results

In view of the dynamic rate of change and development both in China itself and in terms of the EU-China relationship, it is not presently possible to estimate the quantitative results that can be expected from this action. In general terms however, and across a broad range of areas, the anticipated results would include policy advice provided, relevant legislation and regulations drafted and adopted in harmony with international standards, and capacity developed to implement and monitor policy. The programme may also provide opportunities for technical discussion and the transfer of best practices.

2.3.4.4 Activities

The programme activities will take place mainly in priority areas where technical support does not exist, and will thus be complementary to other co-operation activities.

The activities to be undertaken will vary according to the specific area and objective of the dialogue or exchange to be supported, and could include short to medium-term technical assistance; exchanges of experts; training of Chinese staff; and the organisation of workshops and seminars.

Subject to human resource and management requirements, the programme could include grant funding for calls for proposals in support of its objectives.

Continued support for the training of Chinese language interpreters could also be provided under the programme.

2.3.4.5 Implementation

The financing of this action will follow the prior identification of priority areas for intervention, lead partners on both the Chinese and EU sides, and the types of intervention to be undertaken. A single financing agreement will be signed with the Chinese Government.

Responsibility for the implementation of the action will lie with the Commission Delegation in Beijing. The preparation and implementation of specific support activities will be carried out in close liaison with the relevant Chinese authorities and with the Commission's central services that are directly involved with the dialogues and exchanges in question.

Recourse will be made to established framework contacts with specialised consultancy services for the provision of services under the action. Where such framework contracts do not cover the required services, other competitive selection procedures will be undertaken.

The Chinese partners participating in the dialogues and exchanges to be supported will be actively involved in all aspects of the preparation and implementation of the actions.

2.3.4.6 Cross-cutting issues

Cross-cutting issues such as the environment and gender will be addressed where appropriate in the individual support actions. The environment is the subject of a specific dialogue in its own right, and other dialogues are directly related to issues of good governance.

2.3.4.7 Risks and assumptions

The risks and assumptions associated with this action are that:

- the dialogues and exchanges in areas related to the CSP continue, and
- the dialogues and exchanges continue to need support to enhance their impact
- the necessary technical expertise and input can be identified
- the support can be provided in a timely, flexible, and responsive manner

- the transfer of expertise and experience is effective.

2.3.4.8 Main indicators

The main indicators by which the impact and effectiveness of the support programme may be assessed are as follow:

- conformity of support actions with mandates for dialogues and exchanges
- feedback from dialogue stakeholders on effectiveness and efficiency
- the number of calls for support activities in relation to the financing possibilities
- the number of support activities successfully implemented.

2.3.4.9 Estimated EC contribution

The EC contribution to the support programme shall be between €4 and €6 million.

Complementary financing for activities to be supported may be provided by Member States, and other stakeholders. Government counterpart funding is at present hard to assess, but will be provided for individual activities on a case by case basis, and will be substantial.

2.3.4.10 Co-ordination

Overall responsibility for the co-ordination of activities under this action will lie with the Commission Delegation in Beijing. The preparation and implementation of project activities will be the subject of exchanges between the Delegation and the Chinese authorities, and with the Member States representatives and other donors in China in the framework of established co-ordination mechanisms. The Delegation will furthermore liaise directly with the central Commission Services concerned.

Co-ordination within Commission Headquarters will be assured through established and regular inter-service and external co-ordination mechanisms, in particular with the Member States in the framework of the China Experts Meetings.

2.3.4.11 Indicative timeframe

It is foreseen that the funds allocated for this action will be committed in 2005.

## 3 ANNEXES

### *3.1 SUMMARY OF THE OBJECTIVES OF THE CSP*

Principles and objectives for co-operation

The overall objective of EC co-operation with China is to further the Union's key overall aims in relations with China, by supporting the transition process and the sustainability of the economic and social reforms, while integrating China further in the international community and the world economy.

In supporting broader EU policies towards China, the co-operation strategy transcends the more 'traditional' approach of development assistance focussing more narrowly on activities which directly aim to reduce poverty. This strategy constitutes a response to China's needs and takes into consideration the EC's comparative strengths among donors, thus making the most of the EC's limited resources.

China has shown a genuine capacity to absorb foreign aid and is particularly keen to develop co-operation with the EU, given the unique nature of the European Union and the broad expertise it can provide. Co-operation programmes should therefore concentrate on areas where EC action is the most efficient, effective and visible, and where the EC can offer the highest added value, compared to other donors.

At the same time, the present EC co-operation budget of around EUR 250 million over 5 years is undoubtedly low, compared to the size of the challenges that China faces, and to the resources available to other donors. The total EC co-operation budget represents only 1% of net ODA devoted to China. With regard to grant aid, the figure stands at 2%.

In this respect, and within the overall objective mentioned above, support to reform (mainly through institutional support, changes to the legal framework and regulations, development of human resources, market opening), co-operation on the environment, and on issues related to the rule of law, good governance and human rights are areas where the EC has, or can, mobilise unique expertise and thus has a comparative advantage among donors.

Poverty reduction will remain an important consideration which will be taken into account in the design of all EC projects. However, in view of the level of resources allocated by China to its own successful poverty reduction programme, as well as the significant activities in this area especially by the international financing institutions, EC co-operation can add more value in the areas referred to above. This approach is in line with China's own strategy, which stresses that the economic and social reform process is key to economic growth and, ultimately, to poverty reduction.

Within the above priority areas, concentration will be essential in order to preserve the Commission's project delivery capacities. Given the problems experienced in the past over managing numerous projects simultaneously, the Commission will continue its policy, started in 1999, to focus on fewer, larger-budgeted, projects.

Given its limited resources, the EC will seek close co-operation with other donors, such as Member States, the World Bank and others, in the priority areas identified above, in order to enhance the effectiveness of its assistance.

This approach is coherent with EC development policy. The priority areas for intervention are among the strategic areas proposed in the Commission's April 2000 Communication, having been adapted to the specific Chinese context.

In addition to co-operation programmes designed particularly for China, China will also continue to participate in regional projects, where appropriate. Moreover, the EC has several specific global policy initiatives, not exclusively targeted at China, but which China either already participates in or could benefit from. These include the Framework Programme for RTD and humanitarian aid from ECHO, programmes which follow their own objectives and procedures, different from the ones outlined in the present paper. Nonetheless, these programmes constitute an important complement to the general EC co-operation programme, and in many ways help to further the objectives of the latter. This is true in particular for RTD co-operation with China, which promotes two-way exchanges and transfer of knowhow, as well as equitable sharing of results between all partners, in areas which are key to China's economic and technological development, and which aims to foster common analyses of, and solutions to, common problems that both the EU and Chinese societies face.

Priorities and specific objectives for co-operation

In line with the Commission's overall policy objectives towards China, and considering the available financial and human resources, as well as the challenges posed by China's reform process and the added value the EC can provide when compared with other donors, the Commission's co-operation budget should address three specific objectives:

- Support for the social and economic reform process to ensure sustainable economic development and the fight against poverty, and China's integration in the world economy, with special emphasis on WTO implementation;
- Prevention of environmental degradation; conservation of the natural environment; integration of environmental considerations into other policy areas; actions to pursue improved balance between environmental protection and social development in the context of rapid economic growth;
- Support for the transition to an open society based on the rule of law and respect of human rights, through the promotion of good governance and democracy and human rights-related policies.

It should be noted that a number of programmes already designed or ongoing are cross-sectoral and address simultaneously a number of the above objectives.

### *3.2 CHINA'S ENVIRONMENTAL PRIORITIES: INTRODUCTION AND OVERVIEW*[6]

Introduction

The 1990s was another decade of significant economic and social change in China. The country progressed further in the process of transforming itself from a command or planned economy to a market-based and increasingly less-planned economy. It continued the process of structural reform which is seeing it change from a predominantly agricultural economy, to a mixed economy with substantial industrial and service sectors. Finally, and perhaps most remarkably, it continued its assault on poverty by reducing the number of people living in poverty from nearly 90 million (1989) to 42 million by the end of 1998.

As a result, China is now a very different place than it was in 1992 when the World Bank formulated and published its China: Environmental Sector Strategy (World Bank, 1992) and the range and significance of environmental issues which have to be confronted have widened significantly as a consequence. This report has been prepared to take account of these changes, to assess how they are affecting the environmental agenda, and to identify environmental management strategies and priorities to take China into the future and, more particularly, the period covered by the 10$^{th}$ Five Year Plan (2001 – 2005). It was prepared collaboratively between the World Bank, the State Environmental Protection Administration and a wide range of research and other institutes who are working on environmental management problems in China.

The report has been structured to mirror, to a substantial degree, the main priority issues addressed in SEPA's 10$^{th}$ Five Year Plan for Environmental Protection which commenced preparation at about the same time. It does not cover every issue on the environmental agenda; for example, it says nothing about nuclear environmental management or biosafety (genetic engineering) which are two new responsibilities for SEPA. It also says very little about solid waste management or the management and disposal of toxic and hazardous wastes. Instead, it focuses on the main generic issues which have been the prime focus of attention in recent years, which remain issues of priority concern, and will require continued and even heightened attention over the next 10 years, namely; land and biodiversity resources management, water management, air pollution and issues surrounding environmental management and regulation in general. At the request of SEPA, the report also addresses two emerging issues which are potentially of environmental significance, namely; China's pending accession to the World Trade Organization, and, the government's recently announced "Great Western Development Plan".

Overview

In response to requests made by participants at review workshops held during preparation, this review is consciously technical in its analysis and detailed in its prescriptions. However, there are three cross-cutting issues which keep recurring throughout the analysis and these help to characterize the environmental management problem which is being confronted:

- **First**, the environmental agenda is becoming so complex and of such a large scale that it cannot and will not be adequately dealt with by one agency (SEPA and its counterparts at lower levels) working on its own. This is particularly true with regard to the natural resources management, or the "green" environmental agenda, which is emerging as a major challenge for the 21st Century. Effective solutions will require the combined and coordinated efforts of many different branches of government and the rethinking of many development policies. Much of the environmental degradation being experienced in China can be attributed to implementation of policies which were either directly inimical to environmentally sustainable development or inadvertently had the same effect. New development concepts need to be developed which take account of externalities, the multiple potential benefits of natural resources and also the views of different stakeholders in those natural resources.
- **Second**, the systemic fiscal and budgetary problems facing the country as a whole are making it particularly difficult for environmental institutions to effectively do their work. There is a disconnect between assigned responsibilities and resources provided which is growing rather than shrinking. This applies not only to environmental protection agencies but also to other ministries and units within them who have a vital role to play in the promotion and application of environmentally sustainable development including the agricultural research services, agricultural extension services, nature reserve management units within the State Forestry Administration, and so on. This issue is of particular importance in the context of continued market reform where government's role as an environmental regulator is increased. Of course, this is a problem that extends far beyond the question of environmental management and protection but it provides one more reason for continued aggressive reform of government tax and financial management procedures.
- **Third**, government has to continue to diversify the approaches it takes and the tools it uses in the interests of environmentally sustainable development to provide a better fit between the solutions developed and the problems being experienced in different parts of the country. The "one size fits all" approach is proving inadequate to the demands. The concept of developing many tools to deal with many problems is particularly relevant for the management of natural resources where greater attention needs to be paid to addressing the underlying causes of problems not just their symptoms.

Over the coming decade, the government is projecting a continuation of quite strong growth in GDP, industrial output, energy consumption, urbanization and agricultural intensification. This scenario suggests that the challenges and complexities of the environmental agenda will increase rather than decrease.

Given this context, the Government's environmental objectives during the 10$^{th}$ FYP are ambitious. The plans and programs are expected to result in "*improved environmental performance in pollution control while the deteriorating trend in the ecological environment will be halted*". Its success in achieving these objectives will be determined substantially by its success in managing growth within a development framework which is heavily constrained in terms of land, water and other essential natural resources.

Taking account of the development framework, the government's environmental objectives, and the cross-cutting environmental issues discussed above, the environmental strategy for the immediate future has to be built on three main pillars:

- **Institutions: Strengthening the Institutional Base for Environmental Protection and Management.** Work to strengthen existing institutions responsible for pollution control needs to continue and intensify. But, bearing in the mind the growing complexity and crosscutting nature of the problem, the government also needs to mainstream environmentally sustainable development in all of its relevant institutions.
- **Instruments: Developing More Effective Policies and Implementation Mechanisms.** The effectiveness of existing pollution control policies and instruments can be improved significantly and efforts in this regard need to be continued. However, there is also a need to develop new policies and instruments to deal with emerging issues in both pollution control and natural resources management, and to respond to the effects of market reforms and decentralization.
- **Investments: Setting Realistic Agendas and Investment Priorities.** More money needs to be invested in environmental improvement but the resources need to be used more efficiently and effectively. Government needs to set realistic environmental goals, prioritize its investments and maintain focus.

## *3.3 OVERVIEW OF CHINA'S MDG STATUS*

MDGs: China's Progress

Below is a summary of the UN System in China's collective assessment of China's situation *vis a vis* the MDGs.

**OVERVIEW OF CHINA MDG STATUS**

| **GOALS** and Targets | **STATE OF GOAL ACHIEVEMENT** | **STATE OF SUPPORTIVE ENVIRONMENT** |
|---|---|---|
| **Eradicate Extreme Poverty & Hunger by 2015** | | |
| Halve the proportion of people living in extreme poverty | On track | Well developed |
| Halve the proportion of population below minimum level of dietary energy consumption<br>Halve the proportion of underweight children under five years old by 2015 | On track | In place |
| **Universal primary education by 2015** | | |
| Achieve universal primary education by 2015 | On track | In place |
| **Gender equality** | | |
| Achieve equal access for boys and girls to primary and lower secondary schooling by 2005 | Maybe not on track | In place |
| Achieve equal access for boys and girls to upper secondary education by 2005 | Maybe not on track | In place |
| **Under-five mortality** | | |
| Reduce under-five mortality by two-thirds by 2015 | On track | In place |
| **Reproductive health** | | |
| Reduce maternal mortality ratio by three-quarters by 2015 | On track | In place |
| Universal access to safe/reliable reproductive health services (contraceptive methods) by 2015 | On track | Well developed |
| **Combat disease (HIV/AIDS, TB & Malaria)** | | |
| Halt and reverse the spread of HIVS/AIDS by 2015 | Maybe not on track | Maybe not on track |
| Halve the prevalence of TB by 2015 | Maybe not on track | In place |
| Reduce the incidence of malaria | On track | In place |
| **Environment** | | |
| Implement national strategies for sustainable development by 2005 so as to reverse the loss of environmental resources by 2015 | Maybe not on track | Well developed |
| **Basic amenities** | | |
| Halve the proportion of people unable to reach or afford safe drinking water by 2015 | On track | Well developed |
| Improve the proportion of rural people with access to improved sanitation | On track | In place |

40

## 3.4 OVERVIEW OF THE ONGOING PROGRAMME, FINANCED MAINLY BEFORE THE 2002–2004 NIP

EU-CHINA CO-OPERATION PROJECTS UNDER IMPLEMENTATION

This list includes projects financed under the following budget chapters:

| | |
|---|---|
| B7-3 | Co-operation with Asian Developing Countries |
| B7-7 | European Initiative for Democracy and Human Rights (EIDHR)* |
| B7-6000 | NGO co-financing |
| B7-6212 | Health, Population, Fight against HIV/AIDS |

**PROJECTS AND PROGRAMMES UNDER IMPLEMENTATION (1)**

| Category | Project | EC Grant (€ million) | Subtotal |
|---|---|---|---|
| General | Small Project facility | 8,00 | 8,00 |
| Human Resource Development | China Europe International Business School (Phase II) | 10,95 | 69,51 |
| | Junior Managers Programme | 11,64 | |
| | China Europe Public Administration Project | 5,70 | |
| | Vocational Training | 15,10 | |
| | Basic Education | 15,00 | |
| | STD/AIDS Training Project | 0,40 | |
| | Chinese Interpreters Training Programme 2001–2004 | 0,39 | |
| | European Studies Programme | 10,33 | |
| Rule of Law and Good Governance | Legal and Judicial Co-operation | 13,20 | 32,31 |
| | Village Governance | 10,67 | |
| | Intellectual Property Rights | 5,60 | |
| | Human Rights Small Project Facility * | 0,84 | |
| | EU-China Network on Human Rights Covenants * Strengthening the defence of death penalty cases * | 0,88 0,52<br>0,60 | |
| | Economic, Social and Cultural Rights in Yunnan * | | |
| Economic and Social Reform | WTO Accession Project | 3,60 | 48,17 |
| | Financial Services | 8,50 | |

| | | | |
|---|---|---|---|
| | Enterprise Reform | 8,50 | |
| | Civil Aviation | 12,57 | |
| | Support for China's integration into the world trading system | 15,00 | |
| Environment | Liaoning Integrated Environment Project | 37,00 | 87,80 |
| | Environmental Management Co-operation Project | 13,00 | |
| | Vehicle Emmission Control | 0,84 | |
| | Natural Forest Management | 16,50 | |
| | Energy and Environment | 20,00 | |
| | Solid Waste Disposal Project | 0,46 | |
| Rural and Agricultural | Pa-Nam Integrated Poverty Alleviation Project | 7,60 | 7,60 |
| NGO Co-Financing and Health/Population | Access to STD Services in Urban Areas | 1,07 | 4,36 |
| | Maternal and Child Health Care, Mid-West China | 0,88 | |
| | Child Welfare in Communities | 1,00 | |
| | Support to Health Policy in Disfavoured Regions of Wester China | 0,80 | |
| | Rural Poverty Alleviation and Capacity Building | 0,50 | |
| | Sershul County Health Initiative, Sichuan Province | 0,11 | |
| Total: | | | 257,75 |

(1) Pre-2002–2004 NIP (except the Programme to support China's integration into the world trading system -2002)

*3.5 SUMMARY OF PROGRESS ON AND MODIFICATIONS TO THE 2002–2004 NIP*

**CHINA NIP 2002 – 2004. COMMITMENTS AS ORIGINALLY PLANNED AND AS NOW FORESEEN**

| Projects and Programmes by sector | NIP (1) | 2002 | | 2003 | | 2004 | | NIP 2 | Comments |
|---|---|---|---|---|---|---|---|---|---|
| | **150M** (1) | (2) | (3) | (4) | (5) | (6) | (7) | (8) | |
| **Support to Social and Economic Reforms** | (75) | | | | | | | (76.2) | |
| EU-China WTO co-operation | 15 | 15 | 15 | | | | | 15 | |
| Social security reform | 20 | 20 | | | | | 20 | 20 | |
| Information society | 15 | 15 | | | | | 15 | 15 | |
| Human resources development: | 25 | | | 25 | | | | | |
| (a) Managers Exchange and Training Programme | | | | | | | 17.2 | 17.2 | |
| (b) Scholarships linked to Erasmus Mundus | | | | | | | 9 | 9 | |
| | | | | | | | | | |
| **Environment and Sustainable Development** | (45) | | | | | | | (55) | |
| Environment Programme Policy Advice | 15 | | | | | 15 | | | Programme to be integrated into the two other programmes in this sector. |
| Biodiversity protection | 15 | | | 15 | | | 30 | 30 | See comment above |
| Water Resources Conservation | 15 | | | | | 15 | 25 | 25 | See comment above |
| | | | | | | | | | |
| **Good Governance/Strengthening Rule of Law** | (30) | | | | | | | (11) | |
| Fight against illegal immigration | 10 | 10 | | | | | 1 | 1 | |

**CHINA NIP 2002 – 2004. COMMITMENTS (continued)**

| Projects and Programmes by sector | NIP (1) | 2002 | | 2003 | | 2004 | | NIP 2 | Comments |
|---|---|---|---|---|---|---|---|---|---|
| | **150M** (1) | (2) | (3) | (4) | (5) | (6) | (7) | (8) | |
| Support to civil society | 20 | | | | | 20 | 10 | 10 | |
| | | | | | | | | | |
| **Totals** | 150 | 60 | 15 | 40 | 0 | 50 | 127.2 | 142.2 | |

spalpha@TFN = (1) initial 2002–2004 NIP allocations by sector/programme
(2) amount envisaged to be committed in year 2002 as per NIP
(3) amount committed as per financing decision in year 2002
(4) amount envisaged to be committed in year 2003 as per NIP
(5) Commitment in 2003
(6) amount envisaged to be committed in year 2004 as per NIP
(7) Commitment in 2004 (forecast)
(8) Proposed revised NIP allocations by sector/programme

## *3.6 MEETING BETWEEN THE MEMBER STATES' DEVELOPMENT COUNCELLORS AND THE EUROPEAN COMMISSION*

BEIJING, 23 July 2003

Venue: Embassy of Italy, Beijing.

Participants: See Annex II.

Pasqualino Procacci (IT) opened the meeting on behalf of the Presidency.

Richard Wilkinson (China Desk, DG RELEX) explained that the main purpose of the meeting was to allow for an exchange of views between the current and future Member States' representatives in China and representatives from DG RELEX and the Delegation (DEL) on the National Indicative Programme (NIP) 2002–2004. His mission and this discussion were part of a process that had started in May 2003 with a meeting of the EU-China Economic and Trade Working Group. The review involves assessing to which extent actions and indicative allocations were to be maintained, replaced or adjusted. Following formal consultations with the EU Member States (MS), the review would be concluded by a formal decision by the European Commission later in 2003 on an adapted NIP.

Jose Bustamante (DEL) explained that the scope of the meeting was limited to actions under the NIP, but that the EU used a wider set of co-operation instruments (research, regional programmes, etc.).

Micha Ramakers (DEL) made a brief presentation about the EU approach to programming and the 2002–2006 Country Strategy Paper (CSP) and the NIP. Copies of the slides were handed out.

Uwe Wissenbach, Françoise Collet and Josef Margraf (DEL) provided updates on the current state of implementation of the NIP actions in their respective sectors (social and economic reform, environment and sustainable development, good governance and rule of law. The discussion on each section was followed by an exchange of questions and answers. A summary is contained in Annex I.

Richard Wilkinson stated that there had been some delays in implementing the NIP, so that the final period of the programme was now quite heavy. This was due to the sensitivity and the complexity of the issues covered, SARS, and other elements. It was unclear to which extent the PRC had taken on board the EU's multi-annual approach to programming (considering ad hoc "shopping lists" were still occasionally produced). There was also a need for increased inter-ministerial co-ordination.

He summarised the likely direction of the Mid-Term Review as follows:

Priority 1: maintain the indicative allocation at 75 M EUR; keep 10 M EUR from Action 4 available for development of a second project;

Priority 2: increase the indicative allocation by 10 M EUR to 55 M EUR due to greater than anticipated absorption capacity;

Priority 3: reduce the indicative allocation by 9 M EUR for Action 1 (with a follow-up action under the 2005–6 NIP) and Action 2 possibly by 10 M EUR to 10 M EUR (absorption capacity exists, but political will unclear). 19 M EUR available may in full or in part be redistributed to other Priorities.

The initial review process is to be finalised by September. MS in-country representatives may be approached by their capitals for feedback. The review will be fully completed by the end of 2003. Later this year, discussions on the 2005–6 NIP will start.

Other business It was agreed that the next meeting would focus on the legal recognition of NGOs. A speaker from Xinhua University would be invited. The meeting would take place in mid-October.

Denmark was considering making a limited amount available for the recent Red Cross flood appeal. ECHO was studying the situation. Further information would be provided when available.

The Presidency closed the meeting.

Annex I

*Overview of state of implementation NIP 2002–2004*

**Priority 1**: Support to the Social and Economic Reform Process (75 M EUR)

Action 1: EU-China WTO Co-operation 15 M EUR
A project has already been financed for this amount and an FA signed. This needs to be amended. The amendment is currently being finalised by the EC following earlier discussions with the Ministry of Commerce (MOFCOM) and could be signed by both parties in the near future.

Action 2: Information Society 15 M EUR
Progress is being made on developing a project. Initial discussions are progressing well. 15 M EUR to remain. A three-month EC appraisal mission would start in August-September. The State Council Informatisation Office (SCITO), a prospective implementation partner, is sending a mission to the EU.

Action 3: Social Security Reform 20 M EUR
Contents and logframe are being developed with the Ministry of Labour and Social Security (MOLSS). After initial difficulties, good progress is now being made. A proposal for appraisal would be submitted to EC HQ this week for feedback. A 20 M EUR commitment is envisaged for end 2003 or early 2004.

Action 4: EU-China Human Resources Development Programme 25 M EUR
A project outline has recently been discussed by the DEL. This involves a two-way exchange programme. Feedback from HQ is expected to arrive in August/September, following which more detailed discussions could start. It is possible that 15 M EUR could suffice for this project. If so, the remaining 10 M EUR could be available for another project, possibly a training/scholarships initiative linked to the new Erasmus Mundus programme. The two proposals could be completed within the present NIP.

*Discussion*

Place of the Pa-Nam project in this priority

Pa-Nam is a pre-NIP poverty alleviation project, recently extended to 2005.

*Co-ordination with other donors*

Ongoing projects often co-operate closely with those funded by other donors (e.g. Gansu Basic Education w. DIFID, Village Governance w. UNDP). As concerns project preparation, for example, on Action 1 there had been co-operation with AUSAID, Japan and others. On Action 2 with the ILO (but they had withdrawn since their focus was different). Project preparation takes into account reports, studies by other donors.

Feasibility of implementing the new scholarship programme

The reasons for cancelling Scholarship 2000 were explained (lengthy revision, RAL, etc). The new commitment could be managed in sync with Erasmus Mundus.

**Priority 2**: Environment and Sustainable Development (45 M EUR)

Action 1: Environment Programme Policy Advice
This crosscutting action is being integrated into the two other projects foreseen under this priority.

Action 2: Bio-diversity Protection
An identification/formulation mission is ongoing (to be completed within two months). The approach envisaged is multi-faceted, bottom-up and crosscutting, involving various types of projects (with a focus on local levels and western areas), local actors, and the State Environment Protection Agency (SEPA) in a co-ordinating role (not necessarily with implementation responsibility). There is major scope for co-operation with the MS, who had already been closely involved in preparations. Details on the method of implementation (calls for proposals) and co-funding arrangements (Germany) were given. An amount of 30 M EUR, rather than the initial 15 M EUR, is envisaged. A financing decision is foreseen for end 2003/early 2004.

Action 3 Water Resources Conservation
The project being prepared will focus on both the Yangtze and the Yellow rivers. The initially planned amount will most likely be increased from 15 to 25 M EUR.

*Discussion*

How many projects really follow SEPA's policy, since many other actors are involved in the sector?

This is one of the loopholes in the system, leading to parallel activities. The EU wants to take a pro-active approach in breaking through this situation with the biodiversity programme.

SEPA is not in charge of all environmental projects. How to address this?

Line agencies would maintain their current reporting lines and funds, but the purpose of the programme was to stimulate co-ordination and co-operation. There would be no flow of funds to SEPA and overlapping would be avoided.

**Priority 3**: Good Governance and strengthening the Rule of Law (30 M EUR)

Action 1: Fight against Illegal Migration (10 M EUR)
Following initially difficult discussions with the Chinese authorities, a stakeholders meeting in November 2002, and several meetings of a working group with the MS, a financing proposal has been drafted for a commitment by the end of 2003, with a reduced budget of just under 1 M EUR. A larger project is envisaged following this first phase, which will have an implementation period of 16 months starting in early 2004. An overview of activities and topics covered was provided (copy of the proposal would be distributed by e-mail). The project will involve both the central government and certain provinces.

Action 2: Support to Civil Society (20 M EUR)
A brainstorming session with the MS has taken place at a recent Round Table meeting on Human Rights. Three fields of co-operation are envisaged (capacity building, networking of NGOs, grants). Terms of Reference for an identification mission have been submitted to MOFCOM and the Ministry of Civil Affairs s(MOCA) last April, but these have not been accepted to date, despite MOCA's initially positive reaction (there have also been difficulties with MOCA concerning the EC Human Rights Small Project Facility). It is not clear if a 20 M EUR allocation can be maintained for this action and/or if another implementing partner should be identified.

*Discussion*

How does the allocation of budgets in the NIP take place? What about actions that cut across more than one priority?

The NIP is indicative. The process starts with an overall allocation for a programme of co-operation. Then sectors and ideas for action are identified. There are almost by definition issues that cut across various sectors (cf. Biodiversity: environment and good governance). All of this is indicative, and that is one of the reasons for the MTR.

Extent to which the Government is open to working with civil society. Is there opposition to doing so, and if so, where and at what level?

Recent MOFCOM meetings have for the first time included NGO representatives (AIDS, Global Funds, etc.). There have also been recent statements about the importance of NGOs for the future success of China. It was suggested that this topic should be the main focus of a future meeting.

### *3.7 MEETING WITH THE MEMBER STATES ON THE PREPARATION OF THE 2002–2004 NIP*

Meeting with the EU Member States' Development Counselors

Beijing, 27 November 2003

Participants:

Richard Wilkinson (DG Relex), Lars-Erik Larsson (DG AIDCO)

Jose Bustamante, Francoise Collet, Micha Ramakers, Sven Ernedal, Jolanda Jonkhart (DEL)

Peter Grec (Hungary), Pekka Kaihilahti (Finland), Jacob Scott (Denmark), Remi Lambert, Emmanuel Lenain (France), Sylvia Pfanner (Germany), Ales Uchytil (Czech Republic), Mark van de Vloet (Netherlands), Pasqualino Procacci, Francesca Ciccomartino (Italy).

The aim of the meeting was to brief the MS on the state of play concerning the 2005–2006 NIP preparation and to obtain their initial feedback. RW explained that the Permanent Representatives in Brussels would also be consulted and that the preparation process should be completed in the first quarter of 2004. As concerns the Mid-Term Review of the 2002-2004 NIP, which had been the subject of a meeting in June 2003, this was now being completed.

The Country Strategy Paper 2002–2006 had three focal areas (social-economic reform, environment and sustainable development, good governance and rule of law) which remained valid for the 2005–2006 NIP. Three basic criteria were underpinning the current exercise, namely (a) programming should stay within the CSP areas, (b) there should be Chinese ownership and (c) there should be a limited number of new interventions.

RW stated that it was his impression that the donor community in China was moving away from an approach based on discreet projects with limited impact towards a more strategic approach which linked aid to policy objectives and which had policy impact.

For the 2005–2006 NIP, there were a number of areas for which extensions of current actions could be envisaged. These could include an extension of the Legal and Judicial Programme with a fresh orientation, and further action on intellectual property rights. Sanitary and phyto-sanitary standards and food safety, and initiatives in the field of higher education, possibly with a focus on the Western areas were other possibilities. The latter could be framed within the context of a need for balanced regional development and could be linked to the Erasmus Mundus programme and possibly to World Bank actions in this area.

For the post-2006 period, the EC would be very keen to move away from projects altogether in favour of a broader approach linked to policy development which would minimise implementation complications and would maximise policy support. In this context, it was worth noting that during the recent EU-China Summit, it had been agreed that there would be a follow-up Seminar in February 2004 to examine both the EU and China Strategy Papers in order to explore means of moving the relationship forward. The notion of balanced regional development and EU expertise in this respect could, inter alia, be a subject for discussion in the seminar. Fiscal reform was also an issue which could become important for the post 2006 period.

RW then invited the MS representatives to share their views on the 2005–2006 programming exercise, with a view to avoiding overlap and ensuring complementarity.

The Netherlands stated that it would soon phase out its assistance to China, with only a biodiversity programme remaining. This should be linked into the current EU initiative in this field. SE confirmed that this was being discussed already.

Italy stated that it is shifting its co-operation to soft loans, for which it had recently negotiated a programme of 170 M EUR. There would be no more projects, but only programme aid on the environment, health, SMEs, vocational training and cultural heritage. 85% of IT funding went to the Western regions. The concessionality of the loans was 60% over 27 years with a five-year grace period at 0.1% interest.

IT perceived a discrepancy between Chinese and EU priorities. For example, as concerns good governance, this is a major issue for the EU but there is little Chinese willingness. IT did agree that this was a very important area. IT also asked if, for the period after 2006, there was the intention to change the modus operandi and/or the priority sectors.

RW responded that there was nonetheless a certain convergence between the Chinese and EU agendas concerning good governance, citing the human rights dialogue, the civil society identification mission and the Legal and Judicial and IPR projects as examples of areas where good progress was being made. As concerns the period 2005–6, there would be no changes to priority sectors; over the longer term the EC was contemplating a move towards a broader, more programmatic approach to co-operation than was presently the case.

NL said that, despite phasing out aid, it would also continue with a small good governance programme for NGOs in China. It considered the EU selection very relevant for China. As concerns fiscal policies, NL wanted to know if that also included the financial system, e.g.

banking and SMEs. JJ replied that the EU already had ongoing projects on financial services (banking, securities, insurance) and SME development.

HU said it had no real co-operation programme yet, but any programme that would be set up, would be closely linked to its human rights dialogue with China, particularly focusing on the judicial field. Experiences from Hungary's own transition process could be valuable to China.

FI welcomed the EU approach. Although China was not a focus country for Finnish cooperation, there was co-operation in the judicial field and on minority rights. FI welcomed continued funding for combating IPR infringements, which were a hindrance to development and innovation. It inquired about future EU action in the environmental field, and was keen to see a component developed to promote Chinese participation in the emission trade (Kyoto Protocol). SE clarified that this was part of the ongoing Energy/Environment Programme, which had various instruments and substantial funds available for the coming five years.

FR supported the EU approach, which had to continue. It fully supported the focus on the present three priorities and strongly supported the EU's orientation. Good governance and the rule of law were FRs greatest priority. It considered that the current focus of EU efforts in social and economic reform should be reconsidered in the light of SARS and HIV/AIDS. It considered that the sanitary problems in China are a global challenge related to social stability. More action was needed in this field.

FR considered that the general idea of evolving towards a valorization of EU experience in regional development could be a good axis for future co-operation and could substitute poverty reduction for a more modern approach at a higher political level.

CZ considered balanced development very important. This should include the issue of unemployment. It could also have an impact on internal and external migration.

RW emphasized that the EU policy was based on mutual interests. Balanced regional development could indeed be interesting if this meant impact at the policy level. It could include addressing fiscal reform. HIV/AIDS was an issue of debate, also within the EC. There was indeed a paragraph on this matter in the CSP, but at the same time it was not possible to become actively involved in all issues. FC clarified that the EC was already very active in this field through the Global Fund. A first Chinese proposal worth 100 M USD on AIDS treatment had just been approved and a second proposal on prevention was being considered.

FR acknowledged that the NIP had its limits, and that it should be seen in the context of the overall EU policy mix, including e.g. research funds.

IT said EU action rightly did not focus on poverty reduction and that the EU should not be afraid to said so. China has lifted 90 million people out of poverty by itself and knows how to do that successfully. This is not where EU co-operation is needed.

RW concluded by setting out the next steps of the programming process, which would include a consultation with the Chinese Government (28/11/03), internal consultations, consultations with the Member States and finally a Commission Decision within the first four months of 2004.

Micha Ramakers
10 December 2003

Note: Bilateral meetings with UK and D had been held prior to the meeting

## *3.8 CONSULTATIONS WITH THE GOVERNMENT ON THE MID-TERM REVIEW OF THE 2002–2004 NIP*

MEETING BETWEEN THE MINISTRY OF COMMERCE AND THE EUROPEAN COMMISSION
Beijing, 24th July 2003

Participants:

Mr Wang Xinggen, Deputy Director General, Mr Peng Bin, Deputy Division Director, (Ministry of Commerce – MOFCOM)

Mr Richard Wilkinson, China Co-operation Desk Officer, European Commission Directorate general for External Relations; Mr José Bustamante, First Counsellor, Mr Micha Ramakers, Second Secretary (EC Delegation).

### *1. Mid-Term Review*

The main purpose of the meeting was to discuss the Mid-Term Review (MTR) of the National Indicative Programme (NIP) 2002–2004, which is scheduled to be completed by the end of 2003. This would involve assessing to which extent actions and allocations were to be maintained as originally foreseen, replaced or adjusted. Following consultations with the EU Member States, the review would subsequently be concluded by a formal decision of the European Commission.

Each action foreseen in the NIP was reviewed as follows (the indicative figures are given):

1.1 Priority 1: Support to the Social and Economic Reform Process (€75 million)

1.1.1. Action 1: EU-China WTO Co-operation – €15 million

A project had already been financed for this amount and the Financing Agreement signed. This needed to be amended. The amendment was currently being finalised by the EC following earlier discussions with MOFCOM and could be signed by both parties in the near future.

1.1.2. Action 2: Information Society – €15 million

Progress was being made on developing a project to implement this NIP action. The allocation of €15 million should be maintained. Initial discussions were progressing well. A three-month EC appraisal mission would start in August-September. MOFCOM proposed that the project should involve both SCITO for e-government aspects and MOFCOM's Informatisation Division for e-commerce aspects.

1.1.3. Action 3: Social Security Reform – €20 million

Content and logframe were presently being developed in co-operation with MOLSS. After initial difficulties good progress was now being made. A proposal for appraisal would be submitted to EC HQ this week for feedback. A commitment for €20 million was envisaged for the end of 2003 or 2004. MOFCOM proposed the focus should be on the field level and not the central level. It was agreed that the new MOLSS training centre was not a priority for this project. The Minister of labour had written to Commissioner Patten. An EC reply confirming the above would be forthcoming. MOFCOM would be provided with a copy.

1.1.4 Action 4: EU-China Human Resources Development Programme – €25 million

A project outline had recently been discussed by the EC. This involved a two-way exchange as foreseen in the NIP and as requested by MOFCOM. Feedback from HQ was expected to arrive in August/September, following which more detailed discussion could start. It was possible that €15 million could suffice for this project. If so, the remaining €10 million could be available for another project, possibly a training/scholarship initiative linked to the new Erasmus Mundus programme. This was agreeable to MOFCOM. The two proposals could be completed within the present NIP, with the managers project to be committed by end 2003 and the Erasmus-linked project in 2004.

1.2 Priority 2: Environment and Sustainable Development

1.2.1. Action 1: Environment Programme Policy Advice

It was confirmed that there was agreement to integrate this action, which is of a cross-cutting nature, into the projects foreseen for implementing the two other actions contained in the NIP under this priority.

1.2.2. Action 2: Biodiversity Protection

An identification/formulation mission was ongoing and was to be completed within two months from now. The approach envisaged was multi-faceted, involving various types of projects (with a focus on local levels and Western areas) and involving the participation of SEPA in a co-ordinating role, but not necessarily with direct responsibility for implementation. Discussions were underway with various actors. The precise mode of implementation was still being discussed. A financing decision was foreseen for end 2003/early 2004. An amount of €30 million rather than the initially planned €15 million was now envisaged. There was general agreement on this action.

1.2.3. Action 3: Water Resources Conservation

It was agreed that the project being prepared for implementing this action would focus on both the Yangtze and Yellow rivers. The initially planned amount would most likely be increased from €15 to €25 million.

1.3 Priority 3: Good Governance and Strengthening the Rule of Law – €30 million

1.3.1. Action 1: Fight against Illegal Migration – €10 million

Since the agreement at the ETWG on a phased approach, a financing proposal had been drafted for a commitment by the end of 2003 for an amount just under €1 million. The project would have an implementation period of 16 months. This implied that any new funding for possible follow-up actions would be mobilised under the 2005–2006 NIP. It was proposed to re-allocate the remaining €9 million to Priority 2 (environment – see above). This was agreeable to MOFCOM.

1.3.2. Action 2: Support to Civil Society – €20 million

Terms of reference (ToRs) for an identification mission had been submitted to MOFCOM and MOCA last April, but these had not been accepted to date. It was agreed that MOFCOM would re-visit the ToRs for the identification mission with MOCA and that alternatives for project models would be considered. The EC announced it considered reducing the allocation foreseen by €10 million, without re-allocating the surplus amount. MOFCOM would provide feedback on possible project models during August.

1.4 Summary

The discussions concluded as follows:
Priority 1: maintain the indicative allocation at €75 million with €10 million from action 4 available for the development of a second project;
Priority 2: increase the indicative allocation by €10 million to €55 million;
Priority 3: reduce the indicative allocation by €19 million to €11million.

*2. Other Matters*

MOFCOM subsequently raised a number of general co-operation related issues, including the size of projects (considered too large), the cancellation of the Scholarships 2000 project, the implementation of current projects (too slow), and the submission of new proposals (comparison with other donors).

The EC side explained the reasons for cancelling the scholarships programme, its approach to programming, its striving for economies of scale, and project management processes. Within the general framework of the CSP there would be a consultation with MOFCOM before the end of 2003 on the type of project or programme foreseen for the future. This would focus on finding agreement on clear areas for action, on the basis of which project proposals should then be developed.

### *3.9 CONSULTATIONS WITH THE GOVERNMENT ON THE PREPARATION OF THE 2005–2006 NIP*

Meeting with the Ministry of Commerce, Department of International Trade and Economic Affairs 28/11/03

Between:

Mr Xingen Wang, Deputy Director General
Mr Zhao Zhongui, Division Director
Delegation: Mr Bustamante and Sector Heads from the Co-operation SectionDG RELEX/H/2: Mr Wilkinson (the undersigned)

I explained the objectives of the programming exercise for 2005/6, pointing out that the Commission believes that the objectives of the 2002–2006 CSP remain valid, and that planned activities for the new NIP should be consistent with those objectives. We should also take account of the need to focus on a very limited number of activities in order to maximise impact and to facilitate programme implementation.

Possibilities that had so far been identified could include an extension of the Legal and Judicial Programme, further assistance with IPR enforcement (the necessary legislation already being in place), assistance with sanitary and phytosanitary standards (SPS) and food safety in the context of trade and the environment, and possible further specific funding for China's participation in the Erasmus Mundus programme.

A further possibility for co-operation could be in the area of balanced regional development, a theme that had been taken up by President Hu and President Prodi during the previous month's Summit.

MOFCOM appreciated consultation on the NIP preparation, and attaches much importance to its co-operation with the EC, as witnessed in the government's recent policy paper on its relations with the EU. Continued support was particularly appreciated at a time when the donor community is considering reductions to its co-operation programme with China.

China suffers considerably from regional growth disparities, with poverty a major concern, not only in the western regions, but also in the north-east. For example, while efforts are being made to re-vitalise the old industrialised areas in the three north eastern provinces, unemployment remains high, and poverty persists.

While Chinese per capita income is around US$900, 28 million Chinese live in absolute poverty with incomes of less than US$80 million per year, and there could be up to 150 million living on less than $1 per day. The challenges are massive, but China is facing them, and will do so with self-reliance, though donor support is appreciated.

On the proposals for the new NIP, Mr Xingen agreed that we must be guided by the established CSP, and subscribed to the areas of co-operation suggested, in particular to SPS and human resource development. He nevertheless wished to inform the meeting that the government also has its ideas and priorities which he wished to share.

Poverty reduction remains a major priority for China, particularly in the western areas. The World Bank will be hosting a meeting on the subject in Shanghai in May 2004 to which the EC will be invited.

Environmental issues represent a growing problem for China as the economy expands. EC programmes in this area have met with success (he cited the Liaoning programme) and the government is keen that they should continue. He considered that the EC was experienced in this area and that an effort should be made to build upon the experience gained in the Chinese context.

Water supply and management programmes, and waste disposal interventions in the urban context were also called for as urbanisation expands rapidly. The whole of the northern part of the country lacks water.

Also of interest to government were the areas of HIV/AIDS, vocational training, social security in the rural context, and the problem of rural to urban migration.

On this latter point Mr Xingen stated that there are 900 million Chinese living in the rural areas, of which approximately half are labourers. But rural labour needs amount to only around 100 million workers. The remaining 350 million are in the process of, or will, migrate to urban areas in search of employment. In spite of the government's policy in respect of small town development (an area covered by a call for proposals under the small projects facility), much remained to be done.

All this being said, MOFCOM agreed for the need for a focused approach, and the need to maximise programme impact.

In response, I and the Delegation colleagues reviewed the financing that was already being provided in some of the areas raised by MOFCOM, and re-iterated the need for a rational and consolidated approach to the next programming exercise. We would remain in touch with MOFCOM on the matter.

MOFCOM closed the meeting by sharing a number of concerns (expressed on a number of previous occasions). They consider that EC-funded projects are too large, and consider that smaller interventions have more impact. Other donors projects are smaller and more manageable. Smaller projects may involve more management, but they can be managed by the Chinese, without undue reliance on technical assistance. Local staff are cheaper, and their use implies a capacity building element. TA procedures are complicated and result in excessive delays.

MOFCOM considers that the deconcentration of responsibilities to the Beijing delegation has not been only partial. Canada, DFID and AUSAID activities have been fully deconcentrated, and this has resulted in improved implementation rates. The Beijing DFID office, as an example, can take financing decisions up to £7.5 million. The government hopes that the EC performance can be improved.

On counterpart funding a discussion is ongoing with the delegation on what inputs can and cannot be considered as acceptable government contributions to programme financing.

Finally, on the matter of project preparation, MOFCOM insists that all discussions take place through its offices. The Ministry has been mandated by the State Council to manage and coordinate grant aid, and wishes to be more closely associated with preparatory work.

R.H. WILKINSON 28/11/03

## 3.10 OVERVIEW OF EXTERNAL ASSISTANCE

**OVERVIEW OF ONGOING EXTERNAL ASSISTANCE TO CHINA 2003 (1)**

| | Theme I: Improving the Business Environment and Accelerating the Transition to a Market Economy | | | | | Theme II: Addressing Needs of Poorer and Disadvantaged People and Regions | | | | | Theme III: Facilitating an Environmentally Sustainable Development Process | | | | |
|---|---|---|---|---|---|---|---|---|---|---|---|---|---|---|---|
| | Strengthening Macroeconomic Management | China's Post-WTO Integration in Global Economy | Reforming the Financial Sector | Promoting Private Sector Development and Enterprise Reform | Public Sector Governance, Urban & Utility Management | Increasing Employment and Productivity | Strenghtening Transport Links for Lagging Regions | Developing Human Resources | Strengthening Social Protection | Improving Targeted Poverty Reduction Programs | Strengthening Environmental Institutions | Improving Air Quality | Managing Water Resources | Managing Land and Natural Resources | Protecting the Global Commons |
| **Member States and EC** | | | | | | | | | | | | | | | |
| Austria | | | | | | | | | | | | | | | |
| Belgium | | | | | | | | X | | | | | | | |
| Denmark | | | | | X | | | X | | | | X | X | | |
| Finland | | | | | X | X | | | X | | | | | | |
| France | | X | | | X | X | | X | | | X | | X | | |
| Germany | X | X | X | X | X | X | X | X | X | X | X | X | X | X | X |
| Greece | | | | | | | | | | | | | | | |
| Ireland | | | | | | | | | | | | | | | |
| Italy | | | | X | | X | | X | | | X | X | X | | |
| Luxembourg | | | X | | | X | | X | | | | | | | |
| Netherlands | | | | | X | | | | | | X | X | X | X | |
| Portugal | | | | | | | | | | | | | | | |
| Spain | X | | | | X | | | X | | | | | | | |
| Sweden | | X | | | X | | | X | X | | X | X | X | X | |
| United Kingdom | X | X | | X | X | X | | X | | X | X | X | X | X | |
| EC | X | X | X | X | X | X | | X | X | X | X | X | X | X | X |
| **Other Bilateral Donors** | | | | | | | | | | | | | | | |
| Australia | | X | | X | X | X | | X | | X | X | X | X | | |
| Canada | X | X | | | X | X | X | X | | X | X | | | X | X |
| Japan | | X | | | X | X | X | X | X | | X | X | X | X | |
| Norway | | | | | | | | X | | | X | X | X | X | |
| **Multilateral Donors** | | | | | | | | | | | | | | | |
| ADB | X | X | X | X | X | X | X | X | X | X | X | X | X | X | X |
| IMF | X | X | X | | X | | | | | | | | | | |
| OECD | X | X | X | X | X | X | | X | X | | X | | | | |
| UN Agencies | X | X | | X | X | X | | X | X | X | X | X | X | X | X |
| World Bank | X | X | X | X | X | X | X | X | X | X | X | X | X | X | X |
| **Other Institutions** | | | | | | | | | | | | | | | |
| Ford Foundation | | X | | | X | X | | X | | X | | | | X | |

(1) Basic source, World Bank Country Assistance Strategy 2003-2005

## *3.11 ONGOING AND PLANNED DIALOGUES AND EXCHANGES*

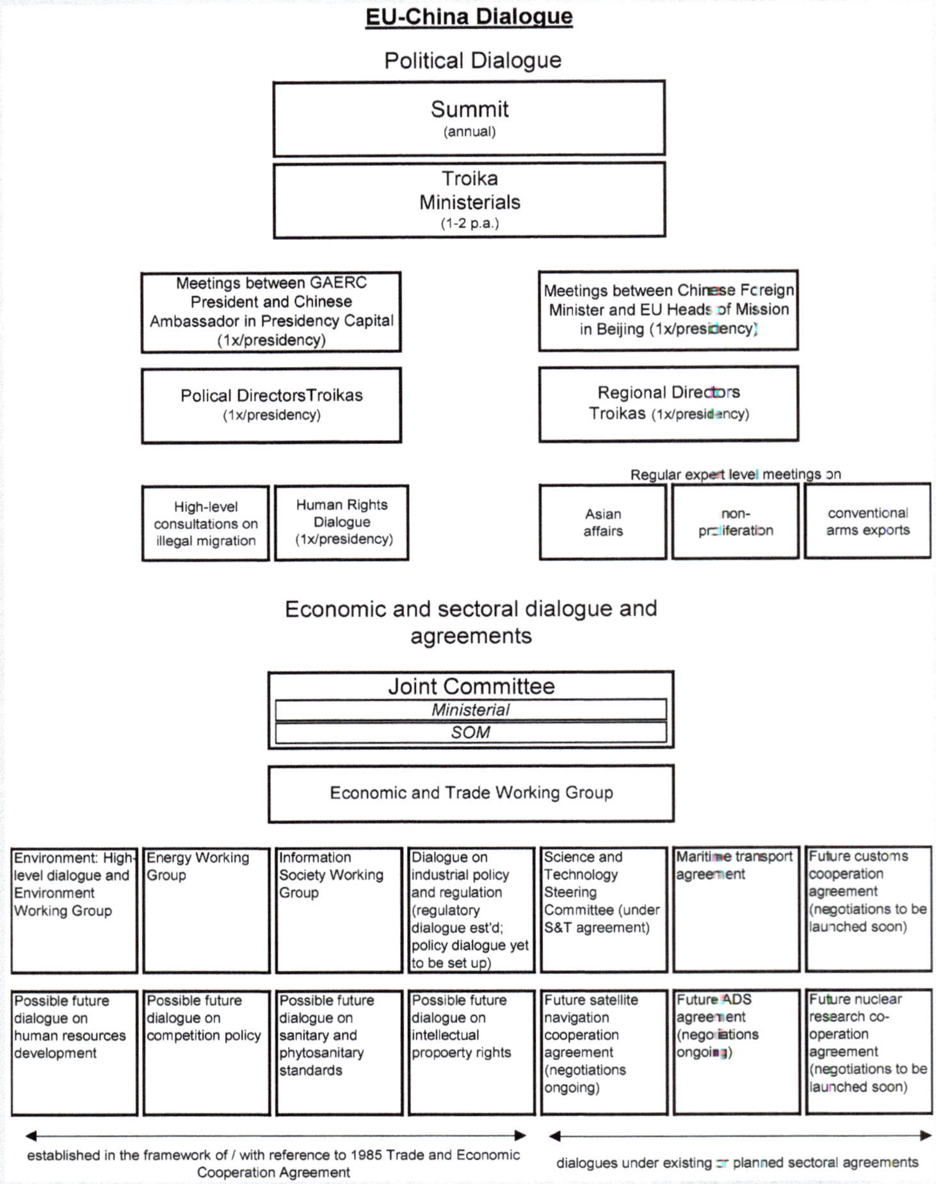

[1] 'Building a comprehensive partnership with China' , COM (1998) 181 of 25/03/98 and 'EU strategy towards China: implementation of the 1998 Communication and future steps for a more effective EU policy', COM (2001) 265 final of 15/05/01

[2] 'A maturing partnership – shared interests and challenges in EU-China relations', COM (2003) 533 of 10/09/03.

[3] Note: China also participates in Asia-wide programmes financed under the ALA Regulation. For 2005–2006 these will involve calls for proposals in the areas of trade and investment, higher education, and the environment with indicative funding of 55to 85 million. China is presently participating in approximately one third of proposals approved for financing. EU-China research co-operation under the 1999 S&T Agreement has become increasingly successful, with China participating in research projects launched since 2000 with total budgets amounting to over 94 million.

[4] Official Journal L345/1 of 13/12/03

[5] Extract from the EU-China Joint press Statement of 6th May 2004 during the visit to the Commission of Chinese Premier Wen Jibao

[6] Extract from the Executive Summary of World Bank 2001 report entitled 'China: Air, Land, and Water. Environmental priorities for a new millenium'.

## MANAGING PARTNERSHIP AND COMPETITION, 2006 AND BEYOND

In 2006, the EU–China strategic partnership entered a new phase. The EU and China relationship had become increasingly dense and complex, but at the same time the maturing of the partnership was accompanied by new tensions. A revised policy framework was required to take account of the rapid development of EU–China relations and the changing domestic, regional and international contexts for the both partners. On 8 May 2006, the European Commission's Directorate-General for Trade launched a public consultation as part of its strategic review of EU–China trade relations for the coming years (see Document 3.14). It revealed that most EU industries think that they can compete with China, but consider that they suffer a competitive disadvantage as a result of numerous barriers and obstacles. In their view, the main obstacles concern intellectual property rights, standards and certification, unfair competition, and an uncertain investment climate and bureaucracy.

### Document 3.14: European Commission, Directorate-General for Trade, 'Summary of the Results of the Public Consultation on the China Communication'

SUMMARY OF THE RESULTS OF THE PUBLIC CONSULTATION ON THE CHINA COMMUNICATION
Brussels, 7.9.2006

**1. Introduction:**

On 8 May Trade Unit G3 launched a public consultation designed to form part of its forthcoming strategic review of trade economic relations between the EU and China in the years to come. We received 102 contributions of interested parties e.g: private companies (21), NGO's (9), academics (2), regional governments (3), consultants (1), trade unions (2) business associations and industry federations(58) and citizens (6) commented, often in detail and with strong recommendations, on how they wish the Commission should react on the opportunities and challenges that one of the EU's top trading partner offers.

The consultation has given excellent results, with an important number of replies, generally of high quality. While most industries believe that they can compete with China, when China is playing by the rules, the general opinion is that they are facing an excessive number of barriers and obstacles which put them at a competitive disadvantage.

Notwithstanding all barriers and obstacles, the overall attitude vis-à-vis China is fairly positive and entails a stronger call for constructive rather than defensive measures. Almost all submissions are convinced that the EU disposes of the potential and resources to cope with the rise of China. They see China also as an opportunity, but only provided that China plays by the rules, opens her market and creates an open investment climate– which is seen as not being the case now. On the contrary, several submissions highlight the rise of Chinese economic nationalism by increasingly protecting its industrial base.

**2. Key obstacles identified:**

The most important obstacles are:

- IPR, counterfeiting and technology transfers which are by far the biggest problem;
- standards, regulations and the China Compulsory Certification (CCC):
- unfair competition (not playing by the rules);
- lack of a predictable, transparent and stable investment climate, and to much red tape is curtailed.

The number of specific issues raised in the submissions is considerable, each of them with an important impact for a given sector. Due to the export strength of China, these obstacles have a global impact on the competitiveness of EU firms.

Other issues often mentioned are: animal welfare, use of trade defence mechanism, subsidies, MES, services liberalisation, minimum standards in the field of labour and environment, non-respect for non-implementation of WTO obligations, improved cooperation and dialogue between the EU and China at all levels of bureaucracy, public procurement, technical barriers to trade, market access limitations (in particular for services), access to raw materials, collusion between the government and Chinese business, absence of rule of law and lack of transparency / due process.

Tariffs are also often mentioned (EU tariffs much lower than China's). Also references to currency issues, but generally moderate and in line with our policy (gradual move to flexible exchange rate) and the enormous untapped potential with regard to agricultural quality products from Europe.

Finally, many calls for involving business more closely in our trade related dialogues. The IPR working group is often mentioned as best practice. There are calls for an Annual Report on China Trade Barriers similar to the USTR one. Quite many industry submissions ask formally for more resources on China in particular the reinforcement of our trade section in Beijing.

A number of contributions had a much wider focus than trade policy – animal welfare in China for instance being often mentioned (6 submissions).

**3. Proposed solutions:**

The replies show a very high level of expectation that the EU can play a considerable role in redressing the situation. The tendency is in general to call for a continuation of our positive engagement vis-à-vis China and develop new initiatives, but also to have a more robust and assertive trade policy that should be based on reciprocity.

Dialogues should seek to deliver concrete results under real deadlines. China should be considered as an equal partner, i.e. no asymmetry of preferences, strict reciprocity for bilateral agreements and China should no longer be treated as a developing country. Many submissions call for the Commission to play a role going beyond trade policy: supporting operators on the ground in particular SMEs (including trade promotion), creation of an export helpdesk to China, better border controls, promoting the impetus of entrepreneurs and aid in reconversion of sectors affected by Chinese competition, disseminating information and, promoting tourism to Europe, promoting learning of China language and (business) culture and training executives. But also helping the Chinese to address internal problems (infrastructure, social policy, access to modern technology, improve quality of goods, modern management etc).

Many submissions not only point out that the traditional trade irritants should be properly addressed, but (industry in particular) also favour a stable, predictable, transparent, nondiscriminatory and rule-based environment to invest in. The EU should stimulate the Chinese authorities to establish such an environment by good governance, transparency, democracy and human rights. Furthermore the EU should extend their relations and cooperation agreements. Not only at governmental level, but also via training programmes and research and innovation schemes. This intensified cooperation could lay the foundations for good future relations at all levels. The EU itself should be able to make more use of opportunities offered by focusing more on R&D and excellence by producing goods and services with a high added value. Some submissions express the fear of an excessive reliance on China imports and the need to diversify our supplies.

**4. Positions of specific industries:**

Industries that do business with China or encounter currently the consequences of China's economic growth can be distinguished in:

Even the industries that are currently in the defensive, such as traditional industries as textiles and ceramics, and who have to cope with fierce and often unfair competition, think they can compete with their Chinese counterparts. By reshuffling their product range towards specialised products with a high added value they create the potential to enter the Chinese market. However, this market is still hardly open for their products due to often high import tariffs and the introduction of Non Trade Barriers (NTBs), amongst others expensive Chinese certification requirements. Massive counterfeiting of designs and brand names is also common practice and hampers further market access.

Although SMEs accept the consequences of globalisation, they feel less equipped to face competition, counterfeiting and difficulties in accessing the Chinese market which have a disproportionate impact on them. Faced with these unfair practices these industries deem Trade Defence Instruments (TDI) often as the only solution to protect the future of their industry, or at least ask, like the textile industry, for more specific calls to extend quotas to 2008 and beyond.

Amongst those industries that profit to a large extent from China's economic rise are: retailers, machinery, electronics, port authorities, ship owners, food and drink industries, sporting goods industries, chemical industry, digital technology industry, pharmaceutics, automotive industry and members of the European Express Association. These had or still have excellent opportunities. Nevertheless it is worth mentioning that in analysing their submissions, there is a general appreciation that the situation has recently deteriorated rather than improved, even though their exports are still increasing due to their capacity for innovation, contribution of quality products, brand potential and contributions of technology. Problems they encounter are: bureaucracy, corruption, burdensome regulations, lack of enforcement of IPR rules, use of national standards, non-respect of national treatment, the China Compulsory Certification system, no consistency in implementing Chinese regulations in different parts of the country, numerous distortions in the economy, and lack of compliance with WTO obligations.

Finally, remains a group of companies that intrinsically has the potential to enter the Chinese market but is at this stage not able to obtain a significant market share due to legal Chinese restrictions, massive piracy, discrimination between domestic and foreign goods, protectionism and GPA not being in force e.g. cultural media markets, law firms, recording industry, insurers and banks. Services will be one of the most promising sectors for the EU where EU companies have a competitive advantage and should be able to redress the growing imbalances of trade with China. Therefore, China should accept all its WTO obligations and opens its financial services sector under favourable conditions (no burdensome capital requirements) to foreign participants.

**5. Details on the most important issues raised:**

Intellectual Property Rights (IPR) is a recurrent key issue in almost all submissions and one of the main problems in trade relations with China. The EU is called upon to ensure innovation protection in China through strong enforcement of IP rules. This lack of enforcing IP rules by the Chinese authorities, at all levels, is creating widespread frustration for EU companies. EU industry insists that the Chinese government takes its responsibilities and implements IPR accordingly to its WTO commitment, adopts meaningful administrative measures, legal action and increases penalties and border controls (taking counter measures e.g. by suing infringers is currently costly and often not effective). As a consequence abuse of IPR and counterfeiting of designs and brands is massive. Protection of patents is insufficient. A submission even indicated that Chinese partners are running parallel factories and e.g. the European recording industry is exposed to the highest piracy levels in the world as; the textile industry is stripped off of their design and models.

The EU is therefore asked to take a vigorous standpoint on IPR, and deliver results on the ground.

Suggested actions are:

- putting more pressure on the Chinese (follow the US example);
- ensuring stronger presence of (a team of specialists of) the EC in Beijing to enforce IP;
- adopting a common European position on IPR vis-à-vis China;
- supporting SMEs via a European Protection Agency;
- supporting SMEs in suing Chinese offenders.

Market Economy Status (MES) Approximately 15% of the submissions mention MES. It is clear that divergent views exists between those definitively opposed to market economy status and those in favour of it. Some submissions take a relatively cautious stance and are not really outspoken. They consider that MES should only be granted when EU criteria are fully met. The distribution sector is more positive about this issue. The general tendency is not in favour of using market economy as a political tool.

On TDI as well exist divergent views between the more traditional industries, who see TDI as an important instrument as a safeguard against unfair practices of China, while others, mainly distributors / retailers ask for a review of the AD system. For them the trading environment should be predictable and not create uncertainty. Others are against misuse and support the amendments of WTO rules to ensure a more harmonised implementation of these rules.

*Services*

Business and Industry federations put in general strong emphasis on full compliance with WTO commitments, but also on the need to go beyond existing commitments. They urge the EU to persuade China to implement its WTO commitments to open wholesale services, insurance, telecom, retail sectors and banking sectors during 2006. The Doha round was hardly mentioned.

Standards, regulations are also high on the agenda. The existence of Chinese standards, which feature Chinese technology, is strongly disapproved and considered as a significant technical barrier to trade for EU companies. They are seen in a way to exclude foreign companies from participation in standardisation activities. Therefore industry puts strong emphasis on enforcement of international accepted standards. China should recognise ISO certification and abandon double testing. Furthermore, mutual recognition of testing and certification would help to achieve more transparency and a level playing-field.

The China Compulsory Certification is heavily criticised. Not only is it considered as a TBT but also as burdensome, lengthy and expensive. List of products for which CCC certificates and labels are required is often without further notice modified. An option proposed, to eliminate some of the most negative effects of the CCC scheme, could be to establish European testing laboratories which are to be accredited by Chinese authorities.

The regulatory framework/legislation is also severely criticised. In general there is no consistency in implementation of regulations in different parts of the country and procedures are considered to be too long compared to the EU. Moreover, the Chinese legislation is opaque and inconsistently enforced by a unreliable and non transparent administration. There is a lack of compliance with international standards, trade and customs regulations. EU should strive towards regulatory convergence.

Several submissions addressed public procurement as an important issue to be followed-up. China committed as part of its WTO commitments to join the General Procurement Agreement (GPA). Recently China has taken the decision to start negotiations on accession to the GPA by December 2007. Despite this announcement and the ongoing EU-China Government Procurement Dialogue there is a strong feeling that GPA accession should proceed expeditiously and that pressure needs to be maintained on China in order to ensure EU access to public procurement in China.

Priorities are given for work to de done on the new EU-China Trade and cooperation agreement that will replace the existing one of 1985. The new agreement should address: better market access, liberalisation of trade and facilitation of investment flows; trade facilitation and regulatory cooperation, IPR, sustainable trade and natural resources. clearer information on custom procedures, simplify SPS and facilitate procedures linked to certification of products.

Environmental issues such as: transparent natural resource management, are often addressed by NGOs. The EU should also take into account the impact of China on countries that provide natural resources and the industry also raises the issue of disruptive nature of the Chinese intervention on the commodity market. Sources should be used in a sustainable way in order to minimize the results of climate change. Special attention is drawn to illegal logging by China as one of the largest importers of illegal timber. The new EU-China Agreement should focus on sustainable trade, production and consumption patterns. The EU should share best practices with China in order that they catches-up quickly with Europe (by the use of environmental-friendly technologies). An important number of replies address animal welfare e.g. trade in dog and cat fur, spread of industry farming.

Labour issues and human rights are often mentioned. A decent labour-market regulation to protect workers and implement fundamental ILO rights is strongly recommended. The best way of establishing such a market is via a civil society. Further issues raised are: freedom of association, corporate social responsibility, collective bargaining, identical behaviour of EU companies in and outside the EU as well as child and forced labour. The issue of human rights is important in relation to trade and should be incorporated in that context. Low labour, environment, health and safety standards are often seen by industry as conferring unfair advantages to the Chinese (asymmetry of enforcement in China penalising foreign companies often cited). Climate change and energy issues were as well often mentioned.

An EU–China Summit was held in Helsinki in September 2006 (see Chapter 4). On the occasion of his visit to Europe, Chinese Premier Wen Jiabao made three significant speeches. On 10 September 2006, he gave a speech at the Sixth ASEM Summit on 'Deepening Asia–Europe Cooperation to Jointly Meet Challenges' (see Document 3.15). He made a number of proposals, including responding better to security threats, deepening cultural exchanges, intensifying financial cooperation, expanding cooperation on energy security, supporting the multilateral trading system, encouraging business participation and cooperation, addressing new security threats such as communicable diseases, and narrowing the rural–urban development gap in Asia, with developed countries' policy support, for example concerning agricultural trade policies.

## Document 3.15: HE Premier Wen Jiabao, Speech at the Sixth ASEM Summit, Helsinki, 10 September 2006, 'Deepening Asia–Europe Cooperation to Jointly Meet Challenges'

**Deepen Asia-Europe Cooperation to Jointly Meet Challenges**

Premier of the State Council of the People's Republic of China

The 6th ASEM Summit

Helsinki, 10 September 2006

Mr. Chairman,

This year marks the 10th anniversary of ASEM. Over the past decade, guided by the principles of mutual respect, conducting dialogue on an equal footing, making gradual progress and building consensus through consultation, Asia and Europe have carried out extensive and diversified cooperation and deepened political dialogue. We enjoy closer economic links, rapidly growing cooperation in social areas and expanding cultural and people-to-people exchanges. ASEM has become a strategic platform for Asia and Europe to strengthen coordination, further cooperation and pursue common development.

The world today is moving towards multi-polarity and economic globalization is gaining momentum, accompanied by rapid progress in science and technology and ever-closer regional cooperation. Peace, cooperation and development are the general trend of our times. On the other hand, there is growing instability and discord, as seen in mounting traditional and non-traditional security threats, unbalanced global economic development and a widening gap in wealth. Facing these new developments, people naturally place higher expectations on the ASEM summit, and it is imperative that we adopt a long-term strategy to plan our future cooperation. We should set the following goals for ASEM: Making Asia and Europe more influential in addressing major global issues through expanding dialogue and cooperation; promoting diversified development of culture and civilization through enhanced mutual political trust; furthering economic cooperation in substantive terms on the basis of equality and mutual benefit; advancing institutional building for cooperation that meet long-term needs as called for; and maintaining ASEM's openness by increasing its outreach. To consolidate and further develop the new Asia-Europe partnership in the interest of global peace and prosperity, I wish to propose the following:

1. **Enhancing political dialogue and better responding to security threats.** Safeguarding peace and security and promoting prosperity and development is the common responsibility of Asia and Europe. We ASEM members should increase consultation in multilateral mechanisms and support the leading role of the United Nations in international affairs. We should strengthen coordination on international and regional issues and intensify our effort in solving the nuclear issue on the Korean Peninsula, the Iranian nuclear issue, the Middle East crisis and other regional issues. We should also intensify cooperation in practical terms in fighting terrorism and proliferation, and combating transnational crimes in a joint effort to maintain global peace and security. China is ready to increase consultation and coordination with other ASEM members through our respective missions to the United Nations and other international agencies, and such channels as the ASEM Conference on Counter-terrorism.

2. **Deepening cultural exchanges to promote harmonious co-existence.** The ASEM Declaration on Dialogue among Cultures and Civilizations adopted at the 5th ASEM Summit is of guiding importance in promoting intercultural and interfaith dialogues. We ASEM members should respect the diversity in our cultural traditions, values and development models, conduct candid exchanges on an equal footing and make joint progress by drawing upon each other's strengths and expanding common understanding while setting aside differences. We should also expand educational and cultural interactions to build an Asia-Europe partnership of peace, amity and harmony. China calls on ASEM to give more support to the Asia-Europe Foundation so as to help it play a greater role in promoting cultural and people-to-people exchanges between Asia and Europe.

3. **Intensifying financial cooperation to promote balanced economic development.** Financial security is crucial for ensuring steady economic development in Asia and Europe. ASEM members should strengthen fiscal and financial policy coordination, promote the reform and improvement of the international financial system and give developing countries greater say in the system. We should work for the reform of the international monetary system, enhance regional monetary cooperation and improve the capacity to ward off risks. We should also work to steadily improve the investment environment and encourage two-way investment. High priority should be given to boosting cooperation in human resources development and capacity building in the financial sector, especially financial

capacity building for developing countries. China supports exploring the possibility of setting up a new financing mechanism for cooperation on the basis of the Asia-Europe Trust Fund to provide funding for future financial dialogue and capacity building.

4. **Expanding dialogue and cooperation to ensure energy security.** Energy security has become an increasingly pressing issue directly affecting global economic stability and prosperity. ASEM members should, through enhanced dialogue and cooperation, work to improve the global energy market mechanism, develop traditional energies in a rational way and vigorously develop renewable energies to ensure globalized and diversified energy supply and maintain stability in the global energy market. We should boost the research, development and application of advanced energy technologies to enhance energy conservation and energy efficiency. A proper technology transfer system should be set up to help developing countries use energy more efficiently. Moreover, we should ensure a sound political environment for energy security and stability. Geopolitical disputes should not stand in the way of global energy supply and energy issues should not be politicized. China calls on ASEM to conduct more dialogue on energy security.

5. **Supporting the multilateral trading system to achieve common development.** Maintaining order in global trade is in the interest of both Asia and Europe. A healthy and stable multilateral trading system is critical to ensuring economic prosperity of all countries, developing countries in particular. The suspension of the Doha Round is in no one's interests. Countries concerned should reflect upon their respective negotiation positions. Major developed members are urged to show their political will and demonstrate greater flexibility in cutting agricultural subsidies and tariffs in order to create conditions for the resumption of the negotiations. Asian and the European economies enjoy respective strengths and complement each other. We should deepen policy dialogue and coordination, further open market to each other, share experience of regional integration and expand intra-regional and inter-regional economic cooperation. China calls on all ASEM members to fight protectionism, properly handle trade disputes, refrain from politicizing trade issues, improve trade and investment environment, enhance economic cooperation and realize common development.

6. **Encouraging business participation and expanding channels of cooperation.** As the importance of small and medium enterprises (SMEs) in Asian and European economies is increasing, there is a growing call for more government support. We ASEM members should enhance inter-governmental cooperation and give key support to SMEs in international exchanges. We should bring into play the role of non-governmental institutions and encourage the Asia-Europe Business Forum (AEBF) to serve as a bridge for SME cooperation. We should provide better public services to SMEs and expand channels of consultation and cooperation between governments and the business community. China proposes to host the ASEM Small and Medium Enterprises Ministerial Meeting and Trade and Investment Fair in 2007.

7. **Addressing non-traditional security issues and effectively preventing and controlling avian influenza.** Communicable diseases and other non-traditional security threats greatly undermine the economic and social development of all countries. We ASEM members should take part in extensive international cooperation, promote the building of a global communicable diseases surveillance and early-warning system and further enhance the international community's capacity in early-warning and emergency response. We should also support the initiatives taken by the United Nations and the World Health Organization, strengthen policy coordination and provide greater financial and technical support for developing

countries. China proposes to host the ASEM Workshop on Avian Influenza Control next year to further promote Asia-Europe cooperation in this field.

**8. Narrowing the urban-rural gap to realize balanced economic development.** Underdevelopment in rural areas is a problem in quite a number of Asian and European countries. We ASEM members should formulate comprehensive strategies for rural development in light of our national conditions to meet targets set for the Millennium Development Goals. Developed countries should adopt measures more favorable to developing countries in agricultural trade policies. We should draw upon each other's successful experience and devise new modalities of cooperation through exchanges on food security and poverty reduction. China also proposes to host the ASEM Forum on Rural Development at an appropriate time to share experience in achieving coordinated development between urban and rural areas.

Mr. Chairman,

China attaches great importance to and has taken an active part in the process of Asia-Europe cooperation. Over the past 10 years, China has carried out many follow-up activities in counter-terrorism, the judicial sector, economy and trade, finance, science and technology, customs, environment and cultural exchanges. We have actively promoted multilateral cooperation, economic exchanges and dialogue between different cultures and civilizations. In 2008, China will host the 7th ASEM Summit, and we are ready to make greater contribution to peace, cooperation and development of Asia and Europe.

China firmly pursues an independent foreign policy of peace and strictly adheres to the purposes of the UN Charter and universally recognized norms of international relations. We are committed to pursuing peace, cooperation and development. China's development of relations with other countries is not based on consideration of ideology or social system, and differences in the modes of development do not affect our cooperation. We are guided by the principle of mutual respect and equality in developing relations with other countries, and we endeavor to develop friendly relations and cooperation with all the other countries on the basis of the Five Principles of Peaceful Co-existence.

China is committed to making the international political and economic order fairer and more equitable. We honor in good faith our international obligations and are assuming greater responsibility in the United Nations, the WTO and other multilateral institutions. China handles international issues in a responsible way. China has mediated in the Korean nuclear issue and the Iranian nuclear issue and urged the parties involved to reach peaceful solutions through negotiations. China has taken an active part in international peacekeeping operations to safeguard world and regional stability. China strictly honors its WTO commitments and observes WTO rules, and is opening its market in phases. It supports free trade based on equality and makes positive efforts to promote progress in the Doha Round multilateral trade talks. China calls for the settlement of trade disputes through consultation on an equal footing within the framework of the multilateral trading system.

China has actively participated in international cooperation against terrorism. We are opposed to associating terrorism with a particular nation or religion and are against applying double standard. We should take a comprehensive approach in fighting terrorism and address both symptom and root causes. In particular, high priority should be given to alleviating poverty and resolving regional conflicts so as to remove the causes of terrorism.

China pursues a transparent defense policy. The policy is defensive in nature, and it is aimed at safeguarding China's national security and unity. China is firmly committed to international arms control, disarmament and non-proliferation. It is a party to relevant international conventions on non-proliferation and supports their implementation. Moreover, China has put in place a comprehensive export control legal regime covering all aspects of non-proliferation and has taken effective steps to enhance law enforcement in this regard.

China is committed to meeting the UN Millennium Development Goals. While not a rich country itself, China has provided selfless assistance with no political strings attached to other developing countries. In the fight against SARS, avian influenza and natural disasters, China has participated in international cooperation in a responsible manner. And we have provided financial and technical assistance to countries struck by the Indian Ocean tsunami and the South Asian earthquake and to the international cooperation programs on combating avian influenza.

Mr. Chairman,

One thing we in China have learned from the reform and opening-up drive in the past 20 years and more is that China cannot develop itself in isolation from the world. Only by actively participating in international cooperation can China make greater progress in its development endeavor. We will continue to develop friendly relations and cooperation with our Asian and European partners and other countries in the world and work with them to build a world of harmony, durable peace and common prosperity. I look forward to seeing you again in China at the 7th ASEM Summit in 2008.

On 12 September Premier Wen Jiabao gave a speech at the 2006 China–Europe Business Summit entitled 'Enhance Cooperation to Promote Win–Win Progress' (see Document 3.16). He gave special attention to the promotion of cooperation concerning technology, energy, the environment and agriculture, and especially to the promotion of cooperation between SMEs in Europe and China.

## Document 3.16: HE Premier Wen Jiabao, Speech and the 2006 China–Europe Business Summit, 12 September 2006, 'Enhance Cooperation to Promote Win–Win Progress'

**Enhance Cooperation to Make Win-win Progress**
2006/09/12
Premier of the State Council of the People's Republic of China
2006 China-Europe Business Summit
Helsinki, 12 September 2006

Honorable Prime Minister Vanhanen,

Ladies and Gentlemen,

It gives me a great pleasure to attend the 2006 China-Europe Business Summit in the beautiful city of Helsinki. I wish to begin by thanking the organizers for their warm invitation and thoughtful arrangement. Today, about 500 Chinese and European business leaders are gathered here to discuss strategies for boosting China-EU economic and technological cooperation. This in itself testifies to the vibrant growth of China-EU Comprehensive Strategic Partnership.

I know you are all keenly interested in China's economic development and particularly, its market prospect. So I will give you a brief overview and then share with you my thoughts on what we should do to enhance our business ties.

Over the past 28 years of reform and opening-up, China's economy has grown rapidly, at an average annual rate of 9.6%. Its GDP reached US$ 2.23 trillion last year, ranking the fourth in the world. The Chinese economy continued to maintain fast yet steady growth in the first half of this year, with GDP increasing by 10.9% over the same period last year. This has led to fast expansion of China's trade, both internal and external, and brought about fundamental change in the size and structure of China's market. China's foreign trade last year amounted to US$ 1.42 trillion, making China the third largest trading nation in the world. China's market is thriving and holds tremendous potential for growth.

**China's market is increasingly open.** Opening-up is a basic policy to which China is committed. Since its WTO entry, China has honored its commitments in good faith. It has increased market openness, ended all non-tariff measures and lowered tariffs on industrial goods to 9.9%. If processing trade is included, China's average tariff level is now below 5%, even lower than that of some developed countries. In service trade, tourism, telecommunications, transportation, accounting, auditing and legal service are now open to foreign investment, and the banking sector will also be fully open by the end of this year. In Central and Western China, we have relaxed restrictions on the proportion of foreign equity and the access of foreign investment to some sectors. As a matter of fact, some sectors have been opened even earlier than required by China's WTO commitment. Of the 160-plus service sectors covered by the WTO, China has opened over 100, close to the level of developed countries.

**China's market has huge potential for growth.** To sustain economic growth by stimulating domestic demand is the long-standing strategy pursued by China. China has a population of 1.3 billion. It is in a crucial period of accelerated industrialization, urbanization and modernization. The rise of income of the urban and rural population and the change in patterns of consumption have generated a huge market demand. Housing, automobiles, electronic communication products, tourism and education are increasingly becoming priorities for urban and rural consumers. According to one estimate, by 2010, China's demand for automobiles will exceed nine million units and the number of mobile phone users will surpass 600 million.

**China's market has enhanced win-win cooperation.** China is both a major exporter and a major importer. By carrying out trade and economic cooperation with other countries, China has obtained capital, technologies and management expertise to meet its own needs and facilitated economic restructuring. Foreign investors, on their part, have also gained big profits from such cooperation. Between 1990 and 2005, foreign companies in China remitted over US$ 280 billion of profits back home. By entering the China market, EU companies have secured favorable a strategic position in global competition. China is now the biggest market for Airbus in Asia and the biggest market for Nokia mobile phones in the world. France has been in China's nuclear energy market for 20 years. Many British banks have equity in Chinese commercial banks. Last year, the sales revenue of Philips China and Siemens China accounted for 10% and 7% of their respective global sales. China-EU cooperation in science and technology, culture and tourism has also yielded fruitful results.

**China's market environment is being steadily improved.** In keeping with China's WTO commitments, we have conducted a general review and check of all foreign-related laws and regulations. The new Foreign Trade Law of the People's Republic of China has been in force for two years. Laws governing foreign investment have been brought into compliance with

WTO rules. At present, the prices of over 90% of commodities are fully determined by the market. As China's economy is increasingly becoming market-oriented, markets for the full range of production factors have taken shape, market intermediary organizations have grown, and market competition unfolds in a more orderly way. All this has provided a level playing field for both Chinese and foreign companies.

China's sustained economic growth and its growing market have both brought benefits to the Chinese people and created tremendous business opportunities for the international business community. The development of China is, therefore, an opportunity for and contribution to the world. It is not a challenge, still less a threat.

Ladies and Gentlemen,

After over 30 years of growth, China-EU relations and business relations in particular have become more mature and wider in scope. The EU is now China's largest trade partner, top technology supplier and fourth largest source of foreign investment. China is EU's second largest trade partner. China-EU trade exceeded US$ 100 billion in 2003. And in just two years, it doubled and reached US$ 217.3 billion in 2005. Between January and July this year, it rose to US$ 143.5 billion, a year-on-year increase of 21%. By the end of last June, the EU had set up over 24,000 companies in China, with a total net investment of over US$ 50 billion. China-EU business ties, being mutually beneficial in nature, have delivered real benefits to our peoples. More importantly, these ties have constituted a solid foundation of China-EU relations and greatly boosted their growth.

As China-EU business ties expand in scope and scale, differences, misunderstanding and even frictions between the two sides over some issues are hardly avoidable. To resolve these problems, we need to deepen mutual trust and understanding. Now, I wish to address several issues of concern to you.

**1. Trade imbalance.** According to EU statistics, the EU ran a deficit of US$ 131.6 billion in its trade with China in 2005. A number of factors have contributed to the deficit. Ninety-five percent of the deficit occurred in processing trade and 81% was caused by foreign invested companies in China. Global relocation of industries has led to significant change in the flow of international trade. In looking at China's surplus in its trade with the EU, to just apply the current rule of origin does not give one the complete and real picture of interests and balance in our trade. China's policy is to maintain basic balance between import and export. It does not seek excessive surplus. At present, China's overall trade surplus only accounts for 4.6% of its GDP, much lower than that of some European countries, such as Germany, Norway, the Netherlands and Ireland. China will endeavor to increase import from the EU. Meanwhile, we hope the EU will relax its restrictions on the export of high-tech and dual use products to China and work with us to bring about balance in China-EU trade.

**2. IPR protection.** IPR protection is necessary, both for China to fulfill its international obligations and to promote its development and enhance its capacity of independent innovation. China is firmly committed to IPR protection. China has adopted the Copyright Law, the Patent Law, the Trademark Law and other IPR-related laws. It is a party to major international conventions on IPR protection and has signed bilateral agreements and established dialogue mechanisms on IPR protection with EU member states and many other countries. The Chinese Government has set up a task force on IPR protection, opened 50 centers for handling IPR violation complaints across the country and strengthened government IPR protection agencies. We have stepped up law enforcement, lowered the threshold for imposing criminal penalty on IPR violations and intensified efforts to crack down on

IPR-related offences. We hope to strengthen cooperation with the EU by giving full play to the role of China-EU Dialogue Mechanism on IPR. On the other hand, we are critical of the practice of maintaining technology monopoly by abusing IPR agreements and rules. Knowledge of mankind should be used to better serve mankind.

**3. Energy consumption.** The main thrust of China's energy strategy is to rely mainly on domestic supply and lay equal emphasis on conservation and development while giving top priority to conservation. We will promote technological progress and pursue a new path of industrialization to ease shortage in energy supply. China is both a major energy consumer and a major energy producer. Since the 1990s, China has always been able to meet over 90% of its total energy needs by itself. China is rich in coal resources. Two-thirds of China's hydropower remains untapped, and the use of renewable energy such as nuclear energy, wind energy, solar energy and biogas has just started. We will work even harder to save energy. In the coming five years, China's per unit GDP energy consumption will be cut by 20%. This is no easy task, but we are confident to meet the goal. China can certainly blaze a new trail in sustainable development. Meanwhile, we are also actively seeking international cooperation to jointly safeguard global energy security.

**4. Trade frictions.** Recent years have seen some increase in China-EU trade frictions. However, China-EU trade relations as a whole remain sound. China runs both a big surplus and a big deficit in trade. To maintain a good trading environment serves the common interests of both parties in trade. Trade frictions are natural. The principle of mutual respect and consultation based on equality should be followed in addressing these problems. Each side should accommodate the concern of the other side while pursuing its own interests, and should refrain from politicizing trade issues. Through addressing textile products and other bilateral trade disputes, we have gained much experience for ensuring mutual benefit and win-win outcome. We should bear in mind the overall interests of China-EU cooperation, continue dialogue and consultation, respect and trust each other and seek common ground while shelving differences. By doing so, we can surely guide the ship of China-EU economic cooperation to cleave waves and charge ahead.

Ladies and Gentlemen,

The theme of this Summit, namely, "Boosting Innovations, the Era of EU-China Economic Cooperation" is an important one. Economically, China and the EU are highly complementary, with great potential for cooperation. We have now reached a new stage in boosting our business ties. We should expand the scope of cooperation, explore new cooperation models, raise level of cooperation and elevate our business relations to a new height. To this end, I would like to propose the following:

**1. Expanding technological cooperation in various fields.** China's modernization endeavor is driven by science and technology. We encourage both independent innovation and introduction of technology through enhanced international cooperation. Europe, which is strong in information technology, bio-medicine, machinery, automobile, electronics, chemistry and energy sector, will find ample opportunities for further development in China. China and the EU should explore new areas, projects and modalities of cooperation and carry out scientific and technological cooperation in diversified forms and at various levels.

**2. Strengthening cooperation in energy and environment protection.** China is endeavoring to build an energy-conserving and environment-friendly society. As a result, it has a growing demand for new energy and environment-friendly products. Europe leads the world in waste treatment, energy-conserving building, environmental management and renewable energy, such as wind energy, solar energy and bio energy. It is thus well positioned to establish itself on the China market. We hope to work with the EU to strengthen cooperation in energy conservation and environmental protection.

**3. Deepening cooperation in agriculture and service sector.** China is working to build a new rural area. Europe has advanced agricultural technologies and has much to offer to China in greenhouse technology and industrial management of agriculture. China and the EU can deepen cooperation in rural development, poverty alleviation, agricultural ecology, quality of agricultural products and animal health. China's service sector, which is opening wider to the outside world, has a broad prospect for development. As the EU has an advanced service sector, the two sides have great potential for cooperation in this field.

**4. Promoting cooperation between small and medium-sized enterprises (SME).** The EU is renowned as a "kingdom" of SMEs. Chinese and European SMEs are mutually complementary in capital, technology, business model and management. The Chinese Government has adopted a series of policies to support SMEs. Industrial parks for European SMEs have been opened in some Chinese cities. We encourage SMEs from both sides to make full use of the existing platform and expand cooperation in technology transfer, market sharing, processing trade and human resources.

Ladies and Gentlemen,

Both China and Europe have long history and splendid cultures, and our peoples have time-honored friendship. In the new century, our peoples can surely, through hard work and drawing on their wisdom, create a more splendid future. Let us join hands and work together to raise China-EU economic cooperation and trade to a new height!

Thank you all.

Then at the official opening of the Hamburg Summit on 13 September, Premier Wen Jiabao gave a speech on 'The Hamburg Summit: China Meets Europe' (see Document 3.17). In this speech he stressed that China was committed to pursuing peaceful development, was a responsible member of the international community, is pursuing a policy of opening up its domestic economy which would benefit its trading partners, relies mainly on domestic energy supplies and takes part in international energy cooperation on the basis of mutual benefit, places high importance and has made important progress in protecting intellectual property rights, and provides sincere assistance to developing countries.

## Document 3.17: HE Premier Wen Jiabao, Speech at the Opening of the Hamburg Summit, 13 September 2006, 'The Hamburg Summit: China Meets Europe'

**"The Hamburg Summit: China meets Europe"**
Speech at the official opening of the conference (translation)
by Wen Jiabao
Premier of the State Council of the People's Republic of China
Hamburg City Hall, 13th September 2006

Dear Mr. Ole von Beust, Mayor of Hamburg, Dear Dr. Karl-Joachim Dreyer, President of the 2nd Hamburg Summit, Dear Mr. Michael Glos, Federal Minister of Economics and Technology, Dear Chancellor Helmut Schmidt, Ladies and Gentlemen, Friends,

It gives me a great pleasure to join you at the 2nd Hamburg Summit: China meets Europe in this golden autumn. Since its inception, the Summit has played an important role in enhancing cooperation and friendship between China and the European Union. I would like to take this opportunity to express my sincere thanks to all of you who have worked over the years to advance EU's friendly cooperation with China.

China-EU relationship is stronger than ever before. We have put in place a mechanism of annual meetings between our leaders, establishing a comprehensive strategic partnership and cooperation. The EU has been China's largest trade partner for two years and China is the first non-EU country to participate at the Galileo program. They epitomize the extensive and multi-dimensional China-EU cooperation and mark a new stage of sound and stable growth of our relationship.

China-EU relations are based on a solid foundation. Politically, we share much in common as we both believe in multilateralism, pursue democracy in international relations and work for safeguard the authority of the United Nations.

Economically, China and the EU complement each other. China has maintained sustained and fast economic growth and has a huge market and abundant supply of labor. The EU is developed, advanced in technology and rich in capital resources. China and the EU both have a strong history and are endowed with splendid cultures, and we are both committed to upholding the diversity of global

civilizations. We are therefore important forces for enhancing dialogue among civilizations. Mutual interests are common need have enables us to strengthen cooperation in the pursuit of the goal of enhancing mutual political trust, economic exchange, cultural interaction and common development.

Four days ago in Helsinki, I had an in-depth exchange of views and reached broad consensus with EU leaders on strengthening China-EU comprehensive strategic partnership. The European business community has played a key role in building strong EU ties with China. If China –EU relationship is likened to a huge ship in the ocean, the business community would be its powerful engine. Let's move into high gear work as one and propel this huge ship to sail forward, braving wind and waves.

Ladies and Gentleman,

During this visit, I have been once again struck by the friendship the European people have towards Chinese people and their keen interest in China. This fills me with even greater confidence about the future of China's relations with the EU. To help you better appreciate developments in China, I would like to address several issues of common interests to you. First, China is committed to pursuing peaceful development. It has not posed , does not and will never pose any threat to other countries.

In pursuing peaceful development, China aims at only one thing, that is, to secure a peaceful international environment for its development and to promote world peace through its development. We mainly rely on our own efforts in our development endeavor. We still meet the growing material and cultural needs of the people by expanding domestic demand. China has the largest population in the world, vast land, fairly rich resources and a market with a huge potential. All this enables China to develop itself mainly through its own efforts. In the course of development, China has also met with challenges in energy, resources and environment. However, after years of hard work, we have succeeded in embarking on a path of realizing comprehensive, coordinated and suitable development, that is, to form and pursue scientific outlook on development and build a resource-conserving and environment-friendly society. At the same time, we will continue to promote economic and political reform, open wider to the outside world and remove institutional obstacles to develop and ensure steady progress in China's modernization drive.

In international affairs, China will continue to adhere to its independent foreign policy of peace, strictly observe the UN Charter and the generally recognized norms governing international relations and foster friendship with all other countries according to their ideologies and social systems. We do not seek to impose our values on others. We do not interfere in the internal affairs of other countries. We oppose hegemonism and power politics and will never seek hegemony. China's defense policy, as it's name clearly suggests, is defensive in nature. We do no engage in arms race or military expansion. Having suffered from foreign aggression and bullying, the Chinese people know only too well what it means to be subjected to aggression and oppression. That is why we are both sincere and determined in pursuing peaceful development.

Second, China is a responsible country. The Chinese people will remain trustworthy friends and reliable partners of the world people.

Being a member of the international system, China is committed to upholding and building it. China is a member of over 130 intergovernmental organizations and a party to over 300 international treaties. China firmly opposes terrorism and the proliferation of weapons of mass destruction. It takes an active part in international counter-terrorism cooperation and has developed a comprehensive legal regime for nonproliferation export control. China strives to work with all other countries to make the international political and economic order more just and equitable. It stands for peaceful resolution of international disputes through diplomacy and opposes the use or threat of force. On the Iranian nuclear issue, China is against the proliferation of nuclear weapons and calls for a negotiated solution to the dispute. On the Korean nuclear issue, China has worked hard to ensure denuclearization as well as peace and stability on the Peninsula by urging parties concerned to enter into negotiation. On the Middle East issue, China has worked with other members of the international community to bring about ceasefire between Lebanon and Israel. China calls on Palestine and Israel to settle their dispute through political negotiation in accordance with the relevant UN resolutions and the principle of "land for peace" so that Israel and Palestine and other Arab countries will live in peace at an early date. China has also taken active part in international cooperation in combating non-traditional security threats such as avian influenza and in providing relief in major natural disasters.

Third, China pursues a strategy of opening-up for mutual benefit, and its development will bring more opportunities to the world.

To open itself to the outside world is a long-term and basic state policy pursued by China. Since 1978, China's economy has maintained fast growth, contributing over 10% and 12% respectively to the growth of global economy and international trade. Since its accession to the World Trade Organization in 2001, China's annual import has averaged about US$ 500 billion, creating nearly 10 million jobs for the exporting countries and regions. China's export of inexpensive but quality goods Offers more choices and benefits to consumers in other countries and helps ease inflation pressure there. China's foreign trade volume exceeds US$ 1,4 trillion last year. China adheres to a policy of free trade and the principle of equality and mutual benefit. It does not seek trade surplus. We are ready to work together with our trading partners to address trade imbalance through development. China has consistently supported active international cooperation, trade and investment liberalization and facilitation and the removal of all trade barriers. We call on all countries to open markets, lift restrictions on technological export, boost international investment and establishing an international multilateral trading system that is open, fear reasonable, transparent and nondiscriminatory. China will continue to reform the RMB exchange rate floating flexibility on the basis of giving due consideration to the development of its economy, financial stability and the resilience of Chinese enterprises as well as the impact of such move on its neighbors, its region and the global economy and finance.

Fourth, China mainly relies on domestic supply to meet its energy need and has taken an active part in international energy development cooperation on the basis of mutual benefit.

China is a major energy consumer, but more importantly, it is a major energy producer. China is rich in coal deposit. Two thirds of its hydropower potential remains untapped, and the development of nuclear, wind and biomass power has just started. Ins hort, it has a huge potential in domestic energy supply. China's energy policy calls for integrating energy development and conservation while giving priority to energy conservation. Our goal is to build a stable, economical and clean energy supply system. In drawing up China's plan for economic development we have set a target of cutting energy consumption per unit GDP of 2005 of 20% by 2010. To safeguard global energy security, we call on the international community to develop a new energy security concept featuring mutually-beneficial cooperation, diversified development and coordinated guarantee. China will use the global energy market as necessary and strengthen cooperation with other energy producers and consumers including the European countries on the basis of equally and mutual benefit in a common effort to enhance global energy security.

Fifth, China places high importance on protecting intellectual property rights and the interests of IPR proprietors.

China is firm in its resolve to protect intellectual property rights and has made important progress in this regard. To us in China, to protect IPR is both an international obligation and a requirement for promoting China's own development and enhancing its capacity for independent innovation. To protect IPR is to respect knowledge, encourage innovation and protect productivity. We must make sure that in China, steps taken to protect IPR are as hard as steel rather than something that are soft like bean curd. We will improve mechanisms for IPR protection, strengthen law enforcement, provide both administrative and legal protection on a mutually reinforcing basis, crack down hard on IPR violation and truly protect the interests of IPR proprietors. We will intensify our outreach efforts to the public and raise their awareness of the importance of IPR protection. We will also take an active part in international exchange and cooperation and wor for more progress in the international effort of IPR protection.

Sixth, China provides sincere and selfless assistance to other developing countries and will contribute its share to realizing the UN Millennium Development Goals.

China is not an affluent country. But as permanent member of the UN Security Council and the biggest developing country, China takes it as its bounden duty to provide assistance to other developing countries to help them achieve sustainable a development. China's assistance to Africa, which is home to the largest number of developing countries, is a good example. Over the years, China has undertaken close to 900 infrastructure and social development projects in Africa and provides 18,000scholarships and sends 16,000 medical personnel to Africa. During the past three years, China has cancelled the debt incurred by 31 African countries totaling RMB 10,5 billion Yuan, extended zero-tariff treatment to 190 types of export products from 29 least developed countries to China and trained 10,000 professionals in various fields. China supports developing countries in strengthening democracy, but it never imposes its own will on others. Nor does it interfere in the internal affairs of other countries.

China's overseas assistance is provided by government and operated by companies based on market rules. We give top priority to ensuring the cost-effectiveness of preferential loans. We follow international practices and endeavor to ensure openness, fairness, effectiveness and transparency of the assistance. China's assistance is focused on social development, agriculture, medical care, education, poverty reduction and environmental protection. We put emphasis on technological cooperation and professional training to help recipient countries with streghten theis capacity for self-development. China's cooperation with other developing countries does not affect their respective cooperation with third parties and wilnot undermine the interests of any other country.

Ladies and Gentlemen, Over 300 years ago, the great German scholar Leibniz, known as the "walking encyclopedia of Europe", once commented on the exchanges between China and Europe, the two great civilizations. He observed that we need to build a bridge for the exchange of knowledge and skills between faraway nations and finally reach new harmony. Today, 300 years later, China and Europe need all the more such a bridge to jointly build an harmonious world of lasting peace and common prosperity.

In conclusion, let us join hands to usher in new phase of win-win cooperation and harmony in China-Europe relations! And I wish the Hamburg Summit full success!

Thank you all!

Between October and December 2006, with the renegotiation and replacement of the 1985 Agreement on Trade and Economic Cooperation in view, the European Commission issued a two policy papers about EU–China relations. Their respective titles revealed a good deal about their contents. First, on 24 October 2006, the European Commission issued a communication entitled 'EU–China: Closer Partners, Growing Responsibilities' (see Document 3.18). The policy paper was designed to presage the new Partnership and Cooperation Agreement to be negotiated between the EU and China. Its point of departure was: 'Europe needs to respond effectively to China's renewed strength'. This formulation in itself indicates the substantial evolution of the relationship between the EU and China since the first EU policy paper in 1995. In this new context, two pillars can be identified. First, the EU and China should work together to offer joint solutions to international problems. Secondly, if the EU is to open its markets to Chinese products, the reverse must also be true. In the words of the policy paper:

> Adjusting to the competitive challenge and driving a fair bargain with China will be the central challenge of EU trade policy in the decade to come.

## Document 3.18: Communication from the Commission to the Council and the European Parliament, 24 October 2006, 'EU–China: Closer Partners, Growing Responsibilities'

COMMUNICATION FROM THE COMMISSION TO THE COUNCIL AND THE EUROPEAN PARLIAMENT

**EU – China: Closer partners, growing responsibilities**

{COM(2006) 632 final}

### 1. What is at stake?

China has re-emerged as a major power in the last decade. It has become the world's fourth economy and third exporter, but also an increasingly important political power. China's economic growth has thrown weight behind a significantly more active and sophisticated Chinese foreign policy. China's desire to grow and seek a place in the world commensurate with its political and economic power is a central tenet of its policy. Given China's size and phenomenal growth, these changes have a profound impact on global politics and trade.

The EU offers the largest market in the world. It is home to a global reserve currency. It enjoys world leadership in key technologies and skills. The EU plays a central role in finding sustainable solutions to today's challenges, on the environment, on energy, on globalisation. It has proved capable of exerting a progressive influence well beyond its borders and is the world's largest provider of development aid.

Europe needs to respond effectively to China's renewed strength. To tackle the key challenges facing Europe today – including climate change, employment, migration, security – we need to leverage the potential of a dynamic relationship with China based on our values. We also have an interest in supporting China's reform process. This means factoring the China dimension into the full range of EU policies, external and internal. It also means close coordination inside the EU to ensure an overall and coherent approach.

To better reflect the importance of their relations, the EU and China agreed a strategic partnership in 2003. Some differences remain, but are being managed effectively, and relations are increasingly mature and realistic. At the same time China is, with the EU, closely bound to the globalisation process and becoming more integrated into the international system.

The EU's fundamental approach to China must remain one of engagement and partnership. But with a closer strategic partnership, mutual responsibilities increase. The partnership should meet both sides' interests and the EU and China need to work together as they assume more active and responsible international roles, supporting and contributing to a strong and effective multilateral system. The goal should be a situation where China and the EU can bring their respective strengths to bear to offer joint solutions to global problems.

Both the EU and China stand to gain from our trade and economic partnership. If we are to recognise its full potential, closing Europe's doors to Chinese competition is not the answer. But to build and maintain political support for openness towards China, the benefits of engagement must be fully realised in Europe. China should open its own markets and ensure conditions of fair market competition. Adjusting to the competitive challenge and driving a fair bargain with China will be the central challenge of EU trade policy in the decade to come. This key bilateral challenge provides a litmus test for our partnership, and is set out in more detail in a trade policy paper entitled "Competition and Partnership" which accompanies the present Communication.

Europe and China can do more to promote their own interests together than they will ever achieve apart.

**2. Context: China's revival**

Internal stability remains the key driver for Chinese policy. Over recent decades, stability has been underpinned by delivery of strong economic growth. Since 1980 China has enjoyed 9% annual average growth and has seen its share of world GDP expand tenfold to reach 5% of global GDP. China's growth has resulted in the steepest recorded drop in poverty in world history, and the emergence of a large middle class, better educated and with rising purchasing power and choices.

But the story of this phenomenal growth masks uncertainties and fragility. The Chinese leadership treads a complex daily path, facing a range of important challenges, primarily domestic, but which increasingly resonate beyond national boundaries:

- Disparities continue to grow. The wealth gap is significant and growing, as are social, regional and gender imbalances; there is huge stress on healthcare and education systems; and China is already facing significant demographic shifts and the challenges of a rapidly ageing population;
- China's demand for energy and raw materials – China is already the world's second largest energy consumer – is already significant and will continue to grow; and the environmental cost of untrammelled economic and industrial growth is becoming more and more apparent. At the same time growth patterns have not been balanced, with a focus on exports to the detriment of domestic demand.

Growth remains central to China's reform agenda, but increasingly is tempered with measures to address social inequality and ensure more sustainable economic and political development. Paradoxically, in a number of areas, the conditions for stability improve as the Party and State relax control. A more independent judiciary, a stronger civil society, a freer press will ultimately encourage stability, providing necessary checks and balances. Recognition of the need for more balanced development, building a "harmonious society", is encouraging. But further reform will be necessary.

China's regional and international policy also supports domestic imperatives: a secure and peaceful neighbourhood is one conducive to economic growth; and China's wider international engagement remains characterised by pursuit of very specific objectives, including securing the natural resources needed to power growth. At the same time we have seen China's desire to build international respect and recognition. The 2008 Olympic Games in Beijing and the 2010 World Expo in Shanghai will focus the world's attention on China's progress.

China has traditionally described its foreign policy as one of strict non-interference, but as it takes on a more active and assertive international role, this becomes increasingly untenable. The Chinese government is beginning to recognise this, and the international responsibilities commensurate to its economic importance and role as a permanent member of the UN Security Council as illustrated by its increasingly active diplomatic commitments.

The EU and China benefit from globalisation and share common interests in its success. It presents challenges to both and brings further responsibilities. We also share a desire to see an effective multilateral system. But there remain divergences in values, on which dialogue must continue.

As the partnership strengthens, expectations and responsibilities on both sides increase. As China's biggest trading partner, EU trade policy has an important impact on China, as do China's policies on the EU. Increasingly, both sides expect that impact to be taken into account in their partner's policy formulation.

**3. The way forward**

The EU should continue support for China's internal political and economic reform process, for a strong and stable China which fully respects fundamental rights and freedoms, protects minorities and guarantees the rule of law. The EU will reinforce co-operation to ensure sustainable development, pursue a fair and robust trade policy and work to strengthen and add balance to bilateral relations. The EU and China should work together in support of peace and stability. The EU should increase co-ordination and joint action and improve co-operation with European industry and civil society.

Until now the legal basis for relations has been the 1985 Trade and Co-operation Agreement. This no longer reflects the breadth and scope of the relationship and at the 9$^{th}$ EU-China Summit leaders agreed to launch negotiations on a new, extended Partnership and Cooperation Agreement (PCA) to update the basis for our co-operation. This new agreement presents an important opportunity. It will provide a single framework covering the full range and complexity of our relationship, and at the same time should be forward-looking and reflect the priorities outlined in this Communication.

*3.1. Supporting China's transition towards a more open and plural society*

The Chinese leadership has repeatedly stated its support for reform, including on basic rights and freedoms. But in this area progress on the ground has been limited. The EU must consider how it can most effectively assist China's reform process, making the case that better protection of human rights, a more open society, and more accountable government would be beneficial to China, and essential for continued economic growth.

Democracy, human rights and the promotion of common values remain fundamental tenets of EU policy and of central importance to bilateral relations. The EU should support and encourage the development of a full, healthy and independent civil society in China. It should support efforts to strengthen the rule of law – an essential basis for all other reform.

At the same time, the EU will continue to encourage full respect of fundamental rights and freedoms in all regions of China; freedom of speech, religion and association, the right to a fair trial and the protection of minorities call for particular attention – in all regions of China. The EU will also encourage China to be an active and constructive partner in the Human Rights Council, holding China to the values which the UN embraces, including the International Covenant on Civil and Political Rights.

The twice-yearly human rights dialogue was conceived at an earlier stage in EU-China relations. It remains fit for purpose, but the EU's expectations – which have increased in line with the quality of our partnership – are increasingly not being met. The dialogue should be:

- more focussed and results-oriented, with higher quality exchanges and concrete results;
- more flexible, taking on input from separate seminars and sub-groups;
- better co-ordinated with Member State dialogues.

*3.2. Sustainable development*

One of today's key global challenges is to ensure our development is sustainable. China will be central to meeting this challenge. China's domestic reform policy is important and the Commission will continue to support this through its co-operation programme, including corporate social responsibility. On issues such as energy, the environment and climate change, respect for international social standards, development assistance, as well as wider macroeconomic issues, the EU and China should ensure close international co-operation. Both sides should:

**Ensure secure and sustainable energy supplies**. As important players in world energy markets, the EU and China share a common interest and responsibility in ensuring the security and sustainability of energy supplies, improving efficiency and mitigating the environmental impact of energy production and consumption. The EU's priority should be to ensure China's integration into world energy markets and multilateral governance mechanisms and institutions, and to encourage China to become an active and responsible energy partner. On that basis both sides should work together to:

- increase international co-operation, in particular efforts to improve transparency and reliability of energy data and the exchange of information aimed at improving energy security in developing countries, including Africa;
- strengthen China's technical and regulatory expertise, reducing growth in energy demand, increasing energy efficiency and use of clean renewable energy such as wind, biomass and bio fuels, promoting energy standards and savings through the development and deployment of near zero emission coal technology;
- commit to enhance stability through a market-based approach to investment and procurement; dialogue with other major consumers; encouragement of transparent and non-discriminatory regulatory frameworks, including open and effective energy market access; and by promoting the adoption of internationally recognised norms and standards.

**Combat climate change and improve the environment**. We already have a good basis for co-operation on environment issues and on climate change through the Partnership established at the 2005 EU-China Summit.

- The EU should share regulatory expertise, working with China to prevent pollution, safeguard biodiversity, make the use of energy, water and raw materials more efficient, and improve transparency and the enforcement of environmental legislation. Both sides should work together to tackle deforestation and illegal logging, sustainable management of fisheries resources and maritime governance;
- Both sides should build on the Climate Change Partnership, reinforcing bilateral cooperation, and strengthening international co-operation, meeting shared international responsibilities under the Climate Change Convention and Kyoto Protocol and engage actively in the dialogues on international climate change co-operation post-2012. We should strengthen the use of emissions trading and clean development mechanisms.

**Improve exchanges on employment and social issues**. China is committed to tackle social disparities and promote more balanced development. The EU and China should:

- intensify co-operation on employment and social issues reinforcing and expanding bilateral dialogue to include issues such as health and safety at work, decent work standards, and meeting the challenges of an ageing population;
- work together to ensure that international commitments on labour and social issues are upheld.

**Improve co-ordination on international development.** Closer co-operation on international development issues would benefit the EU, China and partners in the developing world. There are significant downsides if we are not able to co-ordinate effectively, particularly in Africa but also in other developing countries. The EU and China should:

- engage in a structured dialogue on Africa's sustainable development. There should be transparency on the activity and priorities of both sides, providing a basis for full discussion;
- support regional efforts to improve governance in Africa;
- explore opportunities for improving China's integration into international efforts to improve aid efficiency, co-ordination and opportunities for practical bilateral co-operation on the ground.

**Build sustainable economic growth.** China has become a source growth for the EU and the world, but China's current growth model is also the source of important imbalances in EU-China trade. The Chinese government has recognised the importance of meeting macro economic challenges, of forward-looking fiscal, monetary and structural policies, boosting consumption and reducing inequalities. Increasing exchange rate flexibility will be an important factor, helping rebalance growth towards domestic demand and increasing Chinese households' purchasing power. Policies which would lead to a reduction of its current account surplus would increase China's control of its economy and contain risks of overheating, and at the same time meet China's shared responsibility to ensure a stable and balanced world economy.

As key economic powers, the EU and China should further develop their partnership and work together to tackle global economic issues; they should:

- deepen co-operation and share experience in formulating and implementing monetary, fiscal, financial, exchange rate and structural policies;
- co-operate towards the orderly unwinding of global imbalances;
- strengthen and upgrade their macro-economic dialogue.

*3.3. Trade and economic relations*

China's integration into the global trading system has benefited both Europe and China. The EU is China's largest trading partner, representing more than 19% of China's external trade. European companies trading with and investing in China have contributed to China's growth, bringing capital goods, knowledge and technology that have been instrumental to China's development.

An economically strong China is in Europe's interest. China, especially its rapidly increasing middle class, is a growing market for EU exports. EU exports to China increased by over 100% between 2000 and 2005, much faster than its exports to the rest of the world. EU exports of services to China expanded six-fold in the ten years to 2004. European companies and consumers benefit from competitively priced Chinese inputs and consumer goods. Openness brings benefits to both China and the EU.

Nevertheless, in Europe there is a growing perception that China's as yet incomplete implementation of WTO obligations and new barriers to market access are preventing a genuinely reciprocal trading relationship. Imports from China have added to pressure to adjust to globalisation in Europe. This trend is likely to continue as China moves up the value chain.

For the relationship to be politically and economically sustainable in the long term, Europe should continue to offer open and fair access to China's exports and to adjust to the competitive challenge. The EU needs to develop and consolidate areas of comparative advantage in high-value and high-tech design and production and to help workers retrain. China for its part should reciprocate by strengthening its commitment to open markets and fair competition. Both sides should address concern over the impact of economic growth on natural resources and the environment. The EU will:

**Insist on openness**. The EU will continue working with China towards the full implementation of its WTO obligations and. will urge China to move beyond its WTO commitments in further opening its market to create opportunities for EU companies. The EU will accept that it cannot demand openness from China from behind barriers of its own. The EU will urge China to honour its commitment to open accession negotiations on the Government Procurement Agreement in 2008 and work to bring them to a successful conclusion as rapidly as possible.

**Level the playing field**. Better protection of intellectual property rights in China and ending forced technology transfers are EU priorities, including through implementation by China of WTO obligations and will help create a better investment climate in China. The EU will press China to stop granting prohibited subsidies and reform its banking system, and encourage China to allow market forces to operate in its trade in raw materials.

**Support European companies**. The Commission will make a major effort to assist companies doing business with China, in particular small and medium sized enterprises while urging them to respect decent work standards. The EU will extend and strengthen the existing information, training and advice on protecting and defending IPR in China. A European Centre in Beijing should be opened. The EU-China Managers Exchange and Training Programme should be extended.

**Defend the EU's interests: dialogue first**. The EU has a clear preference for resolving trade irritants with China through dialogue and negotiation. The existing EU-China trade related dialogues should be strengthened at all levels, their focus should be sharpened on facilitating trade and improving market access and their scope extended. The EU and China also have an interest in joining their efforts in international rule making and global standard setting bodies. The EU will actively pursue global supervisory and regulatory solutions, promoting open markets and regulatory convergence, and build on co-operation with China through EU-China regulatory dialogues. This will also help to ensure compliance of Chinese imports with EU standards for food and non-food products.

But where other efforts have failed, the Commission will use the WTO dispute settlement system to ensure compliance with multilaterally agreed rules and obligations. Trade defence measures will remain an instrument to ensure fair conditions of trade. The EU is actively working with China with a view to creating the conditions which would permit early granting of MES. Recent progress has been made on some of the conditions. The Commission will continue to work with the Chinese authorities through the mechanisms we have established and will be ready to act quickly once all the conditions are met.

**Build a stronger relationship**. A key objective of the negotiations for a new Partnership and Cooperation Agreement, which will also update the 1985 Trade and Co-operation Agreement, will be better access to the Chinese market for European exporters and investors, going beyond WTO commitments, better protection of intellectual property and mutual recognition of geographical indications. China is already a major beneficiary of the international trading system and should assume a responsibility commensurate with those benefits, making a substantial contribution to reviving and completing the WTO Doha Round.

Many of these steps are not only in EU's interest. They are strongly in China's interest and an integral part of China's progress towards balanced and sustainable growth and development and global leadership and responsibility. The accompanying trade policy paper sets out a comprehensive approach to EU-China trade and investment relations for the medium term.

*3.4. Strengthening bilateral co-operation*

Bilateral co-operation spans a wide range of issues, including 7 formal Agreements, 22 sectoral dialogues, covering diverse and important issues from aviation and maritime transport to regional and macro-economic policy. Further development of the structured dialogue to exchange experiences and views on competition matters, as well as technical and capacity-building assistance as regards competition enforcement, remains important. Cooperation has been successful and positive. But more must be done to focus co-operation and ensure balance and mutual benefit, in all areas, but particularly on flagship areas such as science and technology co-operation. More should be done to strengthen co-operation on migration issues, people-to-people links, and the structures governing our official relations. Both sides should:

**Ensure quality and increased co-operation in science and technology**. Science and technology co-operation is a priority area for the Chinese government. China spends 1.5% of its GDP on a dynamic and growing research and development programme. Bilateral cooperation is also strong: China is one of the most important third countries participating in more EU research projects under the 6$^{th}$ Research Framework Programme, giving it access to 600 million euros of research, and China is an important partner on key projects such as ITER and Galileo. EU participation in Chinese programmes should be increased.

The Joint Declaration from the Science and Technology Forum in May 2005 set the context for taking co-operation forward, based on mutual benefit and reciprocal access and participation. Both sides should:

- consolidate and improve the visibility of co-operation. This will allow both sides to focus and set priorities effectively and to respond to dynamic issues such as emerging pandemics
- or work on clean energy technologies; make it easier to examine scope for increased reciprocity; and provide a basis for more effective co-ordination with Member States;
- improve joint planning to ensure mutual benefit, and increase flexibility to fund the participation of European researchers in Chinese research programmes. Both sides should facilitate researchers' mobility which in the case of the EU is promoted through specific grants under the Framework Programme.

**Build an effective migration relationship**. Chinese and other migrants enrich the EU culturally and bring with them important skills and expertise. But there is a significant downside if the process is not managed effectively. There has to be an effective legal framework to facilitate people-to-people exchanges. But we need effective mechanisms to deal with those who abuse the system, with a focus on prevention and return. Both sides should work towards the early conclusion of an effective Readmission Agreement.

- The existing consultation mechanism should continue and be extended to cover both legal and illegal migration, and with renewed political commitment to make progress;

- Both sides should agree and push forward specific co-operation projects on e.g. the exchange of officials and training; and there should be exchanges on biometric technology;
- There should be a dedicated dialogue with the Ministry of Public Security covering migration and the fight against organised crime, terrorism and corruption;
- The EU-China Tourism Agreement (ADS) will need continued proactive and practical cooperation to ensure it functions effectively.

**Expand people-to-people links**. We should strengthen the full range of people-to-people links which underpin our relations through significant and sustained action on both sides, from cultural exchanges and tourism to civil society and academic links.

- Civil society and institutional links should provide direct support and impetus for political and trade relations. Both sides should facilitate direct links between civil society groups in the EU and China in all areas, and include them in sectoral dialogues where possible. Official non-governmental links should be strengthened and expanded. The European Parliament plays a central role and should expand co-operation with the Chinese National People's Congress. The EU should also strengthen links between ECOSOC and the Chinese Economic and Social Committee, political parties, and between other semi-official bodies.
- Education has been an area of particular success, with 170 000 Chinese students studying in the EU in 2005. We should continue to build on existing co-operation through programmes run by individual Member States and through the China-specific strand of the Erasmus Mundus programme. There have been positive examples of work to set up joint degree courses and joint campuses. We should also implement specific projects such as a European Law School. Both sides will continue to encourage EU students to study in China. To strengthen language capability, the Commission will support a specific programme to train Chinese language teachers to teach in Europe.
- Academic expertise in the EU on China needs to be improved and co-ordinated more effectively. Action is needed by both sides to support effective interaction between European and Chinese academia. The Commission should continue to support an academic network on China, drawing together academic expertise to inform EU policy and coordinating information-sharing within the academic community; and there should be a small number of prestigious professorships on Chinese studies created and made available to European universities. There should be a permanent regular dialogue between European and Chinese think tanks.

**Make bilateral structures more effective**. Both sides should reflect on the structures which govern relations and consider whether they should be streamlined, improved or upgraded. The Commission's 2003 Policy Paper sought to expand sectoral dialogue between the EU and China. This has been very successful, and the majority function well and make an important contribution to our partnership. But progress should be reviewed. Both sides should also consider whether there are new bodies or mechanisms which would further contribute to EU-China relations.

- Annual Summits provide a good framework for maintaining contacts at head of government level. This should be supported by regular cross-cutting exchange and dialogue at technical, ministerial and more senior level. In addition, both sides should explore further options for flexible and informal opportunities to meet and exchange views;

- The recently agreed strategic dialogue at Vice Foreign Minister level should be a key mechanism covering regional and geo-political issues and adding focus, impact and value to the relationship;
- Both sides should undertake a thorough examination of the rationale, interrelationship and performance of the sectoral dialogues with the aim of maximising synergies and ensuring mutual benefit, and ensure interested stakeholders are involved where possible. The Commission will produce a series of Working Documents on specific sectoral challenges;
- A new independent EU-China Forum should be set up. On the EU side it should be at arms length from the institutions and should draw on civil society, academic, business and cultural expertise, providing policy input to political leaders and impetus to bilateral relations.

The EU should ensure that it speaks with one voice on the panoply of issues related to its relations with China. Given the complexity of the relationship and the importance of continuity, regular, systematic and cross-cutting internal co-ordination will be essential.

The EU's co-operation programme, delivered through the country strategy paper (CSP) and national indicative programmes, should continue to play a role in supporting the partnership between the two sides and China's reform process. But as China moves further away from the status of a typical recipient of overseas development aid, the EU must calibrate its cooperation programme carefully and keep it under review. Co-operation must be in both sides' interests, reflect the EU's own principles and values, and serve to underpin the partnership.

*3.5. International and regional co-operation*

The EU and China have an interest in promoting peace and security through a reformed and effective multilateral system. They should co-operate closely in the framework of the UN, working to find multilateral solutions to emerging crises, and to combat terrorism and increase regional co-operation, including through involvement by both in emerging regional structures. This common interest, in strong multilateralism, peace and security should also be reflected in closer co-operation and more structured dialogue on the Middle East, Africa and East Asia, and on cross-cutting challenges such as non-proliferation.

**East Asia**. It is clear the EU has a significant interest in the strategic security situation in East Asia. It should build on the increasing effectiveness of its foreign and security policy and its strategic interest in the region by drawing up public guidelines for its policy.

China has a key role to play in the region and has been working to improve relations with its neighbours, including Russia and India, and with central Asia through the Shanghai Cooperation Organisation. But there remains scope for improvement in Sino-Japanese relations. The EU has an interest in strong relations between the region's major players and in continued regional integration.

**Taiwan**. The EU has a significant stake in the maintenance of cross-straits peace and stability. On the basis of its One China Policy, and taking account of the strategic balance in the region, the EU should continue to take an active interest, and to make its views known to both sides. Policy should take account of the EU's:

- opposition to any measure which would amount to a unilateral change of the status quo;
- strong opposition to the use of force;
- encouragement for pragmatic solutions and confidence building measures;

- support for dialogue between all parties; and,
- continuing strong economic and trade links with Taiwan.

**Transparency on Chinese military expenditure and objectives**. There is increasing concern caused by the opacity of China's defence expenditure. As expenditure continues to increase, China needs to be convinced of the importance of improving transparency. At the same time, the EU should improve its analytical capacity on China's military development.

**Arms embargo**. The arms embargo was put in place as a result of events in Tiananmen Square in 1989. The EU has agreed to continue to work towards embargo lift, but further work will be necessary by both sides:

- Current and incoming Presidencies should finalise technical preparations to ensure lift would not lead to a qualitative or quantitative increase in arms sales, and continue to explore possibilities for building a consensus for lift. The EU should work with China to improve the atmosphere for lift, making progress on China's human rights situation; working to improve cross-straits relations; and by improving the transparency of its military expenditure.

**Non-proliferation**. Non-proliferation represents a key area for the strategic partnership. International and bilateral co-operation is based on UNSCR 1540 and the Joint Declaration on Non-Proliferation agreed at the 2004 EU-China Summit. The EU is supportive of China's central role in work on the Korean peninsula and continued Chinese support will be crucial to progress on the Iranian nuclear issue. There has been a good start on dialogue and practical co-operation to strengthen and enforce export controls. The EU should build on this, working with Chinese officials to encourage China to:

- comply with all non-proliferation and disarmament treaties and international instruments, and to promote compliance with them regionally and internationally;
- strengthen export controls of WMD-related materials, equipment and technologies as well as of conventional weapons and small arms and light weapons.

Both sides should work together to share practical experience in implementing and enforcing export controls, including through training for Chinese customs officials. They should consider scope for joint EU/Asia initiatives in the context of the ASEAN Regional Forum.

## 4. Conclusion

China is one the EU's most important partners. China's re-emergence is a welcome phenomenon. But to respond positively and effectively, the EU must improve policy coordination at all levels, and ensure a focussed single European voice on key issues.

We have a strong and growing bilateral relationship. But we must continue build on this. The recommendations in this Communication, which the Council is invited to endorse and complement through Council Conclusions, represent a challenging agenda for the EU to do so, and the Partnership and Co-operation Agreement provides an important practical mechanism to move this agenda forward.

A closer, stronger strategic partnership is in the EU's and China's interests. But with this comes an increase in responsibilities, and a need for openness which will require concerted action by both sides.

On the same day, the European Commission published a companion policy paper, focused specifically on trade and investment (see Document 3.19). Essentially conceived as an EU response to China's revival, it reviewed the EU–China trade relationship, in which the EU was China's largest export market and China was the EU's largest source of imports. Though both parties had gained, competition from China was a severe challenge to a number of EU manufacturing sectors. The EU answer was to insist on market opening on both sides. This was to be the basis of the EU approach in the negotiations for a new Partnership and Cooperation Agreement, including but going beyond the 1985 Agreement on Trade and Economic Cooperation.

## Document 3.19: European Commission Working Document, Policy Paper, 24 October 2006, 'EU–China Trade and Investment: Competition and Partnership'

COMMISSION WORKING DOCUMENT
**Accompanying COM(2006) 631 final: Closer Partners, Growing Responsibilities**
**A policy paper on EU-China trade and investment:**
**Competition and Partnership**
COM(2006) 631 final

**Executive summary**

China is the single most important challenge for EU trade policy. EU-China trade has increased dramatically in the past few years, doubling between 2000 and 2005. Europe is China's largest export market; China is Europe's largest source of imports. This trade policy paper addresses the economic and competitive challenges that flow from this change and the responses the EU should adopt in the area of trade and investment. It is part of the broader partnership with China and the approach set out by the Commission in its Communication on relations with China: "*Closer Partners, Growing Responsibilities*".

The EU's open market has been a large contributor to China's export-led growth. The EU has also benefited from the growth of the Chinese market: EU exports to China have more than doubled in the past five years. Competitively priced Chinese products have helped keep inflation and interest rates in Europe lower. European companies have gained from their investments in China. But competition from China has raised serious challenges for Europe in some important manufacturing sectors.

If we strike the right balance, there is ample scope for a continued mutually beneficial trade partnership between Europe and China. Political leaders on both sides should continue to argue for open economic engagement. Europe should continue to offer open and fair access to China's exports and to adjust to the competitive challenge, while pursuing policies to support those bearing the burden of economic adjustment at home. China itself should reciprocate by strengthening its commitment to economic openness and market reform. It should strengthen legal protection for foreign companies and the enforcement of this protection and reject anti-competitive trading practices and policies.

In pursuing this relationship the European Commission will strongly defend openness in European trade with China. But it will also seek to ensure that China meets its WTO obligations and continues to liberalise access to its goods, services, investment and public procurement markets. It will seek the end of forced technology transfers for European investors and imposed export requirements. The EU will seek tougher protection of the legal rights of EU companies, especially in the area of intellectual property and urge China to end the unfair subsidisation or protection of strategic industries. It will seek to ensure that these issues are taken forward within the overall process of dialogue and co-operation between Europe and China and are clearly and comprehensively covered in the new Partnership and Cooperation Agreement including the updating of the 1985 Trade and Co-operation Agreement. To assist European businesses in China, the Commission will oversee the establishment of new commercial resources in China and Europe to support European business and promote language learning.

## 1. CHINA'S ECONOMIC REVIVAL

### China's economic return

Two hundred years ago, China was the largest economy in the world. But, by 1978, its share of global GDP had fallen to 0.5%. Since then, China's policy of reform and economic openness has unlocked unprecedented levels of growth and development. Reforms increased the role of the private sector, channelled high levels of savings into investment, increased the level of education, favoured a move away from agriculture into manufacturing and unlocked the potential of China's large pool of 700 million workers. Since 1980 China has enjoyed annual average growth of 9% and has seen its share of world GDP expand tenfold to reach 5% of global GDP.

### The benefits of growth

China's growth has resulted in the steepest recorded drop in poverty in world history. Per capita income has doubled; doubled and then doubled again reaching a fifth of current EU level in purchasing power parity. China reduced by 170 million the number of people living on a dollar per day between 1990 and 2000. At the same time, a large middle class with rising purchasing power has emerged.

### A new trading power

The progressive integration of China into the international trading system – spurred by its membership of the WTO in 2001 – has provided China with secure, open and predictable export markets. China has become the world's third largest exporter. Its total external trade is now more than three times the combined trade of India and Brazil. Exports represent more than one third of China's economy. However, the majority of China's exports focus on processed goods with limited added value.

### A major recipient of foreign investment

China is one of the world's largest recipients of foreign direct investment (FDI) and operates incentives for foreign investment. In 2005, foreign invested companies accounted for more than half of total Chinese exports.

### A stable, growing China is in Europe's interest

Europe has a critical interest in China's transition to a stable, prosperous and open economy. It recognises that the openness of the EU market to Chinese exports will be a key factor in China's further development. But Europe also stands to benefit from China's growing market for advanced technology, high-value goods and complex services. European consumers will continue to benefit from competitively priced imports from China. The macro-economic benefits of China's export strength for European competitiveness and growth are significant. These gains outweigh the losses suffered in particular areas.

The only sustainable approach for Europe is to welcome China's growth and seek to benefit from it through open trade. To build and maintain political support in Europe for this policy and the adjustment it requires, the benefits of openness and change must be fully realised. This means China must show that it is committed to embracing globalisation as a two way street. China should use its growing influence to champion open markets and fair competition.

The challenges of sustainable growth

Moreover, despite its economic success, China faces serious challenges. Its competitiveness as an exporter cannot hide the structural problems it faces. Rapid growth has been accompanied by environmental costs, social inequalities and human health challenges. For growth to continue, China will need to maintain the momentum of domestic reform and rebalance its pattern of growth away from the export sector and towards domestic demand. China should continue its efforts to develop a more sustainable approach to the exploitation of natural resources. In these areas Europe should offer recognition of the challenges and support for reform in China to balance legitimate demands on China's behaviour towards its trading partners and the international system.

## 2. THE EU-CHINA TRADE AND ECONOMIC RELATIONSHIP

### *2.1. The benefits of openness*

Mutual benefits

China's integration into the global trading and investment system has been beneficial for both Europe and for China. The EU represents more than 19% of China's external trade. European companies trading in China have brought capital goods, knowledge and technology that have helped China develop its productive capacity. Reciprocally, trade with China helps to promote growth and jobs in Europe through increasing exports, continuing specialisation in high-value products and services and strengthening the global competitiveness of EU companies.

EU exports

EU exports to China increased by more than 100% between 2000 and 2005, much faster than its exports in the rest of the world. In the services sector EU exports to China expanded six fold in the period 1994-2004, based particularly on its strengths in the financial, construction, distribution and educational services sectors.

EU investments in China

Investments in China have allowed EU firms to remain competitive by gaining access to lower-cost inputs. A significant part of the value added of products "made in China" accrues to European companies. It has also helped European business maintain jobs and viable economic activities in the EU such as research, design, marketing, global management and complex manufacturing. Some investments in China have allowed EU firms to gain market share in the China market and supported our exports.

Chinese investments in Europe

China's direct investment abroad remains modest but is increasing rapidly. Total Chinese foreign investment in 2004 was 3billion with a strong emphasis on securing access to natural resources. Europe only receives a fraction (2%) of this. However, as this investment increases with Chinese commercial expansion beyond its domestic market, European companies will benefit from selling their experience and knowledge in distribution, sales and logistics networks.

The price effect

Competitively priced imports from China have resulted in lower input prices for EU businesses and lower prices for manufactured products in Europe which have generally translated into lower prices for consumers. The total effect on inflation was estimated by the OECD to be -0.2% for the euro zone for the period 2001-2005. This in turn has helped keep low global interest rates. Savings generated as a result of cheaper goods and inputs have been invested in other parts of the European economy.

***BOX 1: Opportunities for EU businesses to compete in China***

*The evolution of EU-China trade reflects the evolution in overall EU trade with emerging economies. While the latter, and China in particular, are making significant gains in some segments of high technology products (such as laptop computers, mobile phones and DVD players), the EU is strengthening its specialisation in high-quality products in preference to low- and middle-quality goods.*

*Commission studies indicate that the expansion of the Chinese market will continue to bring important benefits to EU operators. Although Chinese companies will become competitive in more market segments (for example in basic chemicals or some types of vehicles), other segments will expand rapidly (for example, specialty chemicals, demand for capital-intensive car components) offering new opportunities to EU operators.*

*The EU is particularly strong in exports of machinery and vehicles which account for two thirds of all EU's goods exports and one third of all Chinese imports of machinery. EU exports to China of chemicals have doubled in the last five years, making China the EU's second export market. The EU market share in China in 2005 was 16% – similar to that in Japan and ASEAN countries but lower than its market share in the USA (20%), India (21%) or in Brazil (31%). There is potential to increase EU market share in line with EU performance in other markets. As China develops, its demand for high-end branded European consumer products will increase.*

*In order to succeed, EU operators will need to develop a more thorough knowledge of the Chinese market and play on their comparative advantage. Europe's chief assets in its trade relationship with China are innovation, specialisation, quality, related services and brand identity. High unit labour costs are not necessarily an impediment to export success: the strongest performing European exporters to China have some of the highest labour costs in Europe.*

*2.2. The impact of competition*

Adjustment in Europe

Competitively priced imports from China have added to the pressure on the European economy to adjust to new sources of global competition, in particular in traditional low value-added manufacturing. Chinese products compete with EU products not just at home but in emerging markets in Asia, Africa and Latin America. This competition is an inevitable and important spur to European competitiveness. In particular, Europe needs to develop and consolidate areas of comparative advantage in high value and high-tech design and production, foster innovation and help workers adjust and retrain. This makes it all the more urgent to make further progress on the Lisbon reform agenda and to pursue the right competitiveness and adjustment policies at home.

Delocalisation

Delocalisation to China has had a negative impact on certain sectors and regions. This remains, however, a limited phenomenon. Current EU investment in China represents a fraction of total EU foreign investments (only 1% of total EU outflows, excluding indirect investment). The total stock of EU direct investments in China represents 5.5% of overall foreign investment in China.

The technological challenge

China's research efforts are developing rapidly and China has the potential to move up the value chain into traditional areas of EU expertise. However, China has yet to develop a coherent policy on innovation, and is hampered in its efforts by its inadequate protection of intellectual property. While China has become the world's first exporter of information technology products, a large proportion of these exports come from foreign companies established in China that import research-intensive, high value-added components. Europe cannot, however, afford to be complacent.

The trade deficit

Europe runs a steep trade deficit with China: in 2005, Chinese exports to the EU reached 158billion and EU exports to China 52billion, resulting in a trade deficit of 106billion. However, approaching the EU-China trade deficit in isolation is misleading. Asia's share of EU imports has remained relatively stable at 20-25% over the last decade. The trade deficit with China hides to some extent the fact that its exports have partly replaced exports from other Asian countries.

While the Chinese competitive challenge needs to be put clearly in perspective, it is unquestionably real and has important consequences for companies and individual workers in Europe. This is why securing reciprocal free and fair market in access in China is crucial. Here, a range of obstacles to market access and skewed conditions of competition need urgent attention.

*2.3. Obstacles to market access*

While Chinese tariffs have gone down significantly as a result of China's WTO accession, EU exports still face a number of tariff and non-tariff barriers to trade and restrictions on investment in manufacturing and in services. There is a growing perception that incomplete implementation of WTO obligations and barriers to market access are preventing a genuinely reciprocal trading relationship between Europe and China.

Tariffs

In the course of WTO accession China's tariffs were reduced to an average of 8.8% for non-agricultural products. However, China has maintained a number of tariff peaks in some industries of particular importance for the EU such as textiles and clothing, leather and fur, footwear, ceramics, steel and vehicles.

Non-tariff barriers

European exporters and investors are facing an increasing number of unjustifiable non-tariff barriers in the form of product certification, labelling standards, import approval requirements and customs clearance delays. The application of laws is often not uniform and regional variations in customs procedures have a negative impact on trade. Unreasonable sanitary and health requirements can create barriers that hamper exports to China, in particular for agricultural products. Chinese national standards often differ significantly from international standards. This results in high compliance costs and extended delays for business which impact on their ability to sell on the China market, affecting in particular EU small and medium-sized enterprises.

Government procurement

China committed itself to opening its procurement market and acceding to the multilateral Government Procurement Agreement as soon as possible after its accession to the WTO. China has now committed to start accession negotiations in 2008. However, many procurement markets remain closed to European businesses. In some sectors, technology transfers have been made a condition for foreign companies to participate in international bids.

New policies discriminating foreign operators

In key sectors such as automobiles, steel, semiconductors or shipbuilding, new policies are emerging which appear to be based on a 'China first approach' contrary to the non-discriminatory principles of the WTO. In a number of industries China has been imposing local content requirements, either through direct legislation or investment authorisation, limiting EU exports and unfairly aiding local industry. There is a growing risk that competition policy will be used against foreign operators and that the lack of independence or transparency of many regulators results in decisions favouring Chinese operators.

Investment restrictions

In the manufacturing and services sectors European investors are still prevented from setting up wholly owned foreign enterprises and are required to establish joint ventures with Chinese partners. In the telecoms and financial services sector, EU firms have been unable to expand significantly because of high capital requirements and complex approval procedures. In the manufacturing sector, China continues to maintain investment restrictions on some key industries for Europe such as automobiles, petrochemicals or steel.

*2.4. Conditions of competition*

EU companies often find themselves competing on unfair terms in China. The absence of conditions of fair market competition and inadequate legal protection pose serious problems. China's policies on the environment, social standards, currency valuation and natural resources can distort trade.

Intellectual property and legal rights, forced technology transfers

The adequate protection of intellectual property rights such as patents, copyrights and trademarks is central to the exercise of Europe's comparative advantage in innovation, design and high-value production. Insufficient protection of intellectual property represents a pressing challenge for EU businesses in China. China is by far the largest source of counterfeit and pirated products seized at the EU's borders. While China has made welcome progress in setting up an intellectual property regime, loopholes remain and effective implementation and enforcement of laws remains uneven or lacking. EU companies also face an opaque and burdensome legal and judicial system that offers insufficient guarantees of legal protection of the rights of EU companies.

Subsidies

China has channelled significant subsidies to favoured national industries, in particular companies destined to become national or regional champions. These companies have also benefited from preferential policies such as privileged access to the banking sector. In some cases, such as the automotive and steel sectors, whole sectors benefit from an integrated industrial policy intended to support domestic production and boost exports. China has also developed a taxation system granting tax preferences contingent on the use of local content or export performance.

Flexible Exchange Rate

China's exports to the EU have also benefited from the currency alignment of the Chinese renminbi to the dollar, which has given them an important competitive advantage. China is now moving towards increased flexibility in its currency regime, which should help shift the balance to higher levels of domestic consumption.

Excessive saving depresses demand for imports

Demand for EU products in China is also suppressed by low domestic demand resulting from high savings as a result of limited public provision of health and social security services. Enterprises' savings are also very large and account for about half of China's savings. This both suppresses domestic demand, including for EU goods and services and ensures that the bulk of domestic production is exported.

Environment, social and safety conditions

China's regulatory regime for the protection of the environment remains incomplete and implementation on the ground inadequate or discriminatory in favour of local producers. This is contributing to the rapid deterioration of China's environment. China has also maintained restrictions on investment or imports of certain environmentally friendly products and services. China has yet to ratify, transpose and implement into domestic legislation four of the eight core ILO conventions relating to freedom of association, collective bargaining and forced labour and other important conventions on labour inspection, health and safety at work and social protection. Chinese companies also often fail to meet reasonable safety standards for their products; half of the alerts in Europe for dangerous non-food products are for products manufactured in China. The lower environmental, social and safety standards applied in China confer a competitive advantage to production in China.

Distorting the market for global trade in natural resources

China's race for natural resources abroad has become a major phenomenon. China is now the second biggest fuel importer globally: this is a clear indication that global competition for resources is set to increase. China's export performance also relies on imports of resources from many developing countries. In some cases, China is subsidising the import of raw materials conferring advantages to its industry. At the same time, China limits exports of certain domestically abundant natural resources such as coal, coke, rare earth, hides and silk, which can distort availability and price of raw materials in world markets.

## 3. THE EU'S RESPONSE AND PRIORITIES FOR ACTION

### *3.1. Insisting on openness*

Europe should pursue a fair and robust trade policy on China. It should insist that openness benefits both Europe and China, and that an economically strong China is in Europe's interests. It cannot call for openness from China from behind walls of its own.

Enforcing China's WTO obligations

The EU continues to monitor closely China's implementation of its WTO accession obligations. Substantial work remains to be done by China. This will remain a central priority for the EU in the years to come. The non-accession to the WTO Government Procurement Agreement leaves important Chinese markets closed and China should honour its commitment to open accession negotiations in 2008 and to work to bring these to a rapid conclusion. In 2007, the Commission will undertake a comprehensive review of market openness in China and China's implementation of its WTO commitments. It will strengthen its links with EU business to help identify key areas of concern.

Liberalising beyond WTO obligations

The EU will continue to urge China to move beyond its WTO commitments in improving market access for EU companies. The EU market is one of the most open markets in the world and will continue to pursue further opening of the Chinese market to create reciprocal opportunities for EU and Chinese operators. The EU will work with Chinese authorities at all levels to achieve this goal. In 2007 the EU will also reshape its overall market access strategy. It will increase cooperation with Member States to improve EU exports to China.

### *3.2. Levelling the playing field*

The EU will continue to press China to improve its record in protecting the rights of EU companies through a transparent legal and judicial system where the regulators are fully independent.

Combating forced technology transfers, piracy and counterfeiting

Following a global enforcement survey this year, China is now the EU's first priority for intellectual property enforcement worldwide. China should implement its WTO commitments both in law and on the ground and impose effective deterrents against counterfeiting and piracy. The EU will create a set of concrete benchmarks against which to measure China's progress. The EU will work with China on the creation of a special risk assessment system for customs controls to fight counterfeiting more effectively and set up contacts between EU and Chinese ports and airports. The EU will address as a priority requirements for technology transfer that are not based on voluntary business decisions and the non-payment of royalties to EU right-holders. The EU will launch a substantial programme in China to improve IPR implementation and to curb the production and trade in China of counterfeit and pirated goods and their export to Europe. The EU will cooperate more closely with key international partners in joint efforts in this field.

Subsidies, banking reform and trade restrictions on raw materials and energy goods

The Commission will press China for improved transparency in its subsidy regimes and will insist that China abide by its WTO commitment to end the granting of prohibited subsidies. The Chinese banking system should be reformed to work on a commercial basis, and soft loans and other forms of unviable lending should be discontinued. The Commission will urge China to allow market forces to operate in its trade in raw materials and energy goods such as coal, coke and rare earths.

*3.3. Supporting European companies*

The Commission will take action to assist EU companies on the ground, in particular small and medium-sized enterprises. In doing so, the Commission should complement rather than duplicate initiatives taken by Member States or private operators.

Protecting European IPR

Working through existing structures, such as the IPR helpdesk and the network of European Information Centres, the EU will extend and strengthen the existing intellectual property rights helpdesk to provide training and advice on protecting and defending European intellectual property rights in China. The EU will also work to develop private-public partnerships with EU industry federations and others to improve the protection of IPR in China.

Supporting EU businesses in China

The Commission will seek partners to establish a European Centre in Beijing to provide support for companies wishing to start exporting or investing in China. Preparatory work should start in 2006 to analyse the feasibility and possible structures for such support.

Language training

In July 2006 the Commission launched the EU-China Executive Managers Exchange and Training Programme which will provide the opportunity for 200 European managers to learn Chinese in the next five years. The Commission will press for this programme to be extended beyond 2010.

Strengthening the Commission on the ground

The Commission will further strengthen the focus on trade activity of the Commission Delegation in Beijing. It will seek to reinforce its activity in Shanghai and Guangzhou in order to be closer to Chinese authorities and EU business in key commercial centres.

*3.4. Defending the EU's interests: dialogue first*

WTO dispute settlement

Where trade irritants arise between China and the EU, the EU will always seek to resolve them through dialogue and negotiation. However, where this fails, the Commission will use the WTO dispute settlement system to resolve trade issues with China and to ensure compliance with multilaterally agreed rules and obligations. This is not a question of replacing cooperation with confrontation but of creating a sound relationship based on objective application of agreed multilateral rules.

Using anti-dumping and anti-subsidy instruments

Trade defence measures will remain an instrument to ensure fair conditions of trade between China and the EU, as with other countries. The EU will use these instruments carefully but rigorously where they are justified. At present, the conditions for granting Market Economy Status (MES) to China for anti-dumping investigations are not fulfilled. The EU is actively working with China with a view to creating the conditions permitting an early granting of MES. Recent progress has been made on some of the conditions. The Commission will continue to work with the Chinese authorities through the mechanisms we have established and will be ready to act quickly once all the conditions are met. An improving bilateral trade relationship should help create the environment in which this happens. China's policy of reform will be instrumental in fulfilling the technical criteria for granting MES.

***BOX 2: The role of dialogue***

*In recent years the European Commission has established a number of important economic dialogues with China that have trade implications. The Commission, the European Parliament and the Economic and Social Committee have been at the forefront of this activity.*

*These dialogues cover issues such as intellectual property, market access, macroeconomic and financial sector issues, agriculture, competition, regulatory and industrial policy, and general product and food safety. The EU has also concluded sectoral agreements with China such as the Customs Cooperation Agreement which provides for reinforced EU China cooperation on IPR controls and supply chain security.*

*These dialogues help promote regulatory cooperation and convergence and are important in managing an increasingly complex relationship. They can also play a crucial role in preventing difficulties before they become trade disputes. The Commission will maintain the focus on trade and economic issues. Some areas where further dialogue is important include: decent work, sustainable trade, China's policy on raw materials and energy, illegal logging, China's need to improve environmental protection and statistics.*

*When it is useful and appropriate, EU and Chinese business, trade unions, NGOs and other stakeholders should be involved in technical and high-level meetings. European companies should play an active role in implementing the decent work agenda and improving social and environmental standards by adopting European norms, eco-technologies and standards of corporate social responsibility in their operations in China.*

*The cooperation programmes which support these dialogues should be continued. The EU China Trade Programme which supports capacity building in China on trade policy issues with 15million for the period 2004-2009 should be renewed after 2009. Its scope should be extended beyond the Central Government to include local and regional government.*

*3.5. Building a stronger global relationship*

The EU's partnership with China should be used to draw the two economies closer together and to engage China on global issues.

Concluding a new EU-China bilateral agreement

At the heart of that partnership will be the new Partnership and Cooperation Agreement (PCA) with China. This Agreement will include a specific focus on trade and investment issues. A key objective of the PCA will be building on China's WTO commitments to remove restrictions on investment and foreign ownership in China, obtain better protection of intellectual property and negotiate mutual recognition of geographical indications. The EU will also seek to address with greater intensity sustainability and environmental aspects and impacts of its economic and trade relations with China and enhance cooperation on safety and health standards.

Increasing China's engagement with the multilateral system

China is already a major beneficiary of the international trading system and would stand to gain even more from a successful conclusion of the negotiations under the WTO Doha Development Agenda, particularly in the area of trade in industrial goods. But for the negotiations to succeed, greater leadership from China is necessary. The EU calls on China to assume a responsibility commensurate with the benefits it derives from the multilateral trading system and to make a substantial contribution to reviving and completing the WTO Doha round. China should take the lead in offering better access to its own markets, including for key developing country imports like textiles and manufacturing inputs. The EU and China should strengthen their cooperation in the WTO and in other multilateral rule-making organisations.

Addressing macroeconomic challenges

A major issue for the stability of the world economy is to ensure an orderly correction of the large current account imbalances of the major economic zones. The US current account deficit reached the unprecedented level of 6.4% of GDP in 2005, while current account surpluses have continued to widen in the Middle-East oil-exporting countries and in Asia. China's current account surplus reached 7.2% of GDP in 2005. The EU, drawing on our own experience, will, in the appropriate fora, continue to encourage China to implement fiscal, monetary and structural policies that would rebalance its growth pattern and ensure long-term sustainable growth.

**Conclusion**

China's re-emergence will continue to have a major impact on every part of the global economy. It will be felt in people's daily lives, from the cost of petrol to the price we pay for our clothes. It entails major challenges for global sustainable development. Adjusting to the competitive challenge and driving a fair bargain with China will be a central political and economic challenge of EU trade policy in the decade to come. Europe and China will be increasingly compelled to cooperate on global issues as responsible trade and economic global leaders.

China's WTO accession in 2001 has provided it with extensive and stable access to foreign markets, notably in Europe. However, European companies, while gaining from China's growth, continue to face serious barriers to access China's market. There is a growing risk that the EU-China trading relationship will not be seen as genuinely reciprocal. Political pressure in the EU to resist further openness to Chinese competition is likely to increase if these problems are not addressed, as we are already seeing in the United States.

European trade policy towards China will seek to promote openness and cooperation to mutual benefit, taking into account the significant domestic challenges China faces. Europe seeks reciprocity from China in a trade partnership of equals. It should be accompanied by strong policies to assist those bearing the burden of economic adjustment in Europe. Europe should accept fierce competition. China should ensure that it is fair competition.

The two October 2006 policy papers were part of the preparation for the renegotiation of the main bilateral legal framework of EU–China relations. Shortly thereafter, the European Commission released a detailed study of 'Future Challenges and Opportunities in EU–China Trade and Investment Relations'.[6] It was commissioned by the European Commission's Directorate General on Trade in March 2006. Based on desk research, field studies and interviews, the study analysed specific industrial and services sectors in China, showing how EU business could benefit from trade in the future and making specific recommendations for EU policy in each sector. It concluded that European businesses could benefit from trade with China if Chinese trade barriers were removed, thus complementing the Commission's two 2006 policy papers.

These documents also formed part of a more general review of EC trade policy instruments. In December 2006 the European Commission issued a communication on 'Global Europe: Europe's Trade Defence Instruments in a Changing Global Economy' (see Document 3.20). 'Global Europe' took the form of a Green Paper for public consultation. Leaving aside tariffs and quotas, the traditional legal means by which countries may protect their domestic industries against imports from other countries are antidumping law, protection against subsidies and the use of safeguards, all of which are part of WTO law and of EC law. Globalisation, direct foreign investment and the development of international production networks render these commercial defence measures in some respects out-of-date, because they 'challenge familiar understandings of what constitutes EU production and the EU's economic interests'. The Green Paper asked for public reaction on six themes: the role of trade policy instruments in a global economy; the weighting of different EU interests in trade defence investigations; the launch and conduct of trade defence investigations; the form, timing and duration of trade defence measures; the transparency of investigations; and the institutional structure of investigations. It is designed to enable the EU

6 This document, despite its interest, is not included here because it is a consultancy report and because of its length and detail. It is available at http://ec.europa.eu/trade/issues/bilateral/countries/china/legis/index_en.htm (accessed 15 February 2007).

to carry out policy reforms in a constructive, pragmatic way, attentive to the different EU interests increasingly in conflict in trade disputes. Changing relations between the EU and China are a significant part of the context of these reflections. The outcome of this discussion is likely to have a major effect on EU–China relations.

## Document 3.20: European Commission, Communication on 'Global Europe: Europe's Trade Defence Instruments in a Changing Global Economy

COMMUNICATION FROM THE COMMISSION

**GLOBAL EUROPE**

**Europe's trade defence instruments in a changing global economy**

**A Green Paper for public consultation**

COM(2006) 763 final

### Introduction

The European Union, like most other importing economies, operates a system of trade defence instruments. These instruments – Anti-Dumping, Anti-Subsidy and Safeguard measures – allow the European Union to defend its producers against unfairly traded or subsidised imports and against dramatic shifts in trade flows in so far as these are harmful to the EU economy. It is important that we use these instruments effectively and rigorously to ensure respect of international trade rules and protect European interests against unfair trade.

The EU's use of these instruments is based on rules derived from the WTO agreements that establish trade defence instruments and the principles on which they operate as a legitimate part of the multilateral system of free trade. Like the urgent work to suppress counterfeiting and intellectual property theft, including through the abuse of electronic communications, defending against unfair trade is a politically and economically crucial part of defending free trade. It allows us to support the interests of European workers and European competitiveness, and is therefore an important part of helping Europe manage the consequences of globalisation.

The economic rationale for Anti-Dumping and Anti-Subsidy trade defence measures essentially follows from the fact that the international economy has no mechanism for correcting anti-competitive practice similar to the competition authorities that operate in almost all national economies. Furthermore, very few jurisdictions have formal rules or institutions for subsidy control similar to the European Union's state aid rules. Trade defence instruments have developed in international law as a means of correcting the trade distorting effects of uncompetitive practice at the international level.

European trade defence action over the last decade has eliminated the trade distorting effects of dumping in important sectors such as steel, chemicals and microprocessors that threatened the continued viability of these industries and their thousands of workers in Europe.

The EU has gone further than any other WTO member in unilaterally building on WTO rules to tighten conditions for use and focus the impact of trade defence action in its own market. The EU has produced a system of trade defence instruments that is arguably more open and more balanced than any other WTO member. The EU has also led the debate on reforming WTO rules on trade defence, which has been an integral part of the Doha Round.

The faithful application of those internationally agreed rules by all members of the WTO is crucial for the functioning of the international trading system. This insistence that all must adhere to the agreed rules in this field must remain a guiding objective for our policy in future.

Nevertheless, in the decade since the 1994 Agreement on Anti-Dumping and the last major reform of EU trade defence instruments, there have been far-reaching changes in the global economy and in the structure of the EU economy. These have been an important factor in the overall priorities of this Commission in promoting a new growth and competitiveness agenda. These priorities are set out in the Commission's contribution to the Hampton Court European Council: *European values in a globalised world.*

Many more EU companies now produce goods outside the EU for import into the EU, or operate supply chains that stretch beyond the EU market. These changes challenge familiar understandings of what constitutes EU production and the EU's economic interests. Because it is precisely these things that trade defence instruments are intended to defend, a periodic review can help us to ensure that the EU's trade defence instruments remain an effective response to unfair trading practices. This may also help to maintain strong political support behind the use of these necessary instruments across the EU.

The Commission has recently highlighted a new policy agenda designed to reinforce the EU's capacity to compete in a global economy marked by the growing fragmentation and complexity of the process of production and supply chains and the growth of major new economic actors, particularly in Asia (*Global Europe: Competing in the World*). This reflection on the EU's trade defence instruments is an integral part of that agenda. The Green Paper does not question the fundamental value of trade defence instruments, but invites a public reflection on how the EU can continue to use them to best effect in the European interest.

The Green Paper draws on the European Commission's experience of managing the use of trade defence instruments as well as on the results of a recent evaluation study of them. It also reflects informal contacts with EU Member States and the European Parliament and a series of papers submitted to EU Trade Commissioner Peter Mandelson by experts in the field of trade defence instruments in July 2006[1].

The paper groups the issues into six themes;

(1) the role of trade defence instruments in a changing global economy;

(2) the weighting of different EU interests in trade defence investigations;

(3) the launch and conduct of trade defence investigations;

(4) the form, timing and duration of trade defence measures;

(5) the transparency of trade defence investigations and;

(6) the institutional structure of trade defence investigations.

For each group of issues it raises a series of questions to which participants to the consultation are invited to respond.

**Box 1: Europe's trade defence instruments Anti-Dumping.**

Anti-Dumping rules are the European Union's most used form of trade defence instrument. Anti-Dumping measures address the import of goods to the European Union at less than their normal value in their home market – usually as a result of the lack of competition and/or state interference in the production process that allows an exporter to artificially lower the cost of an export. Dumping harms both EU producers but also other producers in third countries that compete for access to the EU market. Typical examples of distortions leading to dumping include: significant tariff and non-tariff barriers, insufficient enforcement of competition rules, export tax breaks; artificially low raw material and/or energy prices. Where an EU investigation shows that these imports are harming EU producers Anti-Dumping rules allow for remedial measures to correct the injury. Normally this is the imposition of a duty on the dumped import.

**Anti-Subsidy.** Anti-subsidy measures are similar to Anti-Dumping measures except they specifically correct the trade-distorting effect of WTO-actionable subsidies to foreign producers, where these subsidies can be shown to be harming EU producers.

**Safeguards.** Safeguard measures are different in that they do not focus on whether trade is fair or not, but on shifts in the volume of trade that are so swift and on such a scale that EU producers cannot reasonably be expected to adapt to changed trade flows. In these circumstances, WTO and EU rules allow for short-term restrictions on imports to give industry temporary relief in order to adapt to this sudden surge. This temporary breathing space goes hand in hand with the clear obligation to restructure.

Between January 1996 and December 2005, the EU imposed 194 definitive Anti-Dumping measures. The countries most frequently found to be involved in dumping were China (38 measures) and India (16 measures) during this period. As of 31 October 2006, the EU has 12 Anti-Subsidy measures in force. The EU has only ever imposed eight definitive safeguard measures under WTO rules: only one of these is still in force. In the EU, Anti-Dumping and Anti-Subsidy measures against unfair trade represent less than 0.45% of the value of total imports.

In comparison, the US imposed 201 definitive measures and India imposed 309 definitive measures between 1996 and 2005. In the same period the EU initiated 294 investigations, the US 352 and India 419 investigations.

The **European Commission** is responsible for the conduct of Anti-Dumping, Anti-Subsidy and Safeguard investigations, including decisions on whether to open investigations in response to industry complaints, and reviews during the life of current measures. It may also impose provisional measures and proposes definitive measures to the Council, where these are warranted. The **Council** imposes definitive Anti-Dumping/Anti-Subsidy measures by simple majority while Safeguard measures require the support of a qualified majority of Member States.

**PART 1. What is the role of trade defence measures in a global economy?**

The economic justification for **Anti-Dumping measures** derives chiefly from the fact that international markets are imperfectly competitive – there is no international competition authority to regulate anti-competitive behaviour between countries. In contrast to an internal market like the EU, there are few rules that regulate business behaviour on international markets.

Anti-Dumping measures are the only tool provided for in international law to address the effects of unfairly traded imports from such markets on EU industry. Similarly **Anti-Subsidy measures** counter unfair subsidisation of producers in third countries in the absence of fully developed international means of limiting such intervention. **Safeguard measures** are targeted against imports that increase in such quantities as to cause or threaten to cause serious injury to the EU industry.

The EU currently initiates significantly more Anti-Dumping investigations than Anti-Subsidy investigations. One reason why companies are reluctant to request Anti-Subsidy cases is that they fear retaliation by the governments concerned. One solution to this might be for the Commission itself to initiate more Anti-Subsidy cases.

The economic justification for trade defence instruments remains controversial amongst economists. Some argue that trade defence instruments are needed in the absence of internationally agreed competition rules. Others believe trade defence measures cannot be economically justified from the perspective of the overall welfare of a country. Others argue that they could potentially be misused by sectoral interests as a means of obtaining protection from competitive imports. Yet others argue that Anti-Dumping action is only justified if an exporter in a third country benefits from a lack of, or insufficient enforcement of, domestic competition rules.

***Question 1:*** *What is the role of trade defence instruments in the modern global economy? Do trade defence instruments remain essential in order to ensure respect for international trade rules and to protect European interests? Should the EU consider how they might be improved?*

***Question 2:*** *Should the EU make greater use of Anti-Subsidy and Safeguard instruments alongside its Anti-Dumping actions? Should the Commission, in particular circumstances, be ready to initiate more trade defence investigations on its own initiative provided it is in possession of the required evidence?*

***Question 3:*** *Are there alternatives to the use of trade defence instruments in the absence of internationally agreed competition rules?*

**PART 2. Weighing different EU interests in trade defence investigations**

Trade defence measures must serve the overall economic interest of the EU, including that of producers and workers. EU rules need to continue to address situations in which lower import prices are not driven solely by true comparative advantages in labour and production costs in third countries, but reflect the fact that those advantages are topped up by unfair competitive conditions such as subsidies or other state induced distortions.

Changes in the structure of both the global and EU economies have made determining the EU's economic interests more complex. Globalisation increases the international division of labour as transportation and communication costs have substantially decreased. Increasingly, European companies are using production bases outside the European Union whilst maintaining significant operations and employment in Europe. From the perspective of trade defence instruments, the challenge is to consider whether EU rules take sufficient account of the reality of outsourced production by European businesses, which are then in competition with EU-based production and might be negatively affected by trade defence measures.

It is not in the EU's long-term economic interest to tolerate dumping, even where it benefits European companies that have outsourced production to third countries. But we do need to reflect on the fact that action to limit the injury caused by dumping can impact on the employment and viability of EU companies that are operating legitimately through outsourced production. Striking the right balance between free trade and fair trade is crucial. We need clear rules that help us address this situation.

This part of the paper relates to four key issues related to the Community interest test.

**Box 2: Case study – Anti-dumping measures on leather shoes, August 2006**

In October 2006 the European Union imposed duties of 16.5% and 10% on certain leather shoes imported to the European Union. These duties were the result of an investigation that found both dumping of these exports from certain third countries and consequent injury to EU producers. The application of EU and WTO rules in this highly complex case provoked divisions among EU economic operators and EU Member States. The case illustrated two of the important issues that this Green Paper considers.

**Outsourcing by EU producers.** Although many EU companies still produce leather footwear in the European Union, a significant number of EU companies have outsourced the production of footwear to third countries while keeping other parts of their operations in the EU. Those EU companies that produce leather shoes in the third countries concerned are subject to the Anti-Dumping duty. Moreover, under the existing rules for Anti-Dumping investigations, only producers that keep their production within the EU were considered in determining whether the required proportion of Community industry for the case to be initiated was met. Yet the number of EU companies that are moving elements of their production is growing and these companies account for thousands of jobs in the EU.

**Consumer interest.** The footwear case also illustrated another problem in the context of determining what is in the wider economic interest of the EU. In the majority of cases, especially those which do not concern consumer products, the impact of Anti-Dumping measures on the prices paid by the consumer have typically not been significant. Nonetheless, it is important to reflect on the question of whether and how consumer interests can be better reflected in Anti-Dumping investigations, and any measures taken.

**2.1. The Community interest test.** The EU is one of the few trade defence users that applies a public interest test in the form of the Community interest rule before applying Anti-Dumping measures. The Community interest rule states that measures can only be imposed where the Commission determines that imposing them is not against the wider interest of the EU economy. Such a test is not required by the WTO Anti-Dumping

Agreement but it has proved a useful factor in weighing the balance of interests in Anti-Dumping cases.

However, some argue that the Community interest test is too strongly weighted towards EU producers and does not take sufficient account of the impact of measures on importing businesses that have moved some of their production outside the EU. There is also concern that consumer interests are not adequately weighted, especially when trade defence instruments are applied to finished consumer products. While the principal concern of the EU's instruments is responding to the effect of unfair competition, recent cases have also raised the question of using the Community interest test to weigh the impact of measures on the overall coherence of EU policy. For example, the EU might consider whether in some cases Anti-Dumping measures reduce the effectiveness of EU development assistance to a given country.

***Question 4:*** *Should the EU review the current balance of interests between various economic operators in the Community interest test in trade defence investigations? Alongside the interests of producers and their employees in Europe, how should we take into account the interests of companies which have retained significant operations and employment in Europe, even though they have moved some part of their production out of the EU? How should we take into account the interests of importers or producers who process affected imports?*

***Question 5:*** *Do we need to review the way that consumer interests are taken into account in trade defence investigations? Should the Commission be more proactive in soliciting input from consumer associations? How could such input be weighted? How could the impact of trade defence measures on consumers be assessed and monitored?*

***Question 6:*** *Should the EU include wider considerations in the Community interest assessments in trade defence investigations, such as coherence with other EU policies? With regard to development policy, should the EU make a formal distinction between least developed countries and developing countries in the application of trade defence measures?*

***Question 7:*** *What kinds of economic analysis might help in making these assessments?*

**2.2. Using the Community interest test to fine-tune trade defence measures.** Currently the findings of the Community interest test can only conclude that measures should either go ahead or not be imposed. In principle, this "either/or" test does not allow for Community interest analysis to be used as a rationale for adapting or modifying measures. However, it may be appropriate to introduce more flexibility in this respect provided that any adjustment of measures fully reflects the objective findings of the case. Such flexibility would be limited to downward adjustments by the EU's lesser duty rule which requires that duties be set at the injury margin or the dumping margin, whichever is lower. It could also in theory extend to the ability to exempt certain products from duties for Community interest reasons.

***Question 8:*** *Should it be explicitly foreseen that the level of proposed measures might be adjusted downwards following the results of the Community interest test in trade defence investigations? Should the EU explicitly allow for exclusion of certain product types under Community interest considerations? If so, what criteria should be applied?*

**2.3. Deciding when to apply the Community interest test.** Currently, a Community interest test is foreseen only following the initiation of an investigation at the time of determining measures. WTO rules prohibiting the publicizing of anti-dumping complaints prior to launching an investigation currently preclude the use of the Community interest test in assessing the strength of an initial complaint. However some stakeholders have suggested that the EU should press to see these rules changed.

***Question 9:*** *Should the EU seek to have WTO rules changed to allow Community interest tests to be used at the complaints stage in Anti-Dumping and Anti-Subsidy investigations? Are there other situations where the community interest test would be appropriate – for example before the initiation of expiry reviews?*

**2.4. Viability assessments.** The overall viability of the industry in the EU is an element investigated in the Community interest test. Where there are good prospects for the viability of a particular sector this is an important factor in assessing whether to impose trade defence measures.

***Question 10:*** *Are viability assessments relevant in reaching decisions on using trade defence instruments? If so, what criteria should be used in assessing the viability of EU industries in trade defence investigations, e.g. level of production, employment, market share?*

**PART 3. The launching and conduct of trade defence investigations**

Stakeholders have identified a number of technical areas related to the launching and conduct of trade defence investigations where changes could further improve the proportionality, efficacy and fairness of EU trade defence investigations. Eight of these issues are addressed below:

**3.1. Early consultations with the exporting third countries.** While WTO rules prohibit contact with companies that may be investigated prior to the launch of a case, some stakeholders proposed contacts with exporting third countries' governments prior to launching investigations to help to avoid political frictions and discuss the products and practices likely to be implicated in an investigation.

***Question 11:*** *Should the EU consider consultations with exporting third countries after receiving complaints and prior to launching Anti-Dumping investigations?*

**3.2. The use of the Anti-Subsidy instrument in transition economies.** Current practice does not foresee the initiation of Anti-Subsidy investigations in cases involving economies in transition because of the widespread nature of distortions of costs and prices in such economies. However, the use of the Anti-Subsidy instrument could be considered in cases in which individual companies in economies in transition are awarded market economy treatment.

***Question 12:*** *Should the EU more specifically foresee the use of the Anti-Subsidy instrument in cases involving companies in transition economies that receive market economy treatment?*

**3.3. Standing requirements.** The EU imposes certain requirements that must be met for a trade defence investigation to be launched. WTO rules require that an investigation normally be initiated only when producers expressly supporting the complaint account for more than 25% of total production of the product implicated in the market concerned.

Under current rules businesses that both produce and import the allegedly dumped product may be excluded from the standing assessment. This has the effect of lowering the number of companies required to establish standing in a given case, and excluding companies that may object to a complaint. Some stakeholders consider these so-called 'standing requirements' too low.

***Question 13:*** *Should the EU review the 'standing requirements' for the definition of Community industry in Anti-Dumping and Anti-Subsidy cases? Is the level of support needed to endorse a complaint and thus launch an investigation appropriate? Should we review the possibility of excluding companies which themselves import or are related to exporters from standing assessments?*

**3.4. *De-minimis* rules for dumping, subsidy and injury.** Under current rules, thresholds exist below which cases under investigation are not considered of sufficient importance to merit EU intervention. EU Anti-Dumping law stipulates that an investigation shall be terminated if the margin of dumping is less than 2% expressed as a percentage of the export price – this is called the '*de-minimis* threshold'.

A *de-minimis* threshold is also applicable in the determination of injury from dumped goods. Proceedings are not initiated against countries whose imports represent less than 1% of the EU market. The current *de-minimis* thresholds could be higher or lower, depending on the perceived economic impact of low dumping/subsidy margins and injury thresholds.

Besides these percentage thresholds, a second "*de-minimis* test" could be considered by making the opening of a case dependent on the value of imports in Euro.

***Question 14:*** *Should the EU change the de-minimis thresholds (in percentage and absolute terms) that currently apply to dumping and injury in trade defence investigations?*

**3.5. Dumping margin calculations.** An important part of an Anti-Dumping investigation is the determination of the production costs and normal value of a product in the home market. Some stakeholders have suggested that the EU does not take sufficient account of the extent to which low volumes produced and sold at the start-up phase of a product can distort per-unit costs and might make them appear unrealistically high. This in turn could possibly inflate dumping margins.

***Question 15:*** *Should the Commission refine the approach on "start-up costs" for dumping calculations in Anti-Dumping investigations in order to give a longer "grace period" to exporters in start-up situations?*

***Question 16:*** *Are there other changes to the dumping margin calculation methodology in Anti-Dumping investigations – for example existing rules on the "ordinary course of trade-test" – that need to be considered?*

**3.6. Treatment of new exporters.** Stakeholders have proposed refining the provisions on the treatment of new exporters who begin exporting goods while an investigation is underway. New exporters raise the problem of basing findings on a very small number of transactions. The Commission can also currently only address new exporters that start to operate during the investigation through a separate newcomer review.

***Question 17:*** *Should the EU refine the provisions on the treatment of new exporters in Anti-Dumping and Anti-Subsidy investigations? Should the EU introduce the possibility of dealing with newcomers that start to operate during the investigation of the main case more expeditiously?*

**3.7. Restructuring plans.** Some stakeholders think that EU producers should be required to present a restructuring plan before they benefit from Anti-Dumping measures. Others take the view that where the problems of an industry are the direct consequence of unfair trade practices, restructuring is irrelevant.

***Question 18:*** *Is evidence of restructuring by an EU industry in any way relevant in Anti-Dumping and Anti-Subsidy investigations? If yes, in what way, and at what stage?*

**3.8. Involvement of SMEs.** Many stakeholders think that SMEs have difficulties in launching and participating in trade defence investigations because of the complexity and high costs involved.

***Question 19:*** *What are the particular obstacles for SMEs to participate in trade defence investigations and how could they be addressed?*

**PART 4. The form, timing and duration of trade defence measures**

Stakeholders have identified a number of areas related to the imposition, form, duration and expiry of trade defence measures that could be reviewed. We address four issues in this section.

**4.1. Timing of provisional measures.** Some stakeholders have raised the issue of faster adoption of provisional Anti-Dumping measures. At present they are adopted by the Commission between two and nine months after the launch of an investigation, if preliminary evidence points to a finding of injurious dumping.

***Question 20:*** *Bearing in mind that any shortening of deadlines could impose limitations on the conduct and transparency of investigations, should the EU consider shortening the deadlines in Anti-Dumping and Anti-Subsidy investigations within which it must decide whether or not to impose provisional measures? Should these deadlines be made more flexible?*

**4.2. Form, timing and duration of measures.** Many stakeholders have said that the EU should have a greater choice of possible measures at its disposal than the standard *ad valorem* duties, fixed duties, minimum prices and price undertakings. This would give greater flexibility in dealing with complex cases which involve important consumer products. For example, should the Commission, to the extent that the Community's international obligations allow, generally have the possibility to apply a duty that phases in over time or with import volume, so as to give the market time to adapt?

Some stakeholders have also said that measures should take account of the impact on products that may have been ordered long before measures have been adopted or that are being shipped at the time of adoption.

Currently measures are normally in force for five years – the WTO maximum. It has been suggested that the duration of measures could be shorter, depending, for example, on the type of product, the market situation or the characteristics of an industry. The duration of measures imposed following expiry reviews could also be shorter.

***Question 21:*** *Should the EU make greater use of more flexible measures in Anti-Dumping and Anti-Subsidy investigations?*

***Question 22:*** *Do EU measures in Anti-Dumping and Anti-Subsidy investigations need to be adapted so as to take better account of products with a long order or shipment time? If yes, how?*

***Question 23:*** *Should it be made explicitly possible for the duration of definitive measures in Anti-Dumping and Anti-Subsidy investigations to be shorter than 5 years? If yes, in what type of situations would a shorter duration of measures be justified?*

**4.3. Reimbursement of duties after expiry reviews.** Measures currently expire after five years unless an expiry review is initiated before that date. During the ensuing investigation (which can run for up to 15 months beyond the five-year period), measures remain in force. If the expiry review concludes that measures should not be maintained, consideration could be given to paying back any duties collected beyond the 'normal' five year period. An alternative could be to carry out and conclude expiry reviews before the maximum lifetime of measures ends. With this approach reimbursement would not be an issue.

***Question 24:*** *Should duties collected beyond the 5-year duration of the measures in Anti-Dumping and Anti-Subsidy investigations be reimbursed if the expiry review concludes that measures are not to be continued?*

***Question 25:*** *Should expiry reviews in Anti-Dumping and Anti-Subsidy investigations be timed to end on the fifth anniversary of measures rather than to start on that date?*

**4.4. Higher thresholds for expiry reviews.** Some stakeholders think that it is too easy for Anti-Dumping measures to be renewed. Under WTO and EU rules, industry needs to show that there is "likelihood of recurrence of injurious dumping". A higher threshold for industry might be a "clearly foreseeable and imminent threat of injury".

***Question 26:*** *Should the EU increase thresholds for expiry reviews in Anti-Dumping and Anti-Subsidy investigations? For example should the EU consider introducing the "threat of injury"- standard instead of the "likelihood of recurrence"?*

**PART 5. Transparency in trade defence investigations**

Effective transparency is vital to the credibility of trade defence instruments. EU rules represent a balance between openness in managing investigations and the need to respect the confidentiality of commercial information. The quality of analysis and resulting proposals depends strongly on the quality of the confidential information provided during an investigation. Stakeholders have raised a number of possible ways that the European Commission could nevertheless improve the transparency of trade defence investigations. Four of the aspects related to transparency are addressed below:

**5.1. Hearing officer.** Current EU rules foresee the possibility for interested parties to request hearings. Some parties have argued that a hearing officer would be helpful to ensure that parties in trade defence investigations can better exercise their right to be heard and to ensure that the rights of the parties are respected.

***Question 27:*** *The Commission is going to create the position of a hearing officer for trade defence investigations – what precise functions should such a person carry out?*

**5.2. Public hearings for country-wide Market Economy Status decisions.** Certain countries are not considered market economies for the purpose of trade defence investigations – China and Vietnam for example. These countries can be awarded the status of market economy if they fulfil certain technical criteria. In view of the importance, complexity and political sensitivity of decisions to award country-wide Market Economy Status (MES), many stakeholders recommend holding public hearings prior to the Commission proposing to grant MES to a country.

***Question 28:*** *Should the Commission conduct public hearings in Anti-Dumping investigations for decisions to award country-wide Market Economy Status to a country?*

**5.3. A level playing field for information.** Stakeholders have expressed concern about the uncertainty caused by rumours of possible complaints or investigations. The question has been raised whether the work of the advisory Anti-Dumping Committee could be rendered more transparent.

***Question 29:*** *Should there be greater openness regarding the working of the Anti-Dumping Committee, e.g. publication of its agenda and/or the minutes of its meetings?*

**5.4. Better access to non-confidential files.** If parties want to consult the non-confidential file of an Anti-Dumping investigation, they currently have to do this in person at the premises of the European Commission. It would be possible to provide access to these materials online. However, some stakeholders might consider this an undesirably wide dissemination of non-confidential business facts.

***Question 30:*** *Would it be desirable for the non-confidential files in trade defence investigations to be accessible via the internet? Would intermediary solutions be more appropriate – for example the publication of a file index?*

**PART 6. Institutional process**

While the use of trade defence instruments can be politically sensitive, the credibility of those instruments depends on their use being transparent, predictable and subject to stringent review. The decisions which are taken must be based on the results shown by investigations. The current institutional structure, as set out by the EU's Basic Regulations on trade defence instruments, divides responsibilities between the Commission and the Council. Decisions are subject to review by the European Court of Justice, and must also be compliant with the EU's WTO obligations. This institutional framework has worked well, but some stakeholders are concerned that it sometimes allows decisions to be influenced by factors not directly linked to the facts of the investigation itself.

***Question 31:*** *Should current institutional arrangements for adopting Anti-Dumping, Anti-Subsidy and Safeguard measures be maintained? Are there ways to improve the way those decisions are taken?*

**Contributing to this Green Paper consultation**

Comments are invited from all interested parties, including the European Parliament and Member States, on the questions raised in this Green Paper. A structured questionnaire is available on-line to assist those responding and the Commission would welcome the views of all interested actors, including the views of public authorities in third countries.

The Commission invites respondents to raise issues related to the EU's trade defence instruments that are not directly addressed in the preceding questions.

***Question 32:*** *Is there any other aspect of the EU's trade defence instruments that you would like to see addressed?*

The consultation response forms can be found at:

http://ec.europa.eu/trade/issues/respectrules/anti_dumping/comu061206_en.htm

Replies to the questionnaire should reach the Commission by 31 March 2007. Comments received will be made available on-line unless a specific request for confidentiality is made, in which case only an indication of the contributor will be given. Towards the end of the consultation period the Commission's services intend to organise a seminar with stakeholders. Following this public debate, the Commission will communicate the results of this consultation and consider if further action is appropriate.

[1] http://ec.europa.eu/trade/issues/respectrules/anti_dumping/legis/index_en.htm#txts.

Most recently, within the framework of its 2001 Communication on 'Europe and Asia', the European Commission published its regional policy for Asia, including China. The priorities are support for regional cooperation, policy and know-how cooperation in environment, energy and climate change; higher education and support for research institutions and cross-border cooperation in animal and human health; and support to uprooted people.[7] China is eligible for support within this programme.

At the time of writing, the most recent policy documents on EU policy concerning China are the European Commission's CSP for 2007–2013 (see Document 3.21) and the Multiannual Indicative Programme (MIP) for 2007–2010.[8] The CSP identifies three objectives for EU policy on China for the immediately coming years. These are to provide support for China first in areas where the EU and China have established sectoral dialogues, second with regard to the environment and climate change, and third concerning the development of human resources. The CSP also provides a very useful review of cooperation under the 2002–2006 NIP, the existing sectoral dialogues and cooperation projects. Building on the CSP, the MIP sets out priorities, specific activities, risks and assumptions, and indicators of progress for the three main objectives until 2010.

## Document 3.21: European Commission, China Strategy Paper, 2007–2013

**CHINA**
Strategy Paper, 2007–2013
Brussels, 2006

### EXECUTIVE SUMMARY

With 1.3 billion inhabitants, China is the world's most populous country and has in recent years undergone economic growth at constantly high levels. This growth has delivered higher incomes, has had a dramatic impact on the reduction of poverty, and is contributing significantly towards the attainment of global MDG targets. At the same time, however, it has led to considerable income and regional disparities, has resulted in a high degree of environmental degradation, and has created vulnerable groups of the population.

China's development policy guidelines are set out in its llth Five Year Plan (adopted in 2006) which marks a perceptible shift from all-out economic growth to one which places increasing emphasis on the social consequences associated with rapid economic development. China has. also begun to show willingness to shoulder its growing international responsibilities.

Europe has an important economic and political interest in supporting China's sustainable development and successful transition to a stable, prosperous and open country. EU relations with China have developed from a relationship based mainly on trade issues to a partnership based on political dialogue and economic, trade and sectoral relations. The co-operation programme is an important element of this relationship.

[7] See European Commission, Directorate-General for External Relations, 'Regional Programming for Asia: Strategy Document, 2007–2013' (Brussels, 31 May 2007) Revision 1; and European Commission, Directorate-General for External Relations, 'Multiannual Indicative Programme for Asia, 2007–2010' (Brussels, 2007), available at http://www. ec.europa.eu/external_relations/asia/rsp/mip_0710_en.pdf

[8] The MIP is not reprinted here because it partly repeats the CSP and because of its technical nature. It is available at http://www.ec.europa.eu/external_relations/china/csp/2007_mip-en.pdf (accessed 9 October 2007).

China is, however, moving away from the status of a traditional ODA recipient towards that of a strategic partner with whom the EU engages on a wide range of policy issues, and one that is becoming an increasingly important source of ODA to other developing countries.

The response strategy for the future EC co-operation programme therefore needs to take account of the contradiction in China's nature: that of a developing country in terms of certain traditional indicators on the one hand, and that of a significant player on the world stage in economic and political terms on the other.

In recognition of this 'duality' of character, the EC response strategy will be targeted at providing support for China's reform programme in areas covered by sectoral dialogues; assisting China in tackling global concerns and challenges over the environment, energy and climate change; and supporting China's human resource development. Indicative funding for the seven-year period is €224 million. EC assistance in the areas of intervention will be complemented by actions and support to be provided though various thematic programmes and regional budget lines.

## 1 PAST AND ONGOING EC CO-OPERATION AND CO-ORDINATION

### *1.1 Political dialogue*

In May 2005, the EU and China celebrated the 30$^{th}$ anniversary of diplomatic relations. Since these were established in 1975, ties have developed rapidly, from a one-dimensional relationship based mainly on trade issues to a fully fledged partnership which rests on three "pillars": political dialogue; economic, sectoral and trade relations; and the EU-China co-operation programme. Commission Communications in 1998, 2001 and 2003 laid the groundwork for the development of the EU's strategic partnership with China, and a new Communication on China – "EC-China:

Closer Partners, Growing Responsibilities" was adopted in October 2006 (cf. Annex 3.4.2(3)). In 2003 China issued its first policy paper on the EU.

The political dialogue was formalised in 1994. This dialogue has since grown into a series of regular meetings at all levels, including annual Summits at Head of Government level (since 1998) and ministerial and official level dialogue in a range of areas.

This is supported by a regular exchange of visits and meetings. The most important issues currently on the bilateral agenda are the negotiation of a Partnership and Co-operation Agreement, climate change and energy, illegal migration, human rights. Market Economy Status, market access, IPR, and the arms embargo.

The creation of a new dialogue on Africa's peace, stability, and sustainable development was agreed upon at the 9$^{th}$ EU-China Summit in 2006 in order to foster understanding between the partners, to discuss activities and priorities, and to provide an opportunity for integrating China into international efforts to improve and better co-ordinate development co-operation activities.

In the field of co-operation on foreign and security policy, particular attention will be given to combating WMD proliferation, WMD agents, materials and know-how, and conflict prevention. The challenge is to facilitate the booming legitimate exchanges of people, goods and services, while limiting abuse. Co-operation in the area of justice, freedom and security, will focus on combating terrorism, fighting organised crime including money-laundering, corruption, trafficking of human beings, crime prevention, small arms and light weapons, illicit drugs and drugs precursors. Illegal migration is both a humanitarian concern and a politically sensitive issue on which the EU and China have engaged in regular consultations to reinforce administrative co-operation and the facilitation of people-to-people exchanges, for example through the Tourism Agreement (or Authorised Destination Status agreement – ADS).

Relations are presently based on a Trade and Economic Co-operation Agreement signed in 1985. Leaders agreed at the EU-China Summit in 2006 that this should be updated to more accurately reflect the strength and breadth of bilateral relations Commissioner Ferrero-Waldner launched negotiations for a new Partnership and Co-operation Agreement in January 2007.

*1.2 Lessons learned*

An external Country-Level Evaluation of the EC co-operation programme was commissioned in 2006. This was positive overall, but flagged up scope for improvement. It recommended that: more should be done to integrate poverty reduction considerations; climate change issues should be taken into account; co-ordination with and among Member States should be more substantial; and feedback from projects and programmes should be fed into policy dialogues more systematically. The main conclusions and recommendations from the evaluation are given in Annex 3.10. Future projects and programmes will be subject to regular external evaluation, and a mid-term review of the Strategy Paper and Multiannual Indicative Programme will be carried out.

*1.3 Donor co-ordination*

Information exchange between the EU Member States and the Commission takes place primarily in the EU Development Counsellors Group and in the EU Environment Counsellors Group, which each meet four times a year. In this framework, the EC Delegation has been compiling and updating a list of all EU Member State and Commission-financed co-operation activities with China, which is published on the Delegation website.

The Delegation also has regular contacts with important multilateral donor organisations such as the World Bank, UNDP and ADB as well as with non-EU bilateral donors like Canada, Australia, Norway and Japan. In the areas of renewable energy, for example, an informal donor group meets regularly in order to exchange information and discuss specific topics. The Ministry of Commerce (MOFCOM) furthermore convenes annual donor co-ordination meetings.

In some areas, co-operation between donors goes beyond information exchange. Some donors and projects organise joint events or launch joint initiatives and, in a few instances, projects or programmes are jointly implemented. Examples are the EU-China Biodiversity Programme, a joint action between the European Commission, the UNDP and China's State Environmental Protection Administration (SEPA), which will associate further key donors and stakeholders through a co-financing mechanism, and the recently started EU-China River Basin Management Programme, which is implemented jointly by the European Commission, the World Bank and the Government of China. A further joint project with the UNDP, Governance for Equitable Development, was financed in 2006. An example of co-operation with Member States is the NZEC project financially supported by the UK and in part through the EU research budget.

The Commission intends to engage with China on co-ordination regarding China's own co-operation with developing countries.

## 2 THE EC RESPONSE STRATEGY 2007–2013

### *2.1 Justification*

Europe has a major economic and political interest in supporting China's sustainable development and successful transition to a stable, prosperous and open country. The cooperation programme is an important mechanism for supporting this interest and for strengthening the relationship between the Community and China. Given the pace of China's development the response strategy nevertheless has to recognise that the country is increasingly moving away from the status of a traditional ODA recipient towards that of a strategic partner with whom the EU engages on a wide range of policy issues'. China is itself becoming an increasingly important source of ODA, with whom international development partners, the EU included, are looking to co-ordinate and co-operate. Efforts will be made to engage with China on sustainable development, particularly in Africa, in the framework of the co-operation programme.

While China has the resources to cover its own longer-term development needs and is, step-by-step, putting in place the necessary laws, regulations and administrative structures, the response strategy must nevertheless take account of the duality of its character: on the one hand that of a developing country in terms of some traditional indicators, and on the other that of a major player on the world stage in terms of its commercial weight, FDI flows, consumption of natural resources and contribution to global warming. This combination of different and at times contradictory characteristics therefore justifies a particular strategy.

In recognition of the above and of the analysis provided in Annexes 3.2 and 3.3 the objectives of the response strategy are to:

(1) provide support for China's reform programme in areas covered by sectoral dialogues, where EU experience can provide added value;

(2) assist China in her efforts to address global concerns over the environment, energy, and climate change;

(3) provide support for China's human resources development.

Given the limited resources available for the co-operation programme, this strategy can best be achieved through capacity-building, where China's need to innovate in order to attain sustainable development continues to create opportunities for support in areas where the EU has strong experience, and through the formulation of activities to maximise the multiplier effect, through targeting interventions at the appropriate level and through the development of pilot activities to support policy development. In all areas enhanced co-ordination and co-operation with Member States shall be pursued.

Cross-cutting issues including governance, the environment, human rights and gender will be mainstreamed where possible in the programme.

### *2.2 The Strategy*

In order to meet the objectives specified in 2.1 above, three areas of intervention are proposed for the period of the SP. Indicative funding for the seven-year period amounts to €224 million.

2.2.1 Support to Areas covered by Policy Dialogues

Policy dialogues provide a coherent policy mix between development objectives and EU internal and external policies.

*2.2.1.1 Trade co-operation*

In the area of trade, further future intervention will be required to back up the continued engagement with China on the implementation of its commitments associated with WTO membership, to support China's further integration into the world economy, to promote further trade and economic liberalisation, and to support regulatory reform that impacts on trade. China's significance in international trade is now such that the country must demonstrate its ability to ensure competition on a fair and equitable basis, commensurate with its weight as a trading nation.

The current €15 million EU-China Trade Co-operation Programme (EUTCP) will continue until 2009, and supports China in the context of the trade policy dialogue established in 2003 to strengthen bilateral exchanges in the context of the rapid expansion of trade and economic relations. The EUTCP focuses on six areas of activity: customs and import/export regulatory system; agriculture and agro-food; technical barriers to trade/sanitary and phytosanitary measures; services; legislative and legal aspects of domestic implementation, IPR enforcement; and policy development[2]. While a new €10 million programme on the enforcement of IPR legislation, financed in 2006, will in principle run until 2011, continued broad support for the trade-related objectives outlined above will be required from 2009 onwards.

The EUCTP will also temporarily bridge the gap between the current Financial Services co-operation project (EC contribution €8,5 million), which initially ran from 2002 to 2005, later extended to the end of 2006, and a new co-operation programme for the financial services sector starting in 2008.

*2.2.1.2 Transport Co-operation: Civil Aviation*

It is recognised that a well-developed civil aviation sector is an essential platform for development and reform in the area of market and territorial integration. Exchanges with China in this sector have taken place against a background of annual sector growth of 30% to 40% and a strong commitment from the Civil Aviation Authority of China (CAAC) to improve China's regulatory framework for air transport and to maintain safety levels.

China will soon become the largest Asian market and leading hub for air passenger traffic and international air cargo, and the Chinese authorities are keen to develop closer co-operation with major civil aviation partners in order to benefit from their experience and to incorporate it into the national regulatory framework and operations. The CAAC has expressed satisfaction with the assistance provided by the EU so far in this area and wishes to deepen this co-operation.

The EU-China Civil Aviation Co-operation Project, financed before the preparation of the 2002–2006 Country Strategy Paper, aimed at facilitating co-operation in the sector, and focuses on production management, customer support, air traffic management, training in airline and industry management, and pilot inspection. With a total budget of €23.5 million, of which the EC contribution amounted to €12.5 million, the project started in 1999 and terminates in 2006.

The EU-China Aviation Summit held in Beijing in 2005 provided a further opportunity for the EU to demonstrate its substantial capacity and potential to mobilise partners involved in the field of civil aviation and to further develop co-operation in this field. Such co-operation is proposed under the SP and would be complementary to discussions taking place with the Chinese authorities on measures to ensure that existing bilateral civil aviation agreements between Member States and China conform with Community law. The possibility of negotiating a more comprehensive Community-level agreement is also being explored.

Future co-operation could include the exchange of information and technical assistance in a range of areas including aviation security, aviation safety, competition law and economic regulation, and air traffic maintenance. It will take account of international co-operation policy under the EU Research Framework Programme, particularly in the areas of greener air transport and safety.

*2.2.1.3 Financial services*

In the broader area of macroeconomic policy, trade in services between the EU and China has been growing in importance.

The EU-China Financial Services co-operation project which ended in December 2006 aimed to assist the Chinese government in its effort to reform and restructure the financial services sector. The project provided policy advice for the sector's regulators and supervisors and training.

Further intervention will be required to build directly on these achievements and enhance professionalism and competence in the financial services sector, while also creating sector-awareness in the general public. Such co-operation is proposed under the SP and would be complementary to the Chinese government's efforts to implement its WTO commitments in the sector. Experience has shown that cross-sector initiatives produce the best potential for cooperation in this area.

*2.2.1.4 Social Protection*

Current Chinese policymaking concentrates on the development of what the Government refers to as a 'harmonious society', which implies achieving more balance between rich and poor, urban and rural, coastal and inland provinces, and generally between growth and equity. In policy terms, this concerns mainly employment, social security, and regional policies, though health and education policies are also key areas.

The EU can be considered a laboratory of 27 different experiences and models for all these areas, with a wide variety of lessons relevant to China in different ways, including those from countries that have long experience as market economies, and others that have managed transition over the last 20 years.

As China develops its own model of social provision, it is relevant for the country to examine the main European social models and to see how the EU addresses specific issues such as, for example, labour markets, social exclusion, and pension sustainability. This is already proving beneficial in the current 'social security' project treats three specific areas: pensions, unemployment benefit, and medical insurance.

The objective of further co-operation in this area will be to assist China in reducing the negative social side-effects of economic reform, to contribute to poverty alleviation, and to implement the Decent Work Agenda. This could be done through supporting the development of health and safety insurance schemes, the improvement of regional policy, intuitional strengthening of the agencies charged with managing social provision systems, and the extension of pension and unemployment insurance coverage to the urban private and informal sector.

*2.2.1.5 Sectoral Dialogues*

An increasing number of sectoral dialogues have been established with the Chinese Government in a wide range of sectors. A summary of the subjects presently covered by the dialogues is given in Annex 3.12. The number of dialogues has expanded rapidly in recent years, reflecting the opportunities for China and the EU to leam from each other through the exchange of information, and providing common ground for co-operation.

The dialogues and exchanges are supportive of China's reform and development. The Chinese Government shows keen interest in broadening and intensifying these dialogues. They provide a forum for exchange between policymakers. Some are linked to global sustainable development issues, where China and the EU both face challenges, and where China can benefit from strategies developed by the EU.

In the 2005–2006 NIP €6 million was allocated for a Policy Dialogue Support Facility (PDSF) to support policy dialogues and exchanges between the Commission's services and the Chinese authorities. This will create close links between the co-operation programme and the reform-oriented exchanges that take place. Engagement in exchanges at provincial level will be promoted. While the performance and results of the PDSF will be evaluated in due course, follow-up activity will be required during the period of the SP to maintain impetus and support for these activities.

Some successful aspects of EU-China co-operation in the area of governance, carried out in partnership with the national School of Administration, could be consolidated and deepened. China will continue to be engaged in the reform of its public administration system, an element of which is the first (2006) Civil Servant Law. Continued support for the strengthening and modernisation of public administration would help improve governance and the rule of law and enhance the sustainability of China's economic and social development. Bilateral cooperation and dialogue on tax matters should be further enhanced.

An additional element for consideration in the formulation of further PDSF-related activities is the provision of short-term training for senior Chinese nationals from government and civil society who have a potential role to play in the direction of China's future political, economic, social and administrative environment. Some higher education institutions in the EU are well suited to providing high-level exposure to EU policy issues of direct relevance to China.

2.2.2 The environment, energy and climate change

Policymakers in China increasingly see environmental protection as a major challenge, and environmental developments in China frequently have an impact at global level. There is a genuine wish among policymakers in China to leam from EU experience and, over the last decade, contacts and co-operation on environmental and energy issues between the Commission and China have increased substantially through established ministerial-level dialogues, through working group contacts and through the EU-China co-operation programme.

Of particular pertinence is the issue of climate change. As a major emitter of greenhouse gases, China's active participation in the debate on this subject is vital. Much work has been done on projecting China's emissions and their potential impact on global warming, as well as on the likely impacts of climate change in China, and the Chinese Government is aware of its globa responsibilities that are increasing in parallel with the country's economic growth. In recognition of this, the 2005 EU-China Summit established an EU-China Partnership on Climate Change, which now has an agreed Work Programme and has led to a further increase in co-operation. The flagship project under the Partnership is an agreement to develop a NZEC demonstration plant with carbon capture and storage in China by 2020.

At the 2005 EU-China Summit both sides confirmed their commitment to the objectives of the UN Framework Convention on Climate Change and the Kyoto Protocol, and agreed to set up a partnership to strengthen co-operation and dialogue on climate change including clean energy, and to promote sustainable development. In this context it was agreed that key areas for technical co-operation would be energy sector reform (efficiency, conservation, new and renewable energy, clean coal, methane recovery and use, carbon capture and storage, hydrogen and fuel cells, and power generation and transmission); implementation of the Clean Development Mechanism (CDM); adaptation to climate change, and related research and technological development.

Energy sector reform and the effective promotion of energy saving and efficiency would further reduce China's energy demand on the world markets.

In addition to the areas of co-operation indicated above, other areas of key interest would be pollution control and natural resources management, including biodiversity conservation. The issue of water management is high on the Chinese political agenda, where China is considering alternative approaches which may include aspects of the EU Water Framework Directive. There is also potential for co-operation in the area of air pollution since China suffers from severe air pollution problems in its urban areas and makes a significant to hemispheric transport of pollutants such as mercury. Opportunities also exist for co-operation in the area of vehicle emissions, where China has already adopted some EU standards, and in integrated waste management. These are all areas in which the EC has already co-operated with China, and where there are opportunities to build on available experience. More generally, co-operation on environmental legislation and standards, in particular where they impact on trade, should be continued. The Chinese Government is also keen to explore ways to improve the implementation of such legislation, and is actively promoting public awareness, disclosure of environmental information and public participation. There is, furthermore, interest in using economic instruments in environmental and energy policies, where EU experience can be shared with Chinese partners in these areas.

2.2.3 Human Resources Development

*2.2.3.1 Higher Education*

In the higher education sector Chinese postgraduate students have been extremely successful in taking up scholarships to undertake masters courses in the EU under the Erasmus Mundus Programme, through both the worldwide core funding for the programme and a special €9 million 'China Window' financed under the 2004–2006 NIP to provide additional scholarships ' for Chinese students during the academic years 2005/2006 to 2007/2008. The total intake of Chinese Erasmus Mundus masters students for the first three years of programme implementation is approximately 285, of which 120 under the general scheme and 165 under the China Window.

The strong Chinese interest in developing co-operation with the EU in the field of higher education has been demonstrated in the context of the EU-China Higher Education Dialogue which took place in Beijing for the first time in November 2005 as well as, more recently, in the Joint Statement of the Helsinki EU-China Summit where the Chinese side expressed interest in making further progress with the EU on this topic. It is proposed that financial resources continue to be allocated to this sector under the SP to provide scholarships for Chinese students to further promote their studying in the EU. In addition to the purely educational and developmental benefits that this support provides, it would also contribute substantially towards the improvement of people-to-people links between the EU and China.

The scholarships provided will build on the capacity being created through ongoing EC higher education regional co-operation activities such as Asia-Link, the 6[1] Framework Programme for Research and Technological Development (RTD), and EU Member States' promotional exercises geared to the development of partnerships, networks, contacts and student exchanges.

The new €23 million EU-China Managers Exchange and Training Programme (METP) financed under the 2002–2004 NIP (EU contribution €17.2 million) was launched in 2006, and will run until 2010.

## 3 ANNEXES

### *3.1 ACRONYMS*

| | |
|---|---|
| ADS | Approved Destination Status |
| AQSIQ | General Administration for Quality Supervision, Inspection and Quarantine of the People's Republic of China |
| CAAC | Civil Aviation Authority of China |
| CCP | Chinese Communist Party |
| CDM | Clean Development Mechanism |
| CEPA | China-EU Public Administration Programme |
| CSP | Country Strategy Paper (2002–2006) |
| EUTCP | EU-China Trade Co-operation Programme |
| FDI | Foreign Direct Investment |
| FYP | Five Year Plan |
| GDP | Gross Domestic Product |
| HDI | Human Development Index- |
| ICCPR | International Convention on Civil and Political Rights |
| IPR | Intellectual Property Rights |
| MDGs | Millennium Development Goals . |
| MIP | Multiannual Indicative Programme (2007 onwards) |
| MOFCOM | Ministry of Commerce |
| MTR | Mid-Term Review |
| NIP | National Indicative Programme (2002–2004, and 2005–2006) |

| | |
|---|---|
| NZEC | Near Zero Emission Coal Fired Power Plant |
| ODA | Official Development Assistance |
| PCA | Partnership and Co-operation Agreement |
| PDSF | Policy Dialogue Support Facility |
| PPP | Purchasing Power Parity |
| SAR | Special Administrative Region |
| SEPA | State Environment Protection Administration |
| SP | Strategy Paper (2007–2013) |
| UNFCCC | United Nations Framework Convention on Climate Change |
| WMD | Weapons of Mass Destruction |
| WTO | World Trade Organisation |

*3.2 CHINA'S POLITICAL, ECONOMIC, SOCIAL AND ENVIRONMENTAL SITUATION*

3.2.1 The political situation

The Commission has set out a full analysis of the situation in China, China's priorities, and the EU's approach, in its 2006 Communication and Trade Policy Paper[4]. This analysis builds on these papers.

China is the world's 4$^{th}$ economy, its 3$^{rd}$ exporter, the EU's 2$^{nd}$ trading partner, and the world's most populous country.

The present Chinese leadership took over in March 2003 under President Hu Jintao. President Hu's priorities include sustainable economic growth and the strategic restructuring of the Chinese economy. Increased attention is being paid to social and environmental problems, and to fighting corruption.

Internationally, China is increasingly active in the UN and is keen to promote stability and closer regional co-operation within Asia, where she aims at developing trade and economic relations while reassuring neighbours who are concerned about her military and economic power. Stability on her borders, a guaranteed supply of energy and raw materials and access to water are factors which are essential to China's continued economic growth, and which constitute important elements in the shaping other foreign policy and her development co-operation policy towards countries in Africa and other regions.

In recent years, in the political area, the state has reinforced its power of control over individuals. Respect for human rights in China falls short of accepted international standards in regard to both civil and political rights. Freedom of expression, association, religion, internet use and the press are heavily restricted; ideological debate is strictly limited by the state; and concerns persist over the rights of minorities in certain areas. There is strong international pressure on China to ratify the International Convention on Civil and Political Rights (ICCPR), which the country signed in 1998.

Despite these restrictions, most people in China now enjoy greater freedom than at any other time in the past century, and their opportunities in society have increased in many ways.

Social grievances, widespread corruption, land rights issues and pollution have nevertheless sparked frequent riots, particularly in rural areas. Official figures released in 2005 put the number of riots for that year at some 74,000, involving over three million people, a sharp rise from previous years.

**3.2.2 The economic situation including trade**

Economic growth is estimated to have been consistently in excess of 9% in recent years and is considered likely to continue at that pace in the coming years. Such an increase in output represents one of the most sustained and rapid economic transformations seen in the world economy in the past 50 years. This growth has delivered higher incomes, the emergence of a sizeable middle class, and a substantial reduction in the numbers of those living in absolute poverty. It has also led, however, to considerable income disparities and environmental costs.

China's GDP reached over US$ 2,200 billion in 2005, and now exceeds that of most European economies. Chinese GDP measured at Purchasing Power Parity (PPP) is some four times higher than the above figure, and stands at around US$ 8,800 billion. But average incomes per capita in financial terms and at PPP are US$ 1,700 (or 6% of average per capita income in the EU) and US$ 6,800 (25% of the EU) respectively.

While average incomes are still below those in other middle income countries, there are large parts of the country that have reached income levels seen in some developed East Asian countries just one generation ago, and are rapidly catching up. Many of China's industries have become completely integrated into the world supply chain and on current trends China could become the largest exporter in the world by the beginning of the next decade. Since 2004, the EU has been China's largest trading partner, having overtaken the US and Japan. China remains the EU's second largest trading partner after the US. China has a very large trade surplus with the EU (US$132 billion or €105 billion in 2005[5]) and the US (US$ 201 billion in 2005[6]) that partially offsets its trade deficit with other countries, particularly Asian countries (US$ 75 billion in , 2005[7]). Trade with Asian countries – and with Africa – has nevertheless been growing rapidly.

China continues to attract large foreign capital inflows. In 2005, FDI inflows remained stable at around US$ 60 billion (2.7% of GDP), the main sources being Hong Kong, Korea and Japan. China also provides FDI, mainly to Asian countries. In 2005 China's foreign exchange reserves increased by US$ 209 billion to US$819 billion. By the end of 2006, this figure was approaching US$1 trillion, making China the largest official foreign exchange reserve holder in the world.

3.2.3 The social situation

The rapid economic growth that has taken place in China in recent years has resulted in substantial improvements in living standards for many Chinese. The UN estimates that the number of poor living on less than US$ 1 per day fell from approximately 490 million in 1990 to some 88 million in 2002 (6.9% of the population). However, the benefits of this growth have not been equitably distributed, and positive aggregate national figures can mask considerable and growing disparities between coastal provinces and remote inland resource-poor provinces, and between urban and rural areas. New forms of urban poverty have appeared among the estimated 100 million migrant workers who are not fully employed and are not integrated into urban social services. Many have been left outside existing social safety nets, and there is a need to provide improved social protection in the form of social security schemes, unemployment benefits and pensions. Poverty indicators are given in Annex 3.7.

These inequalities are recognised in China's llth Five Year Plan, which acknowledges the need to address these issues, but at the same time avoiding the elimination of incentives for growth.

In terms of human development, the UNDP 2005 Human Development Report places China in the higher range of the 'Medium Human Development' countries, with an HDI index of 0.755 in 2003.

China is considered to be on track to achieve most of its Millennium Development Goals (MDGs) by 2015, and is the world's largest single contributor to global progress on MDGs. Progress has been impressive across a range of social development indicators such as child mortality, illiteracy and life expectancy. MDG targets that require attention have been identified in the areas of gender equality (achieve equal access to primary and secondary education for girls and boys by 2005), combating disease (halt and reverse the spread of AIDS/HIV and halve the prevalence ofTB by 2015), and the environment (implement national strategies for sustainable development by 2005 to reverse the loss of environmental resources by 2015). China's commitment to achieving the MDGs is strong, and MDG targets that are not presently on track are receiving attention. An overview of China's MDG status is given in Annex 3.8.

Sexual inequality remains a challenge for China. Its labour market is highly segregated by gender: layoffs affect women disproportionately, and gender-based wage differences continue. The proportion of female students enrolled in all types of educational institutions is lower than for men, and within the adult population the illiteracy rate for women is 2.6 times the rate for men. In the area of pension insurance, gender differences are notable even in the cities, where three men have insurance coverage for every two women. There is also a gender difference in public health services and medical insurance.

China has signed important UN conventions and resolutions, notably the UN Covenants on Economic, Social and Cultural Rights and on Civil and Political Rights, signed in 1997 and 1998 respectively, which remain the cornerstone for improving the situation of individual rights in China. The former was ratified on 28 February 2001, though with an important reservation concerning the freedom to establish trade unions.

3.2.4 The environmental and energy situation

An estimated 63% of China's energy comes from coal, which contributes significantly to air pollution and carbon emissions. The Government is shifting towards other energy sources through construction of new nuclear energy plants, gas pipeline projects, hydroelectric schemes, and other forms of renewable energy. But China's coal consumption continues to grow rapidly, with a corresponding increase in emissions. Energy conservation and efficiency in industry and in the building and automotive sectors remain very low. In 2004 China was the world's second largest consumer of petroleum products, and, as the source of around 40% of world oil demand growth in recent years, the country's demand is a key factor in world oil markets.

Carbon emissions and air pollution are direct results of the energy consumption of industrial activity, domestic heating and vehicle emissions. Sulphur dioxide and soot caused by coal combustion are two major air pollutants. Industry consumes almost half of China's coal and is the largest source of urban air pollution, resulting in a high level of pollution-related illnesses and a reduction in GDP. Chinese air pollution also affects other countries and regions, and the country contributes significantly to global carbon emissions. China is a non-Annex I country under the UNFCCC, and is not bound by targets for the reduction of carbon dioxide emissions under the Kyoto Protocol. The Government is nevertheless addressing pollution issues through new legislation, pricing reforms, environmental education campaigns and the delegation of environmental responsibility to local governments. China is playing a key role in international negotiations on climate change.

Economic growth is placing a heavy burden on China's water resources in both quantitative and qualitative terms. The current annual net water deficit is around 40 billion $m^3$ Water pollution exacerbates this situation and is leading to the extinction of species and serious and sometimes irreversible degradation of ecosystems. It stems mainly from industrial and municipal sources, but agricultural pollution from fertilisers and pesticides also impacts on water quality and inland and coastal fisheries. Water scarcity problems are being addressed through water engineering projects, but improved management of available water resources is required.

A further impact of China's industrialisation is the annual production of 30–50 million tonnes of hazardous wastes, for which there are currently neither standard procedures for disposal nor industry-to-disposal tracing methods, and for which legislation and technology are needed.

While China's 1998 logging ban introduced in selected provinces has curbed the degradation of the country's forestry resources, economic growth nevertheless continues to fuel high demand for roundwood, timber, pulp and paper. Domestic plantation production has increased but does not cover domestic needs, and the importation of roundwood and timber is increasing, often from countries where illegal logging is prolific. The Commission and China will continue to engage on the sustainable management of global forestry and timber resources as agreed at the EU-China Summit in September 2005.

At the end of 2004, it was estimated that some 27% of China's total land area was desertified. The reduction of desertification is hampered by non-sustainable agricultural and water-use practices.

### *3.3 CHINA'S POLICY AGENDA*

#### 3.3.1 An overview of China's political and economic agenda

China's 11th Five Year Plan (FYP) was approved by the National People's Congress in March 2006 and sets out policy guidelines for the country for the period from 2006 to 2010. Central to these objectives are efforts to balance economic advancement with the sometimes short-term conflicting objectives of social equality and environmental protection. This means redressing some. of the negative factors associated with China's rapid economic growth in recent years:

imbalances in regional growth and income distribution; uncontrolled capital investment; rising energy consumption; environmental degradation; and depletion of the country's resource base.

Priorities for the FYP can be summarised as follows:

- **To transform and rebalance the means by which China grows:** through increased emphasis on domestic demand as a stimulant for growth; expanding the primarily industrial growth base to services and agriculture; promoting human capital and technology as a driver of investment; and through more efficient use of resources.

- **To adjust and optimise the industrial structure:** through improved research and development capacity, and technological innovation; and through promoting industrialisation and employment creation in a regional context.
- **To address the problems associated with rural areas:** agricultural incomes and production to be improved through more efficient use of resources, improved agricultural techniques, better public services and infrastructure investment.
- **To secure a better balance of development between urban and rural areas, and between different regions:** through continued urbanisation and through policy development for the different regions based on analysis of resources, population distribution, etc.
- **Protection of resources and preservation of the environment:** through the promotion of resource-efficiency, environmental sustainability, and recycling.
- **Development of human resources, talent and technology:** to improve the country's innovative capacity; to ensure a more equitable distribution of education resources; and to improve the quality of higher education.
- **Further economic reform:** through placing greater reliance on market forces and deepening reforms in the fiscal, investment and financial systems; through the examination of structures for the pricing of resources.
- **Institutional reform:** through deepened reform of the administration system strengthening "governance by law", information disclosure and public participation in decision-making.

3.3.2 Social Sectors

Building a more harmonious, more socially responsible society is to be achieved through measures to reduce unemployment (limitation of layoffs in state enterprises, social assistance for the unemployed) and the reinforcement of social protection mechanisms such as health insurance for urban workers, revision of the pension system, and social protection for migrant workers. In parallel with these measures the proposals call for more social justice in income distribution ('regulation' of high incomes, progressive broadening and raising of minimum incomes, reduction of social and regional disparities, etc.).

As regards public health, the FYP highlights the need for increased government intervention. Priority will be given to the prevention of communicable and work-related diseases. The need for improved access to health care is recognised, and the question of work safety is given particular attention, notably in high-risk sectors such as mineral extraction.

In the area of education, the new plan targets the modernisation of teaching methods, the broadening of compulsory schooling to the age of fifteen, and the intensification of vocational training.

3.3.3 Environmental and energy policies

The Chinese Government is committed to maintaining economic growth while making the country's economy more sustainable. The production of cleaner energy, increasing energy efficiency and counteracting the deterioration of the environment are key preconditions to the achievement of these objectives. The concepts of the "harmonious society" and the "circular economy" provide overall guidance in relation to this development path.

China's strategy to meet growing energy demand is twofold: to increase supply from all available national and international energy sources, i.e. fossil fuels, renewable energy and nuclear energy; and to increase energy efficiency. By 2020, China plans to produce 15% of its total energy mix from renewable sources and around 4% from nuclear sources. Coal will nevertheless remain the principal energy source, and it will therefore be important for China to use it in a cleaner and more efficient manner. Improved energy efficiency will require massive investment, particularly in the construction and transport sectors, and in energy-intensive industries.

China's commitment to resolving broader environmental issues is also reflected in the FYP. One of the few quantified targets set out in the Plan is a decrease in energy consumption by 20% per unit of GDP over the period of the plan. Targets have also been set for strengthening macro-economic control over environmental issues, improving water resource management, combating air pollution, controlling waste pollution, halting the decline in biodiversity, enhancing the marine environment, and reinforcing environmental monitoring, supervision and enforcement.

There is strong Chinese interest in exploring EU practices and experience in these areas, including the use of regulatory and economic instruments in environmental policy and public participation in policymaking and implementation.

### *3.4 EC CO-OPERATION OBJECTIVES*

#### 3.4.1 The EU Treaty Objectives for External Co-operation

The European Commission's development programme in China is grounded in Article 177 of the Treaty Establishing the European Community[8], which sets out the following broad objectives for development co-operation:

- Sustainable economic and social development of developing countries;
- Smooth and gradual integration of developing countries into the world economy;
- The campaign against poverty in developing countries.

In addition, Article 18 la of the Treaty provides that the Community shall carry out economic, financial and technical co-operation measures with third countries that are complementary to those carried out by the Member States and consistent with the development policy of the Community. The Community's policy shall contribute to the general objective of developing and consolidating democracy and the rule of law, and encouraging respect for human rights and fundamental freedoms. Development co-operation is a multi-dimensional process covering broad-based equitable growth, capacity and institution-building, private-sector development, social services, environment, good governance and human rights.

#### 3.4.2 EU Objectives as laid down in other applicable documents

(1) In accordance with Article 177 of the Treaty Establishing the European Community, the Community's development cooperation policy shall foster the sustainable economic and social development of the developing countries, the smooth and gradual integration of these countries into the global economy and the fight against poverty. The Community's policy in this area shall contribute to the general objective of developing and consolidating democracy and the rule of law, and to that of respecting human rights and fundamental freedoms.

On the basis of Article 179 of the same Treaty, a new Development Cooperation Instrument (DCI) was adopted in December 2006. China is eligible to participate in co-operation programmes financed under the DCI (Regulation (EC) No. 1905/2006 of the European Parliament and of the Council of 18th December 2006 establishing a financial instrument for development co-operation).

(2) The present basis for EU-China co-operation is the 1985 Trade and Economic Cooperation Agreement between the then European Economic Community and the People's Republic of China (PRC), covering trade, economic co-operation and development as a basis for institutionalised dialogue.

However, this Agreement no longer reflects the breadth and scope of the relationship, and at the 9th EU-China Summit leaders agreed to launch negotiations on a new, extended Partnership and Co-operation Agreement (PCA) to update the basis for co-operation. This new agreement will provide a single framework covering the fall range and complexity of the relationship, and it should be forward-looking and reflect EU priorities.

(3) Current EU policy towards China is set out in the Commission's 2006 Communication to the Council and the European Parliament entitled "EU-China: Closer partners, growing responsibilities".[9]

In this document it is proposed that the EU should continue support for China's internal political and economic reform process, for a strong and stable China which fully respects fundamental rights and freedoms, protects minorities and guarantees the rule of law. It states that the EU will reinforce co-operation to ensure sustainable development, pursue a fair and robust trade policy and work to strengthen and add balance to bilateral relations. It recognises that the EU and China should work together in support of peace and stability and that the EU should increase co-ordination and joint action and improve co-operation with European industry and civil society.

A number of key objectives are identified in the Communication, notably: supporting China's transition towards a more open and pluralist society; promoting sustainable development; ensuring secure and sustainable energy supplies; combating climate change and improving the environment; improving exchanges on employment and social issues; improving co-ordination on international development; and building sustainable economic growth.

(4) In its 12 April 2005 Communication on Policy Coherence for Development, the Commission defined coherence commitments in the overall framework of the EU sustainable development strategy and identified the following priority areas with high potential for attaining synergies with development policy objectives: trade; environment; security; agriculture and fisheries; social dimension of globalisation, employment arid decent work; migration; research and innovation; information society; transport and energy. These commitments were endorsed by the General Affairs and External Relations Council (GAERC) on 24 May 2005. The Communication further calls on non-development policies to respect development policy objectives and on development co-operation to also contribute, where possible, to reaching the objectives of other EU policies.

(5) The importance of strengthening the social dimension of globalisation and of promoting productive employment and decent work opportunities was highlighted in §47 of the UN Summit conclusions of September 2005 regarding human and social development. UN member states committed themselves in particular to "strongly support fair globalisation and resolve to make the goals of full and productive employment and decent work for all, including for women and young people, a central objective of our national and international policies as well as our national development strategies, including poverty reduction strategies, as part of our efforts to achieve the MDGs."

(6) At its meeting on 22 November 2005, the General Affairs and External Relations Council adopted the EU Development Policy Statement, also known as "the European Consensus", endorsed by the European Parliament on 15 December, replacing the development commitments of the Joint Declaration of the Council and European Commission adopted in November 2000. The "European Consensus on Development" provides, for the first time, a common vision that guides the action of the EU, both at Member State and at Community level, in development co-operation.

The Statement identifies the eradication of poverty in the context of sustainable development, including pursuit of the MDGs, as the primary and overarching objective of EU development co-operation. The Statement also emphasises that EU partnership and dialogue with third countries will promote common values of respect for human rights, fundamental freedoms, peace, democracy, good governance, gender equality, the rule of law, solidarity and justice and the EU's commitment to effective multilateralism.

*3.5 REVIEW OF PREVIOUS CO-OPERATION*

In 1996 the Commission and the Chinese Government agreed to shift EC development funding from the established focal areas of infrastructure and rural development towards a range of interventions aimed at supporting the country's reform process, placing appropriate emphasis on human resource development. This policy shift reflected China's transformation from a traditional developing country to an economy in transition, and was designed to underpin the Government's strategy of accelerating economic, social and administrative reform.

The China 2002–2006 CSP reinforced this shift of emphasis, and contained three focal areas: support for social and economic reform; the environment and sustainable development; and good governance and the rule of law. A total indicative budget of €250 million was envisaged for the five-year period, initially allocated as €150 million under the first NIP (2002–2004), and €100 million under the second NIP. Out of this €250 million total indicative allocation, financing of programmes and projects has amounted to €181 million (72%). A list of projects and activities under the two NIPs is given in Annex 3.9. In addition there are two key ongoing pre-NIP programmes, the €16.9 million Natural Forest Management Programme and the €20 million Energy and Environment Programme.

A Mid-Term Review (MTR) of the CSP/NIP was carried out in 2003 and concluded that the cooperation objectives defined in the CSP remained valid. The fast pace of change in China highlighted the importance of the focal areas of co-operation in assisting the country with its efforts to ensure that the overall balance in its development is in keeping with its rapid economic growth. The review considered that the previous CSP was appropriate in this respect, and was in line with the Commission's 2003 China Policy Paper.

Certain modifications to the 2002–2004 NIP were required in order to reflect the realities encountered during project preparation, notably in the third focal sector – support for good governance and the rule of law – where political sensitivities were encountered. Neither the €10 million earmarked for the fight against illegal migration nor the €20 million intended for the development of civil society resulted in financing decisions. A programme designed to strengthen the rule of law and civil society was however approved in 2006, together with financing for the EU-China Law School.

This non-commitment in the third sector of intervention was in part used to strengthen the financing for the second sector – the environment and sustainable development – where the initial allocation of €45 million for biodiversity protection and water resources conservation was increased to €55 million.

The second NIP (2005–2006) focused on the CSP priority areas of social and economic reform, and good governance and the rule of law. Under the first sector, interventions have been approved for business management training (€8.15 million), and for the protection of intellectual property rights (€10.85 million). Under the second sector, funding was approved for the creation of an EU-China Law School (€18.2 million) and for "Governance for Equitable Development:

Strengthening the Rule of Law and Civil Society Participation in China" (€6.8 million). An additional cross-sectoral project to provide support for EU-China dialogues is now under implementation.

It had also been intended under the second NIP to provide financing (€50 million) for a second "China Window" under the worldwide Erasmus Mundus programme to enable additional scholarships to be granted to Chinese students to participate in Masters courses in Europe. Pending discussions with the Chinese Government on these funds, they were re-allocated to humanitarian relief and assistance in Asia, though further funding for higher education is proposed under the present Strategy Paper.

From 2002–2006 humanitarian assistance amounting to €10.5 million was allocated to China to assist the victims of flooding, and to support vulnerable groups in Tibet after heavy snowfall.

### *3.6 THEMATIC AND REGIONAL PROGRAMMES*

In addition to the interventions envisaged under the present programming document, and in support of some policy dialogues, the Commission will continue to finance complementary thematic interventions in the following areas[10]:

- Democracy and Human Rights: where activities could be funded to support co-operation and dialogue in the field of governance and human rights.
- Non-State Actors in Development; assistance could be provided to NGOs and other civil society organisations working in areas related to the SP.
- Migration and Asylum: in support of EU-China dialogue on these issues.
- Investing in People: initiatives to complement activities under the SP priority sector of human resources development and public administration co-operation.
- Environment and Sustainable Management of Natural Resources Including Energy: to complement the focal sector environment, energy and climate change.
- These thematic activities will be supported with financial resources that are additional to those provided under the MIP. In addition, China will benefit from activities funded under the Asia-wide programmes.

*3.7 CHINA AT A GLANCE – BASIC FACTS*

| | |
|---|---|
| Territory | 9.6 million sq km |
| Population | 1,300,000,000 (2004) |
| Population Growth rate | 0.6% (2004 estimate) |
| Birth rate | 13.14 births/I,000 population (2005 estimate) |
| Death rate | 7 deaths/I,000 population (2005 estimate) |
| Life expectancy at birth | 72 years (2004) |
| Adult Literacy Rate | 91% |
| Population below inter-national poverty line | 2.8% (2004) |
| Estimate ofHIV/AIDS prevalence | 0.06 to 0.11% (2004) |
| Malaria prevalence | 6.53% (2004) |
| Population with access to clean drinking water in rural areas | 60% (2004) |
| Under-live mortality rate | 25% (2004) |
| Net primary enrolment ratio | 98% (2003) |
| Girls in primary education | 47.2% (2002) |
| Maternal mortality ratio (per 100,000 live births) | 51.3(2003) |
| Ethnic diversity | Han Chinese: 91.9%; 55 other officially recognised minority groups including: Zhuang (16m), Manchu (10m), Hui (9m), Miao (8m), Muslim Uighurs (7m), Yi (7m); Tibetan (5m), Mongolian (5m), Buyi (3m), Korean (2m) |
| GDP | US$ 8.8 trillion (2005 estimate) at Purchasing Power Parity |
| GDP per Capita (PPP) | US$ 6,800 (2005 estimate) |
| Real GDP Growth | 9% (2005) |
| GDP Composition | agriculture 13%, industry 47%, services 40% (2005 estimates) |
| Exports | US$ 750 billion f.o.b. (2005 estimate) |
| Imports | US$ 630 billion f.o.b. (2005 estimate) |
| Bilateral Trade (Eurostat 2005) | EU Imports €126 billion – 12% of global imports EU Exports €48 billion – 5% of global exports |

*3.8 CHINA MDGs*

**OVERVIEW OF CHINA MDGs STATUS (AS AT OCTOBER 2005)**

| GOALS AND TARGETS | STATE OF GOAL ACHIEVEMENT | STATE OF SUPPORTIVE ENVIRONMENT |
|---|---|---|
| Eradicate Extreme Poverty and Hunger by 2015<br>• Halve the proportion of people living in extreme poverty | On track | Well developed |
| • Halve the proportion of population below minimum level of dietary energy consumption<br>• Make the proportion of underweight children under 5 | On track | In place |
| Universal primary education by 2015<br>• Achieve universal primary education by 2015 | On track | In place |
| Gender equality<br>• Achieve equal access for boys and girls to primary and lower secondary schooling by 2005 | On track | In place |
| • Achieve equal access for boys and girls to upper secondary education by 2005 | Maybe not on track | In place |
| Under 5 mortality<br>• Reduce under 5 mortality by two thirds by 2015 | Maybe not on track | In place |
| Reproductive Health<br>• Reduce maternal mortality ratio by three-quarters by 2015 | On track | In place |
| • Universal access to safe/reliable reproductive health services (contraceptive methods) by 2015 | On track | Well developed |
| Combat disease (HIV-AIDS, TB and malaria)<br>• Halt and reverse the spread ofHTVs/AIDS by 2015 | On track | In place |
| • Halve the prevalence of TB by 2015 | Maybe not on track | In place |
| • Reduce the incidence of malaria | On track | In place |
| Environment<br>• Implement national strategies for sustainable development by 2005 so as to reverse the loss of environmental resources by 2015 | Maybe not on track | Well developed |

| | | |
|---|---|---|
| Basic amenities<br>• Halve the proportion of people unable to reach or afford safe drinking water by 2015<br>• Improve the proportion of rural people with access to improve sanitation | On track<br><br>On track | Well developed<br><br>In place |

Source: "China's progress towards the Millennium Development Goals" Ministry of Foreign Affairs/UN- October 2005

*3.9 EC CO-OPERATION WITH CHINA UNDER THE 2002–2006 CSP*

**NIP 2002 – 2004. COMMITMENTS (PLANNED AND ACTUAL)**

| Projects and Programmes by sector | Planned in NIP | Committed 2002 | Committed 2003 | Committed 2004 | TOTAL COMMIT TED |
|---|---|---|---|---|---|
| **Support to Social and Economic Reforms** | | | | | |
| EU-China WTO co-operation | 15,00 | 15,00 | | | 15,00 |
| Social security reform | 20,00 | | | 20.00 | 20,00 |
| Information society | 15,00 | | | 15.00 | 15,00 |
| Human resources development: | 25,00 | | | | |
| (a) Managers Exchange and Training Programme | | | | 17.20 | 17,20 |
| (b) Scholarships linked to Erasmus Mundus | | | | 9,00 | 9,00 |
| **Sector sub-total** | **(75,00)** | | | | **(76,20)** |
| **Environment and Sustainable Development** | | | | | |
| Environment Programme Policy Advice | 15,00 | | | | |
| Biodiversity protection | 15,00 | | | 30.00 | 30,00 |
| Water Resources Conservation | 15,00 | | | 25.00 | 25,00 |
| **Sector sub-total** | **(45,00)** | | | | **(55,00)** |
| **Good Governance and the Rule of Law** | | | | | |
| Fight against illegal immigration | 10,00 | | | 0,00 | 0,00 |
| Support to civil society | 20,00 | | | 0,00 | 0,00 |
| **Sector sub-total** | (30,00) | | | | (0,00) |
| **TOTALS** | 150,00 | 15,00 | 0,00 | 116.20 | 131,20 |

**NIP 2005 – 2006. PLANNED COMMITMENTS**

| Projects and Programmes by sector | Planned in NIP | Committed 2002 |
|---|---|---|
| **Support to Social and Economic Reforms** | | |
| Higher edication: Erasmus Mundus China Window | 50,00 | 0,00 |
| Business Management Training Project | | 8,15 |
| Protection of Intellectual Property Rights | 10,00 | 10.85 |
| **Sector sub-total** | **(60,00)** | **(60,00)** |
| **Good Governance and the Rule of Law** | | |
| Governance Capacity Building | 25,00 | |
| Rule of Law and Civil Society Programme (1) | | 6,80 |
| EU-China Law School | | 18,20 |
| **Sector sub-total** | **(25,00)** | **(25,00)** |
| **Cross-Sectoral** | | |
| Policy Dialogue Support Facility (PDSF) | 5,00 | 6,00 |
| **Reserve** | **10,00** | |
| **TOTALS** | **100,00** | **50,00** |

(1) Governance for Equitable Development: Strengthening Rule of law and Civil Society participation in China

### *3.10 2006 COUNTRY-LEVEL EVALUATION*

An independent Country-Level Evaluation of the EC co-operation programme was commissioned in 2006, from which conclusions have been drawn from past experience, and recommendations made for future co-operation. The evaluation was carried out while taking account of the EU's strategic interests in China and the sectoral policy dialogues.

Based on in-depth reviews of the main areas of co-operation in which the programme has been engaged since 1998, the evaluation concluded that the EC approach to China is generally rated positively, and the following overall conclusions have been reached and recommendations made:

Overall Conclusions

- The EC approach to China is considered relevant to the Chinese policy context and needs, and is consistent with long-term EU policy goals. It is providing opportunities: to engage in institution-building relating to regulation, legislation, standards, best practices, etc., with positive (albeit hard to quantify) impacts on EU-China trade and business relations; to improve China's capacity to deal with environmental problems as well as with its own emerging social reforms; and to engage in human rights dialogue and co-operation.

- While there have been successes at the level of policy processes and regimes (legislation, standards, regulations), concrete results have been limited by problems at the level of policy administration, implementation and enforcement. Many of these arise from poor governance.
- Impact and effectiveness have been adversely affected, though not fatally, by delays in project implementation.
- At the higher level, the Chinese and European sides share a common language and partnership, and are moving towards a dialogue of equals. At the level of implementation, however, there continues to be some friction over the Commission's policy of limiting its financing to technical assistance and expertise.
- Co-ordination between the EC and Member States, and between the EC and multilateral aid organisations, is strong in form but weak in substance.
- Links between the EC-China sectoral dialogues and the co-operation programme are satisfactory as regards the impact of dialogues on the co-operation programme, but more could be done to feed the dialogues with valuable experience gained from the co-operation programme.
- Too many promising pilot projects have not been replicated elsewhere or rolled out to the national level; project follow-up is weak.
- Poverty and the theme of "winners and losers" have not been well integrated into economic and social reform projects, nor into trade projects.
- Given that the 2006 Commission Communication clearly spells out a new vision for cooperation with China, one based more solidly on mutual gains, there is a need to look beyond the time when development co-operation will be an appropriate tool of engagement.

Overall Recommendations:

- Development co-operation with China should be continued, but with greater effort to publicise the mutual benefits accruing.
- Recent policy formulation successes with programmes designed to improve administration, implementation and enforcement should be continued. In order to be successful, however, the theme of governance should be better mainstreamed into all sectors.
- Problems of implementation delays are universally recognised. The problem should be analysed and measures taken to find remedies.
- On partnership issues, taking account of the financial resources available to the Government of China, the EC should maintain its policy of only financing technical assistance in order to provide international best practice and European policy models, in areas where the EC has a unique comparative advantage to deliver.
- The EC Delegation should review, in terms of organisational structures, information flow and human resources policy, the role and functions of the project officers with regard to the sectoral dialogues.
- The follow-up to pilot projects is essentially the responsibility of the Government of China. However, more attention should be paid to replication and roll-out during the project formulation and implementation phases. The current Social Security Project offers a good laboratory for testing ways of promoting follow-up.
- The mainstreaming of poverty, vulnerable groups and losers from reform into EC-financed interventions should be improved.
- While EC engagement has made a significant contribution to integrating China into the world economy, especially in the areas of WTO-related capacity-building, policy advice and awareness-raising, efforts should be made to align trade co-operation more directly with European industry needs. This could be done by bringing all relevant

parties together – the Ministry of Commerce, European industry representatives, and the EC Delegation – to set a programme of work.

- Projects and programmes should concentrate on large, complex problem areas (such as financial services or information society) that demand long-term involvement of European and Chinese counterparts. Such projects have greater lasting impact than smaller-scale interventions, and they also exploit the EC's comparative advantage more successfully. This comparative advantage consists largely in the ability to offer "one-stop shopping" for European policy models.
- Environment should be a consistent component of important EC interventions in China such as the trade sector policy dialogue and trade programmes, and an integrated approach in tackling climate change issues in China should be taken by incorporating aspects of climate change in ongoing and current EC-financed environmental programmes.
- The EC has successfully mainstreamed the issues of disadvantaged hinterland regions such as Western China, the Central Provinces and the North-Eastern 'rust belt' into its approach to development co-operation. However, the EC's project contributions are (unavoidably) lacking in scope and volume to fundamentally redress the issue of regional disparities in China. The sharing of best European practice in the area of regional development seems to be particularly welcomed by national officials.
- It is recommended that continued attention be given to donor co-ordination. A more unified European position in the area of climate change should, in particular, be established. The concept of complementarity should be integrated more effectively into strategic planning. Discussions on complementarity should feature a structural analysis of how the activities of the different actors interact and how and by whom gaps can be filled.
- With GDP per capita in China continuing to grow at near double-digit rates, bilateral cooperation will in the future cease to be an appropriate means of engagement. The new Communication clearly expresses the view that co-operation with China must be more firmly based on mutual benefit, and it would therefore be appropriate to begin a dialogue with the Government and other relevant partners on the form of longer-term, post-co-operation engagement. Not only would such a process improve the quality of development co-operation outcomes in its remaining years, but it would also avoid the possible situation in which China unilaterally decides that development co-operation has outlived its usefulness.

### *3.11 PROJECTS FINANCED UNDER THEMATIC BUDGET LINES AND ASIA-WIDE PROGRAMMES (ongoing or recently completed)*

| **1. THEMATIC BUDGET LINES** | |
|---|---|
| **1.1 Democracy and Human Rights** | 1.989.518 |
| European Initiative on Democracy and Human Rights | 1.989.518 |
| **1.2 NGO Co-financing** | 7.192.508 |
| Maternal & Child Health Care Project, Mid-West China | 883.779 |
| Child Welfare in Communities | 1.000.000 |
| Poverty Alleviation for Older People and Their Communities in Western China | 750.000 |

| | |
|---|---|
| Yunnan Integrated Primary Health Care Project | 713.824 |
| Innovative and Integrated STI/HIV/AIDS interventions targeting vulnerable mobile population in Guangxi Province, PRC | 575.688 |
| Rural Community Development: a microfinance project for poverty alleviation in PRC | 500.000 |
| Yunnan minority basic education project -replication phase | 680.063 |
| Block Grant | 1.000.000 |
| Poverty Alleviation through Capacity Building of Rural populations | 308.705 |
| **1.3 Gender** | 757.246 |
| Employment Promotion and Rights Protection for Migrant Women Workers in Beijing | 757.246 |
| **1.4 Health and Population** | 1.066.922 |
| Access to essential STD services in urban areas in China | 1.066.922 |
| **2. ASIA-WIDE PROGRAMMES** | |
| **2.1 Asia Pro Eco (environment)** | 8.459.304 |
| Oasis-Hydrosphere-Desert Interaction Influencing Overall Economical Development | 386.429 |
| Toward a better environment: implementation of energy-saving buildings in China | 382.599 |
| Feeding China's expanding demand for wood pulp: a diagnostic assessment of plantation development, fibre supply, and impacts on natural forests in China and in the South East Asia Region | 466.585 |
| Marine Investment for Future Prosperity (MARINVEST) | 386.174 |
| Feasibility Study on Demonstration of Voluntary Approaches for Industrial Environmental Management in China | 334.139 |
| Diagnostic on the commercial use ofbiogas recovered from the landfill in Mianyang | 500.000 |
| SBC Conferences Asia | 350.609 |
| $CO_2$ Managers for the Industry in the People's Republic of China | 212.945 |
| Policy Reinforcement for Environmental Sound and Socially Responsible Economic Development in China (PRODEV) | 480.920 |
| Land Amelioration and Desertification Alleviation by Short-Rotation-Plant using Saline/Brackish Water (LADAS) | 244.872 |
| Diagnostic Study for the Promotion of a Sustainable Solid Waste Management Model in the Province of Sichuan | 238.66 |

| | |
|---|---|
| Feasibility study on the extensive utilisation of biodiesel produced from waste and/or pure oils/fats in the public vehicles in Hangzhou and preparation for the implementation of a demonstration plant (biodiesel-Fs) | 244.75 |
| Reducing $CO_2$ emissions in China: economic legal and technical viability for an architectural integration and local production of large photovoltaic modules in China's Yunnan Province | 78.214 |
| Developing Policy Formulation and Implementation Tools for Providing Support for Ecological Forest Management in China's Urban and Peri-Urban Areas | 221.05 |
| Sustainable Urban Housing: strengthening capacity in policy formulation and implementation in the city of Xi'an | 321.012 |
| Building Capacities for Corporate Environmental Management \A Survey of Experiences in the Yunnan and Jiangsu Provinces of the PR China | 214.616 |
| Feasibility study for the design of an industrial park with very low energy consumption and energy [integration between the manufacturing and the residential buildings | 246.766 |
| Capacity Building and Policy Reinforcement in China in the Field of Water Resource Management | 306.90 |
| Sustainable Problem Solutions for Asian Urban Settlements and Developments by Exemplary Analysis of Sewage and Waters of the Urban Settlement "Changde" and its "Chuanzhi" River Basin | 443.98 |
| Supporting Deyang City in achieving the status of a National Environmental Protection Model City by establishing an environmental coordination office – Green City Deyang- and practically demonstrating its role in advising and build structures that secures the solving of the City's hazardous medical waste [management problems. | 202.914 |
| Chinese Learning for Overcoming Barriers in Environment HI (CLOBE III) | 684.422 |
| Ecological use of pig waste in peri-urban towns | 727.595 |
| i0EU-China Network for Capacity Building on -Municipal Waste Management | 196.627 |
| Capacity Building on Business Opportunities for CDM Projects in China | 179.305 |
| **2.2 Asia Urbs (urban development)** | 5.327.300 |
| Suzhou Ecological waste Management | 47.917 |
| Music & Education: a cooperation for the youth | 404530,62 |
| mUrban Revitalisation in me Former European Concession Area in Tianjin | 486.670 |

| | |
|---|---|
| MAIN – Model Application of Intelligent Public Transport Systems and Sustainable Mobility Policies in iNingbo | 435.856 |
| Heritage Conservation in Beijing URBS MODEL BEIJING | 499.999 |
| Environmental Upgrading of urban areas through Tourism (EUTOU) | 499.810 |
| Better Care-Solutions for Elderly in Shanghai | 439.744 |
| Pilot Project In Panzhihua for the Implementation ofECOPROFIT in China | 439.117 |
| Heritage Management and Economic Development | 498.080 |
| Sustainable City Development for Qufu City: Safeguarding Natural and Cultural Heritage and Cultural Tourism Initiatives | 749.922 |
| Sustainable Waste Handling in Hefei | 723.572 |
| **2.3 Asia Invest (business co-operation)** | 7 953.210 |
| Small Mushrooms – Big Business | 142507 |
| Cleaner Production in the Foundry Industry of the P.R. of China | 150000 |
| EU-Hunan Asia-INTERPRISE 2004 | 2[illegible]3569 |
| Asia-Invest ALLIANCE, Improving Investment & Business Promotion in Sichuan (IIBPS) | 9[illegible]892 |
| Asia-Invest ALLIANCE, Sino-European Network for Better Training Capacities in Intermediary business Organisations (IBOs) | 151425 |
| Asia-Invest TECHNICAL ASSISTANCE, Project Management Training for Chinese SMEs of the Electrical Engineering Sector | 74725 |
| China Food 2004: co-operation in the food industry | 98804 |
| Asia-INTERPRISE, Toy Manufacturing and Industry China 2004 | 104178 |
| Asia-INTERPRISE Vinitech China 2004/2005 | 123,480 |
| Asia-INTERPRISE, EU-China Business Encounters for Analytical, Biotechnology, Diagnostics and Laboratory Technology Sectors | 98,927 |
| Asia-INTERPRISE – “Scandinavia-China Partnership 2004” | 263101 |
| Asia-INTERPRISE – EU-China Business Meeting in the Photonics Industry | 121568 |
| Asia-INTERPRISE – EU-China Chemical Industries Partnership 2004 | 124,290 |
| Asia-INTERPRISE – EU-Sichuan SMEs Business Meeting | 116904 |
| SELECT – Sino-European Liaison enabling collaborations and trade in information technology | 87456 |
| SME Match-making in China for cooperation in the textile and clothing industry | 143618 |

| | |
|---|---|
| Developing Sino-European cooperation by improving Chinese IBOs' services | 104652 |
| U3U-China automotive industry cooperation in the Yangtze river region | 135054 |
| Asia Interprise Medical Devices Business Meeting EU-China | 149091 |
| ChinaEsNET | 173895 |
| Asia Interprise PROPAK CHINA 2005 | 194000 |
| EU-Asia Equipment Manufacturing Alliance 2005 | 132032 |
| PROSYS | 176073 |
| Strengthening the institutional capacity for FDI attraction and European networking linkages to Shanxi region, China | 172573 |
| Capacity Building of Chinese Technological Intermediary Business Organisations (TIBOs) for international Technological Co-operations | 182018 |
| Stiftung für wirtschaftliche Entwicklung und berufliche Qualifizierung (SEQUA) | 143123 |
| ECOPROFIT for Sustainable Mongolian Entrepreneurship | 173704 |
| Asia-Invest Alliance: Strengthening the Photonics Industry, EU-China | 176043 |
| To improve Market Access for European and Chinese SMEs involved in the manufacture and supply of electrical and electronic components, by building their awareness and providing practical training on compliance strategies for the European Environment Directive ROHS, which concerns the Removal of Hazardous Substances from electrical and electronic products | 272216 |
| lEU – China Yellow River Delta Interprise | 295079 |
| EUROASIA 2006 | 314793 |
| Asia Interprise EU-China packaging 2006 | 176,500 |
| Institutional strengthening in support of the enforcement of Copyright protection in China, through capacity building of collection management societies (CMS) and exchange of European best practices in CMS | 146318 |
| Corporate Social Responsibility- A Response to the Social Dimension of Globalisation in China | |
| COSMEC – Cooperation programme for a Sustainable Partnership between SMEs of the Mechanical Industry (Machinery for Mechanics: Wood/Glass-Working Machinery, Construction Machinery, Agriculture Machinery) from the European Union and China | 238959 |
| Embedded Software Quality Assurance and Testing: provision of Training & Technical Assistance to Chinese Software SMEs | 147931 |
| CASE EU-China Matchmaking for Camping Facilities and Services | 397026 |

| | |
|---|---|
| EU-China Business Encounters in the Agricultural and Food Sector | 185899 |
| Euro-Chinese T.O.U.R. (Tourism Operators Utter Reunion) | 360807 |
| EU-Chengdu SMEs Business Matchmaking & Cooperation Incubation | 332692 |
| EU-China Partenariat 2006 | 1.182.944 |
| **2.4 Asia Link (networking between higher education institutions)** | 5.220.131 |
| The development of a core curriculum on European Studies to be used in China for MA students with supplementary Elements for PhD students | 299.233 |
| European Multimedia Curriculum for studying Modem Chinese language and Society | 291.190 |
| An integral approach to curriculum development for nature conservation in China | 242.030 |
| Promoting and Assisting Product Engineering Design Education in China | 300,000 |
| Euro-China Exchange: Technology and Culture of Generative Design Approach | 298,502 |
| Professional Joint European Chinese Cooperation in Tourism | 282.500 |
| Development of a Curriculum for Standardisation in Companies and markets | 300.000 |
| Promoting Illuminating Engineering Studies, Research and Continuing Co-operation between Europe and China | 299.783 |
| Nottingham Trent-Lappeenranta-Chongqing Universities' collaboration for human resource development in mechanical and manufacturing engineering | 222.715 |
| ECLEE – European-Chinese Link in Electrical Engineering | 298.647 |
| Masterclass among FDU, SJU, TUE and QMUL in Materials Science and Engineering | 300.000 |
| Curriculum and Module Development in Asian European Economics and Business Studies | 299.373 |
| Developing an International Master Programme on Entrepreneurship and Innovation | 299.390 |
| EMERSION – Education to Meet the Requirements of Software Industry and Beyond | 300.000 |
| Curricula Development of Technology Oriented Sustainable Resource Management in China and Thailand | 299.585 |
| Interpreting Asia Interpreting Europe | 273.795 |
| Algebra and Representations in China and Europe | 300.000 |

| | |
|---|---|
| Development of Multi-Discilinary Management Strategies for Conservation and Use of Heritage Sites in Asia and Europe | 299,895 |
| Sino-European Design Management Network | 299.895 |
| Asian Studies in Europe and China | 300.000 |
| Knowledge transfer on shi design, production and operation – towards safety, efficiency and low environmental impact | 300,000 |
| Social entrepreneurship in Asia and Europe | 300,000 |
| Academic exchange of soil biophysics: the fundamental science behind the improvement of degraded soils | 300,000 |
| Integrated Watershed Management (INWAMA): a new synergetic training course for Asian – European master degree education and training in Integrated Watershed Management | 300,000 |
| EU-Asia university exchange and cooperation and cooperation in the field of telecommunication technologies | 300,000 |
| Design and Implementation of a Curriculum on Curriculum Development (DCCD) | 298,893 |
| Innovation by Universitary Vocational Training – Curriculum Development for Competence promotion in the building automation | 298,889 |
| Curriculum development for brand building and fashion management in China and the EU | 300,000 |
| Asia-Europe link in nuclear physics and astrophysics | 300,000 |
| Comparing European and Asian studies: towards the renewal of curricular programmes | 299,957 |
| Geo-environmental engineering training programme in China | 300,000 |
| Center for Sino-European sustainable building design and construction | 262,623 |
| A multidisciplinary approach to curriculum development in sustainable built environment | 300,000 |
| STARTSIM (Training of the entrepreneurial skills by networked start up simulation) | 287,608 |
| SECER – Sino-Euro Centre of Education & Research on SoC | 199,990 |
| IMSt&E – Innovative Management Strategies & Education | 300,000 |
| Development of Higher Education Teaching and Training Modules for Energy Saving and Environment protection in process Industries | 287,138 |
| Educating Multi-Cultural Multi-National Future Leaders in Electronic Engineering | 219,604 |
| Executive MBA/ MBA Programme "Conventions and Trade Fair Management" | 298,362 |

| | |
|---|---|
| Development of a joint course module in high performance computing and grid computing | 298,783 |
| Development of Master level Teaching and Professional Training Modules in Managing Implementation of Enterprise Information Systems (Mi-EIS) | 295,945 |
| EA-Grid: Euro-Asia United Establishment of Double Degree Master's Programme in Grid Computing | 296,647 |
| New Intel-university Network For Energy and Environment – NINFEE | 410,597 |
| A Framework Approach to Strengthening Asian Higher Education on Advanced Design and Manufacture | 730,585 |
| Human Resources Development for the improvement and protection of environment in Asia | 635,305 |
| URO – A new curriculum to improve the "quality of life" for people with URinary incOntinence | 299,872 |
| A EU-China Campus for Energy and Environment (EEC) | 354,885 |
| Organic Farming: Social, Ethical, Economical, Scientific and Technical aspects in a global perspective | 648,491 |
| Capacity building and establishing new Master-level curricula on mobile, wireless and Internet technologies | 573,058 |
| Joint Development of a Core Curriculum with printed and Multi-Media Teaching and Learning Material for an Innovative European-Chinese MA Double Degree in Intercultural Studies | 605,028 |
| International OM – International Operations Management | 605,873 |
| Development of an International Curriculum of landscape knowledge in architecture and urban planning education | 294,817 |
| 2.5 Asia IT & C (information technology and communication) | 5.296,230 |
| EDECAD: Education and Ecommerce Task Force for Asia-EU small firm Development | 371,235 |
| Adapting to the Chinese context a software dedicated to design and simulation of the thermal behaviours of buildings | 184,000 |
| Generic Epidemiological network in Nephrology and Rheumatology (GENNERE) | 400,000 |
| SIN-ASIA Sintronic INnovative Technologies for ASIA | 400,000 |
| ELVIS: E-leaming virtual interactive synthetic characters | 387,370 |
| WECIDM (Web-Enabled Collaboration in Intelligent Design and Manufacture) | 381,501 |
| Sino-European Systems Usability project | 370,000 |

| | |
|---|---|
| Enhancing Vegetable Supply Chain Management with Internet Technologies | 327,000 |
| Cybernetic technologies for cars in the Chinese Cities | 400,000 |
| Application of Information technologies for the sustainable management of ectractive industry activities | 343,000 |
| Corp Growth Monitoring and Yield Forecasting in the North China lain (Huabei) | 313,000 |
| Broadband for Barefoot Bankers | 235,000 |
| (TELEATH) Transfer of IT&C e-learning skills to China | 199,000 |
| (DYNASTY) Demonstrating a platform for Dynamic Traffic Information Services for the CITY of Beijing | 398,000 |
| (JEAGAL) Joint European-Asian educational and application development programme on GALileo | 392,000 |
| (Tele-Imaging in Medicine, TIME) a cyber-bridge interfaces China with Europe on collaborative health care | 195,124 |

### *3.12 THE SECTORAL DIALOGUES*

An Overview of Sectoral Dialogues between China and the European Commission

Relations between the European Union and China have intensified in recent years, partly as a consequence of China's economic growth and increasing importance on the world stage. But the rapid development of the relationship also stems from shared interests between the two sides.

In addition to the complementarity of interests in the political arena, in areas such as multilateralism and global sustainable development, further evidence is found in the flourishing area of exchanges on sectoral policies and technical issues or 'sectoral dialogues'. These have grown considerably in recent years and now cover a wide range of areas where China and the EU favour similar approaches.

China today is experiencing challenges which Europe started to tackle a number of years ago in areas such as the environment, the internal market and competition, where the EU has demonstrated its willingness to share its experience with China, and China has shown a corresponding interest in using some of the best practices of the "EU models".

In other areas both Europe and China are confronted with new challenges, such as rapid advances in science and technology and problems associated with health protection. These are two-way exchanges, and cover some areas where Europe can benefit from Chinese experience. Peaceful nuclear research is an example: the use of experimental reactors; nuclear safety; nuclear technology for both existing and future reactors; and radiation protection-Under the 2004 Euratom agreement China is prepared to share her technology with European researchers.

The dialogues take place at various hierarchical levels, from working to ministerial level, and constitute an effective tool for deepening EU relations with China. A "Policy Dialogue Support Facility" financed under the Commission's 2005–2006 National Indicative Programme for China (€6 million) has been prepared and will shortly become operational.

The areas covered by the dialogues

*Agriculture*

The EU-China Dialogue on Agriculture covers bilateral trade in agriculture, non-tariff barriers including in particular sanitary and phytosantitary issues, quality policies including geographical indications and organic products, exchange of policy information, and other topics of mutual interest including food technologies and rural development. The first meeting was held in November 2006 in Brussels.

*Civil aviation*

The need to develop a new framework for China-EU civil aviation relations was highlighted by a judgement of the European Court of Justice in 2002 stating that the bilateral air services agreements between EU Member States and third countries such as China are contrary to European law if they discriminate against carriers from other Member States. This is the case under practically all existing bilateral air services agreements between EU Member States and third countries. China has agreed to restore legal conformity through negotiating a single agreement that would bring bilateral agreements into line with Community law. Negotiations on this agreement started in 2005.

The Chinese side has shown strong interest in enhancing technical co-operation in a broad range of areas including aviation safety, security and air traffic management. A successful co-operation project in this area financed by the Commission and European and Chinese industry was in 2005 extended until 2006. An EU-China Aviation Summit, organised by the European Commission and the Chinese civil aviation authority (CAAC), took place in mid-2005 in Beijing.

*Competition policy*

Competition policy is a crucial issue in the context of China's efforts to restructure its economy. China's large economy needs a sound competition regime. The fragmented domestic Chinese market needs. improved regulation to create a level playing field for market operators and to accompany the reform of large inefficient state-owned enterprises. In the medium term, improved regulation should also alleviate the current risks of trade dumping and economic instability emanating from China. With this in mind, in May 2004 China and the EU agreed upon a permanent mechanism for consultation in this area. The dialogue will enhance the EU's technical and capacity-building assistance to China in the area of competition policy with the aim of developing a proper Chinese competition regime which is shaped in the right way to fit the Chinese reality. The process is facilitated by the fact that the emerging Chinese competition system follows the "European model".

*Consumer product safety*

China is one of the EU's most important trading partners when it comes to consumer goods, and this relationship can only be expected to grow in the coming years. By developing a common understanding between Europe and China on product safety issues, a culture of mutual understanding and trust can be developed. The 2006 Memorandum of Understanding between the European Commission's DG for Health and Consumer Protection (SANCO) and the Chinese General Administration for Quality Supervision, Inspection and Quarantine (AQSIQ) aims at enhancing the co-operation on these issues and establishing better communication and collaboration between the responsible authorities on general product safety. A Working Group has been established between DG SANCO and AQSIQ to implement the different actions under the agreement.

An agreement on a Roadmap for safer toys was concluded with AQSIQ in September 2006 with the aim of ensuring that toys exported to the EU from China are safe. It outlines a strategy for improving the safety of Chinese toys, focusing on training and technical assistance, exchanges of information between EU and Chinese authorities, and tracing, feedback and follow-up mechanisms for dangerous products. It puts in place a framework, supported by both the European and Chinese toy manufacturers' associations, for continuous exchanges of information on unsafe toys. It also contains a commitment from AQSIQ on tightening up inspection and supervision of toys exported to Europe.

*Customs co-operation*

Close co-operation between customs authorities is vital to facilitate trade and to help combat illegal activities such as fraud and counterfeiting. An agreement for EU-China customs co-operation entered into force in April 2005 with the objective to increase operational co-operation usefal for the control of the trade flows and the fight against fraud and illegal activities, to provide mutual technical assistance and to conduct joint EU/China customs actions. Additionally, in order to combat terrorist threats, there is an undergoing pilot project on smart and secure trade lanes to test exchange of information and many other aspects of supply chain security whose long term objective would be mutual recognition of customs controls, security standards and business partnership programs, as advocated by the World Customs Organisation' Framework of Standards and as requested by the tradecommunity.

*Education and Culture*

The European Commission's new Erasmus Mundus programme came into force in 2004. It provides financing for students from third countries to pursue post-graduate studies in Europe. Special 'windows' for China and other Asian countries have been set up to attract significant numbers of students from this region to study in Europe. Further ways of enhancing dialogue and co-operation in the field of education and culture are currently being explored.

*Employment and Social Affairs*

*On* 5 September 2005, at the EU-China Summit in Beijing, Commissioner Vladimir Spidia signed with the Chinese Minister of Labour and Social Security, Tian Chengping, a Memorandum of Understanding (MoU) on EU-China co-operation on Labour, Employment and Social Affairs. This provides the framework for EU-China dialogue in areas such as social protection, social cohesion, labour legislation, employment, labour relations and social dialogue. The first event under the MoU, a seminar on "Employment Promotion and Vocational Training", took place the day after the signing of the MoU. The second event took place in Brussels in November 2006 on the theme of "Labour Mobility in the EU and China". The EU is furthermore assisting China with the reform of social protection systems through a five-year Social Security Reform Co-operation Project.

*Energy – including nuclear energy*

China's increasing appetite for energy has significant repercussions on global markets and on the environment. The energy dialogue has been in existence since 1994 and is one of the earliest sectoral dialogues. It takes the form of annual working group meetings and a bi-annual Conference on EU-China Energy Co-operation. Current subjects of discussion include energy policy and development strategy, the evolution of energy markets, and security of supply and sustainable development.

On 4 March 2005, the Commission's Directorate General for Transport and Energy (TREN) and the MOST signed an Action Plan on Clean Coal and terms of reference for an Action Plan on Industrial Cooperation on Energy Efficiency and Renewable Energies.

A Memorandum of Understanding establishing an "EU-China Dialogue on Energy and Transport Strategies" between DG TREN and the NDRC was signed on the occasion of the EU-China Summit on $5^{th}$ September 2005 in Beijing. The first meetings took place in Brussels on $21^{st}$ March 2006, with the energy discussions focussing on: Energy policies, Energy efficiency, energy savings and the environmental impact of energy. Technology co-operation and renewables.

The 2004 EURATOM agreement with China focuses on research into the peaceful use of nuclear energy and grants researchers from both sides access to each other's facilities, and the EU and China are both participating in the international ITER programme for the construction of an experimental controlled fusion reactor.

*Environment*

Chinese policymakers increasingly see environmental protection as a major challenge and China has an important global role to play in this field. Over the last decade, contacts between the European Commission and the Chinese State Environmental Protection Agency (SEPA), the Ministry of Science and Technology (MOST), the National Development and Reform Council (NDRC) and other key ministries have intensified. The dialogue with SEPA on environmental issues was recently upgraded to ministerial level.

A substantial part of the EU-China financial assistance budget is allocated to environmental support projects. Co-operation and exchanges cover issues such as biodiversity, river basin management, forest protection, climate change and waste management; water and air pollution, vehicle emissions, environmental indicators, sustainable consumption and production and environmental impact assessments. The Joint EU-China Declaration on Climate Change, adopted at the September 2005 Summit, served to identify steps for tackling climate change.

*Food safety – Sanitary and Phytosanitary (SPS) issues*

Co-operation between China and the EC in this field can bring benefits to consumers both in the EU and China, and facilitate trade in agricultural goods. A Joint Technical Group was established in 2002 to deal with regulatory questions in this area. The recent Memorandum of Understanding between the European Commission's DG for Health and Consumer Protection (SANCO) and the Chinese General Administration for Quality Supervision, Inspection and Quarantine (AQSIQ) aims at considerably enhancing co-operation on these issues and at establishing better communication and collaboration between the responsible authorities on food safety and SPS issues.

*Galileo global satellite navigation services*

The European Galileo programme will provide high-precision global satellite navigation services, an area in which China is keen to develop links with the EU. A co-operation agreement was concluded in October 2003 under which China has pledged to contribute €200 million to the programme, the estimated total cost of which amounts to some €3–4 billion. A follow-up agreement between the Chinese Remote Sensing Centre and the Galileo Joint Undertaking was signed in October 2004, for the first time opening this Community undertaking to the full participation of a non-EU country. Chinese participation in the programme paves the way for tangible scientific and industrial collaboration projects.

*High-Level Consultations on the Fight against Illegal Migration and Trafficking of Human Beings*

Following the June 2000 tragedy in Dover where 58 Chinese illegal migrants suffocated in a container, the EC and China agreed to cooperate more closely in the fight against illegal migration. High-Level Consultations on the Fight against Illegal Migration and Trafficking of Human Beings started in October 2000 and have been held regularly since then. At the 7th round in July 2006 it was agreed to broaden the scope of these consultations and also include wider migration-related issues, for example ways of facilitating legitimate people-to-people exchanges and reinforced administrative cooperation. The conclusion ofaReadmission Agreement with China remains a priority for the EU.

*Information Society*

The dialogue on information society started in 1997 and all exchanges in this wide area (Information Technology, telecoms, audiovisual) have now been grouped under one umbrella dialogue, covering both research co-operation and policy discussions. On the co-operation side the aim is to promote collaboration between European and Chinese research teams. This is seen as essential to ensure exploitation of research results at a global level and to build interoperable technology and standards solutions. It is of high value for the competitiveness of European industry, and is of great interest to the Chinese government. It also offers a means of reaching a consensus on global critical issues such as security and dependability. Key issues on the policy side include the respective developments in telecom policy and activities in areas such as e-Govemment, security of networks, and the promotion of e-Commerce. At the same time, the Dialogue offers the possibility for both sides to pursue concerns – for example, for the EU this includes issues such as the assignment of 3G licences (third-generation mobile communications) in China, delays in the emergence of a transparent regulatory framework for telecommunications, difficulties in accessing telecom services markets, and a number of standards issues. The dialogue is being backed up with a considerable number of technical assistance activities under the development co-operation programme (China-EU Information Society project, EU-China Trade Project) and has developed links to the Regulatory and Industrial Policy Dialogue (eg for telecom equipment certification issues) and the Intellectual Property Dialogue (for IP issues regarding telecom equipment).

*Intellectual Property Rights (IPR)*

China has made considerable efforts to adapt its IPR legislation to the 'Trade-Related aspects *of* Intellectual Property Rights Agreement' (TREPs) – a cornerstone of the World Trade Organisation's (WTO) legal framework. China became a WTO member ift 2001. Further concrete action is, however, needed on the Chinese side to update its legislation on IPR and in particular to establish a more effective enforcement system for IPR. A formal dialogue on this was signed in October 2003. The Commission has been financing an important IPR technical co-operation programme. A follow-up programme, which includes many enforcement issues, is being prepared for funding under the 2005–06 financial assistance programme.

*Macro-economic policy and the regulation of financial markets*

At the EU-China Summit in December 2004, an EU-China dialogue on macroeconomic and financial regulatory issues was launched. The first meeting took place in Brussels, on 22 February 2005, jointly chaired by, on the Commission side, Mr. Regling, Director-General for Economic and Financial Affairs, and Mr. Schaub, Director-General for Internal Market and Services, and on the Chinese side Mr. Li Yong, Vice Minister of Finance. On 15 May 2006, Commissioner McCreevy and Chinese Finance Minister Jin Renquing participated in the second dialogue, in Beijing. At both meetings the European Central Bank was represented by a board member.

This dialogue brings together in one single venue all the key Chinese authorities on these matters for a thorough discussion with officials of the European Commission and the European Central Bank. Concerned on the Chinese side are the Ministry of Finance, the People's Bank of China (China's Central Bank) and the key Regulatory Commissions respectively for Banking, Insurance and Securities. On the macroeconomic side, issues discussed concern the macroeconomic situation, global imbalances and monetary and fiscal policies. On the regulatory side, the main topics are China's financial sector reform and further integration of the financial sector in the EU. Other issues that have been addressed during these full-day meetings concern accounting standards and corporate governance. The two sides have agreed to continue and further develop this dialogue, and a third meeting will be held in Brussels in 2007.

In addition, in view of the importance of the EU and China as key global economic players and the need to further enhance bilateral economic relations, the European Commission and the National Development and Reform Commission (NDRC) agreed to launch a dialogue on macroeconomic policies. This dialogue is expected to deepen mutual understanding and foster further cooperation between the two sides. The first meeting of this process took place in Beijing, on 7th December 2006.

At this first meeting, the Chinese delegation was headed by Mr. Zhu Zhixin, Vice Chairman of the National Development and Reform Commission of China while Mr. Klaus Regling, Director General for Economic and Financial Affairs represented the European Commission. The in-depth discussions between the participants focused on their respective policies to promote long-term sustainable economic growth. The Chinese participants presented their policies to increase domestic consumption, to limit income inequalities, to induce more environment friendly growth, to reform social security in order to broaden medical, education and pension coverage and to promote development in the rural areas. All this is captured in the development of a harmonious society. DG ECFIN presented the recent favourable EU macroeconomic developments, the progress with respect to the implementation of structural reforms in the framework of the Lisbon Agenda and the need for additional measures to better cope with the ageing population. The Chinese participants showed a deep interest in EU macroeconomic developments and policies, as shown by their numerous questions.

The discussions helped create a better understanding of the two sides' perspectives on economic issues and laid a solid foundation for future cooperation. Both sides will continue discussions on these topics, identify specific issues for future discussion and deepen cooperation for the next dialogue to be held in Brussels in 2008. They agreed to proceed to an exchange of letters to further work out the concrete details of the structure and organization of the dialogue as well as to develop more permanent channels of communication between the two sides.

*Maritime transport*

In 2002, a maritime agreement was signed between the EC and its Member States and China to improve conditions for maritime transport carried out by EU and Chinese companies between the EU and China and to third countries. The agreement, later amended to cover the 10 new EU Member States who joined in 2004, promotes in particular the freedom for both sides to provide maritime transport services and to have unrestricted access to ports and auxiliary services. It also deals with the commercial presence of shipping companies. Co-operation, relating mainly to safety, security and training, will now be extended to inland waterways and ports. Annual monitoring of the implementation of the agreement is taking place alternately in China and the EU.

*Regional Policy*

China is facing considerable regional development disparities between the booming coastal regions, the underdeveloped western parts of the country and the north-east with its declining traditional heavy industry. There is a more general issue of income disparities, in particular the urban/rural divide.

The dialogue on regional policy provides a basis for sharing the EU's experiences in developing and implementing its regional policy, governance and partnership issues and other related topics of mutual interest. In addition, the role ofEU regional policy in areas such as competition policy and state aid rules, public procurement, transport and environment contributes to co-operation with China in these policy areas. The EU-China dialogue on regional policy should also help in contributing to other dialogue topics as presented in this paper related, for instance, to trade, sustainable development and good governance. A first China-EU Regional Policy Seminar took place in Beijing, in May 2006.

*Regulatory and Industrial Policy*

The objective of the Regulatory Dialogue is to ensure regulatory convergence between the EU and China in the long term. This should help to eliminate obstacles to trade and investment. Both sides try to achieve this through a comprehensive system of consultation and information on technical regulation, standards, certification procedures and market surveillance systems implemented by the two parties. Exchanges take place on best regulatory practices. As a result, trade should be facilitated and the quality and safety of goods sold on both markets and elsewhere should further improve. The dialogue provides for annual meetings where major issues of common interest are discussed and future co-operation is planned. A wide range of technical issues is dealt with in greater detail in 13 Working Groups, covering conformity assessment, standardisation, technical barriers to trade (TBT/WTO), electrical and mechanical products, toys, textiles, lighters, medical devices, pressure equipment, automobile standards, cosmetics and mobile phone radiation. Good governance in the tax area is vital as fair trade conditions and a level playing field in business taxation need to be ensured in both the Chinese and EU markets. Close cooperation is required to eliminate harmful tax competition.

The Industrial Policy Dialogue promotes and enhances mutual understanding and awareness of current and forthcoming policy approaches including sustainable development, legislation and related issues in the industrial sector with a view to increase coherence between EU and Chinese industrial policy. The Parties promote consultations, mutual understanding and transparency. Working groups have been established in three sectors (automobile, metals and textile).

*Science and technology (S&T)*

The EU-China dialogue on Science and Technology started in the early 1990s and was one of the first areas of co-operation between the European Commission and China. The first EU-China S&T agreement entered into force in late 1999 and was renewed in December 2004. Co-operation has increased substantially since the first S&T agreement was signed. Its aim was to promote mutually beneficial research activities in a variety of areas, such as food and environmental safety, the management of natural resources, the control of infectious diseases, etc. Today, this co-operation shows growing dynamism as is demonstrated, for instance, by the participation of Chinese partners in 134 research projects funded by the Commission's 6th Framework Programme for Research and technological Development (RTD).

China is rapidly becoming one of the most active players on the international research scene and in several areas it is a world leader – examples of the latter are nano materials and energy components. The momentum gathered from both the launch of the 7th Framework Programme on the EU side (2007–2013) and China's 11th Five Year Plan (2006–2011) together with the forthcoming EU-China "S&T Year" may be used to review the present co-operation scheme. It would also seem a good occasion to launch new strategic projects in areas of mutual interest and to seek to increase the number of Europeans in projects funded by China.

*Space co-operation*

The Commission and the Chinese government also launched a dialogue on co-operation in space science, applications and technology. Managers of aerospace companies and research institutions attended a workshop in April 2004. High-level meetings took place in July 2006 to explore ways of implementing the dialogue among the various parties concerned. Different fields of co-operation were reviewed, for instance earth observation, with particular regard to the Global Monitoring for Environment and Security (GMES).

*Trade policy dialogue*

This dialogue covers multilateral issues of strategic interest such as the Doha Development Agenda, issues" related to regional integration and free-trade areas, and key bilateral issues. The dialogue focuses on strategic issues and therefore complements the institutional bilateral meetings (which cover, inter alia, trade), such as the Economic and Trade Working Group and the Joint Committee. The first high-level Trade Policy Dialogue took place in June 2004, the second in July 2006.

*Textile trade dialogue*

To pre-empt potential conflicts after the abolition of textile quotas on 1 January 2005, the textiles trade dialogue examines ways in which a smooth transition to the quota-free textiles trade environment can be assured. The process contributed to the textiles agreements forged in the summer of 2005. The Commission expects the dialogue to lead to practical results which will have tangible and positive effects on trade in textiles and clothing between the two sides, based on fair and healthy competition in the marketplace. In addition to the government-to-government dialogue, an EU-China business dialogue is also being set up.

*New dialogues are being launched in the following areas:*

*Transport (in general)*

A Memorandum of Understanding on transport and energy strategies has been concluded with the Chinese National Development and Reform Commission, which will allow for the institutionalisation of cooperation in the transport sector. In particular, it has been agreed that co-operation on road and railway transport would be launched.

*Development cooperation and Africa*

During the $9^{th}$ EU-China summit it was agreed to pursue a structured dialogue on Africa and explore avenues for practical cooperation on the ground in partnership with the African side, including with the support of NEPAD initiatives and with the aim of attaining the Millennium Development Goals. Both the EU and China are signatories of the Paris Declaration on aid effectiveness and the Commission expects the dialogue to lead to practical results which will have tangible and positive effects in promoting the effectiveness principles contained in the Paris Declaration. Dialogue agenda and working methods will be further developed in 2007.

### *3.13 COUNTRY ENVIRONMENTAL PROFILE SUMMARY*

Key Environmental Issues

Undertaking an environmental profile of China, including critical environmental issues, in a short report is a formidable task. Not least is the scale of the country, which under different historical circumstances might be as many as ten or twenty separate nations. It is often remarked that the backward western provinces and regions might be viewed as separate developing countries on their own, while the coastal provinces would easily fit a model of middle income countries. Chinese cities such as Hong Kong and Shanghai have quarters which would make many parts of European cities look dilapidated and quaint.

With this scale comes inevitably an enormous diversity in livelihood systems. These range from extensive pastoral modes in the north and west, where overgrazing is a sustainability factor, to intensive rice land production; here excess biocides and fertilisers have serious environmental consequences. In the south and east there are arable wheat lands, while in the far west in Tibet-Qinghai special mountain adaptations and cultural systems are now being eroded by social change. In central regions of China, inland fishing and aquaculture practices are being seriously affected by water abstraction and drainage projects, and also by the pollution that has damaged river and coastal marine fisheries.

The urban environment sees water-short cities and towns in the north, with a polluting heavy industry, while in the rural interior village textile and intensive livestock enterprises too often function without any reasonable consideration of local environmental and health impacts. Model light technology industries of the south-east may offer desirable models for 'limited environmental impact' development, but exploitative labour conditions and poor waste disposal practice may equally apply. Waste disposal and water treatment by municipalities is an area where poor practice outside the most progressive centres is universally reported.

Sustainable Development Policy

The 2001–2005 Five Year Plan provided for an "improved environmental performance in pollution control while the deteriorating trend in the ecological environment will be halted." At his speech to the National People's Congress of 2004, President Hu Jintao called for balanced growth with the objective of *Xiaokang,* an 'all round, well-off society'. Policy statements at the highest level have therefore recognised the environmental – and possible social — consequences of the legacy of past policies which focused on economic growth. While investment in environmental management in the early 1990s was restricted to 0.8% ofGNP, today the figure is 1.3% ofGNP and is programmed to increase to 1.7%.

China has subscribed to all the major Multilateral Environmental Agreements (MEAs) which, with international encouragement and development co-operation, has seen positive responses in domestic policy-making, not least in tightening up the environmental assessment of new projects. Severe difficulties remain, however, in implementation of policy in the context of weak environmental governance. The 1992 UN Conference on Environment and Development (UNCED), requiring a national response through implementation of 'Agenda 21' policy areas and a 'mainstreaming' of environmental criteria in development policy, was met with a positive and significant policy response in China.

The Chinese leadership is committed, and is well placed to achieving most of its UN Millennium Development Goals (MDGs) in the areas of poverty alleviation, health and education, but a notable possible exception is in Goal 7: Environmental Sustainability. These goals indeed reflect key elements of the '*Xiaokang Society*' to be achieved by 2020, which include a balanced development between a) urban and rural areas, b) different regions, c) economic and social factors, d) humans and nature, and e) domestic security and an open society.

Assessment of Environmental Management

Certain particular factors which have to be taken into consideration in a study of the state of the environment and its management in China are worth emphasising at the outset. These relate to the quality of available research and scientific information. The following points are therefore salient.

- There is a special history of isolation from the West and a dearth of documented and independent social and scientific research on land use change and environmental pollution parameters – never a priority for decision-makers;
- Such scientific data as exists, and is now being increasingly generated, needs to be treated with considerable caution because there is a past history of data which has been falsified or is politically construed – even recent trends are difficult to establish because of this and a lack of consistency and care in the use of statistical data, combined with the fact that change is happening so fast; and
- First-hand social science research still cannot be freely undertaken to understand the nature of poverty and social deprivation, even in the environmental context, because this too may be associated with corruption in local government. The best social science insights depend on individual stories, whereas broader studies tend to represent untested generalisations.

Yet the research context is not universally gloomy; there is an acknowledgement at the highest levels of the seriousness of environmental sustainability issues. There is also an increased readiness to publish environmental data however dire, along with more widespread sharing of such data with civil society through the media. This is seen to bring pressure to bear on key decision-makers in provincial and county offices of government who have responsibility for controlling environmental pollution and managing and implementing the law. As will be seen, the law is not well implemented and is often ambiguous and even unrealistic or over-demanding. In this context the World Bank, in its 2001 report "China – Air, Land and Water", nevertheless acknowledges the law's completeness.

Environmental Decision-Making

China has a top-down administrative culture and an inherited belief in regulation by law, even if its interpretation might seem relativistic. In the event of an accident or a pollution incident, for example, the first appeal is to the law – it was not implemented, or even that new legislation is required. However, the critical problem lies in too many permissive decisions being taken to achieve a consensus of the interests of social stability, lack of resources and, also, vested personal interests. Greater recourse to courts is considered desirable, but there are certain operational deficiencies requiring rectification: a) judges need to be better trained, b) costly evidence to support a case needs to be resourced, and c) court decisions must be implemented – and seen to be implemented. This is much more likely to happen with increasing private-sector ownership and citizen participation drawing public attention to environmental transgressions.

Past decision-making with negative environmental consequences has happened behind closed doors; social connections are invoked *(guanxi)* to avoid taking tough decisions. In any case decisions with financial implications (penalties) where the state owns all the means of production simply involve a transfer from one service to another. Private-sector abuse of the law should become easier to control in the future, provided that local companies are not part-owned by government officials, which is unfortunately too often the case following privatisation initiatives.

One significant positive development is an apparent reinvigoration of EIA with a new law, in 2003, which requires that investors design projects in such a way as to mitigate their potential environmental impacts more significantly. Developers are also to be required to consult civil society. Despite this, controversial projects and factory location decisions may not be so open to challenge. EIAs are conducted by certified government scientific departments, some of which are becoming privatised and more independent of government.

There is an apparent lack of research into the quality and realism of such EIAs, or to what extent wider public interests as opposed to narrow industry interests are taken into account. It is reported, however, that EIA statements are available for consultation in local government offices. Whether any serious challenge might be made is doubtful; indeed there is not enough information in the public domain or enough of a culture of questioning government decisions to lead to meaningful counterproposals.

Environmental Policy Development

Environmental Impact Assessment, and Strategic EIA, is also required of government plans which would incorporate policy EIAs in the natural resource sector. Indeed there has been policy research undertaken on the potential environmental impact of China's entry into the WTO, whose work is drawn on in relation to certain sector impacts in this report (CCICED, 2004). Potentially greater growth rates and therefore energy use are expected, along with more intensive horticulture and livestock in the east coastal areas with accompanying environmental risks. The comparative disadvantage of the Western Regions for new industry is expected to be more marked.

European countries are involved in the massive foreign capital inflows into new industries in China. Such firms mostly come to take advantage of a stable business (and political) environment and cheap and disciplined labour. They also come with a culture of environmental and labour law compliance; and, in the case of internationally known companies, with a reputation (public image) to defend, with company policies and international standards of environmental due diligence (EDD) and corporate social responsibility (CSR). Five thousand companies in China are approved as ISO 1400 certified. Promotion of voluntary instruments such as CSR may indeed be an area where the EU can bring pressure for improved environmental performance.

Chinese businessmen exporting to Europe are certainly conscious of their legal requirements to fulfil product health and safety regulations of the EU. That labour is paid on time and not abused or that wood products might have a history of unsustainable or illegal sourcing raises other questions. But if free trade and competition has any meaning, it would require at least one element of 'fair trade' which is that employees of participating countries and companies are paid according to their contracts – and that these are not themselves abused, as is widely reported in China (see, for example, *China Development Brief*, vol DC No 3, April 2005). Also it is axiomatic that signed international treaties on labour and Multilateral Environmental Agreements (MEAs) be respected.

## Future Scenarios

Although the volume of production and consumption is rapid, with GNP recently reported to be rising last year at 9.5%, China is now allocating 1.5 % of GNP to environmental management. Some Chinese experts and the World Bank (2001) say this should be nearer 2%. This figure in the early 1990s was just 0.8%. China is nevertheless trying to introduce a system of green accounts which may highlight the environmental cost of its development path. A much-quoted calculation referred to in the above World Bank report suggests that pollution of air and water and land degradation is costing China 8–12% of its 1.4 trillion GDP in direct damage to crops and buildings from acid rain, from fishery losses, medical bills and lost work for illness, from money spent on disaster relief following floods aggravated by forest destruction and from soil erosion, the human-induced part of 'natural' disasters.

The UNDP Human Development Report 2002 foresees two scenarios for future environmental change and development sustainability in China: a) The Perilous Path Scenario and b) The Green Reform Path Scenario.

### *The Perilous Path Scenario*

The perilous scenario sees a continued rapid growth in the economy but a failure to control greenhouse gas emissions which could be, by 2050, three times 1995 levels. Urban environmental degradation and massive uncontrolled migration into cities puts pressure on sanitation and physical infrastructure, and vehicle emissions are not significantly improved because of a lack of political will. It sees irreversible losses in biodiversity and in the quality of natural resources (water and soil), and eventual social conflict which destabilises society as increased protest is engendered against corruption and poor environmental governance.

### *The Green Reform Path Scenario*

In the green scenario market-based instruments are allowed to function, promoting efficiency, for instance in water allocation and pollution mitigation. Improvements in energy efficiency in industry by application of new technologies are successfully facilitated. Emission standards continue to be upgraded for vehicles as is already happening in Beijing. With continued economic growth and rule of law the government is able to raise revenues (taxes, user charges and realistic fines) for environmental management and provide valued services to citizens, not least better environmental information.

The public are in turn enfranchised through an opening to civil society whose support for better environmental management, and better governance, is harnessed by political leaders committed to the environmental agenda. The quality of marine and coastal environments is improved and biodiversity fostered and protected in and outside reserves, and these are increasingly valued by citizens who have increased leisure time. The impact of consumption growth is contained by changing demand for environmentally benign (eco-labelled) products and foods produced under acceptable and openly scrutinised responsible social and environmental practices.

Opportunities/or Reform

The role of the international community, and the EU in particular, might then be to help the Chinese authorities to create the framework for development along the green path. A long-term view will be required.

*3.14 DONOR MATRIX*

**COMMUNITY ASSISTANCE TO CHINA (1)**

| (Figures in € million) | MS | | | | | | | | | | | | |
|---|---|---|---|---|---|---|---|---|---|---|---|---|---|
| CATEGORY/SECTOR | AU | D | DK | EC | ES | F | Fl | I | L | NL | SW | UK | TOTALS |
| Agriculture and forestry | | 110,4 | | 17,7 | | | 15,5 | | | 1,0 | | | 144,6 |
| Banking and financial services | | 52,0 | | 8,7 | | | | | | | | | 80,7 |
| Business and other services | | | | 21,8 | | | | | | | | | 21,5 |
| Communications | | | | 1,5 | | | | | | | | | 1,5 |
| Education | 3,7 | 26,2 | | 34,8 | | | 0,3 | 43,6 | | | | 102,4 | 211,0 |
| Energy | | 154,0 | 8,2 | 21.1 | 1,5 | 214,7 | 20,5 | 31,9 | | 5,3 | 2,0 | | 459,2 |
| General environment protection | 0,1 | 93,4 | 2,5 | 36,4 | | 4,3 | 0,0 | 11,2 | | 19,1 | 6,1 | 12,1 | 185,1 |
| Government and civil society | 0,3 | 10,1 | | 1,9 | | 3.5 | 1,7 | | | 0,0 | 7,3 | 4,8 | 29,5 |
| Health | 0,0 | 167,5 | | 3,4 | | 8,0 | 18,5 | 14,8 | 0,2 | | 7,0 | 190,9 | 410,2 |
| Industry and SME development | | 158,0 | | 20,6 | | | 0,2 | | | 3,7 | | 4,8 | 187,3 |
| Multisector/crosscutting | 0,1 | 38,8 | | 1,0 | | | 0,1 | 12,4 | | 13,1 | | 13,6 | 78,7 |
| Other/unspecified | | 22,5 | | 3,7 | | 0,4 | 0,9 | 7,1 | | | | 7,6 | 42,2 |
| idctlparPopulation programmes and reproductive health | | | | | | | | | | | | | |
| Rural and urban development | | 0,0 | | 8,0 | | | | | | | | 9,0 | 17,0 |
| Social infrastructures and services | | | | 0,8 | | | | | | | | 31,3 | 32,1 |
| Support to NGO | | | | | | | 0,1 | | | | | | 0,1 |
| Trade policy and regulations | | | | 15,2 | | | | | | | | | 15,2 |
| Transport | | 348,7 | | 0,9 | | 143,5 | | | | | | | 493,1 |
| Water supply and sanitation | | 154,8 | | 25,8 | | 32,1 | 6,8 | | | 0,2 | 5,0 | 33,9 | 258,6 |
| Women in development | | | | | | | | | | | 0,4 | 0,7 | 1,0 |
| TOTALS | 4,1 | 1.336,2 | 10,7 | 222,8 | 1,5 | 406,5 | 64,4 | 121,0 | 0,2 | 42,4 | 27,7 | 411,0 | 2.648,5 |

(1) Based on information provided by Member States through the Development Counsellors' Group In Beijing. January 2007

[1] While the level of ODA to China between 2000 and 2005 remained stable at around US$ 6 billion per year, FDI during the same period grew from some US$ 300 billion to around US$ 960 billion per year, thus reducing the ODA share of GDP from 2,0 to 0,6%.

[2] Activities have also been undertaken with the Ministry of Commerce (MOFCOM) in the framework of trade cooperation projects to analyse the statistical discrepancies highlighted in section 2.2 of the CP, and offer a possibility for more formal policy dialogue on the subject.

[3] Of which €1.4 million for the continuation of the EU-China Interpreter Training Programme (EUCIPT)

[4] COM(2006) 631 and 632 of 24/10/06

[5] Eurostat: compiled from aggregated EU Member State data. USS70 billion according to Chinese data. The discrepancies are partly explained by the fact that the latter include imports arriving in the EU from China via Hong Kong. Similar methodological problems exist with EU exports to China and highlight the major divergences between EU (and other developed countries') and Chinese methodological approaches. There could be a case for co-operation in the statistical area under the Policy Dialogue Support Facility.

[6] US statistics. China's statistics indicate a trade surplus with the US ofUS$ 114 billion in 2005.

[7] Chinese statistics.

[8] http://europa.eu.mt/eur-lex/lex/en/treaties/index.htm

[9] COM (2006) 631 of 24/10/06.

[10] A list of projects being implemented under thematic budget lines and Asia-wide programmes is given in Annex 3.11

# 4

# Political Dialogues, 1994–Present: Summits, Human Rights and Arms

## INTRODUCTION

In the early 1990s, the European Union and China began to undertake other forms of communication, and for this purpose they created new institutions. Initially these new arrangements concerned trade, but eventually they grew to encompass a wide range of other subjects. The 1985 Agreement on Trade and Economic Cooperation provided the basic legal framework; the central institution was the EU–China Joint Committee. By the late 1990s, however, the 1985 Agreement was inadequate and outdated. Increasingly it served mainly as a general umbrella for the new institutions and forms of communication which at first developed within it, then were elaborated in its interstices and finally, in essence though not legally, supplanted it.

The result of this process of development and differentiation was a new architecture of EU–China relations. Document 4.1 shows the architecture of EU–China relations as of 1 December 2005, the most recent overview available. This architecture consists of a wide range of 'soft' institutions based on 'soft law', measures which are not legally binding but which may have practical or even legal effects, together with a limited number of legally binding agreements on subjects other than trade in general or textile trade in particular. Leaving bilateral agreements for Chapter 6, this chapter and the following chapter focus on dialogues, an especially important type of soft law institutions and measures.

# Document 4.1: Current Architecture of EU–China Relations as of 1 December 2005

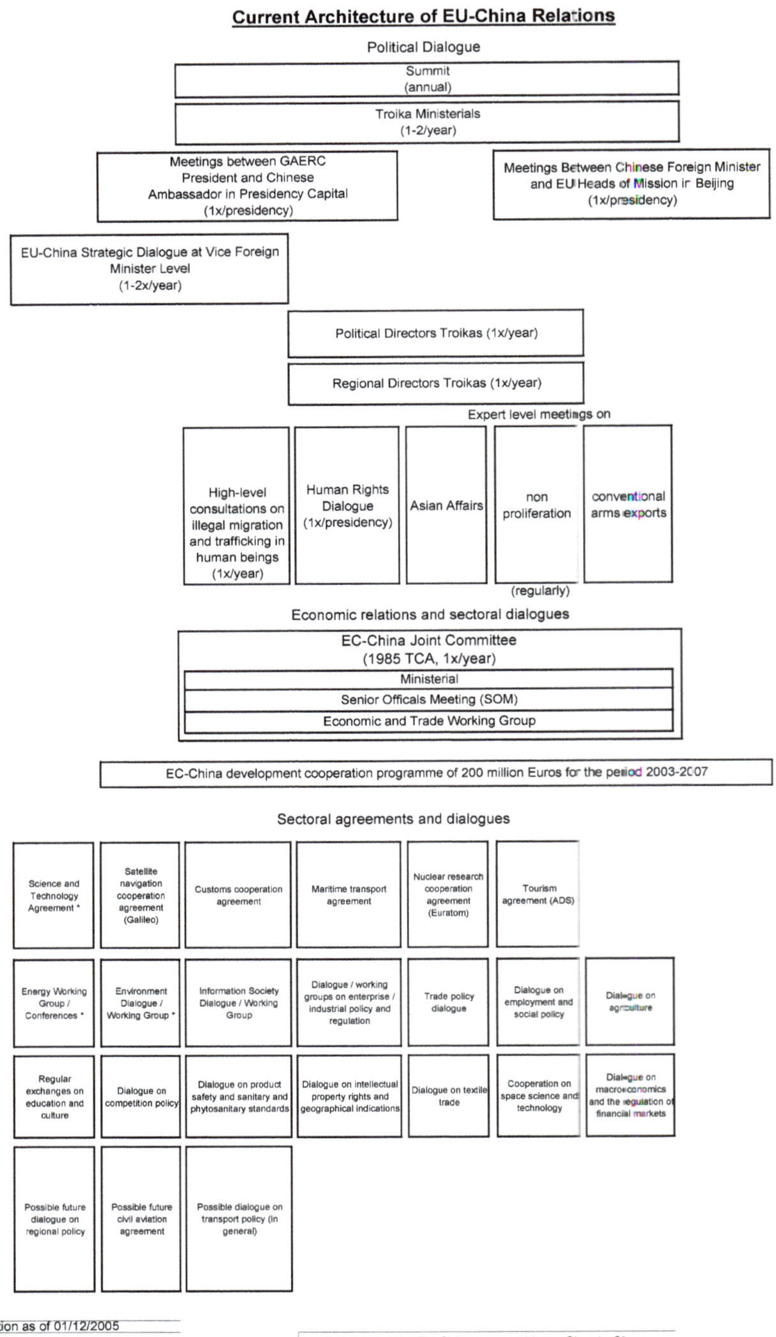

In view of the importance of 'soft law' and 'soft institutions' in EU–China relations, it is useful to introduce them briefly. Non-legally binding norms are well known in EU law, Chinese law and international law. Less well known in these contexts are soft institutions, which do not always have a precise legal basis or even legally recognised form, notwithstanding the fact that they have stable structures and functions on which the parties have agreed. In the context of EU–China relations, however, soft institutions and soft law have been developed to an unusually high degree. This is due to a multitude of reasons, including: the expansion in the competences of the European Community since the conclusion of the 1985 Agreement; the rapid development of China and the transformation of the Chinese economy and society since 1985; the corresponding expansion of EU–China relations from an interconnection focused on trade into a very broad-based relationship; the wish of both parties to discuss a variety of topics despite very different perspectives stemming from differences in history, culture, political systems and societies; and the fact that the bilateral 1985 Trade and Economic Cooperation Agreement is out of date but still in force and only now being renegotiated.

Two types of dialogues can be distinguished in EU–China relations: political dialogues and sectoral dialogues. The distinction is used here for several reasons. First, it follows the conceptualisation and terminology used by both the EU and China in the context of EU–China relations. Both conceptualisation and the terminology are embedded in the current architecture of EU–China relations, as indicated in Document 4.1. From this standpoint, political dialogues include summit meetings and troika meetings, as well as more specialised expert meetings.

Secondly, from a functional standpoint, the distinction between political and sectoral dialogues reflects the fact that, at least in theory, the two types of dialogue differ in their subject matter. Political dialogues, whether at the level of summit meetings or of expert-level meetings, concern subjects which are deemed to be political, concerned with the allocation of power and authority. Sectoral dialogues concern economic relations, namely specific economic sectors or sub-sectors, or issues directly related to them. Though easy to criticise in theoretical terms, the distinction reflects a commonly held view that distinguishes between politics and economics as two different spheres of social life. In the present context, the distinction has a general political significance. It serves to separate highly controversial topics, such as human rights or the arms embargo, from what often are considered to be less controversial topics, such as trade, environmental protection and domestic regulation.

Thirdly, the distinction reflects legal arrangements within the EU. Political dialogues may embrace not only areas of shared competence between the EC and its Member States, such as development, but also areas which in the EU currently fall within the framework of the intergovernmental Common Foreign and Security Policy (CFSP). Hence the European Council (via its Presidency) and the CFSP (via the High Representative for the Common Foreign and Security Policy) are always represented on the EU side at summit meetings. In contrast, the legal framework for sectoral dialogues is the 1985 Agreement on Trade and Economic Cooperation. Within this framework, the EC has exclusive competence for trade matters; the EC and the Member States share competence in matters of economic cooperation. The internal distribution of competences within the EU is mirrored in the distinction between political dialogues and sectoral dialogues in the EU's relations with China.

A fourth, related reason for the distinction between policy dialogues and sectoral dialogues concerns internal institutional arrangements for official decision-making both in the EU and in China. From the EU perspective, political dialogues are concerned with topics which are deemed to fall within the jurisdiction of the European Commission's Directorate-General for External Relations (DG Relex), together with that of the High Representative for the Common Foreign and Security Policy. Sectoral dialogues fall under the jurisdiction of more specialised directorates-general of the European Commission, such as those for Trade or Internal Market. From the Chinese perspective, political dialogues are within the scope of the Ministry of Foreign Affairs. Sectoral dialogues are dealt with by other ministries, notably the Ministry of Commerce (Mofcom, formerly Moftec: Ministry of Trade and Economic Cooperation) and various line ministries or similar organisations connected directly to the State Council.

The remainder of this chapter concentrates on two types of political dialogues. First, it discusses summit meetings involving top leaders. Then it considers examples of policy dialogues, which are meetings of lower-level official experts concerned with policies cutting across the entire range of EU–China relations. Table 4.1 shows relevant documents from the range of meetings encompassed by the term 'political dialogue' in the broad sense. The following chapter, Chapter 5, examines the new High-Level Mechanism and sectoral dialogues, namely meetings of lower-level official experts concerned with economic and social regulation involving specific economic sectors or sub-sectors, or particular areas of social policy.

## SUMMITS

The EU and China first established a structured political dialogue in 1994.[1] It was upgraded to annual summit meetings in 1998. In 2002 it was updated by an exchange of letters that gave it a formal legal basis.[2] Today the EU–China political dialogue embraces a wide variety of meetings at different levels (see Document 4.2). At the top of the hierarchy are the annual summits and one or two troika ministerial meetings each year. The summits bring together top leaders of the People's Republic of China and the European Union. The troika previously consisted of the EU Member State currently presiding over the European Council, its immediate predecessor in that role and the Member State next in line.[3] Since the 1997 Treaty of Amsterdam it has been composed of the European Commissioner for External Relations, the Foreign

[1] Much of this and the following paragraph is based on Delegation of the European Commission to China, 'EU–China Political Dialogue', http://www.delchn.cec.eu.int/en/Political/Political_Dialogue.htm (accessed 31 October 2006).

[2] According to the European Commission, there does not appear to be any document establishing the structured political dialogue. Early summit meetings, eg the 4th Summit (2001), refer to the importance that both sides attached to the political dialogue. The 2002 Exchange of Letters upgrading the Political Dialogue is not publicly available: European Commission, 14 December 2007.

[3] The acronym GAERC in the table stands for the EC General Affairs and External Relations Council.

**Table 4.1: Documents concerning Political Dialogues**

| Document | Place and periodicity | Date of agreement / date | Level | Source |
|---|---|---|---|---|
| EU-China Political Dialogue: Exchange of Letters: Framework [document not available] | | 1994, 2nd exchange of letters April 2002 | | http://www.delchn.cec.eu.int/Political/Political-Dialogue.htm, accessed 14.1.2005 |
| Political dialogue (see Documents 4.3–4.12) | Annual Summits | | Heads of State or Government | http://ec.europa.eu/comm/external_relations/china/summit/index.htm,accessed 28.3.2007 |
| Political dialogue* | Alternates between Beijing and EU; meetings as necessary | | EU Troika Foreign Ministers and their Chinese counterpart, in addition to annual meetings in the margins of the UN General Assembly | http://www.delchn.cec.eu.int/Political/Political-Dialogue.htm, accessed 14.1.2005 |
| Political dialogue* | Alternates between Beijing and EU; annual meetings | | EU Troika political directors with their Chinese counterpart | http://www.delchn.cec.eu.int/Political/Political-Dialogue.htm, accessed 14.1.2005 |
| Political dialogue* | Meetings at least once a year | | EU Troika and Chinese experts on international security, arms control, non-proliferation and export controls issues | http://www.delchn.cec.eu.int/Political/Political-Dialogue.htm, accessed 14.1.2005 |
| Political dialogue* | Beijing, meeting every six months | | Minister of Foreign Affairs of PRC and Ambassadors from the EU posted in Beijing | http://www.delchn.cec.eu.int/Political/Political-Dialogue.htm, accessed 14.1.2005 |

**Table 4:1 (continued)**

| Document | Place and periodicity | Date of agreement / date | Level | Source |
|---|---|---|---|---|
| Political dialogue* | Meeting every six months | | Minister of Foreign Affairs of the country holding the EU Presidency and the Ambassador of China posted in the Presidency's capital | http://www.delchn.cec.eu.int/Political/Political-Dialogue.htm, accessed 14.1.2005 |
| Joint declaration on Non-Proliferation and Arms Control (see Document 4.13) | | 8.12.2004 | | http://ec.europa.eu/comm/external_relations/china/summit_1204/memo04_284.htm, visited 6.4.2007; http://www.fmprc.gov.cn/eng/wjdt/2649/t173749.htm |
| European Union guidelines on Human rights dialogues (see Document 4.14) | Council of the European Union, Brussels | 13.12.2001 | | http://ec.europa.eu/comm/external_relations/human_rights/doc/ghd12_01,htm, accessed 6.2.2006; also http://www.consilium.europa.eu/uedocs/cmsUpload/14469EN.HR.pdf, accessed 21.11.2007 |
| EU-China Human Rights Dialogue | General Affairs Council, 2327th Council meeting, 22–23 January 2001 | | | http://ec.europa.eu/external_relations/humanrights/news/gac_jan_01.htm |

**Table 4:1 (continued)**

| Document | Place and periodicity | Date of agreement / date | Level | Source |
|---|---|---|---|---|
| Resolution on the functioning of the human rights dialogues and consultations on human rights with third countries (P6-TA(2007)20070381) (see Document 4.16) | European Parliament, Strasbourg | 6.9.2007 | | http://www.europarl.europa.eu/sides/getDoc.do?Type=TA&Reference=P6-TA-2007, accessed 22.11.2007 |
| Declaration on China (see Document 4.17) | European Council, Madrid | 26–27.6.1989 | | http://wwcontents/expcon/euchidec.html, accessed 30.11.2007 |
| Renewal of Human Rights Dialogue after interruption | | June 1996 | | http://ec.europa.eu/comm/external_relations/human_rights/doc/ghd12_01.htm |
| EU Code of Conduct on Arms Exports (see Document 4.18) | | 25.5.1998 | | http://consilium.europa.eu/uedocs/cmsUpload/08675r2en8.pdf, visited 30.11.2007, plus http://www.fco.gov.uk/servlet/Front?pagename=OpenMarket/Xcelerate/ShowPage&c=Page&cid=1…, accessed 30.1.2005, http://www.grip/org/bdg/g1655.html, accessed 30.1.2005 |

**Table 4:1 (continued)**

| Document | Place and periodicity | Date of agreement / date | Level | Source |
|---|---|---|---|---|
| User's Guide to the European Union Code of Conduct on Arms Exports [not included in this book] | | | | Council of the European Union, Brussels, Note from the Secretariat to the Working Party on Conventional Arms Exports, 6 November 2003, PESC 637/ COARM 10 |
| Lifting of the arms embargo on China: The Rueda Report on Arms Exports (The Rt Hon Chris Patten, Commissioner for External Relations) (see Document 4.19) | Strasbourg | 16.11.2004 | | http://ec.europa.eu/external_relations/news/patten/sp04_483.htm, accessed 30.11.2007; http://www.europarl.europa.eu/sides/getDoc.do?pubRef=-//EP//NONSGML+REPORT+A6-2004-0022+0+DOC+PDF+V0//EN, visited 30.11.2007 |
| Report on the 24th Human Rights Dialogue (see Document 4.15) | | 19.10.2006 | | |

*Included in EU–China Political Dialogue, Annex: Framework of the EU–China Political Dialogue.

Minister of the EU Member State holding the Presidency of the Council of the European Union and the EU High Representative for Foreign and Security Policy. The troika ministerial meetings take place at the level of ambassadors and heads of mission, and there is one additional meeting per year between political directors and regional directors of the troikas. Among these high-level meetings, this chapter is concerned only with the annual summits.

## Document 4.2: EU–China Political Dialogue

### EU-China Political Dialogue

The EU and China first established in 1994 the framework of a structured political dialogue on issues of common concern. This political dialogue was upgraded in 1998 with the agreement to hold regular EU-China Summits. In 2002, China and the EU decided to formally update the framework of their political dialogue through an exchange of letters, which constitutes the legal basis for the current dialogue. The scope of the EU-China political dialogue has gradually broadened to cover issues ranging from non-proliferation to the security situation in Asia, from global warming to the fight against illegal migration and trafficking in human beings. There is great potential to expand further this dialogue, notably as China shows more and more interest in the reinforcement of the European security and defence capabilities as well as the consequences of EU enlargement.

The commitment of the EU to the strengthening of its political dialogue with China is notably based upon a recognition that China, as a UN Security Council member, a growing economic and political power, and an increasingly assertive member of the international community, can exert a significant influence on a wide series of issues of global concern. In a world increasingly bound together by the forces of globalisation, co-operation with China, bilaterally or within multilateral structures, is crucial to achieve progress in many important areas.

The European Commission, as a full member of the EU Troika, participates in all meetings of the EU-China political dialogue.

Annex: Framework of the EU-China Political Dialogue

- Annual Summits, at the level of the Heads of State or Government, between China and the EU, their location alternating between China and the EU.
- Meetings when needed between the EU Troika Foreign Ministers and their Chinese counterpart, in addition to annual meetings in the margins of the Untied Nations General Assembly.
- Annual meetings of EU Troika political directors with their Chinese counterpart, the location of the meeting alternating between China (Beijing) and the EU.
- Annual meetings (in Beijing) between EU Troika Asia Pacific directors and their Chinese counterpart on Asian and Pacific issues, the location of the meeting alternating between China and the EU.
- Meetings at least once a year between EU Troika and Chinese experts on international security, arms control, non-proliferation and export controls issues.
- A meeting every six months between the Minister of Foreign Affairs of China and the Ambassadors from the European Union posted in Beijing.

- A meeting every six months between the Minister of Foreign Affairs of the country holding the EU Presidency and the Ambassador of China posted in the Presidency's capital.

Summits are at the apex of EU–China political (and sectoral) dialogues today. The EU–China summits began in 1998 and take place alternately in China and Europe (see Table 4.2). The main participants almost invariably include the Premier of the State Council of the People's Republic of China, the Head of State or Government of the EU Member State holding the EU Presidency and the President of the Commission. However, a meeting with the President of the People's Republic of China concluded the second, sixth and tenth summits. Summits are also attended by the highest specialised Chinese or EU officials concerning a specific subject matter under discussion. Summits cover a wide range of topics, notably those concerning EU–China relations, international affairs or regional affairs which require discussion and possible agreement at the highest level. Sometimes they consolidate existing policies or lead to changes in policy. They may also result in new agreements, whether legally binding or 'soft law', or lead to the creation of new institutions, policy dialogues or cooperation programmes. At the end of each summit, the parties have issued a joint press statement or joint statement summarising the results of their discussion; the nomenclature does not appear to have any effect on the content or the significance of the document. The following discussion gives special emphasis to the interrelationship between summits and dialogues, in other words to the extent to which summits have contributed to the establishment of new institutions.

The 1st EU–China Summit was held in London on 2 April 1998. As reflected in the Joint Press Statement (see Document 4.3), its content followed closely the Commission's 1998 Communication on 'Building a Comprehensive Partnership with China', the second major EU policy paper on China, which had been published a week before. The parties agreed on the importance of dialogue between them in a rapidly changing world situation, emphasised their commitment to Chinese accession to the WTO, welcomed the resumption of the China–EU human rights dialogue and agreed to consider holding summits on an annual basis.

**Document 4.3: Joint Press Statement of the 1st EU–China Summit**

EU-CHINA SUMMIT: JOINT PRESS STATEMENT THURSDAY 2 APRIL 1998

On April 2 1998, HE Zhu Rongji, Premier of the People's Republic of China, the Rt Hon Tony Blair, Prime Minister of The United Kingdom - the current EU Presidency - Jacques Santer, President of the European Commission, held the first China-EU Summit in London. The two sides held an in-depth exchange of views on the further development of China-EU relations and international issues of mutual interest in a friendly atmosphere, and reached broad consensus.

Both sides agreed that with a great and profound change of the world's situation, an increase in dialogue and cooperation between the EU and China is not only in the fundamental interests of both sides but is also conducive to world peace, stability and development.

**Table 4.2: EU–China Summits, 1998–Present**

| Topic | Document | Participants | Place | Date | Reference | Source |
|---|---|---|---|---|---|---|
| 1st Summit | EU-China Summit: Joint Press Statement | Prime Minister Zhu Rongji, Prime Minister Tony Blair of the UK, President Jacques Santer of the European Commission | London | 2.4.1998 | | http://www.chinese-embassy.org.uk/eng/wjzc/t27058.htm, accessed 12.12.2006 |
| 2nd Summit | Press Statement of the EU | Prime Minister Zhu Rongji, Prime Minister Paavo Lipponen of Finland, President Romano Prodi of the European Commission (+ meeting with President Zhang Zemin) | Beijing | 21.12.1999 | | http://news.xinhuanet.com/english/2003–10/30/content_1151166.htm; also at http://delchn.cec.eu.int?en/whatsnew/second_summit.htm, accessed 12.12.2006 |
| 3rd Summit | Press Release [Joint Statement not available] | Prime Minister Zhu Rongji, Foreign Minister Tang Jiaxuan, Governor of the People's Bank of China Mr Dai Xianglong, Minister for Foreign Trade and Economic Cooperation Shi Guangsheng, President Jacques Chirac of France + two French Cabinet Ministers, President Romano Prodi of the European Commission, Commissioner for Foreign Trade Pascal Lamy, Commissioner Pedro Solbes Mira, EU High Representative for Foreign and Security Policy Javier Solana | Beijing | 23.10.2000 | | http://ec.europa.eu/comm/external_relations/news/2000/10–00/ip-00–1191.htm, accessed 13.12.2006 |

**Table 4.2 (continued)**

| Topic | Document | Participants | Place | Date | Reference | Source |
|---|---|---|---|---|---|---|
| 4th Summit | Joint Press Statementof the Fourth EU-China Summit | Premier Zhu Rongji, Prime Minister Guy Verhofstadt of Belgium, High Representative for the EU's Common Foreign and Security Policy Javier Solana, President Romano Prodi of the European Commission, with the participation of Minister of Foreign Affairs Tang Jiaxuan, Minister of Foreign Trade and Economic Cooperation Shi Guangsheng, Commissioner for External Relations Chris Patten, Commission for Foreign Trade Pascal Lamy | Brussels | 5.9.2001 | | http://ec.europa.eu/comm/external_relations/china/summit/index.htm, accessed 12.12.2006 |
| 5th Summit | Joint Press Statement of the Fifth EU-China Summit | Premier Zhu Rongji, Prime Minister Fogh Rasmussen of Denmark, President Romano Prodi of the European Commission, with the participation of Minister of Foreign Affairs Tang Jiaxuan, Minister of Foreign Trade and Economic Cooperation Shi Guangsheng, Danish Minister for Foreign Affairs Per Stig Møller, Commissioner for External Relations Chris Patten, Commission for Trade Pascal Lamy | Copen-hagen | 24.9.2002 | | http://ec.europa.eu/enterprise/enterprise_policy/gov_relations/china_regul_coop_dialogue/f1742.pdf, accessed 12.12.2006 |

**Table 4.2 (continued)**

| Topic | Document | Participants | Place | Date | Reference | Source |
|---|---|---|---|---|---|---|
| 6th Summit | Joint Press Statement of the 6th EU-China Summit | Premier Wen Jiabao, Prime Minister Silvio Berlusconi, President Romano Prodi of the European Commission, High Representative for the Common Foreign and Security Policy Javier Solana (plus meeting of EU leaders with President Hu Jintao), plus participation by Minister of Foreign Affairs Li Zhaoxing, Minister in charge of the State Development and Reform Commission Ma Kai, Minister of Science and Technology Xu Guanhua, Vice Minister of Commerce Wei Jianguo, Italian Minister for Foreign Affairs Franco Frattini, Commissioner for Trade Pascal Lamy | Beijing | 30.10.2003 | | http://ec.europa.eu/com/external_relations/china_summit_index.htm, accessed 12.12.2006 |
| 7th Summit | Joint Statement of the 7th EU-China Summit | Premier Wen Jiabao, Prime Minister Jan Peter Balkenende, President of the European Commission José Manuel Barroso, Secretary General/High Representative for the EU Common Foreign and Security Policy Javier Solana, plus participation by Netherlands Minister of Foreign Affairs Bernard Bot, External Relations Commissioner Benita Ferrero-Waldner, European Trade Commissioner Peter Mandelson, Chinese Minister of Foreign Affairs Li Zhaoxing, Chinese Minister of Commerce Bo Xilai | The Hague | 8.12.2004 | | http://ec.europa.eu/comm/external_relations/china/sumit/index.htm, accessed 12.12.2006; also at http://www.fmprc.gov.cn/eng/wjdt/2649/t174512.htm |

**Table 4.2 (continued)**

| Topic | Document | Participants | Place | Date | Reference | Source |
|---|---|---|---|---|---|---|
| 8th Summit | Joint Statement of the 8th EU-China Summit | Premier Wen Jiabao, Prime Minister Tony Blair, European Commission President José Manuel Barroso, Secretary General of the Council of the EU and High Representative for the EU Common Foreign and Security Policy Javier Solana | Beijing | 5.9.2005 | IP/05/478 | http://ec.europa.eu/comm/external_relations/news7barroso/sp05_478.htm |
| 9th Summit | Joint Statement of the Ninth EU-China Summit | Premier Wen Jiabao, Prime Minister Matti Vanhanen of Finland, President José Manuel Barroso of the European Commission | Helsinki | 9.9.2006 | Council of the European Union, 12642/06 (Presse 249), Brussels, 11.9.2006 | http://ec.europa.eu/comm/external_relations/china/summit/index.htm, accessed 12.12.2006; also at http://www.eu2006.fi/news_and_documents/other_documents/vko36/en_GB/1157828673423/, accessed 1.11.2006; http://en.chinabroadcast.cn/2946/2006/09/10/272@137175.htm, accessed 31.10.2006 |
| 10th Summit | Joint Statement of the 10th EU-China Summit | Premier Wen Jiabao, Prime Minister José Socrates of Portugal, President José Manuel Barroso of the European Commission | Beijing | 28.11.2007 | | http://www.eu2007.pt/ue/ven/noticias_documentos/20071202china.htm, accessed 25.1.2008 |

China expressed keen interest in the process of EU integration and welcomed and supported the launching of the Euro. The EU welcomed China's strong commitment to market reform and the impressive way it has undertaken the economic restructuring process. In particular, the EU commended the Chinese Government's bold agenda of specific initiatives announced at the Ninth People's Congress last month.

The EU side briefed the Chinese on the Commission's recent Communication on China. China welcomed the Commission's proposal, which aims to upgrade the status and substance of the China-EU relationship. The two sides expressed their hope to build a long-term, stable and constructive partnership between China and the EU for the twenty-first century.

The two sides stressed that stronger economic and trade ties between China and the EU are an important foundation for the continued development of their relations.

Both sides reaffirmed their shared commitment to securing China's entry into the World Trade Organisation on terms that will be of mutual benefit and reinforce the world trading system. The Chinese side appreciated the EU's support for China's entry into the WTO and reiterated its desire to become a member at an early date on the basis of balanced rights and obligations. The two sides agreed to make a concerted effort to make continued progress on the WTO negotiations over the coming months, focusing on the task of securing agreement on a package that would give substantial market access for goods and services.

The two sides welcomed progress made in the China-EU human rights dialogue since its resumption last year. The EU welcomed China's decision to ratify the UN Covenant on Social, Economic and Cultural Rights and its intention to sign the UN Covenant on Civil and Political Rights. Both sides agreed on the importance of achieving further progress through a continued EU-China dialogue covering all aspects of human rights, and supported by a wide range of cooperation projects.

The EU praised China's steadfast reaction to the financial troubles in Asia, particularly its continued determination not to devalue its currency and its commitment to maintaining the pace of economic and financial reform. Both sides expressed their conviction that Asia will not only overcome the temporary difficulties caused by the financial turmoil, but with effective implementation of the necessary reforms Asia should emerge even stronger than before.

The two sides will strengthen their exchanges and cooperation in the international financial and monetary field. The EU offered China a package of technical assistance measures aimed at facilitating the creation of a sound financial system, an offer which was welcomed by China.

The two sides believe that this successful and productive Summit is of great significance to EU-China relations. They agreed to sustain the momentum of high-level exchanges and to consider holding such Summits on an annual basis.

The EU and China held their second summit in Helsinki, Finland on 21 December 1999. The Press Statement of the EU issued after the summit (see Document 4.4) expressed more directly certain EU concerns about negotiations with China about its WTO accession, the development of the rule of law and greater respect for human rights. Reflecting China's economic transformation, the parties identified the strengthening of private sector links as important to trade and investment. Among other topics, they discussed increased cooperation projects, gave a positive evaluation to Asia–Europe meetings (ASEM) and discussed stability in the Korean Peninsula.

These issues mirrored the increasing significance of China for the EU and vice versa, and the transformation of China and its international role.

## Document 4.4: 2nd EU–China Summit, 1999: Press Statement of the EU

First EU-China Summit, 1998

The first EU-China summit took place in London on April 2, 1998.

Second EU-China Summit, 1999

Press Statement of the EU

1. The second European Union-China Summit was held in Beijing on December 21, 1999, between the Prime Minister of Finland, Mr Paavo Lipponen, representing the Presidency of the European Union, the President of the European Commission, Mr Romano Prodi and the Prime Minister of the People's Republic of China, Mr Zhu Rongji. The Summit concluded with a meeting with the President of the People's Republic of China, Mr Jiang Zemin.

2. The discussions were held in an open and friendly atmosphere, reflecting the strong momentum created by the first EU-China Summit in April 1998. Both sides agreed to build upon this momentum to further strengthening and deepening their multi-faceted relations.

3. The EU welcomes China's determination to continue on the path of reforms and stands ready to share experience and assist China in this process. The EU welcomes the steps already taken by China to enter the WTO but nevertheless underlines the issues that are of great importance to Europe. Bearing this in mind the EU stands ready to negotiate when the Chinese side has completed the examination of the EU positions.

4. The EU expressed concern about the pace of China's evolution towards a more open and transparent society, based on the rule of law and internationally recognised human rights standards. It further urged China to ratify the 2 UN covenants already signed, and stands ready to share experience concerning their ratification and implementation. The EU also encouraged the Chinese authorities to abolish capital punishment.

5. The EU reviewed its co-operation programs with China, notably legal co-operation, education, environment and Science and Technology. The possibilities offered for future co-operation by new information and communication technologies were also discussed: the information society and knowledge-intensive economy open up a wide spectrum of new contacts in the different fields of high technology and learning.

6. Both sides agreed that the strengthening of links between their private sectors would be of great importance to increase the trade and investment flows particularly during the post WTO accession period.

7. The EU briefed China on the results of the Helsinki Summit; on the EU enlargement process; on the strengthened EU crisis management capabilities; and on the successful introduction of the Euro. China informed the EU on the recent developments, both political and economic, in their country. The EU welcomed the smooth transfer of sovereignty in Macao and stressed the importance it attaches to the effective implementation of the "one country two systems" in the new Special Administrative Region.

8. Both the EU and China highly evaluated what the ASEM (Asia-Europe meetings) had achieved in closer regional integration and co-operation as one of the channels bringing the EU and China together.

In regional affairs, stability in the Korean Peninsula was discussed.

The third summit (see Document 4.5) was held in Beijing on 23 October 2000. By this time the EU–China Summit was firmly established as a very significant annual high-level meeting, in many respects the cornerstone of EU–China institutional relations. The third summit consolidated earlier political developments, notably by upgrading the pre-existing political dialogue. It noted the signature of the bilateral EU–China agreement on Chinese accession to the WTO. It also signalled the intention of the parties to deepen and expand the relationship, building on the European Commission's September 2000 Report on the implementation of its 1998 Communication. The EU placed special importance on human rights. The range of topics was expanded to cover other topics, for example trafficking in human beings and illegal migration, partly in response to two tragic incidents involving loss of life of Chinese immigrants into the UK.[4] This had been suggested earlier in the Commission's 1998 Communication, but it gained salience as a result of the end of internal border controls within the Schengen area. The summit also noted a range of new EU–China cooperation projects.

**Document 4.5: 3rd Annual EU–China Summit Press Release (Joint Statement Not Available)**

Third annual EU- China Summit

The Third Annual EU-China Summit will take place in Beijing on Monday 23rd October, this year. President Prodi will represent the Commission and will be accompanied by Commissioners Lamy and Solbes. President Chirac will represent the EU Presidency and will be accompanied by two French Cabinet Ministers and the EU's High Representative Solana. Chinese Prime Minister, Zhu Rongji, will lead for the Chinese. He will be accompanied by Foreign Minister, Tang Jiaxuan, and Governor of the Peoples' Bank of China, Mr Dai Xianglong and Minister for Foreign Trade and Economic Co-operation, Shi Guangsheng.

[4] On 18 June 2000, 58 Chinese immigrants were discovered to have suffocated in a container on a lorry disembarking at Dover. The Dutch lorry driver and a Chinese intermediary were jailed for 14 years and 6 years, respectively. See *R v Perry Wacker*, Court of Appeal (Criminal Division), on appeal from the Maidstone Crown Court, Case No 200102556 S2/200102476R2, 31 July 2002 [200] *EWCA Crim* 1944. Among numerous press reports, see 'Driver jailed for Chinese deaths', *CNN.com/WORLD*, 5 April 2001, available at http://archives.cnn.com/2001/WORLD/europe/04/05/dover.verdict.02/index.html (accessed 16 September 2007); 'Dutch Company Compensates Families of Chinese Immigration Victims', *People's Daily Online*, 5 February 2005, available at http://english.peopledaily.com.cn/200502/05/eng20050205_173039.html (accessed 16 September 2007). This is not unique: in February 2004, 19 Chinese workers were drowned while picking cockles during heavy tides at Morecambe Bay, Lancashire. See F Lawrence, H-H Pai, V Dodd, H Carter, D Ward and J Watts, 'Victims of the Sands and the Snakeheads', *The Guardian*, 7 February 2004, available at http://www.guardian.co.uk/uk_news/story/0,3604,1143060,00.html (accessed 16 September 2007). The Morecambe Bay disaster was also the subject of the 2006 film *Ghosts*, directed by Nick Broomfield.

This Third Annual EU-China summit will consolidate the important developments in EU-China relations over the last three years. Both sides have been able to upgrade the political dialogue and their economic and trade relations, and to take increasingly bold steps in broadening and deepening EU-China co-operation. The very welcome signature of the EU-China WTO agreement on 19 May this year will obviously ensure that China's WTO accession arrangements will also feature highly on the agenda.

In September 2000, the European Commission issued a Report concerning the implementation of its 1998 Communication entitled *"Building a Comprehensive Partnership with China"*, which commented positively on the progress made since the Communication was endorsed by the European Council of Ministers in June 1998. It concluded that although significant developments had taken place, there was much scope to expand the relationship further.

The aim of this year's Summit will be to build on these solid achievements recorded in recent years, to increase and deepen existing co-operation and to expand it into new areas.

Subjects on the agenda will include developments in the EU and in China since the First Annual Summit in 1998, WTO accession, Co-operation, including combating the trafficking in human beings and illegal immigration, Human Rights and the overall EU-China Co-operation programme. The last Summit took place in December 1999, in Beijing, and this was followed up by the successful visit to the Commission by Prime Minister Zhu Rongji, in July this year.

Discussions will also cover global and regional issues, for example, the Korean Peninsula, the Western Balkans, Disarmament and Non-proliferation.

More detailed information is attached concerning China's accession to the WTO.

The EU will raise with particular attention the issue of human rights and will again stress the need to achieve results and improvements of the human rights situation in China (see detailed note on cooperation projects in this field).

Further discussions are also expected in new areas of co-operation such as combating illegal migration. This follows the tragic event in Dover last June, when 58 Chinese illegal immigrants lost their lives. When President Prodi and Prime Minister Zhu Rongji met in Brussels in July this year, they agreed that co-operation in this area was a high priority. As a result of this initiative, a delegation of Chinese immigration experts visited Brussels on 13th October (background information attached).

EU-China co-operation projects totalling around Euro 60 million per year in each of the past five years, have been committed successfully, as part of the EU's overall co-operation programme. These projects have focused on education and training, science and technology, energy and the environment, agriculture, civil aviation, telecommunications, legal co-operation and public administration training, village governance and human rights. All these projects are aimed at supporting China's wide-ranging social and economic reforms.

The fourth summit was held in Brussels on 5 September 2001 (see Document 4.6). The parties agreed to promote the development of a comprehensive partnership. They also agreed to strengthen and widen the political dialogue, to continue the human rights dialogue and to strengthen cooperation in combating illegal migration and trafficking in human beings. They also agreed to start formal negotiations on an EU–China maritime transport agreement and to expand dramatically the number of sectoral dialogues. They agreed on discussions to lead ultimately to a bilateral agreement on customs cooperation. On trade, especially trade conflicts, they agreed to treat these issues 'in accordance with' WTO rules. China would soon be a member of the WTO; the EU has continuously supported Chinese accession.

## Document 4.6: Joint Press Statement of the 4th Annual EU–China Summit

**Joint Press Statement of the Fourth EU-China Summit**
Brussels, 5 September 2001

The Fourth Summit Meeting between China and the European Union was held in Brussels, Belgium on 5 September 2001. Premier Zhu Rongji of the People's Republic of China, Prime Minister Guy Verhofstadt of Belgium in his capacity as President of the European Council, assisted by the High Representative for the EU's Common Foreign and Security Policy Javier Solana, and the President of European Commission Romano Prodi attended the Summit.

The Chinese Minister of Foreign Affairs Tang Jiaxuan, the Chinese Minister of Foreign Trade and Economic Co-operation Shi Guangsheng, the European Commissioner for External Relations Christopher Patten and the European Commissioner for Trade Pascal Lamy participated in the Summit.

Leaders had an in-depth exchange of views on China-EU relations and international and regional issues of common interest. Both sides expressed their resolve to expand and deepen further China-EU cooperation in all areas on the basis of equality and mutual benefit and to promote the development of a comprehensive partnership between China and the EU. Leaders expressed their satisfaction with the positive results of this Summit Meeting. Leaders underlined the significant developments in both China and the EU since the first China-EU summit, held in London in 1998. They welcomed the new progress made in developing China-EU relations over the last three years. They considered a number of ways to enhance the relationship, including through greater exchanges, contact and cooperation between the peoples of China and the EU.

The two sides briefed each other on developments in China and the EU. The Chinese side welcomed the progress of the EU integration and enlargement process. The EU acknowledged and expressed support for the progress made so far in China's economic and social reform.

The EU side reaffirmed that it would continue to adhere to the one China principle and hoped for a peaceful resolution of the Taiwan question through constructive dialogue. The Chinese side appreciated the EU's commitment to the one China principle and reiterated its principled position on the settlement of the Taiwan question in accordance with the basic principle of "peaceful reunification and one country, two systems".

Leaders agreed, in particular, to strengthen China-EU political dialogue and widen its scope. They agreed that China and the EU should conduct more in-depth consultations and exchange of views at all levels, with more regular meetings of senior officials and experts, on China-EU relations and on international and regional security issues of mutual concern, including non-proliferation, arms control and disarmament.

The two sides agreed to continue their dialogue on human rights and reaffirmed their commitment to work towards meaningful and positive results. Both sides reaffirmed that the dialogue would continue on the basis of mutual respect and equality, and agreed that the dialogue should help promote their compliance with international human rights standards and cooperation with U.N. bodies and mechanisms in this field. Leaders emphasized the political importance of China-EU co- operation in combating illegal migration and trafficking in human beings. They expressed satisfaction with the fruitful co-operation that had developed between the sides on these issues over the past year. They agreed to continue to strengthen their co-operation in this area.

Leaders agreed that negotiations for a China-EU maritime transport agreement would be opened formally on 13 September. Leaders stressed the importance of reinforcing dialogue on trade issues and of strengthening and expanding sectoral dialogues on enterprise policy and regulation, the information society, the environment, energy, science and technology, and satellite navigation. They instructed their officials to pursue discussions on customs with a view to negotiating bilateral agreements in this area. They also welcomed the intensification of contacts and co- operation in areas such as competition policy, securities, and quality supervision, inspection and quarantine.

Leaders welcomed the continued growth in China-EU trade and the rising levels of direct investment by EU companies in China. They discussed the issue of EU trade deficit with China and agreed that it was important to exert further efforts to expand China-EU trade and, in the process, improve the balance of trade. They also discussed trade issues such as anti-dumping and quantitative restrictions. Leaders indicated that the two sides would handle these issues in accordance with WTO rules in view of accession and agreed that they would consult on these issues as appropriate.

Leaders expressed their satisfaction that the work for China's accession to the WTO was proceeding smoothly and reaffirmed their shared commitment to securing China's entry into the WTO as soon as possible. Leaders agreed that China's accession would benefit both sides. The Chinese side reiterated that after its accession to the WTO it would, while enjoying its full rights in the multilateral trading system, fully implement its commitments. China expressed its thanks to the EU for its long-standing support for China's entry into the WTO. China also welcomed the EU's willingness to continue existing, and undertake additional, efforts to help China in this area, both through cooperation programs and through dialogue in key areas. Leaders expressed their full support for a broad-based new round of multilateral trade negotiations under the principle of balanced interests for the benefit of all WTO members. Leaders emphasized the significance of further strengthening cultural exchanges. Leaders also agreed that China and the EU should continue their efforts to promote stability, peace and development in the world. They hoped to see an early, just and fair settlement of the conflicts in the Middle East, the Western Balkans and Central Africa, and agreed to continue their common efforts to support the reconciliation process on the Korean peninsula. Leaders looked forward to the next China-EU Summit meeting, to be held in 2002, and agreed to ensure early and full follow-up to the discussions at this fourth Summit.

The fifth summit was held in Copenhagen on 24 September 2002 (see Document 4.7). Topics of discussion included EU enlargement, implementation of Chinese reform and WTO obligations and the forthcoming 16th Congress of the Chinese Communist Party, together with a wide range of other subjects. Sensitive topics included human rights and a possible readmission agreement concerning illegal migrants; on both of these, the Joint Press Statement used diplomatic and relatively non-committal language. The parties agreed to expand the environmental dialogue, created at the 2001 Summit, as well as eventual cooperation on food safety. They agreed to discuss future cooperation on satellite navigation within the framework of the Galileo programme and to expand sectoral dialogues in several new areas, including education.

### Document 4.7: Joint Press Statement of the 5th Annual EU–China Summit

**Joint Press Statement of the Fifth EU-China Summit**

The fifth Summit meeting between the European Union and China was held in Copenhagen on 24 September 2002. Premier Zhu Rongji of the People's Republic of China, Prime Minister Anders Fogh Rasmussen of Denmark in his capacity as President of the European Council, and the President of the European Commission Romano Prodi attended the Summit.

The Chinese Minister of Foreign Affairs Tang Jiaxuan, the Chinese Minister of Foreign Trade and Economic Cooperation Shi Guangsheng, the Danish Minister for Foreign Affairs Per Stig Møller, the European Commissioner for External Relations Christopher Patten and the European Commissioner for Trade Pascal Lamy participated in the Summit.

Leaders had an in-depth exchange of views on EU-China relations and international and regional issues of common interest. They welcomed the progress made since the last Summit meeting in Brussels in September 2001 and expressed their satisfaction with the positive results of this Summit meeting. They stressed their resolve to expand and deepen further EU-China co-operation in all areas on the basis of equality and mutual benefit and to promote the development of a comprehensive partnership between the EU and China.

The two sides briefed each other on developments in the EU and China, with a particular emphasis on the EU integration and enlargement process, the implementation of China's on-going economic and social reform, particularly in light of China's recent accession to WTO, and the forthcoming 16th Congress of the Chinese Communist Party.

Leaders welcomed the recent strengthening of the EU-China political dialogue.

Leaders reaffirmed the EU and China's strong commitment to promoting peace, security and sustainable development throughout the world. They expressed concern about the destabilising effect of regional conflicts and agreed to continue supporting, in particular, the reconciliation process in the Korean Peninsula as well as the peace process in the Middle East. Special attention was also given to developments in Afghanistan and the relations between India and Pakistan.

The EU side reaffirmed that it would continue to adhere to the one China principle and hoped for a peaceful resolution of the Taiwan question through constructive dialogue. The EU side took note of recent developments across the Taiwan Straits, as briefed by the Chinese side. The Chinese side appreciated the EU's commitment to the one China principle and reiterated its principled position on the settlement of the Taiwan question in accordance with the basic principle of "peaceful reunification and one country, two systems".

The two sides agreed to continue their dialogue on human rights on the basis of equality and mutual respect and reconfirmed their commitment to work towards achieving meaningful and positive results. Furthermore, both sides reaffirmed their commitment to respect international human rights standards and to co-operate fully with UN human rights mechanisms. They welcomed the recent developments in bilateral project co-operation, in particular with respect to the establishment of an EU-China academic network related to the ratification and implementation of the UN covenants on human rights. They also welcomed the successful establishment of the Human Rights Small Project Facility, as well as steps towards closer co-operation between European and Chinese non-governmental organisations and academic institutions. The two sides confirmed their ambition of further enhancing co-operation in the field of human rights.

Leaders reaffirmed their commitment to multilateral non-proliferation, arms control and disarmament and emphasised the importance of strengthening the bilateral dialogue on these issues. The two sides considered fight against terrorism as an issue of common concern, which would require a higher degree of co-ordination and cooperation. Leaders stressed the importance of the continued full play of the United Nations' leading role in counterterrorism and of universal implementation of the international counter-terrorism conventions and relevant UN Security Council resolutions. Leaders agreed that in the aftermath of September 11th it was more important than ever to improve international co-operation and co-ordination in a spirit of mutual trust, benefit and equality, and to address the challenges of development and peaceful resolution of disputes. In this context, the EU side noted with interest China's "new security concept".

Leaders emphasised the need to enhance co-operation in facing trans-national challenges. In line with the consensus reached between the Chinese Premier Zhu Rongji and Commission President Prodi in July 2000, Leaders stressed the importance of EU-China co-operation to combat illegal migration and trafficking in human beings. Leaders took note of the progress made in this field and reiterated their commitment to further deepen this co-operation, notably by encouraging further collaboration between relevant departments in Europe and China. The EU side expressed the hope to open soon exploratory discussions on a possible readmission agreement. Leaders stressed the importance of promoting people-to-people contacts between China and the EU, in particular through an increased number of visits by organised travel groups of Chinese citizens to Europe. To achieve this objective, they instructed their officials to pursue discussions on an agreed destination status for the EU, with a view to rapidly negotiating a bilateral agreement in this area. The EU side expressed the view that this agreement would also take into account the issue of returns. The Chinese side expressed the need for the competent authorities of the two sides to increase their communication.

Leaders reaffirmed their commitment to environmental issues and endeavoured to expand the dialogue, which had been initiated at the time of the last bilateral Summit in Brussels in September 2001. They acknowledged the progress, which had been achieved since then, and in particular in the framework of ASEM. Both sides stressed the importance they attach to the work carried out at the World Summit on Sustainable Development recently held in Johannesburg and endeavoured to co-operate closely, with a view to making its follow-up a success. Leaders reaffirmed their commitment to the UN Framework Convention on Climate Change as well as the Kyoto Protocol as the framework for international co-operation on this issue and stressed the importance of the latter's early entry into force.

The two sides expressed their satisfaction with China's accession to the WTO, and their belief that this will be to the mutual benefit of China and all its WTO partners. The Chinese side reiterated that it would, while enjoying its full rights in the multilateral trading system, fully implement its commitments. The EU side re-affirmed its will to continue and intensify its efforts to support China in this, both through co-operation programmes and through dialogue in key areas, including on how to ensure an appropriate degree of transparency.

The two sides affirmed their shared interest in strengthening the multilateral trading system, and, in particular, their commitment to a successful conclusion of the multilateral trade negotiations of the Doha Development Agenda. They pledged to intensify their dialogue in this sphere and to work together for an ambitious result that fulfilled the expectations of all WTO members. In particular, they would consult with each other and with other WTO members to ensure respect of the deadlines foreseen in the Doha Ministerial Declarations and Decisions and to prepare a successful 5th WTO Ministerial Conference in Cancun, Mexico, in September 2003.

Leaders welcomed the continued growth in EU-China trade and agreed to exert further efforts to expand it. They stressed the importance of foreign direct investment and the need for investment flows in both directions to increase further. Leaders expressed the wish to resolve recent food and consumer safety problems as quickly as possible, to open the way for more fruitful co-operation on sanitary and phytosanitary issues.

Leaders welcomed the progress achieved in the field of transport, and, in particular, the forthcoming signature of an EU-China maritime transport agreement. Leaders welcomed that both sides had started specific co-operation activities in the area of satellite navigation and expressed their intention to discuss the possibility of future cooperation in the framework of the recently launched Galileo programme. The two sides expressed their satisfaction with progress in EU-China scientific and technological co-operation and for its expansion under the EU's 6th Framework Programme on research and technological development (2002-2006).

The two sides expressed hope for a rapid conclusion of a customs co-operation agreement. Leaders stressed the importance of strengthening and expanding sectoral dialogues on a wide range of issues, including information society, enterprise policy and education.

On 30 October 2003 the sixth annual summit was held in Beijing (see Document 4.8). The increased number of participants testified to the wide range of topics that were discussed. The parties noted the success of the high-level political dialogues, and the expansion of the dialogue format to other areas, such as regulation for industrial products and industrial policy. They also welcomed progress on two important new agreements, the Galileo Satellite Navigation Cooperation Agreement (signed) and the memorandum of understanding (MOU) on Approved Destination Status for Chinese tourist groups. The International Thermonuclear Experimental Reactor nuclear fusion project, then under negotiation, was discussed for the first time. Topics such as non-proliferation, the one China policy, human rights, terrorism, environmental protection and WTO commitments remained on the agenda. Immediately prior to the summit, each side had issued an important policy paper to set the direction for the future and expand and deepen their cooperation, for example with regard to security strategy. On this basis, the parties emphasised their intention to develop an overall strategic partnership between China and the EU.

### Document 4.8: Joint Press Statement of the 6th EU–China Summit

**Joint Press Statement of the Sixth EU-China Summit**
Beijing, 30 October 2003

1. The Sixth Summit meeting between China and the European Union was held in Beijing on 30 October 2003. The event was hosted by Premier of the State Council Wen Jiabao of

the People's Republic of China. The EU was represented by Prime Minister Silvio Berlusconi of Italy in his capacity as President of the European Council, President of the European Commission Romano Prodi and High Representative for the EU Common Foreign and Security Policy Javier Solana. President Hu Jintao of the People's Republic of China met with the visiting European leaders.

2. Chinese Minister of Foreign Affairs Li Zhaoxing, Minister in charge of National Development and Reform Commission Ma Kai, Minister of Science and Technology Xu Guanhua, Vice-Minister of Commerce Liao Xiaoqi, Italian Minister for Foreign Affairs Franco Frattini and European Commissioner for Trade Pascal Lamy also participated in the Summit.

3. Leaders briefed each other on developments in China and the EU and had an in-depth exchange of views on China-EU relations and international and regional issues of common interest, and reached a broad consensus.

4. Leaders reviewed the development of China-EU relations and welcomed the progress made since the Fifth Summit meeting in Copenhagen in September 2002. The two sides agreed that their high-level political dialogues had been fruitful and the dialogues and consultations at other levels had also further expanded in intensity and scope and such multi-layered structure of China-EU relations is an indicator of the increasing maturity and growing strategic nature of the partnership.

5. Leaders welcomed the signing of the GALILEO Satellite Navigation Cooperation Agreement and the initialling of the Memorandum of Understanding on Approved Destination Status.

Leaders considered both to be significant milestones in their expanding bilateral relations and looked forward to their early implementation. The Agreement on GALILEO opens the way to the participation of China in this strategic programme and the Memorandum of Understanding on Approved Destination Status, including the Joint Declarations concerning Denmark, United Kingdom and Ireland, opens the way to facilitating Chinese group tourism in the EU.

6. Underlining the success of the existing dialogue on regulation for industrial products, leaders also welcomed the newly established dialogue on industrial policy that aims at ensuring a business-friendly level playing field for industrial operators and at contributing to smooth and sustainable trade relations between the EU and China. The dialogue will encourage contributions from both Chinese and European companies.

7. Leaders welcomed the recent issuing of policy papers on China-EU relations by both sides. The two policy papers recognise the satisfaction of both sides with the dynamic progress of their relationship, identify their respective policy objectives and propose new initiatives in many areas. Leaders believe that the two policy papers, which set the agenda for the future direction of China-EU relations, will provide considerable additional momentum to the relationship. A considerable number of common priorities were identified including further strengthening the exchange of high-level visits and political dialogue, reinforcing cooperation on economic and trade and major international and regional issues, and increasing cooperation at the multilateral level. They also noted the draft European Security Strategy Paper, in which China features as one of the key partners for the EU's strategic security relationships.

8. Leaders reaffirmed China and the EU's commitment to promoting peace, security and sustainable development throughout the world, and stood for a strengthened UN role in this

regard. Leaders expressed concern about the destabilising effect of regional conflicts. They reaffirmed their active support for the peace process in the Middle East and stressed the need for Iraq's early resumption of sovereignty and reconstruction. Leaders exchanged the views about the political situation in Myanmar.

9. China and the EU attach high importance to multilateral non-proliferation, arms control and disarmament and leaders emphasised the need for bilateral dialogue on these issues. Both sides expressed, in particular, their support for efforts to promote non-proliferation of WMD in the Korean Peninsula. In this context, the EU side welcomed China's important role in the six-party Beijing talks on DPRK nuclear issue, which was held in August 2003, and fully supports China and all parties involved in their efforts to facilitate a peaceful solution to the issue. The EU stressed its readiness to contribute to this process. Both sides also stressed their support to the International Atomic Energy Agency safeguards.

10. The EU side reaffirmed that it continues to adhere to the one China policy and expressed its hope for a peaceful resolution of the Taiwan question through constructive dialogue. The Chinese side appreciated the EU's commitment to the one China policy and reiterated its principled position on the settlement of the Taiwan question in accordance with the basic principle of "peaceful reunification and one country, two systems".

11. The two sides welcomed the achievements of their human rights dialogue and agreed to continue their ongoing dialogue on human rights on the basis of equality and mutual respect and reconfirmed their commitment to work towards achieving more meaningful and positive results on the ground. They also underlined their respect for international human rights standards provided for in relevant international human rights instruments and to cooperate with UN human rights mechanisms. They also noted the importance of the International Criminal Court in the global fight against genocide, war crimes and crimes against humanity.

Furthermore, leaders confirmed their commitment to further enhance cooperation in the field of human rights.

12. The two sides reiterated their commitment to the fight against terrorism and agreed that this is an issue of common concern, requiring coordination and cooperation both bilaterally and multilaterally, while stressing the need to comply with the basic principles governing international relations and safeguarding human rights. In this context, they referred to the recent successful ASEM seminar on Anti-Terrorism held on 22-23 September 2003 in Beijing. Leaders stressed the key role of the United Nations with respect to counter-terrorism, and the importance of universal implementation of the international counter-terrorism Conventions and relevant UN Security Council resolutions.

13. Following their discussions at the ASEM Summit in Copenhagen in September 2002 on the "Dialogue of Cultures and Civilisations" from Asia and Europe, leaders welcomed the ASEM Ministerial Meeting on this subject to be hosted by China in December 2003.

14. Leaders reaffirmed their commitment to environmental protection and endeavoured to expand the dialogue. They acknowledged the progress which had been achieved since the last Summit. Both sides stressed the importance of further follow-up on the World Summit on Sustainable development and of enhancing cooperation in the context of the United Nations Framework Convention on Climate Change and its Kyoto Protocol. They expressed the hope for strengthening cooperation in the protection of ecological environment in the course of the development of China's western region, and

reaffirmed their support for the China-EU Environmental Ministers' Dialogue Mechanism.

15. Leaders emphasised the need to enhance cooperation in facing trans-national challenges in the field of justice and home affairs. They acknowledged the importance of China-EU operational cooperation to combat illegal migration and trafficking in human beings. Leaders took note of the progress made in this field, in particular the positive result of the fourth round of the China-EU High Level Consultations on the fight against illegal migration and trafficking in human beings held in Beijing on 28 October 2003, and reiterated their commitment to deepen this cooperation and make it more results-oriented. The EU side stressed the need of an early launch of exploratory discussions on a future China-EU readmission agreement.

16. On the China-EU cooperation programme they welcomed the progress being made in several areas, notably with regard to China's reform process. The EU side expressed its wish to see more rapid progress in other areas of the programme, particularly those concerning cooperation on combating illegal migration and support for NGOs. With timely communication, the Chinese side encourages the EU side to establish closer cooperation with relevant Chinese ministries in an effort to enhance efficiency.

17. Leaders welcomed the continued growth of China-EU trade and agreed that its further expansion should take place in a balanced and mutually beneficial manner. The two sides reiterated their willingness to address in a positive spirit bilateral trade problems through increased exchange of views and consultation and welcomed in this context the contribution of enhanced bilateral sectoral dialogues.

18. The two sides stressed the importance of foreign direct investment and the need for further increase of investment flows in both directions.

19. Leaders shared their regret that the WTO Ministerial Meeting in Cancun had not produced a successful outcome. They reaffirmed their commitment to a strong rules-based and equitable multilateral trading system and to a successful conclusion of the multilateral trade negotiations launched in Doha. They agreed to pursue and deepen the bilateral dialogue on WTO issues.

20. The two sides stressed the importance of full and timely implementation of WTO obligations, which serves the common interests of China, the EU and all their WTO partners. The EU side reaffirmed its will to continue and intensify its efforts to support China, both through cooperation programmes and through dialogue in key areas.

21. Leaders noted the need to promote smooth adjustment to imbalances in global trade and capital flows and.

22. Leaders welcomed the recent progress achieved on several sectoral agreements and expressed particular satisfaction with the China-EU maritime transport agreement which had been signed in December 2002 and has now been ratified by the Chinese side and endorsed by the European Parliament in its opinion.

23. The two sides expressed their satisfaction with progress in China-EU scientific and technological cooperation and its expansion under the EU's Sixth Framework Programme on Research and Technological Development (2002-2006). They especially welcomed the new initiatives launched to fight against SARS and other infectious diseases.

24. Both sides hoped that start-up of negotiations on an agreement between the Government of the People's Republic of China and the European Atomic Energy Community

(EURATOM) on cooperation in peaceful uses of nuclear energy would soon make progress. They further welcomed the ongoing negotiations for the establishment of the ITER organization (international fusion energy organisation) between the EU, China and the other international partners.

25. Both sides expressed their hope for an early conclusion of a customs cooperation agreement, and looked forward to starting negotiations very soon, with the common aim of concluding the agreement in the first half of 2004. They agreed that such an agreement should cover mutual administrative assistance on customs matters, particularly in the field of combat against commercial frauds, a major concern for both sides.

26. The EU side emphasised the need to develop a new framework for EU-China civil aviation relations in order to take account of recent legal developments. Both sides looked forward to widening and deepening their relations and cooperation.

27. Leaders stressed the importance of strengthening and expanding sectoral dialogues on a wide range of other issues. Existing dialogues cover key sectors such as energy, the environment, regulatory and industrial policy, the information society and exchanges on the "Digital Olympics". Increasing interest in this type of cooperation has led to plans for new dialogues on competition, intellectual property rights, macro-economic questions, health, employment and education. Both sides underlined the mutual benefits of such exchanges between their experts.

28. Leaders expressed their satisfaction with the positive outcome of this Sixth Summit meeting. They stressed their resolve to further expand and deepen China-EU relations, guided by the two policy papers, which promote the development of an overall strategic partnership between China and the EU.

On 8 December 2004, the seventh summit was held in London. As Document 4.9 attests, it dealt with a very wide range of topics. The parties agreed to explore the feasibility of a new bilateral agreement to replace the outdated 1985 Trade and Cooperation Agreement. They signed new agreements (the Joint Declaration on Non-proliferation and Arms Control and the EU–China Customs Cooperation Agreement), renewed the EU–China Science and Technological Cooperation Agreement, and discussed the possibility of a future EU–China Civil Aviation Agreement. Four new financing agreements for new cooperation projects were endorsed: EU–China Information Society Project, EU–China Managers Exchange and Training Programme, EU–China Social Security Reform Project and the Erasmus Mundus China Window Project. For the first time, discussion of the EU arms embargo against China and the issue of China's market economy status in EC antidumping investigations appeared in the summit, or at least in the Joint Statement. Similarly, on the basis of the very successful EU–China Legal and Judicial Cooperation Programme, the EU and China agreed to explore further cooperation in the legal field, for example the establishment of a 'bilateral training and education institute', a project which today has become the Europe–China School of Law. Extensive discussion of international and regional political issues testified to the increasing importance of China on the international political stage.

## Document 4.9: Joint Statement of the 7th EU–China Summit

**Joint Statement of the 7th EU-China Summit**
8 December 2004

1. The Seventh Summit meeting between the European Union and China was held in The Hague, The Netherlands, on 8 December 2004. The EU was represented by the President of the European Council, Prime Minister of the Netherlands, Mr Jan Peter Balkenende, President of the European Commission, Mr Jose Manuel Barroso and the Secretary General/High Representative for the EU Common Foreign and Security Policy, Mr Javier Solana. China was represented by the Premier of the State Council of the People's Republic of China, Mr Wen Jiabao.

2. Minister of Foreign Affairs of The Netherlands, Mr Bernard Bot, the European Commissioner in charge of External Relations, Ms Benita Ferrero-Waldner, the European Commissioner for Trade, Mr Peter Mandelson, Chinese Minister of Foreign Affairs, Mr. Li Zhaoxing and Chinese Minister of Commerce, Mr Bo Xilai also participated in the Summit.

3. The Leaders reviewed the development of EU-China relations and welcomed the progress made since the Sixth Summit meeting. The two sides agreed that there had been frequent high-level visits and effective dialogues and co-operation in all fields between the two sides, guided by the two policy papers issued by both sides and further defined at the EU-China Seminar in February 2004. The two sides looked forward to celebrating their bilateral achievements on the occasion of the 30th Anniversary of official relations between the EU and China in 2005.

4. The Leaders briefed each other on developments in the EU and China. China welcomed the new European Commission and European Parliament, the enlargement of the EU and the agreement by EU Heads of State and Government on the treaty establishing a Constitution for Europe. The two sides affirmed that the deepening and widening of the EU should contribute to further strengthening Sino-EU relations. The EU recognized China's achievements made under the ongoing social and economic reform.

5. The two sides affirmed that, due to the continuous development of EU-China relations in recent years, the EU and China will explore actively the feasibility of concluding a new EU-China framework agreement.

6. The two sides signed the Joint Declaration on Non-proliferation and Arms Control whereby they recognise each other as major strategic partners in the area of disarmament and non-proliferation. Both sides agreed that enhanced co-operation between the EU and China in the non-proliferation area will be conducive to advancing the multilateral non-proliferation process, as well as to expanding and deepening their comprehensive strategic partnership. They identified, in this context, priority areas for co-operation between the two sides.

7. The EU and China confirmed that EU-China relations in all aspects have developed significantly in the last years. In this context they discussed the issue of the EU arms embargo against China. The EU side confirmed its political will to continue to work towards lifting the embargo. The Chinese side welcomed the positive signal, and considered it beneficial to the sound development of the comprehensive strategic partnership between China and the EU.

Both sides reiterated their positions and agreed to continue consultations on this issue. China reaffirmed that political discrimination on this issue was not acceptable and should be immediately removed. The EU reaffirmed that work on strengthening the application of the European Union Code of Conduct on arms exports was continuing.

8. The EU side reaffirmed its continued adherence to the one China policy, and expressed its hope for a peaceful resolution of the Taiwan question through constructive dialogue. The Chinese side appreciated the EU's commitment to the one China policy and reiterated its principled position on the Taiwan question.

9. The Leaders believed that the EU-China human rights dialogue promoted mutual understanding and agreed to continue this dialogue, while making efforts to achieve more meaningful and positive results on the ground, as well as the related bilateral co-operation programme. They underlined their respect for international human rights standards provided for in relevant international human rights instruments, including on the rights of minorities, and their commitment to co-operate with UN human rights mechanisms. In this respect, China is committed to the ratification of the International Covenant on Civil and Political Rights (ICCPR) as soon as possible. They also noted the importance of the International Criminal Court in the global fight against genocide, war crimes and crimes against humanity. The Leaders underlined the importance of concrete steps in the field of human rights and reaffirmed their commitment to further enhance co-operation and exchanges in this field on the basis of equality and mutual respect.

10. The Leaders underlined that activities on facilitating people-to-people exchanges and co-operation in combating illegal migration are a priority for both sides. In the spirit of full reciprocity, leaders discussed issues of readmission and visa facilitation. They hoped for an early opening of negotiations on these issues, as soon as technically andjuridically possible. Entry procedures were also discussed. The EU reaffirmed the importance of EU-China operational co-operation on combating illegal migration and trafficking in human being.

11. The Leaders, in welcoming the entry into force of the milestone Memorandum of Understanding on Visa and Related Issues Concerning Tourist Groups from the People's Republic of China (ADS), agreed that tourism would enhance people-to-people contacts between the EU and China and deepen mutual understanding. They stressed the need to ensure an efficient and smooth implementation of the modalities of the Memorandum of Understanding.

12. Both sides welcomed the dynamism of their trade relations, best illustrated by the EU becoming China's largest trading partner and China becoming the EITs second largest trading partner in 2004. The Leaders welcomed the EU-China Business Summit held on the sidelines of the Summit. They reiterated their commitment to maximize mutual benefits of such relation by improving market access and increasing investment opportunities for both sides.

The Leaders reiterated the importance of fully implementing their WTO commitments and strengthening the multilateral trading system. The EU agreed to continue to assist China's efforts in capacity building and both sides welcomed the launching of the second WTO support programme for China in 2004.

The Leaders welcomed the progress made in the DDA in July and the new momentum in the Doha Round of negotiations. They agreed to intensify their co-operation with a view to successfully preparing the WTO Ministerial Meeting in Hong-Kong.

The two sides underlined that increased bilateral consultations have helped to make substantial progress in a number of trade issues, in particular the lifting of trade restrictions as a result of their increased co-operation regarding sanitary and phytosanitary measures and technical barriers to trade and pledged to further intensify their trade dialogue mechanisms with a view to solving remaining trade problems. The Leaders expressed their intention to continue and intensify the efforts made to fight violations of Intellectual Property Rights.

13. China reiterated its concern on the issue of full market economy status and underlined the significance it attaches to resolving this issue for deepening EU-China relations. The EU welcomed the positive orientation of China towards building a market economy. Both sides welcomed the creation of a working group aimed at actively identifying a practical solution to this issue.

14. During the Summit, the two sides signed the EU-China Customs Co-operation Agreement which is vital to facilitate trade and help combat customs violations and fraud such as counterfeiting, and renewed the EU-China Science and Technological Co-operation Agreement. The signing of the agreement on R&D co-operation on the peaceful use of nuclear energy between the European Atomic Energy Community (Euratom) and the Government of the People's Republic of China launches research co-operation on the peaceful use of nuclear energy and gives access to research facilities for researchers from both sides.

The Leaders also endorsed four financing agreements for new co-operation projects: the EU-China Information Society Project, the EU-China Managers Exchange and Training Programme, the EU-China Social Security Reform Project, and the Erasmus Mundus China Window project. These projects are under the programme of support for economic and social reform in China within the EU-China development co-operation, with EU funding amounting to €61 million.

15. The Leaders noted with satisfaction progress of co-operation in all fields. The follow-up agreement on technical co-operation in satellite navigation (Galileo) signed in October 2004 enabled China to become the first non-EU country enjoying full participation in the Community framework. China's participation opens the doors for more tangible scientific and industrial collaboration projects. The two sides welcomed the new momentum in the energy dialogue after the successful 5th EU-China Energy Conference. The Leaders expressed their hope that the EU-China High-level Forum on Science and Technology (S&T) Policy and Strategy to be held in Beijing in May 2005 will promote the mutual understanding on S&T development strategy and deepen the S&T co-operation relations between China and EU and that the dialogue on co-operation in space science, applications and technology will lead to co-operation in joint projects between aerospace companies and research institutions from both sides.

16. The Leaders encouraged to promote EU-China inter-sectoral dialogue and co-operation. They welcomed the initiative on establishing an EU-China dialogue and co-operation mechanisms on employment and social affairs. The Leaders also welcomed first contacts since the last Summit on issues relating to macro-economic policy and the regulation of financial markets and agreed on a process of dialogue in related areas.

They expressed satisfaction with the first talks and exchanges of views on issues related to balanced development, regional policies and rural development, and agreed to hold an EU-China seminar on regional economic development next year. The Leaders welcomed the EU-China Dialogue on Intellectual Property (IP), and on industrial competition policy. They agreed to further explore possibilities for strengthening their co-operation in the IP area in particular through further consultation and co-operation between governments and enterprises, and through a closer co-operation of IP-related institutions, including staff exchanges. They supported the continued dialogue on the Information Society at a high level.

They noted with satisfaction the results of the second implementation meeting of the EU-China Maritime Agreement, at which both sides showed a significant convergence of views in respect of handling current and future challenges within the maritime policy context, and looked forward to further enhancing their bilateral co-operation on trade and maritime issues in the international fora.

The Leaders, in welcoming the dialogue progress and the closer EU-China co-operation in civil aviation, agreed to further deepen co-operation in this field, including civil aviation industry and technology, and to solve as a matter of priority outstanding issues thereby opening the way for a potential future EU-China Civil Aviation Agreement. Progress will be reported at the next Summit. China expressed strong interest in strengthening technological co-operation and its willingness to participate in projects other than those in the EU-China civil aviation co-operation programme. An EU-China Aviation Summit will be jointly organised in the first half of 2005.

The Leaders expressed their hope that the European Economic and Social Committee and the China Economic and Social Council establish a regular dialogue between the civil society organisations of both sides, which should be based on the protocol signed by the Presidents of both institutions in 2002.

Both sides believed that, on the basis of the EU-China Legal and Judicial Co-operation Programme, strengthening the exchanges in the judicial field should be further explored, particularly in the co-operation of training legal professionals and seeking to establish a bilateral education and training institute.

17. The Leaders welcomed the fact that many Chinese students are following graduate studies in Europe through the EU-China education co-operation mechanism, particularly the recently launched Erasmus Mundus programme. They also welcomed the launching in the next academic year of a specific "China Window" within Erasmus Mundus. The two sides encouraged and supported further actions to strengthen education co-operation between the EU and China.

18. The Leaders welcomed the progress in the EU-China development co-operation programme, notably in the areas of economic and social reform, as well as environment and sustainable development. The EU side expressed its wish to see more rapid progress in other areas, particularly the support for the development of civil society. The two sides noted with satisfaction the substantial increase in the budget of the 2004 programme.

19. The Leaders underlined their close and productive dialogue on the ongoing negotiations for the establishment of the ITER Organisation among China, EU, Japan, the Republic of Korea, Russia, and the US. The EU expressed its satisfaction and gratitude to China for its continuing support of the EU ITER site. The Leaders looked forward to a rapid conclusion of the ITER site negotiation.

20. The Leaders reaffirmed their shared commitment to environmental protection and encouraged efforts to extend and deepen the high level dialogue in this area. They stressed that biodiversity conservation and integrated river basin management are fruitful areas for co-operation. They also agreed on the health and environmental benefits arising from reducing emissions from motor vehicles and agreed to continue to support China's introduction of the 'Euro[9] emission standards. Technology transfer, exchange of information on methodologies, policy tools and means of implementation as well as staff exchanges and the

implementation of projects can all be used to develop a dynamic partnership on environmental issues. Both sides stressed the importance of further follow-up on the World Summit on Sustainable Development and of enhancing co-operation in the context of the United Nations Framework Convention on Climate Change and its Kyoto Protocol and welcomed the Protocol's entry into force in 2005.

21. The Leaders underlined the importance of the implementation of the Declaration of the Commitment on HIV/AIDS adopted at the General Assembly of the United Nations in 2001. In face of the truly global nature of the epidemic, both sides recognised the importance of increased co-operation to combat HIV/AIDS as well as other newly emerging infectious diseases, appreciated the constructive resolutions on strengthening the capability of global public health adopted at the General Assembly of the United Nations. They underlined the importance of the increasing availability of anti-retro viral drugs and the necessity of preventive measures, including development of vaccines and microbicides, harm reduction approaches and promotion of safer and responsible sexual behaviour. The EU welcomed China's recent adoption of the newly revised "Law on Diseases Prevention and Control" covering non-discrimination against persons with infectious diseases, pathogeny carriers and persons with suspected infectious diseases as an important step to counter stigmatisation and judgmental approaches to persons at risk or infected. The EU welcomed that the HIV/AIDS programme of the Global Fund recently started in China. China appreciated the EU role as a major contributor for this Fund, and encouraged EU's continuous and vigorous financial assistance to China's efforts in HIV/AIDS prevention and treatment.

22. The Leaders had an in-depth exchange of views on international and regional issues of common interest. Leaders reaffirmed the commitment of China and the EU to promoting peace, security and sustainable development throughout the world, with the United Nations at its core. They expressed their strong support for revitalisation and reform of the UN in order to be able to cope with existing and new challenges and threats, and underlined that the report of the UN High-Level Panel should serve as a basis for discussions in this regard and the need for any plan of reform to be decided by consensus through consultation. The two sides stressed the importance of achieving the Millennium Development Goals and attached considerable importance to enhancing bilateral and multilateral co-operation in this area. In this regard, they underlined their strong desire to make the UN Major Event 2005 a success, and agreed to support a comprehensive, balanced approach in the implementation of the Millennium Declaration and of the Millennium Development Goals, as well as in handling issues related to peace and security. A successful outcome of the 13th session of the Commission for Sustainable Development (April 2005) would be of importance in this regard.

23. The two sides reaffirmed their commitment to the fight against terrorism and reiterated that anti-terrorism action must accord with the purpose and principles of the UN Charter and the norms of relevant International Law and fully respect human rights. The two sides underlined the leading role of the United Nations with respect to counter-terrorism, and the importance of the universal implementation of all UN Security Council resolutions, UN conventions and protocols related to counter-terrorism. They undertook to support the work for a draft Comprehensive Convention on International Terrorism. The two sides underlined the importance of enhanced regional and interregional co-operation and referred in particular to the co-operation developed in the framework of ASEM and of the ASEAN Regional Forum.

24. The Leaders expressed deep concern over the destabilising effect of regional conflicts. They welcomed the restoration of full sovereignty to Iraq and expressed their commitment to the implementation ofUNSCR 1546 in support of the political process in Iraq, including elections in 2005. They agreed to work together in the multilateral effort for Iraq's reconstruction and the restoration of peace and prosperity.

The EU and China appreciated their respective efforts in facilitating a political resolution of the Iran nuclear issue. The EU and China welcomed the agreement reached between France, Germany and the UK, supported by the High Representative, and Iran on Iran's suspension of enrichment related and reprocessing activities. Both the EU and China hoped that progress will be made in the negotiations of the EU with Iran on a mutually acceptable agreement on long-term arrangements, that should include objective guarantees that Iran's nuclear program is exclusively for peaceful purposes, and that the Iran nuclear issue will be resolved within the framework of the IAEA at the earliest opportunity.

The two sides stressed their firm commitment to the reconstruction and stabilisation of Afghanistan, in co-operation with the Afghan Government. They welcomed the October presidential elections. The Leaders agreed on the goal of a nuclear-weapons free Korean Peninsula and expressed the conviction that the issue could be settled peacefully through dialogue.

The EU praised China's crucial and active role in promoting the continuation of the Six-Party Talks. The Leaders expressed the hope that the DPRK would continue to take positive steps to participate more fully in the international community.

The Leaders exchanged views on the situation in Burma/Myanmar.

25. The Leaders expressed their satisfaction with the excellent atmosphere and the substantial results achieved at this Seventh Summit meeting. They stressed their resolve to further expand and deepen EU-China relations, towards a rapidly maturing comprehensive strategic partnership between the EU and China.

The eighth summit was held in Beijing on 5 September 2005, marking the thirtieth anniversary of the establishment of diplomatic relations (see Document 4.10). At the meeting, the EU and China endorsed a number of new agreements, for example on labour, employment and social affairs and cooperation in space exploration, science and technology. They signed a memorandum of understanding to create a dialogue on energy and transport. They set in motion the preparation for negotiations on a new China–EU Framework Agreement, while also agreeing to start negotiations on a horizontal aviation agreement to resolve legal issues raised by bilateral air services agreements between China and the EU Member States. As in previous summits, they emphasised their commitment to the protection and promotion of human rights and to the EU–China human rights dialogue, while stressing, especially on the part of the EU, the importance of practical results. The importance given to international and regional political issues testified, as in previous summits, to China's rapidly growing international political importance. This was crystallised in the establishment of a high-level coordination mechanism and a regular vice foreign ministerial strategic dialogue mechanism to be established by the end of 2005.

## Document 4.10: Joint Statement of the 8th EU–China Summit

**Joint Statement of the 8th EU-China Summit**
Brussels, 05 September 2005 IP/05/478

**EU-China Summit**
**Beijing, 5 September 2005**

1. The eighth China-EU Summit was held in Beijing on 5 September 2005. Premier Wen Jiabao of the State Council of China attended the meeting on behalf of the People's Republic of China. The EU was represented by the President of the European Council, Prime Minister Tony Blair of the UK, President of the European Commission, Mr. José Manuel Barroso, and Secretary General of the Council of the EU and High Representative for the EU Common Foreign and Security Policy, Mr. Javier Solana.

2. Leaders of the two sides reviewed the development of China-EU relations and celebrated the 30th anniversary of the establishment of diplomatic relations. Both were of the view that the past three decades had seen great changes in China and the EU and a progressive deepening of the relationship, which is fast maturing into a comprehensive strategic partnership. They believed that the strengthening of the relationship had been of great value to the long-term interests of China and the EU, to cooperation between Asia and Europe, as well as to peace, stability and development in the world at large. The leaders now wished to look ahead to the future, developing the strategic relationship through concrete actions.

3. During the Summit, the two sides endorsed:

- a memorandum of understanding on labour, employment and social affairs
- a joint statement on cooperation in space exploitation, science and technology development
- a memorandum of understanding on China-EU dialogue on energy and transport strategies
- a maritime protocol extending the existing maritime agreement to new member states and
- two major financing agreements for the China-EU bio-diversity and river basin management programmes

Furthermore, leaders witnessed the signing of a 500 million Euro loan from the European Investment Bank for the extension of Beijing airport.

4. During the meeting, a Joint Declaration on Climate Change between China and the EU was issued, which confirmed the establishment of a China-EU partnership on climate change. The two sides were determined to tackle the serious challenges of climate change through practical and results-oriented cooperation. This partnership will fully complement the UN Framework Convention on Climate Change and the Kyoto Protocol. It will strengthen cooperation and dialogue on climate change including clean energy, and will promote sustainable development. It will include cooperation on the development, deployment and transfer of low carbon technology, including advanced near-zero-emissions coal technology through carbon capture and storage.

5. The two sides emphasised the importance of high-level political dialogue and consultations at all levels in enhancing understanding, expanding common ground and advancing bilateral relations. Leaders of the two sides welcomed the recently established high-level coordination mechanism and agreed to launch a regular vice foreign ministerial strategic

dialogue mechanism by the end of 2005 to discuss important international and regional issues and exchange views on bilateral issues of common concern.

6. The two sides agreed to move towards early negotiations on a new China-EU Framework Agreement. The leaders instructed their respective services to expedite preparatory work with a view to concluding at an early date an agreement that will reflect the full breadth and depth of the strategic partnership between China and the EU.

7. The EU side reaffirmed its continued adherence to the one China policy and expressed its hope for a peaceful resolution of the Taiwan question through constructive dialogue. The Chinese side appreciated EU's commitment to the one China policy and reiterated its principled position on the Taiwan question.

8. Leaders discussed the EU arms embargo. The Chinese side was of the view that lifting the arms embargo would be conducive to the sound development of the China-EU comprehensive strategic partnership and urged the EU to lift the arms embargo at an early date. The EU side reaffirmed its willingness to continue to work towards lifting the embargo on the basis of the Joint Statement of the 2004 EU-China Summit and the subsequent European Council Conclusions on this subject.

9. As strategic partners, the two sides reiterated their cooperation in the fields of non-proliferation and disarmament. They will continue to maintain and enhance dialogue and cooperation on the basis of the Joint Declaration of the People's Republic of China and the European Union on Non-proliferation and Arms Control which was adopted at the 2004 China-EU Summit.

10. The two sides underlined their commitment to the protection and promotion of human rights and continued to place a high value on the EU-China human rights dialogue. They underlined the importance of concrete steps in the field of human rights and reaffirmed their commitment to further enhance co-operation and exchanges in this field on the basis of equality and mutual respect, while making efforts to achieving more meaningful and positive results on the ground. The EU welcomed China's commitment to ratifying the International Covenant on Civil and Political Rights (ICCPR) as soon as possible. Both sides confirmed their commitment to co-operate with UN human rights mechanisms and their respect for international human rights standards provided for in relevant international human rights instruments, including the rights of minorities. In respect of the global fight against genocide, war crimes and crimes against humanity, they also noted the importance of the International Criminal Court.

11. Both sides reiterated that China and the EU were committed to efforts to promote world peace, security and sustainable development, with the United Nations at its core. The two sides expressed support for UN reform aimed at improving its ability to cope with the existing and new threats and challenges. The two sides reiterated that any model of reform should be decided upon by consensus through consultations.

12. The two sides will continue to cooperate in international and regional affairs, including through ASEM and the ASEAN Regional Forum. The two sides shared a desire to enhance and promote security and stability in East Asia. The EU reiterated its support for achieving a nuclear-weapon-free Korean Peninsula and maintaining peace and stability there. It expressed its appreciation for China's active role in this and stood ready to provide necessary help when appropriate.

13. The two sides agreed to further strengthen mutual cooperation and sectoral dialogues to deepen and broaden trade and investment flows, which should take place in a balanced and

mutually beneficial way. The two sides welcomed the first China-EU Financial Dialogue that took place in Brussels in February 2005.

14. The EU side welcomed the achievements China has made towards building a market economy. The two sides agreed to launch high-level dialogues to address outstanding issues with a view to achieving positive progress on the issue of MES.

15. Both sides welcomed the China-EU Business Summit being held here today. They recognised the vital importance of transparency in commercial decision making, robust corporate governance, effective implementation of protection of intellectual property and safeguarding the interest of consumers in creating a positive business environment for continued economic growth and individual prosperity. With this in mind China and the EU agreed to deepen the dialogue on intellectual property rights, strengthen cooperation in the field of sanitary and phytosanitary (SPS) and consumer product safety and in particular welcomed the recently established intellectual property rights working group.

16. Both sides were determined to honour and implement their WTO commitments, and work together closely to achieve a successful Hong Kong Ministerial Conference that will deliver an ambitious and balanced package allowing completion of the Doha Development Agenda in 2006.

17. Both sides confirmed their intention to strengthen the China-EU Science and Technology partnership, which is based on substantial achievements of mutual benefit. They recognised that the Joint Declaration and the Vision Paper adopted in Beijing in May 2005 and the CO-REACH initiative laid a strategic foundation for further cooperation. They will create the appropriate conditions for a series of high impact Science and Technology events in China and Europe starting in 2006 to prepare for a "China-EU science and technology year".

18. Both sides expressed their satisfaction at China-EU cooperation within the framework of the Galileo programme. They stressed their full commitment to making Galileo a commercial and technical success worldwide, and called for detailed talks on the conditions related to China's joining of the European GNSS Supervisory Authority and the participation of Chinese enterprises in the Galileo Operation Concessionaire.

19. The two sides looked forward to the early implementation of the ITER scheme and further strengthening of their cooperation in the relevant fields.

20. Leaders of the two sides also pledged to work together to tackle the problem of illegal logging in the Asian region.

21. The two sides welcomed the Memorandum of Understanding launching a dialogue between China and the EU on their strategies in the energy and transport sectors. Both sides highlighted the importance of continuing and intensifying their cooperation in the energy and transport sectors.

22. Leaders of the two sides noted that they would take active measures to expand education cooperation and exchanges through intensified dialogues. They also welcomed the strengthening of cooperation in higher education through the Erasmus Mundus programme and planned to hold a China-EU forum on higher education in Beijing in 2005.

23. The two sides agreed to start negotiations before the end of 2005 on a China-EU horizontal aviation agreement. This will aim to resolve outstanding legal issues in bilateral air services agreements between China and EU Member States. The two sides also agreed to engage in negotiations in the coming months with a view to concluding an agreement

relating to technical cooperation in civil aviation. The two sides believed that the successful China-EU Aviation Summit held in Beijing on 30 June-1 July 2005 marked the beginning of a new era in China-EU civil aviation.

24. The two sides will intensify their cooperation in order to guarantee the smooth and efficient implementation of the Approved Destination Status (ADS) Memorandum of Understanding.

25. The leaders underlined that activities on facilitating people-to-people exchanges and cooperation in combating illegal migration are a priority for both sides. In the spirit of full reciprocity, leaders discussed issues of readmission and visa facilitation. The two sides planned to open negotiations on issues of their respective concern.

26. Leaders of the two sides welcomed the exchanges between scholars and think- tanks of China and the EU, including the cooperation and exchanges between the China Institute of International Studies, the Chinese Academy of Social Sciences and the relevant European research institutions.

On 9 September 2006, in Helsinki, the EU and China held their ninth summit (see Document 4.11). They had established a regular strategic dialogue mechanism for high-level discussions on international and regional as well as significant bilateral issues. Regarding negotiations for a new bilateral agreement, the parties agreed to start negotiations on a new Partnership and Economic Cooperation Agreement to update the 1985 Agreement on Trade and Economic Cooperation (TEC); reflecting Chinese concerns in particular, the updating of the 1985 TEC was to 'be administered in a relatively independent manner' from the incorporation of other, more controversial issues into a legally binding text. Human rights, the arms embargo, illegal migration and readmission, and market economy status in antidumping cases also figured again on the agenda; the parties noted progress in particular on the last issue. Recognising China's increasing links with African countries, the parties each affirmed their own positions at the time, the EU emphasising the importance of good governance and human rights, and China stressing especially the importance of national sovereignty and the principle of non-interference in others' internal affairs. New issues included bird flu, while recently recognised issues such as illegal logging were also discussed. The parties gave great significance to sustainable development and environmental cooperation. With regard to China's implementation of its WTO commitments, also discussed at previous summits, the parties noted that most transition periods would have expired in December 2006, and they emphasised that, instead of immediate recourse or threats of recourse to the WTO, dialogue and cooperation would be used to resolve bilateral issues 'with due regard to their international rights and obligations'. The issues of domestic regulation and standards, though previously on summit agendas, were given special emphasis, due notably to increasing trade of foodstuffs and consumer goods. The EU and China had recently signed an MOU on cooperation between their respective administrative authorities for health and consumer protection—the Chinese General Administration of Quality Supervision, Inspection and Quarantine in China and the Directorate-General for Health and Consumer Protection in Europe—and agreed to establish an EU–China Food and Consumer Goods Safety Joint Committee. The summit also noted the great importance of the numerous dialogues already established between the EU and China. Discussions on educational cooperation had matured into cooperation in establishing a Europe–China School of Law.

### Document 4.11: Joint Statement of the 9th EU–China Summit

**Joint Statement of the Ninth EU-China Summit,**
Helsinki 9 September 2006

1. The Ninth EU-China Summit was held in Helsinki, Finland on 9 September 2006. The EU was represented by the President of the European Council, Prime Minister Matti Vanhanen of Finland, President of the European Commission, Mr. Jose Manuel Barroso. Premier Wen Jiabao of the State Council of China attended the meeting on behalf of the People's Republic of China.

2. Leaders of the two sides agreed that the past decade had seen significant changes In the EU and in China and a progressive deepening of the relationship, which was maturing into a comprehensive strategic partnership. They believed that the strengthening of the relationship had been of great value to the long-term interests of the EU and China, to cooperation between Asia and Europe, as well as to peace, stability, and development in the world at large.

3. Leaders of the two sides emphasized the importance of high-level political dialogue and consultations at all levels in enhancing understanding and trust, expanding common ground, and advancing bilateral relations. They welcomed the recently established regular strategic dialogue mechanism, which had proven to be a valuable tool in the frank and in-depth discussions of important international and regional issues and the exchanges of views on bilateral issues of common concern.

4. In order to reflect the full breadth and depth of today's comprehensive strategic partnership between the EU and China, the two sides agreed to launch negotiations on a new Partnership and Co-operation Agreement which will encompass the full scope of their bilateral relationship, including enhanced co-operation in political matters. These negotiations will also update the 1985 EEC-China Trade and Economic Co-operation Agreement, which will be administered in a relatively independent manner, taking into consideration the global objectives of the EU-China strategic partnership.

5. The EU side reaffirmed its continued adherence to one China policy and expressed its hope for a peaceful resolution of the Taiwan question through constructive dialogue. The Chinese side appreciated EU's commitment to the one China policy and reiterated its principled position on the Taiwan question.

6. Leaders also discussed the EU arms embargo. The Chinese side reiterated its view that lifting the arms embargo would be conducive to the sound development of the EU-China relations and urged the EU to lift the arms embargo at an early date. The EU side recognized the importance of this issue and confirmed its willingness to carry forward work towards lifting the embargo on the basis of the Joint Statement of the 2004 EU-China Summit and subsequent European Council Conclusions.

7. Leaders reiterated their willingness to develop their cooperation in the fields of non-proliferation and disarmament, in particular in the preparation for a successful review conference on Biological and Toxin Weapons Convention in November 2006 and the upcoming Preparatory Committee for the next review conference of the Treaty on the

Non-Proliferation of Nuclear Weapons. They will continue to maintain and enhance dialogue and cooperation on the basis of the Joint Declaration of the European Union and the People's Republic of China on Non-proliferation and Arms Control which was adopted at the 2004 EU-China Summit. The two sides noted with great satisfaction their ongoing practical cooperation in the area of export control.

8. Leaders emphasized the importance of efforts to reform the United Nations system and their strong support for a fair, just and rules-based multilateral international system with the UN playing a central role. They reiterated their commitment to promote world peace, security, sustainable development, and human rights, as recognized in the 2005 UN World Summit outcome document. The two sides expressed their support for reform which would improve the UN's ability to cope with new and existing threats and challenges. They will engage in achieving progress on the reform by consensus and will be committed to ensuring full implementation of the outcome of the 2005 UN World Summit, including by cooperating with the newly established UN bodies such as the Peace Building Commission and the Human Rights Council.

9. The two sides underlined their commitment to the protection and promotion of human rights and continued to place a high value on the EU-China human rights dialogue. They underlined the importance of concrete steps in the field of human rights and reaffirmed their commitment to further enhance co-operation and exchanges in this field on the basis of equality and mutual respect, while making efforts to achieving more meaningful and positive results on the ground. The EU welcomed China's commitment to ratifying the International Covenant on Civil and Political Rights (ICCPR) as soon as possible. Both sides confirmed their commitment to co-operate with UN human rights mechanism and their respect for international human rights standards provided for in relevant international human rights instruments including the rights of minorities. In respect of the global fight against genocide, war crimes and crimes against humanity, they also noted the importance of the International Criminal Court. The two sides were committed to supporting the work of the UN Human Rights Council and undertook to strengthen their communication and coordination in this regard in line with UN General Assembly Resolution 60/251.

10. Summit Leaders welcomed the adoption of United Nations Security Council Resolution 1701 which led to the cessation of hostilities between Israel and Hezbollah. United Nations Security Council Resolution 1701 sets the required framework for a political settlement of the crisis supported by the reinforced UNIFIL forces in which the EU Member States are playing a leading role. Summit leaders urged all parties in the region to play a constructive role in helping to swiftly implement this resolution. They also stressed their determination to bring humanitarian assistance to the people of Lebanon.

11. Summit leaders emphasized the need for a comprehensive peace plan for the Middle East. They reaffirmed their support for a negotiated settlement of the Israeli-Palestinian conflict based on existing agreements which include the relevant UN Security Council Resolutions and the principles laid down in the Road Map.

12. Leaders noted the reports by the IAEA Director General on Iran's nuclear programme and the UNSC Resolution 1696 (2006). They called on Iran to implement UNSC Resolution 1696 (2006) and the resolutions of the IAEA Board of Governors. Leaders welcomed the proposals put forward by France, Germany, the United Kingdom, endorsed by the United States, the Russian Federation and China, with the support of the European Union's High Representative, for a long-term and comprehensive arrangement with Iran based on mutual respect and mutual confidence.

13. Leaders reaffirmed their strong commitment to work towards lasting peace and stability on the Korean Peninsula, including the peaceful resolution of the North Korean nuclear issue. Leaders emphasised their wish to see the Six Party talks process resume as soon as possible and make progress on implementing the Joint Statement of 19 September 2005. They also expressed their grave concern over DPRK's recent multiple launch of missiles. They strongly called on all the parties to take a flexible and pragmatic approach in creating conditions for an early resumption of Six-Party Talks.

14. Leaders expressed their serious concern about the deteriorating security and humanitarian situation in Darfur. Leaders emphasized that transition from an AU to a UN led operation would be conducive to the peace in Darfur.

15. Leaders reiterated their commitment to the Millennium Development Goals (MDGs) and sustainable global development. Meeting the MDGs will require urgent action on all sides, among other more ambitious national development strategies and efforts backed by increased and more effective international support particularly in Africa.

Leaders also stressed the importance of their relations with Africa, and stated their commitment to work together in favour of Africa's peace, stability and sustainable development. The EU reaffirmed its attachment to the principles of good governance and human rights, as embodied in its Africa Strategy. The Chinese side emphasized the upholding of the five principles of peaceful coexistence, in particular the principle of non-interference into others' internal affairs.

The Leaders agreed to pursue a structured dialogue on Africa and explore avenues for practical cooperation on the ground in partnership with the African side, including with the support of NEPAD initiatives and with the aim of attaining the Millennium Development Goals. The leaders welcomed China's structured cooperation with Africa through the Forum on China-Africa Co-operation (FOCAC). Both the EU and China are signatories of the Paris Declaration on aid effectiveness. The two parties will continue to promote the effectiveness principles contained in the Paris Declaration.

16. They also looked forward to a successful 6th ASEM Summit on 10 and 11 September 2006. They viewed ASEM as a valuable framework for Asia-Europe dialogue and cooperation and believed that this Summit, which would also mark the 10th anniversary of ASEM, would take the process forward. They agreed to continue their close cooperation in promoting ASEM and welcomed China's role as the host of the 7th ASEM Summit in 2008.

17. The two sides reaffirmed their commitment to the fight against terrorism and reiterated that anti-terrorism action must accord with the purpose and principles of the United Nations Charter and the norms of relevant International Law and fully respect human rights. The two sides underlined the leading role of the United Nations with respect to counter-terrorism, and the importance of the universal implementation of all UN Security Council resolutions, UN conventions and protocols related to counter-terrorism. Both sides remain committed to achieving consensus on the UN Comprehensive Convention on International terrorism and call upon the UN General Assembly to adopt the counter-terrorism strategy without delay, as mandated by the World Summit.

18. The two sides expressed their concern over the spreading of avian influenza in the world and their high appreciation for the International Pledging Conference on Avian and Human Pandemic Influenza held by China, the European Commission, and the World Bank in Beijing at the beginning of this year. They promised to carry out relevant follow-up actions and agreed to further the cooperation in the prevention and control of such infectious diseases as avian influenza and welcomed the recent WHO resolution on the international

health regulations. In addition to the avian flu and to other newly emerging infectious diseases like SARS, the leaders underlined the importance of increased cooperation to combat HIV/AIDS. They especially stressed the need for transparency and non-discrimination on these issues.

19. Sustainable development is one of the major areas in EU-China cooperation. The leaders agreed to step up the exchange of experiences with a view to building a resource-efficient and environment-friendly society. In this vein, the EU will enhance its cooperation with China, backing its efforts in her rapid economic development, to introduce a circular economy and to safeguard natural resources, including biological diversity. Leaders agreed that many challenges remained, including in the areas of sustainable production and consumption, and energy efficiency. Leaders agreed to intensify cooperation on these areas and on specific issues such as illegal logging, as an important contribution to the preservation of natural resources.

20. Leaders welcomed the progress on the implementation of the EU-China partnership on climate change. The partnership has provided a good foundation for strengthening dialogue and cooperation between the EU and China in the areas covered by the partnership. They agreed to further strengthen the dialogue and cooperation in this regard including the United Nations Framework Convention on Climate Change (UNFCCC) processes launched to promote further development of international climate change policies. They also agreed to work positively towards a rolling work plan to further implement the partnership, covering the period 2007-2010. They welcomed closer cooperation on the implementation of the Kyoto Protocol's Clean Development Mechanism and the start of cooperation on the research of near-zero emission power generation technology through carbon dioxide capture and storage. They underlined the importance of reducing significantly the cost of key technologies and of their transfer, deployment and dissemination, as well as of taking steps to encourage and promote sustainable patterns of consumption and production to lessen the causes and adverse impacts of climate change. To this end, they also stressed the importance of enhancing cooperation in capacity building. They believed that an integrated approach to climate change and energy is crucial, and particularly underlined the need to exploit the synergies between the promotion of energy security, sustainable energy supply, innovation and reduction of greenhouse gas emissions to ensure consistency between meeting the ultimate objectives of the UNFCCC and energy policy goals.

21. Global energy security is crucial to ensuring economic growth and livelihood of people, maintaining world peace and stability and promoting development worldwide. The EU and China share a common concern for ensuring reliable, economical and sustainable energy supply. In this respect the leaders affirmed that they will take appropriate measures to further strengthen dialogue and cooperation on energy in an effort to create a stable, secure, efficient and clean energy environment to support sustainable economic and social development.

The Leaders emphasized the strategic significance of the EU-China High Level Working Group on Energy and the regular industrial conferences on EU-China energy cooperation. The two sides underlined the importance of continuing to strengthen practical cooperation, particularly in the framework of the action plan on clean coal and the action plan on energy efficiency and renewable energy.

22. Both sides were determined to work closely together to resume the WTO Doha Development Agenda negotiations as soon as possible with a view to achieve agreement on an ambitious and balanced outcome. Both sides emphasized the importance of reaching such

an agreement, recalling strongly the need for all WTO Members to make their due contribution.

23. Leaders underlined the importance of a complete implementation of WTO commitments. They noted that most transition periods for China will have expired in December 2006, recognized with satisfaction the progress already made, and acknowledged the importance of remaining work ahead. Both sides underlined the importance of dialogue and cooperation to solve bilateral trade issues with due regard to their international rights and obligations.

They recalled that a transparent, open, and predictable regulatory environment is important in the area of services, as open and efficient services markets serve as a launch-pad for broader economic activity.

24. They reiterated their commitment to their dialogue to maximize mutual benefits of such relation by improving market access and increasing investments opportunities for both sides.

25. Both sides expressed their satisfaction over the progress of the Market Economy Status (MES) dialogue and the working group and they noted the joint report on MES to the summit. Both sides look forward to the update of the June 2004 MES report to be issued by the Commission before the end of 2006 with a view to deepen the communication of both sides on the outstanding issues which will be helpful in resolving the MES issue.

26. Leaders reiterated the importance of protecting intellectual property rights (IPR). In particular, both sides agreed on the need for appropriate deterrence against piracy and to the effective enforcement of IPR legislation. Both sides expressed their satisfaction over the communication and cooperation of the past year under the EU-China IPR Dialogue and the IPR working group and stood ready to further the exchanges and cooperation in this field. Both sides also reiterated that they would strengthen the cooperation and exchanges in the field of geographical indications.

The two sides recognised the importance of technology for their economic development and expressed the willingness to strengthen exchanges and co-operation on IPR protection in this area and support the contractual freedom between enterprises in the field of technology transfers under the condition of fairness, reason and non-discrimination.

27. Leaders underlined the importance of a transparent, open, and predictable regulatory environment. Both sides stressed the value of involving actively stakeholders in the drafting of technical regulations and in related work. They welcomed the signature of the Memorandum of Understanding (MoU) on Administrative Cooperation Arrangements between the General Administration of Quality Supervision, Inspection and Quarantine of the People's Republic of China (ADSIQ) and the European Commission's Directorate General for Health and Consumer Protection (DG SANCO) in January 2006 and the subsequent agreement to establish the "EU-China Food and Consumer Goods Safety Joint Committee" with a view to facilitating the implementation of the MoU. Leaders expected that the Memorandum of Understanding together with the consultation mechanism and other established forms of cooperation between the two sides in the fields of food safety/Sanitary and Phytosanitary (SPS) issues and TBT/industrial product safety would advance sustainable bilateral trade flows. For this purpose, leaders also agreed to actively work to reduce technical barriers and obstacles to trade in TBT and SPS areas by, for example, the use of international standards.

28. Leaders welcomed the EU-China Business Summit to be held in Helsinki on 12 September 2006. They were of the view that the Business Summit would provide a key opportunity to enhance economic relations and the business environment between the EU and China. Both sides underlined the importance of involving more actively stakeholders in EU-China trade and investment related dialogues. The leaders welcomed the discussions taking place between Chinese and EU industry during the business summit and their recognition of the importance of EU-China cooperation in promoting innovations, and sustainable development, including the development of environmental technologies and services.

29. The two sides expressed the common wish to further the EU-China science and technology partnership and recognized that the China National Long and Medium Term Plan for Science and Technology Development and the 7th EU Framework Program provided a new opportunity to carry out cooperation of strategic importance. In this respect, they appreciate the involvement of Chinese organizations in the EU funded five year CO-REACH project, launched in Beijing in May 2005, to help identify priorities and appropriate channels for future S&T collaborations between China and Europe. The two sides announced that the "China-EU Science and Technology Year" activities will be launched in October 2006 in Brussels, to further promote S&T cooperation for sustainable mutual benefit. Both sides will create necessary conditions to make the event a success.

The two sides continued to emphasize and highlight the importance of the cooperation agreement on Galileo between the European Community and its Member States and the People's Republic of China.

The two sides looked forward to the early implementation, with other parties, of ITER and the further expansion and strengthening of their cooperation in the relevant fields.

30. Leaders encouraged relevant authorities of the EU and China to enhance dialogue and cooperation. The two sides will make good use of the current dialogues to continue exchanges and cooperation in various fields including environmental protection, labour and social affairs, development of agriculture and rural areas as well as the customs.

The two sides fully recognized the Memorandum of Understanding on China-EU Dialogue on Energy and Transport Strategies signed in September 2005 and the first plenary meeting of China-EU Strategic Dialogue on Energy and Transport Strategies held in March 2006. They stressed the importance of continuing to foster EU-China cooperation in this field.

Leaders expressed their satisfaction over the cooperation between the EU and China in the field of transport. They emphasized the need to continue the policy dialogue in the framework of the EU-China maritime agreement and they supported the efforts of shipping companies of both sides to run business in each other's territory. They were of the view that the two sides needed to strengthen position coordination and cooperation in international organizations including the International Maritime Organization and the WTO. The two sides expected the transport services of the EU-China to deepen exchanges and cooperation in the above-mentioned fields in the framework of Memorandum of Understanding on Cooperation in the fields of Road Transport and Inland Waterways.

Leaders welcomed the second round of the EU-China Financial Dialogue that was held in Beijing on 25 May 2006. They reiterated the importance of strengthening cooperation and coordination in the macroeconomic, financial, and regulatory areas and agreed that the third round would be held in Brussels in 2007.

Leaders welcomed the newly established sectoral dialogue on regional policy cooperation and expressed their satisfaction over the EU-China Regional Economic Development Seminar held in Beijing. They stressed that practical cooperation should be carried out within the framework of the Memorandum of Understanding on Regional Policy Cooperation between the National Development and Reform Commission (NDRC) and the European Commission and looked forward to the next EU-China meeting within this framework which would take place in Brussels in 2007.

The two sides expressed satisfaction over the progress achieved in the EU-China Information Society Dialogue and they hoped to step up joint efforts, especially in the strategic cooperation on high-speed e-infrastructure and its major application, to promote the development of the information society in the EU and China.

The leaders welcomed the start of the negotiations for a bilateral agreement on drug precursors chemical control.

31. Leaders took note of the progress achieved in the area of civil aviation cooperation since the 8th Summit and reiterated the significant prospects of strengthening cooperation in the aviation sector. In this respect, leaders stressed the necessity of restoring legal certainty to the existing bilateral air services agreements between the People's Republic of China and EU Member States. To this effect, the leaders called for discussions to continue as a matter of priority as agreed between the parties. Leaders also stressed the importance and mutual interest in enhancing technical co-operation in such fields as aviation safety, security, air traffic management, and air transport market supervision.

32. Leaders underlined that facilitating people-to-people exchanges and combating illegal migration were a priority for both sides. They emphasized the good mutual understanding reached at the EC-China High-Level Consultations in July. Leaders also discussed issues of readmission and visa facilitation. They reiterated their willingness to open negotiations on issues of their respective concern and agreed to start concrete cooperation on related issues as soon as possible. Leaders also welcomed significant progress in the implementation of the tourism agreement (ADS) and encouraged the further intensification of cooperation at appropriate level.

33. The two sides recognized that the strengthening of educational cooperation served as the social and cultural foundation for the sustainable development of the EU-China comprehensive strategic partnership. The two sides will conduct deeper and wider cooperation, jointly discuss the mechanism and priorities for future cooperation, and make an effort to institutionalize such cooperation. The Chinese side expressed interest in concluding in the future an EU-China Education Cooperation and Exchanges Agreement. Leaders endorsed cooperation in establishing an EU-China Law School and welcomed the contribution from the EU side. The relevant departments of the two sides will continue to conduct consultations in this regard with a view to reaching agreement at an early date. The Chinese side will launch a five-year Chinese Government Scholarship Program (EU Window) from year 2007 on, to provide 100 scholarships per year to young students from the EU in a bid to provide more opportunities for European students to study Chinese.

34. The leaders also recognised the significance of cultural diversity for sustainable development, and welcomed the UNESCO Convention on the Protection and Promotion of the Diversity of Cultural Expressions. The leaders supported increasing cultural interaction and visits between the EU Member States and China and especially encouraged visits by performing groups and artists as a way to strengthen links between the Chinese and European cultural circles.

35. Leaders recognised the importance of a healthy and developing civil society for the sustainability of the reform process both in the EU and China. Leaders were of the view that the exchanges and cooperation between the China Economic and Social Council (CESC) and the European Economic and Social Committee (EESC) constituted a part of the relationship. To reinforce existing ties, they endorsed and encouraged the establishment of a regular roundtable to contribute to the enrichment and development of the EU-China comprehensive strategic partnership.

36. Leaders of the two sides supported the enhancement of exchanges between the National People's Congress of China and the European Parliament and between the parties, media circles, and think-tanks of the two sides. They also supported the expansion and deepening of exchanges between young people including, inter alia, within the framework of the ASEM-process, and encouraged cooperation between youth organizations in the EU and China.

The ninth summit was held before the most recent EU policy papers on China in autumn 2006 (see Chapter 3). These policy papers reflected the significance of China in economic and political terms on the international stage, as well as with regard to the EU. They also were designed to inform and signal the EU position in the negotiations then soon to begin between the EU and China to replace the 1985 Trade and Economic Cooperation Agreement.

On 28 November 2007 in Beijing the EU and China held their tenth summit (see Document 4.12). The successful 17th National Congress of the Communist Party of China in October 2007, the foreseen adoption of the Treaty of Lisbon in the EU in December 2007 and increased tension in EU–China relations over trade provided the context for outlining the future development of EU–China relations. Chinese Premier Wen Jiabao, Prime Minister Jose Socrates of Portugual, the current holder of the EU Presidency, and European Commission President Jose Manuel Barroso participated in the meeting. Prime Minister Socrates and President Barroso also met the same day with Chinese President Hu Jintao. President Hu outlined three priorities:

1. to strengthen strategic mutual trust, be aware of the general situation and grasp the future;
2. expand pragmatic cooperation and realise mutual benefit, win–win and common development; and
3. in the spirit of mutual respect and negotiation on an equal footing, properly handle new circumstances and problems emerging from the development of bilateral ties so as to expand common ground, narrow discord and create a much better internal and external environment for further pushing forward the China–EU all-round strategic partnership.[5]

At the summit meeting, in addition to reviewing the EU–China strategic partnership, the parties discussed the Renminbi exchange rate, the trade imbalance, energy, climate change, higher education and the current negotiations to replace the 1985 Agreement. Other issues on the agenda were the arms embargo, the issue of

[5] See Yao Siyan (ed), 'President Hu highlights Priorities for China–EU Relations', *China View, Beijing*, 28 November 2007 (Xinhua), available at http://news.xinhuanet.com/english/2007-11/28/content_7162545 (accessed 30 November 2007).

market economy status for China in EC antidumping cases, Taiwan and the EU's trade deficit with China. Chinese Premier Wen Jiabao made several important proposals:

1. to advance negotiations on the trade and economic chapter of the China–EU Partnership and Cooperation Agreement (PCA), now being negotiated;
2. to strengthen cooperation in multilateral organisations such as the WTO;
3. to promote high-tech and services trade;
4. to expand bilateral cooperation on environmental protection and energy conservation; and
5. to increase cooperation in scientific research and education.[6]

This included a proposal to establish a vice-premier level of dialogue to resolve trade disputes and a financial cooperation mechanism to deal with specific financial issues.[7]

## Document 4.12: Joint Statement of the 10th EU–China Summit

### Joint Statement of the 10th China-EU Summit Beijing, 28 November 2007

The Tenth China-EU Summit was held in Beijing on 28 November 2007. Premier Wen Jiabao of the State Council of China attended the meeting on behalf of the People's Republic of China. The EU was represented by the President of the European Council, Prime Minister Jose Socrates of the Portuguese Republic and the President of the European Commission, Mr. Jose Manuel Barroso.

Leaders of the two sides had an overall review of the development of the bilateral relations since the establishment of the mechanism of China-EU Summit in 1998. They agreed that over the decade, China-EU relations have made a historical progress. Leaders expressed their satisfaction with the comprehensive cooperation between the two sides in broad fields and at all levels, and with the growing maturity of the China-EU comprehensive strategic partnership.

Leaders welcomed the development of China-EU political relations. They hold that the full and effective political dialogue mechanism established between the two sides had played a positive role in enhancing mutual understanding and trust, and expanding common ground and cooperation, and serves as an important foundation for stronger China-EU political mutual trust.

Leaders of China and the EU recalled the deepening and expanding economic cooperation and trade between the two sides, and emphasized that China and the EU are becoming each other's most important economic and trade partners thanks to efforts by both sides over the past 10 years, and that bilateral economic cooperation and trade had become one of the most important driving forces behind further strengthening of the China-EU

6 See Yao Siyan (ed), 'Chinese Premier Raises Proposal for Promoting China–EU Economic Co-op', *China View, Beijing*, 28 November 2007 (Xinhua), available at http://news.xinhuanet.com/english/2007–11/28/content-7163313.htm (accessed 29 November 2007).

7 See Mu Xuequan (ed), 'China, EU Outline Future Strategic Partnership', *China View, Beijing*, 29 November 2007 (Xinhua), available at http://news.xinhuanet.com/english/2007–11/29/content-7164194.htm (accessed 30 November 2007).

comprehensive strategic partnership. Leaders discussed the necessary actions to be taken to achieve a more balanced trade and economic partnership.

Leaders made a comprehensive summing up of the achievements made in China-EU all round cooperation in all fields, and pointed out that the increasingly closer sectoral dialogues had become an effective platform for policy coordination between the two sides, and had contributed significantly to stronger mutually beneficial cooperation.

Leaders stated that China-EU consultation and coordination on major international and regional issues – in particular Africa, Myanmar, the Korean peninsula, Iran, the Middle East and Kosovo, as well as ASEM – as an important part of the overall China-EU comprehensive strategic partnership, had played an important role in promoting world peace, stability and sustainable development.

The two sides briefed each other on their respective latest developments. China welcomed the new and significant progress made in EU integration, as a result of the EU agreement on a new Reform Treaty, which further strengthens Europe as a global player. The EU welcomed the Seventeenth National Congress of the Chinese Communist Party, and the application of its Scientific Outlook on Development, pursue a win-win strategy of opening up, and follow unswervingly the path of peaceful development. Leaders stated that the current world is now undergoing extensive and profound changes, and that as comprehensive strategic partners, both at a crucial stage of development, China and the EU would, upholding the spirit of democracy, harmony and collaboration for win-win results, continue to work together to promote democracy in international relations, advance a more balanced development of economic globalization to ensure mutual benefit and win-win progress. They would work to promote human civilization, be committed to the peaceful settlement of international disputes, support each other and make concerted efforts to jointly safeguard planet Earth for the benefit of all mankind. Reaffirming their commitment in favour of preserved environment and sustainable development, they would work to promote the building of a harmonious world of durable peace, common prosperity. This not only serves the fundamental interests of the two sides, but also world peace, stability, and development and human rights.

To this end, leaders of the two sides agreed:

1. The two sides will further enhance political dialogue and consultation at all levels, and continue to maintain consultation and coordination on major international and regional issues to enhance political mutual trust and expand strategic common ground.

2. Leaders expressed their mutual satisfaction on the successful launch and start of negotiations on a Partnership and Co-operation Agreement which will encompass the full scope of their bilateral relationship, including enhanced co-operation on political matters. These negotiations will also update the 1985 EEC-China Trade and Economic Co-operation Agreement, which will be administered in a relatively independent manner, taking into consideration the global objectives of the EU-China strategic partnership.

3. The EU reaffirmed its commitment to one China policy and expressed its hope for a peaceful resolution of the Taiwan question through constructive dialogue. The EU reiterated its concern over the intended referendum on UN membership in the name of Taiwan as this could lead to a unilateral change of the status quo across Taiwan straits to which the EU is opposed. In this context, the EU expressed its concern over the Taipei authorities' intentions about the future status of the island.

4. Leaders also discussed the EU arms embargo. The Chinese side reiterated its view that lifting the arms embargo would be conducive to the sound development of the EU-China relations and urged the EU to lift the arms embargo at an early date. The EU side recognised the importance of this issue and confirmed its willingness to carry forward work towards lifting the embargo on the basis of the Joint Statement of the 2004 EU-China Summit and subsequent European Council Conclusions.

5. Leaders reiterated their willingness to carry out cooperation in the fields of non-proliferation and disarmament. On the basis of the Joint Declaration of the European Union and the People's Republic of China on Non-proliferation and Arms Control, the two sides will continue to enhance dialogue and deepen practical cooperation, building on the successful record in several areas, such as export control.

6. The two sides emphasised their commitment to the promotion and protection of human rights and continued to place a high value on the EU-China human rights dialogue, including the accompanying legal seminar. They underlined the importance of concrete steps in the field of human rights and reaffirmed their commitment to further strengthen dialogue and cooperation in this field on the basis of equality and mutual respect, while making efforts to achieve more meaningful and positive results on the ground. The EU welcomed China's commitment to ratifying the International Covenant on Civil and Political Rights (ICCPR) as soon as possible. In respect of the global fight against genocide, war crimes, and crimes against humanity, they also noted the importance of the International Criminal Court.

Both sides confirmed their commitment to cooperate with UN human rights mechanism and their respect for international human rights standards provided for in relevant international human rights instruments including the rights of minorities. The two sides were committed to supporting the UN Human Rights Council in performing its function to address human rights issues in a credible, objective and non-selective manner. Both sides undertook to strengthen their communication and coordination in this regard in line with UN General Assembly Resolution 60/251.

7. Emphasising the paramount need for effective multilateralism, leaders stressed their strong support for a fair, just and rules-based multilateral international system with the UN playing a central role. They reiterated their commitment to promote peace and security, development and human rights, as recognized in the 2005 UN World Summit outcome document. The two sides expressed their support for reform of the United Nations system which would improve the UN's strength, efficiency and effectiveness to cope with new and existing threats and challenges. The two sides maintained that multilateralism served as an important means to resolve international disputes. They will remain committed to promoting the establishment of a fair and effective collective security mechanism in the spirit of mutual trust, mutual benefit, equality and coordination, and the settling of differences and disputes in a peaceful manner through diplomatic channels. The two sides support the United Nations, and recognize its primacy in international affairs through the Security Council which has the primary responsibility for the maintenance of international peace and security.

8. The two sides reaffirmed their condemnation of terrorism in all its forms and manifestations without qualification, committed by whomever, whenever and for whatever purposes. They also reaffirmed their recognition of the United Nations as the only truly global forum for the fight against terrorism. By adopting the United Nations Global Counter-Terrorism Strategy by consensus on 8 September 2006, the General Assembly and the Member States of the UN demonstrated their unity and resolve in combating terrorism. The EU and China

both expressed support for the Counter Terrorism Implementation Task Force in coordinating the implementation of the Global Strategy. They looked forward to the review which would take place in 2008 to strengthen the consensus achieved to date. Leaders also emphasized their continued commitment to reaching an agreement on the Comprehensive Convention on International Terrorism (CCIT) as soon as possible.

The two sides stressed the importance of multilateralism in the fight against terrorism and underlined the importance of universal adherence to, and full implementation of, all UN Conventions and Protocols related to acts of terrorism.

Both sides expressed the need to address the conditions conducive to the spread of terrorism and supported the view that terrorism should not be linked to any religion or culture, and there should be consistency in the fight against terrorism.

Leaders recognized that any measures undertaken to prevent and combat terrorism must comply with obligations under international law, in particular international human rights law, refugee law and humanitarian law. Effective counter-terrorism measures and the protection of human rights are not conflicting, but complementary and mutually reinforcing goals.

9. Leaders gave a positive assessment of the progress made by Africa in the fields of peace and development and of the efforts of African countries and the African Union in promoting African integration. They reiterated their commitment to the Millennium Development Goals (MDGs) and global sustainable development in a balanced and coordinated way.

Leaders recalled the successful cooperation since the last Summit, at all levels, in the efforts of the international community to facilitate a solution to the Darfur crisis and underlined the need to make further progress as regards the Darfur peace negotiations as well as the implementation of the Comprehensive Peace Agreement. The leaders expressed the objective to see the Africa Union/UN hybrid peace keeping operation UNAMID soon to be deployed; they noted the progress in preparation of the operation MINURCAT and EUFOR Chad/RCA recalling the common aim of contributing to peace and stability in Darfur and the neighbouring regions.

10. Leaders welcomed more practical cooperation by the two sides through their respective existing cooperation mechanisms with Africa, such as the Forum on China-Africa Cooperation and the EU-Africa Summit, so as to contribute to Africa's peace, stability and sustainable development on the basis of equality and mutual benefit. The two sides agreed to continue their dialogue on African issues, and actively explore effective ways and channels of cooperation among China, the EU and Africa in appropriate areas. The EU invited China to attend the EU-Africa Summit as an observer. China invited the EU Commissioner for Development to visit China.

11. The EU and China confirmed their full support for the good offices efforts of Prof. Ibrahim Gambari, Special Advisor of the UN Secretary General, with a view to advancing democracy in Myanmar. Both sides agreed on the need to see tangible progress in the domestic process, with dialogue among the parties concerned.

12. Leaders reaffirmed their strong commitment to work towards lasting peace and stability on the Korean Peninsula, including the effective denuclearisation of the Korean Peninsula. Leaders welcomed the important progress that has been made in the Six Party talks process with a view to implementing the Joint Statement of 19 September 2005 through the steps agreed in February and October 2007. They welcomed the shutdown of the Yongbyon

facility and look forward to its full disablement and dismantlement as well as the complete and correct declaration by DPRK of all its nuclear programmes. Leaders also welcomed the steps agreed at the Inter-Korean Summit in October and the follow-up steps envisaged regarding an eventual peace treaty, economic integration, and Korean unification.

13. Leaders noted the latest report by the IAEA Director General on Iran's nuclear programme and the implementation of UNSC Resolutions 1696 (2006), 1737 (2006) and 1747 (2007). They reiterated their commitment to seek a comprehensive, long-term and proper solution by diplomatic means and through negotiation and dialogue. They reaffirmed the Statement by the Foreign Ministers of China, France, Germany, Russia, the United Kingdom and the United States with the support of the High Representative of the European Union, 28 September 2007 and they urged Iran to fully comply with Resolutions 1737 and 1747.

14. Leaders reaffirmed their support for a negotiated settlement of the Israeli-Palestinian conflict based on existing agreements which include the relevant UN Resolutions and the principles laid down in the Road Map. In that context, leaders welcomed the ongoing bilateral discussions between Prime Minister Olmert and President Abbas. They expressed their hope that this would allow the Parties to move forward to the creation of an independent, democratic and viable Palestinian state living side by side in peace and security with Israel and its other neighbours. Leaders expressed their support for the recent international meeting in Annapolis, which they hope will provide the first step towards a comprehensive solution to the Arab-Israeli conflict. The EU and China confirmed that the international community stands ready to support the political process, including support for the crucial implementation period.

15. Leaders discussed the issue of Kosovo, and reiterated support for the mediating efforts of the international community including the EU.

16. On the emerging regional architecture in Asia, the EU welcomes China's contribution to strengthen open and transparent regional cooperation in Asia, and appreciates China's constructive and active role in this respect. China welcomes the EU's constructive contributions to the regional political architecture in Asia-Pacific. Both the EU and China express their support for further regional cooperation as demonstrated by the Association of South East Asian Nations (ASEAN) and the ASEAN Regional Forum, as well as the enhancement of EU-ASEAN relations. China welcomes the EU's interest in contributing to the East Asia regional cooperation process and its intention to join the Treaty of Amity and Cooperation (TAC).

17. The two sides recognized ASEM as an important framework for multilateral dialogue and political, economic, social and cultural cooperation between Asia and Europe. They recognised the intensifying economic cooperation as a key component of Asia-Europe relations. Leaders reaffirmed their commitment to strengthen the process through constructive dialogues and action-oriented programmes, to ensure the implementation of the 2006 Helsinki Declaration on the Future of ASEM and the success of the 7th ASEM Summit to be held in China in 2008.

18. Leaders agreed to enhance cooperation to ensure smooth progress of the 2008 Beijing Olympics.

19. Leaders agreed to strengthen cooperation in and dialogue on sustainable economic and social development, especially in areas of trade and business exchanges, climate change, environment and energy, human resources development and public administration. Both parties will increase efforts to support corporate social responsibility and sustainable

development, including through sustainable production and consumption patterns and a more efficient use of natural resources.

20. Leaders agreed to enhance cooperation on environment protection, focusing on cooperation in areas such as sustainable production and consumption, pollution control and management, natural resource management, river basin management, biodiversity conservation, international environment governance, emergency response to environmental accidents, chemicals management, and disposal and management of dangerous wastes. They also agreed to promote clean technology transfer conducive to their cooperation, and encouraged the adoption of stricter environmental standards in mutual investment. The two sides are determined to continue their joint effort to tackle illegal logging as an important contribution to the preservation of natural resources and biodiversity, mitigation of climate change, and the economic development in the timber-producing countries.

21. Leaders stressed the great importance they attached to the issue of climate change, and their willingness to strengthen cooperation to jointly meet the serious challenge of climate change, the urgency of which was unequivocally confirmed by the latest scientific findings of the Intergovernmental Panel on Climate Change (IPCC). China and the EU are committed to the stabilization of greenhouse gas concentrations in the atmosphere at a level which would prevent dangerous anthropogenic climate interference with the climate system, in accordance with their common but differentiated responsibilities and respective capabilities.

The leaders reviewed the bilateral cooperation under the China-EU Partnership on Climate Change and called for progress to be made, including on research of near-zero emissions coal power generation technology through carbon capture and storage, as well as development of concrete cooperation projects to strengthen China's participation in the Kyoto Protocol's Clean Development Mechanism.

They agree to step up their efforts to further enhance the bilateral cooperation, including their cooperation on technology development and transfer. China and the EU agreed to actively implement the rolling work plan of China-EU Partnership on Climate Change covering the period 2008-2009, including cooperation on province-level climate change programmes in China, climate change adaptation strategies and public awareness initiatives.

The two sides reaffirmed their commitment to the United Nations Framework Convention on Climate Change and the Kyoto Protocol. They reiterated, in accordance with their common but differentiated responsibilities and respective capabilities, the need for developed countries to continue to take the lead in reducing GHG emissions beyond 2012 and to assist developing countries in enhancing their contributions to addressing climate change. They are committed to moving forward in the UN forum and called on all parties to actively and constructively participate in UNFCCC Conference in Bali in December 2007. They welcomed the progress achieved in the "Dialogue on long-term cooperative action to address climate change by enhancing the implementation of the Convention" and agreed to work towards launching a process on a comprehensive post-2012 arrangement at this year's UNFCCC Conference of the Parties in Bali so as to enhance the implementation of the Convention and aim to complete work under this process as soon as possible but no later than 2010. They also emphasized the importance of speedy and substantive progress in the negotiations of the Ad hoc Working Group on Further Commitments for developed countries beyond 2012 under the Kyoto Protocol and aim to complete work under this process before the end of 2009. They underlined their belief that an integrated approach to climate change and energy is crucial, and particularly stressed the need to exploit the synergies between the promotion of energy security, improved air quality and addressing greenhouse gas emissions to ensure consistency between meeting the ultimate objectives of the UNFCCC and their respective energy policy goals. They agreed on the importance of the engagement, investment of and provision of incentives to private sector in tackling climate change and on the significant potential economic opportunities of China-EU cooperation in this area.

22. Leaders recognized the crucial role of technology in addressing the issue of climate change in particular for the mitigation of greenhouse gas emissions and for adaptation. Both sides consider technology as a major instrument to address climate change. They emphasised the importance of a post-2012 agreement to help within the context of the UNFCCC and the Kyoto Protocol to make clean technologies accessible and affordable to developing countries by technology transfer, deployment and dissemination as well as to strengthen the global carbon market and to intensify cooperation on the adaptation to the increasing adverse impacts of climate change. Leaders witnessed the signing of a €500 million framework loan to the People's Republic of China from the European Investment Bank to support projects that contribute to combating climate change.

23. The two sides maintained that the energy issue is a global issue which is closely related to the economical and social development of all nations. Both China and the EU recognized the importance of enhancing bilateral communication and cooperation on this issue, and agreed to take effective measures and continue to promote their mutually beneficial and practical cooperation in the energy field. The two sides will actively prepare for the Seventh EU-China Conference on Energy Cooperation in 2008 and work together to ensure positive progress of the second China-EU Dialogue on Energy and Transport Strategies. The leaders expressed their support for closer co-operation on increasing efficiencies along the entire coal value chain and for making further progress on the development including research of near zero emissions coal technology. This would assist both sides in securing the economic and environmental benefits of recent developments in coal technologies and practice.

Leaders endorsed cooperation in establishing a China-EU Clean Energy Centre. The two sides will continue to conduct consultations in this regard with a view to reaching agreement and opening the Centre in 2008. Projects and initiatives pertaining to increased energy efficiency could be part of such future cooperation.

24. Both sides agreed to establish by the end of March 2008 a High Level Economic and Trade Dialogue between the European Commission and the State Council of China at the level of Vice-Premier which will discuss strategies in EU-China trade, investment and economic cooperation and coordinate bilateral projects, studies and develop plans in priority sectors. It will cover issues affecting the trade imbalance, including *inter alia* effective market access, intellectual property rights, environment, high technology and energy in order to find concrete means to increase trade in a balanced way. To this end, the Chinese Minister of Commerce and the EU Trade Commissioner will meet as necessary to prepare this mechanism and its agenda.

25. The High Level Economic and Trade Dialogue will review the concerns of China including progress on the issue of Market Economy Status (MES) made in other fora.

26. The two sides agreed to enhance their cooperation in macroeconomic policy, and promote exchange of best practice in economic and social management and public service among their government departments. The two sides will continue to deepen financial dialogue, and conduct exchange and cooperation in China-EU macroeconomic situation, fiscal and financial policies, reforms and regulation of financial sectors.

27. The Parties welcomed the discussions held in Beijing on 27-28 November between the Chinese representatives and their counterparts from Eurogroup on macroeconomic issues. During these discussions, the two sides believed that it was necessary to make concerted efforts to adopt comprehensive measures, intensify structural adjustment, and avoid drastic movement of exchange rates, so as to make due contribution to the orderly adjustment of global imbalances. They took note that a working group involving the People's Bank of China (PBOC) and European Central Bank (ECB) will deal with the exchange rates related issues.

28. Leaders share the view that a high level of product safety is key to consumer confidence and reciprocal trade. To this end, the competent authorities of both sides have established a comprehensive cooperative relationship in recent years and carried out good, close and fruitful cooperation and exchanges. Both sides are willing to continue and deepen their constructive dialogue, regularly exchange information and aim at measurable, continuous improvements.

29. The two sides will take full advantage of the China-EU dialogue mechanism on agriculture and rural areas, and continue to strengthen their cooperation in the fields of prevention and control of animal diseases, quality and safety of agricultural products, agricultural trade as well as management of safety of genetically modified organisms.

30. Leaders agreed to maintain close consultation and dialogue through the competition policy dialogue mechanism, and strengthen cooperation in the field of enforcement of anti-monopoly law and international competition policies. The European Union congratulated China on the adoption of the Anti-Monopoly Law in August 2007. The EU values the competition dialogue greatly and will continue its support to the relevant Chinese competition bodies and authorities in the implementation of the Anti-Monopoly Law.

31. Leaders welcomed the China-EU Business Summit held in Beijing on 27–28 November 2007. Both sides underlined the importance of involving more actively stakeholders in China-EU trade and investment-related dialogues, and expressed their commitment to continue to support the cooperation between the two business communities, with a view to creating more business opportunities and expanding the scope of development for enterprises.

32. The two sides agree that further facilitation is needed for EU SMEs to operate in China and Chinese SMEs to operate in the EU, to contribute to an enabling trade environment. The two sides, therefore, welcome the European initiative of conducting a feasibility study on a European Centre in China to assist European SMEs investing in or exporting to China by providing information and assistance and promoting exchanges with Chinese government agencies, business associations and economic operators.

33. Leaders emphasized the positive results of the China-EU Science and Technology Year (CESTY), gathering researchers, industry, including SMEs and academics, and expressed the willingness to continue to strengthen the existing scientific and technological cooperation, explore new bilateral cooperation mechanisms and jointly identify priority areas of cooperation. They reiterated the recognition of the importance of Science and Technology cooperation for sustainable mutual benefit.

The leaders welcomed the conclusions of the 6th Steering Committee meeting of the EU-China Science & Technology Agreement, which was held in Beijing on 14 November 2007. The two parties agreed to move towards a more strategic scientific cooperation through the launch of EU-China joint research projects. These projects will be co-funded by both parties, in full respect of the EU and China funding principles, laws and rules.

The leaders acknowledged the very important participation of Chinese researchers in the first calls of the 7th Research Framework Programme. They agreed to facilitate also the participation of European researchers in Chinese funded programmes. The leaders encouraged programmes to assist the mobility of researchers.

Both sides will take all necessary steps to renew in due course the China-EU Science and Technology Agreement that will expire by December 2009 and, as a first step in this direction, announced that they will carry out an assessment of their cooperation prior to the renewal as foreseen in the present Agreement.

34. The two sides expressed their satisfaction on the entry into force of the ITER agreement on 24 October 2007 and on the first official meeting of the ITER Council on 27-28 November 2007. The two sides have agreed to start the discussions towards the establishment of a bilateral agreement between EURATOM and China in the field of fusion energy research to complement the ITER Agreement.

The two sides expressed their satisfaction for having concluded the discussions on the R&D agreement for the peaceful uses of nuclear energy. They hope that the agreement will enter into force very soon, allowing cooperation in the area of nuclear fission. In this context they note that EURATOM and China are now active members of the Generation IV International Forum, a situation that should foster bilateral cooperation.

35. The two sides will continue to advance practical cooperation through the China-EU dialogue on the Information Society.

36. The two sides agreed to work within the framework of the Agreement between the Government of the People's Republic of China and the European Community on Cooperation and Mutual Administrative Assistance in Customs Matters, to further standardize and strengthen customs cooperation that reflects the principle of reciprocity. They will continue to enhance customs cooperation regarding intellectual property enforcement, and implement the Smart and Secure Trade Lanes Pilot Project which is aimed at ensuring security and facilitation of the China -EU trade supply chain.

37. Leaders expressed their satisfaction over the recent signing of the Memorandum of Understanding in the fields of road transport and inland waterways and expressed the hope for quick implementation. The two sides welcomed the ratification by EU Member States and China of the Maritime Agreement and the successful results of the 4th meeting on the implementation of the 2002 China-EU maritime transport agreement held in Rotterdam and supported the further deepening of their cooperation in all the relevant areas.

38. Leaders took stock of progress in the area of civil aviation and stressed the need for closer cooperation between China and the EU in this vital area in order to jointly promote solutions to the important common challenges facing the global aviation community.

Leaders reiterated the need to restore legal certainty to the existing bilateral air service agreements through joint efforts and intensified consultations, taking into account the concerns of both sides. Leaders also agreed to strengthen technical and technological cooperation in a broad range of fields in aviation and called for a swift conclusion of an agreement laying down a comprehensive framework for future China-EU technical cooperation in areas including aviation safety, security, environment, economic regulation and air traffic management, including the possible participation of China in Europe's SESAR programme for a new generation of air traffic management systems.

39. The EU and China underlined the importance of cultural relations between the EU and China, especially in the context of the process of implementation of the UNESCO

Convention on the Protection and Promotion of the Diversity of Cultural Expressions. Both sides welcomed the Joint Declaration on culture, signed by the European Commission and China in October 2007, which clearly expresses a strong convergence of views on the role of culture in our societies and in a globalizing world and which reaffirms a strong commitment of both sides to further enhance cooperation and establish a structured policy dialogue in the field of culture.

40. The two sides stressed that they would implement the WHO International Health Regulations (2005) in real earnest, safeguard public health and continue to follow with concern the spread of HIV/AIDS, human infected highly pathogenic avian influenza and other new epidemics. They will maintain and promote information and technology exchanges and cooperation in this field, and enhance cooperation and exchanges in areas of food sanitation and safety, and health personnel training. The two sides looked forward to the signing by China and the European Commission of a Memorandum of Understanding in the fields of animal health and the exchange of avian influenza viruses between reference laboratories in China and the EU for the purpose of improving scientific knowledge on this important disease.

41. Leaders expressed their satisfaction on the cooperation between the EU and China in the field of employment and social affairs, as an important element of the dialogue on sustainable development and decent work. They emphasized the outcomes of the 2nd High Level Round Table on Social Security which took place in Berlin in June 2007, and highlighted its contribution to the current reforms in China. They are encouraged by the ongoing cooperation in the field of labour law, and in particular by the exchange of experience in labour dispute settlement, with a bilateral event taking place in Beijing in November 2007. They strongly support the intention to establish a structured dialogue in the field of health and safety at work, and encourage the establishment of a Memorandum of Understanding to be signed early 2008.

The two sides agreed to strengthen cooperation in the field of social assistance, social welfare and social affairs.

42. Leaders recognised the importance of a healthy and developing civil society for the sustainability of the reform process both in the EU and China. Leaders were of the view that the continued exchanges and pragmatic cooperation between the China Economic and Social Council and the European Economic and Social Committee constitute a part of the relationship. Leaders welcomed the strengthening of the civil society dialogue between the two sides and encouraged the implementation of the Joint Statements of the two Round Tables.

43. The two sides will remain committed to further enhancing and expanding their exchanges and cooperation in legal and judicial areas with a view to enhancing mutual understanding and friendship.

44. The two sides agreed to strengthen cooperation in areas such as anti-terrorism, combating transnational organized crimes, human smuggling and trafficking in persons and drug-related crimes.

45. Leaders underlined that facilitating people-to-people exchanges and combating illegal migration remained a priority for both sides. Leaders also discussed issues of readmission and visa facilitation. They reiterated their willingness to open negotiations on issues of their respective concern and agreed to start concrete cooperation on related issues as soon as possible. Leaders also welcomed significant progress in the implementation of the tourism agreement (ADS) and encouraged the further intensification of cooperation.

46. Leaders agreed to speedily initiate the meeting mechanism of China-EU on youth affairs at ministerial level.

Leaders supported and encouraged the enhancement of exchanges and cooperation between scholars and think tanks of the two sides. The EU and China emphasised their commitment to strengthen China-EU academic cooperation and exchanges by further stimulating the participation of their academic institutions, students and scholars in the Erasmus Mundus programme External Cooperation Window and Chinese Government Scholarship Programme (EU Window). The EU welcomed the launch of the China- EU Language Exchange Project (EU Window).

Both sides welcomed the Joint Declaration on education and vocational training which was signed in October 2007 and which will set the basis for a structured policy dialogue that will allow for regular exchanges of best practice, reviews of policy developments and challenges, and promoting knowledge-building and sharing on horizontal and sectoral issues of common interest for the European Community and China.

Leaders welcomed the cooperation on establishing a Europe-China School of Law in China.

The leaders welcomed the successful launch of the China-Europe Business Management Training Project.

47. The Leaders welcomed the progress in the EU-China development co-operation programme. The two sides noted with satisfaction that the recently finalised Multiannual Indicative Programme for 2007-2010 makes €128 million available, from the EC budget, for support in areas covered by sectoral dialogues, the environment, energy and climate change and human resources development.

## POLICY DIALOGUES

In addition to summits and troika meetings, there are numerous other institutional settings for EU–China cooperation. Among the most significant are policy dialogues. We can define policy dialogues as institutionalised, periodic and more or less well-structured meetings between European and Chinese authorities, involving staff at approximately the same levels in their respective administrative or political hierarchies, and dealing with general subjects which cut across EU–China relations as a whole. They have diverse origins, such as general political decisions reached at summits, negotiations on issues related to but outside legally binding bilateral agreements or mutual concerns about subjects not covered by other arrangements. Regardless of their origins, dialogues are more frequent and more specialised than summits. They have developed their own dynamics and momentum, distinct from that of summits or troika meetings. The widespread use of dialogues illustrates how the EU and China have used innovative institutional forms to develop a multi-faced relationship and then a strategic partnership going far beyond trade.

Examples of policy dialogues include expert meetings on illegal migration and trafficking in human beings, human rights, Asian affairs, non-proliferation and conventional arms exports. For example, on 28 April 2004 the EU and China adopted a Joint Declaration on Non-proliferation and Arms Control (see Document 4.13). It followed China's White Paper on 'China's Non-proliferation Policy and Measures' and the EU's policy paper on 'Strategy against Proliferation of Weapons of Mass Destruction'.[8] From the European standpoint, the subject matter fell clearly within the Common Foreign and Security Policy, which, under the Maastricht Treaty and its successors, has so far been a weakly integrated, mainly intergovernmental domain in which the EC has far less power than the Member States. In the Joint Declaration, the EU and China recognised each other as major strategic partners in the fields of disarmament and non-proliferation. The Joint Declaration set out priority areas for specific cooperation, such as enhancing the role of the United Nations, nuclear non-proliferation, biological and chemical weapons, export control and conventional weapons.

## Document 4.13: EU–China Joint Declaration on Non-proliferation and Arms Control

### Joint declaration of the People's Republic of China and the EU on non-proliferation and arms control

1. The proliferation of weapons of mass destruction (WMD) and their means of delivery poses a serious threat to international peace and security, as it was underlined by the United Nations Security Council in its Resolution 1540. Therefore the People's Republic of China and the European Union welcome this Resolution which was unanimously adopted on 28 April 2004.

2. The possibility of the proliferation of WMD, and their means of delivery as well as related materials and technology, to terrorists and other non-state actors is real and adds a new dimension to this threat, as well as a renewed urgency of concerted and more focused actions and cooperation.

3. The fundamental purpose of non-proliferation is to maintain international and regional peace, security and stability, which is in the interests of China and the EU as well as the entire human kind. Therefore, efforts should be made to address proliferation issues through political and diplomatic measures and international cooperation within the framework of international law.

4. China and the EU agree that prevention of proliferation of nuclear, chemical and biological weapons should not hamper international cooperation in materials, equipment and technology for peaceful purposes while goals of peaceful utilization should not be used as a cover for proliferation.

5. The EU welcomes China's white paper on "China's Non-proliferation Policy and Measures" issued in December 2003. China welcomes the EU "Strategy Against Proliferation of Weapons of Mass Destruction" adopted in December 2003. China and the EU have identified many common elements in these two documents and are resolved to work together, within their strategic partnership, to strengthen the international non-proliferation system, by promoting the universalisation of, and the compliance with, all international

[8] Available at http://www.mfa.gov.cn/eng/wjb/zzjg/jks/jkxw/t54978.htm or http://news.xinhuanet.com/english/2003-12/03/content_6765331.htm; and http://register.consilium.europa.eu/pdf/en/03/st15/st15708.en03.pdf, respectively (accessed 23 November 2007).

non-proliferation and disarmament treaties and instruments, by supporting the role and ability of the international verification agencies (International Atomic Energy Agency, Organisation on the Prohibition of Chemical Weapons) to fulfill their responsibilities and by fostering the specific role and responsibilities of the United Nations Security Council, in accordance with the Charter of the United Nations.

6. The illicit trade of WMD-related materials, equipment and technology is a matter of serious concern for China and the EU. The international community must be united in its endeavor to strengthen international cooperation in that area. The active and positive engagement and cooperation of as many countries as possible are indispensable. We must reinforce our efforts to tackle illicit trafficking in materials, equipment and technology related to WMD and means of delivery and fight against all illicit procurement networks.

7. China and the EU are both underlining the importance of a regional approach in the implementation of our strategies for fighting the proliferation of WMD, and regard in this respect ASEAN Regional Forum (ARF) as one of the important fora for consultation on regional, political and security issues. China and the EU will explore possibilities to launch joint initiatives in the area of non-proliferation in the framework of the ARF.

8. Positive and active efforts must also be made to strengthen controls over exports of conventional weapons. The arms control regimes concerning certain conventional weapons like landmines, need to be strengthened. Efforts to prevent illicit trade of small arms and light weapons and flows of those weapons that would impair regional peace and stability, should be enhanced. Early ratification by states parties to the Convention on Certain Conventional Weapons (CCW), which have not yet done so, of its Protocol V, on Explosive Remnants of War (ERW), and its speedy entry into force would be welcomed.

9. China and the EU, as important forces in the field of international security, bear significant responsibility for the maintenance of international and regional peace, security and stability, and will continue to play a positive role in promoting the international non-proliferation process. Strengthening cooperation between China and the EU will be conducive to the multilateral non-proliferation process, as well as to expanding and deepening our comprehensive strategic partnership.

10. Guided by the shared concerns and aims described above, China and the EU will work together to achieve their common goals, collectively and individually through the identification of concrete measures, including the following:

(a) Recognising each other as a major strategic partner in the area of disarmament and nonproliferation, China and the EU will deepen their cooperation in these pursuits and promote close policy dialogues at various levels at opportunities presented by the major international conferences and other fora.

(b) Reaffirming their commitment to the international treaty system, China and the EU will promote the universalisation, entry into force, implementation and strengthening of the treaties, conventions and norms in the area of disarmament and non-proliferation, such as the Non-Proliferation Treaty (NPT), the Biological and Toxic Weapons Convention (BTWC), the Chemical Weapons Convention (CWC), the Comprehensive Test Ban Treaty (CTBT), the Convention of Certain Conventional Weapons (CCW) and the IAEA Comprehensive Safeguards Agreements and Additional Protocols. Both China and the EU stress the importance of universalisation of the Hague Code of Conduct against Ballistic Missile Proliferation (HCOC) and the Mine Ban Treaty (MBT).

(c) Stressing their determination to support international institutions and agencies charged with the verification and upholding of compliance with these treaties and agreements, China and the EU will work together to ensure strict compliance with the obligations under disarmament and non-proliferation treaties. China and the EU support further effective measures to strengthen and improve the functioning of the above institutions and agencies.

(d) Reaffirming their support of the United Nations to play an important role in non-proliferation, China and the EU will work actively together to ensure the full implementation of UN Security Council Resolution 1540.

(e) China and the EU appreciate their respective efforts in facilitating a political resolution of the Iran nuclear issue. China and the EU welcome the agreement reached between France, Germany and the UK, supported by the High Representative, and Iran on Iran's suspension of enrichment related and reprocessing activities. Both China and the EU hope that progress will be made in the negotiations of the EU with Iran on a mutually acceptable agreement on long-term arrangements, that should include objective guarantees that Iran's nuclear program is exclusively for peaceful purposes, and that the Iran nuclear issue will be resolved within the framework of IAEA at the earliest opportunity. China appreciates the efforts of EU members in encouraging Libya's denunciation of its WMD programs through diplomatic negotiations. The EU appreciates and supports China's positive and constructive role in facilitating a peaceful resolution of the nuclear issue on the Korean peninsula. China and the EU reaffirm in this context their support for a Korean peninsula free of nuclear weapons.

(f) Realising the contribution of political cooperation with partners in the fight against WMD proliferation, China and the EU affirm their intention to mainstream non-proliferation policies into our wider relations with other countries.

(g) Recognising the importance of strengthening the export control of WMD-related materials and technologies and promoting international cooperation to this end, China and the EU agree to take effective measures to improve their respective export control system and enforcement measures. The EU welcomes China's efforts and progress made in enhancing export control legislation, as well as its entry into Nuclear Suppliers Group (NSG) and its efforts in developing relations with other multilateral export control regimes, such as Missile Technology Control Regime (MTCR), Australia Group (AG) and Wassenaar Arrangement (WA).

(h) Recognising the importance of treaty based arms control and disarmament, China and the EU will work together to ensure the expeditious adoption of a programme of work in the Conference on Disarmament in Geneva.

(i) Recognising the need for regular and focused consultations, China and the EU identified priority areas for specific cooperation in the list attached hereto. This list will be revised, as necessary, through regular consultations at the China-EU Troika Working Group or other designated channels.

11. This statement was signed in The Hague, 8 December 2004.

| | |
|---|---|
| For the People's Republic of China<br>Minister of Foreign Affairs | For the European Union<br>President of the Council of Ministers of the European Union |

Secretary General of the Council of the European Union, High Representative for the Common Foreign and Security Policy

## ANNEX: PRIORITY AREAS FOR SPECIFIC COOPERATION

With respect to paragraph 10(i) in the Joint Declaration, the priority areas for specific cooperation are identified as follows.

*Enhancing the role of the United Nations*

- Consultation and coordination within the framework of the United Nations and other multilateral fora aimed at enhancing the important role of the United Nations, and the Security Council in particular, in non-proliferation. China and the EU will actively work together to ensure effective implementation of United Nations Security Council Resolution 1540.

*Nuclear non-proliferation*

- Consultation and coordination on proposals to strengthen international nuclear non-proliferation system.
- Promotion of the universalisation of the IAEA Comprehensive Safeguard Agreements and Additional Protocols.
- Early entry into force of the CTBT.
- Promotion of the early commencement of negotiations on the Fissile Material Cut-off Treaty (FMCT) in the Conference on Disarmament.
- Cooperation on enhancement of the physical protection of nuclear and radiological materials including in the context of the Convention on the Physical Protection of Nuclear Material (CPPNM).

*Biological and chemical weapons*

- Promotion of the universalisation of the BTWC and more effective functioning the BTWC through active participation in the BTWC programme of work, exchange of views and cooperation on strengthening the BTWC.
- Exchange of information, sharing expertise and cooperation in fields related to BTWC, such as bio-security and the surveillance of epidemic diseases.
- Promotion of the universalisation of the CWC and cooperation to help strengthen its national implementation.

*Export control and other non-proliferation measures*

- Exchange of experiences, information and cooperation in export controls of WMD-related materials, equipment and technologies, on a bilateral basis and in the context of nonproliferation regimes (e.g. NSG).
- Cooperation on specific problems related to controls of the export of weapons or WMD-related materials, equipment and technologies with a view to avoiding the risk that they could fall into the hands of terrorists and/or have a destabilising effect on international and regional peace and security.
- Cooperation in strengthening of law enforcement, customs, border controls capabilities including, inter alia, information sharing, experience exchange and personnel training to prevent proliferation of WMD and their means of delivery. A first concrete step in this context is the organization of an EU-China export control workshop which will take place in China shortly after the Summit.
- The EU supports China's entry into MTCR and further dialogue between China and AG as well as WA, which is conducive to the cause of international non-proliferation.

*Conventional weapons*

- Exchange of views on the implementation and expansion of the participation to the United Nations Register of Conventional Arms.
- Exchange of views on existing and possible future mechanisms dealing with the humanitarian effects of landmines.
- Exchange of views on the implementation of the United Nations programme for combating the illicit trade of small arms and light weapons.
- Promotion of the early entry into force and universalisation of CCW Protocol V on ERW.

Another important and particularly controversial topic is the subject of the EU–China Human Rights Dialogue. The EU has general dialogues including human rights with numerous countries, but the only regular, institutionalised and highly structured dialogue on human rights is with China. Such a focused human rights dialogue is used by the EU only concerning countries with which the EC has no agreement (as with the former dialogue with Iran) or where the agreement does not contain a 'human rights' clause (as with the 1985 EEC–China Agreement on Trade and Economic Cooperation).[9] The EU–China Human Rights Dialogue began in January 1996.[10] It was interrupted in 1997 when Denmark and nine other EU Member States tabled a resolution critical of China at the 1997 session of the UN Commission on Human Rights, and then it was resumed at China's decision later in 1997. It is held twice each year, most recently on 17 October 2007 in Beijing.[11]

In 2001 the EU published guidelines on human rights dialogues (see Document 4.14). The guidelines were drafted by the Council Working Party on Human Rights,

> in consultation with geographical working parties, the Working Party on Development Cooperation (CODEV) and the Committee on measures for the development and consolidation of democracy and the rule of law, and for the respect of human rights and fundamental freedoms.[12]

The EU approach is based on pragmatism and flexibility, with some (but relatively limited) participation by civil society, notably in the assessment of the dialogue. The objectives, issues covered and criteria for measuring progress depend on the parties and are determined on a case-by-case basis. The EU considers that the human rights dialogue and resolutions submitted to the UN human rights bodies 'are two entirely separate forms of action',[13] which are not necessarily linked or interdependent.

9 See Council of the EU, 'European Union Guidelines on Human Rights Dialogues' (13 December 2001), available at http://ec.europa.eu/comm/external_relations/human_rights/doc/ghd12_01.htm (accessed 6 February 2006).

10 According to the European Commission, there is no formal document establishing this Dialogue.

11 See Presidency of the European Union, Portugal 2007, 'Press release of the 24th Round of the EU–China Dialogue on Human Rights' (17 October 2007), available at http://www.eu2007.pt/UE/vEN/Noticias-Documentos/20071017UEChina.htm (accessed 22 November 2007).

12 Council of the EU, 'European Union Guidelines on Human Rights Dialogues' (13 December 2001), available on the website of the European Commission, Directorate-General for External Relations, http://ec.europa.eu/comm/external_relations/human_rights/doc/ghd12_01.htm (accessed 6 February 2006).

13 Council of the EU, 'European Union Guidelines on Human Rights Dialogues' (13 December 2001), available at http://ec.europa.eu/comm/external_relations/human_rights/doc/ghd12_01.htm (accessed 6 February 2006).

Starting in 2001, however, the EU reaffirmed the principle that 'the dialogue is an acceptable option only if progress is achieved on the ground'.[14]

**Document 4.14: Guidelines on Human Rights Dialogues**

**EUROPEAN UNION GUIDELINES ON HUMAN RIGHTS DIALOGUES**

**1. Introduction**

In its conclusions of 25 June 2001 the Council welcomed the Commission communication of 8 May 2001 on the European Union's role in promoting human rights and democratisation in third countries, which represents an invaluable contribution towards strengthening the coherence and consistency of the EU's policy on human rights and democratisation. In its conclusions the Council reaffirmed its commitment to the principles of coherence and consistency, integration of human rights into all its actions, openness of its policies and identification of priority areas. As part of the process of implementing those Council conclusions, the Working Party on Human Rights (COHOM) undertook to establish guidelines on human rights dialogues in consultation with the geographical working parties, the Working Party on Development Cooperation (CODEV) and the Committee on measures for the development and consolidation of democracy and the rule of law, and for the respect of human rights and fundamental freedoms.

**2. Current situation**

The European Union is engaged in human rights dialogues with a number of countries. Those dialogues are in themselves an instrument of the Union's external policy. That instrument is one of a range of measures which the EU may use to implement its policy on human rights, and constitutes an essential part of the European Union's overall strategy aimed at promoting sustainable development, peace and stability. However, there are at present no rules to determine at what point it should be applied. It should also be said that there is room for greater consistency in the EU's current approach towards dialogues, which at present employs several different types:

2.1. dialogues or discussions of a rather general nature based on regional or bilateral treaties, agreements or conventions dealing systematically with the issue of human rights. These include in particular:

2.1.1. relations with candidate countries;

2.1.2. the Cotonou Agreement with the ACP States and the Trade, Development and Cooperation Agreement with South Africa;

2.1.3. relations between the EU and Latin America;

2.1.4. the Barcelona process (Mediterranean countries);

2.1.5. political dialogue with Asian countries in the context of ASEAN and ASEM;

2.1.6. relations with the Western Balkans;

14 Council of the EU, 'EU–China Dialogue on Human Rights', General Affairs Council, 2327th Council Meeting, Brussels, 22–23 January 2001, available at http://ec.europa.eu/comm/external_relations/human_rights/news7gac-jan-01.htm (accessed 6 February 2006).

2.1.7. bilateral relations in the framework of association and cooperation agreements.

2.2. dialogues focusing exclusively on human rights. At present there is only one regular, institutionalised dialogue devoted solely to human rights between the European Union and a third country, namely that with China. This is a highly structured dialogue held at the level of senior human rights officials. At one time the European Union also maintained a human rights dialogue with the Islamic Republic of Iran. This type of dialogue, focusing solely on human rights, has so far only been used with countries with which the European Community had no agreement and/or where the agreement contained no "human rights" clause. The fact that such dialogue exists does not preclude discussion of the human rights issue at any level of the political dialogue;

2.3. *ad hoc* dialogues extending to CFSP-related topics such as that of human rights. For instance, the EU currently maintains dialogues with Cuba and Sudan at the level of heads of mission;

2.4. dialogues in the context of special relations with certain third countries, on the basis of broadly converging views. With the United States, Canada and the associated countries these take the form of six-monthly meetings of experts, with the Troika representing the EU, before the Commission on Human Rights and the annual United Nations General Assembly. The main objective of these dialogues is to discuss issues of common interest and the possibilities for cooperation within multilateral human rights bodies.

In addition to dialogues at EU level, a number of Member States also maintain dialogues with various third countries at national level.

The guidelines on human rights dialogues would have several aims, namely to:

- identify the role played by this instrument in the global framework of the CFSP and the EU's policy on human rights;
- strengthen the coherence and consistency of the European Union's approach towards human rights dialogues;
- facilitate use of that instrument by defining the conditions in which it is to be applied and made effective;
- notify third parties (international organisations, non-governmental organisations, the academic world, the European Parliament, third countries) of this approach.

Political dialogues with the ACP countries under the Cotonou Agreement have their own detailed arrangements and procedures as laid down in Article 8 of the Agreement. However, for consistency's sake, exchanges of news and experience will be held on a regular basis in the COHOM Working Party framework.

**3. Basic principles**

3.1. The European Union undertakes to intensify the process of integrating human rights and democratisation objectives ("mainstreaming") into all aspects of its external policies. Accordingly, the EU will ensure that the issue of human rights, democracy and the rule of law will be included in all future meetings and discussions with third countries and at all levels, whether ministerial talks, joint committee meetings or formal dialogues led by the Presidency of the Council, the Troika, heads of mission or the Commission. It will further ensure that the issue of human rights, democracy and the rule of law is included in programming discussions and in country strategy papers.

3.2. However, in order to examine human rights issues in greater depth, the European Union may decide to initiate a human rights-specific dialogue with a particular third country.

Decisions of that kind will be taken in accordance with certain criteria, while maintaining the degree of pragmatism and flexibility required for such a task. Either the EU itself will take the initiative of suggesting a dialogue with a third country, or it will respond to a request by a third country.

**4. Objectives of human rights dialogues**

The objectives of human rights dialogues will vary from one country to another and will be defined on a case-by-case basis. These objectives may include:

(a) discussing questions of mutual interest and enhancing cooperation on human rights inter alia, in multinational fora such as the United Nations;

(b) registering the concern felt by the EU at the human rights situation in the country concerned, information gathering and endeavouring to improve the human rights situation in that country.

Moreover, human rights dialogues can identify at an early stage problems likely to lead to conflict in the future.

**5. Issues covered in human rights dialogues**

The issues to be discussed during human rights dialogues will be determined on a case-by-case basis. However, the European Union is committed to dealing with those priority issues which should be included on the agenda for every dialogue. These include the signing, ratification and implementation of international human rights instruments, cooperation with international human rights procedures and mechanisms, combating the death penalty, combating torture, combating all forms of discrimination, children's rights, women's rights, freedom of expression, the role of civil society, international cooperation in the field of justice, promotion of the processes of democratisation and good governance, and the prevention of conflict. The dialogues aimed at enhancing human rights cooperation could also include – according to the circumstances – some of the priority issues referred to above, (in particular the implementation of the main international human rights instruments ratified by the other party), as well as preparing and following up the work of the Commission on Human Rights in Geneva, of the Third Committee of the UN General Assembly in New York and of international and/or regional conferences.

**6. Procedure for the initiation of human rights dialogues**

6.1. Any decision to initiate a human rights dialogue will first require an assessment of the human rights situation in the country concerned. The decision to embark on a preliminary assessment will be made by the Working Party on Human Rights (COHOM), together with the geographical working parties, the Working Party on Development Cooperation (CODEV) and the Committee on measures for the development and consolidation of democracy and the rule of law, and for the respect of human rights and fundamental freedoms. The assessment itself will be made by COHOM in coordination with the other Working Parties. Amongst other things the assessment will look at developments in the human rights situation, the extent to which the government is willing to improve the situation, the degree of commitment shown by the government in respect of international human rights conventions, the government's readiness to cooperate with United Nations human rights procedures and mechanisms as well as the government's attitude towards civil society. The assessment will be based, *inter alia*, on the following sources: reports by heads of mission, reports by the UN and other international or regional organisations, reports by the

European Parliament and by the various non-governmental organisations working in the field of human rights, and Commission strategy papers for the countries concerned.

6.2. Any decision to initiate a human rights dialogue will first require the defining of the practical aims which the Union seeks to achieve by initiating dialogue with the country concerned, as well as an assessment of the added value to be gained from such dialogue.

The European Union will also, on a case-by-case basis, establish criteria for measuring the progress achieved in relation to the benchmarks and also criteria for a possible exit strategy.

6.3. Exploratory talks will be held before a human rights dialogue with the country concerned is initiated. The aim of those talks will be twofold: first to define the objectives to be pursued by any country accepting or requesting a human rights dialogue with the EU and to determine possible ways of increasing that country's commitment towards international human rights instruments, international human rights procedures and mechanisms and the promotion and protection of human rights and democratisation in general; and subsequently to update the information in the reports following the preliminary assessment. The talks will also provide an opportunity to explain to the country concerned the principles underlying the EU's action, as well as the Union's aims in proposing or accepting a human rights-specific dialogue. The exploratory talks will preferably be led by an EU Troïka team of human rights experts representing the capitals, in close consultation with the Heads of Mission accredited in the country concerned. An assessment of the exploratory talks will then carried out. The European Union will decide in the light of that assessment whether or not it wishes to continue on a more structured and institutionalised basis.

6.4. Any decision to initiate a human rights-specific dialogue will require discussion within the Working Party on Human Rights and its prior agreement. The final decision to initiate a human rights dialogue lies with the Council of Ministers.

6.5. The geographical working parties, the Working Party on Development Cooperation (CODEV) and the Committee on measures for the development and consolidation of democracy and the rule of law, and for the respect of human rights and fundamental freedoms should also be involved in this decision-making process.

6.6. Should the assessment be a negative one and/or the European Union decide not to initiate a human rights dialogue, the European Union will consider whether other approaches might be appropriate, such as emphasis on the human rights aspect of the political dialogue with the country concerned, inter alia by including specialist human rights knowledge in the political dialogue team.

The Working Party on Human Rights (COHOM) will be responsible for following up the dialogue, where necessary together with the other bodies concerned, viz. the geographical working parties, the Heads of Mission, the Working Party on Development Cooperation (CODEV) and the Committee on measures for the development and consolidation of democracy and the rule of law, and for the respect of human rights and fundamental freedoms.

**7. Practical arrangements for human rights dialogues**

Flexibility and pragmatism are the keywords in the context of the practical arrangements for human rights dialogues, which should thus be determined on a case-by-case basis, by joint agreement with the country concerned. The arrangements will cover aspects such as where and how often the dialogue is to be held and the level of representation required.

To ensure that the discussions are as fruitful as possible, the dialogues should, as far as feasible, be held at the level of government representatives responsible for human rights. For the sake of continuity, the European Union should be represented by the Troika – at the level either of representatives from the capitals or of Heads of Mission.

The European Union will ensure that dialogue meetings are regularly held in the country concerned. This approach has the advantage of giving the EU delegation a better opportunity to gauge for itself the situation on the spot and, subject to the agreement of the country's authorities, to contact the people and institutions in which it is interested. Traditionally, dialogues whose primary purpose is to discuss issues of mutual interest and to strengthen human rights cooperation are held in Brussels. That tradition should preferably be maintained.

As far as possible, the European Union will ask the authorities of countries involved in the human rights dialogue to include in their delegations representatives of the various institutions and Ministries responsible for human rights matters, such as the Justice and Interior Ministries, the police, prison administration etc. Likewise, civil society could become involved under the most suitable arrangement in the preliminary assessment of the human rights situation, in the conduct of the dialogue itself (particularly by organising meetings with civil society at local level in parallel with the formal dialogue), and in following up and assessing the dialogue. The European Union could thus signify its support for defenders of human rights in countries with which it maintains exchanges of this kind.

The EU will as far as possible give the human rights dialogues a degree of genuine transparency vis-à-vis civil society.

**8. Consistency between Member States' bilateral dialogues and EU dialogues**

Information exchange is essential if maximum consistency between Member States' bilateral dialogues and EU dialogues is to be ensured. Exchanges of this kind, particularly on the issues discussed and the outcome of discussions, could be conducted by COREU or the Working Party on Human Rights (COHOM). The diplomatic post of the current Presidency in the country concerned could also gather relevant information on the spot. Where appropriate, informal ad hoc meetings between the members of the Working Party on Human Rights (COHOM), the relevant geographical working parties, and the European Parliament could be considered. It would also be possible to consider holding informal ad hoc meetings with other countries which maintain human rights dialogues with the country concerned (as in the case of the current dialogue with China). Such meetings should involve the COHOM Working Party, and the geographical working parties or study groups.

The technical assistance afforded by the European Union in the area of human rights and democratisation in the countries with which it maintains a dialogue should take into account developments in the dialogue and its outcome.

**9. Consistency between human rights dialogues and EU Resolutions to the UNGA and the CHR.**

Human rights dialogues and Resolutions submitted by the European Union to the UNGA or the CHR on the human rights situations in certain countries are two entirely separate forms of action. Accordingly, the fact that there is a human rights dialogue between the EU and a third country will not prevent the EU either from submitting a Resolution on the human rights situation in that country or from providing support for an initiative by the third country. Nor will the fact that there is a human rights dialogue between the EU and a third country prevent the European Union from denouncing breaches of human rights in that country, inter alia in the appropriate international fora, or from raising the matter in meetings with the third countries concerned at every level.

**10. Assessing human rights dialogues**

All human rights dialogues will be assessed on a regular basis, preferably every year.

The assessment will be made by the current Presidency, assisted by the Council Secretariat, and be submitted for discussion and decision to the Working Party on Human Rights (COHOM) in cooperation with the geographical working parties, the Working Party on Development Cooperation (CODEV) and the Committee on measures for the development and consolidation of democracy and the rule of law, and for the respect of human rights and fundamental freedom.

Civil society will be involved in this assessment exercise. The task will involve assessing the situation in relation to the objectives which the Union set itself before initiating the dialogue, and will examine how much added value has been provided by the dialogue. The examination will look particularly closely at the progress made on the priority areas of the dialogue. If progress has indeed been made, the assessment should, if possible, analyse how far the European Union's activities have contributed to that progress. If no progress has been made, the European Union should either adjust its aims, or consider whether or not to continue the human rights dialogue with the country concerned. Indeed, a dialogue assessment must allow for the possibility of a decision to terminate the exercise if the requirements given in these guidelines are no longer met, or the conditions under which the dialogue is conducted are unsatisfactory, or if the outcome is not up to the EU's expectations. Likewise, a decision may be taken to suspend a dialogue which has proved successful and has therefore become redundant. Such matters will be dealt with by the Working Party on Human Rights (COHOM) as a matter of priority.

As for dialogues aimed at strengthening human rights cooperation, particularly those held within international and regional bodies, the assessment will focus on those areas in which cooperation could be further improved.

**11. Managing human rights dialogues**

Given the prospect of increasing numbers of dialogues, the Working Party on Human Rights (COHOM) will have to consider the problem of how these should be managed. Continuity is a very important factor, as is the strengthening of the structures supporting the current Council Presidency in the preparations for the dialogues and their follow-up. To prepare each dialogue properly will also require input from the geographical working parties, the Working Party on Development Cooperation (CODEV) and the Committee on measures for the development and consolidation of democracy and the rule of law, and for the respect of human rights and fundamental freedoms. The Council Secretariat's support is essential in terms of centralising all the data, preparing both the content and the logistics, and following up the dialogues. The European Union could also consider, on a case-by-case basis, the possibility of associating a private foundation or organisation specialised in the field of human rights with one or more dialogues. In this connection, Sweden's experience (the Wallenberg Institute) in the context of the exploratory talks with North Korea (Brussels, June 2001) could be assessed.

**12. The human rights position in political dialogues**

As indicated in paragraph 3, the European Union will ensure that the issue of human rights, democracy and the rule of law is incorporated into all meetings and discussions it has with third countries, at every level, including political dialogue. The European Union undertakes to include human rights experts in the EU delegations. The decision on who will provide the expert knowledge will be taken on a case-by-case basis, but with an eye to continuity. Although this type of discussion does not afford the possibility of dealing with human rights issues in any great depth, the European Union will endeavour to raise the priority issues referred to in paragraph 5 with the country concerned.

Both the EU and China wish to continue the human rights dialogue.[15] However, they have different perceptions of its importance (see Document 4.15). These differences reflect divergent conceptions of human rights, the relative importance of different human rights, different historical and cultural circumstances, different economic and political systems and contrasting conceptions of national sovereignty.

### Document 4.15: Report on the 24th Human Rights Dialogue

Press release of the 24th Round of the EU-China Dialogue on Human Rights

Date: 2007-10-17

On 17 October 2007 the European Union and the People's Republic of China held the 24th round of the «EU-China Dialogue on Human Rights» in Beijing.

The Dialogue provided a platform for a substantive and frank exchange of views between the People's Republic of China and the EU on a wide range of human rights issues. Taking place at the same time as the 17th National Party Congress, the dialogue was conducted in a constructive atmosphere and was an occasion to express concerns and differences of opinion with regard to the implementation of international human rights standards in China and the EU.

Key issues for the EU were reform of the criminal justice system in China, freedom of expression, freedom of religion in Tibet and labour rights. The EU and China discussed a number of specific items tied to the reform of the criminal justice system, including the need for China to ratify the UN Covenant on Civil and Political Rights and to implement the recommendations of the UN Special Rapporteur on Torture. The EU welcomed the reduction in the number of executions in China following the review of death sentences by the People's Supreme Court. The EU was pleased to note on going progress in the field of labour rights and employment. In a discussion that spurred the most robust debate of the session, the EU and China discussed freedom of religion in Tibet, specifically new measures tightening state control over approval of reincarnated lamas. China raised the follow-up to the Durban Declaration and Plan of Action, as well as racism in the EU, as issues of concern, pointing to a number of alleged incidents of racial discrimination in some Member States.

Concerning cooperation in international organisations, the EU attached special importance to the renewal of special procedures in the Human Rights Council (HRC).and to possible

[15] For a recent assessment by the EU, see Council of Ministers and European Commission, *EU Annual Report on Human Rights 2006* (Luxembourg, Office for Official Publications of the European Communities, 2006).

visits of Special Rapporteurs to China. Both sides looked forward to close coordination on issues for the current session of the UN General Assembly. The EU welcomed China's cooperation in the HRC Special Session on Burma/Myanmar and called on China to continue playing a constructive role in support of Ibrahim Gambari's efforts.

In the framework of the dialogue, the EU troika undertook a field visit to Shanxi Province where it visited a legal aid centre, observed a murder trial, and discussed religious freedom with monks and provincial government representatives at a Chinese Buddhist temple. It also visited the Taiyuan television station and met with local representatives of the Communist Party of China.

In a side meeting, the EU and China expressed their commitment to continue the legal seminar, which both sides agreed added value to the Dialogue process by opening it up to academic and civil society participation. The Parties will now start preparations for the next seminar to be held during the first semester of 2008.

The «EU-China Human Rights Dialogue» has, with short interruptions, taken place bi-annually since 1995. The next regular meeting will be held in the first half of 2008 in Ljubljana under the Slovene Presidency.

Non-governmental organisations in the EU and the USA have continually been critical of the lack of concrete progress on human rights in China resulting from the EU–China Human Rights Dialogue. They have proposed specific improvements, such as a clear agenda, transparency and accountability, participation by non-governmental organisations (NGOs) and other organisations, coordination with other dialogues, such as those between the UK and China and between Sweden and China, cooperation with UN human rights mechanisms and an integrated strategy with no compromises on human rights standards.[16] In September 2007, the European Parliament (see Document 4.16) adopted a resolution on the functioning of human rights dialogues and consultations on human rights with third countries. It called for greater coherence among the different EU human rights dialogues and proposed more stringent criteria and monitoring mechanisms, such as the adoption by the Council of the European Union of specific indicators of progress concerning human rights.[17] So far,

16 These proposals are made by Human Rights in China, 'Human Rights Situation in China and the Dialogue on Human Rights', submitted to the Foreign Affairs Committee of the House of Commons, United Kingdom, 28 July 2000, available at http://hrichina.org/public/contents/article?revision%5fid=14289&item%5fid=2577 (accessed 3 February 2007). See also Fédération Internationale des Droits de l'Homme (FIDH), 'Preliminary Assessment of the EU–China Human Rights Dialogue', submitted to the EU–China Human Rights Dialogue meeting, February 2004, available at http://www.fidh.org/IMG/pdf/cn2502a.pdf (accessed 3 February 2007); Free Tibet Campaign, Human Rights in China and the International Campaign for Tibet, 'Behind Closed Doors: Bilateral Dialogues on Human Rights' (2003) 23 *China Rights Forum* (section on International Interventions) 2, available at http://hrichina.org/public/PDFs/CRF.2.2003/bilateral.pdf (accessed 3 February 2007); 'Promoting Human Rights in China: Report by the China Human Rights Strategy Group', sponsored by the Open Society Institute and Human Rights in China (November 2001), full version on file, previously available at http://www.hrichina.org/fs/view/downloadables/pdf/downloadable-resources/Strategy_Report_FINAL.pdf (accessed 3 February 2007); executive summary now available at http://hrichina.org/public/contents/article?revision%5fid=14514&item%5fid=14261 (accessed 21 November 2007).

17 Since 1992, the European Parliament has adopted numerous resolutions on human rights in China, notably in Tibet. See European Parliament, 'Resolution on the Situation in Tibet', Resolution A3-0369/92, available at http://www.yale.edu/laweb/avalon/tibet.htm (accessed 22 November 2007); and recently European Parliament, 'Resolution on Tibet and Hong Kong', P6_TA(2005) 0533 (15 December 2006), available at http://www.europarl.europa.eu/sides/getDoc.do?pubRef=-//EP//TEXT+TA+P6-TA-2005-0533+0+DOC+XML+V0//EN (last accessed 22 November 2007); European Parliament, 'Resolution on the

however, the EU and China have not accepted these proposals in their bilateral dialogue.

### Document 4.16: European Parliament Resolution on Human Rights Dialogues

European Parliament resolution of 6 September 2007 on the functioning of the human rights dialogues and consultations on human rights with third countries (2007/2001(INI))

The European Parliament,

– having regard to all agreements between the EU and third countries and the human rights and democracy clauses contained in those agreements,

– having regard to Articles 177, 178, 300 and 310 of the EC Treaty and Articles 3, 6, 11, 19 and 21 of the EU Treaty,

– having regard to the European Union Guidelines on Human Rights and in particular those on Human Rights Dialogues, adopted in December 2001, and the evaluation of the implementation of those Guidelines, adopted in December 2004, and having regard also to the European Union Guidelines on Human Rights Defenders, adopted in June 2004,

– having regard to its resolution of 14 February 2006 on the human rights and democracy clause in European Union agreements(1) and to the follow-up provided by the Commission to that resolution,

– having regard to the Council's document of 7 June 2006 entitled "Mainstreaming human rights across CFSP and other EU policies",

– having regard to the Framework Agreement of 26 May 2005 between the European Parliament and the Commission,

– having regard to its resolution of 25 April 2002 on the Commission communication to the Council and the European Parliament on the European Union's role in promoting human rights and democratisation in third countries(2),

– having regard to its previous resolutions on the situation with regard to human rights in the world,

– having regard to its previous debates and urgency resolutions on cases of breaches of human rights, democracy and the rule of law,

– having regard to its specific guidelines for human rights and democracy actions of MEPs in their visits to third countries,

– having regard to Regulation (EC) No 1889/2006 of the European Parliament and of the Council of 20 December 2006 on establishing a financing instrument for the promotion of democracy and human rights worldwide(3),

– having regard to the conclusions reached during the debates held in its Foreign Affairs Committee's Subcommittee on Human Rights, at the meetings of 3 May 2007 on human rights in China and in Uzbekistan and of 23 April 2007 on human rights in Russia,

Situation in Tibet', available at http://www.europarl.europa.eu/news/expert/infopress_page/015-11960-293-10-42-902-20061021IPR11916-20-10-2006-2006-false/default_en.htm (accessed 22 November 2007).

– having regard to its resolutions of 10 May 2007 on the EU-Russia Summit to be held in Samara on 18 May 2007[(4)], of 26 April 2007 on the recent repression of demonstrations in Russia[(5)], of 18 January 2007 on the conviction and imprisonment by Libya of five Bulgarian nurses and a Palestinian doctor[(6)], of 16 November 2006 on Iran[(7)], of 26 October 2006 on Uzbekistan[(8)] and of 7 September 2006 on EU-China relations[(9)],

– having regard to the conclusions on Central Asia reached at the 2796th External Relations Council meeting held in Luxembourg on 23 April 2007; to the Partnership and Cooperation Agreements with Kyrgyzstan, Kazakhstan and Uzbekistan, which have already entered into force; to the Partnership and Cooperation Agreements with Tajikistan and Turkmenistan, which have been signed but not yet ratified; and to the Commission's Strategy Paper on Central Asia 2002-2006,

– having regard to Articles 8, 9, 96 and 97 of, and Annex VII to, the Partnership Agreement between the members of the African, Caribbean and Pacific Group of States and the European Community and its Member States, signed in Cotonou on 23 June 2000[(10)] and amended in Luxembourg on 25 June 2005[(11)] (the Cotonou Agreement),

– having regard to the resolutions of the ACP-EU Joint Parliamentary Assembly (ACP-EU JPA) and, in particular, its resolution of 25 November 2004, adopted in The Hague, on the ACP-EU political dialogue (Article 8 of the Cotonou Agreement)[(12)],

– having regard to the bilateral Action Plans adopted by the Commission under the European Neighbourhood Policy (ENP) with the ENP partner countries, with the exception of Algeria, Belarus, Libya and Syria,

– having regard to the Communication from the Commission to the Council and the European Parliament on strengthening the ENP (COM(2006)0726) and to its forthcoming resolution thereon,

– having regard to its recommendations to the Council of 15 March 2007 on the negotiating mandates for association agreements between the European Union and its Member States, of the one part, and the Andean Community and its member countries, of the other part[(13)], and between the European Union and its Member States, of the one part, and the countries of Central America, of the other part[(14)],

– having regard to its resolutions of 12 October 2006 on economic and trade relations between the EU and Mercosur with a view to the conclusion of an Interregional Association Agreement[(15)] and of 27 April 2006 on a stronger partnership between the European Union and Latin America[(16)],

– having regard to Rule 45 of its Rules of Procedure,

– having regard to the report of the Committee on Foreign Affairs and the opinion of the Committee on Women's Rights and Gender Equality (A6-0302/2007),

A. whereas human rights dialogues are one of a range of instruments which the EU may use to implement its policy on human rights, and constitute an essential part of the European Union's overall strategy aimed at promoting sustainable development, peace and stability,

B. whereas the universality, individuality and indivisibility of human rights, meaning not only civil and political rights but also social, environmental, economic and cultural rights, must be upheld and promoted, and whereas the EU continues to establish meaningful instruments to that end,

C. whereas any decision to initiate a human rights dialogue is taken on the basis of certain criteria adopted by the Council which notably take into consideration the major concerns on the part of the EU about the human rights situation on the ground in the country concerned, a genuine commitment on the part of the authorities of the country concerned, with regard to such dialogue, to improve the human rights situation on the ground, and the positive impact which a human rights dialogue may have on the human rights situation,

D. whereas the European Union Human Rights Guidelines call for human rights issues to be addressed adequately and systematically within the framework of the overall political dialogue conducted with third countries at all levels,

E. whereas the Council decided in 2004 to examine twice each year the overall status of the dialogues on the basis of an overview and an updated timetable, and whereas, at the same time, the Council underlined that dialogues should not be engaged in for an indefinite period but rather for a certain time-frame, with an exit strategy also being borne in mind,

F. whereas human rights dialogues and consultations are conducted using a wide variety of structures, formats, and procedures, without sufficient regard for the necessary consistency, whereas this lack of consistency may undermine the credibility of EU human rights policy on the international stage, and whereas greater transparency and democratic control over the application of the abovementioned EU Guidelines on Human Rights Dialogues would be desirable,

G. whereas the Council's current practice is to provide a debriefing on the agenda and the objectives of the forthcoming round of structured human rights dialogues/consultations, and to invite a Parliament official to participate along with representatives of non-governmental organisations,

H. whereas the Cotonou Agreement is directed towards sustainable development and centred on the individual as the main protagonist and beneficiary of development policy; whereas this entails respect for, and promotion of, all human rights and fundamental freedoms, and whereas the abovementioned revision of the Agreement of 25 June 2005 resulted in more intensive political dialogue under Article 8, particularly with regard to human rights,

I. whereas failure by one of the parties to fulfil an obligation stemming from the principle of respect for human rights, democratic principles and the rule of law as referred to Article 9 of the Cotonou Agreement results in the initiation of a consultation procedure under Article 96 to redress the situation,

J. whereas, although Article 8 of the Cotonou Agreement, which provides for political dialogue between ACP countries and the EU, and also for a regular assessment concerning respect for human rights, democratic principles, the rule of law and good governance, is to be welcomed, concern remains that this provision is used to circumvent the consultation procedure under Article 96 in cases of human rights violations,

K. whereas the implementation of ENP Action Plans is monitored by several subcommittees, and whereas, under the bilateral Association Agreements, the EU has launched a process of extending subcommittees for human rights, democratisation and governance to all ENP countries; whereas, to date, Morocco, Jordan and Lebanon have approved the creation of such subcommittees, which have held meetings, Egypt has approved the creation of a subcommittee although it has not yet held a meeting, and Tunisia is in the process of approving a subcommittee,

L. whereas, as a short-term measure in various ENP Action Plans, it is recommended that a subcommittee be set up under Article 5 of the Association Agreement, with a view to developing structured political dialogue on democracy and the rule of law; whereas the subcommittee in question has no decision-making power but may submit proposals to the relevant Association Committee or to bodies at a higher level in the political dialogue,

M. whereas, as a result of the reform of the financial instruments on external assistance, Parliament has acquired the right to carry out democratic scrutiny of the relevant strategic documents, and is at the same time one of the budgetary authorities,

N. whereas the rights of women and children form an inalienable, integral and indivisible part of universal human rights, as laid down in the Beijing Declaration and Platform for Action of 1995,

**A. Enhancing the coherence of human rights dialogues and consultations**

1. Stresses that the promotion of human rights is a fundamental part of the EU's external policy making; urges the Council and the Commission to systematically include human rights issues in the agenda of the EU's political dialogues and consultations with third countries, and increasingly to mainstream human rights into all external EU policies, including the external aspects of the internal EU policies, and insists on the use of all available instruments with a view to attaining those objectives;

2. Takes the view that human rights issues should be placed at the highest political level in order to give more political weight to human rights concerns; recalls that the promotion and defence of human rights in third countries should not be conditioned by geopolitical or geo-strategic alliances; stresses that, within the framework of political, economic and trade-related dialogues, respect for human rights should be fundamental to strategic and privileged relations with the EU;

3. Calls on the Council to fully apply the abovementioned EU Guidelines on Human Rights Dialogues;

4. Endorses the conclusions of the first review of the implementation of the EU Guidelines on Human Rights Defenders, which point out that the situation pertaining to human rights defenders and the environment in which they work should be systematically integrated into the EU's political dialogues and consultations with third countries, including bilateral dialogues and consultations conducted by EU Member States;

5. Welcomes the newly adopted decision of the Council to draft EU Guidelines on the Rights of the Child, to be finalised during the Portuguese Presidency in 2007; stresses, in this regard, the necessary complementarity to be respected with the existing Guidelines on Children in Armed Conflicts and the need to consider the Paris commitments of 6 February 2007 to protect children from unlawful recruitment or use by armed forces or armed groups;

6. Calls on the Council once again to systematically apply in full the Human Rights and Democracy Clause in all EU agreements and relations with third countries; reaffirms its call for a transparent procedure to be laid down for the purpose of assessing the human rights situation and the application of the human rights clause; calls for the findings of such an assessment to be systematically taken into account in the human rights dialogues and consultations with third countries and vice versa;

7. Points out that the main purpose of dialogue and consultation is to encourage the consolidation of democracy, the rule of law, good governance, and respect for fundamental freedoms and human rights in third countries, meaning not only civil and political rights but

also social, environmental, economic and cultural rights; emphasises that these objectives will be pursued in observance of the general principles established by the Universal Declaration of Human Rights, and any other universal instrument on human rights adopted within the framework of the United Nations, and taking into account the Millennium Development Goals;

8. Maintains that the fact of conducting a human rights dialogue or consultations with a third country has to lead to systematic mainstreaming of human rights in every sphere of EU cooperation with the country concerned, including the Community's development policy and economic, financial and technical cooperation with third countries, so that the existence of a human rights dialogue or consultations does not constitute an end in itself;

9. Welcomes the Council's efforts to bring coherence to the human rights dialogue and consultation with the aid of the abovementioned EU Guidelines on Human Rights Dialogues; maintains that the flexibility and pragmatism required to ensure that dialogue and consultation are effective must not undermine the coherence needed to prevent the dialogues and consultations being reduced to a matter of free choice;

10. Notes that there is a wide variety of dialogues and consultations, each based on different structures, formats, frequencies, and methodologies, thus obscuring the picture and creating confusion as regards EU action in this area; deplores the fact that whatever information may exist concerning the agendas, aims, benchmarks, or outcome of the dialogues and consultations based on agreements, of ad hoc dialogues and consultations, of dialogue and consultation with like-minded countries, or of the political dialogue and consultation, the information does not extend to human rights; notes that neither the Council nor the Commission has devised a method for organising and systematising these dialogues and consultations, making the results impossible to view from an overall perspective; calls on the Commission and Council to bring a systematic approach to bear on the human rights dialogues and consultations with third countries, classifying them by methodology and subject so as to provide a basis for objective assessment and monitoring of the human rights situation, the breakthroughs achieved, and so on;

*Increased interinstitutional coherence*

11. Considers it essential to find ways of improving coordination among the different EU institutions (the Council, the Commission, and Parliament) by establishing an interinstitutional trialogue on the political dialogue and the human rights dialogues and consultations; also calls for avenues to be explored immediately with a view to improving internal communication within those institutions;

12. Welcomes the Council Working Party on Human Rights (COHOM) initiative whereby all of the EU's human rights dialogues and consultations are to be periodically reviewed in order to maintain a global perspective in the light of twice-yearly debates based on an updated general framework and a timetable for human rights dialogues and consultations in progress; calls for the review to be duly carried out and for information to be passed on as a matter of course to the other Council working parties, to the Commission and its delegations in third countries, and to Parliament, as part of the above-mentioned interinstitutional trialogue;

*Recommendations to the Council*

13. Calls on the Council to implement the COHOM mandate so as to ensure coherence between the dialogues or consultations and the other ways in which the EU seeks to

promote human rights in the countries concerned (whether those dialogues or consultations result from work in international bodies or originate from obligations laid down in the EU's own instruments);

14. Renews its call for the Council to consider making COHOM a working party with representatives based in Brussels, and to cooperate closely with the European Parliament's competent committee; believes that this would allow more time for meetings and ensure better coordination and hence, possibly, closer supervision of EU human rights policies in the broad sense and human rights dialogues and consultations in particular, as well as for mainstreaming of human rights to give coherence to the EU's policies;

15. Calls on the Council to enhance the role of the Human Rights Unit of its General Secretariat by allowing it to be involved in the conduct of the political dialogues, including the dialogues and consultations based on cooperation agreements under the responsibility of the Commission, and to set up, within its Human Rights Unit, a permanent coordination system for each structured human rights dialogue or consultation, in order to ensure the innovativeness of the dialogue and consultation topics, the selection of relevant participants and continuity, proceeding on the basis that such coordination should contribute to the establishment of bilateral networks of organisations, institutions and academics between Europe and the country in question, so as to ensure the requisite mainstreaming of human rights and democracy in all EU policies, especially following the reforms of the financial instruments for external EC aid; calls, to that end, for the necessary steps to be taken to enable the unit to perform the above tasks, including an increase in financial resources and personnel;

16. Calls on the Council to increase coherence among the bilateral human rights dialogues and consultations conducted by individual Member States and by the EU, and to increase the role of COHOM in coordinating the activities of Member States" embassies with those of the Commission's delegations;

*Recommendations to the Commission*

17. Calls on the Commission and the Council to include in each Country Strategy Paper and other strategy documents a specific strategy on human rights and the situation pertaining to democracy, and to use it as a framework for political dialogue;

18. Renews its call on the Commission to ensure that, within the staff serving at any given time in each Commission delegation in a third country, an EU official is in charge of the human rights dialogue and consultations, and requests it to ensure that the persons responsible for such matters are present whenever any form of political dialogue is being conducted; to this end, calls for the adoption of the necessary measures in order to enable the Commission to fulfil this task, including increasing its financial and human resources;

19. Calls on the Commission to ensure coherence between Election Observation Missions (especially as regards the post-electoral strategy) and the process of human rights dialogues and consultations; calls on the Commission to put in place, together with the European Parliament and third countries concerned, a post-electoral protocol mechanism to monitor and support the democratisation process, which includes the involvement of civil society at all stages, in the implementation of post-electoral recommendations;

20. Calls on the Commission to apply and use the results of human rights dialogues and consultations in drawing up yearly strategies providing a basis for implementation of projects under the European Instrument for Democracy and Human Rights (EIDHR)

established pursuant to Regulation (EC) No 1889/2006, and systematically to link those two tools;

21. Calls on the Commission and the Council to mainstream the human rights dialogue and consultations results into projects and programmes, notably for development aid and technical, trade and financial cooperation;

*Increasing coherence with other states and international organisations*

22. Welcomes the Council's stipulation that the existence of bilateral human rights dialogues or consultations should not have the effect of reducing the international pressure exerted by the EU when human rights violations occur in a given country, and points out that it is essential for dialogue or consultation to be backed up by appropriate diplomatic and political pressure at every level, extending to United Nations bodies and its Human Rights Council, in particular;

23. Calls on the Council and the Commission to analyse, support and coordinate the setting of benchmarks for EU human rights dialogue or consultation with actions of other donors and international organisations, with a special focus on the UN mechanisms in place (reports of the Special Rapporteurs, expert committees, the Secretary-General, the Human Rights Council, the High Commissioner for Human Rights, etc.); considers that, in their overall approach to raising human rights issues in the context of political dialogue, the Council and the Commission should systematically refer to the pledges made upon election by the Member States of the UN Human Rights Council;

24. Recommends that appropriate arrangements be put in place to enable indicators and objectives to be harmonised with other third countries and international bodies carrying on a human rights dialogue or consultation with the same given country or group of countries; recommends that such arrangements be modelled on the Berne Process, established by Switzerland for relations with China, and that, to that end, informal forums be set up in which to exchange information and good practice;

**B. Increasing the transparency of, and publicity given to, human rights dialogues and consultations**

25. Considers that the human rights dialogue and consultations should be conducted in a more transparent and coordinated way, and calls for appropriate means to be sought to achieve this aim without jeopardising the effectiveness of the dialogue and consultation;

26. Understands the need to respect a certain level of confidentiality in the dialogues and consultations and calls for a favourable response to the request to set up a system, in collaboration with Parliament, whereby selected Members of Parliament could be supplied with information about confidential activities connected with the human rights dialogue or consultation and related procedures; proposes once again that such a system be modelled on the criteria already established by the inter-institutional agreement of 20 November 2002 between the European Parliament and the Council concerning access by the European Parliament to sensitive information of the Council in the field of security and defence policy[(17)];

27. Calls on the Council to ensure that, before the EU sets the specific goals to be attained by entering into a dialogue or consultation with the country in question, or lays down the criteria for analysing the progress achieved in the light of the predetermined benchmarks, and the criteria regarding a possible exit strategy, consultations are first held with all interested parties, especially with Parliament and with NGOs;

28. Believes that specific objectives need to be laid down for each dialogue and consultation, using all the documents drawn up by the Council, the Member States, the Commission and Parliament, and reports from international and local human rights organisations, to identify the objectives of a human rights dialogue or consultation with a third country, and calls for the best courses of action to obtain concrete results to be analysed; believes that dialogues and consultations should be conducted in such a way as to ensure that those objectives are effectively met;

29. Maintains that dialogue and consultation objectives should be based on the principle that human rights are universal, indivisible and interdependent, and recommends that the criteria to be established should encompass not only civil and political rights but also economic, social, environmental and cultural rights;

30. Stresses the need to send a delegation of the EU Troika, comprising high-level experts, to a country under consideration with a view to the possible initiation of a human rights dialogue and consultation, to be followed by a presentation of the delegation's report to COHOM and to Parliament;

31. Calls on the Council to set clear criteria for the initiation, suspension or termination of a dialogue or consultation, to conduct an impact assessment before giving the reasons for its initiation or suspension (dealing with its expected period and the steps to be taken in order to restart the dialogue and consultation) and to make sure that the delegation of the country in question does not perceive the EU as viewing the dialogue or consultation as an end in itself that must be maintained at all costs;

32. Calls on the Council, in cases where a third country rejects the initiation or continuation of a human rights dialogue or consultation, to consider specific action with regard to human rights and democratisation, in particular through support to civil society;

33. Calls on the Council and the Commission to publish dialogue and consultation agendas sufficiently in advance for the benefit of all interested stakeholders, especially for Parliament and NGOs, so as to ensure that they are able to make a contribution;

34. Believes that, in the interests of effectiveness, the selection of dialogue and consultation topics on the agenda should be more clear-cut and substance-oriented, involving both sides in their formulation; reminds the Commission and the Council that the development of the dialogues and consultations is based on reciprocity and within the framework of mutual respect;

35. Urges the Council and the Commission to press third-country authorities to allow the participation of representatives of the ministries and other public institutions concerned by the topics selected for the agenda of the human rights dialogue or consultation;

36. Calls on the Council and the Commission, with the involvement of Parliament and NGOs, to draw up indicators for each given objective/benchmark; considers that such indicators must be realistic and aimed at achieving practical results that could be supported through other EU foreign policy tools; strongly believes that it is important to recognise that results of dialogues and consultations should be evaluated in the long term;

37. Takes note of the efforts made by the Council to harmonise key areas of concern regarding EU human rights dialogues and consultations so that those areas of concern may be used as a basis for setting up benchmarks to measure progress, with the aim of enhancing coherence and consistency between human rights dialogues and consultations and all instruments of EU human rights policy;

38. Calls on the Council and the Commission to publish the objectives and benchmarks laid down in the dialogues and consultations, in order to enable them to be analysed not just by the institutions organising the dialogue and consultation but also by actors – whether institutional or non-governmental – not taking part, thus ensuring that the EU can be made publicly accountable for the outcome of, and developments in, the dialogues and consultations;

39. Stresses the need to establish effective follow-up mechanisms to deal with the points raised in the dialogues and consultations and in the final recommendations; calls on the Council and the Commission to follow up the outcome of the dialogues and consultations by devising and implementing programmes and projects designed to improve the human rights situation on the ground;

40. Calls on the Council and the Commission to publish the conclusions of each dialogue and consultation, or at any rate a summary thereof if certain procedures have to be treated as confidential in the interests of effectiveness;

41. Believes that joint public communiqués, applying to both partners, should be issued after every round of dialogue or consultation in order to ensure that there is a greater impact and increased coherence;

42. Calls on the Council and the Commission to increase the transparency and visibility of, and thus to improve, the EU's communications in the field of human rights actions, and in this regard to broaden the scope of the information on COHOM's work that can be accessed via the European Union's website;

43. Calls on the Commission and the Council to ensure the active participation of civil society in the various phases involved in preparing, following up and assessing the human rights dialogues and consultations; supports, in this respect, the decision of the Council to involve human rights defenders in the preparation of dialogue and consultation meetings and to consult local human rights defenders and NGOs when establishing human rights priorities in the context of political dialogues and consultations; recommends that experts" seminars, an arrangement employed for structured dialogues and consultations, should likewise be organised for other forms and types of dialogue and consultation;

44. Calls on the Council and the Commission to promote cooperation by the human rights defenders of the country concerned by the human rights dialogue or consultations, in order to allow them a place and a voice in the procedure, in application of the Council guidelines and following the campaign to promote women who defend human rights;

45. Stresses that, in order to guarantee their freedom of expression, participating NGOs should not be chosen by the authorities of the country concerned;

46. Calls on the Commission to provide, within the framework of the EIDHR, for the financing of the costs of participants from civil society, including NGOs, in experts" seminars;

**C. Enhancing the role of the European Parliament**

47. Calls on the Council to conduct and forward to Parliament and its competent committee the human rights fact sheets regarding third countries, as well as bi-annual assessments of each dialogue and consultation; calls on the Council to clarify the evaluation by explaining how the benchmarks are to be applied, setting time limits for attaining them and placing the emphasis on trends rather than on isolated results; stresses that, should this information

include confidential material, it should be forwarded to Parliament in accordance with the system described in paragraph 26 of this resolution;

48. Calls on the Commission to forward to Parliament periodic assessments of the human rights situation in respect of third countries and regular information on the situation regarding political dialogues and consultations on human rights with third countries or regions, including their timetable and the points raised in the negotiations, and agrees that, if this information includes confidential material, it should be forwarded to Parliament in accordance with the system described in paragraph 26 of this resolution;

49. Calls on the Council and the Commission, as a matter of course whenever a round of dialogue or consultation has taken place, to hold a consultation session and a debriefing with Members of Parliament, and repeats its call for Parliament to be involved in decisions to continue or suspend a dialogue and consultation;

50. Points to the need for Parliament to be involved in the decision to start a new dialogue and consultation and to be provided with all the information required for that purpose; calls for its opinion to be taken into account as regards the mandate, objectives, format, procedures, etc. of the projected dialogue and consultation;

51. Urges the Council and the Commission to allow Members of Parliament to attend the experts" seminars held in connection with structured dialogues and consultations;

52. Calls on the Council and the Commission to use their influence to ensure that members of the national parliament of the third country concerned are involved in the official dialogue or consultation; believes that this would confer greater legitimacy on the dialogue or consultation as such and enable Members of Parliament to take part in it more readily;

53. Considers it essential to increase the role of interparliamentary assemblies and interparliamentary delegations in the human rights dialogues and consultations;

54. Recommends that Parliament's specific guidelines for human rights and democracy actions of MEPs in their visits to third countries be fully applied; accordingly calls for briefings to be held as a matter of routine with the members of the parliamentary delegations, standing and ad hoc, on the human rights dialogue and consultation being conducted with the third country in question, so as to reduce cases of interinstitutional incoherence and increase the impact of the negotiations; believes that Members of Parliament should be invited to take part in the visits on the ground organised in conjunction with certain official dialogues and consultations;

### D. Functioning of the various forms of human rights dialogues and consultations

*1. Structured dialogues*

– Structured dialogue with China

55. Emphasises the need to considerably strengthen and improve the EU-China human rights dialogue; stresses that China's human rights record remains a matter of serious concern;

56. Considers that the matters discussed in the successive rounds of dialogue with China, such as ratification of the United Nations International Covenant on Civil and Political Rights, reform of the criminal justice system, including the death penalty and the system of re-education through work, freedom of expression, particularly on the internet, freedom of the press, freedom of conscience, thought and religion, the situation of minorities in Tibet

and Xinjiang and in Mongolia, the release of detainees following the events in Tiananmen Square, and workers" and other rights, must continue to be raised in the context of the dialogue, in particular with regard to the application of the recommendations resulting from previous dialogues and seminars on legal affairs; to this end, calls on the Council to consider extending the time period of the dialogue and to allow more time for discussion of the issues raised;

57. Calls on China and the EU to increase the opportunities for two-way exchanges of information and strategies on the protection and promotion of human rights; considers that China is today facing an ever growing demand for democracy and human rights from among its own people, and stresses that slight progress has been made in some fields, although it is difficult to gauge precisely what impact the EU-China human rights dialogue has had on the changes that have taken place; emphasises the need to reframe the dialogue so as to make it more results-oriented and to focus on implementation of China's obligations under international law;

58. Stresses the need for the Council to identify and use specific indicators for each of the eight broader benchmarks in order to measure and assess progress;

59. Recommends that the human rights dialogue should not be treated as separate from the rest of Sino-European relations; to that end, urges the Commission to ensure that its trading relationship with China is linked to human rights reforms, and calls in this regard on the Council to carry out a comprehensive evaluation of the human rights situation before finalising any new partnership and cooperation framework agreement;

60. Deplores the fact that the experts" seminar that was to take place in Berlin on 10 May 2007 was postponed because the Chinese authorities did not agree to the participation of two independent NGOs invited by the EU; applauds the insistence of the Commission and the German Council Presidency that these representatives should be allowed to participate fully in the seminar, inasmuch as the representation of NGOs and other civil actors should be regarded as a valuable resource for all the parties involved in the dialogue;

– Structured dialogue with Iran

61. Is very concerned that the human rights dialogue with Iran has been interrupted since 2004 due to Iran's lack of cooperation; regrets that, according to the Council, no progress had been made and calls on the Council to report back to Parliament on the assessment of the human rights dialogue and the further steps that could be taken as regards the promotion of democracy and human rights in Iran;

62. Encourages the Commission to continue financing projects aimed at supporting good governance, including the protection of human rights defenders, reform of the judiciary and educational programmes for children and women; in the same spirit, calls on the Commission to implement all actions required within the framework of the EIDHR, so as to promote contacts and cooperation with Iranian civil society and to further support democracy and human rights, focusing mainly on the protection and promotion of women's and children's human rights;

*2. Consultations with Russia*

63. Notes the continuation of the EU human rights consultations with Russia; supports the Council in its aim of developing those consultations into a frank and genuine EU-Russia human rights dialogue, and calls for the involvement of Parliament and of European and

Russian NGOs in such a process; calls, with that end in view, for the NGOs to be consulted beforehand, while the consultations are still in preparation, so as to enable them to assess the progress achieved and to ascertain the practical results produced on the ground;

64. Calls on the Council and the Commission to request the participation in the consultations of Russian ministry officials whose fields of expertise are related to the topics on the agenda, to insist on the consultations being organised in Moscow and the regions, and to request the participation of their Russian counterparts in a public meeting with NGOs;

65. Deplores that fact that Russia, as a partner, at the end of the consultations, usually issues its own separate communiqué, and renews the call for the communiqués to be drawn up jointly by both delegations;

66. Calls on the Commission to improve communication with independent Russian civil society and to help boost its ability to act within the extremely narrow framework afforded by Russian law by involving the Russian regions and organising a rotation system for NGO participation;

67. Reiterates the need to integrate the consultations on human rights observance with the rest of the issues falling within the sphere of Russo-European relations; calls for the consultations to be integrated with the other political dialogues, negotiations and documents resulting from EU-Russia relations and stresses that the realisation of human rights in Russia has a crucial effect, especially in connection with the four "common spaces" for cooperation or under a future partnership and cooperation agreement; is convinced that a common space of freedom, security and justice cannot be built while human rights issues do not present an essential part of that work, including a consultation mechanism;

68. Urges the Council and the Commission to lay down concrete obligations and establish efficient mechanisms for monitoring and checking the fulfilment of the obligations Russia has taken on, in addition to the human rights clause, in order to achieve a real improvement in the worrisome human rights situation in Russia, such as that relating to freedom of association, freedom of speech and the freedom of the press and the media; urges that the recommendations and conclusions put forward by international and regional institutions, and NGOs' assessments regarding Russia's observance of the main international human rights agreements that it has signed, be followed;

*3. Dialogues based on an agreement*

– Dialogues based on the Cotonou Agreement

69. Stresses the need to systematically consider issues of human rights and democracy in the political dialogue pursuant to Article 8 of the Cotonou Agreement; points out, in this regard, the need to set up a clear and transparent mechanism and benchmarks for a political dialogue under Article 8; expresses its concern that, in the absence of such a mechanism, the risk of circumvention of Article 96, in the event of a special human rights emergency, is real;

70. Calls on the Council and the Commission to respect their commitments under Article 8 (on political dialogue), Article 9 (regarding human rights, democratic principles, the rule of law and good governance) and Articles 96 and 97 (on consultations) of the Cotonou Agreement; calls for the participation of civil society in the dialogues under Article 8, and for the informal involvement of civil society in the preparation of the consultations under Article 96, which should lead to an improvement as regards transparency and democratic control;

71. Calls on the Commission to present to Parliament and to the ACP-EU Joint Parliamentary Assembly a report defining a clear and transparent mechanism in order to enable the positive results and shortcomings of the political dialogue with ACP countries to be assessed;

72. Notes the positive results of the process of consultations under Article 96 of the Cotonou Agreement, which are due in part to its institutionalised and transparent nature, and also to its direct link with EU development aid, and notes that they are particularly evident when constructive steps, stemming from the dialogue, are taken to help the ACP countries comply with democratic standards and to respect human rights; repeats its call for this example to be likewise applied to the other dialogues;

– Dialogues with Central Asia

73. Welcomes the strengthening of political dialogue with the Central Asian countries: Kazakhstan, Kyrgyzstan, Tajikistan, Turkmenistan and Uzbekistan, and calls on the Commission to ensure that social and human rights issues do not take second place to the economic and financial interests of the countries of Central Asia and the European Union in the fields of energy, construction and commerce;

74. Welcomes the adoption of the draft EU-Central Asia strategy by the European Council in June 2007, which includes a strategy on human rights and democratisation that can be used as a framework for political dialogue;

75. Calls on the Council and the Commission to establish a comprehensive and coherent short- and medium-term approach towards the Central Asian region as a whole, but also towards individual countries separately, that includes the above mentioned strategy on human rights and democratisation;

76. Welcomes the Council's request to the authorities of Uzbekistan to institute a regular dialogue on human rights, and notes that a first round was held in Tashkent on 8 and 9 May 2007, and that two meetings of experts were held on the Andijan massacre; considers that the establishment of a regular dialogue should not in itself constitute sufficient justification for lifting the sanctions;

77. Calls for Parliament to be involved in the decision to initiate this dialogue, and for the other proposals contained in this resolution to be taken into account as this dialogue continues;

78. Calls on the Council to establish specific indicators directed towards attaining the objectives sought in the dialogue with Uzbekistan, paying particular attention to the situation of human rights defenders;

– Dialogues based on a partnership and cooperation agreement under the ENP

79. Calls on the Council and the Commission to take advantage of the present situation whereby Partnership and Cooperation Agreements with several neighbourhood countries have expired, and to negotiate new agreements, in order to mainstream human rights and effective dialogue on them into future agreements, including a follow-up mechanism;

80. Points out that the main purpose of the ENP is to establish a privileged relationship with the EU's eastern and southern neighbours on the basis of a mutual commitment to common values, principally in the fields of the rule of law, good governance and respect for human rights; believes that the EU dialogues could have a greater impact on reform in the ENP

neighbours, taking into account the existence of a human rights subcommittee and the outcome of the dialogue within that Subcommittee; points out that, in the case of non-democratic regimes or serious human rights violations, dialogue on human rights should be combined with a stronger reaction, such as public criticism and other appropriate measures;

81. Calls on the Commission to use clearer language and to introduce specific and measurable commitments made by the neighbourhood partners in the Action Plans and in the mandate of the human rights subcommittees, and underlines the need for the Council and the Commission to seek greater active participation by civil society, both in Europe and in the neighbourhood partner countries, in the production and monitoring of ENP Action Plans and in the application of the human rights and democracy clause; welcomes the possibility, under the EIDHR, of providing financial support to projects aimed at the monitoring of ENP Action Plans;

82. Requests the Commission to make greater efforts to set up human rights subcommittees for all ENP countries that do not have them, and to put into operation those that are not yet active in order to ensure an effective and sophisticated monitoring procedure as regards the implementation of the human rights and democracy objectives drawn up in the Action Plans;

83. Takes note of the fact that human rights issues have been examined within the Justice, Freedom and Security Subcommittees set up with Moldova and Ukraine; reiterates, none the less, the final objective, consisting in the establishment of stand-alone human rights subcommittees for all ENP countries, including those of the South Caucasus; draws attention to the continual deterioration of the human rights situation in Azerbaijan and therefore underlines the particular need to establish a human rights subcommittee as soon as possible with that country;

84. Calls on the Commission and the Council to ensure genuine cooperation among subcommittees on human rights and those involved in the field of justice and home affairs, all these issues being closely connected; calls, in this respect, for Parliament to be kept fully informed of the preparation and the follow-up process in this matter;

85. Calls on the Council and the Commission to consider the possibility of establishing a human rights dialogue or consultation mechanisms with Libya;

86. Calls on the Council, pending the signing of an association agreement, to consider the possibility of establishing a human rights dialogue mechanism with Syria;

87. Stresses the need to set up an institutionalised human rights subcommittee with Israel, replacing the current provisional mechanism;

88. Calls on the Council to inform and involve the Euro-Mediterranean Parliamentary Assembly and Parliament's Delegations to the Parliamentary Cooperation Committees existing between the EU and the countries of the eastern neighbourhood;

– Dialogues with Latin America

89. Calls on the Council and the Commission to consider introducing some form of specific mechanism to monitor the human rights clause in the EU's agreements with Latin America and Central America, for instance by supplementing human rights clauses with operational action plans (similar to ENP action plans) and by setting up human rights subcommittees, and stresses in this respect the need to fully inform the relevant Joint Committees and Joint

Councils of the outcome of these dialogues, so as to enhance the integration of human rights into the EU's political dialogues with countries in those regions;

90. Calls therefore on the Commission to make an annual evaluation of the human rights situation in the Latin American countries on the basis of the action plans and the human rights subcommittees to be set up;

91. Calls on the Council and the Commission to involve civil society in the conduct of the human rights dialogues, with adequate participation by the non-profit sector, and considers that the dialogue with Mexico needs to be enhanced and restructured and could provide a reference point for other Latin American countries;

92. Calls on the Commission and the Council to include human rights in the ongoing negotiations on the association agreements with the Andean Community, Central America and Mercosur, and to brief the EP on the progress made in this area;

93. Calls on the Council to inform the EU-Latin America Parliamentary Assembly of,, and to involve it in, the human rights dialogues and consultations;

– Dialogues based on trade and cooperation agreements

94. Points out that EU trade and cooperation agreements with third countries provide that implementation should be regularly monitored by joint committees; notes that specific joint committee working groups on human rights, good governance, the rule of law and administrative reform were set up in 2003, on an experimental basis, with Bangladesh, Vietnam and Laos;

95. Considers that these dialogues should be initiated by the Council on the basis of the same criteria and that their outcome should be discussed within the political dialogue so as to enhance the coherence and consistency of the EU's human rights policy with third countries; in this regard, calls on the Council and the Commission to debrief Parliament on the outcome of these dialogues;

96. Calls once again for the human rights and democracy clause to be extended to all new agreements between the EU and third countries, both industrialised and developing, including sectoral agreements such as those on fisheries, agriculture, textiles, trade and technical or financial aid, along the lines of what has been done with the ACP States;

*4. Ad hoc dialogues*

97. Calls on the Council, and especially the Troika, to apply the recommendations set out in this resolution to all ad hoc human rights dialogues, so as to ensure that they are conducted more transparently and more consistently with other EU external policies, and, before and after such dialogues take place, to provide information to the other institutions and to Parliament and NGOs in particular;

98. Calls on the Commission to apply the recommendations set out in this resolution to the dialogues established as part of the external dimension of the area of freedom, security and justice, and, in the interests of interinstitutional coherence, to keep the other institutions, especially the Parliament, and NGOs informed regarding developments in, and the substance and outcome of, those dialogues;

*5. Dialogues with like-minded countries (Canada, United States, Japan, New Zealand)*

99. Calls on the Council to apply the above proposals also to the Troika consultations with like-minded partners, and to augment transparency and coherence with other EU policies, and recommends that those consultations on human rights issues be used to seek synergies and share experiences, while addressing human rights concerns, with regard to like-minded countries;

100. Welcomes the recent moves to inform civil society of the agenda for these dialogues and requests the Council to adopt the same attitude vis-à-vis Parliament; calls for regular debriefings with Parliament on their substance and outcome to be established on a formal footing;

*6. Political dialogues with third countries in which a human rights component is to be incorporated*

101. Calls on the Council to apply the above proposals also to all political dialogues with third countries, especially as regards the agenda and content of the dialogue;

102. Calls on Parliament's departments to intensify internal coordination among parliamentary bodies by supplying updated information on the human rights situation in third countries, and to that end calls for Parliament's Human Rights Unit to be provided with more substantial financial and human resources in order to enable it to perform this task;

103. Requests the Council and the Commission to mainstream, in the agenda of human rights dialogues and consultations, the recommendations and conclusions contained in Parliament's resolutions, especially those concerning human rights, and the reports of European Parliament delegations;

Women's rights in the human rights dialogues and consultations

104. Insists that women's rights are an integral part of human rights and urges the Commission to include the promotion and protection of women's rights explicitly and systematically in all EU human rights dialogues and consultations on human rights with third countries; emphasises, in this regard, the need to set up a transparent mechanism specifically concerning women's rights for the monitoring of the human rights clause in the EU's external agreements and to take appropriate action should that clause be breached;

105. Draws attention to the importance of civil society, particularly NGOs working to promote women's rights, and recommends that it be fully involved in human rights dialogues between the EU and third countries;

106. Calls on the Council and the Commission to improve interaction between gender and civil society initiatives under the existing European human rights instruments and to encourage third countries to ensure the collaboration and coordination of the work of all human rights bodies and mechanisms;

107. Calls on the Commission to monitor systematically the ratification and implementation of the Convention on the Elimination of All Forms of Discrimination against Women (CEDAW) and the optional protocol thereto within the framework of the human rights dialogue with third countries and to report on this in regular briefings to its Committee on Women's Rights and Gender Equality; calls on the Commission and the Council to ensure that the rights guaranteed by the Convention are respected in those third countries, in order to close the gap between the existence of women's rights and the effective exercise of those rights;

108. Recommends that the Commission list gender-specific discrimination in accordance with the CEDAW and the Human Rights Pacts as production and process methods (PPMs), as defined in the framework of the World Trade Organization, in order to set up a database of products and brands that could eventually be banned from importation into the EU;

109. Insists that women's rights be explicitly addressed in the human rights dialogues, and in particular the combating and elimination of all forms of discrimination and violence against women and girls, including all forms of harmful traditional or customary practices, for example female genital mutilation and early or forced marriage, all forms of trafficking in human beings, domestic violence and feminicide, exploitation at work and economic exploitation;

110. Insists on the explicit inclusion of women's rights in, and a gender-based approach to, the fight against trafficking in human beings and particularly trafficking in women and children for sexual and labour exploitation and organ removal;

111. Stresses that specific measures should be taken to encourage more vigorous participation of women in the labour market, in economic and social affairs, political life and decision-making and in conflict prevention and resolution, peace-building and reconstruction; recommends the broad, gender-balanced participation of Members of Parliament in the evaluation of EC-funded human rights projects and greater involvement of the European Parliament in human rights dialogues with third countries;

112. Urges the Commission to provide training in order to educate Commission delegation personnel and officials, especially those involved in human rights and humanitarian relief activities, about the human rights of women;

113. Urges the Commission to put forward a proposal for a code of conduct for officials of the Community institutions and bodies, particularly while on EU missions to third countries, similar to the code of conduct issued by the UN; considers that the code should express clear disapproval of the purchase of sexual services, other forms of sexual exploitation and gender-based violence and should contain necessary sanctions in the event of misconduct, and that officials should be given detailed information on the content of the code of conduct before being sent on a mission;

114. Recommends the adoption of measures to enhance the physical security of women and girls in refugee camps and to safeguard and protect the human rights of displaced persons;

115. Calls on the Council and the Commission to ensure the implementation of the Beijing Declaration and Platform for Action; urges the Council and the Commission to encourage third countries to incorporate a gender perspective into national programmes of action and to integrate human rights and gender mainstreaming in national policies;

116. Urges the Commission to ensure, in its human rights dialogues with third countries, the development of a comprehensive human rights education programme to raise awareness among women of their human rights and to raise awareness generally of the human rights of women;

117. Urges the Council and the Commission to encourage third countries to incorporate the principle of equality of men and women into their legislation, to ensure, through law and other appropriate instruments, that this is achieved and to guarantee respect for these rights in all areas;

118. Instructs its President to forward this resolution to the Council (including its Secretary-General/High Representative for the Common Foreign and Security Policy, Mr Javier

Solana, and his Permanent representative for Human Rights, Ms Riina Kionka, and the members of COHOM) and the Commission (including the heads of its delegations to third countries), to the governments and parliaments of the Member States, and to the Co-Presidents of the ACP-EU Joint Parliamentary Assembly, the President of the Euro-Mediterranean Parliamentary Assembly and the Co-Presidents of the EU-Latin American Parliamentary Assembly, as well as to the Co-Presidents of the Parliamentary Cooperation Committees and of the Interparliamentary Delegations between the EU and the countries concerned.

(1) OJ C 290 E, 29.11.2006, p. 107.
(2) OJ C 131 E, 5.6.2003, p. 147.
(3) OJ L 386, 29.12.2006, p. 1.
(4) Texts adopted, P6_TA(2007)0178.
(5) Texts adopted, P6_TA(2007)0169.
(6) Texts adopted, P6_TA(2007)0007.
(7) OJ C 314 E, 21.12.2006, p. 379.
(8) OJ C 313 E, 20.12.2006, p. 466.
(9) OJ C 305 E, 14.12.2006, p. 219.
(10) OJ L 317, 15.12.2000, p. 3.
(11) OJ L 287, 28.10.2005, p. 1.
(12) OJ C 80, 1.4.2005, p. 17.
(13) Texts adopted, P6_TA(2007)0080.
(14) Texts adopted, P6_TA(2007)0079.
(15) OJ C 308 E, 16.12.2006, p. 182.
(16) OJ C 296 E, 6.12.2006, p. 123.
(17) OJ C 298, 30.11.2002, p. 1.

At least from the EU standpoint, the issue of human rights has frequently been linked with arms control. In late June 1989, following the Tian'anmen Square events, the European Council at its meeting in Madrid issued a Declaration on China, establishing an embargo on all exports of arms to China (see Document 4.17).

## Document 4.17: European Council Declaration on China, June 1989

THE EUROPEAN COUNCIL
MADRID
26–27 JUNE 1989

Documents in the dossier include:

*European Council: Madrid, 26 and 27 June*
Reproduced from the Bulletin of the European Communities, No. 6/1989

...

**1. European Council**

*Madrid, 26 and 27 June*

...

**Annex II**

...

**Political cooperation**

...

*Asia*

*1.1.21.* The European Council has expressed its deep concern over the situation in China and has approved the attached declaration (—point 1.1.24).

...

**Annex II**

*Declaration on China*

*1.1.24.* The European Council, recalling the Declaration of the Twelve of 6 June (—point 2.3.2), strongly condemns the brutal repression taking place in China. It expresses its dismay at the pursuit of executions in spite of all the appeals of the international community. It solemnly requests the Chinese authorities to stop the executions and to put an end to the repressive actions against those who legitimately claim their democratic rights.

The European Council requests the Chinese authorities to respect human rights and to take into account the hopes for freedom and democracy deeply felt by the population. It underlines that this is an essential element for the pursuit of the policy of reforms and openness that has been supported by the European Community and its Member States.

The Twelve are aware that the recent events have caused great anxiety in Hong Kong.

In the present circumstances, the European Council thinks it necessary to adopt the following measures:

(i) raising of the issue of human rights in China in the appropriate international forums; asking for the admittance of independent observers to attend the trials and to visit the prisons,

(ii) interruption by the Member States of the Community of military cooperation and an embargo on trade in arms with China,

(iii) suspension of bilateral ministerial and high-level contacts,

(iv) postponement by the Community and its Member States of new cooperation projects,

(v) reduction of programmes of cultural, scientific and technical cooperation to only those activities that might maintain a meaning in the present circumstances,

(vi) prolongation by the Member States of visas to the Chinese students who wish it.

Taking into account the climate of uncertainty created in the economic field by the present policy of the Chinese authorities, the European Council advocates the postponement of the examination of new requests for credit insurance and the postponement of the examination of new credits of the World Bank.

...

Subsequently, after intensive lobbying by European NGOs, the EU on 8 June 1998 adopted a Code of Conduct on Arms Exports (see Document 4.18). The Code of Conduct, which is not legally binding, sets down criteria which should be met by any proposal for export of arms to China.[18] The criteria were

1. respect for the international commitments of the EU Member States, such as respect of UN Security Council or Community sanctions;
2. respect of human rights in the country of final destination of the exported arms;
3. the internal situation in the country of destination, notably the existence of tensions or armed conflicts;
4. preservation of regional peace, security and stability;
5. the national security of the EU Member States and of territories whose external relations are the responsibility of a Member State as well as that of friendly and allied countries;
6. the behaviour of the buyer country with regard to the international community, notably its attitude to terrorism, the nature of its alliances and respect for international law;
7. the existence of a risk that the equipment will be diverted within the buyer country or re-exported under undesirable conditions; and
8. the compatibility of the arms exports with the technical and economic capacity of the recipient country, taking into account the desirability that states should achieve their legitimate needs of security and defence with the least diversion for armaments of human and economic resources.

EU Member States were to assess applications for licenses to export arms against these criteria.

The Code includes a notification and consultation mechanism to increase transparency while seeking to discourage Member States from undercutting its provisions.[19] EU Member States are required to submit annual reports on their use of the Code, and the EU itself produces an annual review of the operation of the Code.[20] As these

[18] On equipment covered by the Code, see Common Military List of the European Union (equipment covered by the European Union Code of Conduct on Arms Exports) (updating and replacing the Common Military List of the European Union adopted by the Council on 25 April 2005) (Act adopted pursuant to Title V of the Treaty on European Union, 2006/C66/01), [2006] OJ C66/1.

[19] For further details, see Council of the European Union, *The Users Guide to the EU Code of Conduct on Arms Exports*, PESC 748, COARM 40 (10684/07) (Brussels, 12 June 2007), available at http://register.consilium.europa.eu/pdf/en/07/st10/st10684.en07.pdf (last accessed 16 September 2007). See also Council Common Position 2003/468/CFSP of 23 June 2003 on the control of arms brokering (Act adopted pursuant to Title V of the Treaty on European Union), [2003] OJ L156/79. The Council Secretariat in Brussels has a central database for all Member State denials of licenses to export arms.

[20] All annual reports since the first one in 1999 are available on the website of the Stockholm International Peace Research Institute (SIPRI), at http://www.sipri.org/contents/expcon/annrep.html (last accessed 16 September 2007). All reports are published in the Official Journal of the European Union. For the eighth and most recent report, see 'Eighth Annual Report According to Operative Provision 8 of the European Union Code of Conduct on Arms Exports', [2006] OJ C250, 1. See also the European Parliament resolutions. Among the most recent are 'European Parliament Resolution on the Council's Sixth Annual Report according to Operative Provision 8 of the European Union Code of Conduct on Arms Exports', 2005/2013(INI) (P6_TA(2005)0436), available at http://www.europarl.europa.eu/sides/getDoc-do?pubRef=//EP//NONSGML+TA+PG-TA-2005–0436+0+DOC+WORD+VO//EN (accessed 27 September 2007); and 'European Parliament Resolution on the Council's Seventh and Eighth Annual Reports According to Operative Provision B of the EU Code of Conduct on Arms Exports', available at http://europa.eu/bulletin/en/200701/p127018.htm (accessed 30 October 2007).

reviews indicate, the Code of Conduct has stimulated the harmonisation of the laws of the EU Member States and led to a change in national policies. It is questionable, however, whether it has been very successful in achieving its stated objectives.[21] The EU remains a major player in the global arms trade.[22]

### Document 4.18: EU Code of Conduct for Arms Exports

#### SANCTION REGIMES, ARMS EMBARGOES AND RESTRICTIONS ON THE EXPORT OF STRATEGIC GOODS

**EU Code of Conduct on Arms Exports**

The Council of the European Union,

BUILDING on the Common Criteria agreed at the Luxembourg and Lisbon European Councils in 1991 and 1992,

RECOGNISING the special responsibility of arms exporting states,

DETERMINED to set high common standards which should be regarded as the minimum for the management of, and restraint in, conventional arms transfers by all EU Member States, and to strengthen the exchange of relevant information with a view to achieving greater transparency,

DETERMINED to prevent the export of equipment which might be used for internal repression or international aggression, or contribute to regional instability,

WISHING within the framework of the CFSP to reinforce their cooperation and to promote their convergence in the field of conventional arms exports,

NOTING complementary measures taken by the EU against illicit transfers, in the form of the EU Programme for Preventing and Combating Illicit Trafficking in Conventional Arms,

ACKNOWLEDGING the wish of EU Member States to maintain a defence industry as part of their industrial base as well as their defence effort,

21 See Amnesty International, *Undermining Global Security: The European Union's Arms Exports* (London, Amnesty International, 2004).

22 The export of dual-use goods is a sensitive issue. The current EC legislation is Council Regulation (EC) No 394/2006 amending and updating Regulation (EC) No 1334/2000 setting up a Community regime for the control of exports of dual-use items and technology, [2006] OJ L74/13. For a general discussion from the EU perspective, see http://ec.europa.eu/trade/issues/sectoral/industry/dualuse/index_en.htm (accessed 26 September 2007). For further background, see Commission of the European Communities, 'Communication from the Commission on the Review of the EC Regime of Controls of Exports of Dual-use Goods and Technology', COM(2006)828 final [SEC(2006)1826] (Brussels, 18 December 2006); the Commission proposal for reform of the current legislation in Council of the European Union, 'Proposal for a Council Regulation Amending and Updating Regulation (EC) 1334/2000 Setting Up a Community Regime for the Control of Exports of Dual-use Goods and Technology', Interinstitutional file 2007/0157 (ACC), 12005/07 [COMER 130, PESC 926, CONOP 61, ECO 106, UD 83, ATO 101] (Brussels, 19 July 2007). On the broader framework, see the Wassenaar Arrangement on Export Controls on Conventional Arms and Dual-use Goods and Technologies, Guidelines & Procedures, including the Initial Elements (as amended and updated in December 2003 and July 2004) (WA Secretariat, Vienna, 2004); the list of restricted technologies can be found at http://jya.com/wa/watoc.htm. See also 'A Secure Europe in a Better World: European Security Strategy', document proposed by Javier Solana and adopted by the Heads of State and Government at the European Council in Brussels on 12 December 2003 (The European Institute for Security Studies, Paris, 2003).

RECOGNISING that states have a right to transfer the means of self-defence, consistent with the right of self-defence recognised by the UN Charter,

Have adopted the following Code of Conduct and operative provisions:

*CRITERION ONE*

Respect for the international commitments of EU member states, in particular the sanctions decreed by the UN Security Council and those decreed by the Community, agreements on non-proliferation and other subjects, as well as other international obligations.

An export licence should be refused if approval would be inconsistent with, inter alia:

a) the international obligations of member states and their commitments to enforce UN, OSCE and EU arms embargoes;

b) the international obligations of member states under the Nuclear Non-Proliferation Treaty, the Biological and Toxin Weapons Convention and the Chemical Weapons Convention;

c) their commitments in the frameworks of the Australia Group, the Missile Technology Control Regime, the Nuclear Suppliers Group and the Wassenaar Arrangement;

d) their commitment not to export any form of anti-personnel landmine.

*CRITERION TWO*

The respect for human rights in the country of final destination

Having assessed the recipient country's attitude towards relevant principles established by international human rights instruments, Member States will:

a) not issue an export licence if there is a clear risk that the proposed export might be used for internal repression.

b) exercise special caution and vigilance in issuing licences, on a case-by-case basis and taking account of the nature of the equipment, to countries where serious violations of human rights have been established by the competent bodies of the UN, the Council of Europe or by the EU;

For these purposes, equipment which might be used for internal repression will include, inter alia, equipment where there is evidence of the use of this or similar equipment for internal repression by the proposed end-user, or where there is reason to believe that the equipment will be diverted from it stated end-use or end-user and used for internal repression. In line with operative paragraph 1 of this Code, the nature of the equipment will be considered carefully, particularly if it is intended for internal security purposes. Internal repression includes, inter alia, torture and other crue, inhuman and degrading treatment or punishment, summary or arbitrary executions, disappearances, arbitrary detentions and other major violations of human rights and fundamental freedoms as set out in relevant international human rights instruments, including the Universal Declaration on Human Rights and the International Covenant on Civil and Political Rights.

*CRITERION THREE*

The internal situation in the country of final destination, as a function of the existence of tensions or armed conflicts

Member States will not allow exports which would provoke or prolong armed conflicts or aggravate existing tensions or conflicts in the country of final destination.

*CRITERION FOUR*

Preservation of regional peace, security and stability

Member States will not issue an export licence if there is a clear risk that the intended recipient would use the proposed export aggressively against another country or to assert by force a territorial claim.

When considering these risks, EU Member States will take into account inter alia:

a) the existence or likelihood of armed conflict between the recipient and another country;

b) a claim against the territory of a neighbouring country which the recipient has in the past tried or threatened to pursue by means of force;

c) whether the equipment would be likely to be used other than for the legitimate national security and defence of the recipient;

d) the need not to affect adversely regional stability in any significant way.

*CRITERION FIVE*

The national security of the member states and of territories whose external relations are the responsibility of a Member State, as well as that of friendly and allied countries

Member States will take into account:

a) the potential effect of the proposed export on their defence and security interests and those of friends, allies and other member states, while recognising that this factor cannot affect consideration of the criteria on respect of human rights and on regional peace, security and stability;

b) the risk of use of the goods concerned against their forces or those of friends, allies or other member states;

c) the risk of reverse engineering or unintended technology transfer.

*CRITERION SIX*

The behaviour of the buyer country with regard to the international community, as regards in particular to its attitude to terrorism, the nature of its alliances and respect for international law

Member States will take into account inter alia the record of the buyer country with regard to:

a) its support or encouragement of terrorism and international organised crime;

b) its compliance with its international commitments, in particular on the non-use of force, including under international humanitarian law applicable to international and non-international conflicts;

c) its commitments to non-proliferation and other areas of arms control and disarmament, in particular the signature, ratification and implementation of relevant arms control and disarmament conventions referred to in sub-para b) of Criterion One.

*CRITERION SEVEN*

The existence of a risk that the equipment will be diverted within the buyer country or re-exported under undesirable conditions.

In assessing the impact of the proposed export on the importing country and the risk that exported goods might be diverted to an undesirable end-user, the following will be considered:

a) the legitimate defence and domestic security interests of the recipient country, including any involvement in UN or other peace-keeping activity;

b) the technical capability of the recipient country to use the equipment;

c) the capability of the recipient country to exert effective export controls;

d) the risk of the arms being re-exported or diverted to terrorist organisations (anti-terrorist equipment would need particularly careful consideration in this context).

*CRITERION EIGHT*

The compatibility of the arms exports with the technical and economic capacity of the recipient country, taking into account the desirability that states should achieve their legitimate needs of security and defence with the least diversion for armaments of human and economic resources.

Member States will take into account, in the light of information from relevant sources such as UNDP, World Bank, IMF and OECD reports, whether the proposed export would seriously hamper the sustainable development of the recipient country. They will consider in this context the recipient country's relative levels of military and social expenditure, taking into account also any EU or bilateral aid.

**OPERATIVE PROVISIONS**

1. Each EU Member State will assess export licence applications for military equipment made to it on a case-by-case basis against the provisions of the Code of Conduct.

2. This Code will not infringe on the right of the Member States to operate more restrictive national policies.

3. EU Member States will circulate through diplomatic channels details of licences refused in accordance with the Code of Conduct for military equipment together with an explanation of why the licence has been refused. The details to be notified are set out in the form of a draft pro-forma at Annex A. Before any Member State grants a licence which has been denied by another Member State or States for an essentially identical transaction within the last three years, it will first consult the member State or States which issued the denial(s). If

following consultations, the Member States nevertheless decides to grant a licence, it will notify the Member State or States issuing the denial(s), giving a detailed explanation of its reasoning.

The decision to transfer or deny the transfer of any item of military equipment will remain at the national discretion of each Member State. A denial of a licence is understood to take place when the member state has refused to authorise the actual sale or physical export of the item of military equipment concerned, where a sale would otherwise have come about, or the conclusion of the relevant contract. For these purposes, a notifiable denial may, in accordance with national procedures, include denial of permission to start negotiations or a negative response to a formal initial enquiry about a specific order.

4. EU Member States will keep such denials and consultations confidential and not to use them for commercial advantage.

5. EU Member States will work for the early adoption of a common list of military equipment covered by the Code, based on similar national and international lists. Until then, the Code will operate on the basis of national control lists incorporating where appropriate elements from relevant international lists.

6. The criteria in this Code and the consultations procedure provided for by paragraph 3 of the operative provisions will also apply to dual-use goods as specified in Annex 1 of Council Decision 94/942/CFSP as amended, where there are grounds for believing that the end-user of such goods will be the armed forces or internal security forces or similar entities in the recipient country.

7. In order to maximise the efficiency of this Code, EU Member States will work within the framework of the CFSP to reinforce their cooperation and to promote their convergence in the field of conventional arms exports.

8. Each EU Member State will circulate to other EU Partners in confidence an annual report on its defence exports and on its implementation of the Code. These reports will be discussed at an annual meeting held within the framework of the CFSP. The meeting will also review the operation of the Code, identify any improvements which need to be made and submit to the Council a consolidated report, based on contributions from Member States.

9. EU Member states will, as appropriate, assess jointly through the CFSP framework the situation of potential or actual recipients of arms exports from EU Member States, in the light of the principles and criteria of the Code of Conduct.

10. It is recognised that Member States, where appropriate, may also take into account the effect of proposed exports on their economic, social, commercial and industrial interests, but that these factors will not affect the application of the above criteria.

11. EU Member States will use their best endeavours to encourage other arms exporting states to subscribe to the principles of this Code of Conduct.

12. This Code of Conduct and the operative provisions will replace any previous elaboration of the 1991 and 1992 Common Criteria.

**ANNEX A**

........(name of Member State) has the honour to inform partners of the following denial under the EU Code of Conduct:

Destination country:........

Short description of equipment, including quantity and where appropriate, technical specifications:........

Proposed consignee:........

Proposed end-user (if different):........

Reason for refusal:........

Date of denial:........

The lifting of the arms embargo, proposed by France and Germany, provoked considerable controversy among EU Member States, as well as a strong reaction from the USA.[23] The 2004 Rueda Report for the European Parliament (see Document 4.19) proposed that the arms embargo be lifted in conjunction with the adoption of a legally binding set of rules, replacing the Code of Conduct, with the aim of permitting but controlling arms exports to China.[24] The Council has prepared a Draft Common Position to update the Code of Conduct but this has not yet been adopted.[25] As noted in Chapter 5, the EU and China adopted a Joint Declaration on non-proliferation and arms control in December 2004.

**Document 4.19: The Rueda Report on Arms Exports**

European Parliament Report on the Council's Fifth Annual Report according to Operative Provision 8 of the European Union Code of Conduct on Arms Exports (2004/2103(INI))
Committee on Foreign Affairs
Rapporteur: Raül Romeva Rueda

Motion for a European Parliament Resolution on the Council's Fifth Annual Report according to Operative Provision 8 of the European Union Code of Conduct on Arms Exports (2004/2103(INI))

The European Parliament,

—having regard to the Council's Fifth Annual Report according to Operative Provision 8 of the European Union Code of Conduct on Arms Exports[1],
—having regard to the User's Guide to the European Union Code of Conduct on Arms Exports, as agreed at the Working Party on Conventional Arms Exports on 28 October 2003 (14283/03),

[23] See, eg US Department of State, 'United States Summarises EU Arms Embargo against China', fact sheet, released 17 November 2004, http://usinfo.state.gov/is/Archive/2004/Nov/18–661185.html (accessed 25 November 2004).

[24] See European Parliament, Committee on Foreign Affairs, 'Report on the Council's Fifth Annual Report According to Operative Provision 8 of the European Union Code of Conduct on Arms Exports', 2004/2103(INI) (Rapporteur: Raül Romeva Rueda), European Parliament Session Document, Final A6-0022/2004 (19 October 2004); see also The Rt Hon C Patten, External Relations Commissioner, 'Lifting of the Arms Embargo on China: The Rueda Report on Arms Exports', speech at the European Parliament, Strasbourg (16 November 2004), available at http://europa.eu.int/comm/external_relations/news/patten/sp04_483.htm (accessed 8 February 2005).

[25] See World Security Institute (Brussels), 'EU Arms Exports /Code of Conduct' (19 March 2007), available at http://wsibrussels.org/showarticle.cfm?id=201 (accessed 21 November 2007).

—having regard to the Council Common Position 2003/468/CFSP of 23 June 2003 on the control of arms brokering[2],

—having regard to the European Security Strategy, adopted by the Council on 12 December 2003,

—having regard to the EU Strategy against Proliferation of Weapons of Mass Destruction, adopted by the Council on 12 December 2003 and which aims inter alia to strengthen export control policy and practices,

—having regard to Article 17 of the EU Treaty and Article 296 of the EC Treaty,

—having regard to its resolution of 25 September 2003[3] on the Council's Fourth Annual Report according to Operative Provision 8 of the European Union Code of Conduct on Arms Exports[4],

—having regard to its resolution of 20 November 2003 on the communication from the Commission to the Council, the European Parliament, the European Economic and Social Committee and the Committee of the Regions - European Defence - Industrial and Market Issues - Towards an EU Defence Equipment Policy[5],

—having regard to its resolution of 22 April 2004 on human rights in the world in 2003 and the European Union's policy on the matter[6],

—having regard to its resolution of 18 December 2003[7] on the removal of the EU embargo on arms sales to China,

—having regard to its previous resolutions of 6 July 2000 on the abduction of children by the Lord's Resistance Army (LRA)[8] and of 3 July 2003 on trafficking in children and child soldiers[9],

—having regard to Rule 45 of its Rules of Procedure,

—having regard to the report of the Committee on Foreign Affairs and the opinion of the Committee on International Trade (A6-0022/2004),

A. whereas, specifically against the background of a post Cold War security climate characterised by a high level of regional instability, failing States, non-state players using child soldiers, terrorist networks and organised crime, observance of stringent controls on arms exports is of the highest importance,

B. whereas the Council has identified some of these characteristics of a post Cold War security climate as amongst the key threats in the above-mentioned European Security Strategy,

C. whereas organised crime and international arms smugglers have expanded their illegal activities in the area of small arms, the free and uncontrolled availability of which has been a major factor in the increase in the number of conflicts, and are trafficking weapons along routes which pass through the territory of the enlarged EU, and also through the new neighbouring countries of the enlarged EU and countries in the western Balkan region,

D. whereas around half a million people die every year as a result of violence related to light arms, both in armed conflicts and in connection with criminal activity,

E. whereas the last decade has seen a marked increase in the use of private security or military companies, which calls for the introduction of legislation to control and monitor the activities of private providers of military, police and security services,

F. whereas the EU should fulfil its increased responsibility with regard to peace and security in Europe and throughout the world by means of further arms limitation and disarmament initiatives,

G. whereas maximum transparency in this field, including the production of comprehensive Annual Reports, is an essential prerequisite for democratic accountability as the best guarantee of peace and stability,

H. whereas the User's Guide to the European Union Code of Conduct on Arms Exports is an important step forward in clarifying the denial notification and consultation provisions of the Code and in helping to prevent diverging interpretations in different Member States,

I. whereas the Council Common Position on the control of arms brokering presents a first step in the control of illegal arms brokering but a number of weaknesses still need to be corrected in order for its effectiveness not to be undermined,

J. whereas despite the progress made, it appears that EU weapons, their components, EU licences to produce arms overseas, private EU military and security services, EU military personnel, expertise and training and equipment for capital punishment, torture and other cruel, inhuman and degrading treatment continue to be supplied to regions of the world in which the standards laid down by the Code of Conduct are undoubtedly being flouted,

K. whereas, in order to combat illegal arms trading and effectively prevent the supply of arms to inappropriate end-users, it is essential that arms shipments, end-users of arms exports, other military and security equipment, licensed production and arms brokering should be subject to more effective controls,

L. whereas, specifically in the context of the development of a European armaments industry and a common security and defence policy, there needs to be greater harmonisation of EU arms export control policy,

M. whereas its above-mentioned resolution of 20 November 2003 emphasises that the internal opening-up of military markets should be accompanied by stringent export controls at the external borders of the EU,

N. whereas the EU's share of the international arms trade in general and of exports of small and light weapons in particular has increased with the accession of ten new Member States on 1 May 2004, some of which have significant arms production and exporting activities; whereas some of the new Member States still lack sufficient capacity to meet the existing obligations of the Code immediately and would therefore need assistance to implement them,

O. whereas approximately 80 percent of EU arms exports between 1999 and 2003 went to countries outside Europe,

P. whereas the adoption of the Code of Conduct by the ten new Member States has increased the number of arms exports subject to the Code of Conduct,

Q. whereas, in the context of the further enlargement of the EU, it is particularly important that the candidate countries Croatia, Bulgaria, Romania and Turkey also prepare annual reports on their arms export policy, improve controls on their arms exports and ensure that fundamental standards relating thereto are observed; convinced that the Member States should not only actively support this process, but should also set a positive example with regard to strict observance of the Code of Conduct and production of comprehensive Annual Reports on their arms exporting activities,

R. convinced that further harmonisation of Member States' arms export policy would represent an important contribution to the development of the ESDP and would also contribute to a strengthened common foreign policy approach by the Member States,

S. convinced that the EU's arms export control policy must be such as to ensure coherence in terms of the Community's external policy action, including its goals in the areas of crisis prevention, combating of poverty, strengthening of democracy and promotion of human rights,

T. convinced that only an international arms trade regime centring on an international Arms Trade Treaty based on States' existing responsibilities under international law would be truly effective within a global context,

1. Considers that, in the fight against international terrorism and in the interest of conflict prevention and regional stabilisation and respect for human rights, a clear and efficient common arms export control policy is very decisive;

2. Welcomes, therefore, the progress referred to in the Fifth Annual Report on the implementation of the Code of Conduct, and in particular the continuation of the compendium of Member States' agreed practices published in Annex I and the table in Annex II containing data on the number and value of export licences issued and the value of arms exports;

3. Welcomes in particular the improvements in the information provided by both old and new Member States in regard to their respective arms exports; but is, nevertheless, concerned about the value of the data provided in some instances;

4. Considers that the provision of timely, complete and compatible data by all Member States is essential to ensure the transparency of the data provided;

5. Is delighted that the process of harmonising reporting procedures has been continued and that further steps have been taken towards achieving fully comparable statistics between EU Member States;

6. Wishes, therefore, despite the progress made in achieving greater harmonisation of statistical data, to see that each Member State provides data on the type and quantity of arms supplied and on the total value of exports and the number of licences refused, stating the reasons for refusal, and more precise information on the country of destination and classification of end-users, in order, on the basis of such fuller and more harmonised data, to improve transparency;

7. Welcomes in this regard the establishment of a central database of denial notifications at the Council Secretariat in Brussels and stresses its usefulness, since it will immediately give all Member States a source of information enabling them to investigate specific denials; calls for the expansion, in due course, of this database to include information on consultations under the Code of Conduct as well as on end-users who are known or suspected to have engaged in the re-export, diversion or misuse of arms and other controlled goods;

8. Wishes, furthermore, that information be included in the national arms exports reports on informal denials of arms exports before an official application for obtaining a licence;

9. Stresses the usefulness of this central database of denial notifications, since it will immediately give all Member States a source of information enabling them to investigate specific denials;

10. Welcomes the new and updated version of the EU Common Military List and its publication in the Official Journal; calls on Member States to make their reporting on "dual-use" exports more detailed and transparent because they have been frequently used for human rights abuses;

11. Considers that the wording of the Code of Conduct is leading to diverging interpretations by different Member States and welcomes, therefore, the User's Guide to the Code, which defines and clarifies the operative provisions of the Code; calls on Member States to amend the export criteria to improve their clarity and comprehensiveness and to ensure they fully reflect States' existing responsibilities under international law;

12. Welcomes the fact that a survey on how to apply criterion 8 (compatibility of arms exports with the technical and economic capacity of the recipient country) was initiated, representing a significant contribution to crisis prevention and sustainable development in socially less developed countries, whilst urging Member States to repeat the exercise with regard to the application of the remaining seven criteria;

13. Considers uniform EU rules on controls on arms brokering activities to be essential, and despite the welcome EU Common Position on arms brokering of 2003 there is still a lack of operative provisions for Member States to specifically control arms brokering, arms transporting and arms financing activities by EU nationals and residents when such activities, and the related arms deliveries, take place through "third countries";

14. Welcomes in particular the efforts of Austria, Belgium, Finland, France, Germany, the Netherlands, Sweden and the UK to control the brokering of conventional arms, and calls on the other Member States to speed up national processes for the implementation of the brokering controls provided for in the Council Common Position on the control of arms brokering;

15. Reiterates its view that a compulsory register and authorisation system should be introduced for the brokering of arms transactions, which should also apply to EU citizens and companies outside the territory of the EU in the same way as US legislation;

16. Calls on Member States to include arms transporting and arms financing services into their arms brokering legislation;

17. Calls on Member States to prohibit the brokering of equipment for capital punishment, torture and other cruel, inhuman and degrading treatment; and to criminalise violations, wherever committed, by EU nationals and EU-registered brokers and companies of the UN, EU or OSCE arms embargoes, as well as the national arms embargoes of the relevant EU Member State;

18. Welcomes the fact that the "indication of the end-use of the goods" was included in the minimum details to be set out in an end-user certificate; at the same time calling for the inclusion of a non-misuse clause, declaring that the material will not be used for proscribed uses; reiterates, however, its demand to set up a transfer verification and post-export monitoring system that should include systematic physical inspections at points of transfer and of stockpiles by the competent national authorities, with the possibility of imposing penalties;

19. Calls, therefore, again on Member States to examine the possibility of setting up a common monitoring system at EU level, and recommends that consideration be given to a European arms export control agency model;

20. Calls on the Council and the Member States to maintain the EU embargo on trade in arms with the People's Republic of China and not to weaken the existing national limitations on such arms sales;

21. Calls on the candidate countries - Croatia, Bulgaria, Romania and Turkey - to tighten their national legislation and above all their practices in the areas of arms exports on the basis of the Code, and to report on this practice in accordance with Annexes I and II to the Fifth Annual Report, calls on the Commission to follow the progress closely in the accession negotiation process and calls on all current Member States to compile and publish national annual reports for the calendar year 2004, and for each year thereafter;

22. Considers that the new neighbours of the enlarged EU and countries with which the EU has concluded, or intends to conclude, a stabilisation and association agreement should also be asked to observe the Code of Conduct; particular attention should be paid to Kaliningrad which has in the past served as a transit point for shipments of military equipment and arms from other parts of Russia for illicit end-users; calls on the Council and Commission to prioritise in their cooperation with the Russian Federation measures to combat illicit trafficking, including regular information exchange on export and transit controls and licences;

23. Calls upon Member States to provide in a co-ordinated way sufficient assistance to all states that do not have the necessary means to properly implement the Code of Conduct;

24. Welcomes in this regard the fact that the governments of Poland and Sweden initiated five informal COARM meetings between old and new Member States on arms exports controls, with the recommendation that this system of COARM meetings be maintained and also that it be made more representative and regular, and welcomes the efforts of the government of the Netherlands to introduce candidate countries and other interested states to the practical application of the Code of Conduct;

25. Reiterates its call for legally binding provisions and full harmonisation of Member States' arms export control policy as a short-term goal, and urges Member States to make progress in this direction, penalising any violation by enterprises registered in the EU of the arms embargoes of the UN, the EU, the OSCE or any Member State;

26. Recommends that, in the interim period, the following steps be taken

    (a) full pre-consultation between the Member States with regard to transfers to regions susceptible to crises, together with the development of an EU checklist of "red flag" early warning indicators to indicate when there are serious concerns with regard to a particular end-user which could impact upon the licensing of arms exports;

    (b) a full multilateral approach to the consultation process in connection with decisions to grant or refuse licences, with, as a first step, a commitment by Member States to circulate to all other Member States the substance and result of any consultation to which they are party, particularly in the case of undercutting;

(c) incorporation into national law of all the principles, criteria and operative provisions of the Code of Conduct, on the understanding that this does not affect the right of Member States to operate more restrictive national policies;

(d) all future EU embargoes to refer to those categories of equipment on the Common Military List or in the Annexes to the Dual-Use Regulation to which an embargo is to apply;

27. Calls, with regard to the establishment of a common European armaments market, for controls on the movement of armaments within the European Union to be removed step by step, in the context of a common EU arms export control policy through, for example, the agreement on a no-undercutting rule under the EU Code of Conduct;

28. Strongly supports the proposal for a Council Trade Regulation imposing an export ban on all equipment for the death penalty, for torture or any other degrading or inhuman treatment, prohibiting specific arms such as anti-personnel mines and laying down strict controls for equipment that might be used for internal repression;

29. Calls, with regard to export controls in relation to third countries, for particular attention to be paid to products which may be used for both civilian and military purposes such as surveillance technology and similarly to spare parts and products suitable for use in cyber warfare or for non-lethal human rights abuses;

30. Shares the concerns of COARM on the desirability of permitting the export of regulated goods for humanitarian ends in circumstances where an export permit would otherwise be refused; accepts that in conflict regions certain types of regulated goods may contribute to the security and welfare of the civilian population, but stresses that this must be investigated very strictly on a case by case basis, with the Member States being given sufficient guarantees against abuses;

31. Calls upon Member States to acknowledge that the Code also applies to the licensing of items intended for incorporation by the importing country into a sub-assembly or finished weapons system for subsequent export to a third country;

32. Calls upon Member States to approve legislation requiring the licensing of the production of EU licensed arms (or their components) in third countries;

33. Calls upon Member States to acknowledge that the Code of Conduct also applies to all forms of "government to government" transfers, in particular to the transfer of surplus arms; reiterates that the export or transfer of surplus arms to countries where they will be used for human rights violations, breaches of international humanitarian law or other violations of international law is in violation of the Code;

34. Calls upon Member States to acknowledge that the Code of Conduct also applies to the transfer of military, security and police personnel, expertise and training and to private military and security services;

35. Calls upon Member States to agree on a list of countries involved in armed conflicts to which arms exports should be banned in principle, drawing upon the reports and recommendations of the UN Security Council monitoring mechanisms on arms embargoes;

36. Stresses the importance of research aimed at guaranteeing legal supervision and controls on the electronic transfer of knowledge, software and technology having a

potential link to goods on the Community list of goods for which an export licence is required;

37. Calls on non-EU arms-exporting countries, too, to give their support to the principle and criteria of the Code of Conduct, so that through the Code a genuine contribution can be made to world arms export control, conflict prevention and the promotion of peace in the world;

38. Considers that the effective global control of arms exports can only be achieved by an international arms trade control regime and calls, therefore, upon Member States to promote stringent international rules on arms exports in view of the 2006 UN Review Conference on Small Arms and to work towards a legally binding, international Arms Trade Treaty, including measures for the conversion and restructuring of enterprises producing military goods;

39. Calls on the Council and the Member States to strictly monitor compliance with end user certificates, and in particular with notifications concerning the country of final destination, the ban on re-export and the declaration that the goods will not be used for purposes other than the stated use;

40. Calls for the introduction in the EU of a special tax on the arms trade, and for the EU to carry on active diplomacy with a view to such a tax being levied worldwide, as is being suggested by the United Nations General Assembly as well as by the Presidents of Brazil, Chile and France, and by the Spanish Head of Government, with the revenue from these taxes being paid into funds for victims of armed conflicts in particular and poverty alleviation more generally;

41. Calls on the governments of Member States to conduct a thorough review of the Code of Conduct, taking into account the demands and recommendations mentioned above and consulting relevant parties such as parliaments and non-governmental organisations;

42. Instructs its President to forward this resolution to the Council and Commission, and to the parliaments and governments of the Member States and of third countries which have agreed to observe the principles of the Code of Conduct.

EXPLANATORY STATEMENT

**I. Introduction**

The EU Code of Conduct on Arms Exports adopted on 8 June 1998 laid down minimum standards for the issuing of export licences for conventional armaments by the Member States. It consists of 8 determination criteria and 12 operative provisions. Up to the present day, it is the most comprehensive international arms export control regime.

The Council, in particular its COARM Working Party, and the Member States try continuously to find ways to strengthen transparency, dialogue and convergence in the area of the export control of conventional arms. The major achievements mentioned in the Fifth Annual Report and the attached Compendium are a User's Guide to the Code of Conduct, the establishment of a central database for denial notifications, the Common Position on arms brokering, a revised list of military equipment and the intention to initiate a review of the Code in 2004.

As in previous years, the European Parliament welcomes the improvements of the Code. It is concerned, however, about the continuous lack of implementation of its recommendations. In particular, the European Parliament's call for the Code to be legally binding still remains relevant. Moreover, the Annual Report on human rights of 22 April 2004 stresses that "EU human rights policies have been undermined by (...) Member States systematically not maintaining a restrictive application of the EU Code of Conduct on Arms Exports"[10].

The European Security Strategy of December 2003 identifies regional instability, failing states, organised crime and international terrorism as key threats for the EU. Although the strategy paper does not mention it specifically, uncontrolled arms exports to recipients outside of the EU can increase significantly these threats. In this context, it is necessary to take into consideration that 80 per cent of EU arms exports goes to non-European countries[11]. Moreover, enlargement has increased the EU's share in the international arms trade in general and in the production of small and light weapons in particular. Thus, a clear common arms export policy is very important.

The harmonisation of the EU's arms export policy vis-à-vis third countries will also strengthen the Common Foreign and Security Policy (CFSP) framework, in which it takes place. This is particularly relevant in regard to enlargement on 01 May 2004, when 10 new Member States joined the EU.

**II. Assessment of the fifth year of implementation of the Code**

*1) Harmonisation of national reports*

The Member States' national reports form the basis of the annual report. However, little progress has been achieved in the harmonisation of these reports since the publication of the fourth annual report. Although all Member States should provide data for each recipient country on the number of licences issued, on the value of licences issued in Euros (if available), on the value of arms exports in Euros (if available), on the number of licence refusals and on the criteria numbers on which refusals are based, the SIPRI Yearbook 2004 highlights that some governments are still unwilling or unable to submit the necessary data. Table A in the Annex shows that Denmark, France, Germany, Greece and Ireland do not provide data on the value of arms exports, whereas the Netherlands and Portugal do not submit data on the value of licences issued. This is a clear obstacle to complete transparency and parliamentarian control of EU arms exports. Another problem is the lack of compatibility of the data provided by each Member State. For example, Austria only provides data on 'war material', but not on 'non-war material'[12]. The breakdown of the denials by geographical region in the national reports of Italy, Portugal, Spain, Sweden and the United Kingdom is a welcome development. The SIPRI Yearbook, however, points out correctly that the value of the data provided is problematic, as in some instances the sum of denials per region does not fit the total number of denials[13]. After intra-Community trade, the second largest number of export licences concerned are still the Balkan countries, Russia, the Ukraine and the Caucasus region. The total number of consultations initiated, at 68, and of consultations received, at 48, appear low in relation to the 411 denials and more than 36000 licences granted. Moreover, the number of denials decreased by 54, whereas the number of licences issued increased by more than 11000.

*2) End-user certificates*

The only noteworthy development is that the "indication of the end-use of the goods" was included into the minimal details to be set out in an end-user certificate. However, the more ambitious recommendations of the previous annual report of the European Parliament have not been implemented. Yet, the setting up of a delivery verification and post-export monitoring regime for all exports under the Code of Conduct, including the possibility to impose penalties, remains important in order to control effectively the end-use of arms, of other military and security equipment and of licensed production abroad. As such a monitoring system may exceed the capacities of small states and of some of the new Member States, the Member States should again give serious consideration to the possibility of setting up a common EU monitoring system. A European arms export control agency could still be a suitable counterpart to the planned armaments agency in the area of production and procurement.

*3) Arms brokering*

The Common Position on the control of arms brokering, which was adopted by the Council in June 2003, is an outstanding achievement. It includes a definition of brokering activities, the obligation to obtain a licence or written authorisation for brokering activities by the competent authorities, the exchange of information on arms brokering and the establishment of adequate sanctions. In order to improve the effectiveness of the Common Position, the authorisation to act as an arms broker and the registration of arms brokers should be compulsory. Moreover, the provisions of the Common Position, following the example of US legislation, should also be applicable to EU citizens and companies outside the territory of the EU. In this regard, the efforts of Austria, Belgium, Finland, France, Germany, the Netherlands and Sweden can serve as examples of best practice. However, Member States have not included arms transporting and arms financing services into their arms brokering legislation, which has prevented in several cases the interception of arms exports to recipients, where the standards laid down in the Code are clearly not respected. Even more worryingly, the Common Position does not prohibit explicitly the brokering of equipment for capital punishment, torture and other cruel, inhuman and degrading treating.

*4) The Denial Circulation System*

The User's Guide to the Code of Conduct has significantly improved the system of denial notifications and consultations, as it interprets and clarifies the operative provisions of the Code of Conduct. Diverging interpretations of the provisions by different Member States are, therefore, less likely and loopholes have been closed. The four major parts of the Guide are the definition of a denial, the necessary information for a denial notification, the revocation of denial notifications and the clarification of the procedures for denial notifications and consultations. Furthermore, it has been decided to set up a central denial database at the Council Secretariat in Brussels. It represents a valuable information resource for Member States and is a first step towards more co-ordinated EU arms exports policies. The next step should be the automatic circulation of the substance and outcomes of consultations to all Member States.

*5) Dialogue with candidate countries and third countries*

Although ten new Member States joined the European Union on 01 May 2004 and, thus, were fully incorporated into the system of the Code of Conduct, the dialogue between the EU and the remaining candidate countries - Bulgaria, Romania and Turkey - has to continue. This could take, for example, the form of the informal COARM meetings between old and new Member States as initiated by the Polish and Swedish governments. Denial notifications should be forwarded to these countries, and the EU should exchange national reports on arms exports with them. The candidate countries should, for their part, adopt national legislation to duly transpose the Code. Furthermore, the promotion of the Code of Conduct in associated and the new neighbouring countries, e.g. Ukraine, Belarus or Serbia and Montenegro, has to be intensified. Unfortunately, the Fifth Annual Report does not provide concrete improvements in this regard. As in the past, countries in Central and Eastern Europe have been an important point of departure and transit route for the arms trade and have significant capacity for producing light and also heavier weapons, sufficient assistance must be given to those countries inside and outside the EU, which do not have the means to fully implement the Code of Conduct and to adopt their practices to the standards established between the old Member States. Member States can follow, for instance, the example of the government of the Netherlands, which has introduced candidate and other interested countries to the practical implementation of the Code of Conduct.

*6) EU Common List of Military Equipment*

The first update of the EU common military list since June 2000 and its publication in the Official Journal is an important contribution to the harmonisation and strengthening of the Code of Conduct. It will be based on the numbering system of the Wassenaar Arrangement Munitions List. Unfortunately, certain "dual-use" items, which may well be used for human rights abuses, and certain parts of weapon systems are not included.

*7) Implementation of Criterion 8 of the Code of Conduct*

Criterion 8 is the so-called "sustainable development" criterion and determines the compatibility of arms exports with the technical and economic capacity of the recipient country. As this criterion is particularly important with regard to crisis prevention and sustainable development in socially less developed countries, the survey that was initiated to develop guidelines for its application is welcome. The objective should be to prevent too high a level of arms imports from jeopardising the social and economic development of a country.

*8) Priority Guidelines for the Near Future*

The Fifth Annual Report has identified in total 9 priority guidelines, of which guideline number 7 ("development of dialague [sic!] with the European Parliament") and number 9 ("Review of the Code of Conduct") are of particular importance for the European Parliament. Increasing the dialogue with the Parliament will be a significant step towards more parliamentarian scrutiny of EU arms exports and will enhance the democratic legitimacy of the Code of Conduct. The review of the Code can lead to clear improvements, if it takes the recommendations of the European Parliament resolution into account and if the review will be conducted in a broad and open way - including both parliaments and non-governmental organisations. In general, however, the vague formulation of the priority guidelines suggests that Member States are not fully committed to them.

**III. Recommendations regarding tighter controls of arms exports, legally binding provisions and greater transparency**

A recent report by Amnesty International on the EU's Arms Exports[14] has analysed numerous instances, in which loopholes, undercutting or insufficient clarifications and definitions have lead to EU weapons, their components, EU licences to produce arms overseas, private EU military and security services, EU military personnel, expertise and training and equipment for capital punishment, torture and other cruel, inhuman and degrading treating being - often secretly - exported to countries where the EU standards for democracy, human rights and sustainable development are clearly not respected. Particularly from the point of view of the broad principles underlying the EU's external policy, such as human rights, conflict prevention and sustainable development, a strict arms export control regime at European and international level is very important. Therefore, additional measures for more stringent controls, for legally binding provisions and for greater transparency are urgently needed.

*1) More stringent controls*

First of all, the Council should adopt the European Commission's proposal for a Council Trade Regulation imposing an export ban on all equipment for torture and laying down strict controls for equipment that might be used for internal repression. Furthermore, the Member States should also agree on a common list of countries involved in armed conflicts, to which arms exports should be banned in principle ('presumption of denial'). It is also necessary to systematise physical controls of arms shipments at point of import, transit and export. Finally, the Member States should interpret the Code of Conduct in the strictest way possible. In particular, they should acknowledge the application of the Code in the following cases:

- products which may be used for both civilian and military purposes such as surveillance technology and products or parts thereof which are suitable for cyber warfare or for nonlethal human rights abuses;
- items destined for incorporation by the importing country into a sub-assembly or finished weapons system;
- the production of EU licensed arms (or its components) in third countries;
- all forms of "government to government" transfers, in particular the transfer of surplus arms;
- military, security and police personnel, expertise and training and private military and security devices.

*2) Legally binding provisions*

Parliament has reiterated calls for the Code to be made legally binding and for EU Member States' arms export policy to be fully harmonised. It welcomes, therefore, the possibility that the Code of Conduct will be transformed into a Common Position. However, further substantial improvements and individual steps, which the European Parliament already outlined in its last report, are possible:

(a) The Member States should consult amongst each other to a greater extent prior to decisions being taken to refuse licences or with regard to transfers to regions susceptible to crises. Closer co-operation between the COARM Working Party and the Council's various regional working parties would also contribute to achieving that end.

(b) Whilst exchanges of information and consultation have to date only taken place on a bilateral basis, steered by respective Council Presidencies, a more multilateral approach to the consultation process in connection with decisions to grant or refuse licences would represent an important step in the direction of harmonisation.

(c) As a further interim step towards making the Code of Conduct legally binding, the European Parliament recommends to all Member States that the Code be transposed into national law.

*3) Greater transparency*

The inclusion of 10 acceding countries has made the harmonisation of future national annual reports a pressing issue. This provides also the opportunity to improve, in qualitative terms, the statistics in the annual report.

Member States should not only provide full information according to the agreed criteria (see II. 1), but also on the following points:

- type of arms (e.g. helicopter or machine gun), type of arms components and type of product which may be used for both civilian and military purposes (e.g. surveillance or intelligence technology) per destination;
- quantity (e.g. number of rifles, etc. supplied) per destination;
- transfer of military, security and police personnel, expertise and training;
- detailed data on end-users per destination;
- informal denials of licences for certain arms exports, which were given before a formal licence application. Fuller, more harmonised data of this kind would make the annual report more transparent and a very valuable instrument for parliamentarian scrutiny and, thus, for democratic accountability.

*4) Tackling the brokering*

Many EU states still do not have national brokering legislation, and even in countries where they exist, there is not always a criminalisation of violations of arms embargoes by national or registered individuals and entities when committed abroad. This means that an unscrupulous broker of EU nationality or residence, would simply have to step outside the EU to broker an arms deal in violation of a, for example, UN arms embargo without facing the risk of legal sanctions upon returning to the EU. This needs to be tackled also more seriously.

**IV. Conclusion**

The EU Code of Conduct has evolved significantly since its adoption in 1998 and many new provisions and clarifications have been implemented in one form or another, although the Code in itself has not been changed. The review of the Code in 2004 is a great chance to leap forward and to implement additional measures, as proposed by the European Parliament. Furthermore, the EU and its Member States have to recognise the global dimensions of the problem of illicit arms exports and should, therefore, work with their partner countries, above all the United States, towards a legally binding international Arms Trade Treaty. In the short term and in view of the 2006 UN Review Conference, they should promote at least stringent international norms on arms exports. This will reduce regional instability, organised crime, international terrorism and human rights abuses all over the world and will turn Europe into 'a more secure place in a better world.'

Opinion of the Committee on International Trade for the Committee on Foreign Affairs on the Council's Fifth Annual Report according to Operative Provision 8 of the European Union Code of Conduct on Arms Exports (2004/2103(INI))

Draftsman: Jacky Henin

**SUGGESTIONS**

The Committee on International Trade calls on the Committee on Foreign Affairs, as the committee responsible, to incorporate the following suggestions in its motion for a resolution:

1. Considers that arms control is essential for conducting coherent policies that meet EU objectives on peace, development, respect for human rights and democracy;

2. Notes that some progress has been made in implementing the EU Code of Conduct on Arms Exports, but nevertheless deplores the fact that massive quantities of European arms continue to be supplied, in violation of the Code; hopes that a European instrument can be adopted which will make the Code of Conduct legally binding;

3. Notes a slight drop in expenditure on armaments within the EU in recent years, but is concerned that this is more than offset by an increase in exports of manufactured arms to non-member States; considers that the EU and the Member States should not only implement the Code of Conduct but also help to reduce militarisation and levels of armaments in the world;

4. Supports Parliament's earlier call for legally binding provisions and a full harmonisation of the Member States' arms export policy in the medium term, and calls on the Member States to make progress to this end;

5. Considers that arms manufacturers should be encouraged to diversify and redirect their enterprise towards other products;

6. Considers that the EU should continue to encourage other countries, in particular the United States, Russia, Ukraine and China, to adhere to the Code of Conduct on the arms trade, and to limit arms exports and expenditure on arms;

7. Stresses the importance of research aimed at guaranteeing legal supervision and controls on the electronic transfer of knowledge, software and technology having a potential link to goods on the Community list of goods for which an export licence is required;

8. Considers that, in order to combat illegal arms sales and to ensure that arms do not end up in the hands of inappropriate end-users, it is essential to reinforce controls on shipping cargoes, arms end-users, other military and security equipment, manufacture under licence and brokerage; specifically calls, as far as end-users are concerned, for the inclusion of a non-misuse clause in end-user certificates declaring that the material will not be used for proscribed uses;

9. Supports the call on the Member States to investigate once again the possibility of setting up a Community supervision system; further recommends that consideration be given to the model of a European arms export control agency;

10. Calls on the Member States to introduce criminal sanctions for violations, wherever these take place, by European brokers or EU-registered brokers or enterprises, of arms embargoes laid down by the UN, the EU, the OSCE or any Member State;

11. Calls for the introduction in the EU of a special tax on the arms trade, and for the EU to carry on active diplomacy with a view to such tax being levied worldwide as is being suggested by the United Nations General Assembly as well as by the Presidents of Brazil, Chile and France, and by the Spanish Head of Government, with the revenue

from these taxes being paid into funds for victims of armed conflicts in particular and poverty alleviation more generally;

12. Calls upon Member States to agree on a list of countries involved in armed conflicts to which arms exports should be banned in principle, drawing upon the reports and recommendations of the UN Security Council monitoring mechanisms on arms embargoes;
13. Calls upon Member States to initiate surveys, as carried out for criterion 8, on how to apply the remaining seven criteria;
14. Calls for the expansion, in due course, of the database of denial notifications at the Council Secretariat in Brussels to include information on consultations under the Code of Conduct as well as on end-users who are known or suspected to have engaged in the reexport, diversion or misuse of arms and other controlled goods;
15. Calls on Member States to amend the export criteria in the Code of Conduct to improve their clarity and comprehensiveness and to ensure that they fully reflect States' existing responsibilities under international law;

**PROCEDURE**

| | |
|---|---|
| **Title** | Council's Fifth Annual Report according to Operative Provision 8 of the European Union Code of Conduct on Arms Exports |
| **Procedure number** | 2004/2103(INI) |
| **Committee responsible** | AFET |
| **Enhanced cooperation** | – |
| **Draftsman**<br>Date appointed | Jacky Henin<br>14.9.2004 |
| **Discussed in committee** | 30.9.2004 11.10.2004 |
| **Date suggestions adopted** | 11.10.2004 |
| **Result of final vote** | for: 22 against: 0 abstentions: 0 |
| **Members present for the final vote** | Enrique Barón Crespo, Daniel Caspary, Françoise Castex, Jean-Marie Cavada, Giulietto Chiesa, Christofer Fjellner, Béla Glattfelder, Jacky Henin, Erika Mann, Helmuth Markov, Javier Moreno Sánchez, Pasqualina Napoletano, Georgios Papastamkos, Peter Štastný, Johan Van Hecke, Zbigniew Franciszek Zaleski |
| **Substitutes present for the final vote** | Margrietus J. van den Berg, Reimer Böge, Danute Budreikaite, Harlem Désir, Maria Martens |
| **Substitutes under Rule 178(2) present for the final vote** | Carl Schlyter |

| | |
|---|---|
| **Title** | The Council's Fifth Annual Report according to Operative Provision 8 of the European Union Code of Conduct on Arms Exports |
| **Procedure number** | 2004/2103(INI) |
| **Basis in Rules of Procedure** | Rule 45 |
| **Committee responsible**<br>Date authorisation announced in plenary | AFET 14.10.2004 |
| **Committee(s) asked for opinion(s)**<br>Date announced in plenary | INTA<br>14.10.04 |
| **Not delivering opinion(s)**<br>Date of decision | |
| **Enhanced cooperation**<br>Date announced in plenary | |
| **Motion(s) for resolution(s) included in report** | |
| **Rapporteur(s)**<br>Date appointed | Raül Romeva Rueda<br>13.9.2004 |
| **Previous rapporteur(s)** | |
| **Discussed in committee** | 1.9.04 22.9.04_> 11.10.04 |
| **Date adopted** | 12.10.2004 |
| **Result of final vote** | for: 57<br>against: 4<br>abstentions: 3 |

| | |
|---|---|
| **Members present for the final vote** | Elmar Brok, Toomas Hendrik Ilves, Geoffrey Van Orden, Vittorio Emanuele Agnoletto, Angelika Beer, Panagiotis Beglitis, Bastiaan Belder, Monika Beňová, André Brie, Simon Coveney, Ryszard Czarnecki, Massimo D'Alema, Véronique De Keyser, Giorgos Dimitrakopoulos, Anna Elzbieta Fotyga, Maciej Marian Giertych, Ana Maria R.M. Gomes, Klaus Hänsch, Richard Howitt, Anna Ibrisagic, Jelko Kacin, Georgios Karatzaferis, Ioannis Kasoulides, Helmut Kuhne, Joost Lagendijk, Vytautas Landsbergis, Armin Laschet, Edward H.C. McMillan-Scott, Francisco José Millán Mon, Annemie Neyts-Uyttebroeck, Raimon Obiols i Germà, Cem Özdemir, Alojz Peterle, Tobias Pflüger, João de Deus Pinheiro, Mirosław Mariusz Piotrowski, Paweł Bartłomiej Piskorski, Poul Nyrup Rasmussen, Raül Romeva Rueda, José Ignacio Salafranca Sánchez-Neyra, György Schöpflin, Marek Maciej Siwiec, István Szent-Iványi, Konrad Krzysztof Szymański, Charles Tannock, Jan Marinus Wiersma, Karl von Wogau, Francis Wurtz |
| **Substitutes present for the final vote** | Laima Liucija Andrikienė, Irena Belohorská, Árpád Duka-Zólyomi, Carlo Fatuzzo, Michael Gahler, Anneli Jäätteenmäki, Glenys Kinnock, Jaromír Kohlíček, Miguel Angel Martínez Martínez, Pasqualina Napoletano, Borut Pahor, Józef Pinior, Rihards Pīks, Luís Queiró, Mechtild Rothe, Aloyzas Sakalas, Pierre Schapira, Inger Segelström, Jean Spautz, Marcello Vernola |
| **Substitutes under Rule 178(2) present for the final vote** | |
| **Date tabled – A6** | 19.10.0000 A6-0022/2004 |
| **Comments** | ... |

1 OJ C 320, 31.12.2003, p. 1.
2 OJ L 156, 25.6.2003, p. 79.
3 P5_TA(2003)0418.
4 OJ C 319, 19.12.2002, p. 1.
5 P5_TA(2003)0522.
6 P5_TA(2004)0376.
7 P5_TA(2003)0599.
8 OJ C 121,24.4.2001, p. 401.
9 OJ C 74 E, 24.3.2004, p. 854.
10 P5_TA(2004)0376, paragraph 30.
11 SIPRI Yearbook 2004, p. 458.
12 SIPRI Yearbook 2004, p. 471-472.
13 SIPRI Yearbook 2004, p. 471.
14 Amnesty International: Undermining Global Security: The European Union's Arms Exports, 2004.

# 5

# Sectoral Dialogues, Joint Declarations and Memoranda of Understanding, 1990–Present

## INTRODUCTION

In addition to political dialogues, the EU and China have also established a wide range of sectoral dialogues. The latter are meetings of lower-level official experts concerned with economic and social regulation involving specific economic sectors or sub-sectors or particular areas of social policy. On the EU side, they are the responsibility of the European Commission; on the Chinese side, they are dealt with by the Ministry of Commerce, line ministries or similar organisations such as the Chinese General Administration of Quality Supervision, Inspection and Quarantine (AQSIQ) linked directly to the State Council of the People's Republic of China. The European Commission's website currently states that such dialogues cover 24 different areas,[1] but the term 'sectoral dialogue' is rather ambiguous and fluid, except in indicating a domain about which the EU and China hold regular discussions. These dialogues cover virtually all the areas of cooperation between the EU and China. They vary widely in subject matter and structure. Some are more formal, or 'structured', than others, with institutional arrangements, an agenda, defined objectives and means to achieve them. Their legal or other normative basis also varies, from legally binding agreements, summit meetings, memoranda of understanding or informal frameworks for discussions, or even varying combinations of these different elements. In fact, some dialogues identified by the Commission take place within the framework of legally binding agreements, such as those concerning customs cooperation, global

[1] See European Commission, Directorate-General for External Relations, 'An Overview of Sectoral Dialogues between China and the European Commission', available at http://ec.europa.eu/comm/external_relations/china/intro/sect.htm (last accessed 22 December 2007). The website gives a brief description of each dialogue. Though there are 22 separate entries, the text distinguishes within a single entry between the Regulatory Dialogue and the Industrial Policy Dialogue, making a total of 23 dialogues. To this should be added a regulatory dialogue on public procurement, established on 2 November 2005: see Europa, 'Public Procurement: EU and China Strengthen Cooperation', press release IP/05/1378 (7 November 2005), available at http://europa.eu/rapid/pressReleasesAction.do?reference=IP/05/1378&format=HTML&aged=1&language=EN&guiLanguage=en (accessed 22 November 2007). This makes a total of 24. I have added the Government Procurement Dialogue, which does not figure as a separate dialogue in the Commission list. The 10th EU–China Summit in 2007 established one or two additional dialogues on trade imbalance and the RMB exchange rate, now merged into the much broader new High Level Mechanism (HLM), also included here.

satellite navigation services and maritime transport, rather than having a less formal origin.[2] From the legal standpoint, all have been created within the framework of the 1985 Agreement on Trade and Economic Cooperation. In practice, however, their range, diversity and dynamism reveals the extent to which the 1985 Agreement no longer reflects the reality of EU–China relations, hence the current negotiations on a new agreement.

Dialogues have often developed in symbiosis with memoranda of understanding (MOUs). In this context, MOUs, like joint declarations, are usually not legally binding, but they may have practical and even legal effects. Viewed from a general legal standpoint, an MOU may be legally binding on the parties; it may not be legally binding but nevertheless create legal effects; or it may be a political agreement with no legal effects. The intention of the parties is a (if not the) determining element. In EU–China relations, most, if not all, MOUs fall into the second category. In other words, usually they are soft law. They can crystallise common interests, provide the basis for more detailed cooperation and have the advantage of being easily adaptable to policy developments and changes in circumstances. In principle, MOUs would appear to have a more legal or normative character than dialogues. In practice, the MOUs and dialogues are often closely related, if not indistinguishable. For example, an MOU can establish a dialogue; a dialogue can also be established without an MOU; or an MOU can establish a form of cooperation which, though not called a dialogue, resembles a dialogue in every other respect. A single normative device thus can be used as a point of departure or as a framework for a range of different types of cooperation.

We can identify five main functions of dialogues, while recognising that a specific dialogue usually has more than one function and that the functions of a specific dialogue may change over time. First, dialogues are used as a device for mutual learning and the transfer of knowledge, notably in areas in which the EU and China have many common interests, whether domestically and internationally. Mutual learning is an important feature of most, if not all, dialogues. From the EU standpoint, such dialogues are frequently a regular feature of international relations with other trading partners. Secondly, dialogues may be employed to establish cooperation in specific sectors, perhaps as a prelude to more formal cooperation. Thirdly, dialogues are also used as a means of stimulating or enhancing policy development in China. This may occur, for example, in sectors for which EU regulatory regimes are highly developed or in areas in which the development of new policies could enhance China's fulfilment of its obligations under WTO law, including plurilateral agreements such as the Agreement on Public Procurement, to which China is not yet a party. Fourthly, dialogues can be used as a device for market access, especially by the EU to the Chinese market. Finally, dialogues can be established to allow discussion of specific sensitive issues, though not so sensitive as not to be amenable to organised or official discussion. Dialogues frequently perform this function, usually in the context of other broader discussions. Sometimes, however, a dialogue is established specifically for this purpose. For example, following their 10th Summit, the EU and China established a kind of 'super-dialogue', the EU–China High Level Economic and

[2] On these measures, see chapter 6.

Trade Mechanism (HLM). It will serve as a discussion forum and coordinate policy and practice in many fields.[3]

This chapter considers such dialogues, joint declarations and MOUs from the early 1990s to the present. Table 5.1 gives a list of the new HLM and sectoral dialogues. The remainder of the chapter presents first the HLM and the sectoral dialogues, together with related joint declarations and MOUs, according to sector in alphabetical order. This order is used here to facilitate consultation of the documents, even though it is less useful than a chronological presentation in revealing the pattern of development of EU–China relations.[4] Documents establishing the dialogue are presented whenever possible; if not possible, another document is given to show the structure and function of the dialogue.

## HIGH LEVEL MECHANISM (HLM)

On 25 April 2008 the EU and China inaugurated the HLM (see Document 5.1). Proposed by China at the 10th EU–China Summit, it was originally to serve as a forum for discussing outstanding issues such as trade imbalance and exchange rates. As currently established, however, it has a much wider mandate. Its remit includes the multilateral global trading system, strategic bilateral trade and trade-related issues, investment, innovation, including IPR and technology, and EU–China economic cooperation. It is intended to be a continuous forum for ministerial-level cooperation and a means of resolving difficulties that arise in EU–China economic and trade relations, with periodic high-level steering meetings. Such bodies already exist in other contexts in the form of the EU–US Transatlantic Council and the US–China Strategic Economic Dialogue. The HLM is the analogue in the context of EU–China relations.

[3] See 'China, EU Set Up Joint Panels on Trade, RMB', *China Daily*, 29 November 2007, available at http://english.mofcom.gov.cn/article/counselorsreport/westernasiaandafricareport/20 (accessed 29 November 2007); and T Barber and M Dickie, 'Bilateral Group Set Up to Tackle Trade Imbalance', *Financial Times*, 29 November 2007, 8. The two sources present different perspectives on the number and scope of the dialogues. The former source distinguishes 'two separate high-level dialogue mechanisms on trade and finance', while the latter reports that the EU and China agreed to set up 'a high-level "mechanism" for officials to discuss economics and trade issues'. It is likely that these differences reflect the parties' respective desires to separate or merge the issues in question.

[4] The order is the same as the 'Overview of Sectoral Dialogues', above n 1. However, dialogues which occur within the framework of legally binding agreements are not described in detail here. For documents concerning those dialogues, the reader is referred to chapter 6.

**Table 5.1: High Level Mechanism and Sectoral Dialogues**

| Dialogue | Document | Place and date | Parties | Normative framework | Meetings, activities | Results | Reference or source[a] |
|---|---|---|---|---|---|---|---|
| HLM | Inaugural Meeting of the EU-China High Level Economic and Trade Dialogue Mechanism (HLM) [see Document 5.1] | Beijing, 25.4.2008 | 8 EU Commissioners, 10 Chinese Ministers | | periodic | | http://www.delchn.ec.europa.eu/Upload/News/1209127467.38847.pdf, accessed 2.5.2008 |
| Agriculture | Joint Declaration on the EU-China Dialogue in Agriculture (see Document 5.2) | 15.7.2005 | European Commission DG Agriculture and Rural Development and Ministry of Agriculture, PRC | | 4 Technical Working Groups: Agriculture Trade, Quality Products, Policy Information, Food Technologies; regular meetings; 2-day meeting in Brussels in October 2006 | | http:/ec.europa.eu/external_relations/china/introd/sect.htm |

**Table 5.1: continued**

| Dialogue | Document | Place and date | Parties | Normative framework | Meetings, activities | Results | Reference or source[a] |
| --- | --- | --- | --- | --- | --- | --- | --- |
| Civil aviation | Communication from the Commission, 'A Community civil aviation policy towards the People's Republic of China—strengthening cooperation and opening markets' (see Document 5.3) | Brussels, 11.3.2005 | Commission of the European Communities | | | | COM(2005)78 final |
| | Joint Declaration on EU-China Cooperation in Civil Aviation (see Document 5.4) | Beijing, 29.6.2005 | Mr Yang Yuanyuan, Minister of Civil Aviation, PRC, and Mr Jacques Barrot, Vice-President of the European Commission | EU-China Civil Aviation Summit, Beijing, 29.6-1.7.2005 | negotiation of comprehensive air services agreement, also linked to EU-China MOU on Tourist Groups (ADS) | | http://ec.europa.eu/transport/air_portal/international/pillars/global_partners/doc/china/2005_07_06_ey-china_joint_declaration_en.pdf, accessed 24.12.2007:see also http://ec.europa.eu/comm/external_relations/china/intro/sect.htm, accessed 28.3.2007 |

**Table 5.1: continued**

| Dialogue | Document | Place and date | Parties | Normative framework | Meetings, activities | Results | Reference or source[a] |
|---|---|---|---|---|---|---|---|
| Competition policy | Terms of Reference of the EU-China Competition Policy Dialogue (see Document 5.5) | 6.5.2004 | DG Competition, European Commission; and Treaty and Law Department, Ministry of Commerce, PRC | Joint Statement, 4th EU-China Summit, 5.9.2001 | meetings at least once each year, alternating between Brussels and Beijing; ad hoc working groups as necessary | | http://ec.europa.eu/comm/competition/international/bilateral/cn2b_en.pdf |

**Table 5.1: continued**

| Dialogue | Document | Place and date | Parties | Normative framework | Meetings, activities | Results | Reference or source[a] |
|---|---|---|---|---|---|---|---|
| Consumer product safety | Minutes of the Meeting for Establishing the Consultation Mechanism on Industrial Products and WTO/TBT (see Document 5.6) | 30.10.2002 | General Administration of Quality Supervision, Inspection and Quarantine (AQSIQ), PRC; and DG Enterprise, European Commission | Sino-EU Terms of Reference on Industrial Products Safety (not available to the public) | High Level Steering Committee (Vice Minister of AQSIQ, Director-General DG Enterprise), Coordination Committee on industrial product safety, Coordination Committee on other issues, contact points, Emergency Consultation Working Groups for electrical safety, medical devices, toys, lighters, conformity assessment (including certification and accreditation), standardisation, WTO/TBT, technical regulations, pressure equipment, automotive, cableway transportation, textile, EMF for mobile phones | see also Li Yuanping, AQSQ, 'Believe in China-made, Believe in Chinese products', speech at European Policy Centre, Brussels, 16.10.2007, available at www.chinamission.be/chn/sgxx/t374818.htm, visited 27.12.2007 | http://ec.europa.eu/enterprise/enterprise_policy/gov_relations/china/agreement_30-10-2002.pdf, accessed 22.11.2007 |

**Table 5.1: continued**

| Dialogue | Document | Place and date | Parties | Normative framework | Meetings, activities | Results | Reference or source[a] |
|---|---|---|---|---|---|---|---|
| | Memorandum of Understanding (MOU) on Administrative Cooperation Arrangements (see Document 5.7) | 1.2006 | DG Health and Consumer Protection (SANCO), European Commission; AQSIQ, PRC | Consultation Mechanism on Industrial Products and WTO/TBT | regular meetings, working groups, contact points: covers food safety and general product safety | EU-China Consumer Goods and Food Safety Joint Committee | http://ec.europa.eu/enterprise/enterprise_policy/gov_relations/china/agreement_30-10-2002.pdf, accessed 22.11.2007 |
| | Road Map on Safer Toys: Guideline for Action on Cooperation for Strengthening EU-China Toys Safety (see Document 5.8) | 19.9.2006 | EC Health and Consumer Protection Commissioner Markos Kypriano and Chinese Minister Li Changjiang, in charge of Administration for Quality Supervision, Inspection and Quarantine (AQSIQ) | Memorandum of Understanding (MOU) on Administrative Cooperation Arrangements | transparency, supervision, monitoring, rapid alert system (RAPEX) | | See also http://ec.europa.eu/dgs/health_consumer/dyna/consumervoice/create_cv.cfn?cv_id=213; http://www.chinadaily.com.cn/china/2006-04-27/content_577967.htm: both accessed 6.4.2007 |

**Table 5.1: continued**

| Dialogue | Document | Place and date | Parties | Normative framework | Meetings, activities | Results | Reference or source[a] |
|---|---|---|---|---|---|---|---|
| Customs cooperation | Agreement between the European Community and China on Cooperation and Mutual Assistance in Customs Matters (see Document 6.5 in Chapter 6) | | | | | Smart and Safe Lanes' Pilot Project, http://europa.eu/rapid/pressReleasesAction.do?reference=IP/06/1206&format=HT, visited 27.12.2007 | |
| Education and culture | see Chapter 8 for cooperation programmes | | | | | | |
| Employment and social affairs | Memorandum of Understanding (MOU) on Cooperation in Labour, Employment and Social Affairs (see Documnet 5.9) | 5.9.2005 | | 8th EU-China Summit, 2005 | meetings at least once a year, alternating between Brussels and Beijing; link with technical assistance project on social security reform | | http://ec.europa.eu/employment_social/emplweb/news/news_en.cfm?id=64; www.europa.eu/…/05/296&format?PDF&aged=1&language=EN&guiLanguage=en, accessed 22.12.2007 |

**Table 5.1: continued**

| Dialogue | Document | Place and date | Parties | Normative framework | Meetings, activities | Results | Reference or source[a] |
|---|---|---|---|---|---|---|---|
| | Press Release: 'The European Commission strengthens dialogue with China on employment and social affairs | | | MOU on Cooperation in Labour, Employment and Social Affairs, in force for 4 years | | | www.europa.eu/.../05/296&format?PDF&aged=1&language=EN&guiLanguage=en, accessed 22.12.2007 |
| Energy | Energy Dialogue | 1994 | European Commission DG for Transport and Energy (TREN), Chinese Ministry for Science and Technology (MOST) | | annual meetings of working groups, bi-annual EU-China Energy Cooperation Conference | (1) MOU on transport and energy strategies (2006), (2) Euratom Agreement with China, (3) Action Plan on Clean Coal, (4) terms of reference for Action Plan on Industrial Cooperation on Energy Efficiency and Renewable Energies | http://ec.europa.eu/external_relations/china/intro/sect.htm, accessed 22.12.2007 |

**Table 5.1: continued**

| Dialogue | Document | Place and date | Parties | Normative framework | Meetings, activities | Results | Reference or source[a] |
|---|---|---|---|---|---|---|---|
| | Partnership on Climate Change | | | 8th EU-China Summit, 2005 | high-level political framework | | |
| | EU-China Action Plan on Clean Coal (not available to the public) | | | | | | http://ec.europa.eu/dgs/energy_transport/international/bilateral/china/energy/index…, accessed 26.12.2007 |
| | EU-China Action Plan on Energy Efficiency and Renewable Energies (not available to the public) | | | | | | http://ec.europa.eu/dgs/energy_transport/international/bilateral/china/energy/index…, accessed 26.12.2007 |
| | Joint Declaration on Climate Change (see document 5.10) | | | | | | |

**Table 5.1: continued**

| Dialogue | Document | Place and date | Parties | Normative framework | Meetings, activities | Results | Reference or source[a] |
|---|---|---|---|---|---|---|---|
| | Memorandum of Understanding on Energy and Transport Strategies (not available to the public) | | | 8th EU-China Summit, 2005 | EU-China Dialogue on Transport and Energy Strategies, began on 21.3.2006 | | See http://ec.europa.eu/dgx/energ_transport/international/bilateral/china/energy/index ; see also http://ec.europa.eu/comm/external_relations/china/intro/sect.htm, accessed 29.3.2007, |
| | Memorandum of Understanding on Cooperation on Near-zero Emissions Power Generation Technology through Carbon Dioxide Capture and Storage (see Document 5.11) | Shanghai, 20.2.2006 | European Commission; Ministry of Science and Technology PRC | 8th Summit, 2005; Joint Declaration on Climate Change; MOU on the EU-China Dialogue on Energy and Transport Strategies | Phase 1: exploration by collaborative cooperation programme of feasibility and options for near-zero technology in China through carbon dioxide capture and storage; further phases to be defined | | |

**Table 5.1: continued**

| Dialogue | Document | Place and date | Parties | Normative framework | Meetings, activities | Results | Reference or source[a] |
|---|---|---|---|---|---|---|---|
| Environment | Partnership on Climate Change | | | See above p 776 | | | http://ec,europa.eu/comm/external_relations/china/intro/sect,htm, accessed 28.3.2007; http://europa.eu/rapid/pressReleasesAction.do?reference=MEMO/05/298&format=HTML&aged=1&language=EN&guiLanguage=en, accessed 15.9.2007; http://ec.europa.eu/dgs/energy_transport/international/bilateral/china/energy/index, accessed 26.12.2007 |
| | Joint Declaration on Climate Change (see Document 5.10) | | | | | | |

**Table 5.1: continued**

| Dialogue | Document | Place and date | Parties | Normative framework | Meetings, activities | Results | Reference or source[a] |
|---|---|---|---|---|---|---|---|
| | Minutes of the Meeting between Mrs. Margot Wallstron (Commissioner for Environment, European Commission) and Mr. Xie Zhenhua (Minister, State Environmental Protection Administration, China) (see Document 5.12) | Beijing, 12.11.2003 | DG Environment, European Commission; State Environmental Protection Administration (SEPA), PRC | 4th EU-China Summit, 2001; 6th EU-China Summit, 2003 | capacity building; designation of coordinators, consultations | initiation of EU-China Dialogue on Environmental Policy | European Union, Delegation of the European Commission in China, Press Release, Beijing, 12.11.2003 |
| Food safety | Minutes of the Meeting for Establishing the Consultation Mechanism on Industrial Products and WTO/TBT (see Document 5.6) | 30.10.2002 | General Administration of Quality Supervision, Inspection and Quarantinc (AQSIQ), PRC; and DG Enterprise, European Commission | Sino-EU Terms of Reference on Industrial Products Safety (not available to thc public) | discussions linked with discussions of food safety | | |

**Table 5.1: continued**

| Dialogue | Document | Place and date | Parties | Normative framework | Meetings, activities | Results | Reference or source[a] |
|---|---|---|---|---|---|---|---|
| | Memorandum of Understanding (MOU) on Administrative Cooperation Arrangements (see Document 5.7) | 1.2006 | DG Health and Consumer Protection (SANCO), European Commission; AQSIQ, PRC | Consultation Mechanism on Industrial Products and WTO/TBT | regular meetings, working groups, contact points: covers food safety and general product safety | EU-China Consumer Goods and Food Safety Joint Committee | |
| | Arrangement for the Cooperation on Joint Prevention of Illegal Action for Import and Export of Food (see Document 5.13) | 19.9.2006 | DG SANCO; AQSIQ | | information exchange; provision for disposal of illegal food; preventive measures, designation of contact departments | | |
| Global satellite navigation services | see the Cooperation Agreement on a Global Civil Navigation Satellite System (GNSSS)—GALILEO in Chapter 6 | | | | meetings and other forms of cooperation | | |

**Table 5.1: continued**

| Dialogue | Document | Place and date | Parties | Normative framework | Meetings, activities | Results | Reference or source[a] |
|---|---|---|---|---|---|---|---|
| Government procurement | Memorandum of Understanding (MoU) on Government Procurement Cooperation (see Document 5.14) | Beijing, 2.11.2006 | Alexander Schaub, Director-General, DG Internal Market and Services, European Commission; Zhang Hongli, Assistant Minister, Ministry of Finance, PRC | | consultation and discussion, information exchange, capacity building | | |
| Information society | Information Society Dialogue | 1997 | | | | | http://ec.europa.eu/external_relations/china/intro/sect.htm |
| | Description: 'High-level information society dialogue' (see Document 5.15) | | | closely linked to Regulatory Policy Dialogue and Intellectual Property Rights Dialogue and to cooperation projects | meetings, annual conference, forum on citizen-centric services in e-government | | http://www.eu-china.infso.org/TrainigList.asp?ClassID=2 [EU-China Information Society Project, Training and Capacity Building, accessed 22.11.2007 |

**Table 5.1: continued**

| Dialogue | Document | Place and date | Parties | Normative framework | Meetings, activities | Results | Reference or source[a] |
|---|---|---|---|---|---|---|---|
| Intellectual property rights | EU-China Dialogue on Intellectual Property (see Document 5.16) | 30.10.2003 | DG Trade, European Commission; Ministry of Commerce, PRC | | horizontal discussions covering all sectors, sectoral discussions on individual IP sectors | | http://ec.europa.eu/comm/external_relations/china/intro/sect.htm#Intellectual_property_rights_(IPR), accessed 28 03 07 |
| Macro-economic policy and regulation of financial markets | Dialogue on Macro-economic Policy and Regulation of Financial Markets (see following document) | 12.2004 | European Commission, European Central Bank; Ministry of Finance, People's Bank of China, Regulatory Commissions for Banking, Insurance and Securities, PRC | 7th EU-China Summit | meetings 22.2.2005, 15.5.2006, 4.7.2007 | | |
| | Joint Statement of the 3rd EU-China Economic and Financial Dialogue (see Document 5.17) | Brussels, 4.7.2007 | | EU-China Dialogue on Macro-economic Policy and Regulation of Financial Markets | | | http://2006.chinataiwan.org/web/webportal/W5023951/Ushaotian/A498914.html, accessed 22.11.07 |

**Table 5.1: continued**

| Dialogue | Document | Place and date | Parties | Normative framework | Meetings, activities | Results | Reference or source[a] |
|---|---|---|---|---|---|---|---|
| Maritime transport | Agreement on Maritime Transport between the European Community and its Member States, on the one hand, and the People's Republic of China, on the other hand (see Document 6.2 in Chapter 6) | | | | | | |
| Regional policy | Memorandum of Understanding on Regional Policy Cooperation between the European Commission and the National Development and Reform Commission of the People's Republic of China (see Document 5.18) | 15.5.2006 | Directorate General Regional Policy, European Commission; National Development and Reform Commission, PRC | | information exchange, meetings, contact points, ad hoc technical working groups | establishes a structured dialogue on regional policy | See also: http//europa.eu/rapid/pressReleaseAction.do?reference=IP/06/1502&format=html, accessed 30.11.2007 |

**Table 5.1: continued**

| Dialogue | Document | Place and date | Parties | Normative framework | Meetings, activities | Results | Reference or source[a] |
|---|---|---|---|---|---|---|---|
| Regulatory and industrial policy | Minutes of the Meeting for Establishing the Consultation Mechanism on Industrial Products and WTO/TBT (see Document 5.6) | EC Council approval 25.6.2001, agreement to launch 17.9.2003, framework agreement and launch 30.10.2003 | European Commission and Chinese National Development and Reform Commission (NDRC) | | | 2nd Enterprise and Regulatory Dialogue, Brussels, 8-10.10.2002 | http://ec.europa.eu/enterprise/enterprise_policy/gov_relations/china/minutes_117-09-2003.pdf; see also: http://ec.europa.eu/enterprise/enterprise_policy/gov_relations/china_indpol_dialogue/, accessed 31.10.2006 |
| | Memorandum of Understanding (MOU) on Administrative Cooperation Arrangements (see Document 5.7) | 1.2006 | DG Health and Consumer Protection (SANCO), European Commission; AQSIQ, PRC | Consultation Mechanism on Industrial Products and WTO/TBT | regular meetings, working groups, contact points: covers food safety and general product safety | EU-China Consumer Goods and Food Safety Joint Committee | |

**Table 5.1: continued**

| Dialogue | Document | Place and date | Parties | Normative framework | Meetings, activities | Results | Reference or source[a] |
|---|---|---|---|---|---|---|---|
| | Minutes of the meeting for establishing the Framework of the Industrial Policy Dialogue between the European Commission and China (see Document 5.19) | Beijing, 17.9.2003 | Mr Erkki Liikanen, European Commission; Mr Ma Kai, Chairman, National Development and Reform Commission, PRC | Enterprise Working Group of the EU-China Trade and Economic Cooperation Agreement | annual meetings, alternating between Brussels and Beijing; discussion of horizontal issues on industrial competitiveness and of sector-specific industrial policies; sector-specific working groups as necessary | establishes an Industrial Policy Dialogue | |
| Science and technology | Science and Technology Dialogue | early 1990s | | | | resulted in EU-China S&T Agreement (entered into force late 1999, renewed December 2004) | http://ec.europa.eu/comm/external_relations/china/intro/sect.htm, accessed 28.3.2007 |
| | Agreement for Scientific and Technological Cooperation (see Document 6.1 in Chapter 6) | | | | | | |

**Table 5.1: continued**

| Dialogue | Document | Place and date | Parties | Normative framework | Meetings, activities | Results | Reference or source[a] |
|---|---|---|---|---|---|---|---|
| | Joint Declaration on EU-China Research Cooperation: Building a Knowledge for Growth Pact (see Document 5.20) | Beijing, 12-13.5.2005 | | EU-China High Level Forum on S&T Policy and Development, Beijing, 12-13.5.2005 | preparation of strategic research agenda, stimulate projects, mobility of researchers, information exchange, network and scoreboard | | |
| Space cooperation | Joint Statement on EU-China Dialogue on Space Cooperation (see Document 5.21) | Beijing, 7.4.2004 | Mr Philippe Busquin, Commissioner for Research, European Commission; Mr Xu Guanhua, Minister for Science and Technology, PRC | EU-China Agreement on Science and Technology; Galileo Agreement; visit of Mr Busquin to Beijing, 6-11-.4.2004 | high-level forum, workshops,research cooperation | | http://www.delchn.cec.eu.int/en/whatsnew/jointstatementEnglishpdf. |
| Trade policy | EU-China Trade Policy Dialogue (see Document 5.22) | Brussels, 6.5.2004 | Mr Pascal Lamy, Commissioner for Trade, European Commission; Mr Bo Xilai, Minister of Commerce, PRC | complements institutional dialogue (Joint Committee) under 1985 Trade and Economic Cooperation Agreement | annual meetings, alternating between Brussels and Beijing; contact points | | http://trade-info.cec.eu.int/doclib_section.cfm?sec=120&lev=2&order=date, accessed 12.12.2006 |

**Table 5.1: continued**

| Dialogue | Document | Place and date | Parties | Normative framework | Meetings, activities | Results | Reference or source[a] |
|---|---|---|---|---|---|---|---|
| Textiles trade | China-EU Textiles Trade Dialogue (see Document 5.23) | Brussels, 6.5.2004 | Mr Pascal Lamy, Commissioner for Trade, European Commission; Mr Bo Xilai, Minister of Commerce, PRC | | ad hoc government-to-government working group of senior level officials; supplemented by Sino-EU Forum on T&C trade for business dialogue | | http://trade.ec.europa.eu/doclib/docs/2004/may/tradoc_117079.pdf; see also: http://www.europa.eu.int/comm/trade/issues/bilateral/countries/china/pr231104_en.htm, accessed 12.12.2006 |

**Table 5.1: continued**

| Dialogue | Document | Place and date | Parties | Normative framework | Meetings, activities | Results | Reference or source[a] |
|---|---|---|---|---|---|---|---|
| Transport in general | Memorandum of Understanding on Cooperation in the Fields of Road Transport and Inland Waterways (see Document 5.24) | Brussels, 18.9.2007 | | | Ministerial Meeting mechanism, working group on road construction and transport, working group on inland waterway transport and infrastructure development, each working group to meet once each year or as required; information exchange, visits and study tours, joint organisation of symposiums, personnel training | valid for 5 years, with automatic extension unless otherwise notified | |

[a]Source is the European Commission unless otherwise indicated.

## Document 5.1: High Level Economic and Trade Mechanism (HLM)

Inaugural meeting of the EU-China High Level Economic and Trade Dialogue Mechanism (HLM): 25 April 2008

The EU-China High Level Economic and Trade Dialogue Mechanism is a new joint body that aims to enlarge and deepen cooperation on trade and economic issues between the EU and China. It will focus coordination of policy and practice on the most important issues.

Both sides agree that the HLM will demonstrate progress by delivering regular and concrete results. The HLM will complement the many other dialogues that exist between the EU and China. It will strengthen their work and give them additional political impetus.

Like the EU-US Transatlantic Economic Council and the US-China Strategic Economic Dialogue, the HLM is a continuous process that enhances cooperation at Ministerial level and also provides a forum for resolving frictions that may arise in the relationship. Periodic high level meetings will take stock of the process and steer it.

The HLM met for the first time in Beijing on 25 April 2008. The participation of 8 Commissioners on the EU side made this the largest delegation of European Commissioners to China in the Commission's history. The presence of 10 Ministers on the Chinese side signalled the high level of political commitment to making the new mechanism a useful forum for candid and productive work. It is chaired by Chinese Vice Premier Wang Qishan and EU Trade Commissioner Mandelson.

At the inaugural meeting the EU and China agreed a master work plan for the HLM, and a timetable for review of work. They began exchanges on trade and investment cooperation, balanced economic development, innovation and technology transfer and international economic development. They had focussed discussions on:

- **Energy**, including the removal of investment caps for EU investors in the Chinese energy sector;
- **Trade in high technology**, including a working group to look into barriers to high tech trade and the need to improve intellectual property protection;
- **Intellectual Property Rights protection**, including the agreement to adopt an Action Plan at the next EU-China summit enhancing custom cooperation on seizures of counterfeit goods and concrete measures to reduce counterfeit sales;
- **Trade facilitation,** including concrete steps to improve import and export procedures and increase supply chain security.

*For Europe:*

**Peter Mandelson**, EU Commissioner for Trade; Chair

**László Kovács,** EU Commissioner for Taxation and Customs

**Vladimir Spidla,** EU Commissioner for Social Affairs

**Louis Michel,** EU Commissioner for Development

**Andris Piebalgs,** EU Commissioner for Energy

**Meglena Kuneva,** EU Commissioner for Consumer Protection

**Janez Potocnik,** EU Commissioner for Research

**Stavros Dimas,** EU Commissioner for Environment

*For China:*

**Chair: Vice Premier Wang**

Minister of Commerce **Chen Denming**

Minister of General Administration of Quality Supervision, Inspection and Quarantine (AQSIQ) **Li Changjiang**

Minister of State Administration of Industry and Commerce (SAIC) **Zhou Bohua**

Minister for Human Resources and Social Security **Yin Wenmin**

Minister of General Customs Office **Sheng Guangzu**

Minister for Environmental Protection **Zhou Shengxian**

Vice Chairman of National Development and Reform Commission (NRDC) **Zhang Xiaoqiang**

Vice Minister for Science and Technology **Shang Yong**

Assistant Minister for Foreign Affairs **Wu Hongbo**

Assistant Minister for Finance **Zhu Guangyao**

**The meeting: General exchange on key issues**

*Trade and investment cooperation*

Discussions focused on the need to work towards a more balanced trading relationship. The EU and China agreed that the focus of work will be on creating new trade and investment opportunities. The EU will continue to offer support and technical assistance in improving customs processes and China will aim for tangible progress in the fight against counterfeiting and improving product safety and supply chain security.

*Sustainable development and the environment*

Discussions focussed on the mutual supportiveness of trade and environmental policies and on the need for the EU and China jointly to address the environmental and social challenges associated with globalisation. In particular, the need for trade and social policies together to promote economic growth and improve living standards and quality of life for all. Both sides agreed on the importance of boosting trade in environmentally-friendly goods and to encourage strongly more sustainable production and consumption patterns. The EU urged China to lower tariffs on environmental goods and to widen market access for environmental services.

*Consumer protection and product safety*

Discussions focussed on the importance of enhancing consumer product safety through close cooperation between the EU and China. The EU and China agreed that while primary responsibility for ensuring that products are safe rests with the businesses making and selling them, the EU and China should step up their cooperation in improving product safety standards.

*Development and Aid*

The EU and China agreed on the importance of effective coordination on global development issues, especially in Africa. With their different experiences and approaches to development, the EU and China are committed to intensify their dialogue and explore concrete cooperation in development projects in Africa in areas such as infrastructure, governance, renewable energy, health and education.

**The meeting: Focussed discussions on specific issues**

*Energy*

Led by the EU. Discussions focused on the importance of enhancing bilateral dialogue and cooperation on energy. The EU stressed that important investments, improved energy efficiency and greater use of renewable energy are needed to meet China's climate change targets. Trade in the energy sector should thus foster the use of better, cleaner technologies for energy production.

- The EU and China underlined the need to cooperate on standards in order to facilitate technology transfer.
- The EU raised concerns regarding local content requirements in the Chinese power generation and transmission sectors, that restrict greater EU involvement in the Chinese energy sector.
- The EU and China exchanged information on best practice for approving energy projects and feed-in tariff policies.
- The EU and China stressed the importance of their shared objectives to enhance energy efficiency, and improve the current framework to allow optimal allocation of energy resources in the domestic and global economy.

These issues will be followed up in specialised fora and the next HLM and EU-China Summit will review progress

*Technology cooperation*

Led by China. The EU and China have set themselves the goal of becoming technology and innovation-driven economies. The HLM agreed to step up efforts to encourage high-tech trade. It agreed that for innovation and creativity to prosper, and for increased cooperation and trade in technology to be possible, the environment for technology trade should be improved. There are clear links in particular between trade in technology and effective protection of Intellectual Property Rights. China is an active third country partner in EU research. The HLM will aim to support this further.

- The EU and China agree to further intensify their excellent cooperation in science and technology, based on mutual interest and equal partnership.
- The EU and China discussed the working group on barriers to high tech trade.
- The EU and China agreed to explore strengthened cooperation in civil aviation, maritime and civil nuclear and space technology areas.

The HLM will pursue these issues.

*IPR protection*

Led by the EU. IPR protection is the key to encourage trade in technology and to safeguard the legitimate rights of the inventors and right holders. The EU and China agreed that IPR is an issue of core strategic importance.

- Both sides endorsed the signing of a Joint Customs Action Plan on IPR at the next EU-China Summit and welcomed the establishment of a Roadmap to ensure rapid progress in the preparatory technical discussion. The plan will include exchange of information on customs seizures that would lead to concrete action in stopping the traffic of counterfeit goods.
- The EU and China discussed new ways to encourage Chinese companies to enter into negotiation for licensing agreements for patented technologies.
- The EU and China underlined the importance to improve the enforcement of trademarks in retail and wholesale markets, and looked into how to clean out counterfeit products from markets.
- The EU and China reviewed the need to improve copyright enforcement for online piracy, and to facilitate access to the Chinese judicial system, especially through simplified procedural requirements.

The HLM will pursue these issues.

*Trade Facilitation*

Led by China. The EU and China agreed on the practical benefits of trade facilitation measures for simplifying and modernising import, export and transit procedures, particularly customs requirements.

- The HLM reviewed customs cooperation in this field, including the Smart and Secure Trade Lanes pilot project, and the related broader issues of supply chain security.
- Both sides welcomed progress made in the Working Group on mutual administrative assistance tasked to improve information exchange to counter fraud.
- The EU and China agreed to work closely in the WTO Doha negotiations on trade facilitation which aim to improve global standardisation of customs procedures.

The HLM will pursue these issues

**Background: The EU-China High Level Economic and Trade Dialogue Mechanism**

The High Level Economic and Trade Dialogue Mechanism (HLM) was agreed on at the November 2007 Summit by President Barroso and Premier Wen, signalling the agreement to address the imbalance in bilateral trade flows between the EU and China. The 2007 EU-China Summit Joint Statement states that the Dialogue Mechanism will: "*discuss strategies in EU-China trade, investment and economic cooperation and coordinate bilateral projects, studies and develop plans in priority sectors. It will cover issues affecting the trade imbalance, including inter alia effective market access, intellectual property rights, environment, high technology and energy in order to find concrete means to increase trade in a balanced way.*" The HLM is

The broad remit of the HLM is to examine the following issues

*1. The multilateral global trading system*

In particular, the HLM will focus on the role of EU-China economic and trade relations in the wider framework of the global trading system.

*2. Strategic bilateral trade and trade-related issues*

These will include market access for goods and services, and consumer protection. At the 2007 EU-China Summit the two sides agreed on the need to work towards more balanced trade flows. While recognising that part of the imbalance is caused by global economic factors, the HLM can deliver results to unlock new business opportunities. The HLM will look at ways to enhance cooperation in addressing technical and regulatory barriers to trade. This will cover issues ranging from product standards to restrictions on service providers. The HLM will also provide for a review of China's progress on achieving Market Economy Status.

*3. Investment issues*

This will include strategic discussions on the bilateral investment issues including both portfolio investments and specific sectors. Focus will be on open investment environment and conditions in the respective markets and will look closely at investment restrictions, ownership caps, and local partner restrictions in order to enable greater investment flows in both directions.

*4. Innovation, including IPR, and technology*

For innovation, research and creativity to prosper, both the legal and the practical environment need to encourage those areas. The effective protection of Intellectual Property Rights is therefore key for both the EU and China and necessary for China's efforts to transform its economy. China has made efforts to set up the right legal framework for this. The HLM will focus on ways to improve effective enforcement of this framework, benchmark progress, enhance customs cooperation and foster technology transfer through better intellectual property protection. In the short term, concrete steps are needed to enhance the efficiency and effectiveness of the judicial process, ensure royalty payments, and guarantee effective copyright and trademark enforcement in retail and wholesale markets.

*5. EU-China economic cooperation*

This will include close coordination on energy, sustainable development, including environmental and social pillars and regulatory and sectoral policy issues, transportation, and cross cutting issues such as better regulation.

For more information on the EU-China trade relationship visit: http://ec.europa.eu/trade/

## SECTORAL DIALOGUES

### Agriculture

The EU–China Dialogue on Agriculture was established on 15 July 2005 by a Joint Declaration between the European Commission Directorate-General on Agriculture and Rural Development, on the one hand, and China's Ministry of Agriculture, on the other (see Document 5.2). It aims to promote cooperation, facilitate communication and resolve problems if necessary. The range of topics discussed include agricultural trade, new technologies relating to agricultural development and quality policies for agricultural products, including geographical indications and organic production. Its work is organised in four Technical Working Groups on Agricultural Trade, Quality Products, Policy Information and Food Technologies.

The EU–China Dialogue on Agriculture is often closely linked to other dialogues and meetings, such as the EU-China Trade Dialogue and/or the Memorandum of Understanding on administrative cooperation Arrangements between the European commission's Directorate-General for Health and Consumer Protection (DG SANCO) and China's General Administration of Quality Supervision, Inspection and Quarantine (AQSIQ) (see below).

## Document 5.2: Dialogue on Agriculture

Joint Declaration Establishing A Dialogue on Agriculture between the Directorate-General for Agriculture and Rural Development of the European Commission and the Ministry of Agriculture of the People's Republic of China

On 15 July, 2005, Mr Du Qinglin, Minister of Agriculture of the People's Republic of China and Ms. Fischer Boel, Commissioner for Agriculture and Rural Development, met in Beijing to discuss the creation of a dialogue on agriculture and rural development between the Ministry of Agriculture of the People's Republic of China and the Directorate General for Agriculture and Rural Development of the European Commission and reached the following consensus on the principles, objectives, content and organisation of this dialogue:

**1. Principles**

It is agreed to set up a structured dialogue on agriculture and rural development between the Ministry of Agriculture of the People's Republic of China and the Directorate General for Agriculture and Rural Development of the European Commission (hereafter referred to as both sides) where all related agriculture, bilateral and multilateral agricultural issues can be discussed.

**2. Objectives**

(1) Promote mutual understanding, trust and bilateral co-operation between both sides in the field of agriculture and rural development.

(2) Establish communication channels between so as to strengthen the exchange of information, timely notification of any issues arising and facilitate their efficient resolution.

**3. Content**

(1) Exchange information on our experiences in setting up and implementing agriculture and rural development policies, lawand regulations.

(2) Exchange information on agriculture production and trade (import–export). Assess respective market developments for agricultural products.

(3) Discuss new technologies relating to agricultural development.

(4) Exchange views on quality policies for agricultural products (including geographical indications and organic production, etc.).

(5) Any other topics of mutual interest relating to agriculture.

**4. Organisation**

(1) Both sides agree to establish contact points in Ministry of Agriculture of the Peoples Republic of China and the Directorate General for Agriculture and Rural Development of the European Commission. Both sides will be responsible for the co-ordination of the dialogue. According to needs, both sides may decide to set up technical working groups to work together on specific issues.

(2) The level and composition of the delegations in the meetings will be decided by each side in consultation with the other. At least one meeting of at least one day shall take place each year. The precise agenda for each meeting shall be agreed beforehand between both sides. Both sides may invite other Ministries and Directorates Generals to take part in the meetings subject to need and agreement by both sides. There should be mutually agreed minutes in English and Chinese after every meeting.

(3) The venue for the meetings will alternate between the EU and China.

The precise content, structure and other of the dialogue details will be finalised by both sides in the near future.

This Joint Declaration is signed in Beijing on 15 July, 2005 in duplicate in both English and Chinese

Minister Du Qinglin
Ministry of Agriculture of the
People's Republic of China

Commissioner Fischer Boel
Member of the European Commission
responsible for Agriculture and Rural
Development

## Civil Aviation

In the 2002 'Open Skies' cases,[5] the European Court of Justice decided that bilateral air service agreements between an EU Member State and third countries were incompatible with the EC law principle prohibiting discrimination on grounds of nationality if they discriminated against air carriers from other Member States. Consequently, the European Commission began to negotiate civil aviation agreements with third countries, including China. The EU established a cooperation project to provide technical assistance to China about aviation safety, security and air traffic management. In March 2003 the European Commission published a Communication entitled 'A Community Civil Aviation Policy towards the People's Republic of

[5] Case C–467/98 *Commission v Denmark* [2002] ECR I–9519; Case C–468/98 *Commission v Sweden* [2002] ECR I–9575; Case C–469/98 *Commission v Finland* [2002] ECR I–9627; Case 471/98 *Commission v Belgium* [2002] ECR I–9681; Case C–472/98 *Commission v Luxembourg* [2002] ECR I–9741; Case C–475/98 *Commission v Austria* [2002] ECR I–9797; Case C–477 *Commission v Germany* [2002] ECR I–9855.

China—Strengthening Cooperation and Opening Markets' (see Document 5.3).[6] It requested a mandate from the Council to negotiate a comprehensive civil aviation agreement with China. Subsequently, the 1st EU–China Aviation Summit was held in Beijing on 29 June to 1 July 2005. The Joint Declaration (see Document 5.4) established the Civil Aviation Dialogue. Its aims are to lead to the conclusion of a bilateral agreement on air services, to conclude a similar agreement on technical cooperation in civil aviation and to engage in a broad dialogue on the application of competition law and environmental protection.[7]

## Document 5.3: Commission Communication,' A Community Civil Aviation Policy towards the People's Republic of China—Strengthening Cooperation and Opening Markets'

COMMUNICATION FROM THE COMMISSION
A Community civil aviation policy towards the People's Republic of China – strengthening co-operation and opening markets
COM(2005) 78 final, Brussels 11.2.2005

### 1. INTRODUCTION AND SUMMARY

1.1 The People's Republic of China, the world's most populous nation, has emerged over the past 15 years as a key player in world affairs, reflecting its extraordinary growth and economic development. China is becoming an increasingly important partner for the European Union - and vice versa - both economically and politically.

China is making continued progress in the reform of its economy. China's accession in December 2001 to the World Trade Organisation was significant and will pave the way for further market opening and foreign direct investment. In 2003, China became the EU's second largest trading partner after the US and the EU became China's second largest export market. Following EU enlargement in 2004, the EU is now China's largest trading partner.

1.2 The Chinese air traffic market is among the fastest growing in the world. The average annual growth rate of air travellers in China has been approximately 16% between 1958 and 2002 and high growth rates are expected to prevail until 2020.[1]

China therefore offers a strong potential for growth also for airlines, aircraft manufacturers and service providers in Europe.

The 2008 Olympic Games in Beijing and the 2010 World Expo in Shanghai will provide major impetus to the restructuring and investments in the aviation sector to allow China to use these events to demonstrate an efficient and modern image to the world. However, China is facing significant challenges in this respect, notably in matching continued safety developments with the spectacular growth rates in air traffic.

6 Commission of the European Communities Communication, 'A Community Civil Aviation Policy towards the People's Republic of China—Strengthening Cooperation and Opening Markets', COM(2005) 78 final (Brussels, 11 February 2005).

7 See also European Commission, Directorate-General Transport, Air Transport Portal of the European Commission, International Transport, 'A Policy Built on Three Key Pillars: Global Partners: China', available at http://ec.europa.eu/transport/air_portal/international/pillars/global_partners/china_en.htm (accessed 22 December 2007).

1.3 China is taking a gradual and selective yet determined approach to market opening in civil aviation. As a consequence of the "open skies" judgements of the European Court of Justice on 5 November 2002, the bilateral agreements between Member States and China are unsustainable and need to be amended. The Commission has been given a "horizontal" mandate to negotiate with third countries such necessary corrections to bilateral agreements.

However, in view of (i) the growing importance of the Chinese aviation market, (ii) the difficulties encountered by individual Member States in seeking to bring bilateral agreements into conformity with Community law and (iii) the benefits of replacing the fragmented European approach in its relations with China with a co-ordinated and liberal approach, the Commission is of the view that it is now time to develop a wider range of opportunities between China and the Community in air transport.

1.4 In parallel to this Communication, the Commission therefore recommends that the Council would authorise the Commission to negotiate, on behalf of the European Community, a comprehensive Open Aviation Agreement with China. Positive exploratory contacts between the General Administration of Civil Aviation of China (CAAC) and the services of the European Commission were initiated in May 2004, which may serve as a good basis for entering into formal negotiations with China.

## 2. THE GROWING IMPORTANCE OF EU-CHINA POLITICAL AND ECONOMIC COOPERATION

2.1 In recent years, the Chinese economy has performed spectacularly well with economic growth rates above 7% in 14 consecutive years. In 2003, China's economy grew by 9.1%, the highest level for seven years. Economic growth in some of the large urban centres, which leads China's economic development, even far out-strips the average economic growth rates.

It is generally recognised that the demand for air transport is closely linked with the development of GDP. Against this background, and in view of the improved spending basis of the growing urban middle class representing an important potential for tourist travelling, continuously growing demand for air transport in China is expected.

2.2 EU-China trade is growing faster than China's trade with its other two main trading partners (Japan and the US). Total trade for 2003 between China and the EU was estimated to be worth a total of 135billion, up more than 15% on 2002. Following EU enlargement in 2004, the EU is now China's largest trading partner.

2.3 Buoyed by its sheer size and its nearly 1.3 billion population (22% of World population), extraordinary economic growth rates and immense potential in general, China's economic weight and political status in the world today is very different from what it was as recently as in the 1990s. A broad political dialogue between China and the EU was formally established in 1994.

Enhancing China-EU relations is an important component of China's foreign policy. In its first-ever "*EU Policy Paper*", the Chinese Government outlined in October 2003 its priority areas and plans for strengthening the China-EU political, economic and trade relations.

Improving market access and investment conditions in China is a key objective for the EU. In particular, further reform and liberalisation will help China attract foreign investment and technological know-how, and to sustain economic growth. This is true for any sector of the economy but for civil aviation in particular.

2.4 The Sixth EU-China Summit held in October 2003 clearly demonstrated that China now recognises the Community as such as a primary interlocutor for Europe. With EU enlargement and the process of European integration, Community-level contacts and co-ordination with the EU will become increasingly important for China as well as for the Union. This also applies to civil aviation in relation to which the EU and China agreed at the Sixth Summit that co-operation should be widened and deepened. This was confirmed in May 2004 during the visit of Chinese Prime Minister Wen Jiabao to the EU Headquarters in Brussels and further emphasised during the Seventh EU-China Summit held in December 2004. At the Seventh Summit, the possibility of a future EU-China Civil Aviation Agreement was envisaged.

## 3. CHINA'S GROWING IMPORTANCE IN INTERNATIONAL AVIATION – A MARKET PROFILE

*China – a strategic civil aviation market in rapid growth*

3.1 Over the past decade, the Chinese air traffic market has been among the fastest growing in the world. The average annual growth rate of domestic and international air traffic in China has been around 16% between 1958 and 2002. Total number of air traffic passengers was expected to exceed 100 million in 2004 while cargo was forecasted to reach 2.5 million tons.

Since 1990, the number of seats available on scheduled non-stop flights between the EU and China has increased from 250,000 to nearly 3 million in 2003 (+1150%).[2] The growth in available seats on scheduled non-stop flights to Japan, which is still the EU's largest air traffic market in Asia, "only" grew by 378% over the same period.

3.2 Until as recently as 10 years ago, Beijing was the only destination for European flights to China. Since then and until 2003, all flights to China have been to Beijing and Shanghai with Shanghai experiencing an extremely rapid growth now receiving more than 35% of all air passenger traffic from Europe. New routes are now being opened to a number of other Chinese cities.

Eight EU carriers currently fly passengers to China on scheduled routes while all three main Chinese airline groups (Air China, China Eastern and China Southern) fly to Europe. A total of 21 routes are now operated between China and the EU. The largest share of the non-stop traffic between the EU and China is with Germany with 38% of the total traffic, while France has 23% and the UK 9%. Of a total number of weekly frequencies between the EU and China of 141 in April 2004, Air China had a share of 28% while Lufthansa had a share of 17% and Air France 15%.

*Looking forward*

3.3 While future growth rates in Chinese air passenger traffic may be less spectacular than in recent years, they will still be impressive. The International Air Transport Association, IATA, forecasts an average annual growth of 8.6% in passenger traffic in China over the period 2003-2007. This is nearly three times the world average growth rate forecast by IATA. Cargo is generally expected to grow faster than passenger traffic.

The CAAC expects even higher growth rates for air traffic with an expected average annual increase until 2020 of 15%.

China is therefore expected over the next 10 years to become the largest Asian market and leading hub for air passenger traffic as well as for international cargo traffic thereby taking over Japan's current leading position. China's total passenger traffic is expected to increase from approx. 100 million passengers in 2004 to 215 million passengers in 2014 thereby increasing its total share of Asian-Pacific air passenger traffic to 25% up from 10% in 1985.[3]

*Approved destination status*

3.4 One of the key drivers in Chinese air traffic demand and development will be tourism. International tourist arrivals to China grew by 11% in 2002, making China the fifth largest recipient of tourists in the world. Chinese outbound tourism amounted to 20 million tourists in 2003 (+22% year-on-year) overtaking Japan to become Asia's largest source of tourists. It is estimated that by 2020 the number of Chinese outbound travellers will have reached 100 million.

To facilitate and attract visits of Chinese tourist groups to Europe, the Community and the Chinese government signed in February 2004 a Memorandum of Understanding under which the Community will enjoy an "Approved Destination Status" (ADS). Chinese tourist groups are only allowed to travel to countries which have been granted ADS by China. Until now, private tourism from China to the EU has not been possible.

The ADS scheme will ease the process of visa applications for Chinese tourist groups wishing to visit Europe.

The implementation of the ADS scheme is expected to generate significant numbers of new Chinese tourists visiting Europe. This will have profound implications on airline and airport capacity with airlines already adding capacity to China to meet increasing demand.

## 4. TRENDS IN CHINESE AVIATION POLICY - OPENING SKIES

4.1 China's civil aviation sector is undergoing considerable change these years. The transformation of the Chinese civil aviation sector appears to be a gradual move away from central planning towards a combination of decentralisation and globalisation.

Aviation developments and policies in China are characterised notably by the following key features:

- *Consolidation* of the airline industry into three main airline groups
- Emerging liberalisation and *market opening* both internally and externally
- Development of new airport *infrastructure* and air traffic management technology

Each of these features will briefly be examined in the following.

*Consolidation*

4.2 In the mid 1990s, Chinese aviation industry was characterised by poor safety records with serious accidents. In addition, over-capacity led to intense price-cutting and fierce competition in the domestic market which restricted international expansion. This led the government to pursue a policy of consolidation and price control of the largely state-controlled airline industry. Following only modest progress in the restructuring in the late 1990s, the CAAC announced in July 2000 that the 10 carriers under its direct administration would be merged into the three main airline groups. As a result of this, three airline groups with similar numbers of aircrafts (ca. 100) and assets (ca. USD6bn) have emerged centred around three main geographical centres: Air China (Beijing), China Eastern Airlines (Shanghai) and China Southern Airlines (Guangzhou).

4.3 The three main airline groups account for about 80% of flights in China. The consolidation of the airline industry has created profitable operators with strong balance sheets, which have been able to expand and compete internationally and attract foreign investment and partners. Chinese airlines have traditionally had a domestic focus with only 13% of total passengers carried by the top 5 Chinese airlines in 2002 being international traffic.

4.4 The once fully state-owned airlines are now listed on the stock markets and being partly privatised. The direct control over the state shareholding in the airlines has been transferred from the CAAC to other government agencies and the CAAC is now solely focusing on its regulatory role.

*Market opening*

4.5 China is clearly signalling its intention and willingness to open its domestic and international air transport markets to more competition. The CAAC has announced that it will progressively open mainland China air traffic rights to foreign carriers including more cabotage rights and encouragement of more foreign carriers to fly to China and more mainland carriers to serve foreign cities.

4.6 CAAC intends to liberalise the Chinese aviation market in three phases which by 2010 should have led to an opening of 70-80% of the air transport industry.

CAAC is also progressively deregulating air fare pricing to give airlines greater flexibility in setting fares according to market demand.

Reports that the CAAC is also welcoming low-cost airlines as a strategy for boosting middle class tourism and economic development in Western China is a further significant sign of liberalisation.

As a result of its new policy, CAAC has signed a series of increasingly liberal air services arrangements with third countries including Singapore, Thailand, Australia and most recently the US. Often the cargo services are leading the way in liberalisation but are followed by similar moves in passenger traffic.

4.7 China is also liberalising rules for foreign investment in civil aviation. In 2002 a new Decree on "*Provisions on Foreign Investment in Civil Aviation*" entered into force designed to reinforce the opening of the civil aviation industry of China and stimulate foreign investment both in airports, airlines and other projects and services. Foreign investors can, however, not take control over Chinese airports or airlines.

*Infrastructure – airports, aircraft and air traffic management*

4.8 In order to meet the growing demand for air transport services in China, massive investments in air transport infrastructure are required both in airports, aircrafts, air traffic management technology and supporting facilities.

Since 1990, China has built more than 25 new airports and had in 2002 a total of 160 civilian airports. The number of airports is expected to increase to 260 by 2015.

The new projects include a new airport in Guangzhou; expansion of Beijing's Capital International Airport including a new runway for planned completion in 2007 in time for the 2008 Olympic Games; and expansion of Shanghai's Pudong airport with a new runway for planned completion by 2005-2006. Total investments at these three designated international hubs alone are estimated at more than 5 billion USD over the next four years.

Ownership and control over airports has recently been decentralised to the provincial and municipal authorities, which now have a strong incentive to develop their regional aviation market and attract private capital to support this.

4.9 The CAAC forecasts that Chinese airlines will need to add nearly 1800 new passenger aircraft to their fleets over the next two decades. This offers the European aerospace industry significant business opportunities, particularly in the important market segment of large civil aircraft.

China will also require new air traffic management technology to manage the steadily increasing air traffic. It is expected that China will need to invest more than

1.1 billion USD over the next decade in improving its air traffic management (ATM) infrastructure. Virtually all of this equipment will need to be imported and European industry is well placed to provide this technology.

In addition, China will need to modernise a wide range of support facilities and services such as ground handling, refuelling etc. China should make efforts to remove obstacles to market entry in these sectors including in relation to fuel supply and computer reservation systems, where current practices are discriminatory against foreign suppliers.

*Key challenges facing China's civil aviation sector*

4.10 The spectacular growth in Chinese civil aviation has its own negative side effects and matching the rapid growth in demand for air transport with aviation safety developments and the implementation and management of modern technology is proving very demanding.

CAAC has therefore identified the following main challenges for further developing safe and market-driven civil aviation in China:

- Improve safety and security regulation and oversight capabilities
- Further expansion of infrastructure
- Optimise utilisation of air space
- Better training of personnel
- Develop market mechanisms and competition laws
- Adapt airlines and airports to become more competitive

In view of these challenges, there is a very strong Chinese interest in learning from the European experiences in developing safe and competitive air transport services. In this context, the EU co-financed "EU-China Civil Aviation Co-operation Project" has been seen by the Chinese as a very valuable project. The project started in 1999 and has enjoyed a total of more than 15 million in Community funding. Both the Chinese authorities and industry as well as European industrial interests have expressed a strong interest in a continuation on a longer-term basis of this project or similar co-operation structures.

## 5. WHY A COMMUNITY APPROACH IN EXTERNAL AVIATION RELATIONS?

5.1 Since the 1960s, EU-China relations in civil aviation have been based on bilateral air services agreements between individual Member States and China with little, if any, coordination at Community level. 19 out of the 25 EU Member States have bilateral air services agreements with China (all except Cyprus, Ireland, Lithuania, Malta, Portugal and

Slovenia). All these bilateral agreements are based on national designation at Member State level of a single (or in a few cases more) national carriers which are allowed to operate on routes to China. Moreover, traffic rights allowed under the bilateral agreements are also limited hence restricting the scope for competition.

Following the judgements of the European Court of Justice on 5 November 2002, existing bilateral air services agreements based on national designation urgently need to be amended to include Community designation clauses permitting designation of any Community air carrier established in a Member State.

5.2 A dialogue between the Chinese civil aviation authorities and the services of the European Commission was initiated in May 2004 during which the Commission services informed CAAC about the need to amend existing air services agreements. Both sides expressed their interest in continuing discussions with the aim of resolving this matter as soon as possible.

The two sides agreed to continue the dialogue and to further develop co-operation with the objective of reaching a comprehensive agreement between China and the Community. The services of the European Commission informed the Chinese side of their intention to take the necessary steps to request a mandate from the Council authorising it to negotiate such an agreement with China.

During the May 2004 meeting, CAAC presented a wide range of proposals for closer technical co-operation and EU assistance in civil aviation including in relation to safety management, air traffic control, airworthiness certification, regulation of market access and application of competition law and flight standards.

5.3 This Communication requesting a mandate for negotiating a Community-wide air services agreement with China follows naturally from the judgements of the European Court of Justice and the political agreement reached by the 5 June 2003 Transport Council. It also reflects the acceptance of the Community as negotiator of international agreements in many economic sectors including in air transport.

The Commission is currently negotiating air transport agreements under the "horizontal mandate" with a number of countries and has initialled agreements with some countries already. Such agreements could be the first step towards a more comprehensive open aviation agreement between the Community and these countries. In 2004, the Commission issued a Communication on a "*Community aviation policy towards its neighbours*"[4], which recommended further more comprehensive Community negotiations with a number of neighbouring countries. In December 2004, the Commission was given a comprehensive mandate for negotiating with Morocco and the Western Balkans.

5.4 As the EU has developed a strong Community dimension of its internal aviation market it would be illogical if such a dimension was not pursued also in the EU's external relations. Moreover, the experiences which the EU has gained in this respect are considered highly valuable by third countries.

The European Commission's White Paper "*European transport policy for 2010: time to decide*"[5] stressed the need for the Union to increase its ability to assert itself in international relations and speak with a single voice in international arena in defence of its industrial, social and environmental interests. The EU has demonstrated in several areas that it can obtain and deliver more when it acts in strong unity and as one.

5.5 However, the European Union remains - unlike the US - fragmented in its relations with third countries.

The conduct and outcome of bilateral negotiations in recent months between Member States and third countries have not yet led to the necessary alignment of existing agreements with Community law. The Community and Member States therefore must act together to regulate access, ensure the development of industry and achieve compliance with Community legislation.

5.6 There is no reason why the benefits of opening market access and investment rules in third countries such as China in principle should not be similar to the benefits of an EU-US Open Aviation Area. Indeed, a recent study commissioned by the European Commission has made an indicative assessment of the potential longer-term economic benefits for both sides involved in a fully liberalised EU-China aviation market, which could be in the order of several hundred million {EUROS} per year.

Obviously, it will be of paramount importance to ensure that opening and integration of markets is undertaken in a balanced manner that takes into account other important policy objectives and mitigates potential adverse impacts, be it in competition, environmental protection or other areas. Flexibility for the EU to apply the economic or regulatory instruments that are necessary to counter-balance adverse environmental impacts from the expected growth in traffic volumes should also be ensured.

5.7 Proposing a comprehensive mandate for the negotiations with China that more adequately reflects the EU's position in the world today would clearly strengthen the negotiating position of the Community and also signal the determination of the Community to resolve outstanding infringements of Community law and competence and demonstrate Europe's commitment to open markets and sustainable development.

**6. REQUEST FOR AND SCOPE OF A NEGOTIATING MANDATE**

6.1 As this Communication has shown, China has embarked on profound changes in its civil aviation sector including restructuring of its domestic aviation industry and gradual market reform and opening.

Significant efforts will continue to be necessary for the development of the Chinese air traffic sector to meet China's aspirations as well as international standards. Closer co-operation between the EU and China is paramount and will be mutually beneficial and be able to contribute to the development of an efficient, robust and safe aviation sector.

The Commission therefore considers it important to offer China a comprehensive scope for strengthened co-operation in civil aviation.

Such co-operation must address and resolve the legal issues in relation to existing bilateral agreements between China and Member States.

6.2 However, an agreement with China should not be limited to agreeing on Community designation clauses. It should go further and establish an ambitious framework integrating industrial co-operation and wider aviation issues such as co-operation in the fields of aviation safety, security, air traffic management, technology and research as well as "doing-business" issues.

While ambitions should be high, a fully open aviation area with China may take time to develop and may best be developed in stages to allow a smooth transition and market integration based on a gradual implementation of new rules.

6.3 The scope of the mandate that the Commission is proposing is outlined in a proposed separate draft Council Decision.

6.4 To the extent that restrictions on traffic rights may remain under a future Community-China agreement, or indeed any other Community-wide agreement with a third country, the Community will need to develop transparent and nondiscriminatory procedures for allocation of such limited traffic rights as negotiated at Community level. Such procedures are under preparation and a proposal will be submitted in the near future.

**7. CONCLUSIONS**

7.1 The civil aviation sector offers significant new opportunities for further strengthening transport sector co-operation and mutual benefits of China and the EU. Efforts should therefore now be made for air transport to become the next key area of closer co-operation between the EU and China in the transport sector.

7.2 In the light of this, the Commission proposes the negotiation and conclusion of a comprehensive open aviation agreement with the People's Republic of China and invites the Council to authorise the Commission to enter into negotiations on behalf of the European Community on such an agreement.

The Commission will work closely together with Member States and all relevant stakeholders in further developing and achieving the objectives set out in the proposed Council Decision.

1 The General Administration of Civil Aviation of China (CAAC), 2004.
2 Source: OAG schedules.
3 "Asia/Pacific Air Traffic – Growth and Constraints", Air Transport Action Group (ATAG), 2001.
4 COM(2004)74, "A Community aviation policy towards its neighbours", 9 February 2004.
5 COM(2001)370.

## Document 5.4: Civil Aviation Dialogue Joint Declaration on EU–China Cooperation in Civil Aviation

Joint Declaration by Mr. Yang Yuanyuan, Minister of Civil Aviation of China and Mr. Jacques Barrot, Vice-President of the European Commission
on
EU-China Co-operation in Civil Aviation
Signed at the occasion of the EU-China Aviation Summit,
Beijing, 29 June–1 July 2005.

1. The first EU-China Aviation Summit was held on 29 June–1 July 2005 in Beijing, jointly organised by the General Administration of Civil Aviation of China ("CAAC") and the European Commission. It brought together more than 250 leading representatives of the European Union and Chinese aviation sectors representing public authorities, airlines, aerospace industries and service providers. The EU delegation was led by Mr. Jacques Barrot, Vice President of the European Commission responsible for transport and the Chinese side was led by Mr. Yang Yuanyuan, Minister for Civil Aviation. Mr. Huang Ju, Vice Premier of the State Council of the People's Republic of China, attended the opening session of the aviation summit.

2. The EU-China Aviation Summit was highly successful in bringing together all key stakeholders and in serving as a platform for identifying priority areas and ways forward in closer EU-China aviation co-operation for the future.

3. The Aviation Summit demonstrated the growing importance of the EU-China relations in civil aviation and the excellent collaboration between EU and Chinese industries. EU-China

air traffic has increased significantly in recent years. Since 1990, the number of seats available on scheduled non-stop flights between the EU and China has increased from approx. 275,000 to nearly 5.4 million in 2004 (+1950%). The Chinese air transport market is among the world's fastest growing markets with an average annual growth in air travel between 1978 and 2004 of 18% with high growth rates expected to continue in the coming decades. China is now effectively the largest Asian aviation market and the EU-China market is therefore of increasing strategic importance to both European and Chinese carriers and industry in general.

4. China has granted an "Approved Destination Status" for its tourists to the EU. This has led to a steady increase of Chinese travellers to Europe with a growing demand for air transport capacity between China and the EU. Total Chinese outbound tourism is expected to increase from more than 28 million in 2004 to 100 million by 2020. China's hosting of the Olympic Games in Beijing in 2008 and the World Expo in 2010 in Shanghai will provide further impetus and challenges to the Chinese aviation sector in terms of development ot infrastructure and technology to match growing demand with safety and security.

5. The EU-China Aviation Summit addressed a wide range of areas of mutual interest including notably:

- Market trends and political and regulatory developments in China and the EU including the increasing emphasis on market opening and consumer benefits arising from competition
- Infrastructure plans and investment opportunities
- Aviation safety and security policies and scope for regulatory cooperation and convergence
- Air traffic management and in this respect the potential for co-operation in the EU's Single European Sky technology and industrial programme SESAME
- Enabling doing business and making sustainable investment in both markets
- Future EU-China co-operation in civil aviation including technical assistance and industrial co-operation

6. In this context of growing interdependence, the two sides reiterated their desire to deepening and strengthening co-operation between the EU and China on a broad range of issues in order to support the safe development of rapidly growing air traffic services between China and the EU.

7. Both EU and Chinese aviation sectors are undergoing significant economic as well as regulatory change in a fast growing environment. The two sides confirmed their general interest in gradually opening up their aviation markets by increasing capacity entitlements in relation to market access and through regulatory co-operation facilitating airline operations. This will create significant benefits to passengers and users and significant opportunities for operators both in China and in the European Union.

8. The two parties confirmed their intention to further strengthen the EU-China aviation dialogue notably through:

i. Engaging, as a matter of priority, in formal negotiations with a view to resolve outstanding legal issues in bilateral air services agreements between EU Member States and China. In anticipation of such formal negotiations, a preparatory meeting will be held in early September 2005 between the services of the European Commission, the representatives of CAAC and Chinese carriers, during which the European Commission will provide further clarification in this regard. Following this meeting and the completion of extensive analysis of this issue, CAAC expects to be in a position to start negotiations with the Community in the fourth quarter of 2005. The parties will seek to conclude an agreement at the earliest possible date thereafter based on the principles of equality and mutual benefits.

ii. Engaging in negotiations in the coming months with a view to conclude an agreement relating to technical co-operation in civil aviation including matters such as safety, security and air traffic management and the related SESAME programme.

iii Engaging in a broad dialogue on application of competition law and environmental protection.

9. The European Commission has requested a mandate from the Council of the European Union authorising the European Commission to negotiate on behalf of the Community and its Member States such a comprehensive air services agreement with China. This request will be considered under the UK Presidency of the EU during the coming six months. China will follow the developments in this respect closely and the European Commission will keep CAAC directly informed.

An exploratory dialogue between China and the EU in this respect will start when considered most appropriate by both sides.

10. The General Administration of Civil Aviation of China and the European Commission have agreed to set-up a steering group that will monitor progress in the entire range of areas of co-operation and regularly report progress to the EU-China Summits.

For the European Commission
Jacques Barrot
Vice President

For the General Administration of Civil Aviation of China
Yang Yuanyuan Minister

Done at Beijing, 29 June 2005

## Competition Policy

A structured Competition Policy Dialogue (see Document 5.5) began in 2004. It was presaged by the Joint Statement adopted at the 2001 EU–China Summit, which earmarked competition policy as an area where dialogue should be intensified. Its main objective is to establish a consultation forum and to enhance EU assistance to China in the field. The administrative partners are DG Competition in the European Commission and the Treaty and Law Department of the Chinese Ministry of Commerce. The Dialogue contributed directly to the elaboration of the Chinese Anti-Monopoly Law, enacted 31 August 2007 and intended to enter into force one year later.[8]

[8] Speech given by Mr WU Zhen Guo, Deputy Director General, Anti-Monopoly Office, Department of Treaty and Law, Ministry of Commerce, People's Republic of China, at the International Seminar on Anti-monopoly Law of China, held in Beijing, 14 September 2007.

## Document 5.5: Competition Policy Dialogue

Terms of Reference of the EU-China Competition Policy Dialogue

On 6 May 2004 the Ministry of Commerce of China and the Directorate General for Competition of European Commission reached agreement on a structured dialogue on competition of which the terms of reference are laid down herewith:

### 1. Objectives and scope

The Dialogue comes within the framework of the Joint Statement adopted at the EU-China Summit of 5 September 2001, in which competition policy was earmarked as one of the areas where the EU-China dialogue should be intensified.

China has formulated various competition-related policies, laws and regulations. On its side, the EU has a relatively complete set of competition legislation. This provides a basis for a dialogue between both parties on competition legislation and enforcement.

The increasingly significant role of multilateral forums where competition matters are discussed such as the International competition Network (ICN) should be taken into account in the dialogue between the EU and China on competition policy.

The primary objective of the Competition Policy Dialogue between the authorities in charge of competition policy in China and the services responsible in the European Commission is to establish a permanent forum of consultation and transparency between China and the EU in this area, and to enhance the EU's technical and capacity-building assistance to China in the area of competition policy.

Within this framework, the aim shall be to increase both sides' understanding and awareness of current and forthcoming policy approaches, legislation and related issues, in China and the EU, and to promote exchanges and cooperation between China and the EU in the area of competition policy and legislation.

Both parties understand that competition policy is an important factor in ensuring consumer welfare and it should provide for a level playing field and legal certainty to the business community in the market. The dialogue will promote mutual considerations.

The Dialogue shall also contribute to the establishment of smooth and sustainable trade relations between China and the EU.

### 2. Structure

Treaty and Law Department of MOFCOM and the Directorate for Policy Development and Coordination of Directorate-General for Competition are responsible for coordinating the dialogue. The Dialogue, which will be co-chaired by a senior official (in principle the head of a Department or Directorate) in charge of competition policy and enforcement nominated by each administration, will be comprised of appropriate officials of each party, accompanied by officials from other relevant authorities, as may be appropriate.

The contact points will be the Treaty and Law Department of the Chinese Ministry of Commerce and the Directorate for Policy Development and Coordination of the European Commission Directorate-General for Competition. Any further activity or set up stemming from this dialogue shall be taken by consensus. Each party will also promptly notify the other of all changes of their responsible authorities for competition policy, both for legislation and for enforcement. In particular, parties will make sure that any modifications on the competence of EU or Chinese authorities in charge of competition policy and enforcement will be adequately reflected in the structure of the dialogue.

The Dialogue may establish ad-hoc working groups to facilitate discussions at expert level.

The Dialogue should take place at least once a year. Meetings shall alternate between Beijing and Brussels unless otherwise decided. The parties will take advantage to the maximum of the opportunities to meet granted by forums of dialogue already in place between China and the European Commission such as the China-EU Joint Committee meetings or other present or future forums in which both parties participate.

The working languages will be Chinese and English.

**3. Content**

The Dialogue shall, in particular, deal with:

- Antitrust law and enforcement. Exchange of views on current situations, experience, and new developments on legislation and enforcement of antitrust policies;
- Merger control in a global economy. How can company mergers be regulated? Exchange of views on merger legislations and enforcement;
- Setting up of a competition authority exchange of experiences on the set up of competition authorities, as well as their competition advocacy role;
- Exchange of views with respect to multilateral competition initiatives, with a particular mention to the fight against international «hard-core» cartels;
- Exchange of views on liberalisation of public utility sectors and State interventions into the market process;
- Exchange of experiences on raising companies and public‘s awareness on competition and anti-monopoly laws;
- Engage in cooperation to enhance EU‘s technical and capacity-building assistance to China in the area of competition policy.

**4. Technical assistance and capacity building**

In the framework of the EU-China cooperation projects, both parties will endeavour to support the objectives of the Dialogue with appropriate competition-related technical assistance and capacity building activities such as the organisation of training, seminars, studies etc.

**5. Costs**

Each party will cover its own costs, including transportation costs for international travelling, travelling between cities and accommodation. Each party will provide active support and assistance to the other.

| | |
|---|---|
| Mario Monti, Commissioner | Bo Xilai, Minister |
| European Commissioner for Competition | Minister of Commerce |

**Consumer Product Safety**

On 30 October 2002 the EU and China agreed to establish a Consultation Mechanism on Industrial Products and WTO/TBT (technical barriers to trade) Issues; this was to be complementary to other discussions concerning food safety and WTO/SPS (sanitary and phytosanitary) issues (see Document 5.6).[9] The Consultation Mechanism is the core of the current EU–China Regulatory Cooperation Dialogue, which, as described below, covers consumer product safety and other matters. The second Enterprise Policy and Regulatory Dialogue was held in Brussels on 8–10 October 2002.[10] Building on the Consultation Mechanism on Industrial Products and WTO/TBT Issues, the European Commission's DG SANCO and China's AQSIQ in January 2006 signed an MOU on Administrative Cooperation Arrangements (see Document 5.7). Subsequently they agreed to establish an EU–China Consumer Goods and Food Safety Joint Committee to monitor the MOU.[11] An EU–China Road Map on Safer Toys was signed on 19 September 2006 by EC and Consumer Protection Commissioner Markos Kypriano and Chinese Minister Li Changjiang in charge of AQSIQ (see Document 5.8).

**Document 5.6: Consultation Mechanism on Industrial Products and WTO/TBT**

Minutes of the Meeting for Establishing the Consultation Mechanism on Industrial Products and WTO/TBT between the General Administration of Quality Supervision, Inspection and Quarantine of the People's Republic of China and the Enterprise Directorate-General of the European Commission

With a view to strengthening the cooperation and exchange and enhancing the smooth development between China and the European Commission on October 30, 2002, Mr. Ge Zhirong, the Vice Minister of the General Administration of Quality Supervision, Inspection and Quarantine of the People's Republic of China (AQSIQ), had a discussion with Mr Liikanen, Commissioner of the European Commission (hereafter referred to as "both sides") on the issue of establishing a Consultation Mechanism between both sides and reached consensus as follows (See Annex 1 for the name list of the participants):

1. In order to facilitate Sino-EU trade development, to protect the safety and health of Chinese and EU consumers, both sides agreed to set up a comprehensive consultation mechanism in the areas lying within their respective competencies, so as to establish a smooth channel for communication, technical cooperation, information exchange and personnel training.

2. Both sides agreed that the Consultation Mechanism is the Cooperation and Dialogue on industrial product safely and WTO/TBT in areas lying within AQSIQ and Enterprise DG respective responsibilities.

9 See also European Commission, 'Commission and China Agree to Establish Consultation Mechanism on Industrial Products', press release (Brussels, 30 October 2002), available at http://ec.europa.eu/enterprise/enterprise_policy/gov_relations/china_regul_coop_dialogue/f1753.pdf (accessed 15 September 2007).

10 See European Commission, Directorate-General Enterprise and Industry, External Relations, 'EU–China Regulatory Cooperation Dialogue: Major Documents and Links', available at http://ec.europa.eu/enterprise/enterprise_policy/gov-relations/china-regul-coop-dialogue (accessed 22 November 2007), which also gives the 2003 position papers of the European Chamber of Commerce in Brussels (EUCCC) on different economic sectors in China.

11 See Joint Statement of the 9th EU–China Summit', available at http://www.gov.cn/misc/2006-09/10/content_383505_3.htm (accessed 15 September 2007).

3. Both sides agreed that the *Sectoral Cooperation between the Department of Supervision on Inspection of the State General Administration of the People's Republic of China for Quality Supervision and Inspection and Quarantine (AQSIQ) and Enterprise DG of the Commission of the European Communities (ECC) led by the Enterprise Policy Directorate, concerning the Sino-EU Terms of Reference on Industrial Products Safety Coordination* should be a component of the Consultation Mechanism of which the principles are maintained.

4. Both sides agreed that when the conditions are met, the consultation on Industrial Products and WTO/TBT should be linked, to other discussions dealing with animals and plants, food safety and WTO/SPS issues and should be seen as complementary.

5. Both sides agreed to establish a High Level Steering Committee for industrial products on Sino-EU Quality Supervision, Inspection and Quarantine issues, which can call annual meetings on an irregular time basis, to discuss about major issues on quality supervision, inspection and quarantine and work out the plan of future cooperation. The meetings will be held in turn in China and the EU. For the Chinese side, it will be chaired by the Vice Minister of AQSIQ; for the European Commission side, by the Director-General, Enterprise DG.

6. Both sides agreed to establish a Coordination Committee and working groups (see Annex 2) under the High Level Steering Committee as deemed necessary in each respective area of responsibilities to take charge of the specific liaison work for the consultation on industrial products and WTO/TBT. The work content and the working pattern of the coordination committee and the working groups will be decided through consultation between the two sides.

   A. Both sides have designated a contact point for the Coordination Committee on industrial product safety to be responsible for the general affairs of the safety activities between China and the European Commission.
   For the Chinese side: the Department of Supervision on Inspection, AQSIQ;
   For the EU side: the Director of the Directorate Enterprise policy. Enterprise DG.

   B. Both sides have designated a contact point for the Coordination Committee on other issues beyond industrial products to be responsible for the general affairs 'of regulatory activities between China and the European Commission.
   For the Chinese side: Department of International Cooperation, AQSIQ;
   For the EU side: the Director of the Directorate Enterprise Policy, Enterprise DO.

   C. Both sides agreed to set up Emergency Consultation Working Groups under the Consultation Mechanism for electrical safety, medical devices, toys, lighters, textile, pressure equipment, conformity assessment, standardization, technical regulation, WTO/TBT and etc. Other Working groups under the Mechanism could be established at any time provided both sides agree by exchange of letters.

7. Both sides shared the view that to guarantee the efficiency of our work for the business community, the Mechanism should ensure proper involvement at all levels of our respective industry and standardization bodies.

8. Each party will cover its own costs, including transportation costs for international travelling, travelling between cities and accommodation. Each party will provide active support and assistance to the other.

Both sides share the view that the establishment of such an exchange and cooperation mechanism helps to promote the mutual understanding between China and the EU in the field of quality supervision, inspection and quarantine, and also helps to build a channel to solve trade problems.

This document, signed in Brussels, Belgium on October 30, 2002, is written in Chinese and English, both texts being equally authentic.

| | |
|---|---|
| Representative of the General Administration of Quality Supervision, Inspection and Quarantine | Representative of the European Commission |

**Annex 1: List of participants**

*For the Chinese side:*

| | |
|---|---|
| Mr. GE Zhirong | Vice Minister of AQSIQ |
| Mr.SONG MingChaog | Director-General, Department of Supervision on Health Quarantine (AQSIQ) |
| Mr. QIN ZhenKui | Director-General, Bureau of Import and Export Food Safety (AQSIQ) |
| Mr. LI ShaoQing | Director-General, Office of the WTO Attain (AQSIQ) |
| Ms. QI XiuQin | Deputy Director-General, Department of International Cooperation (AQSIQ) |
| Mr. YU YuanTang | Deputy Division Director, Department of European Affairs (MOFTEC) |
| Mr. ZHANG ChaoHua | Secretary of General Office (AQSIQ) |
| Ms. MA WenXiu | Deputy Division Director, Department of International Cooperation (AQSIQ) |
| Mr. GUAN Chengyuan | Head of the Mission of the People's Republic of China to the European Communities |
| Mr. LIU Yonhou | Minister Councillor of the Chinese Mission to the European Communities |

*For the European Commission side:*

| | |
|---|---|
| Mr E. Liikanen | Member of the European Commission |
| Mrs M. Wörsdörfer | Member of Cabinet of Mr Liikanen |
| Mr D. White | Director, Directorate Enterprise policy. Enterprise DG |
| Mr P. Jean | Head of Unit, Enterprise A3, Enterprise DG |
| Mr M. Coomans | Deputy Head of Unit, Enterprise A2, Enterprise DG |

**Annex 2: Working Groups and contact points**

*1. Co-ordination Committees:*

A. Product safety

For the Chinese side: Department of Supervision on Inspection, Mr. Sun Dawei

For the European Commission side: Mr. David White, Director, Enterprise Policy

B. Other Industrial Products issues

For the Chinese side: Department of International Cooperation, Ms. Qi Xiuqui and Ms. Ma Wenxiu

For the European Commission side: Mr. David White, Director, Enterprise Policy

*2. Group on electrical safety*

For the Chinese side: Department of Supervision on Inspection, Mr. Shan Wei

For the European Commission side: Enterprise DG unit G3, Mr. Luis Montoya

*3. Group on medical devices*

For the Chinese side: Department of Supervision on Inspection, Mr. Yang Wanshan

For the European Commission side; Enterprise DO unit G4, Mr. C. Brekelmans

*4. Group on toys*

For the Chinese side; Department of Supervision on Inspection, Mr. Hao Yilei

For the European Commission side: Enterprise DG unit E5, Mr. Nikita Stampa

*5. Group on lighters*

For the Chinese side: Department of Supervision on Inspection, Mr. Yu Qunli

For the European Commission side: Health & Consumer Protection DG, unit B4, Mr. Erik Hansson

*6. Group on conformity assessment (including certification and accreditation):*

For the Chinese side; Department of International Cooperation, CNCA, Mr. Huang Shouyun

For the European Commission side: Enterprise DO Unit 01

*7. Group on standardization:*

For the Chinese side: State Administration of China for Standardization (SAC), Mr. Su Zhongming and Mr. Wen Shanlin

For the European Commission side: Enterprise DG Unit G2

*8. Group on WTO/IBT:*

For the Chinese side: Department of International Cooperation, Ms. Guo Xueyan

For the European Commission side: Enterprise DG, Unit Gl and Unit A2

*9. Group on technical regulations:*

For the Chinese side: Department of Legislation, Mr. Cao Dahai

For the European Commission side: Enterprise DG Unit Gl and Unit A2

*10. Group on pressure equipment:*

For the Chinese side: Bureau of Safety Supervision on Boilers and Pressure Vessels, Mr. Shi Jiajun

For the European Commission side: Enterprise DG Unit G4, Mr. Cornelis Brekelmans

Groups on automotive, cableway transportation, textile and EMF for mobile phones will be established later.

Specific work of each Working Groups are to be carried out by the groups leaders of both sides in accordance with the present Terms of Reference.

## Document 5.7: MOU on Administrative Cooperation Arrangements between DG SANCO and AQSIQ

MEMORANDUM OF UNDERSTANDING ON ADMINISTRATIVE COOPERATION ARRANGEMENTS BETWEEN
The European Commission's Directorate General for Health and Consumer Protection (DG SANCO) and The General Administration of Quality Supervision, Inspection and Quarantine of the People's Republic of China (AQSIQ)

RECOGNIZING that the Directorate-General Health and Consumer Protection of the European Commission is the European Commission's Department responsible for the EU policies and legislation in the areas of public health, food safety, consumer protection, feed and veterinary matters and other legislation related to SPS-related issues, the General Product Safety Directive (GPSD), for operating Rapid Alert Systems on Food and Feed and on non-food consumer products, and is responsible for promoting and organizing administrative co-operation between the enforcement authorities of the EU Member States for the objectives of these acts; RECOGNIZING that AQSIQ is the Government agency responsible for the supervision and administration of China's import and export commodity inspection including in particular for consumer products, food safety and Sanitary and Phytosanitary (SPS) matters; is in charge of the supervision and administration of certification and standardization, in accordance with the laws and regulations of China and internationally accepted rules; RECOGNISING that in the EU responsibility for some of the aspects covered by this Memorandum belongs to the EU Member States or is shared between the EU Member States and the European Commission and that the EU legislation applicable to some aspects within the scope of the Memorandum is under the responsibility of other European Commission departments; RECALLING that the laws and regulations of both Participants contain certain restrictions on international law enforcement assistance, including information disclosure, and that nothing in this Memorandum requires the

Participants to provide assistance or information if such is prohibited by their respective laws and regulations, enforcement policies or for other important reasons, both sides have reached consensus as follows:

**1. General Principles**

The European Commission Directorate General for Health and Consumer Protection (DG SANCO) and the General Administration of Quality Supervision, Inspection and Quarantine of the People's Republic of China (AQSIQ) agree to establish a consultation and cooperation mechanism with a view to deepen the dialogue on food safety and general product safety of consumer goods and enhance China-EU cooperation on Sanitary and Phytosanitary (SPS) questions related to agricultural and aquatic products and on safety of consumer goods.

**2. Objectives**

Both sides realise that enhancing cooperation in the areas mentioned above will promote mutual understanding, trust and bilateral cooperation between China and the EU. Both sides agree to establish channels of communication so as to promote the development of bilateral trade and to timely notify each other the relevant information and cooperate in shortest time to efficiently search for mutually acceptable solutions if relevant problems are encountered in trade.

The main objectives of bilateral cooperation are as follows:

- Establishment of contact channels
- Timely notification and Exchange of information, consultation for resolution of the relevant problems
- Establishment of a cooperation framework. Specific objectives for certain cooperation frameworks are defined in the annexes.

**3. Work procedures**

Any and all activities under this MOU will be subject to the needs of both Participants based on mutual agreement. The focus of the activities will at each moment of time be agreed between the two sides based on scientific, technical, regulatory or other developments or needs. both sides agree to hold regular meetings according to the current needs of cooperation in order to consult on the main issues of concern to each side and to agree on procedures and a work programme for their further discussion with a view to resolve these issues. The meetings shall be held alternately in the EU and China or, if agreed by both parties, will take place by video or audio conference. Both sides will participate with representatives mandated to discuss the issues identified. The levels of representation shall be equivalent on both sides, taking into account differences in the organisational structure of the administrations. The Directorate General for Trade of the European Commission will participate in the regular meetings under the dialogue. Other Chinese Ministries and Directorates General of the European Commission will be invited to be involved if needed and agreed by both sides. Relevant stakeholders such as business, consumer associations can also be involved if agreed by both sides. Best use will be made of the support that can be obtained under relevant EU-China [arrangements].

**4. Working groups**

At the regular meetings, the two sides may decide when necessary to establish technical working groups to collaborate in the resolution of issues identified. The technical working groups will agree on a suitable work program and a time schedule. Both sides will adequately support the working groups so that they can implement their work programme. Representatives of other Chinese Ministries and Directorates General of the European Commission as well as independent experts can be invited to be involved as appropriate.

**5. Contact points**

Both sides agree to establish a contact point for each area of cooperation to facilitate contacts and carry out applicable items of cooperation.

The European Commission standing point of contact shall be established in DG SANCO. The Chinese standing point of contact shall be established in AQSIQ.

**6. Costs**

Both Participants understand that any and all activities under this MOU will be subject to the availability of funds and resources and the laws governing the respective Participants. Both sides agree to bear expenses relating to cooperation in accordance with the following: unless agreed otherwise, Participants shall be responsible for bearing their own costs, including international and domestic travel and accommodation costs. The respective host should offer appropriate support and assistance to the visiting delegation.

**7. Minutes**

There should be written mutually agreed meeting minutes in English and Chinese for all relevant meetings at every regular meeting.

**8. Revision of terms of cooperation**

This MOU may be modified at any time with the approval in writing of both Participants. This MOU is to become effective on the date of signature and continue in effect for a period of three years from such date, unless one Participant notifies the other of its intention to terminate the MOU sooner. Such notification should be given to the other Participant no later than 90 days before termination of the MOU. The MOU may continue to be extended for another three years from such date unless otherwise terminated by one of the Participants with 90 days advance notice of termination, if possible.

Signed at ............. in the English and Chinese languages, each language being of equal validity.

For the Directorate General Health and Consumer Protection of the European Commission

Markos Kyprianou
EU Commissioner for Health and Consumer Protection

For the Administration of Quality Supervision, Inspection and Quarantine of the People's Republic of China

Li Changjiang
Minister

**ANNEX 1**
**GENERAL PRODUCT SAFETY**

*Cooperation framework foreseen for General Product Safety*

In order to protect the health and safety of consumers, the Participants intend, on the basis of applicable laws and regulations of the EU and China respectively, to cooperate in areas that are within the scope of responsibilities of both Participants and in the scope of consumer products of mutual concern. As far as necessary for the objectives of this Memorandum, the Directorate-General Health and Consumer Protection of the European Commission intends in particular to co-ordinate with the enforcement authorities of the EU Member States, the European Standardisation Organizations and the other competent European Commission departments, and to facilitate contacts to the extent permitted under the laws and regulations of the EU and China respectively between them and the AQSIQ. The co-operation under this Memorandum includes:

- Exchange of scientific, technical, and regulatory information, to help ensure the safety of consumer products;
- Exchange of information on emerging issues of significant health and safety relevance within the scope of the mandate and authority of each Participant. Information regarding products and manufacturers may be provided if necessary and permitted under the laws of the EU and China respectively;
- Exchange and information on standardisation activities and co-operation in comparatively assessing relevant products safety standards and in initiating standardisation activities according to each Participant's rules and procedures;
- Exchange of information on market surveillance, (import and export) inspection and enforcement activities;
- Exchange of information on risks identified and measures taken in respect to products originating from the other Participant's country(ies) and co-operation on measures taken to prevent such risks;
- Exchange of information and co-operation in case of major withdrawal/recall operations of mutual interest; and
- Exchange of information and co-operation on risk assessment and product testing.

For consumer products which are not under the competence of one of the Parties, this Party will facilitate contacts between the other Party and the authorities or departments competent for such products.

Training for technical and regulatory experts and personnel.

**ANNEX 2**
**FOOD SAFETY, SPS Issues**

*Cooperation framework foreseen for questions of Food Safety and Sanitary and Phytosanitary Issues*

The collaboration is established with a view to deepen the dialogue on food safety and enhance China-EU cooperation on Sanitary and Phytosanitary (SPS) questions related to agricultural and aquatic products. Enhancing the EU/China cooperation on these issues will promote mutual understanding, trust and trade in agricultural and fishery products as well as processed food between the EU and China. Both sides agree to establish channels of consultation and communication so as to timely notify each other the relevant information and cooperate in shortest time to efficiently search for mutually acceptable solutions if problems are encountered in trade.

The main objectives of bilateral cooperation are as follows:

- Establishment of SPS consultation and communication channels;
- Exchange and notification of SPS information;
- Discussion and cooperation in the resolution of SPS issues which may arise in trade between the EU and China.

At the regular meetings established under Point 3 of the Memorandum of Understanding, the parties may decide when necessary to establish technical working groups to collaborate in the resolution of issues identified. The technical working groups will agree on a suitable work program and a time schedule. Both sides will adequately support the working groups so that they can implement their work program and report back to the regular meeting within a suitable time period.

## Document 5.8: EU–China Road Map on Safer Toys

Guideline for Action on Co-operation for Strengthening Elf-China Toys Safety between the Directorate-General for Enterprise and Industry of the European Commission (DG ENTERPRISE), the Directorate-General for Health and Consumer Protection (DG SANCO) of the European Commission and the General Administration of Quality Supervision, Inspection and Quarantine of the People's Republic of China (AQSIQ)

**1. Background**

- In October 2001 the Directorate-General for Enterprise and Industry of the European Commission (DG ENTERPRISE) and the General Administration of Quality Supervision, Inspection and Quarantine of the People's Republic of China (AQSIQ) have established a working group on toys in the framework of the EU-China industrial products safety coordination with a view to improving the conformity of toys to the existing safety requirements;
- In January 2006 the Directorate-General for Health and Consumer Protection of the European Commission (DG SANCO) and AQSIQ concluded a memorandum of understanding on administrative co-operation arrangements with the objective of enhancing co-operation i.a. on general product safety of consumer goods;
- Both arrangements share the objective to ensure a high level of consumer safety in general and recognise the need to devote special attention to the safely of children;
- They also share the objective to ensure consumer confidence and ensure the best conditions for trade, in particular in the sector of toys, between the European Union (EU) and China;
- There is a very high volume of trade in toys between the EU and China and a substantial share of the toys sold in the EU are manufactured in China;
- DG ENTERPRISE is responsible for monitoring the application of the EU legislation on the safety of toys including the system of safeguards notification through which the Commission and the EU Member States exchange information on toys that are not in conformity with the EU legislation, whereas DG SANCO operates a rapid alert system (RAPEX) through which the enforcement authorities of the EU Member States exchange information on dangerous non-food consumer products, including in particular dangerous toys;

- AQSIQ is responsible for the import and export commodity inspection and supervision including of consumer goods, in particular toys;
- Toy Industries of Europe (TIE) represent the European toy industry including companies whose toys are partially or totally manufactured in China;
- China Toy Association (CTA) represents Chinese toys manufacturers, including enterprises that produce toys exported to the EU;
- As a consequence of large trade volume, a substantial share of the dangerous toys notified under the safeguard notification and the RAPEX systems are manufactured in China;
- There is therefore a need to confirm and reinforce the activities aimed at ensuring a high level of safety of the toys manufactured in China,

**2. Objectives**

The general aim of this Guideline for Action is to ensure a better understanding of EU toy safety requirements by Chinese manufacturers through all signatories' efforts, thereby providing the basis for conformity of all toys with EU toy safety laws and standards.

The Guideline for Action is complementary and without prejudice to existing formal agreements between the signatories, such as the Consultation Mechanism on Industrial Products and WTO/TBT signed by DG ENTERPRISE and AQSIQ and the Memorandum of Understanding on Administrative Co-operation Arrangements between DG SANCO and AQSIQ.

The specific objectives of this Guideline for Action are

- To provide toys manufacturers in China with adequate, up to date and easy to use information materials on the safety rules and standards applicable to toys and to enhance thereby their capacity to comply with the existing legislation;
- To provide feedback to AQSIQ on the most frequent safety defects discovered in toys manufactured in China, in particular based on the safeguard notifications and RAPEX information;
- To carry out seminars on toys safely in relation to EU requirements and standards and the relevant quality control aspects;
- To ensure a systematic exchange of information between the services of the European Commission and AQSIQ in relation to toy safety, notably on RAPEX notifications, regulatory and standardisation developments and any other relevant issues, as well as co-operation on follow-up to RAPEX and safeguards notifications;
- To identify needs and facilitate training for the personnel of AQSIQ and local CIQ laboratories in the fields of toy safety requirements, testing and market monitoring;
- To jointly monitor and discuss progress and problems encountered and undertake any other initiative that may be agreed to be necessary in order to ensure the general aim of this Guideline.

**3. Activities and Commitments**

- The DG ENTERPRISE will continue making the latest relevant legislation available to AQSIQ, as well as information on toys safeguards notifications as provided for in the current EU legislation.
- The DG SANCO will make RAPEX-data available in a systematic way to AQSIQ. Member States will be requested to, as far as possible trace back the manufacturer of the product and provide more detailed information on the safety risk, including the specific EU requirements that the toys have failed to fulfil;

- AQSIQ will strengthen the inspection and supervision of toys exported to Europe under the Law of the People's Republic of China on Import and Export Commodity Inspection enacted on April 28, 2002 and follow up cases ofnon compliance and circumvention with Chinese producers;
- TIE and CTA, in co-operation with the signatories, have the opportunity to take further steps to share their knowledge of safety requirements and their application with importers of toys to the European Union and manufacturers of toys in China;
- The information sharing can be in the form of activities such as seminars but can also consist of other kinds of information sharing activities;
- The DG ENTERPRISE and DG SANCO will together with AQSIQ facilitate these activities.

**4. Financing**

- The signatories understand that any and all activities under this Guideline will be based on mutual consent and subject to the availability of funds and resources and the laws governing the respective signatories.
- The signatories agree to bear expenses in accordance with the following: unless agreed otherwise, signatories shall be responsible for bearing their own costs, including international and domestic travel and accommodation costs. The respective host should offer appropriate support and assistance to the visiting delegation.
- The DG ENTERPRISE and DG SANCO will, when needs arise, support requests for funding within relevant EU funding mechanisms for supporting activities under this Guideline, such as training of toys administrative and laboratory personnel and printing of information material. The provision of such support is conditional to the availability of funds and the applicable financial rules.

**5. Procedures and monitoring**

The effectiveness of the measures applied will be regularly jointly assessed and in the light of the developments modifications and additional measures may be agreed upon. To that end representatives of the undersigned will meet in conjunction with the annual meeting of the EU-China Working Group on toys safety. In this context, ad hoc meetings for the implementation on the activities can be organised when needs arise.

**6. Contact points**

The contact points for carrying out activities under this Guideline are those designated in the framework of the existing EU-China Working Group on Toys Safety with the addition of contact points to be designated by the remaining signatory.

For Directorate-General for Enterprise and Industry of the European Commission

For the General Administration of Quality Supervision, Inspection and Quarantine of the People's Republic of China

For Directorate-General for Health and Consumer Protection of the European Commission

### Customs Cooperation

An Agreement between the European Community and China on Mutual Assistance and Cooperation in Customs Matters was signed in The Hague on 8 December 2004. Discussions and different forms of cooperation occur within this legal framework (see Chapter 6).

### Education and Culture

The EU and China have long had cooperation programmes in the fields of education and culture. The reader is referred to Chapter 7 for further discussion.

### Employment and Social Affairs

At the 8th EU–China Summit in 2005, the EU and China signed an MOU on Cooperation in Labour, Employment and Social Affairs.[12] It focuses on social protection, social cohesion, employment, labour legislation and corporate social responsibility (see Document 5.9).[13]

#### Document 5.9: Dialogue on Employment and Social Affairs

Memorandum of Understanding
Between
The Ministry of Labour and Social Security
of the People's Republic of China and European Commission

The Ministry of Labour and Social Security of the People's Republic of China and the European Commission (hereinafter referred to as the "Parties"), desiring to strengthen and consolidate ties between the two Parties, promote and enhance mutual understanding and awareness of current and forthcoming policy approaches, legislation and related issues in the labour, employment and social sector, taking into account the need to contribute to the cooperation between the EU and China, have agreed the following through friendly consultation.

1. The Directorate-General for Employment, Social Affairs and Equal Opportunities of the European Commission and the Ministry of Labour and Social Security of the People's Republic of China agree to set up a structured EU-China dialogue on labour, employment, and social affairs. This dialogue includes labour, employment, human resources development, social protection, labour legislation, labour relations and social dialogue.

2. The EU-China dialogue is structured into horizontal and sectoral items. The precise agenda of each session will be decided by joint agreement between the Parlies well in advance.

12 See European Commission, Directorate-General Emplcyment, Social Affairs and Equal Opportunities, 'Commission Vladimir Spidla Signs EU–China Agreement', available at http://ec.europa.eu/employment_social/emplweb/news/news_en.cfm?id=65 (accessed 22 December 2007).

13 Available at http://ec.europa.eu/employment_social/international_cooperation/docs/china_mou.final_signed.pdf (accessed 21 February 2008).

3. Horizontal discussions will consist of exchanges of views on cross-culling issues related to the above areas and will cover institutional, legislative and implementation issues.

4. Sectoral discussions will consists of exchanges of views on specific issues, which are related to the above areas of policies.

5. The Parties agree that specific events can be jointly organi/ed as appropriate. Discussions on the organizations of these events will take place between the parties. The Parties agree that the first event will take place in Beijing in 2005.

6. The precise composition of each delegation will be decided after consultation between the Parties. It is understood that the parties will call upon relevant stakeholders to participate in the dialogue, both horizontal and sectoral as well as in the specific events. In particular, the Parties may invite contribution from the representatives of workers and employers through the respective appropriate mechanisms.

7. The dialogue will take place at least once a year with the venue alternating between Brussels and Beijing—or any other venue agreed by the Parties. The Directorate-General for Employment, Social Affairs and Equal Opportunities of the European Commission and the Ministry of Labour and Social Security of the People's Republic of China will coordinate the dialogue. The Parties shall nominate senior officials as co-chairperson for the dialogue. The Parties will jointly produce agreed conclusions after each session.

8. Both parties bear their own delegation's cost of the participation in the dialogue. The cost o ft he agreed specific events will be decided in consultation between the Parties.

9. This Memorandum will come into force upon the date of signature; it will be valid for 4 years. It will automatically be extended another 4 years unless one party informs the other otherwise in written form three months before the expiry date.

10. Done in Beijing, on the 5th September 2005 in two original copies, each of them in English and Chinese, both of them being equally authentic.

For the European Commission
Vladimir SPIDLA, Commissioner
for Employment, Social Affairs and
Equal Opportunities

For the Ministry of Labour and
Social Security of the People's
Republic of China
TIAN Chengping, Minister of Labour and Social Security

**Energy**

The Energy Dialogue started in 1994. It includes annual meetings of working groups and a biannual EU–China Energy Cooperation Conference.[14] Its scope embraces energy policy, energy markets, energy security and sustainable development, hence the

[14] There does not appear to be a specific document establishing this Dialogue. For a general description, see 'Overview of Sectoral Dialogues', above n 1.

Energy Dialogue and the EU–China Environmental Dialogue are closely linked. In 2005, the EU and China established a Partnership on Climate Change as a framework for cooperation regarding energy and certain aspects of environmental policy. The main objective of the Climate Change Partnership is to develop advanced, zero-emission, clean coal technology. It provides an overall high-level political framework for cooperation in this field, including the China–EU Action Plan on Clean Coal and the China–EU Action Plan on Energy Efficiency and Renewable Energies.[15] Within the framework of the Climate Change Partnership, the EU and China, at the 8th EU–China Summit held in Beijing in September 2005, issued a Joint Declaration on Climate Change (see Document 5.10). Its purpose was 'to address climate change issues through the promotion and development of more environmentally friendly energy technology and sources'. With regard to energy, for example, the EU and China signed an MOU on Energy and Transport Strategies at the 8th EU–China Summit meeting.[16] This MOU was the basis for the EU–China Dialogue on Transport and Energy Strategies, which began on 21 March 2006. Immediately preceding the first Transport and Energy Dialogue, the 6th EU–China Energy Conference was held in Shanghai on 20–21 February 2006. At that time, EU Energy Commissioner Andris Piebalgs and Ma Songde, China's Vice-Minister for Science and Technology, signed an MOU on near-zero power emissions technology[17] (see Document 5.11).

**Document 5.10: Joint Declaration on Climate Change**

Joint Declaration on Climate Change between China and the European Union (EN)

1. We underline our commitment to the objectives and principles of the UN Framework Convention on Climate Change and the Kyoto Protocol and in this context agree to set up a Partnership on Climate Change. This Partnership will strengthen cooperation and dialogue on climate change including clean energy, and promote sustainable development. Follow-up of the Partnership will be carried out regularly at a suitably high level through a bilateral consultation mechanism, including in the context of the China–EU Summits.

2. We will strengthen our dialogue on climate change policies and exchange views on key issues in the climate change negotiations.

3. We will co-operate to realise our respective goals of significantly improving the energy intensity of our economies.

15 See European Commission, Directorate-General Energy and Transport, 'Energy and Transport International Relations: Bilateral Cooperation: China' (16 December 2007), available at http://ec.europa.eu/dgs(energy_transport)/international/bilateral/china/energy/index_en.htm (accessed 26 December 2007). These two Actions Plans are not publicly available.

16 *Ibid.* The MOU is not publicly available.

17 On the conference, see 'Sixth EU–China Energy Conference, Shanghai, 20–21 February 2006', available at http://www.delchn.cec.eu.int/en/whatsnew/pren200206.htm (accessed 15 September 2007). On the MOU, see 'EC and China Increase Cooperation on Clean Technologies', available at http://petrochemical.ihs.com/news-06Q1/eu-en-clean-coal-china.jspf (accessed 15 September 2007. See also 'China, EU to sign pact on clean coal technology', available at http://www.china.org.cn/english/2006/Feb/158652.htm (accessed 15 September 2007).

4. We will strengthen our practical co-operation on the development, deployment and transfer of low carbon technology, to enhance energy efficiency and promote the low carbon economy.

5. We agree on the following key areas for technical co-operation:

- Energy efficiency, energy conservation, and new and renewable energy;
- Clean coal;
- Methane recovery and use;
- Carbon capture and storage;
- Hydrogen and fuel cells;
- Power generation and transmission.

6. We will take strong measures to encourage low carbon technology development, deployment and dissemination and will work jointly to ensure that the technologies become affordable energy options. We will explore financing issues including the role of the private sector, joint ventures, public private partnerships, and the potential role of carbon finance and export credits. We will co-operate to address barriers to the development, deployment and transfer of technology.

7. We will aim to achieve the following co-operation goals by 2020:

- To develop and demonstrate in China and the EU advanced, near-zero emissions coal technology through carbon capture and storage;
- To reduce significantly the cost of key energy technologies and promote their deployment and dissemination.

8. We will enhance our existing co-operation and we welcome the following recent initiatives:

- The China-EU Action Plan on Clean Coal to promote collaboration in the development of clean coal technologies in China;
- The China-EU Action Plan on Industrial Co-operation on Energy Efficiency and Renewable Energies.

9. We will co-operate to strengthen the implementation of the Clean Development Mechanism (CDM), exchange information on CDM projects and encourage our companies to engage in CDM projects co-operation. We will engage in dialogue on improving and further developing the CDM. We will facilitate the exchange of information and experience on the design and practical implementation of other market-based instruments such as emissions trading and on assessing the costs and benefits of their use.

10. We will strengthen co-operation on adaptation to the impacts of climate change through:

- Research and analysis on adverse effects of and vulnerabilities to climate change;
- Research and analysis on assessing the socio-economic impacts and costs of climate change;
- Enhancing the scientific, technical and institutional capacity to predict climate change and its impacts;
- Research and development on technologies and measures to adapt to climate change;
- Raising awareness of integrating vulnerability reduction and adaptation needs into sustainable development strategies and their implementation.

11. We will enhance our co-operation in capacity building and strengthening institutions, including through raising public awareness, exchange of personnel and training.

## Document 5.11: MOU on Near-zero Emissions Power Technology

MEMORANDUM OF UNDERSTANDING
Between
The Ministry of Science and Technology of the People's Republic of China
And
The European Commission
On
Cooperation on Near-zero Emissions Power Generation Technology through Carbon Dioxide Capture and Storage

**Background**

1. The Joint Statement of the Eighth EU-China Summit in Beijing on 5th September 2005 underlined the determination of both parties to tackle the serious challenge of climate change through practical and results-oriented co-operation.

2. A Joint Declaration on Climate Change between China and the EU was issued on the same occasion which established a EU-China partnership on Climate Change designed to strengthen practical cooperation on the development, deployment and transfer of clean fossil fuels technologies, to improve energy efficiency and to achieve a low carbon economy, including cooperation in carbon dioxide capture and storage.

3. This partnership includes co-operation on the development, deployment and transfer of low carbon technologies, including the aim to develop and demonstrate, in the EU and in China, advanced near-zero emission power generation technology, through carbon dioxide capture and storage, by 2020.

4. A memorandum of understanding on the EU-China Dialogue on Energy and Transport Strategies between the European Commission and the National Development and Reform Commission of the People's Republic of China was also endorsed at the Summit.

5. The recent EU-China Action Plan on Clean Coal, as well as the long-standing co-operation in the energy sector between the European Commission and the Chinese Ministry of Science and Technology, are of great importance.

6. The European Commission and the Chinese Ministry of Science and Technology have ,a long-standing co-operation in the research sector in both the non-nuclear and nuclear areas, in particular:

- The 1998 scientific and technological agreement, renewed in 2004, in which the EC and China have privileged relations in research activities.
- The establishment in 2004 of a list of common priorities including hydrogen, fuel cells, renewable energy, energy efficiency and C02 sequestration.
- The participation of Chinese organisations in EU-funded FP6 projects in the area of C02 capture and storage

7. The European Commission and its Chinese counterpart acknowledge the ongoing and foreseen related work in the context of the EU-China Energy and Environment Programme and the importance of ensuring close co-ordination with this work;

The Ministry of Science and Technology of the People's Republic of China, on the one hand, and the European Commission, on the other

1. Agree, based on the Joint Declaration on Climate Change, to co-operate to reduce the impact on global Climate Change of the use of fossil fuels. Agree that Cooperation shall focus on the opportunity for near-zero emissions use of fossil fuels, particularly coal, in power production and industry, through the application of carbon dioxide capture and geological storage. Such Cooperation will have the following objectives:

(a) The assessment of the potential for near-zero emissions coal use through carbon dioxide capture and storage in China

(b) The development of knowledge and expertise.

2. Foresee a first phase of the Cooperation consisting of exploring the feasibility of, and options for, near-zero emissions coal technology in China through carbon dioxide capture and storage. Further phases should be envisaged as a follow up of Phase 1.

**Phase 1- Exploration**

3. Agree that the operational detail of Phase 1 of the Co-operation will be set out in a separate written arrangement that will provide for;

a) The development of knowledge, expertise and experience in carbon dioxide capture and storage;

b) Assessment of the potential for carbon dioxide capture and geological storage in China, including the identification of opportunities for demonstration and deployment of carbon dioxide capture and storage;

c) The review of costs, socio-economics as well as regulatory requirements of near-zero emissions fossil fuel technologies through carbon dioxide capture and storage in China;

d) The identification of options for financing the research and demonstration of carbon dioxide capture and storage;

e) The identification and preparation of the appropriate structures and instruments to establish the co-operation for the following phase.

4. Envisage that Phase 1 of the Cooperation will be a collaborative cooperation programme between European and Chinese researchers with the participation of universities, research institutes and industry. There will be a strong emphasis on joint work for knowledge and technology development and on building capacities, expertise and skills.

5. Will decide how work is shared and will approve the participation of research partners in the Cooperation. Both sides will seek to find appropriate resources to implement the Cooperation.

6. Will share non-confidential information on relevant research and development activity, and agree that if a particular activity under their cooperation may lead to the exchange of confidential information, they will consult with each other and make appropriate written arrangements for the protection of the confidential information.

7. Agree that if a particular activity may lead to the creation of intellectual property[1], they will consult with each other and make appropriate written arrangements for the protection and allocation of such intellectual property, in the framework and in accordance with the particular contractual obligations which may apply.

8. Aim to complete the first Phase of the Cooperation by 2008.

**Final considerations**

9. Both sides agree to form a joint steering committee to facilitate, monitor and steer cooperation. Members will be appointed by both sides.

10. Any Member State of the European Union may also be associated with the activities under this initiative by providing concrete and practical support.

11. The UK has offered to provide concrete and practical support to assist the first phase of this co-operation.

12. Both sides commit to ensuring close co-operation with initiatives underway in this field.

13. The present document records political intent alone and provides for no legal commitment.

Signed in two copies in both English and Chinese languages, on February 20, 2006, in Shanghai.

For The Ministry of Science and Technology of the People's Republic of China

For the European Commission

[1] Intellectual property is as defined in Article 2 of the Convention establishing the World Intellectual Property Organisation, done at Stockholm on 14th July 1967.

## Environment

The 6th EU–China Summit called for a strengthened environmental dialogue, and on 12 November 2003 the EU and China signed a 'political agreement' on strengthening environmental cooperation.[18] The subsequent Environmental Policy Dialogue (see Document 5.12) was partly a response to the environmental side-effects of China's rapid economic development, but it also met increasing domestic EU and international concerns about protection of the environment, as reflected in particular in EU environmental law on imports. Environmental policy is currently a very sensitive subject in China as well as in the EU.

At the 8th EU–China Summit in 2005, the EU and China established a Partnership on Climate Change.[19] The Climate Change Partnership, as already noted, provides a high-level political framework for EU–China cooperation concerning the environment and energy. The EU and China also issued a Joint Declaration on Climate Change (see Document 5.10 above). This Joint Declaration sets out the basic commitments in the Partnership.[20]

[18] See European Union, Delegation of the European Commission in China, 'EU–China: Agreement on Strengthened Environmental Cooperation', press release (Beijing, 12 November 2003).

[19] See Europa, 'EU and China Partnership on Climate Change', press release, available at http://europa.eu/rapid/pressReleasesAction.do?reference=MEMO/05/298&format=HTML&aged=1&language=EN&guiLanguage=en (accessed 15 September 2007).

[20] The Joint EU–China Declaration on Climate Change and Partnership was adopted at the September 2005 EU–China Summit. It is available at http://ec.europa.eu/comm/external_relations/china/intro/sect.htm (accessed 28 March 2007).

## Document 5.12: Environmental Policy Dialogue

Minutes of the Meeting between
Mrs. Margot Wallström (Commissioner for Environment, European Commission) and
Mr. Xie Zhenhua (Minister, State Environmental Protection Administration, China)
Beijing, 12 November 2003

At the invitation of Mr. Xie Zhenhua, Minister of State Environmental Protection Administration (SEPA) of China, Mrs. Margot Wallstrom, Environment Commissioner of the European Commission, visited China from 10 to 13 November, 2003. This visit marked the initiation of the EU-China Dialogue on Environmental Policy at Ministerial level. The two sides exchanged their views on furthering EU-China cooperation in the field of environmental protection.

### I. Initiation of the EU-China Dialogue on Environmental Policy at Ministerial level

The EU-China Summit of September 2001 agreed to establish an environment policy dialogue between China and the European Commission. During the 6th EU-China Summit held in Beijing on 30 October 2003, leaders reaffirmed their commitment to environmental protection and to an expanded dialogue in this area. At today's meeting both sides agreed that the meeting between European Commissioner for Environment and the Minister of the State Environmental Protection Administration symbolized the formal initiation of the China -EU Dialogue on Environmental Policy at Ministerial level.

It was recognized by both sides that strengthening dialogue between senior officials in China and the EU on environmental policy was necessary and agreed that further discussion regarding content, format and participants of the EU-China Dialogue on Environmental Policy would be conducted as soon as possible.

It was also agreed that political leaders' support for EU-China environmental cooperation was essential and that the results of the EU-China Dialogue on Environmental Policy should be reported to leaders on both sides.

### II. Global Environmental Issues

It was recognized that both sides are facing the challenge of addressing global environmental issues in order to achieve sustainable development and that the implementation of sustainable development policy was a common objective.

Both sides stressed the tremendous challenges that lie ahead in order to accomplish the follow-up actions to the World Summit on Sustainable Development as well as the objectives and principles set out in the Rio de Janeiro Declaration on Environment and Development, and were willing to make every effort to achieve them.

Both China and the EU have signed the Kyoto Protocol and have made concrete efforts to address global climate change. Under the framework of Asia Europe Meetings (ASEM), both sides have successfully convened the first and second ASEM Environment Ministers' Meeting and promoted environmental dialogue between Asia and Europe.

China and the EU have a common goal in addressing global environmental issues such as biodiversity conservation, climate change and ozone layer protection, and are both willing to strengthen communication, consultation and coordination in this regard. Both sides support the international community in the pursuit of fair and equitable solutions and in the implementation of relevant international conventions.

They agreed to cooperate to further develop and implement multilateral environmental agreements and to make contributions to global environmental protection by strengthening coordination. China appreciated the cooperative approach pursued by the European Union and supported its efforts in the field of international environment and development. Both agreed to strengthen consultation and coordination in important international institutions and organizations and to make joint efforts to promote synergies, between environmental protection and economic development goals.

**III. Review of Bilateral Environmental Cooperation**

Environmental protection and sustainable development is one of the key areas of EU-China cooperation. China attaches great importance to cooperation with the EU in this area as it believes that it is a critical component in furthering the EU-China relationship. The strengthening of environment dialogue is underlined in "China's EU Policy Paper" adopted by China on 13 October 2003.

The EU side recalled that in its long "Long-Term Policy for EU-China relations" (issued by the European Council in 1995) and in its communication of 1998 "building comprehensive partnership with China" and in the follow up communication on policies to China (issued by the European Union in May 2001), that strengthening dialogue on environment was an important measure and the promotion of sustainable development and environmental protection was seen as one of the three major fields for the EU's assistance to China.

In its latest policy paper on China, "A maturing partnership – shared interests and challenges in EU-China relations", adopted on 13 October 2003, the EU proposes to promote EU-China collaboration on global environmental challenges, to strengthen existing policy dialogue on environment and complement it by implementing planned cooperation projects on environmental capacity-building and sustainable development.

The EU side proposed a policy dialogue and information exchange on international environmental issues in the interest of both sides, and possibly the establishment of fruitful partnerships. The Chinese side expressed its appreciation of this proposal.

With regard to bilateral cooperation, both sides reviewed a series of joint cooperation projects and agreed that these projects had obtained very positive results. For instance, the ongoing 5-year Liaoning EU Integrated Environment Project aims at restructuring the mixture of the industrial energy, improving energy efficiency and promoting local industrial restructuring through capacity building in local governments and implementation of cleaner production. The EU-China Environmental Management Project aims at raising China's environmental management capacity by implementing sustainable development policy, and the EU-China Automobile Exhaust Pollution Control Project has provided direct support to China in the formulation of related regulations and criteria.

Both sides believed that cooperation in the field of the environment would have a positive influence by addressing global environmental issues, including climate change, biodiversity conservation, freshwater conservation and forest protection, and would serve as an example for regional cooperation on related issues. Both also believed that with the elaboration of China's environmental protection legislation and law enforcement management, increased market demand for advanced environmental protection technologies, and the impact of China's entry into the WTO, cooperation between the two sides would have much broader prospects.

China expected to improve its abilities in decision-making, management and technical support in dealing with national, regional and global environmental issues. Further involvement by the EU in China's environmental protection market was welcomed in order to achieve the mutually beneficial objectives of environmental protection and joint development.

**IV. Cooperation Priorities and further actions**

China welcomed EU significant contribution to capacity building on environmental protection of China.

Taking into account the basic attitudes of mutual respect, strengthened communication, priority focusing and mutual benefits, and building on the current favourable climate of EU-Chma environmental cooperation, both sides were willing to add new vigour to their cooperation through increased joint efforts.

Both sides made positive comments on the results of EU environmental assistance projects in China and welcomed the development of new cooperation projects. China underlined its priorities, inter alia in the following fields: environmental protection capacity building and human resources training; environmental protection in the Western Development of China; biodiversity conservation; watershed water resources programming; joint programs on automobile emission standards; and, studies on trade and environment.

Both sides agreed to designate the coordinators as the focal points ofEU-China Environmental Policy Dialogue. A Director General level official of the International Cooperation Department, SEPA, was designated as the Coordinator on the Chinese side and the Director for International Affairs DG Environment was designated as his counterpart on the EU side. They will be in charge of consultations and future arrangements, including the EU-China environmental Dialogue at Ministerial level.

Both sides agreed to continue to encourage exchanges and cooperation between civil environmental protection organizations, to give full support to public participation and to encourage staff exchanges and visits.

| | |
|---|---|
| Mrs. Margot Wallström<br>Commissioner for Environment<br>European Commission | Mr. Xie Zhenhua<br>Minister<br>SEPA, China |

## Food Safety

Cooperation between the EU and China concerning food safety is closely linked to cooperation on agriculture, product safety and regulatory policy. The main reasons lie in the Chinese accession to the WTO, Chinese economic reforms and development of the Chinese domestic market, the character and volume of Chinese exports to the EU, and the impact of EC food safety and product safety legislation on Chinese exports: all stimulate greater concern and demand for food safety regulation. The 30 October 2002 Consultation Mechanism on Industrial Products and WTO/TBT Issues was to be complementary to discussions on food safety and WTO/SPS issues. In January 2006, on the basis of this MOU, the DG SANCO of the European Commission and the China's AQSIQ signed an MOU on Administrative Cooperation Arrangements (see Document 5.7 above). Subsequently they agreed to establish an EU–China Consumer Goods and Food Safety Joint Committee to monitor the MOU.[21] This, in turn, led to an Arrangement to fight the trade of illegal food products, which was signed by EC Health and Consumer Protection Commissioner Markos Kypriano and Chinese Minister Li Changjiang, in charge of AQSIQ on 19 September 2006 (see Document 5.13). The Arrangement provides for information exchange, disposal of illegal food, preventive measures and contact departments. Issues not covered are to be resolved by 'mutual negotiation'. The Arrangement expressly states that its provisions 'are not designed to create legal rights or obligations under international law'.

## Document 5.13: Arrangement on Joint Prevention of Illegal Action for Import and Export of Food

An Arrangement for the cooperation on joint prevention of illegal action for import and export of food between the European Commission's Directorate General for Health and Consumer protection (DG SANCO), and the General Administration of Quality Supervision, Inspection and Quarantine of the People's Republic of China (AQSIQ)

In order to import and export food safely between Europe and China and promote the efficient operation of the system for the import and export of food, The European Commission's Directorate General for Health and Consumer Protection (DG SANCO) and the General Administration of Quality Supervision, Inspection and Quarantine of the People's Republic of China (AQSIQ) (hereinafter "Both Parties"), through friendly negotiations on an arrangement for cooperation on joint prevention of illegal action for import and export of food between Europe and China, have decided as follows within the framework of the Memorandum of Understanding on Administrative Co-Operation Arrangements Between DG SANCO and AQSIQ:

### 1. Objectives

Both Parties are committed to jointly prevent illegal export of foodstuffs of animal and plant origin and pre-packaged foodstuffs arising from fraud, adulteration, illegal entry & exit, illegal transit and smuggling. This objective should be pursued through the seaport and airport inspection notification systems, strengthened technical communication and cooperation (including port and airport inspection measures, anti-fraud measures, applied standards etc). Coordinated preventive actions will be taken where necessary following mutual negotiation to tackle specific illegal food trade in order to maintain the normal food trade system between the European Union and China.

### 2. Information exchanges

Information concerning illegal food actions detected during the inspection and quarantine of import and export food will be notified to the designated contact points as soon as possible, preferably within 48 hours. This will include the following items:

[21] See 'Joint Statement of the 9th EU–China Summit' (Document 4.11 in this book).

2.1. nature of illegal food action: fraud, adulteration, illegal transit, illegal irradiation, smuggling and other types of illegal food actions;

2.2. information related to the illegal food: the basic information such as product name, origin, producer, exporter and its registration number, importer, name of ship, container number, number and weight of boxes, date of import /export, entry/transit/exit port, transportation etc;

2.3. inspection and quarantine information related to the illegal food: sanitary certificate numbers of inspection and quarantine (if available), issuing authorities (if available) etc;

2.4. other information: such as basic information of importer, the reason behind the illegal food action, suggested preventive measures against the specific illegal food action.

**3. Disposal of illegal food**

In accordance with the relevant laws and regulations of the EU and China, the illegal food will be returned or destroyed and the related fees also attributed to the importer or exporter as appropriate.

**4. Preventive measures against illegal food actions**

4.1. Both parties with the cooperation where necessary of exporting authorities, will conduct trace investigation and take corresponding corrective measures to deter and prevent reoccurrence of similar problems, after receiving the notification by importing authorities. The parties will inform the importing authorities of the result of the investigation and corrective measures as soon as possible.

4.2. Both parties with the co-operation where necessary of importing authorities will give 3 months grace period for the investigation, rectification and submission of the report by exporting authorities. Pending the outcome of the above investigation, the importing authorities will not take unreasonable or disproportionate restrictive measures against the specific enterprises and their products in order to avoid unnecessary impact on relevant trade.

4.3. For especially sensitive illegal food actions which are mutually concerned, both parties will jointly conduct investigations, analyze the reasons that cause the illegal food actions and stipulate the technical measures to fight against illegal food actions. If necessary, other measures will be taken into consideration, such as seminars, mutual expert visits or joint specific preventive actions, etc.

4.4. Both parties will speed up the approval of the legal accession procedure for food, especially for mutual inspection and quarantine accession for foods of animal origin.

4.5. Both parties accept to co-operate on the mutual development and implementation of a system of electronic certification for import and export of food aimed especially to stop completely fraudulent food actions using falsified certificates.

4.6. As for the problem beyond the role and responsibilities of the Parties, the relevant issues will be referred to the corresponding competent authorities respectively.

**5. Designation of responsible contact department**

The contact department for The European Commission is the Directorate General for Health and Consumer Protection (SANCO) Unit D/3, Tel: +32-2-2993364, Fax: +32-2-2998566, e-mail: sanco-D3-import@ec.europa.eu. The contact department for the General Administration of Quality Supervision, Inspection and Quarantine of the People's Republic of China is Import Export Food Safety Bureau, Tel: +86-10-82262013, Fax: +86-10-82260174, e-mail: fvd@aqsiq.gov.cn.

**6. Other issue**

Any other relevant issue not covered in the Arrangement will be solved by mutual negotiation. The provisions of this arrangement are not designed to create legal rights or obligations under international law.

This Arrangement is signed in Brussels on 19th September 2006 in duplicate, English and Chinese, both language versions being equally authentic.

The European Commission's Directorate General for Health and Consumer Protection

The General Administration of Quality Supervision, Inspection and Quarantine of the People's Republic of China

## Global Satellite Navigation Services

EU–China cooperation concering global satellite navigation services occurs within the framework of the Galileo Agreement, as to which the reader is referred to Chapter 7.

## Government Procurement

A Dialogue on Government Procurement was established on 2 November 2005 by an exchange of letters between the DG Internal Market and Services of the European Commission and the Chinese Ministry of Finance (see Document 5.14).[22] It is oriented to achieving regulatory convergence between the EU and China in the field. Of special importance is the preparation of China for negotiations to accede to the WTO Government Procurement Agreement (GPA).[23]

22 See European Commission Spokesman's Briefing for 5 November 2007, 'Public Procurement: EU and China Strengthen Cooperation', available at http://www.hri.org/cgi-bin/brief?/news/europe/midex/2005/05-11-07.midex.html (accessed 22 December 2007).

23 See 'EU–China Conference on Government Procurement', available at http://www.euchinawto.org/index.php?option=com_content&task=view&id=100&Itemid=62 (accessed 22 December 2007). For a comparative study of EU and China in the field, see C Fugao, J Colling and P Trepte, 'China's Accession to the WTO Government Procurement Agreement and Opportunities for Domestic Reform: A Study in the Light of EU Experience', EU–China Trade Project (Beijing, June 2007), available at http://www.euchinawto.org/index.php?option=com_content&task=view&id=100&Itemid=62 (accessed 22 December 2007).

## Document 5.14: Dialogue on Government Procurement

Memorandum of Understanding on Government Procurement Cooperation between the Ministry of Finance of the People's Republic of China and the European Commission Directorate-General for the Internal Market and Services

Recognizing that government procurement policy is an important instrument to improve economic welfare, by ensuring that taxpayers obtain best value for the money spent on government procurement through increased competition between suppliers, leading to lower prices and improved performance;

Recognizing the importance of carrying out government procurement in a transparent and impartial manner in order to ensure fair conditions of competition for suppliers;

Recognizing that transparency in government procurement is also a prerequisite for fighting corruption in the public sector;

Given that China has formulated various policies, laws and regulations concerning government procurement, and that the EU has had extensive experience in legislating and implementing government procurement rules for the past thirty years, including a new EC legislative framework adopted 'in 2004;

The Ministry of Finance of the People's Republic of China and the European Commission Directorate-General for the Internal Market and Services agree to have a dialogue between the authorities in charge of government procurement policy in China and the services responsible in the European Commission on government procurement legislation and enforcement, as one of the key cooperation areas within the umbrella of the China-EU Financial Dialogue, which was launched in February, 2005 in Brussels;

Under the following terms and conditions:

### Article I Objectives and Scope

The objective of a government procurement dialogue between the authorities in charge of government procurement policy in China and the services responsible in the European Commission is'to establish a forum of consultation and transparency between regulators in this area, and to enhance Chinese technical expertise and capability in the area of government procurement policy.

Within this dialogue, the aim shall be to increase mutual understanding and awareness of current and forthcoming policy approaches, legislation and related issues, both in China and in the EU, and to promote exchanges and cooperation between China and the EU in the area of government procurement policy and legislation. The dialogue will promote consideration of points of mutual interest.

### Article II Structure

The Treasury Department of the Chinese Ministry of Finance and the Directorate for Public Procurement Policy of the European Commission Directorate-General for the Internal Market and Services shall lead the dialogue. The dialogue will be co-chaired by a senior official (in principle the head of a Department or Directorate) in charge of government procurement policy from each administration and will be composed of officials from each administration, accompanied by officials from other relevant authorities, as may be appropriate.

The contact points will be the Treasury Department of the Chinese Ministry of Finance and the Directorate for Public Procurement Policy of the European Commission Directorate-General for Internal Market and Services.

A meeting should be held once a year in principle. Meetings shall alternate between Beijing and Brussels unless otherwise decided. The two administrations should also take advantage of the opportunities to meet provided by other fora in which both administrations participate.

**Article III Content**

The dialogue should, in particular, consider:

1. exchange of views on current situations, experiences and new developments in legislation and enforcement of government procurement rules (including the use of electronic procurement);
2. exchange of best practice in government procurement;
3. exchange of views on policy and legislation for Public Private Partnerships;
4. exchange of experience on setting up efficient remedies' systems in the field of government procurement ;
5. exchange of views on experience and new developments in international fora for government procurement.

**Article IV Technical Assistance and Capacity Building**

In the framework of EU-China cooperation projects, both administrations will undertake best endeavours to support the objectives of the dialogue where appropriate, with technical assistance related to government procurement and capacity building activities such as the organization of training, seminars, studies, etc.

**Article V Exchange of Officials**

Within this dialogue, both administrations will endeavour to increase mutual understanding and awareness of current and forthcoming policy approaches, legislation and related issues, both in China and in the EU by proceeding to exchanges of respective officials in charge of government procurement, in conformity with their respective internal staff regulations.

**Article VI Costs**

Each administration will cover its own costs, including transportation costs for travelling and accommodation.

**Article VII Validity**

The Memorandum of Understanding shall become effective upon its signature and shall remain in force for five years. Thereafter, it will be automatically extended for further periods of five years, unless one of the two administrations gives a written notice to the other administration of its intention to terminate the Memorandum at least six months before the expiry of the period of validity.

Done in Beijing on November 2, 2005 in two originals, in Chinese and English, all texts being equally authentic.

For the Ministry of Finance of The People's Republic of China

For the European Commission Directorate-General for the Internal Market and Services

## Information Society

An Information Society Dialogue began in 1997 (see Document 5.15). It embraces research collaboration and policy discussion about information technology, telecoms and audiovisual, including market access and technical standards. It is closely linked to cooperation projects (see Chapter 7), the Regulatory Policy Dialogue and the Intellectual Property Dialogue.[24]

### Document 5.15: Description of the Information Society Dialogue

High-level Information Society Dialogue

EU-China Information Society dialogue is approached in a wide and practical manner. It is not limited to the annual high-level conference but includes current issues across Information Society in China and the EU. The impact of a high-quality dialogue is considerably strengthened if it is based on a broad mutual understanding between the EU and China, involving all levels and sectors engaged in the shaping and development of Information Society. The PTF will arrange project activities to strengthen this dialogue to ensure a meaningful cooperation between China and the EU.

One of these activities will be a high-level study tour to Europe to meet policy-makers in the European Commission and selected Member States to discuss the overall development of Information Society in China. This high-level study tour is designed to strengthen contacts at policy-making level between Chinese and European officials. At the same time, the project will support the EU-China Dialogue on Information Society through organizing a high-level seminar in Brussels.

The PFT will continue to encourage the development of networks, links and cooperation activities between the EU and China, not just between experts working in the project, but also between the various stakeholders involved in the development of Information Society in the EU and China. The development of these links will create the necessary conditions for a high quality dialogue, and will allow this dialogue to continue beyond project termination. The various activities will provide valuable feedback to the policy dialogue and to draw to the attention of the participants of the high level dialogue concrete issues and difficulties in building the Information Society in China and its possible implications for cooperation between the EU and China. In addition, a high-level seminar will be held in Europe between senior Chinese and European officials & experts to support the annual dialogue. The focus of the seminar will be on specific topics of direct relevance to both sides and is an opportunity to deepen high-level links initiated by the project in AWP 1.

Information Society dialogue under the project will encourage greater efficiency and transparency as part of economic and social reform. This will be achieved by encouraging government officials at all levels to formulate sound informatisation policies, and to work more closely with citizens and businesses. The PTF will contribute to Information Society

[24] See also 'Overview of Sectoral Dialogues', above n 1.

dialogue between the EU and China, and to contribute to enhanced cooperation between the EU and China in the sectors concerned with developing technologies, services and contents.

In addition, it is planned to hold the second Annual Information Society conference in China to develop a high-level platform for information exchange, to obtain best practices of EU with respect to regulatory developments, e-government best practises and innovation in ICT. The annual high-level dialogue will draw on the results of on-going project regulatory and e-government activities. The numerous existing links and relations between the EU and China will be enhanced and strengthened through the conference.

The first major expert forum will be on e-Commerce and will link in closely in with the research work in component A Regulatory Dialogue above. The forum will bring together leading e-Commerce researchers, practitioners and officials from China and Europe to asses the state of the art in Europe, the status quo in China, assess the bottlenecks in developing e-commerce in China and recommend strategies for an improved e-commerce environment. The results of the forum will be of use to both policy-makers in China as well as the business community on both sides.

The second major event under the Dialogue theme will be a forum on Citizen Centric services in e-Government. The event will address the issue of improving awareness, understanding and visibility of government services based and facilitate efficient and organized e-Government. Citizen-centric approaches to government service development have become a central feature of national and municipal e-Government policies and solutions in Europe. The forum will discuss the latest scenarios for developing citizen-centric e-Government, moving from a government to government (G2G) approach to a more government to citizen (G2C) focus. The forum will assess how to integrate involve the various levels of Government, managing high quality services and focusing on the needs and requirements of end-user citizens both in urban and rural areas.

## Intellectual Property Rights

Clearly the number and variety of dialogues between the EU and China have increased during the past five years, with a dramatic expansion in the past few years. The use of the dialogue mechanism was stimulated in particular by China's accession to the WTO; much impetus came from the EU and China's other WTO trading partners. The Intellectual Property Dialogue (see Document 5.16) was established by the European Commission and the Chinese Ministry of Commerce on 30 October 2003. It is a structured dialogue, covering both bilateral and multilateral (e.g. WTO) matters. It is divided into horizontal discussions covering specified issues such as institutional issues, legislation and enforcement for all intellectual property (IP) sectors together with sectoral discussions on individual IP sectors, such as patent, copyright and trademark. It meets once a year, alternating between Brussels and Beijing.

### Document 5.16: Intellectual Property Dialogue

EU-CHINA DIALOGUE ON INTELLECTUAL PROPERTY

On 30 October 2003 both sides reached agreement on a structured dialogue of which objective, content, structure as well as frequency and participation are laid down herewith:

DG Trade and the Ministry of Commerce agree to set up a structured EU-China dialogue on intellectual property rights where all-encompassing issues, bilateral and multilateral, related to the protection and the enforcement of intellectual property can be discussed.

The dialogue is structured into horizontal and sectoral items, addressing respectively the following issues:

1. **Horizontal discussions** covering all IP sectors, between the Ministry of Commerce which is coordinator from the Chinese side and DG Trade which is the coordinator from the EU side, will cover inter alia the following issues:

a) *Institutional issues*: exchange of experiences in EU and China on IPR enforcement, co-ordination with sub-central levels, inter-agency coordination, institutional reform, human and financial resources, etc.;

b) *Horizontal legislative issues*: exchange of experiences in EU and China on legislative progress;

c) *Horizontal enforcement issues*: exchange of experiences in EU and China on central and sub-central enforcement by customs, police, administrative and judiciary bodies. Co-ordination with other countries on exports of counterfeit goods.

d) Public awareness of consumers and right-holders.

2. **Sectoral discussions** on each individual IP sector.

The precise agenda of each session will be decided by joint agreement between the parties.

It is understood that the co-ordinator on each side will call upon all relevant IPR-related agencies to participate in the discussions, both horizontal and sectorial.

The dialogue will consist of one-day sessions at least once a year with the venue alternating between Brussels and Beijing. DG Trade and MOFCOM will co-ordinate the dialogue. The precise composition of each delegation will be decided by each party in consultation with the other one. The dialogue will report progress at the Economic and Trade Working Group (ETWG).

Pascal Lamy, Commissioner for Trade
DG Trade of European Commission

Lu Fuyuan, Minister
(p.o. Wei Jianguo, Vice Minister)
Ministry of Commerce

## Macro-economic Policy and Regulation of Financial Markets

A Dialogue on Macro-economic Policy and Regulation of Financial Markets was created by the 7th EU–China Summit in December 2004.[25] Officials of the European Commission and the European Central Bank meet with the Chinese Ministry of Finance, the People's Bank of China and Regulatory Commissions for Banking, Insurance and Securities. The Dialogue aims to promote mutual understanding and cooperation on macroeconomic policy and financial market issues, such as financial sector reform, accounting and auditing. So far, meetings have been held in Brussels on 22 February 2005, in Beijing on 15 May 2006 and in Brussels again on 4 July 2007.

[25] On the 7th Summit, see chapter 4. For further details, see 'Overview of Sectoral Dialogues', *ibid.*

The Joint Statement of the 3rd Dialogue (see Document 5.17) illustrates the range of issues, the viewpoints of each party and the links between this Dialogue and related dialogues, such as that on Government Procurement.[26] The EU has regulatory dialogues on financial markets not only with China but also with the USA, Japan, India and Russia.[27]

**Document 5.17: Joint Statement of the 3rd EU–China Economic and Financial Dialogue**

Joint Statement of the 3rd EU-China Economic and Financial Dialogue

BRUSSELS, July 5 (Xinhua) – The 3rd EU-China Economic and Financial Dialogue was held in Brussels on Wednesday. The following is the full text of the joint statement of the meeting:

The 3rd EU-China Economic and Financial Dialogue meeting took place in Brussels on 4 July 2007. The Dialogue was opened by Joaquin Almunia, Commissioner for Economic and Monetary Affairs. Directors General (Jorgen) Holmquist and (Claus) Regling and Vice Finance Minister Zhu Zhigang co-chaired the dialogue. The EU delegation included representatives from Directorate General for Economic and Financial Affairs, Directorate General for Internal Market and Services, Directorate General for External Relations, the EU delegation to China and a representative of the European Central Bank. The Chinese delegation consisted of representatives from Ministry of Finance (MOF), Ministry of Foreign Affairs (MOFA), Ministry of Commerce (MOFCOM), China Banking Regulatory Commission (CBRC), China Securities Regulatory Commission (CSRC), China Insurance Regulatory Commission (CIRC) and Mission of the P. R. China to the European Communities.

Both sides emphasized the important role of this EU-China Economic and Financial Dialogue in strengthening the EU-China comprehensive strategic partnership, promoting mutual understanding and cooperation in macroeconomic and financial areas. The Dialogue complements other economic dialogues covering, among others, trade, investment and intellectual property rights. This exchange of expertise – as also witnessed at the expert meeting on accounting in the margins of the dialogue - has been welcomed by both parties. Both sides agree that a regular exchange of information, including through ad-hoc technical meetings, should be pursued also between the annual Dialogue meetings.

**MACROECONOMIC ISSUES AND POLICIES**

*Global and domestic macroeconomic situation.* The two sides reviewed the global macroeconomic situation as well as the outlook for the two economies. They noted that notwithstanding high oil prices, global growth remains robust, aided by still benign

[26] The document is available at http://xxhs2.mofcom.gov.cn/aarticle/commonnews/200707/20070704861445.html (accessed 22 December 2007).

[27] See European Commission, Internal Market and Services DG, 'International Regulatory Dialogues Concerning the Policies of DG Internal Market and Services', DG Internal Market and Services Working Document, DG Markt/200.05.2005, available at http://ec.europa./internal-market/ext-dimension/docs/dialogues/work-doc-reg-dialog-20-05-2005_en.pdf (accessed 22 November 2007); and European Commission, Internal Market—External Dimension—Regulatory Dialogues, 'Regulatory Dialogues', available at http://ec.europa.internal_market/ext-dimension/dialogues/index_en.htm (accessed 22 November 2007).

financial market conditions and buoyant global trade growth. The Chinese side noted that the Chinese economy has grown faster than expected. The EU side pointed out that economic growth continued to remain above potential. The two sides agreed that this benign environment provides a good opportunity for the two economies to implement structural reforms so as to lay a strong foundation for sustained growth. At the same time, downside risks, including rising prices, global imbalances, reassessment of risk in financial market and growing protectionism, require continued vigilance.

*Addressing global imbalances.* As representatives of two major economies in the world, the two sides reaffirmed their commitment to an orderly adjustment of global imbalances. The Chinese side reiterated its commitment to undertake policies that would lead to sustained, rapid and more balanced growth of its economy. In this context, the Chinese side affirmed its intention to make efforts to boost domestic demand. The EU side outlined the determination of member states to continue comprehensive structural reforms with the aim to strengthen growth and employment.

*Fiscal and monetary policies.* The Chinese side pointed out that, in view of the current economic situation, the government will continue to implement appropriate macroeconomic policies including prudent fiscal policy as well as prudent and moderately tight monetary policy, deepen structural reforms and speed up the transformation of economic growth patterns so as to maintain a sustainable growth momentum. China will continue to improve the formation of a RMB exchange rate mechanism in a principle of self-initiated, controllable and gradual way.

The EU side emphasized that efforts are needed in many EU Member States to further improve budgetary positions. Because of the impact of ageing, a sound budgetary situation is crucial to enhance the long-term sustainability of public finances. The EU also noted that the first experiences with the revised Stability and Growth Pact are encouraging, but that the real challenge will come now as favorable cyclical conditions and rising tax revenues increase pressures for higher spending in some Member States. The EU emphasized its commitment to the comprehensive structural reform strategy adopted under the Lisbon Agenda, which might already have increased the EU's potential growth rate. The EU side pointed out that the monetary stance in the euro area continues to be supportive of growth, as real interest rates are still low by historical standards even after substantial withdrawal of monetary stimulus by the ECB.

**FINANCIAL SECTOR REFORM**
**CHINA'S FINANCIAL SECTOR REFORM**

Both sides stressed the importance of well-functioning and gradual opening up capital and financial services markets to promote economic growth, to reduce financing costs and to foster efficient allocation of capital. The two sides agreed to work towards greater global regulatory convergence including sound international standards and principles-based regulation with a view to promote efficiency, competition and to strengthen investor protection and financial stability. The two sides agreed to strengthen their cooperation in financial sector reform and supervision. Concerning foreign participation, the two sides reaffirmed their commitment that any prudential measure should be non-discriminatory. Both sides expressed their willingness to work together closely, to develop their financial relations and to expand cooperation whenever possible.

Chinese participants described measures taken to strengthen financial sector reforms, including increasing capital adequacy ratio, improving corporate governance of financial institutes, promoting information disclosure, strengthening market order and reforming the non-tradable shares, consolidating securities companies and promoting financial innovation. The Chinese side also reaffirmed its commitment to advance financial sector reforms by keeping opening up policies, strengthening prudential supervision and risk prevention, enhancing transparency and improving the legal framework of financial sector supervision.

**EU'S FINANCIAL SECTOR ISSUES**

EU participants reported on the progress achieved in the EU's financial sector integration and the development of its financial markets. They presented the EU initiatives towards an integrated, open, more competitive and efficient European financial services markets. The EU financial services policy aims at dynamically consolidating progress, ensuring sound implementation and enforcement of existing rules, and transparent and evidence-based policy making, following" better regulation principles". The EU participants stressed the importance of enhanced supervisory convergence, of creating more competition between service providers, and of better positioning the European Union in the global context.

**ACCOUNTING**

Both sides acknowledged the progress made on bilateral communication and cooperation in the development and implementation of accounting standards since the last meeting of the Financial Dialogue in May 2006. The EU side commended China on the adoption of 39 new accounting standards, with a view to achieve substantial convergence of those standards with the International Financial Reporting Standards (IFRS) and to improve transparency of financial information. This is a major step in the direction of convergence with IFRS. Both sides recognized that this was an important step for the development of the Chinese economy and its place in the world's increasingly integrated capital markets. Both sides agreed in a monitoring session on accounting held on 2 July 2007 in Brussels, to continue cooperation on a political and technical level in view of the final decision by the EU on equivalence in mid 2008 as well as on international convergence of accounting. They agreed to create on both sides working groups which will start to work after this meeting in order to develop measures with a view to a final decision on equivalence in 2008.

**AUDITING**

The EU provided an update on its current and forthcoming activities in the field of audit regulation, in particular on the treatment of third countries. Both sides agreed on the main steps leading to close cooperation in auditing matters. In the monitoring session held on 2 July 2007 it was also agreed to create on both sides working groups on EU and China audit regulation and oversight, which will start to work after this meeting in order to pave the way for future close cooperation and mutual recognition in this field.

**GOVERNMENT PROCUREMENT**

Both sides acknowledged the importance of regular discussions and information sharing in promoting mutual understanding of their respective government procurement systems, especially in view of China's forthcoming accession negotiation to the WTO Government Procurement Agreement (GPA). The Chinese side reaffirmed its commitment to start its accession to the GPA by December later this year. The EU side commended China for its commitment and stressed the need to speed up its domestic procurement reforms. Further to the last EU-China Government Procurement Seminar held a couple of weeks ago in

Beijing, both sides expressed desire to deepen their cooperation within the framework of the EU-China Government Procurement Dialogue. As a result, both sides agreed to organize later this year a government procurement study tour by Chinese officials in Europe to see EU state-of-art practices.

**NEXT MEETING**

Both sides reiterated that this dialogue is an effective means in exchanging views on macro-economic and financial services and promoting cooperation in areas of mutual interests and growing relevance in the current global economic framework. The two sides agreed that the 4th Meeting of this Dialogue will be held next year in China. Where appropriate, also in order to prepare the next Dialogue's meeting, Expert meetings should be arranged to identify topics of mutual interest.

## Maritime Transport

In 2002, the EC and its Member States on the one hand and China on the other signed an Agreement on Maritime Transport. EU–China cooperation in the field of maritime transport occurs within the framework of the Agreement, as to which the reader is referred to Chapter 7.

## Regional Policy

Regional policy, in which both the EC and its Member States are competent on the EU side, is another policy area in which the EU and China share common interests. In the EU, regional policy is a matter of shared competence between the EC and its Member States. It is one of the main redistributive policies in the EU. Since recent enlargements, it has assumed even greater significance. In China, economic transformation has led to considerable regional disparities; reducing the gap in incomes, services and growth is a priority for the government. In May 2006, the EU and China launched a Regional Policy Dialogue, crystallised in the 15 May MOU on Regional Policy Cooperation (see Document 5.18). On this basis, the EU and China agreed in October 2006 on a roadmap for detailed cooperation in the field of regional policy.[28] Though apparently not expressed in a specific formal document, this includes high-level seminars, a comprehensive study on the definition of Chinese regions, regional statistics, multi-level governance and partnership mechanisms, and exchange of officials, all topics of great interest and importance to both the EU and China.

[28] There is no document for the roadmap as such. For further information, see Europa Rapid, 'Danuta Hübner Agrees with Chinese National Development and Reform Commission an Ambitious Roadmap for Cooperation in Regional Policy', press release IP/06/1502 (Brussels, 31 October 2006), available at http://europa.eu/rapid/pressReleasesAction.do?reference=IP/06/1502&format=HTML&aged=0&language=EN&guiLanguage=en (accessed 15 September 2007). See also 'EU and China Deepen Dialogue on Regional Challenges at OPEN DAYS on 8 October', press release IP/07/1458 (Brussels, 8 October 2007).

## Document 5.18: MOU on Regional Policy Cooperation

MEMORANDUM OF UNDERSTANDING ON REGIONAL POLICY COOPERATION BETWEEN THE EUROPEAN COMMISSION AND THE NATIONAL DEVELOPMENT AND REFORM COMMISSION OF THE PEOPLE'S REPUBLIC OF CHINA

Directorate General for Regional Policy of the European Commission and the National Development and Reform Commission of the People's Republic of China have decided to set up a Structured Dialogue on Regional Policy with the following principles, objectives, content and organisation:

### 1. PRINCIPLES

The structured dialogue on regional policy between the Directorate General for Regional Policy of the European Commission and the National Development and Reform Commission is the forum where all related regional policy issues can be discussed.

### 2. OBJECTIVES

(1) Promote mutual understanding and bilateral co-operation in the field of regional policy;

(2) Establish communication channels so as to strengthen the exchange of information.

### 3. CONTENT

(1) Exchange information on policies contributing to growth, competitiveness and employment and to achieve a better territorial balance.

(2) Exchange information of our experiences in setting up and implementing regional policy

(3) Exchange views on governance and partnership issues.

(4) Any other topics of mutual interest relating to regional policy

### 4. ORGANISATION

(1) Both sides nominate senior officials as co-chairperson for the dialogue and establish contact points in the Directorate General for Regional Policy of the European Commission and the National Development and Reform Commission. Both sides will be responsible for the co-ordination of the dialogue. According to the needs, both sides may decide to set up ad-hoc technical working groups to work together on specific issues and to facilitate discussions at expert level.

(2) The level and composition of the delegations in the meetings will be decided by each side in consultation with the other. It is understood that both sides will call upon relevant stakeholders to participate in the dialogue. At least one meeting will take place each year. The precise agenda for each meeting will be decided beforehand between both sides. Both sides may invite other Ministries and Directorates Generals to take part in the meetings subject to need and agreement by both sides. There should be mutually agreed minutes in English and Chinese after every meeting.

(3) The venue for the meetings will alternate between the European Union and China unless otherwise decided.

(4) Specific events can be jointly organised as appropriate.

(5) Both sides bear their own delegation's cost of the participation in the dialogue. One side will provide active support and assistance to the other. The cost of the agreed specific events will be decided in consultation between both sides.

This Memorandum of Understanding records political intent alone and provides for no legal commitment.

Done in Beijing on the 15th May 2006 in two original copies, each of them in English and Chinese.

| | |
|---|---|
| Commissioner Danuta Hübner<br>Member of the European Commission<br>Responsible for Regional Policy | Mr. Zhu Zhixin<br>Vice Chairman of<br>National Development and Reform Commission |

**Regulatory and Industrial Policy**

On 25 June 2001, the EU General Affairs Council approved a proposed EU–China Industrial Policy and Regulatory Cooperation Dialogue.[29] As already mentioned, the EU and China on 30 October 2002 established a Consultation Mechanism on Industrial Products and WTO/TBT Issues.[30] The Mechanism became the core of the current EU–China Regulatory Cooperation Dialogue, covering consumer product safety and other matters. The second Enterprise Policy and Regulatory Dialogue was held in Brussels on 8–10 October 2002.[31] In January 2006 the European Commission's DG SANCO and China's AQSIQ signed an MOU on Administrative Cooperation Arrangements (see Document 5.7 above). The Regulatory Dialogue encompasses 13 working groups that, according to the European Commission, deal with:

> conformity assessment, standardisation, technical barriers to trade, electrical and mechanical products, toys, textile, lighters, medical devices, pressure equipment, automobile standards, cosmetics and radiation of mobile phones.[32]

An agreement to begin a Dialogue on Industrial Policy and Regulation was signed on 17 September 2003[33] (see Document 5.19). Its aims include the exchange of views

[29] For background, see European Commission, DG Enterprise, 'EU–China Industrial Policy and Regulatory Dialogue', available at http://ec.europa.eu/enterprise/enterprise_policy/gov_relations/china/eu_china_dialogues (accessed 22 November 2007).

[30] See the discussion above on the Dialogue on Consumer Product Safety. See also European Commission, 'Commission and China Agree to Establish Consultation Mechanism on Industrial Products', press release (Brussels, 30 October 2002).

[31] See 'EU–China Regulatory Cooperation Dialogue', above n 10, which also gives the 2003 position papers of the European Chamber of Commerce in Brussels (EUCCC) on different economic sectors in China.

[32] See 'Overview of Sectoral Dialogues', above n 1.

[33] See also European Commission, 'EU and China Launch a Political Dialogue on Industrial Policy and Regulation', press release IP/03/1260 (Beijing, 17 September 2003).

on policies and strategies concerning competitiveness and productivity, discussion of related strategies to comply with WTO law, and the review and discussion of sector-specific industrial policies. In the long term, it seeks to achieve regulatory convergence between the EU and China.[34] The Dialogue meets once a year. Complementing the dialogue between the European Commission and AQSIQ, it is implemented by DG Enterprise in the European Commission and the relevant departments of the National Development and Reform Commission in China. The Framework Agreement for the Dialogue on Industrial Policy stated expressly that the Dialogue was being created within the legal framework of the 1985 Trade and Economic Cooperation Agreement.[35] There are three working groups, which deal with the automobile, metals and textile sectors.[36]

## Document 5.19: Dialogue on Industrial Policy

Minutes of the meeting for establishing the Framework of the Industrial Policy Dialogue Between the European Commission and the People's Republic of China

On 17 September 2003, Erkki Liikanen, Member of the European Commission and Mr. Ma Kai, Chairman of the National Development and Reform Commission of the People's Republic of China (hereinafter referred to as the "Parties"), desiring to strengthen and consolidate ties between the two Parties, promote and enhance mutual understanding and awareness of current and forthcoming policy approaches, legislation and related issues in the industrial sector, taking into account the need to contribute to the establishment of smooth and sustainable trade relations between the EU and China, have agreed the following.

**I.** The Parties agree to establish a permanent dialogue in the industrial sector for promoting consultation and mutual understanding. The Dialogue should address issues of common interest to the Parties. These include horizontal issues relating to framework conditions favorable to industrial competitiveness as well as sector-specific industrial policies. The Dialogue comes within the framework of the Enterprise policy and regulation Working Group of the EU-China Trade and Economic Cooperation Agreement.

**II.** The Parties intend to contnbute to the improvement of'the competitiveness of businesses from both sides, by ensuring a business-friendly level playing field for industry operators. The Dialogue shall, in particular:

- on the horizontal level, exchange views on policies and related implementation strategies aiming at strengthening the determinants of competitiveness and productivity (ensure conditions are there for development: technology, skilled workforce, finance and other to form a competitive and innovative business environment),
- review and discuss policies ensuring an efficient functioning of the framework, the institutions and instruments that business depends on,

34 See 'Overview of Sectoral Dialogues', above n 1.

35 See also 'Minutes of the Meeting for Establishing the Framework of the Industrial Policy Dialogue between the European Commission and the People's Republic of China, Beijing, 17 September 2003', available at http://ec.europa.eu/enterprise/enterprise_policy/gov_relations/china/minutes_17-09-2003.pdf (accessed 22 November 2007).

36 See 'Overview of Sectoral Dialogues', above n 1.

- discuss strategies to comply with WTO rules and disciplines that directly and indirectly impact on competitiveness and productivity,
- review and discuss sector-specific industrial policies,
- discuss the strategy of EU-China cooperation in the field of industrial policy, and
- enable businesses and other interested parties from both sides to contribute actively to the Dialogue.

**III.** The implementing organizations of the Dialogue are the European Commission Enterprise DG and relevant departments of the National Development and Reform Commission of the People's Republic of China.

Either organization shall nominate a senior official as co-chairman for the Dialogue.

The implementing organizations will comprise appropriate officials, accompanied by officials from other relevant authorities, as may be appropriate.

In addition, the Parties share the view that to guarantee the efficiency of the Dialogue, it should ensure proper involvement at all levels of the respective industries and other interested parties.

**IV.** The Dialogue should meet once a year. Meetings shall alternate between Beijing and Brussels unless otherwise decided. The working languages will be English and Chinese.

Either side will cover its own costs, including transportation costs for international traveling, traveling between cities and accommodation. One side will provide active support and assistance to the other.

**V.** The Parties agree that sector-specific Working Groups could be established at any time, if necessary, provided that both sides indicate their agreement by exchange of letters.

**VI.** Within the limits of the laws of the two Parties, the Minutes are subject to modification following written consent by the Parties.

**VII.** The Dialogue shall be carried out on the day when the Parties sign the Minutes.

Done in Beijing on September 17, 2003 in duplicate in the English and Chinese languages, both texts being equally authentic.

| | |
|---|---|
| Erkki Liikanen<br>Member of the European Commission | Ma Kai<br>Chairman<br>National Development and<br>Reform Commission |

**Science and Technology**

The early dialogues were concerned with technical matters, presaging the 1999 Science and Technology Agreement. The earliest was the Science and Technology Dialogue in the early 1990s. It presaged the 1999 Science and Technology Agreement (see Chapter 6). Today the Dialogue embraces numerous activities and, together with the Agreement, has led to substantial cooperation between the EU and China in the field of scientific research. A prominent example is CO-REACH, which is a network of European science and technology funding organisations which promote research cooperation with China in numerous fields of science, including social science.[37] In May 2005, the EU and China issued a 'Joint Declaration on EU–China Research Cooperation: Building a Knowledge for Growth Pact' (see Document 5.20). The basic principles are to expand the scope of cooperation to the knowledge-based economy and to ensure mutual interest and overall balance between China and Europe. Its objectives include developing large research infrastructures in key technology areas such as biotechnology and nanotechnology, and increasing public and private investment in cooperation projects.[38]

## Document 5.20: Joint Declaration on EU–China Research Cooperation

Joint Declaration on EU-China Research Cooperation: Building a Knowledge for Growth Pact

The European Commission and the Government of China held a High Level Forum on S&T Policy and Development in Beijing on 12/13 May 2005. This major event coincides with the 30th anniversary of diplomatic relations between China and the European Union. Both sides agreed on guidelines for the future cooperation in research and technological development (RTD), thus giving a further boost to the rapidly developing strategic partnership. Leading personalities representing the governments, science, and industry reviewed the RTD relations between China and Europe and made recommendations for future developments.

### 1. A new political and economic paradigm for our RTD cooperation

The partnership that links China and Europe has a long history. This history has always included a significant scientific research and technological dimension. Through the signing of a science and technology (S&T) cooperation agreement in 1998, the EU-China cooperation received a strong impetus and significant progress was recorded in research fields such as ITER, SARS, Galileo, energy, new materials, biotechnology, aeronautics, space, hydrogen economy and information technology. Our cooperation i s a success and is growing in vigour and stature.

S&T relations between Europe and China are contributing to mutual understanding of their people. Based on common goals and understanding, cultural values and scientific goals, the S&T relations reached a level such as to make a significant contribution to the overall good relations between Europe and China.

We feel that the present cooperation should be further developed in the spirit of mutual benefit and progressive convergence of research policies so t hat it contributes directly to the improvement of economic competitiveness and to the achievement of common solutions to problems faced by our societies. The EU-China RTD cooperation is entering a new development stage due first, to the continuous improvement of China's comprehensive national strength and remarkable enhancement of its S&T capacity, and taking into account the fact that China will face deeper reform and a more opened market, and second, considering the

[37] See the CO-REACH website, http://www.co-reach.org/output/homepage.cfm?CFID=131097&CFTOKEN=49429968&jsessionid=4830ddfd95a33387756e (accessed 22 December 2007), from which this description is drawn.

[38] For further information on cooperation in nanotechnology, see Cordis, Nanotechnology, International Cooperation, 'Opening to the World: the EU–China Cooperation', available at http://cordis.europa.eu/nanotechnology/src/intlcoop-cn.htm (accessed 22 December 2007).

development of the European Research Area along with the Lisbon strategy and Barcelona objective and following the enlargement of the European Union.

Demonstrating our political willingness to address together global issues, we are determined to adopt a strategy of "reaching out" for RTD co operation and to promote thriving EU-China exchanges with research and technological innovation.

The convergence of formerly separate forces such as research users and creators, public and private stakeholders, intellectual property ownership and open collaboration, small and large businesses, has profound implications for public research policies and for business strategy as well as for scientific development.

These changes create a real urgency for a new and comprehensive approach to strengthen the EU China RTD cooperation. It is the rationale behind the EU-China RTD cooperation for sustainable and environment friendly growth and the key to understanding why we need both a quantitative and a qualitative change in our cooperation to promote our common interests.

Our pact is our determined commitment to bring Europe and China together. It is the formal translation of European and Chinese expression of a common willingness to lay the basis for a dynamic and harmonious cooperation that ensures sustainable prosperity and welfare for our societies.

**2. Guiding principles**

Our research cooperation will be based on two guiding principles:

*Expanding the scope of our RTD cooperation to the knowledge based economy*

In the 21st century, the engine for growth is the process through which an economy creates, applies and extracts value from knowledge. Scientific research and technological innovation, as the main source of new knowledge and a major field for its application, are at the heart of the knowledge-based economy and society which is currently developing rapidly on a global scale.

To become together more competitive, Europe and China must capitalise on a balanced and intense cooperation to better produce, transmit and exploit knowledge, and turn it into new products, new services and economically successful applications for the well being of their citizens.

The economic growth of China and the EU and their increasing integration in the world economy represents a positive development. Their important domestic markets and prospects of rising incomes offer great and long term opportunities to economic cooperation. At the same time, China's lower labour costs and increasingly qualified workforce make it a tough competitor and an ever expanding commercial power. Hence the importance of ensuring that the EU-China RTD cooperation brings mutual and well balanced benefits.

*Ensuring mutual interest and overall balance between China and Europe*

In a global knowledge-based economy, it is becoming more and more necessary to engage globally, in order to keep up with the frontiers of knowledge and attract the best talent.

Location of plants, R&D activities and investment will inevitably have to take into account where the growing markets are. We do not live in a zero-sum global economy where someone's gain is necessarily someone else's loss. We live in a positive -sum economy, where, through cooperation, the standard of living is rising for everyone. In a world that is global, the best way to increase innovative capacity is that Europe and China engage actively and collaboratively with each other.

Prosperity in China and the EU creates multiplier effects that are positive for both. Our economic opportunities are enhanced by growing economies around the world. The focus of the China-EU RDT cooperation is therefore to foster "win-win" situations that improve our own research, technological innovation capacity and national competitiveness while engaging actively and collaboratively with each other. S&T advancement has become increasingly dependent on extensive international cooperation, such as in the fields of marine, atmosphere and environmental protection that relate to the present and future habitat of mankind, and in the "mega-science" field that call for close cooperation of different countries in the world.

Equality and reciprocal benefits, results sharing, protection of intellectual property (IP) rights, observance of international norms are the basis for RTD cooperation. In this perspective, to enhance and diversify our RTD cooperation, particular attention will be paid to the issue of intellectual property rights.

**3. Objectives and actions**

We believe that Europe and China have an ever greater interest to work together as strategic partners for creating wealth from knowledge. It implies overall objectives, an action plan and a mechanism enabling the evaluation for results and possible adaptation to a fast changing world. Success of the EU-China cooperation depends on our capacity to mobilise talent (in people), the enterprises (large and small ones) investment (public and private) and research capacities (research infrastructures).

The scale of changes needed to adapt the EU-China S&T cooperation to a knowledge based economy cooperation will require that a broader range of policies and instruments are mobilised and coordinated more closely than has been the case until now (such as intellectual property rights, standards, regulations of products, and human resources).

*Objectives*

- Developing joint EU-China RTD projects and large research infrastructures in key technology areas such as information technology, biotechnology, nanotechnology etc…;
- Developing global scientific knowledge, through mobilising a wide range of stakeholders from research, industry and financial institutions in Europe and China, and a more proactive use of the EU-China S&T Cooperation Agreement;
- Increasing public and private investment in EU-China RDT cooperation projects;
- Accelerating and leveraging the implementation of China's and Europe's internal RTD strategies;
- Mobilising all EU Member States to get critical mass and improve coordination between national and Community actions;
- Ensuring mutual interest and balance of the EU-China RTD cooperation and its proper adaptation to scientific, environmental, social and economic evolution;
- Ensuring protection of IPR.

*A non exhaustive list of actions*

- Prepare strategic research agenda for EU-China cooperation on global issues and in key scientific and technological sectors, in particular taking into account the need for research and innovation to tailor products and services of common interest and benefit specifically to the sustainable evolution of our world;
- Fully exploit the possibilities of the EU RTD Framework Programme and of the Ch inese programmes (863/973) for international cooperation, joint activities in priority research and global issues and research infrastructure domains;
- Stimulate and develop common initiatives in fields such as environment, nanotechnologies, hydrogen, aeronautics etc...through e.g. an increased cooperation of China in the European Technology platforms.
- Increase mobility of researchers between China and Europe, including through improved visa conditions for long and short term stays, formulating an EU-China Scientists Exchange and Access Programmes, and facilitating the procedures for Joint degrees between European and Chinese universities and institutions.
- Based on improved scientific and technological knowledge, promote standardisation for the development of key technologies and approaches, as an essential enabling factor for sustainable development including for environment, safety, health, consumer protection purposes, etc...;
- Mobilise the EU and Chinese financial institutions to support EU-China RTD cooperation projects and joint research infrastructures;
- Inform and mobilise the European and Chinese S&T communities;
- Set up a network of European researchers in China and Chinese researchers in Europe;
- Set up a scoreboard to monitor the EU-China RTD cooperation and its impact.

## Space Cooperation

The EU–China Dialogue on Space Cooperation was launched at the joint EU–China High Level Workshop on Space Cooperation on 7 April 2004 (see Document 5.21).[39] Its objective is to build on the many existing forms of cooperation between the EU and China in the field in order to establish a long-term partnership in space activities. So far its main activities have been high-level exploratory meetings, but the Dialogue is closely linked to other aspects of EU–China cooperation, such as the International Thermonuclear Experimental Reactor project, a project to use nuclear fusion as a means of power production.[40]

### Document 5.21: Dialogue on Space Cooperation

Joint Statement

At the invitation of Mr. Xu Guanhua, Chinese Minister for Science and Technology, Mr. Philippe Busquin, European Commissioner for Research, visited the People's Republic of

[39] Available at http://europa.eu.int/rapid/start/cgi/guestfr.jsk?p_action.gettxt=gt&doc=IP/04/460%7C=%7CRAPID&lg=EN&display (accessed 22 December 2007). See also http://fire.pppl.gov/iter_busquin_china_040604.pdf (accessed 22 December 2007).
[40] On ITER, see chapter 6.

China between 6 and 11 April 2004. This visit constitutes a unique opportunity to take stock of EU-China S&T cooperation over the past few years, to broaden and deepen EU-China Cooperation relations and to explore concrete avenues to reinforce this cooperation in future, both in terms of policy dialogue and of partnership.

Both sides recognise that the common emphasis on building a knowledge-based society and on the key role of science and technology in it constitute one of the pillars of EU-China cooperation. This cooperation, initiated over two decades ago, received considerable impetus with the signing of the Science: and Technology Agreement in 1998. Significant progress has recorded in the implementation of this Agreement, reflected in a growing number of joint-research activities as well as continuing policy dialogue and convergence. The ongoing joint-evaluation of the S&T Agreement is expected to yield important information to increase its operational efficiency and lead to its renewal later this year.

China and the EU value highly the results of cooperation on science and technology and while noting the successes already achieved with the 2003 calls for proposals of FP6, have expressed their wish to significantly increase this participation in the near future. Existing cooperation in fields such as biotechnology, information society technology, food safety, SARS, energy or new materials will continue to be strengthened. Both sides have praised China-EU agreement on civil satellite navigation system (the Galileo Programme). In addition, it was also decided to explore relations in new areas, such as space, hydrogen energy and emerging diseases common to man and animals.

Both sides discussed the opening of an EU-China dialogue on space cooperation through the high-level space workshop in Beijing on April 7th, 2004. The workshop was attended by high-level representatives from the European and Chinese space sector. Participants identified navigation/positioning, earth observation and satellite telecommunication as main areas for future co-operation between Europe and China. Under the framework of China-EU Science and Technology Agreement, both sides agreed to establish a High-Level EU-China Steering Group on Space Science & Technology and Application Co-operation, which shall support the development of long-term perspectives for co-operation in the space domain.

Both sides agreed that sustainable development is a common objective and in this framework securing the energy supply, while at the same time protecting the environment, is a major challenge for both China and the EU. It was noted that the 5th China-EU Energy Cooperation Conference will take place in May 2004and provide an excellent opportunity for exchange and partnership on these major challenges, in parallel with the Hyforum Conference in Beijing that will explore the potential of hydrogen as a new source of energy. The Commission recognises the very high standards reached by Chinese research in the field of nuclear fusion and thanks China for its cooperation in the negotiation of the International Thermonuclear Experimental Reactor (ITER).

Both sides note with concern that animal and human diseases as well as new human diseases spreading over from domestic animals or wildlife are a topical problem and an important recurrent challenge to research and scientific cooperation. These diseases represent severe risks not only for human health, but also for international and regional trade flows including tourism, and the economy as a whole. More research is needed to better understand these new diseases. The upcoming projects on SARS research are an encouraging first step and cooperation should be extended to other areas in view of a more comprehensive approach. China is interested to participate in a symposium on bird flu which the Commission intends to organise in 2004.

China is drawing up its medium and long-term S&T development plan. Preparations of the upcoming 7th RTD Framework Programme have already begun, heralding a major evolution in its thematic scope and financial resources. The Chinese side has expressed interest in contributing suggestions already at this early stage, given that the construction of the International Dimension of European Research Area is likely to lead in FP7 to considerably reinforced international scientific cooperation. In this context, both sides are positive to hold an EU-China High-level Forum on Science and Technology Policy and Strategy in 2005, to further promote policy convergence.

Both sides also addressed the importance of bi-regional cooperation under the aegis of ASEM. Both sides expressed satisfaction with the progress made in establishing ASEM S&T Networking Platforms in Water, Food Quality, and Safety and Aquaculture, as well as emerging ones in Forestry and Livestock Health.

Done in Beijing, on 7 April 2004 in both English and Chinese languages.

| | |
|---|---|
| Mr. Philippe Busquin<br>Commissioner for Research<br>European Commission | Mr. Xu Guanhua<br>Minister for Science and Technology<br>The People's Republic of China |

## Trade Policy Dialogue

The Trade Policy Dialogue (see Document 5.22) was established in 2004. It was among several dialogues which were established relatively soon after China's accession to the WTO. It focuses mainly on strategic issues concerning bilateral, regional and multilateral trade agreements and changes in the domestic regulatory environment, in the EU or in China, which might have 'an important impact on bilateral trade'.

### Document 5.22: Trade Policy Dialogue

EU-CHINA TRADE POLICY DIALOGUE

With a view to facilitating the exchange of views between China and the EU on trade issues and creating a better understanding about each other's views and positions on multilateral, regional and bilateral economic and trade issues, the Directorate General for Trade (DG Trade) of the European Commission and the Ministry of Commerce (Mofcom) of the People's Republic of China have hereby decided to establish a Trade Policy Dialogue at China's Vice Minister level / Commission's Director General level, as from the year 2004.

#### Terms of Reference

This dialogue shall meet annually in Brussels and Beijing on a rotating basis. The interlocutors on both sides shall respectively be the Vice Minister responsible for European Affairs of Mofcom and the Director General of DG Trade. This dialogue should complement the institutional dialogue established under the 1985 Trade and Economic Agreement and should focus on strategic issues.

Possible topics to be covered in this dialogue include, but are not limited to, the following:

1. Multilateral trade issues;

2. Regional trade agreements;
3. Key bilateral trade issues;
4. Modifications of the regulatory environment in the EU and China which might have an important impact on bilateral trade;
5. Other trade-related issues of mutual interest.

In an effort to enhance such a dialogue both sides will, to the best extent possible, make full use of the technical assistance provided by the EU to China.

To facilitate the day-to-day communication between the two sides in the context of the Trade Policy Dialogue, the contact points will be the Directorate in charge of China affairs within DG Trade and the Department in charge of EU affairs within Mofcom respectively.

| | |
|---|---|
| Bo Xilai<br>Minister of Commerce<br>The People's Republic of China | Pascal Lamy<br>Commissioner for Trade European<br>Commission |

Done in Brussels, 6 May 2004

## Textiles Trade Dialogue

Soon after the Trade Policy Dialogue, the Textiles Trade Dialogue (see Document 5.23) was established on 6 May of the same year during the visit of Chinese Premier Wen Jiabao to Brussels. It includes both an intergovernmental dialogue and the Sino-EU Forum on Textiles and Clothing Trade for Business Dialogue. At that time, the EU announced the creation of a monitoring system for Chinese textiles; China also introduced measures to control its textiles exports. The Textiles Dialogue played an important role in managing the effects on the EU, its regional trading partners and China of the abolition of textile quotas after 2004, following the end of the ten-year transitional period under the WTO Agreement on Textiles and Clothing.

### Document 5.23: Textiles Trade Dialogue

China-EU Textiles Trade Dialogue

Representatives of the Government of China and of the European Commission have agreed to set up a high level Sino-EU textiles trade dialogue, with the objective of addressing specifically a number of important textiles trade issues of common Sino-EU interest. This dialogue will take place at senior Government official level; an industry to industry dialogue may also run in parallel.

**1. Sino-EU Textile and Clothing Trade Dialogue**

The ad-hoc government to government working group will comprise senior level officials from both sides (Director for the Commission and DG for Mofcom). The topics it will address will be:

- Regular exchange of information and statistics on textiles trade between the EU and China

- Discussion of textile trade issues of concern to either side, including obstacles to textiles and clothing entering each other's markets
- Analysis of trends of production and investment in the sector, including aspects related to sustainable development
- Promotion of possibilities for cooperation between the EU and China in textiles and clothing
- Examination of how to deal with the new situation of international textiles and apparel trade after 2004.

Such a working group will meet with the frequency necessary to address those issues, and can set up as appropriate sub-working groups to deal with specific issues. Both sides will remain in close contact to monitor developments in this area. To assist in that process Mofcom and the Commission will respectively nominate contact persons.

**2. Sino-EU Forum on T&C trade for business dialogue**

A forum for textiles and clothing business dialogue could be set up to examine issues of common interest, with a focus on identifying opportunities for cooperation, and providing for a regular exchange of information on concerns of each other's industries, and to explore how these issues could be dealt with. Such a forum could interact with the governmental working group, in the form for instance of joint sessions on particular topics.

The objectives and precise tasks of such a dialogue would be established by common agreement between the industries of both sides.

| | |
|---|---|
| Bo Xilai<br>Minister of Commerce<br>The People's Republic of China | Pascal Lamy<br>Commissioner for Trade European Commission |

Done in Brussels, 6 May 2004

**Transport in General**

An MOU on Cooperation in the Fields of Road Transport and Inland Waterways resulted from the 9th EU–China Summit on 11 September 2007 (see Document 5.24).[41] It exemplifies a different pattern of relationship between MOUs and dialogues. The name 'dialogue' is not used in the MOU, but the mechanism is essentially the same. Signed on 18 September 2007, it set up ministerial meetings and two working groups, one for road transport and one for inland waterways, with the possibility of extension to other fields by mutual agreement. The MOU includes provision for confidentiality of information.[42] It remains valid for five years unless otherwise notified. The eventual termination of the MOU is not intended to affect specific programmes or activities undertaken under the MOU. As this document

[41] See 'Joint Statement of the 9th EU–China Summit', above n 11.

[42] Para 7 states: 'Neither party will make available any confidential information, documents and data derived from the cooperative activities under this Understanding to a third party unless the other Party gives permission in writing for this to happen.' This appears to take precedence over EU rules on access to documents, contained in Reg (EC) No 1049/2001 of the European Parliament and of the Council of 30 May 2001 regarding public access to European Parliament, Council and Commission documents, [2001] OJ L145/43, and implementing legislation. Such priority might justified by the international relations exception contained in Art 4(1)(a) of Reg 1049/2001.

indicates, current MOUs can be very formal and detailed, and can contain provisions similar to those in legally binding documents, even though in principle such an MOU does not have legally binding force.

**Document 5.24: MOU on Cooperation in the Fields of Road Transport and Inland Waterways**

MEMORANDUM OF UNDERSTANDING BETWEEN THE EUROPEAN COMMISSION
AND
THE MINISTRY OF COMMUNICATIONS OF THE PEOPLE'S REPUBLIC OF CHINA
ON
COOPERATION IN THE FIELDS OF ROAD TRANSPORT AND INLAND WATERWAYS

The European Commission, Directorate-General for Energy and Transport, and the Ministry of Communications of the People's Republic of China (hereinafter referred to as the Parties),

Wishing to deepen and expand the cooperation in the field of transport between the European Union.and the People's Republic of China,

Have reached the following understanding:

**PARAGRAPH 1 OBJECTIVES**

The Parties agree to expand and deepen cooperation in the field of transport under each other's competence on the basis of equality, reciprocity and mutual benefit.

**PARAGRAPH 2 AREAS OF COOPERATION**

The Parties agree that the cooperation may include the following fields:

1. Road safety, road construction and transport

a. The development planning, designing, construction and maintenance of highways, bridges and tunnels;

b. Policies, laws and regulations on road construction and transport;

c. Security and anti-terrorism in highway transport;

d. Intelligent transportation systems (ITS);

e. Euro-Asia land transport corridors ;

f. Policies on and practices in the facilitation of cross-border and transit road transport;

g. Logistics;

h. Road vehicles standards.

2. Inland waterway transport and infrastructure development

i. The development planning, designing, construction and maintenance of inland river ports and navigation channels;

j. Policies, laws and regulations on inland waterway transport;

k. The standardization of the types of vessels in inland waterway transport;

l. Environmental protection in inland waterway transport;

3. Other fields as mutually agreed upon.

**PARAGRAPH 3 MECHANISM OF COOPERATION**

1. For the effective implementation of this Understanding, the Parties agree to establish a Ministerial Meeting mechanism. The Meetings could be held regularly or as required by the needs of cooperation.

2. The Parties agree to establish under the Ministerial Meeting mechanism two Working Groups, one responsible for cooperation in the field of road construction and transport, the Other for that in inland waterway transport and infrastructure development. The Working Groups will have regular meetings once per year, or meetings as required by the needs of cooperation, to decide on specific details of cooperation and to implement specific cooperative projects.

**PARAGRAPH 4 FORMS OF COOPERATION**

The Parties agree that cooperation may be pursued, apart from the above-mentioned Ministerial and Working Group Meetings, through the following approaches:

1. Information exchanges;

2. Exchanges of visit and study tours of officials and experts of both Parties;

3. Joint organization of symposiums, seminars and other forms of activities to share ideas and practices concerning relevant policies, laws, regulations, and technical matters;

4. Personnel training;

5. The provision of facilitation for the cooperation between the enterprises and private organizations of both countries.

**PARAGRAPH 5 COSTS OF PARTICATION**

Each Party will bear the costs of its own participation in activities under this Understanding.

**PARAGRAPH 6 IMPLEMENTATION BODIES**

1. The implementation bodies of this Understanding of both Parties are, for the European side, the Directorate-General for Energy and Transport of the European Commission, and for the Chinese side, the Department of International Cooperation of the Ministry of Communications of the People's Republic of China.

2. The liaison and coordination work for the implementation of this Understanding will be the responsibilities of the implementation bodies of both Parties.

**PARAGRAPH 7 CONFIDENTIALITY OF INFORMATION**

Neither Party will make available any confidential information, documents and data derived from the cooperative activities under this Understanding to a third party unless the other Party gives permission in writing for this to happen.

**PARAGRAPH 8 AMENDMENT**

Amendment to this Understanding may be made at any time by an arrangement in writing and mutual agreement between the Parties.

**PARAGRAPH 9 SETTLEMENT OF DISPUTES**

Differences that may arise between the Parties relating to the interpretation or application of the provisions of this Understanding will be settled amicably by means of consultations.

**PARAGRAPH 10 ENTRY INTO FORCE, DURATION AND TERMINANTION**

1. This Understanding will come into effect from the date of its signature and remain valid for a period of five years. It will automatically be extended for successive periods of five years thereafter, unless either Party notifies the other Party of its intention to terminate this Understanding in writing at least thirty days before the end of the respective period.
2. Unless mutually determined otherwise, the termination of this Understanding will not affect the specific programs or activities being undertaken under this Understanding.

Signed in Brussels, on 18th September 2007, in two originals in the English and Chinese languages, both texts being equally authentic.

| | |
|---|---|
| For the European Commission<br>Jacques Barrot<br>Vice President in charge of Transport | For the People's Republic of China<br>LI Shenglin<br>Minister for Communications |

## CONCLUSION

The EU and China thus cooperate today not only within the framework of legally binding bilateral agreements but also on the basis of a relatively dense network of soft law agreements and arrangements. The choice of normative instrument reflects numerous factors, such as the sensitivity of the issues, the distribution of competences within the EU, the interests of political leaders, the distribution of power among different ministries in China and the extent of existing EU–China cooperation in different fields of policy. Even more than most soft law instruments, sectoral dialogues are chameleon-like. In theory at least, we should be able to site them on a spectrum, running from legally binding instruments at one end to purely political declarations at the other end. Dialogues based on MOUs could be situated near the former end; indeed, some MOUs are legally binding, even though the MOUs examined here usually are not. In contrast, most dialogues would belong in the middle of the spectrum. Moreover, their normative status is not necessarily static. A dialogue may be part of a process of normative development, beginning with very informal discussions based on a summit meeting, then moving to a more structured form of cooperation and finally to legally binding agreement. As this chapter shows, the terminology currently used to refer to these instruments is rather indeterminate. Any presentation of dialogues can be only a snapshot of the situation at a given time; witness the addition of one or two dialogues at the recent 10th EU–China Summit. Nevertheless, this chapter provides a basis for further research on the form and content of these instruments, the processes by which they develop, their normative character and their implementation or other effects in practice.

# 6

# Bilateral Agreements other than Trade and Textiles, 1994–Present

## INTRODUCTION

Starting in the early 1990s, the burgeoning number of dialogues, policy documents and summits between the EU and China frequently invited the conclusion of new bilateral agreements to crystallise common interests. The Commission's 1998 Communication, 'Building a Comprehensive Partnership with China', called expressly for the conclusion of bilateral agreements in areas of common interest.[1] Consequently, beginning in 1999, the EU and China expanded their relations by means of a series of bilateral agreements in areas other than trade and textiles, which previously had been the only subjects of EU–China bilateral agreements since 1978 (see Chapter 2). Whereas the trade and textiles agreements were always legally binding, the new agreements included legally binding measures, memoranda of understanding and numerous dialogues.

Alongside summits and dialogues, new bilateral agreements have become one of the principal means of policy development within the framework of EU–China relations. They reflect domestic developments within each of the trading partners, for example the EU and EC's increasing competences as a result of the 1992 Treaty on European Union (Maastricht Treaty), or the economic and social reforms in China. Together with soft law measures, the new bilateral agreements testify to the rapid development and expansion of the scope of EU–China relations. Soft law measures were discussed in the preceding two chapters. This chapter focuses on legally binding agreements.

## LEGALLY BINDING AGREEMENTS BETWEEN THE EC AND CHINA

Since 1994 the EU and China have concluded seven legally binding bilateral agreements on subjects other than trade and textiles (see Table 6.1). They concern science and technological cooperation, maritime transport, the civil global navigation satellite

[1] Commission of the European Communities Communication, 'Building a Comprehensive Partnership with China', COM(1998) 181 final (Brussels, 25 March 1998).

system (GALILEO), tourist groups, customs cooperation and mutual assistance, and the peaceful use of nuclear energy. In addition to these bilateral agreements, the chapter also includes the agreement on the ITER[2] project. This is a multilateral agreement, to which both the EU and China are parties. It is included here because of its general international significance among non-trade EU–China agreements and because it is likely to be very important for EU–China relations in the future.

The first non-trade, non-textile agreement was the Agreement for Scientific and Technological Cooperation (see Document 6.1). Concluded in 1998, it established a legal framework for existing collaboration and the development of further cooperation in these fields. It also regulated the distribution of intellectual property rights within its sphere of application.

**Document 6.1: Agreement for Scientific and Technological Cooperation**

AGREEMENT
for scientific and technological cooperation between the European Community and the Government of the People's Republic of China

THE EUROPEAN COMMUNITY, hereinafter referred to as the 'Community',

on the one part, and

THE GOVERNMENT OF THE PEOPLE'S REPUBLIC OF CHINA,

on the other part,

hereinafter referred to as the 'Parties';

CONSIDERING the 1985 Agreement on trade and economic cooperation between the European Economic Community and the People's Republic of China;

CONSIDERING the importance of science and technology for their economic and social development;

CONSIDERING the ongoing scientific and technological cooperation between the Community and China;

CONSIDERING that the Community and China are currently pursuing research and technological activities, including demonstration activities, in a number of areas of common interest and that participation in each other's research and development activities on a basis of reciprocity will provide mutual benefits;

DESIRING to establish a formal basis for cooperation in scientific and technological research which will extend and strengthen the conduct of cooperative activities in areas of common interest and encourage the application of the results of such cooperation to their economic and social benefit;

CONSIDERING that this Agreement for scientific and technological cooperation is within the context of the global cooperation between China and the Community,

[2] ITER is an acronym for International Thermonuclear Experimental Reactor. It means 'trail' or 'path' in Latin.

**Table 6.1: Legally Binding Agreements between the EU and China, other than Trade and Textiles Agreements, 1994–Present**

| Document/Title | Place and date of signature | Entry into force | Approval by EC | Source | Other relevant documents |
|---|---|---|---|---|---|
| Agreement for scientific and technological cooperation between the European Community and the Government of the People's Republic of China, OJ L6, 11.1.2000, p. 40 [see document 6.1] | 1999 | 2000, renewed 8.12.2004 | Council Decision 2000/16/EC of 2 December 1999 concluding the Agreement for scientific and technological cooperation between the European Community and the Government of the People's Republic of China, OJ L6, 11.1.2000, p. 39 | http://ec.europa.eu/research/iscp/eu-china/pdf/agreement_en.pdf | See also European Parliament legislative resolution on the proposal for a Council Decision concluding the Agreement for scientific and technological cooperation between the European Community and the People's Republic of China (COM(1999)287 - C5-0038/1999 - 1999/0123(CNS)), OJ C158, 7.6.2000, p. 33 |

**Table 6.1: continued**

| Document/Title | Place and date of signature | Entry into force | Approval by EC | Source | Other relevant documents |
|---|---|---|---|---|---|
| Agreement on Maritime Transport [see document 6.2] | 2002 | expected beginning 2007; amended after EC enlargement | See Proposal for a Council Decision concerning the conclusion of the Agreement on maritime transport between the European Community and its Member States, on the one hand, and the People's Republic of China on the other hand, COM(2002)97 final - CNS 2002/0048, OJ 181E, 30.7.2002, p. 176; Proposal for a Council Decision on the conclusion of a Protocol amending the Agreement on Maritime Transport between the European Community and its Member States, of the one part, and the People's Republic of China, of the other part, to take account of the accession of the Czech Republic, the Republic of Estonia, the Republic of Cyprus, the Republic of Hungary, the Republic of Latvia, the Republic of Lithuania, the Republic of Malta, the Republic of Poland, the Republic of Slovenia, and the Slovak Republic to the European Union, COM(2004)864 final - CNS 2004/0290 | http://ec.europa.eu/comm/external_relations/china/intro/sect.htm, visited 28.3.2007; http://www.official-documents.gov.uk/document/cm66/6621/6621.pdf | European Parliament legislative resolution on the proposal for a Council decision concluding an agreement on maritime transport between the European Community and the People's Republic of China (6049/1/2003 - COM(2002)97 .- C5-0062/2003 - 2002/0048/CNS), OJ C76E, 25.3.2004, p. 102; European Parliament legislative resolution on the proposal for a Council decision on the conclusion of a Protocol amending the Agreement on Maritime Transport between the European Community and its Member States, of the one part, and the People's Republic of China, of the other part, to take account of the accession of the Czech Republic, the Republic of Estonia, the Republic of Cyprus, the Republic of Hungary, the Republic of Latvia, the Republic of Lithuania, the Republic of Malta, the Republic of Poland, the Republic of Slovenia and the Slovak Republic to the European Union (COM(2004)864 - C6-0810/2005 - 2004/0290(CNS)), OJ C157E, 6.7.2006, p. 53 |

**Table 6.1: continued**

| Document/Title | Place and date of signature | Entry into force | Approval by EC | Source | Other relevant documents |
|---|---|---|---|---|---|
| Agreement on Cooperation in EU's Galileo Satellite Navigation Programme (2003); Agreement between the Chinese Remote Sensing Centre and the Galileo Joint Undertaking (2004) [see document 6.3] | 30.10.2003 [Cooperation Agreement], follow-up agreement signed October 2004 | not yet | Proposal for a Council Decision on the signing of the Cooperation Agreement on a Civil Global Navigation Satellite System (GNSS)-GALILEO between the European Community and its Member States and the People's Republic of China (presented by the Commission), Brussels, 3.10.2003, COM(2003)578 final | http://ec.europa.eu/comm/external_relations/china/intro/sect.htm; http://ec.europa.eu/external_relations/china/docs/galileo_agreement_06-13324.pdf [source used in this book] | |
| Memorandum of Understanding (MOU) on Visa and Related Issues concerning Tourist Groups from the People's Republic of China (ADS Agreement) [see document 6.4] | | May 2004 | Council Decision 2004/265/EC of 8 March 2004 concerning the conclusion of the Memorandum of Understanding between the European Community and the National Tourism Administration of the People's Republic of China on visa and related issues concerning tourist groups from the People's Republic of China (ADS), OJ L83, 20.3.2004, p. 12 | http://www.enit.it/adscina/mou_291003_en.pdf | Proposal for a Council Decision concerning the signing of the Memorandum between the European Community and the National Tourism Administration of the People's Republic of China on visas and related issues concerning tourist groups from the People's Republic of China (ADS) [presented by the Commission]. COM(2003) 790 final, Brussels, 15.12.2003, http://eur-lex.europa.eu/LexUriServ/site/en/com/2003/com2003_0790en01.pdf |

**Table 6.1: continued**

| Document/Title | Place and date of signature | Entry into force | Approval by EC | Source | Other relevant documents |
|---|---|---|---|---|---|
| Agreement betrween the European Community and the Government of the People's Republic of China on cooperation and mutual assistance in customs matters, OJ L375, 23.12.2004, p. 20 on Customs Cooperation and Mutual Assistance [see document 6.5] | 8.12.2004 | 1.4.2005 (OJ L110, p. 80). | Council Decision 2004/889/EC of 16 November 2004 on the conclusion of an Agreement between the European Community and the Government of the People's Republic of China on cooperation and mutual administrative assistance in customs matters, OJ L375, 23.12.2004, p. 19 | http://ec.europa.eu/com m/external_relations/chi na/intro/sect.htm, accessed 28.3.2007 | |
| Agreement on Research and Development Cooperation on the Peaceful Use of Nuclear Energy [see document 6.6] | 8.12.2004, | | | Council of the European Union, Cover Note from the Secretary-General of the European Commission to Mr Javier Solana, Secretary-Genera / High Representative, 19 November 2004, subject: Communication from the Commission [see adjacent column], ATO 137 ( RECH 252), (15249/04, Brussels, 25.11.2004 [Agreement is annexed to the Commission Communication] | Communication from the Commission to the Council concerning the conclusion of an agreement for R&D cooperation in the peaceful uses of nuclear energy between the European Atomic Energy Community (Euratom) and the government of the People's Republic of China, COM(2004)755 final |

**Table 6.1: continued**

| Document/Title | Place and date of signature | Entry into force | Approval by EC | Source | Other relevant documents |
|---|---|---|---|---|---|
| Agreement on the Establishment of the ITER International Fusion Energy Organization for the Joint Implementation of the ITER Project, OJ 16.12.2006 L358/62 [see document 6.7] | | | Commission Decision 2006/943/Euratom of 17 November 2006 on Provisional Application of the Agreement for the Establishment of the ITER International Fusion Energy Organization for the Joint Implementation of the ITER Project and of the Agreement on Privileges and Immunities of the ITER International Fusion Energy Organization for the Joint Implementation of the ITER Project, OJ 16.12.2006 L358/60 | OJ EC 16.12.2006 L358/62 | Proposal for a Council Decision concerning the conclusion, by the Commission, of the Agreement on the Establishment of the ITER International Fusion Energy Organization for the Joint Implementation of the ITER Project, of the Arrangement on Provisional Application of the Agreement on the Establishment of the ITER International Fusion Energy Organization for the Joint Implementation of the ITER Project and of the Agreement on the Privileges and Immunities of the ITER International Fusion Energy Organization for the Joint Implementation of the ITER Project (COM 2006/0240) |
| Arrangement on Provisional Application of the Agreement on the Establishment of the ITER International Fusion Energy Organization for the Joint Implementation of the ITER Project, OJ 16.12.2006 L358/81 | | | | | |

**Table 6.1: continued**

| Document/Title | Place and date of signature | Entry into force | Approval by EC | Source | Other relevant documents |
|---|---|---|---|---|---|
| Agreement on the privileges and immunities of the ITER International Fusion Energy Organization for the Joint Implementation of the ITER Project, OJ 16.12.2006 L358/82 | | | | | |

HAVE AGREED AS FOLLOWS:

**Article 1 Purpose**

The Parties shall encourage, develop and facilitate cooperative activities between the Community and China in fields of common interest where they are pursuing research and development activities in science and technology.

**Article 2 Definition**

For the purpose of this Agreement:

(a) 'cooperative activity' means any activity which the Parties undertake or support, pursuant to this Agreement, and includes joint research;

(b) 'information' means scientific or technical data, results or methods of research and development stemming from joint research and any other data deemed necessary by the participants to cooperative activities; including, as necessary, by the Parties themselves;

(c) 'intellectual property' shall have the meaning defined in Article 2 of the Convention a establishing the World Intellectual Property Organisation, done at Stockholm, 14 July 1967;

(d) 'joint research' means research, technological development or demonstration that is implemented with or without financial support from one or both Parties and that involves collaboration by participants from both the Community and China and is designated as joint research in writing by the Parties or their scientific and technological activities organisations and agencies implementing the scientific research programmes. In the case where there is funding by only one Party the designation is made by that Party and the participant in that project;

(e) 'Participant' or 'research entities' means any person moral or private, any research institute or any other legal entity or firm established in the Community or in China involved in cooperative activities including the Parties themselves.

**Article 3 Principles**

Cooperative activities shall be conducted on the basis of the following principles:

(a) mutual benefit based on an overall balance of advantages;

(b) reciprocal access to the activities of research and technological development undertaken by each Party;

(c) timely exchange of information which may affect cooperative activities;

(d) appropriate protection of intellectual property rights.

**Article 4 Areas of cooperative activities**

Cooperation under this Agreement may cover all the activities of research, technological development and demonstration, hereinafter referred to as 'RTD', included in the first activity of the framework programme under Article 130g of the Treaty establishing the European Community and all similar RTD in China in the corresponding scientific and technological fields.

This Agreement does not affect the participation of China, as a developing country, in Community activities in the field of research for development.

**Article 5 Forms of cooperative activities**

(a) Subject to their applicable laws, regulations and policies, the Parties shall foster, to the fullest extent practicable, the involvement of participants in cooperative activities under this Agreement with a view to providing comparable opportunities for participation in their scientific and technological research and development activities.

(b) Cooperative activities may take the following forms:

- participation of Chinese research entities to RTD projects under the first activity of the framework programme and reciprocal participation of research entities established in the Community to Chinese projects in similar sectors of RTD. Such a participation is subject to the rules and procedures applicable in each Party,
- pooling of RTD projects already implemented according to the procedures applicable in the RTD programmes of each Party,
- visits and exchanges of scientists and technical experts,
- joint organisation of scientific seminars, conferences, symposia and workshops, as well as participation of experts to those activities,
- concerted actions,
- exchanges and sharing of equipment and materials,
- exchanges of information on practices, laws, regulations and programmes relevant to cooperation under this Agreement,
- any other modality that would be recommended by the Steering Committee and deemed in conformity with the policies and procedures applicable in both Parties.

The joint RTD projects shall be implemented when the participants have developed a technology management plan, as indicated in the Annex to this Agreement.

**Article 6 Coordination and facilitation of cooperative activities**

(a) The coordination and facilitation of cooperative activities under this Agreement shall be accomplished on behalf of China, by the Ministry of Science and Technology and, on behalf of the Community, by the services of the Commission of the European Communities, acting as executive agents.

(b) The executive agents shall establish a Steering RTD Cooperation Committee, hereinafter referred to as the 'Steering Committee' for the management of this Agreement; this Committee shall consist of an equal number of official representatives of each Party; it shall establish its own rules of procedure.

(c) The functions of the Steering Committee shall include:

1. promoting and overseeing the different cooperative activities as mentioned in Article 4 as well as those that would be implemented in the framework of RTD cooperation for development;

2. indicating, for the following year, pursuant to Article 5(b), first indent, among the potential sectors for RTD cooperation, those priority sectors or subsectors of mutual interest in which cooperation is sought;

3. proposing, pursuant to Article 5(b), second indent, to the scientists of both Parties the pooling of their projects which would be of mutual benefit and complementary;

4. making recommendations pursuant to Article 5 (b), seventh indent;

5. advising the Parties on ways to enhance and improve cooperation consistent with the principles set out in this Agreement;

6. reviewing the efficient functioning and implementation of this Agreement;

7. annually providing a report to the Parties on the status, the level reached and the effectiveness of cooperation undertaken under this Agreement. This report will be transmitted to the Joint Committee established under the 1985 Agreement on trade and economic cooperation between the European Economic Community and the People' Republic of China.

(d) The Steering Committee shall, as a general rule, meet annually, preferably before the meeting of the Joint Committee established under the 1985 Agreement on trade and economic cooperation between the European Economic Community and the People's Republic of China, and according to a jointly agreed schedule; the meetings should be held alternatively in the Community and in China. Extraordinary meetings may be organised at the request of either Party.

(e) The costs incurred by the Steering Committee or in its name shall be borne by the Party to whom members relate. The costs other than those for travel and accommodation which are directly associated with meetings of the Steering Committee shall be borne by the host Party.

**Article 7 Funding**

(a) Cooperative activities shall be subject to the availability of appropriated funds and to the applicable laws and regulations, policies and programmes of the Parties. The costs incurred by the participants to cooperative activities will not lead to any transfer of funds from one Party to the other.

(b) When specific cooperative schemes of one Party provide for financial support to participants from the other Party, any such grants, financial or other contributions from one Party to the participants of the other Party in support of those activities shall be granted tax and customs exemption in accordance with the laws and regulations applicable in the territories of each Party.

**Article 8 Entry of personnel and equipment**

Each Party shall take all reasonable steps and use its best efforts, within the laws and regulations applicable in the territories of each Party, to facilitate entry to, sojourn and exit from its territory of persons, material, data and equipment involved in or used in cooperative activities identified by the Parties under the provisions of this Agreement.

**Article 9 Diffusion and utilisation of information**

The research entities established in China which are involved in Community RTD projects shall follow, as regards the ownership, diffusion and utilisation of information and as regards the intellectual property stemming from this involvement, the rules of diffusion of research results stemming from the Community RTD specific programmes as well as the provisions of the Annex to this Agreement.

The research entities established in the Community which are involved in Chinese RTD projects have, as regards the ownership, diffusion and utilisation of information and as regards the intellectual property stemming from this involvement, the same rights and the same obligations as the Chinese research entities and are subject to the provisions of the Annex to this Agreement.

The Annex on intellectual property rights is an integral part of this Agreement.

**Article 10 Territorial application**

This Agreement shall apply, on the one hand to the territories in which the Treaty establishing the European Community is applied and under the conditions laid down in that Treaty, and on the other hand to the territory of the People's Republic of China. This shall not prevent the conduct of cooperative activities on the high seas, outer space, or the territory of third countries, in accordance with international law.

**Article 11 Entry into force, termination and dispute settlement**

(a) This Agreement shall enter into force on the date on which the Parties have notified each other in writing that their respective internal procedures necessary for its entry into force have been completed.

(b) This Agreement shall be concluded for an initial period of five years and may be renewed by common agreement between the Parties (tacit renewal) after evaluation during the penultimate year of each successive period.

(c) This Agreement may be amended by agreement of the Parties. Amendments shall enter into force on the date on which the Parties have notified each other in writing that their respective internal procedures necessary for amending this Agreement have been completed.

(d) This Agreement may be terminated at any time by either Party upon six months' written notice. The expiration or termination of this Agreement shall not affect the validity or duration of any arrangements made under it, or any specific rights and obligations that have accrued in compliance with the Annex.

(e) All questions or disputes related to the interpretation or implementation of this Agreement shall be settled by mutual agreement between the Parties.

In witness whereof, the undersigned, being duly authorised thereto, have signed this Agreement.

Done at, Brussels on 22 december 1998, in two copies, in the Danish, Dutch, English, Finnish, French, German, Greek, Italian, Portuguese, Spanish, Swedish, and Chinese languages, with each text being equally authentic.

For the Council of the European Union

For the Government of the People's Pepublic of China

**ANNEX INTELLECTUAL PROPERTY RIGHTS**

Rights to intellectual property created or furnished under the Agreement shall be allocated as provided for in this Annex.

*I. Application*

This Annex is applicable to joint research undertaken pursuant to the Agreement, except as otherwise agreed by the Parties.

*II. Ownership, allocation and exercise of rights*

1. For purposes of this Annex 'intellectual property' is defined in Article 2(c) of the Agreement.

2. This Annex addresses the allocation of rights and interests of the Parties and their participants. Each Party and its participants shall ensure that the other Party and its participants may obtain the rights to intellectual property allocated to it in accordance with this Annex. This Annex does not otherwise alter or prejudice the allocation of rights, interests and royalties between a Party and its nationals or participants, which will be determined by the laws and practices applicable to each Party.

3. The Parties will also be guided by, and contractual arrangements should provide for, the following principles:

(a) effective protection of intellectual property. The Parties shall ensure that they and/or their participants notify one another within a reasonable time of the creation of any intellectual property arising under the Agreement, of implementation arrangements and seek protection for such intellectual property in a timely fashion;

(b) effective exploitation of results, taking into account the contributions of the Parties and their participants;

(c) non-discriminatory treatment of participants from the other Party as compared with the treatment given to its own participants;

(d) protection of business-confidential information.

4. The participants shall jointly develop a technology management plan (TMP) in respect of the ownership and use, including publication of information and intellectual property to be created in the course of joint research. The TMP will be approved by the responsible funding agency, or department of the Party involved in financing the research before the conclusion of the specific research and development cooperation contracts to which they are attached. The TMP shall be developed within the rules and regulations in force at each Party taking into account the aims of the joint research, the relative financial or other contributions of the Parties and participants, the advantages and disadvantages of licensing by territory or for fields of use, the transfer of export-controlled data, goods or services, requirements imposed by the applicable laws and other factors deemed appropriate by the participants. The rights and obligations concerning the research generated by visiting researchers (i.e. researchers not coming from a Party or a participant) in respect of intellectual property will also be addressed in the joint TMP.

The TMP is a specific agreement to be concluded between the participants about the implementation of joint research and the respective rights and obligations of the participants.

With respect to intellectual property, the TMP will normally address, among other things, ownership, protection, user rights for research and development purposes, exploitation and dissemination, including arrangements for joint publication, the rights and obligations of visiting researchers and dispute settlement procedures. The TMP may also address foreground and background information, licensing and deliverables.

5. Information or intellectual property created in the course of joint research and not addressed in the TMP will be allocated, with the approval of the Parties, according to the principles set out in the TMP. In case of disagreement, such information or intellectual

property will be owned jointly by all the participants involved in the joint research from which the information or intellectual property results. Each participant to whom this provision applies will have the right to use such information or intellectual property for his own commercial exploitation with no geographical limitation.

6. Each Party will ensure that the other Party and its participants may have the rights to intellectual property allocated to them in accordance with these principles.

7. While maintaining the condition of competition in areas affected by the Agreement, each Party will endeavour to ensure that rights acquired pursuant to the Agreement and arrangements made under it are exercised in such a way as to encourage, in particular (i) the dissemination and use of information created, disclosed or otherwise made available, under the Agreement, and (ii) the adoption and implementation of international standards.

8. The termination or expiry of the Agreement will not affect rights or obligations under this Annex.

*III. Copyright works and scientific literary works*

Copyright belonging to the Parties or to their participants will be accorded treatment consistent with the Berne Convention (Paris Act 1971). Copyright protection will extend to expressions and not to ideas, procedures, methods of operation or mathematical concepts as such. Limitations or exceptions to exclusive rights will be confined to certain special cases which do not conflict with a normal exploitation of the work and do not reasonably prejudice the legitimate interests of the right holder.

Without prejudice to Section II, and unless otherwise agreed in the TMP publication of results of research shall be made jointly by the Parties or participants to that joint research. Subject to the foregoing general rule, the following procedures shall apply

1. In the case of publication by a Party, or public bodies of that Party of scientific and technical journals, articles, reports, books, including video and software arising from joint research pursuant to the Agreement, the other Party will be entitled to a worldwide, non-exclusive, irrevocable, royalty-free licence to translate, reproduce, adapt, transmit and publicly distribute such works.

2. The Parties will ensure that literary works of a scientific character arising from joint research pursuant to the Agreement and published by independent publishers will be disseminated as widely as possible.

3. All copies of a copyright work to be publicly distributed and prepared under this provision shall indicate the names of the author(s) of the work unless an author explicitly declines to be named. They shall also bear a clearly visible acknowledgement of the cooperative support of the Parties.

*IV. Inventions, discoveries and other science and technology achievements*

Inventions, discoveries and other science and technology achievements created under cooperative activities between the Parties themselves will be owned by the Parties unless otherwise agreed by the Parties.

*V. Undisclosed information*

A. Documentary undisclosed information

1. Each Party, its agencies or its participants, as appropriate, will identify at the earliest possible moment and preferably in the TMP the information that they wish to remain undisclosed in relation to the Agreement, taking into account inter alia the following criteria:

(a) secrecy of the information in the sense that it is not, as a body or in the precise configuration or assembly of its components, generally known among or readily accessible by lawful means to experts in the fields;

(b) the actual or potential commercial value of the information by virtue of its secrecy;

(c) previous protection of the information in the sense that it has been subject to steps that were reasonable under the circumstances by the person lawfully in control, to maintain its secrecy.

The Parties and their participants may in certain cases agree that, unless otherwise indicated, parts or all of the information provided, exchanged or created in the course of joint research pursuant to the Agreement may not be disclosed.

2. Each Party shall ensure that it and its participants clearly identify undisclosed information, for example by means of an appropriate marking or restrictive legend. This also applies to any reproduction of the said information, in whole or in part.

A Party receiving undisclosed information pursuant to the Agreement will respect the privileged nature thereof. These limitations will automatically terminate when this information is disclosed by the owner into the public domain.

3. Undisclosed information communicated under the Agreement may be disseminated by the receiving Party to persons within or employed by the receiving Party and other concerned departments or agencies in the receiving Party authorised for the specific purposes of the joint research under way, provided that any undisclosed information so disseminated shall be pursuant to an agreement of confidentiality and shall be readily recognisable as such, as set out above.

4. With the prior written consent of the Party providing undisclosed information, the receiving Party may disseminate such undisclosed information more widely than otherwise permitted in point 3. The Parties shall cooperate in developing procedures for requesting and obtaining prior written consent for such wider dissemination, and each Party will grant such approval to the extent permitted by its domestic policies, regulations and laws.

B. Non-documentary undisclosed information

Non-documentary undisclosed or other confidential information provided in seminars and other meetings arranged under the Agreement, or information arising from the attachment of staff, use of facilities, or joint projects, shall be treated by the Parties or their participants according to the principles specified for documentary information in the Agreement; provided, however, that the recipient of such undisclosed or other confidential or privileged information has been made aware of the confidential character of the information communicated at the time such communication is made.

C. Control

Each Party shall endeavour to ensure that undisclosed information received by it under the Agreement will be controlled as provided herein. If one of the Parties becomes aware that it will be, or may be reasonably expected to become, unable to meet the non-dissemination provisions of Sections A and B, it shall immediately inform the other Party. The Parties will thereafter consult to define an appropriate course of action.

In 2003 the EC and China concluded an Agreement on Maritime Transport (see Document 6.2). EU–China maritime transport relations had increased substantially during the previous decade. Eleven of the then EU Member States already had bilateral maritime agreements with China. The 2003 Agreement replaced the 'trade' provisions of these bilateral agreements.[3] It was a mixed agreement, signed on the European side by both the European Community and its Member States. The Agreement was agreed for a period of five years, renewable on a yearly basis. The main purpose is to improve the conditions of maritime transport to and from the EU and China, as well as to and from the partners and third countries. It applies to international maritime cargo transport and logistic services between Chinese ports and EU Member States' ports, international maritime cargo transport between the ports of EC Member States, and cross trades and the movement of equipment, such as empty containers, between Chinese ports or between EC Member States' ports. Its basic principles are freedom to provide maritime transport services, free access to cargoes and cross trades, and unrestricted access to and non-discriminatory treatment in the use of ports and auxiliary services, as well as regarding commercial presence. Moreover, it covers all aspects of door-to-door services.[4] Its aims include promoting multimodal transport involving a sea leg and developing further a flexible and market-oriented approach to maritime transport. This involves, for example, permitting the shipping companies of the other party to establish wholly owned or jointly invested subsidiaries, branches or representative offices and, for subsidiaries and branches, to engage in economic activities in accordance with its laws and regulations. Consistent with WTO rules, technical standards and licensing requirements and procedures are to be based on objective, non-discriminatory, pre-established and transparent criteria.

[3] It did not replace the provisions of national agreements regarding matters such as the status of crew or taxation. See 'Proposal for a Council Decision Concerning the Conclusion of the Agreement on Maritime Transport between the European Community and its Member States, on the one hand, and the People's Republic of China on the other hand', COM/2002/0097 final (CNS 2002/0049), [2002] OJ 181E, 176.

[4] *Ibid.*

**Document 6.2: Agreement on Maritime Transport between the European Community and its Member States, on the one hand, and the People's Republic of China, on the other hand**

AGREEMENT ON MARITIME TRANSPORT BETWEEN THE EUROPEAN COMMUNITY AND ITS MEMBER STATES, OF THE ONE PART, AND THE GOVERNMENT OF THE PEOPLE'S REPUBLIC OF CHINA, OF THE OTHER PART

THE KINGDOM OF BELGIUM,

THE KINGDOM OF DENMARK,

THE FEDERAL REPUBLIC OF GERMANY,

THE HELLENIC REPUBLIC,

THE KINGDOM OF SPAIN,

THE FRENCH REPUBLIC,

IRELAND,

THE ITALIAN REPUBLIC,

THE GRAND DUCHY OF LUXEMBOURG,

THE KINGDOM OF THE NETHERLANDS,

THE REPUBLIC OF AUSTRIA,

THE PORTUGUESE REPUBLIC,

THE REPUBLIC OF FINLAND,

THE KINGDOM OF SWEDEN,

THE UNITED KINGDOM OF GREAT BRITAIN AND NORTHERN IRELAND,

Parties to the Treaty establishing the European Community[1], hereinafter referred to as "Member States of the Community", and THE EUROPEAN COMMUNITY,

hereinafter referred to as "the Community", of the one part, and

THE GOVERNMENT OF THE PEOPLE'S REPUBLIC OF CHINA,

hereinafter referred to as "China",of the other part,

TAKING INTO ACCOUNT the Trade and Economic Cooperation Agreement between the European Economic Community and the People's Republic of China of May 1985[2];

TAKING INTO ACCOUNT the importance of the maritime relations existing between the Community and its Member States and China;

BELIEVING that cooperation in the international maritime field between the Parties will be beneficial for the development of the trade and economic relations between China and the Community and its Member States;

WILLING to further strengthen and consolidate the relations, on the basis of equality and mutual benefit, in the field of international maritime transport;

RECOGNISING the importance of maritime transport services and wishing to promote even further multimodal transport involving a sea leg in order to increase efficiencies in the transport chain;

RECOGNISING the importance of further developing a flexible and market-oriented approach and the benefits to economic operators of both Parties of controlling and operating their own international cargo transport services in the context of an efficient international maritime transport system;

TAKING INTO ACCOUNT the existing bilateral maritime agreements between the Member States of the Community and China;

SUPPORTING multilateral negotiations on maritime transport services in the World Trade Organisation;

HAVE DECIDED to conclude this Agreement and to this end have designated their plenipotentiaries:

THE KINGDOM OF BELGIUM:
Isabelle DURANT
Deputy Prime Minister and Minister for Mobility and Transport

THE KINGDOM OF DENMARK:
Bendt BENDTSEN
Minister for Economic Affairs, Trade and Industry

THE FEDERAL REPUBLIC OF GERMANY:
Manfred STOLPE
Federal Minister for Transport, Building and Housing

Wilhelm SCHÖNFELDER
Ambassador, Permanent Representative of the Federal Republic of Germany

THE HELLENIC REPUBLIC:
Georgios ANOMERITIS
Minister for Mercantile Marine

THE KINGDOM OF SPAIN:
Francisco ÁLVAREZ-CASCOS FERNÁNDEZ
Minister for Internal Development

THE FRENCH REPUBLIC:
Pierre SELLAL
Ambassador, Permanent Representative of the French Republic

IRELAND:
Peter GUNNING
Deputy Permanent Representative of Ireland

THE ITALIAN REPUBLIC:
Pietro LUNARDI
Minister for Infrastructure and Transport

THE GRAND DUCHY OF LUXEMBOURG:
Henri GRETHEN
Minister for Economic Affairs, Minister for Transport

THE KINGDOM OF THE NETHERLANDS:
Roelf Hendrik de BOER
Minister for Transport, Communications and Public Works

THE REPUBLIC OF AUSTRIA:
Mathias REICHHOLD
Federal Minister for Transport, Innovation and Technology

THE PORTUGUESE REPUBLIC:
Luís Francisco VALENTE DE OLIVEIRA
Minister for Public Works, Transport and Housing

THE REPUBLIC OF FINLAND:
Kimmo SASI
Minister for Transport and Communications

THE KINGDOM OF SWEDEN:
Ulrica MESSING
Minister of Communications

THE UNITED KINGDOM OF GREAT BRITAIN AND NORTHERN IRELAND:
David JAMIESON
Parliamentary Under-Secretary of State for Transport

THE EUROPEAN COMMUNITY:
Bendt BENDTSEN
Minister for Economic Affairs, Trade and Industry of the Kingdom of Denmark
President-in-Office of the Council of the European Union

Loyola de PALACIO
Vice-President of the Commission of the European Communities

THE GOVERNMENT OF THE PEOPLE'S REPUBLIC OF CHINA:
Chunxian ZHANG
Minister for Communications of the People's Republic of China

WHO, having exchanged their full powers, found in good and due form,

HAVE AGREED AS FOLLOWS:

**ARTICLE 1 Aim**

This Agreement is aimed at improving the conditions under which maritime cargo transport operations are carried out to and from China, to and from the Community, as well as to and from the Community and China on the one hand and third countries on the other, for the benefit of economic operators of the Parties. It is based on the principles of freedom to provide maritime transport services, free access to cargoes and cross trades, unrestricted access to, and non-discriminatory treatment in, the use of ports and auxiliary services as well as regarding commercial presence. It covers all aspects of door to door services.

**ARTICLE 2 Scope**

1. This Agreement applies to the international maritime cargo transport and logistic services, including multimodal operations involving a sea leg, between the ports of China

and of the Member States of the Community as well as to the international maritime cargo transport between the ports of the Member States of the Community. It also applies to cross trades and to the movement of equipment such as empty containers, not being carried as cargo against payment, between ports of China or between ports of a Member State of the Community.

If vessels of one Party sail from one port of the other Party to another or from one port of a Member State of the Community to another to load cargo for foreign countries or discharge cargo from abroad, it shall be regarded as a part of the international maritime transport.

This Agreement shall not apply to domestic transport purely between the ports of China or between the ports of any particular Member State of the Community.

2. This Agreement shall not affect the application of the bilateral maritime agreements concluded between China and the Member States of the Community for issues falling outside the scope of this Agreement.

3. This Agreement shall not affect the right of vessels of third parties to engage in cargo and passenger transport between the ports of the Parties or between the ports of either Party and a third party.

**ARTICLE 3 Definitions**

For the purpose of this Agreement:

(a) "international maritime cargo transport and logistic services" cover the supply of services of international maritime transport of cargo, and the related cargo handling, storage and warehousing services, customs clearance services, container station and depot services, port and inland located, shipping agency services and freight forwarding services;

(b) "multimodal transport operations" is the carriage of goods using more than one mode of transport including a sea-leg under a single document;

(c) "shipping agency services" means activities consisting in representing, within a given geographic area, as an agent, the business interests of one or more shipping lines or shipping companies, for the following purposes:

- marketing and sales of maritime transport and related services, from quotation to invoicing, and issuance of bills of lading on behalf of the companies, contracting of the necessary related services, preparation of documentation, and provision of business information;
- acting on behalf of the companies organising the call of the ship or taking over cargoes when required;

(d) "freight forwarding services" means the activity consisting of organising and monitoring shipment operations on behalf of shippers, through contracting related services, preparation of documentation and provision of business information;

(e) "shipping company" means a company which meets the following conditions:

(i) being constituted in accordance with the public or private laws of China, or the Community or a Member State of the Community;

(ii) having its registered office or central administration or principal place of business in China or the Community respectively,

(iii) engaging in international shipping service with its owned or operated vessels.

Shipping companies established outside the Community or China and controlled by nationals of a Member State of the Community or of China respectively, shall also be beneficiaries of the provisions of this Agreement, if their vessels are registered in that Member State or in China in accordance with their legislation;

(f) "subsidiary" means a company owned by a shipping company and having legal personality;

(g) "branch office" means a place of business owned by a shipping company and not having legal personality;

(h) "representative office" means a representative office of a shipping company of one Party established in the other Party;

(i) "vessel" means any merchant ship registered in accordance with the laws of China, or the Community or its Member States in the vessel registration office of either Party under the national flag of that Party and engaged in international maritime transport, including vessels flying the flag of a third country but owned or operated by a shipping company of China or a Member State of the Community. However, this term does not include warships and any other non-commercial ships.

**ARTICLE 4 Supply of services**

1. Each Party shall continue to grant non-discriminatory treatment to vessels flying the flag of the other Party or operated by nationals or companies of the other Party, as compared to the treatment accorded to its own vessels, with regard to access to ports, the use of infrastructure and auxiliary maritime services of those ports, as well as related fees and charges, customs formalities and assignment of berths and facilities for loading and unloading.

2. The Parties undertake to apply effectively the principle of unrestricted access to the international maritime market and traffic on a non-discriminatory and commercial basis.

3. In applying the principles of paragraphs 1 and 2, the Parties shall:

(a) not introduce cargo sharing clauses in future agreements with third countries concerning maritime transport services and terminate such provisions in the case they exist in previous bilateral agreements within a reasonable period of time;

(b) abolish, upon entry into force of this Agreement, all unilateral administrative, technical, or other measures, which could constitute an indirect restriction and have discriminatory effects on the free supply of services in international maritime transport;

(c) abstain from implementing on entry into force of this Agreement administrative, technical or legislative measures which could have the effect of discriminating against nationals or companies of the other Party in the supply of services in international maritime transport.

4. One Party shall allow shipping companies of the other Party to have access to and use of, on a non-discriminatory basis and on agreed terms between the companies concerned, feeder services provided by shipping companies registered in the former Party for the international cargo between the ports of China or between the ports of a Member State of the Community.

**ARTICLE 5 Commercial presence**

In respect of activities for the provision of international maritime cargo transport and logistic services, including door-to-door multimodal transport operations, each Party shall permit the shipping companies of the other Party, to establish wholly-owned or jointly-invested subsidiaries, branch or representative offices and, as regards subsidiaries and branch offices to engage in economic activities, in accordance with its laws and regulations. Such activities include, but are not limited to:

1) cargo soliciting and booking of space;

2) making, confirming, handling and issuing of the bill of lading, including the commonly accepted through bill of lading in the international maritime transport; preparation of documentation concerning transport documents and customs documents;

3) fixing, collecting and remitting freight and other charges incurred on the basis of the service contracts or tariff rates;

4) negotiating and signing service contracts;

5) signing contracts for trucking, railway transport, cargo dealing and other related auxiliary services;

6) quoting and publishing tariff rates;

7) engaging in marketing activities related to their service;

8) owning the equipment necessary for the economic activities;

9) provision of business information by any means, including computerised information systems and electronic data interchange, subject to any non-discriminatory restrictions concerning telecommunications;

10) setting up joint ventures with any locally established shipping agency to engage in agency-related businesses, such as organising the call of the vessels or taking delivery of cargoes for shipment.

**ARTICLE 6 Transparency**

1. Each Party shall, after prior consultation and appropriate pre-notice, publish promptly all relevant measures of general application, which pertain to or affect the operation of this Agreement.

2. Where publication as referred to in paragraph 1 is not practicable, such information shall be made otherwise publicly available.

3. Each Party shall respond promptly to all requests by the other Party for specific information on any of its measures of general application within the meaning of paragraph 1.

**ARTICLE 7 Domestic regulation**

1. The Parties shall ensure that all measures of general application affecting trade in international maritime transport services are administered in a reasonable, objective and impartial manner.

2. In those cases where authorisation is required, the competent authorities of a Party shall, within a reasonable period of time after the submission of an application considered complete under domestic laws and regulations, inform the applicant of the decision concerning the application. At the request of the applicant, the competent authorities of a Party shall provide, without undue delay, information concerning the status of the application.

3. To ensure that measures relating to technical standards and licensing requirements and procedures do not constitute unnecessary barriers to trade, requirements shall be based on objective, non-discriminatory, pre-established and transparent criteria, such as the ability to supply the service; and in the case of licensing procedures, not in themselves be a restriction on or a barrier to the supply of the service.

**ARTICLE 8 Key Personnel**

The wholly-owned or jointly-invested subsidiaries, branch or representative offices of the shipping companies of one Party established in the other Party shall be entitled to employ key personnel, in accordance with the legislation in force in the host country, irrespective of their nationality. Each Party shall facilitate the acquisition of work permits and visas for foreign employees.

**ARTICLE 9 Payments and Capital movements**

1. Revenues of nationals or companies of one Party derived from international maritime transport and multimodal operations in the other Party may be settled in freely convertible currencies.

2. The revenues and expenses of the economic activities of the subsidiaries and branch and representative offices of the shipping companies of a Party established in the other Party may be settled in the currency of the host country. The balance after the payment of the local fees by the abovementioned shipping companies, subsidiaries, branch or representative offices may be freely remitted abroad at the exchange rate of the bank on the date of remittance.

**ARTICLE 10 Maritime Cooperation**

The Parties shall, for the purpose of promoting the development of their maritime industry, encourage their competent authorities, shipping companies, ports, relevant research institutions, universities and colleges to cooperate, including, but not limited to, the following fields:

1) exchange of views related to their activities in the framework of international maritime organisations;

2) formulate and perfect the legislation relating to maritime transport and market administration;

3) promote efficient transport service for international sea trade by the effective exploitation of the ports and fleets of the Parties;

4) guarantee shipping safety and prevent marine pollution;

5) promote maritime education and training, especially the training of seafarers;

6) exchange personnel scientific information and technology;

7) enhance their efforts to combat piracy and terrorism.

**ARTICLE 11 Consultations and settlement of disputes**

1. The Parties shall establish appropriate procedures to ensure the proper implementation of this Agreement.

2. Should any dispute between the Parties arise from the interpretation or application of this Agreement, their competent authorities shall seek to resolve the dispute through friendly consultation. In the event that no agreement is reached, it shall be settled through diplomatic channels.

**ARTICLE 12 Amendment**

This Agreement may be amended by a written agreement between the Parties and the amendment will come into force in accordance with the procedures specified in Article 15(2).

**ARTICLE 13 Territorial application**

This Agreement shall apply, on the one hand, to the territories in which the Treaty establishing the European Community is applied and under the conditions laid down in that Treaty and, on the other hand, to the territory of China.

**ARTICLE 14 Authentic text**

This Agreement is drawn up in duplicate in the Danish, Dutch, English, Finnish, French, German, Greek, Italian, Portuguese, Spanish, Swedish and Chinese languages, each of these texts being equally authentic.

**ARTICLE 15 Duration and entry into force**

1. This Agreement is concluded for a period of five years. It shall be tacitly renewed on a yearly basis unless one of the Parties denounces it in writing six months before the date of expiry.

2. This Agreement will be approved by the Parties in accordance with their own procedures.

This Agreement shall enter into force on the first day of the second month following the date on which the Parties notify each other that the procedures referred to in the first subparagraph have been completed.

3. If this Agreement is less favourable on certain issues than existing bilateral agreements between individual Member States of the Community and China, the more favourable provisions shall prevail without prejudice to Community obligations and taking into account the Treaty establishing the European Community. The provisions of this Agreement replace those of previous bilateral agreements concluded between Member States of the Community and China, if the latter provisions are either inconsistent with the former, save for the situation referred to in the preceding sentence, or identical to them. Provisions of existing bilateral agreements not covered by this Agreement shall continue to apply.

Done at Brussels on the sixth day of December two thousand and two.

IN WITNESS WHEREOF the undersigned Plenipotentiaries have signed this Agreement.

[1] Treaty Series No. 52 (1999) Cm 4434 and Treaty Series No. 47 (1988) Cm 455.
[2] European Communities No. 3 (1986) Cmnd 9723.

The next agreement to be concluded was the Cooperation Agreement on a Civil Global Navigation Satellite System (GNSS)—GALILEO between the European Community and its Member States and the People's Republic of China (see Document 6.3). After the Commission's 1998 communication on the development of a European strategy for global navigation satellite systems,[5] its 1998 Commission Communication on China[6] and its 1999 communication proposing to open up GALILEO to third countries,[7] the Council of the European Union encouraged contacts with non-EC countries.[8] Then, following a further 2002 Commission communication,[9] the Council invited the Commission to open negotiations, which led to a Cooperation Agreement in 2003 and a follow-up Agreement in October 2004.

The objective of the Agreement is to encourage, facilitate and enhance cooperation between the parties, within their respective contributions, to the GALILEO programme. Basic principles include mutual benefit based on an overall balance of rights and obligations, including contributions, partnership in the programme, reciprocal opportunities to cooperate in European and Chinese projects, exchange of information and protection of intellectual property rights. A wide range of sectors are open for cooperation, and the list may be extended by separate agreement. An extension to system security features, critical control features and exchange of classified GALILEO information, if requested, would be subject to a separate agreement. The Agreement does not affect the EC rules on the establishment of GALILEO and its institutional structure, or applicable rules and policies on non-proliferation, export control on dual-use goods, and national domestic measures on security and controls of intangible transfers of technology. Exports of sensitive items by China to third countries must be submitted for prior authorisation by the competent GALILEO security authority if the authority has recommended to EU Member States that such items be subject to export authorisation. The parties agreed to coordinate international approaches on technical standards and promote the application of GALILEO standards worldwide. The Agreement provides measures to protect security, establishes a cooperation mechanism in the form of a joint committee and provides for a financial contribution by China, which is to be subject to a separate agreement. The Agreement is effective for five years, automatically extended for further periods of five years unless either party gives advance notice.

[5] European Commission Communication, 'Towards a Trans-European Positioning and Navigation Network together with a European Strategy for a Global Navigation Satellite System (GNSS)', COM(1998) 29 final (Brussels, 21 January 1998).

[6] European Commission Communication, 'Building a Comprehensive Partnership with China', COM(1998) 181 final. For more on this, see chapter 3.

[7] European Commission Communication, 'GALILEO—Involving Europe in a New Generation of Satellite Navigation Services', COM(1999) 54 final (Brussels, 10 February 1999).

[8] Council Resolution of 5 April 2001 (2001/C157/01) on GALILEO, [2001] OJ C157/1.

[9] European Commission Communication from the Commission to the European Parliament and the Council, 'State of Progress of the Galileo Programme', COM(2002) 518 final (Brussels, 24 September 2002).

## Document 6.3: Cooperation Agreement on a Global Civil Navigation Satellite System (GNSS)—GALILEO between the European Community and its Member States and the People's Republic of China

COOPERATION AGREEMENT ON A CIVIL GLOBAL NAVIGATION SATELLITE SYSTEM (GNSS) - GALILEO BETWEEN THE EUROPEAN COMMUNITY AND ITS MEMBER STATES AND THE PEOPLE'S REPUBLIC OF CHINA

THE PEOPLE'S REPUBLIC OF CHINA hereinafter also referred to as "China", of the one part, and

THE EUROPEAN COMMUNITY hereinafter referred to as the "Community",

and

Parties to the Treaty establishing the European Community, hereinafter referred to as "Member States of the Community", of the other part,

CONSIDERING the common interests in the development of a global navigation satellite system for civil use,

RECOGNISING the importance of GALILEO as a contribution to navigation and information infrastructure in Europe and China,

CONSIDERING the increasing development of GNSS applications in China, Europe and other areas in the world,

DESIRING to strengthen the cooperation between China and the Community,

HAVE AGREED AS FOLLOWS:

### ARTICLE 1 Objective of the Agreement

The objective of the Agreement is to encourage, facilitate and enhance cooperation between the Parties within European and Chinese contributions to a civil global navigation satellite system (GNSS) – GALILEO programme.

### ARTICLE 2 Definitions

For the purposes of this Agreement:

(a) "Augmentation" means regional or local mechanisms such as the European Geostationary Navigation Overlay System (EGNOS), or China's wide Area Differential Satellite Navigation System (CWADSNS). They provide the users of satellite-based navigation and timing signals with input information, extra to that derived from the main constellation(s) in use, and additional range/pseudo-range inputs or corrections to, or enhancements of, existing pseudo-range inputs. These mechanisms enable users to obtain enhanced performance;

(b) "Beidou" means a satellite navigation system including an augmentation system that is designed, developed and operated by the People's Republic of China;

(c) GALILEO local elements are local mechanisms that provide the users of GALILEO satellite-based navigation and timing signals with input information, extra to that derived from the main constellation in use. Local elements may be deployed for additional performance around airports, seaports and in urban or other geographically challenging environments. GALILEO will provide generic models for local elements;

(d) "GALILEO" means an autonomous civil European global satellite navigation and timing system under civil control, for the provision of GNSS services designed and developed by the Community and its Member States. The operation of GALILEO may be transferred to a private party. GALILEO envisages one or more services for open, commercial and safety of life purposes;

(e) "Global navigation, positioning and timing equipment" means any civil end user equipment designed to transmit, receive, or process satellite-based navigation or timing signals to provide a service, or to operate with a regional augmentation;

(f) "Regulatory measure" means any law, regulation, rule, procedure, decision, administrative action or similar action by a Party;

(g) "Interoperability" means at user level a situation where a dual-system receiver can use signals from two systems together for equal or better performance than by using only one system;

(h) "Intellectual property" shall have the meaning given in Article 2 of the Convention Establishing the World Intellectual Property Organisation, done at Stockholm, 14 July 1967;

(i) "Liability" means the legal accountability of a person or legal entity to compensate for damage caused to another person or legal entity in accordance with specific legal principles and rules. This obligation may be prescribed in an agreement (contractual liability) or in a legal norm (non-contractual liability);

**ARTICLE 3 Principles of the cooperation**

The Parties agreed to apply the following principles to cooperation activities covered by this Agreement:

(a) mutual benefit based on an overall balance of rights and obligations including contributions;

(b) partnership in the GALILEO Programme in accordance with the procedures and rules governing the management of GALILEO;

(c) reciprocal opportunities to engage in cooperative activities in European and Chinese GNSS projects;

(d) timely exchange of information that may affect cooperative activities;

(e) appropriate protection of intellectual property rights.

**ARTICLE 4 Scope of cooperation activities**

1. The sectors for cooperative activities in satellite navigation and timing are: scientific research, industrial manufacturing, training, application, service and market development, trade, radio-spectrum issues, integrity issues, standardisation and certification and security. The Parties may adapt the list in paragraph 1 by decision by the Joint Steering Committee established under Article 14.

2. Extending cooperation, if requested by the Parties, to GALILEO Public Regulated Service, system security features (definition, management, use) and critical control features

of the GALILEO global segment as well as exchange of classified GALILEO-information, would be subject to an appropriate separate agreement to be concluded between European Union and China.

3. This Agreement shall not affect the application of the Council Regulation (EC) No 876/2002 of 21 May 2002 setting up the GALILEO Joint Undertaking and the institutional structure established by it or any other Regulation or rule establishing a successor entity to the GALILEO Joint Undertaking. Nor does this Agreement affect the applicable laws, regulations and policies implementing non-proliferation commitments and export control for dual-use items and national domestic measures regarding security and controls of intangible transfers of technology.

**ARTICLE 5 Forms of cooperation activities**

1. Subject to their applicable laws and regulations, the Parties shall foster, to the fullest extent practicable, the cooperative activities under this Agreement with a view to providing comparable opportunities for participation in their activities in the sectors listed under Article 4.

2. The Parties agree to conduct the cooperative activities as referred to in Articles 6 to 13.

**ARTICLE 6 Scientific research**

The Parties shall promote joint research activities in the field of GNSS through European and Chinese research programmes including the European Community Framework Programme for Research and Development, and the research programmes of European Space Agency, and the Ministry of Science and Technology of China.

The joint research activities should contribute to planning the future developments of a GNSS for civil use.

**ARTICLE 7 Radio spectrum**

1. Building on past successes in the framework of the International Telecommunication Union, the Parties agree to continue cooperation and mutual support in radio-spectrum issues.

2. In this context the Parties shall exchange information on frequency filings and promote adequate frequency allocations for GALILEO and Beidou in order to ensure the availability of their services for the benefit of users world-wide and notably in China and in the Community.

3. Moreover, the Parties recognise the importance to protect radionavigation spectrum from disruption and interference. To this end they shall identify sources of interference and seek mutually acceptable solutions to combat such interference.

4. The Parties agree to task the Committee under Article 14 to define the appropriate mechanism in order to ensure effective contacts and collaboration in this sector.

**ARTICLE 8 Industrial cooperation**

1. The Parties encourage and support the cooperation between the industries of the two sides, including by the means of joint ventures with the objective of setting up of the GALILEO system as well as promoting the use and development of GALILEO applications and services.

2. The Parties will establish a joint advisory group on industrial cooperation under the Steering Committee set up under Article 14 in order to investigate and guide the cooperation on satellite manufacturing, launch services, ground station building, and application products.

3. To facilitate industrial cooperation the Parties shall protect intellectual property in accordance with the relevant international standards.

4. Exports by China to third countries of sensitive items related to the GALILEO programme will have to be submitted for prior authorisation by the competent GALILEO security authority, if the authority has recommended to the EU Member States that these items be subject to export authorisation.

5. The Parties encourage reinforced links between Ministry of Science and Technology of China, the Chinese National Space Administration, and the European Space Agency to contribute to the objectives of this Agreement.

**ARTICLE 9 Trade and market development**

1. The Parties encourage trade and investment in European and Chinese satellite navigation infrastructure, equipment, GALILEO local elements and applications.

2. To this end the Parties shall raise awareness of the public on GALILEO satellite navigation technology, identify potential barriers to growth in GNSS applications and take appropriate measures to facilitate this growth.

3. To identify and respond effectively to user needs the Community and China shall consider establishing a joint GNSS user forum.

4. This Agreement will not affect the rights and obligations of the Parties under the World Trade Organisation, relevant export control rules, Council Regulation (EC) No 1334/2000 and its subsequent amendments, Council Joint Action 2000/401/CFSP and other relevant international instruments such as the Hague International Code Of Conduct on Ballistic Missiles and other relevant EU Member States and Chinese legislation.

**ARTICLE 10 Standards, Certification and Regulatory Measures**

1. The Parties recognise the value of coordinating approaches in international standardisation and certification fora concerning global satellite navigation services. In particular the Parties will jointly support the development of GALILEO standards and promote their application world-wide.

One objective of the coordination is to promote broad and innovative use of the GALILEO services for open, commercial and safety of life purposes as a world-wide navigation and timing standard. The Parties agree to create favourable conditions for developing GALILEO applications.

2. Consequently, to promote and implement the objectives of this Agreement, the Parties shall, as appropriate, cooperate on all satellite navigation related matters that arise in the International Civil Aviation Organisation, the International Maritime Organisation and the International Telecommunications Union.

3. At bilateral level the Parties shall ensure that measures relating to technical standards, certification and licensing requirements and procedures do not constitute unnecessary

barriers to trade. Domestic requirements shall be based on objective, non-discriminatory, pre-established transparent criteria.

4. At expert level the Parties intend to organise cooperation and exchanges through the Committee under Article 14 on standards covering codes, navigation, ground receiver equipment and navigation application security. Moreover, the Parties shall promote the participation of Chinese representatives in European standardisation organisations.

**ARTICLE 11 Development of global and regional GNSS systems**

1. Interoperability of global and regional satellite navigation systems enhances the quality of services available to users. The Parties shall collaborate to define and implement system architectures allowing an optimal guarantee of GALILEO integrity and continuity of GALILEO services.

2. At the regional level the Parties shall cooperate on building a regional augmentation system based on the GALILEO system in China. Such a regional system is foreseen to provide regional integrity services additional to those provided by the GALILEO system globally.

At local level the Parties shall facilitate the development of GALILEO local elements.

**ARTICLE 12 Security**

1. The Parties are convinced of the need to protect Global Navigation Satellite Systems against misuse, interference, disruption and hostile acts.

2. The Parties shall take all practicable steps to ensure the continuity and safety of the satellite navigation services and the related infrastructure in their territories.

3. The Parties recognise that cooperation to ensure security of the GALILEO system and services are important common objectives.

4. Hence the Parties shall establish an appropriate consultation channel to address GNSS security issues. This channel shall be used to ensure the continuity of the GNSS services.

The practical arrangements and procedures are to be defined between the competent security authorities of both Parties.

**ARTICLE 13 Liability and cost recovery**

The Parties will cooperate, as appropriate, to define and implement a liability regime and cost recovery arrangements in order to facilitate the provision of civil GNSS services.

**ARTICLE 14 Cooperative mechanism**

1. The coordination and facilitation of cooperative activities under this Agreement shall be accomplished on behalf of China, by the Ministry of Science and Technology and, on behalf of the Community, by the European Commission.

2. In accordance with the objective in Article 1 these two entities shall establish a GNSS Steering Committee hereinafter referred to as the "Committee" for the management of this Agreement. This Committee shall consist of official representatives of each Party and it shall establish its own rules of procedure.

The function of the Steering Committee shall include:

(a) promoting, making recommendations to and overseeing the different cooperative activities as mentioned in Articles 4 to 12;

(b) advising the Parties on ways to enhance and improve cooperation consistent with the principles set out in this Agreement;

(c) reviewing the efficient functioning and implementation of this Agreement.

3. The Committee shall, as a general rule, meet annually. The meetings should be held alternatively in the Community and in China. Extraordinary meetings may be organised at the request of either Party.

The costs incurred by the Committee or in its name shall be borne by the Party to whom members relate. The costs other than those for travel and accommodation which are directly associated with meetings of the Committee shall be borne by the host Party. The Committee may set up Joint Technical Working Groups on specific subjects where the Parties consider it appropriate.

4. The Parties welcome the participation of a relevant Chinese entity in the Joint Undertaking (JU) in accordance with the procedure laid out in Council Regulation (EC) No 876/2002 of 21 May 2002.

**ARTICLE 15 Exchange of information**

1. The Parties shall establish administrative arrangements and enquiry points in order to provide for these consultations and the effective implementation of the provisions of this Agreement.

2. The China-Europe GNSS Training and Technical Cooperation Centre established in Beijing shall contribute to preparing and distributing information on satellite navigation activities to industry representatives, scientists, journalists and the public in China and the Community.

3. The Parties shall encourage further information exchanges concerning satellite navigation among the institutions and enterprises of the two sides.

**ARTICLE 16 Funding**

1. China shall provide a financial contribution to the GALILEO Programme through the GALILEO Joint Undertaking. The amount and arrangements of the contribution will be subject to a separate agreement and in accordance with the institutional arrangements of Council Regulation (EC) No 876/2002 or any subsequent regulation.

2. When specific cooperative schemes of one Party provide for financial support to participants from the other Party, any such grants, financial or other contributions from one Party to the participants of the other Party in support of those activities shall be granted tax and customs exemption in accordance with the laws and regulations applicable in the territories of each Party.

**ARTICLE 17 Consultation and dispute resolution**

1. The Parties shall promptly consult, at the request of any of them, on any question arising out of the interpretation or application of this Agreement. Any disputes concerning the interpretation or application of this Agreement shall be settled by friendly consultations between the Parties.

2. Paragraph 1 shall not prevent the Parties from having recourse to dispute settlement under the WTO Agreement.

**ARTICLE 18 Entry into force and termination**

1. This Agreement shall, after its signature by the Parties, enter into force upon the date on which the Parties have notified each other that their respective internal procedures necessary for its entry into force have been completed.

2. The termination of this Agreement shall not affect the validity or duration of any arrangements made under it or any specific rights and obligations that have accrued in the field of intellectual property rights.

3. This Agreement may be amended by mutual agreement of the Parties in writing. Any amendment shall enter into force on the date on which the Parties exchange diplomatic notes informing each other that their respective internal procedures necessary for its entry into force have been completed.

4. This Agreement shall remain in force for a period of five years from the date of its entry into force. Thereafter, it shall be extended automatically for further periods of five years each. Either Party may, by giving three months' notice to the other in writing, terminate this Agreement.

This Agreement is drawn up in duplicate in the Danish, Dutch, English, Finnish, French, German, Greek, Italian, Portuguese, Spanish, Swedish and Chinese languages.

English and Chinese shall be the authentic languages.

In 2004 the EU and China adopted three very important agreements. The first agreement was a Memorandum of Understanding between the National Tourism Administration of the People's Republic of China and the European Community on Visa and Related Issues concerning Tourist Groups from the People's Republic of China (see Document 6.4). The Agreement, set up on 6 May 2004, is known as the Approved Destination Status (ADS) Agreement because it grants Chinese government approved destination status for Chinese tourist groups to EC Member States, with the exception of Denmark, Ireland and the UK, which do not belong to the Schengen system. Its aim is to facilitate organised group travel from China to the EU. It applies to Chinese tourists in a group of at least five people. The Agreement establishes a specific procedure for granting visas for the EC Member States. Through designated and accredited travel agencies in China, couriers are entitled to submit individual 30-day Schengen visa applications for group members to be processed by the main EU destination or, if not, by the first entry Member State. Each group must have a tour leader, tour guides and an established travel programme. The Agreement sets down procedures regarding illegal overstay and readmission. Participating travel agencies are required to report any ADS tourist missing from the group or who does not return to China. They are to cooperate with governmental authorities in locating the tourist, who is to be readmitted by China on the basis of documentary evidence. Airfare costs are to be borne by the tourist or, if this is not possible, by the EU Member State concerned, which then is to recover the cost from the Chinese travel agency concerned, which in turn is to recover the cost from the tourist. So far, however, the EU and China have not yet been able to agree on a separate readmission agreement.[10] Special provisions apply to the new EU Member States, Denmark, the UK and Ireland; there is also a Joint Declaration concerning Iceland and Norway.

**Document 6.4: Memorandum of Understanding between the European Community and the National Tourism Administration of the People's Republic of China on Visa and Related Issues Concerning Tourist Groups from the People's Republic of China (ADS)**

MEMORANDUM OF UNDERSTANDING
between
the National Tourism Administration of the People's Republic of China,
and
The European Community
On Visa and Related Issues concerning Tourist Groups from
the People's Republic of China (ADS)

THE NATIONAL TOURISM ADMINISTRATION OF THE PEOPLE'S REPUBLIC OF CHINA

and

THE EUROPEAN COMMUNITY,

Hereinafter referred to as "the Contracting Parties"

*Desiring* to facilitate organised group travel from the People's Republic of China to the Community;

*Conscious* that such travel will require matters of visa and related issues to be addressed;

*Considering* that such travel will contribute to strengthening the tourism sectors in both China and the Community;

*Determined* to ensure that this Memorandum of Understanding will be applied in strict conformity with the applicable Chinese regulations and the Community's internal market disciplines;

*Considering* that the provisions of this Memorandum of Understanding do not apply to the United Kingdom and Ireland, in accordance with the Protocol on the position of the United Kingdom and Ireland, and the Protocol integrating the Schengen acquis into the framework of the European Union, annexed to the Treaty on European Union and the Treaty establishing the European Community;

*Considering* that the provisions of this Memorandum of Understanding do not apply to the Kingdom of Denmark, in accordance with the Protocol on the position of Denmark annexed to the Treaty on European Union and the Treaty establishing the European Community;

[10] On EU immigration policy, see European Commission, Justice and Home Affairs, 'Developing a Common European Immigration Policy', available at http://ec.europa.eu/justice_home/doc_centre/immigration/doc_immigration_intro_en.htm (accessed 28 November 2007). On Chinese immigrants in France, see Gao Yun and V Poisson, 'Le trafic et l'exploitation des immigrants chinois en France' (Bureau International du Travail, Programme d'action spéciale pour combattre le travail forcé, Geneva, March 2005); F Aizicovici, 'Le BIT en campagne contre l'immigration illegale chinoise', *Le Monde*, 6 March 2007, Economie IV.

HAVE AGREED AS FOLLOWS:

Section I: Subject and Definitions

**Article 1 Definitions**

For the purpose of this Memorandum of Understanding:

(a) *"Member State"* shall mean any Member State of the European Community, with the exception of the Kingdom of Denmark, Ireland, and the United Kingdom.

(b) *"Chinese Citizen"* shall mean any person who holds the passport of the People's Republic of China.

(c) *"Territory of the Community"* shall mean the Territory in which the treaty establishing the European Community is applicable with the exception of the territory of Denmark, of Ireland, of the United Kingdom and of the French overseas departments.

(d) *"Chinese Designated Travel agency"*, shall mean any travel agency selected and designated by the National Tourism Administration of the People's Republic of China (CNTA).

(e) *"Courier"* shall mean the person entitled to submit visa applications for a tourist group to the embassies or consular offices of Member States in China according to the procedure established in Article 4 paragraph 2 of this Memorandum of Understanding.

(f) "*Schengen Visa*" is the uniform visa laid down in Article 10 of the Schengen Application Convention.

**Article 2 Purpose and Scope of Application**

This Memorandum of Understanding shall apply to the travel by tourist groups of Chinese citizens at their own expenses from China to the territory of the Community. For this purpose, the Community shall enjoy the status of an approved destination (ADS).

Such travel will be organised in accordance with the provisions and requirements set out in this Memorandum of Understanding.

**Article 3 Tourist Groups**

Participants in Chinese tourist groups shall enter and leave the territory of the Community as a group. They shall travel within the territory of the Community as a group according to the established travel programme. The minimum number of participants in a tourist group should be no less than five.

Section II: Visa Procedure and Readmission

**Article 4 Visa Procedure**

*4.1. Chinese Designated Travel Agencies*

(a) The Chinese side shall designate travel agencies in China (hereinafter referred to as "Chinese designated travel agencies") which have been authorised by the CNTA to operate outbound travel of Chinese citizens to the Member States. The Member States' embassies and consular offices shall accredit these designated travel agencies to act as authorised representatives of the visa applicants. The CNTA will notify to the Commission and the

Member States' embassies and consular offices the list of the Chinese designated travel agencies, including their addresses, telephone numbers, fax numbers, emails and contact persons.

(b) In case of any violation of EU and/or Chinese regulations by a Chinese designated travel agency in operating the outbound travel of the Chinese citizens, appropriate measures against such agency in accordance with the legislation in force will be taken. This includes, where appropriate, the withdrawal of the travel agency's designation by China, or of its accreditation with the Member States' embassies or consular offices in China.

*4.2. Couriers*

(a) Each Chinese designated travel agency may appoint up to two persons to act on their behalf and account as couriers in the necessary visa application process for Chinese tourist groups wishing to visit the territory of the Community. The couriers are entitled to submit visa applications for such groups to the embassies or consular offices of Member States in China.

(b) They shall be authorised to enter Member States' embassies or consular offices with a badge issued by CNTA and a photo identity badge and certificate issued by Member States' embassies or consular offices, to which the CNTA shall give relevant details of the persons acting as couriers of each travel agency. The certificate will contain at least the name and address of the travel agency and the name of the agent acting as courier.

(c) In case a designated travel agency is no longer accredited with a Member State's embassy or consular office, the travel agency concerned is obliged to return the badges and certificates to the issuing Member State's embassy or consular office for their subsequent invalidation. Furthermore, an accredited travel agency has the obligation to return the badge and certificate to the issuing Member State's embassy or consular office if the person who was acting as its courier is no longer employed in that capacity with that agency.

*4.3. Visa Applications*

(a) When lodging visa applications for a group of clients of an accredited Chinese travel agency with the Member States' embassies or consular offices, the travel agencies shall also submit the following documents: a communication signed by the representative of the said travel agency with information on the planned trip, payment of travel costs, adequate insurance, the names of the tour participants, together with each participant's passport and duly completed application forms signed by each traveller. Where necessary, further documents and/or information may be requested by the Member States' embassies or consular offices.

(b) The visa applications will be processed according to applicable legislation. Visas shall in principle be granted by Member States' embassies or consular offices in whose territory the sole or main destination of the foreseen visit is located. Where it is impossible to determine the main destination, or where visits of equal length are foreseen, the Member State's embassy or consular office of the first entry into Community territory shall be in charge of granting the visa. Member States' embassies or consular offices may foresee personal or telephone interviews with applicants.

(c) The visa to be issued by the Member States' embassies or consular offices shall be a Schengen visa, limited to a maximum of thirty days, issued in conformity with applicable legislation. It shall be an individual Schengen visa carrying the reference "ADS".

(d) If the embassies or consular offices of the Community approve visa applications from travel agencies, other organisations or individuals that are not designated travel agencies by CNTA, CNTA shall not be responsible for any problems arising during the subsequent trip in the territory of the Community.

**Article 5 Illegal Overstay and Readmission**

1. Chinese designated travel agencies and the participating Community travel agencies are required to report, without delay, to their respective authorities, the CNTA and the competent authority of the Member State having issued the visa, any ADS tourist missing from the group as well as any ADS tourist not having returned to China.

2. In case of any illegal overstay of any ADS tourist, the related travel agencies of the Contracting Parties shall work immediately with the competent departments of the Contracting Parties to help sending back and receiving the tourist, who shall be readmitted by the Government of the People's Republic of China. Documentary evidence shall be provided to prove his or her identity as a Chinese citizen for the purpose of readmission. The airfare shall be borne by the tourist. If the tourist cannot afford it, the costs associated with his or her repatriation have to be borne by the competent authority of the Member State concerned, which will then ask the relevant Chinese designated travel agency to pay back the airfare by receipt. In this case, the related Chinese travel agency shall repay the airfare cost to the competent authority of the Member State concerned within 30 days after the readmission of the tourist and recover the costs from the tourist.

Section III: Implementation and Information Exchange

**Article 6 Approved Destination Status Committee**

1. In order to ensure the sound operation of this Memorandum of Understanding, the Contracting Parties shall exchange information and data in good time, and work closely together. In order to monitor the correct implementation of the Memorandum of Understanding, a consultative mechanism will be established.

2. To this end, the Contracting Parties shall set up an Approved Destination Status Committee (hereinafter referred to as "the Committee") which will, in particular, have the task

a) to monitor the application of this Memorandum of Understanding and to draft a report on the implementation of the Memorandum of Understanding every year;

b) to decide on implementing arrangements necessary for the uniform execution of it;

c) to have regular exchanges of information;

d) to recommend amendments to this Memorandum of Understanding to the Contracting Parties.

3. The Committee shall be composed of Representatives of the Contracting Parties. The Community shall be represented by the European Commission; China shall be represented by the National Tourism Administration of the People's Republic of China.

4. The Committee shall meet whenever necessary at the request of one of the Contracting Parties.

5. The Committee shall establish its rules of procedure.

Section IV: Final Provisions

**Article 7 ADS Arrangements of Member States**

Any similar Memorandum of Understanding or arrangement between China and a Member State shall no longer be applied as of the entry into force of this Memorandum of Understanding.

**Article 8 Entry into Force, Duration and Termination**

1. This Memorandum of Understanding shall be ratified or approved by the Contracting Parties in accordance with their respective procedures.

2. This Memorandum of Understanding shall enter into force on the first day of the second month after the date on which the Contracting Parties notify each other that the procedures referred to in the first paragraph have been completed.

3. This Memorandum of Understanding shall remain in force indefinitely, unless terminated in accordance with paragraph 4 of this Article.

4. Each Contracting Party may terminate this Memorandum of Understanding by giving written notice to the other Contracting Party. This Memorandum of Understanding shall cease to apply three months after the date of such notification.

5. This Memorandum of Understanding may be amended by written agreement of the Contracting Parties. Amendments shall enter into force after the Contracting Parties have notified each other of the completion of their internal procedures necessary for this purpose.

6. This Memorandum of Understanding shall be legally binding on the two Contracting Parties.

Done at xxx on the xxx$^{th}$ day of xxx in the year 2003, in duplicate in the Chinese, Danish, Dutch, English, Finnish, French, German, Greek, Italian, Portuguese, Spanish and Swedish languages, each of these texts being equally authentic.

(signed)
For the
National Tourism Administration
of the People's Republic of China

(signed)
For the
European Community

**ANNEXES**

*Protocol on the New Member States*

In accordance with the Act of Accession, the Member States acceding to the European Union on 1 May 2004 (Czech Republic, Estonia, Cyprus, Latvia, Lithuania, Hungary, Malta, Poland, Slovenia, and Slovakia) do not yet issue Schengen visas.

Therefore, by derogation from Article 4 (3) of the Memorandum of Understanding, and until the Council Decision foreseen in Article 3 (2) of the Act of Accession takes effect, the Member State concerned shall issue national visas limited to its own territory.

*Joint Declaration on Implementation Arrangements*

1. Travel Agencies

The Community recommends Member States and their tourism service providers to furnish to CNTA a list of the travel agencies in their territory, including their addresses, telephone numbers, fax numbers, emails and contact persons. These lists should be updated regularly and transmitted to CNTA.

The Contracting Parties furthermore understand that both Contracting Parties' travel agencies shall be entitled to select their own business partners from the other Contracting Party and conclude contracts with them. The said travel agencies are responsible for all business arrangements covering the tour such as the tour programmes, costs, services, and payments in the tour contract with their respective business partners.

2. Protection of Chinese tourist rights

The legitimate rights and interests of the Chinese citizens travelling to the territory of the Community in tourist groups shall be protected by the pertinent legislations of the Community, Member States and China. In case of violation, those regulations shall be applied to the relevant agencies.

The Community encourages the Member States and their tourism service providers to set up hotlines for consultation and emergency assistance to Chinese tourists.

3. Tour Leaders and Tour Guides

The Contracting Parties understand that accredited Chinese travel agencies shall appoint a tour leader or tour leaders for each group.

The tour leader shall ensure that Chinese tourist groups travelling to the territory of the Community in accordance with this Memorandum of Understanding enter and leave the territory of the Community as a group. The tour leader will be required to carry copies of all tickets and passports throughout the trip.

The Contracting Parties take note that, in addition to the obligatory tour leader provided by the Chinese travel agencies, Community travel agencies may provide tour guides for each Chinese tourist group for the duration of the stay on the territory of the Community. These tour guides may accompany the group from the time it enters to the time it leaves the territory of the Community, on the conditions provided by the law applicable in each Member State, and endeavour to solve any problems that may arise in consultation with the Chinese tour leader.

4. Information Requirements

The Community encourages the Member States and their tourism service providers to make relevant information available to the Chinese designated travel agencies, in particular regarding travel possibilities to and within the territory of the Community, important travel services for Chinese travellers and their prices and information which serves to protect the travellers' legitimate rights.

5. Documentary Evidence

The Contracting Parties agree that documentary evidence referred to in Article 5, paragraph 2 of this Memorandum of Understanding, shall include passports, visa applications, EU immigration control records, travel agency documents, or photocopies thereof.

*Joint Declaration concerning Denmark*

The Contracting Parties take note that this Memorandum of Understanding does not apply to the territory of the Kingdom of Denmark. In such circumstances the National Tourism Administration of the People's Republic of China and the authorities of Denmark state their willingness to conclude, without delay, an Approved Destination Status arrangement in the same terms as this Memorandum of Understanding.

*Joint Declaration concerning the United Kingdom and Ireland*

The Contracting Parties take note that this Memorandum of Understanding does not apply to the territory of the United Kingdom and Ireland. In such circumstances it is desirable that the National Tourism Administration of the People's Republic of China and the authorities of the United Kingdom and of Ireland conclude an Approved Destination Status arrangement in similar terms as this Memorandum of Understanding.

*Joint Declaration concerning Iceland and Norway*

The Contracting Parties take note of the close relationship between the European Community and Iceland and Norway, particularly by virtue of the Agreement of 18 May 1999 concerning the association of these countries with the implementation, application and development of the Schengen acquis. In such circumstances it is appropriate that the National Tourism Administration of the People's Republic of China concludes an Approved Destination Status arrangement with Iceland and Norway in similar terms as this Memorandum of Understanding.

A second significant agreement between the European Community and China was an Agreement on Cooperation and Mutual Administrative Assistance in Customs Matters, concluded on 8 December 2004 (see Document 6.5). The Agreement aims to develop customs cooperation between the EU and China, in particular to improve the effectiveness of actions against breaches of customs legislation, including infringements of intellectual property rights. Mutual assistance is the core of the agreement, which provides for appropriate procedures, spontaneous assistance and precautionary measures. The basic principles of the agreement are cooperation and assistance in accordance with the laws of each party, within the limits of their competence and resources. Exceptions concern sovereignty, public order and commercial secrets. The emphasis is on combating illegal trade, for example circumvention. Implementation is to be carried out by the relevant authorities of China and of both the EC and its Members States. The agreement takes precedence over incompatible bilateral EU Member State agreements with China. The Agreement contains a relatively weak clause on coordination in international organisations. By mutual agreement, the parties can expand the scope of their cooperation in customs matters. Within the framework of the Agreement, in September 2006 the EU and China launched a 'Smart and Safe Trade Lanes' Pilot Projet to remove counterfeit goods from sea containers, involving the ports of Rotterdam (the Netherlands), Felixstowe (UK) and Shenzhen (China).[11]

## Document 6.5: Agreement between the European Community and the Government of the People's Republic of China on Cooperation and Mutual Administrative Assistance in Customs Matters

Agreement between the European Community and the Government of the People's Republic of China on cooperation and mutual administrative assistance in customs matters

THE EUROPEAN COMMUNITY,

and

THE GOVERNMENT OF THE PEOPLE'S REPUBLIC OF CHINA

hereinafter referred to as the "Contracting Parties",

CONSIDERING the importance of the commercial links between the European Community and the People's Republic of China, and desirous of contributing to the benefit of both Contracting Parties, to the harmonious development of those links;

BELIEVING THAT, in order to attain this objective, there should be an undertaking to develop customs cooperation;

TAKING into account the development of customs cooperation between the Contracting Parties, concerning customs procedures;

CONSIDERING that operations in breach of customs legislation including infringements of intellectual property rights, are prejudicial to the economic, fiscal and commercial interests of both Contracting Parties, and recognising the importance of ensuring the accurate assessment of customs duties and other taxes, in particular, by a correct application of the rules on customs valuation, origin and tariff classification;

CONVINCED that action against such operations can be made more effective through cooperation between competent administrative authorities;

HAVE AGREED AS FOLLOWS:

### TITLE I GENERAL PROVISIONS

*Article 1 Definitions*

For the purposes of the Agreement:

[11] See Europa, 'Customs Cooperation: Commission and China Strengthen Cooperation on Supply Chain Security', press release IP/06/1206 (Brussels, 19 September 2006), available at http://europa.eu/rapid/pressReleasesAction.do?reference=IP/06/1206&format=HT (accessed 27 December 2007). See also Union des Fabricants pour la protection internationale de la propriété intellectuelle, 'Launch of EU/China Pilot Project: A Customs Cooperation to Remove Counterfeit Products from Sea Containers', available at http://www.euractiv.com/29/images/Unifab%20-%20Launch%20of%20EU–China%20Pilot%20Project%20%5BEN%5D_tcm29-157985.doc (accessed 26 December 2007); http://news.muzi.com/ll/english/10020889.shtml (accessed 26 December 2007).

(a) "customs legislation" shall mean any laws, provisions or other legally binding instruments of the European Community or the People's Republic of China, governing the import, export and transit of goods and their placing under any other customs regime or procedure, including measures of prohibitions, restrictions and control;

(b) "customs authority" shall mean, in the European Community, the competent services responsible for customs matters of the Commission of the European Communities and the customs authorities of the Member States of the European Community and in the People's Republic of China, the General Administration of Customs of the People's Republic of China;

(c) "applicant authority" shall mean a competent customs authority which is designated by a Contracting Party for this purpose and which makes a request for administrative assistance, on the basis of this Agreement;

(d) "requested authority" shall mean a competent customs authority which is designated by a Contracting Party for this purpose and which receives a request for administrative assistance, on the basis of this Agreement;

(e) "personal data" shall mean all information relating to an identified or identifiable individual;

(f) "operation in breach of customs legislation" shall mean any violation or attempted violation of the customs legislation;

(g) "person" shall mean either a human being or a legal entity;

(h) "information" shall mean data, whether or not processed or analysed, and documents, reports, and other communications in any format, including electronic, or certified or authenticated copies thereof. Article 2 Territorial application This Agreement shall apply on the one hand, to the territories in which the Treaty establishing the European Community is applied and under the conditions laid down in that Treaty and, on the other hand, to the customs territory of the People's Republic of China. Article 3 Future developments The Contracting Parties may by mutual consent expand this Agreement with a view to increasing the levels of customs cooperation and supplementing them, in accordance with their respective customs legislation, by means of agreements on specific sectors or matters.

## TITLE II SCOPE OF THE AGREEMENT

*Article 4 Performance of cooperation and assistance*

All cooperation and assistance under this Agreement shall be performed by the Contracting Parties in accordance with their relevant laws, provisions, and other legal instruments. In addition, all cooperation and assistance under this Agreement by either Contracting Party shall be performed within the limits of its competence and available resources.

*Article 5 Obligations imposed under other agreements*

1. Taking into account the respective competencies of the European Community and the Member States, the provisions of this Agreement shall:

(a) not affect the obligations of the Contracting Parties under any other international agreement or convention,

(b) be deemed complementary to agreements on customs cooperation and mutual administrative assistance which have been or may be concluded between individual Member States and the People's Republic of China,

(c) not affect the Community provisions governing the communication between the competent services of the Commission and the customs authorities of the Member States of any information obtained under this Agreement which could be of interest to the Community;

2. Notwithstanding the provisions of paragraph 1, the provisions of this Agreement shall take precedence over the provisions of any bilateral agreement on customs cooperation and mutual administrative assistance which has been or may be concluded between individual Member States and the People's Republic of China, insofar as the provisions of the latter are incompatible with those of this Agreement.

3. In respect of questions relating to the applicability of this Agreement, the Contracting Parties shall consult each other to resolve the matter in the framework of the Joint Customs Cooperation Committee set up under Article 21 of this Agreement.

## TITLE III CUSTOMS COOPERATION

*Article 6 Scope of the cooperation*

1. The Contracting Parties shall undertake to develop customs cooperation. In particular, the Contracting Parties shall seek to cooperate in:

(a) establishing and maintaining channels of communication between their customs authorities to facilitate and secure the rapid exchange of information;

(b) facilitating effective coordination between their customs authorities;

(c) any other administrative matters related to this Agreement that may from time to time require their joint action.

2. The Contracting Parties undertake to develop trade facilitation actions in customs matters taking account of the work done in this connection by international organisations.

3. Under this Agreement, customs cooperation shall cover all matters relating to the application of customs legislation.

*Article 7 Cooperation in customs procedures*

The Contracting Parties affirm their commitment to the facilitation of the legitimate movement of goods and shall exchange information and expertise on measures to improve customs techniques and procedures and on computerised systems with a view towards implementing that commitment in accordance with the provisions of this Agreement.

*Article 8 Technical cooperation*

The customs authorities of the Contracting Parties may provide each other with technical assistance when mutually beneficial in customs matters including:

(a) the exchange of personnel and experts, for the purposes of promoting the mutual understanding of each other's customs law, procedures and techniques;

(b) the training, particularly developing specialised skills of their customs officials;

(c) the exchange of professional, scientific and technical data relating to customs law and procedures.

(d) techniques and improved methods of processing passengers and cargo.

(e) any other general administrative matters that may from time to time require joint actions by their customs administrations.

*Article 9 Coordination in international organisations*

The customs authorities shall seek to develop and strengthen their cooperation on topics of common interest in order to seek a coordinated position when those topics are discussed in the framework of international organisations.

**TITLE IV MUTUAL ADMINISTRATIVE ASSISTANCE**

*Article 10 Scope*

1. The customs authorities shall assist each other by providing appropriate information which helps to ensure the proper application of customs legislation and the prevention, investigation and combating of any breach of customs legislation.

2. Assistance in customs matters, as provided for in this Agreement, shall apply to any administrative authority of the Contracting Parties which is competent for the application of this Agreement. It shall not prejudice the rules governing mutual assistance in criminal matters. Nor shall it cover information obtained under powers exercised at the request of a judicial authority;

3. Assistance to recover duties, taxes or fines, or the arrest or detention of any person or seizure or detention of property is not covered by this Agreement.

*Article 11 Assistance on request*

1. At the request of the applicant authority, the requested authority shall provide it with all relevant information which may enable it to ensure that customs legislation is correctly applied, including information regarding activities detected or planned which are or could be operations in breach of customs legislation. In particular, upon request, the customs authorities shall furnish to each other information regarding activities that may result in offences within the territory of the other Party, for example, incorrect customs declarations and certificates of origin, invoices or other documents known to be, or suspected of being, incorrect or falsified.

2. At the request of the applicant authority, the requested authority shall inform it of:

(a) the authenticity of official documents produced in support of a goods declaration made to the customs authority of the requesting Party;

(b) whether goods exported from the territory of one of the Contracting Parties have been legally imported into the territory of the other Contracting Party, specifying, where appropriate, the customs procedure applied to the goods;

(c) whether goods imported into the territory of one of the Contracting Parties have been legally exported from the territory of the other Contracting Party, specifying, where appropriate, the customs procedure applied to the goods.

3. At the request of the applicant authority, the requested authority shall, within the framework of its laws, provisions or other legally binding instruments, take the necessary steps to ensure special surveillance of:

(a) persons in respect of whom there are reasonable grounds for believing that they are or have been involved in operations in breach of customs legislation;

(b) places where stocks of goods have been or may be stored or assembled in such a way that there are reasonable grounds for believing that these goods are intended to be used in operations in breach of customs legislation;

(c) goods that are or may be transported in such a way that there are reasonable grounds for believing that they are intended to be used in operations in breach of customs legislation;

(d) means of transport that are or may be used in such a way that there are reasonable grounds for believing that they are intended to be used in operations in breach of customs legislation.

*Article 12 Spontaneous assistance*

The Contracting Parties shall assist each other, at their own initiative and in accordance with their laws, provisions or other legally binding instruments if they consider that to be necessary for the correct application of customs legislation, in particular in situations that could involve substantial damage to the economy, public health, public security or similar vital interest of the other Contracting Party pertaining to:

(a) activities which are or appear to be operations in breach of customs legislation and which may be of interest to the other Contracting Party;

(b) new means or methods employed in carrying out operations in breach of customs legislation;

(c) goods known to be subject to operations in breach of customs legislation;

(d) persons in respect of whom there are reasonable grounds for believing that they are or have been involved in operations in breach of customs legislation;

(e) means of transport in respect of which there are reasonable grounds for believing that they have been, are, or may be used in operations in breach of customs legislation.

*Article 13 Form and substance of requests for assistance*

1. Requests pursuant to this Agreement shall be made in writing. They shall be accompanied by the documents necessary to enable compliance with the request. When required because of the urgency of the situation, oral requests may be accepted, but shall be confirmed promptly in writing.

2. Requests pursuant to paragraph 1 shall include the following information:

(a) the formal endorsement of the applicant authority;

(b) the action requested;

(c) the object of and the reason for the request;

(d) the laws, regulations or other legally binding instruments involved;

(e) indications as exact and comprehensive as possible on the persons who are the target of the investigations;

(f) a summary of the relevant facts and of the enquiries already carried out.

3. Requests shall be submitted in an official language of the requested authority or in a language acceptable to that authority. This requirement shall not apply to any documents that accompany the request under paragraph 1.

4. If a request does not meet the formal requirements set out above, its correction or completion may be requested; precautionary measures may be ordered in the meantime.

*Article 14 Execution of requests*

1. In order to comply with a request for assistance, the requested authority shall proceed, within the limits of its competence and available resources, as though it were acting on its own account or at the request of other authorities of that same Contracting Party, by supplying information already possessed, by carrying out appropriate enquiries or by arranging for them to be carried out.

2. Requests for assistance shall be executed in accordance with the laws, regulations or other legally binding instruments of the requested authority.

3. Duly authorised officials of a Contracting Party may, with the agreement of the other Contracting Party and subject to the conditions laid down by the latter, be present at enquiries carried out in the latter's jurisdiction into specific cases.

4. In the event that the request cannot be complied with, the applicant authority shall be notified promptly of that fact, with a statement of the reasons and of any other information that the requested authority considers may be of assistance to the applicant authority.

*Article 15 Form in which information is to be communicated*

1. The requested authority shall communicate results of enquiries to the applicant authority in writing together with relevant documents, certified copies or other items.

2. This information may be in computerised form which shall where necessary be confirmed in writing immediately afterwards.

*Article 16 Exceptions to the obligation to provide assistance*

1. Assistance may be refused or may be subject to the satisfaction of certain conditions or requirements in cases where a Contracting Party is of the opinion that assistance under this Agreement would:

(a) be likely to prejudice the sovereignty of a Member State of the European Community which has been requested to provide assistance under this Agreement or that of the People's Republic of China; or

(b) be likely to prejudice public order, security or other essential interests, in particular in the cases referred to under Article 17(2) or

(c) violate an industrial, commercial or professional secret.

2. Assistance may be postponed by the requested authority on the ground that it will interfere with an ongoing investigation, prosecution or proceeding. In such a case, the requested authority shall consult with the applicant authority to determine if assistance can be given subject to such terms or conditions as the requested authority may require.

3. Where the applicant authority seeks assistance which it would itself be unable to provide if so requested, it shall draw attention to that fact in its request. It shall then be for the requested authority to decide how to respond to such a request.

4. For the cases referred to in paragraphs 1 and 2, the decision of the requested authority and the reasons therefor must be communicated to the applicant authority without undue delay.

*Article 17 Information exchange and confidentiality*

1. Any information communicated in whatsoever form pursuant to this Agreement shall be of a confidential or restricted nature, depending on the rules applicable in each of the Contracting Parties. It shall be covered by the obligation of official secrecy and shall enjoy the protection extended to similar information under the relevant laws of the Contracting Party that received it and the corresponding provisions applying to the Community authorities.

2. Personal data may be exchanged only where the Contracting Party which may receive it undertakes to protect such data in at least an equivalent way to the one applicable to that particular case in the Contracting Party that may supply it. The Contracting Party that may supply the information shall not stipulate any requirements that are more onerous than those applicable to it in its own jurisdiction. The Contracting Parties shall communicate to each other information on their applicable rules, including where appropriate, legal provisions in force in the Member States of the Community.

3. Nothing in this Agreement shall preclude the use of information or documents obtained in accordance with this Agreement as evidence in administrative proceedings subsequently instituted in respect of operations in breach of customs legislation. Therefore, the Contracting Parties may, in their records of evidence, reports and testimonies and in administrative proceedings use as evidence information obtained and documents consulted in accordance with the provisions of this Agreement. The competent authority which supplied that information or gave access to those documents shall be notified of such use.

4. Information obtained shall be used solely for the purposes of this Agreement. Where one of the Contracting Parties wishes to use such information for other purposes, it shall obtain the prior written consent of the authority which provided the information. Such use shall then be subject to any restrictions laid down by that authority.

5. Practical arrangements for the implementation of this Article shall be determined by the Joint Customs Cooperation Committee established under Article 21.

*Article 18 Experts and witnesses*

An official of a requested authority may be authorised to appear, within the limitations of authorisation granted, as an expert or witness in administrative proceedings regarding the matters covered by this Agreement in the territory of the other Contracting Party, and produce such objects, documents or certified copies thereof, as may be needed for the proceedings. The request for appearance must indicate specifically before which administrative authority the official will have to appear, on what matters and by virtue of what title or qualification the official will be questioned.

*Article 19 Assistance expenses*

1. The Contracting Parties shall waive all claims on each other for the reimbursement of expenses incurred pursuant to this Agreement, except, as appropriate, for expenses to experts and witnesses, and those to interpreters and translators who are not public service employees.

2. If expenses of a substantial or extraordinary nature are, or will be, required to execute the request, the Contracting Parties shall consult to determine the terms and conditions under which the request will be executed as well as the manner in which the costs shall be borne.

## TITLE V FINAL PROVISIONS

*Article 20 Implementation*

1. The implementation of this Agreement shall be entrusted to the customs authorities of the Commission of the European Communities and, where appropriate, of the Member States of the European Community on the one hand, and to the customs authority of the People's Republic of China, on the other. They shall decide on all practical measures and arrangements necessary for its application, taking into consideration the rules in force in particular in the field of data protection. They may recommend to the competent bodies amendments which they consider should be made to this Agreement.

2. The Contracting Parties shall consult each other and subsequently keep each other informed of the detailed rules of implementation which are adopted in accordance with the provisions of this Agreement.

*Article 21 Joint Customs Cooperation Committee*

1. A Joint Customs Cooperation Committee is hereby established, consisting of representatives of the customs authorities of the European Community and the People's Republic of China. It shall meet at a place, on a date and with an agenda, fixed by mutual agreement.

2. The Joint Customs Cooperation Committee shall, inter alia:

(a) see to the proper functioning of the Agreement;

(b) examine all issues arising from its application;

(c) take measures necessary for customs cooperation in accordance with the objectives of this Agreement;

(d) exchange views on any points of common interest regarding customs cooperation, including future measures and the resources for them;

(e) recommend solutions aimed at helping to attain the objectives of this Agreement.

3. The Joint Customs Cooperation Committee shall adopt its internal rules of procedure.

4. The Joint Customs Cooperation Committee will where appropriate, keep informed the Joint Commission set up under Article 15 of the Agreement on Trade and Economic Cooperation between the European Economic Community and the People's Republic of China of activities going on under this Agreement.

*Article 22 Entry into force and duration*

1. This Agreement shall enter into force on the first day of the month following the date on which the Contracting Parties have notified each other of the completion of the procedures necessary for this purpose.

2. Each Contracting Party may terminate this Agreement by giving notice to the other in writing. The termination shall take effect three months from the day of notification to the other Contracting Party. Requests for assistance which have been received prior to the termination of the Agreement shall be completed in accordance with the provisions of this Agreement.

*Article 23 Authentic texts*

This Agreement shall be drawn up in duplicate in the Czech, Danish, Dutch, English, Estonian, Finnish, French, German, Greek, Hungarian, Italian, Latvian, Lithuanian, Maltese, Polish, Portuguese, Slovak, Slovenian, Spanish, Swedish and Chinese languages, each text being equally authentic.

In witness whereof, the undersigned, being duly authorised to do so, have signed this Agreement.

Done at The Hague, 8 December 2004.

Por la Comunidad Europea

Za Evropské společenství

For Det Europæiske Fællesskab

Für die Europäische Gemeinschaft

Euroopa Ühenduse nimel

*Για την Ευρωπαϊκή Κοινότητα*

For the European Community

Pour la Communauté européenne

Per la Comunità europea

Eiropas Kopienas vārdā

Europos bendrijos vardu

az Európai Közösség részéről

Voor de Europese Gemeenschap

W imieniu Wspólnoty Europejskiej

Pela Comunidade Europeia

Za Európske spoločenstvo

za Evropsko skupnost

Euroopan yhteisön puolesta

På Europeiska gemenskapens vägnar

Por el Gobierno de la República Popular China

Za vládu Činské lidové republiky

For Folkerepublikken Kinas regering

Im Namen der Regierung der Volksrepublik China

Hiina Rahvavabariigi valitsuse nimel

*Για την κυβέρνηση της Λαϊκής Δημοκρατίας της Κίνας*

For the Government of the People's Republic of China

Pour le gouvernement de la République populaire de Chine

Per il Governo della Repubblica popolare cinese

Kînas Tautas Republikas vārdā

Kinijos Liaudies Respublikos Vyriausybės vardu

A Kínai Népköztársaság kormánya részéről

Voor de Regering van de Volksrepubliek China

W imieniu rz'du Chiñskiej Republiki Ludowej

Pelo Governo da República Popular da China

Za vládu Činskey ľudovej republiky

Za Vlado Ljudske republike Kitajske

Kiinan kansantasavallan hallituksen puolesta

På Folkrepubliken Kinas regerings vägnar

The third important agreement was the Agreement on Research and Development Cooperation on the Peaceful Use of Nuclear Energy, concluded between the European Atomic Energy Community (EAEC, Euratom) and China (see Document 6.6); when the EAEC Treaty expired at the end of 2004, the EAEC became part of the European Community. The Agreement was signed at the 7th EU–China Summit in The Hague in December 2004. It concerns scientific and technological cooperation and covers all fields of research in the 2002–2006 Euratom Framework Programme.[12] Its provisions deal with non-proliferation and control of nuclear materials, physical safety and retransfer, and thus provided a basis for EU–China cooperation in the later ITER agreements.

12 See Council Decision 2002/668/Euratom of 3 June 2002 concerning the sixth framework programme of the European Atomic Energy Community for nuclear research and training activities also contributing to the development of the European Research Area (2002 to 2006), [2002] OJ L232/34.

## Document 6.6: Agreement for Research and Development Cooperation in the Peaceful Uses of Nuclear Energy between the European Atomic Energy Community (Euratom) and the Government of the People's Republic of China

Agreement for R&D co-operation in the peaceful uses of nuclear energy between the European Atomic Energy Community (Euratom) and the government of the People's Republic of China

THE EUROPEAN ATOMIC ENERGY COMMUNITY (EURATOM),

hereinafter referred to as 'the Community',

on the one part, and

THE GOVERNMENT OF THE PEOPLE'S REPUBLIC OF CHINA,

hereinafter referred to as 'China'

on the other part,

hereinafter referred to as the 'Parties';

DESIRING to further develop a long-term, stable co-operation which may benefit to China, the Community and its Member States in the peaceful and non-explosive uses of nuclear energy on the basis of mutual benefit and reciprocity;

CONSIDERING the 1985 Agreement on trade and economic cooperation between the European Economic Community and the People's Republic of China and noting that there has also been active co-operation and information exchange in a number of scientific and technological areas under the Agreement for scientific and technological cooperation between the European Community and the Government of the People's Republic of China signed in 1998;

CONSIDERING the importance of science and technology for their economic and social development and desiring to establish a formal basis for cooperation in scientific and technological research which will extend and strengthen the conduct of cooperative activities in the fields of common interest in the peaceful uses of nuclear energy and encourage the application of the results of such cooperation to their economic and social benefit;

WHEREAS co-operation in the peaceful uses of nuclear energy between the Community and China should further enhance research in areas of common interest as well as economic co-operation;

CONSIDERING that the Community and China are currently pursuing research and development activities in the area of peaceful uses of nuclear energy and that participation in each other's research and development activities on a basis of reciprocity will provide mutual benefits;

CONSIDERING, in particular, the willingness of both the Community and China to strengthen their co-operation in the field of controlled thermonuclear fusion within the present agreement and if appropriate within a dedicated agreement.

REAFFIRMING the strong commitment of the Government of China, the Community and the Governments of its Member States to nuclear non-proliferation including the strengthening and efficient application of the related safeguards and export control regimes under which co-operation in the peaceful uses of nuclear energy between China and the Community should be carried out;

REAFFIRMING the support of the Government of China, the Community and the Governments of its Member States for the objectives of the International Atomic Energy Agency (IAEA, hereinafter referred to as "the Agency"), including its safeguards system and their desire to promote universal adherence to the Treaty on the Non-Proliferation of Nuclear Weapons, done on July 1, 1968 (hereinafter referred to as "the Non-Proliferation Treaty");

NOTING that nuclear safeguards are applied in the Community both under Chapter VII of the Euratom Treaty and under safeguards agreements concluded between the Community, its Member States and the IAEA;

WHEREAS it is appropriate to provide a legal framework for promoting co-operation in all potential peaceful uses of nuclear energy, focusing particularly on present opportunities of mutual benefit,

RECOGNIZING that China, the Community and its Member States have attained a comparably advanced level in the peaceful uses of nuclear energy and in the security afforded by their respective laws and regulations concerning health, safety, the peaceful uses of nuclear energy and the protection of the environment;

CONSIDERING that this Agreement for co-operation in the peaceful uses of nuclear energy is within the context of the global cooperation between China and the Community,

HAVE AGREED AS FOLLOWS:

**Article 1 Purpose**

The overall purpose of this Agreement is to encourage and facilitate cooperation, in fields of common interest in the peaceful, non-explosive, non-military uses of nuclear energy with a view to strengthening the overall co-operative relationship between the Community and China.

The main objective of the Agreement is to foster scientific and technical co-operation between the Community and China and, in particular to facilitate the participation of Chinese research entities in research projects carried out in the framework of the relevant Community research programmes and to ensure a reciprocal participation of research entities of the Community and its Member States in Chinese projects in similar areas of research.

**Article 2 Definitions**

For the purpose of this Agreement:

1. 'Parties' means the Government of China and the European Atomic Energy Community. 'Party' means one of the above 'Parties'.

2. 'The Community' means both:

(a) the legal person created by the Treaty establishing the European Atomic Energy Community (Euratom); and

(b) the territories to which the Euratom Treaty applies.

3. 'cooperative activity' means any activity which the Parties undertake or support, pursuant to this Agreement, and includes joint research;

4. 'information' means scientific or technical data, results or methods of research and development stemming from joint research and any other data deemed necessary by the participants to cooperative activities; including, as necessary, by the Parties themselves;

5. 'intellectual property' shall have the meaning defined in Article 2 of the Convention establishing the World Intellectual Property Organisation, done at Stockholm, 14 July 1967;

6. 'joint research' means research or technological development that is implemented with or without financial support from one or both Parties and that involves collaboration by participants from both the Community and China and is designated as joint research in writing by the Parties or their scientific and technological organisations and agencies implementing the scientific research programmes. In the case where there is funding by only one Party the designation is made by that Party and the participant in that project;

7. 'Participant' or 'research entities' means any person moral or private, any research institute or any other legal entity or firm established in the Community or in China involved in cooperative activities including the Parties themselves;

8. 'Results of intellectual activity' means information and/or intellectual property;

9. The term "nuclear material" means

(a) "source material", namely, uranium containing the mixture of isotopes occurring in nature; uranium depleted in the isotope 235; thorium; any of the foregoing in the form of metal, alloy, chemical compound, or concentrate; any other material containing one or more of the foregoing in such concentration as the Board of Governors of the Agency determines under Article XX of the Statute of the Agency, done on October 26, 1956 (hereinafter referred to as "the Statute"), and the appropriate authorities of both Parties inform each other, in writing, to accept; and such other material as the Board of Governors of the Agency determines under Article XX of the Statute and the appropriate authorities of the Parties inform each other, in writing, to accept.

(b) "special fissionable material", namely, plutonium; uranium-233; uranium enriched in the isotope 233 or 235; any material containing one or more of the foregoing; and such other material as the Board of Governors of the Agency determines under Article XX of the Statute and the appropriate authorities of both Parties inform each other, in writing, to accept. The term "special fissionable material" does not include "source material".

10. "Sensitive nuclear material" means separated plutonium (including plutonium contained in mixed oxide fuel) or uranium enriched to more than 20 % in the isotope 235 and/or uranium 233.

**Article 3 Principles**

Cooperative activities shall be conducted on the basis of the following principles:

1. mutual benefit based on an overall balance of advantages;

2. reciprocal access to the activities of research and technological development undertaken by each Party;

3. timely exchange of information which may affect the actions of participants in cooperative activities;

4. effective protection of intellectual property and equitable sharing of intellectual property rights.

**Article 4 Areas of cooperative activities**

Cooperation under this Agreement may cover all the activities of research, technological development, hereinafter referred to as 'R&D', included in the Framework Programme of the European Atomic Energy Community for nuclear research and training activities under Article 7 of the Treaty establishing the European Atomic Energy Community and all similar R&D activities in China in the corresponding scientific and technological fields.

Co-operation under this Agreement shall be carried out within the scope of the respective competences of each Party, and shall include the following areas:

(a) radiation protection and radiological monitoring;

(b) nuclear safeguards;

(c) nuclear safety and nuclear technology;

(d) innovative concepts;

(e) nuclear metrology and reference materials;

(f) nuclear medicine ;

(g) decommissioning of nuclear installations;

(h) management of radioactive waste;

(i) controlled thermonuclear fusion;

(k) nuclear education and training;

(l) other areas of co-operation as may be mutually agreed upon by the Parties.

**Article 5 Forms of cooperative activities**

1. Subject to their applicable laws, regulations and policies, the Parties shall foster, to the fullest extent practicable, the involvement of participants in cooperative activities under this Agreement with a view to providing comparable opportunities for participation in their scientific and technological research and development activities.

2. Cooperative activities may take the following forms:

(a) participation of Chinese research entities to R&D projects under the Framework Programmes of the European Atomic Energy Community for nuclear research and training activities and participation of research entities established in the Community to Chinese projects in similar sectors of R&D. Such a participation is subject to the rules and procedures applicable in each Party,

(b) pooling of R&D projects already implemented according to the procedures applicable in the R&D programmes of each Party,

(c) visits and exchanges of scientists and technical experts,

(d) joint organisation of scientific seminars, conferences, symposia and workshops, as well as participation of experts to those activities,

(e) exchanges, sharing and transfer of samples, materials, instruments and apparatus for experimental purposes,

(f) exchanges of information on practices, laws, regulations and programmes relevant to cooperation under this Agreement,

(g) any other modality that would be recommended by the Steering Committee, established in accordance with Article 12 of this Agreement, and deemed in conformity with the policies and procedures applicable in both Parties. The joint R&D projects shall be implemented when the participants have developed a technology management plan, as indicated in the Annex B to this Agreement.

Any transfers of nuclear material carried out pursuant to the co-operation referred to this Article shall be made in accordance with the relevant international commitments of the Parties and of the Member States of the Community in relation to peaceful uses of nuclear energy.

**Article 6 Items subject to the Agreement**

1. Nuclear material transferred between China and the Community, whether directly or through a third country, shall become subject to this Agreement upon its entry into the territorial jurisdiction of the receiving Party, provided that the supplying Party has notified the receiving Party in writing of the intended transfer and the receiving Party has confirmed in writing that such item will be held subject to this Agreement and that the proposed recipient, if other than the receiving Party, will be an authorised person under the territorial jurisdiction of the receiving Party.

2. Nuclear material subject to this Agreement shall remain subject to this Agreement until:

(a) such items have been transferred beyond the territorial jurisdiction of the receiving Party in accordance with the relevant provisions of this Agreement;

(b) the Parties agree that such items should no longer be subject to this Agreement; or

(c) in the case of nuclear material, it is determined in accordance with the provisions for the termination of safeguards in the relevant agreements referred to in paragraph 1. of Article 8 of this Agreement, that the nuclear material has been consumed, or has been diluted in such a way that it is no longer usable for any nuclear activity relevant from the point of view of safeguards, or has become practicably irrecoverable.

3. The appropriate authorities of the Parties shall establish and if necessary amend operational procedures for the purpose of the effective implementation of the provisions of this Agreement and in particular the written notifications and confirmations required under paragraphs 1. and 2. above.

**Article 7 Peaceful use**

1. Co-operation under this Agreement shall be carried out only for peaceful and non-explosive purposes.

2.Nuclear material, transferred pursuant to this Agreement shall not be used other than for peaceful purposes; nor shall it be used for any nuclear explosive device, for research on or for development of any such device.

**Article 8 Nuclear Safeguards**

Co-operation under this Agreement shall require the application, as appropriate, of safeguards by the Community and acceptance of the application of safeguards by the Agency. Therefore, nuclear material transferred pursuant to this Agreement shall be subject to safeguards by the Community while on its territory, pursuant to the Euratom Treaty and by the Agency pursuant to the following safeguards agreements (as they may be revised and replaced):

1. the Agreement between the Republic of Austria, the Kingdom of Belgium, the Kingdom of Denmark, the Republic of Finland, the Federal Republic of Germany, the Hellenic Republic, Ireland, the Italian Republic, the Grand Duchy of Luxembourg, the Kingdom of the Netherlands, the Portuguese Republic, the Kingdom of Spain, the Kingdom of Sweden, the Czech Republic, the Republic of Estonia, the Republic of Cyprus, the Republic of Latvia, the Republic of Lithuania, the Republic of Hungary, the Republic of Malta, the Republic of Poland, the Republic of Slovenia and the Slovak Republic, the Community and the Agency in implementation of Article III (1) and (4) of the Treaty on the Non-Proliferation of Nuclear Weapons done on April 5, 1973 (hereinafter referred to as "the Safeguards Agreement for the non-nuclear weapon Member States of the Community"), as supplemented by an Additional Protocol, done on September 22, 1998 (INFCIRC/193);

2. the Agreement between the United Kingdom of Great Britain and Northern Ireland, the Community and the Agency for the application of safeguards in the United Kingdom of Great Britain and Northern Ireland in connection with the Non-Proliferation Treaty, done on September 6, 1976 (hereinafter referred to as "the Safeguards Agreement for the United Kingdom"), as supplemented by an Additional Protocol done on September 22, 1998; and

3. the Agreement between France, the Community, and the Agency for the application of safeguards in France, done on July 27, 1978 (hereinafter referred to as "the Safeguards Agreement for France"), as supplemented by an Additional Protocol done on September 22, 1998.

4. The Agreement between the People's Republic of China and the IAEA (INFCIRC/369), which entered into force on 18 September 1989 and was supplemented, by the Additional Protocol which entered into force in March 2002.

Implementation of relevant provisions of the Agreement shall not impose upon Member States obligations additional to those resulting from the application by the IAEA of the above mentioned agreements or those resulting from their bilateral agreements, where appropriate.

**Article 9 Physical protection**

1. In respect of nuclear material transferred pursuant to this Agreement, the Government of China, the Governments of the Member States of the Community and, as appropriate, the European Commission, shall apply measures of physical protection according to the criteria which they have individually adopted. Furthermore, the Parties recognise that the recommendations laid down in IAEA document INFCIRC/225/rev.4 ('Physical protection of nuclear material and nuclear facilities'), as they may be updated from time to time, serve as useful orientations for setting up systems for the physical protection of nuclear materials coming under this Agreement while in use, storage and transit.

2. In respect of international transport of nuclear material subject to this Agreement, China, the Member States of the Community and, as appropriate, the Community shall act in conformity with the provisions of the Convention on the Physical Protection of Nuclear

Material, which entered into force on February 8, 1987 (INFCIRC/274/Rev 1), to which they are parties.

**Article 10 Nuclear safety**

The provisions of the "Convention on Nuclear Safety" (CSN -IAEA document INFCIRC/449) to which China, EURATOM and its Member States are parties shall apply. No additional obligations to those assumed under the CNS on the parties to the Agreement and the Member States shall arise.

**Article 11 Retransfers**

1. Nuclear material, transferred pursuant to this Agreement shall not be retransferred beyond the territorial jurisdiction of the receiving Party, except into the territorial jurisdiction of the supplying Party, unless the receiving Party is provided with the assurances of fulfilment of the conditions set out in Annex A of this Agreement in an appropriate way, or unless, in the absence of such assurances, the prior written consent of the supplying Party is obtained.

2. In addition to complying with the provisions of paragraph 1 above, the sensitive nuclear material transferred pursuant to this Agreement shall not be retransferred beyond the territorial jurisdiction of the Parties, except into the territorial jurisdiction of the supplying Party, without the prior written consent of the supplying Party unless, in the case of sensitive nuclear material transferred from China to the Community, it will be subject to the appropriate bilateral agreement for co-operation in the peaceful uses of nuclear energy between China and the receiving third country or, in the case of transfers from the Community to China, the receiving third country is included on a list to be drawn up by the Community, and notification of such retransfers has been given by the receiving Party to the supplying Party.

**Article 12 Coordination and facilitation of cooperative activities**

1. The coordination and facilitation of cooperative activities under this Agreement shall be accomplished on behalf of China, by the Ministry of Science and Technology and, on behalf of the Community, by the services of the Commission of the European Communities, acting as executive agents.

2. The executive agents shall establish a Steering R&D Cooperation Committee, hereinafter referred to as the 'Steering Committee' for the management of this Agreement; this Committee shall consist of an equal number of official representatives of each Party; it shall establish its own rules of procedure.

3. The functions of the Steering Committee shall include:

(a) promoting and overseeing the different cooperative activities as mentioned in Article 4 as well as those that would be implemented in the framework of R&D cooperation for development;

(b) indicating, for the following year, pursuant to Article 5.2, first indent, among the potential sectors for R&D cooperation, those priority sectors or sub-sectors of mutual interest in which cooperation is sought;

(c) proposing, pursuant to Article 5.2, second indent, to the scientists of both Parties the pooling of their projects which would be of mutual benefit and complementary;

(d) making recommendations pursuant to Article 5.2, seventh indent;

(e) advising the Parties on ways to enhance and improve cooperation consistent with the principles set out in this Agreement;

(f) reviewing the efficient functioning and implementation of this Agreement;

(g) providing, every three years, a report to the Parties on the status, the level reached and the effectiveness of cooperation undertaken under this Agreement.

4. The Steering Committee shall, as a general rule, meet annually, according to a jointly agreed schedule; the meetings should be held alternatively in the Community and in China. Extraordinary meetings may be organised at the request of either Party.

5. The costs incurred by the Steering Committee or in its name shall be borne by the Party to whom members relate. The costs other than those for travel and accommodation which are directly associated with meetings of the Steering Committee shall be borne by the host Party.

**Article 13 Funding**

1. Cooperative activities shall be subject to the availability of appropriate funds and to the applicable laws and regulations, policies and programmes of the Parties. The costs incurred by the participants to cooperative activities will not lead to any transfer of funds from one Party to the other.

2. When specific cooperative schemes of one Party provide for financial support to participants from the other Party, any such grants, financial or other contributions from one Party to the participants of the other Party in support of those activities shall be granted tax and customs exemption in accordance with the laws and regulations applicable in the territories of each Party.

**Article 14 Entry of personnel and experimental equipment**

Each Party shall take all reasonable steps and use its best efforts, within the laws and regulations applicable in the territories of each Party, to facilitate entry to, sojourn and exit from its territory of persons, material, data, samples, instruments and apparatus for experimental purposes involved in or used in cooperative activities identified by the Parties under the provisions of this Agreement. In particular, goods imported into the territory of one of the parties for the purpose of the agreement shall be exempted from customs duties and levies.

**Article 15 Diffusion and utilisation of information**

The research entities established in China which are involved in Community R&D projects shall follow, as regards the ownership, diffusion and utilisation of information and as regards the intellectual property stemming from this involvement, the rules of diffusion of research results stemming from the Community R&D specific programmes as well as the provisions of the Annex B to this Agreement, which is an integral part of this agreement.

The research entities established in the Community which are involved in Chinese R&D projects have, as regards the ownership, diffusion and utilisation of information and as regards the intellectual property stemming from this involvement, the same rights and the same obligations as the Chinese research entities and are subject to the provisions of the Annex B to this Agreement.

The provisions of this Agreement shall not be used for the purpose of seeking commercial or industrial advantages, nor of interfering with the commercial or industrial interests, whether domestic or international, of either Party or authorised persons, nor of interfering with the nuclear policy of either Party or of the Governments of the Member States of the Community, nor of hindering the promotion of the peaceful and non-explosive uses of nuclear energy, nor of hindering the movement of items subject to or notified to be made subject to this Agreement either within the respective territorial jurisdiction of the Parties or between the Parties.

**Article 16 Confidentiality**

Without prejudice to application of Article 15, each Party undertakes to keep secret, even after the termination or end of this Agreement, any information, facts or events concerning the other Party and not directly related to the subject of the Agreement that they may have become acquainted with in the course of its execution.

**Article 17 Territorial application**

This Agreement shall apply, on the one hand to the territories in which the Treaty establishing the European Atomic Energy Community is applied and under the conditions laid down in that Treaty, and on the other hand to the territory of the People's Republic of China. This shall not prevent the conduct of cooperative activities on the high seas, outer space, or the territory of third countries, in accordance with international law.

**Article 18 Bilateral nuclear co-operation agreements**

This agreement shall be without prejudice to existing bilateral agreements between individual Member States of the Community and China. Furthermore, this Agreement shall be without prejudice to existing agreements or agreements to be concluded in the future between individual Member States of the Community and China covering the transfer of other nuclear items (equipment, non-nuclear material and sensitive technology).

**Article 19 Entry into force, termination and dispute settlement**

1. This Agreement shall enter into force on the date on which the Parties have notified each other in writing that their respective internal procedures necessary for its entry into force have been completed.

2. This Agreement shall remain in force for a period of thirty years and shall continue in force thereafter for additional periods of five years each.

3. This Agreement may be amended by agreement of the Parties. Amendments shall enter into force on the date on which the Parties have notified each other in writing that their respective internal procedures necessary for amending this Agreement have been completed.

4. Either Party may, by giving six months' written notice to the other Party, terminate this Agreement at the end of the initial thirty-year period or at the end of any subsequent five-year period.. The expiry or termination of this Agreement shall not affect the validity or duration of any arrangements made under it, or any specific rights and obligations that have accrued in compliance with the Annex B.

5. If either Party or a Member State of the Community at any time following the entry into force of this Agreement takes action of any kind which results in a material violation of its obligations under this Agreement and in particular its obligations under Articles 7, 8, 9 and 11, the other Party shall have the right to cease further co-operation under this Agreement or to suspend or terminate, in whole or in part, this Agreement.

6. All questions or disputes related to the interpretation or implementation of this Agreement shall be settled by mutual agreement between the Parties.

7. Notwithstanding cessation of further co-operation under this agreement in whole or in part, the termination of this Agreement for any reason, the provisions of Articles 7, 8, 9, 11, 15 and 16 of this Agreement shall continue to apply.

8. This agreement is drawn up in duplicates in 21 languages (Danish, Dutch, English, Finnish, French, German, Greek, Italian, Portuguese, Spanish, Swedish, Czech, Estonian, Hungarian, Lithuanian, Latvian, Maltese, Polish, Slovak, Slovenian and Chinese. English and Chinese shall be the authentic languages.

In witness whereof, the undersigned, being duly authorised thereto, have signed this Agreement.

Done at, .............., in two copies, in the English and Chinese languages.

For the European Atomic Energy Community

For the Government of the People's Republic of China

**ANNEX A**

1. Items retransferred will be used only for peaceful and non-explosive purposes in the receiving third country.

2. If the receiving third country is a non-nuclear weapon state, all nuclear material in that country is and will be subject to the application of safeguards by the Agency.

3. In the case that nuclear material is retransferred, safeguards by the Agency will be applied to the nuclear material in the receiving third country.

4. In the case that nuclear material is retransferred, adequate measures of physical protection of the nuclear material will be maintained in the receiving third country, as a minimum, at levels set out in Article 9 of this Agreement.

5. Items retransferred will not be further retransferred beyond the receiving third country to another country unless the latter country provides assurances equivalent to those set out in this Annex A.

**ANNEX B-1**
**Guiding principles on the allocation of intellectual property rights resulting from joint research activities under the Agreement**

*I. OWNERSHIP, ALLOCATION AND EXERCISE OF RIGHTS*

1. This Annex shall apply to joint research activities under this Agreement except as otherwise agreed by the Parties. The participants shall jointly develop technology management plans (TMPs) in respect of the ownership and use, including publication, of information and intellectual property, hereinafter referred to as results of intellectual activities (RIA), to

be created in the course of joint research. The TMPs shall be approved by the Parties before the conclusion of any specific R & D cooperation contracts to which they refer. The TMPs shall be developed taking into account the aims of the joint research, the relative contributions of the participants, peculiarities of licensing by territory or for a specific field of use, requirements imposed by laws applicable and other factors deemed appropriate by the participants. The rights and obligations concerning the research generated by visiting researchers under this Agreement in respect of RIA shall also be addressed in the joint TMPs.

2. RIA created in the course of joint research and not addressed in the TMP shall be allocated, with the approval of the Parties, according to the principles set out in the TMP. In case of disagreement, such RIA shall be owned jointly by all the participants involved in the joint research from which the RIA results. Each participant to whom this provision applies shall have the right to use such RIA for his own commercial exploitation with no geographical limitation.

3. Each Party shall ensure that the other Party and its participants shall have the rights to RIA allocated to them in accordance with these principles.

4. While maintaining the conditions of competition in areas affected by this Agreement each Party shall endeavour to ensure that rights acquired pursuant to this Agreement and arrangements made under it are exercised in such a way as to encourage in particular:

(i) the dissemination and use of information created, disclosed legally, or otherwise legally made available, under the Agreement;

(ii) the adoption and implementation of international technical standards.

*II. COPYRIGHT WORKS*

1. Copyright belonging to the Parties or to their participants shall be accorded treatment consistent with the Berne Convention for the protection of literary and artistic work (Paris Act 1971).

2. Without prejudice to section III of this Annex, unless otherwise agreed in the TMP, publication of results of research shall be made jointly by the Parties or participants to that joint research. Subject to the foregoing general rule, the following procedures shall apply:

(a) in the case of publication by a Party or its other participants, of scientific and technical journals, articles, reports, books, including video and software, of the results arising from joint research pursuant to this Agreement, the other Party or its other participants shall be entitled to a worldwide, non-exclusive, irrevocable, royalty-free licence to translate, reproduce, adapt, transmit and publicly distribute such works;

(b) the Parties shall ensure that literary works of a scientific character arising from joint research pursuant to this Agreement and published by independent publishers shall be disseminated as widely as possible;

(c) all copies of a copyright work to be publicly distributed and prepared under the provisions of this Agreement shall indicate the names or pseudonyms of the author(s) of the work unless an author or authors expressly declines or decline to be named. The copies shall also bear a clearly visible acknowledgment of the cooperative support of the Parties and/or their representatives and/or organisations.

*III. UNDISCLOSED INFORMATION*

1. Documentary undisclosed information

(a) Each Party or its participants, as appropriate, shall identify at the earliest possible moment and preferably in the TMP, the information that it wishes to remain undisclosed in relation to this Agreement, taking account, *inter alia*, of the following criteria:

- secrecy of the information in the sense that the information is not, as a body or in the precise configuration or assembly of its components, generally known among or readily accessible by lawful means to experts in the field,
- the actual or potential commercial value of the information by virtue of its secrecy for the third party,
- previous protection of the information in the sense that it has been subject to steps that were reasonable under the circumstances by the person lawfully in control, to maintain its secrecy,

the Parties and their participants may, in certain cases, agree, that, unless otherwise indicated, parts of or all the information provided, exchanged or created in the course of joint research pursuant to the Agreement shall not be disclosed;

(b) each Party shall ensure that undisclosed information under this Agreement and its ensuing privileged nature is readily recognisable as such by the other Party, for example by means of an appropriate marking or restrictive legend. This also applies to any reproduction of the said information, in whole or in part;

a Party receiving undisclosed information pursuant to this Agreement shall respect the privileged nature thereof. These limitations shall automatically terminate when this information is disclosed by the owner without restriction to experts in the field;

(c) undisclosed information communicated under this Agreement may be disseminated by the receiving Party to persons within or employed by the receiving Party, and other concerned departments or agencies in the receiving Party authorised for the specific purposes of the joint research under way, provided that any undisclosed information so disseminated shall be pursuant to a specific agreement on confidentiality and shall be readily recognisable as such, as set out above;

(d) with the prior written consent of the Party providing undisclosed information under this Agreement, the receiving Party may disseminate such undisclosed information more widely than otherwise permitted in paragraph (c). The Parties shall cooperate in developing procedures for requesting and obtaining prior written consent for such wider dissemination, and each Party will grant such approval to the extent permitted by its domestic policies, regulations and laws.

2. Non-documentary undisclosed information

Non-documentary undisclosed or other confidential or privileged information provided in seminars and other meetings arranged under this Agreement, or information arising from the attachment of staff, use of facilities, or joint projects, shall be treated by the Parties or their participants according to the principles specified for documentary information in this Annex, provided, however, that the recipient of such undisclosed or other confidential or privileged information has been made aware of the confidential character of the information communicated at the time such communication is made.

Control

Each Party shall endeavour to ensure that undisclosed information received by it under this Agreement shall be controlled as provided therein. If one of the Parties becomes aware that it will be, or may reasonably be, expected to become unable to meet the non-dissemination provisions of paragraphs 1 and 2, it shall immediately inform the other Party. The Parties shall thereafter consult to define an appropriate course of action.

ANNEX B-2

Indicative features of a technology management plan (TMP)

The TMP is a specific agreement to be concluded between the participants, about the implementation of joint research and the respective rights and obligations of the participants. With respect to RIA, the TMP will normally address, *inter alia*: ownership, protection, user rights for R & D purposes, exploitation and dissemination, including arrangements for joint publication, the rights and obligations of visiting researchers and dispute settlement procedures. The TMP may also address foreground and background information, licensing and deliverables.

ITER is an international research and development project aiming to demonstrate the scientific and technological feasibility of fusion energy for peaceful purposes, designed eventually to result in large-scale production of electric power (see Document 6.7). The EU and China also cooperate within the framework of the ITER Agreement. Known formally as the Agreement on the Establishment of the ITER International Fusion Energy Organization for the Joint Implementation of the ITER Project, the international ITER Agreement was signed in Paris on 21 November 2006 between Euratom (representing the EU), the People's Republic of China, Japan, India, the Republic of Korea, the Russian Federation and the USA. ITER is being built at Cadarache in southern France and is expected to be completed in 2015.

The parties to the ITER Agreement are the Members of the ITER Organization. The main organ is the Council, composed of representatives of the Members. The chief executive officer is the Director-General, appointed for a five-year term, which may be extended for another period of five years. The Agreement provides expressly that the ITER Organization will have international and domestic legal personality. With limited exceptions, it is immune from jurisdiction and execution in court, and its staff enjoys privileges and immunities similar to those of other international organisations.[13] Special provision is made for intellectual property rights.

During the period of operation, the ITER Organization is required to generate a fund to provide for the decommissioning of the ITER facilities. Following the final phase of experimental operation, the ITER Organization is to agree conditions with the Host State (France) on decommissioning, after which the ITER Organization is to hand over to the Host State the Fund and ITER facilities for decommissioning. After acceptance by the Host State, the ITER Organization does not bear any

13 See also Agreement on the Privileges and Immunities of the ITER International Fusion Energy Organization for the Joint Implementation of the ITER Project, [2006] OJ L358/82 (not reprinted in this book).

responsibilities or liabilities for the ITER facilities, except as otherwise agreed with the Host State.

The ITER Agreement was subject to ratification, acceptance or approval according to the procedures of each signatory to the Agreement. It was to enter into force within 30 days of the deposit of the instruments of ratification and acceptance of approval by the signatories.[14]

**Document 6.7: Agreement on the Establishment of the ITER International Fusion Energy Organization for the Joint Implementation of the ITER Project**

Agreement on the Establishment of the ITER International Fusion Energy Organization for the Joint Implementation of the ITER Project

**Preamble**

The European Atomic Energy Community (hereinafter "Euratom"), the Government of the People's Republic of China, the Government of the Republic of India, the Government of Japan, the Government of the Republic of Korea, the Government of the Russian Federation and the Government of the United States of America,

RECALLING that the successful completion of the ITER Engineering Design Activities under the auspices of the International Atomic Energy Agency (hereinafter "the IAEA") has placed at the disposal of the Parties a detailed, complete and fully integrated engineering design of a research facility aimed to demonstrate the feasibility of fusion as an energy source;

EMPHASIZING the long term potential of fusion energy as a virtually limitless, environmentally acceptable and economically competitive source of energy;

CONVINCED that ITER is the next important step on the path to develop fusion energy and that now is the appropriate time to initiate the implementation of the ITER Project on the basis of progress of research and development in the field of fusion energy;

HAVING REGARD to the joint declaration by the Representatives of the Parties to the ITER negotiations, on the occasion of the ministerial meeting for ITER on 28 June 2005 in Moscow;

RECOGNIZING that the World Summit on Sustainable Development of 2002 called upon governments to promote increased research and development in the field of various energy technologies, including renewable energy, energy efficiency and advanced energy technologies;

EMPHASIZING the importance of the joint implementation of the ITER Project to demonstrate the scientific and technological feasibility of fusion energy for peaceful purposes and to stimulate the interest of young generations in fusion;

DETERMINED that the ITER Project's overall programmatic objective will be pursued by the ITER International Fusion Energy Organization through a common international

[14] On provisional application of the ITER Agreement, see the Arrangement on Provisional Application of the Agreement on the Establishment of the ITER International Fusion Energy Organization for the Joint Implementation of the ITER Project, [2006] OJ L358, 81 (not reprinted in this book).

research programme organized around scientific and technological goals, developed and executed with participation of leading researchers from all Parties;

EMPHASIZING the importance of safe and reliable implementation of construction, operation, exploitation, de-activation and decommissioning of the ITER facilities with a view to demonstrating safety and promoting social acceptability of fusion as an energy source;

AFFIRMING the importance of genuine partnership in implementing this long term and large scale project for the purpose of fusion energy research and development;

RECOGNIZING that while scientific and technological benefits will be shared equally among the Parties for fusion energy research purposes, other benefits associated with the implementation of the Project will be shared on an equitable basis;

DESIRING to continue the fruitful cooperation with the IAEA in this endeavour, HAVE AGREED AS FOLLOWS:

**Article 1 Establishment of the ITER International Fusion Energy Organization**

1. The ITER International Fusion Energy Organization (hereinafter "the ITER Organization") is hereby established.

2. The headquarters of the ITER Organization (hereinafter "the Headquarters") shall be at St Paul-lez-Durance, Bouches-du-Rhône, France. For the purposes of this Agreement, Euratom shall be referred to as "the Host Party" and France as "the Host State".

**Article 2 Purpose of the ITER Organization**

The purpose of the ITER Organization shall be to provide for and to promote cooperation among the Members referred to in Article 4 (hereinafter "the Members") on the ITER Project, an international project that aims to demonstrate the scientific and technological feasibility of fusion energy for peaceful purposes, an essential feature of which would be achieving sustained fusion power generation.

**Article 3 Functions of the ITER Organization**

1. The ITER Organization shall:

(a) construct, operate, exploit, and de-activate the ITER facilities in accordance with the technical objectives and the general design presented in the Final Report of the ITER Engineering Design Activities (ITER EDA Documentation Series No. 21) and such supplemental technical documents as may be adopted, as necessary, in accordance with this Agreement, and provide for the decommissioning of the ITER facilities;

(b) encourage the exploitation of the ITER facilities by the laboratories, other institutions and personnel participating in the fusion energy research and development programmes of the Members;

(c) promote public understanding and acceptance of fusion energy; and

(d) undertake, in accordance with this Agreement, any other activities that are necessary to achieve its purpose.

2. In the performance of its functions, the ITER Organization shall give special regard to the maintenance of good relations with local communities.

**Article 4 Members of the ITER Organization**

The Parties to this Agreement shall be the Members of the ITER Organization.

**Article 5 Legal Personality**

1. The ITER Organization shall have international legal personality, including the capacity to conclude agreements with States and/or international organizations.

2. The ITER Organization shall have legal personality and enjoy, in the territories of the Members, the legal capacity it requires, including to:

(a) conclude contracts;

(b) acquire, hold and dispose of property;

(c) obtain licenses; and

(d) institute legal proceedings.

**Article 6 Council**

1. The Council shall be the principal organ of the ITER Organization and shall be composed of Representatives of the Members. Each Member shall appoint up to four Representatives to the Council.

2. The Depositary referred to in Article 29 (hereinafter "the Depositary") shall convene the first session of the Council no later than three months after the entry into force of this Agreement, provided that the notifications referred to in Article 12(5) have been received from all Parties.

3. The Council shall elect from among its Members a Chair and a Vice-Chair who shall each serve for a term of one year and who may be re-elected up to three times for a maximum period of four years.

4. The Council shall adopt its Rules of Procedure by unanimity.

5. The Council shall meet twice a year, unless it decides otherwise. The Council may decide to hold an extraordinary session at the request of a Member or of the Director-General. Sessions of the Council shall take place at the Headquarters, unless the Council decides otherwise.

6. When appropriate, the Council may decide to hold a session at the ministerial level.

7. The Council shall be responsible, in accordance with this Agreement, for the promotion, overall direction and supervision of the activities of the ITER Organization in pursuit of its purpose. The Council may take decisions and make recommendations on any questions, matters or issues in accordance with this Agreement. In particular, the Council shall:

(a) decide on the appointment, replacement and extension of the term of office of the Director-General;

(b) adopt and amend where necessary, on the proposal of the Director-General, the Staff Regulations and the Project Resource Management Regulations of the ITER Organization;

(c) decide, on the proposal of the Director-General, the main management structure of the ITER Organization and complement of the Staff;

(d) appoint senior Staff on the proposal of the Director-General;

(e) appoint the Members of the Financial Audit Board as referred to in Article 17;

(f) decide, in accordance with Article 18, on the terms of reference for the undertaking of an assessment of the management of the ITER Organization and appoint a Management Assessor for that purpose;

(g) decide, on the proposal of the Director-General, the total budget for the various phases of the ITER Project and allowable ranges for adjustment for the purpose of the annual updates referred to in subparagraph (j), and approve the initial ITER Project Plan and Resource Estimates referred to in Article 9;

(h) approve changes to the overall cost sharing;

(i) approve, with the consent of the Members concerned, modifications to the procurement allocation without changing the overall cost sharing;

(j) approve the annual updates of the ITER Project Plan and Resource Estimates and, correspondingly, approve the annual programme and adopt the annual budget of the ITER Organization;

(k) approve the annual accounts of the ITER Organization;

(l) adopt the annual reports;

(m) adopt, as necessary, the supplemental technical documents referred to in Article 3(1)(a);

(n) establish such subsidiary bodies of the Council as may be necessary;

(o) approve the conclusion of agreements or arrangements for international cooperation in accordance with Article 19;

(p) decide on acquisition, sale and mortgaging of land and other titles of real property;

(q) adopt the rules on Intellectual Property management and the dissemination of information in accordance with Article 10 on the proposal of the Director-General;

(r) approve, on the proposal of the Director-General, the details of setting up of Field Teams with consent of the Members concerned, in accordance with Article 13. The Council shall review, on a periodic basis, the continuation of any Field Teams established;

(s) approve, on the proposal of the Director-General, agreements or arrangements governing relations between the ITER Organization and the Members or States on whose territory the Headquarters and Field Teams of the ITER Organization are located;

(t) approve, on the proposal of the Director-General, efforts to promote collaboration among the relevant domestic fusion research programmes of the Members and between such programmes and the ITER Organization;

(u) decide on the accession of States or international organizations to this Agreement in accordance with Article 23;

(v) recommend to the Parties, in accordance with Article 28, amendments to this Agreement;

(w) decide on the taking or granting of loans, provision of assurances and guarantees and furnishing collateral and security in respect thereto;

(x) decide whether to propose material, equipment and technology for consideration by international export control for a inclusion on their control lists, and establish a policy supporting peaceful uses and non-proliferation in accordance with Article 20;

(y) approve compensation arrangements referred to in Article 15; and

(z) decide on waivers of immunity in accordance with Article 12(3) and have such other powers as may be necessary to fulfill the purpose and to carry out the functions of the ITER Organization, consistent with this Agreement.

8. The Council shall decide issues under subparagraphs (a), (b), (c), (g), (h), (o), (u), (v), (w), (x), (y) and (z) of paragraph 7, and on the weighted voting system referred to in paragraph 10, by unanimity.

9. On all issues other than as specified in paragraph 8, the Members shall use their best efforts to achieve consensus. Failing consensus, the Council shall decide the issue in accordance with the weighted voting system referred to in paragraph 10. Decisions on issues related to Article 14 shall require the concurrence of the Host Party.

10. The respective weights of the votes of the Members shall reflect their contributions to the ITER Organization. The weighted voting system, which shall include both the distribution of votes and the decision making rules, shall be set out in the Council Rules of Procedure.

**Article 7 The Director-General and the Staff**

1. The Director-General shall be the chief executive officer and the representative of the ITER Organization in the exercise of its legal capacity. The Director-General shall act in a manner consistent with this Agreement and decisions of the Council, and shall be responsible to the Council for the execution of his/her duties.

2. The Director-General shall be assisted by the Staff. The Staff shall consist of direct employees of the ITER Organization and personnel seconded by the Members.

3. The Director-General shall be appointed for a term of five years. The appointment of the Director-General may be extended once for an additional period of up to five years.

4. The Director-General shall take all measures necessary for the management of the ITER Organization, the execution of its activities, the implementation of its policies and the fulfillment of its purpose. In particular, the Director-General shall:

(a) prepare and submit to the Council:

- the total budget for the various phases of the ITER Project and allowable ranges for adjustment;
- the ITER Project Plan and Resource Estimates and their annual updates;
- the annual budget within the agreed total budget, including the annual contributions, and annual accounts;
- proposals on senior Staff appointments and main management structure of the ITER Organization;
- the Staff Regulations;
- the Project Resource Management Regulations; and
- the annual reports;

(b) appoint, direct and supervise the Staff;

(c) be responsible for safety and undertake all organizational measures needed to observe the laws and regulations referred to in Article 14;

(d) undertake, where necessary in conjunction with the Host State, to obtain the permits and licenses required for the construction, operation and exploitation of the ITER facilities;

(e) promote collaboration among the relevant domestic fusion research programmes of the Members and between such programmes and the ITER Organization;

(f) ensure the quality and fitness of components and systems procured for use by the ITER Organization;

(g) submit to the Council, as necessary, the supplemental technical documents referred to in Article 3(1)(a);

(h) conclude, subject to prior approval of the Council, agreements or arrangements for international cooperation in accordance with Article 19 and supervise their implementation;

(i) make arrangements for the sessions of the Council;

(j) as requested by the Council, assist subsidiary bodies of the Council in the performance of their tasks; and

(k) monitor and control the execution of the annual programmes with respect to timing, results and quality, and accept the completion of the tasks.

5. The Director-General shall attend meetings of the Council unless the Council decides otherwise.

6. Without prejudice to Article 14, the responsibilities of the Director-General and the Staff in respect of the ITER Organization shall be exclusively international in character. In the discharge of their duties they shall not seek or receive instructions from any government or from any authority external to the ITER Organization. Each Member shall respect the international character of the responsibilities of the Director-General and the Staff, and shall not seek to influence them in the discharge of their duties.

7. The Staff shall support the Director-General in the performance of his/her duties and shall be under his/her management authority.

8. The Director-General shall appoint the Staff in accordance with the Staff Regulations.

9. The term of the appointment of each Member of the Staff shall be up to five years.

10. The Staff of the ITER Organization shall consist of such qualified scientific, technical and administrative personnel as shall be required for the implementation of the activities of the ITER Organization.

11. The Staff shall be appointed on the basis of their qualifications, taking into account an adequate distribution of posts among the Members in relation to their contributions.

12. In accordance with this Agreement and the relevant regulations, the Members may second personnel and send visiting researchers to the ITER Organization.

**Article 8 Resources of the ITER Organization**

1. The resources of the ITER Organization shall comprise:

(a) contributions in kind, as referred to in the document "Value Estimates for ITER Phases of Construction, Operation, Deactivation and Decommissioning and Form of Party Contributions", comprising: (i) specific components, equipment, materials and other goods and services in accordance with the agreed technical specifications and (ii) staff seconded by the Members;

(b) financial contributions to the budget of the ITER Organization by the Members (hereinafter "contributions in cash"), as referred to in the document "Value Estimates for ITER Phases of Construction, Operation, Deactivation and Decommissioning and Form of Party Contributions";

(c) additional resources received either in cash or in kind within limits and under terms approved by the Council.

2. The respective Members' contributions over the duration of this Agreement shall be as referred to in the documents "Value Estimates for ITER Phases of Construction, Operation, Deactivation and Decommissioning and Form of Party Contributions" and "Cost Sharing for all Phases of the ITER Project" and may be updated by unanimous decision of the Council.

3. The resources of the ITER Organization shall be solely used to promote the purpose and to exercise the functions of the ITER Organization in accordance with Articles 2 and 3.

4. Each Member shall provide its contributions to the ITER Organization through an appropriate legal entity, hereinafter "the Domestic Agency" of that Member, except where otherwise agreed by the Council. The approval of the Council shall not be required for Members to provide cash contributions directly to the ITER Organization.

**Article 9 Project Resource Management Regulations**

1. The purpose of the Project Resource Management Regulations is to ensure the sound financial management of the ITER Organization. These Regulations shall include, inter alia, the principal rules relating to:

(a) the Financial Year;

(b) the unit of account and the currency that the ITER Organization shall use for accounting, budget and resource evaluation purposes;

(c) the presentation and structure of the ITER Project Plan and Resource Estimates;

(d) the procedure for the preparation and adoption of the annual budget, the implementation of the annual budget and internal financial control;

(e) the contributions by the Members;

(f) the awarding of contracts;

(g) the management of contributions; and

(h) the management of the decommissioning fund.

2. The Director-General shall prepare each year, and submit to the Council, an update of the ITER Project Plan and Resource Estimates.

3. The ITER Project Plan shall specify the plan for the execution of all functions of the ITER Organization and shall cover the duration of this Agreement. It shall:

(a) outline an overall plan including time schedule and major milestones, for the fulfilment of the purpose of the ITER Organization and summarise the progress of the ITER Project in relation to the overall plan;

(b) present specific objectives and schedules of the programme of activities of the ITER Organization for the coming five years or for the period of construction, whichever will last longer; and

(c) provide appropriate commentaries, including assessment of the risks to the ITER Project and descriptions of risk avoidance or mitigation measures.

4. The ITER Resource Estimates shall provide a comprehensive analysis of the resources already expended and required in the future to undertake the ITER Project Plan and of the plans for the provision of the resources.

**Article 10 Information and Intellectual Property**

1. Subject to this Agreement and the Annex on Information and Intellectual Property, the ITER Organization and the Members shall support the widest appropriate dissemination of information and intellectual property they generate in the execution of this Agreement. The implementation of this Article and the Annex on Information and Intellectual Property shall be equal and non-discriminatory for all Members and the ITER Organization.

2. In carrying out its activities, the ITER Organization shall ensure that any scientific results shall be published or otherwise made widely available after a reasonable period of time to allow for the obtaining of appropriate protection. Any copyright on works based on those results shall be owned by the ITER Organization unless otherwise provided in specific provisions of this Agreement and the Annex on Information and Intellectual Property.

3. When placing contracts for work to be performed pursuant to this Agreement, the ITER Organization and the Members shall include provisions in such contracts on any resulting intellectual property. These provisions shall address, inter alia, rights of access to, as well as disclosure and use of, such intellectual property, and shall be consistent with this Agreement and the Annex on Information and Intellectual Property.

4. Intellectual property generated or incorporated pursuant to this Agreement shall be treated in accordance with the provisions of the Annex on Information and Intellectual Property.

**Article 11 Site Support**

1. The Host Party shall make available or cause to be made available to the ITER Organization the site support required for the implementation of the ITER Project as summarized and under the terms outlined in the Annex on Site Support. The Host Party may designate an entity to act on its behalf for this purpose. Such designation shall not affect the obligations of the Host Party under this Article.

2. Subject to the approval of the Council, the details of and the procedures for cooperation on site support between the ITER Organization and the Host Party or its designated entity shall be covered by a Site Support Agreement to be concluded between them.

**Article 12 Privileges and Immunities**

1. The ITER Organization, its property and assets, shall enjoy in the territory of each Member such privileges and immunities as are necessary for the exercise of its functions.

2. The Director-General and the Staff of the ITER Organization and the representatives of the Members in the Council and subsidiary bodies, together with their alternates and experts, shall enjoy in the territory of each of the Members such privileges and immunities as are necessary for the exercise of their functions in connection with the ITER Organization.

3. The immunities provided for in paragraphs 1 and 2 shall be waived in any case where the authority competent to waive the immunity considers that such immunity would impede the course of justice and that waiver would not prejudice the purposes for which it was accorded and where, in the case of the ITER Organization, the Director-General, and the Staff, the Council determines that such a waiver would not be contrary to the interests of the ITER Organization and its Members.

4. The privileges and immunities conferred in accordance with this Agreement shall not diminish or affect the duty of the ITER Organization, the Director-General or the Staff to comply with the laws and regulations referred to in Article 14.

5. Each Party shall notify the Depositary in writing upon having given effect to paragraphs 1 and 2.

6. The Depositary shall notify the Parties when notifications have been received from all Parties in accordance with paragraph 5.

7. A Headquarters Agreement shall be concluded between the ITER Organization and the Host State.

**Article 13 Field Teams**

Each Member shall host a Field Team established and operated by the ITER Organization as required for the exercise of the ITER Organization's functions and the fulfillment of its purpose. A Field Team Agreement shall be concluded between the ITER Organization and each Member.

**Article 14 Public Health, Safety, Licensing and Environmental Protection**

The ITER Organization shall observe applicable national laws and regulations of the Host State in the fields of public and occupational health and safety, nuclear safety, radiation protection, licensing, nuclear substances, environmental protection and protection from acts of malevolence.

**Article 15 Liability**

1. The contractual liability of the ITER Organization shall be governed by the relevant contractual provisions, which shall be construed in accordance with the law applicable to the contract.

2. In the case of non-contractual liability, the ITER Organization shall compensate appropriately or provide other remedies for any damage caused by it, to such extent as the ITER Organization is subject to a legal liability under the relevant law, with the details of

compensation arrangements to be approved by the Council. This paragraph shall not be construed as a waiver of immunity by the ITER Organization.

3. Any payment by the ITER Organization to compensate for the liability referred to in paragraphs 1 and 2 and any costs and expenses incurred in connection therewith shall be considered as "operational cost" as defined in the Project Resource Management Regulations.

4. In case the costs of compensation for damage referred to in paragraph 2 exceed funds available to the ITER Organization in the annual budget for operations and/or through insurance, the Members shall consult, through the Council, so that the ITER Organization can compensate, according to paragraph 2 by seeking to increase the overall budget by unanimous decision of the Council in accordance with Article 6(8).

5. Membership in the ITER Organization shall not result in liability for Members for acts, omissions, or obligations of the ITER Organization.

6. Nothing in this Agreement shall impair, or shall be construed as a waiver of, immunity that Members enjoy in the territory of other States or in their territory.

**Article 16 Decommissioning**

1. During the period of operation of ITER, the ITER Organization shall generate a Fund (hereinafter "the Fund") to provide for the decommissioning of the ITER facilities. The modalities for the generation of the Fund, its estimation and updating, the conditions for changes and for its transfer to the Host State shall be set out in the Project Resource Management Regulations referred to in Article 9.

2. Following the final phase of experimental operations of ITER, the ITER Organization shall, within a period of five years, or shorter if agreed with the Host State, bring the ITER facilities into such conditions as are to be agreed and updated as necessary between the ITER Organization and the Host State, following which the ITER Organization shall hand over to the Host State the Fund and the ITER facilities for their decommissioning.

3. Following the acceptance by the Host State of the Fund together with the ITER facilities, the ITER Organization shall bear no responsibilities or liabilities for the ITER facilities, except when otherwise agreed between the ITER Organization and the Host State.

4. The respective rights and obligations of the ITER Organization and the Host State and the modalities of their interactions in respect of the decommissioning shall be set out in the Headquarters Agreement referred to in Article 12, under which the ITER Organization and the Host State shall, inter alia, agree that:

(a) after the handing over of the ITER facilities, the Host State shall continue to be bound by the provisions of Article 20; and

(b) the Host State shall make regular reports to all Members that have contributed to the Fund on the progress of the decommissioning and on the procedures and technologies that have been used or generated for the decommissioning.

**Article 17 Financial Audit**

1. A Financial Audit Board (hereinafter "the Board") shall be established to undertake the audit of the annual accounts of the ITER Organization in accordance with this Article and the Project Resource Management Regulations.

2. Each Member shall be represented on the Board by one Member. The Members of the Board shall be appointed by the Council on the recommendation of the respective Members for a period of three years. The appointment may be extended once for an additional period of three years. The Council shall appoint from among the members the Chair of the Board, who shall serve for a period of two years.

3. The members of the Board shall be independent and shall not seek or take instructions from any Member or any other person and shall report only to the Council.

4. The purposes of the audit shall be to:

(a) determine whether all income/expenditure has been received/incurred in a lawful and regular manner and has been accounted for;

(b) determine whether the financial management has been sound;

(c) provide a statement of assurance as to the reliability of the annual accounts and the legality and regularity of the underlying transactions;

(d) determine whether expenditures are in conformity with the budget; and

(e) examine any matter having potential financial implications for the ITER Organization.

5. The audit shall be based on recognized international principles and standards for accounting.

**Article 18 Management Assessment**

1. Every two years, the Council shall appoint a Management Assessor who shall assess the management of the activities of the ITER Organization. The scope of the assessment shall be decided by the Council.

2. The Director-General may also call for such assessments following consultation with the Council.

3. The Management Assessor shall be independent and shall not seek or take instructions from any Member or any person and shall report only to the Council.

4. The purpose of the assessment shall be to determine whether the management of the ITER Organization has been sound, in particular with respect to management effectiveness and efficiency in terms of scale of staff.

5. The assessment shall be based on records of the ITER Organization. The Management Assessor shall be granted full access to personnel, books and records as he/she may deem appropriate for this purpose.

6. The ITER Organization shall ensure that the Management Assessor shall abide by its requirements relating to the treatment of sensitive and/or business confidential information, in particular its policies concerning Intellectual Property, Peaceful Uses and Non-Proliferation.

**Article 19 International Cooperation**

Consistent with this Agreement and upon a unanimous decision of the Council, the ITER Organization may, in furtherance of its purpose, cooperate with other international organizations and institutions, non-Parties, and with organizations and institutions of non-Parties, and conclude agreements or arrangements with them to this effect. The detailed arrangements for such cooperation shall be determined in each case by the Council.

**Article 20 Peaceful Uses and Non-Proliferation**

1. The ITER Organization and the Members shall use any material, equipment or technology generated or received pursuant to this Agreement solely for peaceful purposes. Nothing in this paragraph shall be interpreted as affecting the rights of the Members to use material, equipment or technology acquired or developed by them independent of this Agreement for their own purposes.

2. Material, equipment or technology received or generated pursuant to this Agreement by the ITER Organization and the Members shall not be transferred to any third party to be used to manufacture or otherwise to acquire nuclear weapons or other nuclear explosive devices or for any non-peaceful purposes.

3. The ITER Organization and the Members shall take appropriate measures to implement this Article in an efficient and transparent manner. To this end, the Council shall interface with appropriate international fora and establish a policy supporting peaceful uses and non-proliferation.

4. In order to support the success of the ITER Project and its non-proliferation policy, the Parties agree to consult on any issues associated with the implementation of this Article.

5. Nothing in this Agreement shall require the Members to transfer material, equipment or technology contrary to national export control or related laws and regulations.

6. Nothing in this Agreement shall affect the rights and obligations of the Parties that arise from other international agreements concerning non-proliferation of nuclear weapons or other nuclear explosive devices.

**Article 21 Application with regard to Euratom**

In accordance with the Treaty establishing Euratom, this Agreement shall apply to the territories covered by that Treaty. In accordance with that Treaty and other relevant agreements, it shall also apply to the Republic of Bulgaria, Romania and the Swiss Confederation, participating in the Euratom fusion programme as fully associated third States.

**Article 22 Entry into Force**

1. This Agreement is subject to ratification, acceptance or approval in accordance with the procedures of each Signatory.

2. This Agreement shall enter into force 30 days after the deposit of instruments of ratification, acceptance or approval of this Agreement by the People's Republic of China, Euratom, the Republic of India, Japan, the Republic of Korea, the Russian Federation and the United States of America.

3. If this Agreement has not entered into force within one year after signature, a meeting of the Signatories shall be convened by the Depositary to decide what course of action shall be undertaken to facilitate its entering into force.

**Article 23 Accession**

1. After the entry into force of this Agreement, any State or international organization may accede to and become a Party to this Agreement following a unanimous decision of the Council.

2. Any State or international organization that wishes to accede to this Agreement shall notify the Director-General, who shall inform the Members of this request at least six months before it is submitted to the Council for decision.

3. The Council shall determine the conditions of accession of any State or international organization.

4. Accession to this Agreement by a State or international organization shall take effect 30 days after the Depositary has received both the instrument of accession and the notification referred to in Article 12(5).

**Article 24 Duration and Termination**

1. This Agreement shall have an initial duration of 35 years. The last five years of this period, or shorter if agreed with the Host State, shall be dedicated to the de-activation of the ITER facilities.

2. The Council shall, at least eight years before the expiry of this Agreement, establish a Special Committee, chaired by the Director-General, that shall advise it on whether the duration of this Agreement should be extended having regard to the progress of the ITER Project. The Special Committee shall assess the technical and scientific state of the ITER facilities and reasons for the possible extension of this Agreement and, before recommending to extend this Agreement, the financial aspects in terms of required budget and impact on the de-activation and decommissioning costs. The Special Committee shall submit its report to the Council within one year after its establishment.

3. On the basis of the report, the Council shall decide by unanimity at least six years before the expiry whether to extend the duration of this Agreement.

4. The Council may not extend the duration of this Agreement for a period of more than 10 years in total, nor may the Council extend this Agreement if such extension would alter the nature of the activities of the ITER Organization or the framework of financial contribution of the Members.

5. At least six years before the expiry of this Agreement, the Council shall confirm the foreseen end of this Agreement and decide the arrangements for the de-activation phase and the dissolution of the ITER Organization.

6. This Agreement may be terminated by agreement of all Parties, allowing the necessary time for de-activation and ensuring the necessary funds for decommissioning.

**Article 25 Settlement of Disputes**

1. Any issue arising among the Parties or between one or more Parties and the ITER Organization out of or in connection with this Agreement shall be settled by consultation, mediation or other procedures to be agreed, such as arbitration. The parties concerned shall meet to discuss the nature of any such issue with a view to an early resolution.

2. If the parties concerned are unable to resolve their dispute in consultation, either party may request the Chair of the Council (or if the Chair has been elected from a Member that

is a party to the dispute, a Member of the Council representing a Member that is not a party to the dispute) to act as a mediator at a meeting to attempt to resolve the dispute. Such meeting shall be convened within 30 days following a request by a party for mediation and concluded within 60 days thereafter, immediately following which the mediator shall provide a report of the mediation, which report shall be prepared in consultation with the Members other than the parties to the dispute with a recommendation for resolution of the dispute.

3. If the parties concerned are unable to resolve their dispute through consultations or mediation, they may agree to submit the dispute to an agreed form of dispute resolution in accordance with procedures to be agreed.

**Article 26 Withdrawal**

1. After this Agreement has been in force for ten years, any Party other than the Host Party may notify the Depositary of its intention to withdraw.

2. Withdrawal shall not affect the withdrawing Party's contribution to the construction cost of the ITER facilities. If a Party withdraws during the period of operation of ITER, it shall also contribute its agreed share of the cost of decommissioning the ITER facilities.

3. Withdrawal shall not affect any continuing right, obligation, or legal situation of a Party created through the execution of this Agreement prior to its withdrawal.

4. The withdrawal shall take effect at the end of the Financial Year following the year the notification referred to in paragraph 1 is given.

5. The details of withdrawal shall be documented by the ITER Organization in consultation with the withdrawing Party.

**Article 27 Annexes**

The Annex on Information and Intellectual Property and the Annex on Site Support shall form an integral part of this Agreement.

**Article 28 Amendments**

1. Any Party may propose an amendment to this Agreement.

2. Proposed amendments shall be considered by the Council, for recommendation to the Parties by unanimity.

3. Amendments are subject to ratification, acceptance or approval in accordance with the procedures of each Party and shall enter into force 30 days after the deposit of the instruments of ratification, acceptance or approval by all Parties.

**Article 29 Depositary**

1. The Director-General of the IAEA shall be the Depositary of this Agreement.

2. The original of this Agreement shall be deposited with the Depositary, who shall send certified copies thereof to the Signatories, and to the Secretary-General of the United Nations for registration and publication pursuant to Article 102 of the Charter of the United Nations.

3. The Depositary shall notify all Signatory and acceding States and international organizations of:

(a) the date of deposit of each instrument of ratification, acceptance, approval or accession;

(b) the date of deposit of each notification received in accordance with Article 12(5);

(c) the date of entry into force of this Agreement and of amendments as provided for under Article 28;

(d) any notification by a Party of its intention to withdraw from this Agreement; and

(e) the termination of this Agreement.

IN WITNESS WHEREOF, the undersigned, being duly authorized thereto, have signed this Agreement.

Done at Paris on 21 November 2006, in a single original, in the English language.

For the European Atomic Energy Community

For the Government of the People's Republic of China

For the Government of the Republic of India

For the Government of Japan

For the Government of the Republic of Korea

For the Government of the Russian Federation

For the Government of the United States of America

**ANNEX I Annex on Information and Intellectual Property**

*Article 1 Subject Matter and Definitions*

1.1. This Annex covers the dissemination, exchange, use and protection of information and intellectual property pertaining to protectable subject matter, in the execution of this Agreement. Unless otherwise provided, the terms used in this Annex shall have the same meaning as in this Agreement.

1.2. Information shall mean published data, drawings, designs, computations, reports and other documents, documented data or methods of research and development, as well as the description of inventions and discoveries, whether or not protectable, which are not covered by the term Intellectual Property as defined in paragraph 1.3 below.

1.3. Intellectual Property shall have the meaning defined in Article 2 of the Convention Establishing the World Intellectual Property Organization, done at Stockholm on July 14, 1967. For the purposes of this Annex, Intellectual Property may include confidential information such as know-how or trade secrets provided that they are unpublished, and in written or otherwise documented form, and

(a) have been held in confidence by their owner,

(b) are not generally known or available to the public from other sources, and/or are not generally available to the public in printed publications and/or other readable documents,

(c) have not been made available by their owner to other parties without an obligation concerning confidentiality, and

(d) are not available to the receiving party without an obligation concerning confidentiality.

1.4. Background Intellectual Property shall mean Intellectual Property that has been or is acquired, developed or produced, before the entry into force of this Agreement, or outside of the scope of this Agreement.

1.5. Generated Intellectual Property shall mean Intellectual Property that is generated or acquired with full ownership by a Member, acting through a Domestic Agency or Entity, or by the ITER Organization or jointly pursuant to and in the course of the performance of this Agreement.

1.6. Improvements shall mean any technological advancement to existing Intellectual Property, including derivative works.

1.7. Entity or Entities shall mean any entity with which a Domestic Agency or the ITER Organization has entered into a contract for the supply of goods or services for the purposes of this Agreement.

*Article 2 General Provisions*

2.1. Subject to the provisions of this Annex, the Members support the widest possible dissemination of Generated Intellectual Property.

2.2. Each Member shall ensure that the other Members and the ITER Organization can obtain the rights to Intellectual Property allocated in accordance with this Annex. Contracts placed by each Member or the ITER Organization with any Entity shall be consistent with the provisions of this Annex. In particular, appropriate public procurement procedures must be followed by all Members and the ITER Organization in order to ensure compliance with this Annex. The ITER Organization shall properly identify in a timely manner the Background Intellectual Property of the contracting Entities with a view to obtaining for the ITER Organization and the Members access to this Background Intellectual Property in conformity with this Annex. Each Member shall properly identify in a timely manner the Background Intellectual Property of the contracting Entities with a view to obtaining for the ITER Organization and the Members access to this Background Intellectual Property in conformity with this Annex. Each Member and the ITER Organization shall ensure access for the ITER Organization and the other Members to inventions and other Intellectual Property generated or incorporated in the execution of the contracts provided that inventors' rights are respected, in conformity with this Annex.

2.3. This Annex does not alter or prejudice the allocation of rights between a Member and its nationals. Whether the rights concerning Intellectual Property shall be held by a Member or its nationals shall be determined as between themselves in accordance with their applicable laws and regulations.

2.4. If a Member generates or acquires full ownership of Intellectual Property in the course of the execution of this Agreement, the Member shall notify all other Members and the ITER Organization in a timely manner and provide details of such Intellectual Property.

*Article 3*
*Dissemination of Information and Scientific Publications whether or not Copyrighted*

Each Member shall be entitled, for non-commercial uses, to translate, reproduce, and publicly distribute Information directly arising from the execution of this Agreement. All publicly distributed copies of a copyrighted work prepared under this provision shall indicate the names of the authors of the work unless an author explicitly declines to be named.

*Article 4*
*Intellectual Property Generated or Incorporated by a Member, a Domestic Agency or Entity*

4.1. Generated Intellectual Property:

4.1.1. If protectable subject matter is generated by a Member, a Domestic Agency or Entity in the course of the execution of this Agreement, the Member, the Domestic Agency or Entity shall be entitled to acquire all rights, title and interest in all countries in and to such intellectual property according to applicable laws and regulations.

4.1.2. Any Member, acting through a Domestic Agency or Entity, which has generated Intellectual Property in the course of the execution of this Agreement shall grant on an equal and non-discriminatory basis an irrevocable, non-exclusive, royalty-free license to such Generated Intellectual Property to other Members and the ITER Organization, with the right of the ITER Organization to sub-license, and the right of the other Members to sub-license within their respective territory, for the purposes of publicly sponsored fusion research and development programmes.

4.1.3. Any Member, acting through a Domestic Agency or Entity, which has generated Intellectual Property in the course of the execution of this Agreement shall make available on an equal and non-discriminatory basis a non-exclusive license to such Generated Intellectual Property to the other Members for commercial fusion use, with the right to sub-license for such use by such Members' own domestic third parties within such Members' own territory on terms no less favorable than the basis upon which such Member licenses such Generated Intellectual Property to third parties within or outside such Member's own territory. As long as such terms have been offered such license shall not be denied. The above license may be revoked only in case the licensee does not fulfil its contractual obligations.

4.1.4. Any Member, acting through a Domestic Agency or Entity, which has generated Intellectual Property pursuant to this Agreement is encouraged to enter into commercial arrangements with the other Members, Domestic Agencies, Entities and third parties in order to allow use of Generated Intellectual Property in fields other than fusion.

4.1.5. Members, and their Domestic Agencies or Entities, that license or sub-license Generated or Background Intellectual Property pursuant to this Annex, will maintain records of any such licensing, which records will be available to other Members, such as through the ITER Organization.

4.2. Background Intellectual Property:

4.2.1. Background Intellectual Property shall remain the property of the party that owns this intellectual property.

4.2.2. Any Member, acting through a Domestic Agency or Entity, which has incorporated Background Intellectual Property, except confidential information such as know-how and trade secrets into the items provided to the ITER Organization which Background Intellectual Property is required:

- to construct, operate, use or integrate technology for research and development in relation to the ITER facilities,
- to maintain or repair the item provided, or
- when decided necessary by the Council, in advance of any public procurement,

shall grant on an equal and non-discriminatory basis an irrevocable, non-exclusive, royalty-free license to such Background Intellectual Property to other Members and to the ITER Organization, with the right of the ITER Organization to sub-license and the right of Members to sub-license to their research institutes and institutes of higher education within their respective territory for the purposes of publicly sponsored fusion research and development programmes.

4.2.3. (a) Any Member, acting through a Domestic Agency or Entity, which has incorporated background confidential information into the items provided to the ITER Organization which background confidential information is required:

- to construct, operate, use or integrate technology for research and development in relation to the ITER facilities,
- to maintain or repair the item,
- when decided necessary by the Council, in advance of any public procurement, or
- for safety, for quality assurance and quality control reasons as required by regulatory authorities,

shall ensure that the ITER Organization has an irrevocable, non-exclusive, royalty-free license available to use such background confidential information including manuals or instructional training materials for the construction, operation, maintenance and repair of the ITER facilities.

(b) When confidential information is made available to the ITER Organization, it must be clearly marked so, and transmitted pursuant to an arrangement for confidentiality. The recipient of such information shall use it only for purposes set forth in 4.2.3 (a) and shall preserve its confidentiality to the extent provided in that arrangement. Compensation for damages arising from the misuse of such background confidential information by the ITER Organization shall be paid by the ITER Organization.

4.2.4. Any Member, acting through a Domestic Agency or Entity, which has incorporated background confidential information such as know how or trade secrets into the items provided to the ITER Organization which background confidential information is required:

- to construct, operate, use or integrate technology for research and development in relation to the ITER facilities,
- to maintain or repair the item provided, or
- when decided necessary by the Council, in advance of any public procurement,

shall use its best efforts to either grant a commercial license to such background confidential information or supply the same items incorporating the background confidential information to the receiving party by means of private contracts with financial compensation for publicly sponsored fusion research and development programmes of a Member on terms no less favorable than the basis upon which such Member licenses such background confidential information or supplies the same items to third parties within or outside such Member's own territory. As long as such terms have been offered, such license or supply of such item shall not be denied. The license, if granted, may be revoked only in case the licensee does not fulfil its contractual obligations.

4.2.5. Any Member, acting through a Domestic Agency or Entity, which has incorporated Background Intellectual Property, including background confidential information, in the execution of this Agreement shall use its best efforts to make sure that the component incorporating the Background Intellectual Property is available on reasonable terms and conditions, or use its best efforts to grant on an equal and non-discriminatory basis a non-exclusive license to the other Members for commercial fusion use, with the right to sub-license for such use by such Members' own domestic third parties within such Members' own territory, on terms no less favorable than the basis upon which such Member licenses such Background Intellectual Property to third parties within or outside such Member's own territory. As long as such terms have been offered, such license shall not be denied. The above license may be revoked only in case the licensee does not fulfil its contractual obligations.

4.2.6. Any Member, acting through a Domestic Agency or Entity, is encouraged to make available for commercial purposes other than those set out in Article 4.2.5 to the other Members, any Background Intellectual Property incorporated into the items provided to the ITER Organization which Background Intellectual Property was required:

- to construct, operate, use or integrate technology for research and development in relation to the ITER facilities,
- to maintain or repair the item provided, or
- when decided necessary by the Council, in advance of any public procurement.

Such Background Intellectual Property, if licensed by the owners to the Members, shall be licensed on an equal and non-discriminatory basis.

4.3. Licensing to Third Parties of Non-Members:

Any license on Generated Intellectual Property granted by the Members to third parties of non-Members shall be subject to the rules on licensing to third parties determined by the Council. Such rules shall be determined by unanimous decision of the Council.

*Article 5 Intellectual Property Generated or Incorporated by the ITER Organization*

5.1. Generated Intellectual Property:

5.1.1. Where intellectual property is generated by the ITER Organization, in the course of the execution of this Agreement, it shall be owned by the ITER Organization. The ITER Organization shall develop appropriate procedures for the recording, reporting and protection of the Intellectual Property.

5.1.2. Such intellectual property shall be licensed by the ITER Organization to the Members on an equal, non-discriminatory, irrevocable, non-exclusive, royalty-free basis, with the right of the Members to sub-license within their territory for the purpose of fusion research and development.

5.1.3. Generated Intellectual Property that has been developed or acquired by the ITER Organization in the course of the execution of this Agreement shall be licensed to the Members on an equal, non-discriminatory, non-exclusive basis for commercial use, with the right to sub-license for such use by such Members' own domestic third parties within such Members' own territory on terms no less favorable than the basis upon which the ITER Organization licenses such Generated Intellectual Property to third parties. As long as such terms have been offered, such license shall not be denied. The above license may be revoked only in case the licensee does not fulfil its contractual obligations.

5.2. Background Intellectual Property:

5.2.1. Provided that it has the pertinent rights, when the ITER Organization incorporates Background Intellectual Property which is required:

- to construct, operate, use or integrate technology for research and development in relation to the ITER facilities,
- to create improvements and derivative works,
- to repair and maintain the ITER facilities, or
- when decided necessary by the Council, in advance of any public procurement,

the ITER Organization shall make the necessary arrangements in order to sub-license that Background Intellectual Property on an equal and non-discriminatory basis by an irrevocable, non-exclusive, royalty-free license to the Members, with the right of the Members to sub-license within their respective territory for the purpose of fusion research and development. The ITER Organization shall make its best efforts to acquire the pertinent rights.

5.2.2. For Background Intellectual Property, including background confidential information, incorporated by the ITER Organization in the course of the execution of this Agreement, the ITER Organization shall use its best efforts to make available on an equal and non-discriminatory basis a non-exclusive license to the Members for commercial fusion use, with the right to sub-license for such use by such Members' own domestic third parties within such Members' own territory on terms no less favorable than the basis upon which the ITER Organization licenses such Background Intellectual Property to third parties. As long as such terms have been offered, such license shall not be denied. The above license may be revoked only in case the licensee does not fulfil its contractual obligations.

5.2.3. The ITER Organization shall use its best efforts to make available to the Members any Background Intellectual Property, including background confidential information, for purposes other than those set out in Article 5.2.2. Such Background Intellectual Property, if licensed by the ITER Organization to the Members, shall be licensed on an equal and non-discriminatory basis.

5.3. Licensing to third parties of a non-Member:

Any license granted by the ITER Organization to third parties of a non-Member shall be subject to the rules on licensing to third parties determined by the Council. Such rules shall be determined by unanimous decision of the Council.

*Article 6*
*Intellectual Property Generated by the ITER Organization's Staff and other Researchers*

6.1. Intellectual Property generated by directly employed and seconded staff of the ITER Organization shall be owned by the ITER Organization and treated in corresponding employment contracts or regulations consistent with the provisions set out herein.

6.2. Intellectual Property generated by visiting researchers who are participating in the activities of the ITER Organization through an arrangement with the ITER Organization for undertaking specific activities and who are directly involved in general programmes of the ITER Organization exploitation, shall be owned by the ITER Organization unless otherwise agreed by the Council.

6.3. Intellectual Property generated by visiting researchers not involved in general programmes of the ITER Organization exploitation shall be subject to an arrangement with the ITER Organization pursuant to conditions established by the Council.

*Article 7 Protection of Intellectual Property*

7.1. When a Member acquires or seeks protection for Generated Intellectual Property developed or acquired by that Member, such Member shall notify in a timely manner and provide details of such protection to all other Members and to the ITER Organization. If a Member decides not to exercise its right to seek protection for Generated Intellectual Property in any country or region, it shall notify the ITER Organization in a timely manner of its decision, and the ITER Organization may then seek to obtain such protection either directly or via the Members.

7.2. For Generated Intellectual Property developed or acquired by the ITER Organization, the Council shall adopt, as soon as practicable, appropriate procedures for the reporting, protection and recording of such Intellectual Property for example through the creation of a database to which the Members may have access.

7.3. In the event of a joint creation, the participating Members and/or the ITER Organization shall have the right to seek to obtain in co-ownership Intellectual Property in any State they choose.

7.4. There shall be co-ownership of Intellectual Property when created by two or more Members or by one or more Members together with the ITER Organization and when the features of such intellectual property are not capable of being separated for the purpose of applying for, obtaining and/or maintaining in force the protection of the relevant intellectual property right. In such a case the joint creators shall agree among themselves by means of a co-ownership arrangement on the allocation of and the terms of exercising the ownership of the said Intellectual Property.

*Article 8 Decommissioning*

8.1. For the decommissioning phase after the transfer of the facilities to the Host State, the Host Party shall provide to the other Members all relevant information, whether published or not, generated or used during the decommissioning of the ITER facilities.

8.2. Intellectual Property generated by the Host State during the decommissioning phase shall not be affected by this Annex.

*Article 9 Termination and Withdrawal*

9.1. The Council shall, as necessary, address any issues relating to the termination of this Agreement or the withdrawal of a Party in so far as they relate to Intellectual Property, that are not fully addressed in this Agreement.

9.2. The Intellectual Property rights conferred and obligations imposed upon the Members and the ITER Organization by the provisions of this Annex, in particular all granted licenses, shall subsist after the termination of this Agreement, or after the withdrawal of a Party.

*Article 10 Royalties*

Royalties received from the licensing of Intellectual Property by the ITER Organization shall be a resource of the ITER Organization.

*Article 11 Settlement of Disputes*

Any dispute arising out of or in connection with this Annex shall be settled in accordance with Article 25 of this Agreement.

*Article 12 Awards to Inventors*

The Council shall determine appropriate terms and conditions for the remuneration of the Staff when such Staff generates Intellectual Property.

*Article 13 Liability*

When negotiating license arrangements, the ITER Organization and the Members shall, as appropriate, include suitable provisions governing their respective liabilities, rights and obligations arising from the execution of those license arrangements.

**ANNEX II Annex on Site Support**

*Article 1 Site Support Agreement*

1. The Host Party shall make or cause to be made available to the ITER Organization land, facilities, buildings, goods and services in support of the site as summarized in this Annex. The Host Party may designate an entity to act on its behalf for this purpose.

2. The details of such support, as well as the procedures for cooperation between the ITER Organization and the Host Party or its designated entity (hereinafter "the Host"), shall be covered by an agreement (hereinafter "the Site Support Agreement") to be concluded between them.

*Article 2 Duration of the Agreement*

The Host shall provide the site support to the ITER Organization throughout the period from the establishment of the ITER Organization to the expiry or termination of this Agreement.

*Article 3 Liaison Committee*

The ITER Organization and the Host shall establish a liaison committee to ensure the effective provision of the support covered by this Annex under the terms of the Site Support Agreement.

*Article 4 Land, Buildings, Facilities and Access*

The Host shall at its own expense provide the ITER site under the conditions set out in the ITER Site Requirements and Site Design Assumptions as adopted in 2000 (hereinafter the "Reference Conditions") by the Council established under the Agreement among the European Atomic Energy Community, the Government of Japan, the Government of the Russian Federation, and the Government of the United States of America on Cooperation in the Engineering Design Activities for the International Thermonuclear Experimental Reactor (hereinafter "the ITER EDA") and other specific facilities and services as set out below:

(a) Land to be put at the disposal free of charge to the ITER Organization allowing for the construction, use and possible extension of all the ITER buildings and auxiliary services which are referred to in the Final Report of the ITER EDA;

(b) Main services to be supplied to the site boundary:- water, electricity, sewage and drainage, alarm systems;

(c) Roads, Paths and Bridges, including adaptations, as necessary, to the route between the Port Autonome de Marseille and the ITER site to provide access to the site boundary for the maximum size and weights of equipment to be delivered for the ITER Project and for Staff and visitors;

(d) Transportation services from the Port Autonome de Marseille or in case of air transport the Marignane airport to the ITER site of components contributed by the Parties;

(e) Temporary accommodation as required for the ITER Organization at or near the ITER site until the final buildings and facilities of the ITER Organization are ready for occupation;

(f) Power supplies: installation and maintenance up to the site boundary of power supplies able to provide up to 500 MW for pulsed loads as well as a capability to draw from the grid 120 MW continuous electrical power without interruption because of connection maintenance;

(g) Water cooling supply to dissipate on average 450 MW (thermal) energy to the environment; and

(h) Connection to computer network and telecommunication lines with large capacity.

*Article 5 Services*

In addition to the items referred to in Article 4 of this Annex, the Host shall supply at its own expense or charged at proven cost, in accordance with the Site Support Agreement, such technical, administrative and general services as are required by the ITER Organization. Such services shall include, but are not limited to:

(a) support staff, in addition to Staff assigned from the Host to the ITER Organization under Article 8 of this Agreement;

(b) medical services facilities;

(c) emergency services;

(d) security-alarm system and its facilities;

(e) cafeteria;

(f) support to licensing process;

(g) support to safety management;

(h) support to language courses;

(i) services for the management and disposal of radioactive wastes arising from ITER operations;

(j) relocation and settlement support;

(k) bus service to and from work;

(l) recreation, social and welfare facilities;

(m) utility services and supplies;

(n) library and multi-media services;

(o) environmental monitoring, including radiation monitoring; and

(p) site services (waste disposal, cleaning and gardening).

*Article 6 Education*

The Host shall, at its own expense, establish an international school for the education of the children of Staff and provide pre-university education according to an international core curriculum to be developed in consultation with the educational authorities of the non-Host Parties, and shall facilitate the implementation of additional curricular elements specific to and supported by non-Host Parties. The non-Host Parties shall use their best efforts to assist the development of the school and the accreditation of its curriculum by their respective authorities.

# 7

# Cooperation Projects, 1985–Present

From 1985 to the present, the EU and China have deepened and broadened their cooperation by concluding a large number of agreements concerning cooperation projects in a wide variety of fields. With respect to the EU, these projects have been within the legal competence initially of the European Economic Community and since 1992 the European Community. In addition, the Member States of the EU have separately concluded numerous bilateral cooperation projects with China. Based on the relatively limited data available to the public, this chapter gives a brief overview of EU–China cooperation projects since 1985. Though it gives some examples, it does not discuss in detail the terms of tender, particular agreements, the results or interim or final reports for specific projects.[1]

Table 7.1 shows the chronological development of cooperation projects between the EU and China. It demonstrates the length of time during which the EU and China have worked together by means of cooperation projects and also indicates the types of projects as exhaustively as possible. The list includes 33 projects, beginning with the Interpreter Training Programmes in the mid-1980s and ending with the Europe–China Business Management Training Project, for which the financing agreement was signed only in January 2007. Whereas the early projects concerned mainly economic and social reform, more recent projects deal with rule of law and good governance, reflecting changing priorities from both the European and the Chinese perspectives.

Three caveats, however, are in order. First, complete information is not publicly available for all projects. Secondly, the projects are sometimes indicated in general terms, so the list in the table substantially under-represents the actual range of particular projects. A number of so-called 'projects' listed in the table are actually 'umbrella' projects, which provide a framework for a number of more specific projects. An example is the EU–China Small Projects Facility under the EU–China Legal and Judicial Cooperation Programme, which included a variety of small projects in the legal field. Thirdly, the table also includes a limited number of EU regional programmes which include China together with other countries; Asia Link is an example.

Table 7.2 shows the cooperation projects that have been completed up to 2006, the latest date for which information is available. Many, if not most, of these projects

[1] The author has participated in several EU–China projects, notably the EU–China Higher Education Cooperation Project as the first Robert Schuman Professor, based at the Chinese Academy of Social Sciences (CASS) in Beijing; the EU–China Legal and Judicial Cooperation Project as a member of the Programme Advisory Group; and the EU–China European Studies Centres Programme in several capacities, including as European Visiting Professor at Peking University, Beijing.

**Table 7.1: Chronological Development of Cooperation Projects between the EU and China, 1985–2007**

| Project | Subject[a] | Parties (if known) | Duration by start date | Budget or type | Source |
|---|---|---|---|---|---|
| Interpreter Training Programmes | economic and social reform, interpreter training | | 1985-present | | www.uibe.edu.cn/yxxl/yyxy/15.htm; http://scic.cec.eu.int/china/Default.htm |
| EU-China Civil Aviation Cooperation Project | economic and social reform, civil aviation | | 1998–2006 | | www.aecma-international.org, |
| Asia Information Technology and Communication Programme (Asia IT&C) | regional programme | | 1999-present | | www.europa.eu.int/comm/europaid/projects/asia-itc |
| EU-China Legal and Judicial Cooperation Programme | rule of law and good governance, professional training | | 2000–2004, renewed to 2005 | 13.5m euro | |
| Asia Urbs | regional programme | | since 2001 for China | | www.europa.eu.int/comm/europaid/projects/asia-urbs |
| Asia Link | regional programme | | 2001–2007 | | www.europa.eu.int/comm/europaid/projects/asia-link/index_en.htm |
| Asia Pro Eco | regional programme | | 2002–2007 | | http://europa.eu.int/comm/europaid/projects/asia-pro-eco/index_en.htm |
| EU-China Small Projects Facility | general | EC Delegation Beijing; Ministry of Commerce MOFCOM, China International Centre for Economic and Technical Exchanges (CICETE) | 25.6.2003–25.4.2006 | 8m euros: grant | http://www.delchn.cec.eu.int/en/Co-operation/Project_Fiches.htm; project website: www.eucnspf.org |

**Table 7.1: continued**

| Project | Subject[a] | Parties (if known) | Duration by start date | Budget or type | Source |
|---|---|---|---|---|---|
| China Human Rights Microprojects Programme | rule of law and good governance | EC Delegation; EU Delegation Beijing | 1.1.2003–31.3.2006 | grant | http://www.delchn.cec.eu.int/en/Co-operation/Project_Fiches.htm |
| China-Europe Public Administration Programme (CEPA) | government | EC Delegation Beijing; MOFCOM, China National School of Administration | 20.1.2003–19.1.2007 | 5.7m euros:grant | http://www.delchn.cec.eu.int/en/Co-operation/Project_Fiches.htm |
| Asia-Invest | regional programme | | 2003–2007 | | www.europa.eu.int/comm/europaid/projects/asia-invest |
| Energy/Environment Programme | environment and sustainable development | EC Delegation Beijing; National Development and Reform Commission/Energy Research Institute, China National Petroleum Corporation and Ministry of Science and Technology | 24.5.2003–24.5.2008 | 20m euros:grant | http://www.eep.org.cn |
| Natural Forest Management Project | agriculture | EC Delegation Beijing: Ministry of Commerce MOFCOM; State Forestry Administration | 1.7.2003–30.6.2008 | 16.9m euros: grant | http://www.delchn.cec.eu.int/en/Co-operation/Project_Fiches.htm |
| EU-China Programme to Support China's Integration into the World Trading System | trade | EC Delegation Beijing; Ministry of Commerce (MOFCOM) WTO Affairs Department | 8.2.2004–30.11.2008 | 15m euros:grant | www.euchinawto.org |

**Table 7.1: continued**

| Project | Subject[a] | Parties (if known) | Duration by start date | Budget or type | Source |
|---|---|---|---|---|---|
| EU-China European Studies Centres Programme (ESCP) | economic and social reform, education and training | EC Delegation Beijing; China Academy of Social Sciences (CASS) | 2004–2008 | 10.33m euros: grant | www.escp.com.cn |
| EU-China Biodiversity Programme | environment and sustainable development | EC Delegation Beijing; State Environmental Protection Administration (SEPA) and UNDP | 7.10.2005–31.3.2010 | 30m euros:grant | http://www.delchn.cec.eu.int/en/Co-operation/Project_Fiches.htm |
| EU-China IPR Cooperation Programme | IPR | | follow-up under 2005–2006 financial assistance programme | | http://ec.europa.eu/comm/external_relations/china/intro/sect.htm, accessed 28.3.2007 |
| Erasmus Mundus China Window Programme | educational scholarships for Chinese students and scholars to study in the UK | DG EAC | 2005–2009 | 9m euros | http://ec.europa.eu/comm/external_relations/china/summit_1204/memo04_284.htm, accessed 6.4.2007 |
| China-EU Information Society Project | regulation, e-government, training, knowledge transfer | European Commission, State Council Information Office (SCITO) | 2005–2009 (preceded by Euro China 2002 Information Society Forum, Beijing, 16.4.2002) | 15m euros: grant | www.eu-china-infso.org; http://ec.europa.eu/comm/external_relations/china/summit_1204/memo04_284.htm, accessed 6.4.2007; project website: www.eu-china.infso.org |
| EU-China Biodiversity Programme | environment and sustainable development | EC Delegation Beijing; State Environmental Protection Administration (SEPA) and UNDP | 7.10.2005–31.3.2010 | 30m euros:grant | http://www.delchn.cec.eu.int/en/Co-operation/Project_Fiches.htm |

**Table 7.1: continued**

| Project | Subject[a] | Parties (if known) | Duration by start date | Budget or type | Source |
|---|---|---|---|---|---|
| EU-China Managers Exchange and Training Programme | management training and internships, language training and seminars, teacher training and exchange | EC Delegation Beijing | 2006–2010 | 17.2m euros (grant) | http://ec.europa.eu/comm/external_relations/china/summit_1204/memo04_284.htm, accessed 6.4.2007 |
| River Basin Management Programme | environment and sustainable development | EC Delegation Beijing: MWR, SEPA | 2006–2010 | 25m euros: grant | http://www.delchn.cec.eu.int/en/Co-operation/Project_Fiches.htm |
| EU-China Social Security Reform Cooperation Project | economic and social reform, support construction of social security system in China | EC Delegation Beijing; Ministry of Labour and Social Security | 1.4.2006–31.12.2010 | 20m euros: grant | http://ec.europa.eu/comm/external_relations/china/intro/sect.htm, accessed 28.3.2007; http://ec.europa.eu/comm/external_relations/china7summit_1204/memo04_284.htm, accessed 6.4.2007 |
| Memorandum of Understanding to build in China a near zero emission coal-fired power plant before 2020 | environment and sustainable development | | signed in Shanghai, February 2006 | | http://ec.europa.eu/comm/external_relations/china/intro/sect.htm, accessed 28.3.2007 |
| Governance for Equitable Development | rule of law and good governance | | 2007–2112 | | http://www.delchn.cec.eu.int/en/Co-operation/Project_Fiches.htm |

**Table 7.1: continued**

| Project | Subject[a] | Parties (if known) | Duration by start date | Budget or type | Source |
|---|---|---|---|---|---|
| Chinese partners participate 'in more than 100 research projects funded by the Commission's Framework Programme for research' | | | | | http://ec.europa.eu/comm/external_relations/china/intro/sect.htm, accessed 28.3.2007 |
| EU-China 'S&T Year' | science and technology | | | | http://ec.europa.eu/comm/external_relations/china/intro/sect.htm, accessed 28.3.2007 |
| Action Plan on Clean Coal | environment and sustainable development | | | | http://ec.europa.eu/comm/external_relations/china/intro/sect.htm, accessed 28.3.2007 |
| Terms of Reference for an Action Plan on Industrial Cooperation, Energy Efficiency and Renewable Energies | environment and sustainable development | | | | http://ec.europa.eu/comm/external_relations/china/intro/sect.htm, accessed 28.3.2007 |
| International Thermonuclear Experimental Reactor (ITER), involving European Community, China, India, Japan, South Korea, United States | energy | | signed in Paris, 21.11.2006 (see Chapter 5 in this book) | | http://ec.europa.eu/comm/external_relations/china/intro/sect.htm, accessed 28.3.2007 |

**Table 7.1: continued**

| Project | Subject[a] | Parties (if known) | Duration by start date | Budget or type | Source |
|---|---|---|---|---|---|
| Europe-China School of Law | rule of law and good governance, education, professional training | | financing agreement signed 17.1.07, Beijing | 18.2m euro (EU contribution) | http://www.delchn.cec.eu.int/en/whatsnew/pren170107b.htm, accessed 6.4.2007 |
| EU-China Project on the Protection of Intellectual Property | IPR enforcement | | financing agreement signed 17.1.07, Beijing | 10.85m euro (EU contribution) | http://www.delchn.cec.eu.int/en/whatsnew/pren170107b.htm, accessed 6.4.2007 |
| Europe-China Business Management Training Project | training | | financing agreement signed 17.1.07, Beijing | 8.15m (EU contribution) | http://www.delchn.cec.eu.int/en/whatsnew/pren170107b.htm, accessed 6.4.2007 |

[a]Classification is based partly on Delegation of the European Commission to China, Index of Projects, available at http://www.delchn.cec.eu.int/eu/Co-operation/Project_Fiches.htm, accessed 24 July 2007.

**Table 7.2: EU–China Cooperation Projects Completed to 2006**

| Project | Subject | Duration (by start date) | Budget or type | Website | Source |
|---|---|---|---|---|---|
| EU-China Higher Education Programme | education | 1997–2001 | | | http://www.delchn.cec.eu.int/en/Co-operation/Project_Fiches.htm |
| EU-China Liaoning Integrated Environmental Programme | environment | 1999–2005 | | http://www.eu-liep.org | http://www.delchn.cec.eu.int/en/Co-operation/Project_Fiches.htm |
| EU-China Legal and Judicial Cooperation Programme | governance and law, professional training | 2000–2005 | 13.5 m euros | www-lawprojectforum.org | http://www.delchn.cec.eu.int/en/Co-operation/Project_Fiches.htm |
| EU-China Intellectual Property Rights Cooperation Programme | IPR | 2000–2005 | | | http://www.delchn.cec.eu.int/en/Co-operation/Project_Fiches.htm |
| EU-China Basic Education Cooperation Programme | education | 2001–2005 | | www.eugs.net | http://www.delchn.cec.eu.int/en/Co-operation/Project_Fiches.htm |
| EU-China Programme for the Development of Vocational Training for the Industry | vocational training | 2001–2005 | | www.eugs.net | http://www.delchn.cec.eu.int/en/Co-operation/Project_Fiches.htm |
| Panam Integrated Rural Development Project | rural development | 2001–2005 | | http://www.pirdp.org | http://www.delchn.cec.eu.int/en/Co-operation/Project_Fiches.htm |
| EC-China Environmntal Management Cooperation Programme (EMCP) | environment | 2001–2005 | | http:emcp.acca21.org.cn | http://www.delchn.cec.eu.int/en/Co-operation/Project_Fiches.htm |
| EU-China Training Programme on Village Governance | governance | 22.5.2001–21.5.2006 | 10.67m euros:grant | www.chinarural.org/euchinaprog/ | http://www.delchn.cec.eu.int/en/Co-operation/Project_Fiches.htm |
| Framework Programme for EU Support to China's Accession to WTO | trade, law, professional training | 2001–2006 | 3.6m euro | | http://www.delchn.cec.eu.int/en/Co-operation/Project_Fiches.htm |
| China-Europe International Business School (CEIBS) | education | Phase II (2001–2006) | | www.jxsme.com | http://www.delchn.cec.eu.int/en/Co-operation/Project_Fiches.htm |

**Table 7.2: continued**

| Project | Subject | Duration (by start date) | Budget or type | Website | Source |
|---|---|---|---|---|---|
| EU-China Enterprise Reform Project | economic reform | 2002–2005 | | www.jxsme.com | http://www.delchn.cec.eu.int/en/Co-operation/Project_Fiches.htm |
| EU-China Financial Services Cooperation Project | financial services | 1.1.2003–31.12.2006 | 8.50m euros: grant | www.eufscp.org | http://www.delchn.cec.eu.int/en/Co-operation/Project_Fiches.htm |
| Human Rights Micro Project Programme | human rights | 2004–2006 | 1.34m euros: grant | www.europa.eu.int/comm/europeaid/projects/eidhr/index_en.htm | http://www.delchn.cec.eu.int/en/Co-operation/Project_Fiches.htm |
| Integrated Pest Management for Cotton in Asia | agriculture | | | | http://www.delchn.cec.eu.int/en/Co-operation/Project_Fiches.htm |
| Human Rights Micro Project Programme | human rights | 2004–2006 | 1.34m euros: grant | www.europa.eu.int/comm/europeaid/projects/eidhr/index_en.htm | http://www.delchn.cec.eu.int/en/Co-operation/Project_Fiches.htm |
| EU-China Junior Managers Training Programme | economic reform, training | | | | http://www.delchn.cec.eu.int/en/Co-operation/Project_Fiches.htm |
| EU-China Cooperation in the Field of Public Procurement – Pilot Project | public procurement, economic reform | | | | http://www.delchn.cec.eu.int/en/Co-operation/Project_Fiches.htm |
| Qinghai Livestock Development | agriculture | | | | http://www.delchn.cec.eu.int/en/Co-operation/Project_Fiches.htm |
| EU-China Qinghai Potato Development Project | agriculture | | | | http://www.delchn.cec.eu.int/en/Co-operation/Project_Fiches.htm |
| EU-China Technical & Commercial Cooperation within the Dairy and Food Processing Sector | agriculture, food | | | | http://www.delchn.cec.eu.int/en/Co-operation/Project_Fiches.htm |

**Table 7.2: continued**

| Project | Subject | Duration (by start date) | Budget or type | Website | Source |
|---|---|---|---|---|---|
| EU-China Cooperation Programme in Statistics | statistics | | | | http://www.delchn.cec.eu.int/en/Co-operation/Project_Fiches.htm |
| Water Buffalo Development Project | agriculture | | | | http://www.delchn.cec.eu.int/en/Co-operation/Project_Fiches.htm |
| adjustrightVocational Training Project for the Disabled | social services, public health | | | | http://www.delchn.cec.eu.int/en/Co-operation/Project_Fiches.htm |
| Vehicle Emission Control Cooperation Project | environment | | | | http://www.delchn.cec.eu.int/en/Co-operation/Project_Fiches.htm |
| Capacity Building for Municipal Solid Waste Management Reform in China | environment, public health | | | | http://www.delchn.cec.eu.int/en/Co-operation/Project_Fiches.htm |

This table is based mainly on the website of the Delegation of the European Commission, Beijing, http://www.del.chn.cec.eu/en/Co-operation/Project_Fiches.htm

were oriented toward specific objectives, such as professional training in law, support for China's accession to the World Trade Organization or targeted types of agricultural cooperation.

On the European side, cooperation projects with China are not limited to the European Community: numerous EU Member States have also entered into bilateral agreements to establish cooperation projects with China. Table 7.3 gives an overview of European cooperation projects with China by the various European partners as of June 2007. The table is intended to be indicative rather than exhaustive, since it does not take account of information from Chinese sources concerning projects with individual EU Member States.

**Table 7.3: Overview of European Cooperation Projects with China by European Partner**

| Country | Number of projects | Total amount (in million euro) | Main sectors by number of projects |
|---|---|---|---|
| Austria | 6 | 4.12 | Education |
| Denmark | 4 | 20.05 | Energy |
| European Commission | 131 | 255.42 | Education, business, environment |
| Finland | 50 | Not available | Not available |
| France | 28 | 348.13 | Water, energy |
| Germany | 138 | 1018.90 | Environment, agriculture, education |
| Italy | 26 | 118.74 | Energy, health |
| Luxembourg | 1 | 0.2 | Health |
| Netherlands | 21 | 46.46 | Government |
| Spain | 2 | 1.45 | Energy |
| Sweden | 25 | 27.96 | Environment |
| UK | 32 | 410.98 | Health,multi-sector |

Source: Delegation of the European Commission, Beijing, available at http://delchn.cec.eu.int (accessed 6 April 2007).

We can draw several conclusions from this table. First, not all EU Member States have cooperation projects with China. Only 11 Member States have such projects, out of a total of 27 current EU Member States.

Secondly, the distribution of China projects among EU Member States is extremely uneven, both in number of projects and in total expenditure. Germany leads the group with 138 projects, compared, for example, to the UK with 32 projects, France with 28, Italy with 26 and Spain with only 2, to mention only EU Member States with roughly the same population as Germany. Note, however, that Finland has 50 projects, even more than the UK. Concerning expenditure, Germany leads with €1,018.90m, followed among Member States by the UK with €410.98m, France with €348.13m and Italy with €118.74m. There is no direct correlation between expenditure and number of projects.

Thirdly, perhaps the most surprising fact to emerge from the table is that Germany, with 138 China projects, has even more cooperation projects with China than the European Commission, which has 131 projects. In fact, German expenditure is almost four times the total expenditure of the European Commission (€255.42m). France and the UK also spend more on China projects than does the European Commission. In this context, it is helpful to recall that Germany is the only EU Member State which has a roughly equal trade balance with China; in other words, the financial value of German exports to China are almost as much as that of Chinese exports to Germany. These are official EU statistics, though it is necessary to bear in mind that 'project' may have many meanings and also that these figures should be taken as an indication of the general order of magnitude rather than as precise accounting data.

Table 7.4 helps us to explore these differences between EU Member States in more detail. It shows a breakdown of Europe–China cooperation projects by Member State (including total expenditure) and by sector. The projects concerned are those financed by the EC or its Member States and ongoing as of April 2007. As well as the European partner of China and the sector in which the project is undertaken, the table also shows the total expenditure by the European Commission and each EU Member State involved in cooperation projects with China, with the exception of Finland, for which expenditure data is not publicly available. This exception is unfortunate because, as the previous table indicated, Finland has 50 projects with China, more than any other single Member State bar Germany. It is also unfortunate that data does not seem to be publicly available on the expenditure by different Member States according to the sectors in which the projects are undertaken.

Of the 389 total projects indicated, the main fields of cooperation projects are education (76 projects, or 19.5% of total projects), environment (66 projects, or 17% of total projects), energy (39 projects, or 10% of total projects) and health (34 projects, or 9% of total projects). The largest share of EU projects concern education (47 projects, or 35.9% of a total of 131 projects).

An example is the Erasmus Mundus programme in higher education.[2] It includes a 'China Window', which in 2006–2007 supported 81 Chinese students under the general Erasmus Mundus programme, an additional 99 students under the 'Asian Windows' section and 32 scholars under the 'China Window.'[3] In 2007–2008, the programme supported 136 Chinese students under the general programme, 37 under the 'Asia Window/China Window' and 21 Chinese scholars.[4]

Another example is the Europe–China School of Law, announced in 2006 and for which €18.2m has been allocated to improve the knowledge and skills of the Chinese legal profession and enhance the stability of economic and social reforms in China.[5] As education is a field in which the EC Treaty provides that both the EC and the Member States have competence, that is, the legal power to make agreements, the

[2] See http://ec.europa.eu/education/programmes/mundus/projects_en.html (accessed 29 September 2007).

[3] See Europa, 'Erasmus Mundus 2006–2007: More than 1600 Graduates to Study and Teach in Europe's Universities', IP/06/789 (Brussels, 15 June 2006), available at www.europa.eu/rapid/pressReleasesAction.do?reference=IP/06/789&format=HTML&aged=0&language=EN&guiLanguage=en (accessed 29 September 2007).

[4] See http://ec.europa.eu/education/programmes/mundus/projects_en.html (accessed 29 September 2007).

[5] For the basic documents, see http://ec.europa.eu/europeaid/cgi/frame12.pl/right?reference=125527&hidden_type=T1 (accessed 29 September 2007).

**Table 7.4: Europe–China Cooperation Projects as of April 2007 by Member State and Sector**

| | European Commission | AUS | DMK | FRA | GER | ITA | LUX | NL | SP | SW | UK | Total amount (million Euros) | Total number of projects |
|---|---|---|---|---|---|---|---|---|---|---|---|---|---|
| Agriculture | 3 | | | | 17 | | | 1 | | | | | 21 |
| Banking | 1 | | | | 5 | | | | | | | | 6 |
| Business | 22 | | | | 1 | | | | | | | | 23 |
| Economic and structural reform and environment | | | | | 1 | | | | | | | | 1 |
| Education | 47 | 2 | | | 17 | 4 | | | | | 6 | | 76 |
| Emergency | | | | 1 | | | | | | | | | 1 |
| Energy | 5 | | 4 | 6 | 12 | 8 | | 1 | 2 | 1 | | | 39 |
| Environment | 14 | | | 1 | 32 | 3 | | 2 | | 11 | 3 | | 66 |
| Gender | | | | | | | | | | 2 | | | 2 |
| Government | 4 | 1 | | 3 | 3 | | | 14 | | | 1 | | 26 |
| Health | 4 | 1 | | 4 | 4 | 8 | 1 | | | 4 | 8 | | 34 |
| Human rights | | | | | | | | | | 3 | | | 3 |
| Industry | 13 | | | | 4 | | | 1 | | | 3 | | 21 |
| Multi-sector | 2 | | | | 7 | | | | | | 7 | | 16 |
| NGO | | | | | 6 | | | | | | | | 6 |
| Population | 1 | | | | 1 | | | | | | | | 2 |
| Project administration | | | | | | | | | | 1 | | | 1 |
| Public administration | | | | | | | | | | 1 | | | 1 |
| Railway | | | | 1 | | | | | | | | | 1 |
| Rural | 4 | | | | 10 | | | 1 | | | | | 15 |
| Social | 3 | | | | 3 | | | | | | | | 6 |

**Table 7.4: continued**

| | European Commission | AUS | DMK | FRA | GER | ITA | LUX | NL | SP | SW | UK | Total amount (million Euros) | Total number of projects |
|---|---|---|---|---|---|---|---|---|---|---|---|---|---|
| Trade | 2 | | | | 3 | | | | | | | | 5 |
| Transport | 3 | | | 3 | 3 | | | | | | | | 9 |
| Water | 3 | | | 9 | 5 | | | 1 | | 1 | 3 | | 22 |
| Women | | | | | 1 | | | | | | 1 | | 2 |
| Unallocated | | 2 | | | 3 | 4 | | | | | | | 9 |
| Unclassified | | | | | | | | | | 1 | | | 1 |
| Total projects | 131 | 6 | 4 | 28 | 138 | 27 | 1 | 21 | 2 | 25 | 32 | | 389 |
| Total amount (million euros) | 255.452 | 4.12 | 20.05 | 348.13 | 1081.9 | 118.74 | 0.20 | 46.64 | 1.45 | 27.96 | 410.98 | 2315.622 | |

Source: Calculated from 'Overview of European Union Ongoing Cooperation Projects in China', available at http://delchn.cec.eu.int (accessed 11April 2007).

agreements concerning these projects would usually involve both the EC and its Member States on the European side. Of the 138 German projects with China, 32 projects concern the environment, 17 (12.3%) concern agriculture and another 17 deal with education (12.3%). Available data do not indicate whether the German projects in education are jointly with or separate from the EC projects in the same sector.

The total expenditure by these European partners for ongoing projects with China as of April 2007 amounts to €2315.62m. Table 7.4 indicates the expenditure for projects by the European Commission or different EU Member States in total, though not by sector. As expected, the largest expenditure is by Germany (€1,081.90m, or 47% of the total expenditure). The UK (€410.98m, or 17.7% of the total) and France (€348.13m, or 15% of the total) also rank above the European Commission (€255.45m). In drawing these provisional conclusions, one must bear in mind the lacunae in the data already noted, and also that the classification of projects is done by the cooperating authorities and some categories overlap.

We can conclude this brief survey of EU–China cooperation projects by referring to recent EU National Indicative Programmes (NIP) for China[6] and the recent Country Stategy Paper for China 2007–2013.[7] The China NIP for 2002–2004 classified programmes at that time into three main categories: support to social and economic reforms, environment and sustainable development, and good governance/strengthening rule of law. Initial allocation of funds provided for €75m, €45m and €30m, respectively, for each category. In contrast, the 2005–2006 NIP classified projects into seven main categories, each with its own financing: general (€8m), human resource development (€69.51m), rule of law and good governance (€32.31m), economic and social reform (€48.71m), environment (€87.80m), rural and agricultural (€7.60m), non-governmental organization financing and health/population (€4.36m). Most were financed mainly before the 2002–2004 NIP, except for the programme to support China's integration into the world trading system, itself part of the category for economic and social reform. The EU's 2007–2013 Country Strategy Paper for China reviewed previous cooperation. It reaffirmed the 2005–2006 priorities as well as the support for policy dialogues and so-called 'thematic interventions', such as democracy and human rights, non-state actors in development, migration and asylum, human resources, and environment and sustainable management of natural resources, including energy.[8] This evolution, together with the tables presented here, demonstrates the development, gradual diversification and, to some extent, increase in expenditure of EU–China cooperation programmes. These changes contribute to and reflect the transformation of the intensity, form and content of EU–China relations.

[6] European Commission, 'National Indicative Programme 2005–2006: China', available at www.europa.eu.int (last accessed 15 June 2007). For further details and recent documents, see chapter 3.

[7] See chapter 3.

[8] See chapter 3 for the EU's China Strategy Paper 2007–2013. A detailed breakdown of ongoing or recently completed projects financed under thematic budget lines or Asia-wide programmes is given at pp 28–32 of the Strategy Paper.

# 8

# Relations between the EU and Hong Kong and Macao, 1989–Present

## INTRODUCTION

The European Union has extensive relations not only with mainland China, but also with Hong Kong and Macao. Hong Kong, as agreed by the UK and the PRC in the 1984 Sino-British Joint Declaration,[1] reverted to Chinese sovereignty on 1 July 1997. Under the principle of 'One Country, Two Systems', it became a Special Administrative Region (SAR) of the PRC. Similarly, Macao, following the terms of the 1987 Sino-Portuguese Declaration on the Question of Macao,[2] became an SAR of the PRC on 20 December 1999. This chapter presents policy papers, related documents and bilateral agreements between the EU and Hong Kong and between the EU and Macao. The first section concerns Hong Kong and the second section considers Macao.

## HONG KONG

Since the reversion of Hong Kong to China, Hong Kong is governed partly by the Basic Law of the Hong Kong Special Administrative Region of the People's Republic of China.[3] According to Article 151 of the Basic Law, the Hong Kong SAR:

> may on its own, using the name 'Hong Kong, China', maintain and develop relations and conclude and implement agreements with foreign states and regions and relevant

[1] Joint Declaration of the United Kingdom of Great Britain and Northern Ireland and the Government of the People's Republic of China on the Question of Hong Kong, signed in Beijing on 19 December 1084, available at http://www.hkbu.edu.hk/~pchksar/JD/jd-full1.htm (accessed 24 November 2007).

[2] Joint Declaration of the Government of the People's Republic of China and the Government of the Republic of Portugal on the Question of Macau, signed in Beijing on 13 April 1987, available at http://www.macau99.org/mo/e_doc_declaracao.html, or http://www.imprensa.macau.gov.mo/bo/i/88/23/dc/en/ (accessed 24 November 2007).

[3] For the text and related material, see http://www.info.gov.hk/basic_law/fulltext/ (accessed 23 September 2007).

international organisations in the appropriate fields, including the economic, trade, financial and monetary, shipping, communications, tourism, cultural and sports fields.

Hong Kong, China is a founder member of the World Trade Organization (WTO).

Since 1997, the EU has issued two policy papers in the form of Commission communications on Hong Kong (see Table 8.1). The first policy paper on Hong Kong was issued on 23 April 1997 (see Document 7.1).

**Table 8.1: EU Policy Papers on Hong Kong, 1997–Present**

| Document | Title | Author | Place and date | Reference |
|---|---|---|---|---|
| Communication from the Commission to the Council | The European Union and Hong Kong: Beyond 1997 | Commission of the European Communities | Brussels, 23.4.1997 | COM(97) 171 final |
| Communication from the Commission to the Council and the European Parliament | The European Union, Hong Kong and Macao: possibilities for cooperation 2007–2013 | Commission of the European Communities | Brussels, 26.10.2006 | COM(2006) 648 final |

## Document 8.1: Communication from the Commission to the Council, 'The European Union and Hong Kong: Beyond 1997' (1997)

### COMMUNICATION FROM THE COMMISSION TO THE COUNCIL THE EUROPEAN UNION AND HONG KONG : BEYOND 1997

1. The Dublin European Council in December 1996 "reiterated the European Union's strong interest in the future peace and prosperity" of Hong Kong. This communication seeks to lay out what the transfer of sovereignty means for the European Union and its many interests in Hong Kong, and how EU-Hong Kong relations will develop in the years to come.

2. On 1 July 1997, Hong Kong reverts to Chinese sovereignty. This peaceful transfer of sovereignty will be a unique event, and will create a unique entity, the Hong Kong Special Administrative Region of the People's Republic of China. Hong Kong has long stood as an example and a model for its neighbours throughout the region. It has always been an international crossroads: it is a trading centre, a magnet for investment, a media hub, a transit point for travellers worldwide. Hong Kong lives by its relations with the outside world, with its strong tradition of openness making it a home for the exchange of goods, finance, people and ideas. Hong Kong's future is therefore of profound importance for the international community.

**European interests in Hong Kong**

3. European interests in Hong Kong have many aspects:

- a deep economic involvement. The importance of Hong Kong as a trading centre is well established: Hong Kong is the EC's tenth largest trading partner, and one with whom the EC maintains a healthy surplus. But economic ties go beyond trade. There are over 100 European companies involved in banking, insurance, and the securities industry in Hong Kong. Some 250 European companies have their regional headquarters in Hong Kong, and some 100 European companies manufacture in Hong Kong. 115 European companies have been involved m the construction of the new Hong Kong airport project, winning almost 40% of the business. Although Hong Kong investment in Europe has been much more slow to develop, investment in the services sector has slowly increased.

  Two particular points are worth noting about these extraordinarily diverse economic ties. First, all Member States are involved, with five Member States enjoying trade of over 2 billion ecu with Hong Kong. Second, recent years have seen an acceleration of economic links, with more trade and more companies settling in Hong Kong. This tends to confirm surveys indicating business' confidence in Hong Kong's future prosperity.

  These economic ties have long been cemented through Hong Kong's autonomous participation in the world trading system. For example, arrangements for Hong Kong's textiles exports to the EC have been settled bilaterally for many years, with a bilateral textiles agreement under the Multi-Fibre Agreement now subsumed into the Agreement on Textiles and Clothing.

- close personal ties. Over 50,000 EU citizens are in Hong Kong at any one time, with some 32,000 settled in Hong Kong. This means there are more Europeans in Hong Kong than in any other city in Asia. This is reflected in the number of cultural and educational contacts between the EU and Hong Kong, with over 60 ongoing research and cooperation actions between European and Hong Kong universities.

  These ties reflect the reality that in many respects, Europeans and Hong Kong people share many of the same values. Hong Kong is renowned for its openness, its willingness to look at new ideas and to debate. As such Hong Kong has always proved an important channel for exchange of all kinds between Europe and Asia. This is an important facet of Hong Kong, and one which will remain a defining characteristic of Hong Kong as an SAR.

- continuing political interests. Although sovereignty over Hong Kong will pass from the United Kingdom, the Joint Declaration deposited as an international agreement at the United Nations will continue to regulate Hong Kong until 1 July 2047. But the EU also has a broader continuing interest in Hong Kong, as a territory of strategic importance in the region, with a developing democracy and freedom of speech and expression.

4. The breadth of these interests is the explanation of the wide range of current European links with Hong Kong, and gives every reason to believe that the ongoing development of relations in the future will be a key element in the EU's future relations with China. The implementation of the "one country, two systems" policy embodied in the Joint Declaration will be central for this continued development to become a reality: the conditions provided in the SAR will preserve the environment required for the successful evolution of European interests in Hong Kong.

**Hong Kong as a Special Administrative Region**

5. The United Kingdom and China agreed to the transfer of sovereignty of Hong Kong under the Sino-British Joint Declaration in 1984. China's policies on Hong Kong and the elaboration of those policies in the Joint Declaration were reflected in the Basic Law of the Hong Kong SAR, promulgated in 1990 and due to take effect on 1 July 1997. The core principle behind Hong Kong's new status was to be "one country, two systems", the idea that Hong Kong would operate under a political, legal and economic system distinct from that of China. As such. Hong Kong will become a "Special Administrative Region" (SAR) of China.

6. As an SAR, Hong Kong falls under Chinese sovereignty, and foreign and defence affairs will be regulated from Beijing. A garrison from the People's Liberation Army will be stationed in Hong Kong.. But in other areas, the "high degree of autonomy" given to Hong Kong makes the SAR a unique experiment. The Hong Kong SAR will have a large degree of economic autonomy, remaining a separate customs territory with an independent currency and financial system. China will levy no taxes in Hong Kong. But the scope of SAR autonomy extends beyond the economic. The SAR will retain executive, legislative and judicial power. The Government will be run by Hong Kong people, laws will be made in the Legislative Council, and the final judicial Court of Appeal will be in Hong Kong. The SAR government will be responsible for maintaining public order. The Joint Declaration also explicitly enshrines rights and freedoms including freedom of speech, assembly, association and religion. A fuller summary appears in Annex 1.

7. A central theme running through the Joint Declaration and the Basic Law is the importance of maintaining Hong Kong's international role. Hong Kong will continue to have a distinct voice as a separate member of numerous international organisations, including the World Trade Organisation, the World Customs Organisation, and APEC. Hong Kong will be able to sign international agreements as a separate party within the areas for which the SAR is responsible. There will also be a separate Hong Kong passport, and Hong Kong will remain host to official representations from across the world.

8. Much of the political debate about and within Hong Kong in recent years has centred on the interpretation of the SAR's autonomy, and how secure the provisions of the Joint Declaration would prove in practice. To some extent, uncertainty is inevitable when entering such uncharted waters. The European Commission pointed to the importance of implementing the principles of the Joint Declaration in its 1995 Communication on China.[1] The blueprint laid out in the Joint Declaration and the Basic Law is designed specifically to ensure that Hong Kong continues to thrive. Its effective implementation remains the best guarantee for Hong Kong in the future. This will also reinforce confidence in the transfer of sovereignty in Macau in 1999, and could provide some useful pointers to settling other disputes where the issues of practical autonomy and legal sovereignty need to be tackled.

9. Most of the differences which have arisen between the United Kingdom and China in the run-up to the transfer of sovereignty have now been settled. A major exception is the issue of the Legislative Council ("LegCo"). China has not agreed to the concept of a "through train" for the LegCo elected under new electoral arrangements in 1995. In December 1996, the members of a "provisional Legislature" were selected. It is intended that this body will replace the existing LegCo on 1 July 1997, and will itself be replaced after new elections within a year. There is a clear danger that the work of the provisional Legislature before the transfer of sovereignty will create confusion about responsibility for legislation, which would be damaging for the rule of law in Hong Kong. It is essential that the procedures adopted to enact new or amended laws to govern the SAR do not open those laws to lengthy

legal challenge in the months and years to come. Early elections for a new LegCo, on a free and fair basis, would be the best way to ensure that the LegCo can play its part in the governance of the SAR fully and effectively.

10. The provisions of the Joint Declaration and the Basic Law confirming individual rights and liberties in Hong Kong are not only of importance to individual Hong Kong people. Respect of key freedoms such as free speech, the right of assembly, data protection and the right to form active political parties will be critical to confidence in the governance of Hong Kong as an SAR, and to the maintenance of the rule of law. Hong Kong's role as a regional hub would make any restrictions on the Press, news agencies or other information channels particularly damaging.

**Working to support European interests in Hong Kong**

11. Confidence in Hong Kong's future, both within Hong Kong and in the international community, is based on the conviction that the SAR model will preserve the features of Hong Kong government and society which lie behind its current success. Making the SAR a reality and a success is therefore critical. Primary responsibility for achieving this must lie with the Hong Kong government and with the Chinese authorities. The unique nature of the SAR makes this a challenging task, but all parties seem convinced that this goal is in their mutual interests.

12. The international community also has a role to play in ensuring that the SAR lives up to its task and to the responsibilities it has been given under the Joint Declaration. Europe can play its part in helping the SAR government as an autonomous administration to operate as foreseen:

- In areas within the responsibility of the SAR government, the EU should continue to deal directly with Hong Kong. These areas are clearly laid out in the Joint Declaration, and this will mean maintaining a dialogue with the SAR government in these areas, including direct liaison with Hong Kong in international organisations to which it is a separate party. The Commission established an Office in Hong Kong in 1993, which has proved an effective voice for European interests in Hong Kong. The Chinese authorities responsible for official representations in Hong Kong have agreed in principle that the Office may continue to liaise directly with the SAR government. The Commission is currently finalising with the Chinese authorities agreement on the privileges and immunities that the Office will enjoy after 30 June of this year.

  One of the areas of SAR government responsibility is trade policy. Hong Kong will continue to be a wholly separate entity for trade policy purposes. As a separate customs territory, it will continue to be treated in its own right in terms of origin, GSP and anti-dumping rules, and in respect of the remaining quotas on textiles as we move towards elimination in 2005. The few' quantitative restrictions still maintained on exports from China will not apply to products manufactured in Hong Kong. Hong Kong will continue to be an important partner within the World Trade Organisation.

- The SAR concept is not limited to trade and economic matters. Its provisions cementing an independent administration, a distinct legal system guaranteeing the rule of law, a separate elected legislature, a free Press, and a series of fundamental rights and privileges are all core elements in the package. All the different aspects of Hong Kong as an SAR are interrelated: the business community relies on the rule of law in Hong Kong; the financial markets need to be guaranteed accurate and free access to all types of information; maintaining Hong Kong's entrepreneurial dynamism means keeping open the free flow of ideas and debate.

The Dublin European Council underlined the EU's continuing support for and commitment to the principle that all the rights granted to Hong Kong citizens under the SAR should be fully respected. The EU should ensure permanent vigilance and keep-a watching brief on developments in Hong Kong. We welcome the recent announcement that China will sign, before the end of 1997, the UN Covenant on Economic, Social and Cultural Rights, and that China is considering also signing the Covenant on Civil and Political Rights. We hope that China will also soon accept the proposition that the maintenance of the two UN human rights covenants in Hong Kong implies that the reporting requirements under those covenants should also be maintained. The international community will in any case have other ways of monitoring the situation in Hong Kong. In the case of the EU, this should mean regular consideration of the situation in Hong Kong, and active use of the instruments – common positions, joint actions, political dialogue, cooperation – at the EU's disposal. As a basis for such discussions, the Commission intends to publish an annual report on EU-Hong Kong relations across the board, beginning in 1998. The issue will clearly figure in the EU's political dialogue with China, and Hong Kong could be included in any future initiatives to develop cooperation in the human dimension in the region.

Both the Commission and the Member States should ensure that contact is in no way diminished after the handover: high level visits to Hong Kong should be a priority. Hong Kong depends on confidence, and alertness in the international community is an important guarantee to sustain this confidence. The interests of the international community in Hong Kong's future are very similar: the EU should work together with key international partners to pursue a common approach.

- Another important way in which the EU can recognise the autonomy of Hong Kong is (o reaffirm clearly that, for the purposes of the common visa list. Hong Kong should be assessed after the handover as it is now, on it own merits. This would reflect our confidence in the arrangements Hong Kong is making to ensure that the new Hong Kong SAR passport is secure. The SAR will control temporary or permanent movement into its territory, whether from the rest of the PRC or elsewhere. Hong Kong SAR passports will be issued under SAR authority, and will incorporate the most up-to-date anti-forgery 'technology available. The decision about whether 10 grant visa-free access lies with each Member State- But the benefits which easy travel gives to developing economic and other contacts, and the importance of demonstrating confidence in Hong Kong's future, suggest (hat freer access to the EU would be in the interests of both the EU and of Hong Kong.

13. At the same time as helping to ensure that autonomy is a reality, the EC should do more to encourage the continued development of ties with Hong Kong. More formal and structured cooperation would be of benefit to both sides, for example in the area of customs cooperation and anti-fraud matters, where Council directives for the negotiation of an agreement already exist. The Commission will explore ways to put trade, investment and cooperation relations between the EC and the SAR on a more permanent footing, including through formal legal agreements in areas within SAR responsibility. Providing more systematic support to the development of such contacts would benefit both Europe and Hong Kong.

14. There are many fields where tangible cooperation could be developed with a real mutual benefit. The autumn 1997 IMF/World Bank meeting in Hong Kong will serve as a useful reminder of Hong Kong's global financial importance, and Hong Kong is to take its place in the "G-6" of key financial players in the Pacific. Hong Kong's communications infrastructure has cemented its role as an Asian hub for Europeans. So Hong Kong's particular experience in the fields of services or the media would make these obvious starting points for further collaboration. Cooperation in the environmental field could also be to real mutual advantage, whilst the growing cooperation in areas such as business to business contact between small and medium sized enterprises, and research and technology, should be developed further. European universities increasingly see Hong Kong as a natural home for research collaboration in Asia. In all these areas, as well as in other sectors of cooperation, there is every reason to see Hong Kong continuing to act as a pivotal point of communication between Europe and Asia.

15. For many Europeans, Hong Kong is the natural first point of contact with Asia. Hong Kong therefore has a particular role to play in the EU's rapidly developing policy towards Asia as a whole. Ever since the 1994 Asia strategy[2], ties have been intensified with Asia both on a bilateral and plurilateral level, with the first-ever Asia-Europe Meeting (ASEM) held at summit level in Bangkok in March 1996. Hong Kong is not an ASEM participant, and the political side of ASEM activity goes beyond the competence of the SAR government. But as a range of different activities emerges from the Asia strategy process, with Asia in general and with China in particular. Hong Kong can be expected to play an important part. In cooperation programmes with developing Asia, for example. Hong Kong could have a useful role in providing local knowledge and contacts from a developed and open perspective.

**Conclusion**

16. The depth and breadth of European interests in Hong Kong make it inevitable that Hong Kong will continue to be a key partner for the EU in Asia, playing a central part in our relations with China. The EU should look forward to a vigorous and effective engagement with the SAR government within its areas of responsibility. This should involve:

- dealing directly with the Hong Kong government as an international partner, and maintaining regular and close contacts;
- continuing to treat Hong Kong as an independent entity for trade policy purposes, as an important partner within the WTO;
- monitoring closely the situation in Hong Kong and the respect for the rights granted to Hong Kong citizens under the SAR, working together with the international community and bringing EU instruments into play if necessary;
- acknowledging that the case for granting visa-free access for Hong Kong people should be treated on its own merits;
- exploring ways to put trade, investment and cooperation relations between the EC and the SAR on a more permanent footing;
- developing active cooperation with Hong Kong as an Asian hub.

Far from being a time to downgrade links with Hong Kong, 1997 should mark another step forward in the progressive enhancement of ties between the European Union and Hong Kong.

17. The Council is invited to note and to endorse the contents of this communication.

## ANNEX I HONG KONG AS A SPECIAL ADMINISTRATIVE REGION

**Background**

In 1841, British forces seized Hong Kong island. Kowloon was ceded in 1860 and a 99 year "lease" on the New Territories and some 235 islands was signed in 1898. With the land covered by the lease amounting to some 92% of Hong Kong's total land area, it became clear that Hong Kong's future would have to be clarified well ahead of the 1997 termination of the lease. China had consistently claimed full sovereignty over the whole of Hong Kong, but had also stressed its wish for a peaceful settlement. In 1982, negotiations between the United Kingdom and China began with the common aim of maintaining the long-term stability and prosperity of Hong Kong. The result was the Sino-British Joint Declaration of 1984, an international agreement deposited in the United Nations.

**Hong Kong as a Special Administrative Region**

The underlying principle behind the Joint Declaration is the idea of "one country, two systems", which means that whilst Hong Kong will fall under Chinese sovereignty, it will retain its current social, administrative, legal and economic characteristics. The "one country, two systems" approach represents an explicit desire by China for Hong Kong to remain different from the rest of the PRC. As such. Hong Kong will become a Special Administrative Region (SAR) of the People's Republic of China (PRC) on 1 July 1997, and this status will remain unchanged for at least 50 years. The Joint Declaration was transposed into Chinese law by the Basic Law of the Hong Kong Special Administrative Region (April 1990). The National People's Congress retains the power to amend the Basic Law.

A UK-China Joint Liaison Group (JLG) was set up to help implement the Joint Declaration and to flesh out the details. This will continue to meet until 2000. The JLG has often been bedevilled by political friction and disagreements, on issues including the legislative system, infrastructure projects, and the civil service. But the number of outstanding issues is now relatively small.

The SAR model grants Hong Kong a "high degree of autonomy", and "executive, legislative and independent judicial power". The only areas explicitly placed within the responsibility of Beijing are foreign and defence affairs.

(i) Executive. The SAR will be headed by a Chief Executive, whose functions include signing legislation, making appointments to government and the judiciary, conducting external affairs' for the SAR, granting pardons, and acting as a channel of communication to the Chinese government. The chief executive must be a permanent resident of Hong Kong, a Chinese citizen with no right of abode in a foreign country, and resident in Hong Kong for ,at least 20 years. The term of office is 5 years, renewable only once. The original method of selecting the Chief Executive is appointment by China after "selection by elections or through consultations held locally", but the ultimate aim is selection by universal suffrage after nomination by a "broadly representative nominating committee in accordance with democratic procedures".

The Chief Executive will appoint an Executive Council, made up of permanent Hong Kong residents, who are to be consulted about most major policy decisions. The Chief Executive is obliged to explain if he goes against the will of the majority in the Council.

A Commission Against Corruption is a formal institution of the SAR.

Principal officials of the Hong Kong SAR Government must be Hong Kong residents with no right of abode elsewhere, and should have been resident in Hong Kong for 15 years.' The Government must act within the law, and be accountable to the Legislative Council (Legco). Civil servants above a certain rank must be permanent residents, and all swear an oath to uphold the Basic Law and the Special Administrative Region. English can continue, alongside Chinese, as an official language.

(ii) Legislature. Under the terms of the Joint Declaration and the Basic Law, the Legislative Council will be responsible for lawmaking in Hong Kong. This includes the right to overrule a veto from the Chief Executive with a two-thirds majority: though the National People's Congress in Beying also has the power to annul Legco laws it considers contrary to the Basic Law in areas of central government responsibility. Legco also approves budgets and taxation, ratifies senior judicial appointments, conducts debates on matters of public interest, and scrutinises the executive (including mandating a commission of enquiry if the Chief Executive is suspected of serious wrongdoing).

Legco members again have to be permanent residents, though up to one-fifth of Legco members can have right of abode overseas or be non-Chinese citizens. The question of the method of choosing Legco members has been controversial, but the Basic Law includes some specific indications for the future. For example, in the SAR Legco's second term, 24 of the 60 members should be elected by geographical constituencies through direct elections, rising to 30 members for the third term. The ultimate aim is described as the election of all the members by universal suffrage.

The Basic Law also provides for the election of deputies from the SAR to the National People's Congress.

(iii) Legal System and Public Order. The Joint Declaration stated that the "laws currently in force in Hong Kong will remain basically unchanged". The judiciary will operate independently, the system of trial by jury will continue, and basic principles such as the right to a fair trial and presumption of innocence will be maintained. Hong Kong will have its own final Court of Appeal, and have jurisdiction over all cases except "acts of state such as defence and foreign afiairs".

The Joint Declaration lays out that the SAR government is responsible for public order, and the Chinese garrison to be stationed in Hong Kong "shall not interfere" in the local affairs of the region, and will abide by SAR law. The SAR is responsible for enacting laws against "any act of treason, secession, sedition, or subversion" against the PRC government, as well as against political activities by or links with foreign political organisations.

(iv) Individual Rights. The Basic Law lays out the rights and duties of permanent and non-permanent residents of Hong Kong, including "freedom of -speech, of the press and of publication; freedom of association, of assembly, of procession and of demonstration; and the right and freedom to form and join trade unions, and to strike." Also listed are freedom to vote and stand in elections for all permanent residents, freedom of the person, against arbitrary arrest, privacy of communications; freedom of movement, travel and emigration, freedom of conscience and religious belief, freedom to engage in academic research, and access to legal advice and to legal remedy.

The provisions of the International Covenant on Civil and Political Rights, the International Covenant on Economic, Social and Cultural Rights, and international labour conventions applying to Hong Kong are to remain in force, although China has made clear that it does not consider itself obliged to continue reporting requirements in respect of Hong Kong under international instruments to which it is not a party.

(v) The Economy. The Basic Law explains that "the socialist system ... shall not be practised" in the SAR, and that the "previous capitalist system" shall remain unchanged. Hong Kong's status as an international financial centre should be protected. The right to private property will be maintained, and land leases issued before me transfer of sovereignty respected.

Public finances will be independent. No taxes raised in Hong Kong will be remitted to Beijing (even the costs for the Chinese garrison in Hong Kong will be met by Beijing). Public finances will pursue a policy of a balanced budget, with the current policy of low taxation as a point of reference. Budget growth should keep within GDP growth.

Hong Kong will have autonomous economic, monetary, and financial policies, with a separate currency and reserve fund, and freedom of capital movements. Hong Kong will remain a free port with a free trade philosophy and free access for shipping. It will be a separate customs territory. Export quotas, tariff preferences and other arrangements obtained by the SAR will be used exclusively by the SAR. The SAR will issue its own certificates of origin.

The SAR will participate in relevant international organisations and international trade agreements as an independent entity, such as the World Trade Organisation and the World Customs Organisation.

(vi) External Relations. Though Beijing will be responsible for foreign affairs and defence, and will open a branch of the Chinese Ministry of Foreign Affairs in Hong Kong to conduct foreign relations, the SAR will conduct "relevant external relations" on its own, in areas such as the economy, trade, finance and monetary affairs, shipping, communications, tourism, culture and sport. SAR representatives can have a separate voice in PRC delegations to organisations reserved for states, identifying themselves as "Hong Kong, China". It can participate autonomously in organisations not limited to states. International agreements to which Hong Kong is a party and the PRC is not can continue in force in the SAR.

The SAR has the authority to issue passports and other travel documents and to apply immigration controls.

The SAR can maintain official or semi-official economic and trade missions in third countries.

Consulates and other official missions established in Hong Kong by states which have diplomatic relations with China will be maintained.

(vi) Other signs of autonomy. Chinese people will require permission to enter the SAR from other parts of the PRC. The Basic Law states that central and local government should not interfere in the running of the SAR, and need approval from both the SAR and Beijing to set up an office in Hong Kong. Hong Kong will have a regional flag and emblem.

The Basic Law also emphasises the SAR's autonomy in other areas, such as education, health, science and technology, culture and copyright, professional qualifications, sport, social welfare, and labour law. Special mention is made of the continuing work of non-governmental organisations in these fields.

## ANNEX II EUROPEAN ECONOMIC INTERESTS IN HONG KONG

Not only is Hong Kong a major trading partner of the EC (see statistics attached). The scale of European economic activity within Hong Kong is considerable. Of the 2,068 companies which have established regional headquarters or offices in Hong Kong, 597 (29%) have EU-based parent companies. This compares to 501 from Japan, and 344 from the United States. The EC's interests also range across many fields of economic activity:

(i) Trading. Trading still represents the major European economic interest in Hong Kong, reflecting its continued place at the heart of the Hong Kong economy (the trading and retail sector accounts for a quarter of the Hong Kong economy). Some 43% of the EU companies which have established regional headquarters or offices in Hong Kong are engaged in trade.

(ii) Manufacturing. In spite of the shift in the Hong Kong economy away from manufacturing towards the services industries, there remain some 91 EU-invested industrial establishments in Hong Kong. The EU is the third largest investor in manufacturing in Hong Kong, responsible for investments totalling some HK$6.5 billion (0.65 billion ecu) at the end of 1994, with the United Kingdom, the Netherlands and Germany the main investors.

(iii) Communications. Ten EU-based air carriers currently operate at Hong Kong international airport. As for shipping, major EU shipping interests are well established in Hong Kong. In addition, European brands have captured a significant share of the portable phone market in Hong Kong.

(iv) Financial Services. With Hong Kong now established as one of the world's major financial centres, EU financial services institutions have a major stake in Hong Kong. Out of the 151 licensed banks incorporated in Hong Kong in August 1996, 47 were incorporated in the EU, with another 57 EU banks maintaining representative offices in Hong Kong. Over the period 1990-95, EU banks ranked third in Hong Kong in terms of both assets and lending, following local and Japanese banks.

As for insurance, more EU insurance companies are established in Hong Kong than from any other part of the world: 82 of the 222 registered insurance companies in Hong Kong in August 1996 were incorporated in the EU. EU-based companies also play an important part in securities and commodities trading, and in investment services.

(v) Construction. EU companies have been major beneficiaries of the enormous construction works linked to the construction of the new Hong Kong airport. EU companies have been awarded around one-third of the contracts for the New Airport Programme, with some 41 contracts and 147 consultancies totalling some HK$35 billion (3.5 billion ecu) by March 1996. Companies from the United Kingdom, the Netherlands, France, Belgium and Spain have been the major beneficiaries.

**Trade trend between the EC and Hong Kong (Ecu millions – Eur 12)**

| Year | Imports | Exports | Total trade | Balance |
|---|---|---|---|---|
| 1980 | 3674 | 2166 | 5840 | –1508 |
| 1984 | 5172 | 3981 | 9153 | –1191 |
| 1985 | 4819 | 4551 | 9370 | –268 |
| 1986 | 5300 | 4229 | 9529 | –1071 |
| 1987 | 5507 | 4777 | 10284 | –730 |

| | | | | |
|---|---|---|---|---|
| 1988 | 6320 | 6769 | 13089 | 449 |
| 1989 | 6431 | 7022 | 13453 | 591 |
| 1990 | 5909 | 6597 | 12506 | 688 |
| 1991 | 6404 | 7409 | 13813 | 1005 |
| 1992 | 5908 | 8782 | 14690 | 2874 |
| 1993 | 6428 | 11390 | 17818 | 4962 |
| 1994 | 6571 | 13170 | 19741 | 6599 |
| 1995 | 6675 | 14683 | 21358 | 8008 |

From 1980 until 1995, EC imports almost doubled, exports increased sevenfold, total trade increased more than three times and the EC balance of trade was transformed from a deficit of 1 508 mecu in 1980 to a surplus of 8 008 mecu in 1995. Source: EUROSTAT.

1 "A long term policy for China-Europe relations", Brussels 5.7.1995, COM(95) 279 final.
2 "Towards a new Asia strategy", Brussels 13.7.1994, COM(94) 314 final.

The EU was concerned to maintain and develop its trade and other relations with Hong Kong in the future, to monitor so far as possible respect for citizen's rights under the Basic Law and to maintain Hong Kong's international role. For example, during 2003 the Hong Kong government proposed a draft national security bill which sparked considerable controversy. It was based on Article 23 of the Basic Law, which provides that the Hong Kong SAR shall enact laws on its own to protect national security.[4] The EU Presidency issued three declarations on the behalf of the EU, expressing concern over the proposed legislation,[5] which eventually was withdrawn by the Hong Kong government.

On 26 October 2006 the EU issued a second policy paper (see Document 8.2). Covering both Hong Kong and Macau, it was entitled 'The European Union, Hong Kong and Macao: Possibilities for Cooperation 2007–2013'. It emphasised that relations were 'practical and built on mutual interest'. It identified the following as key areas for further cooperation: trade and customs, finance, people-to-people links, transport, environment, health and food safety. Putting forward a strong case for further engagement with the Hong Kong SAR, the Commission proposed the establishment of a regular structured dialogue for matters within Hong Kong's competence.

4 Art 23 provides that 'The Hong Kong Special Administrative Region shall enact laws on its own to prohibit any act of treason, secession, sedition, subversion against the Central People's Government, or theft of state secrets, to prohibit foreign political organizations or bodies from conducting political activities in the Region, and to prohibit political organizations or bodies of the Region from establishing ties with foreign political organizations or bodies'. See www.info.gov.hk/basic_law/fulltext (accessed 23 September 2007).

5 'Statement by the EU on the Hong Kong SAR Government's Proposal to Implement Article 23 of the Basic Law' (Hong Kong and Brussels, 23 December 2002). 'Declaration by the Presidency on behalf of the European Union on Article 23 of Hong Kong Basic Law', 8474/03(Presse 115) (P48/03) (Brussels, 15 April 2003); 'Declaration by the Presidency on Behalf of the European Union on Article 23 of the Basic Law of Hong Kong', 11454/1/03 REV1 (Presse 213) (Brussels, 16 July 2003); all available at http://ec.europa.eu/comm/external_relations/hong_kong/doc/index.htm.

## Document 8.2: Communication from the Commission to the Council and the European Parliament, 'The European Union, Hong Kong and Macao: Possibilities for Cooperation 2007–2013' (2006)

COMMUNICATION FROM THE COMMISSION TO THE COUNCIL AND THE EUROPEAN PARLIAMENT

The European Union, Hong Kong and Macao: possibilities for cooperation 2007-2013

**Executive summary**

The European Union's relations with the Hong Kong and Macao Special Administrative Regions (SARs) have continued to develop since they returned to Chinese sovereignty.

The EU has a strong interest in the continued autonomy and freedoms enjoyed by the two SARs, and supports early and substantial progress towards universal suffrage. The Commission has issued annual reports on the constitutional, political, trade, economic and bilateral developments in the two SARs and will continue to do so.

Relations are above all practical and based on mutual interest. There is substantial and growing cooperation, both direct and indirect, as Hong Kong and Macao continue to provide a platform for deepening cooperation with mainland China.

The EU should continue to build on the strong base of existing cooperation and dialogue. There should be a regular structured dialogue between the Commission and the Hong Kong SAR on matters under its competence, and the annual Joint Committee meetings between the Commission and the Macao SAR should continue.

Following agreement of a new financing instrument for industrialised countries, there should be a review and new agenda for cooperation between the two sides. This Communication sets a number of challenging objectives for moving forward cooperation in seven key areas: trade and customs; finance; people-to-people links (including academia); transport; the environment; health; and food safety.

### THE EUROPEAN UNION, HONG KONG AND MACAO: POSSIBILITIES FOR COOPERATION 2007-2013

The Commission's policy towards the Hong Kong Special Administrative Region (SAR) was set out in a 1997 Communication to the European Council. That Communication, which was issued in the context of Hong Kong's handover to Chinese sovereignty, underlined the importance of smooth implementation of the 'one country, two systems' principle and set out ways in which the EU could contribute to Hong Kong's political and economic development. The Commission has since issued annual reports on developments in the Hong Kong SAR, most recently with the eighth annual report on developments in 2005. The Commission has also engaged with the SAR Government on a number of policy dialogues, notably on trade and economic policy, signed important bilateral agreements in areas such as customs cooperation and the readmission of illegal immigrants, and, when the need has arisen, made declarations on political developments in Hong Kong.

Policy towards the Macao Special Administrative Region was set out in a Communication to the European Council in 1999. The Commission has issued annual reports on developments in the Macao SAR and held annual meetings of the Joint Committee with the SAR authorities.

The European Union's relations with both Hong Kong and Macao have developed considerably since they returned to Chinese sovereignty. During his visit to Macao and Hong Kong on 18 July 2005, President Barroso agreed with the Chief Executives of both SAR Governments that "the European Commission should develop, broaden and deepen cooperation" with the two Special Administrative Regions in areas of mutual interest. Accordingly, this Communication evaluates the current relationships and makes a number of recommendations for improving and deepening the EU's cooperation with the two SARs.

*1. Political and Constitutional Developments*

Since the transfer of Hong Kong and Macao to Chinese sovereignty, both Special Administrative Regions have been governed according to the principle of 'one country, two systems', set out in detail in a separate Basic Law for each.

In general the 'one country, two systems' principle has been respected and is working well for the people of Hong Kong and Macao. The EU supports this principle, and in particular the respect for human rights and individual freedoms enshrined in the Basic Laws, which should be enjoyed by the citizens of both SARs. Both SAR governments continue to enjoy a high degree of autonomy in economic, trade, fiscal, financial and regulatory matters, and the people of Hong Kong and Macao benefit from their own legal systems, an independent rule of law, individual property rights, freedom of speech, and market economic systems.

In both SARs, the specific constitutional development measures envisaged in their Basic Laws have been implemented fully and on schedule.

However, the Basic Law of Hong Kong also states: "The ultimate aim is the selection of the Chief Executive by universal suffrage upon nomination by a broadly representative nominating committee in accordance with democratic procedures"[1]. (There is no analogous article in Macao's Basic Law[2].) Neither Hong Kong nor Macao has yet achieved universal suffrage nor defined a road map towards full democracy.

The European Union supports democracy throughout the world as the best means of creating legitimate, stable, accountable and transparent government, protecting rights and freedoms, and upholding the rule of law. The EU supports early and substantial progress towards the ultimate goal of universal suffrage in Hong Kong as set out in the Basic Law, and also in Macao, in line with the wishes of the people of Hong Kong and Macao.

The Commission has commented at length on Hong Kong's constitutional development and interpretations by the National People's Congress of the SAR's Basic Law in its previous annual reports (see the 2004 and 2005 annual reports in particular)[3] . It has also commented on developments in Macao in its previous annual reports on the Macao SAR[4].

On the international stage, both the Hong Kong and Macao SAR Governments have quickly become accepted as, and remain, autonomous international partners on economic, trade, fiscal, financial, sports, research, educational, cultural, and people-to-people matters, for which they retain legal competence under their Basic Laws. They continue to be active members of international organisations such as the World Trade Organisation (WTO) and the World Customs Organisation and are parties to a number of international treaties. As recently as December 2005, Hong Kong successfully hosted the Sixth WTO Ministerial meeting, and in the same month Macao hosted the 2005 East Asian Games.

*2. Economic Developments*

Mainland China's rapid growth and increasing economic prosperity has created new opportunities for Hong Kong and Macao. The SARs' close relationships with south China, and Guangdong province in particular, have become key to their economic success. Hong Kong and Macao are benefiting as liberal, open gateways to and from China. The Closer Economic Partnership Arrangements with mainland China and the Individual Visit Schemes, which relax travelling restrictions for mainland residents wishing to visit, have made significant contributions to economic growth.

Hong Kong

In the period immediately following handover, the Hong Kong SAR Government was faced with unprecedented challenges in financial, economic and fiscal management. It is to the credit of the SAR Government that Hong Kong has now recovered from the recession that followed the negative economic impacts of the Asian financial crisis in 1997-98 and the outbreak of SARS (Severe Acute Respiratory Syndrome) in 2003.

Hong Kong's 2005 economic and financial figures have now regained their 1997 levels. GDP grew in 2005 at 7.3 % (and the government's forecast for 2006 is for 4 to 5% growth). Unemployment in December 2005 was at a four-year low of 5.2%. Fiscal balance was finally restored for 2005-06, the first time in eight years after the handover, as the economy picked up and public expenditure was restrained.

Helped by the financing needs of mainland China, Hong Kong is consolidating its position as the international financial centre for East Asia. Mainland Chinese enterprises are using Hong Kong as a fund-raising and investing centre, creating a growing demand for Hong Kong's financial, legal and business services. China-related companies accounted for over 80% of the IPO (initial public offering) funds raised in Hong Kong, helping to make Hong Kong the fourth largest equity fund raising centre in the world in 2005 and a globally important funds trading and asset management centre. Hong Kong's success as an international financial centre hinges on its ability to play an increasing role in intermediating Mainland China's large domestic savings. Given the competition from other regional financial centres, Hong Kong will need to continue to increase competitiveness by maintaining flexible labour and product markets, strong institutions and sound macroeconomic policies.

Hong Kong's businesses and people have also demonstrated a remarkable capacity to adjust to competitive and external challenges. They have been able to move up the value-added chain to higher-price and higher-margin activities in financial services, business services, trade, high-value manufacturing, tourism, retail and other services. But Hong Kong still faces the challenges of increasing cost and supply-side constraints resulting from the challenges of congestion and environmental pollution. Its ambition to remain "Asia's World City" will depend on meeting these challenges.

Macao

The explosive growth of Macao's small, open economy since 2000 has been due primarily to the gaming and tourism sectors. In 2002 the gaming sector was liberalised, and the 40-year-old casino monopoly abolished. Coupled with the Individual Visit Scheme from mainland China, this has attracted a growth in visitors, which in turn has provided impetus for wider economic growth. With rising demand, Macao should continue to grow rapidly, though this could be affected if there were problems with or a challenge to its gaming monopoly for China.

Macao is a small but dynamic urban centre, which is seeking to build itself as a strategic services hub for the Pearl River Delta. With gaming and tourism as its basic economic pillars, the SAR Government aims to diversify Macao into a regional entertainment, exhibition and conference service centre. But it will face stiff competition, squeezed between Hong Kong's highly developed services economy and the low wages of the mainland. The key challenges for Macao will be to: reinforce its legal and financial systems to support future growth and avoid erosion of the integrity of its financial and social systems; and effective training of a local labour market (or importing and integration of qualified labour).

*3. Case for Greater Engagement*

Hong Kong

EU interests in Hong Kong are substantial: Hong Kong is the EU's sixteenth bilateral trading partner by volume, and if the huge transit trade via Hong Kong to China is taken into account, ranks as high as sixth. Two-way trade, although declining slightly in recent years (due primarily to a number of Hong Kong industries moving to the mainland) remains close to €30 billion. Hong Kong continues to play a 'gateway' function for a number of EU newcomers looking for access to the mainland Chinese market. Increasingly, mainland Chinese companies are using Hong Kong as a base and a source of knowledge — a gateway for business opportunities in Europe. The EU is Hong Kong's third largest supplier after the mainland and Japan, and the third largest investor.

Thousands of EU companies maintain regional HQs or offices in the SAR and over 45 000 EU citizens are resident there. EU financial services institutions continue to have a leading stake in Hong Kong. In 2005, 34 of the 132 licensed banks in Hong Kong were incorporated in the EU; and of the 175 insurance companies authorised in Hong Kong 30 are incorporated in the EU, putting them top of the list in terms of the number of overseas insurers operating in Hong Kong.

European business activity within Hong Kong accounts for the largest foreign non-Chinese presence. EU companies constitute the largest number of foreign companies with regional headquarters and regional offices based in Hong Kong (1083 or 28% of the total, as at June 2005). In addition to a European Chamber of Commerce, there are 14 EU Member State bilateral Chambers of Commerce in Hong Kong. The EU/Hong Kong Business Council also meets annually to provide a forum for a strategic dialogue between Hong Kong and EU business leaders.

Hong Kong is a key East Asian transportation hub for European Union traders, service providers and individuals. Hong Kong's container port remains the largest in the world in terms of the number of containers passing through. The EU also has strong civil aviation relations with Hong Kong: most Member States have bilateral air services agreements. Hong Kong is a major airfreight and passenger hub for onwards traffic to the wider Asia-Pacific region as well as an important gateway to the Chinese mainland. Hong Kong's open English-speaking environment means it is also a key tourism, education and conference destination.

Overall, our bilateral relationship with Hong Kong is good across the board, with highlights including:

- the strength of trade relations and shared priorities for multilateral trade engagement through the WTO process;

- our Customs Cooperation Agreement, signed in 1999, which facilitates co-operation to combat fraud, piracy and other forms of illegality, and the exchange of information and coordination between the customs authorities of Hong Kong and the EU's Member States.
- and our agreement on 'readmission of persons residing without authorisation', which entered into force in 2004, and which provides a good basis to take forward co-operation on wider immigration issues.

But there are also areas where we would like to see improvements. Two key areas are:

- competition policy, where European companies often complain about the lack of a level playing field in certain key sectors;
- and IPR violations, where Hong Kong has worked hard in recent years, but nonetheless remains the source of some 8 % of all recorded violations in the EU.

Since 1993, the EU has maintained a permanent Office in Hong Kong (which is accredited to both Hong Kong and Macao). It is staffed and operated by the European Commission and is active in a number of areas, with the focus on economic and trade issues. 16 EU Member States are represented by resident missions accredited to Hong Kong and to Macao (the mission of Portugal is located in Macao and the other missions are located in Hong Kong).

In February 2006 the Hong Kong Government proposed to reinforce its representation offices in Europe, opening a new trade office in Berlin to serve Germany and the eastern European Member States of the EU. The existing Hong Kong Office in Brussels is to be upgraded to become the Hong Kong head office in Europe, with the London and Berlin offices reporting to Brussels.

Macao

The EU is Macao's third largest trading partner. While there are only a few EU companies based in Macao, those that are there express satisfaction with the infrastructure and communications.

Macao retains close links with Portuguese culture, and Portuguese remains one of the official languages of Macao. This contributes to the strength of the EU's relations with Macao and its attractiveness as a tourism, education and conference destination.

The EU concluded a Trade and Cooperation Agreement with Macao in 1992 and the EC-Macao Joint Committee, established under this agreement, meets annually. Since signature of the agreement, the EU has funded cooperation projects with Macao worth around 1 million euros per annum. Projects have included: training for the tourism industry (1999-2001); a European studies programme (1999-2001); a services development programme (1999-2001) advising Macao on ways to improve Macao's services sector; and the Asia-Invest programme (2001 and 2002). The EU-Macao Legal Cooperation Programme (2001-2005) is ongoing and provides training, workshops and seminars to develop Macao's legal system and to promote the rule of law in the SAR. The European Union's interpretation service (SCIC) is providing translation and interpretation training in 2006, financed by the Government of Macao.

The EU–Macao Readmission Agreement signed in 2002 is working well, and constructive annual bilateral meetings are held to review progress.

The Macao representative in Europe, based in Lisbon, Geneva and Brussels, plays a very useful and positive role in EU-Macao relations.

*4. Delivering Closer Cooperation: Objectives*

The existing policy and regulatory dialogues and cooperation between the EU and the Hong Kong and Macao SARs have provided an excellent base for relations. To move relations further forward, this base needs to be built upon and strengthened, and at the same time widened to include other sectors and take account of the much greater EU cooperation with mainland China. Hong Kong and Macao are indeed platforms for deepening cooperation with mainland China. The EU should now widen and deepen the scope for greater EU involvement in the ongoing trilateral cooperation between Hong Kong, Macao and mainland China.

Accordingly, this section sets a number of challenging new objectives for moving forward cooperation in seven key areas: trade and customs; finance; people-to-people links (including academia); transport; the environment; health; and food safety.

Trade and customs cooperation

Trade and customs cooperation remains the cornerstone for a strong bilateral relationship between the EU and both partners. This should be built upon by:

- Improving informal consultation and coordination on multilateral trade and economic regulation, particularly within the framework of the WTO as and where appropriate;
- Continuing close consultation on bilateral trade issues, in particular on trade facilitation, and strengthening customs cooperation on IPR. The EU should consider programmes to disseminate and explain measures on regulations, standards, customs procedures, phytosanitary requirements and other regulations that may affect the trade in goods and services between the EU, Hong Kong, Macao and China;
- Building on the framework of the Customs Cooperation Agreement to strengthen action against copyright infringement; combating transnational smuggling of counterfeit cigarettes by sharing information and intelligence; and working towards a more secure global shipping system by electronically scrutinizing containers, without slowing the flow of international commerce.
- Exchanging views and best practice on competition policy and public procurement procedures as appropriate;
- Greater support for business (particularly SMEs), including provision of information on greater China markets. The European Chambers of Commerce in Hong Kong and the Offices of Hong Kong and Macao in Europe could be involved and more closely integrated with the work of the EU-Hong Kong Business Council Cooperation Committees;
- Encouraging universities and business schools in the EU, Hong Kong, Macao and the Chinese mainland to cooperate on management education and training.

With the establishment of Closer Economic Partnership Arrangements between both SARs and China (CEPAs) since July 2003, companies in the SARs are benefiting from widening access to the Mainland Chinese market. This is a positive development, but the EU will continue to monitor the CEPAs' WTO compliance and any potential negative impact on foreign invested companies.

Financial cooperation

The financial, banking and investment relationship between the EU and the SARs is already strong, but there is scope for:

- Improved regulatory dialogue and convergence on financial regulation matters, in particular on issues like anti-money laundering legislation and its implementation, investment fund regulation, corporate jurisdiction and governance issues, and accounting and financial reporting standards.
- Improved dialogue, cooperation and convergence on issues relating to good governance in tax matters, taking account of the fiscal autonomy of the Hong Kong and Macao SARs within a sovereign China. In line with its stated tax policy of promoting internationally accepted good governance principles as widely as possible, the Commission proposes work with both SARs to improve transparency and the exchange of information, strengthening enforcement measures to prevent the avoidance or evasion of taxes, and in particular promoting application of measures equivalent to those applied within the EU on taxation of income from savings. In addition the Commission will encourage both SARs to adopt the principles of the Code of conduct on business taxation which aims to develop a fair, transparent and cooperative tax environment that favours business, growth and jobs on both sides.

People-to-people and academic links

- The education and research sectors provide a rich area for possible EU/Hong Kong and EU/Macao cooperation. The Commission should consider the scope for improving relations through contacts between think tanks and journalists, parliamentary exchanges, student and teacher exchanges, institutional twinning arrangements, joint research and debate on public policy, cultural exchanges, and language training (building on the current Commission support to enhance capacity for Portuguese/Chinese interpretation in Macao); the EU should also continue to encourage civil society and non-governmental debate and dialogues.
- Both the Erasmus exchange scholarships and the Jean Monnet Programme are relevant and should be made accessible;
- A more substantial visitors programme should be built upon the existing European Union Visitors Programme (EUVP), which is successful but of limited scope at present;
- Hong Kong and Macao universities and research institutes are already bidding jointly with European institutions for access to funding from the EU Framework Programmes for Research Technology and Development. Measures should be developed to enhance this trend and in parallel to encourage deeper cooperation — possibly though twinning and cooperation agreements (and possibly including mainland Chinese institutions) — to provide opportunities for information exchanges and networking;
- Immigration cooperation should continue. The EU and Hong Kong and Macao maintain a regular dialogue through the Joint EC-Hong Kong Readmission Committee, which last met in January 2005 in Hong Kong. This should form a basis for moving toward greater cooperation on wider immigration issues;
- The current legal cooperation and training project in Macao is a good example and should be built upon; international cross-border legal issues could form an interesting area for cooperation on the rule of law, good governance, human rights issues, civil law and commercial law;

- EU visibility should be enhanced in Hong Kong and Macao. This should be done mainly through practical actions, including through the possibility of setting up a "Europe Centre" or "Europe House". But there is also a need to reinforce EU visibility more generally and directly. There should be a concerted public diplomacy strategy for the EU in Hong Kong and Macao and for the wider region.

Transport cooperation

- There is significant shared expertise on maritime security and regulation, and this should form the basis for further cooperation. The ongoing pilot project for the security of maritime containers, involving the Commission and ports in the UK (Felixstowe), Netherlands (Rotterdam), Shanghai and Hong Kong, provides a good example.
- The EU has strong aviation relations with Hong Kong: most Member States have bilateral air services agreements with the SAR. Hong Kong is in itself a major hub in Asia for onwards traffic to the wider Asia-Pacific region as well as an important gateway to mainland China. The EU wishes to strengthen aviation relations with Hong Kong as well as with Macao, which are key partners in the region for the EU aviation industry.
- Joint efforts are underway, and need to be reinforced, to conclude horizontal agreements at Community level with Hong Kong and Macao, which would restore legal certainty for air carriers on each side under existing bilateral agreements. This would represent an important first step in developing closer cooperation between the EU and Hong Kong and Macao in civil aviation. Broader areas of cooperation, including technical, industrial and regulatory cooperation in areas such as air traffic management, aviation safety and security as well as in other areas, should also be explored.

Health, food and product safety

The EU and Hong Kong and Macao have shared interests in international health, food and product safety issues.

- On internationally transmittable diseases the informal consultations already begun between the European Commission and Hong Kong in January 2006 should form the basis for future discussions and possible co-operation with both SARs.
- Both sides should consider scope for strengthening cooperation on the Rapid Alert System for Food and Feed.
- Given the importance of Hong Kong's role in the export of consumer products and the importance of combating seriously dangerous consumer products, both sides should cooperate closely to ensure that products produced in or transited through Hong Kong are safe and are monitored against EU safety standards.

Environmental cooperation

- The Commission welcomes the deepening EU dialogue with mainland China on the environment and climate change. The Commission should also explore with Hong Kong and Macao the scope for cooperation on air and water pollution and industrial emissions to help the Hong Kong and Macao SARs better carry out their pollution control strategies, to take into account and influence cross-border issues and to work on solutions at regional and global level where relevant.
- Among other things, this should have the aim of promoting business cooperation for SMEs and dialogue on air and water pollution and industrial emissions. Hong Kong's

and Macao's universities, business associations and training facilities could serve as a platform for engagement on these issues.

*5. Delivery Mechanisms*

Consultations and transparency

In July 2005 President Barroso and the Chief Executives of Hong Kong and Macao — Donald Tsang and Edmund Ho — agreed it was important to have structured, regular dialogue between the European Commission and the two SAR governments on matters within the competence of the two governments under their respective Basic Laws.

As far as Hong Kong is concerned, this would best be achieved through regular dialogue, for which the arrangements might be as follows: (a) meetings should be held annually; (b) there should be an adequate level of representation from the European Commission and the Hong Kong government; and (c) the agenda for each meeting should cover the full range of practical issues in the relationship and be agreed in advance by both sides. These arrangements, which would compliment and not replace existing sector-specific dialogue, should be implemented as soon as possible, with the first annual meeting taking place before the end of 2006.

The Commission believes that the existing EC/Macao Joint Committee mechanism works well and should continue, and positive lessons drawn from it might inform the establishment of dialogue with Hong Kong.

There should be public and transparent reporting of the annual meetings and the ongoing cooperation, which could be achieved through a combination of Joint Statements and the existing mechanism of the Commission's Annual Reports.

The Commission will continue to maximise policy coordination with all EU partners (both with Member States and the European business community) in Hong Kong, Macao, and Europe — as well as in mainland China, as appropriate. Making available information and ensuring open communication on initiatives for future cooperation should help ensure that these actions complement and support the strategies of EU Member States, the Hong Kong and Macao governments, and private entities and individuals.

Already during 2005 and early 2006, in order to discuss and explore possible content and means to deepen, develop and broaden cooperation between the EU and Hong Kong and Macao in areas of mutual interest, a series of informal, open, brainstorming consultative seminars were arranged by the Office of the European Commission in Hong Kong and Macao with over 200 representatives of various sectors of Hong Kong and Macao society: trade and economic operators, EU Heads of Mission, environment and health professionals, and representatives of civil society, NGOs, and the academic and research community. A sixth seminar was held in November 2005 with representatives of various sectors of Macao society in Macao.

Financing cooperation

Hong Kong and Macao are important partners that share many values and institutional structures with the EU in the economic, regulatory, social and cultural spheres.

Dialogue and cooperation should therefore be backed up and reinforced by an EU financing instrument, such as the new Industrialised Countries Instrument under the future Financial Perspectives of the EU. This could provide funding for meetings, conferences, and other actions fostering economic partnerships, business collaboration and science and technology cooperation, as well as people-to-people exchanges and the development of policy dialogues in the areas detailed in this Communication. The overall aim of such action would be to promote better mutual understanding and co-operation and stimulate further development in bilateral trade, investment flows and customs cooperation between the EU and both partner SARs. The Commission should explore potential synergies for trilateral cooperation with mainland China including under the Development Cooperation Instrument.

1 Article 45.

2 For Macao, the Basic Law stipulates that "if there is a need to change the method for forming the Legislative Assembly of the Macao SAR in and after 2009, such amendments must be made with the endorsement of two-thirds majority of all the members of the Assembly and the consent of the Chief Executive", and there is no reference to universal suffrage.

3 The Commission's annual reports on Hong Kong are available on the internet website: http://www.delhkg.cec.eu.int/en/index.htm and are listed in annex to this Communication.

4 The Commission's annual reports on Macao are available on the internet website: http://www.delhkg.cec.eu.int/en/index.htm and are listed in annex to this Communication.

For each year since 1998 the Commission has also issued an annual report on the Hong Kong SAR (see Table 8.2).

The EU and Hong Kong have long had bilateral agreements concerning trade in textiles. Table 8.3 shows the bilateral agreements on textiles between the EU and the Hong Kong SAR since 1980.[6] Since 1 January 1995 textile trade between the EU and the Hong Kong SAR has been governed by the WTO Agreement on Textiles and Clothing (ATC). According to the ATC, EU quotas on textile exports from the Hong Kong SAR expired on 31 December 2004.

In addition to textiles, the EU and the Hong Kong SAR have concluded bilateral agreements on assistance in customs matters and readmission of persons residing without authorisation (see Table 8.4).

On 13 May 1999, the EU and the Hong Kong SAR signed an agreement on cooperation and mutual assistance in customs matters which came into effect on 1 June 1999 (see Document 8.3). As with the similar agreement between the EU and China, it is intended to prevent circumvention. It provides for assistance on request and spontaneous assistance. It also provides that, in suspect cases, special surveillance may be applied to any natural or legal person, place, movement of goods or transport which is or may be linked to, or used to commit operations in breach of, customs legislation.

6 These agreements are not included in the book because most are very long, they are no longer in force and they are readily available on the internet. For the evolution of EC law on textiles imports since the end of the period of liberalisation under the WTO Agreement on Textiles and Clothing, see chapter 2.

**Table 8.2: Commission Annual Reports on the Hong Kong SAR, 1998–Present**

| Short title of document | Official title of document | Author | Place and date of issue | Reference number | Location |
|---|---|---|---|---|---|
| First Annual Report | First Annual Report by the European Commission on the Special Administration Region of Hong Kong | Commission of the European Communities | Brussels, 8.1.1999 | COM(1998)796 final | http://ec.europa.eu/comm/external_relations/hong_kong/doc/index.htm |
| Second Annual Report | Report from the Commission to the Council and the European Parliament, 'Second Annual Report by the European Commission on the Special Administrative Region of Hong Kong' | Commission of the European Communities | Brussels, 18.5.2000 | COM(2000)294 final | http://ec.europa.eu/comm/external_relations/hong_kong/doc/index.htm |
| Third Annual Report | Report from the Commission to the Council and the European Parliament, 'Third Annual Report by the European Commission on the Hong Kong Special Administrative Region' | Commission of the European Communities | Brussels, 25.7.2001 | COM(2001)431 final | http://ec.europa.eu/comm/external_relations/hong_kong/doc/index.htm |
| Fourth Annual Report | Report from the Commission to the Council and the European Parliament, 'Fourth Annual Report by the European Commission on the Hong Kong Special Administrative Region' | Commission of the European Communities | Brussels, 5.8.2002 | COM(2002)431 final | http://ec.europa.eu/comm/external_relations/hong_kong/doc/index.htm |
| Fifth Annual Report | Report from the Commission to the Council and the European Parliament, 'Annual Report by the European Commission on the Hong Kong Special Administrative Region' | Commission of the European Communities | Brussels, 15.9.2003 | COM(2003)544 final | http://ec.europa.eu/comm/external_relations/hong_kong/doc/index.htm |

**Table 8.2: continued**

| Short title of document | Official title of document | Author | Place and date of issue | Reference number | Location |
|---|---|---|---|---|---|
| Annual Report 2003 | Report from the Commission to the Council and the European Parliament, 'Hong Kong Special Administrative Region (SAR): Annual Report 2003' | Commission of the European Communities | Brussels, xxx [in original] | COM(2004)yyy final [in original] | http://ec.europa.eu/comm/external_relations/hong_kong/doc/index.htm |
| Sixth Annual Report | Report from the Commission to the Council and the European Parliament, 'Hong Kong Special Administrative Region: Annual Report 2003' | Commission of the European Communities | Brussels, 28.6.2004 | COM(2004)414 final [SEC(2004)791] | http://ec.europa.eu/comm/external_relations/hong_kong/doc/index.htm |
| Annual Report 2004 | Report from the Commission to the Council and the European Parliament, 'Hong Kong Special Administrative Region: Annual Report 2004' | Commission of the European Communities | Brussels, 8.7.2005 | COM(2005)308 final | http://ec.europa.eu/comm/external_relations/hong_kong/doc/index.htm |
| Annex to 2004 Report | Commission Staff Working Document, 'Annex to the Report from the Commission to the Council and the European Parliament, Hong Kong Special Administrative Region: Annual Report 2004' | Commission of the European Communities | Brussels, 8.7.2005 | SEC(2005)922 | http://ec.europa.eu/comm/external_relations/hong_kong/doc/index.htm |
| Annual Report 2005 | Report from the Commission to the Council and the European Parliament: Hong Kong Special Administrative Region (SAR): Annual Report 2005' | Commission of the European Communities | Brussels, 7.9.2006 | COM(2006)482 final | http://ec.europa.eu/comm/external_relations/hong_kong/doc/index.htm |

**Table 8.2: continued**

| Short title of document | Official title of document | Author | Place and date of issue | Reference number | Location |
|---|---|---|---|---|---|
| Accompanying Document 2005 | Commission Staff Working Document, 'Accompanying Document to the Report from the Commission to the Council and the European Parliament, Hong Kong Special Administrative Region (SAR): Annual Report 2005' | Commission of the European Communities | Brussels, 7.9.2006 | SEC(2006)1098 | http://ec.europa.eu/comm/external_relations/hong_kong/doc/index.htm |
| Annual Report 2006 | Report from the Commission to the Council and the European Parliament, 'Hong Kong Special Administrative Region (SAR): Annual Report 2006' | Commission of the European Communities | Brussel, 20.6.2007 | COM(2007)341 | http://ec.europa.eu/comm/external_relations/hong_kong/doc/index.htm |

**Table 8.3: EU–Hong Kong SAR Bilateral Agreements on Textiles 1989–Present**

| Title | Reference |
|---|---|
| Agreement between the European Economic Community and Hong Kong on trade in textile products | OJ 11.4.1980 L95/2 |
| Agreement between the European Economic Community and Hong Kong on trade in textile products | OJ 14.4.1988 L97/2 |
| Agreement Minute modifying the Agreement between the European Economic Community and Hong Kong on trade in textile products | OJ 29.9.1988 L269/57 |
| Agreed Minute modifying the Agreement between the European Economic Community and Hong Kong on trade in textile products | OJ 31.12.1988 L382/45 |
| Agreed Minute modifying the Agreement between the European Economic Community and Hong Kong on trade in textile products | OJ 4.10.1989 L286/21 |
| Agreed Minute modifying the Agreement between the European Economic Community and Hong Kong on trade in textile products | OJ 30.12 1989 L396/15 |
| Agreed Minute modifying the Agreement between the European Economic Community and Hong Kong on trade in textile products (Unofficial translation) | OJ 12.4.1990 L96/85 |
| Agreement in the form of an exchange of letters amending the Agreement between the European Economic Community and Hong Kong on trade in textile products | OJ 4.[illegible].1992 L90/3 |
| Agreement in the form of an exchange of letters amending the Agreement between the European Economic Community and Hong Kong on trade in textile products – Agreed Minutes – Notes verbales – Exchanges of notes (Unofficial translation) | OJ 31.12.1992 L410/2 |
| Agreement in the form of an Exchange of Letters between the European Community and Hong Kong amending the Agreement between the European Economic Community and Hong Kong on trade in textile products to take into account the expected accession of the Republic of Austria, the Republic of Finland, the Kingdom of Norway and the Kingdom of Sweden to the European Union – Exchange of Notes (Unofficial translation) | OJ 26.4.1995 L94/155 |
| Administrative arrangements on trade in textile products between the European Community and Hong Kong – Agreed Minute | OJ 11.7.1996 L17377 |
| Corrigendum to: Administrative arrangements on trade in textile products between the European Community and Hong Kong – Agreed Minute | OJ 24.10.1996 L271/43 |

**Table 8.4: EU–Hong Kong SAR Bilateral Agreements other than Textiles**

| Title | Approval by the EC | Other relevant documents |
|---|---|---|
| Agreement between the European Community and Hong Kong, China on cooperation and mutual assistance in customs matters, OJ 18.6.1999 L151/21 | Council Decision 1999/400/EC of 11 May 1999 concerning the conclusion of the Agreement between the European Community and Hong Kong on cooperation and mutual assistance in customs matters, OJ 18.6.1999 L151/20 | |
| Agreement between the European Community and the Government of Hong Kong Special Administrative Region of the People's Republic of China on the readmission of persons residing without authorisation, OJ 24.1.2004 L17/25 | Council Decision 2004/80/EC of 17 December 2003 concerning the conclusion of the Agreement between the European Community and the Hong Kong Special Administrative Region of the People's Republic of China on the readmission of persons residing without authorisation, OJ 24.1.2004 L17/23 | European Parliament legislative resolution on the proposal for a Council decision on the conclusion of the Agreement between the European Community and the Government of the Special Administrative Region of Hong Kong of the People's Republic of China on the readmission of persons residing without authorisation (SEC)(2002) 412 - C5 - 0263/2002 - 2002/0092(CNS), OJ 5.2.2004 C31E/252 |

## Document 8.3: Agreement between the European Community and Hong Kong, China, on Cooperation and Mutual Administrative Assistance in Customs Matters

### AGREEMENT

**between the European Community and Hong Kong, China on cooperation and mutual administrative assistance in customs matters**

The EUROPEAN COMMUNITY and HONG KONG. CHINA [(1)] (hereinafter referred to as the 'Contracting Parties'),

CONSIDERING the importance of the commercial links between the European Community and Hong Kong, China and desirous of contributing, to the benefit of both Contracting Parties, to the harmonious development of those links;

BELIEVING THAT, in order to attain thi* objective, there should be an undertaking to develop customs cooperation;

TAKING into account the development of customs cooperation between the Contracting Parties, concerning customs procedures;

CONSIDERING that operations in breach of customs legislation are prejudicial to the economic, fiscal and commercial interests of both Contracting Parties, and recognising the importance of ensuring the accurate assessment of customs duties and other taxes;

CONVINCED that action against such operations can be made more effective by cooperation between their competent administrative authorities;

HAVING regard to obligations imposed under international conventions already accepted by, or applied to the Contracting Parties; and having regard also to the recommendation of the Customs Cooperation Council on mutual administrative assistance of 5 December 1953,

HAVE AGREED AS FOLLOWS:

## TITLE I GENERAL PROVISIONS

*Article 1 Definitions*

For the purposes of this Agreement:

(a) 'customs legislation' shall mean any laws, regulations or other legally binding instruments of the European Community or Hong Kong, China governing the import, export and transit of goods and their placing under any other customs regime or procedure, including measures of prohibition, restriction and control falling under the competence of the customs authorities and other administrative authorities;

(b) 'customs authority' shall mean, in the European Community, the competent services of the Commission of the European Communities and the customs authorities of the Member States of the European Community, and in Hong Kong, China, the Customs and Excise Department;

(c) 'applicant authority' shall mean a competent administrative authority which has been designated by a Contracting Party for this purpose and which makes a request for assistance on the basis of this Agreement;

(d) 'requested authority' shall mean a competent administrative authority which has been designated by a Contracting Party for this purpose and which receives a request for assistance, on the basis of this Agreement;

(e) 'personal data' shall mean all information relating to an identified or identifiable human being;

(f) 'operation in breach of customs legislation' shall mean any violation or attempted violation of the customs legislation;

(g) 'person' shall mean either a human being or a legal entity.

*Article 2 Territorial application*

This Agreement shall apply, on the one hand, to the territories in which the Treaty establishing the European Community is applied and under the conditions laid down in that Treaty and, on the other hand, to Hong Kong, China.

*Article 3 Future developments*

The Contracting Parties may by mutual consent expand this Agreement with a view to increasing and supplementing customs cooperation, in accordance with their respective customs legislation, by means of agreements on specific sectors or matters.

*Article 4 Scope of the cooperation*

1. The customs authorities undertake to develop customs cooperation. In particular, the Contracting Parties shall seek to cooperate in:

(a) establishing and maintaining channels of communication between their customs authorities to facilitate the secure and rapid exchange of information;

(b) facilitating effective coordination between their customs authorities;

(c) any other administrative matters related to this Agreement that may from time to time require their joint action.

2. Under this Agreement, customs cooperation shall cover all matters relating to the application of customs legislation.

*Article 5 Scope of assistance*

1. The Contracting Panics shall assist each other, in the areas within their competence and within the limits of available resources, and in the manner and under the conditions laid down in this Agreement, to ensure the correct application of customs legislation, in particular by preventing, investigating and combating operations in breach of that legislation.

2. Assistance in customs matters under this Agreement shall be provided between the customs and other administrative authorities of the Contracting Parties which are competent for the application of this Agreement. It shall not prejudice the rules governing mutual assistance in criminal matters. Nor shall it cover information obtained under powers exercised at the request of a judicial authority.

3. Assistance to recover duties, taxes or fines is not covered by this Agreement.

*Article 6 Obligations imposed under other agreements*

1. Taking into account the respective competences of the European Community and the Member States, the provisions of this Agreement shall:

(a) not affect the obligations of the Contracting Parties under any other international agreement or convention,

(b) be deemed complementary with agreements on customs cooperation and mutual administrative assistance which have been or may be concluded between individual Member States and Hong Kong, China, and

(c) not affect the Community provisions governing the communication between the competent services of the Commission and the customs authorities of the Member States of any information obtained under this Agreement which could be of interest to the Community.

2. Notwithstanding the provisions of paragraph 1, the provisions of this Agreement shall take precedence over the provisions of any bilateral agreement on customs cooperation and

mutual administrative assistance which has been or may be concluded between individual Member States and Hong Kong, China insofar as the provisions of the latter are incompatible with those of this Agreement.

3. In respect of questions relating to the applicability of this Agreement, the Contracting Parties shall consult each other to resolve the matter in the framework of the Joint Customs Cooperation Committee set up under Article 21 of this Agreement.

## TITLE II CUSTOMS COOPERATION

### *Article 7 Cooperation in customs procedures*

The Contracting Parties affirm their commitment to the facilitation of the legitimate movement of goods and shall exchange information and expertise on measures to improve customs techniques and procedures and on computerised systems with a view towards implementing that commitment in accordance with the provisions of this Agreement.

### *Article 8 Technical assistance*

1. The customs authorities may provide technical assistance to each other and exchange personnel when mutually beneficial, and according to the availability of resources, for the purpose of advancing their understanding of each other's customs techniques, procedures and computerised systems.

2. They may also, when appropriate, exchange information about technical assistance to any other customs administrations.

### *Article 9 Discussions in international organisations*

The customs authorities shall seek to develop and strengthen their cooperation on topics of common interest with a view to facilitating discussions on customs matters in the framework of international organisations, such as the Customs Cooperation Council.

## TITLE III MUTUAL ADMINISTRATIVE ASSISTANCE

### *Article 10 Assistance on request*

1. At the request of the applicant authority, the requested authority shall provide it with all relevant information which may enable it to ensure that customs legislation is correctly applied, including information regarding activities detected or planned which are or could be operations in breach of customs legislation.

2. At the request of the applicant authority, the requested authority shall inform it:

(a) whether goods exported from one of the Contracting Parties have been properly imported into the other, specifying, where appropriate, the customs procedure applied to the goods;

(b) whether goods imported into one of the Contracting Parties have been properly exported from the other, specifying, where appropriate, the customs procedure applied to the goods.

3. At the request of the applicant authority, the requested authority shall, within the framework of its laws, regulations or other legally binding instruments, take the necessary steps to ensure special surveillance of;

(a) persons in respect of whom there are reasonable grounds for believing that they are or have been involved in operations in breach of customs legislation;

(b) places where stocks of goods have been or may be assembled in such a way that there are reasonable grounds for believing that these goods are intended to be used in operations in breach of customs legislation;

(c) goods that are or may be transported in such a way that there are reasonable grounds for believing that

they are intended to be used in operations in breach of customs legislation;

(d) means of transport that are or may be used in such a way that there are reasonable grounds for believing that they are intended to be used in operations in breach of customs legislation.

*Article 11 Spontaneous assistance*

The Contracting Parties shall assist each other, at their own initiative and in accordance with their laws, regulations or other legally binding instruments, if they consider that to be necessary for the correct application of customs legislation, particularly by providing information obtained pertaining to:

(a) activities which are or appear to be operations in breach of customs legislation and which may be of interest to the other Contracting Party,

(b) new means or methods employed in carrying out operations in breach of customs legislation;

(c) goods known to be subject to operations in breach of customs legislation;

(d) persons in respect of whom there are reasonable grounds for believing that they are or have been involved in operations in breach of customs legislation;

(e) means of transport in respect of which there are reasonable grounds for believing that they have been, are, or may be used in operations in breach of customs legislation.

*Article 12 Delivery, notification*

1. At the request of the applicant authority, the requested authority shall, in accordance with laws, regulations or other legally binding instruments applicable to the latter, take all necessary measures in order:

(a) to deliver any documents of an administrative nature, or

(b) to notify any decisions,

emanating from the applicant authority and falling within the scope of this Agreement, to an addressee residing or established in the jurisdiction of the requested authority.

2. Requests for delivery of documents or notification of decisions shall be made in writing in an official language of the requested authority or in a language acceptable to that authority. This requirement shall not apply to any documents that are to be delivered under paragraph 1.

*Article 13 Form and substance of requests for assistance*

1. Requests pursuant to this Agreement shall be made in writing. They shall be accompanied by the documents necessary to enable compliance with the request. When required because of the urgency of the situation, oral requests may be accepted, but must be confirmed in writing immediately.

2. Requests pursuant to paragraph 1 shall include the following information:

(a) the applicant authority;

(b) the action requested;

(c) the object of and the reason for the request;

(d) the laws, regulations or other legally binding instruments involved;

(e) indications as exact and comprehensive as possible on the persons who are the target of the investigations;

(f) a summary of the relevant facts and of the enquiries already carried out.

3. Requests shall be submitted in an official language of the requested authority or in a language acceptable to that authority. This requirement shall not apply to any documents that accompany the request under paragraph 1.

4. If a request does not meet the formal requirements set out above, its correction or completion may be requested; precautionary measures may be taken in the meantime.

*Article 14 Execution of requests*

1. In order to comply with a request for assistance, the requested authority shall proceed, within the limits of its competence and available resources, as though it were acting on its own account or at the request of other authorities of that same Contracting Party, by supplying information already possessed, by carrying out appropriate enquiries or by arranging for them to be carried out. This provision shall also apply to any other authority to which the request has been addressed in accordance with this Agreement by the requested authority when the latter cannot act on its own.

2. Requests for assistance shall be executed in accordance with the laws, regulations or other legally binding instruments of the requested Contracting Party.

3. Duly authorised officials of a Contracting Party may, with the agreement of the other Contracting Party and subject to the conditions laid down by the latter, be present to obtain in the offices of the requested authority or any other concerned authority in accordance with paragraph 1, information relating to activities that are or may be operations in breach of customs legislation which the applicant authority needs for the purposes of this Agreement.

4. Duly authorised officials of a Contracting Party may, with the agreement .of the other Contracting Party and subject to the conditions laid down by the latter, be present at enquiries carried out in the latter's jurisdiction into specific cases.

5. In the event that the request cannot be complied with, the applicant authority shall be notified promptly of that fact, with a statement of the reasons and of any other information that the requested authority considers may be of assistance to the applicant authority.

*Article 15 Form in which information is to be communicated*

1. The requested authority shall communicate results of enquiries to the applicant authority in writing together with relevant documents, certified copies or other items.

2. This information may be in computerised form.

3. Original files and documents shall be transmitted only upon request in cases where certified copies would be insufficient. These originals shall be returned at the earliest opportunity. The rights of the requested authority or of third parties relating to the originals shall remain unaffected.

*Article 16 Exceptions to the obligation to provide assistance*

1. Assistance may be refused or may be subject to the satisfaction of certain conditions or requirements, in cases where a Party is of the opinion that assistance under this Agreement would:

(a) be likely to prejudice the vital interests of Hong Kong, China or those of a Member State which has been requested to provide assistance under this Agreement; or

(b) be likely to prejudice public order, security or other essential principles, in particular those referred to under Article 17(2); or

(c) violate an industrial, commercial or professional secret.

2. Assistance may be postponed by the requested authority on the ground that it will interfere with an ongoing investigation, prosecution or proceeding. In such a case, the requested authority shall consult with the applicant authority to determine if assistance can be given subject to such terms or conditions as the requested authority may require.

3. Where the applicant authority seeks assistance which it would itself be unable to provide if so requested, it shall draw attention to that fact in its request. It shall then be for the requested authority to decide how to respond to such a request.

4. For the cases referred to in paragraphs 1 and 2, the decision of the requested authority and the reasons therefor must be communicated to the applicant authority without undue delay.

5. Practical arrangements for the implementation of this Article shall be determined by the Joint Customs Cooperation Committee established under Article 21.

*Article 17 Information exchange and confidentiality*

1. Any information communicated in whatsoever form pursuant to this Agreement shall be of a confidential or restricted nature, depending on the rules applicable in each of the Contracting Parties. It shall be covered by the obligation of official secrecy and shall enjoy the protection extended to similar information under the relevant laws of the Contracting Party that received it and the corresponding provisions applying to the Community authorities.

2. Personal data may be exchanged only where the Contracting Party which may receive it undertakes to protect such data in at least an equivalent way to the one applicable to that particular case in the Contracting Party that may supply it. The Contracting Party that may supply the information shall not stipulate any requirements that are more onerous than those applicable to it in its own jurisdiction.

Contracting Parties shall communicate to each other information on their applicable rules, including, where appropriate, legal provisions in force in the Member States of the Community.

3. Nothing in this Agreement shall preclude the use of information or documents obtained in accordance with this Agreement as evidence in proceedings or charges subsequently instituted before the courts or tribunals in respect of operations in breach of customs legislation. Therefore, the Contracting Parties may, in their records of evidence, reports and testimonies and in proceedings and charges which may subsequently be brought before the courts or tribunals, use as evidence information obtained and documents consulted in accordance with the provisions of this Agreement. The competent authority which supplied that information or gave access to those documents shall be notified of such use.

4. Information obtained shall be used solely for the purposes of this Agreement. Where one of the Contracting Parties wishes to use such information for other purposes, it shall obtain the prior written consent of the authority which provided the information. Such use shall then be subject to any restrictions laid down by that authority.

*Article 18 Experts and witnesses*

An official of a requested authority may be authorised to appear, within the limitations of the authorisation granted, as an expert or witness before an authority in the other Contracting Party regarding the matters covered by this Agreement, and produce such objects, documents or certified copies thereof as may be needed for this purpose. The request for appearance must indicate specifically before which authority the official will have to appear, on what matters and by virtue of what title or qualification the official will be questioned.

*Article 19 Assistance expenses*

The Contracting Parties shall waive all claims on each other for the reimbursement of expenses incurred pursuant to this Agreement, except, as appropriate, for expenses payable to experts and witnesses, and those to interpreters and translators who are not public service employees.

## TITLE IV FINAL PROVISIONS

*Article 20 Implementation*

1. The implementation of this Agreement shall be entrusted on the one hand to the competent services of the Commission of the European Communities and, where appropriate, the customs authorities of the Member States of the European Community and on the other hand to the Customs and Excise Department of Hong Kong, China. They shall decide on all practical measures and arrangements necessary for its application, taking into consideration the rules in force in particular in the field of data protection. They may recommend to the competent bodies amendments which they consider should be made to this Agreement.

2. The Contracting Parties shall consult each other and subsequently keep each other informed of the detailed rules of implementation which are adopted in accordance with the provisions of this Agreement.

*Article 21 Joint Customs Cooperation Committee*

1. A Joint Customs Cooperation Committee is hereby established, consisting of representatives of the European Community and of Hong Kong, China. It shall meet at a place, on a date and with an agenda, fixed by mutual agreement.

2. The Joint Customs Cooperation Committee shall see to the proper functioning of the Agreement and shall examine all issues arising from its application. In fulfilling this role, its main functions will be to:

(a) review the progress of the customs cooperation in accordance with this Agreement and identify new areas and specific sectors for further customs cooperation;

(b) exchange views on any points of common interest regarding customs cooperation, including future measures and the resources for them; and

(c) in general terms, recommend solutions aimed at helping to attain the objectives of this Agreement.

3. The Joint Customs Cooperation Committee shall adopt its internal rules of procedure.

*Article 22 Entry into force and duration*

1. This Agreement shall enter into force on the first day of the month following the date on which the Contracting Parties have notified each other of the completion of the procedures necessary for this purpose.

2. Each Contracting Party may terminate this Agreement by giving notice to the other in writing. The termination shall take effect three months from the date of notification to the other Contracting Party. Requests for assistance which have been received prior to the termination of the Agreement shall be completed in accordance with the provisions of this Agreement.

*Article 23 Authentic texts*

This Agreement shall be drawn up in duplicate in the Danish, Dutch, English, Finnish, French, German, Greek, Italian, Portuguese, Spanish, Swedish and Chinese languages, each text being equally authentic.

In witness whereof, the undersigned, being duly authorised to do so, have signed this Agreement.

Done at Hong Kong, China on the thirteenth day of May in the year one thousand nine hundred and ninety-nine.

For the European Community For Hong Kong, China

(1) In accordance with Article 151 of the Basic Law of the Hong Kong Special Administrative Region of the People's Republic of China.

The EU–Hong Kong SAR agreement on readmission of persons residing without authorisation (see Document 8.4) was signed on 27 November 2002 and came into effect on 1 March 2004. Intended to combat illegal immigration, it is the first readmission agreement ever signed by the EU, which for some time has been trying to negotiate a similar agreement with the PRC. It requires Hong Kong or the EU to readmit permanent residents or former permanent residents (in the case of Hong Kong) or nationals or former nationals of an EU Member State (in the case of the EU) without any formalities other than those provided in the Agreement.

## Document 8.4: Agreement between the European Community and the Hong Kong SAR on the Readmission of Persons Residing without Authorisation

**AGREEMENT**

**between the European Community and the Government of the Hong Kong Special Administrative Region of the People's Republic of China on the readmission of persons residing without authorisation**

THE CONTRACTING PARTIES,

THE EUROPEAN COMMUNITY,

hereinafter referred to as 'the Community',

and

THE GOVERNMENT OF THE HONG KONG SPECIAL ADMINISTRATIVE REGION OF THE PEOPLE'S REPUBLIC OF CHINA,

hereinafter referred to as 'the Hong Kong SAR',

DETERMINED to strengthen their cooperation in order to combat illegal immigration more effectively,

REFERRING to Council Regulation (EC) No 539/2001[(1)], and in particular Article 1(2) in conjunction with Annex II thereof, exempting holders of a 'Hong Kong Special Administrative Region' passport from the requirement, for stays of no more than three months in all, to be in possession of a visa when crossing the external borders of the Member States of the European Union,

DESIRING to establish, by means of this Agreement and on the basis of reciprocity, rapid and effective procedures for the identification and return of persons who do not, or no longer, fulfil the conditions for entry to, presence in, or residence on the territories of the Hong Kong SAR or one of the Member States of the European Union, and to facilitate the transit of such persons in a spirit of cooperation,

CONSIDERING that the provisions of this Agreement, which falls within the scope of Title IV of the Treaty establishing the European Community, do not apply to the Kingdom of Denmark, in accordance with the Protocol on the position of Denmark annexed to the Treaty on European Union and the Treaty establishing the European Community,

HAVE AGREED AS FOLLOWS:

*Article 1 Definitions*

For the purpose of this Agreement:

(a) 'Member State' shall mean any Member State of the European Union, with the exception of the Kingdom of Denmark;

(b) 'national of a Member State' shall mean any person who holds the nationality, as defined for Community purposes, of a Member State;

(c) 'permanent resident of the Hong Kong SAR' shall mean any

person who has the right of abode, that is the right to reside permanently, in the Hong Kong SAR;

(d) 'person of another jurisdiction' shall mean any person who is neither a permanent resident of the Hong Kong SAR, nor a national of a Member State. This shall include third-country nationals and stateless persons;

(e) 'stateless person' shall mean any person who does not hold a nationality;

(f) 'residence authorisation' shall mean a permit of any type issued by the Hong Kong SAR or one of the Member States entitling a person to reside on its territory. This shall not include an application for a residence authorisation or temporary permissions to remain on its territory as a visitor or in connection with the processing of an asylum application;

(g) 'visa' shall mean an authorisation issued or a decision taken by the Hong Kong SAR or one of the Member States which permits a person's entry in, or transit through, its territory and which has been issued or taken prior to the person's arrival at its border. This shall not include an airside transit visa.

**SECTION I READMISSION BY THE HONG KONG SAR**

*Article 2 Readmission of permanent residents and former permanent residents*

1. The Hong Kong SAR shall readmit, upon application by a Member State and without any formalities other than those specified in this Agreement, all persons who do not, or who no longer, fulfil the conditions in force for entry to, presence in, or residence on, the territory of the requesting Member State provided that it is proved, or may be validly assumed on the basis of prima facie evidence furnished, that they are permanent residents of the Hong Kong SAR. The same shall apply to persons who, since entering the territory of a Member State, have lost their right to permanent residence in the Hong Kong SAR, unless such persons have at least been promised naturalisation by that Member State.

2. At the request of a Member State, the Hong Kong SAR shall, as necessary and without delay, issue the person to be readmitted with the travel document required for his or her return that is of a period of validity of at least six months. If, for legal or factual reasons, the person concerned cannot be transferred within the period of validity of the travel document that was initially issued, the Hong Kong SAR shall issue a new travel document with the same period of validity within 14 days. if the Hong Kong SAR does not issue the travel document requested within 15 days of the date of the request it shall be deemed to accept use of the EU standard travel document for the purposes of readmission.

*Article 3 Readmission of persons of another jurisdiction*

1. The Hong Kong SAR shall readmit, upon application by a Member State and without any formalities other than those specified in this Agreement, all persons of another jurisdiction who do not, or who no longer, fulfil the conditions in force for entry to, presence in, or residence on, the territory of the requesting Member State provided that it is proved, or may be validly assumed on the basis of prima facie evidence furnished, that such persons:

(a) at the time of entry held a valid visa or residence authorisation issued by the Hong Kong SAR; or

(b) after having entered the territory of the Hong Kong SAR, proceed to enter unlawfully the territory of the Member States, coming directly from the territory of the Hong Kong SAR.

2. The readmission obligation in paragraph 1 shall not apply if:

(a) the person of another jurisdiction has been in airside transit via the Hong Kong International Airport; or

(b) the requesting Member State has issued to the person of another jurisdiction a visa or residence authorisation before or after entering its territory, which has a longer period of validity than any visa or residence authorisation issued by the Hong Kong SAR; or

(c) the person of another jurisdiction enjoyed visa-free access to the territory of the requesting Member State.

3. At the request of a Member State, the Hong Kong SAR shall, as necessary and without delay, issue the person to be readmitted with the travel document required for his or her return that is of a period of validity of at least six months. If, for legal or factual reasons, the person concerned cannot be transferred within the period of validity of the travel document that was initially issued, the Hong Kong SAR shall issue a new travel document with the same period of validity within 14 days. If the Hong Kong SAR does not issue the travel documents requested within 15 days of the date of the request it shall be deemed to accept use of the EU standard travel document for the purposes of readmission.

**SECTION II READMISSION BY THE COMMUNITY**

*Article 4 Readmission of own and former own nationals*

1. A Member State shall readmit, upon application by the Hong Kong SAR and without any formalities other than those specified in this Agreement, all persons who do not, or who no longer, fulfil the conditions in force for entry to, presence in, or residence on, the territory of the Hong Kong SAR provided that it is proved, or may be validly assumed on the basis of prima facie evidence furnished, that they are nationals of that Member State.

The same shall apply to persons who have been deprived of, or who have renounced, the nationality of a Member State since entering the territory of the Hong Kong SAR unless such persons have at least been promised permanent residence in the latter.

2. At the request of the Hong Kong SAR, a Member State shall, as necessary and without delay, issue the person to be readmitted with the travel document required for his or her return that is of a period of validity of at least six months. If, for legal or factual reasons, the person concerned cannot be transferred within the period of validity of the travel document that was initially issued, the Member State concerned shall issue a new travel document with the same period of validity within 14 days.

*Article 5 Readmission of persons of another jurisdiction*

1. A Member State shall readmit, upon application by the Hong Kong SAR and without any formalities other than those specified in this Agreement, all persons of another jurisdiction who do not, or who no longer, fulfil the conditions in force for entry to, presence in, or residence on, the territory of the Hong Kong SAR provided that it is proved, or may be validly assumed on the basis of prima facie evidence furnished, that such persons:

(a) at the time of entry held a valid visa or residence authorisation issued by the requested Member State; or

(b) after having entered the territory of the requested Member State, proceed to enter unlawfully the territory of the Hong Kong SAR, coming directly from the territory of the requested Member State.

2. The readmission obligation in paragraph 1 shall not apply if:

(a) the person of another jurisdiction has been in airside transit via an international airport of the requested Member State; or

(b) the Hong Kong SAR has issued to the person of another jurisdiction a visa or residence authorisation before or after entering its territory, which has a longer period of validity than any visa or residence authorisation issued by the requested Member State; or

(c) the person of another jurisdiction enjoyed visa-free access to the territory of the Hong Kong SAR.

3. If two or more Member States issued a visa or residence authorisation, the readmission obligation in paragraph 1 is for the Member State that issued the document with a longer period of validity or, if one or several of them have already expired, the document that is still valid. If all of the documents have already expired, the readmission obligation in paragraph 1 is for the Member State that issued the document with the most recent expiry date.

4. At the request of the Hong Kong SAR, a Member State shall, as necessary and without delay, issue the person to be readmitted with the travel document required for his or her return that is of a period of validity of at least six months. If, for legal or factual reasons, the person concerned cannot be transferred within the period of validity of the travel document that was initially issued, the Member State concerned shall issue a new travel document with the same period of validity within 14 days.

## SECTION III READMISSION PROCEDURE

### *Article 6 Principle*

1. Subject to paragraph 2, a transfer of a person to be readmitted on the basis of one of the obligations contained in Articles 2 to 5 shall require the submission of a readmission application to the competent authority of the requested Contracting Party.

2. The readmission application may be replaced by a written communication to the requested Contracting Party within a reasonable time period prior to the return of the person concerned provided that

(a) the person to be readmitted is in possession of a valid travel document and, where applicable, a valid visa or residence authorisation of the requested Contracting Party; and

(b) the person to be readmitted is willing to return to the requested Contracting Party.

### *Article 7 Readmission application*

1. Any readmission application is to contain the following information:

(a) the particulars of the person to be readmitted (e.g. given names, surnames, date of birth, and, where possible, place of birth, and the last place of residence);

(b) copies of documents which provide proof or prima facie evidence of nationality or permanent residence.

2. To the extent possible, the readmission application should also contain the following information:

(a) statement indicating that the person to be transferred may need help or care, provided the person concerned has explicitly consented to the statement;

(b) any other protection or security measure which may be necessary in the individual transfer case.

3. A common form to be used for readmission applications is attached as Annex 5 to this Agreement.

*Article 8 Means of evidence regarding nationality and permanent residence*

1. Proof of nationality or permanent residence pursuant to Article 2(1) and Article 4(1) can be furnished through the documents listed in Annex 1 to this Agreement, even if their period of validity has expired. If such documents are presented, the Member States shall recognise the nationality, and the Hong Kong SAR shall recognise the permanent residence, without further formalities. Proof of nationality or permanent residence cannot be furnished through false documents.

2. Prima facie evidence of nationality or permanent residence pursuant to Article 2(1) and Article 4(1) can be furnished through the documents listed in Annex 2 to this Agreement, even if their period of validity has expired. If such documents are presented, the Member States shall deem the nationality, and the Hong Kong SAR shall deem the permanent residence, to be established unless they can prove otherwise.

3. If none of the documents listed in Annexes 1 or 2 can be presented, the competent authorities of the Hong Kong SAR or the Member State concerned shall, upon request, make the necessary arrangements in order to establish his or her nationality or permanent residence.

*Article 9 Means of evidence regarding persons of another jurisdiction*

1. Proof of the conditions for the readmission of persons of another jurisdiction laid down in Article 3(1) and Article 5(1) can be furnished through the means of evidence listed in Annex 3 to this Agreement; it cannot be furnished through false documents. Any such proof shall be mutually recognised by the Contracting Parties without further formalities.

2. Prima facie evidence of the conditions for the readmission of persons of another jurisdiction laid down in Article 3(1) and Article 5(1) can be furnished through the means of evidence listed in Annex 4 to this Agreement. Where such prima facie evidence is presented, the Contracting Parties shall deem the conditions to be established unless they can prove otherwise.

3. The unlawfulness of entry, presence or residence may be established by means of the travel documents of the person concerned in which the necessary visa or other residence authorisation for the territory of the requesting Member State or the Hong Kong SAR are missing. A statement by the competent authority of the requesting Contracting Party that the person concerned has been found not having the necessary travel documents, visa or residence authorisation shall likewise provide prima facie evidence of the unlawful entry, presence or residence.

*Article 10 Time limits*

1. The application for readmission must be submitted to the competent authority of the requested Contracting Party within a maximum of one year after the requesting authority has gained knowledge that a person of another jurisdiction does not, or does no longer, fulfil the conditions in force for entry, presence or residence. Where there are legal or factual obstacles to the application being submitted in time, the time limit shall, upon request, be extended but only until the obstacles have ceased to exist.

2. A readmission application must be replied to without undue delay, and in any event within a maximum of one month; reasons shall be given for refusal of a readmission request. This time limit begins to run with the date of receipt of the readmission request. Upon expiry of this time limit the transfer shall be deemed to have been agreed to.

3. After agreement has been given or, where appropriate, upon expiry of the one month time limit, the person concerned shall be transferred without undue delay and, at the most, within three months. Upon application, this time limit may be extended by the time taken to deal with legal or practical obstacles.

*Article 11 Transfer modalities and modes of transportation*

1. Before returning a person, the competent authorities of the Hong Kong SAR and the Member State concerned shall make arrangements in writing in advance regarding the transfer date, the border crossing point and possible escorts.

2. No means of transportation, whether by air, land or sea, shall be prohibited but, as a rule, return shall take place by air. Return by air is not restricted to the use of national carriers or security staff of the requesting Contracting Party, and may take place by using scheduled flights as well as charter flights.

**SECTION IV TRANSIT OPERATIONS**

*Article 12 Principles*

1. The Hong Kong SAR shall allow the transit of persons of another jurisdiction through its territory if a Member State so requests, and a Member State shall authorise the transit of persons of another jurisdiction through its territory if the Hong Kong SAR so requests, if the onward journey in possible other States of transit and the readmission by the State of destination is assured.

2. The Member States and the Hong Kong SAR shall endeavour to restrict the transit of persons of another jurisdiction to cases where such persons cannot be returned to the State of destination directly.

3. Transit can be refused by the Hong Kong SAR or a Member State:

(a) if the person of another jurisdiction runs the risk of persecution, or could be subjected to criminal prosecution or sanctions in another State of transit or in the State of destination, or could be threatened by criminal prosecution on the territory of the requested Member State or the Hong Kong SAR;

(b) on grounds of public health, domestic security, public order or other national interests.

4. The Hong Kong SAR or a Member State may revoke any authorisation issued if circumstances referred to in paragraph 3 subsequently arise or come to light which stand in the way

of the transit operation, or if the onward journey in possible States of transit or the readmission by the State of destination is no longer assured.

*Article 13 Transit procedure*

1. An application for transit must be submitted to the competent authorities in writing and is to contain the following information:

(a) type of transit (by air, land or sea), possible other States of transit and intended final destination;

(b) the particulars of the person concerned (e.g. given name, surname, date of birth, and — where possible — place of birth, nationality, type and number of travel document);

(c) envisaged border crossing point, time of transfer and possible use of escorts;

(d) a declaration that in the view of the requesting Contracting Party the conditions pursuant to Article 12(2) are met, and that no reasons for a refusal pursuant to Article 12(3) are known of.

A common form to be used for transit applications is attached as Annex 6 to this Agreement.

2. The competent authority of the requested Contracting Party shall, without undue delay and in writing, inform the requesting competent authority of the admission, confirming the border crossing point and the envisaged time of admission, or inform it of the admission refusal and of the reasons for such refusal.

3. If the transit takes place by air, the person to be readmitted and possible escorts shall be exempted from having to obtain an airport transit visa.

4. The competent authorities of the requested Contracting Party shall, subject to mutual consultations, assist in the transit, in particular through the surveillance of the persons in question and the provision of suitable amenities for that purpose.

**SECTION V COSTS**

*Article 14 Transport and transit costs*

Without prejudice to the right of the competent authorities to recover the costs associated with the readmission from the person to be readmitted or third parties, all transport costs incurred in connection with readmission and transit pursuant to this Agreement as far as the border of the State of final destination shall be borne by the requesting Contracting Party.

**SECTION VI DATA PROTECTION AND NON-AFFECTION CLAUSE**

*Article 15 Data protection*

The communication of personal data shall only take place if such communication is necessary for the implementation of this Agreement by the competent authorities of the Hong Kong SAR or a Member State as the case may be.

The processing and treatment of personal data in a particular case shall be subject to the domestic laws of the Hong Kong SAR and, where the controller is a competent authority of a Member State, to the provisions of Directive 95/46/EC[(2)] and of the national legislation of that Member State adopted pursuant to this Directive. Additionally the following principles shall apply:

(a) personal data must be processed fairly and lawfully;

(b) personal data must be collected for the specified, explicit and legitimate purpose of implementing this Agreement and may not be further processed by the communicating authority nor by the receiving authority in a way incompatible with that purpose;

(c) personal data must be adequate, relevant and not excessive in relation to the purpose for which they are collected and/ or further processed; in particular, personal data communicated may concern only the following:

- the particulars of the person to be transferred (e.g. surname, given name, any previous names, nicknames or pseudonyms, date and place of birth, sex, current and any previous nationality),
- identity card or passport (number, period of validity, date of issue, issuing authority, place of issue),
- stop-overs and itineraries,
- other information needed to identify the person to be transferred or to examine the readmission requirements pursuant to this Agreement:

(d) personal data must be accurate and, where necessary, kept up to date;

(e) personal data must be kept in a form which permits identification of data subjects for no longer than is necessary for the purpose for which the data were collected or for which they are further processed;

(f) both the communicating authority and the receiving authority shall take every reasonable step to ensure as appropriate the rectification, erasure or blocking of personal data where the processing does not comply with the provisions of this article, in particular because that data are not adequate, relevant, accurate, or they are excessive in relation to the purpose of processing. This includes the notification of any rectification, erasure or blocking to the other Party;

(g) upon request, the receiving authority shall inform the communicating authority of the use of the communicated data and of the results obtained therefrom;

(h) personal data may only be communicated to the competent authorities. Further communication to other bodies requires the prior consent of the communicating authority;

(i) the communicating and the receiving authorities are under an obligation to make a written record of the communication and receipt of personal data.

*Article 16 Non-affection clause*

1. This Agreement shall be without prejudice to rights, obligations and responsibilities arising from International Law applicable to the Community, the Member States and the Hong Kong SAR.

2. Nothing in this Agreement shall prevent the return of a person under other formal or informal arrangements.

## SECTION VII IMPLEMENTATION AND APPLICATION

*Article 17 Readmission Committee*

1. The Contracting Parties shall provide each other with mutual assistance in the application and interpretation of this Agreement. To this end, they shall set up a Readmission Committee which will, in particular, have the task:

(a) to monitor the application of this Agreement;

(b) to decide on implementing arrangements necessary for the uniform application of this Agreement;

(c) to have regular exchanges of information on any implementing Protocols drawn up by individual Member States and the Hong Kong SAR pursuant to Article 18;

(d) to recommend amendments to this Agreement.

2. Recommendations of the Readmission Committee for amendment of the annexes to this Agreement may be approved by the Parties through a simplified procedure.

3. The Readmission Committee shall be composed of representatives of the Community and the Hong Kong SAR; the Community shall be represented by the Commission of the European Communities, assisted by experts from Member States.

4. The Readmission Committee shall meet where necessary at the request of one of the Contracting Parties.

5. The Readmission Committee shall establish its rules of procedures.

*Article 18 Implementing protocols*

1. The Hong Kong SAR and a Member State may draw up implementing protocols which shall cover rules on;

(a) designation of the competent authorities, border crossing points and exchange of contact points;

(b) conditions for transit of persons of another jurisdiction under escort;

(c) means and documents additional to those listed in Annexes 1 to 4 to this Agreement.

2. The implementing protocols referred to in paragraph 1 shall enter into force only after the Readmission Committee referred to in Article 17 has been notified.

3. The Hong Kong SAR agrees to apply any provision of an

implementing protocol drawn up with one Member State also in its relations with any other Member State upon request of the latter.

*Article 19 Relation to bilateral readmission agreements or arrangements of Member States*

The provisions of this Agreement shall take precedence over the provisions of any bilateral agreement or arrangement on the readmission of persons residing without authorisation which have been or may, under Article 18, be concluded between individual Member States and the Hong Kong SAR, in so far as the provisions of the latter are incompatible with those of this Agreement.

**SECTION VIII FINAL PROVISIONS**

*Article 20 Entry into force, duration and termination*

1. This Agreement shall be ratified or approved by the Contracting Parties in accordance with their respective procedures.

2. This Agreement shall enter into force on the first day of the second month following the date on which the Contracting Parties notify each other that the procedures referred to in the first paragraph have been completed.

3. This Agreement is concluded for an unlimited period.

4. Each Contracting Party may denounce this Agreement by officially notifying the other Contracting Party. This Agreement shall cease to apply six months after the date of such notification.

*Article 21 Annexes*

Annexes 1 to 6 shall form an integral part of this Agreement.

Done at Brussels on the twenty-seventh day of November in the year two thousand and two in duplicate in the Danish, Dutch, English, Finnish, French, German, Greek, Italian, Portuguese, Spanish and Swedish languages, each of these texts being equally authentic

Por la Comunidad Europea

For Det Europæiske Fællesskab

Für die Europäische Gemeinschaft

*Για την Ευρωπαική Κοινότητα*

For the European Community

Pour la Communauté européenne

Per la Comunità europea

Voor de Europese Gemeenschap

Pela Comunidade Europeia

Euroopan yhteisön puolesta

För Europeiska gemenskapen

Por el Gobiemo de la Region Administrativa Especial de Hong Kong de la República Popular China

På regeringen for Folkerepublikken Kinas saerlige administrative region Hongkongs vegne

Im Namen der Regierung der Sonderverwaltungsregion Hongkong der Volksrepublik China

*Για την κυβέρνση της ειδικής περιοχής Χονγκ της Λαϊκής Δημοκρατίας της Κίνας*

For the Government of the Hong Kong Special Administrative Region of the People's Republic of China

Pour le gouvemement de la région administrative spéciale de Hong Kong de la République populaire de Chine

Per il governo della regione ad amministrazione speciale di Hong Kong della Repubblica popolare cinese

Voor de regering van de Speciale Administratieve Regio Hong Kong van de Volksrepubliek China

Pelo Governo da Regiao Administrativa Especial de Hong Kong da Republica Popular da China

Kiinan kansantasavallan erityishallintoalueen Hongkongin hallituksen puolesta

För regeringen i Folkrepubliken Kinas sarskilda administrativa region Hongkong

ANNEX 1

**Common list of documents the presentation of which is considered as proof of nationality or permanent residence**

**(Article 2(1), Article 3(1), Article 4(1) and Article 5(1))**

Member States:

- passports of any kind (national passports, diplomatic passports, service passports, collective passports and surrogate passports including children's passports);
- identity cards of any kind (including temporary and provisional ones);
- service books and military identity cards;
- seaman's registration books and skippers' service cards;
- official documents indicating the nationality of the person concerned.

Hong Kong:

- Hong Kong Special Administrative Region Passports;
- Hong Kong Certificate of Identity;
- Hong Kong Permanent Identity Card;
- official documents indicating the permanent residence status of the person concerned.

ANNEX 2

**Common list of documents the presentation of which is considered as prima facie evidence of nationality or permanent residence**

**(Article 2(1), Article 3(1), Article 4(1) and Article 5(1))**

- photocopies of any of the documents listed in Annex 1 to this Agreement;
- driving licenses or photocopies thereof;
- birth certificates and photocopies thereof;
- company identity cards or photocopies thereof;
- statements by witnesses;
- statements made by the person concerned and language spoken by him or her, including by means of an official test result;
- any other document which may help to establish the nationality or the permanent residence status of the person concerned.

ANNEX 3

**Common list of documents which are considered as proof of the conditions for the**

**readmission of persons of another jurisdiction**
**(Article 3(1), Article 5(1))**

- entry/departure stamps or similar endorsement in the travel document of the person concerned;
- tickets as well as certificates and bills of any kind (e.g. hotel bills, appointment cards for doctors/dentists, entry cards for public/private institutions, etc.) which clearly show that the person concerned stayed on the territory of the requested Member State or the Hong Kong SAR;
- railway tickets and tickets and/or passenger lists of air or boat passages which show the itinerary on the territory of the requested State;
- information showing that the person concerned has used the services of a courier or travel agency.

ANNEX 4

**Common list of documents which are considered as prima facie evidence of the conditions for the readmission of persons of another jurisdiction**
**(Article 3(1), Article 5(1))**

- official statements made, in particular, by border authority staff and other witnesses who can testify to the person concerned crossing the border;
- description of place and circumstances under which the person concerned has been intercepted after entering the territory of the requesting Member State or the Hong Kong SAR;
- information related to the identity and/or stay of a person which has been provided by an international organisation;
- reports/confirmation of information by family members, travelling companions, etc.;
- statement by the person concerned.

ANNEX 5

..............................................................................................................

..............................................................................................................

(Designation of requesting authority)

..............................................................................................................

(Place and date)

Reference

..............................................................................................................

To

..............................................................................................................

..............................................................................................................

..............................................................................................................

(Designation of receiving authority)

**READMISSION APPLICATION**

pursuant to Article 7 of the Agreement of 27 November 2002 between the European Community and the Government of the Hong Kong SAR on the readmission of persons residing without authorisation

A. **PERSONAL DETAILS**

Photograph

1. Full name (underline surname):

..............................................................................................................

2. Maiden name:

..............................................................................................................

3. Date and place of birth:

..............................................................................................................

4. Sex and physical description (height, color of eyes, distinguishing marks etc.):

..............................................................................................................

5. Father's and mother's name:

..............................................................................................................

6. Also known as (earlier names, nicknames or pseudonyms):

..............................................................................................................

7. Nationality and language:

..............................................................................................................

8. Last residence in the requesting State:

..............................................................................................................

9. Address in the requested State:

..............................................................................................................

B. **SPECIAL CIRCUMSTANCES RELATING TO THE TRANSFEREE**

1. State of health (e.g. possible reference to special medical care ; latin name of contagious disease):

.......................................................................................................................................

2. Indication of particularly dangerous person (e.g. suspected of serious offence ; aggressive behaviour):

.......................................................................................................................................

C. **MEANS OF EVIDENCE ATTACHED**

1. ........................................ (type of document) ........................................ (serial number, date and place of issue)

........................................ (issuing authority) ........................................ (expiry date)

2. ........................................ (type of document) ........................................ (serial number, date and place of issue)

........................................ (issuing authority) ........................................ (expiry date)

3. ........................................ (type of document) ........................................ (serial number, date and place of issue)

........................................ (issuing authority) ........................................ (expiry date)

4. ........................................ (type of document) ........................................ (serial number, date and place of issue)

........................................ (issuing authority) ........................................ (expiry date)

5. ........................................ (type of document) ........................................ (serial number, date and place of issue)

........................................ (issuing authority) ........................................ (expiry date)

D. **OBSERVATIONS**

.......................................................................................................................................

.......................................................................................................................................

.......................................................................................................................................

.......................................................................................................................................

........................................

(Signature) (Seal/stamp)

ANNEX 6

..........................................................................

..........................................................................
(Designation of requesting authority)

..........................................................................
(Place and date)

Reference

..........................................................................

To

..........................................................................

..........................................................................

..........................................................................
(Designation of receiving authority)

**TRANSIT APPLICATION**

pursuant to Article 13 of the Agreement of 27 November 2002 between the European Community and the Government of the Hong Kong SAR on the readmission of persons residing without authorisation

A. **PERSONAL DETAILS**

Photograph

1. Full name (underline surname):

..........................................................................

2. Maiden name:

..........................................................................

3. Date and place of birth:

..........................................................................

4. Sex and physical description (height, color of eyes, distinguishing marks etc.):

..........................................................................

5. Also known as (earlier names, nicknames or pseudonyms):

..........................................................................

6. Nationality and language:

..........................................................................

7. Type and number of travel document:

..........................................................................

B. **TRANSIT OPERATION**

1. Type of transit

☐ by air ☐ by sea ☐ by land

2. State of final destination

.....................................................................................................................................................

3. Possible other States of transit

.....................................................................................................................................................

4. Proposed border crossing point, date, time of transfer and possible escorts

.....................................................................................................................................................

.....................................................................................................................................................

.....................................................................................................................................................

5. Admission guaranteed in any other transit State and in the State of final destination (Article 12(2))

☐ yes ☐ no

6. Knowledge of any reason for a refusal of transit (Article 12(3))

☐ yes ☐ no

C. **OBSERVATIONS**

.....................................................................................................................................................

.....................................................................................................................................................

.....................................................................................................................................................

.....................................................................................................................................................

.....................................................................................

(Signature) (Seal/stamp)

JOINT DECLARATION ON ARTICLE 1(f)

The Contracting Parties take note that, under the Hong Kong SAR's current immigration laws, a 'residence authorisation' in the meaning of Article 1(f) is, in particular, issued in all cases where a person is given permission to land in Hong Kong:

- as a student at a specified and officially approved school, university or other educational institution, or
- for paid employment and self-employed economic activities (professionals, investors, talents, imported workers, domestic helpers etc.), or
- for the purpose of joining residents in Hong Kong as dependants (family reunion).

JOINT DECLARATION CONCERNING DENMARK

The Contracting Parties take note that this Agreement does not apply to the territory of the Kingdom of Denmark. In such circumstances it is appropriate that the Hong Kong SAR and Denmark conclude a readmission agreement in the same terms as this Agreement.

JOINT DECLARATION CONCERNING ICELAND AND NORWAY

The Contracting Parties take note of the close relationship between the European Community and Iceland

and Norway, particularly by virtue of the Agreement of 18 May 1999 concerning the association of these countries with the implementation, application and development of the Schengen acquis. In such circumstances it is appropriate that the Hong Kong SAR concludes a readmission agreement with Iceland and Norway in the same terms as this Agreement.

(1) Council Regulation (EC) No 539/2001 of 15 March 2001 listing the third countries whose nationals must be in possession of visas when crossing the external borders and those whose nationals are exempt from that requirement (OJ L 81, 23.3.2001, p. 1).

(2) Directive 95/46/EC of the European Parliament and of the Council of 24 October 1995 on the protection of individuals with regard to the processing of personal data and on the free movement of such data (OJL 281, 23.11.1995, p. 31).

The EU and the Hong Kong SAR are also parties to the multilateral agreement on trade in information technology products (ITA).[7] The ITA implements the WTO Ministerial Declaration on Trade in Information Technology Products, signed in Singapore on 13 December 1996. It eliminates customs duties and other taxes on information technology (IT) products among 63 parties to the agreement, representing 93% of world trade in IT products.

## MACAO

Macao, like Hong Kong, is a SAR of the PRC. Its institutional arrangements and relation to the PRC are set down in a Basic Law.[8] According to the Macao Basic Law,

[7] The text of the ITA is not included here. For further information and the text of the ITA, http://www.wto.org/english/docs_e/legal_e/itadec_e.htm (accessed 24 September 2007).

[8] For the Basic Law of Macao SAR, see http://www.umac.mo/basiclaw/english/main.html (accessed 24 September 2007).

Macao conducts external relations in a variety of fields, including trade. It is a founding Member of the WTO.

The relations of Macao with the EU differ from those of Hong Kong in being based on a Trade and Cooperation Agreement (TCA) (see Document 8.5). Concluded on 14 December 1992 and coming into effect on 1 January 1993, the Agreement for Trade and Economic Cooperation between the European Community and Macao was concluded before the resumption of Chinese sovereignty but continued in force after 1999. It aims to extend and deepen trade and economic relations between the parties and reinforce existing links through cooperation in fields of mutual interest. It provides for cooperation concerning trade and other fields, notably industry, investment, science and technology, information, communication and culture, training, environmental protection, social development, the fight against drugs, and tourism. It also established a joint committee to promote cooperation and oversee the functioning of the Agreement. The EC–Macao TCA is a 'third generation' EC agreement providing that respect for democratic principles and human rights is an integral part of the Agreement. A Joint Committee oversees the operation of the Agreement.

**Document 8.5: Agreement for Trade and Economic Cooperation between the European Community and Macao**

AGREEMENT for trade and cooperation between the European Economic Community and Macao

THE COUNCIL OF THE EUROPEAN COMMUNITIES,

of the one part

and

THE GOVERNMENT OF MACAO,

of the other part,

CONSIDERING that the European Economic Community, hereinafter referred to as the "Community" and Macao wish to develop, extend and deepen economic and trade relations between them;

CONSIDERING that it would be timely to reinforce existing links between the parties by means of cooperation between Macao and the Community in matters of mutual interest;

REAFFIRMING the importance they attach to democratic values and to respecting human rights;

DECLARING that the basic aim of this Agreement shall be to consolidate, intensify and diversity relations between the Parties, to the benefit of both;

DESIROUS of stepping up and diversifying trade and actively developing cooperation in an evolutionary and pragmatic manner;

CONVINCED of the importance of the rules and principles of the General Agreement on Tariffs and Trade (GATT) for the purposes of open and continually expanding international trade, and reaffirming their commitments under that Agreement,

HAVE AGREED AS FOLLOWS:

*Article 1 Basis for cooperation*

The two parties undertake to strengthen their relations and resolve to promote cooperation between them, taking account of Macao's special situation and of its level of development.

Cooperation between the Community and Macao and the implementation of this Agreement are based on respect for the democratic principles and human rights which inspire the policies of both the Community and Macao.

## CHAPTER I TRADE COOPERATION

*Article 2*

1. The Contracting Parties reaffirm their reciprocal commitments under the terms of the General Agreement on Tariffs and Trade (GATT) and shall accord each other most-favoured-nation treatment in all trade matters regarding:

(a) customs duties and charges of any kind imposed on or in connection with imports, exports, re-exports or transit of goods, including the method of levying such duties and charges;

(b) methods of payment and the transfer of such payments;

(c) rules and regulations, procedures and the formalities connected with imports and exports, including provisions relating to customs clearance, transit, warehousing and transhipment of imports or exports;

(d) administrative formalities relating to import and export licences;

(e) taxes and other internal charges levied directly or indirectly on imported or exported goods and services;

(f) laws, rules and regulations and requirements relating to the sale, offering for sale, purchase, transportation, distribution and use of goods on the domestic market.

2. In accordance with the GATT, this treatment shall not apply to:

(a) advantages accorded by one of the two Contracting Parties with the aim of creating a customs union or a free-trade area or pursuant to the creation of such a union or area;

(b) other advantages accorded under the GATT.

*Article 3*

The Contracting Parties undertake to promote trade between them to the greatest possible degree, taking into account their respective economic situations and granting each other the widest possible opportunities.

## CHAPTER II OTHER FIELDS OF COOPERATION

*Article 4*

With the particular aims of bringing about the development of their economies and standards of living, diversifying their links with each other, encouraging scientific and technological progress, opening up new sources of supply and new markets, promoting investment, protecting the environment and improving living condition, the Contracting

Parties agree to develop cooperation, within the bounds of their respective powers and on the basis of mutual interest, in all areas in which they have responsibility for policy, notably the following:

- industry,
- trade,
- science and technology,
- energy,
- transport,
- telecommunications,
- data-processing,
- intellectual and industrial property, standards and specifications,
- protection of the environment,
- social development,
- tourism,
- financial services,
- fisheries,
- customs matters,
- statistics.

*Article 5 Industrial cooperation*

The Contracting Parties shall encourage the use of the various forms of industrial and technical cooperation to benefit their firms and entities, within the bounds of the needs and capabilities of the Parties.

With the aims of the Agreement in mind, the Contracting Parties shall endeavour to facilitate and promote the following, inter alia:

- the establishment of joint ventures,
- the transfer of technology,
- cooperation between financial institutions,
- measures such as visits, contacts and activities to promote cooperation between persons and delegations representing firms or economic organizations,
- the organization of seminars and symposia.

*Article 6*

The Contracting Parties shall promote the development and diversification of Macao's production base in industry and services, in particular by targeting cooperation activities at small and medium-sized enterprises and by encouraging steps to facilitate access on the part of such enterprises to sources of capital, markets and appropriate technology. Such measures could include the joint establishment of suitable mechanisms and institutions.

*Article 7 Investment*

The Contracting Parties agree:

(a) to promote an increase in mutually beneficial investment, within the limits of their responsibilities, rules and policies;

(b) to improve the climate for investment on both sides, notably by means of agreements between the Community Member States and Macao for the protection and promotion of investment, on a basis of non-discrimination and reciprocity.

*Article 8*

Cooperation in science and technology Taking into account their mutual interest and the objectives of their development strategies, the Contracting Parties shall undertake to promote cooperation in science and technology in such a manner as to improve Macao's potential for development.

*Article 9 Cooperation in the field of information, communication and culture*

The Contracting Parties shall establish cooperation in the field of information and communication, taking account of the cultural dimension of relations between them. Such cooperation could include conservation of objects of historic and cultural interest.

*Article 10 Training*

1. Cooperation under this Agreement shall include appropriate provision for training. The Contracting Parties shall furthermore implement individual training programmes in areas of mutual interest.

2. The measures concerned shall be targeted first and foremost at teachers, trainers and executive personnel in positions of responsibility in firms, government, public services and other educational, economic and social entities. They could include promotion of cooperation agreements between institutions of higher education and training in Europe and in Macao, notably with regard to science, technology and vocational training.

*Article 11 Cooperation in the field of the environment*

The Contracting Parties shall undertake to cooperate in the field of environmental protection, particularly with regard to legislation and standards, research, training, technical assistance, the implementation of environmental improvement projects and the organization of seminars and meetings in this field.

*Article 12 Cooperation in the field of social development*

1. The Contracting Parties shall establish cooperation in the field of social development in Macao in order to improve the standard of living and quality of life of the most disadvantaged sections of the population.

2. Measures to attain this aim could include technical assistance concentrating on vocational training, the administration and improvement of social services, job creation, improvement of housing and preventive medicine.

*Article 13 Cooperation in the fight against drugs*

Within the bounds of their respective powers, the Contracting Parties undertake to coordinate and intensify their efforts to prevent and reduce the production, trafficking and consumption of drugs. They shall exchange relevant information in this regard.

*Article 14 Cooperation in the field of tourism*

Within the bounds of their legislation, the Contracting Parties shall encourage cooperation in Macao's tourist industry through targeted action, notably the development of promotion, an exchange of information and statistics, exchanges of experts and training focused on a transfer of technology and improved administration in the industry.

*Article 15 Resources for undertaking cooperation*

In order to facilitate the achievement of the aims set out in this Agreement, the Contracting Parties shall make available, within the limits of their abilities and through their own channels, the appropriate resources, including financial resources.

## CHAPTER III JOINT COMMITTEE

*Article 16*

1. The Contracting Parties shall establish under this Agreement a Joint Committee consisting of representatives of the Community, on the one hand, and representatives of Macao, on the other.

The role of the Joint Committee shall be to promote cooperation as proposed by the Contracting Parties, and in particular:

- to oversee and verify the functioning of this Agreement,
- to study the development of trade and cooperation,
- to propose measures of forestalling problems which might arise in areas covered by the Agreement,
- to propose measures suitable for the development and diversification of trade and cooperation,
- to exchange opinions and make suggestions on any issue of common interest within the fields covered by this Agreement.

2. The Joint Committee shall meet at least once a year, in Brussels and Macao alternately. Special meetings may be convened by mutual agreement, at the request of either Contracting Party.

3. The Joint Committee shall adopt its own rules of procedure and programme of work. The agenda for meetings of the Joint Committee shall be determined by agreement between the Parties.

## CHAPTER IV FINAL PROVISIONS

*Article 17*

Without prejudice to the provisions of the Treaties establishing the European Communities, neither this Agreement nor any action taken under it shall in any way affect the powers of the Member States of the Communities to undertake bilateral activities with Macao in the field of economic cooperation or where appropriate to conclude new economic cooperation agreements with Macao.

*Article 18 Territorial application*

This Agreement shall apply, on the one hand, to the territories in which the Treaty establishing the Community is applied and under the conditions laid down in that Treaty and, on the other hand, to the territory of Macao.

*Article 19 Entry into force and duration*

1. This Agreement shall enter into force on the first day of the month following the date on which the Contracting Parties have notified each other of the completion of the procedures necessary for this purpose.

2. This Agreement is concluded for a period of five years. It shall be renewed tacitly on a yearly basis unless one of the Contracting Parties denounces it to the other Party in writing six months before the date of expiry.

*Article 20 Authentic texts*

This Agreement is drawn up in duplicate in the Danish, Dutch, English, French, German, Greek, Italian, Portuguese, Spanish and Chinese languages, each text being equally authentic.

*Article 21 Future developments*

1. The Contracting Parties may by mutual consent expand this Agreement with a view to enhancing the levels of cooperation and supplementing them, within the bounds of their respective laws, by means of agreements on specific sectors or activities.

2. With regard to the implementation of this Agreement, either of the Contracting Parties may put forward suggestions for widening and strengthening mutual cooperation, taking into account the experience gained in its application.

Hecho en Luxemburgo, el quince de junio de mil novecientos noventa y dos.

Udfærdiget i Luxembourg, den femtende juni nitten hundrede og toghalvfems.

Geschehen zu Luxemburg am fünfzehnten Juni neunzehnhundertzweiundneunzig.

Done at Luxembourg on the fifteenth day of June in the year one thousand nine hundred and ninety-two.

Fait à Luxembourg, le quinze juin mil neuf cent quatre-vingt-douze.

Fatto a Lussemburgo, addì quindici giugno millenovecentonovantadue.

Gedaan te Luxemburg, de vijftiende juni negentienhonderd tweeënnegentig.

Feito no Luxemburgo, em quinze de Junho de mil novecentos e noventa e dois.

In addition to the 1998 Communication, 'Building a Comprehensive Partnership with China' (see Chapter 3), the European Commission has adopted two policy papers concerning Macao. First, the communication entitled 'The EU and Macao: Beyond 2000' (see Document 8.6) was adopted on 12 November 1999. It identified the bases of EU–Macao relations as being common values, a shared legal tradition, sound economic relations and the fact that Macao was a promising economy with good links to the mainland. It emphasised the necessity of ensuring full implementation of the Macao Basic Law and the integrity of the 'One Country, Two Systems' principle. The second policy paper concerned with Macau was the 2006 Commission Communication entitled 'The European Union, Hong Kong and Macao: possibilities for cooperation 2007–2013' (see Document 8.2 above). Its overall priorities are similar to those already discussed for Hong Kong.

## Document 8.6: Communication by the European Commission to the Council and the European Parliament, 'The EU and Macao: Beyond 2000' (1999)

COMMUNICATION FROM THE COMMISSION TO THE COUNCIL AND THE EUROPEAN PARLAMENT
THE EUROPEAN UNION AND MACAU: BEYOND 2000

### 1: Introduction

On 20th December 1999 Macau will revert to China after more than four centuries under Portuguese administration. The EU, as one of Macau's major international partners, has a key role to play in contributing to a smooth handover and a stable, prosperous development of the territory thereafter. The links that exist between Europe and Macau – a similar legal system, common rights, liberties and values, and vibrant trade and investment and in particular the extremely solid relationship in terms of culture and civilisation– make Europe uniquely placed to fulfil this role.

The key to Macau's future stability lies in the full implementation of the Sino-Portuguese Joint Declaration, which guarantees the rights and freedoms of the Territory. It enshrines the concept of "one country, two systems", and guarantees a high degree of autonomy for the Macau SAR within the People's Republic of China. The EU will use all the instruments at its disposal – political dialogue, trade, investment, cooperation and cultural relations – to help underscore Macau's autonomy within China and its particular way of life which the Joint Declaration is committed to preserve. The EU believes this will strengthen Macau and the mainland, rooting them both more firmly in the world community. It will also boost economic and social development in Macau as a vital bridgehead into neighbouring Chinese regions.

In June 1999, the European Council of Cologne stated very clearly the support of Europe to Macau in following terms:

> "The European Council looks forward to the transition process in Macau being concluded in the same positive atmosphere which has hitherto marked it throughout. It is confident that full implementation of the 1987 Sino-Portuguese joint declaration will ensure a harmonius transfer of responsibilities on 20 December 1999 and believes that a high degree of autonomy of the future Special Administrative Region and continuity of Macau's specific social, economic, legal and cultural identity will provide a basis for its stability and prosperity. The European Council is confident that existing relations and ongoing cooperation between the Union and Macau will improve, thus favouring the further development of the area."

### 2: The basis of EU-Macau relations

*2.1: Rights, liberties and values*

The EU and Macau share similar rights and values. For Macau, these have been enshrined in the Joint Sino-Portuguese Declaration signed by both Governments in April 1987. This calls for the creation of a Special Administrative Region in accordance with the "one country, two systems" principle with a distinct social and economic system for 50 years beyond 20th December 1999.

The Joint Declaration states that the SAR of Macau will enjoy a high degree of autonomy, except in foreign and defence affairs; it will retain executive, legislative and judicial power.

The Government will be run by the people of Macau, its Legislative Council will make laws, and the final judicial Court of Appeal will be in Macau. The laws currently in force will remain basically unchanged. The current social and economic systems will also remain unchanged, and so will the life-style.

The Joint Declaration also states that: "The Macau SAR will guarantee, in accordance with the law, all the rights and freedoms of those living in Macau, including personal liberties, the freedom of expression, press freedom, freedom of association and of movement, the right to strike and to choose a profession, freedom of academic research, of religion and belief, freedom of communication and the right to own private property."

The terms of the Joint Declaration are embodied in the Basic Law -or mini-constitution - of the future SAR, approved by the Chinese National People's Congress in 1993. It will enter into force on the day of the handover.

Cultural tolerance and freedom of religion and worship feature prominently as an integral part of Macau's identity. Western and Chinese traditions are jointly preserved.

All of these rights, freedoms and values must be safeguarded. Autonomy and respect for freedom and fundamental rights are inseparable from the "one country, two systems" concept, and the EU will take a close interest in monitoring its full implementation.

European presence in the territory and strong personal ties between Europe and Macau are also some of the main features which help to make Macau a natural springboard for the EU in the region.

*2.2: A shared legal system*

Macau's legal system is rooted in Europe's own continental law structure, which recognises the primacy of the law. It will be succeeded upon the handover by a system, localised after consultations with China in the Joint Liaison Group, which directly transposes Macau's law as it was under Portuguese administration. The Joint Declaration and Basic Law state that the laws in force in Macau before the transfer to China will not change.

Macau's legal system also recognises the primacy of international law over domestic law. In case of conflict the rule of self-sufficient treaty will prevail over the rule of domestic law. This also applies to international conventions in force in Macau but not in China itself. Local rules cannot limit or impede the implementation of international ones.

The basic Law also guarantees the SAR a high degree of autonomy and independence for its executive, legislature and judiciary. All these important principles must be preserved in the future and will be strongly supported by the EU.

*2.3: Sound economic relations*

Economic relations are already firmly based on open trade and investment. This is underpinned by the EU-Macau Trade and Cooperation Agreement, in force since 1993. The EU is Macau's second largest trading partner, and absorbs roughly 30% of its total annual exports, while 11% of Macau's imports came from the EU in 1998. Macau ran a trade surplus of US$ 447 million with the EU in 1998.

The EU is the third biggest investor in Macau, after China and Hong Kong. Portugal is by far the most active EU investor in Macau (27 investing firms), followed by France (5) and the United Kingdom (4).

Macau enjoys several cooperation programmes with the EU in key areas such as business management, public administration, financial services, tourism and European studies. Macau is also eligible for the Asia Invest programme, providing EU expertise and funding to promote investment.

The continuity of the current economic system is also fostered by the renewal, after consultations in the Joint Liaison Group, of the most important franchise contracts in areas of public service, many of which involve the participation of European companies.

*2.4: A promising economy with good links to the mainland*

The per capita income in Macau is around 17,000 Euros a year, one of the highest in Asia. Macau borders Guangdong province and is close to Hong Kong. It has developed from a manufacturing economy focused on particular sectors like textiles and toys into a service provider dominated by, but not limited to, tourism. It continues to develop its specialisation in services, and acts as a bridgehead for foreign investors looking to trade with China.

China's investment in Macau is considerable, particularly in infrastructure, tourism and trade. Macau offers China a basis for manufacturing, distribution and shipment for export and re-export. Macau offers foreign investors a familiar legal and cultural environment in which to trade with the Chinese mainland.

It also enjoys political stability, a free port, low taxation and fiscal advantages, low operating costs, a large supply of housing and office space, modern infrastructure, a sophisticated telecommunications system, a sound fiscal and monetary system, and well trained personnel, all of which give it a competitive lead over other economies in the region.

**3. Furthering EU-Macau relations**

*3.1: Making a success of "one country, two systems"*

In order to help ensure that "one country, two systems" is fully implemented, the European Union will further develop and reinforce its relations with Macau in areas which fall within the responsibility of the SAR government. In these areas the EU will continue to deal directly with the Macanese authorities.

The European Union will follow closely the implementation of the principles enshrined in the Joint Declaration and in the Basic Law, as well as the agreements reached in the Joint Liaison Group. It will make active use of the instruments at its disposal, including political dialogue, joint actions, common positions and cooperation. The Commission intends to publish an annual report on EU-Macau relations across the board, beginning in the year 2000. The issue of Macau will clearly figure in the EU's political dialogue with China.

All interested parties -China, the EU, Portugal and Macau - have already agreed to extend the implementation of the trade and co-operation Agreement between the EC and Macau beyond the handover. The Agreement constitutes a permanent framework for direct dialogue between the Macau SAR and the European Union. The structures embodied in the agreement, such as the annual Joint Committee, will be maintained.

The European Union reiterates the need for the principles of the Agreement to be fully maintained after the handover, including the provision that "the implementation of the present agreement is based on respect for the democratic principles and human rights that inspire the policy of the Community and Macau."

In particular, the EU strongly supports the development of democracy in the territory.

Macau's political system, as enshrined in the Basic Law, does not provide for election by universal suffrage of all members of the Legislative Assembly. The EU believes that it would ultimately be in the best interest of Macau and of all China that the territory's democratic process be constantly improved.

The successful implementation of one country two systems requires the continued development of a well-trained and efficient public administration.

The EU is committed to the full application of the provisions of the UN Covenants on Economic, Social and Cultural Rights, and of the UN Covenant on Civil and Political Rights and core labour standards set out in the relevant ILO conventions in Macau. The EU welcomes the fact that China is committed to reporting regularly on the implementation of these Covenants in Macau.

### *3.2: Strengthening economic relations*

The European Union reiterates the Trade and Cooperation Agreement's key objective of intensifying and diversifying trade and bilateral economic relations with Macau mainly in favour of the services sector in support of the priorities fixed by the Government of Macau.

The EU is confident that trade relations will continue to improve after the handover. Macau is a separate customs territory as provided in the Basic Law and will continue to be treated as such by the European Union in its trade relations.

The EU supports the creation by Macau of a Trade and Economic Office accredited to the European Communities as a means of ensuring a regular dialogue on trade, economic and co-operation issues.

The European Union takes note of the economic potential that Macau offers in the field of services. The EU will make efforts to encourage European investment in the territory. To this end it will actively use the instruments currently at its disposal, notably Asia Invest, as well as future instruments. Direct dialogue among EU and Macau private businessmen will also be promoted.

Another important way in which the EU can recognise the autonomy of Macau is to reaffirm clearly that, for the purposes of the common visa list, Macau should be assessed after the handover as it is now, on its own merits. This would reflect our confidence in the arrangements Macau is making to ensure that the new SAR of Macau passport is secure. Freer access for Macau residents into European countries would certainly help to reinforce and facilitate economic and other contacts, and to demonstrate European confidence in the future of Macau. It would be in the interest of both the EU and Macau.

### *3.3: Promoting multilateral trade*

Macau, as a founding member of the WTO, can convey to China the advantages of a membership and provide experience on the way in which the rules of the world trade system are applied. The EU encourages Macau actively to participate in WTO sectoral agreements such as those applying to the telecoms and financial services sectors.

### *3.4: Supporting Macau's international status*

The European Union will support Macau in preserving its way of life as it is guaranteed in the Basic Law of the territory. This way of life comprises the continuity of a European presence and the reinforcement of personal ties with Europe.

The European Union will also support Macau in continuing its participation in international organisations and fora as it corresponds to its international status.

*3.5: Macau as a regional hub for training and cultural exchange*

The European Union intends to support Macau as a regional centre for training and cultural exchange, as well as in law, tourism, public administration, management and European studies. The EU also encourages Macau to promote knowledge of Europe in Asia and vice-versa. This will contribute to mutual understanding and facilitate economic co-operation between the two continents.

In addition, Macau will remain eligible for regional co-operation projects involving the EU and Asia. It will be able to be involved in bilateral projects with China, in particular those that correspond to its own particular characteristics such as development of human resources, education and training, and university co-operation schemes.

An EC-Macau cooperation officer will be located in Macau in order to assist the coordination of bilateral cooperation for a limited period and under the responsibility of the European Commission Office accredited to Hong Kong and Macau

**4: Conclusions**

The European Union considers that Macau has a vital role as a bridge between Asia and Europe, notably in the following areas:

- Democracy, human rights, individual freedoms and related issues
- Economic and trade issues, including WTO
- Cultural issues, as a regional hub for training and exchange.

The EU looks forward to maintaining and developing its friendly relations with Macau before and after the transfer of sovereignty. The EU believes it has an important and distinct role to play in helping Macau fully to implement the Basic Law, thereby securing a prosperous and stable future for the territory after the handover. With this in mind, the EU will:

- Continue to deal directly with Macau in areas stipulated by the Basic Law.
- Closely monitor and promote the implementation of "one country, two systems" in order fully to support Macau's political, economic and cultural autonomy, and the preservation of the rights and freedoms set out in the Sino-Portuguese Joint Declaration.
- Ensure full implementation of the bilateral EC-Macau trade and co-operation Agreement as an instrument through which to reinforce bilateral relations.
- Deal directly with Macau as an international partner, and maintain regular and close contacts.
- Facilitate European investment in the territory, in particular in the field of services, by using existing or future Community instruments, and by promoting direct dialogue between business representatives.
- Welcome the accreditation to the European Communities of a Trade and Economic Office of Macau as a means of ensuring a regular dialogue in trade, economic and co-operation issues.
- Encourage Macau to impart its experience of WTO membership to China as and when the latter accedes to the WTO.
- Follow the implementation of those international conventions of which Macau is a member and encourage it to broaden its participation in other conventions.

- Help reinforce Macau's regional role in the field of human resources through training, information activities and exchange, in particular involving media, cultural exchanges, civil society entities and higher education institutions. This aim should be fulfilled through actions involving directly the authorities of the SAR and the EU and through the inclusion of the SAR in regional projects.

In addition to communications, the European Commission issues annual reports about EU–Macao relations (see Table 8.5).[9]

The EC and Macao have concluded a number of bilateral agreements (see Table 8.6). A number concern trade in textiles[10]; these agreements are similar to those between the EC and Hong Kong. Trade in textiles between the EU and Macau is now governed by the WTO Agreement and Textiles and Clothing.

In addition to textiles, the EU and Macao have also concluded an agreement on the readmission of persons residing without authorisation (see Document 8.7). This agreement is virtually identical to the analogous agreement with Hong Kong. Its stated aim is to help the EU and Macao combat illegal immigration.

### Document 8.7: EC–Macao Agreement on the Readmission of Persons Residing without Authorisation

**AGREEMENT**

**between the European Community and the Macao Special Administrative Region of the People's Republic of China on the readmission of persons residing without authorisation**

THE EUROPEAN COMMUNITY,

hereinafter referred to as 'the Community',

and

THE MACAO SPECIAL ADMINISTRATIVE REGION OF THE PEOPLE'S REPUBLIC OF CHINA,

hereinafter referred to as 'the Macao SAR', duly authorised to conclude this Agreement by the Central People's Government of the People's Republic of China,

hereinafter referred to as the 'Contracting Parties',

DETERMINED to strengthen their cooperation in order to combat illegal immigration more effectively,

REFERRING to Council Regulation (EC) No 539/2001 of 15 March 2001, listing the third countries whose nationals must be in possession of visas when crossing the external borders and those whose nationals are exempt from that requirement (0) L 81, 21.3.2001, p. 1), and in particular Article 1(2) in conjunction with Annex II thereof, exempting holders of a 'Região Administrativa Especial de Macau' Passport from the requirement, for stays of no more than three months in all, to be in possession of a visa when crossing the external borders of the Member States of the European Union,

[9] The annual reports are available at www.delhkg.cec.eu.int/en/index.htm (accessed 24 September 2007).
[10] The EC–Macao textiles agreements are not included here.

**Table 8.5: Commission Annual Reports on EU–Macao Relations**

| Short title | Official title | Author | Reference | Place and date |
|---|---|---|---|---|
| Annual Report 2000 | Report from the Commission to the Council and the European Parliament, 'First Annual Report by the European Commission on the Macao Special Administrative Region' | European Commission | COM(2001) 432 final | Brussels, 25.7.2001 |
| Annual Report 2001 | Report from the Commission to the Council and the European Parliament, 'Second Annual Report by the European Commission on the Macao Special Administrative Region' | European Commission | COM(2002) 445 final | Brussels, 31.7.2002 |
| Annual Report 2002 | Communication from the Commission to the Council and the European Parliament, 'Macao Special Administration Region: third Annual Report - 2002' | European Commission | COM(2003) 415 final | Brussels, 10.7.2003 |
| Annual Report 2003 | Report from the Commission to the Council and the European Parliament, 'Macao Special Administrative Region: Annual Report 2003' | European Commission | COM(2004) 506 final | Brussels, 16.7.2004 |
| Annual Report 2004 | Report from the Commission to the Council and the European Parliament, 'Macao Special Administrative Region: Annual Report 2004' | European Commission | COM(2005) 363 final | Brussels, 12.8.2005 |
| Annex to the Annual Report 2004 | Commission Staff Working Paper, Annex to the Report from the Commission to the Council and the European Parliament, 'Macao Special Administrative Region: Annual Report 2004', COM(2005)363 final | European Commission | SEC(2005) 1040 | Brussels, 5.8.2005 |
| Annual Report 2005 | Report from the Commission to the Council and the European Parliament, 'Macao Special Administrative Region: Annual Report 2005' | European Commission | COM(2006)480 final | Brussels, 6.9.2006 |
| Annual Report 2006 | Report from the Commission to the Council and the European Parliament, 'Macao Special Administrative Region: Annual Report 2006' | European Commission | COM(2007)471 final | Brussels, 14.8.2007 |

**Table 8.6: Bilateral Agreements between the EU and Macao, 1979–Present**

| Title | Reference |
|---|---|
| Agreement between the European Economic Community and Macao on trade in textile products | OJ 26.11.1979 L298/107 |
| Agreement between the European Economic Community and Macao on trade in textile products | OJ 16.10.1986 L293/186 L298/107 |
| Additional Protocol to the Agreement between the European Economic Community and Macao on trade in textile products consequent to the accession of the Kingdom of Spain and the Portuguese Republic to the Community | OJ 29.11.1986, L338/53 |
| Agreement between the European Economic Community and Macao on trade in textile products – Protocol A – Protocol B – Protocol C – Protocol D – Protocol E– Protocol F – Agreed Minutes – Exchanges of notes | OJ 9.10.1987 L287/47 |
| Agreement in the form of an exchange of letters amending the Agreement between the European Economic Community and Macao on trade in textile products | OJ 4.4.1992 L90/11 |
| Agreement for trade and cooperation between the European Economic Community and Macao | OJ 31.12.1992 L404/27 |
| Agreement in the form of an exchange of letters amending the Agreement between the European Economic Community and Macao on trade in textile products | OJ 31.12.1992 L410/53L90/11 |
| Agreement in the form of an Exchange of Letters between the European Community and Macao amending the Agreement between the European Economic Community and Macao on trade in textile products to take into account the expected accession of the Republic of Austria, the Republic of Finland and the Kingdom of Sweden to the European Union – Exchange of notes | OJ 26.4.1995 L94/237 |
| Administrative arrangements on trade in textile products between the European Community and Macao – Note Verbale | OJ 11.7.1996, L173/26 |
| Agreement between the European Community and the Macao Special Administrative Region of the People's Republic of China on the readmission of persons residing without authorisation | OJ 30.4.2004 L143/99 |

DESIRING to establish, by means of this Agreement and on the basis of reciprocity, rapid and effective procedures for the identification and return of persons who do not, or no longer, fulfil the conditions for entry to, presence in, or residence on the territories of the Macao SAR or one of the Member States of the European Union, and to facilitate the transit of such persons in a spirit of cooperation,

CONSIDERING that the provisions of this Agreement, which falls within the scope of Title IV of the Treaty establishing the European Community, do not apply to the Kingdom of Denmark, in accordance with the Protocol on the position of Denmark annexed to the Treaty on European Union and the Treaty establishing the European Community,

HAVE AGREED AS FOLLOWS:

*Article 1 Definitions*

For the purpose of this Agreement:

(a) 'Member State' ' shall mean any Member State of the European Union, with the exception of the Kingdom of Denmark;

(b) 'National of a Member State' shall mean any person who holds the nationality, as defined for Community purposes, of a Member State;

(c) 'Permanent resident of the Macao SAR' shall mean any person who has the right to reside permanently in the Macao SAR;

(d) 'Person of another jurisdiction' shall mean any person who is neither a permanent resident of the Macao SAR, nor a national of a Member State;

(e) 'Residence authorisation' shall mean a permit of any type issued by the Macao SAR or one of the Member States entitling a person to reside on its territory. This shall not include temporary permissions to remain on its territory in connection with the processing of an asylum application or an application for a residence authorisation;

(f) 'Visa' shall mean an authorisation issued or a decision taken by the Macao SAR or one of the Member States which is: required for entry in, or transit through, its territory. This shall not include airport transit visa.

**SECTION I READMISSION OBLIGATIONS BY THE MACAO SAR**

*Article 2 Readmission of permanent residents and former permanent residents*

1. The Macao SAR shall readmit, upon application by a Member State and without any formalities other than those specified in this Agreement, all persons who do not, or who no longer, fulfil the conditions in force for entry to, presence in, or. residence on, the territory of the requesting Member State provided that it is proved, or may be validly .presumed that they are permanent residents of the Macao SAR.'

The same shall apply to persons who, since entering the territory of a Member State, have lost their right to permanent residence in the Macao SAR, unless such persons have been naturalised by that Member State.

2. At the request of a Member State, the Macao SAR shall, as necessary and without delay, issue the person to be readmitted with the travel document required for his or her return that is of a period of validity of at least 6 (six) months. If, for legal or factual reasons, the person concerned cannot be transferred within the period of validity of the travel document that was initially issued, the Macao SAR shall issue a new travel document with the same period of validity within 14 (fourteen) days. If the Macao SAR has not replied to the request by a Member State within 15 (fifteen) days, it shall be deemed to accept the use of the EU standard travel document for expulsion purposes.

*Article 3 Readmission of persons of another jurisdiction*

1. The Macao SAR shall readmit, upon application by a Member State and without any formalities other than those specified in this Agreement, all persons of another jurisdiction who do not, or who no longer, fulfil the conditions in force for entry to, presence in, or residence on, the territory of the requesting Member State provided that it is proved, or may be validly presumed, that such persons:

(a) at the time of entry in the Member State concerned held a valid residence authorisation issued by the Macao SAR; or

(b) after having entered the territory of the Macao SAR, proceed to enter unlawfully the territory of the Member States, coming directly from the .territory of the Macao SAR.

2. The readmission obligation in paragraph 1 shall not apply if:

(a) the person of another jurisdiction merely transited without entering the territory of the Macao SAR; or

(b) the requesting Member State has issued to the person of another jurisdiction a residence authorisation before or after entering its territory unless that person is in possession of a residence permit, issued by the Macao SAR, which has a longer period of validity.

3. At the request of a Member State, the Macao SAR shall, as necessary and without delay, issue the person to be readmitted with the travel document required for his or her return that is of a period of validity of at least 6 (six) months. If, for legal or factual reasons, the person concerned cannot be transferred within the period of validity of the travel document that was initially issued, the Macao SAR shall issue a new travel document with the same period of validity within 14 (fourteen) days. If the Macao SAR has not replied to the request by a Member State within 15 (fifteen) days, it shall be deemed to accept the use of the EU standard travel document for expulsion purposes.

## SECTION II READMISSION OBLIGATIONS BY THE COMMUNITY

*Article 4 Readmission of own and former own nationals*

1. A Member State shall readmit, upon application by the Macao SAR and without any formalities other than those specified in this Agreement, all persons who do not, or who no longer, fulfil the conditions in force for entry to, presence in, or residence on, the territory of the Macao SAR provided that it is proved, or may be validly presumed, that they are nationals of that Member State. The same shall apply to persons who have been deprived of, or who have renounced, the nationality of a Member State since entering the territory of the Macao SAR unless such persons are permanent residents of the latter.

2. At the request of the Macao SAR, a Member State shall, as necessary and without delay, issue the person to be readmitted with the travel document required for his or her. return that is of a period of validity of at least 6 (six) months. If, for legal or factual reasons, the person concerned cannot be transferred within the period of validity of the travel document that was initially issued, the Member State concerned shall issue a new travel document with the same period of validity within 14 (fourteen) days. If the Member State has not replied to-the request by the Macao SAR within 15 (fifteen) days, it shall be deemed to accept the use of the Travel Permit of Exceptional Use' of the Macao SAR.

*Article 5 Readmission of persons of another jurisdiction*

1. A Member State shall readmit, upon application by the Macao SAR and without any formalities other than those specified in this Agreement, all persons of another jurisdiction who do not, or who no longer, fulfil the conditions in force for entry to, presence in, or residence on, the territory of the Macao SAR provided that it is proved, or may be validly presumed, that such persons:

(a) at the time of entry in the Macao SAR held a valid residence authorisation issued by the requested Member State; or

(b) after having entered the territory of the requested Member State, proceeded to enter unlawfully the territory of the Macao SAR, coming directly from the territory of the requested Member State.

2. The readmission obligation in paragraph 1 shall not apply if:

(a) the person of another jurisdiction has been in airside transit via an International airport of the requested Member State; or

(b) the Macao SAR has issued to the person of another jurisdiction a residence authorisation before or after entering its territory unless that person is in possession of a residence permit, issued by the requested Member State, which has a longer period of validity.

3. If two or more Member States issued a residence authorisation, the readmission obligation in paragraph 1 is for the Member State that issued the document with a longer period of validity or, if one or several of them have already expired, the document that is still valid. If all of the documents have. already expired, the readmission obligation in paragraph 1 is for the Member State that issued the document with the most recent expiry date.

4. At the request of the Macao SAR, a Member State shall, as necessary and without delay, issue the person to be readmitted with the travel document required for his or her return that is of a period of validity of at least 6 (six) months. If, for legal or factual reasons, the person concerned cannot be transferred within the period of validity of the travel document that was initially issued, the Member State concerned shall issue a new travel document with the same period of validity within 14 (fourteen) days. If the Member State has not replied to the request by the Macao SAR within 15 (fifteen) days, it shall be deemed to accept the use of the 'Travel Permit of Exceptional Use' of the Macao SAR.

## SECTION III READMISSION PROCEDURE

*Article 6 Principle*

1. Subject to paragraph 2, a transfer of a person to be readmitted on the basis of one of the obligations contained in Articles 2 to 5 shall require the submission of a readmission application to the competent authority of the requested Contracting Party.

2. The readmission application may be replaced by a written communication to the requested Contracting -Party within a reasonable time period prior to the return of the person concerned provided that:

(a) the person to be readmitted is in possession of a valid travel document and, where applicable, a valid residence authorisation of the requested Contracting Party; and

(b) the person to be readmitted is willing to return to the requested Contracting Party.

*Article 7 Readmission application*

1. Any readmission application is to contain the following information:

(a) the particulars of the person to be readmitted (e.g. given names, surnames, date of birth, and, where possible, place of birth, and the last place of residence);

(b) indication of the means which provide proof or valid presumption of nationality or permanent residence and, where possible, copies of documents.

2. To the extent possible, the readmission application should also contain the following information:

(a) a statement indicating that the person to be transferred may need help or care, provided the person concerned has explicitly consented to the statement;

(b) any other protection or security measure which may be necessary in the individual transfer case.

3. A common form to be used for readmission applications is attached as Annex 5 to this Agreement.

*Article 8 Means of evidence regarding nationality and permanent residence*

1. Proof of nationality or permanent residence pursuant to Article 2(1) and Article 4(1) can be furnished through the documents listed in Annex 1 to this Agreement, even if their period of validity has expired. If such documents are presented, the Member States shall recognise the nationality, and the Macao SAR shall recognise the permanent residence, without further formalities. Proof of nationality or permanent residence cannot be furnished through false documents.

2. Valid presumption of nationality or permanent residence pursuant to Article 2(1) and Article 4(1) can be furnished through the documents listed in Annex 2 to this Agreement, even if their period of validity has expired. If such documents are presented, the Member States shall deem the nationality, and the Macao SAR shall deem the permanent residence, to be established unless they can prove otherwise.

3. If none of the documents listed in Annexes 1 or 2 can be presented, the competent authorities of the Macao SAR or the Member State concerned shall, upon request, make arrangements to interview by any means the person to be readmitted without undue delay in order to establish his or her nationality or permanent residence.

*Article 9 Means of evidence regarding persons of another jurisdiction*

1. Proof of the conditions for the readmission of persons of another jurisdiction laid down in Article 3(1) and Article 5(1) can be furnished through the means of evidence listed in Annex 3 to this Agreement; it cannot be furnished through false documents. Any such proof shall be mutually recognised by the Contracting Parties without farther formalities.

2. Valid presumption of the conditions for the readmission of persons of another jurisdiction laid down in Article 3(1) and Article 5(1) can be furnished through the means of evidence listed in Annex 4 to this Agreement. Where such prima facie evidence is presented, the Contracting Parties shall deem the conditions to be established unless they can prove otherwise.

3. The unlawfulness of entry, presence or residence may be established by means of the travel documents of the person concerned being missing, or in which the necessary visa or other residence authorisation for the territory of the requesting Member State or the Macao SAR are missing. A statement by the competent authority of the requesting Contracting Party that the person concerned has been found not. having the necessary travel documents, visa or residence authorisation shall likewise provide valid presumption of the unlawful entry, presence or residence.

*Article 10 Time limits*

1. The application for readmission must be submitted to the competent authority of the requested Contracting Party within a maximum of one year after the requesting authority has gained knowledge that a person of another jurisdiction does not, or does no longer, fulfil the conditions in force for entry, presence or residence. Where there are legal or factual obstacles to the application being submitted in time, the time limit shall, upon request, be extended but only until the obstacles have ceased to exist.

2. A readmission application must be replied to without undue delay, and in any event within a maximum of one month; reasons shall be given for refusal of a readmission request. This time limit begins to run with the date of receipt of the readmission request. Upon expiry of this time limit the transfer shall be deemed to have been agreed to.

3. After agreement has been given or, where appropriate, upon expiry of the one month time limit, the person concerned shall be transferred without undue delay and, at the most, within three months. Upon application, this time limit may be extended by the time taken to deal with legal or practical obstacles.

*Article 11 Transfer modalities and modes of transportation*

1. Before returning a person, the competent authorities of the Macao SAR and the Member State concerned shall make arrangements in writing and in advance regarding the transfer date, the border crossing point and possible escorts.

2. No means of transportation, whether by air, land or sea, shall be prohibited but, as a rule, return shall take place by air. Return by air is not restricted to the use of national carriers or security staff of the requesting Contracting Party, and may take place by using scheduled flights as well as charter flights.

## SECTION IV TRANSIT OPERATIONS

*Article 12 Principles*

1. The Macao SAR shall allow the transit of persons of another jurisdiction through its territory if a Member State so requests, and a Member State shall authorise the transit of persons of another jurisdiction through' its territory if the Macao SAR so requests, if the onward journey in possible other States of transit and the readmission by the State of destination is assured.

2. The Member States and the Macao SAR should restrict the transit of persons of another jurisdiction to cases where such persons cannot be returned to the State of destination directly.

3. Transit can be refused by the Macao SAR or a Member State:

(a) if the person of another jurisdiction runs the risk of persecution, or could be subjected to criminal prosecution or sanctions in another State of transit or in the State of destination, or could be threatened by criminal prosecution on the territory of the requested Member State or the Macao SAR;

(b) on grounds of public health, domestic security or other fundamental interests of the legal order.

4. The Macao SAR or a Member State may revoke any authorisation issued if circumstances referred to in paragraph 3 subsequently arise or come to light which stand in the way of the transit operation, or if the onward journey in possible States of transit or the readmission by the State of destination is no longer assured.

*Article 13 Transit procedure*

1. An application for transit must be submitted to the competent authorities in writing and is to contain the following information:

(a) type of transit (by air, land or sea), possible other States of transit and intended final destination;

(b) the particulars of the person concerned (e.g. given name, surname, date of birth, and — where possible — place of birth, nationality, type and number of travel document);

(c) envisaged border crossing point, time of transfer and possible use of escorts;

(d) a declaration that from the viewpoint of the requesting Contracting Party the conditions pursuant to Article 12(2) are met, and that no reasons for a refusal pursuant to Article 12(3) are known of.

A common form to be used for transit applications is attached as Annex 6 to this Agreement.

2. The competent authority of the requested Contracting Party shall, without undue delay and in writing, inform the requesting competent authority of the admission, confirming the border crossing point and the -envisaged time of admission, or inform it of the admission refusal and of the reasons for such refusal.

3. If the transit is effected by air, the person to be readmitted and possible escorts shall be exempted from having to obtain an airport transit visa.

4. The competent authorities of the requested Contracting Party shall, subject to mutual consultations, support the transit, in particular through the surveillance of the persons in question and the provision of suitable amenities for that purpose.

## SECTION V COSTS

*Article 14 Transport and transit costs*

Without prejudice to the right of the competent authorities to recover the costs associated with the readmission from the person to be readmitted or third parties, all- transport costs incurred in connection with readmission and transit pursuant to this Agreement as far as the border of the State of final destination shall be borne by the requesting Contracting Party.

## SECTION VI DATA PROTECTION AND NON-AFFECTION CLAUSE

*Article 15 Data protection*

1. The communication of personal data shall only take place if such communication is necessary for the implementation of this Agreement by the competent authorities of the Macao SAR or the Member States.

2. The processing and treatment of personal data in a particular case shall be subject to the Macao SAR law and, where the controller is a competent authority of a Member State, to the provisions of Directive 95/46/EC of the European Parliament and of the Council of 24 October 1995 on the protection of individuals with regard to the processing of personal data and on the free movement of such data (OJ L 281, 23.11.1995, p. 31) and of national legislation adopted pursuant to this Directive.

3. Additionally, the following principles shall apply:

(a) personal data must be processed fairly and lawfully;

(b) personal data must be collected for the specified, explicit and legitimate purpose of implementing this Agreement and not farther processed by the communicating or by the recipient in a way incompatible with that purpose;

(c) personal data must be adequate, relevant and not excessive in relation to the purpose for which they are collected and/or farther processed; in particular, personal data communicated may concern only the following:

- the particulars of the person to be transferred (e.g. surname, given name, any previous names, nicknames or pseudonyms, date and place of birth, sex, current and any previous nationality),
- identity card or passport (number, period of validity, date of issue, issuing authority, place of issue),
- stopping places and itineraries,
- other information needed to identify the person to be transferred or to examine the readmission requirements pursuant, to this Agreement.

(d) personal data must be accurate and, where necessary, kept up to date;

(e) personal data must be kept in a form which permits identification of data subjects for no longer than is necessary for the purpose for which the data were collected or for which they are farther processed;

(f) both the communicating authority and the recipient shall take every reasonable step to ensure as appropriate the rectification, erasure or blocking of personal data where the processing does not comply with the provisions of this Article, in particular because the data are not adequate, relevant, accurate, or they'are excessive in relation to the purpose of processing. This includes the notification of any rectification, erasure or blocking to the other Party;

(g) upon request, the recipient shall inform the communicating authority of the use of the communicated data and of the results obtained therefrom;

(h) personal data may only be communicated to the competent authorities. Further communication to other bodies requires the prior consent of the communicating authority;

(i) the communicating and the receiving authorities are under the obligation to make a written record of the communication and receipt of personal data.

*Article 16 Non-affection clause*

1. This Agreement shall be without prejudice to the rights, obligations and responsibilities arising from International Law applicable to the Community, the Member States and the Macao SAR.

2. Nothing in this Agreement, shall prevent the return of a person under other formal or informal arrangements.

## SECTION VII IMPLEMENTATION AND APPLICATION

*Article 17 Readmission Committee*

1. The Contracting Parties shall provide each other with mutual assistance in the application and interpretation of this Agreement. To this end, they shall set up a Readmission Committee which will, in particular, have the task:

(a) to monitor the application of this Agreement;

(b) to decide on implementing arrangements necessary for the uniform execution of it;

(c) to have a regular exchange of information on the implementing Protocols drawn up by individual Member States and the Macao SAR pursuant to Article 18;

(d) to recommend amendments to this Agreement.

2. Recommendations of the Readmission Committee for amendment of the Annexes to this Agreement may be approved by the Parties through a simplified procedure.

3. The Readmission Committee shall be composed by representatives of the Community and the Macao SAR; the Community shall be represented by the Commission of the European Communities, assisted by experts from Member States.

4. The Readmission Committee shall meet where necessary at the request of one of the Contracting Parties.

5. The Readmission Committee shall establish its rules of procedures.

*Article 18 Implementing Protocols*

1. The Macao SAR and a Member State may draw up implementing Protocols which shall cover rules on;

(a) the designation of the competent authorities, the border crossing points, the exchange of contact points and the languages in communication;

(b) the conditions for transit of persons of another jurisdiction under escort;

(c) means and documents additional to those listed in Annexes 1 to 4 to this Agreement.

2. The implementing Protocols referred to in paragraph 1 will enter into force only after the Readmission Committee, established by Article 17, has been notified.

3. The Macao SAR agrees to apply any provision of an implementing Protocol drawn up with one Member State also in its relations with any other Member State upon request of the latter.

*Article 19 Relation to bilateral readmission agreements or arrangements of Member States*

The provisions of this Agreement shall take precedence over the provisions of any bilateral agreement or arrangement on the readmission of persons residing without authorisation which have been or may, under Article 18, be concluded between individual Member States and the Macao SAR, in so far as the provisions of the latter are incompatible with those of this Agreement.

## SECTION VIII FINAL PROVISIONS

*Article 20 Entry into force, duration and termination*

1. This Agreement shall be ratified or approved by the Contracting Parties in accordance with their respective procedures.

2. This Agreement shall enter into force on the first day of the second month after the date on which the Contracting Parties notify each other that the procedures referred to in the first paragraph have been completed.

3. This Agreement shall remain in force indefinitely, unless terminated in accordance with paragraph 4 of this Article.

4. Each Contracting Party may terminate this Agreement by giving written notice to the other Contracting Party. This Agreement shall cease to apply six months after the date of such notification.

*Article 21 Annexes*

Done at Luxembourg on the thirteenth day of October in the year two thousand and three in duplicate in the Danish, Dutch, English, Finnish, French, German, Greek, Italian, Portuguese, Spanish, and Swedish languages, each of these texts being equally authentic.

Por la Comunidad Europea

For Det Europæiske Fællesskab

Fur die Europäische Gemeinschaft

*Για την Ευρωπαική Κοινότητα*

For the European Community

Pour la Communauté européenne

Per la Comunità europea

Voor de Europese Economische Gemeenschap

Pela Comunidade Europeia

Euroopan yhteisön puolesta

För Europeiska gemenskapen

Por la Région Administrativa Especial de Macao de la República Popular de China

For Folkerepublikken Kinas særlige administrative region Macao

Für die Sonderverwahungsregion Macau der Volksrepublik China

*Για την Ειδικής Διοιητική Περιφέρεια Μακάο της Λαϊκής Δημοκρατίας της Κίνας*

For the Macao Special Administrative Region of the People's Republic of China

Pour la région administrative spéciale de Macao de la République populaire de Chine

Per la Regione ad amministrazione speciale di Macao della Repubblica popolare cinese

Voor de Speciale Administratieve Regio Macao van de Volksrepubliek China

Pela Região Administrativa Especial de Macau da República Popular da China

Kiinan kansantasavallan Macaon erityishallintotalueen puolesta

För folkrepubliken Kinas sarskilda administrativa region Macao

## ANNEX 1

**Common list of documents the presentation of which is considered as proof of nationality or permanent residence**
**(Article 2(1), Article 3(1), Article 4(1) and Article 5(1))**

Member States:

- passports of any kind (national passports, diplomatic passports, service passports, collective passports and surrogate passports including children's passports),
- identity cards of any kind (including temporary and provisional ones),
- service books and military identity cards,
- seaman's registration books and skippers' service cards,
- official documents indicating the nationality of the person concerned.

Macao:

- Macao Special Administrative Region Passports (Passaporte da Regiao Administrativa Especial de Macau),
- Permanent Resident Identity Card of the Macao Special Administrative Region. (Bilhete de Identidade de Residente Permanente da Regiao Administrativa Especial de Macau),
- Official documents indicating the permanent residence status of the person concerned.

## ANNEX 2

**Common list of documents the presentation of which is considered as valid presumption of nationality or permanent residence**
**(Article 2(1), Article 3(1), Article 4(1) and Article 5(1))**

- photocopies of any of the documents listed in Annex 1 to this Agreement,
- Macao Resident Identity Card carrying date of first issue at least seven years ago,
- birth certificates and photocopies thereof,
- statements by witnesses,
- statements made by the person concerned and language spoken by him or her, including by means of an official test result,
- any other document which may help to establish the nationality or the permanent residence status of the person concerned, such as driving licences and company identity cards.

## ANNEX 3

**Common list of documents which are considered as proof of the conditions for the readmission of persons of another jurisdiction**
**(Article 3(1) and Article 5(1))**

- visa, entry/departure stamps or similar endorsement in the travel document of the person concerned,
- tickets as well as certificates and bills of any kind (e.g. hotel bills, appointment cards for doctors/dentists, entry cards for public/private institutions, etc.) which clearly show that the person concerned stayed on the territory of the requested Member State or the Macao SAR,
- railway tickets and tickets and/or passenger lists of air or boat passages which show the itinerary on the territory of the requested state,
- information showing that the person concerned has used the services of a courier or travel agency.

## ANNEX 4

**Common list of documents which are considered as prima fade evidence of the conditions for the readmission of persons of another jurisdiction**
**(Article 3(1) and Article 5(1))**

- official statements made, in particular, by border authority staff and other witnesses who can testify to the person concerned crossing the border,
- description of place and circumstances under which, the person concerned has been intercepted after entering the territory of the requesting Member State or the Macao SAR,
- information related .to the identity and/or stay of a person which has been provided by an International organisation,
- reports/confirmation of information by family members, travelling companions, etc,
- statement by the person concerned.

ANNEX 5

[Emblem of the Macao SAR]

.............................................. ..............................................
(Place and date)

..............................................
(Designation of requesting authority)

Reference

..............................................

To

..............................................

..............................................

..............................................
(Designation of receiving authority)

**READMISSION APPLICATION**

pursuant to Article 7 of the Agreement of 13 October 2003 between the European Community and the Macao SAR on the readmission of persons residing without authorisation

A. PERSONAL DETAILS

Photograph

1. Full name (underline surname):

..............................................

2. Maiden name:

..............................................

3. Date and place of birth:

..............................................

4. Sex and physical description (height, colour of eyes, distinguishing marks, etc.):

..............................................

5. Father's and mother's name:

..............................................

6. Also known as (earlier names, nicknames or pseudonyms):

..............................................

7. Nationality and language:

..............................................

8. Last residence in the requesting State:

..............................................

9. Address in the requested State:

..............................................

B. SPECIAL CIRCUMSTANCES RELATING TO THE TRANSFEREE

1. State of health

(e.g. possible reference to special medical care; Latin name of contagious disease):

.....................................................................................................

2. Indication of particularly dangerous person

(e.g. suspected of serious offence; aggressive behaviour):

.....................................................................................................

C. MEANS OF EVIDENCE ATTACHED

| | | |
|---|---|---|
| 1. | .................................... (type of document) | .................................... (serial number, date and place of issue) |
| | .................................... (issuing authority) | .................................... (expiry date) |
| 2. | .................................... (type of document) | .................................... (serial number, date and place of issue) |
| | .................................... (issuing authority) | .................................... (expiry date) |
| 3. | .................................... (type of document) | .................................... (serial number, date and place of issue) |
| | .................................... (issuing authority) | .................................... (expiry date) |
| 4. | .................................... (type of document) | .................................... (serial number, date and place of issue) |
| | .................................... (issuing authority) | .................................... (expiry date) |
| 5. | .................................... (type of document) | .................................... (serial number, date and place of issue) |
| | .................................... (issuing authority) | .................................... (expiry date) |

D. OBSERVATIONS

.....................................................................................................

.....................................................................................................

.....................................................................................................

........................................

(Signature) (Seal/stamp)

ANNEX 6

[Emblem of the Macao SAR]

. . . . . . . . . . . . . . . . . . . . . . . . . . . . . . . . . . . . . . . . . . . . . . . . . . . . . . . . . . . . . . . . . . . . . . . . . . . . . . . . . . . . . . .

(Place and date)

. . . . . . . . . . . . . . . . . . . . . . . . . . . . . . . . . . . . . . . . . . .

(Designation of requesting authority)

Reference

. . . . . . . . . . . . . . . . . . . . . . . . . . . . . . . . . . . . . . . . . . .

To

. . . . . . . . . . . . . . . . . . . . . . . . . . . . . . . . . . . . . . . . . . .

. . . . . . . . . . . . . . . . . . . . . . . . . . . . . . . . . . . . . . . . . . .

. . . . . . . . . . . . . . . . . . . . . . . . . . . . . . . . . . . . . . . . . . .

(Designation of receiving authority)

TRANSIT APPLICATION

pursuant to Article 13 of the Agreement of 13 October 2003 between the European Community and the Macao SAR on the readmission of persons residing without authorisation

A. PERSONAL DETAILS

Photograph

1. Full name (underline surname):

. . . . . . . . . . . . . . . . . . . . . . . . . . . . . . . . . . . . . . . . . . . . . . . . . . . . . . . . . . . . . . .

2. Maiden name:

. . . . . . . . . . . . . . . . . . . . . . . . . . . . . . . . . . . . . . . . . . . . . . . . . . . . . . . . . . . . . . .

3. Date and place of birth:

. . . . . . . . . . . . . . . . . . . . . . . . . . . . . . . . . . . . . . . . . . . . . . . . . . . . . . . . . . . . . . .

4. Sex and physical description (height, colour of eyes, distinguishing marks, etc.):

. . . . . . . . . . . . . . . . . . . . . . . . . . . . . . . . . . . . . . . . . . . . . . . . . . . . . . . . . . . . . . . . . . . . . . . . . . . . . . . . . . . . . . . . . . .

5. Also known as (earlier names, nicknames or pseudonyms):

. . . . . . . . . . . . . . . . . . . . . . . . . . . . . . . . . . . . . . . . . . . . . . . . . . . . . . . . . . . . . . . . . . . . . . . . . . . . . . . . . . . . . . . . . . .

6. Nationality and language:

. . . . . . . . . . . . . . . . . . . . . . . . . . . . . . . . . . . . . . . . . . . . . . . . . . . . . . . . . . . . . . . . . . . . . . . . . . . . . . . . . . . . . . . . . . .

7. Type and number of travel document

. . . . . . . . . . . . . . . . . . . . . . . . . . . . . . . . . . . . . . . . . . . . . . . . . . . . . . . . . . . . . . . . . . . . . . . . . . . . . . . . . . . . . . . . . . .

B. TRANSIT OPERATION

1. Type of transit

☐ by air ☐ by sea ☐ by land

2. State of final destination

.............................................................................................................

3. Possible other States of transit

.............................................................................................................

4. Proposed border crossing point, date, time of transfer and possible escorts

.............................................................................................................

.............................................................................................................

.............................................................................................................

5. Admission guaranteed in any other transit State and in the State of final destination

(Article 12 paragraph 2)

☐ yes ☐ no

6. Knowledge of any reason for a refusal of transit

(Article 12 paragraph 3)

☐ yes ☐ no

C. OBSERVATIONS

.............................................................................................................

.............................................................................................................

.............................................................................................................

..............................................
(Signature) (Seal/stamp)

JOINT DECLARATION ON STATELESS PERSONS

The Contracting Parties take note that, at present, no International Convention or agreement dealing with stateless persons is applicable to the Macao SAR. They therefore agree that this category of persons shall be covered by the definition of 'person of another jurisdiction' in Article l(d).

JOINT DECLARATION ON VISAS

The Contracting Parties take note that, under Macao's current laws, visas are issued upon arrival only, and expire upon departure from Macao. Consequently, it is legally impossible for a third country national to enter an EU Member State while holding a valid visa for Macao.

The Parties agree to consult each other in due time, should this legal situation change.

JOINT DECLARATION ON ARTICLE 3(2)(a)

The Contracting Parties agree that persons of another jurisdiction who are 'merely transiting without entering' in the meaning of Article 3(2)(a) are persons whose transit is taking place with the knowledge or under the escort of the competent authorities of the Macao SAR.

JOINT DECLARATION CONCERNING DENMARK

The Contracting Parties take note that this Agreement does not apply to the territory or to the nationals of the Kingdom of Denmark. In such. circumstances it is appropriate that the Macao SAR and Denmark conclude a readmission agreement in the same terms as this Agreement.

JOINT DECLARATION CONCERNING ICELAND AND NORWAY

The Contracting Parties take note of the close relationship between the European Community and Iceland and Norway, particularly by virtue of the Agreement of 18 May 1999 concerning the association of these countries with the implementation, application and development of the Schengen acquis. In such circumstances it is appropriate that the Macao SAR concludes a readrnission agreement with Iceland and Norway in the same terms as this Agreement.

The EU and Macao have established a number of cooperation projects for training in the tourism industry, European studies, services development, funding of companies in partnership and legal training.[11]

Recently Macao has become an important platform for relations between China and Portuguese-speaking countries, in addition to Portugal and Macao (see Table 8.7). The first Forum for Trade and Economic Cooperation between China and Portuguese-speaking Countries was held in Macao on 12–14 October 2003.[12] The Portuguese-speaking member countries of the ministerial-level Forum include

[11] For a brief description, see http://ec.europa.eu/comm/external_relations/macau/intro/index.htm (accessed 4 June 2007).

[12] See http://english.peopledaily.com.cn/200310/12/print20031012_125848.html (accessed 30 October 2006). For more complete information on cooperation between the countries involved, see http://english.mofcom.gov.cn/subject/chinaportuguese/index.shtml (accessed 24 October 2007).

Angola, Brazil, Cape Verde, Guinea Bissau, Mozambique, Portugal and East Timor. At the first Forum they signed an Action Plan for Economic and Trade Cooperation (see Document 8.8). The Action Plan included general principles, and provisions on intergovernmental cooperation, trade, investment and business cooperation and cooperation in agriculture and fisheries, engineering and infrastructure construction, natural resources, development of human resources and accompanying measures. The Forum has a permanent secretariat in Macao. The 2nd Ministerial Conference of the Forum was held in Macao in September 2006. It also resulted in an Action Plan for Economic and Trade Cooperation for 2007–2009 (see Document 8.9). The provisions expanded on those of the 2003 Action Plan and added new provisions concerning development, new areas of cooperation, such as finance, tourism and transport, and the active role of Macao as a bridge between China and the Portuguese-speaking countries.

## Document 8.8: Action Plan for Economic and Trade Cooperation (2003)[13]

Forum for Economic and Trade Co-operation between China and the Portuguese-speaking Countries (Macao)
2003 Ministerial Conference
Action Plan for Economic and Trade Co-operation

The Ministers who were present at the Forum for Economic and Trade Co-operation between China and Portuguese-speaking Countries (Macao), held between 12th and 14th October 2003, in the Macao Special Administrative Region of the People's Republic of China, considered that this Forum will contribute positively to the development of economic, trade and investment relations between the participating countries, and recognise the platform role that Macao may perform in the deepening of economic ties between China and the Portuguese-speaking Countries.

Ministers from Angola, Brazil, Cape Verde, China, Guinea-Bissau, Mozambique, Portugal and East-Timor were present at the Forum.

**1 – General Principles**

1.1 The Ministers appreciated positively the current level of bilateral co-operation between China and the Portuguese-speaking Countries and expressed conviction that, with the efforts of the respective Governments, there exist a great potential for their development.

1.2 The Ministers registered the existing peculiarities in terms of the level of economic development between China and the Portuguese-speaking Countries and agreed to establish partnership relations in terms of economic and trade co-operation, based on principles of mutual confidence equality, reciprocity and barter of resources, diversification of means of co-operation, as well as the exchange of interests.

1.3 The Ministers considered that China and the Portuguese-speaking Countries have common interests in relation to opportunities and challenges encountered in the process of economic globalisation.

[13] Translated from Portuguese.

**Table 8.7: Forum for Economic and Trade Cooperation between China and the Portuguese-Speaking Countries, based in Macau**

| Document | Author | Place | Date | Source |
|---|---|---|---|---|
| Discursos Efectuados na 1a Conferência Ministerial de Fórum para a Cooperação Económica e Comercial entre a China e os Países de Língua Portuguesa (Macau) | Secretaríado Permanente do Fórum para a Cooperação Económica e Comercial entre a China e os Países de Lingua Portuguesa | Macao | 12–14.10.2003 | Governo da Região Especial do Macau, Gabinete de Apoio ao Secretariado Permanente do Fórum para a Cooperação Económica e Comercial entre a China e os Países de Língua Portuguesa, Avenida Governador Jaime Silvério Marques, no. 415, Edifício Comecial Tai Fung, R/C-2°, andar "N", Macau |
| Plano de Acçao para a Cooperação Económica e Comercial (2003) (see Document 8.8) | Conferência Ministerial de 2003, Fórum para a Cooperação Económica e Comercial entre a China e os Países de Lingua Portuguesa | Macao | 13.10.2003 | Governo da Região Especial do Macau, Gabinete de Apoio ao Secretariado Permanente do Fórum para a Cooperação Económica e Comercial entre a China e os Países de Língua Portuguesa, Avenida Governador Jaime Silvério Marques, no. 415, Edifício Comecial Tai Fung, R/C-2°, andar "N", Macau |
| Textos do Seminário sobre o Desenvolvimento do Fórum para a Cooperação Económica e Comercial entre a China e os Países de Língua Portuguesa | Secretaríado Permanente do Fórum para a Cooperação Económica e Comercial entre a China e os Países de Lingua Portuguesa | Macao | published in May 2006 by Tipografia Macau Hung Heng Lda, Macau | Governo da Região Especial do Macau, Gabinete de Apoio ao Secretariado Permanente do Fórum para a Cooperação Económica e Comercial entre a China e os Países de Língua Portuguesa, Avenida Governador Jaime Silvério Marques, no. 415, Edifício Comecial Tai Fung, R/C-2°, andar "N", Macau |
| Plano de Acçao para a Cooperação Económica e Comercial /2007-2009) (see Document 8.9) | Conferência Ministerial de 2006, Fórum para a Cooperação Económica e Comercial entre a China e os Países de Lingua Portuguesa | Macao | 13.10.2003 | Governo da Região Especial do Macau, Gabinete de Apoio ao Secretariado Permanente do Fórum para a Cooperação Económica e Comercial entre a China e os Países de Língua Portuguesa, Avenida Governador Jaime Silvério Marques, no. 415, Edifício Comecial Tai Fung, R/C-2°, andar "N", Macau |

1.4 The Ministers agreed that, within the scope of the Forum, the economic and trade co-operation between China and the Portuguese-speaking Countries, shall be directed by the present Action Plan, safeguarding the negotiated actions and programmes, by each country, in the scope of the respective processes of regional integration or deriving from other international obligations.

**2. Inter-governmental Co-operation**

2.1 The Ministers agreed in intensifying and improving the mechanism of bilateral consultations between China and the Portuguese-speaking Countries through the promotion of visits and high level inter-governmental exchanges, as well as visits from high-ranking representatives, with the objective of finding new areas and new means of economic and trade co-operation.

2.2 The Ministers agreed that the mechanisms to be established at the Forum will be complementary to those already existing in bilateral consultations, so as to increase inter-governmental contacts more and more, to share experiences, to make partnerships and strengthen the ties of co-operation.

2.3 The Ministers reaffirmed their commitment to the development of bilateral relations in the economic area, through the forum of the existing Mixed Commissions for Economic and Trade, with the objective of energising bilateral economic co-operation.

**3. Trade**

3.1 The Ministers considered that the increase in trade between China and the Portuguese-speaking Countries, constitutes a common objective for all, making the progress of bilateral trade possible, on a basis of equality and reciprocity, harmonious development and respect for international trade regulations.

3.2 The Ministers agreed to use the mechanisms of consultations established by the Forum as a platform to facilitate exchange of businesses between the different Countries and create favourable conditions for trade.

3.3 The Ministers agreed to support the holding of fairs and exhibitions of specific products from the Countries participating in the Forum, as well as other forms of co-operation, with a view to facilitate the entry of those products into the respective markets.

3.4 The Ministers expressed conviction that the strengthening of contacts between entities and organisations of the participating Countries, and the increase in information exchanges about their products and markets as well as evolution of the commercial flow, will contribute to the expansion of bilateral trade.

3.5 The Ministers agreed to stimulate the co-operation relating to technical standards, looking towards overcoming the barriers from the adoption of differentiated regulations, whilst safeguarding compromises negotiated for each country in this matter.

**4. Investment and Enterprise Co-operation**

4.1 The Ministers considered the improvement of the investment climate in their Countries to be of great importance and therefore pledged to undertake efforts by way of encouraging a suitable legal entity for carrying out and protecting investments as well as to promote the sealing of bilateral agreements for the protection and promotion of investments.

4.2 The Ministers agreed to promote and encourage the creation of partnerships between enterprises of their Countries, search for means of co-operation and exploitation of projects of common interest that can contribute to the development of the local economy, through the establishment of "joint-venture" enterprises or equity capital.

4.3 The Ministers agreed to favour the development of relations between enterprises of their Countries, through the exchange of information having recourse to the latest information technologies, concerning opportunities for business and investment.

**5. Agricultural and Fishery Co-operation**

5.1 The Ministers, cognisant that the development of agriculture and fishery plays a significant role in the eradication of poverty, considered that a great potential exists in the area of agricultural and fishery co-operation between China and the Portuguese-speaking Countries, and expressed their availability to take the necessary measures to promote co-operation in this area.

5.2 The Ministers agreed to co-operate in the various areas of the agricultural and fishery activity, giving priority to the study and preparation of agricultural development programmes, cultivation and breeding, construction of infrastructure, production of machinery, transformation of products as well as exchange and transfer of agricultural and fishery technology, amongst others.

5.3 The Ministers expressed their availability to share the experiences of their countries in the development of agriculture and fishery, with the objective of facilitating the capture of investments and the development of entrepreneurial and technological co-operation.

**6. Co-operation in the Areas of Engineering and Construction of Infrastructures**

6.1 The Ministers recognised the existence of a high technological level and productive capacity of plant and equipment in some participating Countries, in the areas of engineering and infrastructure construction, and proposed to stimulate the enterprises in their Countries to participate in projects for infrastructures in the transport, electrical energy, telecommunications, water supply and treatment and urban planning sectors, amongst others.

6.2 The Ministers agreed to intensify the exchange of experiences in the technological area and in the material for administration of contract work, as well as the exchange of information about project bids and construction of infrastructures to be developed, whenever possible, resorting to projects financed by International Financing Institutions.

**7. Co-operation in the Natural Resources Area**

7.1 The Ministers agreed to strengthen exchange and co-operation in the area of natural resources, with the objective of favouring sustainable management and a rational utilisation from it.

7.2 The Ministers agreed to intensify co-operation in the area of exploitation and use of natural resources, according to the principle of reciprocity and barter of resources.

8. Co-operation in the Area of Development of Human Resources

The Ministers agreed to intensify and improve, within the framework of the Forum, co-operation and bilateral exchange between China and the Portuguese-speaking Countries in terms of human resources, in order to promote economic and trade exchange between the parties, as well as to increase mutual understanding and friendship.

The Ministers, cognisant of the importance of education on the quality of human resources, agreed to strengthen co-operation in area of education and professional training, proposing to prepare specific projects in this field, through devising definitive training programmes in the various areas of the Forum.

**9. Follow Up Mechanism**

9.1 The Ministers agreed with the establishment of a follow up mechanism, through the constitution of a permanent Secretariat in Macao, who guarantees the necessary logistic and financial support as well as the indispensable link to execute the initiatives and the projects to implement, which definition will be assured, previously and exclusively, by the network of focal points created by the participating Countries. The network of focal points will also assure the follow up and the evaluation of the execution of the initiatives agreed to in the present Forum, which may include the holding of periodic meetings, at various levels.

9.2 The Ministers agreed to hold a 2$^{nd}$ Ministerial Conference of the Forum for Economic and Trade Co-operation between China and Portuguese-speaking Countries, in 2006, in the Macao Special Administrative Region of the People's Republic of China, at which conference the summary of the results of the economic and enterprise co-operation between China and the Portuguese-speaking Countries will be discussed and new means of co-operation will be evaluated.

**Pelo Governo da República de Angola**
Victorino Domingos Hossi
Ministro do Comércio

**Pelo Governo da República Federativa do Brasil**
Luiz Fernando Furlan
Ministro do Desenvolvimento, Indústria e Comércio Exterior

**Pelo Governo da República de Cabo Verde**
Avelino Bonifácio Fernandes Lopes
Ministro da Economia, Crescimento e Competitividade

**Pelo Governo da República Popular da China**
An Min
Vice Ministro do Comércio

**Pelo Governo da República da Guiné-Bissau**
João José Silva Monteiro
Ministro dos Negócios Estrangeiros, da Cooperação Internacional e das Comunidades

**Pelo Governo da República de Moçambique**
Carlos Alberto Sampaio Morgado
Ministro da Indústria e Comércio

**Pelo Governo da República Portuguesa**
José Luís Fazenda Arnaut Duarte
Ministro Adjunto do Primeiro Ministro

**Pelo Governo da República Democrática de Timor-Leste**
Abel da Costa Freitas Ximenes
Vice-Ministro do Desenvolvimento e Ambiente

## Document 8.9: Action Plan for Economic and Trade Cooperation (2007–2009)[14]

2nd Ministerial Conference
Action Plan for Co-operation in Business and Trade

### Preface

The 2nd Ministerial Conference of the Forum on Economic and Trade Co-operation Between China and Portuguese-Speaking Countries (Macao) – hereunder referred to as 'the Forum' – was hosted by the Macao Special Administrative Region (hereunder referred to as 'Macao') of the People's Republic of China on 24th and 25th September 2006. It was attended by Ministers responsible for business and trade affairs of Portuguese-speaking countries (i.e.) the Republic of Angola, the Federal Republic of Brazil, the Republic of Cape Verde, the Republic of Guinea-Bissau, the Republic of Mozambique, the Republic of Portugal, and the Democratic Republic of East Timor.

In line with the principles and objectives agreed upon by the Forum of strengthening, consolidating, and enhancing bilateral consultation and co-operation in business and trade affairs, Ministers reviewed the development of the said co-operation between China and Portuguese-speaking countries since the first Ministerial Conference and positively appraised the success achieved over the past three years in business and trade within the framework of the Action Plan laid out in Macao in 2003.

Ministers appreciated and acknowledged Macao's role as the platform for strengthening and elaborating business and trade relations between China and Portuguese-speaking countries and conveyed their gratitude to the government of the Macao Special Administrative Region for its generous support for the follow-up actions taken subsequent to the Forum.

Ministers believed that the Action Plan adopted in 2003 had facilitated work seeking to strengthen and expand co-operative relations between China and the Portuguese-speaking countries.

Ministers were confident that the Action Plan would promote mutual understanding and communication between the member countries of the Forum and further advance co-operation in business and trade as well as bilateral investment in addition to further strengthening Macao's role as a bridge between China and Portuguese-speaking countries.

Ministers were aware of the different stages of socio-economic development achieved by member countries and hold on the basis of equality and mutual benefit that each member state should identify its own problems and devise corresponding policies, strengthen co-operation and advance mutual development.

Ministers were determined to promote practical partnership relations between member countries. They unanimously agreed to expand the scope of co-operation and adopt the following measures to implement this Action Plan:

[14] Translated from Portuguese.

**1. Inter-governmental Co-operation**

1.1 Ministers fully endorsed the importance of high-level exchange visits in advancing mutual consultation and co-operation, agreeing to strengthen the existing bilateral mechanism of governmental co-operation between China and the Portuguese-speaking countries and continuously improve the mechanism in order to promote exchanges at high official levels between member countries.

1.2 Ministers acknowledged that business and trade exchange are the foundation and core of the current exchanges between the participating countries and unanimously agreed to further develop the bilateral and multilateral relations between China and the Portuguese-speaking countries, especially in areas such as foreign direct investment, tourism, transport, and co-operation between businesses.

1.3 Ministers were aware that inter-governmental co-operation is not to be limited to the scope of business and trade but may well be expanded to other sectors of common interest in addition to areas complementary to the principal operations of the Forum.

**2. Trade**

2.1 Ministers praised the success achieved in implementing the Action Plan of Forum 2003, and took note of the rapidly expanding trade between China and the Portuguese-speaking countries with increasing annual trade volumes. It was agreed that there was huge potential yet to be realised in business and trade between the parties and that further expanding bilateral trade would be in every party's interests. It was unanimously agreed that active measures be taken to promote bilateral trade between China and the Portuguese-speaking countries with a view to achieving bilateral trade in the amount of US$45-50 billion by 2009 and increasing the volume of exports from Portuguese-speaking countries to the Chinese market.

2.2 In accordance with the international pledge made by participating countries, free trade is to be actively advocated and promoted and measures that are conducive to increasing the volume of trade between China and the Portuguese-speaking countries are to be encouraged.

2.3 In accordance with the *Protocol on Co-operation between Trade Promotion Institutions or Chambers of Commerce* signed in October 2003, co-operation is to be strengthened; a mechanism of regular consultation is to be established as soon as possible and the mutual and prompt flow of information about trade and market demands is to be realised in order that trade between China and the Portuguese-speaking countries may be enhanced.

**3. Investment and Co-operation between Enterprises**

3.1 It was acknowledged that investment plays an important role in trade relations between the participating countries and it was unanimously agreed that measures were to be taken to promote mutual direct investment between China and the Portuguese-speaking countries, especially Chinese investment in Portuguese-speaking countries. It is planned that the volume of bilateral investment between China and Portuguese-speaking countries be at least doubled in the three years from 2007 to 2009.

3.2 In order to encourage and attract investment, it was agreed that the laws and regulations concerning investments currently in effect in participating countries be publicised and presented to target audiences. Meanwhile, participating countries were encouraged to conclude agreements on the protection of mutual investment.

3.3 It was agreed that participating countries establish an Investment Work Group co-ordinated by the Secretariat of the Forum, which should undertake to facilitate the implementation of bilateral and multi-lateral investment projects between the participating countries.

3.4 It is agreed that trade and business information continue to be publicised, that the annual Trade Fair of China and the Portuguese-Speaking Countries – held in participating countries on a rotational basis – be better conducted, and that exchange visits between enterprises be encouraged in addition to participation in other exhibitions, expositions and trade fairs in participating countries.

3.5 It is agreed that co-operation in various economic domains between enterprises from participating countries be supported in such enterprises as infrastructure construction, transport, information and communication, energy and agriculture in addition to the exploitation and utilisation of natural resources.

3.6 It is agreed that participating countries mutually inform and update information regarding market openness in terms of industries open to enterprise, and enact laws and policies of financial protection that are conducive to business.

**4. Co-operation in Agriculture and Fishery**

4.1 It was acknowledged that the development of agriculture and fishery plays an extremely important role in eradicating poverty and that huge potential exists in co-operating in agriculture and fishery between China and the Portuguese-speaking countries. Participating countries reiterated their intention to adopt specific measures to promote co-operation in this area.

4.2 It was reiterated that promoting co-operation in domains such as agriculture and fishery was necessary, with the exchange of personnel and training a top priority. Development plans regarding agriculture and fishery between China and Portuguese-speaking countries are to be studied and established and relevant work initiated. Enterprises are to be encouraged and supported to engage in the construction of infrastructure of fishery, agricultural cultivation, propagation of cultivation techniques, mechanised production, and the processing of agricultural and food products.

**5. Co-operation in Infrastructure Construction**

5.2 It was acknowledged that some of the participating countries were in a period of technical transition in the construction of infrastructure and that they had a certain capability in the manufacture of equipment. It is reiterated that participating countries are willing to promote and actively participate – both bilaterally and multilaterally – in projects of infrastructure construction.

5.2 It is reiterated that, in terms of the management of contracted construction projects, the exchange of techniques and experience be enhanced and that information related to infrastructure construction projects be promoted.

5.3 It is to be encouraged that enterprises from China and Portuguese-speaking countries, via various modes such as planning, design, consultation, provision of merchandise and facilities, construction and operation etc., search for and identify appropriate modes of funding, and facilitate enterprises from both parties.

**6. Co-operation in Natural Resources**

In view of the importance of natural resources to the sustainable development of participating countries, it was reiterated that different projects be continued in compliance with the principle of 'mutual benefit and development' and that co-operation be conducted in various forms to enhance the exploitation and utilisation of natural resources.

**7. Co-operation in Human Resources**

7.1 It was acknowledged that developing human resources and creating employment opportunities were important to the socio-economic development of participating countries. It was also noted that China had, since the ministerial conference of 2003, increased its efforts related to co-operation in human resource development with Portuguese-speaking countries.

7.2 It was reiterated that greater effort should continue to be made in co-ordination activities, human resources training planning, and in establishing priority training subjects and the number of trainees.

7.3 It was agreed that based on the potential of each participating country co-ordination and co-operation be strengthened by identifying training projects, broadening training scope and promoting the internationalisation of trainers as well as increasing the number of trainees. It was also agreed that on the basis of multilateral co-operation the feasibility of establishing a Forum training centre be studied and promoted in order to facilitate personnel training in trade, tourism and hotel management as well as economic co-operation.

7.4 To facilitate the training of workers necessary for further expanding trade and business exchanges, it was emphasised that the Forum take active measures to provide facilities and trainers, among other necessary steps, in order to promote the teaching of the Chinese and Portuguese languages.

7.5 It was appreciated that China was willing to enhance co-operation in higher education with Portuguese-speaking countries within the framework of the Action Plan of the Forum (e.g.) in organising undergraduate and post-graduate programmes as well as increasing the quota of scholarships, etc.

7.6 It was appreciated that China was willing, within the framework of the Action Plan of the Forum, to expand the number of training personnel of developing Portuguese-speaking countries. China would, based on the needs of developing Portuguese-speaking countries and the realities of conducting such activities, organise training courses to address specific needs and endeavour to train some 900 officials and technicians in various disciplines for developing Portuguese-speaking countries in the three years from 2007 to 2009.

7.7 It was appreciated that China had proposed, within the framework of the Action Plan of the Forum, to help build a certain number of village primary schools in Portuguese-speaking countries in Asia and Africa over the next three years and would send young volunteers to such countries to work in healthcare, culture and education, etc.

**8. Co-operation and Development**

8.1 It was appreciated that the participating countries would support co-operation conducive to the development of Portuguese-speaking countries in Asia and Africa, to be embodied in specific actions within the framework of the Action Plan of the Forum in the three years from 2007 to 2009.

8.2 It was appreciated that China and Portugal had decided, within the bilateral framework, to respectively provide Portuguese-speaking countries in Africa and Asia with RMB800 million in loans on favourable terms and no less than EUR100 million in credit for funding prioritised public investment projects in accordance with their development strategies for the eradication of poverty.

8.3 It was noted that some countries such as Brazil have, within the bilateral framework, forgiven the debt of certain Portuguese-speaking countries in Africa the amount exempted by Brazil totalled US$471 million.

8.4 It was appreciated that China had decided to waive its governmental interest-free loans due by the end of 2004 and still outstanding owed by participating Portuguese-speaking countries which are heavily in debt.

8.5 It was appreciated that China would continue to provide aid to projects as agreed under the bilateral framework.

**9. Co-operation in New Sectors**

9.1 In view of the fact that the Forum plays an increasingly important role in strengthening bilateral and multilateral co-operation between the participating countries, and in order to be conducive to implementing related business and trade activities, it was unanimously agreed that China and the Portuguese-speaking countries initiate work in the following areas:

9.2 Promotion of co-operation between financial institutions of participating countries to identify and establish commonly attractive projects and their funding sources within the multilateral framework in order to examine the feasibility of establishing a mechanism for financial co-operation within the Forum.

9.3 Encouragement of co-operation in tourism between China and Portuguese-speaking countries; that exchange between tour institutions and personnel be promoted and that tourist infrastructure and tourism promotion products be enhanced. China will actively enlist Portuguese-speaking countries as outbound tour destinations for its citizens.

9.4 Initiation of co-operation in transportation in order to establish a logistics network between China and Portuguese-speaking countries; urging concerned departments of participating countries to examine the feasibility of opening direct flights and sailing routes thereby facilitating tourism and trade between China and Portuguese-speaking countries.

9.5 Making full use of the existing bilateral and multilateral co-operation mechanisms, especially those regarding medicine between China and the Portuguese-speaking countries, and expanding co-operation in public health. Establishing protocols to establish various co-operative schemes to prevent and treat malaria, AIDS, tuberculosis and other infectious diseases for public and private institutions. It was appreciated that China had proposed the establishment of a malaria control demonstration centre in Portuguese-speaking countries in Africa and Asia.

9.6 Promoting co-operation in science and technology; encouraging participating countries to undertake further exchanges in sci-tech projects, including the transfer of technology and training.

9.7 Initiating co-operation in TV and radio broadcasting via programme production – personnel as well as technique exchange and training – enhancing mutual understanding and experience sharing; via news report on radio and TV, faithfully presenting the partner countries.

9.8 Promoting cultural exchanges between China and the Portuguese-speaking countries; further improving existing co-operation in culture, sharing experiences, enhancing mutual understanding of governments and enterprises between participating countries, and facilitating exchange.

**10. Macao's Role as Platform**

10.1 It was reiterated that Macao should continue to play an active role as a platform for enhancing co-operation on trade and business between China and the Portuguese-speaking countries. To this end, Macao would continue to conduct related tasks and enhance and deepen mutual understanding, in addition to attempting to establish various partnerships between governments and enterprises of participating countries.

10.2 It was emphasised that co-operation between enterprises from Macao, Mainland China and Portuguese-speaking countries be promoted in various forms in areas such as trade, transport, investment, agriculture and fishery, exploitation of resources, construction of infrastructure, healthcare and communication, etc.

10.3 It is agreed to encourage Macao to participate in and expand its involvement in training personnel for Portuguese-speaking countries and to facilitate the training of Forum personnel in, for example, languages, trade, tourism, finance, business administration and management, etc.

**11. Follow-up Mechanism**

11.1 The role of the Macao-based Secretariat of the Forum was positively regarded in implementing the 2003 Action Plan of Economic and Business Co-operation as well as in providing logistical and financial backing to projects designed by the participating countries. It was reiterated that this co-ordination mechanism, which includes a network of liaison officers, be further improved.

11.2 It was agreed that the organisational structure and functions of the Forum's Secretariat be further improved in order to better undertake the initiatives planned by the 2$^{nd}$ Ministerial Conference.

**12. Next Ministerial Conference**

It was agreed that the 3$^{rd}$ Ministerial Conference of China and Portuguese-Speaking Countries Economic Co-operation Forum (Macao) be hosted by the Macao Special Administrative Region of the People's Republic of China in 2009.

Minister of Commerce of the Republic of Angola
Joaquim Muafumba

Executive Secretary of Ministry of Development, Industry and Foreign Trade of the Federal Republic of Brazil
Ivan Ramalho

Minister of Economy, Development and Competitiveness of the Republic of Cape Verde
João Pereira da Silva

Minister of Commerce of the People's Republic of China
Bo Xilai

Minister of Commerce, Industry and Handicrafts of the Republic of Guinea-Bissau
Domingos Pascoal Baticã

Minister of Energy of the Republic of Mozambique
Salvador Namburete

Minister of Public Works, Transport and Communications of the Republic of Portugal
Mário Lino

Minister of Development of the Democratic Republic of East Timor
Arcanjo da Silva

# 9

# EU, China and the World Trade Organization

## INTRODUCTION

China became a member of the World Trade Organization (WTO) on 11 December 2001. The accession of the People's Republic of China to the WTO was the culmination of a long and difficult series of negotiations for policy-makers and many others in China, as well as in other WTO members, such as the USA, the European Community and the EC Member States. At the same time it reinforced China's domestic economic and social reforms and engagement in the world economy. On the one hand, it was merely another phase in the adaptation of China to the WTO,[1] though of course a crucial one. On the other hand, it marked the beginning of the adaptation of the WTO to the PRC, the implications of which stretch far into the future. Both before and after the date of accession, China's principal trading partners, especially the USA and the EU, played a major role in shaping the basic parameters of China's relationship to the WTO. This chapter focuses on the relations between the EU and China with regard to China's membership of the WTO. Table 8.1 gives a list of the basic documents. The table does not include bilateral agreements on textiles, for which the reader is referred to Chapter 2.

## NEGOTIATIONS

China was an original signatory and a founding Contracting Party to the General Agreement on Tariffs and Trade (GATT 1947). After the Chinese revolution and the founding of the People's Republic of China, the Kuomintang government, having been expelled to Taiwan, announced in 1950 that China would leave the GATT. However, the PRC never recognised this decision. In 1984 the PRC was granted

[1] For basic Chinese legal instruments, see Ministry of Commerce of the People's Republic of China, 'Compilation of the Legal Instruments on China's Accession to the World Trade Organization', available at http://english.mofcom.gov.en/aarticle/topic/2to/200501/20050100012779.html (accessed 8 February 2005).

**Table 9.1: Documents on EU–China Relations in the WTO Framework**

| Document | Author | Subject | Place and date if applicable | Source | Approval or implementation by the EC |
|---|---|---|---|---|---|
| Overview of Sino-EU Agreement on China's Accession to the WTO [see document 9.1] | European Commission | China's Accession to the WTO | Brussels, 20.6.2001 | reference?http://trade.ec.europa.eu/doclib/docs/2003/april/tradoc_111851.pdf | |
| Resolution on the inclusion of China and Taiwan in the General Agreement on Tariffs and Trade (GATT) [see document 9.2] | European Parliament | | | OJ C 176, 28.6.1993, p. 221 | |
| European Commission Overview of the Terms of China's Accession to WTO [see document 9.3] | European Commission | China's Accession to the WTO | 1.10.2001 | http://trade.ec.europa.eu/doclib/docs/2003/october/tradoc_111955.pdf | |
| Proposal for a Council Decision establishing the Community position within the Ministerial Conference set up by the Agreement establishing the World Trade Organization on the accession of the People's Republic of China to the World Trade Organization, COM (2001) 517 final [see document 9.4] | European Commission | | 19.10.2001 | OJ C51E, 26.2.2002, p. 314 | |

**Table 9.1: continued**

| Document | Author | Subject | Place and date if applicable | Source | Approval or implementation by the EC |
|---|---|---|---|---|---|
| Report on the proposal for a Council decision establishing the Community position within the Ministerial Conference set up by the Agreement establishing the World Trade Organization on the accession of the People's Republic of China to the World Trade Organization (O (2001) 517 – C5-=$(//2001 – 2001/0218/CNS) [see document 9.5] | European Parliament | | report 18.10.20001; resolution adopted 25.10.2001 | OJ C112E, 9.5.2002, p. 313 | |
| Adoption of Council Decision establishing the Community position within the Ministerial Conference set up by the Agreement establishing the World Trade Organization [not included in this book] | Council of the European Union | | 19.10.2001 | Council of the European Union, Interinstitutional File: 2001/0218(CNS), 2001/0216(CNS), Brussels, 19.10.2001 (23.10) (OR.en,fr), 12557/01, WTO 106 | |

**Table 9.1: continued**

| Document | Author | Subject | Place and date if applicable | Source | Approval or implementation by the EC |
|---|---|---|---|---|---|
| Council Decision establishing the Community position within the Ministerial Conference set up by the Agreement establishing the World Trade Organization on the accession of the People's Republic of China to the World Trade Organization | Council of the European Union | China's Accession to the WTO | 29.10.2001 | http://europa.eu/bulletin/en/200110/p106026.htm | |
| Decision of 10 November 2001 and Protocol on the Accession of the People's Republic of China [see document 9.6] | Ministerial Conference of the World Trade Organization | China's Accession to the WTO | Doha, Qatar, 10.11.2001 | http://docsonline.wto.org/DDFDocuments/t/WT/L/432.doc | Council Regulation (EC) No 427/2003 of 3 March 2003 on a transitional product-specific safeguard mechanism for imports originating in the People's Republic of China and amending Regulation (EC) No 519/94 on common rules for imports from certain third countries, OJ 8.3.2003 L65/11; see also Notice on the application of Article 10a [next item] |
| Report of the Working Party on the Accession of China to the World Trade Organization [not included in this book] | | China's Accession to the WTO | 1.10.2001 | OJ C 51 E, 26.2.2002, p. 314–315 | |
| Notice on the application of Article 10a of Council Regulation (EEC) No 3030(93 concerning a textiles specific safeguard clause [see Chapter 2 of this book] | Council of the European Union | | 27.4.2005 | OJ C 101, 27.4.2005, p. 2–15 | |

**Table 9.1: continued**

| Document | Author | Subject | Place and date if applicable | Source | Approval or implementation by the EC |
|---|---|---|---|---|---|
| EU-China textile agreement (Shanghai Agreement) [see Chapter 2 of this book] | | | Shanghai, 10.6.2005 | http://ec.europa.eu/trade/issues/sectoral/industry/textile/mou_tex_china_en.htm | Commission Regulation (EC) No 1084/2005 of 8 July 2005 amending Annexes II, III and V to Council Regulation (EEC) No 3030/93 on common rules for imports of certain textile products from third countries, OJ 9.7.2005 L177(19 |
| Minutes of the consultations regarding the establishment of transitional flexibility measures on the Memorandum of Understanding between the European Commission and the Ministry of Commerce of the People's Republic of China on the export of certain Chinese textile and clothing products to the EU [see Chapter 2 of this book] | | | Beijing, 1.9.2005 | http://trade.ec.europa.eu/doclib/docs/2005/september/tradoc_124580.pdf%20sans%20signature%20bis.pdf | Commission Regulation (EC) No 1468/2005 of 12 September 2005 amending Annexes V, VII and VIII to Council Regulation (EEC) No 3030/93 on common rules for imports of certain textile products from third countries, OJ 13.9.2005 L236/11 |

**Table 9.1: continued**

| Document | Author | Subject | Place and date if applicable | Source | Approval or implementation by the EC |
|---|---|---|---|---|---|
| Agreement in the form of an Exchange of letters between the European Community and the People's Republic of China pursuant Article XXIV:6 and Article XXVIII of the General Agreement on Tariffs and Trade (GATT) 1994 relating to the modification of concessions in the schedules of the Czech Republic, the Republic of Estonia, the Republic of Cyprus, the Republic of Latvia, the Republic of Lithuania, the Republic of Hungary, the Republic of Malta, the Republic of Poland, the Republic of Slovenia and the Slovak Republic in the course of their accession to the European Union [not included in this book] | European Community, People's Republic of China | modification of GATT schedules of new Member States acceding to the EC | | OJ L154, 8.6.2006, p. 24 | Council Regulation (EC) No 838/2006 of 20 March 2006 concerning the implementation of the Agreement in the form of an Exchange of letters between the European Community and the People's Republic of China pursuant Article XXIV:6 and Article XXVIII of the General Agreement on Tariffs and Trade (GATT) relating to the modification of concessions in the schedules of the Czech Republic, the Republic of Estonia, the Republic of Cyprus, the Republic of Latvia, the Republic of Lithuania, the Republic of Hungary, the Republic of Malta, the Republic of Poland, the Republic of Slovenia and the Slovak Republic in the course of their accession to the European Unon, amending and supplementing Annex I to Regulation (EEC) No 2658/87 on the tariff and statistical nomenclature and on the Common Customs Tariff, OJ L154, 8.6.2006, p. 1; Council Decision 2006/398/EC of 20 March 2006 on the conclusion of an Agreement in the form of an Exchange of Letters between the European Community and the People's Republic of China pursuant to |

observer status in GATT. In 1986, it notified GATT of its intention to renegotiate terms of membership, initially for 'resumption' of its status as a GATT Contracting Party. A GATT Working Party to consider China's membership was established in 1987 and became a WTO Working Party after the WTO agreements entered into force in 1995.

Accession to the WTO involves both bilateral and multilateral negotiations. China concluded bilateral negotiations on market access with its major trading partners, particularly but not only the USA and the EU. Following the conclusion of the bilateral agreement between the USA and China on 19 November 1999,[2] the EU and China concluded their bilateral agreement in Beijing on 19 May 2000. Document 8.1 presents an overview of this bilateral agreement. It covers telecommunications, insurance, monopoly state import and export restrictions, tariffs, motor vehicles, distribution, agriculture, horizontal measures and certain other issues.

## Document 9.1: Overview of the Sino-EU Agreement on Chinese Accession to the WTO

The Sino-EU Agreement On China's Accession To The WTO: Results Of The Bilateral Negotiations

The following is an overview of the results achieved by the EU since the signature of the Sino-US accord. Some of the issues covered are unique to the EU, while others had already been the subject of negotiations between China and other partners. In both cases, the list below is confined to commitments which were secured explicitly by the European Union.

### INDUSTRIAL GOODS

*Import tariffs*

As for specific EU priorities not covered by China's previous bilateral Agreements, these were concentrated on 150 specific products varying from gin to building materials. On these EU-specific priorities, an additional reduction of 40% on top of earlier offers was obtained (the tariff average falling from 18.6% to 10.9%).

Tariffs on all **spirits** will be aligned to a level of 10%. There will be no difference in the treatment of whisk(e)y, Cognac, Gin etc. The presently applied tariff level is still at 65%.

Tariffs on key **cosmetics** products will come down to a level of 10% (currently up to 30%). This implies good prospects for a sector which already exports up to EUR 7 billion worldwide.

On **leather and leather articles** negotiations focused on 13 specific products which account for 60% of total EU exports in this sector. China agreed a reduction on these products from 20-25% to 10%.

[2] For a summary, see The White House Office of Public Liaison, 'Briefing on the Clinton Administration Agenda for the World Trade Organization Material' (19 November 2004), available at http://www.uschina.org/public/991115a.html (accessed 24 November 2007). See also http://www.ustr.gov/Document_Library/Press_Releases/2001/June/USTR_Releases_Details_on_US-China_Consensus_on_China's_WTO_Accession.html (accessed 24 November 2007).

On **textiles** China made some further improvements to the previous offer. China's textiles tariffs are very close to the levels of the EU and far lower than almost all other textile exporting countries.

Tariffs on 5 particular **footwear** products which account for more than 70% of EU footwear exports will be reduced from 25% to 10%.

**Marble/building stones** are popular articles in China's enormous construction market. On the 5 most important products tariffs will also be reduced from 25% to 10%.

On **ceramics** China agreed to reduce tariffs on 11 key ceramics products from 24.5-35% to 10-15%. And tariffs on 6 particular **glass** products will be reduced from 24.5% to 5%.

On 52 particular products in the important **machinery and appliances** sector, which accounts for 26% of total EU exports, tariffs will be cut to 5-10% from levels up to 35%.

- **Quotas:** China's quota on Europe's fertilizer exports (NPK) will be liberalised upon accession, and restrictions in place this year will be immediately relaxed.
- **State Trading:**

**Liberalisation of import monopolies on oil and fertiliser** - China has agreed to open the crude and processed oil sectors, as well as NPK fertiliser, to private traders through a process of gradual liberalisation. This means that firms will no longer be obliged to go exclusively through China's state importers when shipping oil and fertiliser to China. The oil (petroleum) and fertiliser sectors are the most significant domains where a state import monopoly has been in place.

**Liberalisation of export monopoly on silk** ¨C EU firms will be able to buy raw silk directly from Chinese producers (who make 70% of the world total). Until now all purchases had to go through state export channels. This will bring substantial benefits to the EU's numerous manufacturers of ties, scarves and other high value silk garments and accessories.

- **Motor vehicles:** the EU and China agreed on a range of improvements for EU firms which produce cars, vans and trucks in China. For those who have invested in joint-venture manufacturing operations (or will do so in the future), there are 3 key points:
  - all restrictions regarding the category, type and models of vehicle produced will be lifted within 2 years, leaving the car-maker free to make such decisions on a purely commercial basis;
  - provincial authorities alone will be able to approve investments in the sector up to $150 million (ceiling raised from $30m), substantially reducing red-tape for car manufacturers;
  - for the manufacture of engines, China's joint-venture requirement will be removed, allowing wholly foreign owned production.

**AGRICULTURE**

- **Market access (tariffs and tariff quotas):** Improvements have been made on the tariff quota for rape oil, as well as on tariffs on products such as: rape oil (down from 85% to 9%), pasta (down from 25% to 15%), butter (down from 30% to 10%), milk powder (down from 25% to 10%), mandarins (down from 40% to 12%), wine (down from 65% to 14%), olives (down from 25% to 10%) and wheat gluten (down from 30% to 18%).
- **Sanitary and Phytosanitary measures:** The EU and China signed an SPS Agreement that will provide for compliance by China with the WTO's SPS Agreement, as well as

resolving a number of bilateral SPS trade frictions. This agreement will be supplemented by subsequent agreements with individual EU Member States, to be concluded before China's formal entry into the WTO.

## SERVICES

- **Telecommunications:** The telecommunications offer has been considerably enhanced. China will open its mobile telephony market 2 years ahead of schedule. Upon accession, foreign operators will be permitted a 25% share, rising to 49% 3 years after accession. China has agreed to allow operations between Chinese cities (where the biggest business is located, covering more than 75% of current traffic) and not to restrict them to activity within each city. The liberalisation of domestic leased circuit services has also been obtained, which is a key commitment for foreign telecom companies to allow them to sell their spare capacity. Furthermore, the access of user firms (usually large foreign corporations) to international corporate telecommunications has also been improved. Finally, China and the EU have agreed to a satisfactory settlement concerning the mobile investments of EU telecommunication companies (France Telecom, Siemens/Deutsche Telekom and Telecom Italia) in the 2$^{nd}$ Chinese carrier, China Unicom.
- **Insurance:** Effective management control has been negotiated for foreign participants in life insurance joint ventures, through choice of partner, and a legal guarantee of freedom from any regulatory interference in privately negotiated contracts on a 50-50 equity basis. Foreign insurers will see their scope of business advanced by 2 years in life and non-life activities, selling the same products their Chinese competitors. This includes health, pension and group insurance in life, and all non-life activities except for mandatory 3$^{rd}$ party liability auto insurance. Geographic expansion of cities open to foreign insurers has also been accelerated. Brokers (insurance intermediaries) will have access to the Chinese market through local establishment for the first time. A number of new licences, for both life and non-life business, will be immediately provided to EU companies.
- **Banking:** The banking offer has been improved. Non-financial institutions will be able to give credit facilities for the purchase of all motor vehicles, including trucks, buses, tractors, motorcycles etc, rather than just cars. China has also agreed to allow foreign banks in the city of Zhuhai to advance their operations in local currency. Zhuhai, which is just off Macao, holds several EU banks.
- **Distribution:** China has agreed to lift the specific joint venture restriction applicable to large department stores, as well as for virtually all chain stores, as well as lifting the 20,000m$^2$ size limit for foreign-owned stores.
- **Securities:** China and the EU have agreed to establish a regulatory dialogue on the development of the securities market in China. The EU welcomes the opportunity to contribute its expertise to the expansion of the Chinese securities market.
- **Dredging:** Dredging activities, related to infrastructure construction, are now open to foreign firms.
- **Tourism:** The tourism offer has been extended from holiday services to also cover corporate travel business. The establishment requirements for travel agencies and tour operators have been eased to the benefit, in particular, of SMEs specialised in the Chinese market. The capital requirement will be gradually reduced to the same level as that applied to Chinese firms. The minimum turnover requirement has also now been further reduced, upon accession, by 20% (down to 40 million USD).
- **Legal services:** foreign law firms will, for the first time, be able to also offer services on Chinese law. In particular they will be able to provide information to their clients on

the Chinese legal environment. Concerning other activities in Chinese law (representations before the Courts etc.), the arrangements with local law firms have been improved by allowing foreign firms directly to instruct individual Chinese lawyers in these firms. Improvements have also been obtained on the prior experience requirements for lawyers ¨C prior experience will no longer have to be consecutive, and the requirement for all lawyers, other than the Chief representative has been reduced from 3 to 2 years. Finally, it has been recognised for the first time that solicitors (although not members of a bar) will also be covered by the agreement.

- **Accountancy:** Accountants will be able to provide taxation and management consultancy services under the same conditions as accounting services, and will no longer be required to partner.
- **Architects:** Architects will now have an extended access on a cross-border basis, by allowing them to provide scheme design services.
- **Market research:** The Chinese Decree imposing extremely burdensome requirements that might affect the confidentiality of market research reports will be substantially amended. Reports will no longer be pre-examined by Chinese authorities before being given to the client, but firms will merely have send copies of questionnaires to the authorities (not of the replies and results).

**HORIZONTAL ISSUES**

- **Government Procurement:** China has agreed to full transparency and non-discrimination (MFN) in government purchases.
- **Trade-distorting investment-related measures:** The EU and China have agreed on commitments similar to those included in the Sino-US agreement but also incorporating an obligation to eliminate industrial export subsidies, and offset requirements in the civil aircraft sector.
- **National treatment:** This is a basic GATT obligation. China has now given specific commitments to phase out legislation that gives unfair advantages to domestic producers in the field of pharmaceutical pricing, after-sales services of imported goods, chemical import registration requirements, control of imported boilers, and retail of imported cigarettes and spirits. In some cases China will have one or two years to make her legislation WTO compliant.

Multilateral negotiations within the WTO Working Party took place concurrently with bilateral negotiations. The EU strongly supported the accession of China to the WTO, though official documents reveal differences of opinion concerning modalities. In 1993, the European Parliament had adopted a resolution on the inclusion of China and Taiwan in the GATT (see Document 9.2). It favoured the resumption by China of its status as a GATT Contracting Party. It also supported the request of the government of Taiwan to become a GATT member as the separate customs territory of Taiwan, Penghu, Kinmen and Matsu under Article XXXIII GATT, thus not requiring PRC sponsorship as under Article XXVI 5(c).[3] Taiwan later joined the WTO as such a separate customs territory.

[3] See also European Parliament, 'Resolution on GATT Membership for Taiwan', A3-0139/93, [1993] OJ C176/225 and European Parliament, Committee on Industry, External Trade, Research and Energy, 'Report on the Proposal for a Council Decision Establishing the Community Position within the Ministerial

## Document 9.2: European Parliament Resolution on the Inclusion of China and Taiwan in the General Agreement of Tariffs and Trade (GATT)

Admission of China and Taiwan to GATT

**(a) A3-0092/93: Resolution on the inclusion of China and Taiwan in the General Agreement on Tariffs and Trade (GATT)**

*The European Parliament,*

having regard to its resolution of 9 September 1986 on the new round of multilateral trade negotiations in GATT, especially paragraph 20 (I),

having regard to its resolution of 17 March 1989 on economic and trade relations between the EC and the People's Republic of China (2),

having regard to the motions for resolutions by:

(a) Mr De Clercq and others on the inclusion of China and Taiwan in the General Agreement on Tariffs and Trade (GATT) (B3-0613/92),

(b) Mr Pasty on strengthening links between the EC and Taiwan (B3-1315/92),

having regard to the report of the Committee on External Economic Relations (A3-oo92/93),

A. whereas China was one of the original founding contracting parties of the GATT in 1947,

B. whereas the Government of the Republic of China (ROC), having been expelled from the mainland in 1949, withdrew from the GATT in 1950 - a withdrawal which the People's Republic of China (PRC) has not accepted as having validity regarding the PRC's status in GATT,

C. whereas Taiwan had been granted observer status in GATT from 1965 to 1971, which was then revoked due to a UN Resolution recognizing the PRC as the sole lawful representative of China,

D. whereas the PRC embarked in the early 80's on major economic reforms in the context of its 'open-doors-policy' during which it demonstrated a growing interest in the work of GATT and subsequently obtained a special observer status in the GATT in 1984,

E. whereas the PRC in 1986 formally notified to the GATT its intention to resume its status as a contracting party; whereas a working party to examine this request was established in 1987,

F. whereas the PRC participates fully in the multilateral trade negotiations of the Uruguay Round,

Conference Set Up by the Agreement Establishing the World Trade Organization on the Accession of the Separate Customs Territory of Taiwan, Penghu, Kinmen and Matsu (Chinese Taipei) to the World Trade Organization (Rapporteur: Per Gahrton)', COM(2001) 518-C5-0488/2001–2001/0261/CNS, A5-0367/2001 final (18 October 2001), available at http://www.europarl.europa.eu/sides/getDoc.do?pubRef=-//EP//NONSGML+REPORT+A5-2001–0367+0+DOC+PDF+V0//EN&language=EN (accessed 28 November 2007).

G. whereas the GATT provides for the possibility for separate customs territories to become a contracting party whether they are sovereign states or not

H. whereas Hong Kong and Macao have become Contracting Parties of the GATT as separate customs territories under Article XXVI(5c) of the GATT,

I. whereas in 1990 the Government of Taiwan applied for GATT membership, under Article XXXIII of the GATT, as the separate customs territory of Taiwan, Penghu, Kinmen and Matsu; whereas a working party to examine this application was established in 1992,

J. whereas Taiwan's economy has been restructured - in 1992, Taiwan achieved a per capita GNP of US$ 10 000, giving it industrialized country status - and trade reforms implemented in such a way as to remove all objective barriers to immediate accession by Taiwan to the GATT,

1. Is in favour of a resumption of China's status as a Contracting Party of GATT by the PRC but points out that this resumption will necessitate extraordinary transitional arrangements;

2. Believes, therefore, that the re-integration of China into the GATT system will only formally be a resumption, but substantially a new accession with the result that the PRC will have to enter into negotiations on new tariff concessions and that the Contracting Parties will remain entitled to invoke the non-application clause under Article XXXV of the GATT, if they are not satisfied with the concessions offered by the PRC for its new accession;

3. Accepts that for the resumption of the PRC's rights and obligations in the GATT a gradual approach, which allows a balance of advantages to be maintained between' China and the Contracting Parties, will be the most appropriate;

4. Suggests that according to such an approach the formal resumption of GATT membership could come into effect quite soon, whereas for the actual integration a transitional period should be instituted, during which neither the PRC nor the other contracting parties would be obliged mutually to apply the Most-Favoured-Nation Treatment;

5. Stresses the importance of the economic reforms undertaken by the PRC for its resumption of GATT membership, which will be easier the more market-oriented these reforms are;

6. Regards the extent of the PRC state's involvement in economic affairs, particularly trade, as highly problematic; the degree to which the PRC can still be regarded as a state trading nation will have to be more fully clarified before the PRC's exact GATT arrangements can be defined;

7. Takes the view that during the transitional period the contracting parties should be entitled to take specific safeguard measures against Chinese exports if these create or threaten to create a serious injury for their economies;

8. Points out that one of the major comparative advantages of China in an open multilateral trade system will be its abundance of cheap labour, which will make it highly competitive with regard to labour-intensive products on the world markets;

9. Insists that the PRC and Taiwan, like all the other industrialized and developing countries, must respect the minimum labour standards worked out by the International Labour

Organization (ILO) as for instance the ban on child or slave labour and respect for the right to establish free trade unions;

10. Points to the interdependence between economic reforms seeking to introduce certain market economy elements into the Chinese economic system and political reforms designed to ensure greater respect for human and democratic rights, which if neglected could lead to problems similar to those which culminated in the Tiananmen events;

11. Welcomes the fact that Hong Kong and Macao have become Contracting Parties of GA TT and takes the view that they should keep their GATT status after 1997 and 1999 respectively, when both territories will be handed over to the PRC;

12. Supports the request of the government of Taiwan to become a GATT member;

13. Is aware of the political implications of Taiwan's application for GATT membership, but realizes that the GATT has at its disposal the appropriate instruments to accept Taiwan as a contracting party without prejudging the main political issue;

14. Believes that the pertinent legal base for Taiwan's accession to the GATT is to be found in Article XXXIII, and not Article XXVI(5c), of the GATT, since the latter requires the sponsorship of an existing Contracting Party which, in the case of China and Taiwan, would mean touching upon the main political problem between both;

15. Supports both applications, which should be examined strictly on their own respective merits;

16. Underlines that the application of Taiwan does not pose major difficulties in economic terms for it has long enjoyed a market economy system;

17. Recalls that Taiwan belongs to the newly industrialized economies (NIB) and to the so-called 'five Tigers' of the Far East, which precludes Taiwan being given developing country status in GATT;

18. Believes that the integration of Taiwan's economy into the multilateral trading system will not only reflect its importance as one of the major trading entities of the region but will be to the advantage of all other GATT members including the PRC;

19. Firmly believes that the membership of both China (PRC) and Taiwan in GATT is manifestly in the European Community's interests and will stabilize further trading relations in East Asia and between East Asia and Europe;

20. Strongly recommends that GATT pay particular attention to the delicate political issue of the timing of the entry of the PRC and Taiwan to GATT;

21. Instructs its President to forward this resolution to the Commission, the Council, the governments of the Member States, the PRC and the ROC and the GATT Secretariat.

At the concluding state of the multilateral negotiations, the European Commission in October 2001 published an overview of the terms of Chinese accession to the WTO (see Document 9.3). On this basis, it made a proposal on 19 October for a Council decision establishing a Community position within the WTO Ministerial Conference to be held at Doha (see Document 9.4). Concurrently, the European Parliament prepared a report and on 25 October adopted a legislation resolution approving the Commission's proposal. In its Explanatory Statement, however, the European

Parliament criticised the Commission's view concerning Chinese attitudes toward and China's position vis-à-vis the WTO (see Document 9.5).[4] The Council of the European Union at its meeting on 29–30 October 2001 approved the Commission proposal as the official Community position within the WTO Ministerial Conference supporting China's accession to the WTO.[5]

## Document 9.3: European Commission Overview of the Terms of China's Accession to WTO

Overview of the Terms of China's Accession to WTO

### I Introduction

1. Members of the World Trade Organisation (WTO) and the People's Republic of China have reached the concluding stage of agreement on the terms for China's accession to the organisation. This comes after fifteen years of negotiations, which began when China applied to join the General Agreement on Tariffs & Trade (GATT) in 1986. There must now be a Council Decision approving the terms of China's entry, before the EU can formally support China's entry.

2. There follows an outline of the implications of China's membership for the EU, the WTO system, and for China herself, and a summary of the terms themselves.

### II Implications of China's WTO Membership

*China's legally binding commitment to open trade*

3. The terms of an accession take two basic forms. First there are the schedules of commitments, which set out the full range of market access obligations which China will be legally bound to grant to every Member when it enters the WTO. The schedules cover tariffs and non-tariff measures applicable to agricultural trade and industrial goods (commitments under the GATT), and services (commitments under the General Agreement on Trade in Services, or GATS).

4. Second there are the Protocol and Working Party Report on the accession of China to the WTO. These documents, which also include legally binding commitments, essentially set out *how* China promises to fulfil her new WTO obligations.As well as containing detailed descriptions of, and obligations relating to, China's current and planned trade and investment régimes, they detail a number of special provisions to which China will be subject during the first years of her WTO Membership. These temporary derogations from normal

[4] For the adopted Resolution, see 'European Parliament Legislative Resolution on Proposal for a Council Decision Establishing a Community Position within the Ministerial Conference Set Up by the Agreement Establishing the World Trade Organization on the Accession of the People's Republic of China to the World Trade Organization', COM(2001) 517-C5-0487/2001–2001/0218(CNS), [2002] OJ C112E/313.

[5] See *Bulletin of the European Union,* 10–2001, point 1.6.26; Europa-Rapid-Press Releases, General Affairs, PRES/01/390 (29 October 2001), available at http://europa.eu/rapid/pressReleasesAction.do?reference=PRES/01/390&format=HT (accessed 21 February 2008). For the entire procedure of adoption, see PreLex, 'Monitoring of the Decision-making Process between Institutions', COM(2001) 517-2001/0218/CNS, http://ec.europa.eu/prelex/detail_dossier_real.cfm?CL=en&DosId=167920 (accessed 21 February 2008).

WTO rules are intended to reflect the unique challenge of incorporating China into the world trading system. This is an economy in the midst of transition from state ownership to the market based system; a country that has taken many measures to introduce market economics, but where certain features of a state led economy still prevail. Most notably, the protocol affords other Members special protection for their own industries against damaging surges of exports from China.

*A one-way market opening process*

5. The entire negotiation revolved around how, and in some cases to what extent, China will adopt the WTO 'acquis' of rules and agreements. These govern international trade in goods, agriculture and services, and include provisions on many related areas such as trade related investment measures, technical barriers to trade, sanitary and phytosanitary measures, intellectual property protection, and government procurement. This means that the process consisted in the WTO Membership securing "concessions" or market opening improvements from China, without themselves altering their obligations within the WTO.

6. For the EU, which ensured that the interests of European industries and firms were fully represented, China's entry will therefore signal an enormous gain in enforceable rights, with no significant change in our own commitments towards China. The long (and arduous) series of bilateral negotiations held between European Commission and Chinese officials resulted in terms of accession which will substantially benefit those sectors and interests of greatest value to the all Member States of the EU (details provided below).

7. The only obligation for WTO Members is that they must accord China so-called permanent MFN ('most favoured nation') status, entitling it to be treated in the same way as every other WTO Member, unless exceptions are specified in the protocol of accession. As the EU has always accorded China this status in any event, there will be virtually no practical impact. The only notable consequence of according China the same treatment as other WTO Members will be the requirements to phase out China-specific quantitative restrictions (quotas) by 2005. This applies to the EU's remaining textile quotas applied to China , which must be dismantled in line with the Agreement on Textiles and Clothing. It also applies to the three industrial products for which the EU still maintains China-quotas: footwear, ceramic tableware and porcelain tableware. In recognition of these changes, until 2008 a specific safeguard instrument for countering injurious imports of textile products from China will be available. And for up to 12 years after accession, product specific safeguard provisions will allow remedial action to be taken against surges of imports from China which damage, or threaten to damage, competing EU industries.

8. Of course, once a WTO member, China will have a full seat at the negotiating table whenever further steps to multilateral liberalisation are agreed. Arguably, this is the most important change that WTO membership will engender.

*Impact on the WTO system*

9. The entry of China into the WTO will mean that the organisation itself takes a huge step closer to becoming genuinely global. It should be recalled that China was in fact a contracting party to the GATT in 1947, but withdrew from the organisation shortly thereafter. It has long been the unanimously agreed policy of EU Member States to support China's entry bid.

10. As the world's most populous country, China will very likely immediately become a key player in the organisation. China has a fundamental interest in both the promotion and the proper regulation of trade at the global level. Increased trade has been a major contributor to the country's phenomenal growth rates since the open door policy was launched in 1978. And it sees WTO membership as a lever for continuing domestic reforms which are a now an established priority of the leadership.

11. Also important in this respect is the high standard of commitments given by China to open its economy to foreign imports, investors and businesses. China's trade regime will be significantly more liberal than most existing WTO Members of a comparable level of development. One of the reasons the talks lasted so long was the concern of the EU and others that China's entry should in no way lower the average standard of openness to trade in WTO. The tariff average will be low, quotas will be phased out quickly, service providers from virtually all sectors will have good market access, protection for intellectual property rights will be guaranteed in law. As explained below, the final results constitute an extremely substantial market opening package.

## III The benefits of bringing China into the multilateral trading system

*Good for EU business*

12. First of all, the deal will secure vastly improved access for EU firms to China's market. Import tariffs and other non-tariff restrictions will be sharply and permanently reduced. And investments by foreign companies will take place in a more attractive, and more predictable, business environment. WTO membership will consolidate and accelerate China's own efforts to promote transparency, fairness and openness in its trade régime across the board. And the WTO's independent and legally binding dispute settlement system will enable both sides to resolve trade problems. In short, this agreement greatly enhances the climate for European companies to export to, and do business in, China.

*Good for China's economy*

13. As with all important liberalisation agreements, China's WTO commitments will in the first place benefit her own economy and people. But beyond the commercial opportunities it will offer, WTO accession will have a substantial impact on economic reform and development in China. The EU has been concerned throughout the negotiations to come up with a package which fosters gradual but lasting reform and sustainable development in China, at a rate which is intended to run in parallel with the domestic reform programme. Together, we have agreed to step-by-step market opening in many areas, with implementation typically taking place within a three to five year period, rather than overnight exposure of China's firms and service providers to foreign competition. WTO accession provides an unrivalled anchor for reform. Entering the world trading system will be a catalyst for Chinese firms to become more efficient, to show that they can compete on fair terms with the rest of the world. This agreement will therefore also be good for Chinese companies and workers, as they draw the benefits of increasing foreign investment, and take on the most modern management practices and legal structures.

*Good for the future of EU-China relations*

14. China's entry into WTO will contribute to steady and sustainable economic development, not only in China, but for her neighbours in Asia, and indeed for the rest of the

world. On top of this, the agreement reached, when it is implemented as part of the multilateral system, will boost the rule of law in China. The fundamental principles of transparency, nondiscrimination, efficient administration and independent judicial review which the WTO upholds will contribute to the positive evolution of China's economic, legal and social systems.

15. In reality, China's accession can only lock in and deepen market reforms, empowering those in the leadership who support further and faster moves towards economic freedom. The opening up of telecommunications, the internet and satellite services will inevitably expose the Chinese people to information, ideas and debate from around the world. The rule of law will be strengthened as China finds herself obliged to play by the global trade rules. The spillover of economic freedom and respect for commercial law into the political and social sphere will be gradual, but the contribution made by WTO entry will be positive. Many human rights activists and members of the foreign policy community agree that bringing China into the world trading system will be a push in the right direction in these spheres also.

*Implementation through partnership – EU assistance*

16. As China enters the WTO, it will of course be vital that all of the changes to her trade regime described below are implemented as promptly and accurately as possible. In order to make this process as smooth as possible, the EU is committed to working in partnership with China, and determined to share its experience in the WTO, assisting as far as possible with the changes which China will have to introduce and sustain in its continuing economic transition. Technical assistance will clearly have a role to play, and the EU has a number of co-operation projects in place, or lined up for the near future, with a budget totalling around EUR 24 million, which are either designed specifically, or may henceforth be used, to help build the capacity of China's government and administration to implement its impending commitments under the WTO.

17. In addition, support for the transition required by WTO accession, and related economic reforms has been earmarked by the European Commission as a focal area for future funding. Projects will be proposed in consultation with China, to ensure that help is targeted where it is most useful. This broad-based assistance programme will accompany the efforts of the European Commission, Member States and business groups to monitor China's adherence to her new international commitments. Indeed, the WTO Membership as a whole has recognised the particular attention which will need to be paid to implementation of the WTO rules by China. A "transitional review mechanism" will require annual progress reviews to be conducted in Geneva for eight years after accession, to be followed by a bi-annual review thereafter.

## IV Summary of terms of China's WTO Accession by Sector

*Industrial goods*

18. China will reduce its tariffs on all goods to an average of 9%, down from around 17% at present. All import tariffs will be bound. Notably, tariff "peaks" above 15% -which are the most restrictive of trade -will be very significantly reduced. As well as tariffs coming down, China has committed itself to removing all of its import quotas -restricting the volume of goods which can enter China from abroad -by 2005. The gains this represents for EU exporters are clear. Coupled with the right to trade and distribute freely within China, which will also become widespread, the opportunities for EU manufacturers to participate in one of the world's largest markets will become real at last.

Industrial tariffs in detail

19. On motor vehicles, the tariff on cars will fall from 80-100% today to 25% by July 1, 2006 (with the greatest reductions in the first years). Additionally, as a result of its negotiations with the EU, China agreed on a range of improvements which will benefit EU firms which produce cars, vans and trucks through direct investment in China (see paragraph 50 for details).

20. Tariffs on Information Technology products, beer, toys and furniture will be eliminated. These sectors account for almost 10% of total EU exports of industrial products. Sectoral averages on other 'double-zero sectors' range between 4.2% for pharmaceuticals and 6.2% for construction equipment. Chemical tariff 'harmonisation' will be implemented, with limited exceptions, so that the sectoral average will be reduced by 40% to 7.1%.

21. As for EU priorities not covered in China's bilateral negotiations with any other WTO members, these were concentrated on 150 specific products varying from gin to building materials. On these EU priorities, an additional reduction of 40% on top of earlier offers was obtained (the tariff average here falling from 18.6% to 10.9%). The following is a breakdown by category.

22. Tariffs on all spirits will be aligned to a level of 10%. There will be no difference in the treatment of whisk(e)y, Cognac, Gin etc. The presently applied tariff level is still at 65%.

23. Tariffs on key cosmetics products will come down to a level of 10% (currently up to 30%). This implies good prospects for a sector which already exports up to EUR 7 billion world-wide.

24. On leather and leather articles negotiations focused on 13 specific products which account for 60% of total EU exports in this sector. China agreed a reduction on these products from 20-25% to 10%.

25. On textiles China made some further improvements to the rates offered during other bilateral negotiations. China's textiles tariffs will now be very close to the levels of the EU and far lower than almost all other textile exporting countries.

Tariffs on 5 particular footwear products which account for more than 70% of EU footwear exports will be reduced from 25% to 10%.

26. Marble/building stones are popular articles in China's enormous construction market. On the 5 most important products tariffs will also be reduced from 25% to 10%.

27. On ceramics China agreed to reduce tariffs on 11 key ceramics products from 24.5-35% to 10-15%. And tariffs on 6 particular glass products will be reduced from 24.5% to 5%.

28. On 52 particular products in the important machinery and appliances sector, which accounts for 26% of total EU exports, tariffs will be cut to 5-10% from levels up to 35%.

*Agriculture*

29. On agricultural goods, China will cut its tariffs on the 60 products most exported by the EU to an average of 10% by 2005. Improvements have been made on the tariff quota for rape oil, as well as on tariffs on products such as: rape oil (down from 85% to 9%), pasta (down from 25% to 15%), butter (down from 30% to 10%), milk powder (down from 25% to 10%), mandarins (down from 40% to 12%), wine (down from 65% to 14%), olives (down from 25% to 10%) and wheat gluten (down from 30% to 18%).

30. On the domestic side, China has committed to eliminating all agricultural export subsidies for her producers. Additionally, using the leverage of the negotiations on WTO accession, the EU and China have drawn up a bilateral accord on sanitary and phytosanitary issues (SPS) to ensure that market access for animal and plant based goods is not hampered on any nonscientific grounds. It now rests on EU Member States to make this agreement operational by negotiating bilateral SPS protocols for the products they export.

*Trading rights and liberalisation of state trading monopolies*

31. Vitally, these improvements in market access for industrial and agricultural goods will be accompanied by the right for foreign firms to import and export freely within three years, and to distribute, retail, transport, repair and service their products within China within 3 years after accession (see under Services below). This represents a major break with the past, and will allow exporters to participate in every aspect of business right through to sales to final consumers in China.

32. The key sectors of crude and processed oil, as well as fertiliser, will be gradually opened to non-state importers, including foreign importers. This means that companies will no longer have to channel all oil or fertiliser going into China through state importers. The growth of the volumes open for private import is steady, allowing China's own industry to adjust gradually to liberalisation.

33. The right for foreign, private firms to import silk directly from China, which was previously subject to a state run export monopoly, has also been secured. This means that EU clothing firms will have improved access to raw silk from China which can then be processed and finished in Europe. EU exports of silk products in 1999 amounted to 3,000 million Euros. China produces 70% of the world's raw silk.

*Services*

34. A large part of the accession negotiations focused on services, of paramount importance to the EU in particular as the world's leading exporter in this field. China's commitments cover a wide range of service sectors, with access for foreign providers guaranteed by transparent and automatic licensing procedures which have been set out in detail in the Protocol of Accession.

Insurance

35. Access for foreign insurance companies to China's market will be significantly improved when China enters the WTO. Operating licences will be granted on the basis of transparent prudential criteria. Effective management control has been negotiated for foreign participants in life insurance joint ventures, through choice of partner, and a legal guarantee of freedom from any regulatory interference in privately negotiated contracts on a 50-50 equity basis. Foreign insurers will be able to sell the same products as their Chinese competitors 3 years (life) or one year (non-life) after accession. This scope of business includes health, pension and group insurance in life, and all non-life activities except for statutory 3$^{rd}$ party liability insurance.

36. Geographic expansion of cities open to foreign insurers has also been accelerated. Brokers (insurance intermediaries) will have access to the Chinese market through local establishment for the first time. Subsequent to the EU's agreement with China, foreign brokers will also be able to conduct large-scale commercial risk, and reinsurance business in

China, with majority control of operations 3 years after accession, and complete ownership after 5 years.

37. Outside the terms of the WTO accession Agreement itself, China agreed to grant EU firms seven new licences (five for life and two for non-life business), and two sub-branch licences for firms already present in China, before she enters the WTO - the intention being to ensure that EU firms are on the same footing as their rivals when China enters the WTO.

Telecommunications

38. As a result of its WTO accession negotiations, China has agreed to open a significant part of its telecommunications market to foreign firms. It was as a result of her bilateral negotiations with the EU – home of some of the world's most competitive telecommunications companies – that China committed to some of the most significant opportunities in this sector.

39. A vital area where China will offer improved conditions for foreign telecommunications investors is in the field of mobile telephony, where non-Chinese firms will be allowed to hold a 25% share of operations on accession, rising to 35% one year later, and 49% 3 years after China joins WTO. Negotiated by the EU, this is a significant acceleration of the phasing-in of business first agreed in the Sino-US bilateral Accord. China currently allows no foreign investment in telecommunications services.

40. Foreign firms will also be allowed to provide private leased circuits to businesses in China which wish to get better value for money in their own communications, both throughout China and internationally. The right to provide telecommunications services in China's leading cities is now accompanied by the right to provide services between them.

Distribution

41. As mentioned already, the right to distribute imported products, whether goods or services, has been severely restricted in China until now. This includes the right to carry out sales, marketing and advertising, packaging and warehousing, customer support and maintenance. Clearly this is of vital importance to the service industries as well as manufacturers which export to China. China's market will thus be gradually opened at every level from wholesale to retail, with all products being available for distribution by foreigners, except salt and tobacco. At the retail end, the EU secured improved opportunities – the size restriction of 20.000 m$^2$ will be lifted, allowing large European supermarkets or furniture retailers to be set up, for example. And there will no longer be a limit to the number of shops in a chain which can be foreign-owned, as the specific joint venture restriction for large department stores and chain stores is also lifted.

Banking & Securities

42. European banks or other foreign banks will be able to establish and conduct local currency business with Chinese companies within 3 years of accession, and with private individuals all over China within 5 years of accession. The phase-in periods vary for different cities, but the EU succeeded in bringing forward the date for the city bordering the special administrative region of Macao (Zhuhai). In an important deregulatory step, motor vehicle distributors and other non-financial institutions will be able to give credit facilities for the purchase of cars, trucks & buses.

43. Fund management firms will be able to engage in joint ventures (up to 49% share by 3 years after accession) – and underwrite and trade debt and equity in foreign currency denominated securities (B-shares), as well as underwriting domestically denominated securities (A-shares).

44. The banking sector is one in which China has made extremely significant commitments, set to make capital available to China's entrepreneurs on an unprecedented scale.

Professional Services

45. Foreign law firms, accountancy firms and other professional service providers will be able to hold majority control of businesses in China. Importantly, the EU successfully negotiated the right for foreign owned firms to have entrustment relations with Chinese lawyers, thereby enabling their practices to cover Chinese legal business as well as advising on foreign law.

46. The EU also ensured that recently introduced Chinese laws which placed restrictions on the conduct of market research in China will be relaxed, opening the way for European companies freely to carry out vital pre-investment research before entering the Chinese market.

Tourism

47. Within 3 years of accession, foreign firms will be able to hold the full 100% ownership stake in their hotels in China. EU business will also benefit from improved opportunities for foreign firms in the tourism trade, by reducing the minimum capital and turnover requirements so that small firms – which covers many of the China specialists in Europe – can provide the full range of tourism services.

*Protocol commitments*

48. As explained above, in the final, multilateral stage of the accession process, WTO Members collectively sought to ensure the basic compatibility of China's trade laws and institutions with WTO rules and agreements, setting these out in the Protocol of accession and Working Party Report. In advance of this stage, the EU also discussed certain horizontal issues directly with China, to make certain that the interests of EU firms would be properly safeguarded. As a result of these discussions, commitments of particular value to the EU were given by China on the following subjects:

National treatment

49. Any measures and practices which are the cause of legal or practical discrimination between Chinese and imported products will be illegal when China is in the WTO. This is a fundamental principle. But as a result of negotiations with the EU, China has explicitly committed herself to eliminate a number of existing such practices. For example, those who provide after-sales service on Chinese goods will equally be able to cover imported goods, the special pricing rules and profit ceilings imposed on imported pharmaceuticals will be removed, the special registration procedures applicable to imported chemicals will be repealed, the different retail licences required to sell foreign and domestic spirits, and imported and domestic cigarettes will be unified, and differences in standards verification and inspection procedures for boilers & pressure vessels will be reduced so that they do not constitute an illegal barrier to trade. On a broader front, China has agreed to end the potentially discriminatory dual system for pre-market testing and certification of new products,

whereby until now one agency dealt with all imported goods, and another with all home-produced items.

Trade related investment measures (TRIMs) and other investment conditions

50. The EU secured additional commitments in receiving Chinese assurances that foreign investors will not be subject to mandatory export performance or technology transfer obligations. China has also agreed to implement the TRIMs Agreement upon accession, and to remove trade and foreign exchange balancing requirements, local content requirements. China will therefore not condition investment approvals, import licenses, or other import approvals on any such requirements. With specific reference to motor vehicle production by foreign invested enterprises, restrictions regarding the category, type and models of vehicle produced will be lifted; the ceiling above which investments have to be approved by both central and provincial authorities will rise from $30 million to $150 million, and for the manufacture of engines, China's joint-venture requirement will be removed, allowing wholly foreign owned production.

Protection of intellectual property rights

51. From the date of her accession to the WTO, China has committed to abide fully to the rules of the TRIPs Agreement. This will provide a welcome boost to the ability of the holders of copyrights, trademarks, patents and other recognised categories of intellectual property to enforce their rights within China. In a country where abuse and counterfeiting are still prevalent, foreign companies can look forward to improved safeguards for their rights, and have been promised reinforced co-operation from the Chinese authorities, as proper protection becomes an international, legally binding obligation. In recognition of the scale of the current problem in this field, China has agreed to go some way beyond the requirements of the TRIPs Agreement. This includes, for example, undertakings to enact legislation which will protect commercially sensitive information which is disclosed for testing and certification purposes for a minimum of six years, and to decrease the minimum financial thresholds for bringing infringement lawsuits to the criminal courts.

Export subsidies

52. In addition to the above, China also gave commitments regarding export subsidies on industrial goods. On accession, China will eliminate all forms of export subsidies as defined by Articles 1 and 3 of the WTO Subsidies Agreement, including not only direct grants but also, in particular, tax breaks linked to export performance.

Government procurement

53. The EU also broke new ground in securing commitments from China regarding public procurement. China has expressed her wish to join the GPA at a future date and – pending the completion of those GPA negotiations – has undertaken to procure in a transparent and nondiscriminatory manner. This undertaking applies not only to central and provincial government agencies, but also to all state-owned enterprises, unless they are engaged in exclusively commercial activities.

Trade defence instruments

54. Finally, in China's Protocol of Accession there are key provisions specifying how the trade defence instruments (anti-dumping, anti-subsidy, safeguards) may be used to deal with

imports specifically from China. In reflection of the fact that China's economy is still in transition, there will be derogations from the WTO rules, available for a certain period of time, which will permit Members to maintain tighter control over injurious inflows of goods from China (whether due to their high volume or low-price) than would normally be the case.

55. The EU's present legislation which provides specific procedures for dealing with cases of alleged dumping by Chinese exporters, which may not yet be operating in normal market economy conditions, will remain available for up to fifteen years after China enters the WTO. The China-specific safeguard provision, allowing safeguard action to be taken only with respect to imports from China (in contrast to the normal requirement for *erga omnes* action against all sources of imports) will be available for up to twelve years after China's accession. And a further sector specific mechanism has been put in place to provide added protection in the textiles field, until 2008.

### V Recommendation

56. In submitting the terms of Accession of the People's Republic of China to the WTO for approval by the Council, and for the opinion of the European Parliament, the Commission commends these terms as representing a balanced but ambitious package of market opening commitments, which will bring substantial benefits to China and her WTO trading partners alike.

## Document 9.4: Proposal for a Council Decision Establishing the Community Position within the WTO Ministerial Conference

Proposal for a Council Decision establishing the Community position within the Ministerial Conference set up by the Agreement establishing the World Trade Organization on the accession of the People's Republic of China to the World Trade Organization
(2002/C 51 E/10)
COM(2001) 517 final—2001/0218(CNS)
*(Submitted by the Commission on 19 October 2001)*

THE COUNCIL OF THE EUROPEAN UNION,

Having regard to the Treaty establishing the European Community, and in particular Articles 37, 44, 47, 55, 71, 80(2), 95, 133 and 308, in conjunction with the first subparagraph of Article 300(3) thereof,

Having regard to the proposal from the Commission,

Having regard to the opinion of the European Parliament,

Whereas:

(1) On 10 July 1986 the Government of the People's Republic of China applied to resume its status as a contracting party to the General Agreement on Tariffs and Trade (GATT 1947).

(2) On 7 December 1995 the Government of the People's Republic of China applied for accession to the Agreement establishing the World Trade Organization (WTO), pursuant to Article XII of that Agreement.

(3) A Working Party on China's status as a GATT 1947 Contracting Party was established on 4 March 1987, and was transformed into a WTO Accession Working Party on 7 December 1995, in order to reach agreement on terms of accession acceptable to the People's Republic of China and all WTO Members.

(4) The Commission, on behalf of the Community and its Member States, negotiated a comprehensive series of market opening commitments on the part of the People's Republic of China which are of particular importance to the Community, provided for in the bilateral agreement between the People's Republic of China and the Community authenticated by signature on 19 May 2000.

(5) These commitments are now embodied in the Protocol of Accession of the People's Republic of China to the WTO.

(6) Accession to the WTO is expected to make a positive and lasting contribution to the process of economic reform and sustainable development in the People's Republic of China.

(7) It will also bring trade relations between the People's Republic of China and the Community into a stable and legally binding framework.

(8) The Protocol of Accession should therefore be approved.

(9) Article XII of the Agreement establishing the WTO provides that the terms of accession are to be agreed between the acceding Member and the WTO, and that the Ministerial Conference of the WTO approves the terms of accession on the WTO side.

(10) Accordingly, it is necessary to establish the position to be taken by the Community within the Ministerial Conference.

(11) For some of the objectives of the Community which accession of China to the WTO will help achieve the Treaty does not provide powers other than those under Article 308.

HAS DECIDED AS FOLLOWS:

**Sole Article**

The position to be taken by the Community within the Ministerial Conference set up by the Agreement establishing the WTO on the accession of the People's Republic of China to the WTO, is to support the draft Decision of the Ministerial Conference which supports the accession (see attachment).

**ANNEX**
**Draft Decision**
**ACCESSION OF THE PEOPLE'S REPUBLIC OF CHINA**
**Decision of [. . . November 2001]**

[The Ministerial Conference,

*Having regard* to paragraph 2 of Article XII and paragraph 1 of Article IX of the Marrakesh Agreement Establishing the World Trade Organization, and the Decision-Making Procedures under Articles IX and XII of the Marrakesh Agreement Establishing the World Trade Organization agreed by the General Council (WT/L/93),

*Taking note* of the application of the People's Republic of China for accession to the Marrakesh Agreement Establishing the World Trade Organization dated 7 December 1995,

*Noting* the results of the negotiations directed toward the establishment of the terms of accession of the People's Republic of China to the Marrakesh Agreement Establishing the World Trade Organization and having prepared a Protocol on the Accession of the People's Republic of China (WT/ACC/. . ./. . .),

*Has decided as follows:*

The People's Republic of China may accede to the Marrakesh Agreement Establishing the World Trade Organization on the terms and conditions set out in the Protocol annexed to this decision.][(1)]

(1) Das Dokument ist nur in englisch verfügbar.

## Document 9.5: European Parliament Report on the Proposal for a Council Decision Establishing the Community Position within the WTO Ministerial Conference

Report on the proposal for a Council decision establishing the Community position within the Ministerial Conference set up by the Agreement establishing the World Trade Organization on the accession of the People's Republic of China to the World Trade Organization (COM (2001) 517 – C5-0487/2001 – 2001/0218(CNS))
Committee on Industry, External Trade, Research and Energy
Rapporteur: Per Gahrton

**PROCEDURAL PAGE**

By letter of 12 October 2001 the Council consulted Parliament, pursuant to the first subparagraph of Article 300(3) of the EC Treaty, on the proposal for a Council decision establishing the Community position within the Ministerial Conference set up by the Agreement establishing the World Trade Organization on the accession of the People's Republic of China to the World Trade Organization (COM (2001) 517 - 2001/0218 (CNS)).

At the sitting of 22 October 2001 the President of Parliament will announce that she has referred this proposal for consideration to the Committee on Industry, External Trade, Research and Energy as the committee responsible (C5-0487/2001).

The Committee on Industry, External Trade, Research and Energy appointed Per Gahrton rapporteur at its meeting of 10 October 2001.

The committee considered the draft Council decision and draft report at its meeting of 15 October 2001.

At that meeting it adopted the draft legislative resolution by 18 votes with 3 abstentions.

The following were present for the vote: Carlos Westendorp y Cabeza, chairman; Nuala Ahern, vice-chairman; Peter Michael Mombaur, vice-chairman; Per Gahrton, rapporteur; Felipe Camisón Asensio (for Jaime Valdivielso de Cué), Concepció Ferrer, Francesco Fiori (for Umberto Scapagnini), Neena Gill (for Glyn Ford), Alfred Gomolka (for Werner Langen), Michel Hansenne, Rolf Linkohr, Caroline Lucas, Eryl Margaret McNally, Erika Mann, Elly Plooij-van Gorsel, John Purvis, Mechtild Rothe, Jacques Santer (for Paul Rübig), Konrad K. Schwaiger, Claude Turmes and W.G. van Velzen.

The report was tabled on 18 October 2001.

**DRAFT LEGISLATIVE RESOLUTION**

**European Parliament legislative resolution on the proposal for a Council decision on establishing the Community position within the Ministerial Conference set up by the Agreement establishing the World Trade Organization on the accession of the People's Republic of China to the World Trade Organization (COM (2001) 517 œ C5-0487/2001 œ 2001/0218 (CNS))**

*(Consultation procedure)*

The European Parliament,

- having regard to the proposal for a Council decision (COM (2001) 517[1]),
- having regard to Articles 37, 44, 47, 55, 71, 80(2), 95, 133 and 308 of the EC Treaty,
- having been consulted by the Council pursuant to the first subparagraph of Article 300(3) of the EC Treaty (C5-0487/2001),
- having regard to Rule 67 and Rule 97(7) of its Rules of Procedure, œ having regard to the report of the Committee on Industry, External Trade, Research and Energy (A5-0366/2001),

1. Approves the Community position;

2. Instructs its President to forward its position to the Council and Commission, and to the governments and parliaments of the Member States.

**EXPLANATORY STATEMENT**

The Proposal for a Council decision by the EC describes the implications of China's WTO membership from a number of aspects, such as China's legally binding commitment to open trade, the impact on the WTO system and the terms of China's WTO accession by sectors.

*1. A one-sided EU victory?*

According to the EC, China's WTO accession is 'a one-way market opening process'. For the EU, the EC says, 'which ensured that the interests of European industries and firms were fully represented, China's entry will therefore signal an enormous gain in enforceable rights, with no significant change in our own commitments towards China'. The very few concessions the EU had to accept, such as the phasing-out of China-specific quantitative restrictions by 2005, will be softened by specific safeguard instruments against injurious imports or surges of imports from China for up to 12 years after accession. The final result, the EC says, is 'an extremely substantial market opening process'.

Thus, it is obviously a very one-sided affair, where China has had to accept requirements to 'open its economy to foreign imports, investors and businesses' (EC par 11). One might call it an important EU victory. The question is, of course, if trade agreements in a world of international cooperation should be judged as if they were football matches. The rapporteur thinks not and is rather sceptical about the victorious language in the proposal by the EC.

*2. Chinese criticism of WTO accession*

The Chinese Government has accepted the conditions for WTO accession which have triggered the jubilant wordings by the EC. However, WTO accession is not undisputed in China, a fact that the EC does not mention by a single word, although it should be known to it through the EC representation in Beijing, which must have been able to deliver full information about the ongoing Chinese debate on the matter.

During a visit last year to Beijing the rapporteur met the authors of two books (in Chinese) that both maintain that the accession to the WTO constitutes a threat to the social and economic development and political cohesion of China. Interestingly enough these books are not part of a forbidden underground literature, but published by Chinese publishers in China and available at bookstores all over the country.

One of the books, 'Collision: Globalisation and China's reality choice', is written by a young economist at Beijing Aeronautic University, Han Deqiang. He considers China to be the weaker part that will lose to a system that is dominated by transnational companies. He denies being 'conservative', he is closer to the Western brand of criticism of 'neo-liberal globalisation'. His sympathies are with the lower classes, he says. He believes that Chinese companies will be outflanked or swallowed by transnational giants. At the same time he is a supporter of the opening-up policy of Deng Xiao Ping. He believes in a market economy in a politically controlled framework. His main argument against WTO accession is that the Chinese economy is not strong enough and that the poorest classes of China will have to pay a heavy price in the form of unemployment and social insecurity.

Our chat, he says, could not have taken place six to seven years ago. The climate is more open now. Han Deqiang visited Brussels as guest speaker at a seminar on China and the WTO this summer. Asked why the Chinese leadership, despite criticism such as his own, is so keen to join the WTO he answered: join the WTO so the wallet of the rich won't be under threat.

Han Deqiang's book received quite extensive attention in China when it was published in 2000. The Central Policy Research Institute published a long summary and the journal 'International Trade', belonging to the Ministry of Foreign Trade, published an article based upon the book. Several other magazines published abstracts or comments.

The other book, 'China in the shadow of globalisation', has a map on its cover which shows how China has been split up in five parts, apart from 'traditional' China, also Tibet, Xinjiang, Inner Mongolia and Manchuria. The authors, the political scientist Fang Nin and the economic journalist Wang Xiaodong, pretend that such a partition is one of the possible effects of WTO accession, which may release internal tensions which may end up in a division of the country, a result that they consider to be the intention of the USA and the EU. Also in 'traditional' China there is tension. According to Fang and Wang, south China is more positively inclined towards integration into the world market, while there is hesitation in the north and in the interior. The reason is, of course, that the economy in Guangdong and other southern coastal provinces is more competitive, while the northern provinces are dominated by outdated heavy industries of the Soviet type and the interior by primitive small-scale agriculture, which despite, or because of, its lower technological level has a higher price level than imported food from large-scale industrial agriculture in the West. Thus, the USA will control the agricultural market of China, says Fang.

These two books give a picture of China close to explosion. Nothing is predictable. The Western belief that WTO accession automatically will lead to political liberalisation, is not accepted by any of the three authors. They say it may also turn the opposite way, but they admit everything is uncertain. If WTO accession creates tensions and conflicts that destroy one-party rule, the alternative may be some kind of democracy, but it may also be a worse dictatorship. Or chaos and civil war.

The rapporteur finds it extremely surprising that the EC, not with a single word, is even hinting at the existence in China of these types of general critical views concerning China's WTO accession. There are several reasons why it would be logical for the EU to take this kind of criticism into account:

a) China is not a parliamentary democracy. The Chinese people may or may not agree with its government about WTO accession. From a EU point of view it should be clear that the EU has a special responsibility to take into consideration alternative opinions in China.

b) The cited criticism is not of the 'dissident' or 'underground' type. The fact that the cited criticism is neither outlawed or made by 'dissidents', but published in books available in bookstores in China, shows that it most probably represents much wider circles than its authors. There is a much more widespread uneasiness about the implications of WTO accession in China than is represented in the fact that the political elite has decided to go for membership. It is obviously a very hazardous affair for the political leaders. In this perspective it appears to the rapporteur rather inappropriate to present the China–EU agreement on WTO accession in such jubilant and victorious terms as the EC has chosen to do in its document. Any Chinese reader of the EC proposal must get the impression that the whole affair is a series of one-sided concessions by China to open its market to EU business.

c) If there is anything valid in the general criticism of the type cited above the effects may be very serious upon stability in China, with repercussions not only for global security but also for the security of EU business in China. Shouldn't the EC, apart from praising itself for its victories at the negotiating table, give some thought to the problems that may arise ahead, how the EU should act in order to avoid the exploitation by EU business of the opportunities given by China's WTO accession leading to negative effects of the type described in the above-quoted books?

*3. Special implications for the Chinese economy of WTO accession*

The EC document outlines on 14 lines how WTO accession is 'good for China's economy' (par 13). There is no indication whatsoever in the EC document that problems or negative effects may arise in China. For information about this, other sources are needed. The rapporteur will not try to give any extensive picture of the abundant reports by journalists, sinologists, social scientists and economists that exist on possible problems in China because of WTO entry. Just some examples:

Problems in the state sector

One of the most severe problems includes the non-performing state-owned enterprises (SOEs), with the entire sector showing a net loss from 1996 through to 1998. The financial sector has remained mostly a policy tool to channel resources to the SOEs causing a serious credit crunch for the private sector. At the same time, the banks are plagued with bad loans from the SOEs. Production terms, excessive capacity and bloated administrations afflict the state sector. Over half the SOEs reported idle capacity of at least 50%. An estimated 18% of total employees in the state sector are redundant workers. These problems will lead to serious unemployment and more bad loans as reform continues.

Of course, some of China's plate will be quite bitter to swallow. It may be good to let inefficient SOEs die; jobs will also disappear. The estimated unemployment rate in cities and towns is already above 15% and this number is likely to increase. Re-employment prospects are very bleak because those who are laid off are often older and unskilled. Furthermore, decades of the iron rice bowl have formed poor attitudes toward working that are not welcomed in a profit-oriented business. To make the picture worse, an estimated 30% of the agricultural labour force is redundant, meaning 120 million farmers will have to look for jobs in the cities. This creates another source of unemployment pressure.

While the picture looks bleak, there is hope that if China survives this radical transformation, a new economy will emerge that is much more affluent, market-oriented, rules-based, transparent, orderly and efficient. (From China Online 14/8-01).

Weed attack risk heightened with WTO entry, says expert

China faced a higher risk of damage from introduced weeds when opening its doors to foreign agricultural imports under its entry to the World Trade Organization, an agricultural expert warned yesterday.

Xinhua quoted Shi Zhicheng, vice-chairman of the China Agricultural Society, as saying Beijing needed to tighten regulations against the importation of foreign plant species. Mr Shi's warning came after negotiators in Geneva said on Friday that they had reached an informal agreement on China becoming a full member of the WTO later this year. Earlier state media reports said Chinese farmers would face increased competition from foreign imports once the country was a full member of the WTO. Mr Shi said non-indigenous weeds had already caused considerable damage to China's ecology. (From South China Morning Post 17/9-01)

Debate over farm subsidies toughest of hurdles

With more than 900 million of its 1.3 billion population working in agriculture, China's leaders were understandably concerned about how they would cope with the flood of farm imports when the average tariff on agricultural products fell to 17% by 2004. Official Chinese estimates say that because of cheaper grain imports, 9.7 million farmers will lose their jobs within seven years after Beijing joins the WTO. A US$ 2 billion-a-year increase in United States agricultural exports to the Middle Kingdom could be seen, according to US Agriculture Department estimates. (From South China Morning Post 18/9-01)

From these sample reports it is clear that to describe the implications of WTO accession without reservations as 'good for China's economy' is simply not correct. The picture is much more multifaceted and complicated. Implications will be quite different for different regions, different social groups, different individuals.

## Conclusion

The Chinese Government has accepted the terms and conditions for accession to the WTO which the EU Council is asked to accept in the proposal for a decision. Although this rapporteur is convinced that internal Chinese criticism made important points and that several of the negative effects of WTO entry, such as rising unemployment, reinforced flight from the countryside into the big cities, social insecurity and widening of the social and economic gaps between different regions and social groups in China, will in effect take place, it would be to go too far to recommend that the EU Council ought to reject the agreements negotiated and oppose China's entry because of considerations about what is the best solution for the Chinese people. The EU cannot replace the Chinese Government. Also the implications of WTO entry for China are not given from the start, but will be decided by its implementation and by accompanying measures undertaken both by the Chinese authorities and by the EU and its businesses.

If EU businesses choose to abstain from exploiting cheap labour and weak labour and environmental regulations and instead decide to set good examples in accordance with the required behaviour in their home countries, several possible negative effects will be avoided and a basis established for long-term confidence between these firms and Chinese civil society. But the main responsibility for coping with all possible problems in order to avoid social and ecological deteriorations remains, of course, with the Chinese political system. The challenges of WTO accession will undoubtedly test the ability of the present authoritarian system to adapt to new conditions in close contact with the popular will. The accession of an at least nominally Communist regime, at the same time the most populous country of the world with the second largest economy, into the core of market liberalism is a unique experiment.

1 Not yet published in the Official Journal. RR\452249EN.doc 5/10 PE 302.160

## ACCESSION

Subsequently, the WTO Decision of 10 November 2001 decided that the People's Republic of China may accede to the Marrakesh Agreement Establishing the World Trade Organization.[6] China became a WTO Member on 11 December 2001. On accession, China became legally bound by the results of the Uruguay Round of multilateral trade negotiations. These results comprised the Final Act of the Uruguay Round negotiations, the Marrakesh Agreement establishing the WTO and the annexes of the Marrakesh Agreement. These annexes included the multilateral agreements on trade in goods, such as the General Agreement on Tariffs and Trade 1994 (GATT) and numerous other agreements on goods; the General Agreement on Trade in Services (GATS); the Agreement on Trade-related Intellectual Aspects of Intellectual Property Rights (TRIPS); the Understanding on Rules and Procedures Governing the Settlement of Disputes (Dispute Settlement Understanding, or DSU); and the Trade Policy Review Mechanisms (TPRM).[7]

In addition to the Marrakesh Agreement, the multilateral agreements concerning Chinese accession to the WTO include two other documents agreed formally by the WTO Ministerial Conference in Doha.[8] The first was the Decision of 10 November 2001 and the annexed Protocol on the Accession of the People's Republic of China, which include a number of general provisions and the schedules on goods and services agreed by China.[9] The WTO Decision of 10 November 2001 and the Protocol (without annexes) are reproduced as Document 9.6. Paragraph 15 on antidumping

6 See World Trade Organization, Decision of 10 November 2001, Accession of the People's Republic of China, WT/L/432 (23 November 2001), available on the WTO website, www.wto.org.

7 The agreements are also available in World Trade Organization, *The Legal Texts: The Results of the Uruguay Round Multilateral Trade Negotiations* (Cambridge, Cambridge University Press, 2000). See also the WTO website, www.wto.org.

8 A useful bilingual (English and Chinese) collection of relevant texts is *Compilation of the Legal Instruments on China's Accession to the World Trade Organization* (Beijing, Law Press China, 2002), also available on the website of the WTO, www.wto.org.

9 WT/L/432, 23 November 2001, reprinted in *Compilation of the Legal Instruments on China's Accession to the World Trade Organization* (Beijing, Law Press China, 2002) 1 (including Annexes).

and Paragraph 16 on the product-specific safeguard clause are controversial elements in EU–China trade relations.

## Document 9.6: Decision of 10 November 2001 and Protocol on the Accession of the People's Republic of China (Annexes Excluded)

ACCESSION OF THE PEOPLE'S REPUBLIC OF CHINA
*Decision of 10 November 2001*

The Ministerial Conference,

*Having regard to* paragraph 2 of Article XII and paragraph 1 of Article IX of the Marrakesh Agreement Establishing the World Trade Organization, and the Decision-Making Procedures under Articles IX and XII of the Marrakesh Agreement Establishing the World Trade Organization agreed by the General Council (WT/L/93),

*Taking note* of the application of the People's Republic of China for accession to the Marrakesh Agreement Establishing the World Trade Organization dated 7 December 1995,

*Noting* the results of the negotiations directed toward the establishment of the terms of accession of the People's Republic of China to the Marrakesh Agreement Establishing the World Trade Organization and having prepared a Protocol on the Accession of the People's Republic of China,

*Decides* as follows:

The People's Republic of China may accede to the Marrakesh Agreement Establishing the World Trade Organization on the terms and conditions set out in the Protocol annexed to this decision.

PROTOCOL ON THE ACCESSION OF THE PEOPLE'S REPUBLIC OF CHINA

**Preamble**

The World Trade Organization ("WTO"), pursuant to the approval of the Ministerial Conference of the WTO accorded under Article XII of the Marrakesh Agreement Establishing the World Trade Organization ("WTO Agreement"), and the People's Republic of China ("China"),

*Recalling* that China was an original contracting party to the General Agreement on Tariffs and Trade 1947,

*Taking note* that China is a signatory to the Final Act Embodying the Results of the Uruguay Round of Multilateral Trade Negotiations,

*Taking note* of the Report of the Working Party on the Accession of China in document WT/ACC/CHN/49 ("Working Party Report"),

*Having regard* to the results of the negotiations concerning China's membership in the WTO,

*Agree as follows:*

***Part I – General Provisions***

*1. General*

1. Upon accession, China accedes to the WTO Agreement pursuant to Article XII of that Agreement and thereby becomes a Member of the WTO.

2. The WTO Agreement to which China accedes shall be the WTO Agreement as rectified, amended or otherwise modified by such legal instruments as may have entered into force before the date of accession. This Protocol, which shall include the commitments referred to in paragraph 342 of the Working Party Report, shall be an integral part of the WTO Agreement.

3. Except as otherwise provided for in this Protocol, those obligations in the Multilateral Trade Agreements annexed to the WTO Agreement that are to be implemented over a period of time starting with entry into force of that Agreement shall be implemented by China as if it had accepted that Agreement on the date of its entry into force.

4. China may maintain a measure inconsistent with paragraph 1of Article II of the General Agreement on Trade in Services ("GATS") provided that such a measure is recorded in the List of Article II Exemptions annexed to this Protocol and meets the conditions of the Annex to the GATS on Article II Exemptions.

*2. Administration of the Trade Regime*

(A) Uniform Administration

1. The provisions of the WTO Agreement and this Protocol shall apply to the entire customs territory of China, including border trade regions and minority autonomous areas, Special Economic Zones, open coastal cities, economic and technical development zones and other areas where special regimes for tariffs, taxes and regulations are established (collectively referred to as "special economic areas").

2. China shall apply and administer in a uniform, impartial and reasonable manner all its laws, regulations and other measures of the central government as well as local regulations, rules and other measures issued or applied at the sub-national level (collectively referred to as "laws, regulations and other measures") pertaining to or affecting trade in goods, services, trade-related aspects of intellectual property rights ("TRIPS") or the control of foreign exchange.

3. China's local regulations, rules and other measures of local governments at the sub-national level shall conform to the obligations undertaken in the WTO Agreement and this Protocol.

4. China shall establish a mechanism under which individuals and enterprises can bring to the attention of the national authorities cases of non-uniform application of the trade regime.

(B) Special Economic Areas

1. China shall notify to the WTO all the relevant laws, regulations and other measures relating to its special economic areas, listing these areas by name and indicating the geographic boundaries that define them. China shall notify the WTO promptly, but in any case within 60 days, of any additions or modifications to its special economic areas, including notification of the laws, regulations and other measures relating thereto.

2. China shall apply to imported products, including physically incorporated components, introduced into the other parts of China's customs territory from the special economic areas, all taxes, charges and measures affecting imports, including import restrictions and customs and tariff charges, that are normally applied to imports into the other parts of China's customs territory.

3. Except as otherwise provided for in this Protocol, in providing preferential arrangements for enterprises within such special economic areas, WTO provisions on non-discrimination and national treatment shall be fully observed.

(C) Transparency

1. China undertakes that only those laws, regulations and other measures pertaining to or affecting trade in goods, services, TRIPS or the control of foreign exchange that are published and readily available to other WTO Members, individuals and enterprises, shall be enforced. In addition, China shall make available to WTO Members, upon request, all laws, regulations and other measures pertaining to or affecting trade in goods, services, TRIPS or the control of foreign exchange before such measures are implemented or enforced. In emergency situations, laws, regulations and other measures shall be made available at the latest when they are implemented or enforced.

2. China shall establish or designate an official journal dedicated to the publication of all laws, regulations and other measures pertaining to or affecting trade in goods, services, TRIPS or the control of foreign exchange and, after publication of its laws, regulations or other measures in such journal, shall provide a reasonable period for comment to the appropriate authorities before such measures are implemented, except for those laws, regulations and other measures involving national security, specific measures setting foreign exchange rates or monetary policy and other measures the publication of which would impede law enforcement. China shall publish this journal on a regular basis and make copies of all issues of this journal readily available to individuals and enterprises.

3. China shall establish or designate an enquiry point where, upon request of any individual, enterprise or WTO Member all information relating to the measures required to be published under paragraph 2(C)1 of this Protocol may be obtained. Replies to requests for information shall generally be provided within 30 days after receipt of a request. In exceptional cases, replies may be provided within 45 days after receipt of a request. Notice of the delay and the reasons therefor shall be provided in writing to the interested party. Replies to WTO Members shall be complete and shall represent the authoritative view of the Chinese government. Accurate and reliable information shall be provided to individuals and enterprises.

(D) Judicial Review

1. China shall establish, or designate, and maintain tribunals, contact points and procedures for the prompt review of all administrative actions relating to the implementation of laws, regulations, judicial decisions and administrative rulings of general application referred to in Article X:1 of the GATT 1994, Article VI of the GATS and the relevant provisions of the TRIPS Agreement. Such tribunals shall be impartial and independent of the agency entrusted with administrative enforcement and shall not have any substantial interest in the outcome of the matter.

2. Review procedures shall include the opportunity for appeal, without penalty, by individuals or enterprises affected by any administrative action subject to review. If the initial right

of appeal is to an administrative body, there shall in all cases be the opportunity to choose to appeal the decision to a judicial body. Notice of the decision on appeal shall be given to the appellant and the reasons for such decision shall be provided in writing. The appellant shall also be informed of any right to further appeal.

*3. Non-discrimination*

Except as otherwise provided for in this Protocol, foreign individuals and enterprises and foreign-funded enterprises shall be accorded treatment no less favourable than that accorded to other individuals and enterprises in respect of:

(a) the procurement of inputs and goods and services necessary for production and the conditions under which their goods are produced, marketed or sold, in the domestic market and for export; and

(b) the prices and availability of goods and services supplied by national and sub-national authorities and public or state enterprises, in areas including transportation, energy, basic telecommunications, other utilities and factors of production.

*4. Special Trade Arrangements*

Upon accession, China shall eliminate or bring into conformity with the WTO Agreement all special trade arrangements, including barter trade arrangements, with third countries and separate customs territories, which are not in conformity with the WTO Agreement.

*5. Right to Trade*

1. Without prejudice to China's right to regulate trade in a manner consistent with the WTO Agreement, China shall progressively liberalize the availability and scope of the right to trade, so that, within three years after accession, all enterprises in China shall have the right to trade in all goods throughout the customs territory of China, except for those goods listed in Annex 2A which continue to be subject to state trading in accordance with this Protocol. Such right to trade shall be the right to import and export goods. All such goods shall be accorded national treatment under Article III of the GATT 1994, especially paragraph 4 thereof, in respect of their internal sale, offering for sale, purchase, transportation, distribution or use, including their direct access to end-users. For those goods listed in Annex 2B, China shall phase out limitation on the grant of trading rights pursuant to the schedule in that Annex. China shall complete all necessary legislative procedures to implement these provisions during the transition period.

2. Except as otherwise provided for in this Protocol, all foreign individuals and enterprises, including those not invested or registered in China, shall be accorded treatment no less favourable than that accorded to enterprises in China with respect to the right to trade.

*6. State Trading*

1. China shall ensure that import purchasing procedures of state trading enterprises are fully transparent, and in compliance with the WTO Agreement, and shall refrain from taking any measure to influence or direct state trading enterprises as to the quantity, value, or country of origin of goods purchased or sold, except in accordance with the WTO Agreement.

2. As part of China's notification under the GATT 1994 and the Understanding on the Interpretation of Article XVII of the GATT 1994, China shall also provide full information on the pricing mechanisms of its state trading enterprises for exported goods.

*7. Non-Tariff Measures*

1. China shall implement the schedule for phased elimination of the measures contained in Annex 3. During the periods specified in Annex 3, the protection afforded by the measures listed in that Annex shall not be increased or expanded in size, scope or duration, nor shall any new measures be applied, unless in conformity with the provisions of the WTO Agreement.

2. In implementing the provisions of Articles III and XI of the GATT 1994 and the Agreement on Agriculture, China shall eliminate and shall not introduce, re-introduce or apply non-tariff measures that cannot be justified under the provisions of the WTO Agreement. For all non-tariff measures, whether or not referred to in Annex 3, that are applied after the date of accession, consistent with the WTO Agreement or this Protocol, China shall allocate and otherwise administer such measures in strict conformity with the provisions of the WTO Agreement, including GATT 1994 and Article XIII thereof, and the Agreement on Import Licensing Procedures, including notification requirements.

3. China shall, upon accession, comply with the TRIMs Agreement, without recourse to the provisions of Article 5 of the TRIMs Agreement. China shall eliminate and cease to enforce trade and foreign exchange balancing requirements, local content and export or performance requirements made effective through laws, regulations or other measures. Moreover, China will not enforce provisions of contracts imposing such requirements. Without prejudice to the relevant provisions of this Protocol, China shall ensure that the distribution of import licences, quotas, tariff-rate quotas, or any other means of approval for importation, the right of importation or investment by national and sub-national authorities, is not conditioned on: whether competing domestic suppliers of such products exist; or performance requirements of any kind, such as local content, offsets, the transfer of technology, export performance or the conduct of research and development in China.

4. Import and export prohibitions and restrictions, and licensing requirements affecting imports and exports shall only be imposed and enforced by the national authorities or by sub-national authorities with authorization from the national authorities. Such measures which are not imposed by the national authorities or by sub-national authorities with authorization from the national authorities, shall not be implemented or enforced.

*8. Import and Export Licensing*

1. In implementing the WTO Agreement and provisions of the Agreement on Import Licensing Procedures, China shall undertake the following measures to facilitate compliance with these agreements:

(a) China shall publish on a regular basis the following in the official journal referred to in paragraph 2(C)2 of this Protocol:

- by product, the list of all organizations, including those organizations delegated such authority by the national authorities, that are responsible for authorizing or approving imports or exports, whether through grant of licence or other approval;
- procedures and criteria for obtaining such import or export licences or other approvals, and the conditions for deciding whether they should be granted;

- a list of all products, by tariff number, that are subject to tendering requirements, including information on products subject to such tendering requirements and any changes, pursuant to the Agreement on Import Licensing Procedures;
- a list of all goods and technologies whose import or export are restricted or prohibited; these goods shall also be notified to the Committee on Import Licensing;
- any changes to the list of goods and technologies whose import and export are restricted or prohibited.

Copies of these submissions in one or more official languages of the WTO shall be forwarded to the WTO for circulation to WTO Members and for submission to the Committee on Import Licensing within 75 days of each publication.

(b) China shall notify the WTO of all licensing and quota requirements remaining in effect after accession, listed separately by HS tariff line and with the quantities associated with the restriction, if any, and the justification for maintaining the restriction or its scheduled date of termination.

(c) China shall submit the notification of its import licensing procedures to the Committee on Import Licensing. China shall report annually to the Committee on Import Licensing on its automatic import licensing procedures, explaining the circumstances which give rise to these requirements and justifying the need for their continuation. This report shall also provide the information listed in Article 3 of the Agreement on Import Licensing Procedures.

(d) China shall issue import licences for a minimum duration of validity of six months, except where exceptional circumstances make this impossible. In such cases, China shall promptly notify the Committee on Import Licensing of the exceptional circumstances requiring the shorter period of licence validity.

2. Except as otherwise provided for in this Protocol, foreign individuals and enterprises and foreign-funded enterprises shall be accorded treatment no less favourable than that accorded to other individuals and enterprises in respect of the distribution of import and export licences and quotas.

*9. Price Controls*

1. China shall, subject to paragraph 2 below, allow prices for traded goods and services in every sector to be determined by market forces, and multi-tier pricing practices for such goods and services shall be eliminated.

2. The goods and services listed in Annex 4 may be subject to price controls, consistent with the WTO Agreement, in particular Article III of the GATT 1994 and Annex 2, paragraphs 3 and 4 of the Agreement on Agriculture. Except in exceptional circumstances, and subject to notification to the WTO, price controls shall not be extended to goods or services beyond those listed in Annex 4, and China shall make best efforts to reduce and eliminate these controls.

3. China shall publish in the official journal the list of goods and services subject to state pricing and changes thereto.

*10. Subsidies*

1. China shall notify the WTO of any subsidy within the meaning of Article 1 of the Agreement on Subsidies and Countervailing Measures ("SCM Agreement"), granted or

maintained in its territory, organized by specific product, including those subsidies defined in Article 3 of the SCM Agreement. The information provided should be as specific as possible, following the requirements of the questionnaire on subsidies as noted in Article 25 of the SCM Agreement.

2. For purposes of applying Articles 1.2 and 2 of the SCM Agreement, subsidies provided to state-owned enterprises will be viewed as specific if, inter alia, state-owned enterprises are the predominant recipients of such subsidies or state-owned enterprises receive disproportionately large amounts of such subsidies.

3. China shall eliminate all subsidy programmes falling within the scope of Article 3 of the SCM Agreement upon accession.

*11. Taxes and Charges Levied on Imports and Exports*

1. China shall ensure that customs fees or charges applied or administered by national or sub-national authorities, shall be in conformity with the GATT 1994.

2. China shall ensure that internal taxes and charges, including value-added taxes, applied or administered by national or sub-national authorities shall be in conformity with the GATT 1994.

3. China shall eliminate all taxes and charges applied to exports unless specifically provided for in Annex 6 of this Protocol or applied in conformity with the provisions of Article VIII of the GATT 1994.

4. Foreign individuals and enterprises and foreign-funded enterprises shall, upon accession, be accorded treatment no less favourable than that accorded to other individuals and enterprises in respect of the provision of border tax adjustments.

*12. Agriculture*

1. China shall implement the provisions contained in China's Schedule of Concessions and Commitments on Goods and, as specifically provided in this Protocol, those of the Agreement on Agriculture. In this context, China shall not maintain or introduce any export subsidies on agricultural products.

2. China shall, under the Transitional Review Mechanism, notify fiscal and other transfers between or among state-owned enterprises in the agricultural sector (whether national or sub-national) and other enterprises that operate as state trading enterprises in the agricultural sector.

*13. Technical Barriers to Trade*

1. China shall publish in the official journal all criteria, whether formal or informal, that are the basis for a technical regulation, standard or conformity assessment procedure.

2. China shall, upon accession, bring into conformity with the TBT Agreement all technical regulations, standards and conformity assessment procedures.

3. China shall apply conformity assessment procedures to imported products only to determine compliance with technical regulations and standards that are consistent with the provisions of this Protocol and the WTO Agreement. Conformity assessment bodies will determine the conformity of imported products with commercial terms of contracts only if authorized by the parties to such contract. China shall ensure that such inspection of

products for compliance with the commercial terms of contracts does not affect customs clearance or the granting of import licences for such products.

4. (a) Upon accession, China shall ensure that the same technical regulations, standards and conformity assessment procedures are applied to both imported and domestic products. In order to ensure a smooth transition from the current system, China shall ensure that, upon accession, all certification, safety licensing, and quality licensing bodies and agencies are authorized to undertake these activities for both imported and domestic products, and that, one year after accession, all conformity assessment bodies and agencies are authorized to undertake conformity assessment for both imported and domestic products. The choice of body or agency shall be at the discretion of the applicant. For imported and domestic products, all bodies and agencies shall issue the same mark and charge the same fee. They shall also provide the same processing periods and complaint procedures. Imported products shall not be subject to more than one conformity assessment. China shall publish and make readily available to other WTO Members, individuals, and enterprises full information on the respective responsibilities of its conformity assessment bodies and agencies.

(b) No later than 18 months after accession, China shall assign the respective responsibilities of its conformity assessment bodies solely on the basis of the scope of work and type of product without any consideration of the origin of a product. The respective responsibilities that will be assigned to China's conformity assessment bodies will be notified to the TBT Committee 12 months after accession.

### *14. Sanitary and Phytosanitary Measures*

China shall notify to the WTO all laws, regulations and other measures relating to its sanitary and phytosanitary measures, including product coverage and relevant international standards, guidelines and recommendations, within 30 days after accession.

### *15. Price Comparability in Determining Subsidies and Dumping*

Article VI of the GATT 1994, the Agreement on Implementation of Article VI of the General Agreement on Tariffs and Trade 1994 ("Anti-Dumping Agreement") and the SCM Agreement shall apply in proceedings involving imports of Chinese origin into a WTO Member consistent with the following:

(a) In determining price comparability under Article VI of the GATT 1994 and the Anti-Dumping Agreement, the importing WTO Member shall use either Chinese prices or costs for the industry under investigation or a methodology that is not based on a strict comparison with domestic prices or costs in China based on the following rules:

  (i) If the producers under investigation can clearly show that market economy conditions prevail in the industry producing the like product with regard to the manufacture, production and sale of that product, the importing WTO Member shall use Chinese prices or costs for the industry under investigation in determining price comparability;

  (ii) The importing WTO Member may use a methodology that is not based on a strict comparison with domestic prices or costs in China if the producers under investigation cannot clearly show that market economy conditions prevail in the industry producing the like product with regard to manufacture, production and sale of that product.

(b) In proceedings under Parts II, III and V of the SCM Agreement, when addressing subsidies described in Articles 14(a), 14(b), 14(c) and 14(d), relevant provisions of the SCM Agreement shall apply; however, if there are special difficulties in that application, the importing WTO Member may then use methodologies for identifying and measuring the subsidy benefit which take into account the possibility that prevailing terms and conditions in China may not always be available as appropriate benchmarks. In applying such methodologies, where practicable, the importing WTO Member should adjust such prevailing terms and conditions before considering the use of terms and conditions prevailing outside China.

(c) The importing WTO Member shall notify methodologies used in accordance with subparagraph (a) to the Committee on Anti-Dumping Practices and shall notify methodologies used in accordance with subparagraph (b) to the Committee on Subsidies and Countervailing Measures.

(d) Once China has established, under the national law of the importing WTO Member, that it is a market economy, the provisions of subparagraph (a) shall be terminated provided that the importing Member's national law contains market economy criteria as of the date of accession. In any event, the provisions of subparagraph (a)(ii) shall expire 15 years after the date of accession. In addition, should China establish, pursuant to the national law of the importing WTO Member, that market economy conditions prevail in a particular industry or sector, the non-market economy provisions of subparagraph (a) shall no longer apply to that industry or sector.

*16. Transitional Product-Specific Safeguard Mechanism*

1. In cases where products of Chinese origin are being imported into the territory of any WTO Member in such increased quantities or under such conditions as to cause or threaten to cause market disruption to the domestic producers of like or directly competitive products, the WTO Member so affected may request consultations with China with a view to seeking a mutually satisfactory solution, including whether the affected WTO Member should pursue application of a measure under the Agreement on Safeguards. Any such request shall be notified immediately to the Committee on Safeguards.

2. If, in the course of these bilateral consultations, it is agreed that imports of Chinese origin are such a cause and that action is necessary, China shall take such action as to prevent or remedy the market disruption. Any such action shall be notified immediately to the Committee on Safeguards.

3. If consultations do not lead to an agreement between China and the WTO Member concerned within 60 days of the receipt of a request for consultations, the WTO Member affected shall be free, in respect of such products, to withdraw concessions or otherwise to limit imports only to the extent necessary to prevent or remedy such market disruption. Any such action shall be notified immediately to the Committee on Safeguards.

4. Market disruption shall exist whenever imports of an article, like or directly competitive with an article produced by the domestic industry, are increasing rapidly, either absolutely or relatively, so as to be a significant cause of material injury, or threat of material injury to the domestic industry. In determining if market disruption exists, the affected WTO Member shall consider objective factors, including the volume of imports, the effect of imports on prices for like or directly competitive articles, and the effect of such imports on the domestic industry producing like or directly competitive products.

5. Prior to application of a measure pursuant to paragraph 3, the WTO Member taking such action shall provide reasonable public notice to all interested parties and provide adequate opportunity for importers, exporters and other interested parties to submit their views and evidence on the appropriateness of the proposed measure and whether it would be in the public interest. The WTO Member shall provide written notice of the decision to apply a measure, including the reasons for such measure and its scope and duration.

6. A WTO Member shall apply a measure pursuant to this Section only for such period of time as may be necessary to prevent or remedy the market disruption. If a measure is taken as a result of a relative increase in the level of imports, China has the right to suspend the application of substantially equivalent concessions or obligations under the GATT 1994 to the trade of the WTO Member applying the measure, if such measure remains in effect more than two years. However, if a measure is taken as a result of an absolute increase in imports, China has a right to suspend the application of substantially equivalent concessions or obligations under the GATT 1994 to the trade of the WTO Member applying the measure, if such measure remains in effect more than three years. Any such action by China shall be notified immediately to the Committee on Safeguards.

7. In critical circumstances, where delay would cause damage which it would be difficult to repair, the WTO Member so affected may take a provisional safeguard measure pursuant to a preliminary determination that imports have caused or threatened to cause market disruption. In this case, notification of the measures taken to the Committee on Safeguards and a request for bilateral consultations shall be effected immediately thereafter. The duration of the provisional measure shall not exceed 200 days during which the pertinent requirements of paragraphs 1, 2 and 5 shall be met. The duration of any provisional measure shall be counted toward the period provided for under paragraph 6.

8. If a WTO Member considers that an action taken under paragraphs 2, 3 or 7 causes or threatens to cause significant diversions of trade into its market, it may request consultations with China and/or the WTO Member concerned. Such consultations shall be held within 30 days after the request is notified to the Committee on Safeguards. If such consultations fail to lead to an agreement between China and the WTO Member or Members concerned within 60 days after the notification, the requesting WTO Member shall be free, in respect of such product, to withdraw concessions accorded to or otherwise limit imports from China, to the extent necessary to prevent or remedy such diversions. Such action shall be notified immediately to the Committee on Safeguards.

9. Application of this Section shall be terminated 12 years after the date of accession.

*17. Reservations by WTO Members*

All prohibitions, quantitative restrictions and other measures maintained by WTO Members against imports from China in a manner inconsistent with the WTO Agreement are listed in Annex 7. All such prohibitions, quantitative restrictions and other measures shall be phased out or dealt with in accordance with mutually agreed terms and timetables as specified in the said Annex.

*18. Transitional Review Mechanism*

1. Those subsidiary bodies[1] of the WTO which have a mandate covering China's commitments under the WTO Agreement or this Protocol shall, within one year after accession and in accordance with paragraph 4 below, review, as appropriate to their

mandate, the implementation by China of the WTO Agreement and of the related provisions of this Protocol. China shall provide relevant information, including information specified in Annex 1A, to each subsidiary body in advance of the review. China can also raise issues relating to any reservations under Section 17 or to any other specific commitments made by other Members in this Protocol, in those subsidiary bodies which have a relevant mandate. Each subsidiary body shall report the results of such review promptly to the relevant Council established by paragraph 5 of Article IV of the WTO Agreement, if applicable, which shall in turn report promptly to the General Council.

2. The General Council shall, within one year after accession, and in accordance with paragraph 4 below, review the implementation by China of the WTO Agreement and the provisions of this Protocol. The General Council shall conduct such review in accordance with the framework set out in Annex 1B and in the light of the results of any reviews held pursuant to paragraph 1. China also can raise issues relating to any reservations under Section 17 or to any other specific commitments made by other Members in this Protocol. The General Council may make recommendations to China and to other Members in these respects.

3. Consideration of issues pursuant to this Section shall be without prejudice to the rights and obligations of any Member, including China, under the WTO Agreement or any Plurilateral Trade Agreement, and shall not preclude or be a precondition to recourse to consultation or other provisions of the WTO Agreement or this Protocol.

4. The review provided for in paragraphs 1 and 2 will take place after accession in each year for eight years. Thereafter there will be a final review in year 10 or at an earlier date decided by the General Council.

**Part II – Schedules**

1. The Schedules annexed to this Protocol shall become the Schedule of Concessions and Commitments annexed to the GATT 1994 and the Schedule of Specific Commitments annexed to the GATS relating to China. The staging of concessions and commitments listed in the Schedules shall be implemented as specified in the relevant parts of the relevant Schedules.

2. For the purpose of the reference in paragraph 6(a) of Article II of the GATT 1994 to the date of that Agreement, the applicable date in respect of the Schedules of Concessions and Commitments annexed to this Protocol shall be the date of accession.

**Part III – Final Provisions**

1. This Protocol shall be open for acceptance, by signature or otherwise, by China until 1 January 2002.

2. This Protocol shall enter into force on the thirtieth day following the day of its acceptance.

3. This Protocol shall be deposited with the Director-General of the WTO. The Director-General shall promptly furnish a certified copy of this Protocol and a notification of acceptance by China thereof, pursuant to paragraph 1 of Part III of this Protocol, to each WTO Member and to China.

4. This Protocol shall be registered in accordance with the provisions of Article 102 of the Charter of the United Nations.

Done at Doha this tenth day of November two thousand and one, in a single copy, in the English, French and Spanish languages, each text being authentic, except that a Schedule annexed hereto may specify that it is authentic in only one or more of these languages.

1 Council for Trade in Goods, Council for Trade-Related Aspects of Intellectual Property Rights, Council for Trade in Services, Committees on Balance-of-Payments Restrictions, Market Access (covering also ITA), Agriculture, Sanitary and Phytosanitary Measures, Technical Barriers to Trade, Subsidies and Countervailing Measures, Anti-Dumping Measures, Customs Valuation, Rules of Origin, Import Licensing, Trade-Related Investment Measures, Safeguards, Trade in Financial Services.

The second significant WTO document for China, in addition to the Uruguay Round agreements, was the Report of the Working Party on the Accession of China. It analysed China's foreign trade regime and set out China's specific commitments concerning economic policies, the framework of making and enforcing policies, policies affecting trade in goods, the trade-related intellectual property regime, policies affecting trade in services and other issues.[10] In addition to the standard obligations accepted by all WTO members, China accepted certain additional obligations, known as 'WTO plus'. The Protocol on China's Accession (in Article 15) provided for a special transitional provision lasting 15 years on price comparability in determining dumping. It also (in Article 16) established a transitional product-specific safeguard mechanism (SSC: special safeguard clause) available to other WTO members for 12 years on imports from China. The Working Party Report (in paragraph 242) established a specific safeguard clause (TSSC: textiles-specific safeguard clause) for imports of textile products from China, which could be used by other WTO members until the end of 2008.

Trade in textiles has long been a subject of regulation and a source of disagreement between the EU and China. The WTO Agreement on Textiles and Clothing provided for a ten-year period for the removal of textile quotas among WTO members, starting on 1 January 1995. This transitional period ended on 31 December 2004. Consequently, trade in textiles among WTO members was liberalised as of 1 January 2005, except for the potential application of textiles-specific safeguard clause set out in paragraph 242 of the China Accession Protocol. The result was a dispute between the EU and China concerning trade in textiles, which was resolved in September 2005. Chapter 2 of this book presents the main documents on the EU–China textiles dispute between January and September 2005, including a Notice by the European Commission that interpreted the TSSC in paragraph 242 of the WTO Working Party Report on Chinese accession.

The enlargement of the EU in 2005 required the modification of concessions in the market-access schedules of the new EU Member States. This was achieved by an Agreement in the form of an exchange of letters between the European Community and China. The Agreement is listed in Table 9.1, but the text is not included here.[11]

10 WT/ACC/CHN/49 (1 October 2001), Restricted, reprinted in *Compilation of the Legal Instruments on China's Accession to the World Trade Organization* (Beijing, Law Press China, 2002) 755 (English and Chinese). Due to its length, the Report of the Working Party is not reproduced here. It is available on the WTO website at http://www.wto.org/english/thewto_e/countries_e/china_e.htm.

11 For further information on relations between the EU and China within the WTO, see the WTO website, www.wto.org.

# Index

www.ingramcontent.com/pod-product-compliance
Ingram Content Group UK Ltd.
Pitfield, Milton Keynes, MK11 3LW, UK
UKHW051448290926
15471UKWH00008B/1086

9 781841 137247